1973
CATHOLIC
ALMANAC

FELICIAN A. FOY, O.F.M.
Editor

Our Sunday Visitor, Inc.
Huntington, Indiana 46750

Acknowledgments: NC News Service for coverage of news and documentary texts; *America* Press for quotations from *The Documents of Vatican II,* Walter M. Abbott, S.J., general editor; *Annuario Pontificio, 1972; The Official Catholic Directory, 1972,* P. J. Kenedy & Sons, Charles R. Cunningham, editor; The United States Mission Council, 1325 Massachusetts Ave. N.W., Washington, D.C. 20005, for US foreign missionary compilations and statistics; *Britannica Book of the Year,* 1972 edition, for religious population of the world. Other sources are credited in various entries.

ISBN: 0-87973-814-6

Library of Congress Catalog Card Number: A43-2500

Published, printed and bound in U.S.A. by
OUR SUNDAY VISITOR, INC.
Huntington, Indiana 46750

814

TABLE OF CONTENTS

3

INDEX

A

S

TEN YEARS AFTER THE START OF VATICAN II

(The following article was written by James C. O'Neill, Rome correspondent of NC News Service.)

October 11, 1972, marked the 10th anniversary of the opening of what Pope John XXIII hoped would become "a revolutionary event not merely for the well-being of the Church but for the progress of human society."

On Oct. 11, 1962, a total of 2,540 bishops and other Church officials marched into St. Peter's Basilica to hear Pope John proclaim the opening of the Church's 21st ecumenical council.

Looking back across the past 10 years, there is little doubt that Vatican II contained the seeds of a modern revolution within the Church. But it is legitimate to ask what specific changes and innovations the council has brought about in the thinking and approach of the Vatican and its central administrative offices.

Certainly the council had a great effect on the Vatican offices through which the Pope administers the affairs of the Church. Many critics, however, maintain that the effects were not great enough, nor did they go deep enough.

Anti-institutionalists protest that the council did not have the desired effect of reducing the number of Vatican offices. In fact, there are more new offices and secretariats today than there were 10 years ago — witness the establishment of the Pontifical Commission on Justice and Peace, the Council of the Laity, the Vatican Secretariats for Non-Christians and for Non-Believers, the Synod of Bishops, all of which are outgrowths of the council.

Curial Reform

Pope Paul's reform of the Roman Curia, however, is also a direct outgrowth of the council. In announcing its reform in 1967, Pope Paul flatly told critics that "certainly there can be no doubt about the need for the Roman Curia."

While granting the need for a general reform to make the curial offices "better adapted to the needs of the times," Pope Paul repeated an earlier statement on the reform at which the council had aimed. He recalled his words opening the second session of the council in 1963, when he said:

"The reform at which the council aims is not a turning upside down of the Church's present way of life or a breaking with what is essential and worthy of veneration in her tradition. It is, rather, an honoring of tradition by stripping it of what is unworthy or defective so that it can be rendered firm and faithful."

The reform of the Curia has required all the central administrative offices to work out new norms governing their operating procedures in order to bring them more in line with the desires expressed by Vatican II.

Bishops, representative of various parts of the world, have been added as members of the congregations and other offices that in the past had their membership limited only to cardinals. It should be added, however, that this gesture to the collegial concept of all bishops being responsible for the whole Church has had varying success in the actual day-to-day operation of the Vatican offices.

Decentralization

Again reflecting the desire of Vatican II, Pope Paul has called more and more non-Italian cardinals and bishops to top administrative jobs in the Vatican.

Advisory bodies such as the Synod of Bishops, the Justice and Peace Commission and the Laity Council have been established by Pope Paul as a means of providing a platform and the possibility of two-way communications of ideas and needs of the Church today.

They are specific attempts not only to remedy a one-sided conversation dominated by the Vatican but also to provide offices outside the traditional structure of the Curia in order to keep going the "aggiornamento" called for by Pope John.

Efforts toward decentralization of authority and of decision-making as called for by the council are best exemplified by the strengthening of national bishops' conferences. More and more, decisions, that in the past were made in the Vatican, are now being passed on for action to the national conferences and through them to the local bishops.

New Attitude

Officials who work in the Curia insist that there has also been a shift in the thinking and spirit guiding the work of the central offices. The shift is from the older mentality of giving strict orders and specific instructions to a new and freer concept of service.

As one Vatican monsignor put it: "Today we want to know what we can do to help the bishops and the faithful, and not to tell them what they must do."

Certainly today's flow of bishops from all parts of the world coming and going in Vatican offices in which they are now consultors, members or simply interested parties, is far greater than in the past. Not only are more people, bishops, priests and laymen coming to Rome for consultation and to air their points of view, but they are being seen and heard by Vatican officials.

For instance, American Cardinal John Wright's Congregation for the Clergy reports an ever-increasing number of visitors. An official of that office said that "the number of diocesan priests from all over the world and of study groups of various nations who take advantage of the congregation's invitation to visit and learn at first hand its operations has increased annually."

Up to October, he said, "an estimated 2,000 priests have visited the congregation individually or in groups" in 1972.

Consultation by mail has also increased. There is hardly a new instruction or document coming out of the Vatican these days that has not been debated and consulted on back and forth for years by local bishops and other interested parties.

Consultation

In fact, the amount of time spent in consultation by mail and committee study has prompted the criticism that by the time the Vatican finally does issue new guidelines or norms, they have already been superseded by developing events.

Many of the officials in the Curia also report a less juridical or legalistic attitude to situations and persons than in the past. For instance, in the Doctrinal Congregation, which is charged with guarding faith and morals, new regulations have been drawn up giving a fairer hearing to those whose writings are questionable or suspect.

Under the reform of the Doctrinal Congregation, a qualified scholar is appointed as the defender of the writings under question.

The regulations also provide for a personal encounter with the writer to permit him to explain his views before a judgment is reached.

Moreover, the old hard words such as "heresy" and "excommunication" are not used any more in the congregation's public comments or warnings.

Although bureaucracies are slow and difficult to change, there are signs that Vatican II has already had a real impact on the Church's central administrative offices. Despite the encumbrances of centuries of tradition and an in-built tendency to consolidate and preserve what has proved valid in the past, the "signs of the times" have already left their mark on the Roman Curia.

But the question remains: "Has that revolutionary event intended by Pope John for the well-being of the Church gone far enough?"

The Pope, Central Figure

Of all Vatican offices, institutions and personalities stamped with the "signs of the times" of the Second Vatican Council, Pope Paul is the most central and significant.

It can be fairly stated that the pontificate of Giovanni Battista Montini has been shaped by and lived in the revolutionary event of the 21st ecumenical council.

It was Pope Paul who presided over three of the four annual sessions, after Pope John XXIII died. More importantly, it has been Pope Paul's fate and role in history to put into practice the mandates of that council in what has come to be called the post-conciliar Church.

In the nine years that he has been Pope, Paul VI has had an unequaled view from that "window of the council, opened wide to the world," as he described that event at the beginning of the council's second session in 1963.

There have been times when the winds blowing through that window have been cold and chilling, so biting that it once caused the Pope to weep when talking to a group of Latin American bishops of disaffection and strife within the Church.

Peace Initiatives

From the window of the council and with the whole-hearted backing of the assembled bishops from around the world, Pope Paul has made his pontificate a pilgrimage of peace and pledge of reconciliation.

Pope Paul's peace-making efforts are notable, even among Popes. His dramatic one-day flight in 1964 to New York to stand before the United Nations to declare "Never again war; war, never again," is unparalleled in history.

He has used his diplomatic channels unceasingly to open the way for negotiations, peaceful exchanges and personal pleas for peace. Most recently, British Prime Minister Edward Heath was at the Vatican to discuss the nagging horrors of Northern Ireland.

The British Prime Minister came despite the fact Pope Paul has in the past been publicly critical of British policies in Northern Ireland. American leaders, from President Nixon down, as well as Soviet President Nikolai Podgorny, Yugoslavia's Marshall Josip Broz (Tito) have passed through the Vatican halls and have stayed for private talks in the Pope's library.

Development

But Pope Paul's peace initiatives have by no means been confined to the strictly diplomatic level. His 1967 encyclical *Populorum Progressio* ("On the Development of Peoples") embodied much of Vatican II's teachings on the Church in the modern world.

In that encyclical, which has won praise for its open awareness of world problems, the Pope proclaimed the concept that "development is another word for peace."

In the same year, he established his Commission for Justice and Peace, again responding to a definite call of the council.

Through this international office the Pope hopes to reach down to the grass-root level of every nation to stimulate Catholics and to help them think and act in the world in support of the ideals to which their faith is committed.

Practical Problems

Pope Paul has always linked his peace programs and efforts with the practical problems of the world. This concern with the Church in the world and its responsibility to the world has put the Pope aboard planes girdling the globe.

Flights to India, Latin America, Africa and Asia have become commonplace. But they too are gestures of Pope Paul's interpretation of the council.

On almost every one of his major flights, Pope Paul has met with the bishops from the Third World of underdeveloped nations. He has talked to them of their area's needs, both spiritual and social.

While always linking his trips with some religious or international concern of justice and peace, Pope Paul has also centered his interest on the needs of the times, economic development and the better apportionment of wealth.

He has not failed to warn the rich nations of their duty to their younger and poorer partners in the world community. He told the Australians to open their rich and vital world to the less fortunate of the Pacific — a message not entirely welcomed by all "down under." At the United Nations he pleaded both for the inclusion of all countries — interpreted rightly as a reference to the exclusion of Red China — and for the feeding of all at the table of life — interpreted rightly as a firm stand against the UN's favorable policies toward international birth control.

Firm Teacher

Although the Pope has been a powerful voice for peace and reconciliation, he nevertheless has not pulled his punches when it comes to the defense of what he considers the basic teachings of the Church and the fundamental defenses of mankind. Most pointedly his 1968 encyclical *Humanae Vitae,* which reaffirmed the Church's traditional opposition to artificial birth control, flew in the face of public opinion.

Although inflexible in doctrinal matters, Pope Paul has shown himself to be among the most advanced leaders in the search for the reunion of Christendom. His pontificate initiated a series of "firsts" in the ecumenical world that had not been equalled in history.

Ecumenism

Expressing, again dramatically, the council's desire for a new approach to reunion, Pope Paul in his first year as Pope announced his first pilgrimage — to the Holy Land to meet with the late Ecumenical Orthodox Patriarch Athenagoras I.

In that one flight he began the ending of a bitter isolation of the two great Christian churches and opened the way for still other landmarks of ecumenical action with Protestantism.

Today, only 10 short years after the council, it is almost taken for granted that two Anglican archbishops of Canterbury have made their visits to Rome. The Pope himself went to Geneva to visit the World Council of Churches headquarters, and its leaders these days make their visits to the Vatican as a matter of course.

The period of ecumenical "firsts" has now passed. Vatican theologians and historians are meeting frequently with Anglicans, Methodists, Lutherans, Orthodox and other religious bodies in the hard, slogging work of trying to find out what they hold in common and what points are really at the heart of their disunion.

The fact that the joint Roman Catholic-Anglican commission could draw up a common statement about the Eucharist is in itself one of the major significant developments of the ecumenical "firsts" chalked up by Pope Paul.

The effects of Vatican II are by no means over, but in the few years that have elapsed since its solemn opening, Pope Paul has embodied in his acts his own description he gave of the council's entire four-year period, when he said:

ADDITIONS AND CHANGES

Cardinals (pp. 196-207): Cardinal Paul Leger is also a member of the Sacred Congregation for the Evangelization of Peoples.

Cardinal Humberto Quintero resigned as Archbishop of Caracas, Venezuela, in late September at the age of 70.

Nuncios and Delegates (pp. 209-10): Ivory Coast, Giovanni Mariani, pro-nuncio.

Diplomats at the Vatican (pp. 211-12): Belgium, Prince Zerner De Merude, Ambassador.

Costa Rica, Julian Zamora Dobles, Ambassador.

Nicaragua, Enrique F. Sanchez Salinas, Ambassador.

Sudan, Sala-El-Din Osman Hashim, Ambassador.

PUBLICATION HISTORY

The Catholic Almanac originated, remotely, from *St. Anthony's Almanac,* a 64-page annual with calendar, feature and devotional contents, published by the Franciscans of Holy Name Province from 1904 to 1929.

Completely revised and enlarged, the publication was issued under the title, *The Franciscan Almanac,* by *The Franciscan Magazine* from 1931 to 1933 and by St. Anthony's Guild from 1936 to 1971. From 1940 to 1968 its title was *The National Catholic Almanac;* the present title was adopted in 1969. The 1959 to 1971 editions were produced jointly by St. Anthony's Guild and Doubleday & Co., Inc.

The Almanac was acquired in 1971 by Our Sunday Visitor, Inc., Huntington, Ind. 46750, publisher of this 1973 edition.

NOVEMBER 1971

VATICAN

World Needs Religion — Pope Paul told a general audience Nov. 3 that the world needs religion more than ever before. He said religion is the foundation and cornerstone of human life, and provides man with light, sustenance, and a chance of happiness in the world. To offer it to the world, he stated, "the Church is organized, exists, loves, suffers, and is always developing its . . . conversation with God and man."

Right to Religious Education — Every child has a right to religious education, and the lack of it handicaps his personal freedom. These were two of the points stated in a letter written for the Pope by Secretary of State Cardinal Jean Villot and addressed to a Nov. 12 to 14 congress of parents' associations in Angers, France. The letter noted that an education "worthy of the name" must help youths "establish a real hierarchy of values . . . judge their first experiences . . . acquire a true conception of life."

Daily Newspapers — The Catholic daily press in Italy should be the "clear and honest mirror" of life as it is lived today, Pope Paul told a gathering of thousands in St. Peter's Square Nov. 14. Speaking in observance of Catholic Daily Newspaper Day, he said the role of the five Italian Catholic dailies is to give a "Christian interpretation" to "daily reality. . . . This is what the Catholic paper proposes to do, since it is its reason for being. Unfortunately, it is generally the only newspaper that does."

The Voice of Christ — Christians must listen to the "mysterious voice of Christ," Pope Paul declared at a general audience Nov. 17. "The ear of modern man," he said, "is deafened by the roar of material progress or bewitched by the magic of our loquacious culture. Man does not hear, he does not heed the mysterious voice of Christ. . . . Even if his profane ear faintly hears something of the Gospel echo, he often wants to interpret it by himself. That is, he listens to himself rather than to the authentic appeal of the Spirit." As a result, "man in fact does not have, on his own, a secure awareness of his reason for living."

Church-State Collaboration — The Holy Father stressed the importance of close collaboration between Church and state for the service of humanity at a meeting Nov. 18 with Austrian President Franz Jonas. He said: "Although the state and Church are each independent in their own sphere, a trusting collaboration between the two institutions can only benefit the people, who can then develop their own capacities." President Jonas stated:

"The Church has great tasks to fulfill in the interest of human promotion. . . . Collaboration between Church and state, which is afforded by a pluralistic society, is not only useful but necessary."

Right to Life — Twenty years after Pius XII delivered a landmark address to midwives in which he upheld the sacredness of procreation and the right of the unborn to life, Pope Paul reminded another group of midwives that the Church still holds sacred the right to life. In a Nov. 24 address, he said: "The Church's teaching authority has never ceased to refer, with consistent constancy, to the primary moral demands of man and to the mystery which becomes part of every creature born to life. . . . Where there is life, there is the spirit of God the creator . . . there is his mark, his strength, and his voice which fills us with admiration."

Church Structures and the Holy Spirit — The role of the Holy Spirit in the Church cannot be isolated from church structures, the Pope declared at a general audience Nov. 24. He said that "one of the most lively problems discussed in our time is exactly that which seeks to make a distinction between the just relation between the visible, human and sacramental structure of the Church and the mystery of the Spirit, of which the Church is the sign and instrument, and from which we derive our Christian life." Many contend that the church "structure is allegedly an illegitimate or at least an unnecessary derivation from the authentic formula of the apostolic Church. It is allegedly authoritative, juridical, formalistic, and polluted by tendencies toward power, wealth and traditional immobility . . . in a word, it is anti-Gospel and anti-historical." The Pope emphasized, however, that in concentrating on the charism of the Spirit "one cannot prescind from the divine design . . . one cannot isolate the economy of the Spirit — even though . . . it blows where it will — from the so-called structures, both ministerial and sacramental, instituted by Christ."

The Pope Also:
• Met privately with members of the council of the five-year-old Anglican Center in Rome, Nov. 17.
• Met with Apollo 15 astronauts David Scott, James Irving and Alfred Worden, Nov. 17.
• Urged 80 members of an Italian women's organization to press forward with efforts to make women "always more aware of their specific and irreplaceable function in society," Nov. 22.
• Told Niger's first Ambassador to the Vat-

ican, Ibra Kabo, that the Church encourages its missionaries "to contribute with all their efforts to the teaching and education which open the door to human development as demanded by our time," Nov. 25.

• Advised a group of Italian workers in the mass media that their responsibility is to "inform and form right consciences toward sound judgments," Nov. 27.

• In a message to Jordanian officials, deplored the assassination of Prime Minister Wasfi Tal Nov. 28 in Cairo.

Vatican-Poland Talks — The Vatican and the Polish government "recognized the usefulness" of continuing talks on "problems of mutual interest," according to an announcement made Nov. 20 following the return to the Vatican of Archbishop Agostino Casaroli, secretary of the Council for the Public Affairs of the Church, from his third trip to Poland in four years. Alexander Skarzynski, director of the Polish Bureau of Cult, stated publicly several weeks earlier that a "lasting normalization" of Church-state relations would have to be built on two foundations:

• unequivocal recognition by the Church and the Polish bishops of the socialistic character of the Polish nation;

• recognition by the nation not only of the Church's religious activity, strictly speaking, but also of its role in the education of believers, "including the religious education of children and of youth."

Taize Representative at the Vatican — With the appointment of Brother Max Thurian, the Protestant monastery of Taize, France, became the first organization of its kind to have a representative at the Vatican.

Vatican Briefs:

• In a decree dated Nov. 11, the Congregation for Divine Worship authorized the use of traditional Latin chants of the Divine Office and Mass by members of religious orders until the adoption of new versions of the chants.

• An unnamed Vatican official confirmed rumors that a new law for the election of popes was being drafted.

Synod '71

The third meeting of the Synod of Bishops, in session since Sept. 30, was adjourned Nov. 6 after referring to Pope Paul the results of discussions on the ministerial priesthood and justice in the world. The Holy Father told the participants that he considered the meeting a "very important event."

Reports submitted to the Pope and published later disclosed that the delegates voted: to stand by the discipline of celibacy for Roman-Rite clergy and to reaffirm traditional norms concerning the sacramental and pastoral ministry of priests; to make work for justice and peace an integral element of pastoral activity and to stress the responsibility of powerful nations to promote justice among their own people and in other countries.

The Synod got mixed ratings, ranging from failure to limited success, depending on the expectations of various critics.

DOMESTIC

Priest Mayor — Father Roland H. St. Pierre, O.M.I., was elected mayor of Plattsburgh, N.Y., Nov. 2 in an easy victory over a Democratic incumbent. He ran for the office with the permission of his religious superiors after resigning his pastorate in the city.

Foreign Aid Rejection Disappointing — Initial Senate rejection, Oct. 29 by a vote of 41 to 27, of the US foreign aid program was disappointing, declared Msgr. Marvin Bordelon, director of the Department of International Affairs, US Catholic Conference. In a statement released Nov. 2, he said the action brought out "the worst elements in American society — isolationism, selfishness, greed, and the exaggerated nationalism that prompts this nation to opt narrowly for our own good, at the expense of others."

Prayer Amendment Defeated — A proposed constitutional amendment to permit voluntary prayer in public schools was defeated Nov. 8 in the House of Representatives. Although the vote was 240 to 162 in favor of overturning Supreme Court anti-prayer rulings in 1962 and 1963, the tally was 28 votes short of the two-thirds majority required for approval of a constitutional amendment. The text on which the House voted read: "Nothing contained in this constitution shall abridge the right of persons lawfully assembled, in any public building which is supported in whole or in part through expenditure of public funds, to participate in voluntary prayers and meditation."

Nearly all major religious groups in the country opposed the amendment. The US Catholic Conference did so "on the conviction that it (the amendment) would accomplish nothing on behalf of the goals it purports to serve and would represent a threat to the existing legality of denominational prayer."

Amnesty for COs — Father William A. Toohey, director of campus ministry at Notre Dame University, urged President Nixon to grant amnesty for young Americans who were in prison or in other countries because of conscientious objection to the war in Vietnam. Amnesty, he said, "would afford those in exile an opportunity to return to worthwhile citizenship in their native land. . . . would help bring together and reconcile the various parts of our disunited country . . . would also brighten the image of America on the international scene." In making his appeal, Father Toohey cited a request made by the US bishops in October that the President consider the amnesty question.

Inadequate Enforcement of Civil Rights —

Inadequate ratings were given 29 federal agencies by the US Civil Rights Commission in a past-year review of enforcement and compliance policies. Father Theodore M. Hesburgh, C.S.C., chairman of the commission, said at a news conference Nov. 16 that "most agencies seem determined to avoid upsetting the status quo for the sake of assuring equal rights and, if changes must be made, they often will be changes in form, but not in substance — changes in structure, but not in performance."

Catholic Educational "Establishment" — Father Albert J. Nevins, M.M., editor of *Our Sunday Visitor*, asked the American bishops to save Catholic education "by destroying the insidious and closed establishment that has developed since Vatican II." Writing in the Nov. 14 edition of the national weekly, Father Nevins disgreed with press accounts that all the problems affecting Catholic education today "boil down to money." He said: "Money is . . . certainly not the root problem. Catholics will find the money to keep their schools open — but only if they see these schools have a value. We are suffering today not a loss of money but a loss of confidence." He wrote that parents do not object to modern teaching methods. They suspect, however, that many teachers "do not transmit the faith because they no longer have it themselves." Father Nevins told NC News that he intended to stress in his column the need for each bishop to examine the schools in his diocese "to determine how Catholic they are" and what their philosophical foundation really is.

National Council of Catholic Laity — Three hundred delegates from about 60 lay organizations with 20 million members formally established the National Council of Catholic Laity at a two-day meeting in Cincinnati. They elected H.G. Rountree and Miss Margaret Mealey president and executive director, respectively, and seated a 24-member board of directors.

Teacher Strikes — Members of the Independent Secondary Teachers' Association struck the high schools of the Archdiocese of San Francisco in the middle of the month after rejecting a salary offer of four per cent raises each year in 1972-73 and 1973-74.

In the Archdiocese of New York, the Federation of Catholic Teachers struck the Association of (314) Catholic Schools Nov. 22 in a dispute over salary demands and insurance-pension-medical benefits. Forty-five per cent of about 2,800 lay teachers belonged to the union, which authorized the strike by a vote of 481 to 198.

CRS Aid — Catholic Relief Services disclosed that it had airlifted 37 tons of supplies worth $245,000 to aid cyclone and tidal-wave victims in the Bay of Bengal area. It was also reported that the agency had provided more than 65,000 tons of aid supplies valued at $8.7 million to East Pakistani refugees in India.

Msgr. Neighbor Resigns — Ill health forced the resignation of Msgr. Russell J. Neighbor from the office of director of the National Center of Religious Education — Confraternity of Christian Doctrine. The 50-year-old priest, who had been director since 1967, was suffering from virulent lateral sclerosis.

Anti-Poverty Grants — William R. Schumacher, chairman of the planning and budget commission, reported that the Archdiocese of Cincinnati had allocated $1,046,511 in grants to 112 local organizations in three and one-half years. Many of the organizations had been sponsored by other-than-Catholic bodies and by regional, community and neighborhood groups.

Rockville Centre's Diocesan Task Force on Poverty, Race and Allied Problems announced that it had funded 19 local aid projects with $35,924 from February to November, 1971.

Fetus Not a Person — So ruled the Ohio Supreme Court Nov. 24 in overturning the conviction of a man charged with vehicular homicide in the death of a seven-month-old fetus. In interpreting an Ohio law stating that "no person shall unlawfully and unintentionally cause the death of another" while operating a vehicle, the court held that "another" meant "another person," specifically, "a person existing or present from birth."

No Merger Now — Notre Dame University and St. Mary's College called off indefinitely plans announced in May, 1971, to merge the two schools. Officials said in a joint statement Nov. 30 that the schools "were unable to solve financial and administrative problems" connected with the proposed merger. They announced, however, that joint programs and collaboration, dating from 1965, would be "preserved and strengthened."

Sister Deputy Attorney General — Sister Mary Ann Burgess, of the Sisters of Charity of St. Elizabeth, was sworn in as a deputy attorney general of New Jersey Nov. 30. She was assigned to the state's Department of Community Affairs.

Domestic Briefs:
• Georgetown University Medical School announced the start of a program of research and clinical work to fight sicle cell anemia, a hereditary disease afflicting about 50,000 black Americans.
• Three thousand youths attended the convention of the National Catholic Youth Organization Federation in Washington, Nov. 11 to 14.
• It is impossible to be a Christian without caring for people's needs, Archbishop Humberto S. Medeiros of Boston said at a White House prayer service Nov. 14.
• Bishop Vincent S. Waters, who had earlier directed sisters in the Raleigh diocese to wear identifiable religious garb, made the same demand of priests in a letter addressed to secular and religious priests in the diocese.

Meeting of NCCB and USCC

More than 250 bishops attended the semi-annual meeting of the National Conference of Catholic Bishops and the United States Catholic Conference Nov. 15 to 19 in Washington, D. C.

The bishops, among other actions, elected Cardinal John J. Krol to succeed Cardinal John F. Dearden as president of the conferences; voted for admission of the press to future meetings; approved a set of *Ethical and Religious Directives for Catholic Health Facilities;* issued statements seeking tax credits for parents with children in Catholic schools and calling for a speedy end to US involvement in the war in Southeast Asia; stated policy regarding population problems.

(See Bishops' Meetings.)

FOREIGN

Anglican Dean Convicted — The Very Rev. Gonville A. ffrench-Beytagh of Johannesburg, an outspoken opponent of apartheid in South Africa, was sentenced Nov. 1 under the Terrorism Act to a minimum of five years in prison.

In a related development, the South African government rejected a call by churchmen, politicians, students and newspapers for an official inquiry into allegations of torture in government prisons.

Vietnamese Chaplains — One hundred and four of nearly 2,000 Vietnamese priests were serving as chaplains for 200,000 Catholics among the million members of the armed forces of South Vietnam.

Bolivian Police Excommunicated — Following an Oct. 15 police search of a Carmelite convent near Santa Cruz for Communists and subversive literature, Bishop Luis Rodriguez declared that the "main persons involved" in the raid had been excommunicated. He called police charges made in connection with the raid — that three extremists had fled the scene and that subversive material had been found — "a lie and a calumny." The raid was the latest incident in a series of harassments of priests and lay persons engaged in work for social reform.

All-Africa Conference — Members of the executive committee of the All-Africa Conference of Churches said in a "Declaration of Kinshasa" that they "are convinced that God has called the ecumenical movement in Africa to grow out into a religion of hope for our peoples." The statement also said: "We earnestly beg the Church to work with God for the liberation and salvation of the entire African people."

Terrorists of the Church — Theologians who attack the faith are "terrorists of the Church," Cardinal Jean Danielou, S.J., told a meeting of European Catholic intellectuals in Strasbourg, France. He said: "We now read that it is necessary to destroy the Church to liberate the Gospel. We reject that totally. Because, if we separate the Church from the Gospel, the Gospel becomes mad. . . . Let us have the will to defend the faith against all those who attack it."

Red China in UN — Delegates of the People's Republic of China, headed by Chiao Kuan-hua, were seated in the United Nations Nov. 15, taking places formerly held by officials of recently expelled Nationalist China, a charter member of the organization.

Celibacy — Bishop Johann Weber of Graz-Seckau said at a news conference in Vienna that it was a mistake to believe that elimination of celibacy requirements would gain many new priests for the Church. "Other churches that permit their priests and pastors to marry are experiencing the same problems in the recruitment of new priests as we are," he said. The Austrian bishops, he declared, "accept the Synod's recommendation to maintain celibacy without exception."

Five Jesuits to Sudan — Jesuit headquarters in Rome announced Nov. 18 that three priests and two brothers were en route from India to southern Sudan to take up duties as seminary instructors in Juba. Only three foreign missionaries had been in the area since 1964. The number of Sudanese priests there was 27.

Justice Probe in Canada — The Social Action Office of the Canadian Catholic Conference was conducting a "justice probe" of clerical and lay opinion concerning policies approved at the September, 1971, meeting of the bishops. The policies in question included greater openness in reporting church finances, revision of pastoral priorities, rights and responsibilities of youth and women, and action against the root causes of violence, excessive nationalism, and abuse of justice by multi-national corporations. Survey findings were to be used in preparing action proposals for a future meeting of the Canadian bishops.

Mason Praises Church — Jaime Fernandez, foreign minister of the Dominican Republic and head of the Inter-American Masonic Confederation, praised the Church at a continent-wide Masonic convention in Tampico, Mexico. He said that Masonry "fully backs the new social efforts of the Catholic Church" in Latin America.

Assembly of the Silent — Nearly 3,000 Catholics attended the third meeting of the Assembly of the Silent Members of the Church in Strasbourg, France. The central problem of the meeting was how to resolve tensions between reactionaries, who refused to accept the decrees of the Second Vatican Council, and conservatives, who accepted the council but felt that the nature and pace of certain reforms were endangering the faith. The assembly claimed 350,000 members in Europe.

Pakistani Refugee Situation Desperate — The plight of 9.5 million East Pakistani refugees was called the "greatest tragedy of modern history" by the Rev. Dr. J. Harry Haines, executive secretary of the United Methodist Committee for Overseas Relief. In a report to his church's board of missions after returning from India, he said that the continued pressure of caring for refugees could devastate the Indian economy and force the country into a full-scale war with Pakistan.

Priest Killed in East Pakistan — Father William P. Evans, C. S. C., 52, a native of Pittsfield, Mass., and a missionary in Pakistan since 1947, was beaten, stabbed and shot to death Nov. 13 near Nawabgonj, 25 miles south of Dacca, while traveling by boat to a mission station.

Radio Veritas — Canadian-born Bishop Gerard Mongeau was named head of a three-member committee in charge of a newly formed Asian section of Radio Veritas in Manila, The Philippines. The facility, for island and general Asiatic programming, was subsidized for a one-year trial period by Misereor, a German Catholic aid agency.

Compton Report — Cardinal William Conway of Armagh was joined by the bishops of five other dioceses in branding as "immoral and inhuman" methods used by the British Army and the Royal Ulster Constabulary in interrogating suspected terrorists in Northern Ireland. He condemned IRA violence as well as brutality by the military in a statement issued Nov. 21 after publication of the controversial Compton Report. The Cardinal stressed his "abhorrence of violence as a means to political ends," and said that those responsible for it "are bringing shame and distress on noble and just causes, and are acting contrary to the law of Christ." He said it was also his duty to condemn another form of violence—"the process known as 'interrogation in depth' as it has been practiced in Northern Ireland in recent months" by British forces.

Congregational-Presbyterian Merger Vote — The final phase of voting was underway for a merger of the Congregational Church in England and Wales (2,280 parishes and 166,000 members) and the Presbyterian Church in England (more than 300 congregations with approximately 80,000 active members). Voting trends pointed in the direction of merger.

Two Women Ordained Anglican Priests — Two deaconesses — Jane Hwang and Joyce Bennett, both unmarried and in their 50's — were ordained Anglican priests Nov. 28 in the Diocese of Hong Kong. Their bishop, Gilbert Baker, said the ordinations were in line with a decision reached by the Anglican Consultative Council earlier in the year.

Dutch Bishops Uneasy — Cardinal Bernard Alfrink of Utrecht said the bishops of The Netherlands "are uneasy about a possible legalization in this country of abortion." At the opening of a hospital in Deventer, he declared: "If we are not very careful about our respect for human life, there is danger that decisions will be made to eliminate human lives on the grounds of deficiency or uselessness ... Respect for the still unborn human life is not only a Christian principle but a general human attitude based on human values that man cannot neglect without abandoning his human dignity. ... The unborn life has its own rights, and for that reason one cannot say that a mother can decide about the life of the unborn child by appealing to her rights alone." In the background of the Cardinal's remarks was a statement made by the Dutch bishops at the beginning of 1971 in which they stressed respect for the unborn while also asking concern for mothers bearing the unborn.

Foreign Briefs:

• At the invitation of government officials, two leading churchmen — Cardinal Raul Silva and Archbishop Sotero Sanz, papal nuncio — attended ceremonies of welcome for Fidel Castro at the start of a generally uneventful 10-day fisit to Chile.

• Twenty'five Christian, Hindu and Moslem delegates participated in the Caribbean Ecumenical Consultation for Development Nov. 15 to 21 in Port of Spain, Trinidad.

• The International Catholic Film Office awarded its grand prize for 1971 to the English film, "One Day in the Life of Ivan Denisovich."

• The Swedish Council of Churches, meeting Nov. 16 in Stockholm, decided to invite the Catholic Church to full membership as of Jan. 1, 1972.

• Nearly 300 persons took part in the first National Catholic Biblical Seminar in Toronto, Canada.

• Good Shepherd Sister Rose Goodear, 63, was made a Member of the Order of the British Empire by order of Queen Elizabeth in recognition of her 30 years of work for the rehabilitation of delinquent girls.

• Freedom to conduct the affairs of their rite in a patriarchal system was the subject of discussion at several meetings of Ukrainian bishops in Rome. (See Ukrainian Bishops.)

No Place for Church

A proposal by Senator Danton Jobim, that the Church be represented in the Brazilian Council for the Defense of Human Rights, was turned down by the military government.

The council, despite its title and responsibility, has refused to conduct investigations of more than 100 publicly known cases of torture of political prisoners.

Bishop Ivo Lorscheiter, on learning of the defeat of Jobim's proposal, said that "it doesn't matter anyhow. In the council or out of it," the bishops' conference of which he was secretary general, "will continue its determined defense of human rights. In fact, it is better to keep out; once in, it might be difficult to bypass political pressure."

DECEMBER 1971

VATICAN

Lay Persons Must Act — Catholic lay persons must act to meet the demands of those who are oppressed and who thirst for justice, Pope Paul told about 50 members and consultors of the Council of the Laity Dec. 2, at the conclusion of a four-day plenary meeting that marked the end of the cuncil's first five-year experimental period. The Holy Father, who authorized the council to continue its work on an experimental basis, said that a vast field of action awaits lay persons in confronting social, economic and political problems, and that "the announcement of the Gospel is more necessary than ever. And it is important to announce it in such a way that all men may receive it and understand it." Lay action was stressed by the Pope during the year.

Offer to Mediate India-Pakistan Conflict — A news story in the Dec. 4 edition of *L'Osservatore Romano* reported: "In the past days the Holy Father has sent to the presidents of India and Pakistan his own personal message . . . Paul VI has appealed to both governments not to overlook any effort that would avoid a recourse to arms, which would be a bloody trial. . . . His Holiness has expressed his own willingness to help reach a just and honorable arrangement among negotiators and said that the Holy See is always ready to offer its own cooperation."

Original Sin and Mary — To understand and enjoy the "extraordinarily beautiful" feast of the Immaculate Conception, Pope Paul told a noonday crowd Dec. 8, one must keep in mind "the entire theological, moral and historical background of mankind. . . . For us believers, the scene to be contemplated is immense and dramatic. It consists of the dark background of the fall of man and of his entire progeny, including all of us. It is the history of the original sin that caused existing man to be no longer the true and perfect man God had planned and created him to be. . . . We do not think enough about this general misfortune which has altered and degraded the human figure and which lies at the root of our misfortunes and of the humiliating and troubled experiences of our moral psychology. But, behold, in the center of this scene of universal misery there appears an exception, an ideal figure . . . Mary . . . the favored óne, the blessed among all women, excelling in goodness, in beauty, in immaculate purity, the unique grace-full woman. . . ."

"I Love Jesus" — Even hippy "I love Jesus" T-shirts seem to testify that Christ is not dead, Pope Paul stated before a general audience Dec. 15. Referring to the Jesus Movement in the US, the Pope said: "American magazines recently published photographs of young hippies wearing T-shirts on which are printed in large letters the words, 'I Love Jesus.' Why, it is not clear. But, then, many attitudes of this paradoxical youth are not clear." He observed, nevertheless, that "an interest in Christ exists in our modern world, which is so marked by denying or at least forgetting him."

Pastoral Purpose of Canon Law — In an address to a group of canon lawyers, the Holy Father said that the "business of law" is "that the life of the Church's members individually or collectively be properly disposed and directed to the supernatural end which shines forth in them. If this principle is kept in mind, and if matters are dealt with in accordance with this purpose, then law would not be regarded as something foreign to the vital human condition, as something repugnant to human freedom. Law would be regarded as a safeguard, ever at hand for Christians to help them achieve their calling."

Ideals of Womanhood — To attain the "purest ideals of womanhood," women must be faithful to the "principles of a healthy morality," declared Pope Paul at an audience with some 150 members of the National Congress of the Italian Women's Center. He urged his hearers to oppose "principles that undermine women's morals and values, which have to be regarded as sacred and fundamental because they hold the real human and Christian features of women."

Desire for Knowledge of God — "There exists in the human spirit a deep desire, a mystical nostalgia, a certain predisposition to know more about God, a secret hope of reaching him in some way." The Pope told a pre-Christmas audience Dec. 22 that this is true despite the opinion of some persons that "scientific awareness of the nature of things is sufficient."

The Pope Also:

• Met for more than 40 minutes with US Secretary of the Treasury John B. Connally, Dec. 2.

• Received the credentials of Mendi Vakil, new Iranian ambassador to the Vatican, Dec. 16.

• Reminded 33 newly ordained American priests that they are "part of a fellowship, a brotherhood of priests who serve the Lord in every part of the world and in every generation of history," Dec. 18.

• Urged 250 members of the general chapter of the Society cf St. John Bosco Dec. 20 to remain faithful to the goals of their founder — "the education of youth, evangelization of pagans, teaching catechism, love of the pope, and devotion to the Virgin Mary."

Austerity for Priests and Religious — In a Christmas message addressed to the clergy and men and women religious of Rome, Papal Vicar Cardinal Angelo Dell'Acqua urged them to give examples of an austere way of life and to be visibly recognizable for what they are. He said: "It is necessary and indispensable that those who have the privilege and who have assumed the responsibility for a complete consecration to the glory of God and the good of souls give consistent witness by their external behavior and offer an example of the austere life and full separation from every compromise with evil wherever it shows itself."

Vatican Briefs:

• The Vatican announced a contribution of $2,500 to the regular budget of the UN Relief and Works Agency for Palestine Refugees in the Near East. The agency, funded for another year in the amount of nearly $19 million Nov. 30, was established to aid a million or more refugees made homeless by the Arab-Israeli war in 1948; it also provided relief services for later groups of refugees.

• The Vatican Press Office stated that a "substantial agreement on the doctrine of the Eucharist" reached by an Anglican-Catholic commission was strictly a "study document" that "commits for the time being only the (18) members of the commission." The statement said that the agreement "was not yet complete and that there are still essential points to be clarified." (See Doctrine of the Eucharist.)

Christmas Message

In a traditional Christmas message to the Roman cardinals Dec. 23, the Holy Father denounced war and violence against "weak and defenseless men." He referred specifically to hostilities and danger situations in Vietnam, India and Pakistan, the Middle East and Northern Ireland.

The Pope also touched on subjects affecting the Church and the world — the teachings of the Second Vatican Council, events following the council, the 1971 Synod of Bishops, the priesthood and celibacy, and justice in the world. He noted that some currents of thought — that "the council would authorize profound changes in the theological order and destructive constitutional changes" — repudiate tradition and challenge authority. Optimistically, he stated: "We remain open to the greatest confidence . . . that . . . sincere and deep love, with suffering for the Church, will be capable of bringing about constructive and positive results, through the cooperation of all — clergy, religious and laity — under the wise guidance of our brothers in the episcopacy, the successors of the Apostles."

DOMESTIC

Conference for Aging — Thirty-four hundred elderly and near-elderly delegates attended the Nov. 28 to Dec. 2 White House Conference on Aging in Washington. Recommendations approved during the conference asked for a minimum annual income of $4,500 for an aged couple and other assistance to the elderly, including greater food-stamp benefits, liberalized retirement laws, national health insurance, and reduced or no-fare public transit. It was also recommended that institutions caring for the elderly be required to "provide adequate chaplaincy services." Delegates emphasized that efforts to meet the spiritual needs of the aging should be made "by ministering to them in conjunction with people of all ages, as well as in groups with special needs," and noted that "special attention should be given to allowing older persons to share in the planning and implementation of all programs related to them." Catholic delegates included Archbishop Fulton J. Sheen, Bishops Raymond J. Gallagher of Lafayette (Ind.) and Leo T. Maher of San Diego, and Msgr. Lawrence J. Corcoran, secretary of the National Conference of Catholic Charities. The conference was chaired by Dr. Arthur S. Flemming, former secretary of the Department of Health, Education and Welfare.

Pentecostalism — Pentecostalism as a help toward the renewal of spiritual life in the Church was the theme of a conference at San Francisco University attended by 200 representatives of Catholic Pentecostal groups in the Western United States and Canada. Of special significance, in the view of Ralph Martin, a member of the National Catholic Charismatic Service Committee and the Word of God Pentecostal Community, is the Pentecostal stress on the "baptism of the Spirit" — a greater awareness and application to life of the gifts of the Holy Spirit already received in the sacrament of baptism. (See separate entry.)

Meals on Wheels — An ecumenical effort to help older persons in need of assistance, Meals on Wheels was set in motion in North Palm Beach County, Fla., Dec. 6 when volunteers from area churches delivered hot lunches to senior citizens.

Elks and a Priest — The Middleboro, Mass., lodge of the Elks dropped all charges of "violations of his obligations and conduct unbecoming an Elk" against Father William M. McKenzie, who had publicly opposed a "white only" clause in the order's national bylaws. The priest was informed that complaints against him were dropped after his accusers failed to press charges.

400 Blacks Get Jobs — A this-man-for-hire ad placed in a daily newspaper by a ghetto pastor, Father George Clements, resulted in jobs for 400 black men in Chicago. Father Clements paid for the ad with $1,000 borrowed from friends.

Black Clergy Aims — Marist Brother Joseph C. Hager told NC News in an interview that his job as executive director of the National Black Catholic Clergy Caucus involved "acting as a liaison between the hierarchy and black priests and brothers in the United States, as well as the black lay community." He said the caucus was seeking "more emphasis on action than rhetoric. We are developing a series of workshops to improve the expertise of the black clergy in the areas of pastoral counseling, community organization, educational development plans, and liturgy, adapting ritual and music to the black experience."

Racial Attitudes — The fourth survey of racial attitudes conducted by the National Opinion Research Center of Chicago disclosed that Jews had the most liberal racial attitudes, followed in order by Irish Catholics, German Catholics, and, collectively, German Protestants, Scandinavian Protestants, Italian Catholics, and Slavic Catholics. The most bigoted groups were white Anglo-Saxon Protestants, according to the report issued by Father Andrew M. Greeley and Paul B. Sheatsley. They predicted, on the basis of emerging and continuing trends, progressive improvement in ethnic attitudes with respect to integrated schools, open housing and racial intermarriage. Commenting on the survey, Msgr. Geno Baroni, of the National Center for Urban Ethnic Affairs, said: "It has been my experience that there is less prejudice than what the media and others want to believe. Therefore, I basically agree with their findings."

Vicar for Spanish-Speaking — Father Joseph T. Morales, a native of Mexico engaged in priestly work in the US since 1953, was appointed the first vicar for the Spanish-speaking in the Diocese of Saginaw. The appointment was announced by Bishop Francis R. Reh at dedication ceremonies for Our Lady of Guadalupe Chapel and Center, Bay City, Mich.

Agnostic Stays on Faculty — Fairfield University announced that Dr. Augustine Caffrey would remain on its faculty as an associate professor of religious studies. His ouster had been sought because he had left the priesthood and Jesuit order, and considered himself an agnostic. The university, his backers claimed, could not fire him in view of stated testimony that it had no religious qualifications for faculty members.

Guardian of Unborn — Fordham University law professor Robert M. Byrn was appointed legal guardian of all human fetuses between the fourth and 24th weeks of gestation scheduled for abortions in New York City municipal hospitals. The appointment was made by the state supreme court in action on a suit, filed by Byrn, charging that New York's abortion law violated the 14th Amendment to the US Constitution by depriving the unborn of the right not to have their lives taken without due process of law.

Byrn later asked the court for an injunction against all abortions in the state pending the settlement of his suit.

Doctors against Abortion — The US Supreme Court agreed to consider medical evidence on abortion from more than 220 physicians across the country. The physicians asked the court in a 79-page brief to recognize the unborn as "developing human persons" entitled to protection under the Fifth and Fourteenth Amendments to the US Constitution.

Capuchins Aid Indians — Land and buildings valued at $250,000 were sold for $1 by the midwest province of the Friars Minor Capuchin to the Keeweenaw Bay Indian community in Baraga, Mich. Father Rupert Dorn, the provincial, said the sale was a sign of practicing rather than talking about social justice.

Bail for Christmas — The Dismas Committee of the St. Vincent de Paul Society of the Diocese of Rockville Centre, N.Y., put up $40,000 in bail for some 80 prisoners awaiting trial so they could spend the Christmas holidays with their families. "The whole thrust of this action was to do something for poor people who were in jail just because they had no money," stated Luke Smith, executive director of the society.

Prison Reform — Archbishop Humberto S. Medeiros of Boston called for a concerned public to support meaningful legislative proposals for prison reform, in a Christmas pastoral letter. He emphasized that "basic to all efforts for penal reform is a realization of the worth and dignity of every human being, however obscured it may have become through circumstances, weakness or even deliberate malice."

Arrest of Lithuanian Priests Protested — Catholic, Protestant and Jewish clergymen marched to the residence of Soviet diplomats in Glen Cove, N.Y., early in the month to protest against the arrest and one-year prison sentences of two priests in Lithuania for giving religious instructions to children in their parishes. The group also sent a letter to Anatoly Dobrynin, Soviet ambassador to the US, in which they called the government's action "unjust, inhuman and contrary to the guarantees of religious liberty found in the Soviet Constitution and the Universal Declaration on Human Rights adopted by the United Nations, of which the USSR is a charter member."

Priest Reclassified for Draft — Both the mayor of Memphis and the deputy director of the Selective Service System in Tennessee denied any intent to attack Bishop Carroll T. Dozier by reclassifying a priest as immediately available for induction into the armed forces. A local draft board had switched the classification of Father Joseph Umphries, principal of Bishop Byrne Catholic High School, Memphis, from 4-D to 1-A less than a week after the Bishop had issued a pastoral letter calling for the immediate withdrawal of US forces from Vietnam. A spokesman for the board said the reclassification was made because it had been decided that Father Umphries' duties were primarily educational rather than religious. Bishop Dozier objected:

"It smacks of interference of state and religion when they tell me who is a priest and who's not." He maintained that the board was trying to "strike back at me because of my pastoral letter."

Vietnam Bombing — In a statement they described as "unique in the history of the congregation," 128 of 140 Holy Cross priests and brothers expressed "outrage by the decision of the United States government to renew the bombing of North Vietnam" during the Christmas holidays. The statement said: "We felt that this decision was wrong and violates the convictions of a growing number of American citizens. This decision represents a continuing pattern of violence, unrestrained force and deception which characterizes our nation's foreign policy and exceeds all acceptable moral limits."

Domestic Briefs:

• Father Clarence J. Rivers was appointed head of the newly established Department of Culture and Worship of the National Office for Black Catholics.

• Cardinal Terence Cooke received the USO's Gold Medal Distinguished Service Award for his ministry as military vicar for Catholics in the armed forces. On Dec. 22, he left New York for his fourth annual visit to service personnel overseas.

• Golfing immortal Bobby Jones, 69, was baptized and given the last rites of the Church three days before his death.

• Father John L. Wessel, moments after an hour-long visit with a mentally disturbed veteran of the Vietnam war, was shotgunned to death by the man in Mount Holly, N.J.

Teacher Strikes

A month-long strike against 314 Catholic schools in the Archdiocese of New York, resulting in the closing of two schools and inadequate supervision of several others, ended Dec. 21 when members of the Federation of Catholic Teachers voted 214 to 109 to ratify a two-year contract with the Association of Catholic Schools. Terms of the settlement were: raises of $200 and $400 for teachers with bachelor degrees in elementary and high schools, respectively, and of $600 for non-degreed teachers in both types of schools; tenure after three years; increased health and other benefits. The strike had less than enthusiastic support from lay teachers belonging to the federation (nearly 1,400 of approximately 2,800).

In San Francisco, a three and one-half week strike against seven archdiocesan high schools ended with agreement by lay teachers to accept pay hikes of 11 percent over a two-year period.

FOREIGN

Rhodesian Plan — The British House of Commons approved a plan Dec. 1 for eventual recognition of the independence self-proclaimed by Rhodesia in 1965. Key provisions included political parity of more than five million blacks with 250,000 whites, and ratification of the settlement by black and white Rhodesians and the British government.

Spanish Bishops — In an apparent compromise with Vatican officials seeking a change in Church-state relations, Gen. Francisco Franco's government agreed to the papal appointment of several progressive bishops to dioceses in Spain. The Pope, in exchange, named conservative bishops to other dioceses in a major reshuffling of the hierarchy. Perhaps the most significant appointment was that of Cardinal Vicente Enrique y Tarancon, who favored an end to strong church-state ties, to the Archdiocese of Madrid. Observers in Rome held the view that the new appointments represented a "mid-stream" agreement between the Vatican and the Spanish government as they moved toward revision of a concordat in effect since 1953.

Spanish Human Development Aid — According to a report of 1971 operations, Spanish Caritas collected and disbursed $6 million for human development works in the country, including more than 1,500 projects and services in schools, cooperatives, community and child-care centers, summer camps, youth programs, projects for the elderly and vocational training. Most programs emphasized self-help. An additional $1 million was allocated for relief aid to Peru, Chile, India and Pakistan.

Mutual Recognition of Baptism — In a statement released Nov. 23, Catholics and Protestants in Belgium announced mutual recognition of the validity of baptism administered in the respective churches. Signatories of the declaration were Cardinal Leo Suenens and representatives of the Protestant Church of Belgium, the Reformed Church of Belgium (two divisions, French and Flemish), and the Evangelical Community in Belgium.

Mexican Priest Excommunicated — Father Joaquin Saenz Arriaga, a right-wing extremist and campaigner against church renewal and social reform, was declared excommunicated by Cardinal Miguel Dario Miranda of Mexico City. The cause of the excommunication was a book written by the priest, *The Church a la Montini*. The Cardinal said the book "offers a collection of insults, unfair judgments and heresies against the Pope and the bishops of the Second Vatican Council." The author's principal assertion in the book was that the council and its sponsors, in advocating and moving for changes in the Church, left the Church adrift "and without a visible head." It was also charged that the council made "heretical" pronouncements.

Generation Gap — Bishop G. Emmett Carter told more than 300 school board officials in London, Ont., that adults are primarily responsible for the existing generation gap because of their failure to communicate "values to be loved."

Cassocks and Habits — In a decree issued by Archbishop Giacomo Beltritti, Roman-Rite patriarch of Jerusalem, the bishops of the Middle East forbade the wearing of secular clothes by their own and visiting priests and religious without special authorization of a local bishop.

Bangladesh — East Pakistan, under martial law and ravaged by guerrilla conflict since March, emerged as the new nation of Bangladesh during the Dec. 3 to 16 war between India and the national forces of (West) Pakistan. The war was triggered by Pakistani bombing raids on Indian airfields. Background reasons included hostility between India and the national government of Pakistan and pressure on the Indian economy by nearly 10 million refugees from the East.

Violence in Northern Ireland — In his strongest denunciation to date, Cardinal William Conway of Armagh condemned without qualification all acts of violence of Northern Irish terrorists. Speaking in his cathedral, he said: "To condone (these acts of violence) in the slightest degree, even in thought, would be to become morally soiled oneself. . . . The person who could shoot a man dead in his own sitting-room, in front of his wife and children, is a monster. The person who could plant a bomb among innocent people is a foul murderer. The same thing can be said of all the other horrible killings which have taken place over the past two weeks. Nothing can cloud our cold, clear condemnation of these deeds."

Status of Church in China Unknown — So stated an article circulated by Fides, the news service of the Congregation for the Evangelization of Peoples. The article also reported that the Vatican had tried to make contact with Peking in recent years but had received no encouragement. It added: "Even if Peking were to enter into negotiations with the Holy See, which is unlikely, under the present regime a revival of even minimal religious freedom can hardly be expected." The agency said that even the Patriotic Catholic Church, organized by the government in 1957, had ceased to exist.

Ban on Religious Literature — Czechoslovakia's closed-door policy against religious literature mailed from abroad was provoking a stream of protests from within its own borders, according to reports reaching Vienna. Demands for explanation were being sent to postal authorities by citizens who learned that bibles and other religious books mailed to them had been returned to the senders. The regime's reply, given without explanation as to how it applied to such literature, was that publications contrary to law were refused entry.

Rights Menaced in Chile — The bishops of Chile, eight months after issuing a warning that Marxism could lead to denial of human rights, published a list of rights endangered by the regime of President Salvador Allende. At the same time, however, they criticized opponents of the government who were not joining in efforts to create new opportunities for Chileans. "If you want peace," they said, "work for justice." Government trends, the bishops said, threatened rights to: "participate in economic and political decisions"; "share in goods and services . . . through a fair distribution of income"; "equal opportunity and freedom to choose options"; "education without economic hardships or ideological dictation"; "know the truth and proclaim the truth"; "freedom of association"; "end the perpetuation of monopolies by power groups"; "demand efficient curbing of violence."

Repression in Paraguay — The bishops of Paraguay denounced the repression of Catholic Farm Workers' Leagues by the Stroessner regime, the oldest dictatorship in Latin America. Evidence of the repression, they reported, included the arrest, jailing and torture of some league members, and government interference in league demonstrations and programs. The bishops made the charges public in their monthly bulletin, *Informaciones,* the only uncensored publication in the country.

Canadian Bishops — The editorial staff of the *Canadian Register* named the bishops the top newsmakers of 1971 because of their pronounced openness and dialogue with all levels of Church membership in the country.

Foreign Briefs:

• Jacques Maritain, 89, philosopher and author, joined the religious Congregation of the Little Brothers of Jesus at Rangueil, near Toulouse, France.

• The bishops of Bolivia, headed by Cardinal Clemente Maurer of Sucre, asked the government to grant a Christmas amnesty to its political enemies in order to relieve tensions.

Meaning of Liberation

In an address to the Seventh Caritas Latin American Congress in San Salvador, Bishop Luciano Cabral Duarte of Aracaju, Brazil, said: "We must make two things clear. When a Marxist speaks of liberation and is loyal to his ideology, and when a Christian advocates liberation and is likewise true to his Gospel, both are talking of two entirely different things. Marxist liberation stresses as a forceful line the economic problem of man, and dies out at the earth's horizon. Christian liberation places man in his full perspective, body and soul, draws its inspiration from faith, and its final goal and horizon is God."

In reply to questions from newsmen, the Bishop said the Church "definitely rejects violence" as the solution to socio-economic problems and advocates as an alternative "the determined, steady building of a more human society."

JANUARY 1972

VATICAN

Pope's New Year's Day — Paul VI received congratulations for his fifth annual World Day of Peace Message from UN General Secretary U thant, Orthodox Patriarch Athenagoras, and other political and religious leaders. In the 1,400-word message, which was released before Jan. 1, the Holy Father said that "peace is rooted in a sincere feeling for man . . . (which) we call justice." In line with the theme, he challenged: "If you want peace, work for justice."

The Pope started the day with the celebration of Mass for the 160 residents of Rome's Boystown. He told them that peace is "beautiful but difficult, (yet) it is possible and it is a duty" to work for it.

Cor Unum — The governing body of the Pontifical Council for Human and Christian Advancement held its first meeting Jan. 10 to 14 "to enable the members to hear each other's opinion about how Cor Unum should operate." Two of the 28 members at the meeting were Bishop Edward Swanstrom, head of Catholic Relief Services, and Coadjutor Archbishop Leo C. Byrne of St. Paul and Minneapolis. Cor Unum was established July 22, 1971, to serve as a super-agency for coordinating Catholic relief and development work throughout the world.

Pope Paul told those attending the meeting that he had set up the agency precisely "because the Church cannot permit herself any waste of the modest resources" at her disposal for relief and development work. He also stressed the fact that Cor Unum "is not to take the place of any existing organizations nor to diminish their administrative autonomy." This emphasis, it was observed, was meant to allay allegations that Cor Unum was intended to take over the initiatives, programs and funds of individual organizations.

Religion and Faith — Speaking of religion and faith at a general audience Jan. 12, the Holy Father said: "Man's passage from agnostic or atheistic ignorance to the recognition of a natural and necessary religion is a difficult . . . process, by the nature of things. The second passage — from a religious sense that may be sincere and deep but is vague and uncertain to a determinate religious truth — is still more difficult. It is motivated by an utter honesty of thought and life, hand-in-hand with a secret divine intervention."

Model of Modesty — Pope Paul praised St. Agnes as a model of modesty for modern times, Jan. 16. He noted that the 12-year-old girl had died "in defense of her chastity," whereas today the honor and dignity of women are often offended. He expressed "sorrow at the licentiousness which, through fashions and the press and entertainment, destroys the reserve due one of the loftiest and dearest values of the human person."

Orthodoxy — This is the first concern of the Church, Pope Paul declared at a general audience Jan. 19. "To those who urge it to make its faith easier, more in keeping with the tastes of the changing mentality of the times, the Church replies with the Apostles' *'non possumus'* — we cannot." The Holy Father warned against regarding revelation as "an evolution that is still continuing, changing itself and surpassing itself." He said: "The word of God, finally, is for us the Incarnate Word, the historical Christ, and then the Christ living in the community joined to him through faith and the Holy Spirit, in the Church. . . . That is the way it is. . . . In so affirming, our doctrine detaches itself from the errors that have circulated and still flourish in current culture. These errors could totally ruin our Christian concept of life and of history. Modernism represented the characteristic expression of these errors, and under other names it is still current. . . . Orthodoxy is its (the Church's) first concern, and the pastoral magisterium is its primary and providential function."

First Missionary Priority — Missionaries should give top priority to preaching the message of salvation, Pope Paul told delegates to the general chapter of the Pontifical Institute of Foreign Missions Jan. 21. He acknowledged that new problems had come to the fore in recent years, including the need for missionaries to work for the progress of underdeveloped peoples and to promote justice, and said: "These are problems which the missionary cannot disregard, but which can lead him to accept ideas and to adopt attitudes which are not in perfect harmony with the genuine nature of missionary action. Permit us, therefore, to recommend warmly the priority of the message of salvation in your missionary activity. The presence of missionaries in the human community to which they have been sent, their contribution to the promotion of the complete development of individuals and peoples, the frank and intelligent readiness for dialogue with non-Christian religions, the ecumenical spirit — everything — must be seen in relation to evangelization, which can never be reduced to mere sociological or cultural activity without failing in the essential purpose of missionary activity."

Real Ecumenism Not Halted — Pope Paul granted, in an address Jan. 23, that perhaps a type of "superficial ecumenism," or one that tries to resolve the problems of Christianity merely by fusing religious beliefs, has slowed because it "neglects its (ecumenism's) real demands of true faith and effective communion." Ecumenism "founded on sincere study and common prayer," however, continues to make progress, he said.

Pope and Orthodox Representatives — Pope Paul and representatives of Orthodox Patriarch Athenagoras of Constantinople — led by Metropolitan Meliton of Chalcedon and Metropolitan Damaskinos — exchanged greetings of peace in a ceremony marking the annual Week of Prayer for Christian Unity Jan. 24 in the Basilica of St. John Lateran. During the 50-minute observance, the Pope said: "We are all Christians. We have become through baptism part of the Mystical Body of Christ, which is his Church. . . . All of us have faith in Christ the Lord and all expect through him to be forgiven, redeemed and saved in the same vivifying and sacntifying Holy Spirit. Behold, the basis has already been laid for that ecumenical unity which we are ardently seeking."

The Pope Also:

• Named Father Edward Heston, C.S.C., head of the Pontifical Commission for Social Communication, Titular Archbishop of Numidia, Jan. 7.

• Had a 40-minute conversation with Prime Minister Dom Mintoff of Malta, Jan. 15.

• Named the first Tongan bishop in history, Patrick Finau, 37, coadjutor with right of succession to New Zealand-born Bishop John Rodgers of Tonga.

• Calling Rome a "cement jungle that is spreading endlessly in concentric circles around the central historical nucleus," urged city fathers to protect the physical and moral health of the Eternal City, during a meeting with the mayor and other officials, Jan. 27.

• Told a gathering in St. Peter's Square Jan. 30: "Christian unity is a vain hope if we ourselves do not have esteem and loyalty for the unity we have the good fortune to possess and the duty to live and to bear witness to. . . . It is vain to hope that the separated brothers will unite themselves to us if we are in discord."

Vatican Briefs:

• The Vatican and the Ecumenical Orthodox Patriarchate of Constantinople jointly published the *Volume of Charity*, a documentary chronicle of Catholic-Orthodox relations in recent years.

• The Congregation for Divine Worship stated in an article in *Notitiae* that liturgical regulations prohibited the use of glass tabernacles for "permanent exposition" of the Blessed Sacrament.

• The Vatican, in line with annual practice since 1953, made a symbolic contribution of $1,000 for 1972 to the UN Children's Fund.

Pastoral Canon Law

Pope Paul, in an address Jan. 28 which marked the start of the Roman Rota's legal year, said that canon law has to be revised to show that it is at the "service, ministry and love" of Catholics and aims at "the defense of the human person."

At the same time, the Pontiff challenged the attitude of those who argue for the abolition of canon law "as if faulty expressions of legislative activity in the Church were to justify reproval and abolition of such an activity." Other criticism, he said, stems from "a certain abusive interpretation of the recent (Second Vatican) council, as if it had loosened the juridical and hierarchical bonds which are essential in the Church." He acknowledged the need for "healthy reforms."

Canon law will have to be marked with pastoral concern "in its formulation, in its interpretation, in its implementation . . . but that pastoral note will have to impress on the law of the Church a more human character more manifestly aware of the charity that this law must promote and safeguard in the ecclesial community and in relation to secular society."

DOMESTIC

Priesthood Study — Msgr. Colin A. MacDonald announced that an 11-member consultative committee had been appointed to help an ad hoc committee of US bishops to develop programs geared to the findings of a $500,000 study of the priesthood commissioned by the National Conference of Catholic Bishops. Msgr. MacDonald, secretary of the bishops' study group, also announced the formation of a second committee of nine members to study the spirituality of the priesthood.

Project Equality — Bishop Bernard J. Topel announced that the Diocese of Spokane would participate in Project Equality, a nationwide interfaith effort to obtain equal employment opportunities for minority group members, especially Indians and the Spanish-speaking.

Abortion Prediction — Population expert Dr. Christopher Tietze of New York predicted in an unpublished study prepared for a presidential panel that 1,630,000 women would seek abortions within a one-year period if abortion on demand became legal nationwide.

Pornography and Obscenity — Bishop Ernest J. Primeau of Manchester called on the priests, religious and laity of his diocese to cooperate "toward the development of informed and articulate public opinion" throughout New Hampshire for the control of obscenity and pornography in films, television and printed matter. He said that "obscenity and pornography can only thrive in an atmosphere that is hospitable to them. . . . Our task . . . will be . . . to educate, to motivate, to inspire. It will be to uplift the society we live in through the power of the Word we preach and the example we show."

Fink OSV Executive — John F. Fink, with 19 years of service behind him, was appointed to succeed his deceased father, Francis A. Fink, as executive vice-president of Our Sunday Visitor, Inc.

Aid Law Unconstitutional — A three-judge federal panel declared unconstitutional a New York State law providing financial aid to nonpublic schools for the teaching of secular subjects. The court said in a decision issued Jan. 11 that it found no substantive differences between the New York statute and similar laws already ruled unconstitutional in Pennsylvania, Rhode Island and Connecticut. The law in question, which was adopted in May, 1971, would have provided $33 million to nonpublic elementary and secondary schools; it had been scheduled to go into effect Jan. 15.

Peace Witness — Six hundred Protestants, Catholics, Orthodox and Jews participating in an Ecumenical Witness for Peace Jan. 13 to 16 in Kansas City, Mo., endorsed resolutions urging that service ministries be demilitarized and calling on "denominations, churches and synagogues to announce publicly and transmit to all US Armed Forces personnel their support and sanctuary for all who refuse to fight and who refuse to continue to fight."

Religious Vocations — In the Archdiocese of Philadelphia, the number of women entering religious life decreased about 37 percent in 1971 (from 121 to 76) while the number of men remained the same (143) as in 1970.

Mexican-American Center — A Mexican-American Cultural Center was opened in San Antonio under the auspices of the Texas Catholic Conference. "Among the multi-purposes of the center will be to prepare Mexican-Americans for fusion into the mainstream of United States life while maintaining a sensitivity for their own culture and pride in their customs," stated Father Virgil Elizondo, director of the center.

Catholic Relief Services — Officials of CRS, meeting in New York, said they were finding it difficult to convince US Catholics of the urgency of overseas aid and development programs and of the need to support them. They reported that the ensuing financial pinch had forced them in December to trim a proposed 1972 budget of $6.1 million down to $5.6 million. They also reported that in the 12 months preceding June 30, 1971, CRS had distributed 483,000 tons of aid supplies worth approximately $154 million.

Archbishop Ramsey — Michael Ramsey, spiritual leader of the world's 45 million Anglicans, became the first Archbishop of Canterbury ever to preach in St. Patrick's Cathedral, New York, Jan. 23 when he participated in an ecumenical prayer service with Cardinal Terence Cooke and Greek Orthodox Bishop Iakavos of North and South America. In his sermon, the Archbishop said: "Far and wide we have come to realize what

the ecumenical task really is. It does not mean asking how may we unite our churches just as they are now. It means asking: How may our churches become more Christlike, more obedient to Christ's purpose for them?"

Three days after the service in St. Patrick's, Archbishop Ramsey received an ecumenism award from the Franciscan Friars of the Atonement.

Action toward Peace — Officials of the Leadership Conference of Women Religious drafted a letter urging immediate withdrawal of all American men and war materials from Indochina and "continued efforts to assure release of all prisoners of war." The letter — addressed to President Nixon, Vice-President Agnew, and Speaker of the House of Representatives Carl Albert — was part of a five-phase "action toward peace" resolution passed unanimously by the national board of the conference at a meeting Jan. 16 to 20 in Washington. The letter also urged "multilateral assistance to Indochina in the postwar period," amnesty to self-exiled conscientious objectors, and "generous pardon of those convicted under the Selective Service Act."

Harrisburg Seven Trial — The trial of Father Philip Berrigan, S.S.J., and six other defendants — for conspiracy to blow up heating systems in federal buildings in Washington and to kidnap presidential aide Henry Kissinger — got underway Jan. 24 with the start of jury selection in Harrisburg, Pa.

Berrigan Parole — The US Parole Board ordered the release of Father Daniel Berrigan, S.J., from the Federal Correctional Institution at Danbury, Conn., Feb. 24, 19 months short of the full prison term to which he had been sentenced for burning draft records in Catonsville, Md.

Guardians of Unborn — Two physicians, Maureen Fedeson and Richard Jaynes, were appointed guardians ad litem (for purposes of litigation) "of the class of all the unborn persons in the State of Michigan." The appointment, made by Circuit Judge Charles Kaufman, gave the doctors and their attorney the right to intervene effectively in a test case of the constitutionality of Michigan's anti-abortion law.

Family Planning — Natural family planning techniques are not as successful as they could be because of "ignorance of these methods by lay people and professionals alike," stated Dr. William A. Lynch, science committee chairman of the Human Life Foundation. He made the statement at the conclusion of a three-day research conference on natural family planning, in Washington. The conference was sponsored by the foundation and the Population Research Center of the National Institute of Child Health and Human Development. Co-sponsorship by the institute marked the first specific participation by the federal government in rhythm research.

CICOP — Social communication was the

principal theme of the three-day ninth annual conference of the Catholic Inter-American Cooperation Program in Washington. Some 400 participants agreed that the media had the potential to tell the full story of the struggle for human dignity in Latin America and among the Latins in this country, but were falling short of the mark.

Domestic Briefs:

• McGraw-Hill Book Company announced the acquisition of Herder and Herder of New York, publishers of religious and general trade books. The purchased firm, established in 1957, was a subsidiary of Verlag and Herder of Freiburg, Germany.

• Edward B. McConnell, administrative director of New Jersey courts, announced that public officeholders in the state could, but would no longer be required to, end their oaths of office with the phrase, "so help me God."

• Auxiliary Bishop Patrick Flores of San Antonio put up his episcopal ring as a prize in a fund-raising raffle for the legal defense of Aureliano Silva, a Mexican-American, accused of murder in Houston. The ring was returned to the Bishop after the raffle had raised $2,400.

Playboy Ad

A full-page advertisement in the January issue of *Playboy,* inviting young men to join the Order of the Most Holy Trinity, evoked this comment in the Jan. 13 edition of the *Catholic Standard,* Washington:

"Our main objection is that the entire philosophy of *Playboy* is hedonism, and that by paying some $9,000 for an ad in the magazine a religious order is helping *Playboy* to promote hedonism.

"It is helping to pay for . . . a consistent emphasis that this is the only life there is, so you might as well enjoy it with unlimited sex, good liquor, fast cars, plush apartments and all the other accoutrements that make up what *Playboy* regards as 'the good life.'

"*Playboy* may have spectacular circulation among the college set — the ad may even attract some vocations, though we have our doubts — but at $9,000, or even nine cents, the price is too high for a religious order."

The ad was placed by Father Joseph Lupo, O.SS.T., vocations director for the Trinitarians. He said the cost was covered by the gift of a friend of the Order.

FOREIGN

No Room for Dissent — Gen. Francisco Franco, in a New Year's message televised throughout the nation, warned Spaniards that under his rule there was no room for dissent by progressives, including priests, and that the Church must cooperate with the state. He said: "The state cannot stand idly by in the face of certain attitudes of a temporal order shown by some churchmen. Thus, the state will oppose any interference whatsoever in its sovereign functions. . . ." In the background of Franco's message were tensions which began to grow more intense in 1971 over negotiation of a new concordat that would remove the clergy from state ties; social activism by an increasing number of bishops, priests and lay persons; and a charge made in December by the Spanish bishops' commission on justice and peace, that "peace really does not exist here, because there is no justice."

Dutch Bishop's Views — "People must pay more attention to those priests who remain in the celibate ministry" than to those who leave the priesthood, stated Bishop Adrian J. Simonis of Rotterdam in an interview published in the magazine *Elseviers.* The bishop, whose appointment in December, 1971, aroused heated controversy because of his reputation as a conservative, also said: "We may have paid too much attention to the extreme progressives because they demanded so much attention and because we were afraid of their starting an underground Church. But that may be the reason now for our having a traditionalist underground Church."

Moral Pollution of African Society — The bishops of Kenya, in a statement issued after a recent meeting, called on the government, other authorities and influential persons to protect African society and culture — and especially children — from moral pollution. They cited the dangers of the "exploitation of sex as big business" and the "catastrophic avalanche of pornography, immodest dress and indecent behavior." They said these influences could lead to "the destruction of the cradle of our society — the family." The bishops also noted that "family planning propaganda is an insidious danger . . . and the unspeakable crime of abortion is now being advocated. . . ."

Spree of Eroticism — The French bishops' commission on the family, in a statement published in Paris, urged a political campaign to halt the "spree of eroticism" it said was degrading public morality. The commission attacked the "subtle errors that pretend to justify" eroticism and "the scandalous profits of those who exploit it. . . . The result of all this is a real obsession with the sexual that degrades love, debases emotions, and undermines all mutual respect between man and woman. The woman is especially the victim of this. She loses the sense of dignity that is expressed by modesty and becomes more and more an object of pleasure for man. . . . It is the reign of Eros and Mammon combined to reduce man to slavery."

Intimidation in Argentina — Members of the Third World Priests' Movement accused the rightist government of Gen. Alejandro Lanusse of waging a "campaign of intimidation" to spread fear among the people, following the arrest of one of their leaders. Father Alberto Fernando Carbone was arrested early in the morning of Jan. 6 and accused of collaboration in staging an armed attack three days earlier on the naval base at Zarate. Twelve Third World Priests said in a statement that Father Carbone was falsely charged and was being maligned by the government. He was jailed later without bail.

Church Mergers — Members of the Presbyterian Church of England and the Congregational Church in England and Wales ratified a plan to merge the two churches into United Reformed Church, with a total of nearly 250,000 members. Voting in favor of the merger were 1,668 of 2,280 Congregational churches and 14 Presbyterian regional jurisdictions. Two non-Catholic churches in India announced they had achieved full intercommunion.

Repression in Cuba — In an obvious reaction to recent favorable publicity about conditions in Cuba, exiled Bishop Boza Masvidal of Havana told Cubans in Caracas, Venezuela, that the reports tended to ignore repression and executions still going on in their country. The prime example of repression, he wrote in the bulletin *Mensaje*, was "in the condition of political prisoners there, who are mistreated, humiliated and tortured, especially those who resist all attempts at Marxist indoctrination."

Malta Negotiations — Archbishop Michael Gonzi of Malta was credited with playing a major role in the reopening of negotiations for continued British presence on the island. His flying trips to Rome and London for consultations with the Pope and government officials were considered the major initiative in forestalling a precipitous withdrawal of British naval forces and a related economic crisis for Malta.

Bangladesh Aid — Caritas Internationalis, with participation by 11 national Catholic relief agencies, set up a $30 million aid program for victims of violence in Bangladesh. The program was designed to assist the victims of a cyclone disaster in November, 1970, and some of the nearly 10 million refugees of last month's Indo-Pakistani war.

In a related development, Catholic Relief Services ordered 37.5 tons of relief supplies flown out of New York to Dacca, Jan. 20.

Another "Conservative" Bishop — For the second time in 13 months, Pope Paul appointed Jan. 22 a bishop of conservative reputation to a diocese in The Netherlands, John M. Gijsen, 39, of Roermond. The cathedral chapter reacted negatively to the appointment, saying in a statement that the Vatican had neglected to follow its "carefully prepared advice." The bishop-elect, according to an informed source, was not among the three candidates whose names had been submitted by the chapter to the Holy See. The chapter, however, asked the people of the diocese to have trust in the new bishop. In another statement,

the Dutch bishops expressed confidence that they could collaborate with him. Bishop-elect Gijsen was a friend of Bishop Adrian J. Simonis of Rotterdam, whose appointment in December, 1970, had occasioned controversy.

Funerals for Divorced — A second French Bishop, Gerard Huyghe of Arras, announced permission for the burial of remarried divorced persons. In so doing, he followed the lead of Bishop Armand Le Bourgeois of Autun who had issued a similar directive in March, 1971. Bishop Le Bourgeois told priests of his diocese to "welcome every request for the religious burial of a person who has manifested his attachment to the Church, whatever the person's canonical situation may be." He also said that priests should explain to the family before the funeral rites that the Church's intent is to pray for the deceased and not to go through a social ritual.

Foreign Briefs:
• Lutheran World Relief — the the overseas relief service of the American Lutheran Church, the Lutheran Church in America, and the Lutheran Church-Missouri Synod — reported that it had sent nearly 50 million pounds of clothing, food, medicines, and other supplies to 15 countries in 1971.

• It was announced in Ottawa that new translations of prayers common to the major Christian churches — Glory to God, the Nicene Creed, and Holy, holy holy — would be available for use by English-speaking Catholics at the beginning of Lent. The translations were made by the International Consultation on English Texts, composed of representatives of Catholic and Protestant churches in English-speaking countries.

• Two members of the Swedish Parliament nominated Fathers Philip and Daniel Berrigan for the 1972 Nobel Peace Prize, for their witness to the "right of the individual to criticize a government."

Bloody Sunday

January 30 turned into Bloody Sunday in Londonderry when British troops opened fire on a peaceful rally of 10,000 persons, killing 13 civilians, wounding 17 more, and suffering one wounded in their own ranks.

A British commander, Maj. Gen. Robert Ford, said the troops had opened fire only after having been fired upon. His view was rejected unanimously by spokesmen for the demonstrators, who were protesting the imprisonment without trial of more than 700 alleged terrorists.

Cardinal William Conway of Armagh, "deeply shocked at the news of the awful slaughter in Derry," called on British Prime Minister Edward Heath to hold an "impartial and independent inquiry" into the bloodiest incident of violence in Northern Ireland since British troops were ordered in to maintain order in August, 1969.

FEBRUARY 1972

VATICAN

Secular Institutes — Pope Paul, speaking Feb. 2 on the 25th anniversary of the approval of secular institutes by Pius XII, said that the consecrated lives of their members are "an expression of undivided unity with Christ and the Church." He commended the worldly status of the institutes which "reaches out especially to accentuate — as different from the religious life — your relation with the world." Noting "the destructive threat of secularism which exalts only human values," he said that secular institutes could help bridge "a tragic divorce between faith and life as it is being lived."

Religion and Self-Interest — Man's own self-interest can be used to attract him to the Christian faith because it offers him eternal salvation, Pope Paul told a general audience Feb. 3. He framed the statement in the form of a question: "Does not present-day theology gravitate toward the center of interest, the supreme human interest — the salvation of man, the salvation of the world?"

The Holy Father also spoke about the relationship between faith and love: "We are in the sphere of love if we enter the sphere of faith. There has been much talk of love when preaching Christian devotion. But we have perhaps not always realized, and have not made others realize, how enchanting is the discovery of God's love for us, and how it penetrates and pushes against the threshold of our desires . . . to make us feel again the need and the happiness of being Christians, that is, true men, men who have been saved."

Communicators — Persons in the communications media have a double task as witnesses to truth and as servants of those who listen to and read them, Pope Paul stated Feb. 12 in an address to the staff of Radio Monte Carlo. They have to be witnesses of "the aspirations and needs of men, of the signs of hope growing out of events"; and witnesses of "truth, of justice, and of all the moral and spiritual values which ennoble man." In addition, the Pope said: "They are man's servants not to favor men's passions or to tell them what they want to hear, but rather to educate them and to indicate to them what is useful for their human development, since this is a service that is truly for the good of humanity." The talk was one of several on the subject given by the Pope during the year.

Lenten Penance — On Ash Wednesday, Pope Paul invited all Christians to march in penance down the "tiring but joyous road of Lent" to the glories of Easter morning. He said: "Penance refers to sin and sin to detachment from the living God. This is a very grave theme which should always keep us alert, but particularly during the Lenten season, a time devoted to the reparation of the misfortune of sin." The Holy Father cited what he called the "nothingness of this temporal life," because man must one day die. He emphasized, however, that man saves himself by doing penance, by placing his faith in God.

Priestly Identity — Talking to pastors and Lenten preachers of Rome Feb. 17, the Holy Father said that the identity of priests and their role in the Church could be stated in the words "chosen" (by Christ), "disciples" (and teachers of doctrine given by Christ and through the Church), and "apostles" (with a God-given saving mission). He was critical of those who wanted to throw off "every clerical or religious distinction . . . in short, to laicize themselves" in order to penetrate society more effectively.

Church Wants To Contribute — Pope Paul told an assembly in St. Peter's Square on the first Sunday of Lent that the Church "is a school of religious faith, of honesty, of austerity and of decency. It wants to infuse into human society the sentiments of a noble and strong uprightness, of hard-working and brotherly concord," and to contribute "much needed remedies for social inadequacies."

The Pope Also:

• Received a first-edition copy of the *Judaic Encyclopedia,* in recognition of his spiritual and universal mission, from Amiel Najer, Israeli ambassador to Italy, Feb. 1.

• Praised the North Atlantic Treaty Organization for working to preserve peace and defend civilization, at a meeting with 58 graduates of the NATO Defense College in Rome, Feb. 3.

• Told a Sunday crowd in St. Peter's Square: "We desire that any form of violence be avoided by the parties concerned, from any side," in Northern Ireland, Feb. 6.

• Pledged continuing support of the UN, during an audience with Kurt Waldheim, its new secretary general, Feb. 7.

• Praised Cardinal Slipyi for his constancy, his dynamism, and the justice of his judgments, on the prelate's birthday, Feb. 17.

• While meeting with Stane Kolman, the new ambasador of Yugoslavia to the Vatican, Feb. 28, said: "The Church asks its sons and believers to cooperate loyally with all men of good will in the construction of a better world and of one which is more just and brotherly."

Ecumenical Commission — The Joint Commission for Society, Development and Peace, sponsored by the Pontifical Commission for Justice and Peace and the World Council of Churches, got a new general secretary, Belgian Father Joseph J. Spae, a new mandate "to carry out a role of service for the benefit of local churches," and a two-thirds cut in its budget. The three-year-old commission had been criticized for extending itself in activist educational and development work rather than limiting its efforts to the research and consultation functions for which it was established.

Missionary Think Tank — Delegates representing 29 bishops' conferences met with officials of the Congregation for the Evangelization of Peoples Feb. 23-24 to work out plans for future missionary activity. Archbishop Sergio Pignedoli, secretary of the congregation, said it was "the first time the congregation had ever met with bishops from all the countries of the world precisely as representatives for the missions." Cardinal Agnelo Rossi, prefect, called the meeting "a historic event which opens for the Church and particularly for the missions a new period of hope for evangelization." He added that the new think-tank group represented "a maturing of common action as the result of the dialogue undertaken during the Second Vatican Council and the Synod of Bishops."

Vatican Briefs:
• The Congregation for Divine Worship made public Feb. 17 an *Ordo Initiationis Christianae Adultorum,* for the Christian initiation of adults. The rite, dated Jan. 6, was to take the place of an earlier one approved in 1962. (See separate entry under Baptism.)
• The Congregation for Catholic Education, in an instruction sent to bishops throughout the world, warned that the study of philosophy in seminaries must not be watered down or supplanted by the pursuit of popular sciences. The congregation said it was alarmed at a lack of philosophical interest among seminarians and in seminaries, and stressed the absolute necessity of philosophy for priests as a study that can lead to the "supreme level of knowledge." The 12-page instruction, dated Jan. 20 and released Feb. 17, was entitled *On the Study of Philosophy in Seminaries.*
• Baltimore-born Brother Thomas More Page, 56, former head of the Xaverian Brothers, was named executive director of Agrimissio, a Rome-based service organization aiding missionary groups working in rural development.

Love the Church

The Holy Father urged all Christians to love the Church even when it may not be very lovable, during an afternoon Mass celebrated Feb. 27 in a working-class suburb of Rome. He said: "How did St. Peter Damian (patron of the church in which the Mass was offered) behave toward the faults of the Church which were then (in his time) much graver? He loved it and taught others to love it.

"We must love the Church all the more, the more it seems to us inferior to what it ought to be. Just as we have greater love for a sick person because he needs to be assisted, so too we must have great love for the Church in

spite of its infirmities, its weaknesses and its miseries. . . . The Church is human . . . sometimes even basely human, but it is the Bride of Christ, the beauty of Christ and the virtue of Christ."

DOMESTIC

Aid for Elizabeth Schools — The Board of Education of Elizabeth, N. J., adopted a budget that included an appropriation of $505,000 for nonpublic schools, which enrolled about 50 per cent of the city's students. Board president Albert Kopf indicated that "there might be some question as to the legality of this appropriation," but said he hoped legal questions could be cleared up satisfactorily. The money was designated for a variety of non-religious purposes.

Religious Education — A St. Paul-Minneapolis report disclosed that almost half of the Catholic school-age children in the archdiocese were not receiving any formal religious education. The report covered religious education at elementary, junior and senior high school levels, as well as pre-school, adult and special education.

Ex-Priests and Wives Club — Thirteen priests who had left the ministry, with permission of the Church, and their wives began formation of a new kind of couples' club with the advice and consent of the Brooklyn diocese. One purpose of the group was to influence Catholics to think positively about resigned priests rather than regard them as "misguided or emotionally disturbed" clerics whose marriages should be hushed up.

Black Officeholders in South — Eight hundred and 76 elected black officeholders in 11 southern states were in the following categories: state senators, 6; state representatives, 41; county officials, 111; city officials, 425 (31 of them mayors); law enforcement officers, 117; school board members, 176. Before passage of the Voting Rights Act of 1965, the number of elected black officials in the South was less than 100. The figures were reported by the Voter Education Project, Inc., Atlanta.

Unauthorized Liturgy — Bishop Clarence E. Elwell withdrew from participation in a two-day workshop in Dayton sponsored by the Leadership Conference of Women Religious after a liturgy he described as "wholly unauthorized." He objected to: reading by all attendants at Mass of the Canon, including the words of Consecration; reading of parts of the Gospel by lay persons and religious; in-hand administration of Holy Communion; inclusion in the homily of portions of Leonard Bernstein's *Mass.*

Brother on School Board — Marist Brother John Tevlin, 24, was elected to the Roselle, N.J., school board as head of a three-man ticket that hoped to restore calm to a community divided by controversy over integration policies.

Sacred Heart Devotion — The Center for Applied Research in the Apostolate announced the beginning of a research project designed to identify problems connected with devotion to the Sacred Heart and to develop "a national pastoral strategy" for promoting the devotion. The project, under the direction of Father Adrian Fuerst, O.S.B., was financed by the De Rance Foundation of Milwaukee.

Ash Wednesday Protest — Bishop George H. Guilfoyle of Camden expressed disapproval of the Ash Wednesday anti-war protest action of Father Michael J. Doyle, who burned a copy of the Pentagon Papers in an army helmet and used the ashes to make the Sign of the Cross on the heads of about 50 persons. Father Doyle, who was under indictment for conspiracy in connection with an Aug. 22, 1971, raid on a Camden draft board, was relieved of the associate pastorship of St. Joseph Cathedral he had held for three and one-half years.

Aid Payments Withheld — A three-judge federal panel in Philadelphia handed down a 90-day stay order Feb. 22 on an earlier decision that would have authorized payment by the state of $24 million owed nonpublic schools under a Pennsylvania purchase of services statute. Payment had been sought for services rendered between the time the law went into effect and June 28, 1971, when it was declared unconstitutional. The payment issue was on appeal to the US Supreme Court.

Minority Scholarships — Establishment of a $3 million scholarship fund for minority students at the University of Notre Dame was announced by Father Theodore M. Hesburgh, C.S.C., Feb,. 22. Sources of the endowment included the Ford Foundation, a gift from the Knights of Columbus and an oversubscribed university fund-raising campaign.

Nun School Head — Dominican Sister Elinor Rita Ford, 41, the first woman ever appointed to such a post in a major US diocese, took office Feb. 22 as head of the school system of the Archdiocese of New York.

Berrigan Freed — Father Daniel Berrigan, S.J., was released on parole Feb. 24 after spending 18 months in the federal prison at Danbury, Conn., for participation in a draft board raid in Catonsville, Md.

Divorce and Abortion — The American Bar Association, meeting in New Orleans, voted down, 170 to 72, a recommendation that every state adopt no-fault divorce laws but overwhelmingly approved a resolution for nationwide unrestricted abortion up to the 20th week of pregnancy.

Unborn Child Not a Person — A New York state appeals court ruled that an unborn child cannot be considered a legal person with the right to life guaranteed under the US Constitution. "We have seen no indication that the framers of the Fifth Amendment intended to include fetal life when they provided that no 'person' shall be deprived of life without due process," the appellate board said. The 4 to 1 decision was made on a suit brought by Fordham University law professor Robert M. Byrn, who had challenged the constitutionality of the state's 1970 liberal abortion law. Byrn promised further appeal of the case.

NAL and Catholic Schools — The National Association of Laity called upon the Church in the US to equalize religious education dollars and opportunities for all Catholics instead of concentrating on parochial schools. In a *First Annual Report on Catholic Schools,* the association contended that 96 per cent of church education revenues was benefitting 4.4 million children in parochial schools while only four per cent was being used to finance religious instruction classes for some of the 7.6 million Catholics in public schools.

Domestic Briefs:
• Bishop Sylvester Treinen sold the episcopal residence in Boise, Ia., and moved into a small apartment in a middle-class neighborhood of the city. He said that funds from the sale would be used for diocesan needs.
• TV comedian Dick Van Dyke expressed regret over an episode in his Nov. 13 show in which a nun and a priest renounced celibacy to run away and get married. He said he had received "thousands and thousands" of letters about the incident. "People thought it was mostly tasteless," he said.
• Cardinal Patrick A. O'Boyle was inducted into the French National Order of the Legion of Honor with the rank of commander, Feb. 3.
• Charlie Gehringer, all-time Detroit Tiger great turned local businessman, was named lay chairman of the Detroit Archdiocesan Development Fund Drive for 1972.
• Cardinal John Cody of Chicago was appointed a member of the Prefecture of the Economic Affairs of the Holy See.

Jesus Movement

Religious sociologist Peter L. Berger told an NC News Service interviewer that the Jesus Movement appeared to be "more than a fad" and was "a very strange development among middle-class youths of a secularized culture" because the movement's content of sexual puritanism and taboos "comes right out of the wishful thinking of Baptist home missions officials. . . . It's sort of a Billy Graham with long hair," about which sociologists had little data.

In another comment, Berger said: "Among the middle class there's been a lot of romanticizing that young people are more pure and more honest, that the kids will save us, the Tom Wicker *(New York Times* columnist) type of position. This is absolute nonsense — and also a little pathetic."

FOREIGN

Church Not Crumbling — Any impression that the Church is crumbling under widespread unrest is not accurate, Cardinal Gordon J. Gray of St. Andrews and Edinburgh told the St. Andrews University Theological Society early in the month. In an age of ceaseless questioning, he said, many of the disciplinary laws of the Church are being questioned and sometimes opposed, with the result that a distorted picture can sometimes emerge when the voices of extremists become loud. "The very fact there is controversy does not worry me one little bit," he said, "because surely that is a sign of life. If there were silence, then I would worry."

Abortion Assessment — A significant increase in the number of abortions in England — from 83,849 in 1970 to 126,774 in 1971 — was leading to reassessment of the 1967 law which allowed abortion for a pregnant woman who could get two registered doctors to declare that either she or the fetus was in danger of physical or mental danger if the pregnancy continued. Leo Abse, Member of Parliament, commented: "We are virtually having abortion on demand. It is easy to create consumer demand when one creates the atmosphere which permits easy abortions." Author Malcom Muggeridge said: "The figures are a shameful, a terrible, thing, but they were implicit in the act. The bill was a fake when it was said it would not lead to abortion on demand."

Euthanasia — The same advocacy type of journalism which won support for passage of a liberal abortion law in 1967 was picking up momentum in support of voluntary euthanasia in Great Britain. While the propaganda campaign intensified, many opponents of voluntary euthanasia feared its legalization would simply be a first step toward making it obligatory for persons considered personal or social liabilities.

Ordinations in Poland — The number of priestly ordinations in Poland rose to 480 in 1971, according to figures released by PAX, a government-supported organization. It was also reported that there were 3,131 students for the diocesan priesthood and 1,093 candidates in religious orders. Poland had 381 and 406 ordinations in 1970 and 1969, respectively.

Critics of Pope — Father Pedro Arrupe, superior general of the Society of Jesus, released a letter Feb. 10 in which he called on Jesuits throughout the world to be loyal to the Pope and took to task those who had caused damage to "the public image of the Holy Father." He said that loyalty to the Pope has been one of the special marks of the Society since its foundation. "We should proceed with that love and respect which we owe the Vicar of Christ. It is only natural that our tendency should be to share his preoccupations, accept his directives and collaborate in carrying them out." Father Arrupe did not rule out difficulties in accepting some papal directives, but he suggested that one who disagrees with the Pope should "determine whether a 'respectful silence' might not actually be of greater service." He said that "the use of pressure, public opinion and personal criticism is not an appropriate means to make known one's ideas to the Holy Father."

Social Change in Peru — Cardinal Juan Landazuri of Lima said the Church in Peru "is ready to cooperate with the country's revolutionary regime in its efforts to improve the cultural and material lot of the people." He reassured the regime of support after pressure from business and political groups sought to delay nationalization programs designed to place the country's resources at the service of the people at large.

Archbishop Released — Archbishop Vasil Velechkovsky, a Ukrainian Redemptorist who served as Cardinal Slipyi's successor in Lvov, reached Rome several weeks after being released Jan. 28 from a three-year prison sentence in the Soviet Union. He had been ordained a bishop secretly because of the outlaw status of the Catholic Church in the Ukraine.

Dutch Marriage Tribunals Criticized — The secretariat of the Dutch Bishops' Conference confirmed reports published in Amsterdam that Cardinal Dino Staffa, prefect of the Supreme Tribunal of the Apostolic Signature, had sent a letter to the bishops criticizing the permissiveness of their marriage tribunals in allowing second marriages of divorced or separated Catholics. Commenting on the criticism, the head of one diocesan tribunal said: "The Church has always officially recognized the rule that physical or biological impotence nullifies a marriage, and the Church has recognized that a marriage can be invalid because of serious mental illness at the moment of marriage. In the interpretation used by the Dutch tribunals and by some others elsewhere in the world, there can also be moral impotence in marriage. In this interpretation, a marriage is not merely a legal contract; it must be a real community of love. The mutual declaration of loyalty between the partners is more important than the legal document."

Dutch Statistics — The Dutch Catholic Social Ecclesiastical Institute reported from The Hague that 209 brothers, nuns, deacons and lay persons were engaged in pastoral work in 160 parishes, as of Jan. 1, 1971. The Institute also reported that the number of Dutch priests, in The Netherlands and in foreign missions, decreased by more than nine per cent, from 13,570 to 12,311, between Jan. 1, 1965, and Jan. 1, 1971.

Chinese Rites — Ancestor-honoring ceremonies were held in all churches of Taiwan after the celebration of the Lunar New Year

Mass Feb. 15. It was the first such observance ever ordered by Chinese bishops. Such rites had been forbidden, as fostering superstition, by Benedict XIV in 1742 in the course of the Chinese Rites Controversy which bedeviled the Church for more than a hundred years. The new rites were an expression of the traditional Chinese virtue of filial piety and respect.

Birth Control in Colombia — Archbishop Anibal Muñoz Duque of Bogota, chairman of the Colombian Bishops' Conference, objected to a US sponsored "Godparents' Plan" under which American families help Colombian children whose parents register with birth control clinics. He asked: "Why is it that aid from developed nations is always marked by neo-colonialism? This is an attempt against the dignity and freedom of Colombians." He also denounced priests who endorsed birth-control programs and "ignore the teachings of the Church . . . and instead falsify the Gospel and true concern for the poor."

Don't Forget Taiwan — In a statement released in New York on the eve of President Nixon's Feb. 17 departure for the People's Republic of China, 55 Catholic and Protestant missionaries in Taiwan called on him to "contract no agreement in Peking which does not conform to the rights and wishes of the 15 million citizens of Taiwan."

Support for Allende — Some church leaders in Chile were cautiously supporting President Salvadore Allende's Marxist government in hopes that it would fulfill his promise to help the people, especially the poor, according to Father Renato Poblete, director of a Chilean center for social action and research. He said: "There are some Christians who feel . . . that they must add their efforts to those ideologies that offer an alternative to capitalism."

The auxiliary bishop of Santiago said the Church was sympathetic but wary with respect to programs of the regime. "The Church in Chile," he said, "is watchful of those values in which there cannot be compromise — not to fight over them but to preserve them as essential to a true revolution: freedom, political pluralism, human dignity."

Aid for Raped Women in Bangladesh — Four international Catholic organizations called on the United Nations Status of Women Commission to take "a positive interest" in the plight of women and girls raped during the recent war in East Pakistan. The groups also urged efforts by women's organizations to collect funds for existing programs like that of Mother Teresa and her Missionaries of Charity in Dacca, Pabna, Rajshani and Khulna, for rehabilitation of the women.

Mozambique Bishops — Four episcopal appointments announced by Pope Paul Feb. 24 affected bishops in Mozambique, the Portuguese territory in East Africa from which the White Fathers withdrew 40 of their missionaries in May, 1971. Superiors of the missionaries issued a statement at that time in which they described the bishops of the territory as servile to government policy against basic human rights of the black population.

Anglicans Ordered Out — Anglican Bishop Colin O'Brien Winter of Damaraland in Namibia (South West Africa) and two other Anglicans were under government order to leave the territory by Mar. 4. The three were known opponents of the South African government's official policy of strict racial segregation.

Sudan — The Sudanese government and the South Sudan Liberation Movement signed an agreement Feb. 28 granting self-government to the South Sudan after years of bloody civil war and efforts by the Arab-dominated government to Moslemize the whole country.

Foreign Briefs:

• Bishop Joaquim de Lange and the priests of a mission territory deep in the Amazon region of Brazil refused to celebrate Mass for rubber plantation owners because of their refusal to change the near-slave status of their workers. "For a long time," he said, "we tried to open (the owners') hearts to their obligation of social justice, but to no avail."

• While President Nixon was conferring with government officials in Peking, Maryknoll Bishop James E. Walsh was in Hong Kong to break ground for a new school, started by a group of Chinese nuns he had founded. Bishop Walsh had spent 12 years in prisons in mainland China before being released in 1971.

Crisis in Zaire

Speaking at a mass rally Feb. 13, President Mobutu Sese Seko called Cardinal Joseph Malula of Kinshasa "nothing but a provocateur" and said: "As long as I shall be chief of state, and if the Pope wants to collaborate with the Zairean state, the Archbishop of Kinshasa will no longer be Archbishop Malula."

Mobutu made the statement less than a month after an article by the Cardinal in the January edition of *Afrique Chretienne* criticized his program for a return to African authenticity, especially through changing Christian names to African ones. After publication of the article, the Cardinal was expelled from a national honorary order and evicted from his state-owned residence. He left Zaire Feb. 11 for a visit to Rome and consultations with Cardinal Jean Villot, papal secretary of state, and Pope Paul.

According to some observers, the "African authenticity" issue raised by Mobutu was a mask to a broader move to gain full submission of the Church to his political aims. Others thought the government crackdown was restricted to the Kinshasa archdiocese.

MARCH 1972

VATICAN

Mediocre Ideal — Pope Paul attacked what he called the mediocre ideal of a comfortable life and said that self-sacrifice is the "true and highest measure" of love. He told a general audience Mar. 1 that Lenten penance runs counter to "our habits and our outlook."

Sin Not Mentioned — The Holy Father told a general audience Mar. 8 that there is a modern tendency not only to avoid "consideration of sin as such but even the mention of it," because the "notion of sin implies two other realities that modern man does not intend to deal with . . . the mysterious but undeniable reality of God" and the "metaphysical and moral reality" of the human person. He urged his hearers to restore "the correct awareness of sin . . . the sense of responsibility which rises from our internal moral judgments, which then . . . extends to our personal, social and religious duties."

Christianity Universal — "Christianity is a universal religion" that can enhance rather than destroy the ancient wisdom of other cultures, Pope Paul declared before a group of Japanese university students Mar. 13. He said: "Experience tells us that the light of the Gospel displays to greater effect the treasures of truth and right carefully and lovingly preserved in the heritage of a nation. It brings to sharper focus a people's ancient wisdom and gives it fresh vigor."

Nausea of Life — Pope Paul said that the "nausea of life" found mostly in more developed countries is evidence that "man does not live by bread alone, that is, by depending on those things which come from the earth. Man needs something which comes from on high, which comes from the lips of God: the word of God." He made the remark in a talk Mar. 19 at St. Mary of the Visitation parish in a working class suburb of Rome.

Priests' Associations — Associations of priests working within the system of church authority to foster spirituality and the brotherhood of priests were praised by Pope Paul Mar. 22 in an address to leaders of the Italian National Council of the Apostolic Union of the Clergy. The Pope also observed: "We well realize the difficulties your union is encountering today because of the widespread indifference toward official structures and even joining associations."

Praise for Young — Pope Paul praised young people for looking for new expressions of life and protesting against the "emptiness" passed on to them by their elders. While not approving excesses in the contemporary youth revolution, he made it clear that he saw behind it something more than empty protest and troublemaking. To thousands of young men and women in St. Peter's Basilica on Palm Sunday, the Holy Father said that underlying their anxiety he saw "something profoundly interesting, the sincerity of your spirit."

Passion and Resurrection — No aspect of Christianity reveals the "fiery intensity of Christ's love" more than his death and resurrection, stated Pope Paul on the Wednesday of Holy Week. He said: "Nothing teaches us better the gravity of sin; nothing teaches us in a more persuasive and consoling way that it is possible to turn sorrow into something of value, of worth and merit. But also, and above all, no aspect of Christianity reveals to us equally the fiery intensity of Christ's love for us."

The Pope Also:

• Gave $10,000 to the Faith and Order Commission of the World Council of Churches in support of theological research fostering the unity of churches, Mar. 21.

• Defined conscience as "the judgment that one has of oneself . . . with regard to behavior," not just a "fine, humane word . . . applied to any sort of thing in our minds," at a general audience Mar. 15.

Leadership — Recalling that Christ conceived of authority as a service, Pope Paul urged a group of French industrialists Mar. 22 to have a Christian notion of leadership in their business enterprises.

• Said he hoped relations between the Roman Catholic Church and the Rumanian Orthodox Church would grow in "mutual recognition and mutual trust," Mar. 18, while welcoming a delegation of Rumanian Orthodox leaders to the Vatican. He called their visit "a sign of a new era" in relations between the two churches.

• Met with Doctor Andrew Herron, moderator of the Church of Scotland (Presbyterian) in private audience, Mar. 27.

• Told Francois Guillame, Haiti's new ambassador to the Vatican, that the Catholics of that country "ask nothing else . . . than to enjoy religious liberty." In the background of the statement was a record of repression under the regime of the late "Papa Doc" Duvalier dating to 1964.

• Appointed Cardinal Amleto Cicognani, former apostolic delegate to the US and papal secretary of state, dean of the College of Cardinals.

Doctrinal Warning — The Congregation for the Doctrine of the Faith warned that those who question the full divinity of Jesus Christ are "far from the true faith," in a declaration entitled "Regarding the Safeguarding of Faith in the Mysteries of the Incarnation and of the Most Blessed Trinity." The declaration, which was approved by Pope Paul Feb. 21, was made public Mar. 9 (see Index for text).

Lay Recommendations — In a 124-page report entitled "Dialogue within the Church," the Vatican Council of the Laity recommended open financial reporting in place of secrecy, permanent dialogue that does not shun conflicts, and the shedding of "all triumphalistic, authoritarian and bureaucratic attitudes" in the Church. The report and recommendations, made public early in the month, were compiled during a week-long symposium of the council in 1971.

Drugs — Getting hooked or high on drugs is seriously sinful, according to a staff theologian of the Vatican weekly *L'Osservatore della Domenica*. It is not a matter of "grave guilt to take small doses once in a while that do not lead to addiction, but there is a moral obligation to avoid drugs, alcohol or tobacco that "harm our body and moral faculties," wrote Father Gino Concetti in one of the few moral comments about addiction in 1972.

Synod Suggestions — Major changes in the preparation and procedures of future sessions of adn procedures of future sessions of the Synod of Bishops were suggested by several Americans who attended Synod '71. The recommendations, which were presented at a Feb. 29 to Mar. 3 meeting of the Secretariat of the Synod, were for:
• a greater proportion of delegates from larger episcopal conferences;
• use of vernacular languages for discussions;
• attendance by priest-auditors "elected by the priests of a country" and by ecumenical observers;
• permission for delegates to change their minds about synodal subjects and to be free to vote in their own way.

Anniversary Observances — The Vatican announced plans for two celebrations featuring a panoply of peoples from mission countries, on May 22 and Oct. 22, to mark the 350th anniversary of the Congregation for the Evangelization of Peoples.

Vatican Briefs —
• As of Mar. 1, the 3,000 employees of the Vatican were eligible for both retirement pensions and terminal pay equal to their last month's salary multipled by their number of years in Vatican service.
• With the appointment of a pro-nuncio to Algeria, Mar. 7, and Tunisia, Mar. 22, the Vatican had full diplomatic relations with 16 Moslem nations.
• The Vatican announced plans Mar. 16 to put on display in 1972 about 150 priceless bibles and manuscripts as its contribution to UNESCO's International Book Year.
• International organizations wanting to call themselves "Catholic" must conform to guidelines prepared by the Vatican's Council of the Laity and gain approval from the papal secretariat of state (see separate entry).
• The Vatican's Information Office for Pilgrims and Tourists served more than 200,000 visitors during its first year.

Obligations of Priesthood

Pope Paul told 24 newly ordained priests Mar. 20: "Through the priestly ministry that now is yours you are likened to the Apostles serve the Church and the world with all your strength."

Calling the obligations of the priesthood a "cross you have willingly accepted," he said: "Whatever difficulties and trials you may encounter, you are sure of never-failing help and support, the assistance of God's grace, the communion of the Church, the esteem — and the good example — of the People of God.

"Therefore, we repeat: Never doubt your priesthood. Go forward with confidence."

DOMESTIC

Anti-Busing Amendment — Father Theodore M. Hesburgh, C.S.C., chairman of the US Civil Rights Commission, testified Mar. 1 that a proposed anti-busing amendment before Congress would undermine the "13th, 14th and 15th amendments which made free men out of slaves, gave these men equal protection of the laws of the land, and granted them the specific right to exercise the franchise."

Cardinal Suenens — Belgian Cardinal Leo Suenens made a nine-stop cross-country speaking tour of the US between Mar. 3 and 21. One of his themes was the need for continuing renewal of personal and community life in the Church.

School Aid Law Downed — A US appeals court panel in Burlington declared unconstitutional a year-old state law which would have provided about $800,000 annually in aid to nonpublic schools in Vermont. The Mar. 6 decision affected 19 Catholic elementary and secondary schools serving about 8,000 students.

Farm Workers' Contracts — Cesar Chavez, head of the United Farm Workers Organizing Committee, signed the first contracts of his union with two Florida citrus growers, Coca-Cola's Minute Maid Corp. and J. P. Hood and Sons. The contracts covered more than 1,200 harvesters. The Minute Maid agreement provided that minimum wages would rise from $1.80 to $2.25 an hour and that maximum salaries would range from $2.25 to $3.75 an hour.

Catholics in Philadelphia Public Schools — The number of Catholic children attending public schools passed the 100,000 mark in 1971 for the first time in the history of the Philadelphia archdiocese, according to a report issued Mar. 22 by Father Raymond J. Teller, director of the Confraternity of Christian Doctrine. The report said that 68,275 and 34,989 children were in public elementary and high schools, respectively.

Ethnics — Sixteen hundred black, white and brown residents of some 50 cities met in

Chicago to join forces in doing something about injustices they felt they shared. One of the targets was poor housing, and one of the institutions singled out for reform was the Federal Housing Administration. Msgr. Geno Baroni, director of the National Center for Urban and Ethnic Affairs, said: "The FHA is not responsive. We need a whole new instrument to deal with the housing problems of the central city."

Nixon China Policy — Four priests, who had been missionaries in pre-Communist China, criticized the President's China policy as desertion of "our faithful ally of 30 years" (the Nationalist Chinese Republic of Taiwan), at a St. Louis meeting of the 10th annual national leadership conference of the Cardinal Mindszenty Foundation.

Soviet Jews — Members of a Catholic caucus at the National Interreligious Consultation on Soviet Jewry pledged themselves to seek Pope Paul's intervention on behalf of Jews in Russia. Among Catholics attending the meeting in Chicago were Archbishop Fulton J. Sheen and (Father) Rep. Robert F. Drinan of Massachusetts.

School Closings — The increase in Catholic school closings after 1971 Supreme Court rulings against nonpublic school aid appeared to be less than predicted, reported Dr. George Elford of the National Catholic Educational Association. An initial review of 1971-72 statistics indicated a 3.4 per cent drop, about 386 schools, rather than 4.1 per cent, about 466 schools, as predicted by the NCEA.

Nonpublic School Enrollments Down — The number of children attending US private schools declined 23 per cent between 1965 and 1971, according to the US Census Bureau. "School Enrollment in the United States: 1971" reported 5.4 million students in private elementary and high schools, compared with seven million in 1965. Estimates from the National Catholic Educational Association indicated that 3.9 million of the students were in Catholic schools. In 1965, the Catholic enrollment figure was 5.6 million.

Alhambra Aid to Retarded — The 20,000-member Order of Alhambra, a Catholic fraternal organization, pledged itself to donate $1 million in 1972 to provide scholarships for the training of teachers of the mentally retarded and to help support organizations aiding retarded children. Since 1959, Alhambra had contributed more than $5 million for similar projects in the US and Canada.

More than Mergers — Greek Orthodox Archbishop Iakovos told 300 Catholic seminarians in Douglaston, N.Y., that church mergers do not necessarily advance Christian unity. He said it "cannot be achieved by any kind of Octave of Prayer for Christian Unity," or by decrees, organic unions and the deliberations of ecumenical agencies if its "seal and trademark" of holiness is missing.

US Mission Aid — Pope Paul hailed the "unfailing and most generous" help of American Catholics to the missions throughout the world, in a letter to Cardinal John Krol in connection with the 150th anniversary of the Pontifical Society for the Propagation of the Faith.

Teachers Contract — In a 30-month contract signed with the Secondary Teachers Association, the San Francisco archdiocese recognized the association as the sole bargaining agent for some 160 lay teachers and provided salary increases of four to six per cent in each of the next two school years.

NFPC Convention — Two hundred delegates from more than 120 senates and associations of priests across the country attended the four-day convention of the National Federation of Priests' Councils in Denver at which Father Frank Bonnike was reelected president for a second term. Among a variety of resolutions passed, delegates voted 128 to 70 to continue seeking change in the law of clerical celibacy but refused to admit the Society of Priests for Free Ministry to membership. (See separate entry.)

Two-Child Family Stamp — A US postage stamp celebrating the family planning movement — complete with a sketch of a husband, wife and two children — was called an "an unwarranted interference" in family life matters by Msgr. James T. McHugh, director of the Family Life Division, US Catholic Conference. he said the stamp, which was released Mar. 18, "endorses the two-child family, and thereby supports the position of those who urged the government to adopt policies that will put pressure on married couples to limit family size to two children."

Children's March — Approximately 20,000 children, parents, chaperones and supporters took part in a day-long Children's March for Survival in Washington against what they felt were inadequate welfare programs in force and welfare reform proposals before Congress.

Playboy Ad Results — Nearly three months after his newsmaking vocation ad appeared in *Playboy,* Trinitarian Father Joseph Lupo reported that 27 applicants for the order were under review. More than 500 inquiries were received in response to the ad, he said.

War and Amnesty — A two-day Interreligious Conference on Amnesty in Washington declared that the US government had a moral obligation not only to end all involvement in the Vietnam war but also to grant unconditional amnesty to draft resisters and military deserters. The conference said: "There can be no reconciliation until our government finally and totally ends all involvement, military and financial, in the Indochinese war. . . . Amnesty would demonstrate that America is still capable of a communal moral act."

Domestic Briefs:
• The Burlington (Vt.) Cathedral of the Im-

maculate Conception, New England's oldest, was destroyed by fire Mar. 13. Police said the fire was caused by arson.

• Many of the 100,000 marchers in New York City's St. Patrick's Day parade wore black armbands symbolic of mourning for the 13 Irish civil rights demonstrators slain by British troops Jan. 30 in Londonderry.

• Major Gen. Francis L. Sampson, 60, retired US Army chief of chaplains and an Iowa pastor, was elected president of the United Service Organizations, Inc. (USO).

• The due process system of the Detroit archdiocese, the first in the nation, handled 14 cases in its first two years of operation.

Population Report

Abortion recommendations made in the second of a three-part report of the President's Commission on Population Growth and the American Future drew adverse criticism from Catholic circles and mixed reviews, many of them favorable, from other quarters.

The commission, after releasing Part One findings regarding the impact of population growth and distribution on government services, the economy, environment and natural resources, called in Part Two for funding of abortion in states with liberal laws on the subject and for making abortion available through public and private programs of health insurance. In Part 3 of the report, the commission made recommendations concerning immigration, internal migration, urban development and population research.

FOREIGN

Persecution in Lithuania — More than 17,000 Lithuanian Catholics sent petitions to the United Nations accusing officials of the Soviet government of persecution. The petitioners said:

• Officials limit the number of candidates admitted to seminaries to 10 a year, and control the assignment of priests to parishes.

• Officials do not enforce a law requiring punishment for persons who persecute church-goers.

• Officials have not allowed Catholics to rebuild churches destroyed during World War II and have made it difficult to get permission for religious services in private homes.

Property Reporting in Poland — A decree issued by the ministry of finance annulled a 10-year-old law which required the Catholic Church in Poland to submit to the government reports of income and spending, and to deep detailed records on property, including sacred objects. The law had been a major cause of friction between the Church and the Communist regime.

Rhodesian Catholics — The Catholic bishops of Rhodesia were strongly criticized by many white lay persons for opposing the proposed plan of the British government for set-

tling questions concerning national independence and the rights of the predominantly black majority. One prominent African layman commented: "Our white brothers . . . of themselves as white first and Christians second."

Northern Ireland Conflict Not Religious — So stated Cardinal William Conway of Armagh Mar. 17 in St. Patrick's Church, Washington. He said: "The issues are social and political, civil rights and a united Ireland." In support of his statement, he quoted former prime minister Terence O'Neill: "The basic problem in Northern Ireland was the fear of the Unionist majority that the nationalist minority would one day outbreed and outvote them into a united Ireland."

Family Planning in Canada — Representatives of all segments of the Canadian population should share in policy-making for family planning in the country, stated Bernard M. Daly at a National Family Planning Conference in Ottawa. Daly, the director of the Family Bureau, Canadian Catholic Conference, said general participation is necessary because "policies touching human reproduction are at once the most intimate and global of matters."

Psychological Torment — Amnesty International, an organization that aids political prisoners, accused British-backed security forces in Northern Ireland of psychological torment of Catholic prisoners interned as suspected terrorists. More than 800 of nearly 1,000 interned since Aug. 9, 1971, were still in custody, it was reported.

Renewal in Spain — The Spanish Bishops' Conference voted to put into effect a number of recommendations made in the fall of 1971 by a joint assembly of bishops and priests seeking looser church ties with the government and stronger ones with the poor. The 51 to 10 vote, after a seven-hour meeting, indicated a strengthening of pro-renewal ranks in the conference and the continuance of tension between them and old-line conservatives. The conference voted to "conform to the Church's doctrine and spirit" in implementing the recommendations.

Lebanese Sovereignty — Cardinal Paul Meouchi, Maronite-Rite patriarch of Antioch, urged all Lebanese to uphold their nation's sovereignty and maintain its safety and security. He said he wondered how well these ideals were being realized in Lebanon "after plans have increased to make its land available to all, its gates wide open (even to Palestinian guerrillas), its citizenship easily accessible, its policy aimless, its relations unstable and its goals ambiguous."

Novelist's Lenten Letter — Nobel Prize-winning novelist Alexander I. Solzhenitsyn denounced leaders of the Russian Orthodox Church in the Soviet Union for not opposing anti-religious policies of the country's "atheistic dictatorship." In a letter circulating in

Moscow and addressed to Russian Orthodox Patriarch Pimen and all Russia, the novelist cited restrictions on the rights of priests, church closings and the repression of dissident clergymen as examples of submission by Orthodox officials to the government. He said: "The Russian Church has an indignant opinion about every evil in distant Asia and Africa, but none ever about domestic ills. We are losing our last traces and signs as a Christian people."

Priests Expelled from Peru and Paraguay — The Peruvian ministry of the interior Mar. 1 deported as "social agitators" two foreign priests and a Brazilian sociologist whom the national news magazine *Oiga* said "were simply denouncing rampant social injustices in the country."

Paraguayan police deported Jesuit Father Vicente Barreto on charges of subversion after manhandling and insulting him, according to his superiors. The real charge was his involvement in work for the improvement of conditions among farm workers. He was one of the latest casualties of the strong-arm regime of Gen. Alfredo Stroessner, dictator since 1954.

Argentine Farm Workers — Bishop Alberto Devoto of Goya said that he and six other bishops who were supporting farm workers' leagues in northeastern Argentina were not agitators, as charged in an editorial appearing in *La Prensa,* the Buenos Aires newspaper. Observers said the paper's position reflected anti-change attitudes of those with wealth and power who feared action for social reform.

Christians for Socialism — Chilean Cardinal Raul Silva told a leftist group of priests he definitely could not sponsor their continent-wide efforts in support of a Marxist revolution. Answering an invitation from Jesuit Father Gonzalo Arroyo, a leader of the Christians for Socialism movement in Santiago, he said the group "is out of line with the Church and says and does things totally in conflict with recent teachings of the Chilean Bishops' Conference."

Marxist Revolution — Impressed by economic, sociial and political achievements they observed during three weeks in Cuba, nine priests and three seminarians from Chile appealed to Christians throughout Latin America to join the Marxist revolution. The clerics were members of Christians for Socialism.

Hungarian Appointments — Vatican negotiations with Hungary resulted in the appointment of two apostolic administrators and two auxiliary bishops to dioceses in that country. The nature of the appointments (of administrators rather than bishops) indicated that full agreement had not yet been reached with the Communist regime.

Less Taiwan Conversions — Lack of clear-cut apostolic objectives on the part of many priests and sisters was cited as one reason for the decrease in local conversions in the past few years, according to observers in Taiwan. Conversions were reported falling off quite rapidly from the annual average of 17,000 during the 10 years before 1965.

Foreign Briefs:
• The ecumenical Christian Institute of South Africa reported that the South African government had penalized or acted against more than 80 clergymen since the beginning of 1968.

• About 60 provincial superiors of the Friars Minor, the Capuchins, the Conventuals and the Third Order Regular conferred at Assisi Mar. 7 and 8 on collaboration in pastoral and cultural work and in the education of young Franciscans.

• A Swedish parliamentary commission recommended that the Swedish Lutheran State Church, set up by King Gustav Vasa in 1527, be separated from the state in 1983.

• Views opposing unrestricted abortion in Sweden, which was recommended in a government report, were called "vulgar Christian propaganda" and "hair-splitting" by Lutheran Bishop Ingmar Stroem of Stockholm. Catholic Bishop John E. Taylor, in a letter to the minister of justice, said: "The report cannot possibly be used as a basis for new legislation."

Theologians' Manifesto

In a manifesto issued late in the month and circulated widely in newspapers in several countries, 33 theologians from Europe and North and South America blamed the Church's alleged crisis of leadership and confidence on bishops and ecclesiastical structures they considered obsolete. They urged Catholics to contest the structures and the leadership of the bishops, and to act for change either inside or outside of the institutional Church.

The Madrid daily, *Nuevo Diario,* called the manifesto "as harsh a challenge to the Church as the theses Luther nailed on a church door at Wittenberg four centuries ago." Its contestation thesis was particularly objectionable.

Cardinal Gabriel Garrone, prefect of the Congregation for Catholic Education, viewed the statement as a public appeal for resistance to decisions of the pope and bishops. He also observed in a front-page editorial in *L'Osservatore Romano:* "It takes a good dose of presumption (for the authors) to believe themselves the authentic witnesses of the Gospel against those who are responsible for the faith."

Signers of "Against Discouragement in the Church" included Fathers Hans Kung of Switzerland and Gregory Baum, O.S.A., of Canada, and Americans Richard McBrien of Boston, John L. McKenzie of Chicago, Gerard S. Sloyan and Mr. Leonard Swidler of Philadelphia.

APRIL 1972

VATICAN

Churches of Silence — Pope Paul addressed a special message to the persecuted churches of silence on Easter Sunday, saying: "In many vast regions of the earth there still exist or, rather, there still languish, those humble undaunted communities or individual faithful who are denied a legitimate and by no means subversive existence in the free establishment and expression of their religious and churchly life. Let these individuals know, let those restricted and oppressed churches know ... that they are not forgotten. They are assured of our solidarity in faith and love, together with our prayers and the hope we share in the risen Christ."

Easter Joy — Commenting on the meaning of Easter for Christians, Pope Paul told a gathering in St. Peter's Square Apr. 9: "So many sad things are happening around us. There is still the fury of arms, and organized and overpowering delinquency on all sides. Ideologies of every stripe vie with each other to capture public opinion. Some claim that not only the energies but also the principles and possibilities of good are failing. Indeed, in the very midst of the Catholic people some profess an habitual pessimism while others stir up an intolerance even within the bosom of the Church." Despite all this, pessimism and intolerance have no place in the lives of Christians regenerated by Easter. The Pope concluded by asking that "each of us do all the good we can in concord and peace. Let us intensify our good works! Let us always live happily in Easter joy."

Democracy Is Difficult — This was the reminder given by Pope Paul to representatives of Europe's Christian Democrat parties early in the month. He said: "It is a question principally of giving the right place to liberty, to personal initiative, to the rights of persons and families and intermediary bodies, without ever failing to harmonize them with duties, with the demands of the common good, of order and of solidarity. In sum, a sense of responsibility must be created at every level." The Pope emphasized that neither the Church nor its visible head is "tied to any political system, nor to any political party." He also stressed the mutual independence and autonomy of the church community and the political community.

Church Concerns — The Church is concerned "for the development of the whole man and all men ... is anguished by the drama of world hunger ... is worried as well by the abyss that ... seems to be widening between industrial countries and countries that are still rural economies." So stated Pope Paul at a meeting with scientists, Apr. 15, attending a study week sponsored by the Pontifical Academy of Sciences. He told the scientists that the Church "expects much from your research as contributions to the solution of these problems."

Renewal Tension — The Christian is caught in a two-way tension between continuous renewal and a firm commitment to unchangeable faith, Pope Paul told a general audience of 8,000 persons Apr. 25. For the Christian, he said, continuous renewal is required along with firmness in faith, hope and charity. This "anxiousness for consistency and for Christian authenticity, combined with the tension of exploring the inexhaustible reaches of revealed truth ... must be one of the constant desires of the authentic Christian."

The Pope Also:

• Sent his condolences to the Russian Orthodox community of the Georgian Soviet Socialist Republic on learning of the death Apr. 7 of their Patriarch, Ephrem II.

• Received 400 members of the Catholic Fraternity of the Sick and the Handicapped, from a dozen countries of Europe, Africa and South America, Apr. 8.

• Commended a group of Italian draftees and their chaplains for responding to the service of "the common good of the entire nation," Apr. 12.

• Told a general audience that Christians must give witness to the Resurrection by spreading the Gospel on which faith can be founded, Apr. 12.

• Sent a message of sympathy to the people of Iran, where an estimated 4,000 persons were killed in an earthquake.

• Said justice demands that the world's poor nations be given a voice in decisions affecting their economic life, in a message to the United Nations Conference on Trade and Development (UNCTAD), meeting in Santiago, Chile.

• Sent President Nixon a telegram in which he congratulated "the courageous crew" of Apollo 16 on the completion of their mission to the moon.

Vocation Decline—The decline in priestly and religious vocations is linked to the crisis of the priesthood and the faith in general, said Cardinal Gabriel Garrone, prefect of the Congregation for Catholic Education, in an interview on Radio Vatican. He said that many Catholic young men think about entering the priesthood but that the world in which they live does not help them respond to the call, nor can they conceive it clearly. Despite this, he insisted that those who are engaged in recruiting candidates for the priesthood must realize that "there are no excuses which would authorize us to lose courage." The Cardinal spoke in connection with a Day of Prayer for Vocation Apr. 23.

Sex Education — Current soaring abortion rates cry out for "proper sexual education in the schools" and medical, psychological and social help for "women faced with the problem of an unwanted maternity," according to a commentator on Vatican Radio. The commentator also objected to "an inexplicable kind of false puritanism" that opposed any sexual education in schools.

Vatican Briefs:

• A treaty to ban bacteriological, biological and toxic warfare, signed by 46 nations Apr. 10 in Moscow, was praised by *L'Osservatore Romano* as a "significant step on the road to disarmament." The paper said the treaty "is the foundation stone of that desired, but still far-off, guaranteed and effective peace."

• Federico Alessandrini, veteran staff member and former editor of *L'Osservatore Romano*, was named permanent press spokesman of the Vatican.

• The Vatican gardens were opened to guided tours for the public four days a week.

Resurrection

Christ's Resurrection was not "the ecstatic visionary imagination of some inconsolable women," the Holy Father told a general audience Apr. 5. "He really arose in his very own humanity."

The Pope called attention to two things.

"First, Jesus arose with the same body he had taken from the Virgin Mary, but in a new condition, vivified by a new and immortal animation which imparts to Christ's physical flesh the laws and the energies of the Spirit. This marvel does not nullify the reality, but rather constitutes the new reality.

"Second, this new reality, which is documented in the unimpugnable proofs of the Gospel and then of the Church living through such testimony, is so far above our ability to understand and even to imagine that only through faith can our spirit grasp it."

In another reflection on the meaning of Easter, the Holy Father said at a general audience Apr. 19 that, although a Christian may suffer in this world, his joy in the risen Christ will keep him from being pessimistic.

DOMESTIC

General Absolution — Communal absolution on a limited scale was authorized in several parishes of the Juneau diocese as a way of encouraging people to receive the sacrament of penance. The difficulty "for the penitent in a small isolated community to preserve anonymity" was one of the reasons cited by Bishop Francis T. Hurley in granting the permission. It was made clear that recipients of general absolution had the obligation of confessing serious sins in a subsequent confession. (See separate entry.)

Desegregation Suit — The families of 43 black children asked for court action to force the Alexandria (La.) diocese to integrate its school system by September or lose tax-exempt status and any federal school aid. The

suit maintained tet the diocesan system was segregated, had "served as a haven for white families fleeing public school desegregation orders," and had in effect undermined the public school desegregation orders of federal courts.

In reaction, Msgr. Richard Mouton, Lafayette superintendent, said: "I don't think we should be put on the defensive in this problem. I know how hard we've worked, and I know how much progress we've made." Bishop Robert E. Tracy of Baton Rouge commented: "The diocese of Baton Route has no segregated facilities, no dual school system, no discrimination in its policies, and has never experienced undue delay in acting on these matters."

A presidential commission on school finances reported later in the month that Catholic schools in Louisiana "have been making significant but discouragingly slow progress toward racial integration among students and teachers."

Berrigan Verdict — The 10-week trial of the Harrisburg Seven ended with a deadlocked jury and both sides claiming their own version of victory. Sister Elizabeth McAlister and Father Philip Berrigan, S.S.J., were found guilty April 5 of seven counts of smuggling letters in and out of Lewisburg Federal Prison, but 10 of the 12 jurors rejected the government's key charge of conspiracy to kidnap presidential aide Henry Kissinger and sabotage government facilities in Washington. Five other defendants were set free. The jury was dismissed when it failed to reach a unanimous verdict after 60 hours of deliberation.

President's Promise — President Nixon promised Catholic educators that he would recommend to Congress "specific measures designed to preserve the nonpublic school system in the US," in a surprise address Apr. 6 at the convention of the National Catholic Educational Association in Philadeophia. He said he was "irrevocably committed" to helping religious and private schools stay open and solvent.

In a related development, a presidential panel on nonpublic education recommended that the federal government aid nonpublic schools with construction loans, tuition subsidies for poor families, and tax credits for families of middle-class income.

Clergyman of the Year — Father Theodore M. Hesburgh, C.S.C., was named Clergyman of the Year by Religious Heritage of America, an organization dedicated to preserving America's Judaeo-Christian heritage and working "to instill its principles and ethics into all areas of American life." Father Hesburgh is president of Notre Dame University and a member of the national Commission on Civil Rights and the United Negro College Fund.

Jesuit Land to Indians — The Jesuits gave

nearly 1,200 acres, including the campus and 12 buildings of St. Marys College, to the Prairie Band Pottawatomi Indians in Kansas, for use in developing programs to advance self-determination among Indians.

Boys Town Finances — The Sun Newspapers of Omaha reported in a copyrighted story that Father Flanagan's Boys Town, a tax exempt religious institution, had accumulated stocks, bonds and other assets with an estimated worth of $209 million.

Birth Control — Five Protestant leaders called an "affront to Christians" a statement issued by Archbishop Humberto Medeiros of Boston in criticism of any liberalization of birth control legislation in Massachusetts. The Archbishop's criticism was made known before and after the Mar. 22 Supreme Court ruling that single people had the same right as married couples to birth control devices — a ruling which struck down the Massachusetts law barring the dissemination of contraceptives to single persons. In a letter to the state legislature, Archbishop Medeiros described birth control proponents as "advocates of death."

Bishops' Meeting — Two hundred and thirty-seven bishops attended the semiannual meeting of the National Conference of Catholic Bishops Apr. 11 to 13 in Atlanta. Among other actions, they took sharp exception to pro-abortion and some other recommendations of the National Commission on Population Growth and the American Future; approved plans for developing a National Catechetical Directory; endorsed measures relating to reorganization of the US Catholic Conference and budgetary cutbacks. (See separate entry.)

Abortion Law Unconstitutional — Declaring that a woman has the free choice to decide whether or not she wants to bear a child, a three-judge federal panel ruled two-to-one that Connecticut's abortion statute was unconstitutional. In response, a spokesman for the Hartford archdiocese asked the state to contest the ruling, in order to "defend the absolute God-given right of the child over a mother's false absolute freedom to take her own child's life away."

Uniform Abortion Act — A national convention of diocesan attorneys, meeting in Washington, unanimously condemned the Uniform Abortion Act approved two months earlier by the American Bar Association. The ABA proposal was faulted for encouraging unrestricted abortion up to the 20th week of pregnancy and as a danger to the constitutional rights of the unborn.

Sterilization Suits — The Association for Voluntary Sterilization — in cooperation with the American Civil Liberties Union and Zero Population Growth — was encouraging women to institute suits against hospitals refusing to grant requests for sterilization operations. Suits were already on file against

two hospitals, one in New York and another in Oregon.

WCC Membership — Father Thomas E. Stransky, C.S.P., a consultant to the Vatican Secretariat for Promoting Christian Unity, told Catholic ecumenists in Toledo that he thought the next assembly of the Synod of Bishops would take up the question of Roman Catholic membership in the World Council of Churches. He said the "delay" of the Church in deciding on membership indicated it is seriously interested in joining the WCC.

Savannah Knights Scored — Rejection of a candidate for membership in a Savannah council of the Knights of Columbus, "solely because his skin is black," drew strong criticism from the bishop and the chaplain, both of whom resigned from the council. Strong criticism was registered in other quarters as well.

Sister Board Member — Sister Michelle Olley, the first nun ever to seek public office in Racine, Wis., was elected to the city's public school board in an easy victory which surprised her.

End the War — A "renewed commitment by all governments involved" to end the war in Vietnam was called for by Bishop Joseph L. Bernardin, general secretary of the National Conference of Catholic Bishops and the US Catholic Conference. His statement, which was authorized by NCCB-USCC president Cardinal John Krol, repeated a previous stand taken by the bishops in November, 1971, when they urged a "speedy end of this war as a moral imperative of the highest order." Similar appeals for peace in Southeast Asia were made by the National Council of Churches and the World Council of Churches.

Evangelistic Crusade — Leighton Ford, an associate of Billy Graham, received endorsement in Bishop Joseph L. Hogan's encouragement to Catholics to attend and participate in an Apr. 28 to May 7 evangelistic crusade in Rochester, N. Y. Bishop Hogan said in a letter to pastors: "I have approved of the involvement of our clergy, religious and laity in the crusade which has been endorsed by some of my brother bishops in the United States. It has been their experience that the Catholic community was blessed with a more active and dedicated membership as a result of God's grace working through the program."

Key 73 — The National Association of Evangelicals declined to approve participation in Key 73, a Protestant evangelism campaign already endorsed by some 130 Protestant organizations and a number of Catholic bishops. Key 73 proposed to saturate the US and Canada with evangelism by means of hymn contests, Bible study, prayer meetings, state fair missionary crusades and youth programs. Before the NAE vote, the

Ecumenical Affairs Committee of the National Conference of Catholic Bishops issued a favorable report on Catholic participation in Key 73.

Domestic Briefs:

• Bishop Joseph L. Bernardin, general secretary of the US Catholic Conference endorsed the Apr. 30 National Solidarity Day for Soviet Jews as an observance drawing "Christians and Jews into ever closer fellowship."

• Sister Lourdes Sheehan, 37, was appointed superintendent of schools in the Richmond diocese by Bishop John J. Russell.

Religion of Football

Professional football has become America's new religion, said Rabbi A. James Rudin in the *Christian Century*. With tongue in cheek, he wrote: "The players, both rookies (novices) and veterans (ordained clergy), often train in secluded areas like Redskin Park, Va. (monasteries). . . . The coaches (hierarchy) demand total commitment from their charges. . . . Pro football has its distinctive uniform (religious garb) and its weekly ritual of emotional and violent confrontation with the opposing team (sin). . . . Devout followers . . . witness and participate in these rituals (liturgy) by invoking traditional and hallowed chants.

"It is not unusual for these pilgrims to travel hundreds of miles to witness a game, sometimes braving the bitter cold with the zeal and ardor of ancient martyrs."

FOREIGN

Pakistan Schools — President Zulfiquar Ali Bhutto announced that all private colleges and schools would be nationalized in September and October, respectively. Two hundred and eight Catholic institutions would be affected by the announced policy.

Sacraments for Handicapped — The National Board of Religious Inspectors and Advisors in England and Wales emphatically asserted Apr. 6 the rights of handicapped children to receive the sacraments. They did so in opposition to the practice of some priests who would not allow such children to go to confession and receive Holy Communion because they could not be prepared for the sacraments in a normal way.

Christians? — The Rev. Gerrie Lubbe, a Dutch Reformed clergyman, rebuked his fellow Afrikaners for the "humiliating and unChristian way" in which they treated persons of Indian descent in South Africa. In a newspaper interview, he said that Indians wondered how Afrikaners could be Christian and at the same time deal with Indians as a segregated group of people.

No Nun-Running — The Church has no intention of preventing Indian Catholic girls from going to Europe for nurses' training or to become nuns, said Archbishop Gregorios Varghese Thangalathil of the SyroMalankara Archdiocese of Trivandrum. He denied charges of "nun-running" for money made recently by the British Broadcasting Corporation.

World Council of Youth — Sixteen thousand young delegates from 80 countries, meeting at the Protestant Monastery of the Reconciliation, Taize, France, reached a decision Apr. 13 to establish a World Council of Youth. It was said that the decision, which was two years in the making, would require another two years to translate into action. It was hoped that the council would provide young people with a forum for expressions of view in world religious and social organizations.

Charges Dropped — A military court in Rio de Janeiro dropped 1970 charges of subversion against the Young Christian Workers and the Brazilian Development Institute for lack of evidence and "other difficulties."

A Polish Question — Churchmen in Rome were wondering why the government suddenly bolted the door on eight Polish Catholic lay leaders about to visit West Germany. The members of Znak, a political and intellectual movement with close ties to the bishops, had been scheduled to make the visit in mid-April but had their exit visas revoked by the regime. One theory was that PAX, a governmentlinked nominally Catholic organization in conflict with the Polish hierarchy and the Vatican, had objected to the visit by its rivals because a visit there by its own leaders stirred an outcry from German Catholics.

Priests in Cuba — The Spanish-Latin American Priests Organization reported from Madrid that the number of priests in Cuba declined from 215 in 1969 to 193 by the end of 1971. The organization also reported that only 15 ordinations took place in that time and that the Cuban government was refusing to permit priests from Spain into the country.

Apparitions — Cardinal Jose M. Bueno Monreal banned demonstrations at the sites of alleged apparitions of Mary in Seville and a place near El Palmar de Troya. Of the "apparitions," he said: "There is nothing that shows any supernatural intervention. There are on the contrary strong indications that this is a case of collective superstition very harmful to the faith."

Dean Cleared — The Very Rev. Gonville A. ffrench-Beytaugh, Anglican Dean of Johannesburg who had been found guilty of three violations of South Africa's Terrorism Act in November, 1971, was cleared of charges on appeal and left the country for England.

Nuns Out of Sight — Government agents completed Apr. 13 a roundup of nuns for forced removal from parishes where they had been working to "concentration points" in remote mental hospitals and farms where they could work out of sight. It was not known how many sisters were caught in the dragnet. Communism in the country appeared to have lost the "human face" it had begun to put on during the 1968 regime of Alexander Dubcek.

It was also reported that the government was holding down the number of entrants to seminaries and planning to force all priests out of the active ministry and into retirement at the age of 60.

Chilean Progress, but . . . — The bishops of Chile, in a statement released at the end of their annual meeting, said that the Allende regime was making some progress toward justice and equality in the country, but warned that violence and propaganda were "poisoning the nation" and dividing the people. They appealed to "political leaders in the government and the opposition" to distinguish clearly between the realms of God and Caesar "in building this new society."

Canadian Bishops' Meeting — The bishops of Canada ended a five-day spring meeting in Ottawa with a major statement calling for greater sharing of the national wealth and appealing to bishops, priests, religious and lay persons to practice restraint and "generous sharing" in their life styles. (See separate entry.)

Clerical Celibacy— Leaders among the Canadian bishops suggested in informal conversations at a meeting in Ottawa that the ordination of married men to the priesthood is not a dead issue, even though the 1971 assembly of the Synod of Bishops voted against it. They said, however, that they were committed to the synod's majority view that the values of an unmarried Western clergy were high and that there was need for a deeper understanding throughout the Church of the joy and service of celibacy.

Widgery Report — Cardinal William Conway of Armagh said he disagreed with the findings of the Widgery Report which exonerated British paratroopers of guilt in the killing of 13 Catholic civil rights demonstrators Jan. 30 in Londonderry. He said the findings of the inquiry behind the report did not correspond with the evidence, and called the report "a very extraordinary use of the English language."

Priests' Appeal — Catholic priests in troubled areas of Belfast appealed to the outlawed Irish Republican Army Provisionals for an end to the campaign of terror in Northern Ireland. A statement read at Masses also said that the hostility of Catholics toward the internment of suspected terrorists without trial should not be mistaken for support of bombings and shootings.

Later in the month, an IRA soldier told a news conference in Rome that, while the IRA regretted the killing of innocent victims, it had vowed to continue its all-out war against British troops in Northern Ireland.

Moscow Attacks Religious Broadcasts — Radio Moscow accused foreign radio stations, including Vatican Radio and The Voice of America, of "ideological brainwashing" to incite believers in the Soviet Union against Communism and its whole system. Commentator Boris Maksimovich Maryanov said that religion "is now the only ideology in our country which can in any way be considered to have mass appeal that is alien to Marxist-Leninism and a Communist world outlook."

No Korean Dialogue — Cardinal Stephen Kim of Seoul said in an Easter message that there was an absence of meaningful dialogue and mutual understanding between the Korean people and the government of President Park Chung-hee. This was especially true since the declaration of a state of national emergency in December, 1971. Church-state relations were uneasy and general tension was a fact of life.

Foreign Briefs:

• Catholics and Lutherans in the Philippines announced mutual recognition of the validity of baptism conferred according to the rites of the two churches.

• Parish representatives of the established Swedish Lutheran Church voiced opposition to a parliamentary commission's recommendation that the Church be separated from the state by 1983. One legislator said he feared an independent Church would have millions of dollars at its disposal and would become a weighty factor in the formation of public opinion.

• Cardinal Joseph Parecattil appealed for the Indianization of Christianity, in an address in an ecumenical meeting in Madras. He said the "Western garb" of Christianity inhibited relations between Christians and other Indians.

• Archbishop Michael Gonzi called on Maltese Catholics to join in special thanksgiving ceremonies for the seven-year, $37 million agreement between Great Britain and Malta concerning military bases on the island. The Archbishop figured in negotiations that led to the accord.

Zairean Bishops Yield

The bishops of Zaire announced they were yielding to government demands that youth cells of the People's Revolutionary Movement be established in the country's seminaries. They added a condition — "if the authorities of the party promise to respect the goals, good order and specific character of these institutions."

Party officials announced that Pope John XXIII Seminary, closed in January, would be permittted to reopen.

Meanwhile, Cardinal Joseph Malula, who had rejected Africanization policies of President Mobuto Sese Seko, was in voluntary exile in Rome. The secretary of the bishops' conference was expelled earlier this month.

MAY 1972

VATICAN

Concern for Workingmen — The Church's concern for workingmen was the theme of Pope Paul's address to a general audience on Europe's Labor Day, May 1. He affirmed that the Church has "the greatest sympathy with the workingmen precisely because it sees in him and proclaims for him the dignity of man, the brother who is equal to every other man, the inviolable person upon whose face is impressed a divine likeness."

Appeal for Peace — In response to an appeal from 300 American students at the Rome Branch of Loyola University, Chicago, Pope Paul said at a general audience May 3 that he hoped all sides would terminate the Vietnam conflict with "generous and noble proposals for rapid, sincere and effective negotiations for a ceasefire and for peace." As the representative of Christ, he said, he was "obliged to deplore every war; in its causes, in its inhuman violence, and in its murderous and senseless destruction."

Right to Life — Pope Paul appealed to the "moral sensitivity" of doctors to join the Church in its campaign for the right to life, at a Mass for 1,000 delegates to the 18th world congress of the International College of Surgeons. He also asked "men of medicine" to act on his behalf in teaching that social diseases, drugs and torture, as well as contraception, abortion and euthanasia, offend the "dignity and integrity of human life."

Pride in Confessing Christian Faith — Christians must be confident, strong and "humbly proud" to confess their faith in Christ even when it is unfashionable, the Holy Father told a general audience May 10. Noting that many were urging the Church to accept "ideologies and habits which are current in secular society," he admitted the need for the Church to adopt "life forms and norms in keeping with the needs of the times." He asserted, however, that the faithful must be reminded "of the inalienable demands of a follower of Christ and the paramount and responsible demands that the term implies." He said the Christian "must be consistent, strong and frank. He must be humbly proud to define himself as such and be ready, if need be, to give testimony of his own privileged title of Christian."

Communications — Caught in a "virtually ceaseless flood" of news and entertainment, man must search for truth with "sincerity and diligence," Pope Paul declared in a World Communications Day message May 14. He also said that the obligation to search for truth rests with both communicators and listeners and viewers of news and entertainment.

Structure of the Church — Speaking about the foundation of the Church during a general audience May 17, Pope Paul said that many persons oppose an institutional and hierarchical Church, preferring one that would be democratic in concept and operation. He commented: "We believe that this question, raised within the Catholic Church, is an attempt against the very existence of the Church."

Missionary Anniversary — Pope Paul was the principal celebrant of a multilingual "Mass of the Nations" on Pentecost, May 21, which marked the 350th anniversary of the Congregation for the Evangelization of Peoples. In a brief homily addressed to priests and seminarians of mission countries, the Holy Father said: "In you we see represented all nations. Your task is to proclaim, each in his own tongue, the salvation brought by Christ."

Milquetoasts and Contestors — Pope Paul criticized milquetoast Catholics and constant protesters as underminers of today's apostolate, at a general audience May 24. Too often, he said, Christians are overly concerned about winning the favor of others, and the accompanying "paralyzing fear of the judgment of others" tempts them to forget the teachings of the Church and the promptings of conscience. He also stated plainly that contestation is a "falsification of the apostolate," and added: "We wish that the Holy Spirit by whom they say they are guided — possibly to avoid . . . homage due to those who minister authority—would restore them" to a function of authentic renewal and charity.

Eucharist — Pope Paul recommended five lines of meditation on the meaning of the Eucharist at a general audience May 31: (1) the Real Presence of Christ under the appearances of bread and wine; (2) the significance of the Eucharist not only as spiritual food but also as a true sacrifice; (3) the necessity of a priestly ministry for the Eucharist; (4) the need to be purified of sin before receiving the sacrament; (5) understanding of charity and unity that are the specific effects of the Eucharist.

"It would also be well," the Pope said, "to react against certain denials here and there regarding the permanence of the Real Presence of Christ in the Eucharistic species even beyond the celebration of the Mass during which the bread and wine were consecrated."

The Holy Father Also:

• Received nearly 2,000 Italian children who made their first Communion during the year, May 17.

• Told representatives from more than 40 countries that agricultural cooperatives have the blessing of the Church because they help farmers become "active participants in social and economic life," May 25.

• Praised the American Catholic presence in Rome on the 50th anniversary of the Paulist-staffed Parish of Santa Susanna, May 26.

• Welcomed the first large pilgrimage of 300 persons from Hungary since World War II, late in the month. He expressed the hope that future relations between the Church and government there would be marked by "recognition of respective rights" and by "cooperation in the service of the welfare of the Hungarian people."

Caritas Internationalis — Delegates from 90 national Catholic charity agencies attended the ninth general assembly of Caritas Internationalis May 8 to 12 in Rome. The principal items under study were emergency disaster relief, social action and the integral development of man. Earlier regional meetings of participating agencies gave high priority to the establishment and assistance of Catholic relief organizations in developing nations. Msgr. Karl Vath, founder of the Catholic Relief Center in Hong Kong, was elected president of the organization.

Mission Collection Down — The 1970 worldwide collection for the support of missions ($30.9 million) was slightly less than the $31.4 million raised in 1969. Msgr. Joseph Kempeneers of the Pontifical Society for the Propagation of the Faith said he felt that Catholics, "even in the most generous countries, fell very far short of what might be hoped for, even when one took into account the many demands" on their charity.

Pieta — Without minimizing the difficulties involved, Vatican officials predicted two days after the hammer-mutilation of Michelangelo's Pieta that the sculpture would be restored and would eventually look the same as before. *L'Osservatore Romano* reported that Maszlo Toth, the hammer-wielder, had struck as many as 10 blows in an effort to decapitate the figure of Mary.

Vatican Briefs:

• Diplomatic relations were established with Sudan.

• Twenty-four recruits were sworn into the Swiss Guards May 6 at annual ceremonies commemorating the 147 members of the corps who died defending Pope Clement VII in 1527.

• Recourse to private violence, as in the attempted assassination of presidential candidate George Wallace, threatens to destroy all civil coexistence, stated editor Raimondo Manzini in the May 17 edition of *L'Osservatore Romano..*

A Catholic University

The Pope defended the idea of a Catholic university and said that its dedication to Catholic doctrine is a help rather than a hindrance to scientific research, in an address to officials, faculty members and students of the Gregorian University May. 13.

Explaining the role of a Catholic university, he said: "Now it seems to us a duty to emphasize sharply the general criteria that should distinguish the cultural mission entrusted to every ecclesiastical Catholic university. It is this: that teachers and students must be able to realize ever more expressly, with God's grace, the ideal of a wisdom animated by an ardent spirit of faith, by a sharp awareness of the problems facing the Church. . . . This Catholic atmosphere, stemming from a living and suffering faith, guarantees and respects within the university the seriousness of scientific research rooted in man and in the human world."

Of the university's scientific work, the Pope said: "On the scientific plane it is not just a question of not breaking with but of giving value to, scrutinizing and understanding the living ties with tradition. . . . That does not mean that scientific research is held in check, as certain shortsighted objections of shallow minds would have it. The university is by definition a university of sciences. It is, in the honest freedom of God's children, the ideal place for research along fully scientific lines, where new problems are faced. . . ."

On the theological level, Pope Paul stated that the Catholic university "must assure the orthodoxy of faith, of which the teaching authority of the Church is the guarantor."

DOMESTIC

Catholic Population — *The Official Catholic Directory, 1972,* published by P. J. Kenedy and Sons, reported a 1971 increase of 176,261 Catholics in the US, for a total of 48,390,990, or 23.3 per cent of the total population. Also reported were: 1,054,933 infant baptisms (33,530 less than in 1971); 70,012 adult converts 5,522 less); 57,421 priests (740 less); 22,963 seminarians (2,745 less); 146,914 sisters (6,731 less); 4,067,413 students enrolled in Catholic elementary and high schools (361,910 less).

Rosary Crusade — Father Patrick Peton, C.S.C., announced May 1 that the Family Rosary Crusade and the Crusade for Family Prayer would be concentrated in the US during the next decade.

Public School Applications — Parents of more than 50,000 Catholic school students in the Brooklyn diocese obtained applications needed to transfer their children to public schools. The purpose of the May 1 action was to dramatize the severe strain which would be placed on public schools if nonpublic schools closed for lack of public financial aid.

Boys Town Plans — Administrators of Boys Town reported that they were studying expansion plans that would include programs for girls and the mentally retarded, and research into problems experienced by homeless boys. The board of directors also said it was developing an evaluation of current programs of Boys Town.

Humanist Dialogue — The first formal dialogue in the US between Catholics and humanists may have given participants a clearer view of each other but failed to produce any points of agreement. Two 25-member teams took part in the three days of discussion in New York.

Cathedral Lie-In — Seven nuns and a laywoman were arrested in St. Patrick's Cathedral, New York, for interfering with religious services by lying down in the middle aisle during Mass to protest against the war in Vietnam. Charges against them were dropped by the archdiocese.

Lobbying — A bill designed to clarify the amount of lobbying that public charitable organizations could do and still retain tax exempt status might involve "excessive government entanglement with religion," stated Bishop Joseph L. Bernardin, general secretary of the US Catholic Conference. In written testimony submitted to the Ways and Means Committee of the House of Representatives, he said that the inclusion of churches under the bill's broadened restrictions on influencing public opinion "can only be described as intolerable and quite likely unconstitutional." The excessive entanglement argument was urged against the constitutionality of non-public school aid statutes in Rhode Island and Pennsylvania in June, 1971.

Amish Decision — The US Supreme Court ruled May 15 that forcing Amish parents to send their children to high school violated their constitutionally protected right to practice their religion. In a nearly unanimous decision, the Court said that secondary schooling exposes Amish children to attitudes, goals and values contrary to their beliefs, and substantially hinders "the religious development of the Amish child and his integration into the way of life of the Amish faith community at the crucial adolescent stage of development."

Abortion Law — The New York State Assembly and State Senate voted 79 to 68 and 30 to 27, respectively, for repeal of the nation's most permissive abortion law. Their action was nullified, however, by the veto of Governor Nelson Rockefeller. The bill would have outlawed abortion on demand during the first 24 weeks of pregnancy.

In a related development, President Nixon endorsed repeal of the statute in a letter to Cardinal Terence Cooke. He acknowledged the Cardinal's stand against the law and said he would "personally like to associate myself with the convictions you deeply feel and eloquently express." Governor Rockefeller and others took strong exception to the President's letter.

In Connecticut, Governor Thomas Meskill signed into law a bill permitting abortion only to save a mother's life. The law, which was enacted by the legislature and signed May 23, was essentially the same as the 112-year-old statute struck down as unconstitutional by a federal court in April.

Former Priests — Bishop Edward A. McCarthy of Phoenix said that he planned to set up a council of former priests to explore ways in which men who have left the active ministry can continue to serve the Church. He made the announcement at a dinner meeting of the Phoenix priests' senate and about 40 former priests. He said the latter are also "members of my flock, and I'm not going to let them be lepers."

Archdiocese Sued — A group of Sisters of Notre Dame, 36 children, a priest and the Newark archdiocese were involved in a suit over the disposition of nearly $900,000 willed seven years earlier to St. Peter's Orphanage. The suit charged the archdiocese with improper action in administering the funds, claimed that the children were never informed of the bequest, and sought a court order requiring the archdiocese to turn the funds over to a new corporation which would continue to operate the orphanage.

Niagara University — While acknowledging that Niagara was experiencing financial difficulties, Father Kenneth Slattery, C.M., president, said the school "would never accept" state funds if that meant modifying religious and moral standards. Niagara University, he stated flatly, "would remain Catholic."

School Aid — For the third time in three years, a bill designed to aid nonpublic schools in New York — with more than $40 million going to poor and middle income families with children in such schools — was signed into law and quickly challenged in the courts. The challenger was the Committee for Public Education and Religious Liberty, a coalition of groups opposed to public aid for parochial schools.

Domestic Briefs:

• Msgr. Geno Baroni, director of the National Center of Urban Ethnic Affairs, was named May 2 to receive the 1972 American Heritage Award of the John F. Kennedy Memorial Library.

• Sister Rose Thering, program coordinator of Seton Hall University's Institute for Judaeo-Christian Studies, received the Louise Waterman Wise Award of the American Jewish Congress May 4, for "distinguished services in the field of Christian-Jewish relations."

• Father Daniel J. Berrigan, S.J., antiwar activist, received the 1972 Senior Class Fellow Award of Notre Dame University.

• Shock and dismay were expressed by religious as well as political leaders at the shooting of presidential candidate George Wallace May 15 in Laurel, Md. He was hospitalized at Holy Cross Hospital, Silver Spring, Md.

• Acting individually, more than a dozen US bishops took strong stands against the mining of North Vietnamese waters and intensification of the war. Their various appeals called the continuing war immoral and past the point where any good could come of it for anyone. Several bishops called for a unilateral ceasefire.

• Father Jeremy Harrington, O.F.M., editor of the *St. Anthony Messenger,* received the 1972 St. Francis de Sales Award of the Catholic Press Association.

• The girls' high school of 104-year-old Ursuline Academy, Louisville, closed May 28 with the graduation of its last class of 94 students.

• J. C. Willke, M.D., author of *Handbook on Abortion,* estimated that at least 4,000 babies were aborted alive in New York State since July, 1970.

• Archbishop Fulton J. Sheen, named the "Catholic Man of Action" for 1971 by the Knights of Columbus, was honored by more than 6,000 persons at the National Shrine of Our Lady of Czestochowa, Doylestown, Pa.

Bernstein's Mass

Leonard Bernstein's "Mass," first performed six months earlier in Washington and featured in the Cincinnati May Festival of Music, got mixed reviews in Catholic circles.

Archbishop Paul F. Liebold of Cincinnati said it was "in extremely bad taste and offensive to what we hold in great reverence."

Father John Gallen, S.J., wrote in *America* that it was "a religiously successful work" which "brings us, in the midst of turmoil, to peace." Paul Hume of the *Washington Post* gave it a favorable review.

Father Gilbert V. Hartke, chairman of speech and drama at Catholic University, was highly critical. "One of my dearest Jewish friends," he related, "said to me that, if that was the Torah (instead of the bread and wine used in the Mass), every Jewish person would be up in arms."

FOREIGN

Merger Rejected — For the third time in three years, a proposal for the union of the Anglican and Methodist Churches was rejected May 3 at the Anglican General Synod in London because it failed to pass with a 75 per cent majority vote. Voting in favor of the merger were 85 per cent of the bishops but only 65.62 per cent of the clergy and 62.82 per cent of the laity. Two reasons were given for the rejection:

• A decision to give reconciled Methodist ministers the same status as those in Anglican orders would weaken the case for the validity of Anglican orders.

• The unity proposal was based on argument and bargaining or compromise rather than on basic unity of religious beliefs.

Vocations in France — The National Center for Vocations in Paris reported a continuing decline in the number of French seminarians and priests. The number of seminarians was 2,900, as compared with 3,350 in the previous year. Two hundred and 37 men were ordained to the priesthood in 1971, compared with 384 in 1970 and 346 in 1969.

Population Explosion Fallacy — The population explosion is a fallacy created by a society unwilling to face up to its social responsibilities, author and radio and television personality Malcolm Muggeridge told a Glasgow meeting organized by Pro Fide of Scotland, a Catholic lay group. He said: "The contemporary superstition on which future historians will fasten with most glee and contumely, I feel sure, is the so-called population explosion. . . . It is simply not true that our earth is overcrowded, as of now or in the measurable future. On the contrary, the problem of over-production is a much more pressing one. . . . Nor is it true that world production of food and other necessities is falling behind population growth. On the contrary, the problem is one of overproduction and distribution."

Breakaway Churches in Africa — Observers felt that African "independent" churches — first called schismatic and then "breakaway" churches and "renewal movements" — seemed to be gaining ground, despite the facts that all of them could not be described as Christian and that many had little chance of surviving for very long. The largest group separated from the Catholic Church was called the Legion of Mary Africa Church.

Training Centers in Honduras — The bishops of Honduras told landowners that the Church would not stop its program of education and civic action for farmworkers, and the government that landless peasants had a right to own land. They issued their statement against a background of conflict over land rights and charges by big farmers and cattle growers that the Church was operating "schools for subversion."

Trouble in Yugoslavia — A correspondent of *The Tablet,* the British Catholic weekly, reported that a "bitter personal attack" on Archbishop Franjo Kuharic of Zagreb had appeared in *Vjesnik,* the largest daily in Zagreb. The reason for the attack appeared to be the Archbishop's appeal, in a Lenten pastoral letter, for an end to "the still prevalent forms of discrimination against believers in public life." *Glas Koncila,* a bimonthly Croatian Catholic magazine, reported arrests of Catholic students, searches of church buildings, and administrative measures restricting Catholic publications.

Lithuanian Protest — Thousands of Lithuanian youths rioted May 18 in Kaunas after the funeral of a young Catholic who burned himself to death. The demonstrators were protesting against Soviet domination and restrictions against religious freedom in the predominantly Catholic country.

Two Children Families — The South Korean government was mounting a campaign to keep the national population below 45 million by the year 2000. To achieve this goal, a white paper on population issued by the Ministry of Health and Social Affairs said that 90 per cent of the nation's couples of child-bearing age would have to restrict their families to two children and the other 10 per cent to three children.

No Mass by Married Priest — Cardinal Bernard Alfrink told the student parish at Leyden University, The Netherlands, that the bishops of the country could not approve the continued celebration of Mass by a married priest, Father Henry van Breukelen. He said the celebration of Mass by married priests was not approved by the 1971 Synod of Bishops and was "not accepted by the universal Church."

Feast Days in Zaire — The Congregation for the Evangelization of Peoples granted the request of the bishops of Zaire to shift the celebration of the Ascension, the Assumption and All Saints' Day to Sundays. The change was made because of the removal of the holy days from the list of national holidays by President Mobutu Sese Seko.

Moscow Meeting — The meeting in Moscow of President Nixon and other US officials with leaders of the Soviet Union must produce "a satisfactory answer" to the hopes of the world for peace, said an unsigned editorial in *L'Osservatore Romano*. Quoting the "simple voices" of Soviet citizens in the press as pleading for peace and disarmament, the editorial observed: "These voices are the thought, the preoccupations and the expectations, we can well say, of the whole world."

UNCTAD a Failure — The third meeting of the UN Conference for Trade and Development, called to help underdeveloped nations, ended in "marked pessimism" if not "complete failure," according to Bishop Ramon Torrella Cascante who led the Vatican delegation at the meeting in Santiago, Chile. He cited these items in a Vatican Radio broadcast May 24: "No progress was made in the important question of opening up the markets of developed countries to products of developing nations. Nor was any progress made regarding financial aid for development for the poorer nations. . . . We are still far from granting (as resolved at the second UNCTAD meeting in 1968) to the emerging nations that one per cent of the gross national product that was established in New Delhi."

Troubled Bishop — The latest development in the troubled five-month episcopates of Bishop John Gijsen of Roermond, The Netherlands, was rejection of his authority by the diocesan staff following his decision to dismiss the head of the diocesan personnel department and his announcement that he would make all future appointments to diocesan positions by himself. The deans of the dioceses, the central committee of the diocesan pastoral council, and priests working in diocesan administration said they had decided to end all collaboration with the Bishop.

Press Convention — The first International Religious Press Convention — combining the annual conventions of the Catholic Press Association, the Associated (Protestant) Church Press and the Canadian Catholic Press — was held May 8 to 11 in Banff, Alta. The three organizations voted overwhelmingly to move toward greater structural cooperation but put off the question of merger for more study. Reelected CPA officers were Father Louis G. Miller, C.SS.R., of *The Liguorian,* president, and John F. Fink, executive vice president of Our Sunday Visitor, Inc.

Burundi Massacres — At least 50,000 persons were dead by the end of the month as violence continued to take a horrendous toll in the wake of an abortive revolt in April, the murder of King Ntare on his return to the country, and power struggles between the Tutsi minority and the Hutu majority.

Foreign Briefs:

• Three hundred and 50 experts from 70 countries met at the headquarters of the International Red Cross in Geneva for a month-long effort to update the Geneva Conventions of 1949, the rules by which wars are supposed to be fought and civilians protected.

• Spanish Father Juan Jarque y Jutglar was appointed executive secretary of the International Union of the Catholic Press.

• Pressure from Argentine bishops and priests led to the release of Father Alberto Carbone who had been held in detention on presidential orders after a judge declared him innocent of charges of conspiracy in a guerrilla attack on a naval base at Zarate in January.

• Thirty-one bishops attending the seventh Inter-American Bishops' Meeting in Chateauguay, Que., agreed that the creation of an international conscience to work for justice and peace remained one of the unattained goals of the churches of North and South America.

Burial of Divorced Persons

Eight bishops in southern France announced that religious funerals would no longer be automatically refused to divorced Catholics who had remarried.

Requests for such funerals would be favorably received, they said, on behalf of remarried divorced persons "who have manifested their attachment to the Christian faith not only at the moment of death, by calling a priest to their bedside, for example, but especially during their lifetime, by expressing their spiritual anxiety about their state of life, by giving a religious upbringing to their children, by assisting at Sunday Mass. . . .

"This personal consideration is not at all a questioning of the indissolubility of marriage nor an agreement that remarried divorced persons may receive the sacraments.

"It is intended as an expression of the link that the Church maintains with those who are baptized."

JUNE 1972

VATICAN

Ninth Anniversary — Pope Paul celebrated Mass June 3 at the tomb of his predecessor, John XXIII; in attendance were two of the late Pontiff's brothers, Zaverio and Giuseppe, and other relatives. Tribute was also paid by thousands of pilgrims in St. Peter's Basilica and Sotto Il Monte, Pope John's birthplace.

Canadian Bishops — Pope Paul told three representatives of the Candian Catholic Conference June 5 that he was confident the Canadian bishops "will draw all that is good and positive from new trends" in the Church and the world, and will "reaffirm the doctrine of the Church whenever necessary and with clarity." He also praised Canadian Catholics for their initiatives in the fields of education, social assistance and aid to developing nations, and for their "remarkable contribution, in personnel and resources, to the great work of the missions."

Criticism of the Church — Pope Paul told a general audience June 7 that there are friendly and hostile attitudes behind criticism of the Church. "The friendly attitude," he said, "remains objective, indeed critical, and, if necessary, severe. But this attitude remains filial." It does not seek out the Church's defects in order "to divulge them purposely, or to limit itself to protest and a belittling of functions."

Hierarchical Church — The hierarchical structure of the Church was again the subject of a talk by Pope Paul June 11. He said: "If the Church is the People of God, if it is the Mystical Body of Christ, if it is the human, visible and stable edifice he is building, if it is the temple with the apostolic ministry of the Spirit — it cannot be without that hierarchial organization which Christ willed as its basis and for the service and guidance of the community of believers ... and for those adhering to the one and perfect charity. We must acquire greater awareness of the authentic and historic form which the structures of the Church are assuming, and of the joint and filial interests which we all have in the spiritual and practical vitality of these structures."

Cabinet-Level Meeting — Pope Paul presided over a "cabinet-level" meeting of cardinals June 13 to hear reports on the trial reorganization of the Roman Curia. At the end of the meeting, he noted some problems that still had to be worked out, with respect to:
• the competence of various offices of the Curia;
• the development of ecclesiology;
• the improvement of norms of operation;
• the application of subsidiarity, in order to give bishops and their conferences more authority for independent action while preserving the right of individual recourse to the Holy See.

Sainthood — The Christian surrendering his own freedom to answer God's call to sainthood is the "Christian paradox," Pope Paul told a general audience June 14. He said: "Our Freedom is called to perfection and to love. The encounter of the loving and saving will of God with the obedient and happy will of our human heart is perfection, is sanctity." He insisted that "we cannot involve ourselves with religion without involving ourselves with sanctity; and, vice versa, sanctity makes no sense unless it is grounded in religion." The Pope also stated: "There are many mediocre Christians, not because they are weak or lacking in information but because they wish to be mediocre."

Obligations of Priests — Catholics expect their priests to fulfill the obligations of the ministry, said Pope Paul in an impromptu address to a group of Chicago priests June 16. This was one of two certainties about the priesthood, he declared, the other being the very fact of the ministerial priesthood. The priests were silver jubilarians.

Pastoral Action — The need to work together is the most important pastoral demand being made today on the bishops of Italy, Pope Paul declared June 17 before 200 members of the Italian Bishops' Conference. He said that pastoral action without cooperation and consultation is unthinkable. He admitted that "to work together is certainly more complicated ... but this working together is more in conformity with the spirit of the Church. It calls for a more pastoral exercise of authority."

Pope's Anniversary — On June 21, nine years after he became Pope, Paul VI said that he had "never in the least desired, far less fostered" his election. He added: "Perhaps the Lord has called me to this service not indeed because I have any aptitude for it, or so that I may govern and save the Church from her present difficulties, but so that I may suffer something for the Church, and so that it may be clear that he and not others leads her and is saving her."

Price of Delay — Pope Paul, calling again for peace in Vietnam, said June 23 that each day peace is delayed there "is paid for with terrifying destruction." He also voiced hope for an end to violence in the Middle East, Ireland and Burundi.

Faith in the Church — The Holy Father, speaking at a Mass in St. Peter's Basilica June 29, urged Catholics to have faith in the Church despite "the smoke of Satan" that seemed to be dimming its brilliance. He said: "It was believed that after the (Second Vatican) Council there would be a day of sunshine in the history of the Church. There came instead a day of clouds, storm and darkness, of search and uncertainty. ... One no longer trusts the Church; one trusts in the first profane prophet who comes along. ... Doubt has entered our conscience and it has entered through windows which . . . should have been opened to the light."

The Pope Also:
• Denounced the shooting of more than 20 persons at the Tel Aviv Airport by three Japanese May 30, and sent a message of "deep sorrow" to Israeli President Shazar.
• Praised Buddhism for its "spiritual, moral and socio-cultural treasures" at a meeting with Somdey Phra Vannarat of Thailand, June 5.
• Urged almost 3,000 Conventual Franciscans to meet today's challenges by staying close to the cross of Christ and living a life of true austerity and poverty, at a June 12 audience with officials and participants in the 187th general chapter of the order.
• Forget worries but remember God during the summer holidays, was the theme of advice given to vacationers gathered in St. Peter's Square, June 18.
• Sent a message of sympathy and his promise of prayers for nearly 470 Rhodesian miners trapped underground after an explosion.

Respect Rome — In a letter published in *L'Osservatore Romano,* Cardinal Angelo Dell'Acqua, Pope Paul's vicar for Rome, urged tourists to "respect the sacred character" of Rome and not "to profane the churches with immodest dress which incites to evil." He also said: "Do not waste away your days of a well-earned summer vacation by abandoning yourselves to insane pleasures."

Vatican Briefs:
• A Vatican Radio commentator warned June 8 that critics and reformers of the Church who go so far as to spurn its hierarchical authority run the risk of heresy. The commentary was a follow-up to Pope Paul's earlier remarks in which he said that some critics and Catholic publications seemed to be absorbed in searching out the defects of the Church and publicizing them for purposes of "protest and defamation."
• Work was underway on the installation of a new bronze door, called the "Door of Prayer," at one of the entrances to St. Peter's Basilica.
• Representatives of the Vatican signed the International Treaty for Non-Proliferation of Nuclear Weapons in a symbolic action signifying the Church's support for world disarmament and efforts to achieve peace.

Communicants Must Love

The Christian who takes Communion "at the table of the Lord" is obliged to love all men and to form a world of peace, stated the Holy Father at a Corpus Christi Mass June 1. He said the true follower of Christ cannot approach the Eucharistic table "with hatred in his heart" nor leave it without recalling the precept to love all men.

"We who honor the Eucharist must demonstrate in feeling, thought and practice that we know truly how to love our neighbor, including him who does not join us at the table of the Lord and who still lacks the communion of faith . . . and the unity of the Church.

"We must (also) demonstrate our love for him who lacks the necessities of life, that is, dignity, friendship, hope, aid, education, defense, work and food."

DOMESTIC

Pentecostalism — Catholic Pentecostalism is "not an end in itself, not a substitute for the Church, but truly a tool of Church renewal," Kevin Ranaghan told 11,500 participants in the June 2 to 4 International Conference on the Charismatic Renewal in the Catholic Church at Notre Dame University. He said that the "resources, spiritual energies and very lives of the individuals and communities who are the Catholic Charismatic Renewal are to be laid down in service for the well-being of the whole Church."

Another St. Patrick's Incident — A special Mass for peace June 4 at St. Patrick's Cathedral, New York, was interrupted when a third of the congregation, including Father Daniel Berrigan, S.J., left the church to stage their own liturgy outside. Father Berrigan charged that he had not been allowed to preach as planned. Cathedral officials denied the charge and said that another Jesuit had been invited to give the sermon.

Test-Tube Baby Experiments — Paul Ramsey, Ph. D., writing in the June 5 issue of the *Journal of the American Medical Association,* said that scientists should halt all such experiments on the moral grounds that they may be doing irreparable harm to the child-to-be. He said that artificial fertilization "constitutes unethical medical experimentation on possible future human beings" and "is subject to absolute moral prohibition."

Priest for Congress — Father Armand Moriessette, a parish priest of Lowell who called himself "a liberal in religion but a conservative in politics," opened a campaign to become the second priest-Congressman in the US. He announced his candidacy for the Republican nomination in Massachusetts' Fifth District. He said: "I am not running as a priest. If asked if priests should run for political office, I would say 'no,' but there are exceptions."

Catholic Worker — "My little case is to explain to the court that performing the corporal works of mercy is indeed charitable, even under the standards imposed by our government; and I refuse to apply for tax exemption." With these words Dorothy Day, the 74-year-old founder of the Catholic Worker, summarized what she expected to say July 3 in a federal court in Lewisburg, Pa. She had been called upon to explain why the movement had not paid $296,359 in fines, penalties and income taxes to the Internal Revenue Service for the previous six years. Her contention was that the nonprofit nature of the Catholic Worker movement was self-evident.

School Costs — A committee of Protestant, Jewish and Catholic community leaders predicted that Philadelphia Catholic schools, already $4 million in debt, would be $55 million in debt by 1975. "As a businessman looking at this balance sheet, I'd say let's liquidate the corporation," commented John Gurash, chairman of the committee. The "significant determinant" against such closure, he said, would be the Catholic community.

National Council of Churches — Members of the board were asked to "take the initiative" as individuals in explaining the National Council of Churches to Catholics in their home communities. The Rev. R. H. Edwin Espy, general secretary, gave the reason: "The decision to be made by the National Conference of Catholic Bishops (to join or not to join) . . . will largely depend on the initiatives taken by local and regional denominational and ecumenical people."

Hospital Returns Grant — Mercy Hospital in New Orleans returned a $100,000 grant to the Department of Health, Education and Welfare, stating that it "cannot accept any federal funds which might result in the hospital being forced to liberalize its moral position" on abortion and sterilization. After returning the money, the hospital withdrew from all further participation in the Hill-Burton program of federal construction assistance.

Montezuma Seminary — Officials of Montezuma Seminary announced that, after 35 years of operation and the ordination of 1,500 priests for Mexico, the institution was going to move from New Mexico to Tula, Hidalgo, Mexico. The US bishops, who set up the seminary during the years of Mexican persecution, said they would continue to fund the school.

Doctor Honored — Dr. Patricia Smith, who provided medical care for Montagnards in South Vietnam for 13 years, was named recipient of the 1972 Damien-Dutton Award.

Vocations Center — The National Center for Church Vocations, founded in 1969, announced transfer of its office from Chicago to the Detroit auxiliary chancery building. It was also reported that Father Edward J. Baldwin of Detroit would succeed Father John J. O'Neill as executive director July 15.

Secretary Resigns — Father Thomas A. McDonough, C.SS.R., resigned from the office of national secretary of the National Apostleship of the Sea Conference after serving in the post for more than 25 years. He was succeeded by Father James P. Keating, port chaplain of Chicago and director of Chicago's International Seamens' Center.

Serrans — Fifteen hundred members attending the Serra International convention in St. Louis heard Msgr. Colin MacDonald report that the Church in this country was losing 2.3 priests — through death, retirement and withdrawal from the ministry — for every one newly ordained. He also said that the most turbulent years for the priesthood had been the period from 1966 to 1968. Despite "troubled waters," however, he said he had found "a renewed sense of hope and confidence" among American priests. Msgr. MacDonald was executive director of the US Bishops Office for Priestly Life and Ministry.

Mythologies — Modern mythologies which keep religious persons from fulfilling their potential in the world were the theme of an address by Rabbi Marc Tanenbaum to 1,300 participants in the Ecumenical Institute on Religious Instruction in Cincinnati June 30. Among the mythologies were:

• "the notion that we live in a post-Christian society, a post-Judaeo-Christian world, a post-Western, post-modern world."

• dismissal of the Jewish and Christian experience coupled with what is called a new perception of the solidarity of mankind.

• the "ease with which people in this time of transition and turmoil resort to apocalyptic language."

Tax Credit in Ohio — A bill providing a maximum tax credit of $90 to parents for each child attending a nonpublic school passed both houses of the Ohio General Assembly and was signed into law by Gov. John J. Gilligan. The law, which was retroactive to the 1971-72 school year, was immediately challenged by the American Civil Liberties Union.

Birthright-USA — Mrs. Eunice Kennedy Shriver, speaking at the first annual convention of Birthright-USA in Atlantic City, proposed a "One Million for Life" campaign — as "clear evidence to every mother-to-be that her child, even if undesired by her, is wanted by a family willing and able to raise it as its own." She also said: "If we believe in life, we cannot draw the line of color or intellect or fitness. We must be on the side of life all the way."

In a letter published in the June 6 edition of *The New York Times,* Mrs. Shriver accused the President's population commission of throwing ethics out the window in recommending wider use of abortion, sterilization and dissemination of contraceptives.

Domestic Briefs:

• The Rev. Lawrence Gillick, S.J., 32-years-old and blind from childhood, was ordained to the priesthood.

• Bishop Raymond J. Gallagher of Lafayette (Ind.) told the Democratic Platform Committee that the Church is opposed to "any law or public policy — state or federal — that deprives the weakest members of our society of their basic rights." He warned that "the fundamental dignity of the human person, particularly before he is born and toward the end of his days, is under assault."

• Presidential hopefuls had different views on abortion, President Nixon opposing it and Senators McGovern and Humphrey regarding it as a matter of state rather than federal concern.

• Richard M. Guilderson, Jr., resigned the directorship of NC News Service after three years in the position. A.E.P. Wall, former editor of *The Catholic Review,* was appointed to succeed him Aug. 31.

• *The Monitor,* newspaper of the San Francisco archdiocese, announced that Gerard E. Sherry would take over as editor-manager Aug. 1, two weeks after the shutting down of the *Central California Register* in Fresno. The *Register* was a casualty of an advertising boycott traceable to objectors to the paper's stand for justice to grape-pickers at odds with large California growers.

Encuentro de Pastoral

Two hundred fifty representatives of Spanish-speaking Catholics in the US attended the four-day Hispano Encuentro de Pastoral held in Washington under the sponsorship of the Division for Spanish-Speaking, US Catholic Conference.

The purposes of the assembly were to evaluate the pastoral performance of the Church among the Spanish-speaking and to find ways and means of improving it. Accordingly, the delegates called for:

• establishment of a National Pastoral Institute for the Spanish-Speaking, to function as a study, information and publications center;

• establishment of a Secretariat for the Liturgy, within the USCC, to produce liturgical materials suitable for the Spanish-speaking;

• the assignment of work with and for the Spanish-speaking to "leaders who recognize and understand the permanent reality of this cultural minority in the United States."

FOREIGN

Ecclesiastical Guerrilla Warfare — Cardinal John Heenan attacked the "ecclesiastical guerrilla warfare" of theologians he said had been at loggerheads with the Holy See since the Second Vatican Council. Their chief menace is their rejection of authentic conciliar theology despite their claim that they are teaching it, he said in a letter to the clergy. One target of the Cardinal's criticism was the manifesto issued by thirty-odd theologians in March.

Cuban Tortured to Death — The family of Catholic student leader Luis Boitel disclosed that he died at the Castillo del Principe Prison, Havana, from wounds received during torture, for his refusal to join "the rehabilitation" program of the Castro government. He had been in jail since 1960.

Cursillos — Church leaders defended the Cursillos de Cristianadad against charges of brainwashing, group therapy and political meddling, at the third Latin American gathering of Cursillistas in Sao Paulo, Brazil. Archbishop Avelar Brandao Vilela of Bahia told 2,000 leaders of the movement that Cursillos "are a powerful instrument in the hands of the Spirit to revitalize society."

Mother Teresa — The Indian Council of Cultural Relations conferred the Nehru Award and its accompanying prize of $13,000 on Mother Teresa, foundress of the Missionaries of Charity. The award citation stated: "In serving selflessly, without narrow considerations of nationality, caste or creed, and without expectation of public recognition, Mother Teresa has set an example of how quiet, dedicated effort can contribute to the promotion of good will, friendship and understanding among the peoples of the world."

Paraguayan Government Nervous — Spanish Father Jose Luis Caravias, S.J., expelled from Paraguay for his efforts to aid farmworkers, said the growing strength of their organized movement was regarded "as a serious threat" by the nation's rulers. He said: "The Stroessner government is getting nervous. All of us who work in adult education in the rural areas are being persecuted. Before it was the students, but now the farmworkers are awakening with more force." Most of the league's organizers were members of the Third Order of St. Francis.

Missionary Spirit of Communion — In an open letter to 30,000 diocesan and religious priests in Spain, Bishop Eduardo Pironio, secretary general of the Latin American Bishops' Council, said: "The Church in Latin America is at a critical moment of responsibility and commitment to the whole population; and, within the limitations of our poverty, the Spirit is performing wonders, one of them being our gradual discovery of our own identity and vocation in facing the process of profound change now happening here. We cannot do it alone. More than ever, we need to live in communion with you. Our poverty has something to teach, your missionary wealth can communicate much to other churches. But this must come in the sense of communion, not mere help."

Cardinal Goes Home — Cardinal Joseph Malula, ending four months of exile in Rome, returned to the Kinshasa archdiocese June 12. His return and the appointment of two new bishops to dioceses in Zaire were said to be signs that Church-state difficulties "have been settled to the satisfaction of both sides." At the heart of the troubles were President Mobutu's determination to set up political cells of the Popular Revolutionary Movement seminaries and the substitution of African culture for European culture, including insistence on the use of African names instead of baptismal names.

Greek Orthodox Priests Screened — The Directorate of National Security was reported to be playing a powerful role in screening candidates for ordination in the Greek Orthodox Church. A government circular told bishops that, if a security investigation "shows that the ordinands are loyal, and provided that they have the necessary legal and other qualifications, you can then proceed to their ordination as priests."

Bishops and President Differ — The bishops and president of Uruguay held different views on the causes of violence in the nation. The Uruguayan Bishops' Conference said that "stagnation, dependency and hopelessness" engulfing people in their jobs, homes, schools, health and social security were responsible "for the difficult situation." President Juan Maria Bordaberry said: "I disagree with such justification of the causes of violence." He thought it was caused by a "seditious" plan of guerrilla leaders.

Population Problems — Debate at a session of the Economic and Social Council demonstrated that member countries of the United Nations were not only divided but splintered in attitudes toward population trends and problems. The cleavage was greatest between those who held that the UN had not done enough to meet the challenge of the so-called population explosion and those who protested that it had done far too much — in what they claimed was an over-emphasis on birth control and family planning. The latter members included Latin American, Moslem and some Communist nations.

IRA Provisionals — "Now we've got to find a formula for the future that Catholics and Protestants can live with; that;s going to be a real tough nut to crack," stated Tom Conaty, chairman of Belfast's Central Citizens' Defense Committee, after the militant IRA Provisionals ordered a ceasefire in Northern Ireland. "We've got to learn, first of all, to talk to one another again, not on the old basis of Protestant masters and Catholic vassals, but as equals — as citizens of the same country both wanting the best for the whole citizenry."

Radicals Arrested — In an effort to help bring peace to Northern Ireland, the government of Prime Minister Jack Lynch arrested three leaders in the radical ranks of advocates for a united Ireland — Rory and Sean O'Brady and Joe Cahill. The three were charged, under the Offenses against the State Act, with membership in an illegal organization, the Sinn Fein and the IRA.

Sex Advice — Catholics in London attacked a project of the Family Planning Association to give widespread "safe sex" advice to English teenagers. Under the plan, scheduled to be implemented in July, trained volunteers would encourage youngsters to use contraceptives. "It's monstrous," commented Father George Leonard of the Catholic Information Office. "It's another example of encouraging promiscuity, of separating love and sex. This thing could promote VD."

Environment — "Harmony can be restored between man and nature" only if man is willing to be more instead of wanting to have more, Father Henri De Reidmatten told the UN Conference on the Human Environment in Stockholm. The head of the Vatican delegation said: "The present technological civilization has compromised the basic interrelationship between man and his environment," and has made man want to have more despite dire ecological consequences.

Bangladesh Relief — Catholic Relief Services received $5 million in grants from the US Agency for International Development for relief operations in Bangladesh. CRS, working through the Bangladesh Christian Organization for Relief and Rehabilitation, earmarked the funds for use in housing, road and bridge repair, agricultural development, small business loans and skilled employment programs.

Untouchables Not Eligible — Converts to Christianity from the "untouchable" class were declared ineligible to receive land reform benefits in the State of Kerala. At the request of the national government, the state government amended its land act to annul an existing benefit provision for the Harijans.

Foreign Briefs:

• Billy Graham, on tour in Ireland, offered no easy solutions to troubles in the North. Instead, he stressed that "the love of God" is the only basic basis for brotherhood.

• Two hundred eighty men and women religious and lay persons were authorized to distribute Holy Communion in Eucharistic ceremonies in Rio de Janeiro.

• Archbishop Gerolamo Prigione, nuncio to Gautemala, was criticized by the families of some 600 persons missing after five years of political violence. They charged him with failure to make attempts to find those who were missing.

Church in Czechoslovakia

Facts speak for themselves with silent and sad "eloquence" concerning the condition of the Church in Czechoslovakia, according to an editorial comment in *L'Osservatore Della Domenica* June 18. Federico Alessandrini commented:

• The recent deaths of two aged bishops left only three Catholic bishops in the country.

• Two other priests were acting as "provisional ordinaries" under "always increasingly difficult conditions."

• Other "vicars" had been "imposed" by the government on some dioceses.

• Restrictions on nuns had been tightened.

Alessandrini said: "Things are returning to the situation that existed" before the New Spring of 1968.

JULY 1972

VATICAN

Changeless Things — Commenting on change in an ever-changing world, Pope Paul told a general audience July 5: "There are some things which can and perhaps should be changed (in the Church), but we all know there are other things which are so important . . . and so essential, such as divine truth and the make-up of the Church legitimately and authoritatively founded, that must not be changed." He insisted that these important and essential qualities of the Church "should be defended, preserved, reaffirmed and absolutely renewed both interiorly and exteriorly."

Church's Right To Judge — Pope Paul reiterated the right of the Church "to pass moral judgments, even in matters touching the political order, whenever basic personal rights or the salvation of souls make such judgments necessary." He made the statement at an audience with Enrique Sanchez Salinas, Nicaragua's new ambassador to the Holy See, June 6.

"Enough!" — Pope Paul made one of his most pointed and plaintive pleas for the end of the Vietnam war July 9. "We repeat the groans of so many innocent people," he said. "We make ours the voice of a population driven to exhaustion by massacre and calamity. We cry out . . . to beseech those who can and who ought to discuss and deliberate: Enough!"

Heritage of Athenagoras — A thirst for Christian unity is the heritage Patriarch Athenagoras left us, and now that unfulfilled desire becomes our obligation, Pope Paul told a gathering in St. Peter's Square July 9, two days after his death. "The patriarch's supreme and only wish," the Pope said, "was to be able to drink from the same chalice with us, that is, to celebrate together the Eucharistic Sacrifice, the synthesis and crown of our common ecclesial identification with Christ. Indeed, we desired this so very much."

The Pope delegated four high-ranking prelates to serve as his personal representatives at the funeral of the Patriarch in Istanbul July 11.

"Man, Be A Man" — "Man, be a man. Christian, be a Christian," Pope Paul VI urged the people of the world as he addressed 10,000 tourists and pilgrims at a general audience July 12. He said the moral command that men act like men and Christians act like Christians derived from "the very first insights into the way in which men should conduct themselves."

Brotherhood and Peace — Not armaments but brotherhood among nations is the key to peace, Pope Paul told graduates of the 40th session of the North Atlantic Treaty Organization Defense College.

"Peace in our time," he told the 57 graduates from 12 nations, "is indeed something weak, something not yet perfected, and something circumscribed by the many limitations of our age. We are convinced that you will succeed in this mission if you work to strengthen the bonds of solidarity and union among peoples, the bonds of friendship and the bonds of fraternal collaboration. These — not armaments — are the means adapted to your goal. With these means you are assured of success."

Confession Stays — Pope Paul commented at a general audience July 19 on norms issued by the Congregation for the Doctrine of the Faith concerning the granting of general absolution in certain circumstances. He said: "These norms deal with the sacrament of penance which involves confession, according to the rule which derives from Christ, from the tradition of the Church and from several councils. This rule of private confession remains." The Pope called on priests, "doctors of souls and psychiatrists of grace," to hear confessions "with the interest and enthusiasm for the greatest events of our life."

Call to Youth — Pope Paul continued a campaign to call modern youth to Christ which he began in Australia late in 1970. He dedicated his entire Sunday talk July 23 to the youth of the world, telling them: "Perhaps your search for truth is a prophecy of the coming of one voice which says everything and of an encounter which provides everything. It is Christ. Perhaps you do not know you are turning toward Christ. But we tell you this: He is marching toward you."

Youth is too smart, the Pope declared, to fall for the lie that doing away with the present civilization will solve the world's problems. Youth continues its search for truth, he went on, and hopes to find it in friendships and in returning to nature. Suggesting that this is not sufficient to answer their needs, he added: "Let us pray this day to celebrate the new encounter of Christ with the young."

Praise from Rogers — US Secretary of State William P. Rogers said he personally conveyed to Pope Paul "the very warm thanks of President Nixon and the American people" his attempts to obtain an exchange of prisoners in Vietnam.

The Pope Also:

• Sent a letter of praise and good wishes to Cardinal John P. Cody of Chicago on his 25th anniversary as a bishop, July 2.

• Met for 25 minutes with Gov. Ronald Reagan of California, July 13.

• Began a two-month working vacation at Castel Gandolfo, July 15.

• As millions of Italians fled the cities for seashore and mountains to begin annual August vacations, paid tribute to the "not small minority" of workmen who must stay on the job "to expedite this annual exodus," July 30.

• Assured new Eastern Orthodox Patriarch Dimitrios: "In the Bishop of Rome you will always find a loving brother."

Pentecostal Groups — A delayed report disclosed that representatives of the Vatican Secretariat for Promoting Christian Unity and non-Catholic Pentecostal churches and groups met together for the first time June 20 to 24 in Switzerland. A communique issued by the secratariat said that "areas on which agreement tended to emerge were the role of the Holy Spirit in the life of the believer; the way in which this is experienced, and the manifestations of the experience through those charismata (gifts of the Holy Spirit) which can build up the life and unity of the Christian community. Additional meetings were scheduled over a five-year period, to "focus on the role of the Holy Spirit in the life of the Christian and of the churches."

Vatican Briefs:

• The Congregation for the Doctrine of the Faith made public July 13 norms regulating the granting of general absolution without confession in certain circustances. The norms made it clear that subsequent confession of serious sins remains an obligation of the penitent. (See separate entry.)

• The Secretariat for Promoting Christian Unity issued an instruction stating that a Protestant may be given Communion in a Catholic Church if his belief in the Eucharist conforms to Catholic teaching, if he has serious need of "Eucharistic sustenance," if he is unable to join with members of his own religious community, and if he spontaneously asks for the sacrament. The instruction dealt with the admission of individuals, not groups, to the Eucharist, and was meant primarily for the guidance of bishops' conferences and individual bishops.

• Two Vatican congregations notified the cathedral chapter of the Roermond diocese by letter that they found the acts and statements of controversial Bishop John M. Gijsen "correct in every canonical, doctrinal and pastoral sense."

Discrimination against Women — The Church's former reluctance to let women read the word of God in church was branded narrow and discriminating in *L'Osservatore della Domenica.* "We must frankly recognize that this legislation shows marks of a narrow outlook and of human discrimination, as if man were superior to woman," wrote Father Gaetano Meaolo. His comment concerned a regulation of the 1969 rubrics for the *Roman Missal,* which stipulated that, in the absence of a suitable man, national or regional bishops' conferences could allow "a well-prepared woman, standing outside the sanctuary, to read the lessons preceding the Gospel." He asserted that the rule implied "discrimination against God's word itself, as if it were no longer the word of God when proclaimed by a woman."

Christian Morality

Pope Paul, tackling what he called the "immense problems" of relations between secular life and Christian life, declared July 26 that Christian morality is distinct from natural morality, and defined it "from a practical point of view as a way of living according to the faith, that is, by the light of the truths of Christ and his example."

He drew two conclusions from St. Paul's formula, "the just man lives by faith."

"The first conclusion is that our practical idea of life should keep first place for God, for religion, for faith, for spiritual health. This should not be an honorary first place, purely formal or ritualistic, but rather a first place of principle and of action."

The second conclusion is that religion cannot exonerate man from duties toward human justice and social progress.

"It should be recognized that the primacy of the religious factor in ordering human action does not carry with it an evasion of urgent duties concerning justice and human social progress, as if purely religious observance sufficed to exonerate a man's conscience from the obligations of solidarity and generosity toward his neighbor. Much less does the recognition of religious primacy in morality create a selfish and irrational slow-down in the active quest for remedies for social evils. Quite the contrary."

DOMESTIC

Limited Terms for Pastors — On the recommendation of the Brooklyn Priests' Senate, Bishop Francis J. Mugavero announced July 5 that pastors in the diocese could henceforth serve in that capacity for a maximum of two six-year terms. Similar limitations were announced earlier in Boston and a number of other dioceses across the country.

Help for Agnes Victims — The National Catholic Disaster Relief Committee launched a nationwide appeal for financial aid for victims of tropical storm Agnes. In a letter to all the country's bishops, Msgr. Leo Coady, chairman of the committee, urged them to do everything possible to raise funds to ease the suffering caused by the "unprecedented disaster on the East coast."

Priests Suspended — Information leaked to the press and published early in the month disclosed that six priests of the Buffalo diocese had been suspended by Bishop James A. McNulty. Chancery officials declined comment, stating only that "the reasons for this action come under the classification of privileged information and should not be publicized."

Lettuce Boycott — The Social Development Committee of the US Catholic Conference endorsed the boycott of iceberg lettuce called by Cesar Chavez' United Farm Workers' Union. The committee said that a "fundamental issue of social justice" was at stake in the union's efforts to organize workers and negotiate with growers.

Nativist Attitude — According to Father Edmundo Rodriguez, co-founder of PADRES, an organization of Mexican-American priests, the persistence of "American nativism" is a major barrier in the advancement of Mexican-Americans. In an interview with *The Southern Cross,* the San Diego diocesan newspaper, he said that the main problem facing Mexican-Americans is the "resentment of people who feel we're foreign to their way of life, to their own ethnic and cultural background." He claimed that nativism had excluded Mexican-American participation in business, education, and government.

Cursillo and Ecumenism — Fifty-seven delegates attending a national meeting of the Cursillo Movement in Dallas reaffirmed a policy of adhering to existing discipline regarding ecumenical activities. Noting that some diocesan Cursillo movements were allowing inter-Communion, the delegates agreed unanimously that the Cursillo's ecumenical policy is always to be "consistent with Church discipline."

Former Priests — The Milwaukee Archdiocesan Priests' Senate called for charitable treatment of former priests and recognition by prospective employers of "the broad spectrum of talents and expertise of these men." Stating that priests who leave the active ministry have made "serious and often painful moral decisions," the senate said it respected "the fact that these men have followed the dictates of their consciences," and added: "We hope that they will remain in touch with the Church and join us in worship with their families."

Capital Punishment — Editorial opinion in Catholic newspapers varied widely in reaction to the Supreme Court decision which ruled that the death penalty, as commonly administered, was unconstitutional but that new laws applying the penalty for specific reasons and in a fair manner might meet constitutional tests. The decision affected nearly 700 persons on death rows throughout the country. Thirty-seven nations had already outlawed capital punishment.

Addict Rehabilitation — For the second time in two years, a former Jersey City convent was converted into a halfway house for the rehabilitation of drug addicts. Casa Bonifacio was the name of the house which adopted a program similar to one in operation in Christ the King Parish. It was also reported that St. Patrick's Parish was in the process of setting up a methadon treatment center.

School Aid — A package of bills designed to provide $30 million in aid to nonpublic schools in Illinois was signed into law by Gov. Richard B. Ogilvie. To assure the earliest possible test of the constitutionality of the enactment, the state auditor, aa supporter of nonpublic school aid, refused to release funds appropriated by the bills.

Tax Credit Constitutional — Minnesota's landmark program of income tax credits for the parents of nonpublic school children was ruled constitutional July 6 in a state court in St. Paul. The law was the first of its kind in the US and the ruling was believed to be the first court decision on the tax credit form of nonpublic school aid. The law provided that the parents of nonpublic school pupils could deduct tuition costs — up to $140 per high school student and $100 per elementary school child — from their final state income tax bills.

Similar measures had been passed or were pending in other states, and more than 20 tax credit bills had been introduced in Congress.

No Aid — In New Jersey, hopes for assistance to parents of children attending nonpublic schools were dashed when the State Assembly rejected an income tax proposal and other tax reform measures of Governor William T. Cahill by a margin of 2 to 1. His program would have provided parents with tax credits of $50 and $100 per child enrolled in nonpublic elementary and high schools, respectively. The legislature's action did not affect an existing program under which parents were reimbursed $10 on the elementary level and $20 on the secondary level for textbooks on secular subjects.

No Bishop Title — Delegates attending the sixth biennial convention of the Lutheran Church in America in Dallas rejected, 286 to 218, a proposal to use the "bishop" title when referring to leaders of the church.

Ukrainian Seminar — One hundred and 50 scholars attending a seminar at Fordham University heard Father George A. Maloney, S.J., charge that Pope Paul's refusal to set up a Ukrainian patriarchate under Cardinal Slipyi was blocking unity efforts of the Orthodox, Anglicans and Protestants. He also criticized plans to codify Oriental canon law as a "further Latinization of the Eastern Churches." The seminar was sponsored by the Society for a Patriarchal System in the Ukrainian Catholic Church.

Elderly Religious — An expert on aging urged religious communities to replace "busy work" 2programs for retired religious with creative, community-based social service projects.

Dr. Paul Kerschner, executive director of the Maryland Commission on Nursing Homes, made the recommendation July 25 at an Institute on Retirement and Religious at Georgetown University.

"There is," he said, "a pressing need for innovative, experimental retirement enclaves," for the elderly. He suggested ". . . independent retired religious living in apartments, engaged in teaching, delivering of services to less mobile elderly, and operating shops."

Sister-Senator? — Sister Eleanor Anstey, 46, religious education coordinator for two parishes in Muscatine, filed for the Democratic nomination for the Iowa Senate. She was the first nun in Iowa history to enter politics.

Pastoral Councils — Survey results released late in the month by an advisory group of the US Catholic Conference indicated that 57 of 137 dioceses responding had pastoral councils, 69 were planning to establish them, and 11 had no plans.

Domestic Briefs:

• George Wallace ended a 54-day stay at Holy Cross Hospital, Silver Spring, Md., following attendance and reading of the 23rd Psalm at Mass June 7.

• Joanne Pierce, 31, a former Sister of Mercy, was one of the two first women sworn in as FBI agents July 17.

• Project Equality, a national alliance of religious organizations to promote fair employment policies, was endorsed by Bishop Louis E. Gelineau of Providence.

• Our Sunday Visitor, Inc., assumed control of the Catechetical Guild Educational Society, a St. Paul, Minn., corporation producing audio-visual materials for Catholic schools and after-school religion programs.

• The sacrament of the anointing of the sick was administered to more than 500 persons in Orlando in an unusual liturgy on July 25, the feast of St. James, patron of the sick and aged.

• Catherine Schaefer and Alba Zizzamia, former director and assistant director, respectively, of the UN Affairs Division of the US Catholic Conference, were awarded Benemerenti Medals by Pope Paul.

Key '73

The four dioceses of Missouri announced July 25 that they had decided to participate in Key '73, a year-long (Advent, 1972, through 1973) evangelism crusade involving Catholic and Protestant churches throughout North America.

In line with its purpose of "Calling Our Continent to Christ," the program was to be keyed to sharing the Gospel with every person in North America, employing all modern means of communicating the Gospel, applying the Gospel to modern social issues, and developing new resources for evangelism.

FOREIGN

Athenagoras I Dies — Ecumenical Orthodox Patriarch Athenagoras I, 86, died July 7 at the Bakliki Hospital, Istanbul. Pope Paul called him "a great protagonist of the reconciliation of all Christians." (See separate entry.)

New Patriarch — The Holy Synod of the Eastern Orthodox Church elected Metropolitan Dimitrios, 58, to succeed Athenagoras I as Ecumenical Patriarch. (See separate entry.)

No Visa — The Turkish government refused to grant Archbishop Iakovos of the Greek Orthodox Diocese of North and South America a visa to attend the funeral of Orthodox Patriarch Athenagoras I in Istanbul. In support of the Archbishop, whom the government regarded as *persona non grata*, an ecumenical delegation including Cardinal Terence Cooke of New York cancelled plans to attend the funeral.

Loyola College — Catholic leaders in Montreal expressed suspicion that Quebec's Anglo-Protestant universities had ganged up on Catholic Loyola College in the interest of their own preservation. This was their reaction following publication of a report by the Quebec Province's Council of Universities which recommended that Loyola — Quebec's only Catholic, English-language institution of higher learning — be phased out by 1975.

Confused Image in Peru — The Church must do more in the communications field if it is to project an accurate image of itself in Peru, according to a study made by the journalism school of the Pontifical Catholic University there. Among problems to be overcome, according to the study, were failure of the bishops to take clear-cut stands on moral and social issues, the international wire services' dominant position in the flow of news to Peruvian papers, and the fact that within Peru itself there was no coordinated press effort by the Church.

Vocations Explosion — A vocations explosion was under way among Ibos in the territory that was called Biafra during the Nigerian civil war, according to an Irish priest working there. Father J. C. McGuinness, a missionary at Holy Family College in Abak, South Eastern State, reported in *The Furrow* that seminaries in all the Iboland dioceses were overcrowded and that there was also "a very large increase" in the number of vocations for congregations of nuns.

Church Marriages Down in Africa — A survey being prepared for publication under the auspices of the Anglican Consultative Council showed that there had been a startling decline in the number of church marriages during the past five years. Factors contributing to the decline probably included tribal attitudes and the cost of formal weddings.

Latin American Nuns — A nun in Latin America was said to be undergoing a crisis of identity, often "not understanding her role in society, not knowing who she is . . . and in danger of failing to fulfill her Church mission because of her feelings of insecurity." This was a conclusion of "The Nun in Latin America Today," a survey of the attitudes and aspirations of 131,000 Sisters sponsored by the Latin American Confederation of Religious. The changing role of women in Latin America posed a dilemma for nuns, according to the study, as well as the ambivalence of popular attitudes toward them. "Especially among the young," the study asserted, "there is at once the freakish image of the traditional nun and the expectation that she must adapt herself to the conditions of modern living." The resultant identity crisis was reported to be at the root of a decline in recruitment during the period from 1968 to 1971.

Church Troubles in Yugoslavia — Church-state tensions were erupting in the Serbian area of Yugoslavia, according to reports reaching Vienna. Partial evidence was the imposition by a local court of a 30-day jail sentence on Orthodox Bishop Vasilje of Zica for "activities hostile to the state." The Holy Synod of the Serbian Orthodox Church protests against the sentence and was demanding not only a reversal of the guilty verdict but also dropping of all charges and procedures against the prelate.

Catholic-Lutheran Talks — Talks between representatives of the Catholic Church and the Lutheran World Federation, begun in 1967, ended with some very impressive results, according to one of the participants. Dr. Harding Meyer, one of the Lutheran parties, noted:

• a common affirmation by participants that the world of God is sovereign and not at man's disposition, and that all authority of the Church derives from service to this world;

• a far-reaching consensus in understanding the Lutheran doctrine of justification by faith as an expression of the unconditional nature of God's gift of salvation;

• agreement on points of substance regarding the Eucharist, especially as to the Real Presence and sacrifice of Christ;

• a consensus on the basic understanding and basic structure of the ministry, along with a clear coming together on the "sacramental" character of ordination, the concept of "apostolic succession," and the so-called "priestly character." Results of the talks reflected the views of the participants. Official positions of the Churches were not changed.

Sudan Gets Administrator — Vatican Radio reported July 26 that Msgr. Paolini Doggale had been installed as the newly appointed apostolic administrator of Juba. Another source reported that the 100th Sudanese priest has been ordained in Uganda and that about 40 of 80 active Sudanese priests were engaged in the ministry in their own country.

Young Marriages — Archbishop Anthony Jordan of Edmonton, Canada, issues directives designed to cut down the failure rate of marriages of persons in the 19-and-under age bracket. He ordered persons contemplating marriage to consult a priest at least four months before the intended date and to go through steps considered necessary to assure their maturity, readiness and freedom to marry.

Oder-Neisse Dioceses — Germans in public life, both in the Church and in government, were generally critical of Pope Paul's action in placing formerly German dioceses in Western Poland under Polish bishops, even though the action has been expected for a long time. Prior to the appointment of the Polish bishops, the dioceses had been nominally German but under the actual administration of Poles. The Pope acted after ratification by the government of Poland, East Germany and West Germany of an agreement regarding Polish possession of the Oder-Neisse area.

No Memoirs — A Hungarian-born university professor in Vienna said that publication of Cardinal Mindszenty's memoirs was precluded by the agreement between the Vatican and the Hungarian government which resulted in the Cardinal's leaving the US Embassy in Budapest in September, 1971.

Foreign Briefs:

• By the end of June, 32 voluntary and religious organizations had spent $47.5 million on aid and relief work in Bangladesh. The largest operation was the one sponsored by the Christian Organization for Relief and Rehabilitation, under the direction of two Holy Cross missionaries and with the aid of Catholic Relief Services.

• American Columban Father Patrick McGlinchey was awarded the Order of Industrial Service Merit by President Park Chunghee of South Korea for his role in developing a major cattle-raising industry on Cheju Island.

• The Northern Transvaal Synod of the Dutch Reformed Church asked provincial authorities not to renew the contracts of six nurses at a hospital for blacks in Tembisa because they were all Catholic nuns. The synod also called on all members of the church to boycott Catholic schools, hospitals and maternity institutions as the only effective way to prevent the spread of Catholicism.

Lack of Christianity

The major superiors of seven religious orders in Burundi condemned the lack of Christianity they said that recent bloodshed there revealed. In a "confidential" note to the bishops of Burundi, the superiors said: "Our leaders have never been prepared to assume their political responsibilities in a Christian way." They called for increased efforts to instill the teachings of the Gospel more deeply.

Archbishop Andreas Makarakiza of Kitega, president of the Burundi Bishops' Conference, asked missionaries in the country not to leave in protest against what their superiors called the lack of Christianity in the nation.

He said: "I invite you to reflect on this especially at the time when departures for political motives by certain members of technical assistance teams risk making people believe that your presence and your mission are purely and simply identical to their presence and their mission."

AUGUST 1972

VATICAN

Conscience Not Enough — Pope Paul warned Aug. 2 that conscience alone is not enough for the guidance of moral conduct. "Of itself, conscience does not suffice even though it carries within itself the basic teachings of the natural law," he asserted. "The Christian way would not be known to us with truth and authority if it had not been announced to us by the message of the outer word, by the Gospel and the Church.

Whoever wants to emancipate himself from legitimate authority would find his moral sense mute on many inconvenient and principal teachings which are basic for a Christian. He would finish by losing the exactness of his moral judgment, and by yielding to that elastic and permissive morality which unfortunately seems to prevail today."

Sports — Sports can train man to achieve life's goals, Pope Paul told more than 300 young athletes taking part in the 24th series of competitions sponsored by the International Sports Federation of Catholic Education, Aug. 6. He said: "We hope that your experience in athletics is helping you to understand that in every area of life it is necessary to use all your talents and energies. Only in that way is it possible for you to attain your goals."

Revolution and Duty — Pope Paul spoke about both subjects at a general audience Aug. 9.

He criticized those who try to make revolution a duty, and asked: "Are we not abusing this explosive word 'revolution' to make of it a disastrous myth, or at least a tormenting one?" Noting that revolutionary movements often claim for themselves absolute authority to judge all things, he asked again: "What regime is more rigorously conservative than a revolutionary one?"

Of duty, he said it exists independently of obligations resulting from social legislation. He also stated that, contrary to what some people think, the concept of duty is not in conflict with freedom of action but is a moral guide to action. "We, sons of Christ and the Church, are the defenders of the genuine freedom of the human spirit, and therefore of the social order deriving from that freedom," he said.

Liberty — Pope Paul devoted another of his weekly audiences Aug. 16 to consideration of moral attitudes and behavior. He said, in part: "If we wish to respect man in his integrity, we must educate him to do good, logically, with a sense of responsibility, a capacity for self-control and even with the exterior help of laws and authority, without which every person would be exposed to dangers of every sort and society to anarchy. "But we must not deprive him of his intimate, legitimate and intangible liberty. The game is extremely risky, but this is the fate of man and of society."

Concept of the Will — Speaking in the same vein a week later, the Holy Father stated: "To give to the moral stature of men and Christians its perfect measure, it is not enough to grow passively over the years or simply to assimilate the training one receives in the sphere in which one lives." He continued: "It is most important, especially at a young age, to have an exact concept of the will in the human structure. . . . Good will should express itself in terms of an anxiousness to live, a desire to work and a capacity to love. There are those who speak madly of the 'will to power,' but we prefer to speak humbly of the power to will." The Pope said that stress on the importance of the will and will power flows from the teachings of Christianity: "Christian education tends to form strong and active souls. Laziness is not permitted, nor is sloth accepted by the school of Christ."

The Pope Also:
• Said that building a united Europe can contribute to international harmony so long as the "sense of man" is kept in mind, at a meeting with Prince Werner de Merode, Belgium's new ambassador to the Vatican, Aug. 11.
• Sent his best wishes and assurance of prayers to Dr. William Potter, newly elected secretary general of the World Council of Churches, Aug. 17.
• Said the opening of the Olympic Games "awakens hope" for a world of peace, Aug. 26.

Pastoral Councils — Pastoral councils "by nature" are limited in scope to individual dioceses, and therefore the concept of a national pastoral council "does not fit into the constitutional structure of the Church," an official of the Congregation for the Clergy told NC News. He said that a document on such councils was being prepared by the congregation and that it would be sent to Pope Paul for approval before publication. The Vatican viewed pastoral councils, composed of priests and lay persons, strictly as a means of "personal contact" between the People of God and the bishop of a single diocese, the official said. He explained that this does not exclude setting up an office for the exchange of ideas or information on a level broader than a diocese, but that such an office would not be part of the juridical structure.

Lay Activity in Africa — A papal letter hailed the increasing activity of Catholic lay persons in Africa, and advised: "An apostolic action of the laity cannot be carried out effectively if it is not in strict and permanent communion with the bishops" and if there is not "a trusting and brotherly exchange with their collaborators, the priests and religious." The letter was written for the Pope by Cardinal Jean Villot, secretary of state. It was addressed to Cardinal Paul Zoungrana, president of the Symposium of the Episcopal Conferences of Africa and Madagascar.

Religious Garb — The Congregation for Religious, in a letter made public Aug. 26, called on papal representatives and heads of religious conferences to remind priests and religious, men and women, that "the religious habit is considered by the Second Vatican Council as a sign of their consecration." The directive was the latest of several of the same type which had fallen on deaf ears in some quarters. It was reminiscent of remarks made by Cardinal Ildebrando Antoniutti, head of the congregation, in a 1969 address to 550 major superiors of women. He said: "The increasing trend toward secularization . . . has not only caused necessary changes in religious garb, but also has at times introduced a completely secular style of dress which is not the sign of consecration called for by the (Second Vatican) Council."

Vatican Briefs:
• A Vatican Radio editorial implied that the banning of Rhodesia from the Olympic Games was hypocritical. The key question was: "Are all the nations who are participating in the Olympic Games in Munich immune from racism, the factor which expelled Rhodesia?"
• The ambassador of the Republic of China (Taiwan) to the Vatican said he discounted rumors that the Vatican was planning to downgrade its diplomatic mission on Taiwan in order to clear the way for possible negotiations with Communist China. Rumors of a possible change in diplomatic policy centered on the prolonged absence from Taiwan of the pronuncio, Archbishop Cassidy.
• The Vatican Book Store started sale of *The Teachings of Pope Paul,* a 1,376-page volume of the Pope's 1971 messages, sermons, discourses and other documents.
• The administrative office of the Vatican museums verified reports that electronic gear and other protective devices were in operation to guard art treasures.
• The Vatican began making hooded raincoats available for tourists seeking entrance to St. Peter's Basilica who were judged to be improperly attired.

Authentic Christian Life

Pope Paul told a general audience Aug. 30 that the search for an "authenic interpretation of Christian life today" is endangered by moral uncertainty which places "every moral norm in doubt."

Many persons, he said, are being led to think "that all rules . . . are debatable, even untenable, and can and must be changed."

The Christian answer to this state of affairs is: "Moral norms, those of natural law and also of the Gospel, cannot undergo change."

He explained that he did not mean that man's understanding of these norms could not be deepened or enhanced. But he warned that the desire and goal of renewal must not lead to ethical relativism or situation ethics.

The Pope recommended three remedies for Christians faced with "the spreading and overwhelming moral uncertainty of today leading toward a nihilism that could be catastrophic:

• "first, a right understanding of natural law;
• "second, habitual recourse to a truly good conscience;
• "third, trust in obedience to those in authority over us, in the domestic, civic and ecclesiastical spheres."

The Holy Father concluded by pointing out the special significance of his words for Catholics:

"To pretend to liberate the faithful from the Church's teaching authority established by Christ, both by freeing him from the dogmatism of ecclesiastical teaching and by loosening the bonds of hierarchical authority instituted by Christ in the Church, means to tear the faithful away from the certainty of both the faith and moral norms, from this charisma of certainty of truly Catholic faith, and to prefer senseless torment, spiritual aloneness and apostolic fruitlessness."

DOMESTIC

Complaints Lead to Change — Wahlert High School, Dubuque, responded to criticism of its religion courses by dropping two textbooks and starting a program offering three kinds of courses. The changes resulted from controversy over content and methodology which broke out in February, 1971, when a group of dissatisfied parents charged that "the fundamentals of doctrine" were not being taught.

Genocide — Cardinal Patrick O'Boyle accused municipal officials of predominantly black Washington of promoting genocide through new abortion regulations. Looking at the new regulations, he said: "In a city that is 71 per cent black, and that includes a measurable amount of poor people, no one can ignore the implications of genocide." He added: "The Nuremberg war-crimes tribunals called abortion promoted among the Jews in Germany a 'crime against humanity.' Can it be that what was crime in Germany 30 years ago has become a civilized action in Washington today? Or is it that history is repeating itself?"

Tax Benefits Good Sense — Granting tax benefits to parents of nonpublic school children makes good legislative sense, according to an education study published in Washington. Tax benefits have traditionally been allowed for "special burdens borne by the particular taxpayer," and to promote "activities which are regarded to be in the public interest," said Roger A. Freeman, author of the study. Both factors are present in the case of a parent who sends his children to a nonpublic school, he said. The study — "Income Tax Credits for Tuitions and Gifts in Nonpublic School Education" — was originally prepared for President Nixon's Commission on School Finance.

Advice to Seminarians — Bishop Bernard J. Topel of Spokane told seminarians in his diocese to develop a strong, personal and regular prayer life or to discontinue study for the priesthood. He said in a letter: "If it appears that you are not likely to practice daily mental prayer in the priesthood, I ask that you cease studying for the priesthood." Bishop Topel explained he was not referring to "meditation, strictly speaking," but rather to "personal mental prayer."

Leave for Lindsay Aide — Archbishop Humberto S. Medeiros of Boston granted a one-year leave of absence from the active ministry to Father Mark D. Corrigan, but refused to approve of his work as an aide to New York Mayor John Lindsay. The Archbishop had asked the priest to accept another assignment after learning that officials of the archdiocese did not approve of his work in New York.

Planks Wanted — Bishop William E. McManus of Chicago urged the Republican Platform Committee to commit the party to:

• equal educational opportunities for all;
• racial integration in schools;
• federal assistance to the urban poor, including those with children in nonpublic schools;
• federal income tax credits for a portion of nonpublic school tuition.

The platform writers later opposed school busing, spoke approvingly of tax credits to aid the parents of nonpublic school children, and ignored the abortion issue.

Euthanasia — There is no "death with dignity" when it means ending human suffering through euthanasia, Cardinal Terence Cooke told the first annual American Health Congress in Chicago. "If there is to be any death with dignity," he said, "every person's right to life must be respected."

No Change — The Congregation for the Sacraments refused a request from the US bishops to lower the age for the ordination of married permanent deacons from 35 to 30. The National Conference of Catholic Bishops, by a vote of 182 to 44, had asked for the change in April. The congregation said the most it could do would be to grant dispensations for two and a half years in individual cases.

Black Caucus — More than 600 delegates to the third annual convention of the National Black Lay Catholic Caucus pledged to continue to work for "a black archbishop for Washington, D.C., and other dioceses as a means of obtaining black input in policy-making decisions as they affect the lives of black people." Delegates also said: "We have

by no means exonerated the American hierarchy of racism in the Catholic Church, but we are appealing to them to support us in our struggle for total liberation and survival here in America."

Father Armbruster Leaves — Father Carl J. Armbruster, S.J., 43, theology professor at Boston College, announced he was leaving the priesthood. He said there was no connection between this action and the refusal of the National Conference of Catholic Bishops to publish a study on the priesthood of which he was the principal author.

Abortion and Contraception Views — A Gallup survey showed that 56 per cent of Catholics believed that the decision to have an abortion should be left solely to the woman and her doctor, and that 68 per cent favored birth control information for teenagers. The survey also disclosed that 64 per cent of Americans were in favor of liberalized abortion and that 73 per cent believed that birth control services should be available to sexually active teenagers.

Msgr. James McHugh, spokesman on family life for the US Catholic Conference, charged that the survey was misleading and "raises more questions that it settles."

Change of Mind — A United Methodist pastor who worked in an abortion counseling service in Columbus, O., said he had "30 regrets," one for each abortion that followed his counseling. The Rev. Mike Baldwin said he felt "anguish" for having become involved in the service in the first place and that he hoped to get "some minds turned around" about abortion.

Convictions Upheld — A federal judge in Harrisburg upheld the convictions of antiwar activists Father Philip Berrigan, S.J., and Sister Elizabeth McAlister for smuggling letters in and out of prison.

Hibernian Controversy — Controversy at the convention of the American Ancient Order of Hibernians centered on the issue of support for terrorist tactics of the Irish Republican Army. Judge James J. Comerford of New York, editor of the *National Hibernian Digest,* announced that the AOH unequivocably supported the campaign of violence in Northern Ireland. Officials immediately denied that he spoke for the organization. A spokesman insisted that the AOH did not support unrestrained violence.

Catholic Worker Tax-Free — The Internal Revenue Service dropped its attempt to force Dorothy Day and the Catholic Worker to pay $296,359 in income taxes and penalties for the previous five years.

The IRS had tried to collect the money because the movement had refused to apply for tax exemption as a nonprofit organization. Miss Day said her lawyer and an attorney for the government had reached an agreement. "We reached a verbal settlement couched in more human and satisfactory terms" than the formal notice she later received, said Miss Day.

First Service of Religious — A Vatican official declared that religious who place social service ahead of their Gospel mission "are offering the world a service for which it did not ask, at least not as its first preference." Archbishop Sergio Pignedoli, secretary of the Congregation for the Evangelization of Peoples, said the service the world most desires from religious is their witness as "signs of the Absolute," or God. The prelate made his comments at the fourth national assembly of the Consortium Perfectae Caritatis in St. Louis.

Domestic Briefs:

• Robert Sargent Shriver, Jr., a descendant of a Catholic family who settled in Maryland in 1693, was chosen to take the place of Sen. Thomas Eagleton of Missouri as the Democratic candidate for the vice-presidency.

• Michigan State University archeologists discovered the site where Jesuit Father Jacques Marquette was buried by Huron Indians in the 17th century. The diggers also said they had found a portion of a Huron village located next to his mission near present-day St. Ignace, Mich.

• Archbishop James P. Davis, acting on a request from PADRES, appointed Father Ramon Aragon vicar general for the Hispano-Indian peoples of the Santa Fe archdiocese.

Human Development Grants

More than $1.5 million in self-help grants were awarded by the Campaign for Human Development, the anti-poverty education and action program sponsored by the Church in this country.

Fifty-two organizations of poor people in more than 20 states and Puerto Rico received grants worth an agregate of $1,516,930.

CHD headquarters, which funded 264 projects worth more than $5.6 million in its first two years, announced that 1972 grants were going primarily to projects in economic development, education, legal aid, communications, housing, transportation, health, and social development for the poor.

FOREIGN

Ecumenical Intentions — Newly elected Orthodox Patriarch Dimitrios I repeated his intentions to pursue the unity of all Christians. He told a conference of newsmen in Istanbul that he would follow the direction taken by his predecessor, Athenagoras I: "We will systematically strive to preserve the unity of all Orthodox churches and, through this, the unity of all Christians." Sometime before the conference, Cardinal Jan Willebrands, head of the Vatican Secretariat for Promoting Christian Unity, wrote to the Patriarch, saying: "I hope that we can continue the close collaboration of our churches and draw ever nearer the sought-after full communion."

Israeli Refusal Protested — Jews as well as Christian Arabs demonstrated against the Israeli government's refusal to permit Christian Arabs from resettling two villages near the Lebanese border from which they had been barred since 1948.

Knights' Convention — Among other actions taken at their Aug. 15 to 17 convention in Toronto, the Knights of Columbus unanimously condemned abortion as "without foundation in human reason and opposed to nature," and adopted new admission rules designed to prevent discrimination against black candidates for membership.

Dutch Council Meeting Off — The secretariat of the Dutch Bishops' Conference announced that the first meeting of the new Dutch National Pastoral Council, scheduled for Oct. 6 to 8, would be postponed because of objections from the Vatican. The Roman Curia "thinks that the authority of the bishops and their position within the Church is not sufficiently guaranteed by the regulations of the Dutch National Pastoral Council," stated the secretariat. The Dutch bishops, however, "are convinced that in the regulations for the Dutch National Pastoral Council their own responsibility was guaranteed."

It was reported from the Vatican that the Congregation for the Clergy was expected to discuss the establishment of norms for national pastoral councils at a future meeting, possibly in March, 1973.

Criticism in Korea — Cardinal Stephen Kim of Seoul criticized the government of President Park Chung Hee for "using police methods" in trying to achieve its ends.

In a statement which did not appear in the press, he suggested that it was time to return the nation to a state of normalcy under the country's constitution instead of having all powers concentrated in the presidency.

Campaign Promises No Help — Campaign promises of a quick end to the war in Vietnam and the repatriation of all prisoners were not helping official peace overtures of the US government, according to Federico Alessandrini. He said, in an editorial in *L'Osservatore della Domenica,* that the Communist government of Hanoi was assured of "a weapon of singular efficiency even in the United States where the Democratic candidate for the presidency believes it opportune and useful to promise his possible electors the end of the war in Southeast Asia and the repatriation of all Americans."

South African Black Bishop — A black priest was appointed auxiliary bishop in the Johannesburg diocese, where a group of Catholics in 1971 called for the replacement of Bishop Hugh Boyle by a black bishop. The priest, Oblate Father Peter J. Butelezi, 42, was a member of the Zulu tribe. Bishop Boyle said his new auxiliary bishop "will be a tremendous help for the pastoral care of the flock."

Indian Colleges — Catholic colleges in Kerala State reopened following settlement of a dispute with the government concerning tuition and control issues. It was finally agreed that the government would pay all salaries and would have a voice in faculty appointments, that the colleges would turn tuition income over to the government, and that the Church would remain in control of the schools.

Lutheran View of Papacy — Before Lutherans can accept the papacy "as a visible sign of the unity of the churches," that office must be made subordinate "to the primacy of the Gospel," must be theologically reinterpreted, and must be restructured, according to statements in a "Report of the Lutheran-Roman Catholic Study Commission on 'The Gospel and the Church.' " The report pointed out that the controversial question that still remained between Catholics and Lutherans was "whether the primacy of the pope is necessary, or whether it represents only a fundamentally possible function."

Peace Needs Religious Change — "I believe that radical change within the religious institutions of Ireland is the only kind of force that is essential to a just and lasting peace." This was the view stated by sociologist Anthony Spencer, a lecturer of Queen's University, Belfast, at a social studies conference in Falcarragh, Ireland.

Appeal for Bishop's Release — In a letter addressed to Soviet Prime Minister Alexei Kosygin, 124 Lithuanian priests asked for the release of Bishop Julijonas Steponavicius who was being held in house arrest.

Common Prayer Texts — Common texts for Christian prayers were gaining wider acceptance among Catholics and Protestants in English speaking countries, according to a report of the International Committee for English in the Liturgy. The report focused on texts proposed by the International Consultation on English Texts, an ecumenical group of church authorities and liturgists founded in 1969. According to the report, the Catholic Church in the US had accepted and was using all of the ICET texts except the Apostles' Creed and the Lord's Prayer. Canadian Catholics were using all but the Lord's Prayer.

Pray for Hungary — Cardinal Jozsef Mindszenty, exiled primate of Hungary, told a congregation at a Mass in Brussels that "the Hungarian people are living through the most tragic period in their modern history. In the last 12 years," he said, "two and a half million abortions have taken place in our country, and the statistics for divorce and suicides break almost all world records." Cardinal Mindszenty urged the crowd, especially youths, to avoid "modern errors which erode spiritual values." In closing, he asked the group to pray for "the freedom of oppressed peoples and the freedom of religion in Hungary."

New Pattern — In the month since the British Army eliminated no-go areas in Northern Ireland, violence continued but with a different pattern. More direct confrontation between the hard core of the militant wing of the IRA and the military, with deliberate sniper attacks, appeared to be replacing the stoning and taunting of soldiers and wild firing at military posts.

Olympians at Dachau — Olympic athletes visited the former Nazi concentration camp at Dachau for a memorial service the day before they marched in the opening ceremonies at Olympic stadium in Munich. Sponsored by the Church Service to the Olympic Games, the memorial featured participation by Catholic, Protestant and Jewish clergy and lay persons.

Don't Attack Catholics — An official newspaper in Lithuania warned against "administrative attacks" on Catholics and "insults to believers' sentiments." The article, which appeared in the Communist newspaper *Sovietskaya Litva,* was interpreted by observers as recognition of the strength of traditional religious feelings among Lithuanians who had suffered much for their faith.

Foreign Briefs:

• The North Vietnamese released four French priests captured during their spring offensive in the Central Highlands of South Vietnam.

• The Austrian press was carrying reports that several US religious organizations were calling for volunteers to smuggle bibles — considered contraband by the government — into Czechoslovakia.

• Cardinal Corrado Ursi authorized a new scientific examination of the phenomenon in which the blood of St. Januarius, preserved in the cathedral of Naples, appears to liquefy several times a year.

World Council of Churches

The Catholic Church will not become a member of the World Council of Churches in the near future but ecumenists must not lose hope, because "less than a decade is a very short time to repair the damage and heal the wounds of centuries of conflict and mutual alienation." This was one item in a report submitted to the WCC Central Committee by the Rev. Dr. Eugene Carson Blake, retiring general secretary.

He said that a report of the joint WCC-Catholic working group noted that further discussion of Catholic membership was still necessary. Meanwhile, he described the situation of the two bodies as one of full cooperation without Catholic membership.

The committee elected Dr. Philippe Potter to succeed Dr. Blake as general secretary. Dr. Potter, 51, a Methodist and director of the WCC Committee for World Mission and Evangelism since 1966, was from the Island of Dominica in the British Lesser Antilles.

SEPTEMBER 1972

VATICAN

Olympic Killings — Within hours of the deaths of 11 Israeli Olympic athletes and five of their Arab guerrilla captors near Munich, Pope Paul raised his voice Sept. 6 against "this deed which truly dishonors our times." At the same time, he pleaded against reprisals from the Israeli side: "God grant that nothing like it may come about, as the very nature of our human weakness makes likely. Hate engenders hate, blood lusts for blood, revenge seeks revenge. Where will it end?"

Axioms for Peace — In a carefully worded address Sept. 10, Pope Paul said that, without standing in judgment of the wars around the world, he could recall some axioms which lead to peace. The axioms, one or another of which applied to combatants in current conflicts, were:

• "Without equal justice there cannot be a happy and stable concord between nations and social classes.

• "Vendetta is no remedy, but an evil which tends to duplicate itself and lead to other measures.

• "Terrorism is unworthy of brave and civilized men; it punishes the innocent and destroys faith in peaceful coexistence.

• "War is no solution.

• "The preferable method of solving difficulties between men is frank and honest discussion.

• "Fairness, compromise, generosity, reciprocal forgiveness and respect for the honor of others are the best means of settling differences."

Sexuality — Man today is living in a period in which "human animality is degenerating into an unbridled corruption," and "true love is decaying," Pope Paul declared at a general audience Sept. 13. Sexuality theme," he said, and is no longer treated with great care. Instead, it has been debased, and eroticism, pornography and indecency flourish. "In the place of love, which is the highest value, there is confusion between sensual and passionate egotism and the lyric and generous dream of giving oneself." He added: "If we have a sense of personal dignity and of respect for others, for society and, above all, for our elevation to the level of the Christian, as the sons of God, as persons baptized and sanctified by grace . . . we must put ourselves on guard, to repudiate and to renounce the many exhibitions and manifestations of modern immorality. We must not yield, through acquiescence or out of human respect, to the pollution of social immorality."

Seamen — Pope Paul, declaring that men who sail the sea "constitute their own international world," urged the Christian community to "become aware of its mission to sailors and fishermen whether they be on the seas, in port or with their families." He issued the appeal in a Sept. 13 address to about 300 participants in the 15th World Congress of the Apostleship of the Sea.

Peace Talks — A Vatican press spokesman confirmed that Pope Paul had sent private messages appealing for peace in Vietnam to the four major participants in the Paris peace talks. News of the papal messages of concern was disclosed by the Viet Cong delegation leader, Madame Nguyen Thi Binh. She disclosed that the verbal message was sent by Pope Paul in July through a representative. "The appeal of the Holy Father," the spokesman said, "was addressed to all four participants in the Paris conference on Vietnam (the United States, the Viet Cong, North Vietnam and South Vietnam). All replied."

Rendezvous with History — The unevangelized world offers the Church "a rendezvous with history, a date set by God," and to miss it would mean "incalculable damage" to the Church's future, Pope Paul told about 2,000 persons taking part in an Italian national congress of pontifical missionary undertakings. He urged those connected with missionary work to hold high their hopes, keeping faith in their work and faith in Christ.

Cardinal John J. Wright, prefect of the Congregation for the Clergy, said at the meeting in Rome: "The day when the Roman Catholic Church stops carrying the faith to new lands and new horizons, the faith will die. The reason is simple. Faith without works is dead."

"Venice Must Live!" — This cry of the Pope evoked cheers and applause from some 100,000 persons in St. Mark's Square Sept. 16 when he made the seventh visit in his lifetime to the city threatened by the sea. He voiced the hope: "May Venice, city of ideal beauty, never be corroded by manifestations of aesthetic and moral decadence. But, in harmony with her history and her dignity, may she always shine forth with regal excellence in the heavens of culture and faith."

During his visit en route to a national Eucharistic Nongress at Udine, he made a contribution of $50,000 to a Save Venice Fund.

Pilgrimage for Peace — Peace in the Church was the theme of Pope Paul's main address during the principal Mass of a national Eucharistic congress at Udine Sept. 16. Following a flight from Rome via Venice, he told 100,000 persons that the Eucharist "touches on the unity of the Church," and declared: "We must all be one. We must constitute a society of one mind . . . a society that is living and supernatural (because) it comes from Christ." Because this is so, he continued, members of the Church must not "stir up the defects of small groups, that is, antipathies, jealousies, slanders, spites, contestations, aversions and fights which often tend to grow even in our midst." The Pope said that "it would be a sad fate" for local churches "to lose the catholicity of the one People of God and to give in to the temptation of separatism, self-sufficiency, arbitrary pluralism and schism. Those who would do this forget that it is necessary to be inserted organically in the Mystical Body of Christ to enjoy the authentic fullness of the spirit of Christ."

Later, speaking extemporaneously, the Pope told priests and nuns packed into Udine's cathedral: "What if times are bad? You are consecrated religious, and that is sufficient to combat evil."

No Eucharist without Priests — In what appeared to be a warning against a current theological opinion that the Eucharist can be brought into being by the Christian community without the presence and action of an ordained priest, the Holy Father said Sept. 17: "This reality is not achieved except through a minister, that is, through the ministerial priesthood which is wonderfully and exclusively qualified to bring about the Eucharist, to celebrate Mass."

Love — Love is among the most popular words today, but for that reason it is all the more difficult to define, Pope Paul told the year's last general audience at Castelgandolfo Sept. 20. He said that "true love is a conscious and voluntary act toward good." For the Christian, this means "bringing together all our spiritual and sentimental powers toward the supreme good which is God." This concentration of love for God "is connected to a second love, the love for one's neighbor, both as a means of attaining God's love and as a reason for devoting one's own activity to the service and benefit of others." If this gospel of love were truly grasped, the Pope said, Christians would not doubt that their faith — instead of "economic materialism, class hatred and civil strife" — could deal with social questions of justice and peace and other vexing contemporary problems.

Charitable Activity — Even though "public aid programs have taken over slowly but surely offices entrusted in centuries past to the charity of the Church, . . . the charitable activity of the Church nonetheless has not lost its function in the contemporary world. Charity is always necessary as the complement to and the stimulus of justice itself." This was the theme of an address by the Pope to 300 participants in the first national study meeting of Italian Caritas.

The Day . . . — September 26 was, as one Vatican observer put it, "the day on which the Pope did not resign." Rumors of a possible papal resignation had been floating around the press and Vatican offices ever since Pope Paul recommended that diocesan bishops should tender their resignations at the age of 75. He became 75 on Sept. 26, but did not resign. As in the past, he treated his birthday as a business-as-usual non-event.

The Pope Also:
• Paid tribute to the "riches of the Islamic faith" as he received the credentials of Lt. Gen. Mohammed Yousuf, Pakistan's new ambassador to the Vatican, Sept. 11.
• Without any direct reference to controversy over a national divorce law, told Italian President Giovanni Leone that Italy should be a "model to other nations" in protecting the family, during a state visit Sept. 22.
• Told the 10-member Boy Scouts World Committee that the Scouts have "great potential for good" in a changing world, Sept. 26.
• Told member os the Italian Biblical Association that cooperation between biblical scholars and moral theologians can present the Bible as "the true foundation of man's moral conduct" in today's world of uncertainty, Sept. 29.

Anointing of the Sick — Msgr. Balthasar Fischer, member of a commission of the Congregation for Divine Worship, said that a new rite for administration of the sacrament, formerly called extreme unction, would be released in the near future. He indicated that the revised rite would emphasize the positive aspects of the sacrament and would avoid notions of fear some people had about "the last rites."

Laicization — The Congregation for the Doctrine of the Faith, in a letter circulated during the summer, cautioned bishops that the door must not spring open automatically to priests who want to leave the ministry, but should be opened only after due deliberation and for sound reasons. The letter was written in response to queries from bishops and major superiors of men religious concerning norms issued by the congregation in January, 1971.

The congregation said that the "simple desire to marry" is not a sufficient reason for permitting a priest to become a layman, nor is "contempt for the law of sacred celibacy." It warned that going through a civil marriage ceremony or announcing a wedding date do not in themselves provide grounds for laicization.

The letter urged that priests be given "fatherly" help in moment of crisis "lest they act precipitously" and rush out of the priesthood. To support its warning, the congregation pointed out that "not a few" priests had withdrawn petitions for laicization while they were pending and others had changed their minds after having petitions granted.

Also noted were cases of priests who had proved unfaithful to new obligations after being laicized and validly married.

In reply to one specific query, the congregation said that bishops did not have authority to dispense from the obligation of celibacy. The right to do so is reserved to the pope.

Vatican Briefs:
• Franz Pfyffer von Altishofen of Lucerne

was named captain commander of the Swiss Guards Sept. 15.

• The Vatican announced Sept. 25 that agreement had been reached with the Republic of Bangladesh for the establishment of diplomatic relations "to promote mutual friendly relations."

• The Pontifical Commission for Justice and Peace reported at the end of a week-long plenary meeting that special subjects under study included "hot spots" of war, conflict and violence, and closer collaboration with existing international organizations.

Revision of Orders

Two documents issued by Pope Paul on his own initiative in the form of apostolic letters clarified the clerical order of deacon (*Ad Pascendum*) and revised the structure of other ministries (*Ministeria Quaedam*). The documents were dated Aug. 15, were released for publication Sept. 14, and were scheduled to go into effect Jan. 1, 1973.

According to the letters:

• Ordination to the diaconate marks entrance into the ranks of the clergy. Candidates for the priesthood and unmarried candidates for the permanent diaconate commit themselves to lifelong celibacy before being ordained.

• The orders of subdeacon, exorcist and lector are abolished.

• The orders of acolyte and lector are changed in status to ministries. Candidates for the priesthood must, other men can, be formally installed — rather than ordained — in these ministries, which are functional in connection with divine worship (assisting at Mass, distributing Holy Communion, reading Scripture, and related actions). In line with established practice, women cannot be formally installed in these ministries although they may perform them to the degree that they are delegated to do so.

• Additional ministries may be authorized, as needed, requested and approved by the Holy See.

• The ceremony of tonsure, which formerly marked induction into the ranks of the clergy before the reception of minor orders, is abolished. Taking its place is "a rite of admission for candidates to the diaconate and to the priesthood."

The mandated revisions, under study and preparation since 1965, were in accord with enactments of the Second Vatican Council.

One of the shortest passages in *Ministeria Quaedam* occasioned the loudest comment. It stated: "In accordance with the venerable tradition of the Church, installation in the ministries of lector and acolyte is reserved to men."

DOMESTIC

Youth Masses — The youth Masses which "many a parish bulletin announces with pride" do not really reach young people," according to an article in *Liturgy* by theologian-musician Roy Portier. "The congregation is most often made up of young married people in their late twenties and thirties," he wrote. "The 'folk Mass' . . . has little to do with the religious needs of high school and college-age youth."

Draw — A legal dispute over disposition of a bequest ended in a draw when Judge Max Mehler gave the nuns and children of St. Peter's Orphanage the $70,000 they needed to purchase new facilities and authorized the Newark archdiocese to use other funds for the scholarship program it wanted.

Priests Reinstated — Four of seven priests who had been suspended by the late Bishop James A. McNulty of Buffalo were reinstated by Auxiliary Bishop Bernard J. McLaughlin. Bishop McLaughlin said one of his predecessor's last wishes was for efforts to have the priests restored to the ministry.

Project Equality — This fair employment program expanded operations in New York with the addition of area offices in Albany, Syracuse and Buffalo. Nationally, the program maintained 18 regional offices.

In-Hand Holy Communion — The Administrative Committee of the National Conference of Catholic Bishops voted against conducting a national survey to determine Catholic opinion regarding in-hand reception of Holy Communion. The committee explained in a statement that the decision was based on the idea that a survey would be without meaning unless Catholics first received more information on the subject.

Abortion Law Unconstitutional — For the second time this year, a federal district court ruled against the constitutionality of a Connecticut abortion law. The first decision, handed down in April, struck down a 19th century statute which, substantially, was reenacted in May. The court asserted that the new law violated the rights of a woman "to privacy in matters of sex and family life."

School Aid — Two parts of an Illinois nonpublic school aid program were declared constitutional by a state court in Chicago — a textbook-auxiliary services act funded by an appropriation of $20.5 million, and an innovative program supporting cooperative public-nonpublic school projects funded by an appropriation of $5 million. A third part of the program, which would have aided poor families with children in nonpublic schools, was ruled unconstitutional.

Proposition 22 — The Catholic bishops of California asked voters to reject November ballot Proposition 22, a proposal to restrict unionizing activities of farm laborers and outlaw secondary boycotts of agricultural products.

Masses Stopped — Liturgical violations — of Second Vatican Council norms and the revised Order of the Mass — were the reasons why officials of the Philadelphia archdiocese ordered the end of a series of controversial Masses celebrated since 1968 in the local convent of the Medical Mission Sisters. The archdiocese also revoked the faculties of the celebrant of the Masses.

Elizabeth School Aid — A month after a legal opinion apparently put down a $500,000 aid program to parochial schools in Elizabeth, N.J., state officials said the ruling was concerned only with the method of appropriating the aid and not with the substantive concept of aid to nonpublic schools. The money was earmarked for auxiliary services already declared legal.

Pastoral Letter — Bishop John K. Mussio of Steubenville, concerned over what he considered confusion among laymen over some of the fundamental tenets of Catholicism, issued a three-part pastoral letter to help clear up misconceptions he said were prevalent among some people. He told NC News Service that some priests of the diocese were unwisely using "confusing phraseology" that made some of the young and less educated unsure of what to believe.

Berriganism — Abbot Edmund F. McCaffrey, O.S.B., of Belmont Abbey deplored "Berriganism" as a force that "seeks peace without the firm foundation of justice." In a homily before 3,000 persons at the National Shrine of the Immaculate Conception, Washington, for God Day rally, the Abbot also chided Sen. George McGovern's phrase, "Come home, America," as "harmful to the international common good."

Birth Rate — Reports by two federal agencies showed that the national birth rate had dropped to the replacement level — 2.1 children for each young woman of child-bearing age. The Census Bureau and National Center for Health Statistics, however, did not say that their findings indicated the country had already reached the level of zero-population growth. The end of population growth in this country, experts said, would not come until the 2.1 rate had prevailed for 70 years.

Domestic Briefs:

• NC Publications, Inc., released its first volume of the *American Catholic Who's Who*. The previous 19 editions were published by Walter Romig of Detroit.

• Father Philip Berrigan, S.S.J., (four concurrent two-year terms) and Sister Elizabeth McAlister (one year plus three years of probation) were sentenced to prison terms for smuggling letters in and out of prison.

• British economist and writer Barbara Ward was named to receive the first Woman of Distinction Award ever made by the Leadership Conference of Women Religious.

A Woman's View

A papal decree on ministries open to laymen brought reactions of regret and dismay from several women leaders and a clarification from the general secretariat of the National Conference of Catholic Bishops.

The decree does "not forbid women to serve as lectors and as extraordinary ministers of Communion, said a statement from the secretariat. "Women can continue to perform these functions, just as they have done in increasing numbers in recent years," even though they may not be formally inducted into the ranks of ministers.

One woman's view was stated by Sister Thomas Aquinas Carroll, past president of the Leadership Conference of Women Religious. She called the latter part of the decree "a very regressive action." She said, however, that she was generally "pleased" with the thrust of the decree — "that the offices in the Church are being opened to lay people in a greater way."

FOREIGN

Baptismal Certificate — The Catholic Church and other major Christian churches in Great Britain announced agreement on a common baptismal certificate stating that a person had been baptized with water "in the name of the Father, Son and Holy Spirit."

Missionary Spirituality — "The lack of missionary spirituality among the Oriental Churches is the main cause of their insufficient growth," stated Msgr. Jaroslav Swyschuk of Chicago at the blessing of a Ukrainian-Rite ecumenical center in Nazareth, Israel. "Initiating this spirituality," he said, "would hopefully give them new dimensions, a new orientation, new vigor and a new identity."

Food and Population — World food production rose three per cent while world population increased at a rate of two per cent in 1971, according to preliminary survey findings released by the UN Food and Agriculture Organization. Most of the food gains were registered in the highly developed countries of the West, although improvement of production was also reported in the Third World.

St. Joan's Alliance — A serious shortage of funds appeared to be threatening the future of St. Joan's International Alliance, a 60-year-old Catholic organization seeking equal rights and opportunities for women in the Church and society at large. The problem was slated for discussion at an emergency meeting of the executive council scheduled for the first week of November.

Martial Law — The imposition of martial law in the Philippines stirred protests from a religious group and resulted in the arrest of Father Cornelius Lagerway, a Dutch-born priest accused of producing protest literature. He was behind a manifesto issued by a provincial chapter of Christians for National Liberation which criticized the government of President Ferdinand Marcos and called for a rally to oppose martial law. The manifesto claimed that preparations for martial law had been made by increasing the military budget to more than a billion pesos, "thus imposing more financial burdens on an already impoverished and suffering citizenry."

Troubles Continue — The four-year-old battle between the military regime and the Church continued in Paraguay, this time over the fate of two Catholic political prisoners. The regime of Gen. Alfredo Stroessner, in power for 17 years, said it was fighting Communism; the bishops said the government was making a mockery of the judicial process. As a result of the Church's stand, bishops, religious and lay persons had been harassed and persecuted. In mid-August two young lawyers, Miguel Angel Gauto and Blanca Florentin, were arrested without charges. High officials promised their prompt release, but the two — both active in the apostolate — remained in jail along with 150 other political prisoners.

Interfaith Relations in Scotland — Cardinal Gordon Gray of St. Andrews and Edinburgh said in a magazine article that "happy exchanges" between the Catholic Church and the Church of Scotland "may seem small enough matters but they do indicate movement, and the pace is accelerating."

Religion in Schools — The bishops of Panama asked a convention meeting in Panama City to write into a new constitution a provision guaranteeing the teaching of the Catholic religion in schools as a right of the majority of the people. The request was prompted by publication of a constitutional proposal recognizing the "Catholic religion as that professed by the majority of the Panamanian people" but changing previous provisions regarding religious education in public schools.

South Pacific Concerns — Bishops of Oceania attending a conference on the "Church and the Development of the Peoples of the South Pacific" said in a statement: "We are prepared to become actively involved in helping the peoples of the South Pacific in their struggle for national identity, true freedom and real independence." The conference, which was held in Suva, Fiji, affirmed that being a Christian "means to be involved in the world and to take an active part in change so as to build up a community of peace, love, justice, harmony and freedom."

Secular Institutes — Representatives of secular institutes met at Nemi, near Rome, to establish a world conference of their own. Vatican Radio reported that the new organization would promote studies and research programs concerning the nature and mission of the institutes and would also communicate their needs, interests and opinions to the Holy See.

Eucharistic Statement — Representatives of the Catholic Church and the Anglican Communion reaffirmed the joint 1971 "Windsor Statement" in which they expressed "substantial agreement" on Eucharistic doctrine, despite questions and criticisms concerning the document. They said in a communiqué: "It was felt that some of the objections arose from a misunderstanding of the scope of the document. Other difficulties, it was hoped, would dissolve in the light of a volume of background material . . . which is to be published in due course."

Foreign Briefs:

• Six bishops concelebrated a memorial Mass in La Paz for recently deceased Bishop James A. McNulty of Buffalo, in gratitude for help he had given the archdiocese and the Coroico prelature in Bolivia.

• Maryknoll and other US missionaries in Bolivia were praised by the Latin American Bishops' Council for their "vigorous effort to spread the Catholic faith among the Aymaras." Special citation was made of their work in training more than 1,000 native catechists in the previous five years.

• Radio San Rafael, operated by US Maryknollers in Bolivia, received a medal of merit from the Voice of America for its educational work among Andean Indians.

• Notre Dame University's Ecumenical Institute for Advanced Theological Study in Jerusalem was formally dedicated September 24 to 27.

Northern Ireland

Developments in the murderous see-saw of violence in Northern Ireland were reflected in the following reports.

• The Civil Rights Association of Belfast sent a delegation to Dublin early in the month to try to curb bombings and shootings in Ulster by the militant wing of the IRA. Their purpose was to make clear "the revulsion which the majority of people feel at this murderous activity," said Des O'Hagan, an official of the association. The action demonstrated the strength of Catholic feeling against the continuing terror campaign, a sentiment which, it was hoped, might lead to steps toward peace.

• The hard-line Protestant Vanguard agreed to unite with the paramilitary Ulster Defense Association to make common cause against what they claimed was the British government's ineffective policy in the area. They also agreed that restoration of the parliament of Northern Ireland, which has been suspended by British authorities, was urgent and that this body should have local control over security. The vanguard had some 60,000 members. The UDA said it could muster an army of 50,000 men it it ever had to fight the IRA.

• In talks held late in the month, the Protestant-controlled Unionist Party insisted that Ulster should have a new legislature and that the province should remain part of Great Britain so long as a majority of Ulstermen so wished. Only three of the seven concerned political parties took part in the talks.

OCTOBER 1972

VATICAN

Infidelity — The Church is suffering from the "infidelity of so many of her children," Pope Paul told a general audience Oct. 11, the 10th anniversary of the opening of the Second Vatican Council. The remark was interpreted as a reference to priests and nuns who had left their ministries.

Women in Ministries — Pope Paul will not allow women to share in the sacred orders of bishop, priest or deacon, but will probably institute an "initiation rite" for installing them in lesser ministries, an informed Vatican source told NC News.

Papal Election Rules — There was no doubt that Pope Paul was planning to change rules governing papal elections, but there was great confusion as to what the proposed changes might be and when they would be published.

Lodge at Vatican — The recurring presence of Ambassador Henry Cabot Lodge in Rome was a quiet but persistent reminder of his extraordinary mission as special envoy of President Nixon to the Vatican. The diplomat was in Rome early in October for his eighth regular visit since mid-1970. Specifics of his Vatican conversations were not available from either side. It was understood, however, that subjects included the war in Southeast Asia and international drug traffic. It was known that, thanks at least in part to Vatican intervention, mail to prisoners of the Hanoi government had risen from a trickle of letters a year to more than 150 letters every two months.

Theology — Theology can and must be diversified for differing cultures around the world, according to participants in a week-long study by the Vatican's International Theological Commission. An observer of the meeting said the 28 theologians were prepared to broaden the approach of theological research in matters of faith just as biblical scholars have used diverse methods of study to deepen understanding of the Scriptures.

No Non-Christians — The annual session of the Vatican's Secretariat for Non-Christians had just about everything except the presence of non-Christians. Three of the four non-Christian speakers failed to show up. Observers felt that attendance could be improved if the secretariat would meet with non-Christians on their own ground rather than at the Vatican.

DOMESTIC

School Prayer — The US Catholic Conference, which had opposed one school prayer amendment, was searching for an alternative method of allowing prayer in public schools. USCC officials acknowledged that the requests of "concerned individuals and groups" played a part in its decision to announce a continuing study of the issue. Bishop Joseph L. Bernardin, general secretary, said, however, that the conference still opposed a school prayer amendment offered in the fall of 1971 by Rep. Chalmer P. Wylie of Ohio. The conference's general counsel office and advisory committee on law and public policy were trying to find a different "formula" to resolve the controversy over prayer in public schools, Bishop Bernardin said.

Second Marriages — The Church should not always oppose second marriages after the failure of the first, according to a committee of the Catholic Theological Society of America. Father John R. Connery, committee chairman, reported that "in our judgment the absolute prohibition of a second union in cases of doubt is not a necessary protection of Christian marriage." The committee statement said: "It would be rash to assert that every first marriage that has failed was invalid from the beginning, but there are serious reasons today, that were either not present or not recognized in the past, to question the validity of many of them."

Religious Education — A controversy over religious education in the Portland, Ore., diocese ended with reinstatement of the archdiocesan education director and the withdrawal of several books from circulation. Archbishop Robert Dwyer had dismissed Father Emmet Harrington as education director because the priest's office had issued books which the prelate thought diverged from Vatican norms. The Archbishop reinstated Father Harrington after a meeting with the priest and representatives of the archdiocesan board of education and priests' senate. According to an agreement reached by all parties, Archbishop Dwyer repudiated "any imputation of doctrinal divergency from Catholic orthodoxy" in the priest's case.

Holy Name Society — Two thousand representatives of six million American Holy Name Society members voted to ask all presidential candidates to state clearly their positions on abortion. The representatives also discussed a proposal to allow women to join the society, but postponed action until later.

Tax Credits — The House Ways and Means Committee voted 18 to 6 for a bill granting tax credits to parents of nonpublic school children. The legislation, which would affect parents of about five million students in Catholic and other private elementary and secondary schools, granted a tax credit of up to $200 per pupil for tuition paid to private schools. The bill had been strongly supported by Catholic educators as well as by leaders of several Jewish and Protestant school groups. It was considered the aid method most likely to survive constitutional challenges.

No Money Back — The US Supreme Court

voted,8 to 1, to rule unconstitutional an Ohio law providing tuition reimbursement to parents of nonpublic school students. Despite the ruling, Catholic and other advocates of government aid appeared to be guardedly optimistic. The officials said that parent reimbursement laws in other states might prove to be constitutional, and they pointed out that the Court's brief order had no direct effect on the tax credit form of aid to nonpublic schools.

Decision Postponed — Catholic school officials were encouraged that a federal court in New York had postponed a decision on tax credits while indicating that it was favorably disposed to such assistance for nonpublic school students. The same officials, however, expressed disappointment that the three-judge panel declared unconstitutional two other measures that would have allocated up to $25 million in direct aid to poor families and granted up to $4 million for maintenance of private schools. The third part, providing up to $15 million in tax benefits to parents earning more than $5,000 and less than $25,000, was permitted to stand by a 2-to-1 vote of the judges.

Bishop Donohoe Praised — Pope Paul praised Bishop Hugh A. Donohoe of Fresno for his defense of the rights of farm workers. The words of praise, contained in a letter marking the Bishop's 25th episcopal anniversary, referred to his efforts on behalf of farm workers during the long grape dispute in the San Joaquin Valley. "Besides your other accomplishments of evangelical justice . . . you have striven to protect the rights of farm workers, indeed, most vigorously and without compromise," the Pope wrote.

Nixon Over McGovern — US Catholics favored President Nixon over Sen. George McGovern by 54 to 31 per cent, a poll by seven newspapers revealed. The same poll showed, however, that American Catholics had strong ties to the Democratic party and would have given Sen Edward Kennedy overwhelming support over President Nixon. The survey findings indicated that the President's support among American Catholics was shallow and based upon unfavorable perception of Sen. McGovern rather than upon favorable reaction to the accomplishments of the Nixon administration.

Human Development Campaign — The US bishops' anti-poverty program opened its 1972 fund raising campaign with an announcement of more than $1 million in grants funded by the 1971 campaign. In encouraging Catholics to contribute to the campaign, Auxiliary Bishop Michael R. Dempsey of Chicago pointed out that $16 million had been donated since the campaign began in 1970.

Jail Rather than Payment — Bishop John J. Russell of Richmond declared that he "will go to jail" before he would pay a city "service charge" levied on Catholic schools and convents. His statement came in a meeting between Richmond city officials and representatives of the city's Catholic schools and convents. At issue was a "service charge" for police, fire and sanitation services, levied on all tax exempt properties in the city except "those wholly and exclusively used for religious worship or for the residence of ministers." The charge was being levied on Catholic schools and halls.

Priest Candidate — A 57-year-old priest, running for a New York State senatorial seat, said he decided to enter politics to help counteract the "lawyer domination" in the state legislature. The candidate was Father Joseph B. Dorsey, a member of the Order of Basilian Fathers of Toronto, on leave of absence from John Fisher College, Rochester, where he was executive vice president.

Praise for Archbishop — Participants in an "encounter" for Spanish-speaking Catholics praised retired Archbishop Robert E. Lucey of San Antonio for his pioneering work on behalf of the Spanish-speaking. In praising the Archbishop, Paul Sedillo of the US Catholic Conference cited a 1945 statement in which the prelate told a newspaper: "If a Mexican American is improvident, illiterate, diseased and delinquent, whose fault is it but those who from birth condemned him to the unwholesome atmosphere of poverty and squalor? . . . The truth is that the Mexican American laborers are honest and hard working in a civilized manner."

Abortion Laws — Lawyers for the states and opponents of the Georgia and Texas abortion statutes argued before the US Supreme Court over the rights of the states to enact abortion laws and whether an unborn child had constitutional rights. The Supreme Court had already heard testimony in the cases but postponed a decision so a full nine-member bench could decide the cases. Justices Lewis F. Powell Jr. and William H. Rehnquist did not begin their terms until two months after their first hearing. The Texas law, which forbids abortions except in cases in which the mother's life is endangered, was similar to statutes in more than 30 states. At least 12 states had abortion regulations similar to those of Georgia, where abortions are illegal except when the mother's life is in jeopardy, when the child is likely to be born with a physical and mental defect. and when pregnancy resulted from rape or incest.

The Missouri Supreme Court upheld the constitutionality of the state's stringent abortion law, asserting that "human life is a continuum from conception to death." In a related development, the South Dakota Supreme Court also upheld the constitutionality of that state's abortion statute. The laws of both states permitted abortions only when pregnancy endangered the life of the mother. The Missouri law dated from 1835, with a revision in 1949, while the South Dakota statue was enacted in 1889.

FOREIGN

Dutch Catechism — After almost two years of discussion, the Vatican insisted publicly that two Dutch bishops immediately withdraw a catechism in school use in their dioceses. A Vatican spokesman told a press conference that the catechism was found wanting "in many points" by the Congregation for the Doctrine of the Faith and the Congregation for the Clergy. The ban and its instructions to the bishops of s'-Hertogenbosch and Breda to withdraw the catechism immediately was first reported in September, but the Oct. 12 press conference was the first time the matter was aired publicly at the Vatican.

Church in North Vietnam — The Catholic Church was flourishing in North Vietnam despite US bombing, according to five North Vietnamese Catholics, including three priests. The five spoke at the second international assembly of Christians in Solidarity with the Peoples of Vietnam, Laos and Cambodia, at Cap Rouge, Quebec.

Heath Visits Pope — Violence-ridden Northern Ireland was the focus of British Prime Minister Edward Heath's visit to Pope Paul Oct. 4. Heath publicly avowed his determination not only "to work for the ending of violence in Northern Ireland" but to achieve there "the peace and justice for which Your Holiness hopes and prays."

IRA Ready To Talk — The militant wing of the outlawed Irish Republican Army was ready to talk about new initiatives to stop its bombing and shooting campaign in Northern Ireland, according to Rory O'Brady, head of the Provisionals' political arm, Sinn Fein. O'Brady also said in Dublin that the Provisionals might contest a number of seats in local elections in Ulster in late November or early December. He said that the military campaign had probably reached a stalemate, and that new political moves were vital.

WOMEN IN THE CHURCH

The most recent protest from champions of women's rights in the Church has been raised against the shortest paragraph in two Vatican documents stating that, in line with long-standing tradition, ordination to holy orders is reserved to men.

Earlier protests, still continuing, have been and are being lodged against what is called second-class citizenship for women in the Church — as well as society in general. Targets of the protests are the Church, theological prejudice — attributed especially to Sts. Paul, Augustine and Thomas Aquinas — and sociological subjection to men.

In response to criticism concerning the restriction of holy orders and of formal installation in minor ministries to men, the Vatican pleaded innocent in October, 1972, to the charge that Pope Paul had demoted women in *Ministeria Quaedam,* a document he issued on his own initiative in September.

Although the document reserved to men the formal office of lector (that is, reader), an official clarification in the Vatican daily, *L'Osservatore Romano,* said that women may still read scriptural lessons at Mass.

The clarification recalled that this point had been made expressly by a spokesman, Father Paolo Dezza, S.J., in presenting the *motu proprio* to the press Sept. 14.

Many of the criticisms of the new regulations complained that they failed to provide for the formal admission of women into various liturgical ministries. The Vatican's clarification, however, said it would be "inopportune to anticipate or prejudice what might subsequently be established at the end of the study on women's participation in the Church's community life."

This was the first public indication that the Vatican had accepted the request of several participants in the 1971 Synod of Bishops for serious theological study of the possibility of ordaining women.

The Vatican statement, after noting that the *motu proprio* had opened to the laity certain ministries previously reserved to the clergy, continued:

"Concerning the exercise by women of some liturgical offices, the *motu proprio* did not intend to make innovations, and stood by the norms then in vigor.

"Furthermore, it would be inopportune to anticipate or prejudice what might subsequently be established at the end of the study of women's participation in the Church's community life, a study which some bishops requested during the 1971 Synod.

"Therefore — as Father Dezza stated expressly in his Sept. 14 press conference on the two pontifical documents — nothing prevents women from continuing to be given the task of public reading during liturgical celebrations, as they have in fact been doing for some years on the basis of the General Instruction of the new *Roman Missal,* promulgated April 3, 1969. Nor is a formal and canonical investiture on the bishop's part necessary for this service.

"Likewise, according to the norms in existence, the bishops may still seek from the Holy See authorization for women to distribute Holy Communion, as extraordinary ministers."

Ordination Not Anticipated

Informed sources at the Vatican were of the opinion that the commission studying the role of women in the Church would not recommend to Pope Paul the ordination of women, on the grounds that Christ did not ordain women as priests.

According to many, however, the fact that Christ chose 12 men does not mean he intended that women could never be admitted to the priesthood.

Msgr. Philippe Delhaye, secretary of the International Theological Commission, said in an article in the *Theological Review* of Louvain University that Christ and the Apostles were restrained from ordaining women because of the "environment and times" rather than from any misconception of the "inferiority of women."

Cardinal George Flahiff of Winnipeg told the Synod Oct. 11, 1971, that the reasons Christ did not ordain women were largely "sociological," that the "priesthood of the Old Testament was all-male," and that "Jesus could not change so radically the social perception" of the day.

Cardinal Flahiff asked the Vatican to study the place of women in the Church's "sacred ministries," and this "despite a centuries-old social tradition against a ministry of women in the Church."

Two weeks later, Archbishop Leo Byrne of St. Paul-Minneapolis rose in the synod hall to speak of women's influence in the Church's mission — "an influence," he said, "that up to the present has been sorely underestimated and all too slighted."

Although Archbishop Byrne did not use the term women priests, he did call for a commission to study greater participation by women in the various ministries, declaring:

"Women are not to be excluded from any service to the Church if the exclusion stems from questionable interpretation of Scriptures, male prejudice, or blind adherence to merely human traditions that may have been rooted in the social position of women in other times."

Jesuit Father Paolo Dezza said he held to the idea that Christ had a divine motive in not ordaining women and that the Church cannot alter that despite the changing times.

"The commission appointed by the Pope to study the place of women must keep an essential point in mind," Father Dezza said.

"There is a vast difference between the sacred order in which bishops, priests and deacons share and the nonsacramental ministries to which women can be admitted.

"The Church can do what it wants with these ministries, but the Church must continue to do what Christ did with the divine priesthood."

Msgr. Delhaye, speaking of the fact that Christ did not ordain women, said that the Church is tied to that tradition.

"The reasons for the decisions not to ordain women — whether well-founded or not — don't matter much. These decisions are nevertheless a norm and a limit for a Church which intends to remain faithful to what the Lord has done."

In this context of the Church being tied to 20 centuries of tradition, Vatican sources predicted that Pope Paul would not take the innovative step of allowing the ordination of women to the priesthood.

"Instead, I believe that, upon the recommendation of the commission, the Pope will probably allow women to receive admission to such ministries as lector, acolyte, sacristan or catechist through initiation rites," the source said.

"Whatever you do, please do not call these rites an ordination, or we will just prolong the confusion."

The source was referring to the furor that arose when Pope Paul, in streamlining the various steps leading to the priesthood, stated that the steps involving an ordination were limited to male recipients.

ST. JOAN'S ALLIANCE

St. Joan's Alliance, which developed from the Catholic Woman's Suffrage Society founded in 1911 in London, has for its objective the securing of legal and de facto equality between women and men in the Church and all other sectors of society. Its US Section was formed in 1965. Frances McGillicuddy is president. The US address of the Alliance is 435 W. 119th St., New York, N.Y. 10027.

Purposes

The Alliance pioneered efforts for implementation of the Christian principle of the equality of the sexes within the Church, and has played a leadership role in petitioning for: lay men and women observers and women auditors at the Second Vatican Council, revision of the nuptial liturgy, revision of the canons of the Code of Canon Law affecting women, the admission of women to ordination to the diaconate and priesthood. The Alliance calls on women to exercise their full rights and responsibilities as Christians by fulfilling their vocation of service in the Church.

Full membership in the Alliance is open to Catholic women and men committed to its objectives and activities.

GOOD CONSCIENCE PROCEDURE

The Vatican declared in August, 1972, that "dioceses are not to introduce procedures that are contrary to current discipline" on divorce and remarriage, Cardinal John Krol of Philadelphia, president of the National Conference of Catholic Bishops, said in a statement issued in Washington.

Although Cardinal Krol did not mention individual dioceses, his statement came in the wake of a controversy over the Baton Rouge diocese's initiation of a "good conscience" procedure which allowed some remarried Catholics to receive the sacraments of penance and the Eucharist.

While the question of admitting divorced and remarried Catholics to the sacraments was under study by the Holy See and the NCCB, Cardinal Krol said, "It would be rash to conclude that a study must necessarily lead to change of principles or procedure, or that a study precludes the possibility of reaffirmation of current discipline."

The Holy See's position was expressed in a letter to the NCCB, Cardinal Krol said. An NCCB spokesman said the conference was not authorized to release the letter. He added:

"Neither Cardinal Krol's statement nor the letter from the Holy See makes any comment on individual dioceses. I think it is fair to say that both the letter and the statement were occasioned less by actual practices in particular dioceses — concerning which specific information is lacking at this time — than by the possibility that many sincere people may have been confused by reports about alleged departures in some places from accepted procedures in marriage cases."

Baton Rouge Procedure

In June, Bishop Robert E. Tracy of Baton Rouge announced that the diocese had set up procedures for allowing Catholics who had divorced and remarried to receive the sacraments. By the "good conscience" procedure, recognition was given to the good conscience of a person who sincerely believed that his (her) first marriage was not a true marriage and that his (her) present one is.

Such decisions apply only to cases where annulment of any previous marriage appears impossible, Claretian Father Joseph Peplansky, a member of the Baton Rouge diocesan "Good Conscience Committee," said at the time of the announcement of the procedure's institution.

Informed of Cardinal Krol's statement, Father Joel LaBauve, vice-chancellor of the diocese, said: "As far as I know, we have not been informed that what we instituted is not in conformity" with existing discipline.

Father LaBauve said that officials of the Baton Rouge diocese had not sought permission from the Holy See to set up the good conscience procedure because they believed, after consultation with canon lawyers and theologians, that the local bishop had the right to institute such a procedure.

Following the Baton Rouge announcement, it was learned that several other US dioceses had instituted similar procedures. These included Portland, Ore., Birmingham and Boise. A spokesman for the Chicago archdiocese said that occasional "good conscience" cases were handled there but that no uniform procedure had been instituted.

The Baton Rouge announcement prompted a flurry of statements in dioceses around the nation. Some officials of other dioceses questioned the Baton Rouge procedure, particularly its implications with regard to the Church's teaching on the indissolubility of marriage.

In his original announcement, however, Bishop Tracy repeated his commitment to the Church's teaching on "the sanctity and lifelong character of the marriage vows and married life." The procedure, he said, was based on the "pastoral responsibility of healing and forgiveness."

Cardinal Krol's Statement

Cardinal Krol's statement said:

"The Church's solicitude for the spiritual welfare of all the faithful has been manifested in a special way by her efforts to dispose divorced and remarried Catholics to receive the sacraments worthily. This subject has been discussed in articles, pamphlets and books, and is currently under study by the Holy See and by the Committee on Pastoral Research and Practices of the National Conference of Bishops.

"It would be rash to conclude that a study must necessarily lead to change of principles or procedure, or that a study precludes the possibility of reaffirmation of current discipline. Moreover, the Holy See has made it clear, in a recent letter addressed to the conference, that, since the discipline is of interest to the entire Church, dioceses are not to introduce procedures that are contrary to current discipline.

"The complexity of the problem is illustrated by the variety of circumstances that may exist. In some cases a prior marriage may appear to be invalid, but proof of invalidity according to the rules of evidence cannot be produced. In some cases the current marriage is demonstrably invalid, but for a variety of reasons the parties cannot separate. Grave doctrinal implications, including the indissolubility of marriage and fidelity to the Gospel of Christ, are involved, as are moral issues, such as the dispositions required for the worthy reception of the sacraments.

"The Church is not insensitive to the anxiety and anguish of the individuals involved. The Church responds to the imperative imposed upon it by the ministry of compassion, mercy and reconciliation, but must also respond to the grave imperative imposed by the ministry of correction. The Church must be faithful to her children, by recalling them to fidelity to Christ and his Gospel.

"The problem is not local to any one diocese or nation. It is a problem found in the entire Church. There are no facile solutions and reputable theologians and canonists acknowledge the complexity and gravity of the problem and do not venture any ready solutions. Bishops, motivated by deep pastoral concern for people in difficult marriage situations, continue to explore the question, without presuming to hold out hopes — which could well be disappointed — of finding an easy or early answer."

DEATHS OCT. 1, 1971 TO OCT. 1, 1972

Adrian, Bishop William L., 88, Feb. 13, Nashville, Tenn.; bishop of Nashville from 1936 to 1969 when he retired.

Aggey, Archbishop John Kwao Amuzu, Mar. 13, 65, Lagos, Nigeria; archbishop of Lagos from 1965; president of the Nigerian Episcopal Conference.

Alberione, Don Giacomo, 87, Nov. 26, 1971, Rome, Italy; founder of Pious Society of St. Paul and Daughters of St. Paul for work in the communications fields; also founded several other congregations and institutes.

Athenagoras I. Patriarch. (See Index)

Bergan, Archbishop Gerald T., 80, July 12, Omaha, Nebr.; archbishop of Omaha from 1948 until his retirement in 1969; previously bishop of Des Moines, 1934-48.

Blowick, Rev. John 83, June 19, Navan, Ireland; founder with Rev. (later Bishop) Edward Galvin of the Society of St. Columban in 1916; also founded Missionary Sisters of St. Columban.

Brezanoczy, Archbishop Paul, 60, Feb. 11, Eger, Hungary; archbishop of Eger since 1969; repeatedly urged the departure from Hungary of Cardinal Mindszenty for the betterment of Church-state relations; expert at Vatican II.

Bullion, Rev. Albert J., 50, Nov. 4, 1971, Pittsburgh, Pa.; associate national director of the Pontifical Association of the Holy Childhood.

Budenz, Louis F., 80, May 2, Newport, R.I.; one-time leading figure in American Communist Party; editor of *The Daily Worker;* rejected Communism in 1945 and returned to the Catholic Church; author of *This Is My Story.*

Cahill, Mother Benedict, Apr. 18, Addis Ababa, Ethiopia; superior general of Franciscan Sisters for Africa; killed in plane crash.

Carey, Rev. Thomas, O.P., 68, May 8, New York, N.Y.; director of Blackfriars' Guild and Blackfriars' Theatre (see Index) for 31 years; assistant director of Holy Name Society, 1940-52; founder with Father Urban Nagle, O.P., of the Blackfriars' Institute of the Dramatic Arts, now the Department of Speech and Drama at Catholic University.

Colgan, Msgr. Harold V., 77, Apr. 16, Miami, Fla.; founder and national president of the Blue Army of Our Lady of Fatima.

Colum, Padraic, 90, Jan. 11, Enfield, Conn.; Irish-American poet.

Dell'Acqua, Cardinal Angelo, 68, Aug. 27, Lourdes, France, while leading a pilgrimage of Italians there; vicar general of Rome since 1968; served in the papal secretariat of state, 1950-67; named cardinal, 1967.

Dwinell, Col. John S., 69, Nov. 7, New York, N.Y.; military lawyer for 40 years.

Everett, Millard F. (Leo), 69, June 26, New Orleans, La.; editor of the *Clarion Herald,* New Orleans archdiocesan paper; won numerous awards, especially for work in the areas of civil rights and economic justice.

Fink, Francis A. (Bill), 64, Dec. 4, 1971, Fort Wayne, Ind.; executive vice-president of *Our Sunday Visitor, Inc.,* with which he was associated for more than 40 years; president of the Catholic Press Association, 1950-52.

Fisher, Lord Geoffrey, 85, Sept., Sherborne, England; retired head of the Anglican Communion; his meeting with John XXIII in 1960 marked the first time an archbishop of Canterbury had visited a pope since the Reformation.

Fitzgerald, Bishop Edward A., 80, Mar. 31, Winona, Minn.; bishop of Winona from 1949 to 1969 when he retired; previously auxiliary bishop of Dubuque, 1946-49.

Gallaher, Francis X, 43, Feb. 11, Baltimore, Md., one of the defense lawyers in the trial of the Harrisburg Seven; attorney for the Baltimore archdiocese and prominent figure in Maryland Democratic reform politics.

Garibi y Rivera, Cardinal Jose, 83, May 27, Guadalajara, Mexico; archbishop of Guadalajara from 1936 to 1969 when he retired; first Mexican named to the College of Cardinals, 1958.

Giobbe, Cardinal Paolo, 92, Aug. 14, Rome, Italy; member of the College of Cardinals since 1958; served in the Vatican diplomatic corps as nuncio to Colombia, 1925-35, and internuncio to The Netherlands, 1935-48; datary of the Holy See from 1959 to 1968 when the office was suppressed in reorganization of the Curia.

Grimmelsman, Bishop Henry J., 81, June 26, Evansville, Ind.; bishop of Evansville from 1945 to 1965 when he retired.

Hillinger, Bishop Raymond P., 67, Nov. 14, 1971, Chicago, Ill.; auxiliary bishop of Chicago since 1956; previously bishop of Rockford, 1954-56.

Holzner, Very Rev. Ferdinand, C.M.M., 65, Apr. 16, Rome, Italy; German-born superior general of the Mariannhill Missionaries since 1957.

Jones, Robert T. (Bobby), 69, Dec. 18, 1971, Atlanta, Ga.; golf immortal, lawyer; only player to win the Grand Slam in a single year, 1930 — the National Open, the National Amateur, the British Open and the British Amateur tournaments; became a Catholic a few days before his death.

Kowalski, Bishop Kazimierz, 77, May 6, Czestochowa, Poland; bishop of Chelmno since 1946; chairman of the Polish Episcopal Commission for the Missions.

Kuhn, Sister Alexis, 102, May 1, Normandy, Mo.; Sister of Charity of St. Vincent de Paul for 85 years.

Leibold, Archbishop Paul, 57, June 1, Cincinnati, Ohio; archbishop of Cincinnati since

1969; previously auxiliary of Cincinnati, 1958-65, and bishop of Evansville, 1965-69.

Leverman, Bishop Alfred B., 69, Apr. 28., St. John's, N.B., Canada; bishop of St. John's, N.B., from 1953 to 1968 when he retired.

Ley, Bishop Felix, O.F.M. Cap., 63, Jan. 24, Ryukyu Islands; apostolic administrator of the Ryukyu Islands since 1968.

Loesch, Rev. Francis N., S.J., 75, Feb., Patna, India; US missioner in India for 46 years.

McCarty, Bishop William T., 83, Sept. 14, Rapid City, S.D.; bishop of Rapid City from 1948 to 1969 when he retired; had previously served under Cardinal Spellman as auxiliary in the military ordinariate from 1943 to 1947.

McCormack, Mrs. John W. (Harriet Joyce), 87, Dec. 2, 1971, Washington, D.C.; wife of retired Speaker of the House, John W. McCormack.

McNulty, Bishop James A., 72, Sept. 4, Montclair, N.J.; bishop of Buffalo since 1963; previously bishop of Paterson, 1953-63, and auxiliary of Newark, 1947-53; outspoken advocate of civil rights.

Montini, Msgr. Carlo, 69, Apr. 20, near Bologna, Italy; cousin of Pope Paul VI; priest of Brescia diocese.

Mundy, Msgr. Thomas M., 57, Aug. 3, Rome, Italy; only US judge of the Sacred Roman Rota; Philadelphia archdiocesan priest.

Natucci, Msgr. Salvatore, 100, Dec. 16, 1971, Vatican City; for many years promoter of the faith (devil's advocate) in causes for beatification and canonization.

Neighbor, Msgr. Russell J., 51, July 31, Manchester, N.H.; director of National Center of Religious Education — Confraternity of Christian Doctrine from 1967 to 1971 when he retired because of illness.

Nethisinghe, Rev. Joseph, 44, Dec. 27, 1971, Colombo, Sri Lanka (Ceylon); director of the country's newly established Catholic Information Center.

O'Donnell, Gen. Emmett (Rosy), 66, Dec. 26, 1971, McLean, Va.; president of USO since 1963; retired Air Force officer; commanded major air operations in the Pacific area during World War II and the Korean War.

Olwell, Bishop Quentin C., C.P., 74, Jan. 30, Okinawa; US-born prelate of Marbel, the Philippines, from 1961 to 1969 when he retired.

Perbal, Rev. Albert, O.M.I., 87, Dec. 27, 1971, Rome, Italy; well-known missiologist, spent most of his priestly life in Rome in research and training missionaries, born near Nancy on Franco-Belgian frontier.

Phillips, Msgr. Gerard, 73, July 13, Louvain, Belgium; noted Belgian theologian, author; member of the preparatory Theology Commission of Vatican II; later an under-secretary of the Commission of Faith; played an important role in drafting the constitution *Lumen Gentium;* member of the International Theological Commission.

Quiroga y Palacios, Cardinal Fernando, 71, Dec. 7, 1971, Madrid, Spain; archbishop of Santiago de Compostela, Spain, since 1949; named cardinal, 1953; first president of the Spanish Bishops' Conference.

Rock, Mrs. Ruth Craven, 65, Apr. 19, Washington, D.C.; former executive director of the National Council of Catholic Women; active in Catholic organizations and women's rights movements.

Roncalli, Alfredo, 83, Aug. 8, Sotte il Monte (Bergamo(, Italy; second youngest of the three surviving brothers of Pope John XXIII.

Schuette, Rev. Johannes, S.V.D., 58, Nov. 18, 1971, Rome, Italy; German-born assistant secretary of the Pontifical Commission on Justice and Peace; former superior general of the Divine Word Missionaries; missionary in China from 1940 until his imprisonment and expulsion in 1951.

Skoupy, Bishop Karel, 86, Feb. 24, Brno, Czechoslovakia; bishop of Brno since 1946; impeded from governing his diocese from 1953 to 1968 by the Communist government (10 of these years were spent in prison; the remainder, in a monastery); "rehabilitated" and restored to his diocese in 1969.

Stock, Bishop John, 53, June 29, near Mount Holly, N.J., in an auto accident; auxiliary bishop of the Ukrainian archeparchy of Philadelphia since 1971.

Tisserant, Eugene Cardinal, 87, Feb. 21, Albano, Italy; French-born dean of the College of Cardinals; cardinal since 1936; former administrator of the Vatican Library which he reorganized and modernized; prefect of the Sacred Congregation for the Oriental Churches for more than 20 years; specialist in Oriental languages; awarded honorary Doctorate of Laws by Princeton University in 1947 as "a distinguished scholar and eminent churchman, interpreter of early Christian documents, expert in the liturgical arts of the Eastern Rites, world authority on the Oriental languages, master of manuscripts"; member of the French Academy.

Valencia Cano, Bishop Gerardo, 56, Jan. 21, Colombia, in a plane crash; vicar apostolic of Buenaventura since 1953; social activist; leader of the Golconda Movement (priests attempting to initiate and organize socioeconomic reform in Colombia).

Venini, Rev. Joseph E., 72, May 22, Guatemala; Canadian missionary in Guatemala for almost 20 years; member of Scarboro Mission Society; killed by robbers at his parish.

Wessel, Rev. John L., Dec. 31, 1971, Mount Holly, N.J.; fatally shot by a mentally depressed Vietnam veteran he was counseling.

POPULATION AND THE AMERICAN FUTURE—A RESPONSE

Following is the text of a statement adopted unanimously by the National Conference of Catholic Bishops Apr. 13, 1972, in response to the three-part report published in March by the National Commission on Population Growth and the American Future.

[This text was circulated by the NC Documentary Service, *Origins.*]

The Commission on Population Growth and the American Future has recently issued a report in which it makes recommendations for limiting further population growth in the United States (1). As religious leaders — but also as concerned Americans — we wish to record our objections to this report.

Narrow Vision

Population growth is more than a matter of statistics. In fact, population decisions reflect society's total view of man. We repeat our concern that "one of the dangers of a technological society is a tendency to adopt a limited view of man, to see man only for what he does or produces and to overlook the source of man's dignity, the fact that he is made in the image of God, and that from the moment of conception, he is worthy of the full support of the human family of which he is a member" (2). The Commission's preoccupation with limiting population growth has led to a confined view of the inherent value of every person, and a narrow vision of man's ability to live in peace, justice and charity with his fellowman.

False Solution

We take serious exception to the general approach taken by this Commission — that is, to equate quality of life simply with a lower rate of population growth, on the grounds that a smaller number of people will result in greater affluence and material comfort for all. Experience has already taught us that our social problems — poverty, disease, injustice and violence — are not solved merely by population decrease, but require a change of heart and a re-ordering of priorities for the entire nation.

Principles

Population growth and distribution are serious topics. They deserve careful study and discussion by all Americans. In order to safeguard human rights and the dignity of man, we reaffirm the following principles.

1. "The well-being of the individual person and of human and Christian society is intimately linked with the healthy condition of that community produced by marriage and the family" (3).

2. "It is for the parents to decide, with full knowledge of the matter, on the number of their children, taking into account their responsibilities towards God, themselves, the children they have already brought into the world, and the community to which they belong" (4).

3. "It is certain that public authorities can intervene, within the limit of their competence, by favoring the availability of appropriate information and by adopting suitable measures, provided that these be in conformity with the moral law and that they respect the rightful freedom of married couples" (5).

4. "Abortion, directly willed and procured, even if for therapeutic reasons, is to be absolutely excluded as a licit means of regulating births" (6).

Moral Dissent

Many of the recommendations of the Commission cannot be harmonized with our moral convictions, nor with the values and beliefs of many of our fellow Americans. Without attempting a comprehensive analysis of the Commission's Report, we cite the following instances.

• The Commission recommends nationwide abortion-on-demand as a means of eliminating the unwanted child, "particularly when the child's prospects for a life of dignity and self-fulfillment are limited." This is an immoral and dangerous principle. What constitutes self-fulfillment? How does one arrive at the conclusion that another person's prospects for a life of dignity and self-fulfillment are in fact limited? Who is to make such decisions, and on what basis, especially when the conclusion leads to the death of the child? Furthermore, if this thinking is extended to other persons whose prospects for a life of dignity and self-fulfillment are limited, the lives of the aged, the sick, and the mentally or physically disadvantaged are thereby endangered. This argument — drawn to its ultimate conclusions — could also be used to discriminate against racial and social minorities.

We re-state our teaching that "from the moment of its conception life must be guarded with the greatest care, while abortion and infanticide are unspeakable crimes" (7). We are opposed to the continuing efforts in our society to deprive the unborn child of legal protection for his or her right to life. We also reject the reasoning of some courts that have decided that the right to privacy outweighs the child's right to life.

Family Respect

• The Commission makes a series of recommendations that lead to a population policy. However, policies affecting population —

as well as the administrative guidelines of government agencies — must always respect the well-being and stability of the family unit, the free and voluntary decision-making power of parents, and the good of society. In point of fact, a population policy may be only a positive part of a broader policy that is calculated to support and strengthen family life. We find that the report of the Commission on Population Growth and the American Future is beset with inconsistencies, as the conscientious dissent of individual Commission members records.

Prayer, Study

Because of continuing efforts to deprive the unborn child of legal protection for the right to life, we propose a Week of Prayer and Study dedicated to the sanctity of human life, and the many threats to human life in our world, including war, violence, hunger and poverty. This Week will be held during October, 1972, in all dioceses in the United States, and it will be initiated by the Sunday liturgy. Throughout that Week we will urge that educational programs be conducted on the dignity of human life and the responsibility of society to protect all its members — the un-

BIRTHRIGHT

Birthright, in the words of Dr. Herbert Ratner of Oak Park, Ill, is a telephone and counseling service which "tries to get a woman contemplating abortion through the crisis and panic period so that she can solve her problems" and avoid the abortion decision she really does not want to make.

The service was started by Louise Summerhill who opened the first Birthright office Oct. 15, 1968, in Toronto. Since then, Birthright groups have been set up in more than 35 citites in Canada, the US, Australia and New Zealand, and more are in the process of formation. The movement has been incorporated in Canada and the US, and 125 representatives of independent groups attended the first international meeting in August, 1971, in Toronto.

Birthright is nondenominational, but its program has been adopted by numerous Catholic groups. Allied with other Right-to-Life groups in this country, it has developed into a major counseling service — its first purpose — and a strong force against liberalized abortion laws. Through its own activities and those of other groups, it has slowed down the adoption of liberal statutes in several states.

Directory

Following, by states, is the directory of Birthright group telephone numbers.

California: Grass Valley, 916-273-2738; Los Angeles, 213-724-6436; San Fernando Valley, 213-981-4357; San Francisco, 415-567-8370; Santa Barbara. 805-963-2200.

born child, and also the aged, sick and disadvantaged. In this endeavor we will seek the counsel and advice of scientists and legal scholars, and we will invite the participation and cooperation of all concerned Americans, especially those who have demonstrated deep ethical convictions concerning the sacredness of human life and the good of society.

Footnotes

(1) *Population and the American Future*, 1972, US Government Printing Office, Washington, D. C. (The Commission on Population Growth and the American Future was established by Congress in March, 1970, to conduct a two-year study of population growth in the US and its foreseeable social consequences. The Commission, on completion of this report in March, 1972, terminated its work and was phased out of existence.)
(2) *Statement on Abortion*, National Conference of Catholic Bishops, Apr. 17, 1969.
(3) *Constitution on the Church in the Modern World*. Second Vatican Council, No. 47. (4) and (5) Encyclical *Development of Peoples*. Paul VI, No. 37. (6) Encyclical *Of Human Life*, Paul VI, No. 14. (7) *Constitution on the Church in the Modern World*, No. 51.

Colorado: Colorado Springs, 303-473-1690.
District of Columbia: 202-526-3333.
Georgia: Atlanta, 404-688-4496.
Illinois Chicago, 312-233-0305; Joliet, 815-727-2222; Skokie, 312-359-4919.
Indiana: Evansville, 812-424-2555.
Iowa: Cedar Rapids, 319-398-3543; Des Moines, 515-283-1556.
Kentucky: Louisville, 502-637-9730.
Maine: Portland, 207-773-5678; toll free, 1-800-442-6018.
Maryland: Baltimore, 301-323-7444.
Massachusetts: Worcester, 617-791-9128.
Minnesota: Austin, 507-437-2373; Minneapolis, 612-333-2397; Rochester, 507-288-9374; St. Cloud, 612-252-4848;
Missouri: Kansas City, 816-474-4676.
New Jersey: Neptune, 201-922-9333; Newark, 201-485-1677; New Brunswick, 201-247-5445; North Haledon, 201-427-5142; Woodbury, 609-848-1818.
New York: Buffalo, 716-832-2966; New York City, 212-260-2700; Syracuse, 315-455-5871.
Ohio: Cincinnati, 512-241-5433; Cleveland, 216-228-5998; Dayton, 513-223-3446; Toledo, 419-241-9131.
Oregon: Portland, 503-292-0812.
Pennsylvania: Philadelphia, 215-M07-3910; Pittsburgh, 412-621-1988.
Texas: Dallas, 214-691-8881.
Washington: Snohomish, 206-252-6444, 206-353-7351.
Wisconsin: Beloit, 608-365-2844; Milwaukee, 414-272-5860.
Wyoming: Laramie, 307-742-2723.

HUMAN LIFE FOUNDATION

The Human Life Foundation came into being in 1968 as the bishops of the United States responded to the appeal of Pope Paul VI to world science for the initiation of research to improve methods of child spacing in keeping with the tenets of his encyclical, *Humanae Vitae.*

The foundation, with a grant of $800,000 in seed money provided by the bishops, was incorporated in the District of Columbia in February, 1969, as a non-profit, charitable organization; a year later, it was granted tax-exempt status. The foundation is totally independent and self-governing with a board of 12 directors, all of whom are laymen and scientists.

Purposes

The corporation is organized exclusively for these purposes:

• to sponsor — through funding pursuant to contracts entered into with qualified persons — scientific research, experimentation, investigation and analysis pertaining to the following areas: the generation of human life and reproductive physiology (including ovulation, spermatogenesis, factors influencing the transmission of life at the ovulant stage and at the stage of fertilization; fertilization, nidation, what constitutes the beginning of human life); psychological and physiological ramifications of the human sexual act; medical implications of human fertility in relation to social and economic pressures upon family life and in relation to demographic problems; termination of the existence of the conceptus by and to sponsor or carry out educational programs related to the foregoing areas;

• to make available to the public scientific knowledge and to sponsor or carry out educational programs related to the foregoing areas;

• to cooperate with other organizations and persons performing research and education in the foregoing areas.

Programs

Initial studies sponsored by the foundation have focused almost exclusively on child spacing by means of periodic abstinence.

Between July, 1970, and the end of August, 1971, the foundation funded ($101,255) 10 research and educational projects.

The Human Life Foundation and the population research center of the National Institute of Child Health and Human Development co-sponsored a Jan. 24 to 26, 1972, conference on natural family planning. Co-sponsorship by the institute marked the first specific participation of the federal government in rhythm research.

Dr. William A. Lynch is chairman of the foundation's science committee. Lawrence J. Kane is executive director. Offices are located at 1776 K St. N.W., Washington, D.C. 20006.

ABORTION LAWS AND ACTION

Permissive abortion laws are in effect in 17 states and the District of Columbia.

Twenty-five state legislatures considered more permissive abortion statutes in 1971 but none were passed. The same pattern obtained in 1972.

The main action for liberalization in both years took place in the courts.

Two Connecticut laws against abortion were struck down in 1972. The first one, dating from 1860, was ruled unconstitutional in March in a 2-1 decision of a federal district court. The same court, by the same margin, gave the same ruling to a second law passed in May which restricted abortion to cases in which the life of the mother was at stake.

In the second decision, handed down Sept. 20, the majority opinion stated: "Our conclusion, based on the text and the history of the Constitution and on cases interpreting it, is that a fetus is not a person within the meaning of the 14th Amendment. There is nothing in the history of that amendment nor in its interpretation by the Supreme Court to give any support whatever to the contention that a fetus has constitutional rights."

The dissenting judge said that this ruling was an incursion of the judiciary into the domain of the legislature. He stated: "The legislature, but not the judiciary, was designed by our Founding Fathers to reflect the standards of human decency which must be weighed in any choice between the competing moral values which are to guide governmental policy."

Another federal court ruled, 2-1, in March that New Jersey's 122-year-old abortion law was unconstitutional because it was vague and an invasion of privacy.

Three months later, a three-judge federal panel ruled in Kentucky that a state law on abortion was constitutional, citing "the universal belief in the sanctity of human life" and denying that the statute was vague and infringed on the rights of women. The judges said that "the argument of vagueness is nothing more than a guise for the plaintiff's belief that the law is too restrictive."

In New York, the legislature voted by the narrowest of margins to repeal the most permissive abortion law in the nation — allowing abortion on demand up to the 24th week of pregnancy — but its action was vetoed by Governor Nelson Rockefeller.

In Michigan, the state supreme court ruled, 5-2, on Sept. 9 that a state constitutional amendment liberalizing a 126-year-old abortion law could be placed on the ballot in November.

On June 26, 1972, the US Supreme Court ordered rearguments during its 1972-73 term of appeals challenging anti-abortion statutes in Georgia and Texas on the grounds that they violated the rights of women to privacy and of doctors to practice their profession freely.

MORAL IMPERATIVE TO END VIETNAM WAR

The following statement was adopted nearly unanimously by the National Conference of Catholic Bishops Nov. 19, 1971.
[This text was circulated by the NC Documentary Service, Origins.]

In the light of the urgent appeal for justice in the world pronounced by the recent Synod (of Bishops) in Rome, we Bishops of the United States address ourselves again to the agonizing issue of the American involvement in Southeast Asia. And we feel compelled to make some positive recommendations concerning the long journey ahead to peace with justice in our world.

I. American Involvement

Three years ago, in our Pastoral Letter "Human Life in Our Day," we raised some basic moral questions concerning the Vietnam War:

"In assessing our country's involvement in Vietnam we must ask: Have we already reached, or passed, the point where the principle of proportionality becomes decisive? How much more of our resources of men and money should we commit to this struggle, assuming an acceptable cause and intention? Has the conflict in Vietnam provoked inhuman dimensions of suffering?"

Moral Imperative

At this point in history it seems clear to us that whatever good we hope to achieve through continued involvement in this war is now outweighed by the destruction of human life and of moral values which it inflicts. It is our firm conviction, therefore, that the speedy ending of this war is a moral imperative of the highest priority. Hence we feel a moral obligation to appeal urgently to our nation's leaders, and indeed to the leaders of all the nations involved in this tragic conflict, to bring the war to an end with no further delay.

II. Peace with Justice

It is our prayerful hope that we in America will have learned from the tragedy of Vietnam important lessons for reconstructing a world with justice and a world at peace.

First, we must be determined as never before "to undertake an evaluation of war with an entirely new attitude" (Vatican II, *Pastoral Constitution on the Church in the Modern World,* No. 80). And we reach this new attitude by attending more carefully to the spirit of the Gospel and by heeding the pleas of recent Popes: "Nothing is lost by peace; everything may be lost by war" (Pius XII, Radio Broadcast of 24 August 1939); "In this age of ours which prides itself on atomic power it is irrational to believe that war is still an apt means of vindicating violated rights" (John XXIII, Encyclical *Pacem in Terris,* No. 127); "No

more war, war never again" (Paul VI, Address to the United Nations, 4 October 1965).

Secondly, we realize that "peace is not merely the absence of war, but an enterprise of justice" (Vatican II, *Pastoral Constitution on the Church in the Modern World.* No. 78). In this vein we recognize our nation's moral obligation, together with other nations, to contribute mightily to the restoration and development of Southeast Asia. After World War II our country launched an unprecedented program of economic assistance and social reconstruction of war-torn countries. Certainly we can do no less now.

Thirdly, we are convinced that the United Nations must become more effective in the promotion of world justice and peace. In saying this, we echo the words of Pope Paul VI that "the people of the earth turn to the United Nations as the last hope of concord and peace," and we recognize with the Holy Father that the United Nations "must be perfected and made equal to the needs which world history will present" (Address to the United Nations, 4 October 1965). Only by strengthening the United Nations, as an international forum for peace and as a multilateral instrument for peace-keeping can future Vietnams be averted.

Finally, we recognize a clear need at this point in history to urge upon all Americans a spirit of forgiveness and reconciliation. We recall that at a similarly critical moment in American history, Abraham Lincoln urged his countrymen to act "with malice towards none, with charity towards all." We invite our fellow Americans to let these words guide new efforts to heal wounds in our divided society and to unite our country in the years after the war in Southeast Asia.

Concern

We speak with special concern for those who have borne the heaviest burden of this war: the young men who chose conscientiously to serve in the Armed Forces, many of whom lost life or limb in this conflict. We wish to express our profound sympathy to the wives and families of the soldiers who have died in Southeast Asia. We express our profound concern for our prisoners of war and their families, and promise our prayers for the prisoners' welfare and release. And on behalf of returning veterans we urge strongly that the Government increase the present benefits and educational opportunities afforded by the GI Bill, and that it create new programs of drug rehabilitation, vocational training and job placement wherever necessary.

Conscientious Objectors

Those who in good conscience resisted this war are also subjects of our genuine pastoral concern. They too must be reintegrated as fully as possible into our society and invited to share the opportunities and responsibilities of building a better nation. Hence we repeat our plea of October 21, 1971, that the civil authorities grant generous pardon of convictions incurred under the Selective Service Act, with the understanding that sincere conscientious objectors should remain open in principle to some form of service to the community. Surely a country which showed compassion by offering amnesty after the Civil War will want to exercise no less compassion today.

Conclusion

In setting forth our position at this time, we realize that the task of constructing a just social order and a world genuinely at peace will never be an easy one. But we must reaffirm that followers of Christ and all men of good will must redouble their efforts to achieve this task so worthy of our best efforts.

Otherwise, for all its marvelous knowledge, humanity, which is already in the middle of a grave crisis, will perhaps be brought to that mournful hour in which it will experience no peace other than the dreadful peace of death. But while we say this, the Church of Christ takes her stand in the midst of the anxiety of this age, and does not cease to hope with the utmost confidence. She intends to propose to our age over and over again, in season and out of season, this apostolic message: "Behold, now is the acceptable time" for a change of heart; "Behold, now is the day of salvation!" (Vatican II, *Pastoral Constitution on the Church in the Modern World,* No. 82).

AMNESTY

The issue of amnesty for draft evaders and deserters from the military remained a moot question in 1972, with opinion divided:
• no amnesty, but punishment;
• amnesty but with a stipulation of an alternative form of national service;
• amnesty with no strings.

A majority of the US Catholic bishops—in November, 1968, October, 1971, and April, 1972—stated the view that conscientious objectors (75,000 according to a conservative estimate) who fled the country to avoid military service should not be imprisoned or lose their citizenship "provided they perform some other service to the human community."

This view is rejected outright by those claiming that the Vietnam war is all wrong and that draft resisters and deserters should not be punished for refusing to be involved in it.

Amnesty with no strings was called for in a four-page statement issued in March, 1972, by a two-day Interreligious Conference on Amnesty sponsored by the National Council of Churches. The conferees said:

"We see amnesty not as a matter of forgiveness, but as a blessed act of oblivion, the law's way of undoing what the law itself has done.

"Amnesty would demonstrate that America is still capable of a communal moral act. It would be bitterly ironic if we were to make peace with the peoples of China and Southeast Asia but persisted in vindictiveness toward those of the young generation who refused to share in the brutalities and destruction of the war."

Arguments

A month earlier, arguments for and against amnesty with or without strings were presented by two speakers on the CBS-TV weekly "Lamp Unto My Feet" show.

Father Michael J. Hunt, a teacher in the religion department of Boston University and a draft counselor in the Boston area, said resisters should be honored.

The resisters, he said, took the right stand while US leaders were wrong in pursuing the war in Vietnam.

James Finn, editor of *Worldwide* magazine, said resisters might have fulfilled a "much better political option" by voicing their protest and going to jail in this country.

Father Hunt disagreed with a bill proposed by Sen. Robert Taft, Ohio Republican, that would clear draft dodgers of any offense provided they were willing to perform three years of alternative public service. He said the legislation would in fact take on "the character of being punitive."

"If we're going to resolve some of the dilemma which is inevitably going to come in the period after Vietnam," he said, "we have to do some truth-telling.

"As a matter of fact these young men who, for conscientious reasons, refused to fight were right and our leaders were wrong. And I think we need to make this very concrete. . . . If as a society we have done wrong in Vietnam, then there are some very important ways we can undo the wrong."

One way would be to welcome back the draft resisters, he declared.

Finn said a welcome should be extended, but not "as if they had performed the highest political role when they left the country.

"I think that in leaving the country, they left undone some political role which might well have been their accomplishment. This is purely speculation, but suppose all those people who had left the country as deserters or draft evaders had stayed here and had clogged up the jails or voiced their protest? In my own terms that would have been a much better option, politically and morally."

Father Hunt said that, from the "Pentagon Papers" and other sources, it could be seen that leaders of the US government "consistently deceived the people" about Vietnam.

"I think as a society we ought to honor those who spoke the truth, even if it was not under the best and the most courageous circumstances," he said.

UN CONFERENCE ON THE HUMAN ENVIRONMENT

More than 1,200 delegates from 186 nations attended the United Nations Conference on the Human Environment June 5 to 16, 1972, in Stockholm. The purpose of the conference, the first of its kind, was to generate international agreement and to mobilize action to halt deterioration of the environment and to conserve natural resources.

Concrete results were:

• creation of a new UN agency, to begin work Jan. 1, 1973, on the development of international programs to improve the environment;

• approval of a global early-warning system to monitor climate changes and levels of air pollution;

• agreement on a statement of international concern and purpose with respect to ecological issues.

A Major Issue

One of the major issues at the conference was the effect that environmental clean-up and control measures might have on developing nations. Delegates from 78 such countries made it clear that poverty was more of a problem for them than environmental pollution. They argued that wealthier industrialized nations, which were most responsible for pollution, should pay the bill for ecological improvement. They argued too for a principle of additionality under which wealthier nations would be liable for economic damages caused to poor nations as a result of antipollution programs. The US delegation, unlike some others, did not agree with the argument; neither did it go along with proposals for more developmental aid to poor nations.

The conference, which was four years in the making, did not take any definite action on many of 186 recommendations prepared in advance. It aired them all, however; and this fact, plus its concrete decisions, assured the conference a measure of accomplishment.

Father Henri de Riedmatten, head of the Vatican delegation, said that the conference indicated a "firm effort of governments and people of good will to establish at least a basic outline, a useful instrument of ideas" concerning the human environment.

Father de Riedmatten presented a message from Pope Paul (see below) to Maurice F. Strong, secretary general of the conference.

Christian groups made a number of contributions to the conference. Among them were the participation of the Vatican delegation, on the official side, and the efforts of non-governmental agencies which included: the International Conference of Catholic Charities, the International Federation of Catholic Businessmen, the International Movement of Catholic Students, the World Union of Catholic Women's Organizations, the Christian Democratic World Union, the World Council of Churches, the Lutheran World Federation, the International Association for Religious Freedom, and the Young Women's Christian Association.

Pope Paul's Message

Man and the environment form a totality and share a common future which nations must meet with mutual responsibility, was the theme of a message from Pope Paul VI to the UN Conference on the Human Environment.

[This text was circulated by the NC Documentary Service, Origins.]

On the occasion of the opening of the United Nations Conference on the Environment, for which you have prepared with so much zeal and competence, we would like to tell you and all the other participants that we are following this important undertaking with great interest. The effort to conserve and to improve man's surroundings, and the desire to bring about the beginning of world cooperation in this effort, are answers to needs that are felt profoundly by men of our time.

Man and Environment

Today, in fact, there is an emerging awareness that man and his environment are more than ever inseparable; the environment shapes the life and the development of man, and man improves and elevates his environment by his presence, his work, and his contemplation. But man's capacity for creation cannot bear true and lasting fruit except insofar as man respects the laws that govern nature's dynamism and capacity for regeneration. Man and his environment form a totality and share a common future. And so mankind is warned that it must replace the too often blind and brutal drive of unguided material progress with a global and respectful vision of the world, for — in the striking motto of the Conference — there is "only one earth."

Interdependence

The compression of distance by progress in communication, the formation of always closer bonds between peoples through economic development, the increasing domination of nature's forces by science and technology, the multiplication of human relationships across the frontiers of nations and race — all of these are, for better or for worse, in hope or toward disaster, elements of interdependence. An abuse or a waste in one part of the world has an effect in other parts and can change the quality of life of people who are often unaware of the situation and without fault. Man knows now with certainty that scientific and technical progress, in spite of its promise for all peoples, carries within itself — as does every human work — ambivalent forces that can have good or evil results.

Moral Considerations

Above all, the moral conscience recoils in horror at man's application of the discoveries of science to the production of means of destruction such as atomic, chemical, and bacteriological weapons. And how can we ignore the upheavals in the biosphere provided by the undisciplined exploitation of the planet's physical resources, even when the aim is useful products. Both animal and plant life have been attacked by pollution of the soil, water, and air; and non-renewable natural resources have been wasted. These things deplete and break down man's environment to the point of threatening his survival. We must meet the challenge presented to our generation forcefully by going beyond partial and immediate objectives to build for tomorrow's mankind an earth that will be a home for them.

Mutual Responsibility

From now on, with interdependence must go mutual responsibility, for a community headed into the future must be united.

Solutions will not be found in easy answers. Just as the population problem is not solved by limiting access to life, so the problem of the environment cannot be coped with simply in terms of technology. Technology, of course, is indispensable, and your Assembly will have to study means appropriate to the situation. It is quite clear, for example, that — since industry is one of the principal causes of pollution — it is necessary that industry's leadership develop methods and final avenues, as much as possible without harming production, of reducing and even entirely eliminating pollution. In this work of healing, it is clear too that chemists have an important role, and great hope rests on their professional abilities.

Key Question

But technical measures will be ineffective unless they are accompanied by a radical change of mentality. We are called to lucidity and to courage. Will our civilization, tempted to push its prodigious accomplishments even further by a tyrannical domination of the human environment, discover in time the way to master its material growth, the way of moderation in the use of the earth's goods, the way of real poverty of spirit, so that the necessary and urgent changes can be made? The answer can be yes; the very excesses of progress have led men, and in a significant way the young especially, to see that their rule over nature must be ordered by an authentic ethic. The saturation brought about by some through too great an ease in living, together with the growing consciousness among many of mankind's solidarity, is leading to a restoration of the respectful attitude that is the essential basis of man's right relation to his environment. We cannot fail here to remember the timeless examples of Saint Francis of Assisi and of the great Christian contemplative religious orders; these have shown us an interior harmony worked out in the framework of a happy union with nature's rhythms and laws.

"All that God has created is good," Saint Paul has written (I Tm. 4:4), echoing the Genesis text that tells of God's benevolence toward each of his works. For man to rule over creation means not to destroy but to build up, not to make the world an uninhabitable chaos but a neat and attractive place to be lived in. No one, then, has a right to take over the environment in an absolute and egoistic way. The world man lives in is not a *res nullius*, the property of no one; it is a *res omnium,* the patrimony of mankind. Those responsible for the environment, both private and public agencies, must regulate the environment for the well-being of all men, for man himself is the first and the greatest wealth of the earth.

Fair Sharing

For these reasons, the necessity of offering to all the possibility of a fair sharing in the existing and the potential resources of our planet should weigh heavily on the consciences of men of good will. Development, the integral fulfillment of man, can be seen to be an excellent theme, the keystone of your deliberations, where you will be able to join the search for ecological balance with the search for a just balance of prosperity between those at the industrialized centers of the world and those at the periphery. It has been rightly said that the worst pollution is human misery. The young nations are building a better future for their peoples at the cost of great effort, trying to assimilate the positive gains of technological civilization but rejecting its excesses and its deviations. Is it unrealistic to hope that these young nations become the pioneers of a new world that can be begun at this Conference? It would be very unjust to refuse to these nations the necessary means, for they have often, through no fault of their own, had to pay a heavy price in the degradation adn the depletion of the common biological patrimony. Therefore, instead of understanding the fight for a better environment as a fearful reaction of the rich, we should see it as for the advantage of all, an affirmation of faith and hope in its destiny on the part of the human family united in a common enterprise.

It is with these thoughts that we pray the all-powerful God that in his goodness he bless all the participants and grant them the light of wisdom and the strength of brotherly love that they may succeed in their work.

The foregoing message of Pope Paul was his longest, but not first, statement on the subject. He mentioned it several times in addresses delivered in previous years, with emphasis on moral responsibility.

CATHOLIC CHARISMATIC RENEWAL

More than 11,000 persons from the United States, Canada and several foreign countries attended the sixth International Conference on the Catholic Charismatic Renewal June 2 to 4, 1972, on the campus of Notre Dame University. The number was significant as an indicator of the rapid growth of the movement when compared with the 90 participants in the first such conference held in 1967.

Background

The movement originated with a handful of Duquesne University students and faculty members in the 1966-67 school year and spread from there to Notre Dame, Michigan State University and the University of Michigan, numerous other campuses and cities throughout the United States.

Scriptural keys to the renewal, according to *Newark Advocate* feature writer Anne Buckley, are:

• Christ's promise to send the Holy Spirit;
• a passage in the Acts of the Apostles describing the effects of the coming of the Spirit upon the Apostles on Pentecost;
• St. Paul's explanation, in the Letter to the Romans, of the charismatic gifts the Holy Spirit would bestow on Christians.

Awareness of these gifts, renewalists — or Pentecostalists, as they are also called — is lacking among many Catholics. Father John A. Kakolewski of Rutherford, N. J., observed:

"Christian communities haven't been experiencing the things in Acts. This movement is God calling us in an age when people are saying, 'God is dead.' The Lord is gathering up people, raising up communities, using this to make the world aware of his action and power. For some reason, we haven't been aware."

Noting the importance of this awareness, he said of the movement: "It is a community of young people coming together in faith—faith is essential. It is really believing in God's presence at this moment in time, believing that God's power is alive. They really believe Jesus' promise to give the Holy Spirit to those who ask for him, and they seek fulfillment of that promise in their lives. And they seek the charismatic gifts so that God's action will be manifested in their midst."

Baptism of the Spirit

The seeking starts with prayer for the Baptism of the Spirit, which is regarded as "the initiation of a new life in the Spirit." The prayer is for the "unleashing of the gifts present in a Christian through the sacraments of baptism and confirmation for use in a new life based on repentance and a total commitment to Jesus which is renewed each day."

Pentecostalists make it clear that they regard this Baptism of the Spirit not as a new sacrament but as the actualization of gifts already received with the sacraments.

Reaction to the Baptism of the Spirit, according to Father William O'Brien, a chaplain at Fairleigh Dickinson University, is "an experience of the presence and love of God, an awareness of the presence of God" in one's life. With it comes a new sense of spiritual peace and a desire for reading the Scriptures and sharing Christian life with a group of persons.

Charismatic gifts—such as speaking and interpreting strange tongues (glossalalia), healing, prophecy and the interpretation of events, which are said to manifest themselves in various ways—are secondary in importance to the Baptism of the Spirit and the effects of this experience in daily life.

The gift of tongues, whatever it is, is regarded by leaders of the movement as the least of the gifts. Emphasis on its bizarre features by some has not helped the reputation of the movement.

Pentecostalist practices include the laying-on of hands to communicate and share the gifts of the Spirit, spontaneous prayer, participation in prayer meetings, personal testimony to the action of the Holy Spirit, scriptural reading, meditation, and, for many, vigorous participation in the liturgy.

One of the movement's strongest points of emphasis is on community experience and the sharing of spiritual gifts.

The movement is international and has an estimated participation of at least 100,000 persons of all ages.

A National Renewal Service Committee, for developing services on a national level to foster charismatic renewal in the Church, has the mailing address: P.O. Box 12, Notre Dame, Ind. 46556.

The movement publishes a monthly magazine, *New Covenant*. Its mailing address is Box 102, Main St. Station, Ann Arbor, Mich. 48107.

Critics and Supporters

Pentecostalists have their critics as well as supporters.

Critics charge them with emotionalism and holy-rollerism because of the emphasis they place on the experience of God's presence and action; lack of concern for authentic doctrine because of their stress on spiritual experience and association with Pentecostalists of other faiths; elitism because of the uniqueness of the movement. Some compare them with enthusiasts of the Jesus Revolution.

Supporters, however, demonstrate the doctrinal soundness of the movement and attribute real or alleged excesses on the part of some to their own fault or misconceptions about charismatic renewal and/or authentic Pentecostalism.

1972 Conference

"Jesus is Lord of His People" was the theme of the 1972 conference which, in 140 workshops and seminars, explored aspects of Christian life ranging from the Eucharist in daily life to social action and intense Christian community.

The place of charismatic renewal in the Church was stressed in the main address by Kevin Ranaghan, a member of the service committee. He said:

"The charismatic renewal is not an end in itself, nor can it have an existence separate from that of the Church. Rather the charismatic renewal is part of the Church. Thus, the resources, spiritual energies, and very lives of individuals and communities who are in the Catholic charismatic renewal are laid down in service for the well-being of the whole Church."

Ranaghan also cautioned those at the conference to avoid "any attitude or action which makes the charismatic renewal and its participants look like a special 'in group,' the elect of God, or the select few who have the whole truth." Catholic Pentecostalists "are not members of a small separate body of Christ, but we are a small fraction of a much larger, Spirit-endowed body of Christ, the Church at large."

Father Edward O'Connor, associate professor of theology at Notre Dame University and author of *The Pentecostal Movement in the Catholic Church,* spoke in the same vein. He said that Catholic Pentecostalism "is not an underground movement in the Church," but a movement which "tends to rediscover and follow the traditional doctrines and practices of the faith." It "is not the novelty in the Church that it was" several years ago, but is "still looked at as something alien."

Regarding the attitude of bishops toward the movement, Auxiliary Bishop Joseph McKinney of Grand Rapids said at the conference: "I would guess that 90 per cent of the bishops have the impression that the Catholic charismatic renewal is a good thing for the Church, a few are enthusiastic, and some others would like to know more."

Bishop Charles B. McLaughlin of St. Petersburg said in the Orlando diocesan newspaper: "The charismatic renewal is wonderful for certain people. . . . It is not, of course, the approach all will be attracted to."

Attendants at the spring, 1972, meeting of the National Conference of Catholic Bishops stated that the charismatic renewal "should at this point not be inhibited but allowed to develop."

In addition to the sixth international conference, 1972 developments included a number of regional conferences and the establishment of the first non-territorial Pentecostal parish in the United States — the Community of the Holy Spirit in St. Charles, Ill. — with the approval of Bishop Arthur J. O'Neill of Rockford.

HOUSE OF PRAYER EXPERIENCE

(Source: Sister Ann E. Chester, HOPE Clearing Center, 70 W. Boston Blvd., Detroit, Mich. 48202: *Exploring Inner Space,* published by the Center.)

The purpose of the House of Prayer Experience (HOPE) movement is to help active religious and priests and lay persons to acquire a contemporary style of contemplative life for renewal, inner growth and a more joyful personal and communal life in the light of the Gospel.

The starting point of participation in the movement is an extended period, from several weeks to several years, of concentration on intensive prayer with a community — a house of prayer experience. The result sought is the development of a style of prayer and contemplation with a carry-over that integrates and permeates religion and life.

Background

Ideas for what eventually turned out to be the movement and houses of prayer to carry it on were in the process of development in 1962 in proposals for the renewal of religious life made by the Conference of Major Superiors of Women Religious and various communities of sisters. Real impetus was given by Father Bernard Haring, C.SS.R., who sketched the main outlines of the movement and gave it a name at a meeting of the conference held in the autumn of 1965.

Early in 1968, the Immaculate Heart of Mary Sisters of Monroe, Mich., organized a clearing center to serve as a focal point for idea exchanges which preceded and led up to a national planning conference in the summer of that year. The four-day meeting, held in Monroe, was attended by 156 representatives from 96 congregations of sisters.

The IHM Sisters sponsored the first program of the movement, called HOPE '69, the following summer. Eight more programs — lasting six weeks and for intercommunity groups — were conducted in 1970 and at least 40 in the summer of 1971. By the beginning of 1972 about 45 houses of prayer were in year-long or seasonal operation, offering HOPE programs not only to sisters, who pioneered the movement, but also to priests and lay persons. The first house of prayer for diocesan priests was established in 1970 by the Archdiocese of Detroit.

Underlying the movement are the convictions that prayer is necessary to integrate religion and life, and that institutionalized and long-practiced forms of prayer and prayer life are not adequate for religious and priests engaged in apostolic ministries and of lay persons involved in the multiple concerns of life in the world. Hence the emphasis on new forms of prayer and concentration on them in periods of comtemplation.

Programs

The communities of houses of prayer consist of a relatively stable core of members with an authentic call to a deeper prayer life and of guests who come and go for shorter or longer periods of participation. The stability of the core group, while not a now-and-forever type of commitment, is such as to guarantee continuity in programs and the resources of experienced personnel in conducting them. Experience has shown that the ideal size of a community is relatively small, from seven to nine members; also that, within limits, mixed groups are better than homogeneous ones for realizing the purposes of the movement. The importance of communities bound together by interpersonal relationships of spiritual depth rather than by institutional ties is paramount.

Program elements include the liturgy, meditation, scriptural reading and discussion, shared prayer in the shared life of community, silence and solitude, search for new forms of prayer and for new adaptations of traditional forms — all against the background of existential conditions.

Programs are flexible rather than predetermined, taking shape and finding expression in line with the particular charisms of the participants and their response to the Holy Spirit. In this respect, they differ from conventional retreat exercises and monastic practices.

This flexibility opens the way to particular thrusts with which programs become identified. Thus, some are known for their emphasis on forms of prayer and experience characteristic of charismatic renewal or for the adoption of practices of Eastern spiritual traditions, including yoga as an aid to contemplation. Others are identifiable with programs stressing solitude and silence. One of the strongest thrusts is the ministry of prayer, to spread HOPE and to increase participation

in its abbreviated (day-long, weekend, etc.) as well as extended programs.

All programs represent efforts to develop prayer and prayer experience in a community of interpersonal relationships which is open to dialogue and involvement with the Church and the world at large.

Representative Houses

Following is a partial list of houses representative of the movement and some its thrusts.

Visitation House (Immaculate Heart of Mary Sisters), 529 Stewart Rd., Monroe, Mich. 48161.

Kresge House (intercommunity), 70 W. Boston Blvd., Detroit, Mich. 48202; orientation program, additional thrust.

Community of HOPE (intercommunity), Xavier Center, Convent Station, N.J. 07961; Pentecostal thrust.

St. Joseph Priory (Chicago Province of Priests), 9750 Ferguson Rd., Dallas, Tex. 75228; ministry of prayer.

House of Prayer (St. Joseph Sisters of Kalamazoo), 418 Pearl St., Pinckney, Mich. 48169; parish ministry.

Passionist Prayer Center, 427 Clay St., Hinsdale, Ill. 60521.

Trinity Center (Missionary Servants of the Most Holy Trinity), 1190 Long Hill Rd., Stirling, N.J. 07980; developmental prayer services for priests, religious, lay persons.

House of Peace (Canadian Conference of Religious), R.R. No. 2, Combermere, Ont., Canada.

IHM House, C. P. 550, Recife, Pe., Brazil; mission thrust.

Interest in the HOPE movement has increased steadily not only in this country but also abroad, as indicated by inquiries received at the Clearing Center from places in England, France, Africa, Australia, New Zealand, India and Korea. *Exploring Inner Space,* published by the Center, has been translated into Italian, and work on a German translation is underway.

HUMAN DEVELOPMENT CAMPAIGN

The Campaign was undertaken by the US Catholic Conference in November, 1969, to combat poverty in this country in three significant ways:

• by making people in this country, Catholics in particular, aware of the prevalence of poverty among some 34 million persons through programs of education and information;

• by raising funds to finance programs designed to attack the root causes of poverty:

• by funding self-help programs with participation of the poor.

The campaign got underway with a collection taken up in parishes throughout the country Nov. 22, 1970. The proceeds, the largest ever received in a nationwide collec-

tion, amounted to nearly $8.5 million. Seventy-five percent of the money ($6,262,184.72) was earmarked for allocation to self-help projects by a 40-member national committee; 25 per cent ($2.1 million) remained in dioceses where it was collected for similar allocation by commitees on local levels.

More than 1,100 fund requests were received by the national committee in 1971, and grants were awarded to 231 organizations for a wide variety of projects.

The second nationwide collection in support of the campaign, made in the fall of 1971, raised close to $7 million. More than 2,000 requests for funding were filed for review by July, 1972, and by Sept. 12 more than

50 organizations were awarded grants total-
ing more than $1.5 million.

Campaign grants are made with the approval of a bishops' committee headed by
Bishop Francis J. Mugavero of Brooklyn.
They are first reviewed, with recommendations, by a national committee chaired by

Dr. Albert Wheeler of Detroit and staffed by
40 members.

Auxiliary Bishop Michael R. Dempsey of
Chicago is national director. Rev. Robert V.
Monticello is the executive director.

Offices are located at 1325 Massachusetts
Ave. N.W., Washington, D.C. 20005.

NATIONAL FEDERATION OF PRIESTS' COUNCILS

The National Federation of Priests' Councils was organized by 233 delegates from 127
priests' organizations at a charter meeting
held in Chicago May 20 and 21, 1968.

Its stated purposes are to:

• give priests' councils, official or unofficial, a representative voice in matters of concern to the Church and with respect to problems facing the nation, including racism and
poverty;

• improve communications among priests
all over the country;

• coordinate programs of research and
make recommendations to priests, bishops
and others on specific matters;

• cooperate with lay persons, religious and
bishops in meeting the contemporary needs of
the Church.

Activities

Since its establishment, the NFPC has
sponsored studies of the priesthood, conferences and workshops on prayer and the spiritual life of priests, continuing education, and
personnel officers, policies and practices in
US dioceses. It has supported efforts for developing and establishing due process machinery for handling disputes. It has allied itself with black priests, religious and lay persons in their attempts to make the Church
more present and active in their communities,
and has made recommendations for action by
the Church on peace and other social issues.
Most of all, it has pressed for a larger role for
priests in decision-making and pastoral responsibility, changes in their styles of life, and
freedom to seek and pursue new forms of
ministry.

The representational character of the
NFPC has been questioned. Its influence,
however, has been considerable in voicing
and shaping the attitudes and aspirations of
many individual priests as well as priests' senates and other organizations.

The NFPC has a membership of 131 senates, councils and associations, including several provinces of men religious and the Glenmary Home Missioners. Its programs and
operations are determined by a house of delegates from member bodies, which meets annually, and an elected 27-member executive
board. Its publication is *Priests/USA*, a
monthly.

The president is Father Frank Bonnike of
De Kalb, Ill.

Headquarters are located at 1307 S. Wabash Ave., Chicago, Ill. 60605.

1972 Convention, Developments

Two hundred delegates from 127 member
bodies attending the Mar. 13 to 16, 1972, convention in Denver reelected Father Frank
Bonnike to the presidency over a candidate,
Father Jerome Fraser of Michigan, who criticized his and the NFPC's willingness to be
conciliatory in dealing with the National
Conference of Catholic Bishops.

Father Bonnike, in a 5,000-word state-of-
the-federation address, proposed the establishment of 15 task forces to study and develop action programs relating to justice and
peace, in line with the convention theme,
"Ministry for Justice and Peace: Imperative
for Priests/USA." He and other speakers emphasized the need for priests not to pull back
from the social thrust of their ministry.

Delegates passed a wide range of resolutions of this type, from an appeal to the US
bishops — and the NFPC — to press for an
end to the war in Vietnam, to amnesty for
military dissenters, the end of discrimination
in clubs, the abolition of the death penalty
and the sharing of ministry with lay persons.

In other actions during the year, the federation and/or spokesmen for it came out
strongly against new norms issued by the Vatican for the selection of bishop candidates
and a Vatican letter to bishops and religious
superiors regarding the laicization of priests
(see separate entries).

Stands of this type — including the 1971
"Moment of Truth" statement calling for optional celibacy — have cost the NFPC a
number of members, according to a statement
issued from its headquarters in September,
1972. Dropouts have included senates or
councils from Cleveland, Newark and St. Augustine.

The most recent joiners, bringing membership to its total of 131, were the Fort
Worth senate and the Western Province of
the Servite Fathers.

Father Francis F. Brown, an NFPC official, said in connection with the statement
that Father Bonnike had urged the federation
"to relate to" the National Conference of
Catholic Bishops' ad hoc committee on
priestly life and ministry, of which he was a
member.

Father Brown said that the NFPC is "an
independent group. We haven't made any
overtures to become official. This isn't new in
the Church. This is encouraged, that independent groups be formed."

OBSCENITY LAWS AND THE SUPREME COURT

Between 1967 and the beginning of the 1972-73 term, five Supreme Court Justices handed down 22 or more decisions in which they overturned obscenity convictions in 14 states and overruled 98 jurists of lower courts.

These rulings, along with the following decisions of the entire Supreme Court, served as precedents for scheduled 1972-73 action by the Court on suits in which the constitutionality and related aspects of a number of obscenity and nuisance laws were at issue.

Roth Test

Roth v. United States, Alberts v. California (1957): The Court ruled that obscene literature is not within the area of speech or press protected by the Constitution. The ruling was based on the observation: "Implicit in the history of the First Amendment is the rejection of obscenity as utterly without redeeming social importance. This rejection for that reason is mirrored in the universal judgment that obscenity should be restrained."

The Court gave this test of obscenity: "Whether to the average person, applying community standards, the dominant theme of the material taken as a whole appeals to prurient interest."

In connection with this definition, the Court indicated that material relating to sex is not necessarily obscene. Determiing standards of obscenity were said to be:

• The quality of the material must be of such a nature that it has the inherent "capacity to attract individuals eager for a forbidden look: that is, it must consist of material which goes substantially beyond customary limits of candor in the description or representation of nudity, sex or shameful acts."

• It must be offensive to the community conscience and not merely to a group in the community. This standard, however, does not outlaw the enactment of statutes designed to prevent the deliberate distribution of obscene literature to children.

• The offensive material must constitute the dominant theme. Unrelated excerpts or incidental passages are not sufficient to render a book obscene.

Smith v. California: The Court ruled unconstitutional a Los Angeles ordinance making it a criminal offense to have an obscene book in one's possession for the purpose of sale, on the ground that the ordinance did not make "knowledge" of the obscene contents an essential element of the crime.

Roth Test Modified

Manual Enterprises v. Day (1962): The Court reversed a Circuit Court of Appeals decision which had substantiated findings of the Post Office Department that homosexual material could not be mailed because it was obscene and because the magazine in question indicated where obscene material could be obtained. One opinion supporting the decision held that the allegedly objectionable material was not of such a nature as to be considered "patently offensive" by community standards of the nation. This line of thought represented a modification of the community standards test stated in Roth.

Jacobellis v. Ohio (1964): The Court reversed the conviction of a motion picture operator for exhibiting "The Lovers." The opinion noted that "a work cannot be proscribed unless it is utterly without social importance," and that the term "community standards" used in Roth does not refer to a local standard but rather to a national standard.

Tralins v. Gerstein, Grove Press, Inc., v. Gerstein: The Court ruled that Florida courts had erred in finding two publications obscene, *Pleasure Is My Business* and *Tropic of Cancer.*

Three major decisions were handed down Mar. 21, 1966, when the Court sustained the convictions of **Ralph Ginzburg,** publisher of *Eros* magazine, and **Edward Mishkin,** publisher of books on sadism and masochism, while reversing a Massachusetts ban on John Clelan's 18th century novel, *Fanny Hill.*

In the Ginzburg ruling it said that, when material is neither obviously obscene nor obviously not obscene, courts may take the advertising and promotional activities of distributors into account as an indication of their intentions.

In the Mishkin case, the Court said legal obscenity is present when the material appeals to the prurient interest of the special audience to which it is addressed.

In the *Fanny Hill* decision, the Court declared that the presence of "redeeming social value" can render a work immune to a ban on grounds of obscenity

Trend

The trend of Court decisions since 1957 has been progressively permissive, with modification of the initial Roth test with the concept of national community standards and standards of "redeeming social values."

Outside the Court, a report issued in September, 1970, by the majority of a Congressional Commission on Obscenity and Pornography said: "The Commission does not believe that a sufficient social justification exists for the retention or enactment of broad legislation prohibiting the consensual distribution of sexual materials to adults."

A six-member minority — especially Charles H. Keating, Jr., and Father Morton A. Hill, S.J., heads of the interdenominational Citizens for Decent Literature and Morality in Media, respectively — took exception to the report as well as the composition and procedures of the Commission.

40TH INTERNATIONAL EUCHARISTIC CONGRESS

"Love one another as I have loved you," was the stated theme of the 40th International Eucharistic Congress scheduled for Feb. 18 to 25, 1973, in Melbourne, Australia.

Preparations for the congress were still in progress at the time of writing.

They got underway several months after the priests of the host archdiocese voted in December, 1971, to ratify the proposal to hold the Congress and to focus it on the relevance of Eucharistic worship to daily life and the social concerns of the peoples of Oceania.

In the first vote, taken in October, they had put down the proposal because of anticipated expenses and triumphalist pomp which they feared might obscure the essential purposes of such a congress.

Renewal Program

Those purposes provided the background for a three-part, year-long period of pastoral renewal preceding the congress.

The first phase of the program consisted of study and discussion sessions on the meaning of renewal in the Church and in the lives of Christians. By the end of June, 1972, it was reported that 55,000 persons had taken part in the activity of 4,850 discussion groups.

The second phase shifted attention to the theme, "Good Neighbors in a Global Village." The social thrust of the Gospel and Christian doctrine were the points up for special consideration.

October and November were devoted to rounding out the preparatory program and putting all of its elements together in home discussions of the "Eucharist and Life." The culminating event of this final stage was a general Family Communion Day observed on the feast of Christ the King, Nov. 26.

Other Christians as well as Catholics participated in preparations for and events of the congress.

The renewal program started with an ecumenical service in which the Rev. Dr. Eugene Carson Blake, then secretary general of the World Council of Churches, and other church representatives took part. Two announced features connected with the congress were a national ecumenical seminar to be held in mid-February and an ecumenical service to be held during the week of the congress.

Participants in the seminar were to include Cardinal Jan Willebrands, president of the Vatican Secretariat for Promoting Christian Unity; Dr. Lukas Vischer, head of the Faith and Order Commission of the World Council of Churches; Lutheran theologian Jurgen Moltmann; and representatives of various Christian churches in Oceania.

Ecumenical participation on other levels was reported to be significant, in connection with religious discussions, arrangements for facilities, hospitality and fund-raising.

Congress Events

Events scheduled during the congress included the following:

• Eucharistic and other celebrations attended by the bishops of Australia and the rest of Oceania — who would be holding a joint meeting in Sydney — as well as bishops from many other countries;

• the blessing of new centers of study for candidates for the priesthood, Corpus Christi College and Catholic College, at Clayton;

• a seminar sponsored by the National Missionary Council, with special reference to the civil rights and developmental needs of 150,000 Australian aborigines, New Guineans, Pacific Islanders and Southeast Asians;

• observances for children and youth, with special Masses, a National Altar Servers' Conference and a meeting of Catholic Scouts;

• Mass for the elderly and handicapped;

• Eastern Rite celebrations, to be led by Melkite-Rite Patriarch Maximos V Hakim and Ukrainian-Rite Cardinal Josy Slipyi;

• Masses for migrant communities, the blessing of a new Polish chapel and an ordination ceremony presided over by Cardinal Karol Wojtyla of Cracow;

• study sessions and seminars on: "A Caring Christian Community," the first seminar of its kind in Australia for Catholic social workers; population and economy; family health care; human development; homeless men and seafarers, combined with the opening of new facilities by the Society of St. Vincent de Paul and the Stella Maris Club; problems of poverty.

Congress of the People

Some 300 Australians, most of them lay persons, handled all preparatory work for the congress — as others had done before them for the 1928 congress in Sydney.

Their "Congress of the People," emphasizing Christian and Eucharistic concern for the needy, was symbolized by a medallion depicting the gathering of peoples from many nations against the background of the Eucharistic host and chalice.

The First International Eucharistic Congress was held in 1881 in Lille, France. The idea for the observance originated in 1873 with Marthe Marie Tamisier, the "beggar woman of the Blessed Sacrament," who disclosed the proposal to Philibert Vrau, an industrialist in northern France. He secured the approval of Pope Leo XIII and, in collaboration with Bishop Gaston de Segur, organized the program and proceedings of the first congress. A success from the start, it set the patterns for all such subsequent celebrations, which are planned and held under the auspices of a permanent committee for international Eucharistic congresses.

ADMISSION OF OTHER CHRISTIANS TO THE EUCHARIST

This Instruction outlines conditions under which other Christians may receive the Eucharist in the Catholic Church, and contains what may be the most complete discussion in official documents of the theological principles underlying this question. The instruction was made public July 8, 1972.

The following translation of the text was distributed by the Vatican Secretariat for Christian Unity and was circulated in this country by the NC Documentary Service, *Origins.*]

1. The Question: We are often asked the question: In what circumstances and on what conditions can members of other churches and ecclesial communities be admitted to Eucharistic Communion in the Catholic Church?

The question is not a new one. The Second Vatican Council (in the *Decree on Ecumenism)* and the *Directory on Ecumenism* dealt with it (1).

The pastoral guidance offered here is not intended to change the existing rules but to explain them, bringing out the doctrinal principles on which the rules rest and so making their application easier.

2. The Eucharist and the Mystery of the Church:

There is a close link between the mystery of the Church and the mystery of the Eucharist.

(a) The Eucharist really contains what is the very foundation of the being and unity of the Church: the body of Christ, offered in sacrifice and given to the faithful as the bread of eternal life. The sacrament of the body and blood of Christ, given to the Church so as to constitute the Church, of its nature carries with it:

• the ministerial power which Christ gave to his Apostles and to their successors, the bishops along with the priests, to make effective sacramentally his own priestly act — that act by which once and forever he offered himself to the Father in the Holy Spirit, and gave himself to his faithful that they might be one in him;

• the unity of the ministry, which is to be exercised in the name of Christ, head of the Church, and hence in the hierarchical communion of ministers;

• the faith of the Church, which is expressed in the Eucharistic action itself — the faith by which she responds to Christ's gift in its true meaning.

The sacrament of the Eucharist, understood in its entirety with these three elements, signifies an existing unity brought about by him, the unity of the visible Church of Christ which cannot be lost (2).

(b) "The celebration of Mass, the action of Christ and of the people of God hierarchically ordered, is the center of the whole Christian life, for the universal Church as for the local Church and for each Christian"(3). Celebrating the mystery of Christ in the Mass, the Church celebrates her own mystery and manifests concretely her unity.

The faithful assembled at the altar offer the sacrifice through the hands of the priest acting in the name of Christ, and they represent the community of the people of God united in the profession of one faith. Thus they constitute a sign and a kind of delegation of a wider assembly.

The celebration of Mass is of itself a profession of faith in which the whole Church recognizes and express itself. If we consider the marvelous meaning of the Eucharistic prayers as well as the riches contained in the other parts of the Mass, whether they are fixed or vary with the liturgical cycle; if at the same time we bear in mind that the Liturgy of the Word and the Eucharistic Liturgy make up a single act of worship (4), then we can see here a striking illustration of the principle *lex orandi lex credendi,* ("the law of prayer is the law of belief") (5). Thus the Mass has a catechetical power which the recent liturgical renewal has emphasized. Again, the Church has in the course of history been careful to introduce into liturgical celebration the main themes of the common faith, the chief fruits of the experience of that faith. This she has done either by means of new texts or by creating new feasts.

(c) The relation between local celebration of the Eucharist and universal ecclesial communion is stressed also by the special mention in the Eucharistic prayers of the pope, the local bishop and the other members of the episcopal college.

What has been said here of the Eucharist as center and summit of the Christian life holds for the whole Church and for each of its members, but particularly for those who take an active part in the celebration of Mass and above all for those who receive the body of Christ. Communion during Mass is indeed the most perfect way of participating in the Eucharist, for it fulfills the Lord's command, "take and eat" (6).

3. The Eucharist as Spiritual Food: The effect of the Eucharist is also to nourish spiritually those who receive it as what the faith of the Church says it truly is — the body and blood of the Lord given as the food of eternal life (cf. Jn. 6: 54-58). For the baptized, the Eucharist is spiritual food, a means by which they are brought to live the life of Christ himself, are incorporated more profoundly in him and share more intensely in the whole economy of his saving mystery. "He who eats my flesh and drinks my blood abides in me and I in him" (Jn. 6: 56).

(a) As the sacrament of full union with Christ (7) and of the perfection of spiritual life, the Eucharist is necessary to every Christian: in our Lord's words, ". . . unless you eat the flesh of the Son of man and drink his blood, you have no life in you" (Jn. 6: 53). Those who live intensely the life of grace feel a compelling need for this spiritual sustenance, and the Church herself encourages daily Communion.

(b) Yet, though it is a spiritual food whose effect is to unite the Christian man to Jesus Christ, the Eucharist is far from being simply a means of satisfying exclusively personal aspirations, however lofty these may be. The union of the faithful with Christ, the head of the Mystical Body, brings about the union of the faithful themselves with each other. It is on their sharing of the Eucharistic bread that St. Paul bases the union of all the faithful, "Because there is one loaf, we who are many are one body, for we all partaké of the same loaf" (1 Cor. 10:17). By this sacrament "man is incorporated in Christ and united with his members" (8). By frequent receiving of the Eucharist the faithful are incorporated more and more in the body of Christ and share increasingly in the mystery of the Church.

(c) Spiritual need of the Eucharist is not therefore merely a matter of personal spiritual growth: simultaneously, and inseparably, it concerns our entering more deeply into Christ's Church, "which is his body, the fullness of him who fills all in all" (Eph. 1:23).

4. General Principles Governing Admission to Communion: Where members of the Catholic Church are concerned, there is a perfect parallel between regarding the Eucharist as the celebration of the entire ecclesial community united in one faith and regarding it as sustenance, as a response to the spiritual needs, personal and ecclesial, of each member. It will be the same when, in the Lord's good time, all the followers of Christ are reunited in one and the same Church. But what are we to say today, when Christians are divided? Any baptized person has a spiritual neød for the Eucharist. Those who are not in full communion with the Catholic Church have recourse to the ministers of their own communities, as their conscience dictates. But what about those who cannot do this, and who for that or other reasons come and ask for Communion from a Catholic priest?

The *Directory on Ecumenism* has already shown how we must safeguard simultaneously the integrity of ecclesial communion and the good of souls. Behind the *Directory* lie two main governing ideas:

(a) The strict relationship between the mystery of the Church and the mystery of the Eucharist can never be altered, whatever pastoral measures we may be led to take in given cases. Of its very nature, celebration of the Eucharist signifies the fullness of profession of faith and the fullness of ecclesial communion. This principle must not be obscured and must remain our guide in this field.

(b) The principle will not be obscured if admission to Catholic Eucharistic Communion is confined to particular cases of those Christians who have a faith in the sacrament in conformity with that of the Church, who experience a serious spiritual need for the Eucharistic sustenance, who for a prolonged period are unable to have recourse to a minister of their own community and who ask for the sacrament of their own accord; all this provided that they have proper dispositions and lead lives worthy of a Christian. This spiritual need should be understood in the sense defined above (No. 3, b and c): a need for an increase in spiritual life and a need for a deeper involvement in the mystery of the Church and of its unity.

Further, even if those conditions are fulfilled, it will be a pastoral responsibility to see that the admission of these other Christians to Communion does not endanger or disturb the faith of Catholics (9).

5. Differences, in View of These Principles, between Members of the Oriental Churches and other Christians: The *Directory on Ecumencism* (10) gives different directions for the admission to Holy Communion of separated Eastern Christians, and of others. The reason is that the Eastern Churches, though separated from us, have true sacraments, above all, because of the apostolic succession, the priesthood and the Eucharist, which unite them to us by close ties, so that the risk of obscuring the relation between Eucharistic Communion and ecclesial communion is somewhat reduced (11). Recently the Holy Father recalled that "between our Church and the venerable Orthodox Churches there exists already an almost total communion, though it is not yet perfect: it results from our joint participation in the mystery of Christ and of his Church"(12).

With Christians who belong to communities whose Eucharistic faith differs from that of the Church and which do not have the sacrament of Orders, admitting them to the Eucharist entails the risk of obscuring the essential relation between Eucharistic Communion and ecclesial communion. This is why the *Directory* treats their case differently from that of the Eastern Christians and envisages admission only in exceptional cases of "urgent necessity." In cases of this kind the person concerned is asked to manifest a faith in the Eucharist in conformity with that of the Church, i.e., in the Eucharist as Christ instituted it and as the Catholic Church hands it on. This is not asked of an Orthodox person because he belongs to a church whose faith in the Eucharist is conformable to our own.

6. What Authority Decides Particular Cases? — The Meaning of No. 55 of the *Directory on Ecumenism:*

Number 55 of the *Directory* allows fairly wide discretionary power to the episcopal authority in judging whether the necessary conditions are present for these exceptional cases. If cases of the same pattern recur often in a given region, episcopal conferences can give general directions. More often, however, it falls to the bishop of the diocese to make a decision. He alone will know all the circumstances of particular cases.

Apart from danger of death, the *Directory* mentions two examples, people in prison and those suffering persecution, but it then speaks of "other cases of such urgent necessity." Such cases are not confined to situations of suffering and danger. Christians may find themselves in grave spiritual necessity and with no chance of recourse to their own community. For example in our time, which is one of large-scale movements of population, it can happen much more often than before that non-Catholic Christians are scattered in Catholic regions. They are often deprived of the help of their own communion and unable to get in touch with it except at great trouble and expense. If the conditions set out in the *Directory* are verified, they can be admitted to Eucharistic Communion, but it will be for the bishop to consider each case.

Footnotes

(1) *Decree on Ecumenism* (No. 8):

"Yet worship in common *(communicatio in sacris)* is not to be considered as a means to be used indiscriminately for the restoration of unity among Christians. There are two main principles upon which the practice of such common worship depends: first, that of the unity of the Church which ought to be expressed; and second, that of the sharing in means of grace. The expression of unity very generally forbids common worship. Grace to be obtained sometimes commends it. The concrete course to be adopted, when due regard has been given to all the circumstances of time, place and persons, is left to the prudent decision of the local episcopal authority, unless the bishops' conference according to its own statutes, or the Holy See, has determined otherwise." Cf. also *Decree on the Eastern Catholic Churches*, (No. 27).

Also, *Directory on Ecumenism:*

A. Sharing in liturgical worship with our separated Eastern brothers.

"Besides cases of necessity, there would be reasonable ground for encouraging sacramental sharing of special circumstances make it materially or morally impossible over a long period for one of the faithful to receive the sacraments in his own Church, so that in effect he would be deprived, without legitimate reason, of the spiritual fruit of the sacraments" (No. 44).

B. Sharing in liturgical worship with other separated brethren.

"*Celebration of the sacraments is an action of the celebrating Community, carried out within the Community, signifying the oneness if the Community, signifying the oneness in his unity of sacramental faith is deficient, the participation of the separated brethren with Catholics, especially in the sacraments of the Eu-*

charist, penance and anointing of the sick, is forbidden. Nevertheless, since the sacraments are both signs of unity and sources of grace (cf. Decree on Ecumenism, No. 8), the Church can for adequate reasons allow access to those sacraments to a separate brother. This may be permitted in danger of death or in urgent need (during persecution, in prisons) if the separated brother has no access to a minister of his own Communion, and spontaneously asks a Catholic priest for the sacraments — so long as he declares a faith in these sacraments in harmony with that of the Church, and is rightly disposed. In other cases the judge of this urgent necessity must be the diocesan bishop or the Episcopal Conference.

A Catholic in similar circumstances may not ask for these sacraments except from a minister who has been validly ordained" (No. 55).

(2) *Dogmatic Constitution on the Church* (No. 3); *Decree on Ecumenism* (No. 4).

(3) General Instruction, *Roman Missal* (Chap. I, No. 1).

(4) *Decree on the Life and Ministry of Priests* (No. 4).

(5) Encyclical of Pius XI, *Quas Primas,* Dec. 28, 1925; *Decree on the Life and Ministry of Priests* (No. 5); *Constitution on the Sacred Liturgy* (Nos. 2, 6).

(6) *Constitution on the Sacred Liturgy* (No. 55); Instruction on the Eucharist, *Eucharisticum Mysterium,* May 25, 1967 (No. 12). Also, *Decree on Ecumenism* (No. 22):

"The fact of having received the same baptism does not of itself afford a title of admission to Holy Communion. Eucharistic sharing expresses an integral profession of faith and full insertion in the Church, towards the sacramental bond of unity existing among all who through it are reborn. But baptism, of itself, is only a beginning, a point of departure, for it is wholly directed toward the acquiring of fullness of life in Christ. Baptism is thus ordained toward a complete profession of faith, a complete incorporation into the system of salvation such as Christ himself willed it to be, and finally, toward a complete integration into Eucharistic Communion."

(7) *Decree on the Life and Ministry of Priests* (No. 5).

(8) Council of Florence, *Decree for the Armenians.*

(9) *Decree on the Eastern Catholic Churches* (No. 26).

(10) *Directory on Ecumenism* (Nos. 44, 45).

(11) Two passages from the *Directory on Ecumenism* derived from the *Decree on Ecumenism* (No. 15) and the *Decree on the Eastern Catholic Churches* (Nos. 24 to 29):

"Although these (Eastern) Churches are separated from us, yet they possess true sacraments above all — by apostolic succession — the priesthood and the Eucharist, whereby they are still joined to us in closest intimacy. Therefore some sharing in liturgical worship

(Communicatio in sacris) given suitable circumstances and the approval of Church authority, is not merely possible but is encouraged" (No. 39).

"Between the Roman Catholic Church and the Eastern Churches separated from us there is still a very close communion in matters of faith; moreover, 'through the celebration of the Eucharist of the Lord in each of these Churches, the Church of God is built up and grows in stature' and 'although separated from us yet these Churches possess true sacraments, above all — by apostolic succession — the priesthood and the Eucharist" (No. 40).

(12) Letter to Patriarch Athenagoras, Feb. 8, 1971.

AGREED STATEMENT ON EUCHARISTIC DOCTRINE

Following is the text of a statement on Eucharistic doctrine drawn up by the Anglican-Roman Catholic Commission of 18 delegates under the joint chairmanship of Anglican Bishop H. R. McAdoo of Ossary, Ferns and Leighlin, and Roman Catholic Auxiliary Bishop Alan Clark of Northampton. The statement, under preparation since January, 1970, was agreed upon by the delegates Sept. 17, 1971, and was released for publication the following December 31. Comment on the agreement follows the text. The document has been called the "Windsor Statement."

[This text was circulated by the NC Documentary Service, *Origins*.]

Foreword

The following Agreed Statement evolved from the thinking and the discussion of the International Commission over the past two years. The result has been a conviction among members of the Commission that we have reached agreement on essential points of Eucharistic doctrine. We are equally convinced ourselves that, though no attempt was made to present a fully comprehensive treatment of the subject, nothing essential has been omitted. The document has been presented to our official authorities, but obviously it cannot be ratified by them until such time as our respective Churches can evaluate its conclusions.

We would want to point out that the members of the Commission who subscribed to this Statement have been officially appointed and come from many countries, representing a wide variety of theological background. Our intention was to reach a consensus at the level of faith, so that all of us might be able to say, within the limits of the Statement: this is the Christian faith of the Eucharist.

Agreed Statement

1. In the course of the Church's history several traditions have developed in expressing Christian understanding of the Eucharist. (For example, various names have become customary as descriptions of the Eucharist: Lord's Supper, Liturgy, Holy Mysteries, Synaxis, Mass, Holy Communion. The Eucharist has become the most universally accepted term.) An important stage in progress towards organic unity is a substantial consensus on the purpose and meaning of the Eucharist. Our intention has been to seek a deeper understanding of the reality of the Eucharist which is consonant with biblical teaching and with the tradition of our common inheritance, and to express in this document the consensus we have reached.

2. Through the life, death and resurrection of Jesus Christ God has reconciled men to himself, and in Christ he offers unity to all mankind. By his word God calls us into a new relationship with himself as our Father and with one another as his children — a relationship inaugurated by baptism into Christ through the Holy Spirit, nurtured and deepened through the Eucharist, and expressed in a confession of one faith and a common life of loving service.

I—THE MYSTERY OF THE EUCHARIST:. When his people are gathered at the Eucharist to commemorate his saving acts for our redemption, Christ makes effective among us the eternal benefits of his victory and elicits and renews our response of faith, thanksgiving and self-surrender. Christ through the Holy Spirit in the Eucharist builds up the life of the Church, strenghens its fellowship and furthers its mission. The identity of the Church as the body of Christ is both expressed and effectively proclaimed by its being centered in, and partaking of, his body and blood. In the whole action of the Eucharist, and in and by his sacramental presence given through bread and wine, the crucified and risen Lord, according to his promise, offers himself to his people.

4. In the eucharist we proclaim the Lord's death until he comes. Receiving a foretaste of the kingdom to come, we look back with thanksgiving to what Christ has done for us, we greet him present among us, we look forward to his final appearing in the fullness of his kingdom when "The Son also himself (shall) be subject unto him that put all things under him, that God may be all in all" (1 Cor. 15:28). When we gather around the same table in this communal meal at the invitation of the same Lord and when we "partake of the one loaf," we are one in commitment not only to Christ and to one another, but also to the mission of the Church in the world.

II — THE EUCHARIST AND THE SACRIFICE OF CHRIST: 5. Christ's redeeming death and resurrection took place once and for all in history. Christ's death on the cross, the culmination of his whole life of obedience, was the one, perfect and sufficient sacrifice for the sins of the world. There can be no repetition of or addition to what was then accomplished once for all by Christ. Any attempt to express a nexus between the sacrifice of Christ and the Eucharist must not obscure this fundamental fact of the Christian faith (1). Yet God has given the Eucharist to his Church as a means through which the atoning work of Christ on the cross is proclaimed and made effective in the life of the Church. The notion of *memorial* as understood in the Passover celebration at the time of Christ — i.e., the making effective in the present of an event in the past — has opened the way to a clearer understanding of the relationship between Christ's sacrifice and the Eucharist. The Eucharistic memorial is no mere calling to mind of a past event or of its significance, but the Church's effectual proclamation of God's mighty acts. Christ instituted the Eucharist as a memorial *(anamnesis)* of the totality of God's reconciling action in him. In the Eucharistic prayer the Church continues to make a perpetual memorial of Christ's death, and his members, united with God and one another, give thanks for all his mercies, entreat the benefits of his passion on behalf of the whole Church, participate in these benefits and enter into the movement of his self-offering.

III — THE PRESENCE OF CHRIST: 6. Communion with Christ in the Eucharist presupposes his true presence, effectually signified by the bread and wine which, in this mystery, become his body and blood (2). The real presence of his body and blood can, however, only be understood within the context of the redemptive activity whereby he gives himself, and in himself reconciliation, peace and life, to his own. On the one hand, the Eucharistic gift springs out of the paschal mystery of Christ's death and resurrection, in which God's saving purpose has already been definitively realized. On the other hand, its purpose is to transmit the life of the crucified and risen Christ to his body, the Church, so that its members may be more fully united with Christ and with one another.

7. Christ is present and active, in various ways, in the entire Eucharistic celebration. It is the same Lord who through the proclaimed word invites his people to his table, who through his minister presides at that table, and who gives himself sacramentally in the body and blood of his paschal sacrifice. It is the Lord present at the right hand of the Father, and therefore transcending the sacramental order who thus offers to his Church, in the Eucharistic signs the special gift of himself.

8. The sacramental body and blood of the Saviour are present as an offering to the believer awaiting his welcome. When this offering is met by faith, a lifegiving encounter results. Through faith Christ's presence — which does not depend on the individual's faith in order to be the Lord's real gift of himself to his Church — becomes no longer just a presence *for* the believer, but also a presence *with* him. Thus, in considering the mystery of the Eucharistic presence, we must recognize both the sacramental sign of Christ's presence and the personal relationship between Christ and the faithful which arises from that presence.

9. The Lord's words at the Last Supper, "Take and eat; this is my body," do not allow us to dissociate the gift of the presence and the act of sacramental eating. The elements are not mere signs; Christ's body and blood become really present and are really given. But they are really present and given in order that, receiving them, believers may be united in communion with Christ the Lord.

10. According to the traditional order of the liturgy the consecratory prayer *(Anaphora)* leads to the communion of the faithful. Through this prayer of thanksgiving, a word of faith addressed to the Father, the bread and wine become the body and blood of Christ by the action of the Holy Spirit, so that in Communion we eat the flesh of Christ and drink his blood.

11. The Lord who thus comes to his people in the power of the Holy Spirit is the Lord of glory. In the Eucharistic celebration we anticipate the joys of the age to come. By the transforming action of the Spirit of God, earthly bread and wine become the heavenly manna and the new wine, the eschatological banquet for the new man: elements of the first creation becomes pledges and first fruits of the new heaven and the new earth.

12. We believe that we have reached substantial agreement on the doctrine of the Eucharist. Although we are all conditioned by the traditional ways in which we have expressed and practiced our Eucharistic faith, we are convinced that if there are any remaining points of disagreement they can be resolved on the principles here established. We acknowledge a variety of theological approaches within both our communions. But we have seen it as our task to find a way of advancing together beyond the doctrinal disagreements of the past. It is our hope that in view of the agreement which we have reached on Eucharistic faith, this doctrine will no longer constitute an obstacle to the unity we seek.

Footnotes

(1) The early Church in expressing the meaning of Christ's death and resurrection often used the language of sacrifice. For the Hebrew *sacrifice* was a traditional means of communication with God. The Passover, for example, was a communal meal; the Day of Atonement was essentially expiatory; and the covenant established communion between God and man.

(2) The word *transubstantiation* is common-

ly used in the Roman Catholic Church to indicate that God acting in the Eucharist effects a change in the inner reality of the elements. The term should be seen as affirming the *fact* of Christ's presence and of the mysterious and radical change which takes place. In contemporary Roman Catholic theology it is not understood as explaining *how* the change takes place.

Comment

The theological commission of the English and Welsh bishops said in March, 1972, that the Anglican-Catholic "substantial agreement" on the doctrine of the Eucharist was "an important advance in the mutual understanding of the Eucharist" and contained nothing contrary to the Cahtolic faith.

A minority of the commission, however, said that the statement was inadequate on certain points and therefore could be misleading. The commission asked for amplification and clarification of some sections.

The commission urged a more detailed treatment or thorough commentary in order to bring out "the sacrificial nature of the Eucharist and its relation to the once-for-all atoning work of Christ" and "the role of the Christian people in the abiding offering of Christ."

The commission said that the statement "clearly maintains the real and true presence of Christ. The substantial nature of the change of the bread and wine we consider to be asserted by the phrases in the statement that they 'become his body and blood' . . . and that this change is 'mysterious and radical.' "

Other commentators — all of whom recognized that the document represented only the views of its signatories and had not been given official sanction by the respective churches — approved and/or expressed reservations about the statement.

Some took exception to the footnote reference to transubstantiation.

Others, while acknowledging the limited scope of the statement — describing the present status of Eucharist belief in the respective communions — noted the need for additional study regarding Eucharistic belief in the Anglican Communion in the past and the vital question of the validity of Anglican orders. This need was also apparent to the framers of the "Windsor Statement."

JESUS MOVEMENT

One view of the Jesus Movement, a phenomenon of the late 60's which maintained considerable momentum in 1972, was expressed by Cardinal John Heenan of Westminster in a pastoral letter of May 27, 1972.

He said that the young, while often denying any belief in God, are taking a new interest in religion through protests against the existing materialist order. Disillusioned by pop stars and revolutionaries, contemptuous of material comfort and concerned with the needy and oppressed, they are nearly everywhere in the world rejecting the standards offered by their elders and are ready to revolt against anyone in authority.

"They repudiate existing authority but have not yet found a satisfying substitute. . . . That is where the Church can help them. They must be directed not to Jesus Christ, Superstar, but to Jesus Christ, Son of God.

"Jesus — the gentle bewildered leader persecuted by priests and politicians — may serve as hero in a stage musical but he cannot become the center of their spiritual lives.

"It is of the utmost importance that they should be told the truth about Christ."

Young people "may not read theological books but they enjoy what they regard as religious experiences. These are sometimes no more than hallucinations. . . . They are, nevertheless, a sign that some young people are genuinely searching for guidance.

"Their so-called meditations may be of doubtful spiritual values in themselves but at least they show the spiritual longings of the growing generation. It would be no less wrong to laugh at their efforts than to regard them as proof that youth has rediscovered God.

"Most young people would probably deny that they are turning to God or that they believe in God. Their new-found admiration for Christ need not have a religious explanation. It may be that they have merely become disillusioned with their former heroes."

BLACK CATHOLICS

The National Office for Black Catholics originated from the first meeting of the Black Catholic Clergy Caucus in April, 1968, in Detroit.

According to executive director Brother Joseph Davis, S.M., "The NOBC is an effort to revitalize the Church in the black community as an institution for and about black people. It will be devoted to the liberation of people, black and white. In short, it will give black Catholics — especially black priests and religious — a chance to be about our Father's business."

The National Office for Black Catholics, which has affiliates in several dioceses, is located at 1325 Massachusetts Ave. N.W., Washington D.C. 20005.

Establishment of the office was approved by the US bishops in November, 1969. To date they have allocated nearly $250,000 for support of the office, which conducted its own fund raising campaign in 1972.

Sharing the aims and purposes of the NCOB are the Black Catholic Clergy Caucus, organized in 1968, the National Black Sisters' Conference (see separate entry), the National Black Lay Caucus, their affiliates and other groups.

ADMINISTRATION OF GENERAL ABSOLUTION

(The text of Pastoral Norms concerning the Administration of General Sacramental Absolution, approved by Pope Paul VI June 16, was made public by the Sacred Congregation for the Doctrine of the Faith July 13, 1972.

[The following text appeared in the July 27 English edition of *L'Osservatore Romano.* Subheads and italics have been added.]

Christ our Lord instituted the sacrament of penance in order that the faithful who have sinned might obtain pardon from the mercy of God for the offenses committed against him and at the same time be reconciled with the Church. He instituted it when he gave the Apostles and their lawful successors the power to forgive and retain sins (cf. Jn. 20:22-23).

The Council of Trent solemnly taught that for full and perfect forgiveness of sins three acts are required from the penitent as parts of the sacrament, these acts being contrition, confession and satisfaction. It also taught that absolution is given by the priest, who acts as judge, and that it is necessary by divine law to confess to a priest each and every mortal sin and the circumstances that alter the species of sins that are remembered after a careful examination of conscience.

A number of local Ordinaries have been disturbed at the difficulty of their faithful to go to confession individually because of the shortage of priests in some regions. They have also been troubled at certain erroneous theories about the doctrine of the sacrament of penance and the growing tendency to introduce the improper practice of granting general sacramental absolution to people who have made only a generic confession. They have therefore asked the Holy See to recall to the Christian people, in accordance with the true nature of the sacrament of penance, the conditions needed for the right use of this sacrament and to issue norms in the present circumstances.

This Sacred Congregation has carefully considered these questions and, taking account of the Instruction of the Sacred Apostolic Penitentiary of 25 March 1944, makes the following declarations.

I. Recent Abuse

The teaching of the Council of Trent must be firmly held and faithfully put into practice. This implies a reprobation of the recent custom which has sprung up in places by which there is a presumption to satisfy the precept of sacramentally confessing mortal sins for the purpose of obtaining absolution by confession made only generally or through what is called a community celebration of penance. This reprobation is demanded not only by divine precept, as declared by the Council of Trent, but also by the very great good of souls deriving, according to centuries-long experience, from individual confession and absolution rightly administered. Individual and integral confession and absolution remain the only ordinary way for the faithful to be reconciled to God and the Church unless physical or moral impossibility excuses from such confession.

II. Special Circumstances

It can indeed happen because of particular circumstances occasionally occurring that general absolution may or even should be given to a number of penitents without previous individual confession.

This can happen, first of all, when there is imminent danger of death and, even though a priest or priests are present, they have no time to hear the confession of each penitent.

In this case any priest has the faculty to give general absolution to a number of people after first exhorting them, if there is time, very briefly to make an act of contrition.

III.

Apart from the cases of danger of death, it is lawful to give sacramental absolution collectively to a number of faithful who have confessed only generically but have been suitably exhorted to repent, provided that there is serious necessity; namely, when, in view of the number of penitents there are not enough confessors at hand to hear properly the confessions of each within an appropriate time, with the result that the penitents through no fault of their own would be forced to do without sacramental grace or Holy Communion for a long time. This can happen especially in mission lands, but also in places and within groups where it is clear that this need exists.

This is not lawful, however, when confessors are able to be at hand, merely because of a great concourse of penitents such as can, for example, occur on a great feast or pilgrimage.

IV.

Local Ordinaries and, to the extent that they are concerned, priests are bound in conscience to see that the number of confessors should not become reduced because some priests neglect this noble ministry while involving themselves in secular affairs or devoting themselves to less necessary ministries, especially if these ministries can be performed by deacons or suitable lay people.

V. Bishop's Decision

The judgment as to whether the conditions mentioned above (Art. III) are present and, consequently, the decision as to when it is lawful to grant general sacramental absolution, are reserved to the local Ordinary after he has conferred with other members of the episcopal conference.

If a serious need arises of giving general

sacramental absolution, are reserved to the local Ordinary after he has conferred with other members of the episcopal conference.

If a serious need arises of giving genreal sacramental absolution apart from the cases laid down by the local Ordinary, the priest is obliged, whenever it is possible, to have previous recourse to the local Ordinary in order to grant the absolution lawfully. If this is not possible, he is to inform the Ordinary as soon as possible of the need and of the granting of absolution.

VI. Proper Dispositions

In order that the faithful may take advantage of general sacramental absolution, it is absolutely required that they be suitably disposed; each should repent of the sins he has committed, have the purpose of keeping from sin, intend to repair any scandal or loss caused, and also have the purpose of confessing in due time each serious sin that he is at present unable to confess. Priests should carefully remind the faithful of these dispositions and conditions, which are required for the validity of the sacrament.

VII. Confession Afterwards

Those who have serious sins forgiven by general absolution should make an auricular confession before receiving absolution in this collective form another time, unless a just cause prevents them. They are strictly obliged, unless prevented by moral impossibility, to go to confession within a year. They too are affected by the precept that obliges every Christian to confess privately to a priest once a year at least all his serious sins that he has not yet specifically confessed.

VIII.

Priests are to teach the faithful that those who are aware of being in mortal sin are forbidden to refuse deliberately or by neglect to satisfy the obligation of individual confession, when it is possible to have a confessor, while they wait for an occasion for collective absolution.

IX. Availability of Confessors

In order that the faithful may easily be able to satisfy the obligation of making an individual confession, let care be taken that confessors are available in the churches on days and at hours that are convenient for the faithful.

In places that are remote or difficult to reach, where the priest can come only at rare intervals during the year, let it be arranged that, as far as possible, the priest on each occasion hear the sacramental confessions of a group of penitents and give collective absolution to the other penitents, provided that the conditions mentioned above (Art. III) are present, so that in this way all the faithful, if possible, shall be able to make an individual confession at least once a year.

X. Avoid Confusion

The faithful are to be carefully taught that liturgical celebrations and community rites of penance are of great unefulness for the preparation of a more fruitful confession of sins and amendment of life. Care must be taken, however, that such celebrations or rites are not confused with sacramental confession and absolution.

If in the course of such celebrations the penitents make an individual confession, each is to receive absolution singly from the confessor to whom he goes. In the case of general sacramental absolution, it is always to be given in accordance with the special rite laid down by the Sacred Congregation for Divine Worship. However, until the publication of this new rite, the formula of sacramental absolution now prescribed is to be used, but changed to the plural. The celebration of this rite is to be kept quite distinct from the celebration of Mass.

XI.

If one who is in a situation causing actual scandal to the faithful is sincerely penitent and seriously proposes to remove the scandal, he can indeed receive general sacramental absolution along with others but he is not to go Holy Communion until, in the judgment of a confessor whom he is first to approach personally, he has removed the scandal.

With regard to absolution from reserved censures, the norms of law in force are to be observed, calculating the time for recourse from the next individual confession.

XII. Devotional Confession

Priests should be careful not to discourage the faithful from frequent or devotional confession. On the contrary, let them draw attention to its fruitfulness for Christian living and always display readiness to hear such a confession whenever a reasonable request is made by the faithful. It must be absolutely prevented that individual confession should be reserved for serious sins only, for this would deprive the faithful of the great benefit of confession and would injure the good name of those who approach the sacrament singly.

XIII.

The granting of general sacramental absolution without observing the norms given above is to be considered a serious abuse. Let all pastors carefully prevent such abuse out of awareness of the moral duty enjoined upon them for the welfare of souls and for the protection of the dignity of the sacrament of penance.

General absolution was being given in Juneau in accordance with norms of the instruction.

ETHICAL DIRECTIVES FOR CATHOLIC HEALTH FACILITIES

The following Ethical and Religious Directives for Catholic Health Facilities were approved by the National Conference of Catholic Bishops Nov. 16, 1971, by a vote of 232 to 7 with 2 abstentions. The directives were updated from earlier ones published in 1954.

[The following text was circulated by NC News Service. Footnotes appear at the end of the text.]

Catholic health facilities witness to the saving presence of Christ and his Church in a variety of ways: by testifying to transcendent spiritual beliefs concerning life, suffering and death; by humble service to humanity, and especially to the poor; by medical competence and leadership; and by fidelity to the Church's teachings while ministering to the good of the whole person.

The total good of the patient, which includes his higher spiritual as well as his bodily welfare, is the primary concern of those entrusted with the management of a Catholic health facility. So important is this, in fact, that, if an institution could not fulfill its basic mission in this regard, it would not have justification for continuing its existence as a Catholic health facility. Trustees and administrators of Catholic health facilities should understand that this responsibility affects their relationship with every patient, regardless of religion, and is seriously binding in conscience.

A Catholic-sponsored health facility, its board of trustees and administration face today a serious difficulty as, with community support, the Catholic health facility exists side by side with other medical facilities not committed to the same moral code, or stands alone as the one facility serving the community. However, the health facility identified as Catholic exists today and serves the community in a large part because of the past dedication and sacrifice of countless individuals whose lives have been inspired by the Gospel and the teachings of the Catholic Church.

And, just as it bears responsibility to the past, so does the Catholic health facility carry special responsibility for the present and future. Any facility identified as Catholic assumes with this identification the responsibility to reflect in its policies and practices the moral teachings of the Church, under the guidance of the local bishop. Within the community the Catholic health facility is needed as a courageous witness to the highest ethical and moral principles in its pursuit of excellence.

The Catholic-sponsored health facility and its board of trustees, acting through its chief executive officer, further, carry an overriding responsibility in conscience to prohibit those procedures which are morally and spiritually harmful. The basic norms delineating this moral responsibility are listed in these Ethical and Religious Directives for Catholic Health Facilities. It should be understood that patients and those who accept board membership, staff appointment or privileges, or employment in a Catholic health facility will respect and agree to abide by its policies and these directives. Any attempt to use a Catholic health facility for procedures contrary to these norms would indeed compromise the board and administration in its responsibility to seek and protect the total good of its patients, under the guidance of the Church.

These directives prohibit those procedures which, according to present knowledge, are recognized as clearly wrong. The basic moral absolutes which underlie these directives are not subject to change, although particular applications might be modified as scientific investigation and theological development open up new problems or cast new light on old ones.

The moral evaluation of new scientific developments and legitimately debated questions must be finally submitted to the teaching authority of the Church in the person of the local bishop, who has the ultimate responsibility for teaching Catholic doctrine. (The USCC Committee on Health Affairs should regularly receive suggestions and recommendations from the field.)

I. General Directives

1. The procedures listed in these directives as permissible require the consent, at least implied or reasonably presumed, of the patient or his guardians. This condition is to be understood in all cases.

2. No person may be obliged to take part in a medical or surgical procedure which he judges in conscience to be immoral; nor may a health facility or any of its staff be obliged to provide a medical or surgical procedure which violates their conscience or these directives.

3. Every patient, regardless of the extent of his physical or psychic disability, has a right to be treated with a respect consonant with his dignity as a person (1).

4. Man has the right and the duty to protect the integrity of his body together with all of its bodily functions.

5. Any procedure potentially harmful to the patient is morally justified only insofar as it is designed to produce a proportionate good.

6. Ordinarily the proportionate good that justifies a medical or surgical procedure should be the total good of the patient himself.

7. Adequate consultation is recommended not only when there is doubt concerning the morality of some procedure but also with regard to all procedures involving serious consequences, even though such procedures are

listed here as permissible. The health facility has the right to insist on such consultations.

8. Everyone has the right and the duty to prepare for the solemn moment of death. Unless it is clear, therefore, that a dying patient is already well prepared for death as regards both spiritual and temporal state, it is the physician's duty to inform him of his critical condition or to have some other responsible person impart this information.

9. The obligation of professional secrecy must be carefully fulfilled not only as regards the information on the patients' charts and records but also as regards confidential matters learned in the exercise of professional duties. Moreover, the charts and records must be duly safeguarded against inspection by those who have no right to see them.

10. The directly intended termination of any patient's life, even at his own request, is always morally wrong.

11. From the moment of conception, life must be guarded with the greatest care. Any deliberate medical procedure, the purpose of which is to deprive a fetus or an embryo of its life, is immoral (2).

12. Abortion — that is, the directly intended termination of pregnancy before viability — is never permitted, nor is the directly intended destruction of a viable fetus. Every procedure whose sole immediate effect is the termination of pregnancy before viability is an abortion, which, in its moral context, includes the interval between conception and implantation of the embryo.

13. Operations, treatments and medications, which do not directly intend termination of pregnancy but which have as their purpose the cure of a proportionately serious pathological condition of the mother, are permitted when they cannot be safely postponed until the fetus is viable, even though they may or will result in the death of the fetus. If the fetus is not certainly dead, it should be baptized.

14. Regarding the treatment of hemorrhage during pregnancy and before the fetus is viable: Procedures that are designed to empty the uterus of a living fetus still effectively attached to the mother are not permitted. Procedures designed to stop hemorrhage (as distinguished from those designed precisely to expel the living and attached fetus) are permitted insofar as necessary, even if fetal death is inevitably a side effect.

15. Caesarean section for the removal of a viable fetus is permitted, even with the risk to the life of the mother, when necessary for successful delivery. It is likewise permitted, even with risk for the child, when necessary for the safety of the mother.

16. In extrauterine pregnancy the dangerously affected part of the mother (e.g., cervix, ovary or fallopian tube) may be removed, even though fetal death is foreseen, provided: that (a) the affected part is presumed already to be so damaged and dangerously affected as to warrant its removal; and that (b) the operation is not just a separation of the embryo or fetus from its site within the part (which could be a direct abortion from a uterine appendage); and that (c) the operation cannot be postponed without notably increasing the danger to the mother.

17. Hysterectomy, in the presence of pregnancy and even before viability, is permitted when directed to the removal of a dangerous pathological condition of the uterus of such serious nature that the operation cannot be safely postponed until the fetus is viable.

II. Reproductive Organs and Functions

18. Sterilization, whether permanent or temporary, for men or for women, may not be used as a means of contraception (3).

19. Similarly excluded is every action which, either in anticipation of the conjugal act, or in its accomplishment, or in the development of its natural consequences, proposes, whether as an end or as a means, to render procreation impossible (4).

20. Procedures that induce sterility, whether permanent or temporary, are permitted when: (a) they are immediately directed to the cure, diminution or prevention of a serious pathological condition and are not directly contraceptive (that is, contraception is not the purpose), and (b) a simpler treatment is not reasonably available. Hence, for example, oophorectomy or irradiation of the ovaries may be allowed in treating carcinoma of the breast and metastasis therefrom; and orchidectomy is permitted in the treatment of carcinoma of the prostate (5).

21. Because the ultimate personal expression of conjugal love in the marital act is viewed as the only fitting context for the human sharing of the divine act of creation, donor insemination and insemination that is totally artificial are morally objectionable. However, help may be given to a normally performed conjugal act to attain its purpose. The use of the sex faculty outside the legitimate use by married partners is never permitted even for medical or other laudable purpose; e.g., masturbation as a means of obtaining seminal specimens.

22. Hysterectomy is permitted when it is sincerely judged to be a necessary means of removing some serious uterine pathological condition. In these cases, the pathological condition of each patient must be considered individually and care must be taken that a hysterectomy is not performed merely as a contraceptive measure or as a routine procedure after any definite number of Caesarean sections.

23. For a proportionate reason, labor may be induced after the fetus is viable.

24. In all cases in which the presence of pregnancy would render some procedure illicit (e.g., curettage), the physician must make

use of such pregnancy tests and consultation as may be needed in order to be reasonably certain that the patient is not pregnant. It is to be noted that curettage of the endometrium after rape to prevent implantation of a possible embryo is morally equivalent to abortion.

25. Radiation therapy of the mother's reproductive organs is permitted during pregnancy only when necessary to suppress a dangerous pathological condition.

III. Other Procedures

26. Therapeutic procedures which are likely to be dangerous are morally justifiable for proportionate reasons.

27. Experimentation on patients without due consent is morally objectionable, and even the moral right of the patient to consent is limited by his duties of stewardship.

28. Euthanasia ("mercy killing") in all its forms is forbidden. The failure to supply the ordinary means of preserving life is equivalent to euthanasia. However, neither the physician nor the patient is obliged to the use of extraordinary means (6).

29. It is not euthanasia to give a dying person sedatives and analgesics for the alleviation of pain, when such a measure is judged necessary, even though they may deprive the patient of the use of reason, or shorten his life.

30. The transplantation of organs from living donors is morally permissible when the anticipated benefit to the recipient is proportionate to the harm done to the donor, provided that the loss of such organ(s) does not deprive the donor of life itself nor of the functional integrity of his body.

31. Post-mortem examinations must not be begun until death is morally certain. Vital organs — that is, organs necessary to sustain life — may not be removed until death has taken place. The determination of the time of death must be made in accordance with responsible and commonly accepted scientific criteria. In accordance with current medical practice, to prevent any conflict of interest, the dying patient's doctor or doctors should ordinarily be distinct from the transplant team.

32. Ghost surgery, which implies the calculated deception of the patient as to the identity of the operating surgeon, is morally objectionable.

33. Unnecessary procedures, whether diagnostic or therapeutic, are morally objectionable. A procedure is unnecessary when no proportionate reason justifies it. *A fortiori,* any procedure that is contra-indicated by sound medical standards is unnecessary.

Religious Care of Patients

34. The administration should be certain that patients in a health facility receive appropriate spiritual care.

35. Except in cases of emergency (i.e.,

danger of death), all requests for baptism made by adults or for infants should be referred to the chaplain of the health facility.

36. If a priest is not available, anyone having the use of reason and proper intention can baptize. The ordinary method of conferring emergency baptism is as follows: The person baptizing pours water on the head in such a way that it will flow on the skin, and, while the water is being poured, must pronounce these words audibly: "I baptize you in the name of the Father, and of the Son, and of the Holy Spirit." The same person who pours the water must pronounce the words.

37. When emergency baptism is conferred, the chaplain should be notified.

38. It is the mind of the Church that the sick should have the widest possible liberty to receive the sacraments frequently. The generous cooperation of the entire staff and personnel is requested for this purpose.

39. While providing the sick abundant opportunity to receive Holy Communion, there should be no interference with the freedom of the faithful to communicate or not to communicate.

40. In wards and semi-private rooms, every effort should be made to provide sufficient privacy for confession.

41. When possible, one who is seriously ill should be given the opportunity to receive the sacraments of the sick while in full possession of his rational faculties. The chaplain must, therefore, be notifed as soon as an illness is diagnosed as being so serious that some probability of death is recognized.

42. Personnel of a Catholic health facility should make every effort to satisfy the spiritual needs and desires of non-Catholics. Therefore, in hospitals and similar institutions conducted by Catholics, the authorities in charge should, with the consent of the patient, promptly advise ministers of other communions of the presence of their communicants and affort them every facility for visiting the sick and giving them spiritual and sacramental ministrations (7).

43. If there is a reasonable cause present for not burying a fetus or member of the human body, these may be cremated in a manner consonant with the dignity of the deceased human body (8).

Footnotes

(1) Encyclical *Peace on Earth,* John XXIII, No. 11. (2) *Pastoral Constitution on the Church in the Modern World,* No. 51. (3 and 4) Encyclical *Of Human Life,* Paul VI, No. 14. (5) *Ibid.,* No. 15.

(6) *Pastoral Constitution on the Church in the Modern World,* No. 27. (7) Directory for the Application of the Decisions of the Second Ecumenical Council of the Vatican concerning Ecumenical Matters (*Directory on Ecumenism*), No. 63. (8) *Canon Law Digest,* Vol. 6, p. 669.

CHRISTOLOGICAL AND TRINITARIAN ERRORS

With the approval of Paul VI, the Sacred Congregation for the Doctrine of the Faith issued the following declaration, Mar. 8, 1972, "for safeguarding belief in the mysteries of the Incarnation and of the Most Holy Trinity against some recent errors."

[This text appeared in the Mar. 30, 1972, English edition of *L'Osservatore Romano.* Subheads have been added.]

1. The mystery of the Son of God, who was made man, and the mystery of the Most Holy Trinity, both pertaining to the innermost substance of Revelation, must be in their authentic truth the source of light for the lives of Christ's faithful. But because some recent errors undermine these mysteries, the Sacred Congregation for the Doctrine of the Faith has determined to reaffirm and to safeguard the belief in them that has been handed down to us.

Son of God Made Man

2. **Catholic belief in the Son of God who was made man.** Jesus Christ, while dwelling on this earth, manifested in various ways, by word and by deed, the adorable mystery of his person. After being made "obedient unto death" (1), he was divinely exalted in his glorious resurrection, as was fitting for the Son "by whom all things" (2) were made by the Father. Of him St. John solemnly proclaimed: "In the beginning was the Word and the Word was with God and the Word was God . . . And the Word was made flesh" (3).

The Church reverently preserved the mystery of the Son of God, who was made man, and "in the course of the ages and of the centuries" (4) has propounded it for belief in a more explicit way.

In the Creed of (Nicaea-) Constantinople, which is still recited today during Mass, the Church proclaims her faith in "Jesus Christ, the only-begotten Son of God, born of the Father before all ages . . . true God from true God . . . consubstantial with the Father . . . who for us men and for our salvation . . . was made man" (5).

The Council of Chalcedon laid down to be believed that the Son of God according to his divinity was begotten of the Father before all the ages, and according to his humanity was begotten in time of the Virgin Mary (6). Further, this council called one and the same Christ the Son of God a "person" *(hypostasis),* but used the term "nature" to describe his divinity and his humanity, and using these terms it taught that both his natures, divine and human, together belong, without confusion, unalterably, undividedly and inseparably, to the one person of our Redeemer (7).

In the same way, the Fourth Lateran Council taught for belief and profession that the Son of God, coeternal with the Father, was made true man and is one person in two natures (8). This is the Catholic belief which the recent Vatican Council II, holding to the constant tradition of the whole Church, clearly expressed in many passages (9).

Christological Errors

3. **Recent errors in regard to belief in the Son of God.** The opinions according to which it has not been revealed and made known to us that the Son of God subsists from all eternity in the mystery of the Godhead, distinct from the Father and the Holy Spirit, are in open conflict with this belief; likewise the opinions according to which the notion is to be abandoned of the one person of Jesus Christ begotten in his divinity of the Father before all the ages and begotten in his humanity of the Virgin Mary in time; and lastly the assertion that the humanity of Christ existed not as being assumed into the eternal person of the Son of God but existed rather of itself as a person, and therefore that the mystery of Jesus Christ consists only in the fact that God, in revealing himself, was present in the highest degree in the human person Jesus.

Those who think in this way are far removed from the true belief in Christ, even when they maintain that the special presence of God in Jesus results in his being the supreme and final expression of divine Revelation. Nor do they come back to the true belief in the divinity of Christ by adding that Jesus can be called God by reason of the fact that in what they call his human person God is supremely present.

The Holy Spirit

4. **Catholic belief in the Most Holy Trinity, and especially in the Holy Spirit.** Once the mystery of the divine and eternal person of Christ the Son of God is abandoned, the truth respecting the Most Holy Trinity is also undermined, and with it the truth regarding the Holy Spirit who proceeds eternally from the Father and the Son, or from the Father through the Son (10). Therefore, in view of recent errors, some points concerning belief in the Most Holy Trinity, and especially in the Holy Spirit, are to be recalled to mind.

The Second Epistle to the Corinthians concludes with this admirable expression: "The grace of our Lord Jesus Christ, and the love of God, and the fellowship of the Holy Spirit be with you all" (11). The commission to baptize, recorded in St. Matthew's Gospel, names the Father, and the Son, and the Holy Spirit as the three pertaining to the mystery of God and it is in their name that the converts must be reborn (12). Lastly, in St. John's Gospel, Jesus speaks of the coming of the Holy Spirit: "When the Paraclete comes whom I will send you from the Father, the Spirit of truth who proceeds from the Father, he will give testimony of me" (Jn. 15:26) (13).

On the basis of the indications of divine Revelation, the magisterium of the Church, to which alone is entrusted "the office of authentic interpretation of the word of God, written or handed down" (14), acclaims in the Creed of Nicaea-Constantinople "the Holy Spirit, Lord and giver of life . . . who together with the Father and the Son is adored and glorified" (15). In like manner the Fourth Lateran Council taught what it is to be believed and professed "that there is but one only true God . . . Father and Son and Holy Spirit: three persons indeed, but one essence . . . : the Father proceeding from none, the Son from the Father alone and the Holy Spirit equally from both, without beginning, always, and without end" (16).

Errors

5. **Recent errors concerning the Most Holy Trinity, and especially concerning the Holy Spirit.** The opinion that Revelation has left us uncertain about the eternity of the Trinity, and in particular about the eternal existence of the Holy Spirit as a person in God distinct from the Father and the Son, is out of line with the faith. It is true that the mystery of the Most Holy Trinity was revealed to us in the economy of salvation, and most of all in Christ himself who was sent into the world by the Father and together with the Father sends to the People of God the life-giving Spirit. But by this Revelation there is also given to those who believe some knowledge of God's intimate life, in which "the Father who generates, the Son who is generated, and the Holy Spirit who proceeds" are "consubstantial and co-equal, alike omnipotent and co-eternal" (17).

Immutable Truth of Faith

6. **The mysteries of the Incarnation and of the Trinity are to be faithfully preserved and expounded.** What is expressed in the documents of the councils referred to above, concerning the one and the same Christ the Son of God, begotten before the ages in his divine nature and in time in his human nature, and also concerning the eternal persons of the Most Holy Trinity, belongs to the immutable truth of the Catholic faith.

This certainty does not prevent the Church in her awareness of the progress of human thought from considering that it is her duty to take steps to have the aforesaid mysteries continually examined by contemplation and by theological examination, and to have them more fully expounded in up-to-date terminology. But, while the necessary duty of investigation is being pursued, diligent care must be taken that these profound mysteries not be interpreted in a meaning other than that in which "the Church has understood and understands them" (18).

The unimpaired truth of these mysteries is of the greatest moment for the whole Revelation of Christ, because they pertain to its very core, in such a way indeed that, if they are undermined, the rest of the treasure of Revelation is falsified. The truth of these same mysteries is of no less concern to the Christian way of life both because nothing so effectively manifests the charity of God, to which the whole of Christian life should be a response, as does the Incarnation of the Son of God, our Redeemer (19), and also because "through Christ, the Word made flesh, men have access to the Father in the Holy Spirit and are made partakers of the divine nature" (20).

Responsibility of Pastors

7. With regard to the truths which the present declaration is safeguarding, it pertains to the pastors of the Church to see that there is unity in professing the faith on the part of their people, and especially on the part of those who by mandate received from the magisterium teach the sacred sciences or preach the word of God. This function of the bishops belongs to the office divinely committed to them "of keeping pure and whole . . . the deposit of faith" in common with the successor of Peter and "of proclaiming the Gospel without ceasing" (21); and by reason of this same office they are bound not to permit that ministers of the word of God, deviating from the way of sound doctrine, should pass it on corrupted or incomplete (22). The people, committed as they are to the care of the bishops who "have to render account to God" (23) for them, enjoy "the sacred and inalienable right of receiving the word of God, the whole word of God, into which the Church does not cease to penetrate ever more profoundly" (24).

The faithful, then, and above all the theologians because of their important office and necessary function in the Church, must make faithful profession of the mysteries which this declaration reaffirms. In like manner, by the movement and illumination of the Holy Spirit, the sons of the Church must hold fast to the whole teaching of the faith under the leadership of their pastors and of the pastor of the universal Church (25) "so that, in holding, practicing and professing the faith that has been handed down, a common effort results on the part of the bishops and faithful" (26).

The Supreme Pontiff by divine Providence, Pope Paul VI, in an audience granted on February 21, 1972, to the undersigned Prefect the Sacred Congregation for the Doctrine of the Faith, ratified and confirmed this declaration for safeguarding from certain recent errors the belief in the mysteries of the Incarnation and of the Most Holy Trinity, and ordered it to be published.

Given at Rome, from the offices of the

Sacred Congregation for the Doctrine of the Faith, on the 21st day of February . . . in the year of our Lord, 1972.

(5) *Roman Missal,* Typical Edition, 1970, p. 389; Dz.-Sch. 150. (6) Definition of the Council of Chalcedon, *Conc. Oec. Decr.,* p. 62; Dz.-Sch. 301. (7) *Ibid.;* Dz.-Sch. 302. (8) Fourth Lateran Council, Constitution *Firmiter credimus; Conc. Oec., Decr.,* p. 206; Dz.-Sch. 800, f.

(9) Documents of the Second Vatican Council — *Dogmatic Constitution on the Church,* Nos. 3, 7, 52, 53; *Dogmatic Constitution on Revelation,* Nos. 2, 3; *Constitution on the Church in the Modern World,* No. 22; *Decree on Ecumenism,* No. 12; *Decree on the Bishops' Pastoral Office in the Church,* No. 1; *Decree on the Church's Missionary Activity,* No. 3. Cf. also *Creed of the People of God* (See Almanac Index), Paul VI, No. 11; *Acta Apostolicae Sedis* 60 (1968), 437.

(10) Council of Florence, Bull *Laetentur caeli; Conc. Oec. Decr.,* p. 501, f.; Dz.-Sch. 1300. (11) 2 Cor. 13:14. (12) Mt. 28:19. (13) Jn. 15:26. (14) Second Vatican Council, *Dogmatic Constitution on Revelation,* No. 10.

(15) *Roman Missal,* Typical Edition, 1970; Dz.-Sch. 150. (16) Fourth Lateran Council, Constitution *Firmiter credimus; Conc. Oec. Decr.,* p. 206; Dz.-Sch. 800. (17) *Ibid.*

(18) First Vatican Council, Dogmatic Constitution *Dei Filius,* Chap. 4, Can. 3; *Conc.*

Oec. Decr., p. 787; Dz.-Sch. 3043. See Pope John XXIII, *Allocution at the Inauguration of the Second Vatican Council, Acta Apostolicae Sedis* 54 (1962), 792, and the Second Vatican Council, *Pastoral Constitution on the Church in the Modern World,* No. 62. See also *Creed of the People of God* (see Almanac Index) No. 4.

(19) 1 Jn. 4:9,f. (20) Second Vatican Council, *Dogmatic Constitution on Revelation,* No. 2; cf. Eph. 2:18; 2 Pt. 1:4. (21) Pope Paul VI, Apostolic Exhortation *Quinque iam anni,* in *Acta Apostolicae Sedis* 68 (1971), 99.

(22) 2 Tm. 4:1-5. See Pope Paul VI, *ibid.,* p. 103, f. See also 1967 Synod of Bishops: *Relatio Commissionis Synodalis constitutae ad examen ulterius peragendum circa opiniones periculosas et atheismum,* II, 3: *De pastorali ratione agendi in exercitio magisterii,* Vatican Polyglot Press, 1967, p. 10, f. (*L'Osservatore Romano,* Oct. 30-31, 1967, p. 3).

(23) Pope Paul VI, *ibid.,* p. 103. (24) Pope Paul VI, *ibid.,* p. 100. (25) Second Vatican Council, *Dogmatic Constitution on the Church,* Nos. 12, 25; 1967 Synod of Bishops: *Relatio Commissionis Synodalis . . .* II, 4; *De Theologorum opera et responsabilitatae . . .* p. 11 (*L'Osservatore Romano,* Oct. 30-31, 1967, p. 3). (26) Second Vatican Council, *Dogmatic Constitution on Revelation,* No. 10.

NORMS FOR SELECTING BISHOPS

The document containing these norms was made public by the Vatican May 12, 1972.

[The following text was circulated in the US by NC News Service. Subheads have been added.]

Foreword

The choice of bishops is to be made in such a way as to insure that the Church will be entrusted to pastors who will be "examples to the flock" (1 Pt. 5:3). Thus in the past the Apostolic See has provided for the selection of bishops by issuing particular rules for various countries.

The decisions of the Second Vatican Ecumenical Council, however, must also be applied in this field. Hence, Pope Paul VI, accepting the wishes of many of his brothers in the episcopate, and having sought the views of the competent departments of the Roman Curia, proceeded to give effect to what was laid down in the motu proprio *Ecclesiae Sanctae,* No. 10 (a document which implemented various decisions of the council): "The episcopal conference shall each year, in accordance with the norms made or to be made by the Apostolic See, prudently discuss in private the ecclesiastics to be called to the office of bishop in their territory and propose the names of candidates to the Apostolic

See." He accordingly gave instructions that a document on this subject be very carefully drawn up and placed before the episcopal conferences for their examination.

This having been done, the Pope has approved the annexed norms on the promotion to the episcopacy of ecclesiastics of the Latin Rite. The norms do not affect the laws proper to the Eastern Churches. They are to come into force 21 May 1972, on which date the particular decrees mentioned above will be abrogated. All things to the contrary not withstanding.

From the Vatican, 25 March 1972.

J. Cardinal Villot, Prefect of the Council for the Public Affairs of the Church.

Bishops' Responsibility

Article I: 1. Bishops have the faculty and the duty of making known to the Apostolic See the names of priests whom they consider worthy of the episcopal office and suited for it, whether these priests belong to the diocesan clergy, or are religious performing their sacred ministry in the diocese, or are priests of another jurisdiction who are well known to them.

2. Every diocesan bishop and other local ordinaries, with the exception of vicars general, shall take care to obtain all the informa-

tion needed for carrying out this important and difficult duty. They shall do so either by personal investigation, or by appropriately consulting, within the limits of their jurisdiction, although not collectively, priests of the cathedral chapter or diocesan consultors, or members of the council of priests, or other members of the clergy, diocesan or regular, or members of the laity.

3. With regard to ecclesiastical territories entrusted to missionary institutes, it is recognized that the superiors general concerned have the faculty, in accordance with the present practice of the Sacred Congregation for the Evangelization of Peoples, to propose candidates from their institutes, while the Apostolic See always retains the right to make other provisions, if it considers it opportune to do so.

Meeting Procedures

Article II. 1. The names of candidates for the office of bishop shall as a general rule be examined and proposed by the bishops during their meetings. But every bishop and every other ordinary as above (Art. I, No. 2) can propose candidates directly to the Apostolic See.

2. The meetings or conferences in question shall usually be on a provincial level; in other words, they shall be composed of the bishops and other Ordinaries as above belonging to the same ecclesiastical province, unless special circumstances suggest interprovincial, regional or even national meetings. In these last cases prior notice shall be given to the Apostolic See.

Article III. 1. All the bishops of the province or of the region or nation who, according to the respective statutes, belong to the same episcopal conference and have a deliberative vote take part in the meeting with equal rights.

2. In the case of a provincial meeting, the metropolitan is to prepare the agenda and preside over the meeting; in his absence this is to be done by the senior suffragan. In the case of a regional or national meeting the task is to be carried out by the president of the respective conference.

Article IV: 1. The meetings are to be held at fixed intervals, in accordance with the rule laid down in the motu proprio *Ecclesiae Sanctae,* No. 10. It is fitting that they should be held during the usual assemblies of the bishops.

2. The periodical meetings are convened in order that the bishops may propose candidates, or, if appropriate, supply further information concerning candidates previously proposed. It may also happen that some candidate previously put forward should no longer be kept on the list, because of age, ill health or some other reason making him unfit for the episcopal office.

Article V. 1. At a suitable time before the meeting, the names of the candidates to be proposed shall be sent to the president by those who have the right and duty to be present at the assembly. The president, with proper precautions, shall take care to communicate to them the complete list of names.

2. They shall examine the names of the candidates and consider what they know about each one.

Questions

Article VI: 1. At the meeting the bishops shall share their information and observations on each candidate, indicating whether they are speaking from first-hand knowledge or expressing what they have heard from others.

2. The candidates are to be examined in such a way that it may be seen whether they are endowed with the qualities necessary for a good pastor of souls and teacher of the faith: whether they enjoy a good reputation; whether they are endowed with right judgment and prudence; whether they are even-tempered and of stable character; whether they firmly hold the orthodox faith; whether they are devoted to the Apostolic See and faithful to the magisterium of the Church; whether they have a thorough knowledge of dogmatic and moral theology and canon law; whether they are outstanding for their piety, their spirit of sacrifice and their pastoral zeal; whether they have aptitude for governing. Consideration must also be given to intellectual qualities, studies completed, social sense, spirit of dialogue and cooperation, openness to the signs of the times, praiseworthy impartiality, family background, health, age and inherited characteristics.

Voting

Article VII: 1. When the discussion has been completed, votes, or abstentions, concerning each candidate are to be expressed in writing or in some other suitable manner.

2. Votes are to be cast in secret, to preserve the complete freedom of each one in voting. It is fitting that, apart from the vote itself, a clear indication should be given of the nature of the diocese or office for which each candidate appears more suitable.

3. After the votes have been cast for each candidate, they are to be exactly counted.

4. If it seems advantageous, the president may invite the bishops to hold a further discussion on one or more candidates, and have another vote taken, so that the particular characteristics of each candidate may be clarified.

Article VIII: 1. Before the close of the meeting, a list is to be drawn up of those who, being worthy of and suitable for the episcopal office, are to be proposed to the Apostolic See.

2. Likewise, before the meeting closes everything from which it might be possible to discover how each has voted is to be destroyed. However, the minutes of the meeting are to be drawn up according to the norms of the law.

3. It is very desirable that the bishops should not depart before they have read, approved and signed the minutes.

Article IX: The president of the meeting will send to the Apostolic See through the pontifical representative (e.g., an apostolic delegate) a complete copy of the minutes and of the list of candidates.

Inquiries

Article X: 1. In the case of nations where there is more than one ecclesiastical province, if at least two-thirds of those with a deliberative vote in the national episcopal conference judge it opportune, the list drawn up by a provincial or regional meeting shall be sent for information to the president of the national episcopal conference. He can add comments and information, keeping in mind the needs and circumstances of the Church in the whole country.

2. Likewise, if the majority, specified in the preceding paragraph, of the members of the national episcopal conference consider it opportune, it may be arranged that either a permanent committee of the conference, or a special commission, of restricted size, may add comments and information as in paragraph 1, above. The members of this special commission will be elected for a fixed term by the plenary meeting of the conference; the president of the national conference will preside over the commission.

Article XI: 1. When candidates for a particular episcopal office are to be proposed to the Apostolic See, the lists drawn up by the provincial meetings, or by regional or national meetings in the cases described in Article II, 2, are to be taken into account.

2. These lists, however, do not detract from the liberty of the Roman Pontiff, who in virtue of his office is always free to choose and appoint men who do not appear on the lists.

Article XII: 1. Before any candidate is appointed bishop, the Apostolic See conducts a careful and wide-ranging inquiry about him. It consults individually people who know him very well and who are able to provide the fullest possible information and to make before God a prudent and considered judgment about him.

2. This inquiry is entrusted to the pontifical representative. He submits the questions drawn up for this purpose to ecclesiastics; bishops, priests and religious. Prudent and genuinely reliable lay people who possess useful information about the candidate can also be consulted in the same way.

Papal Representative

Article XIII: 1. When there is a question of appointing someone to a diocese or of naming a coadjutor with right of succession, the pontifical representative will ask the vicar capitular or apostolic administrator or the ordinary himself for a full and careful report on the condition and needs of the diocese. The clergy and laity, especially through their canonically established representative bodies, may also be consulted, es well as religious.

2. Apart from cases legitimately exempted by a particular law or custom or for some other reason, before proposing the *ternae* (list of three candidates) to the Apostolic See, the pontifical representative has the task of requesting, individually, the suggestions of the metropolitan and suffragans of the province to which the vacant diocese belongs, or whose meeting it attends, as well as those of the president of the national episcopal conference. These suggestions, together with his own recommendation, he will then submit to the Apostolic See. The pontifical representative, moreover, will, as may be opportune, hear the opinions of some members of the cathedral chapter, or of the diocesan consultors, and of other members of the clergy, both secular and religious, especially members of the priests' council in existence while the diocese is still filled.

3. With the necessary adjustments, a similar method of procedure is to be followed by those who have the task of proposing candidates for nomination as auxiliary bishops.

Secrecy

Article XIV: In all these matters, the prescribed "papal secret" is to be strictly observed by the bishops, the pontifical representative, the priests and the laity in any way involved. This is demanded by the very nature of the matter and by the respect due to the persons being considered.

Article XV: Maintaining unaltered the desire expressed by the Second Vatican Ecumenical Council in the degree *Christus Dominus* ("On the Bishops' Pastoral Office in the Church"), No. 20, concerning the free election of bishops, the preceding norms neither abrogate nor replace privileges or rights that have been lawfully acquired, or special procedures approved by the Apostolic See by agreement or in some other way.

ADVERSE REACTION

The new rules for the nomination of episcopal candidates embodied provisions already in effect in the United States, Canada and several other countries. They failed, however, to satisfy demands made in some circles for open and democratic participation by all members of the church community.

This was the view stated by a group of theologians and canon lawyers who met with faculty members of the School of Canon Law of the Catholic University May 7 to 11, 1972. They said in a joint statement:

"The procedure for the selection of bishops contained in the norms issued by the Holy See represents a retrogressive development running against the ecclesiological principles of the (Second) Vatican Council and the expressed needs and desires of the faithful."

The statement added: "The increased emphasis upon shared authority, participation of the faithful in the life of the Church, and the real ecclesiological needs of the churches indicate that the direct appointment of bishops by the Holy See, an emergency measure of relatively late origin in the Latin Church, be generally changed. The Holy See as center of unity in the universal Church should retain a role in the acceptance of bishops into the college of bishops. This would imply that the role of the Holy See be more properly one of confirmation, rather than appointment. The juridical act of formal acceptance of an elected bishop into hierarchical communion should be one of confirmation, with right of refusal for serious justifying reasons.

"Thus, the present document must be rejected by the Church for the good of the churches and the progress of the ecumenical movement. The National Conference of Catholic Bishops should provide procedures for the selection of bishops in accord with the promise of *Ecclesiae Sanctae,* for example, such as those proposed by the Canon Law Society of America for local consultation, that will meet the theological demands of the episcopal office in the Church and the needs of the faithful."

Another Plan

Proposals accepted "in substance" by the Canon Law Society of America at a meeting Oct. 11 to 14, 1971, provided for nominating committees in each diocese with a membership of two diocesan priests, two men religious, two women religious, two laymen, two laywomen, and one appointee of the bishop. The committee would study diocesan conditions, determine specific qualifications for episcopal nominees and make nominations, passing lists from parish and diocesan councils through the priests' senate to the local bishop, the bishops of the ecclesiastical province, and eventually the president of the national bishops' conference. Additions, deletions and other changes could be made at each step along the way. A final list of nominees would be sent to the pope by the president of the national episcopal conference. The actual choice and appointment of a bishop would be up to the pope. The plan did not mention any role for the papal representative who, under existing procedures, transmits the names of the candidates to the Holy See.

The adoption of proposals more or less like the plan of the Canon Law Society, or at least

in line with its advocacy of representative and democratic features in the nomination process, has been urged in recent years by a growing number of priests' senates, groups of religious, pastoral councils and others.

NFPC View

The National Federation of Priests' Councils, which favored the plan developed by the Canon Law Society of America, called the new rules "intolerable. . . . This latest promulgation is a retrogression from Vatican II, an insult to the practice of the Eastern Church and to the religious orders of the Western Church, a reversal of the tradition of the early Church and an obstacle to ecumenical yearnings of Christians everywhere."

". . . We urge the People of God in the US to employ the plan offered by the Canon Law Society of America, or any other such plan involving broad participation, before responding to a request from Rome or the Apostolic Delegate for information on any potential candidate for the episcopacy. Such requests should be returned without supplying the information requested if they were consulted and the appointee's name not among those nominated."

The NFPC called for appointees to seek episcopal nomination from the people whom they would serve and not to accept appointment if the people found them unsatisfactory. If an unsatisfactory appointment were made, the people should inform the apostolic delegate that it was in fact unsatisfactory and would result in divisiveness.

RECOMMENDATIONS

Far-reaching changes in the exercise of episcopal authority in the Catholic Church in the US were recommended in a 31-page "initial report" released Oct. 16, 1972, by the bishops' Ad Hoc Committee for Priestly Life and Ministry. The report, sent to all American bishops, recommended:

• Priests and laity should have a far greater say in the selection of bishops.

• Priests should participate and "have a voice" in meetings of bishops.

• An interdisciplinary committee should be set up to consider a "limited term of office" for bishops.

• The inclusion of more Spanish-speaking and blacks among the hierarchy is "of utmost and immediate concern."

• "Consultation" in the Church must be taken much more seriously, and stronger structures of consultation and due process should be set up in all dioceses.

• Structures for the evaluation of priests in their ministry must be established as an integral part of their personal growth and pastoral accountability.

The recommendations were made after wide consultation by the committee with priests throughout the country.

SOCIAL IMPACT OF CHURCH INVESTMENTS

James W. Alsip disclosed in January, 1972, that a special committee of which he was chairman was studying the social impact of deposits and investments of the US Catholic Conference in the areas of minority employment and military production.

Complicity

Earlier in the month, the Corporate Information Center of the National Council of Churches accused 10 Protestant denominations, including some that had outspoken opponents of the Vietnam war, of complicity in the "immoral and socially injurious acts" of major military contractors. The center reported that the 10 denominations, representing about one-fourth of US church membership, and the NCC itself, had a total of nearly $203 million invested in 20 corporations that produced more than $10 billion worth of war material in 1971.

James Jennings, with Alsip a member of the USCC's investment and deposit study committee, said that a similar correlation between investment policies of the Catholic Church and its position on the war was impossible because "the official Catholic position about the war is equivocal" and also because "the level of information about the Catholic Church's investments is minuscule."

The World Council of Churches announced in May that one of its commissions was urging member churches to withdraw all investments in companies operating in southern Africa by way of protest against and refusal to support racist policies of governments there. The commission said that some churches and mission agencies, while supporting liberation movements, continued to "connive" in the "imperialistic and racist activities of countries and . . . regimes by their (investment) policies and practices."

Findings of an inquiry conducted by the Lutheran World Federation indicated, however, that the withdrawal of funds from South Africa by international corporations and banks in which churches had investments would hurt blacks there more than the corporations or the racist government. Banks informed the LWF that threats of a number of churches to withdraw investments from institutions doing business in South Africa would not accomplish their intended purposes.

Oversimplification

If churches are to be condemned for investing in the military-industrial complex — or, by analogy, in firms doing business in racist countries — then it is also complicity to pay taxes and buy US Savings Bonds, stated Dr. Dale A. Fiers, general minister and president of the Christian Church. Speaking in January, 1972, in Indianapolis, he said: "It must be recognized that moral implications of investing money are very complex. To condemn the churches for complicity with the so-called military-industrial complex for war contracts primarily in relation to the conflict in Indo-China is, in my judgment, oversimplification."

A proposal was advanced in England during 1972 for churches to use their investment capabilities for social impact in nations of the Third World, where there was great need of capital for the development and growth of native economies.

DUE PROCESS

The National Conference of Catholic Bishops approved in November, 1969, a set of experimental proposals on due process covering conciliation, arbitration and administrative discretion relating to disputes involving the rights of members of the Church. The proposals, which have since been put into effect in a number of US dioceses with modifications to suit local conditions, were described as a major development at the time they were put forward.

Suggested procedures called for: (1) establishment in each diocese of a five-person council for conciliation whose members would serve as conciliators but would "have no power to force the participants to accept a solution" in a dispute at issue; (2) establishment in dioceses of an office of arbitration with a panel of 10 persons to accept complaints and designate impartial arbitrators for the settlement of disputes; (3) establishment of a court of arbitration in each diocese to serve as a board of review on decisions handed down by arbitrators.

Safeguard Freedoms

Due process is intended to safeguard the "common rights and freedoms" of all persons in the Church. Among such rights are:

• "the right and freedom to hear the word of God and to participate in the sacramental and liturgical life of the Church;

• "the right and freedom to exercise the apostolate and share in the mission of the Church;

• "the right and freedom to speak and to be heard and to receive objective information regarding the pastoral needs and affairs of the Church;

• "the right to education, to freedom of inquiry and to freedom of expression in the sacred sciences;

• "the right to free assembly and association in the Church;

• "and such inviolable and universal rights of the human person as the right to the protection of one's reputation, to respect for one's person, to activity in accord with the upright norm of one's conscience, to protection of privacy."

TITLES AND FORMS OF ADDRESS IN LETTERS

For Churchmen

In general, it has been customary for Catholics to add the words "in Christ" to the appropriate conclusions of formal letters to ecclesiastical dignitaries, priests and religious. "Asking Your Excellency's blessing" and similar forms have also been customary.

Given below are forms of proper address, salutation and conclusion.

Patriarchs: His Beatitude (Christian Name and Surname), Patriarch of (See City); Your Beatitude; Asking the Apostolic Blessing of Your Beatitude, I am, Yours respectfully, (Name).

Cardinals: His Eminence (Christian Name) Cardinal (Surname); (if he is an archbishop or bishop, include Title of the See); Your Eminence; Asking the Blessing of Your Eminence, I am, Yours respectfully, (Name).

Archbishops and Bishops: The Most Rev. (Name), Archbishop or Bishop of (Name of See); Your Excellency; Asking Your Excellency's Blessing, I am, Yours respectfully, (Name).

Abbots: The Right Rev. (Name), Abbot of (Name of Abbey); Right Reverend and dear Abbot; I am, Yours respectfully, (Name).

Monsignors: The Rev. Monsignor or Monsignor (Name); Reverend and dear Monsignor; I am, Yours respectfully, (Name).

Rectors of Seminaries, Heads of Colleges: The Very Rev. (Name); Very Reverend and dear Father; I am, Yours respectfully, (Name).

Provincials of Religious Orders: The Very Rev. Father Provincial, (Name, Title of Order); Very Reverend and dear Father Provincial; I am, Yours respectfully, (Name).

Diocesan Clergy: The Rev. (Name); Reverend and dear Father; Respectfully yours, (Name).

Regular Clergy: The Rev. (Name); Reverend and dear Father (Religious Name); Respectfully yours, (Name). Benedictine and Cistercian Monks and Canons Regular are addressed as The Rev. Dom (Name).

Clerics in Major Orders below the Priesthood: The Reverend (Religious Name) or The Reverend Mr. (Name). Reverend Sir or Dear Mr. (Name); Respectfully yours, (Name).

Brothers and Sisters: Brother or Sister (Name); Dear Brother or Sister (Religious Name); Respectfully yours, (Name).

Protestant Minister: The Reverend (Name), Reverend Sir; Very truly yours, (Name).

Rabbi: Rabbi (Name); Reverend Sir; Very truly yours, (Name).

For Others

President: The President; Dear Mr. President; Yours very truly, (Name).

Vice-President: The Vice-President; Dear Mr. Vice-President; Yours very truly, (Name).

Member of Cabinet: The Honorable (Name), Secretary of (Name of Department); Dear Mr. (or Madam) Secretary; Yours very truly, (Name).

Ambassador: The Honorable, or His Excellency, for Ambassador of foreign country (Name), Ambassador to (Name of Country); Dear Mr. Ambassador (Your Excellency, for ambassador of foreign country); Yours very truly, (Name).

Senator: The Honorable (Name), United States Senate; My dear Senator, Dear Mr. (or Madam) Senator; Yours very truly, (Name).

Congressman: The Honorable (Name), United States House of Representatives, Dear Sir (Madam); Yours very truly, (Name).

Member of Supreme Court: The Honorable (Name), United States Supreme Court; Dear Mr. Justice; Yours very truly (Name).

Judge: TJHE Honorable (Name), Name of Court; Dear Sir, Dear Judge (Name); Yours very truly, (Name).

Governor: The Honorable (Name), Governor of (Name of State); Dear Sir; Yours very truly, (Name).

Mayor: The Honorable (Name), Mayor of (Name of City); Dear Sir; Yours very truly, (Name).

Military and Naval Officers: Rank, for general and commissioned officers, (Name); Dear Sir; Yours very truly, (Name). Warrant officers and flight officers are addressed as Mister; non-commissioned officers, by their titles.

King: His Majesty (Name); Sir, or May it please Your Majesty; Yours very truly, (Name).

Ecclesiastical Titles

According to instructions issued by Pope Paul Mar. 28, 1969, titles used by him with reference to cardinals, bishops and other church dignitaries are limited to: "Our Venerable Brother," "Venerable Brother," "Beloved Son."

Customary titles still stand for cardinals and bishops; e.g., "Eminence," "Excellency," "Most Reverend," "Lord Cardinal," "Monsignor," is used for prelates of honor and chaplains of the pope.

Recent changes in the life styles of religious have been accompanied by changes in titles of superiors. In some institutes, general superiors are known as presidents and the heads of convents as coordinators. Many superiors have relinquished the title of mother. Many institutes no longer require their members to adopt a religious name for use in place of a given name, and it has become customary for religious, sisters and brothers, to use family names.

Pope Paul VI

(See additional entries under News Events, Vatican, Pope Paul, titles of documents, topical headings for coverage of 1972 and other events.)

Cardinal Giovanni Montini was elected Pope June 21, 1963, on the fifth or sixth ballot cast by the 79th and largest conclave of cardinals in the history of the Church. Taking the name Paul VI as the 261st successor to St. Peter as Bishop of Rome, he was crowned June 30 in solemn ceremonies in St. Peter's Square.

Early Career

Giovanni Battista Montini was born Sept. 26, 1897, at Concesio, near Brescia, in the foothills of the Italian Alps. He was the second of the three sons of Giorgio Montini and Giuditta Alghisi.

He suffered from ill health during his boyhood and youth and lived mostly at home while pursuing studies for the priesthood at the Cesare Arici Institute and Christ the King Seminary in Brescia. He was ordained in the cathedral there May 29, 1920. After a short period spent in parish work, he continued studies at the Gregorian University, the University of Rome and the academy for Vatican diplomats. He received degrees in civil and canon law, theology and philosophy.

Named as attaché of the nunciature at Warsaw, he served there for less than a year, returning to Rome for reasons of health in 1923. He then became chaplain of the Catholic Students' Club at the University of Rome and, in 1925, national moderator of the Italian Catholic University Federation's publications program. The student organization was suppressed by Mussolini in 1931.

He became a clerk in the Vatican Secretariat of State in 1933 and was appointed undersecretary three years later. He was named substitute secretary of state in 1944 and prosecretary for ordinary affairs in 1952.

During this period of service in the secretariat, he worked closely with Pius XII, who left the office of secretary vacant following the death of Cardinal Maglione in 1944. With a 10-year background of practical experience in Catholic Action and a longer involvement in diplomatic tasks, he is thought to have been influential in supporting the Christian Democratic parties in Europe, in helping to mobilize action against Communists at the polls in Italy in 1948, and in fostering the priest-worker experiment in France after World War II.

He was ordained archbishop of Milan Dec. 12, 1954, and was installed in the See the following Jan. 6. He was the first of 52 cardinals created by John XXIII Dec. 15, 1958, and served in the Roman Curia as a member of the Consistorial Congregation (Congregation of Bishops), the Congregation for Extraordinary Ecclesiastical Affairs (Secretariat of State, Council for the Public Affairs of the Church), and the Congregation of Seminaries and Universities (Congregation for Catholic Education).

In eight and one-half years in Milan he conducted a two-year visitation of the 1,000 churches in the archdiocese, built or renovated 200 churches and chapels, set up a modern system for social services, established a center for study by his priests of pastoral methods suited to contemporary conditions, stimulated Catholic Action, and made direct and effective contact with the people and their conditions of life in the Communist-affected region of northern Italy.

Renewal Commitment

On the day following his election to the papacy, Paul VI announced on Vatican Radio his intention of carrying on with the Church renewal policy and program of his predecessor. Accordingly and in his own way, he has been seeking to move forward and make last what John XXIII, in his unique and charismatic way, stimulated — despite conflicting and obstructive currents of progressivism and conservatism in the Church.

Vatican II

Immediately on his election, Paul announced he would reconvene the Second Vatican Council, which had completed only one session before the death of John XXIII.

He opened the second session Sept. 29, 1963, and at its conclusion Dec. 4 approved the promulgation of the first two conciliar documents, the *Constitution on the Sacred Liturgy* and a *Decree on Media of Social Communication.* Between the second, third and fourth sessions, he ordered that measures be taken by the various conciliar commissions to simplify and streamline the work load and to modify procedures for the smoother and faster conduct of business. At the end of the third session Nov. 21, 1964, by which time the Council had in work all of the items in its wide-ranging agenda, he approved the promulgation of the *Dogmatic Constitution on the Church.* a *Decree on Ecumenism* and a *Decree on Eastern Catholic Churches.* On Sept. 14, 1965, he opened the fourth and final session by concelebrating Mass with a group of the Council Fathers.

During the last three sessions of the Council, he generally followed the hands-off policy of John XXIII with respect to deliberations and the general conduct of business. Like John, however, who intervened during the first sesssion to prevent fruitless consideration of a draft proposal on revelation which hardly any of the Fathers favored, he took a direct hand in Council affairs on several occasions.

On June 23, 1964, he announced he was reserving to himself for study and decision a number of questions regarding birth control. Assisting him in the study was a mixed commission of some 60 persons including priests, theologians, married men and women, physicians and psychiatrists. Their reports — for and against relaxation of Church teaching and practice on the subject — were submitted to him for decision.

During the third session of the Council, at the request of a large majority of the Council Fathers, he also took under personal advisement a number of questions related to mixed marriages and similar matters.

Several weeks after the fourth session began, he cut off Council discussion of clerical celibacy because of the delicacy of the matter and the emotional manner of its treatment in communications media. His action was hailed by the Fathers of the Council.

Before final action was taken on several documents at the end of the third session, he made 19 changes in the *Decree on Ecumenism* and proclaimed Mary the Mother of the Church in the *Dogmatic Constitution on the Church.*

Another incident worthy of note at the close of the third session was his refusal to order a vote on the proposed *Declaration on Religious Freedom.* A final version of several draftings of the document was proposed for balloting but was withheld by the Council's presiding board. He refused to override their decision, which was in accordance with rules of Council procedure. He stated at the time that the decree would be given first place on the agenda of the fourth session. It was so placed, and was approved.

He brought the Second Vatican Council to a close Dec. 8, 1965. He noted in a final address that the decisive phase of *aggiornamento*-in-action was already underway, and declared a special jubilee of prayer, study and work in the Church for the purpose of realizing in practice the objectives laid down in the 16 documents of the Council. He later extended the period of jubilee from May 29 to Dec. 8, 1966. He also announced at the Council closing that the beatification causes of his predecessors, John XXIII and Pius XII, were being set in motion.

He has implemented enactments of the Council in various documents. The motu proprio *Ecclesiae Sanctae* of Aug. 6, 1966, laid down executive norms for the four decrees on the pastoral office of bishops, the ministry and life of priests, the adaptation and renewal of religious life and the missionary activity of the Church. The motu proprio *Catholicam Christi Ecclesiam* of Jan. 6, 1967, established the Council of the Laity and the Commission for Justice and Peace. The encyclical *The Development of Peoples* represented an effort to implement the *Pastoral Constitution of the Church in the Modern World.* His authorization of activities and publications of the secretariats for interfaith affairs were in line with provisions of the *Decree on Ecumenism.* His approval of the establishment of scores of territorial conferences of bishops, the creation of the Synod of Bishops and the statement of norms in 1967 regarding the reestablishment of the permanent diaconate in the Roman Rite were efforts in pursuit of conciliar objectives regarding the action and composition of the hierarchy in the Church.

Two documents issued in 1966 embodied the thinking and spirit of the Council: the apostolic constitution *Paenitemini* of Feb. 17, a major statement on the revision of penitential discipline; and a decree of Mar. 18, with respect to mixed marriages. In 1967, he issued an apostolic constitution entitled *The Doctrine and Practice of Indulgences* which stated new norms in this area of Church life.

To quicken the spirit of faith in the Church, the Pope ordered observance throughout the world of a Year of Faith from June 29, 1967, to June 29, 1968. He closed the year with the publication of a Creed of the People of God.

Collegiality

The Second Vatican Council completed the work of the First by spelling out, among other things, the doctrine of collegiality of the bishops. With and under the Pope — as the successors of the Apostles with and under the leadership of Peter — the bishops as a body are the pastors of the Church whose mission, while concentrated in the sphere of their own proper jurisdictions, extends also to care, concern, and collective action with each other and the pope for the good of the universal Church.

On Nov. 21, 1964, when the third session promulgated the *Dogmatic Constitution on the Church,* Pope Paul told the assembled bishops that he intended to associate them more closely with himself in the work of the whole Church, through participation in postconciliar commissions and in other ways.

This led to the establishment of the Synod of Bishops on paper Sept. 15, 1965. The initial meeting of the Synod from Sept. 29 to Oct. 25, 1967, represented the first papal effort in modern times to seek the consultation of bishops gathered in a collegial assembly outside of an ecumenical council. Second and third meetings in 1969 and 1971 dealt with questions concerning collegiality, territorial conferences of bishops, clerical celibacy and problems of world justice and peace.

In a move toward decentralizing and delegating authority, he increased the powers of bishops, in virtue of the motu proprio *De Episcoporum Muneribus* of July 11, 1966. In 1967, he extended the same grants of authority to bishops of the Eastern Rites. Additional faculties have since been given to bishops.

Roman Curia

He started a reorganization of the Roman Curia in 1965 by revising the Sacred Congregation of the Holy Office. He gave the body a new name, the Sacred Congregation for the Doctrine of the Faith, made the orientation of its work more positive, and abolished the Index of Forbidden Books. He issued Aug. 15, 1967, the apostolic constitution *Regimini Ecclesiae Universae,* providing for the overall reorganization of the Curia and for the inclusion of diocesan bishops in its various departments. The constitution was put into effect in 1968.

He established an International Theological Commission in 1969, and reconstituted the Biblical Commission in 1971 and the Commission for the Codification of Oriental Canon Law in 1972.

In addition to reorganizing the Curia, he has given it a greater international complexion than it ever had in previous history.

Cardinals

By elevating 27 prelates to the rank of cardinal on Feb. 22, 1965, he increased the membership of the College of Cardinals to the high total of 103 and made it more representative (43 nations) of the Church throughout the world than it had ever been. Of greater significance than the increased geographical representation, however, was the fact that the new cardinals included three major patriarchs of Eastern Rite. Without prejudice to their patriarchal prerogatives, these prelates, and a fourth patriarch already in the Sacred College, became cardinal bishops.

He further increased the membership of the College to the all-time high total of 118 in 1967. The creation of the new cardinals, which took place in ceremonies held between June 26 and June 29, seemed to answer negatively some speculation that the College might be phased out of existence or its functions diminished. He named another group of 35 cardinals in March, 1969.

In November, 1970, he decreed that, as of Jan. 1, 1971, cardinals 80 years of age and older could not take part in a conclave for the election of a Pope or be active in the administration of Church affairs in the Roman Curia. The decree *(Ingravescentem Aetatem)* immediately affected 25 cardinals.

He also asked for the resignation of active bishops at the age of 75.

Liturgical Renewal

He authorized promulgation of the *Constitution on the Sacred Liturgy* Dec. 8, 1963, and ordered some of its provisions into effect as of Feb. 16, 1964. On Jan. 28, 1964, he announced the formation of a post-conciliar commission with responsibility for continuing work in this field.

Progressive liturgical renewal was the sub-ject of several documents issued by the Pope during 1967. The principal ones were instructions on sacred music, dated Mar. 5; the adaptations of rites and ceremonies, May 4; and Eucharistic worship, May 25.

In 1968, through the Consilium for Implementing the Constitution on the Sacred Liturgy, approval was given for three new Canons and eight prefaces in the Mass.

A New Order of the Mass, related to revisions of the universal liturgical calendar and the Liturgy of the Hours (revised in 1970) was decreed in 1969, to take the place of the form of Mass ordered and standardized for the Roman Rite by the Council of Trent in the 16th century. Universal adoption of these reforms has been delayed pending the preparation of vernacular translations of official texts and for other reasons.

Interfaith Relations

He approved promulgation of the *Decree on Ecumenism* at the conclusion of the third session of the Second Vatican Council, and gave the late Cardinal Augustin Bea, head of the Secretariat for Promoting Christian Unity, and his successor, Cardinal Jan Willebrands, a free hand in relations with members and communities of other Christian churches. To supplement interfaith relations among others, he established a Secretariat for Non-Christians May 19, 1964.

While on pilgrimage to the Holy Land Jan. 4 to 6, 1964, he held two conversations with Orthodox Patriarch Athenagoras I. He was the first Pope since St. Peter to visit the Holy Places and the first Pontiff in more than 500 years to hold conversations with an Orthodox Patriarch.

The prelates met on two more occasions, in Istanbul in July and at the Vatican in October, 1967. The visit of Athenagoras to Rome was the first by a Patriarch of Constantinople since 1451.

Between the two sets of visits, the Pope and Patriarch nullified Dec. 7, 1965, mutual Catholic-Orthodox excommunications imposed in 1054.

Also on the personal contact level, the Pope has met with numerous Orthodox prelates, Anglican Archbishop Michael Ramsey in 1966, leaders of the World Council of Churches and representatives of other religious bodies.

He authorized the initiation in May, 1965, of exploratory talks and steps toward dialogue with the World Council of Churches, and has approved of high-level talks with Anglicans and the Lutheran World Federation.

While on a visit to the Geneva headquarters of the World Council of Churches in June, 1969, he told members of the staff that the Church had great interest in the council but that the time was not yet ripe for a request for Catholic membership.

For all of his interest in ecumenism, he has repeatedly cautioned Catholics engaged in interfaith endeavors to stay within the bounds of sound doctrine. Ecumenism at any price is false, he has stated.

Encyclicals

The first of Paul's encyclicals, *Ecclesiam Suam,* dated Aug. 6, 1964, developed four principal themes related to *aggiornamento* and the aims and purposes of the Second Vatican Council: (1) the awareness the Church has of itself, and the need for this to increase and develop in depth; (2) internal renewal in the Church, and external expression of it; (3) the dialogue the Church must conduct internally among its members and externally with all men; (4) an offer of his services for furthering the cause of peace in the world.

Mense Maio, dated Apr. 29, 1965, urged prayer, especially through the intercession of the Blessed Virgin Mary during the month of May, for the success of the Second Vatican Council and for peace in the world.

Mysterium Fidei, dated Sept. 3, 1965, was a strong statement of traditional doctrine concerning the Holy Eucharist.

Prayer for peace, especially the Rosary during the month of October, was the subject of his fourth encyclical, *Christi Matri Rosarii,* Sept. 15, 1966.

The Development of Peoples was the title and subject of his fifth encyclical, dated Mar. 26, 1967. Wide in concept and definite in practical guidelines, the widely hailed document extended the social doctrine of Pope John's *Peace on Earth* and blueprinted the application to the Third World of the contents of the Second Vatican Council's *Pastoral Constitution on the Church in the Modern World.*

Priestly Celibacy dated June 24, 1967, restated the traditional doctrine and practice of the Latin Church on clerical celibacy. The well-documented and backgrounded encyclical was not received favorably by those who were arguing for change in this discipline.

Of Human Life, dated July 25, 1968, restated traditional doctrine concerning the regulation of birth.

Documents published in 1971, with the significance but not the title of encyclicals, were an apostolic letter to Cardinal Maurice Roy, on social questions; a *Pastoral Instruction: The Media, Public Opinion and Human Progress;* and an apostolic exhortation addressed to religious.

Communism

In his first encyclical, *Ecclesiam Suam,* he said he had no intention of excluding Communists from dialogue with the Church even though such dialogue would probably be incomplete and extremely difficult. In February, 1965, he urged members of an Italian workers' association to maintain contact with their fellow workers, including those with Communist leanings, but not to compromise their fidelity to Christian social principles.

One of the purposes of the Secretariat for Non-Believers, authorized and established Apr. 8, 1965, is to study and initiate relations with Communists and others on the subject of atheism. Since that time, some limited dialogue has taken place but hardly any observable results have been noted. In 1967, he approved release by the secretariat of an introductory document on dialogue of this kind. Detailed guidelines were published in October, 1968.

Negotiations with the Hungarian government, in progress for about two months before Paul's election, led to agreement in September, 1964, with respect to some Vatican freedom in making bishops' appointments and to modification of a loyalty oath expected of the clergy. The negotiations, as anticipated, left many problems unsettled, including the status of Cardinal Mindszenty who remained in seclusion in the American Embassy in Budapest until September, 1971.

Four sets of diplomatic conversations over a two-year period were concluded June 25, 1966, with the signing by Vatican and Yugoslav representatives of an agreement designed to regularize Church-State relations. Full diplomatic relations were established in 1970.

Some measure of agreement was reached with the Polish government in 1972 when Polish bishops were appointed to head four jurisdictions formerly held by German prelates in the Oder-Niesse territory.

Negotiations with Czechoslovakia, said to be underway for several years, have been fruitless, and the diplomatic doors of other Communist countries have remained closed.

Peace

From the very beginning of his pontificate, he made known his dedication to the cause of world peace.

In 1963, he spoke in favor of negotiations for a nuclear test ban agreement which was finally signed by nearly 100 nations.

At the very beginning of 1964, while in Jerusalem as a pilgrim visiting the Holy Places, he sent 220 peace messages to heads of state and other international leaders. Eleven months later, while attending the 38th International Eucharistic Congress in Bombay, he again appealed for peace and disarmament, and urged nations to spend for useful and humanitarian purposes — to relieve hunger, misery, illness and ignorance — funds and efforts that could be saved through disarmament. He repeated these ideas in his annual Christmas message to the world a few weeks later.

Time and again during 1965, he raised his voice in pleas for peace — in Vietnam, the Congo, the Dominican Republic, India, Pakistan and Kashmir. In February, he told the bishops of Vietnam in a letter that he had initiated confidential approaches for the sake of peace in the divided nation. On another occasion, he decried the use of terrorist guerrilla tactics under any and all circumstances.

In one of many appeals for the outlawing of nuclear weapons, he prayed on the occasion of the 20th anniversary of the atomic bombing of Japan: "May the world never again see a day of misfortune like that of Hiroshima."

To plead, "No more war; never again war," was the simple and uncomplicated — yet extremely complex — purpose of his visit to the United Nations headquarters Oct. 4, 1965.

With the quickening of the tempo of war in Vietnam from the end of 1965, he escalated his efforts for peace. In many addresses, he pleaded for a Christmas truce, for negotiations and disarmament, and for the humane treatment of prisoners. In the fall of 1966, he sent a special delegation to Vietnam for conversations with the bishops of the country and, probably, for fact-finding purposes. Peace was the subject of many private talks, especially with persons like UN Ambassador Arthur Goldberg, US Ambassador to Vietnam Henry Cabot Lodge, and Soviet Foreign Minister Andrei Gromyko.

In July, 1966, it was reported that a fund-raising campaign begun the previous December in response to a papal appeal had collected almost $7.5 million for the relief of famine, particularly in India and Pakistan.

Throughout 1967, he missed no opportunity to appeal and to offer his services for peace-making in Vietnam, but without results. He made similar appeals to prevent, and then to stop, the Israeli-Arab conflict which erupted during the first week of June and continued sporadically thereafter. The most he could do was to mobilize Vatican relief forces to assist refugees.

Beginning in July, he made peace overtures to leaders of opposing factions in Nigeria where bloody tribal and political warfare took a terrible toll of life.

In 1968 and 1969, strife in these areas continued to preoccupy the Pope. He offered the Vatican as a site for Vietnam peace talks, and coupled pleas for peace in Nigeria-Biafra with appeals for stepped-up relief measures there. In August, with most other world leaders, he decried the Soviet invasion and occupation of Czechoslovakia.

The war in Indochina and Arab-Israeli hostility were subjects of frequent comment in papal talks in 1970 and 1971. He made several appeals in 1971 for the cessation of civil war in East Pakistan and called for international action to relieve the pressing needs of the millions of refugees in India.

He added Northern Ireland to his litany of prayers and appeals for peace as conflict intensified there in 1971 and 1972.

Pilgrimages

While John XXIII was the first Pope to venture outside the Vatican since 1870, Paul VI is the first Pontiff to travel outside of Italy since Pius VII was forced to do so by Napoleon more than 150 years ago.

Paul traveled to the Holy Land as a pilgrim to the Holy Places and to meet Ecumenical Patriarch Athenagoras I from Jan. 4 to 6, 1964.

He went to Bombay, Dec. 2 to 5, 1964, to take part in the 38th International Eucharistic Congress.

He spent nearly 14 hours in New York Oct. 4, 1965, appearing as a pilgrim to plead for peace before representatives of 116 countries at the United Nations.

In December, 1966, he made a short pilgrimage of sympathy so he could be with the people of the Florentine area of Italy which was devastated by a flood of catastrophic proportions.

To pray at the Marian shrine as a pilgrim of peace was the purpose of his one-day flying pilgrimage to Fatima, Portugal May 13, 1967.

On July 25, 1967, he flew to Turkey to see Patriarch Athenagoras I of Constantinople and to visit the ancient city of Ephesus, the locale of the house where, according to an old tradition, the Blessed Virgin Mary lived toward the end of her life, and the place of meeting of the ecumenical council which ratified her title, Mother of God *(Theotokos)*, in 431. The purposes of the pilgrimage were plainly ecumenical and Marian.

On the sixth of his journeys outside Italy, he made a three-day flying visit to take part in the 39th International Eucharistic Congress in Bogota, Columbia, in August, 1968.

He made two visits in 1969: to Geneva, where he delivered addresses at the headquarters of the International Labor Organization and the World Council of Churches, in June; and to Kampala, to honor the martyrs of Uganda, July 31 to Aug. 2.

His ninth trip, Apr. 24, 1970, was a one-day visit to Sardinia, where he joined the islanders for a celebration in honor of their patroness, Our Lady of Bonaria.

The 10th, also in 1970, was the most extensive of all his trips with stops in Teheran, Nov. 26; Manila, the Philippines, Nov. 27 to 29; Samoa, Nov. 29; Sydney, Australia, Nov. 30 to Dec. 3; Djakarta, Indonesia, Dec. 3 and 4; Hong Kong, Dec. 4; Colombo, Ceylon, Dec. 4; and cyclone-ravaged Pakistan. Rome departure and return dates were Nov. 26 and Dec. 5. An attempt was made on the Pope's life in Manila.

He visited Udine, Italy, Sept. 16, 1972, to take part in a Eucharistic congress there. En route, he stopped in Venice.

It appeared unlikely that he would attend the February, 1973, International Eucharistic Congress in Melbourne, Australia.

Dates and Events in Church History

First Century

Early 30's: First Christian Pentecost: gathering together of the Christian community, outpouring of the Holy Spirit, preaching of St. Peter to Jews in Jerusalem, baptism and aggregation of some 3,000 persons to the Christian community.

St. Stephen, deacon, was stoned to death at Jerusalem; he is venerated as the first Christian martyr.

34-36/67: St. Paul, formerly Saul the persecutor of Christians, was converted, baptized and joined to the college of Apostles. After three major missionary journeys, he was martyred in 64 or 67 at Rome.

39: The Gentile Cornelius and his family were baptized by St. Peter.

42: Persecution of Christians in Palestine broke out during the rule of Herod Agrippa; St. James the Greater, the first Apostle to die, was beheaded in 44; St. Peter was imprisoned for a short time; many Christians fled to Antioch and elsewhere.

At Antioch, the followers of Christ were first called Christians.

49: Christians at Rome, who were considered members of a Jewish sect, were adversely affected by a decree of Claudius which forbade Jewish worship there.

51: The Council of Jerusalem, in which all the Apostles participated under the presidency of St. Peter, decreed that circumcision, dietary regulations, and various other prescriptions of Mosaic Law were not obligatory for Gentile converts to the Christian community. The decree was issued in opposition to Judaizers who contended that observance of the Mosaic Law in its entirety was necessary for salvation.

64: Persecution under Nero: The emperor, accusing Christians of starting a fire which destroyed half of Rome, inaugurated the era of major Roman persecutions.

64/65: Martyrdom of St. Peter at Rome during the Neronian persecution. He established his see and spent his last years there after preaching in and around Jerusalem, establishing a see at Antioch, and presiding at the Council of Jerusalem.

70: Destruction of Jerusalem by Titus.

88-97: Pontificate of St. Clement I, third successor of St. Peter as bishop of Rome, one of the Apostolic Fathers. The *First Epistle of Clement to the Corinthians,* with which he has been identified, was addressed by the Church of Rome to the Church at Corinth, the scene of irregularities and divisions in the Christian community.

95: Domitian persecuted Christians, principally at Rome.

c. 100: Death of St. John, Apostle and Evangelist, marking the end of the Age of the Apostles and the first generation of the Church.

Second Century

c. 107: St. Ignatius of Antioch was martyred at Rome. He was the first writer to use the expression, "the Catholic Church."

112: Rescript to Pliny. Emperor Trajan instructed Pliny, governor of Bithynia, not to search out Christians but to punish them if they were publicly denounced and refused to do homage to the Roman gods. The rescript set a pattern of discretionary leniency for Roman magistrates in dealing with Christians.

117-138: Persecution under Hadrian. Many *Acts of Martyrs* date from this period.

c. 125: Spread of Gnosticism.

c. 155: St. Polycarp, bishop of Smyrna and disciple of St. John the Evangelist, was martyred.

c. 156: Beginning of Montanism.

161-180: Reign of Marcus Aurelius. His persecution, launched in the wake of natural disasters, was more violent than those of his predecessors.

165: St. Justin, an important early Christian writer, was martyred at Rome.

c. 180: St. Irenaeus, bishop of Lyons and one of the great early theologians, wrote *Adversus Haereses.* He stated that the teaching and tradition of the Roman See was the standard for belief.

196: Easter Controversy.

The *Didache,* written in the second century, was an important record of Christian belief, practice and government in the first century.

Latin was introduced in the West as a liturgical language.

The Catechetical School of Alexandria, founded about the middle of the century, increased in importance.

Third Century

202: Persecution under Septimius Severus, who wanted to establish one common religion in the Empire.

206: Tertullian, a convert since 197 and the first great ecclesiastical writer in Latin, joined the heretical Montanists. He died in 230.

215: Death of Clement of Alexandria, teacher of Origen and a founding father of the School of Alexandria.

217-235: St. Hippolytus, the first anti-pope. He was reconciled to the Church while in prison during persecution in 235.

232-254: Origen established the School of Caesarea after being deposed in 231 as head of the School of Alexandria; he died in 254. A scholar and voluminous writer, he was one of the founders of systematic theology and exerted wide influence for many years.

c. 242: Manichaeism originated in Persia.

249-251: Persecution under Decius. Many of those who denied the faith *(lapsi)* sought readmission to the Church at the end of the persecution in 251. Pope St. Cornelius had correspondence with St. Cyprian on the subject and ordered that *lapsi* were to be readmitted after suitable penance.

250-300: Neo-Platonism of Plotinus and Porphyry gained followers.

251: Novatian, an antipope, was condemned at Rome.

256: Pope St. Stephen I upheld the validity of baptism administered by heretics, in the Rebaptism Controversy.

257: Persecution under Valerian, who attempted to destroy the Church as a social structure.

258: St. Cyprian, bishop of Carthage, was martyred.

c. 260: St. Lucian founded the exegetical School of Antioch.

Pope St. Dionysius condemned teachings of Sabellius and the Marcionites.

St. Paul of Thebes became a hermit.

261: Gallienus issued an edict of toleration which ended general persecution for nearly 40 years.

c. 266: Sabellianism was condemned and Paul of Samosata deposed.

292: Diocletian divided the Roman Empire into East and West. The division emphasized political, cultural and other differences between the two parts of the Empire and influenced the Church in the East and West. The prestige of Rome began to decline.

Fourth Century

303: Persecution broke out under Diocletian. It ended in the West in 306 but continued for 10 years in the East; it was particularly violent in 304.

305: St. Anthony of Heracles established a foundation for hermits near the Red Sea in Egypt.

306: The first local legislation on clerical celibacy was enacted by a council held at Elvira, Spain; bishops, priests, deacons and other ministers were forbidden to have wives.

310: St. Hilarion established a foundation for hermits in Palestine.

311: An edict of toleration issued by Galerius at the urging of Constantine and Licinius officially ended persecution in the West; some persecution continued in the East.

313: The *Edict of Milan* issued by Constantine and Licinius recognized Christianity as a lawful religion and the legal freedom of all religions in the Roman Empire.

314: The Council of Arles condemned Donatism in Africa and declared that baptism by heretics was valid.

318: St. Pachomius established the first foundation of the cenobitic (common) life, as compared with the solitary life of hermits in Upper Egypt.

325: The Ecumenical Council of Nicaea (I), first of its kind in the history of the Church, condemned Arianism; see separate entry.

326: Discovery of the True Cross on which Christ was crucified.

337: Baptism and death of Constantine.

c. 342: Beginning of a 40-year persecution in Persia.

343-344: A local Council of Sardica reaffirmed doctrine formulated by Nicaea I and declared that bishops had the right of appeal to the pope as the highest authority in the Church.

361-363: Julian the Apostate waged an unsuccessful campaign against the Church in an attempt to restore paganism as the religion of the Empire.

c. 365: Persecution under Valens in the East.

c. 376: Beginning of the barbarian invasion in the West.

379: Death of St. Basil, the Father of Monasticism in the East. His writings contributed greatly to the development of rules for the religious life.

381: The Ecumenical Council of Constantinople (I); see separate entry.

382: The *Decree of Pope St. Damasus* listed the Canon of Sacred Scripture.

382-c. 406: St. Jerome translated the Old and New Testaments into Latin. His work is called the Vulgate Version of the Bible.

396: St. Augustine became bishop of Hippo in North Africa.

397: A local Council of Carthage published the Canon of Sacred Scripture.

Fifth Century

410: Visigoths sacked Rome.

411: Donatism was condemned by a council at Carthage.

430: St. Augustine, bishop of Hippo for 35 years, died. He was a strong defender of orthodox doctrine against Manichaeism, Donatism and Pelagianism. The depth and range of his writings made him a dominant influence in Christian thought for many centuries.

431: The Ecumenical Council of Ephesus; see separate entry.

432: St. Patrick arrived in Ireland. By the time of his death in 461 most of the country had been converted, monasteries founded and the hierarchy established.

438: The *Theodosian Code*, a compilation of decrees for the Empire, was issued by Theodosius II. It had great influence on subsequent civil and ecclesiastical law.

449: The Robber Council of Ephesus, which did not have ecclesiastical sanction, declared itself in favor of the opinions of Eutyches who contended that Christ had only one nature.

451: The Ecumenical Council of Chalcedon; see separate entry.

452: Pope St. Leo the Great persuaded Attila the Hun to spare Rome.

455: Vandals sacked Rome. The decline of imperial Rome dates approximately from this time.

484: Patriarch Acacius of Constantinople was excommunicated for signing the *Henoticon,* a unity law published by Emperor Zeno in 482 to end the turmoil associated with the Monophysite heresy. The document capitulated to the heresy. The excommunication triggered a 35-year-long schism.

494: Pope St. Gelasius I declared in a letter to Emperor Anastasius that the pope had power and authority over the emperor in spiritual matters.

496: Clovis, King of the Franks, was converted and became the defender of Christianity in the West. The Franks became a Catholic people.

Sixth Century

520 and later: Irish monasteries flourished as centers for spiritual life, missionary training and scholarly activity.

529: The Second Council of Orange condemned Semi-Pelagianism.

c. 529: St. Benedict founded the Monte Cassino Abbey. Some years before his death in 543 he wrote a monastic rule which exercised tremendous influence on the form and style of religious life. He is called the Father of Monasticism in the West.

533: John II became the first pope to change his name. The practice did not become general until the time of Sergius IV (1009).

533-534: Emperor Justinian promulgated the *Corpus Juris Civilis* for the Roman world. Like the *Theodosian Code,* it influenced subsequent civil and ecclesiastical law.

c. 545: Death of Dionysius Exiguus who introduced the division of history into periods before and after Christ — B.C., A.D. His calculations were at least four years in error (late).

553: The Ecumenical Council of Constantinople (II); see separate entry.

585: St. Columban founded an influential monastic school at Luxeuil. He died in 615.

589: The most important of several councils of Toledo was held. The Visigoths renounced Arianism, and St. Leander began the organization of the Church in Spain.

590-604: Pontificate of Pope St. Gregory I the Great. He set the form and style of the papacy which prevailed throughout the Middle Ages; exerted great influence on doctrine and liturgy; was strong in support of monastic discipline and clerical celibacy; authored writings on many subjects. Gregorian Chant is named in his honor.

596: Pope St. Gregory I the Great sent St. Augustine of Canterbury and 40 monks to do missionary work in England.

597: St. Columba died. He founded an important monastery at Iona, established

schools and did notable missionary work in Scotland.

By the end of the century, monasteries of nuns were common; Western monasticism was flourishing; monasticism in the East, under the influence of Monophysitism and other factors, was losing its vigor.

Seventh Century

613: St. Columban established the influential Monastery of Bobbio in northern Italy.

622: The Hegira (flight) of Mohammed from Mecca to Medina signalled the beginning of Islam which, by the end of the century, claimed almost all of the southern Mediterranean area.

629: Emperor Heraclius recovered the True Cross from the Persians.

649: A Lateran Council condemned two erroneous formulas *(Ecthesis* and *Type)* issued by emperors Heraclius and Constans II as means of reconciling Monophysites with the Church.

664: Actions of the Synod of Whitby advanced the adoption of Roman usages in England, especially regarding the date for the observance of Easter. (See Easter Controversy.)

680-681: The Ecumenical Council of Constantinople (III); see separate entry.

692: Trullan Synod. Eastern-Church discipline on clerical celibacy was settled, permitting marriage before ordination to the diaconate and continuation in marriage afterwards, but prohibiting marriage following the death of the wife thereafter. Anti-Roman canons contributed to East-West alienation.

During the century, the monastic influence of Ireland and England increased in Western Europe; schools and learning declined; regulations regarding clerical celibacy became more strict in the East.

Eighth Century

711: Moslems began the conquest of Spain.

716: Emperor Leo III, the Isaurian, launched a campaign against the veneration of sacred images and relics; called Iconoclasm (image-breaking), it caused turmoil in the East until about 843.

731: Pope Gregory II and a synod at Rome condemned Iconoclasm, with a declaration that the veneration of sacred images was in accord with Catholic tradition.

731: Venerable Bede issued his *Ecclesiastical History of the English People.*

732: Charles Martel defeated the Moslems at Poitiers, halting farther advance by them in the West.

744: The Monastery of Fulda was established by St. Sturm, a disciple of St. Boniface.

754: A council of more than 300 Byzantine bishops endorsed Iconoclast errors. This council and its actions were condemned by the Lateran Synod of 769.

Stephen II (III) crowned Pepin ruler of the Franks. Pepin twice invaded Italy, in 754 and 756, to defend the pope against the Lombards. His land grants to the papacy, called the Donation of Pepin, were later extended by Charlemagne (773) and formed part of the States of the Church.

c. 755: St. Boniface (Winfrid) was martyred. He was called the Apostle of Germany for his missionary work and organization of the hierarchy there.

781: Alcuin was chosen by Charlemagne to organize a Palace School, which became a center of intellectual leadership.

787: The Ecumenical Council of Nicaea (II); see separate entry.

792: A council at Ratisbon condemned Adoptionism.

The famous *Book of Kells* ("the Great Gospel of Columcille") dates from the early eighth or late seventh century.

Ninth Century

800: Charlemagne was crowned Emperor by Pope Leo III on Christmas Day.

Egbert became king of West Saxons. He unified England and strengthened the See of Canterbury.

813: Emperor Leo V, the Armenian, revived Iconoclasm, which persisted until about 843.

814: Charlemagne died.

843: The Treaty of Verdun split the Frankish kingdom among Charlemagne's three grandsons.

844: A Eucharistic controversy involving the writings of Paschasius Radbertus, Ratramnus and Rabanus Maurus occasioned the development of terminology regarding the doctrine of the Real Presence.

846: The Moslems invaded Italy and attacked Rome

847-852: Period of composition of the *False Decretals,* a collection of forged documents attributed to popes from St. Clement (88-97) to Gregory II (715-731). The *Decretals,* which strongly supported the autonomy and rights of bishops, were suspect for a long time before being repudiated entirely about 1628.

848: The Council of Mainz condemned Gottschalk for heretical teaching regarding predestination. He was also condemned by the Council of Quierzy in 853.

857: Photius displaced Ignatius as patriarch of Constantinople. This marked the beginning of the Photian Schism, a confused state of East-West relations which has not yet been cleared up by historical research. Photius, a man of exceptional ability, died in 891.

865: St. Ansgar, Apostle of Scandinavia, died.

868: Sts. Cyril (d. 869) and Methodius (d. 885) were consecrated bishops. The Apostles of the Slavs devised an alphabet and translat-

ed the Gospels and liturgy into the Slavonic language.

869: The Ecumenical Council of Constantinople (IV); see separate entry.

871-c. 900: Reign of Alfred the Great, the only English king ever anointed by a pope at Rome.

Tenth Century

910: William, Duke of Aquitaine, founded the Benedictine Abbey of Cluny, which became a center of monastic and ecclesiastical reform.

915: Pope John X played a leading role in the expulsion of Saracens from central and southern Italy.

955: St. Olga, of the Russian royal family, was baptized.

962: Otto I, the Great, crowned by Pope John XII, revived Charlemagne's kingdom, which became the Holy Roman Empire.

966: Mieszko, first of a royal line in Poland, was baptized; he brought Latin Christianity to Poland.

989: Vladimir, ruler of Russia, was baptized. Russia was subsequently Christianized by Greek missionaries.

993: John XV was the first pope to decree the official canonization of a saint (Ulrich) for the universal Church.

997: St. Stephen became ruler of Hungary. He assisted in organizing the hierarchy and establishing Latin Christianity in that country.

999-1003: Pontificate of Sylvester II (Gerbert of Aquitaine), a Benedictine monk and the first French pope.

Eleventh Century

1009: Beginning of lasting East-West schism in the Church, marked by dropping of the name of Pope Sergius IV from the Byzantine diptychs (the listing of persons prayed for during the liturgy). The deletion was made by Patriarch Sergius II of Constantinople.

1012: St. Romuald founded the Camaldolese Hermits.

1025: The Council of Arras, and other councils later, condemned the Cathari (Neo-Manichaeans, Albigenses).

1027: The Council of Elne proclaimed the Truce of God as a means of stemming violence. The truce involved armistice periods of varying length, which were later extended.

1038: St. John Gualbert founded the Vallombrosians.

1043-1059: Constantinople patriarchate of Michael Cerularius, the key figure in a controversy concerning the primacy of the papacy. His and the Byzantine synod's refusal to acknowledge this primacy in 1054 widened and hardened the East-West schism in the Church.

1047: Pope Clement II died. He was the only pope ever buried in Germany.

1049-54: Pontificate of St. Leo IX, who inaugurated a movement of papal, diocesan, monastic and clerical reform.

1055: Condemnation of the Eucharistic doctrine of Berengarius.

1059: A Lateran Council issued new legislation regarding papal elections. Voting power was entrusted to the Roman cardinals.

1066: Death of St. Edward the Confessor, King of England from 1042 and restorer of Westminster Abbey.

Defeat, at Hastings, of Harold by William I, who subsequently exerted strong influence on the life style of the Church in England.

1073-1085: Pontificate of St. Gregory VII (Hildebrand). A strong pope, he carried forward programs of clerical and general ecclesiastical reform and struggled against Henry IV and other rulers to end the evils of lay investiture. He introduced the Latin liturgy in Spain and set definite dates for the observance of ember days.

1077: Henry IV, excommunicated and suspended from the exercise of imperial powers by Gregory VII, sought absolution from the Pope at Canossa. Henry later repudiated this action and in 1084 forced Gregory to leave Rome.

1079: The Council of Rome condemned Eucharistic errors of Berengarius, who retracted.

1084: St. Bruno founded the Carthusians.

1097-1099: The first of several Crusades undertaken between this time and 1265. Recovery of the Holy Places and gaining free access to them for Christians were the original purposes, but these were diverted to less worthy objectives in various ways. Results included: a Latin Kingdom of Jerusalem, 1099-1187; a military and political misadventure in the form of a Latin Empire of Constantinople, 1204-1261; acquisition, by treaties, of visiting rights for Christians in the Holy Land. East-West economic and cultural relationships increased during the period. In the religious sphere, actions of the Crusaders had the effect of increasing the alienation of the East from the West.

1098: St. Robert founded the Cistercians.

Twelfth Century

1108: Beginnings of the influential Abbey and School of St. Victor.

1115: St. Bernard established the Abbey of Clairvaux and inaugurated the Cistercian Reform.

1118: Christian forces captured Saragossa, Spain; the beginning of the Moslem decline in that country.

1121: St. Norbert established the original monastery of the Praemonstratensians near Laon, France.

1122: The Concordat of Worms (Pactum Callixtinum) was formulated and approved by Pope Callistus II and Emperor Henry V to settle controversy concerning the investiture of prelates. The concordat provided that the emperor could invest prelates with symbols of temporal authority but had no right to invest them with spiritual authority, which came from the Church alone, and that the emperor was not to interfere in papal elections. This was the first concordat in history.

1123: The Ecumenical Council of the Lateran (I), the first of its kind in the West; see separate entry.

1139: The Ecumenical Council of the Lateran (II); see separate entry.

1140: St. Bernard met Abelard in debate at the Council of Sens. Abelard, whose rationalism in theology was condemned for the first time in 1121, died in 1142 at Cluny.

1148: The Synod of Rheims enacted strict disciplinary decrees for communities of women religious.

1152: The Synod of Kells reorganized the Church in Ireland.

1160: Gratian, whose *Decretum* became a basic text of Canon Law, died.

Peter Lombard, compiler of the *Four Books of Sentences,* a standard theology text for nearly 200 years, died.

1170: St. Thomas Becket, archbishop of Canterbury, who clashed with Henry II over Church-state relations, was murdered in his cathedral.

1171: Pope Alexander III reserved the process of canonization of saints to the Holy See.

1179: The Ecumenical Council of the Lateran (III); see separate entry.

1184: Waldenses and other heretics were excommunicated by Pope Lucius III.

Thirteenth Century

1198-1216: Pontificate of Innocent III, during which the papacy reached its medieval peak of authority, influence and prestige in the Church and in relations with civil rulers.

1208: Innocent III called for a crusade, the first in Christendom itself, against the Albigensians.

1209: Verbal approval was given by Innocent III to a rule of life for the Order of Friars Minor, started by St. Francis of Assisi.

1212: The Second Order of Franciscans, the Poor Clares, was founded.

1215: The Ecumenical Council of the Lateran (IV); see separate entry.

1216: Formal papal approval was given to a rule of life for the Order of Preachers, started by St. Dominic.

The Portiuncula Indulgence was granted by the Holy See at the request of St. Francis of Assisi.

1221: The Third Order of St. Francis for lay persons was founded.

1226: Death of St. Francis of Assisi.

1245: The Ecumenical Council of Lyons (I); see separate entry.

1247: Preliminary approval was given by the Holy See to a Carmelite rule of life.

1270: St. Louis IX, king of France, died.

Beginning of papal decline.

1274: The Ecumenical Council of Lyons (II); see separate entry.

Death of St. Thomas Aquinas, Doctor of the Church, of lasting influence; see separate entry.

1280: Pope Nicholas III, who made the *Breviary* the official prayer book for clergy of the Roman Church, died.

1281: The excommunication of Michael Palaeologus by Pope Martin IV ruptured the union effected with the Eastern Church in 1274.

Fourteenth Century

1302: Pope Boniface VIII issued the bull *Unam Sanctam*, concerning the unity of the Church and the temporal power of princes, against the background of a struggle with Philip IV of France; it was the most famous medieval document on the subject.

1308-1378: For a period of approximately 70 years, seven popes resided at Avignon because of unsettled conditions in Rome and other reasons; see separate entry.

1311-1312: The Ecumenical Council of Vienne; see separate entry.

1321: Dante Alighieri died a year after completing the *Divine Comedy*.

1324: Marsilius of Padua completed *Defensor Pacis*, a work condemned by Pope John XXII as heretical because of its denial of papal primacy and the hierarchical structure of the Church, and for other reasons. It was a charter for conciliarism.

1337-1453: Period of the Hundred Years' War, a dynastic struggle between France and England.

1338: Four years after the death of Pope John XXII, who had opposed Louis IV of Bavaria in a years-long controversy, electoral princes declared at the Diet of Rhense that the emperor did not need papal confirmation of his title and right to rule. Charles IV later (1356) said the same thing in a *Golden Bull*, eliminating papal rights in the election of emperors.

1347-1350: The Black Death swept across Europe, killing perhaps one-fourth to one-third of the total population; an estimated 40 per cent of the clergy succumbed.

1374: Petrarch, poet and humanist, died.

1378: Return of the papacy from Avignon to Rome.

Beginning of the Western Schism; see separate entry.

Fifteenth Century

1409: The Council of Pisa, without canonical authority, tried to end the Western Schism but succeeded only in complicating it by electing a third claimant to the papacy; see Western Schism.

1414-1418: The Ecumenical Council of Constance ended the Western Schism; see separate entry.

1431: St. Joan of Arc was burned at the stake.

1431-1449: The Council of Basle, which began with convocation by Pope Martin V in 1431, turned into an anti-papal forum of conciliarists seeking to subject the primacy and authority of the pope to the overriding authority of an assembly of bishops. It was not an ecumenical council.

1438: The Pragmatic Sanction of Bourges was enacted by Charles VIII and the French parliament to curtail papal authority over the Church in France, in the spirit of conciliarism. It found expression in Gallicanism and had effects lasting at least until the French Revolution.

1438-1443: The Ecumenical Council of Florence affirmed the primacy of the pope in opposition to conciliarism and effected a measure of union with separated Eastern Christians; see separate entry.

1453: The fall of Constantinople to the Turks.

c. 1456: Gutenberg issued the first edition of the Bible printed from movable type, at Mainz, Germany.

1476: Pope Sixtus IV ordered observance of the feast of the Immaculate Conception on Dec. 8 throughout the Church.

1492: Columbus discovered the Americas.

1493: Pope Alexander VI issued a *Bull of Demarcation* which determined spheres of influence for the Spanish and Portuguese in the Americas.

The Renaissance, a humanistic movement which originated in Italy in the 14th century, spread to France, Germany, the Low Countries and England. A transitional period between the medieval world and the modern secular world, it introduced profound changes which affected literature and the other arts, general culture, politics and religion.

Sixteenth Century

1512-1517: The Ecumenical Council of the Lateran (V); see separate entry.

1517: Martin Luther signalled the beginning of the Reformation by posting 95 theses at Wittenberg. Subsequently, he broke completely from doctrinal orthodoxy in discourses and three published works (1519 and 1520); was excommunicated on more than 40 charges of heresy (1521); remained the dominant figure in the Reformation in Germany until his death in 1546.

1519: Zwingli triggered the Reformation in Zurich and became its leading proponent there until his death in combat in 1531.

1524: Luther's encouragement of German princes in putting down the two-year Peasants' Revolt gained political support for his cause.

1528: The Order of Friars Minor Capuchin was approved as an autonomous division of the Franciscan Order; like the Jesuits, the

Capuchins became leaders in the Counter-Reformation.

1530: The *Augsburg Confession* of Lutheran faith was issued; it was later supplemented by the *Smalcald Articles* approved in 1537.

1533: Henry VIII divorced Catherine of Aragon, married Anne Boleyn, was excommunicated. In 1534 he decreed the Act of Supremacy, making the sovereign the head of the Church in England, under which Sts. John Fisher and Thomas More were executed in 1535. Despite his rejection of papal primacy and actions against monastic life in England, he generally maintained doctrinal orthodoxy until his death in 1547.

1536: John Calvin, leader of the Reformation in Switzerland until his death in 1564, issued the first edition of *Institutes of the Christian Religion,* which became the classical text of Reformed (non-Lutheran) theology.

1540: The constitutions of the Society of Jesus (Jesuits), founded by St. Ignatius of Loyola, were approved.

1541: Start of the 11-year career of St. Francis Xavier as a missionary to the East Indies and Japan.

1545-1563: The Ecumenical Council of Trent formulated statements of Catholic doctrine under attack by the Reformers and mobilized the Counter-Reformation; see separate entry.

1549: The first *Book of Common Prayer* was issued by Edward VI. Revised editions were published in 1552, 1559 and 1662.

1553: Start of the five-year reign of Mary Tudor who tried to counteract actions of Henry VIII against the Roman Church.

1555: Enactment of the Peace of Augsburg, an arrangement of religious territorialism rather than toleration, which recognized the existence of Catholicism and Lutheranism in the German Empire and provided that citizens should adopt the religion of their respective rulers.

1558: Beginning of the reign of Elizabeth I, during which the Church of England took on its definitive form.

1559: Establishment of the hierarchy of the Church of England, with the consecration of Matthew Parker as archbishop of Canterbury.

1563: The first text of the *39 Articles* of the Church of England was issued. Also enacted were a new Act of Supremacy and Oath of Succession to the English throne.

1570: Elizabeth I was excommunicated. Penal measures against Catholics subsequently became more severe.

1571: Defeat of the Turkish armada at Lepanto staved off the invasion of Eastern Europe.

1577: The *Formula of Concord,* the classical statement of Lutheran faith, was issued; it was, generally, a Lutheran counterpart of the canons of the Council of Trent. In 1580, along with other formulas of doctrine, it was included in the *Book of Concord.*

1582: The Gregorian Calendar, named for Pope Gregory XIII, was put into effect and was eventually adopted in most countries: England delayed adoption until 1752.

Seventeenth Century

1605: The Gunpowder Plot, an attempt by Catholic fanatics to blow up James I of England and the houses of Parliament, resulted in an anti-Catholic Oath of Allegiance; the Oath was condemned by Pope Paul V in 1606.

1610: Death of Matteo Ricci, outstanding Jesuit missionary to China, pioneer in cultural relations between China and Europe.

Founding of the first community of Visitation Nuns by Sts. Francis de Sales and Jane de Chantal.

1611: Founding of the Oratorians.

1613: Catholics were banned from Scandinavia.

1625: Founding of the Congregation of the Mission (Vincentians) by St. Vincent de Paul. He founded the Sisters of Charity in 1633.

1642: Death of Galileo, scientist, who was censured by the Congregation of the Holy Office for supporting the Copernican theory of the sun-centered planetary system.

Founding of the Sulpicians by Jacques Olier.

1643: Start of publication of the Bollandist *Acta Sanctorum,* a critical work on lives of the saints.

1648: Provisions in the Peace of Westphalia, ending the Thirty Years' War, extended terms of the Peace of Augsburg (1555) to Calvinists and gave equality to Catholics and Protestants in the 300 states of the Holy Roman Empire.

1649: Oliver Cromwell invaded Ireland and began a severe persecution of the Church there.

1653: Pope Innocent X condemned five propositions of Jansenism, a complex theory which distorted doctrine concerning the relations between divine grace and human freedom. Jansenism was also a rigoristic movement which seriously disturbed the Church in France, the Low Countries and Italy in this and the 18th century.

1673: The Test Act in England barred from public office Catholics who would not deny the doctrine of transubstantiation and receive Communion in the Church of England.

1678: Many English Catholics suffered death as a consequence of the Popish Plot, a false allegation by Titus Oates that Catholics planned to assassinate Charles I, land a French army in the country, burn London, and turn over the government to the Jesuits.

1682: The four articles of the *Gallican Declaration,* drawn up by Bossuet, asserted political and ecclesiastical immunities of France from papal control. The articles, which rejected the primacy of the pope, were condemned in 1690.

1689: The Toleration Act granted a measure of freedom of worship to other English dissenters but not to Catholics.

This century is called the age of Enlightenment or Reason because of the predominating rational and scientific approach of its leading philosophers, scientists and writers with respect to religion, ethics and natural law. This approach downgraded the fact and significance of revealed religion. Also characteristic of the Enlightenment were subjectivism, secularism and optimism regarding human perfectibility.

Eighteenth Century

1704: Chinese Rites—involving the Christian adaptation of elements of Confucianism, veneration of ancestors and Chinese terminology in religion — were condemned by Clement XI. Similar bans were issued in 1645 and 1742.

1720: The Passionists were founded by St. Paul of the Cross.

1724: Persecution in China.

1732: The Redemptorists were founded by St. Alphonsus Liguori.

1738: Freemasonry was condemned by Clement XII and Catholics were forbidden to join, under penalty of excommunication; the prohibition was repeated by Benedict XIV in 1751 and by later popes.

1760's: Josephinism, a theory and system of state control of the Church, was initiated in Austria; it remained in force until about 1850.

1764: Febronianism, an unorthodox theory and practice regarding the constitution of the Church and relations between Church and state, was condemned for the first of several times. Proposed by an auxiliary bishop of Trier using the pseudonym Justinus Febronius, it had the effects of minimizing the office of the pope and supporting national churches under state control.

1773: Clement XIV issued a brief of suppression against the Jesuits, following their expulsion from Portugal in 1759, from France in 1764 and from Spain in 1767. Political intrigue and unsubstantiated accusations were principal factors in these developments. The ban, which crippled the Society, contained no condemnation of the Jesuit constitutions, particular Jesuits or Jesuit teaching. The Society was restored in 1814.

1778: Catholics in England were relieved of some civil disabilities dating back to the time of Henry VIII, by an act which permitted them to acquire, own and inherit property. Additional liberties were restored by the Roman Catholic Relief Act of 1791 and subsequent enactments of Parliament.

1789: Religious freedom in the United States was guaranteed under the First Amendment to the Constitution.

Beginning of the French Revolution which resulted in: the secularization of church property and the Civil Constitution of the Clergy in 1790; the persecution of priests, religious and lay persons loyal to papal authority; invasion of the Papal States by Napoleon in 1796; renewal of persecution from 1797-1799; attempts to dechristianize France and establish a new religion; the occupation of Rome by French troops and the forced removal of Pius VI to France in 1798.

Nineteenth Century

1809: Pius VII was made a captive by Napoleon and deported to France where he remained in exile until 1814. During this time he refused to cooperate with Napoleon who sought to bring the Church in France under his own control.

The turbulence in church-state relations in France at the beginning of the century recurred in connection with the Bourbon Restoration, the July Revolution, the second and third Republics, the Second Empire and the Dreyfus case.

1814: The Society of Jesus, suppressed since 1773, was restored.

1817: Reestablishment of the Congregation for the Propagation of the Faith (Propaganda) by Pius VII was an important factor in increasing missionary activity during the century.

1820: Years-long persecution, during which thousands died for the faith, ended in China. Thereafter, communication with the West remained cut off until about 1834. Vigorous missionary work got underway in 1842.

1822: The Pontifical Society for the Propagation of the Faith, inaugurated in France by Pauline Jaricot for the support of missionary activity, was established.

1829: The Catholic Emancipation Act relieved Catholics in England and Ireland of most of the civil disabilities to which they had been subject from the time of Henry VIII.

1832: Gregory XVI, in the encyclical *Mirari Vos,* condemned indifferentism, one of the many ideologies at odds with Christian doctrine which were proposed during the century.

1833: Start of the Oxford Movement which affected the Church of England and resulted in some notable conversions, including that of John Henry Newman in 1845, to the Catholic Church.

Frederick Ozanam founded the Society of St. Vincent de Paul in France. The society, whose objective was works of charity, became worldwide.

1848: The *Communist Manifesto,* a revolutionary document symptomatic of socio-economic crisis, was issued.

1850: The hierarchy was reestablished in England and Nicholas Wiseman made the first archbishop of Westminster. He was succeeded in 1865 by Henry Manning, an Oxford convert and proponent of the rights of labor.

1853: The Catholic hierarchy was reestablished in Holland.

1854: Pius IX proclaimed the dogma of the Immaculate Conception in the bull *Ineffabilis Deus.*

1858: The Blessed Virgin Mary appeared to St. Bernadette at Lourdes, France; see separate entry.

1864: Pius IX issued the encyclical *Quanta Cura* and the *Syllabus of Errors* in condemnation of some 80 propositions derived from the scientific mentality and rationalism of the century. The subjects in question had deep ramifications in many areas of thought and human endeavor; in religion, they explicitly and/or implicitly rejected divine revelation and the supernatural order.

1867: The first volume of *Das Kapital* was published. Together with the Communist First International, formed in the same year, it had great influence on the subsequent development of Communism and Socialism.

1869: The Anglican Church was disestablished in Ireland.

1869-1870: The First Vatican Council; see separate entry.

1870-1871: Victor Emmanuel II of Sardinia, crowned king of Italy after defeating Austrian and papal forces, marched into Rome in 1870 and expropriated the Papal States after a plebiscite in which Catholics, at the order of Pius IX, did not vote. In 1871, Pius IX refused to accept a Law of Guarantees. Confiscation of church property and hindrance of ecclesiastical administration by the regime followed.

1871: The German Empire, a confederation of 26 states, was formed. Government policy launched a Kulturkampf whose May Laws of 1873 were designed to annul papal jurisdiction in Prussia and other states and to place the Church under imperial control. Resistance to the enactments and the persecution they legalized forced the government to modify its anti-Church policy by 1887.

1878: Beginning of the pontificate of Leo XIII, who was pope until his death in 1903. Leo is best known for the encyclical *Rerum Novarum,* which greatly influenced the course of Christian social thought and the labor movement. His other accomplishments included promotion of a revival of Scholastic philosophy and the impetus he gave to scriptural studies.

1881: The first International Eucharistic Congress was held in Lille, France.

Alexander II of Russia died. His policies of Russification — as well as those of his two predecessors and a successor during the century — caused great suffering to Catholics, Jews and Protestants in Poland, Lithuania, the Ukraine and Bessarabia.

1882: Charles Darwin died. His theory of evolution by natural selection, one of several scientific highlights of the century, had extensive repercussions in the faith-and-science controversy.

1889: The Catholic University of America was founded in Washington, D.C.

1893: The US apostolic delegation was set up in Washington, D. C.

Twentieth Century

1901: Restrictive measures in France forced the Jesuits, Benedictines, Carmelites and other religious orders to leave the country. Subsequently, 14,000 schools were suppressed; religious orders and congregations were expelled; the concordat was renounced in 1905; church property was confiscated in 1906. For some years the Holy See, refusing to comply with government demands for the control of bishops' appointments, left some ecclesiastical offices vacant.

1903: Start of the 11-year pontificate of St. Pius X. He initiated the codification of canon law, 1904; removed the ban against participation by Catholics in Italian national elections, 1905; issued decrees calling upon the faithful to receive Holy Communion frequently and daily, and stating that children should begin receiving the Eucharist at the age of seven, 1905 and 1910, respectively; ordered the establishment of the Confraternity of Christian Doctrine in all parishes throughout the world, 1905; condemned Modernism in the decree *Lamentabili* and the encyclical *Pascendi,* 1907.

1908: The United States and England, long under the jurisdiction of the Congregation for the Propagation of the Faith as mission territories, were removed from its control and placed under the common law of the Church.

1910: Laws of separation were enacted in Portugal, marking a point of departure in church-state relations.

1911: The Catholic Foreign Mission Society of America — Maryknoll, the first US-founded society of its type — was established.

1914: Start of World War I, which lasted until 1918.

Start of the eight-year pontificate of Benedict XV. Much of his pontificate was devoted to seeking ways and means of minimizing the material and spiritual havoc of World War I. In 1917 he offered his services as a mediator to the belligerent nations, but his pleas for settlement of the conflict went unheeded.

1917: The Blessed Virgin Mary appeared to three children at Fatima, Portugal; see separate entry.

A new constitution, embodying repressive laws against the Church, was enacted in Mexico. Its implementation resulted in persecution in the 1920s and 1930s.

Bolsheviks seized power in Russia and set up a Communist dictatorship. The event marked the rise of Communism in Russian and world affairs. One of its immediate, and lasting, results was persecution of the Church, Jews and other segments of the population.

1918: The *Code of Canon Law,* in preparation for more than 10 years, went into effect in the Western Church.

1919: Benedict XV stimulated missionary work through the decree *Maximum Illud,* in which he urged the recruiting and training of native clergy in places where the Church was not firmly established.

1922: Beginning of the 17-year pontificate of Pius XI. He subscribed to the Lateran Treaty, 1929, which settled the Roman Question created by the confiscation of the Papal States in 1871; issued the encyclical *Casti Connubii,* 1930, an authoritative statement on Christian marriage; resisted the efforts of Benito Mussolini to control Catholic Action and the Church, in the encyclical *Non Abbiamo Bisogno,* 1931; opposed various Fascist policies; issued the encyclicals *Quadragesimo Anno,* 1931, developing the social doctrine of Leo XIII's *Rerum Novarum,* and *Divini Redemptoris,* 1937, calling for social justice and condemning atheistic Communism; condemned anti-Semitism, 1937.

Ireland was partitioned. All but two of the predominantly Catholic counties were included in the southern part of the country, which eventually attained the status of an independent republic in 1949.

1926: The Catholic Relief Act repealed virtually all legal disabilities of Catholics in England.

1931: Leftists proclaimed Spain a republic and proceeded to disestablish the Church, confiscate church property, deny salaries to the clergy, expel the Jesuits and ban teaching of the Catholic faith. These actions were preludes to the civil war of 1936-1939.

1933: Emergence of Adolf Hitler to power in Germany. By 1935 two of his aims were clear, the elimination of the Jews and control of a single national church. Persecution decimated the Jews over a period of years. The Church was subject to repressive measures, which Pius XI protested futilely in the encyclical *Mit Brennender Sorge* in 1937.

1936: A three-year civil war broke out in Spain between the leftist Loyalists and forces led by Francisco Franco. The Loyalists were defeated and one-man, one-party rule was established. A number of priests, religious and lay persons fell victims to Loyalist persecution.

71939: Start of World War II, which lasted until 1945.

Start of the 19-year pontificate of Pius XII; see separate entry.

1940: Start of a decade of Communist conquest in more than 13 countries, resulting in conditions of persecution for a minimum of 60 million Catholics as well as members of other faiths; see various countries.

Persecution diminished in Mexico through non-enforcement of anti-religious laws still on record.

1950: Pius XII proclaimed the dogma of the Assumption of the Blessed Virgin Mary.

1954: St. Pius X was canonized.

1957: The Communist regime of China attempted to start a national schismatic church.

1958: Beginning of the five-year pontificate of John XXIII; see separate entry.

1962: The Second Vatican Council began the first of four sessions; see separate entry.

1963: Paul VI began his pontificate; see separate entry.

HERESIES

Heresy is the formal and obstinate denial or doubt by a baptized person, who remains a nominal Christian, of any truth which must be believed as a matter of divine and Catholic faith. Formal heresy involves deliberate resistance to the authority of God who communicates revelation through Scripture and tradition and the teaching authority of the Church. Obstinate refusal to accept the infallible teaching of the Church constitutes the canonical crime of heresy.

Formal heretics automatically incur the penalty of excommunication (Canon 1325 of the Code of Canon Law). Material heretics are those who, in good faith and without formal obstinacy, do not accept articles or matters of divine and Catholic faith.

Heresies have been significant not only as disruptions of unity of faith but also as occasions for the clarification and development of doctrine.

Heresies from the beginning of the Church to the 13th century are listed below.

Judaizers: Early converts who claimed that members of the Church had to observe all the requirements of Mosaic Law as well as the obligations of Christian faith. This view was condemned by the Council of Jerusalem held in 51 under the presidency of St. Peter (Acts 15:28).

Gnosticism: A combination of elements of Platonic philosophy and Eastern mystery religions which claimed that its secret knowledge-principle gave its adherents a deeper insight into Christian doctrine than divine revelation and faith. One Gnostic thesis denied the divinity of Christ; others denied the reality of his humanity, calling it mere appearance (**Docetism, Phantasiasm**).

Modalism: A general term covering propositions (**Monarchianism, Patripassianism, Sabellianism**) that the Father, Son and Holy Spirit are not really distinct divine Persons but are only three different modes of being and self-manifestation of the one God. Various forms of Modalism, which appeared in the East in the second century and spread westward, were all condemned.

Marcionism: A Gnostic creation named for its author, who claimed there was total opposition and no connection at all between the Old Testament and the New Testament, between the God of the Jews and the God of the Christians; and that the canon of Scripture consisted only of portions of Luke's Gospel and 10 Epistles of Paul. Marcion was excommunicated in 144 at Rome, and his tenets were condemned again by a Roman council about 260. The heresy was checked at Rome by 200 but persisted for several centuries in the East and had some adherents as late as the Middle Ages.

Montanism: A form of extremism preached about 170 by Montanus of Phrygia, Asia Minor. Its principal tenets were: an imminent second coming of Christ, denial of the divine nature of the Church and its power to forgive sin, excessively rigorous morality. Condemned by Pope St. Zephyrinus (199-217). Tertullian was one of its victims.

Novatianism: A heresy of excessive rigorism named for its author, a priest of Rome and antipope. Its principal tenet was that persons who fell away from the Church under persecution and/or those guilty of serious sin after baptism could not be absolved and readmitted to communion with the Church. The heresy, condemned by a Roman synod in 251, slowly subsided in the West and died in the East by the end of the seventh century.

Subordinationism, Adoptionism: Christological errors and logical antecedents of Arianism. The key tenet was that Christ, while the most excellent of creatures, was subordinate to God whose Son he was by adoption rather than by nature. First proposed at Rome late in the second century, it was condemned by Pope St. Victor in 190 and again in the following century, in 785 by Pope Adrian I, in 794 by a Council of Frankfurt, and in 1177 by Pope Alexander III.

Arianism: Denial of the divinity of Christ, the most devastating of the early heresies, authored by Arius of Alexandria and condemned by the Council of Nicaea I in 325. Arians and several kinds of **Semi-Arians** propagandized their tenets widely, raised havoc in the Church for several centuries, and established their own hierarchies and churches.

Macedonianism: Denial of the divinity of the Holy Spirit, who was said to be a creature of the Son. Condemned by the Council of Constantinople I in 381. Macedonians were also called **Pneumatomachists,** enemies of the Spirit; and **Marathonians,** after the name of one of their leaders, a bishop of Nicomedia.

Nestorianism: Denial of the real unity of divine and human natures in the single divine Person of Christ, proposed by Nestorius, patriarch of Constantinople. He also held that Mary could not be called the Mother of God *(Theotokos);* that is, of the Second Person of the Trinity made Man. Condemned by the councils of Ephesus in 431 and Chalcedon in 451.

Monophysitism: Denial of Christ's human nature; also called **Eutychianism,** after the name of one of its leading advocates. Condemned by the Council of Chalcedon in 451.

Monothelitism: Denial of the human will of Christ. Severus of Antioch and Sergius, patriarch of Constantinople, were leading advocates of the heresy, which was condemned by the Council of Constantinople III in 681.

Priscillianism: A fourth century amalgamation of elements from various sources — Sabellianism, Arianism, Docetism, Pantheism, belief in the diabolical nature of marriage, corruption of Scripture. Condemned by a Council of Braga in 563 on 17 different counts.

Donatism: A development of the error at the heart of the third century **Rebaptism Controversy** (baptism conferred by heretics is invalid because persons deprived of grace are incapable of being ministers of grace to others). Followers of Donatus the Great asserted throughout the fourth century that sacraments administered by sinners were invalid. Condemnation of the heresy is traced to Pope St. Stephen I (254-257) and the principle that sacraments have their efficacy from Christ, not from their human ministers.

Pelagianism: Denial of the supernatural order of things, proposed by Pelagius (360-420), a Breton monk. Proceeding from the assumption that Adam had a natural right to supernatural life, the theory held that man could attain salvation through the efforts of his own free will and natural powers. The theory involved errors concerning the nature of original sin, the meaning of grace and other matters. St. Augustine opposed the heresy, which was condemned by the Council of Ephesus in 431. **Semi-Pelagianism** was condemned by a Council of Orange in 529.

Iconoclasm: An image-breaking campaign which resulted from an edict issued by Eastern Emperor Leo the Isaurian in 726, that the veneration of images, pictures and relics was idolatrous. The theoretical basis of the heresy was the Monophysite error which denied the humanity of Christ. It was denounced several times before its condemnation by the Council of Nicaea II in 787.

Berengarian Heresy: Denial of the Real Presence of Christ under the appearances of bread and wine, the first clear-cut Eucharistic heresy; proposed by Berengarius of Tours (c. 1000-1088). Condemned by various synods and finally by a council held at Rome in 1079.

Waldensianism: Claimed by Peter Waldo, a merchant of Lyons, to be a return to pure Christianity, the heresy rejected the hierarchical structure of the Church, the sacramental system and other doctrines. Its adherents were excommunicated in 1184 and their tenets were condemned several times thereafter.

Albigensianism, Catharism: Related errors based on the old **Manichaean** assumption that two supreme principles of good and evil were operative in creation and life, and that the supreme objective of human endeavor was liberation from evil (matter). The heresy denied the humanity of Christ, the sacramental system and the authority of the Church (and state), and endorsed a moral code which threatened seriously the fabric of social life in southern France and northern Italy in the 12th and 13th centuries. Condemned by councils of the Lateran III and Lateran IV in 1179 and 1215.

ECUMENICAL COUNCILS

An ecumenical council is an assembly of the college of bishops, with and under the presidency of the pope, which has supreme authority over the Church in matters pertaining to faith, morals, worship and discipline.

The Second Vatican Council stated: "The supreme authority with which this college (of bishops) is empowered over the whole Church is exercised in a solemn way through an ecumenical council. A council is never ecumenical unless it is confirmed or at least accepted as such by the successor of Peter. It is the prerogative of the Roman Pontiff to convoke these councils, to preside over them, and to confirm them" (*Dogmatic Constitution on the Church,* (No. 22).

Pope Presides

The pope is the head of an ecumenical council; he presides over it either personally or through legates. Conciliar decrees and other actions have binding force only when confirmed and promulgated by him. If a pope dies during a council, it is suspended until reconvened by another pope. An ecumenical council is not superior to a pope; hence, there is no appeal from a pope to a council.

Collectively, the bishops with the pope represent the whole Church. They do this not as democratic representatives of their faithful in a kind of church parliament, but as the successors of the Apostles with divinely given authority, care and responsibility over the whole Church.

Council participants with a deliberative vote are: cardinals; residential patriarchs, primates, archbishops and bishops, even if they are not yet consecrated; abbots and certain other prelates, an abbot primate, abbot superiors of monastic congregations and heads of exempt clerical religious; titular bishops, on invitation. Experts in theology and canon law may be given a consultative vote. Others, including lay persons, may address a council or observe its actions, but may not vote.

Basic legislation concerning ecumenical councils is contained in Canons 222-229 of the Code of Canon Law. Basic doctrinal considerations were stated by the Second Vatican Council in the *Dogmatic Constitution on the Church.*

Background

Ecumenical councils had their prototype in the Council of Jerusalem in 51, at which the Apostles under the leadership of St. Peter decided that converts to the Christian faith were not obliged to observe all the prescriptions of Old Testament law (Acts 15). As early as the second century, bishops got together in regional meetings, synods or councils to take common action for the doctrinal and pastoral good of their communities of faithful. The expansion of such limited assemblies to general or ecumenical councils was a logical and historical evolution, given the nature and needs of the Church.

Emperors were active in summoning or convoking the first eight councils, especially the first five and the eighth. Among reasons for intervention of this kind were the facts that the emperors regarded themselves as guardians of the faith; that the settlement of religious controversies, which had repercussions in political and social turmoil, served the cause of peace in the state; and that the emperors had at their disposal ways and means of facilitating gatherings of bishops. Imperial actions, however, did not account for the formally ecumenical nature of the councils.

Some councils were attended by relatively few bishops, and the ecumenical character of several was open to question for a time. However, confirmation and de facto recognition of their actions by popes and subsequent councils established them as ecumenical.

Role in History

The councils have played a highly significant role in the history of the Church by witnessing to and defining truths of revelation, by shaping forms of worship and discipline, and by promoting measures for the ever-necessary reform and renewal of Catholic life. In general, they have represented attempts of the Church to mobilize itself in times of crisis for self-preservation, self-purification and growth.

The first eight ecumenical councils were held in the East; the other 13, in the West. The majority of separated Eastern Churches — e.g., the Orthodox — recognize the ecumenical character of the first seven councils, which formulated a great deal of basic doctrine. Nestorians, however, acknowledge only the first two councils; the Monophysite Armenians, Syrians, and Copts acknowledge the first three.

The 21 ecumenical councils in the history of the Church are listed below, with indication of their names or titles (taken from the names of the places where they were held); the dates; the reigning and/or approving popes; the emperors who were instrumental in convoking the eight councils in the East; the number of bishops who attended, when available; the number of sessions; the most significant actions.

The 21 Councils

1. Nicaea I, 325: St. Sylvester I (Emperor Constantine I); attended by approximately 300 bishops; sessions held between May 20 or

June 19 to near the end of August. Condemned Arianism, which denied the divinity of Christ; contributed to formulation of the Nicene Creed; fixed the date of Easter; passed regulations concerning clerical discipline; adopted the civil division of the Empire as the model for the organization of the Church.

2. Constantinople I, 381: St. Damasus I (Emperor Theodosius I); attended by approximately 150 bishops; sessions held from May to July. Condemned various brands of Arianism, and Macedonianism which denied the divinity of the Holy Spirit, contributed to formulation of the Nicene Creed; approved a canon which made the bishop of Constantinople the ranking prelate in the East, with primacy next to that of the pope. Doubt about the ecumenical character of this council was resolved by the ratification of its acts by popes and the Council of Chalcedon.

3. Ephesus, 431: St. Celestine I (Emperor Theodosius II); attended by 150 to 200 bishops; five sessions held between June 22 and July 17. Condemned Nestorianism, which denied the real unity of the divine and human natures in the Person of Christ; defined *Theotokos* ("Bearer of God") as the title of Mary, Mother of the Son of God made Man; condemned Pelagianism, which reduced the supernatural to the natural order of things.

4. Chalcedon, 451: St. Leo I (Emperor Marcian); attended by approximately 600 bishops; 17 sessions held between Oct. 8 and Nov. 1. Condemned: Monophysitism, also called Eutychianism, which denied the humanity of Christ by holding that he had only one, the divine, nature; and the Monophysite Robber Synod of Ephesus, of 449.

5. Constantinople II, 553: Vigilius (Emperor Justinian I); attended by 165 bishops; eight sessions held between May 5 and June 2. Condemned the *Three Chapters,* Nestorian-tainted writings of Theodore of Mopsuestia, Theodoret of Cyprus and Ibas of Edessa.

6. Constantinople III, 680-681: St. Agatho, St. Leo II (Emperor Constantine IV); attended by approximately 170 bishops; 16 sessions held between Nov. 7, 680, and Sept. 16, 681. Condemned Monothelitism, which held that there was only one will, the divine, in Christ; censured Pope Honorius I for a letter to Sergius, bishop of Constantinople, in which he made an ambiguous but not infallible statement about the unity of will and/or operation in Christ. Constantinople III is also called the Trullan Council because its sessions were held in the domed hall, Trullos, of the palace.

7. Nicaea II, 787: Adrian I (Empress Irene); attended by approximately 300 bishops; eight sessions held between Sept. 24 and Oct. 23. Condemned: Iconoclasm, which held that the use of images was idolatry; and Adoptionism, which claimed that Christ was not the Son of God by nature but only by adoption. This was the last council regarded as ecumenical by Orthodox Churches.

8. Constantinople IV 869-870: Adrian II (Emperor Basil I); attended by 102 bishops; six sessions held between Oct. 5, 869, and Feb. 28, 870. Condemned Iconoclasm; condemned and deposed Photius as patriarch of Constantinople; restored Ignatius to the patriarchate. This was the last ecumenical council held in the East. It was first called ecumenical by canonists toward the end of the 11th century.

9. Lateran I, 1123: Callistus II; attended by approximately 300 bishops; sessions held between Mar. 18 and Apr. 6. Endorsed provisions of the Concordat of Worms concerning the investiture of prelates; approved reform measures in 25 canons.

10. Lateran II, 1139: Innocent II; attended by 900 to 1,000 bishops and abbots; three sessions held in April. Adopted measures against a schism organized by antipope Anacletus; approved 30 disciplinary measures and canons, one of which stated that holy orders is an invalidating impediment to marriage.

11. Lateran III, 1179: Alexander III; attended by at least 300 bishops; three sessions held between Mar. 5 and 19. Enacted measures against the Waldenses and Albigensians; approved reform decrees in 27 canons; provided that popes be elected by two-thirds vote of the cardinals.

12. Lateran IV, 1215: Innocent III; sessions held between Nov. 11 and 30. Ordered annual confession and Communion; defined and made first official use of the term "transubstantiation"; adopted measures to counteract the Cathari and Albigensians; approved 70 canons.

13. Lyons I, 1245: Innocent IV; attended by approximately 150 bishops; three sessions held between June 28 and July 17. Confirmed the deposition of Emperor Frederick II; approved 22 canons.

14. Lyons II, 1274: Gregory X; attended by approximately 500 bishops; six sessions held between May 7 and July 17. Accomplished a temporary reunion of separated Eastern Churches with the Roman Church; issued regulations concerning conclaves for papal elections; approved 31 canons.

15. Vienne, 1311-1312: Clement V; attended by 132 bishops; three sessions held between Oct. 16, 1311, and May 6, 1312. Suppressed the Knights Templar; enacted a number of reform decrees.

16. Constance, 1414-1418: Gregory XII, Martin V; attended by nearly 200 bishops, plus other prelates and many experts; 45 sessions held between Nov. 5, 1414, and Apr. 22, 1418. Took successful action to end the Western Schism; rejected the teachings of Wycliff; condemned Hus as a heretic. One decree, passed in the earlier stages of the council, asserted the superiority of an ecumenical council over the pope; this was later rejected.

17. Florence (also called Basel-Ferrara-Florence), 1438-1445: Eugene IV; attended by many Latin-Rite and Eastern-Rite bishops; preliminary sessions were held at Basel and Ferrara before definitive work was accomplished at Florence. Reaffirmed the primacy of the pope against the claims of Conciliarists that an ecumenical council is superior to the pope; formulated and approved decrees of union — with the Greeks, July 6, 1439; with the Armenians, Nov. 22, 1439; with the Jacobites, Feb. 4, 1442. These decrees failed to gain general or lasting acceptance in the East.

18. Lateran V, 1512-1517: Julius II, Leo X; 12 sessions held between May 3, 1512, and Mar. 16, 1517. Stated the relation and position of the pope with respect to an ecumenical council; acted to counteract the Pragmatic Sanction of Bourges and exaggerated claims of liberty by the French Church; condemned erroneous teachings concerning the nature of the human soul; stated doctrine concerning indulgences. The council reflected concern for abuses in the Church and the need for reforms but failed to take decisive action in the years immediately preceding the Reformation.

19. Trent, 1545-1563: Paul III, Julius III, Pius IV; 25 sessions held between Dec. 13, 1545, and Dec. 4, 1563. Issued a great number of decrees concerning doctrinal matters opposed by the Reformers, and mobilized the Counter-Reformation. Definitions covered the rule of faith, the nature of justification, grace, faith, original sin and its effects, the seven sacraments, the sacrificial nature of the Mass, the veneration of saints, use of sacred images, belief in purgatory, the doctrine of indulgences, the jurisdiction of the pope over the whole Church. Initiated many reforms for renewal in the liturgy and general discipline in the Church, the promotion of religious instruction, the education of the clergy through the foundation of seminaries, etc. Trent ranks with Vatican II as the greatest ecumenical council held in the West.

20. Vatican I, 1869-1870: Pius IX; attended by approximately 800 bishops and other prelates; four public sessions and 89 general meetings held between Dec. 8, 1869, and July 7, 1870. Defined papal primacy and infallibility in a dogmatic constitution on the Church; covered natural religion, revelation, faith, and the relations between faith and reason in a dogmatic constitution on the Catholic faith. The council suspended sessions Sept. 1 and was adjourned Oct. 20, 1870.

Vatican II

The Second Vatican Council, which was forecast by Pope John XXIII Jan. 25, 1959, was held in four sessions in St. Peter's Basilica.

Pope John convoked it and opened the first session, which ran from Sept. 11 to Dec. 8, 1962. Following John's death June 3, 1963, Pope Paul VI reconvened the council for the other three sessions which ran from Sept. 29 to Dec. 4, 1963; Sept. 14 to Nov. 21, 1964; Sept. 14 to Dec. 8, 1965.

A total of 2,860 Fathers participated in council proceedings, and attendance at meetings varied between 2,000 and 2,500. For various reasons, including the denial of exit from Communist-dominated countries, 274 Fathers could not attend.

The council formulated and promulgated 16 documents — two dogmatic and two pastoral constitutions, nine decrees and three declarations — all of which reflect its basic pastoral orientation toward renewal and reform in the Church. Given below are the Latin and English titles of the documents and their dates of promulgation.

• *Lumen Gentium* (Dogmatic Constitution on the Church), Nov. 21, 1964.

• *Dei Verbum* (Dogmatic Constitution on Divine Revelation), Nov. 18, 1965.

• *Sacrosanctum Concilium* (Constitution on the Sacred Liturgy), Dec. 4, 1963.

• *Gaudium et Spes* (Pastoral Constitution on the Church in the Modern World), Dec. 7, 1965.

• *Christus Dominus* (Decree on the Bishops' Pastoral Office in the Church, Oct. 28, 1965.

• *Ad Gentes* (Decree on the Church's Missionary Activity), Dec. 7, 1965.

• *Unitatis Redintegratio* (Decree on Ecumenism), Nov. 21, 1964.

• *Orientalium Ecclesiarum* (Decree on Eastern Catholic Churches), Nov. 21, 1964.

• *Presbyterorum Ordinis* (Decree on the Ministry and Life of Priests), Dec. 7, 1965.

• *Optatam Totius* (Decree on Priestly Formation), Oct. 28, 1965.

• *Perfectae Caritatis* (Decree on the Appropriate Renewal of the Religious Life), Oct. 28, 1965.

• *Apostolicam Actuositatem* (Decree on the Apostolate of the Laity), Nov. 18, 1965.

• *Inter Mirifica* (Decree on the Instruments of Social Communication), Dec. 4, 1963.

• *Dignitatis Humanae* (Declaration on Religious Freedom), Dec. 7, 1965.

• *Nostra Aetate* (Declaration on the Relationship of the Church to Non-Christian Religions), Oct. 28, 1965.

• *Gravissimum Educationis* (Declaration on Christian Education), Oct. 28, 1965.

The key documents were the four constitutions, which set the ideological basis for all the others. To date, the documents with the most visible effects are those on the liturgy, the Church, the Church in the world, ecumenism, the renewal of religious life, the life and ministry of priests, the lay apostolate.

The main business of the council was to explore and make explicit dimensions of doctrine and Christian life requiring emphasis for the full development of the Church and the better accomplishment of its mission in the contemporary world.

Popes

LIST OF POPES

(Source: *Annuario Pontificio.*)

Information includes the name of the pope, in many cases his name before becoming pope, his birthplace or country of origin, the date of accession to the papacy, and the date of the end of reign which, in all but a few cases, was the date of death. Double dates indicate times of election and coronation.

St. Peter (Simon Bar-Jona): Bethsaida in Galilee; d. c., 67.

St. Linus: Tuscany; 67-76.

St. Anacletus (Cletus): Rome; 76-88.

St. Clement: Rome; 88-97.

St. Evaristus: Greece; 97-105.

St. Alexander I: Rome; 105-115.

St. Sixtus I: Rome; 115-125.

St. Telesphorus: Greece; 125-136.

St. Hyginus: Greece; 136-140.

St. Pius I: Aquileia; 140-155.

St. Anicetus: Syria; 155-166.

St. Soter: Campania; 166-175.

St. Eleutherius: Nicopolis in Epirus; 175-189.

Up to the time of St. Eleutherius, the years indicated for the beginning and end of pontificates are not absolutely certain. Also, up to the middle of the 11th century, there are some doubts about the exact days and months given in chronological tables.

St. Victor I: Africa; 189-199.

St. Zephyrinus: Rome; 199-217.

St. Callistus I: Rome; 217-222.

St. Urban I: Rome; 222-230.

St. Pontian: Rome; July 21, 230, to Sept. 28, 235.

St. Anterus: Greece; Nov. 21, 235, to Jan. 3, 236.

St. Fabian: Rome; Jan. 10, 236, to Jan. 20, 250.

St. Cornelius: Rome; Mar., 251, to June, 253.

St. Lucius I: Rome; June 25, 253, to Mar. 5, 254.

St. Stephen I: Rome; May 12, 254, to Aug. 2, 257.

St. Sixtus II: Greece; Aug. 30, 257, to Aug. 6, 258.

St. Dionysius: July 22, 259, to Dec. 26, 268.

St. Felix I: Rome; Jan. 5, 269, to Dec. 30, 274.

St. Eutychian: Luni; Jan. 4, 275, to Dec. 7, 283.

St. Caius: Dalmatia; Dec, 17, 283, to Apr. 22, 296.

St. Marcellinus: Rome; June 30. 296, to Oct. 25, 304.

St. Marcellus I: Rome; May 27, 308, or June 26, 308, to Jan. 16, 309.

St. Eusebius: Greece; Apr. 18, 309 or 310, to Aug. 17, 309 or 310.

St. Melchiades (**Miltiades**): Africa; July 2, 311, to Jan. 11, 314.

St. Sylvester I: Rome; Jan. 31, 314, to Dec. 31, 335. (Most of the popes before St. Sylvester I were martyrs.)

St. Marcus: Rome; Jan. 18, 336, to Oct. 7, 336.

St. Julius I: Rome; Feb. 6, 337, to Apr. 12, 352.

Liberius: Rome; May 17, 352, to Sept. 24, 366.

St. Damasus I: Spain; Oct. 1, 366, to Dec. 11, 384.

St. Siricius: Rome; Dec. 15, or 22 or 29, 384, to Nov. 26, 399.

St. Anastasius I: Rome; Nov. 27, 399, to Dec. 19, 401.

St. Innocent I: Albano; Dec. 22, 401, to Mar. 12, 417.

St. Zozimus: Greece; Mar. 18, 417, to Dec. 26, 418.

St. Boniface I: Rome; Dec. 28 or 29, 418, to Sept. 4, 422.

St. Celestine I: Campania; Sept. 10, 422, to July 27, 432.

St. Sixtus III: Rome; July 31, 432, to Aug. 19, 440.

St. Leo I (the Great): Tuscany; Sept. 29, 440, to Nov. 10, 461.

St. Hilary: Sardinia; Nov. 19, 461, to Feb. 29, 468.

St. Simplicius: Tivoli; Mar. 3, 468, to Mar. 10, 483.

St. Felix III (II): Rome; Mar. 13, 483, to Mar. 1, 492.

He should be called Felix II, and his successors of the same name should be numbered accordingly. The discrepancy in the numerical designation of popes named Felix was caused by the erroneous insertion in some lists of the name of St. Felix of Rome, a martyr.

St. Gelasius I: Africa; Mar. 1, 492, to Nov. 21, 496.

Anastasius II: Rome; Nov. 24, 496, to Nov. 19, 498.

St. Symmachus: Sardinia; Nov. 22, 498, to July 19, 514.

St. Hormisdas: Frosinone; July 20, 514, to Aug. 6, 523.

St. John I, Martyr: Tuscany; Aug. 13, 523, to May 18, 526.

St. Felix IV (III): Samnium; July 12, 526, to Sept. 22, 530.

Boniface II: Rome; Sept. 22, 530, to Oct. 17, 532.

John II: Rome; Jan. 2, 533, to May 8, 535.

John II was the first pope to change his name. His given name was Mercury.

St. Agapitus I: Rome; May 13, 535, to Apr. 22, 536.

St. Silverius, Martyr: Campania; June 1 or 8, 536, to Nov. 11, 537 (d. Dec. 2, 537).

St. Silverius was violently deposed in March, 537, and abdicated Nov. 11, 537. His successor, Vigilius, was not recognized as pope by all the Roman clergy until his abdication.

Vigilius: Rome; Mar. 29, 537, to June 7, 555.

Pelagius I: Rome; Apr. 16, 556, to Mar. 4, 561.

John III: Rome; July 17, 561, to July 13, 574.

Benedict I: Rome; June 2, 575, to July 30, 579.

Pelagius II: Rome; Nov. 26, 579, to Feb. 7, 590.

St. Gregory I (the Great): Rome; Sept. 3, 590, to Mar. 12, 604.

Sabinian: Blera in Tuscany; Sept. 13, 604, to Feb. 22, 606.

Boniface III: Rome; Feb. 19, 607, to Nov. 12, 607.

St. Boniface IV: Abruzzi; Aug. 25, 608, to May 8, 615.

St. Deusdedit (Adeodatus I): Rome; Oct. 19, 615, to Nov. 8, 618.

Boniface V: Naples; Dec. 23, 619, to Oct. 25, 625.

Honorius I: Campania; Oct. 27, 625, to Oct. 12, 638.

Severinus: Rome; May 28, 640, to Aug. 2, 640.

John IV: Dalmatia; Dec. 24, 640, to Oct. 12, 642.

Theodore I: Greece; Nov. 24, 642, to May 14, 649.

St. Martin I, Martyr: Todi; July, 649, to Sept. 16, 655 (in exile from June 17, 653).

St. Eugene I: Rome; Aug. 10, 654, to June 2, 657.

St. Eugene I was elected during the exile of St. Martin I, who is believed to have endorsed him as pope.

St. Vitalian: Segni; July 30, 657, to Jan. 27, 672.

Adeodatus II: Rome; Apr. 11, 672, to June 17, 676.

Donus: Rome; Nov. 2, 676, to Apr. 11, 678.

St. Agatho: Sicily; June 27, 678, to Jan. 10, 681.

St. Leo II: Sicily; Aug. 17, 682, to July 3, 683.

St. Benedict II: Rome; June 26, 684, to May 8, 685.

John V: Syria; July 23, 685, to Aug. 2, 686.

Conon: birthplace unknown; Oct. 21, 686, to Sept. 21, 687.

St. Sergius I: Syria; Dec. 15, 687, to Sept. 8, 701.

John VI: Greece; Oct. 30, 701, to Jan. 11, 705.

John VII: Greece; Mar. 1, 705, to Oct. 18, 707.

Sisinnius: Syria; Jan. 15, 708, to Feb. 4, 708.

Constantine: Syria; Mar. 25, 708, to Apr. 9, 715.

St. Gregory II: Rome; May 19, 715, to Feb. 11, 731.

St. Gregory III: Syria; Mar. 18, 731, to Nov., 741.

St. Zachary: Greece; Dec. 10, 741, to Mar. 22, 752.

Stephen II (III): Rome; Mar. 26, 752, to Apr. 26, 757.

After the death of St. Zachary, a Roman priest named Stephen was elected but died (four days later) before his consecration as bishop of Rome, which would have marked the beginning of his pontificate. Another Stephen was elected to succeed Zachary as Stephen II. (The first pope with this name was St. Stephen I, 254-57.) The ordinal III appears in parentheses after the name of Stephen II because the name of the earlier elected but deceased priest was included in some lists. Other Stephens have double numbers.

St. Paul I: Rome; Apr. (May 29), 757, to June 28, 767.

Stephen III (IV): Sicily; Aug. 1 (7), 768, to Jan. 24, 772.

Adrian I: Rome; Feb. 1 (9), 772, to Dec. 25, 795.

St. Leo III: Rome; Dec. 26 (27), 795, to June 12, 816.

Stephen IV (V): Rome; June 22, 816, to Jan. 24, 817.

St. Paschal I: Rome; Jan. 25, 817, to Feb. 11, 824.

Eugene II: Rome; Feb. (May), 824, to Aug., 827.

Valentine: Rome; Aug. 827, to Sept., 827.

Gregory IV: Rome; 827, to Jan., 844.

Sergius II: Rome; Jan., 844 to Jan. 27, 847.

St. Leo IV: Rome; Jan. (Apr. 10), 847, to July 17, 855.

Benedict III: Rome; July (Sept. 29), 855, to Apr. 17, 858.

St. Nicholas I (the Great): Rome; Apr. 24, 858, to Nov. 13, 867.

Adrian II: Rome; Dec. 14, 867, to Dec. 14, 872.

John VIII: Rome; Dec. 14, 872, to Dec. 16, 882.

Marinus I: Gallese; Dec. 16, 882, to May 15, 884.

St. Adrian III: Rome; May 17, 884, to Sept., 885. Cult confirmed June 2, 1891.

Stephen V (VI): Rome; Sept., 885, to Sept. 14, 891.

Formosus: Portus; Oct. 6, 891, to Apr. 4, 896.

Boniface VI: Rome; Apr., 896, to Apr., 896.

Stephen VI (VII): Rome; May, 896, to Aug., 897.

Romanus: Gallese; Aug., 897, to Nov., 897.

Theodore II: Rome; Dec., 897, to Dec., 897.

John IX: Tivoli; Jan., 898, to Jan., 900.

Benedict IV: Rome; Jan. (Feb.), 900, to July, 903.

Leo V: Ardea; July, 903, to Sept., 903.

Sergius III: Rome; Jan. 29, 904, to Apr. 14, 911.

Anastasius III: Rome; Apr., 911, to June, 913.

Landus: Sabina; July, 913, to Feb., 914.

John X: Tossignano (Imola); Mar., 914, to May, 928.

Leo VI: Rome; May, 928, to Dec., 928.

Stephen VII (VIII): Rome; Dec., 928, to Feb., 931.

John XI: Rome; Feb. (Mar.), 931, to Dec., 935.

Leo VII: Rome; Jan. 3, 936, to July 13, 939.

Stephen VIII (IX): Rome; July 14, 939, to

Oct., 942. (See note for enumeration.)

Marinus II: Rome; Oct. 30, 942, to May, 946.

Agapitus II: Rome; May 10, 946, to Dec., 955.

John XII (Octavius): Tusculum; Dec. 16, 955, to May 14, 964 (date of his death).

Leo VIII: Rome; Dec. 4 (6), 963, to Mar. 1, 965.

Benedict V: Rome; May 22, 964, to July 4, 966.

Confusion exists concerning the legitimacy of claims to the pontificate by Leo VIII and Benedict V. John XII was deposed Dec. 4, 963, by a Roman council. If this deposition was invalid, Leo was an antipope. If the deposition of John was valid, Leo was the legitimate pope and Benedict was an antipope.

John XIII: Rome; Oct. 1, 965, to Sept. 6, 972.

Benedict VI: Rome; Jan. 19, 973, to June, 974.

Benedict VII: Rome; Oct. 974, to July 10, 983.

John XIV (Peter Campenora): Pavia; Dec., 983, to Aug. 20, 984.

John XV: Rome; Aug., 985, to Mar., 996.

Gregory V (Bruno of Carinthia): Saxony; May 3, 996, to Feb. 18, 999.

Sylvester II (Gerbert): Auvergne; Apr. 2, 999, to May 12, 1003.

John XVII (Siccone): Rome; June, 1003, to Dec., 1003.

John XVIII (Phasianus): Rome; Jan., 1004, to July, 1009.

Sergius IV (Peter): Rome; July 31, 1009, to May 12, 1012.

The custom of changing one's name on election to the papacy is generally considered to date from the time of Sergius IV. Before his time, several popes had changed their names. After his time, this became a regular practice, with few exceptions; e.g., Adrian VI and Marcellus II.

Benedict VIII (Theophylactus): Tusculum; May 18, 1012, to Apr. 9, 1024.

John XIX (Romanus): Tusculum; Apr. (May), 1024, to 1032.

Benedict IX (Theophylactus): Tusculum; 1032, to 1044.

Sylvester III (John): Rome; Jan. 20, 1045, to Feb. 10, 1045.

Sylvester III was an antipope if the forcible removal of Benedict IX in 1044 was not legitimate.
Benedict IX (second time): Apr. 10, 1045, to May 1, 1045.
Gregory VI (John Gratian): Rome; May 5, 1045, to Dec. 20, 1046.
Clement II (Suitger, Lord of Morsleben and Hornburg): Saxony; Dec. 24 (25), 1046, to Oct. 9, 1047.
If the resignation of Benedict IX in 1045 and his removal at the December, 1046, synod were not legitimate, Gregory VI and Clement II were antipopes.

Benedict IX (third time): Nov. 8, 1047, to July 17, 1048 (d. c. 1055).

Damasus II (Poppo): Bavaria; July 17, 1048, to Aug. 9, 1048.

St. Leo IX (Bruno): Alsace; Feb. 12, 1049, to Apr. 19, 1054.

Victor II (Gebhard): Swabia; Apr. 16, 1055, to July 28, 1057.

Stephen IX (X) (Frederick): Lorraine; Aug. 3, 1057, to Mar. 29, 1058.

Nicholas II (Gerard): Burgundy; Jan. 24, 1059, to July 27, 1061.

Alexander II (Anselmo da Baggio): Milan; Oct. 1, 1061, to Apr. 21, 1073.

St. Gregory VII (Hildebrand): Tuscany; Apr. 22 (June 30), 1073, to May 25, 1085.

Bl. Victor III (Dauferius; Desiderius): Benevento; May 24, 1086, to Sept. 16, 1087. Cult confirmed July 23, 1887.

Bl. Urban II (Otto di Lagery): France; Mar. 12, 1088, to July 29, 1099. Cult confirmed July 14, 1881.

Paschal II (Raniero): Ravenna; Aug. 13 (14), 1099, to Jan. 21, 1118.

Gelasius II (Giovanni Caetani): Gaeta; Jan. 24 (Mar. 10), 1118, to Jan. 28, 1119.

Callistus II (Guido of Burgundy): Burgundy; Feb. 2 (9), 1119, to Dec. 13, 1124.

Honorius II (Lamberto): Fiagnano (Imola); Dec. 15 (21), 1124, to Feb. 13, 1130.

Innocent II (Gregorio Papareschi): Rome; Feb. 14 (23), 1130, to Sept. 24, 1143.

Celestine II (Guido): Citta di Castello; Sept. 26 (Oct. 3), 1143, to Mar. 8, 1144.

Lucius II (Gerardo Caccianemici): Bologna: Mar. 12, 1144, to Feb. 15, 1145.

7Bl. Eugene III (Bernardo Paganelli di Montemagno): Pisa; Feb. 15 (18), 1145, to July 8, 1153. Cult confirmed Oct. 3, 1872.

Anastasius IV (Corrado): Rome; July 12, 1153, to Dec, 3, 1154.

Adrian IV (Nicholas Breakspear): England; Dec. 4 (5), 1154, to Sept. 1, 1159.

Alexander III (Rolando Bandinelli): Siena; Sept. 7 (20), 1159, to Aug. 30, 1181.

Lucius III (Ubaldo Allucingoli): Lucca; Sept. 1 (6), 1181, to Sept. 25, 1185.

Urban III (Uberto Crivelli): Milan; Nov. 25 (Dec. 1), 1185, to Oct. 20, 1187.

Gregory VIII (Alberto de Morra): Benevento; Oct. 21 (25), 1187, to Dec. 17, 1187.

Clement III (Paolo Scolari): Rome; Dec. 19 (20), 1187, to Mar., 1191.

Celestine III (Giacinto Bobone): Rome; Mar. 30 (Apr. 14), 1191, to Jan. 8, 1198.

Innocent III (Lotario dei Conti di Segni); Anagni; Jan. 8 (Feb. 22), 1198, to July 16, 1216.

Honorius III (Cencio Savelli): Rome; July 18 (24), 1216, to Mar. 18, 1227.

Gregory IX (Ugolino, Count of Segni): Anagni: Mar. 19 (21), 1227, to Aug. 22, 1241.

Celestine IV (Goffredo Castiglioni): Milan; Oct. 25 (28), 1241, to Nov. 10, 1241.

Innocent IV (Sinibaldo Fieschi): Genoa; June 25 (28), 1243, to Dec. 7, 1254.

Alexander IV (Rinaldo, Count of Segni): Anagni; Dec. 12 (20), 1254, to May 25, 1261.

Urban IV (Jacques Pantaléon): Troyes; Aug. 29 (Sept. 4), 1261, to Oct. 2, 1264.

Clement IV (Guy Foulques or Guido le Gros): France; Feb. 5 (15), 1265, to Nov. 29, 1268.

Bl. Gregory X (Teobaldo Visconti): Piacenza; Sept. 1, 1271 (Mar. 27, 1272), to Jan. 10, 1276. Cult confirmed Sept. 12, 1713.

Bl. Innocent V (Peter of Tarentaise): Savoy; Jan. 21 (Feb. 22), 1276, to June 22, 1276. Cult confirmed Mar. 13, 1898.

Adrian V (Ottobono Fieschi): Genoa: July 11, 1276, to Aug. 18, 1276.

John XXI (Petrus Juliani or Petrus Hispanus): Portugal; Sept. 8 (20), 1276, to May 20, 1277.

Elimination was made of the name of John XX in an effort to rectify the numerical designation of popes named John. The error dates back to the time of John XV.

Nicholas III (Giovanni Gaetano Orsini): Rome; Nov. 25 (Dec. 26), 1277, to Aug. 22, 1280.

Martin IV (Simon de Brie): France; Feb. 22 (Mar. 23), 1281, to Mar. 28, 1285.

The names of Marinus I (882-84) and Marinus ii)942-46) were construed as Martin. In view of these two pontificates and the earlier reign of St. Martin I (649-55), this pope was called Martin IV.

Honorius IV (Giacomo Savelli): Rome; Apr. 2 (May 20), 1285, to Apr. 3, 1287.

Nicholas IV (Girolamo Masci): Ascoli; Feb. 22, 1288, to Apr. 4, 1292.

St. Celestine V (Pietro del Murrone): Isernia; July 5 (Aug. 29), 1294, to Dec. 13, 1294; d. 1296. Canonized May 5, 1313.

Boniface VIII (Benedetto Caetani): Anagni; Dec. 24, 1294 (Jan. 23, 1295), to Oct. 11, 1303.

Bl. Benedict XI (Niccolo Boccasini): Treviso; Oct. 22 (27), 1303, to July 7, 1304. Cult confirmed Apr. 24, 1736.

Clement V (Bertrand de Got): France; June 5 (Nov. 14), 1305, to Apr. 20, 1314. (First of Avignon popes.)

John XXII (Jacques d'Euse): Cahors; Aug. 7 (Sept. 5), 1316, to Dec. 4, 1334.

Benedict XII (Jacques Fournier): France; Dec. 20, 1334 (Jan. 8, 1335), to Apr. 25, 1342.

Clement VI (Pierre Roger): France; May 7 (19), 1342, to Dec. 6, 1352.

Innocent VI (Etienne Aubert): France; Dec. 18 (30), 1352, to Sept. 12, 1362.

Bl. Urban V (Guillaume de Grimoard): France; Sept. 28 (Nov. 6), 1362, to Dec. 19, 1370. Cult confirmed Mar. 10, 1870.

Gregory XI (Pierre Roger de Beaufort): France; Dec. 30, 1370 (Jan. 5, 1371), to Mar. 26, 1378. (Last of Avignon popes.)

Urban VI (Bartolomeo Prignano): Naples; Apr. 8 (18), 1378, to Oct. 15, 1389.

Boniface IX (Pietro Tomacelli): Naples; Nov. 2 (9), 1389, to Oct. 1, 1404.

Innocent VII (Cosma Migliorati): Sulmona; Oct. 17 (Nov. 11), 1404, to Nov. 6, 1406.

Gregory XII (Angelo Correr): Venice; Nov. 30 (Dec. 19), 1406, to July 4, 1415, when he voluntarily resigned from the papacy to permit the election of his successor. He died Oct. 18, 1417. (See The Western Schism.)

Martin V (Oddone Colonna): Rome; Nov. 11 (21), 1417, to Feb. 20, 1431.

Eugene IV (Gabriele Condulmer): Venice;

Mar. 3 (11), 1431, to Feb. 23, 1447.

Nicholas V (Tommaso Parentucelli): Sarzana; Mar. 6 (19), 1447, to Mar. 24, 1455.

Callistus III (Alfonso Borgia): Jativa (Valencia); Apr. 8 (20), 1455, to Aug. 6, 1458.

Pius II (Enea Silvio Piccolomini): Siena; Aug. 19 (Sept. 3), 1458, to Aug. 15, 1464.

Paul II (Pietro Barbo): Venice; Aug. 30 (Sept. 16), 1464, to July 26, 1471.

Sixtus IV (Francesco della Rovere): Savona; Aug. 9 (25), 1471, to Aug. 12, 1484.

Innocent VIII (Giovanni Battista Cibo): Genoa; Aug. 29 (Sept. 12), 1484, to July 25, 1492.

Alexander VI (Rodrigo Borgia): Jativa (Valencia); Aug. 11 (26), 1492, to Aug. 18, 1503.

Pius III (Francesco Todeschini-Piccolomini): Siena; Sept. 22 (Oct. 1, 8), 1503, to Oct. 18, 1503.

Julius II (Giuliano della Rovere): Savona; Oct. 31 (Nov. 26), 1503, to Feb. 21, 1513.

Leo X (Giovanni de' Medici): Florence; Mar. 9 (19), 1513, to Dec. 1, 1521.

Adrian VI (Adrian Florensz): Utrecht; Jan. 9 (Aug. 31), 1522, to Sept. 14, 1523.

Clement VII (Giulio de' Medici): Florence; Nov. 19 (26), 1523, to Sept. 25, 1534.

Paul III (Alessandro Farnese): Rome; Oct. 13 (Nov. 3), 1534, to Nov. 10, 1549.

Julius III (Giovanni Maria Ciocchi del Monte): Rome; Feb. 7 (22), 1550, to Mar. 23, 1555.

Marcellus II (Marcello Cervini): Montepulciano; Apr. 9 (10), 1555, to May 1, 1555.

Paul IV (Gian Pietro Carafa): Naples; May 23 (26), 1555, to Aug. 18, 1559.

Pius IV (Giovan Angelo de' Medici): Milan; Dec. 25, 1559 (Jan. 6, 1560), to Dec. 9, 1565.

St. Pius V (Antonio-Michele Ghislieri): Bosco (Alexandria); Jan. 7 (17), 1566, to May 1, 1572. Canonized May 22, 1712.

Gregory XIII (Ugo Boncompagni): Bologna; May 13 (25), 1572, to Apr. 10, 1585.

Sixtus V (Felice Peretti): Grottammare (Ripatransone); Apr. 24 (May 1), 1585, to Aug. 27, 1590.

Urban VII (Giovanni Battista Castagna): Rome; Sept. 15, 1590, to Sept. 27, 1590.

Gregory XIV (Niccolo Sfondrati): Cremona; Dec. 5 (8), 1590, to Oct. 16, 1591.

Innocent IX (Giovanni Antonio Facchinetti): Bologna; Oct. 29 (Nov. 3), 1591, to Dec. 30, 1591.

Clement VIII (Ippolito Aldobrandini): Florence; Jan. 30 (Feb. 9), 1592, to Mar. 3, 1605.

Leo XI (Alessandro de' Medici): Florence; Apr. 1 (10), 1605, to Apr. 27, 1605.

Paul V (Camillo Borghese): Rome; May 16 (29), 1605, to Jan. 28, 1621.

Gregory XV (Alessandro Ludovisi): Bologna; Feb. 9 (14), 1621, to July 8, 1623.

Urban VIII (Maffeo Barberini): Florence; Aug. 6 (Sept. 29), 1623, to July 29, 1644.

Innocent X (Giovanni Battista Pamfili):

Rome; Sept. 15 (Oct. 4), 1644, to Jan. 7, 1655.

Alexander VII (Fabio Chigi): Siena; Apr. 7 (18), 1655, to May 22, 1667.

Clement IX (Giulio Rospigliosi): Pistoia; June 20 (26), 1667, to Dec. 9, 1669.

Clement X (Emilio Altieri): Rome; Apr. 29 (May 11), 1670, to July 22, 1676.

Bl. Innocent XI (Benedetto Odescalchi): Como; Sept. 21 (Oct. 4), 1676, to Aug. 12, 1689.

Alexander VIII (Pietro Ottoboni): Venice; Oct. 6 (16), 1689, to Feb. 1, 1691.

Innocent XII (Antonio Pignatelli): Spinazzola; July 12 (15), 1691, to Sept. 27, 1700.

Clement XI (Giovanni Francesco Albani): Urbino; Nov. 23, 30 (Dec. 8), 1700, to Mar. 19, 1721.

Innocent XIII (Michelangelo dei Conti): Rome; May 8 (18), 1721, to Mar. 7, 1724.

Benedict XIII (Pietro Francesco — Vincenzo Maria — Orsini): Gravina (Bari); May 29 (June 4), 1724, to Feb. 21, 1730.

Clement XII (Lorenzo Corsini): Florence; July 12 (16), 1730, to Feb. 6, 1740.

Benedict XIV (Prospero Lambertini): Bologna; Aug. 17 (22), 1740, to May 3, 1758.

Clement XIII (Carlo Rezzonico): Venice; July 6 (16), 1758, to Feb. 2, 1769.

Clement XIV (Giovanni Vincenzo Antonio — Lorenzo — Ganganelli): Rimini; May 19, 28 (June 4), 1769, to Sept. 22, 1774.

Pius VI (Giovanni Angelo Braschi): Cesena; Feb. 15 (22), 1775, to Aug. 29, 1799.

Pius VII (Barnaba — Gregorio — Chiaramonti): Cesena; Mar. 14 (21), 1800, to Aug. 20, 1823.

Leo XII (Annibale della Genga): Genga (Fabriano); Sept. 28 (Oct. 5), 1823, to Feb. 10, 1829.

Pius VIII (Francisco Saverio Castiglioni): Cingoli; Mar. 31 (Apr. 5), 1829, to Nov. 30, 1830.

Gregory XVI (Bartolomeo Alberto — Mauro — Cappellari): Belluno; Feb. 2 (6), 1831, to June 1, 1846.

Pius IX (Giovanni M. Mastai Ferretti): Senigallia; June 16 (21), 1846, to Feb. 7, 1878.

Leo XIII (Gioacchino Pecci): Carpineto; (Anagni); Feb. 20 (Mar. 3), 1878, to July 20, 1903.

St. Pius X (Giuseppe Sarto): Riese (Treviso); Aug. 4 (9), 1903, to Aug. 20, 1914. Canonized May 29, 1954.

Benedict XV (Giacomo della Chiesa): Genoa; Sept. 3 (6), 1914, to Jan. 22, 1922.

Pius XI (Achille Ratti): Desio (Milan); Feb. 6 (12), 1922, to Feb. 10, 1939.

Pius XII (Eugenio Pacelli): Rome; Mar. 2 (12), 1939, to Oct. 9, 1958.

John XXIII (Angelo Giuseppe Roncalli): Sotto il Monte (Begamo); Oct. 28 (Nov. 4), 1958, to June 3, 1963.

Paul VI (Giovanni Battista Montini): Concessio (Brescia); June 21 (June 30), 1963 to —.

(See additional entries under 20th Century Popes and Pope Paul VI.)

ANTIPOPES

(Source: *Annuario Pontificio.*)

This list of men who claimed or exercised the papal office in an uncanonical manner includes names, birthplaces and dates of alleged reigns.

St. Hippolytus: Rome; 217-235; was reconciled before his death.

Novatian: Rome; 251.

Felix II: Rome; 355 to Nov. 22, 365.

Ursinus: 366-367.

Eulalius: Dec. 27 or 29, 418, to 419.

Lawrence: 498; 501-505.

Dioscorus: Alexandria; Sept. 22, 530, to Oct. 14, 530.

Theodore: ended alleged reign, 687.

Paschal: ended alleged reign, 687.

Constantine: Nepi; June 28 (July 5), 767, to 769.

Philip: July 31, 768; retired to his monastery on the same day.

John: ended alleged reign, Jan., 844.

Anastasius: Aug., 855, to Sept., 855; d. 880.

Christopher: Rome; July or Sept., 903, to Jan., 904.

Boniface VII: Rome; June, 974, to July, 974; Aug., 984, to July, 985.

John XVI: Rossano; Apr., 997, to Feb., 998.

Gregory: ended alleged reign, 1012.

Benedict X: Rome; Apr. 5, 1058, to Jan. 24, 1059.

Honorius II: Verona; Oct. 28, 1061, to 1072.

Clement III: Parma; June 25, 1080 (Mar. 24, 1084), to Sept. 8, 1100.

Theodoric: ended alleged reign, 1100; d. 1102.

Albert: ended alleged reign, 1102.

Sylvester IV: Rome; Nov. 18, 1105, to 1111.

Gregory VIII: France; Mar. 8, 1118, to 1121.

Celestine II: Rome; ended alleged reign, Dec., 1124.

Anacletus II: Rome; Feb. 14 (23), 1130, to Jan. 25, 1138.

Victor IV: Mar., 1138, to May 29, 1138; submitted to Pope Innocent II.

Victor IV: Montecelio; Sept. 7 (Oct. 4), 1159, to Apr. 20, 1164; he did not recognize his predecessor (Victor IV, above).

Paschal III: Apr. 22 (26), 1164, to Sept. 20, 1168.

Callistus III: Arezzo; Sept., 1168, to Aug. 29, 1178; submitted to Pope Alexander III.

Innocent III: Sezze; Sept. 29, 1179, to 1180.

Nicholas V: Corvaro (Rieti); May 12 (22), 1328, to Aug. 25, 1330; d. Oct. 16, 1333.

Four antipopes of the Western Schism:

Clement VII: Sept. 20 (Oct. 31), 1378, to Sept. 16, 1394.

Benedict XIII: Aragon; Sept. 28 (Oct. 11), 1394, to May 23, 1423.

Alexander V: Crete; June 26 (July 7), 1409, to May 3, 1410.

John XXIII: Naples; May 17 (25), 1410, to May 29, 1415.

Felix V: Savoy; Nov. 5, 1439 (July 24, 1440), to April 7, 1449; d. 1451.

Avignon Papacy

During the 70 years of papal and curial residence at Avignon in the 14th century, the College of Cardinals began to gain a stronger role in ecclesiastical affairs; the organization of administrative offices and other agencies was improved; influential measures for reform of the clergy were inaugurated; stimulus was given to the mendicant orders for the extension of missionary work to Asia; university education was encouraged; peace feelers and initiatives were made by several popes to settle royal rivalries and end armed conflicts.

Western Schism

The Western Schism was a confused state of affairs which divided Christendom into two and then three papal obediences from 1378 to 1417.

It occurred some 50 years after Marsilius theorized that a general (not ecumenical) council of bishops and other persons was superior to a pope and nearly 30 years before the Council of Florence stated definitively that no kind of council had such authority.

It was a period of disaster preceding the even more disastrous period of the Reformation.

Urban VI, following transfer to Rome of the 70-year papal residence at Avignon, was elected pope Apr. 8, 1378, and reigned until his death in 1389. He was succeeded by Boniface IX (1389-1404), Innocent VII (1404-1406) and Gregory XII (1406-1415). These four are considered the legitimate popes of the period.

Some of the cardinals who chose Urban pope, dissatisfied with his conduct of the office, declared that his election was invalid. They proceeded to elect Clement VII, who claimed the papacy from 1378 to 1394. He was succeeded by Benedict XIII.

Prelates seeking to end the state of divided papal loyalties convoked the Council of Pisa which, without authority, found Gregory XII and Benedict XIII, in absentia, guilty on 30-odd charges of schism and heresy, deposed them, and elected a third claimant to the papacy, Alexander V (1409-1410). He was succeeded by John XXIII (1410-1415).

The schism was ended by the Council of Constance (1414-1418). This council, although originally called into session in an irregular manner, acquired authority after being convoked by Gregory XII in 1415. In its early irregular phase, it deposed John XXIII whose election to the papacy was uncanonical. After being formally convoked, it accepted the abdication of Gregory in 1415 and dismissed the claims of Benedict XIII two years later, thus clearing the way for the election of Martin V on Nov. 11, 1417. The Council of Constance also rejected the theories of John Wycliff and condemned John Hus as a heretic.

20th CENTURY POPES

Leo XIII

Leo XIII (Gioacchino Vincenzo Pecci) was born May 2, 1810, in Carpineto, Italy. Although all but three years of his life and pontificate were of the 19th century, his influence extended well into the 20th century.

He was educated at the Jesuit college in Viterbo, the Roman College, the Academy of Noble Ecclesiastics, and the University of the Sapienza. He was ordained to the priesthood in 1837.

He served as an apostolic delegate to two States of the Church, Benevento from 1838 to 1841 and Perugia in 1841 and 1842. Ordained titular archbishop of Damietta, he was papal nuncio to Belgium from January, 1843, until May, 1846; in the post, he had controversial relations with the government over education issues and acquired his first significant experience of industrialized society.

He was archbishop of Perugia from 1846 to 1878. He became a cardinal in 1853 and chamberlain of the Roman Curia in 1877. He was elected to the papacy Feb. 20, 1878. He died July 20, 1903.

Canonizations: He canonized 18 saints and beatified a group of English martyrs.

Church Administration: He established 300 new dioceses and vicariates; restored the hierarchy in Scotland, set up an English, as contrasted with the Portuguese, hierarchy in India; approved the action of the Congregation for the Propagation of the Faith in reorganizing missions in China.

Encyclicals: He issued 50 encyclicals, on subjects ranging from devotional to social. In the latter category were *Annum Sacrum,* on the Sacred Heart, in 1899, and nine letters on Mary and the Rosary.

Interfaith Relations: He was unsuccessful in unity overtures made to Orthodox and Slavic Churches. He declared Anglican orders invalid in the apostolic bull *Apostolicae Curae* Sept. 13, 1896.

International Relations: Leo was frustrated in seeking solutions to the Roman Question arising from the seizure of church lands by the Kingdom of Italy in 1870. He also faced anticlerical situations in Belgium and France and in the Kulturkampf policies of Bismarck in Germany.

Social Questions: Much of Leo's influence stemmed from social doctrine stated in numerous encyclicals, concerning liberalism, liberty, the divine origin of authority; socialism, in *Quod Apostolici Muneris,* 1878; the Christian concept of the family, in *Arcanum,* 1880; socialism and economic liberalism, relations between capital and labor, in *Rerum Novarum,* 1891. Two of his social encyclicals were against the African slave trade.

Studies: In the encyclical *Aeterni Patris* of Aug. 4, 1879, he ordered a renewal of philosophical and theological studies in seminaries along scholastic, and especially Thomistic, lines, to counteract influential trends of liberalism and Modernism. He issued guidelines for biblical exegesis in *Providentissimus Deus* Nov. 18, 1893, and established the Pontifical Biblical Commission in 1902.

In other actions affecting scholarship and study, he opened the Vatican Archives to scholars in 1883 and established the Vatican Observatory.

United States: He authorized establishment of the apostolic delegation in Washington, D.C. Jan. 24, 1893. He refused to issue a condemnation of the Knights of Labor. With a document entitled *Testem Benevolentiae,* he eased resolution of questions concerning what was called an American heresy in 1899.

St. Pius X

St. Pius X (Giuseppe Melchiorre Sarto) was born in 1835 in Riese, Italy.

Educated at the college of Castelfranco and the seminary at Padua, he was ordained to the priesthood Sept. 18, 1858. He served as a curate in Trombolo for nine years before beginning an eight-year pastorate at Salzano. He was chancellor of the Treviso diocese from November, 1875, and bishop of Mantua from 1884 until 1893. He was cardinal-patriarch of Venice from that year until his election to the papacy by the conclave held from July 31 to Aug. 4, 1903.

Aims: Pius' principal objectives as pope were "to restore all things in Christ, in order that Christ may be all and in all," and "to teach (and defend) Christian truth and law."

Canonizations, Encyclicals: He canonized four saints and issued 16 encyclicals. One of the encyclicals was issued in commemoration of the 50th anniversary of the proclamation of the dogma of the Immaculate Conception of Mary.

Catechetics: He introduced a whole new era of religious instruction and formation with the encyclical *Acerbo Nimis* of Apr. 15, 1905, in which he called for vigor in establishing and conducting parochial programs of the Confraternity of Christian Doctrine.

Catholic Action: He outlined the role of official Catholic Action in two encyclicals in 1905 and 1906. Favoring organized action by Catholics themselves, he had serious reservations about interconfessional collaboration.

He stoutly maintained claims to papal rights in the anticlerical climate of Italy. He authorized bishops to relax prohibitions against participation by Catholics in some Italian elections.

Church Administration: With the motu proprio *Arduum Sane* of Mar. 19, 1904, he inaugurated the work which resulted in the Code of Canon Law; the code was completed in 1917 and went into effect in the following year. He reorganized and strengthened the Roman Curia with the apostolic constitution *Sapienti Consilio* of June 29, 1908. While promoting the expansion of missionary work, he removed from the jurisdiction of the Congregation for the Propagation of the Faith the Church in the United States, Canada, Newfoundland, England, Ireland, Holland and Luxembourg.

International Relations: He ended traditional prerogatives of Catholic governments with respect to papal elections, in 1904. He opposed anti-Church and anticlerical actions in several countries: Bolivia in 1905, because of anti-religious legislation; France in 1906, for its 1901 action in annulling its concordat with the Holy See, and for the 1905 Law of Separation by which it decreed separation of Church and state, ordered the confiscation of church property, and blocked religious education and the activities of religious orders; Portugal in 1911, for the separation of Church and state and repressive measures which resulted in persecution later.

In 1912 he called on the bishops of Brazil to work for the improvement of conditions among Indians.

Liturgy: "The Pope of the Eucharist," he strongly recommended the frequent reception of Holy Communion in a decree dated Dec. 20, 1905; in another decree, *Quam Singulari,* of Aug. 8, 1910, he called for the early reception of the sacrament by children. He initiated measures for liturgical reform with new norms for sacred music and the start of work on revision of the *Breviary* for recitation of the Divine Office.

Modernism: Pius was a vigorous opponent of "the synthesis of all heresies," which threatened the integrity of doctrine through its influence in philosophy, theology and biblical exegesis. In opposition, he condemned 65 of its propositions as erroneous in the decree *Lamentabili* July 3, 1907; issued the encyclical *Pascendi* in the same vein Sept. 8, 1907; backed both of these with censures; and published the Oath against Modernism in September, 1910, to be taken by all the clergy. Ecclesiastical studies suffered to some extent from these actions, necessary as they were at the time.

Pius followed the lead of Leo XIII in promoting the study of scholastic philosophy. He established the Pontifical Biblical Institute May 7, 1909.

His death, Aug. 20, 1914, was hastened by the outbreak of World War I. He was beatified in 1951 and canonized May 29, 1954. His feast is observed Aug. 21.

Benedict XV

Benedict XV (Giacomo della Chiesa) was born Nov. 21, 1854, in Pegli, Italy.

He was educated at the Royal University of Genoa and Gregorian University in Rome. He was ordained to the priesthood Dec. 21, 1878.

He served in the papal diplomatic corps from 1882 to 1907; as secretary to the nuncio to Spain from 1882 to 1887, as secretary to the papal secretary of state from 1887, and as undersecretary from 1901.

He was ordained archbishop of Bologna Dec. 22, 1907, and spent four years completing a pastoral visitation there. He was made a cardinal just three months before being elected to the papacy Sept. 3, 1914, He died Jan. 22, 1922. Two key efforts of his pontificate were for peace and the relief of human suffering caused by World War I.

Canonizations: Benedict canonized three saints; one of them was Joan of Arc.

Canon Law: He published the Code of Canon Law, developed by the commission set up by St. Pius X, June 28, 1917; it went into effect the following year.

Curia: He made great changes in the personnel of the Curia. He established the Congregation for the Oriental Churches May 1, 1917, and founded the Pontifical Oriental Institute in Rome later in the year.

Encyclicals: He issued 12 encyclicals. Peace was the theme of three of them. In another, published two years after the cessation of hostilities, he wrote about child victims of the war. He followed the lead of Leo XIII in *Spiritus Paraclitus*, Sept. 15, 1920, on biblical studies.

International Relations: He was largely frustrated on the international level because of the events and attitudes of the war period, but the number of diplomats accredited to the Vatican nearly doubled, from 14 to 26, between the time of his accession to the papacy and his death.

Peace Efforts: Benedict's stance in the war was one of absolute impartiality but not of disinterested neutrality. Because he would not take sides, he was suspected by both sides and the seven-point peace plan he offered to all belligerents Aug. 1, 1917, was turned down. The points of the plan were: recognition of the moral force of right; disarmament; acceptance of arbitration in cases of dispute; guarantee of freedom of the seas; renunciation of war indemnities; evacuation and restoration of occupied territories; examination of territorial claims in dispute.

Relief Efforts: Benedict assumed personal charge of Vatican relief efforts during the war. He set up an international missing persons bureau for contacts between prisoners and their families, but was forced to close it because of the suspicion of warring nations that it was a front for espionage operations. He persuaded the Swiss government to admit into the country military victims of tuberculosis.

Roman Question: Benedict arranged a meeting of Benito Mussolini and the papal secretary of state, which marked the first step toward final settlement of the question in 1929.

Pius XI

Pius XI (Ambrogio Damiano Achille Ratti) was born May 31, 1857, in Desio, Italy.

Educated at seminaries in Seviso and Milan, and at the Lombard College, Gregorian University and Academy of St. Thomas in Rome, he was ordained to the priesthood in 1879.

He taught at the major seminary of Milan from 1882 to 1888. Appointed to the staff of the Ambrosian Library in 1888, he remained there until 1911, acquiring a reputation for publishing works on palaeography and serving as director from 1907 to 1911. He then moved to the Vatican Library, of which he was prefect from 1914 to 1918. In 1919, he was named apostolic visitor to Poland in April, nuncio in June, and was made titular archbishop of Lepanto Oct. 28. He was made archbishop of Milan and cardinal June 13, 1921, before being elected to the papacy Feb. 6, 1922. He died Feb. 10, 1939.

Aim: The objective of his pontificate, as stated in the encyclical *Ubi Arcano,* Dec. 23, 1922, was to establish the reign and peace of Christ in society.

Canonizations: He canonized 34 saints, including the Jesuit Martyrs of North America, and conferred the title of Doctor of the Church on Sts. Peter Canisius, John of the Cross, Robert Bellarmine and Albertus Magnus.

Eastern Churches: He called for better understanding of the Eastern Churches in the encyclical *Rerum Orientalium* of Sept. 8, 1928, and developed facilities for the training of Eastern-Rite priests. He inaugurated steps for the codification of Eastern-Church law in 1929. In 1935 he made Syrian Patriarch Tappouni a cardinal.

Encyclicals: His first encyclical, *Ubi Arcano,* in addition to stating the aims of his pontificate, blueprinted Catholic Action and called for its development throughout the Church. In *Quas Primas,* Dec. 11, 1925, he established the feast of Christ the King for universal observance. Subjects of some of his other encyclicals were: Christian education, in *Divini Illius Magistri,* Dec. 31, 1929; Christian marriage, in *Casti Connubii,* Dec. 30, 1930; social conditions and pressure for social change in line with the teaching in *Rerum Novarum,* in *Quadragesimo Anno,* May 15, 1931; atheistic Communism, in *Divini Redemptoris,* Mar. 19, 1937; the priesthood, in *Ad Catholici Sacerdotii,* Dec. 20, 1935.

Missions: Following the lead of Benedict XV, Pius called for the training of native clergy in the pattern of their own respective cultures, and promoted missionary developments in various ways. He ordained six native bishops for China in 1926, one for Japan in 1927, and others for regions of Asia, China and India in 1933. He placed the first 40 mission dioceses under native bishops, saw the number of native priests increase from about 2,600 to more than 7,000 and the number of Catholics in missionary areas more than double from nine million.

In the apostolic constitution *Deus Scientiarum Dominus* of May 24, 1931, he ordered the introduction of missiology into theology courses.

Interfaith Relations: Pius was negative to the ecumenical movement among Protestants but approved the Malines Conversations, 1921 to 1926, between Anglicans and Catholics.

International Relations: Relations with the Mussolini government deteriorated from 1931 on, as indicated in the encyclical *Non Abbiamo Bisogno,* when the regime took steps to curb liberties and activities of the Church; they turned critical in 1938 with the emergence of racist policies. Relations deteriorated also in Germany from 1933 on, resulting finally in condemnation of the Nazis in the encyclical *Mit Brennender Sorge,* March, 1937. Pius sparked a revival of the Church in France by encouraging Catholics to work within the democratic framework of the Republic rather than foment trouble over restoration of a monarchy. Pius was powerless before the civil war which erupted in Spain in July, 1936; sporadic persecution and repression by the Calles regime in Mexico; and systematic persecution of the Church in the Soviet Union. Many of the 10 concordats and two agreements reached with European countries after World War I became casualties of World War II.

Roman Question: Pius negotiated for two and one-half years with the Italian government to settle the Roman Question by means of the Lateran Agreement of 1929. The agreement provided independent status for the State of Vatican City; made Catholicism the official religion of Italy, with pastoral and educational freedom and state recognition of Catholic marriages, religious orders and societies; and provided a financial payment to the Vatican for expropriation of the former States of the Church.

Pius XII

Pius XII (Eugenio Maria Giovanni Pacelli) was born Mar. 2, 1876, in Rome.

Educated at the Gregorian University and the Lateran University, in Rome, he was ordained to the priesthood Apr. 2, 1899.

He entered the Vatican diplomatic service in 1901, worked on the codification of canon law, and was appointed secretary of the Congregation for Ecclesiastical Affairs in 1914. Three years later he was ordained titular archbishop of Sardis and made apostolic nuncio to Bavaria. He was nuncio to Germany from 1920 to 1929, when he was made a cardinal, and took office as papal secretary of state in the following year. His diplomatic negotiations resulted in concordats between the Vatican and Bavaria (1924), Prussia (1929), Baden (1932), Austria and the German Republic (1933). He took part in negotiations which led to settlement of the Roman Question in 1929.

He was elected to the papacy Mar. 2, 1939. He died Oct. 9, 1958, at Castel Gandolfo after the 12th longest pontificate in history.

Canonizations: He canonized 33 saints, including Mother Frances X. Cabrini, the first US citizen-Saint.

Cardinals: He raised 56 prelates to the rank of cardinal in two consistories held in 1946 and 1953. There were 57 cardinals at the time of his death.

Church Organization and Missions: He increased the number of dioceses from 1,696 to 2,048. He established native hierarchies in China (1946), Burma (1955), and parts of Africa, and extended the native structure of the Church in India. He ordained the first black bishop for Africa.

Communism: In addition to opposing and condemning Communism on numerous occasions, he decreed in 1949 the penalty of excommunication for all Catholics holding formal and willing allegiance to the Communist Party and its policies. During his reign the Church was persecuted in some 15 countries which fell under Communist domination.

Doctrine and Liturgy: He proclaimed the dogma of the Assumption of the Blessed Virgin Mary Nov. 1, 1950 (apostolic constitution, *Munificentissimus Deus*).

In various encyclicals and other enactments, he provided background for the *aggiornamento* introduced by his successor, John XXIII: by his formulations of doctrine and practice regarding the Mystical Body of Christ, the liturgy, sacred music and biblical studies; by the revision of the Rites of Holy Week; by initiation of the work which led to the calendar-missal-breviary reform ordered into effect Jan. 1, 1961; by the first of several modifications of the Eucharistic fast; by extending the time of Mass to the evening. He instituted the feasts of Mary, Queen, and of St. Joseph the Worker, and clarified teaching concerning devotion to the Sacred Heart.

His 41 encyclicals and nearly 1,000 public addresses made Pius one of the greatest teaching popes. His concern in all his communications was to deal with specific points at issue and/or to bring Christian principles to bear on contemporary world problems.

Peace Efforts: Before the start of World War II, he tried unsuccessfully to get the contending nations — Germany and Poland, France and Italy — to settle their differences peaceably. During the war, he offered his services to mediate the widened conflict, spoke out against the horrors of war and the suffering it caused, mobilized relief work for its victims, proposed a five-point program for peace in Christmas messages from 1939 to 1942, and secured a generally open status for the city of Rome. After the war, he endorsed the principles and intent of the United Nations and continued efforts for peace.

United States: Pius appointed more than 200 of the 265 American bishops resident in the US and abroad in 1958, erected 27 dioceses in this country, and raised seven dioceses to archiepiscopal rank.

John XXIII

John XXIII (Angelo Roncalli) was born Nov. 25, 1881, at Sotte il Monte, Italy.

He was educated at the seminary of the Bergamo diocese and the Pontifical Seminary in Rome, where he was ordained to the priesthood Aug. 10, 1904.

He spent the first nine or 10 years of his priesthood as secretary to the bishop of Bergamo and as an instructor in the seminary there. He served as a medic and chaplain in the Italian army during World War I. Afterwards, he resumed duties in his own diocese until he was called to Rome in 1921 for work with the Society for the Propagation of the Faith.

He began diplomatic service in 1925 as titular archbishop of Areopolis and apostolic visitor to Bulgaria. A succession of offices followed: apostolic delegate to Bulgaria (1931-1935); titular archbishop of Mesembria, apostolic delegate to Turkey and Greece, administrator of the Latin vicariate apostolic of Istanbul (1935-1944); apostolic nuncio to France (1944-1953). On these missions, he was engaged in delicate negotiations involving Roman, Eastern-Rite and Orthodox relations; the needs of people suffering from the consequences of World War II; and unsettling suspicions arising from wartime conditions.

He was made a cardinal Jan. 12, 1953, and three days later was appointed patriarch of Venice, the position he held until his election to the papacy Oct. 28, 1958. He died of stomach cancer June 3, 1963.

John was a strong and vigorous pope whose influence far outmeasured both his age and the shortness of his time in the papacy.

Second Vatican Council: John announced Jan. 25, 1959, his intention of convoking the 21st ecumenical council in history to renew life in the Church, to reform its structures and institutions, and to explore ways and means of promoting unity among Christians. Through the council, which completed its work two and one-half years after his death, he ushered in a new era in the history of the Church.

Canon Law: He established a commission Mar. 28, 1963, for revision of the Code of Canon Law. The work of this commission, still underway, will greatly influence the future course of Catholic life and the conduct of ecclesiastical affairs.

Canonizations: He canonized 10 saints. He also beatified Mother Elizabeth Ann Seton, the first native of the US ever so honored. He

named St. Lawrence of Brindisi a Doctor of the Church.

Cardinals: He created 52 cardinals in five consistories, raising membership of the College of Cardinals above the traditional number of 70; at one time in 1962, the membership was 87. He made the college more international in representation than it had ever been, appointing the first cardinals from the Philippines, Japan and Africa. He ordered episcopal ordination for all cardinals. He relieved the suburban bishops of Rome of ordinary jurisdiction over their dioceses so they might devote all their time to business of the Roman Curia.

Eastern Rites: He made all Eastern-Rite patriarchs members of the Congregation for the Oriental Churches.

Ecumenism: He assigned to the Second Vatican Council the task of finding ways and means of promoting unity among Christians. He established the Vatican Secretariat for Promoting Christian Unity June 5, 1960. He showed his desire for more cordial relations with the Orthodox by sending personal representatives to visit Patriarch Athenagoras I June 27, 1961; approved a mission of five delegates to the General Assembly of the World Council of Churches which met in New Delhi, India, in November, 1961; removed a number of pejorative references to Jews in the Roman-Rite liturgy for Good Friday.

Encyclicals: Of the eight encyclicals he issued, the two outstanding ones were *Mater et Magistra* ("Christianity and Social Progress"), in which he recapitulated, updated and extended the social doctrine stated earlier by Leo XIII and Pius XI; and *Pacem in Terris* ("Peace on Earth"), the first encyclical ever addressed to all men of good will as well as to Catholics, on the natural-law principles of peace.

Liturgy: In forwarding liturgical reforms already begun by Pius XII, he ordered a calendar-missal-breviary reform into effect Jan. 1, 1961. He authorized the use of vernacular languages in the administration of the sacraments and approved giving Holy Communion to the sick in afternoon hours. He selected the liturgy as the first topic of major discussion by the Second Vatican Council.

Missions: He issued an encyclical on the missionary activity of the Church; established native hierarchies in Indonesia, Vietnam and Korea; and called on North American superiors of religious institutes to have one-tenth of their members assigned to work in Latin America by 1971.

Peace: John spoke and used his moral influence for peace in 1961 when tension developed over Berlin, in 1962 during the Algerian revolt from France, and later the same year in the Cuban missile crisis. His efforts were singled out for honor by the Balzan Peace Foundation. In 1963, he was posthumously awarded the US Presidential Medal of Freedom.

CANONIZATIONS BY LEO XIII AND HIS SUCCESSORS

Canonization is an infallible declaration by the pope that a person who suffered martyrdom and/or practiced Christian virtue to a heroic degree is in glory with God in heaven and is worthy of public honor by the universal Church and of imitation by the faithful.

Leo XIII
(1878-1903)

1881: Clare of Montefalco, virgin (d. 1308); John Baptist de Rossi, priest (1698-1764); Lawrence of Brindisi, doctor (d. 1619); Benedict J. Labre (1748-1783).

1888: Seven Holy Founders of the Servite Order; Peter Claver, priest (1581-1654); John Berchmans (1599-1621); Alphonsus Rodriguez, lay brother (1531-1617).

1897: Anthony M. Zaccaria, founder of Barnabites (1502-1539); Peter Fourier, cofounder of Augustinian Canonesses of Our Lady (1565-1640).

1900: John Baptist de La Salle, founder of Christian Brothers (1651-1719); Rita of Cascia (1381-1457).

St. Pius X
(1903-1914)

1904: Alexander Sauli, bishop (1534-1593); Gerard Majella, lay brother (1725-1755).

1909: Joseph Oriol, priest (1650-1702); Clement M. Hofbauer, priest (1751-1820).

Benedict XV
(1914-1922)

1920: Gabriel of the Sorrowful Mother (1838-1862); Margaret Mary Alacoque, virgin (1647-1690); Joan of Arc, virgin (1412-1431).

Pius XI
(1922-1939)

1925: Therese of Lisieux, virgin (1873-1897); Peter Canisius, doctor (1521-1597); Mary Magdalen Postel, foundress of Sisterhood of Christian Schools (1756-1846); Mary Magdalen Sophie Barat, foundress of Society of the Sacred Heart (1779-1865); John Eudes, founder of Eudist Fathers (1601-1680); John Baptist Vianney (Curé of Ars), priest (1786-1859).

1930: Lucy Filippini, virgin (1672-1732); Catherine Thomas, virgin (1533-1574); Jesuit North American Martyrs (see Index); Robert Bellarmine, bishop-doctor (1542-1621); Theophilus of Corte, priest (1676-1740).

1931: Albert the Great, bishop-doctor (1206-1280) (equivalent canonization).

1933: Andrew Fournet, priest (1752-1834); Bernadette Soubirous, virgin (1844-1879).

1934: Joan Antida Thouret, foundress of Sisters of Charity of St. Joan Antida (1765-1826); Mary Michaeli, foundress of Institute of Handmaids of the Blessed Sacrament (1809-1865); Louise de Marillac, foundress of Sisters of Charity (1591-1660); Joseph Benedict Cottolengo, priest (1786-1842); Pompilius M. Pirotti, priest (1710-1756); Teresa Margaret Redi, virgin (1747-1770); John Bosco, founder of Salesians (1815-1888); Conrad of Parzham, lay brother (1818-1894).

1935: John Fisher, bishop-martyr (1469-1535); Thomas More, martyr (1478-1535).

1938: Andrew Bobola, martyr (1592-1657); John Leonardi, founder of Clerics Regular of the Mother of God (c. 1550-1609); Salvatore of Horta, lay brother (1520-1567).

Pius XII
(1939-1958)

1940: Gemma Galgani, virgin (1878-1903); Mary Euphrasia Pelletier, foundress of Good Shepherd Sisters (1796-1868).

1943: Margaret of Hungary, virgin (d. 1270) (equivalent canonization).

1946: Frances Xavier Cabrini, foundress of Missionary Sisters of the Sacred Heart (1850-1917).

1947: Nicholas of Flue, hermit (1417-1487); John of Britto, martyr (1647-1693); Bernard Realini, priest (1530-1616); Joseph Cafasso, priest (1811-1860); Michael Garicoits, founder of Auxiliary Priests of the Sacred Heart (1797-1863); Jeanne Elizabeth des Ages, cofoundress of Daughters of the Cross (1773-1838); Louis Marie Grignon de Montfort, founder of Montfort Fathers (1673-1716); Catherine Laboure, virgin (1806-1876).

1949: Jeanne de Lestonnac, foundress of Religious of Notre Dame of Bordeaux (1556-1640); Maria Josepha Rossello, foundress of Daughters of Our Lady of Pity (1811-1880).

1950: Emily de Rodat, foundress of Congregation of the Holy Family of Villefranche (1787-1852); Anthony Mary Claret, bishop, founder of Claretians (1807-1870); Bartolomea Capitanio (1807-1833) and Vincenza Gerosa (1784-1847), foundresses of Sisters of Charity of Lovere; Jeanne de Valois, foundress of Annonciades of Bourges (1461-1504); Vincenzo M. Strambi, bishop (1745-1824); Maria Goretti, virgin-martyr (1890-1902); Mariana Paredes of Jesus, virgin (1618-1645).

1951: Maria Domenica Mazzarello, cofoundress of Daughters of Our Lady Help of Christians (1837-1881); Emilie de Vialar, foundress of Sisters of St. Joseph "of the Apparition" (1797-1856); Anthony M. Gianelli, bishop (1789-1846); Ignatius of Laconi, lay brother (1701-1781); Francis Xavier Bianchi, priest (1743-1815).

1954: Pius X, pope (1835-1914); Dominic Savio (1842-1857); Maria Crocifissa di Rosa, foundress of Handmaids of Charity of Brescia (1813-1855); Peter Chanel, priest-martyr (1803-1841); Gaspar del Bufalo, founder of Missioners of the Most Precious Blood (1786-1837); Joseph M. Pignatelli, priest (1737-1811).

John XXIII
(1958-1963)

1959: Joaquina de Vedruna de Mas, foundress of Carmelite Sisters of Charity (1783-1854); Charles of Sezze, lay brother (1613-1670).

1960: Gregory Barbarigo, bishop (1625-1697) (equivalent canonization); John de Ribera, bishop (1532-1611).

1961: Bertilla Boscardin, virgin (1888-1922).

1962: Martin de Porres, lay brother (1569-1639); Peter Julian Eymard, founder of Blessed Sacrament Fathers (1811-1868); Anthony Pucci, priest (1819-1892); Francis Mary of Camporosso, lay brother (1804-1866).

1963: Vincent Pallotti, founder of Pallotine Fathers (1795-1850).

Paul VI
(1963-   )

1964: Twenty-two Martyrs of Uganda.

1967: Benilde, lay brother (1805-1862).

1969: Julia Billiart, foundress of Sisters of Notre Dame de Namur (1751-1816).

1970: Maria Della Dolorato Torres Acosta, foundress of Servants Sisters of Mary (1826-1887); Leonard Murialdo, priest, founder of Congregation of St. Joseph (1828-1890); Therese Couderc, foundress of Congregation of Our Lady of the Cenacle (1805-1885); John of Avila, preacher and spiritual director (1499-1569); Sts. Nicholas Tavelic, Deodatus of Aquitaine, Peter of Narbonne and Stephen of Cuneo, martyrs (d. 1391); Forty English and Welsh Martyrs (d. 16th cent.).

English and Welsh Martyrs

Forty Martyrs of England and Wales, victims of persecution from 1535 to 1671, were canonized by Pope Paul Oct. 25, 1970.

The martyrs were prosecuted and executed as traitors for refusal to comply with laws enacted by Henry VIII and Elizabeth I regarding supremacy succession and the prohibition of native-born to study for the priesthood abroad and return to England for practice of the ministry.

John Houghton, prior of the London Charterhouse, was the first of his group to die (1535) for opposing Henry's Acts of Supremacy and Succession. Cuthbert Mayne (d. 1577) was the protomartyr of the English seminary at Douay. Margaret Clitherow (d. 1586) and Swithun Wells (d. 1591) were executed for sheltering priests. Richard Gwyn (d. 1584), poet, was the protomartyr of Wales.

Others in the group were:

John Almond, Edmund Arrowsmith, Ambrose Barlow, John Boste, Alexander Briant, Edmund Campion, Philip Evans, Thomas Garnet, Edmund Gennings;

Philip Howard, John Jones, John Kemble, Luke Kirby, Robert Lawrence, David Lewis, Ann Line, John Lloyd;

Henry Morse, Nicholas Owen, John Paine, Polydore Plasden, John Plessington, Richard Reynolds, John Riggby, John Roberts;

Alban Roe, Ralph Serwin, Robert Southwell, John Southworth, John Stone, John Wall, Henry Walpole, Margaret Ward, Augustine Webster and Eustace White.

ENCYCLICALS ISSUED BY LEO XIII AND HIS SUCCESSORS

An encyclical letter is a pastoral letter addressed by a pope to the whole Church. In general, it concerns matters of doctrine, morals or discipline. Its formal title consists of the first few words of the official text. A few encyclicals, notably *Pacem in Terris* by John XXIII and *Ecclesiam Suam* by Paul VI, have been addressed to "all men of good will" as well as to bishops and the faithful in communion with the Church.

An encyclical epistle, which is like an encyclical letter in many respects, is addressed to part of the Church, that is, to the bishops and faithful of a particular country or area. Its contents may concern other than doctrinal, moral or disciplinary matters of universal significance; for example, the commemoration of historical events, conditions in a certain country.

The authority of encyclicals was stated by Pius XII in the encyclical *Humani Generis* Aug. 12, 1950.

"Nor must it be thought that what is contained in encyclical letters does not of itself demand assent, on the pretext that the popes do not exercise in them the supreme power of their teaching authority. Rather, such teachings belong to the ordinary magisterium, of which it is true to say: 'He who hears you, hears me' (Lk. 10:16); for the most part, too, what is expounded and inculcated in encyclical letters already appertains to Catholic doctrine for other reasons. But if the supreme pontiffs in their official documents purposely pass judgment on a matter debated until then, it is obvious to all that the matter, according to the mind and will of the same pontiffs, cannot be considered any longer a question open for discussion among theologians."

The following list contains the titles and indicates the subject matter of encyclical letters and epistles. The latter are generally distinguishable by the limited scope of their titles or contents.

Leo XIII
(1878-1903)

1878: Inscrutabili Dei Consilio (Evils of Society), Apr. 21.

Quod Apostolici Muneris (Socialism, Communism, Nihilism), Dec. 28.

1879: Aeterni Patris (Scholastic Philosophy, especially of Thomas Aquinas), Aug. 4.

1880: Arcanum (Christian Marriage), Feb. 10.

Grande Munus (Sts. Cyril and Methodius), Sept. 30.

Sancta Dei Civitas (Three French Societies), Dec. 3.

1881: Diuturnum (Origin of Civil Power), June 29.

1882: Etsi Nos (Conditions in Italy), Feb. 15.

Auspicato Concessum (Third Order of St. Francis), Sept. 17.

Cum Multa (Conditions in Spain), Dec. 8.

1883: Supremi Apostolatus Officio (The Rosary), Sept. 1.

1884: Nobilisima Gallorum Gens (Religious Question in France), Feb. 8.

Humanum Genus (Freemasonry), Apr. 20.

Superiore Anno (Recitation of the Rosary), Aug. 30.

1885: Immortale Dei (The Christian Constitution of States), Nov. 1.

Quod Auctoritate (Proclamation of Extraordinary Jubilee Year), Dec. 22.

1886: Quod Multum (Liberty of the Church in Hungary), Aug. 22.

Pergrata Nobis (Needs of the Church in Portugal), Sept. 14.

1888: Libertas (Human Liberty), June 20.

Paterna Caritas (Recalling the Dissenting Armenians), July 25.

Quam Aerumnosa (Italian Immigrants in America), Dec. 10.

1889: Quamquam Pluries (Patronage of St. Joseph and the Blessed Virgin Mary), Aug. 15.

1890: Sapientiae Christianae (Chief Duties of Christian Citizens), Jan. 10.

Ab Apostoli (To the Clergy and People of Italy), Oct. 15.

1891: Rerum Novarum (Condition of the Working Classes), May 15.

Octobri Mense (The Rosary), Sept. 22.

1892: Au Milieu des Sollicitudes (Church and State in France), Feb. 16.

Magnae Dei Matris (The Rosary), Sept. 8.

1893: Ad Extremas (Seminaries in the East Indies), June 24.

Constanti Hungarorum (Conditions of the Church in Hungary), Sept. 2.

Laetitiae Sanctae (The Rosary), Sept. 8.

Providentissimus Deus (Study of Holy Scripture), Nov. 18.

1894: Caritatis, Mar. 19.

Iucunda Semper Expectatione (The Rosary), Sept. 8.

Christi Nomen, Dec. 24.

1895: Adiutricem (The Rosary), Sept. 5.

1896: Satis Cognitum, June 29.

Fidentum Piumque Animum (The Rosary), Sept. 20.

1897: Divinum Illud Munus (The Holy Spirit, doctrine and devotion), May 9.

Militantis Ecclesiae (Third Centenary of the Death of St. Peter Canisius), Aug. 1.

Augustissimae Virginis (The Rosary), Sept. 12.

Affari Vos (The Manitoba School Question), Dec. 8.

1898: Caritatis Studium (The Magisterium of the Church in Scotland), July 25.

Spesse Volte (Catholic Action in Italy) Aug. 5.

1899: Annum Sacrum (Consecration of Mankind to the Sacred Heart), May 25.

Depuis le Jour (Ecclesiastical Education in France), Sept. 8.

1900: Tametsi Futura Prospicientibus (Jesus Christ, Our Redeemer), Nov. 1.

1901: Graves de Communi Re (Christian Democracy), Jan. 18.

1902: Mirae Caritatis (The Most Holy Eucharist), May 28.

Fin dal Principio (Education of the Clergy in Italy), Dec. 8.

Saint Pius X
(1903-1914)

1903: E Supremi (Restoration of All Things in Christ), Oct. 4.

1904: Ad Diem Illum Laetissimum (Jubilee of the Immaculate Conception), Feb. 2.

Iucunda Sane (Thirteenth Centenary of the Death of St. Gregory the Great), Mar. 12.

1905: Acerbo Nimis (Teaching of Christian Doctrine), Apr. 15.

Il Fermo Proposito (Catholic Action in Italy), June 11.

1906: Vehementer Nos (French Separation Law), Feb. 11.

Tribus Circiter (Condemnation of the Mariavites), Apr. 5.

Pieni l'Animo (Clergy in Italy), July 28.

Gravissimo Officio Munere (Forbidding Associations Cultuelles), Aug. 10.

1907: Une Fois Encore (Separation of Church and State in France), Jan. 6.

Pascendi Dominici Gregis (Modernism), Sept. 8.

1909: Communium Rerum (Eighth Centenary of the Death of St. Anselm), Apr. 21.

1910: Editae Saepe (Third Centenary of the Death of St. Charles Borromeo), May 26.

1911: Iamdudum (Separation Law in Portugal), May 24.

1912: Lacrimabili Statu (Indians of South America), June 7.

Singulari Quadam (Labor Organizations in Germany), Sept. 24.

Benedict XV
(1914-1922)

1914: Ad Beatissimi Apostolorum (Appeal for Peace), Nov. 1.

1917: Humani Generis Redemptionem (Preaching), June 15.

1918: Quod Iam Diu (Peace Congress, Paris), Dec. 1.

1919: In Hac Tanta (Twelfth Centenary of St. Boniface), May 14.

Paterno Iam Diu (Christian Charity of the Children of Central Europe), Nov. 24.

1920: Pacem, Dei Munus Pulcherrimum (Peace and Christian Reconciliation), May 23.

Spiritus Paraclitus (Holy Scripture), Sept. 15.

Principi Apostolorum Petro (St. Ephrem the Syrian, declared Doctor), Oct. 5.

Annus Iam Plenus (Child War Victims), Dec. 1.

1921: Sacra Propediem (Seventh Centenary of the Third Order of St. Francis), Jan. 6.

In Praeclara Summorum (Sixth Centenary of Dante's Death), Apr. 30.

Fausto Appetente Die (Seventh Centenary of the Death of St. Dominic), June 29.

Pius XI
(1922-1939)

1922: Ubi Arcano Dei Consilio (Peace of Christ in the Kingdom of Christ), Dec. 23.

1923: Rerum Omnium Perturbationem (Third Centenary of the Death of St. Francis de Sales), Jan. 26.

Studiorum Ducem (Sixth Centenary of the Canonization of St. Thomas Aquinas), June 29.

Ecclesiam Dei (Third Centenary of the Death of St. Josaphat, Archbishop of Polotsk), Nov. 12.

1924: Maximam Gravissimamque (French Diocesan Associations), Jan. 18.

1925: Quas Primas (Feast of Christ the King), Dec. 11.

1926: Rerum Ecclesiae (Catholic Missions), Feb. 28.

Rite Expiatis (Seventh Centenary of the Death of St. Francis of Assisi), Apr. 30.

Iniquis Afflictisque (Persecution of the Church in Mexico), Nov. 18.

1928: Mortalium Animos (Promotion of True Religious Unity), Jan. 6.

Miserentissimus Redemptor (Reparation Due the Sacred Heart), May 8.

Rerum Orientalium (Reunion with the Eastern Churches), Sept. 8.

1929: Mens Nostra (Promotion of Spiritual Exercises), Dec. 20.

Quinquagesimo Ante (Sacerdotal Jubilee), Dec. 23.

Divini Illius Magistri (Rappresentanti in Terra) (Christian Education of Youth), Dec. 31.

1930: Ad Salutem (Fifteenth Centenary of the Death of St. Augustine), Apr. 20.

Casti Connubii (Christian Marriage), Dec. 31.

1931: Quadragesimo Anno (Social Reconstruction), May 15.

Non Abbiamo Bisogno (Catholic Action), June 29.

Nova Impendet (Economic Crisis, Unemployment, Armaments), Oct. 2.

Lux Veritatis (Fifteenth Centenary of the Council of Ephesus), Dec. 25.

1932: Caritate Christi Compulsi (Sacred Heart and World Distress), May 3.

Acerba Animi (Persecution of the Church in Mexico), Sept. 29.

1933: Dilectissima Nobis (Conditions in Spain), June 3.

1935: Ad Catholici Sacerdotii (Catholic Priesthood), Dec. 20.

1936: Vigilanti Cura (Clean Motion Pictures), June 29.

1937: Mit Brennender Sorge (Church in Germany), Mar. 14.

Divini Redemptoris (Atheistic Communism), Mar. 19.

Firmissimam Constantiam (Nos Es Muy Conocida) (Conditions in Mexico), Mar. 28.

Ingravescentibus Malis (The Rosary) Sept. 29.

Pius XII
(1939-1958)

1939: Summi Pontificatus (Function of the State in Modern World), Oct. 20.

Sertum Laetitiae (To the Church in the United States), Nov. 1.

1940: Saeculo Exeunte Octavo (Missions), June 13.

1943: Mystici Corporis Christi (Mystical Body), June 29.

Divino Afflante Spiritu (Biblical Studies), Sept. 30.

1944: Orientalis Ecclesiae Decus (Fifteenth Centenary of the Death of St. Cyril of Alexandria), Apr. 9.

1945: Communium Interpretes Dolorum (Appeal for Prayers), Apr. 15.

Orientales Omnes Ecclesias (Anniversary of the Ruthenian Reunion), Dec. 23.

1946: Quemadmodum (Call for Intensified Aid to Youth), Jan. 6.

Deiparae Virginis Mariae (Proposing to the Bishops the Question of the Definition of the Dogma of the Assumption), May 1.

1947: Fulgens Radiatur (Fourteenth Centenary of the Death of St. Benedict), Mar. 21.

Mediator Dei (Sacred Liturgy), Nov. 20.

Optatissima Pax (Peace and Social Disorders), Dec. 18.

1948: Auspicia Quaedam (Prayer to Blessed Virgin Mary for Peace), May 1.

In Multiplicibus Curis (Crisis in Palestine), Oct. 24.

1949: Redemptoris Nostri (Internationalization of Jerusalem), Apr. 15.

1950: Anni Sacri (Holy Year Call for Public Prayer), Mar. 12.

Summi Maeroris (Renewed Holy Year Call for Public Prayer), July 19.

Humani Generis (Warnings against Attempts to Distort Catholic Truths), Aug. 12.

Mirabile Illud (Call for Renewed Crusade of Prayers for Peace), Dec. 6.

1951: Evangelii Praecones (Call for Greater Missionary Effort), June 2.

Sempiternus Rex (Fifteenth Centenary of the Council of Chalcedon), Sept. 8.

Ingruentium Malorum (Recitation of the Rosary), Sept. 15.

1952: Orientales Ecclesias (Communist Persecution of the Church; Call for Prayers for the Persecuted), Dec. 15.

1953: Doctor Mellifluus (Eighth Centenary of Death of St. Bernard), May 24.

Fulgens Corona (Call for Catholics to Observe Marian Year), Sept. 8.

1954: Sacra Virginitas (Preeminence of Evangelical Chastity), Mar. 25.

Ecclesiae Fastos (Commemoration of St. Boniface), June 5.

Ad Sinarum Gentem (The Church in China), Oct. 7.

Ad Caeli Reginam (Feast of Queenship of Mary), Oct. 11.

1955: Musicae Sacrae (Sacred Music), Dec. 25.

1956: Haurietis Aquas (The Sacred Heart), May 15.

Luctuosissimi Eventus (Prayers for Hungary), Oct. 28.

Laetamur Admodum (Middle East Crisis), Nov. 1.

Datis Nuperrime (Prayers for Peace), Nov. 5.

1957: Fidei Donum (Missionary Effort, especially in Africa), Apr. 21.

Invicti Athletae Christi (Third Centenary of Death of St. Andrew Bobola), May 16.

Le Pelerinage de Lourdes (Centenary of Lourdes Apparitions), July 2.

Miranda Prorsus (Radio, TV and Motion Pictures), Sept. 8.

1958: Ad Apostolorum Principis (Critical Situation of the Church in China), June 29.

Meminisse Juvat (Prayers for Peace and the Persecuted Church), July 14.

John XXIII
(1958-1963)

1959: Ad Petri Cathedram (Appeal to Separated Christians to Reunite with Church), June 29.

Sacerdotii Nostri Primordia (Centenary of the Cure of Ars), Aug. 1.

Grata Recordatio (Rosary), Sept. 26.

Princeps Pastorum (Missions), Nov. 28.

1961: Mater et Magistra (Christianity and Social Progress), May 15.

Aeterna Dei Sapientia (Fifteenth Centenary of the Death of St. Leo the Great), Nov. 11.

1962: Paenitentiam Agere (Appeal for Works of Penance for Success of the Second Vatican Council), July 1.

1963: Pacem in Terris (Peace on Earth), Apr. 11.

Paul VI
(1963-   )

1964: Ecclesiam Suam (Second Vatican Council Themes), Aug. 6.

1965: Mense Maio (Prayer for Success of Vatican II, Peace), Apr. 29.

Mysterium Fidei (The Eucharist), Sept. 3.

1966: Christi Matri Rosarii (The Rosary), Sept. 15.

1967: Populorum Progressio (Development of Peoples), Mar. 26.

Sacerdotalis Caelibatus (Priestly Celibacy), June 24.

1968: Humanae Vitae (Birth Control), July 25.

Problems and Solutions

"Grave problems of our time" and what the Church and Christians can do about them, were the themes of an apostolic letter addressed May 14, 1971, by Paul VI to Cardinal Maurice Roy, president of the Council of the Laity and the Pontifical Commission on Justice and Peace. The occasion for the letter was the 80th anniversary of *Rerum Novarum.*

The Pope said, in part:

"There is, of course, a wide diversity among the situations in which Christians — willingly or unwillingly — find themselves according to regions, socio-political systems and cultures. In some places they are reduced to silence, regarded with suspicion and, as it were, kept on the fringe of society, enclosed without freedom in a totalitarian system. In other places they are a weak minority whose voice makes itself heard with difficulty. In some other nations, where the Church sees her place recognized, sometimes officially so, she too finds herself subjected to the repercussions of the crisis which is unsettling society; some of her members are tempted by radical and violent solutions from which they believe that they can expect a happier outcome. While some people, unaware of present injustices, strive to prolong the existing situation, others allow themselves to be beguiled by revolutionary ideologies which promise them, not without delusion, a definitively better world.

"In the face of such widely varying situations it is difficult for us to utter a unified message and to put forward a solution which has universal validity. Such is not our ambition, nor is it our mission. It is up to the Christian communities to analyze with objectivity the situation which is proper to their own country, to shed on it the light of the Gospel's unalterable words, and to draw principles of reflection, norms of judgment and directives for action from the social teaching of the Church. . . .

"It is up to these Christian communities, with the help of the Holy Spirit, in communion with the bishops who hold responsibility and in dialogue with other Christian brethren and all men of good will to discern the options and commitments which are called for in order to bring about urgently needed social, political and economic changes."

Hierarchy of the Catholic Church

ORGANIZATION AND GOVERNMENT

As a structured society, the Catholic Church is organized and governed along lines corresponding mainly to the jurisdictions of the pope and bishops.

The pope is the supreme head of the Church. He has primacy of jurisdiction as well as honor over the entire Church.

Bishops, in union with and in subordination to the pope, are the successors of the Apostles for care of the Church and for the continuation of Christ's mission in the world. They serve the people of their own dioceses, or local churches, with ordinary authority and jurisdiction. They also share, with the pope and each other, in common concern and effort for the general welfare of the whole Church.

Bishops of exceptional status are Eastern Rite patriarchs who, subject only to the pope, are heads of the faithful belonging to their rites throughout the world.

Subject to the Holy Father and directly responsible to him for the exercise of their ministry of service to people in various jurisdictions or divisions of the Church throughout the world are: resident archbishops and metropolitans (heads of archdioceses), resident bishops (heads of dioceses), vicars and prefects apostolic (heads of vicariates apostolic and prefectures apostolic), certain abbots and prelates, apostolic administrators. Each of these, within his respective territory and according to the provisions of canon law, has ordinary jurisdiction over pastors (who are responsible for the administration of parishes), priests, religious and lay persons.

Also subject to the Holy Father are titular archbishops and bishops (who have delegated jurisdiction), religious orders and congregations of pontifical right, pontifical institutes and faculties, papal nuncios and apostolic delegates.

Assisting the pope and acting in his name in the central government and administration of the Church are cardinals and other officials of the Roman Curia.

THE HIERARCHY

The ministerial hierarchy is the orderly arrangement of the ranks and orders of the clergy to provide for the spiritual care of the faithful, the government of the Church, and the accomplishment of the Church's total mission in the world. Persons belong to this hierarchy by virtue of ordination and canonical mission.

The term hierarchy is also used to designate an entire body or group of bishops; for example, the hierarchy of the Church, the hierarchy of the United States.

Hierarchy of Order: Consists of the pope, bishops, priests and deacons, by divine law. Their purpose, for which they are ordained to holy orders, is to carry out the sacramental and pastoral ministry of the Church.

Hierarchy of Jurisdiction: Consists of the pope and bishops by divine law, and other church officials by ecclesiastical institution and mandate, who have authority to govern and direct the faithful for spiritual ends.

Prelates: Clerics with the authority of public office in the Church — i. e., the authority of jurisdiction in the external forum. They are: the pope, patriarchs, residential archbishops and bishops, certain abbots and prelates, vicars and prefects apostolic, vicars general, certain superiors in clerical exempt religious communities. Titular archbishops and bishops without ordinary jurisdiction are not prelates in the strict sense of the term; neither are pastors, who have very limited jurisdiction in the external forum.

The Pope

His holiness the Pope is the Bishop of Rome, the Vicar of Jesus Christ, the successor of St. Peter, Prince of the Apostles, the Supreme Pontiff who has the primacy of jurisdiction and not merely of honor over the universal Church, the Patriarch of the West, the Primate of Italy, the Archbishop and Metropolitan of the Roman Province, the Sovereign of the State of Vatican City.

Cardinals
(See Index)
Patriarchs

Patriarch, a term which had its origin in the Eastern Church, is the title of a bishop who, second only to the pope, has the highest rank in the hierarchy of jurisdiction. He is the incumbent of one of the sees listed below. Subject only to the pope, an Eastern-Rite patriarch is the head of the faithful belonging to his rite throughout the world. The patriarchal sees are so called because of their special status and dignity in the history of the Church.

The Council of Nicaea (325) recognized three patriarchs — the bishops of Alexandria and Antioch in the East, and of Rome in the West. The First Council of Constantinople (381) added the bishop of Constantinople to the list of patriarchs and gave him rank second only to that of the pope, the bishop of Rome and patriarch of the West; this action was seconded by the Council of Chalcedon (451) and was given full recognition by the Fourth Lateran Council (1215). The Council of Chalcedon also acknowledged patriarchal rights of the bishop of Jerusalem. Since 451, the major patriarchates have been listed in this order of precedence: Rome, Constantinople, Alexandria, Antioch and Jerusalem.

Eastern Rite patriarchs are as follows: one of Alexandria, for the Copts; three of Antioch, one each for the Syrians, Maronites and Melkites (the latter also has the personal title of Melkite patriarch of Alexandria and of Jerusalem). The patriarch of Babylon, for the Chaldeans, and the patriarch of Sis, or Cilicia, for the Armenians, should be called, more properly, *Katholikos* — that is, a prelate delegated for a universality of causes. These patriarchs are elected by bishops of their rites: they receive approval and the pallium, symbolic of their office, from the pope.

Latin Rite patriarchates were established for Antioch, Jerusalem, Alexandria and Constantinople during the Crusades; afterwards, they became patriarchates in name only. Jerusalem, however, was reconstituted as a patriarchate by Pius IX, in virtue of the bull *Nulla Celebrior* of July 23, 1847. In 1964, the Latin titular patriarchates of Constantinople, Alexandria and Antioch, long a bone of contention in relations with Eastern Rites, were abolished.

As of June 1, 1972, the patriarchs in the Church were:

Paul VI, Bishop of Rome, Pope, Patriarch of the West; Cardinal Stephanos I Sidarouss, C.M., of Alexandria, for the Copts; Ignace Antoine Hayek, of Antioch, for the Syrians; Maximos V Hakim, of Antioch, for the Melkites (he also has the titles of Alexandria and Jerusalem for the Melkites); Cardinal Paul Meouchi, of Antioch, for the Maronites; Giacomo Beltritti, of Jerusalem, for the Latin Rite; Paul II Cheikho, of Babylon, for the Chaldeans; Ignace Pierre XVI Batanian, of Cilicia, for the Armenians.

The titular patriarchs (in name only) of the Latin Rite were: Jose Vieria Alvernaz, of the East Indies; Archbishop Antonio Ribeiro, of Lisbon; Archbishop Albino Luciana, of Venice. The patriarchate of the West Indies has been vacant since 1963.

ARCHBISHOPS, METROPOLITANS

Archbishop: A bishop with the title of an archdiocese.

Metropolitan Archbishop: Head of the principal see, an archdiocese, in an ecclesiastical province consisting of several dioceses. He has the full powers of bishop in his own archdiocese and limited supervisory jurisdiction and influence over the other (suffragan) dioceses in the province.

Titular Archbishop: Has the title of an archdiocese which formerly existed in fact but now exists in title only. He does not have ordinary jurisdiction over an archdiocese.

Archbishop ad personam: A title of personal honor and distinction granted to some bishops. They do not have ordinary jurisdiction over an archdiocese.

Primate: A title given to the ranking prelate of some countries or regions.

BISHOPS

Residential Bishop: A bishop in charge of a diocese.

Titular Bishops: Have the titles of dioceses which formerly existed in fact but now exist in title only. They have delegated authority of jurisdiction, by grant in line with their assignments, rather than the ordinary jurisdiction of office which belongs to a residential bishop. An auxiliary bishop (titular) is an assistant to a residential bishop. A coadjutor bishop (titular) is as assistant bishop of higher status; some coadjutors have the right of succession to residential sees.

Episcopal Vicar: An assistant, who may or may not be a bishop, appointed by a residential bishop as his deputy for a certain part of a diocese, a determined type of apostolic work, or the faithful of a certain rite.

Eparch, Exarch: Titles of bishops of Eastern-Rite churches.

Nomination of Bishops: Nominees for episcopal ordination are selected in several ways. Final appointment in all cases is subject to decision by the pope.

In the US, bishops periodically submit the names of candidates to the archbishop of their province. The names are then considered at a meeting of the bishops of the province, and those receiving a favorable vote are forwarded to the apostolic delegate for transmission to the Holy See. Bishops are free to seek the counsel of priests, religious and lay persons with respect to nominees.

Eastern-Rite churches have their own procedures and synodal regulations for nominating and making final selection of candidates for episcopal ordination.

In some countries where concordat or other special arrangements are in effect, civil governments have specified privileges to express approval or disapproval of candidates for the episcopacy.

Ad Limina Visit: Residential bishops and military vicars are obliged to make a periodic *ad limina* visit ("to the threshold" of the Apostles) to the tombs of Sts. Peter and Paul, have audience with the Holy Father and present a written report of conditions in their dioceses or military jurisdictions. European bishops are required to make the visit every five years. The visits may be made every 10 years by bishops of dioceses on other continents, but a report must be submitted every five years.

OTHER PRELATES

Some prelates and abbots, formerly called *nullius,* have jurisdiction over territories (abbacies, prefectures, prelatures) not under the authority of diocesan bishops.

Vicar Apostolic: Usually a titular bishop who has ordinary jurisdiction over a mission territory. A vicar apostolic could also serve as the administrator of a vacant diocese or a diocese whose bishop is impeded from the exercise of his office.

Prefect Apostolic: A prelate with ordinary jurisdiction over a mission territory.

Apostolic Administrator: Usually a bishop appointed to administer an ecclesiastical jurisdiction temporarily. Administrators of lesser rank are also appointed for special and more restricted supervisory duties.

Vicar General: A bishop's deputy for the administration of a diocese. Such a vicar does not have to be a bishop.

HONORARY PRELATES

Honorary prelates belonging to the Pontifical Household are: Apostolic Prothonotaries, Honorary Prelates of His Holiness, and Chaplains of His Holiness. Their title is Reverend Monsignor.

SYNOD OF BISHOPS

The Synod of Bishops was chartered by Pope Paul Sept. 15, 1965, in a document he issued on his own initiative under the title, *Apostolica Sollicitudo*. According to the document:

• The purposes of the Synod are: "to encourage close union and valued assistance between the Sovereign Pontiff and the bishops of the entire world; to insure that direct and real information is provided on questions and situations touching upon the internal action of the Church and its necessary activity in the world of today; to facilitate agreement on essential points of doctrine and on methods of procedure in the life of the Church."

• The Synod is a central ecclesiastical institution, permanent by nature.

• The Synod is directly and immediately subject to the Pope, who has authority to assign its agenda, to call it into session, and to give its members deliberative as well as advisory authority.

• In addition to a limited number of ex officio members and a few heads of male religious institutes, the majority of the members are elective by and representative of national or regional episcopal conferences. The Pope reserved the right to appoint the general secretary, special secretaries and no more than 15 per cent of the total membership.

First Meeting, 1967

The Synod met for the first time from Sept. 29 to Oct. 29, 1967, in Vatican City. Its objectives, as stated by Pope Paul at the first session, were "the preservation and strengthening of the Catholic faith, its integrity, its force, its development, its doctrinal and historical coherence."

One result of synodal deliberations was a recommendation to the Pope to establish an international commission of theologians to assist the Congregation for the Doctrine of the Faith and to broaden approaches to theological research. The commission was sub-

sequently set up by Pope Paul in 1969.

In other actions, the Synod called for the formulation of a Code of Canon Law more pastoral than the one in force since 1918 and more in touch with the mentality, aspirations and needs of people in contemporary circumstances; favored the view that episcopal conferences should have major control over seminaries in their respective areas; suggested some changes in pastoral procedures with respect to mixed marriages, which were authorized in 1970; gave general approval to the New Order of the Mass which was promulgated and put into effect in 1969.

The first meeting of the Synod had 197 participants: 135 representatives of more than 90 episcopal conferences, 13 representatives of Eastern-Rite churches, 13 cardinals of the Roman Curia, 10 representatives of the Union of Superiors General of Religious, 25 members and a secretary general appointed by Pope Paul.

Extraordinary Session

The second Synod of Bishops, meeting in extraordinary session Oct. 11 to 28, 1969, opened the door to wider participation by the bishops with the Pope and each other in the government of the Church.

The business assigned to the meeting by Pope Paul was to seek and examine ways and means of putting into practice the principle of collegiality which figured largely in declarations of the Second Vatican Council on the Church and the pastoral office of bishops.

Accordingly, proceedings were oriented to three main points: (1) the nature and implications of collegiality; (2) the relationships of bishops and their conferences to the Pope; (3) the relationships of bishops and their conferences to each other. The end results were three proposals approved by the bishops and the Pope, and five times that number approved and placed under advisement by the Pope. All proposals pointed in the direction of more cooperative action by all the bishops with the Pope in the conduct of Church affairs.

The three proposals which were approved and moved for action provided for regular meetings of the Synod at two-year intervals, staff organization and operations of the general secretariat in the interim between meetings, and openness of the synodal agenda to suggestions by bishops.

The second meeting had 146 participants: 93 presidents of episcopal conferences — 22 from Europe, 14 from Asia, 29 from Africa, 24 from the Americas, four from Oceania; 13 representatives of Eastern-Rite Churches — six patriarchs, one major archbishop, six metropolitans; three religious, elected by the Union of Superiors General; 19 officials from the various departments of the Roman Curia; secretary general Bishop Ladislaw Rubin, and 17 appointees of Pope Paul.

Between the second and third meetings of the Synod, an advisory council of 15 members (12 elected, three appointed by the Pope) was formed to provide the secretariat with adequate staff for carrying on liaison with episcopal conferences and for drawing up the agenda of synodal meetings. The council, at its first meeting May 12 to 15, 1970, followed the lead of the second assembly by opening the agenda of the 1971 meeting to the suggestions of bishops from all over the world.

Synod '71

The ministerial priesthood and justice in the world were the principal topics of discussion at the third and longest meeting, the Second General Assembly of the Synod, Sept. 30 to Nov. 6, 1971.

Advisory reports on these subjects, compiled from views expressed by the bishops before and during the synodal sessions, were presented to Pope Paul at the end of the meeting. He authorized publication of the reports and said, in a letter made public Dec. 9, that he accepted conclusions reached by the bishops which "conform to the current norms" of church teaching.

The Priesthood

In its report on the priesthood, the Synod described difficulties experienced by priests, stated traditional doctrinal principles on the priesthood, and drew from these principles a set of guidelines for priestly life and ministry in the mission of Christ and the Church, and in the communion of the Church.

The report emphasized the primary and permanent dedication of priests in the Church to the ministry of word, sacrament and pastoral service as a full-time occupation.

The synodal Fathers — with 168 votes in favor without reservations, 21 votes in favor with reservations, and 10 votes against — supported the existing discipline of clerical celibacy. They favored leaving to the discretion of the Pope decisions regarding the ordination of already married men in special circumstances. They did not consider the question of permitting already ordained priests to marry. The majority voted against permitting priests who had left the ministry to resume priestly duties, although they said such priests could serve the Church in other ways and should be treated in a just and fraternal manner.

Justice in the World

In connection with "the mission of the People of God to further justice in the world," a synodal report reviewed a wide range of existing injustices; cited the social-justice imperatives of the Gospel; called for the practice of justice throughout the Church and for greater efforts in education and ecumenical collaboration for justice; and outlined an eight-point program for international action.

Behind the Synod's recommendations were the convictions:

• "The Church . . . has a proper and specific responsibility which is identified with her mission of giving witness before the world of the need for love and justice contained in the Gospel message, a witness to be carried out in church institutions themselves and in the lives of Christians."

• "Action on behalf of justice and participation in the transformation of the world fully appear to us as a constitutive dimension of the preaching of the Gospel; or, in other words, of the Church's mission for the redemption of the human race and its liberation from every oppressive situation."

• "The present situation of the world, seen in the light of faith, calls us back to the very essence of the Christian message, creating in us a deep awareness of its true meaning and of its urgent demands. The mission of preaching the Gospel dictates at the present time that we should dedicate ourselves to the liberation of man even in his present existence in this world. For, unless the Christian message of love and justice shows its effectiveness through action in the cause of justice in the world, it will only with difficulty gain credibility with the men of our times."

State of the Church

At the beginning of the assembly, the Synod received a state-of-the-Church report which pinpointed a number of contemporary problems, including:

(1) scandals and ·disturbances because of the departure of priests from the ministry;

(2) "a certain decline in the tone of the spiritual life of clergy and laity";

(3) "disputes within the Church, which at times take on radical or corrosive forms";

(4) the efforts of some persons to "minimize the institutional aspect of the Church by exalting its mystical, charismatic or prophetic nature" out of proper proportion;

(5) lack of "religious acceptance of the Church's authentic teaching authority";

(6) need for clarification of the relations between local churches and the universal Church.

Another report presented during the Synod concerned progress made by a special commission in drafting a Fundamental Law of the Church.

The assembly had 210 participants: six patriarchs, one major archbishop, seven Eastern-Rite metropolitans (one of whom was listed also as a representative of an episcopal conference), 142 elected representatives of 94 episcopal conferences, 10 men religious elected by the Union of Major Superiors, 19 cardinals of the Roman Curia, and 26 papal appointees — the general secretary, 22 bishops and three priests.

Delegates from the US were: Cardinals John F. Dearden, John J. Krol (who was elected to the advisory council of the permanent secretariat of the Synod), John J. Carberry, and Coadjutor Archbishop Leo C. Byrne — elected by the National Conference of Catholic Bishops; Eastern-Rite Archbishops Ambrose Senyshyn and Stephen Kocisko; papal appointees Bishop William W. Baum, Archbishop Martin J. O'Connor and Father Edward Heston, C.S.C. Cardinal John J. Wright, one of the three presiding legates of the Pope, attended in his official capacity as head of the Congregation for the Clergy. Fathers John F. Cronin and Barnabas Ahern, C.P., were two of 23 priests appointed by Pope Paul to attend the Synod as auditors.

ROMAN CURIA

The Roman Curia consists of the Secretariat of State, the Sacred Council for the Public Affairs of the Church, ten congregations, three tribunals, three secretariats, and a complex of commissions, councils and offices which administer church affairs at the highest level.

Background

The Curia evolved gradually from advisory assemblies or synods of the Roman clergy with whose assistance the popes directed church affairs during the first 11 centuries. Its original office was the Apostolic Chancery, dating from the fourth century. The antecedents of its permanently functioning agencies and offices were special commissions of cardinals and prelates. Its establishment in a form resembling what it is now dates from the second half of the 16th century.

Pope Paul VI gave the following short account of the background of the Curia in the apostolic constitution *Regimini Ecclesiae Universae* ("For the Government of the Universal Church"), dated Aug. 15, 1967.

"The Roman Pontiffs, successors to Blessed Peter, have striven to provide for the government of the Universal Church by making use of experts to advise and assist them.

"In this connection, we should remember both the Presbyterium of the City of Rome and the College of Cardinals of the Holy Roman Church which in the course of centuries evolved from it. Then, little by little, as we know, out of that office (Apostolic Chancery) which was set up in the fourth century to transmit papal documents, many offices developed; to these was added the Auditorium, which was a well-developed tribunal in the 13th century and which was more thoroughly organized by John XXII (1316-1334).

"With an increase in the volume of things to be dealt with, bodies or commissions of cardinals selected to treat of specific questions began to be more efficiently organized in the 16th century, from which eventually arose the congregations of the Roman Curia. It is to the credit of our predecessor Sixtus V that, in the constitution *Immensa Aeterni Dei*

of Jan. 22, 1558, he arranged the sacred councils in an orderly manner and wisely described the structure of the Roman Curia.

"With the progress of time, however, it happened that some of them became obsolete, others had to be added, and others had to be restructured. This is the work our predecessor St. Paul X set out to do with the constitution *Sapienti Consilio* of June 29, 1908. Its provisions, a lasting testimony to that wise and ingenious pastor of the Church, were with a few changes incorporated into the Code of Canon Law" (Canons 242-264).

Reorganization

Pope Paul initiated a four-year reorganization study in 1963 which resulted in the constitution *Regimini Ecclesiae Universae.*

While the study was underway, the Pope took preliminary steps toward curial reorganization by reorienting and changing the title of the Sacred Congregation of the Holy Office (to the Sacred Congregation for the Doctrine of the Faith) and by appointing a number of non-Italians to key curial positions.

The stated purposes of the reorganization were to increase the efficiency of the Curia and to make it more responsive to the needs and concerns of the Universal Church. The pursuit of these objectives involved various modifications.

Curial Departments

• The Office of the Pope, including the Papal Secretariat or Secretariat of State and the Council for the Public Affairs of the Church.

• Ten congregations, instead of twelve as formerly. The functions of the Sacred Congregation of Ceremonies were transferred to the Prefecture of the Pontifical Household; the duties of the Sacred Congregation for Extraordinary Ecclesiastical Affairs were taken over by the Sacred Council for the Public Affairs of the Church; the Sacred Congregation of the Basilica of St. Peter was reduced in rank. In 1969, the Sacred Congregation of Rites was phased out of existence and its functions were assigned to the Sacred Congregation for the Causes of Saints and the Sacred Congregation for Divine Worship.

• Three secretariats, the Council of the Laity and the Pontifical Commission on Justice and Peace.

• Three tribunals.

• Six offices, including the former Apostolic Chancery and Apostolic Chamber, and the newly constituted Prefecture of Economic Affairs, Prefecture of the Pontifical Household, Administration of the Patrimony of the Apostolic See, and Central Statistics Office. Functions of the former Apostolic Datary and the Secretariats of State, of Briefs to

Princes, and of Latin Letters were transferred to the Secretariat of State.

Operational Procedures

• The papal secretary or secretary of state has authority to take initiative in coordinating and expediting curial business through meetings and other cooperative procedures with department heads.

• Officials of departments have five-year terms of office, which may be renewed. Resignation is automatic on the death of a pope. The five-year terms of consultors are renewable.

• Diocesan bishops as well as full-time curial personnel have membership in curial departments, in accordance with provisions of the decree *Pro Comperto Sane* of Aug. 6, 1967. Seven diocesan bishops hold five-year membership in each congregation, with full rights to participation in the more important plenary assemblies scheduled once a year. They are also entitled to take part in routine meetings whenever they are in Rome. Three general superiors of male religious institutes hold similar membership in the Sacred Congregation for Religious and Secular Institutes.

• Lay persons are eligible to serve as consultors to curial departments.

• Close liaison with episcopal conferences is required. They should be given prior notice of forthcoming curial decrees affecting them in any special way.

• In line with customary procedure, matters in which the competence of two or more departments is involved are handled on a cooperative basis, with mutual consultation and decision.

• Although Latin remains the official language of the Curia, communication in any of the widely known modern languages is acceptable.

• Informational and financial services are centralized in the Central Statistics Office and the Prefecture of Economic Affairs, respectively.

• Heads of curial departments are required to notify the pope before conducting any serious or extraordinary business.

• Authority to act and decide on many matters belongs to departmental officials in virtue of delegation from the pope. Some matters, however, have to be referred to the pope for final decision.

Internationalization

The international complexion of personnel in the Roman Curia changed considerably during the decade from 1961 to 1970. The number of non-Italians increased from 570 to more than 1,400, a rise of 145 per cent, while the number of Italians increased from 750 to 850, a rise of only 14 per cent. In 1970, 62 per cent were from other countries, as compared with 44 per cent in 1961.

DEPARTMENTS OF THE CURIA

Secretariat of State

The Secretariat of State provides the pope with the closest possible assistance in the care of the Universal Church and in dealings with all departments of the Curia.

The cardinal secretary is the key coordinator of curial operations. He has authority to call meetings of the prefects of all departments for expediting the conduct of business, for consultation and intercommunication. He handles: any and all matters entrusted to him by the pope, and ordinary matters which are not within the competence of other departments; some relations with bishops; relations with representatives of the Holy See, civil governments and their representatives, without prejudice to the competence of the Council for the Public Affairs of the Church.

The cardinal secretary has been likened to a prime minister or head of government because of the significant role he plays in coordinating curial operations at the highest level.

The secretariat has two offices for preparing and writing letters for the pope (functions formerly performed by the Secretariat of Briefs to Princes and the Secretariat of Latin Letters), and a Central Statistics Office.

It also handles work formerly done by the Apostolic Datary (the dating and countersigning of papal documents, and the management of church benefices).

It has supervisory duties over the Commission for the Instruments of Social Communication, Two Vatican publications, *Acta Apostolicae Sedis* and *Annuario Pontificio*, and the Vatican Personnel Office.

The Prefecture of Vatican City is answerable to the secretary of state.

OFFICIALS: Cardinal Jean Villot, secretary of state (Cardinal Amleto G. Cicognani, secretary emeritus); Most Rev. Giovanni Benelli, substitute secretary and secretary of the Cifra.

Council for Public Affairs

The Council for the Public Affairs of the Church handles diplomatic and other relations with civil governments. With the Secretariat of State, it supervises matters concerning nunciatures, internunciatures and apostolic delegations. It also has supervision of the Pontifical Commission for Russia.

The council has the same head as the Secretariat of State.

OFFICIALS: Cardinal Jean Villot, prefect, secretary of state; Most Rev. Agostino Casaroli, secretary.

BACKGROUND: Originated by Pius VI in 1793 as the Congregation for Extraordinary Affairs from the Kingdom of the Gauls; given wider scope by Pius VII, July 19, 1814; formerly called the Sacred Congregation for Extraordinary Ecclesiastical Affairs.

CONGREGATIONS

Doctrine of the Faith

The function of the Sacred Congregation for the Doctrine of the Faith is to safeguard the doctrine of faith and morals.

Accordingly, it examines doctrinal questions; promotes studies thereon; evaluates theological opinions and, when necessary and after prior consultation with concerned bishops, reproves those regarded as opposed to principles of the faith; examines books on doctrinal matters and can reprove such works, if the contents so warrant, after giving authors the opportunity to defend themselves.

It examines matters pertaining to the Privilege of Faith (Petrine Privilege) in marriage cases, and safeguards the dignity of the sacrament of penance.

It has working relations with the Pontifical Biblical Commission.

In 1969, Pope Paul set up a Theological Commission (see separate entry) as an adjunct to the congregation, to provide it with the advisory services of additional experts in theology and allied disciplines.

OFFICIALS: Cardinal Franjo Seper, prefect; Most Rev. Paul Philippe, O.P., secretary.

BACKGROUND: At the beginning of the 13th century, legates of Innocent III were commissioned as the Holy Office of the Inquisition to combat heresy; the same task was entrusted to the Dominican Order by Gregory IX in 1231 and to the Friars Minor by Innocent IV from 1243 to 1254. On July 21, 1542 (apostolic constitution *Licet*), Paul III instituted a permanent congregation of cardinals with supreme and universal competence over matters concerning heretics and those suspected of heresy. Pius IV, St. Pius V and Sixtus V further defined the work of the Congregation. St. Pius X changed its name to Congregation of the Holy Office.

Paul VI, in virtue of the motu proprio *Integrae Servandae* of Dec. 7, 1965, began reorganization of the Curia with this body, to which he gave the new title, Sacred Congregation for the Doctrine of the Faith. Its orientation is not merely negative, in the condemnation of error, but positive, in the promotion of orthodox doctrine. The right of appeal, judicial representation, and the consultation of their proper regional conference of bishops, are assured to persons accused of unorthodox doctrine. The office for the censorship of books and the Roman Index of Prohibited Books were abolished.

Oriental Churches

The Sacred Congregation for the Oriental Churches has competence in matters concerning the persons and discipline of Eastern Rite Churches. It has jurisdiction over territories in which the majority of Christians belong to Oriental Rites (i. e., Egypt, the Sinai Peninsula, Eritrea, Northern Ethiopia, Southern Albania, Bulgaria, Cyprus, Greece, Iran, Iraq, Lebanon, Palestine, Syria, Jordan, Turkey, Afghanistan, the part of Thrace subject to Turkey); also, over minority communities of Orientals no matter where they live.

To assure adequate and equal representation, it has as many offices as there are rites of Oriental Churches in communion with the Holy See.

It is under mandate to consult with the Secretariat for Promoting Christian Unity on questions concerning separated Oriental Churches, and with the Secretariat for Non-Christians, especially in relations with Moslems.

It has a special commission on the liturgy and an Oriental Church Information Service.

OFFICIALS: Cardinal Maximillen de Furstenberg, prefect; Most Rev. Mario Brini, secretary.

Members include all Eastern Rite patriarchs and the president of the Secretariat for Promoting Christian Unity. Consultors include the secretary of the same secretariat.

BACKGROUND: Special congregations for the affairs of the Greek and other Oriental Churches were founded long before this body was created by Pius IX Jan. 6, 1862 (apostolic constitution *Romani Pontifices*), and united with the Sacred Congregation for the Propagation of the Faith. The congregation was made autonomous by Benedict XV May 1, 1917 (motu proprio *Dei Providentis*), and given wider authority by Pius XI Mar. 25, 1938 (motu proprio *Sancta Dei Ecclesia*). John XXIII appointed six patriarchs, five of Eastern Rites and one of the Roman Rite, to the congregation and gave them the same rights as cardinals belonging to the body, in March, 1963. Paul VI named representatives of all Eastern-Rite bodies to serve as consultors of the congregation, in November, 1963.

Bishops

The Sacred Congregation for Bishops, formerly called the Sacred Consistorial Congregation, has functions related in one way or another to bishops and the jurisdictions in which they serve.

Its concerns are: the establishment and changing of dioceses, provinces, military vicariates and other jurisdictions; providing for the naming of bishops and other prelates; studying things concerning the persons, work and pastoral activity of bishops; providing for the care of bishops when they leave office; receiving and studying reports on the conditions of dioceses; general supervision of the holding and recognition of particular councils and conferences of bishops; publishing and circulating pastoral norms and guidelines through conferences of bishops.

It supervises the Pontifical Commission

for Latin America and the Pontifical Commission for Migration and Tourism.

OFFICIALS: Cardinal Carlo Confalonieri, prefect; Most Rev. Ernesto Civardi, secretary.

Ex officio members are the prefects of the Council for the Public Affairs of the Church, and of the Congregations for the Doctrine of the Faith, for the Clergy, and for Catholic Education. The substitute secretaries and undersecretaries of these curial departments are ex officio consultors.

BACKGROUND: Established by Sixtus V Jan. 22, 1588 (apostolic constitution *Immensa*); given an extension of powers by St. Pius X June 20, 1908, and Pius XII Aug. 1, 1952 (apostolic constitution *Exsul Familia*).

Discipline of the Sacraments

The Sacred Congregation for the Discipline of the Sacraments supervises the discipline of the seven sacraments, without prejudice to the competencies of the Sacred Congregation for the Doctrine of the Faith and other curial departments.

It issues decrees regarding the discipline of the sacraments and the celebration of Mass, and has the power of decision regarding the fact of non-consummation in marriage and concerning questions about the obligations and validity of holy orders.

OFFICIALS: Cardinal Antonio Samore, prefect; Most Rev. Giuseppe Casoria, secretary.

BACKGROUND: The congregation was instituted by St. Pius X June 29, 1908 (apostolic constitution *Sapienti Consilio*).

Divine Worship

The Sacred Congregation for Divine Worship has general competence over the ritual and pastoral aspects of divine worship in the Roman and other Latin Rites. These matters were formerly handled by the Congregation of Rites.

The congregation has three offices.

One office deals with divine worship from the ritual or pastoral point of view and supervises the updating and publication of liturgical books. A second office handles relations with regional episcopal conferences and is responsible for decisions on liturgical adaptations proposed by such conferences. The third office has liaison duties with national liturgical commissions.

OFFICIALS: Cardinal Arturo Tabera Araoz, prefect; Most Rev. Annibale Bugnini, C.M., secretary.

BACKGROUND: The functions and title of the congregation were determined by Paul VI May 8, 1969 (apostolic constitution *Sacra Rituum Congregatio*). Formerly, its duties were performed by the Congregation of Rites, which was established by Sixtus V in 1588 and affected by legislation of Pius XI in 1930.

In 1970 the congregation took over the functions of the Consilium for Implementing the Second Vatican Council's *Constitution on the Sacred Liturgy*, an auxiliary body established in 1964.

Causes of Saints

The Sacred Congregation for the Causes of Saints handles all matters connected with beatification and canonization procedures, and the preservation of relics. These affairs were formerly under the supervision of the Congregation of Rites.

The congregation carries on its work through three sections or offices.

One section is a juridical office with supervisory responsibility over procedures and examinations conducted to determine the holiness of prospective saints. It includes a medical commission for the study of miracles attributed to the intercession of candidates for sainthood.

A second section, headed by the promoter general of the faith, who is popularly called the "Devil's Advocate," serves the purpose of establishing beyond reasonable doubt the evidence of holiness advanced in support of beatification and canonization causes.

Research and evaluation of documentary evidence figuring in canonization causes are the functions of the historic-hagiographical section.

OFFICIALS: Cardinal Paolo Bertoli, prefect; Most Rev. Giuseppe Ferdinando Antonelli, O.F.M., secretary.

BACKGROUND: The functions and title of this congregation were determined by Paul VI May 8, 1969 (apostolic constitution *Sacra Rituum Congregatio*). Formerly, its duties were carried out by the Congregation of Rites, which was established by Sixtus V in 1588 and affected by legislation of Pius XI in 1930.

Clergy

The Sacred Congregation for the Clergy, formerly called the Sacred Congregation of the Council, handles matters concerning the persons, work and pastoral ministry of clerics who exercise their apostolate in a diocese. Such clerics are diocesan deacons and priests, and religious who are engaged in ordinary parochial ministry in a diocese.

It carries on its work through three offices.

One office promotes the spiritual growth and formation as well as the professional competence of priests by encouraging the establishment and operation of pastoral institutes and other study opportunities; oversees the general discipline of the clergy, the establishment and conduct of pastoral councils and senates of priests, and resolves controversies among clerics; has a mandate to draw up a set of general principles to direct a better distribution of priests for pastoral service.

A second office, in view of its primary concern for preaching of the word of God, encourages effective apostolic programs and methods, with special emphasis on catechetical and other forms of religious training and formation for the faithful.

A third office has supervisory responsibility over church property and the temporalities of priestly life; among its functions are efforts to provide for the support of the clergy through suitable salary scales, pensions, security and health insurance programs, and other measures.

OFFICIALS: Cardinal John J. Wright, prefect; Most Rev. Pietro Palazzini, secretary.

BACKGROUND: Established by Pius IV Aug. 2, 1564 (apostolic constitution *Alias Nos*), under the title, Sacred Congregation of the Cardinals Interpreters of the Council of Trent; affected by legislation of Gregory XIII and Sixtus V.

Religious and Secular Institutes

The extension of the title of this congregation, which was formerly known as the Sacred Congregation of Religious or for the Affairs of Religious, indicates its dual competence over institutes of religious, together with societies of the common life without vows, and secular institutes.

One section deals with the affairs of all religious institutes and societies of the common life, and their members. It has authority in matters related to the establishment, general direction and suppression of institutes; general discipline in line with their rules and constitutions; the movement toward renewal and adaptation of institutes in contemporary circumstances; the setting up and encouragement of councils and conferences of major religious superiors for intercommunication and other purposes.

A second section has the same competence over the affairs and members of secular institutes as the first has over religious.

OFFICIALS: Cardinal Ildebrando Antoniutti, prefect; Most. Rev. Augustine Mayer, O.S.B., secretary.

BACKGROUND: Founded by Sixtus V May 27, 1586, with the title, Sacred Congregation for Consultations of Regulars (apostolic constitution *Romanus Pontifex*); confirmed by the apostolic constitution *Immensa* Jan. 22, 1588; made part of the Congregation for Consultations of Bishops and other Prelates in 1601; made autonomous by St. Pius X in 1908.

Catholic Education

The Sacred Congregation for Catholic Education, formerly known as the Sacred Congregation of Seminaries and Universities, has supervisory competence over institutions and works of Catholic education.

It carries on its work through three offices.

One office handles matters connected with the direction, discipline and temporal administration of seminaries, and with the education of diocesan clergy, religious and members of secular institutes.

A second office oversees Catholic universities, faculties of study and other institutions of higher learning inasmuch as they depend on the authority of the Church; encourages cooperation and mutual assistance among Catholic institutions, and the establishment of Catholic hospices and centers on campuses of non-Catholic institutions.

A third office is concerned in various ways with all Catholic schools below the college-university level, with general questions concerning education and studies, and with the cooperation of conferences of bishops and civil authorities in educational matters.

The congregation supervises Pontifical Works for Priestly Vocations.

OFFICIALS: Cardinal Gabriel Garrone, prefect; Most Rev. Joseph Schroeffer, secretary.

BACKGROUND: The title and functions of the congregation were defined by Benedict XV Nov. 4, 1915; Pius XI, in 1931 and 1932, and Pius XII, in 1941 and 1949, extended its functions. Its work had previously been carried on by two other congregations erected by Sixtus V in 1588 and Leo XII in 1824.

Evangelization of Peoples

Propagation of the Faith

This congregation, which has alternative titles, directs and coordinates missionary work throughout the world.

Accordingly, it has competence over those matters which concern all the missions established for the spread of Christ's kingdom. These include: fostering missionary vocations; providing for the training of missionaries in seminaries; assigning missionaries to fields of work; establishing ecclesiastical jurisdictions and proposing candidates to serve them as bishops and in other capacities; encouraging the recruitment and development of indigenous clergy; mobilizing spiritual and financial support for missionary activity.

In general, the varied competence of the congregation extends to most persons and affairs of the Church in areas classified as mission territories.

To promote missionary cooperation, the congregation has a Supreme Council for the Direction of Pontifical Missionary Works. Subject to this council are the general councils of the Missionary Union of the Clergy, the Society for the Propagation of the Faith, the Society of St. Peter the Apostle for Native Clergy, the Society of the Holy Childhood, and the *Fides* news agency.

OFFICIALS: Cardinal Agnelo Rossi, prefect; Most Rev. Sergio Pignedoli, secretary; Most Revs. Bernardin Gantin and Duraisamy S. Lourdusamy, associate secretaries.

The heads of the Secretariats for Promoting Christian Unity, for Non-Christians, and for Non-Believers are ex officio members of the congregation.

BACKGROUND: Originated as a commission of cardinals by Gregory XIII and modified by Clement VIII to promote the reconciliation of separated Eastern Christians; erected as a stable congregation by Gregory XV June 22, 1622 (apostolic constitution *Inscrutabili*).

TRIBUNALS
Sacred Apostolic Penitentiary

This tribunal has jurisdiction for the internal forum only (sacramental and nonsacramental). It issues decisions on questions of conscience; grants absolutions, dispensations, commutations, sanations and condonations; has charge of non-doctrinal matters pertaining to indulgences.

OFFICIALS: Cardinal Giuseppe Ferretto, major penitentiary; Msgr. Giovanni Sessolo, regent.

BACKGROUND: Origin dates back to the 12th century; affected by the legislation of many popes; radically reorganized by St. Pius V in 1569; jurisdiction limited to the internal forum by St. Pius X; Benedict XV annexed the Office of Indulgences to it Mar. 25, 1917.

Apostolic Signatura

The principal concerns of this supreme court of the Church are to resolve questions concerning juridical procedure and to supervise the observance of laws and rights at the highest level. It decides the jurisdictional competence of lower courts and has jurisdiction in cases involving personnel and decisions of the Rota. It is the supreme court of the State of Vatican City.

OFFICIALS: Cardinal Dino Staffa, prefect; Most Rev. Aurelio Sabatini, secretary.

BACKGROUND: A permanent office of the Signatura has existed since the time of Eugene IV in the 15th century; affected by the legislation of many popes; reorganized by St. Pius X in 1908 and made the supreme tribunal of the Church.

Sacred Roman Rota

The Rota is the ordinary court of appeal for cases appealed to the Holy See. It is best known for its competence and decisions in cases concerning the validity of marriage.

OFFICIAL: Most Rev. Boleslaus Filipiak, dean.

BACKGROUND: Originated in the Apostolic Chancery; affected by the legislation of many popes; reorganized by St. Pius X in 1908 and further revised by Pius XI in 1934.

At the start of the judicial year, Pope Paul VI told judges of the Rota Jan. 28, 1972, that "the inviolable laws of family life . . . should have careful and unchanging support for the sake of the common good."

SECRETARIATS
Christian Unity

Promoting unity among Christians is the function and competence of this secretariat.

Accordingly, it handles relations with members of other ecclesial communities; deals with the correct interpretation and execution of the principles of ecumenism; initiates or promotes Catholic ecumenical groups and coordinates on national and international levels the efforts of those promoting Christian unity; undertakes dialogue regarding ecumenical questions and activities with churches and ecclesial communities separated from the Apostolic See; sends Catholic observer-representatives to Christian gatherings, and invites to Catholic gatherings observers of other churches; orders into execution conciliar decrees dealing with ecumenical affairs.

It has competence in the religious aspects of matters pertaining to the Jews.

It has two offices, for the West and for the East. Each office is under the immediate direction of a delegate.

The prefects of the Congregation for the Oriental Churches and of the Congregation for the Evangelization of Peoples are ex officio members of the secretariat. Consultors include the secretaries of these two departments.

OFFICIALS: Cardinal Jan Willebrands, president; Rev. Jerome Hamer, O.P., secretary.

BACKGROUND: Established by John XXIII June 5, 1960, as a preparatory secretariat of the Second Vatican Council; raised to commission status during the first session of the council in the fall of 1962; this status confirmed Jan. 3, 1966.

For Non-Christians

This secretariat is concerned with persons who are not Christians but profess some kind of religious faith. Its function is to promote studies and dialogue for the purpose of increasing mutual understanding and respect between Christians and non-Christians.

It has a special office for handling relations with Moslems.

The prefect of the Congregation for the Evangelization of Peoples is an ex officio member of the secretariat.

OFFICIALS: Cardinal Paolo Marella, president; Very Rev. Peter Humbertclaude, S.M., secretary.

BACKGROUND: Established by Paul VI May 19, 1964.

For Non-Believers

This secretariat studies the background and philosophy of atheism, and initiates and carries on dialogue with non-believers.

OFFICIALS: Cardinal Franz Koenig,

president; Most Rev. Antonio Mauro, vice-president; Rev. Vincenzo Miano, S.D.B., secretary.

BACKGROUND: Established by Paul VI Apr. 9, 1965.

COUNCILS, COMMISSIONS

Council of the Laity: Instituted by Paul VI Jan. 6, 1967, to promote the development of the lay apostolate as a service agency for: coordinating apostolic works, establishing liaison between lay persons and the hierarchy, compiling doctrinal studies on the role of lay persons in pastoral activity, establishing and maintaining a documentation center; Cardinal Maurice Roy, president.

Commission on Justice and Peace: Instituted by Paul VI Jan. 6, 1967, to develop awareness among the People of God of their mission to promote the progress of poor nations, to encourage international social justice, to help underdeveloped nations work for their own improvement, to seek ways and means of establishing peace in the world; Cardinal Maurice Roy, president.

Revision of the Code of Canon Law: Instituted by John XXIII Mar. 28, 1963, to replace a former commission dating from 1917; Cardinal Pericle Felici, president.

Revision of the Code of Oriental Canon Law: Reconstituted by Paul VI in 1972 to replace a former commission dating from July 17, 1935, "to prepare . . . the reform of the Code of Oriental Canon Law, both in the sections already published by . . . four motu proprios" (1,950 canons concerning marriage; processes; religious, church property and terminology; Eastern Rites and persons "and in the remaining sections which have been completed but not published" (the balance of a total of 2,666 canons).

Interpretation of the Decrees of the Second Vatican Council: Cardinal Pericle Felici, president.

Social Communication: Instituted on an experimental basis by Pius XII in 1948; reorganized three times in the 1950's; made permanent commission by John XXIII Feb. 22, 1959; name changed to present title Apr. 11, 1964; authorized to implement the *Decree on the Instruments of Social Communication* promulgated by the Second Vatican Council; under supervision of the Secretariat of State and the Council for the Public Affairs of the Church; Most Rev. Edward L. Heston, C.S.C., president; Most Rev. Martin J. O'Connor, president emeritus.

Latin America: Instituted by Pius XII Apr. 19, 1958; placed under supervision of the Congregation for Bishops July, 1969; Cardinal Carlo Confalonieri, president.

Migration and Tourism: Instituted by Paul VI Mar. 19, 1970, for pastoral assistance to migrants, nomads, tourists, sea and air travelers; placed under the general supervision and direction of the Congregation for Bishops;

Cardinal Carlo Confalonieri, president.

Cor Unum: Instituted by Paul VI July 15, 1971, to provide informational and coordinating services for Catholic aid and human development organizations and projects on a worldwide scale; Cardinal Jean Villot, president.

Theological Commission: Innstituted by Paul VI Apr. 11, 1969, as an advisory adjunct of no more than 30 theologians to the Congregation for the Doctrine of the Faith; Cardinal Franjo Seper, president.

Biblical Commission: Instituted by Leo XIII Oct. 30, 1902; completely restructured by Paul VI June 27, 1971.

Abbey of St. Jerome for the Revision and Emendation of the Vulgate: Instituted by Pius XI June 15, 1933, to replace an earlier commission established by St. Pius X; Rev. Vincent Truijen, superior.

Revision of the New Vulgate: Instituted by Paul VI in 1965 to augment the work of the Abbey of St. Jerome; Most Rev. Edward Schick, president.

Sacred Archeology: Instituted by Pius IX Jan. 6, 1852; Most Rev. Gennaro Verolino, president.

Historical Sciences: Instituted by Pius XII Apr. 7, 1954, as a continuation of a commission dating from 1883; Msgr. Michael Maccarrone, president.

Ecclesiastical Archives of Italy: Instituted by Pius XII Apr. 5, 1955; Msgr. Martino Giusti, president.

Sacred Art in Italy: Instituted by Pius XI Sept. 1, 1924; Most Rev. Giovanni Fallani, president.

Sanctuaries of Pompei and Loreto: Originated by Leo XIII; under supervision of the Congregation for the Clergy; Cardinal Silvio Oddi, president.

Russia: Instituted by Pius XI Apr. 6, 1930, to handle all ecclesiastical affairs of the country; placed under supervision of the Congregation for Extraordinary Ecclesiastical Affairs (now the Council for the Public Affairs of the Church) in 1934, with jurisdiction limited to clergy and faithful of the Roman Rite; under supervision of the Council for the Public Affairs of the Church; Most Rev. Agostino Casaroli, president.

State of Vatican City: Cardinal Jean Villot, president.

Protection of the Historical and Artistic Monuments of the Holy See: Instituted by Pius XI in 1923, reorganized by Paul VI in 1963; Most Rev. Giovanni Fallani, president.

Preservation of the Faith, Erection of New Churches in Rome: Instituted by Pius XI Aug. 5, 1930, to replace a commission dating from 1902.

Works of Religion: Instituted by Pius XII June 27, 1942, to bank and administer funds for works of religion; replaced an earlier administration established by Leo XIII in 1887; Most Rev. Paul C. Marcinkus, president.

OFFICES

Apostolic Chancery

The principal function of the chancery is to transmit such important papal documents as apostolic constitutions and letters. The chancery is also responsible for keeping the leaden seal of the pope (the bulla) and the Fisherman's Ring.

OFFICIALS: Cardinal Luigi Traglia, chancellor of the Holy Roman Church; Msgr. Francesco Tinello, regent.

BACKGROUND: Originated in the fourth century office of notaries of the Roman Church, who drew up pontifical acts and kept the archives; St. Pius X restored the title of Chancellor of the Holy Roman Church.

Prefecture of Economic Affairs

The Prefecture of the Economic Affairs of the Holy See is a financial office which coordinates and supervises administration of the temporalities of the Holy See.

OFFICIALS: Cardinal Egidio Vagnozzi, president; Msgr. Giovanni Angelo Abbo, secretary.

BACKGROUND: Established by Paul VI Aug. 15, 1967.

Apostolic Chamber

This office administers the temporal goods and rights of the Holy See between the death of one pope and the election of another, in accordance with special laws.

OFFICIALS: Cardinal Jean Villot, chamberlain of the Holy Roman Church; Most Rev. Vittorio Bartoccetti, vice-chamberlain.

BACKGROUND: Originated in the 11th century; reorganized by Pius XI in 1934.

Administration of Patrimony

The Administration of the Patrimony of the Apostolic See handles the estate of the Apostolic See under the direction of papal delegates acting with ordinary or extraordinary authorization.

OFFICIALS: Cardinal Jean Villot, president; Most Rev. Giuseppe Caprio, secretary.

BACKGROUND: Some of its functions date back to 1878; established by Paul VI Aug. 15, 1967.

Prefecture of Pontifical Household

This office oversees the papal chapel — which is at the service of the pope in his capacity as spiritual head of the Church — and the pontifical family — which is at the service of the pope as a sovereign. It arranges papal audiences, has charge of preparing non-liturgical elements of papal ceremonies, makes all necessary arrangements for papal visits and trips outside the Vatican, and settles questions of protocol connected with papal audiences and other formalities.

OFFICIALS: Most Rev. Jacques Martin, prefect; Msgr. Dino Monduzzi, regent.

BACKGROUND: Established by Paul VI Aug. 15, 1967, under the title, Prefecture of the Apostolic Palace; it supplanted the Sacred Congregation for Ceremonies founded by Sixtus V Jan. 22, 1588. The office was updated and reorganized under the present title by Paul VI, Mar. 28, 1968.

Central Statistics Office

The functions of this service office are to compile, systematize and analyze information on the status and condition of the Church and the needs of its pastoral ministry, from the parish level on up to the top.

The office is one of the organs of the Secretariat of State.

OFFICIAL: Francesco Norese.

BACKGROUND: Established by Paul VI Aug. 15, 1967.

Eleemosynary Office

This office distributes alms and aid to the aged, sick, handicapped and other persons in need.

OFFICIAL: Most Rev. Antonio M. Travia.

BACKGROUND: The office originated as a charitable office in the time of Bl. Gregory X (1271-1276).

Vatican II Archives

The function of the office is preservation of the acts and other documents of the Second Vatican Council:

OFFICIAL: Cardinal Pericle Felici.

Personnel

This office was set up by Paul VI May 9, 1971, to handle personnel relations in the offices and other agencies of the Vatican.

OFFICIAL: Msgr. Antonio Mazzo.

THEOLOGICAL COMMISSION

Establishment of a Theological Commission as an adjunct to the Congregation for the Doctrine of the Faith was announced by Pope Paul Apr. 28, 1969. The move had been recommended by the Second Vatican Council and proposed by the Synod of Bishops.

The purpose of the commission is to provide the Doctrinal Congregation with the consultative and advisory services of theologians and scriptural and liturgical experts representative of various schools of thought. The international membership is restricted to 30.

Membership

The commission is headed by Cardinal Franjo Seper, prefect of the Doctrinal Congregation. Its members, all of whom were appointed by the Pope, are: Bishops Carlo Colombo, president of the Institute Giuseppe Toniolo (Italy); Tharcisse Tshibangu, auxiliary of Kinshasa (Zaire), and Ignace Abdo Khalife, auxiliary of the Patriarchate of Antioch for the Maronites (Lebanon), and Fathers:

Barnabas Ahern, C.P. (US); Hans Urs von Balthasar (Switzerland); Louis Bouyer, C.O. (France); Walter Burghardt, S.J. (US); Ives Congar, O.P. (France); Philippe Delhaye (Belgium); John Feiner (Switzerland); Andre Feuillet, S.S. (France); Lucio Gera (Argentina);

Olegario Gonzalez de Cardedal (Spain); Franz Lakner, S.J. (Austria); Marie-Joseph Le Guillou, O.P. (France); J. F. Lescrauwaet, Miss. S.C. (Holland); Bernard Lonergan, S.J. (Canada); Henri De Lubac, S.J. (France); Andrew H. Maltha, O.P. (Holland); Jorge Medina (Chile); Peter Nemeshegyi, S.J. (Japan);

Stanislaus Olejnik (Poland); Gerard Philips (Belgium); Karl Rahner, S.J. (Germany); Joseph Ratzinger (Germany); Roberto Roxo Mascarenhas (Brazil); Tomislav Sagi-Bunic, O.F.M. Cap. (Yugoslavia); Rudolf Schnackenburg (Germany); Heinz Schuermann (Germany); Cipriano Vagaggini, O.S.B. (Italy).

Philippe Delhaye of Belgium was appointed executive secretary of the commission in March, 1972.

Meetings

The commission met for the first time Oct. 6 to 8, 1969, for organizational purposes and the assignment of subcommissions to studies on the priesthood, the theology of hope, unity of faith and pluralism in theology, the criteria of moral knowledge, and collegiality.

Twenty-six members attending the second meeting, Oct. 5 to 10, 1970, discussed reports on the priestly ministry and collegiality. Views were exchanged about the utility of ordaining married men, but marriage was ruled out for already ordained priests wanting to continue in the ministry. With respect to collegiality, no doubt was raised about the pope's authority to act independently in the Church; the consensus, however, was that he would be prudent to engage in wide consultation before acting.

By early 1971, the commission had prepared the basis of a feasible working paper on the priesthood for the Synod of Bishops, which met for the third time in the fall. At its own meeting, held at about the same time, the commission went over some of the ground covered in synodal discussions and planned the continuation of its own work.

Theological Pluralism

Msgr. Philippe Delhaye, secretary of the commission, said in a Vatican Radio interview July 21 that "Unity of Faith and Theological Pluralism" — concerning a variety of approaches to understanding of the Catholic faith — would be the main topic of discussion at the fourth general assembly of the commission Oct. 5 to 11, 1972.

The subject had been under study since the first meeting of the body in 1969.

Msgr. Delhaye quoted Pope Paul as saying at that time:

"We willingly admit the development and variety of the theological sciences, that 'pluralism' which seems to characterize modern culture today, not, of course, without recalling the indispensable necessity, always professed by ecclesiastical tradition, of preserving for Catholic doctrine the same intrinsic truth."

The commission's secretary said that, "above all, it is important to study how a certain theological pluralism can be integrated into the unity of Revelation and of the Church."

Msgr. Delhaye was asked for his opinion regarding the most acute questions raised for the Christian community, and particularly for theologians, by the necessity of safeguarding the unity of faith while respecting legitimate theological pluralism. He replied:

"The reconciliation of the unity of the faith and of theological pluralism raises numerous connected problems.

"(a) A hermeneutical problem: what is the meaning of the solemn dogmatic formulas proclaimed by the ecumenical councils and the popes? How can the 'invariable' in Revelation be expressed in a language that evolves with the culture on which it depends?

"(b) An ecclesiological problem: In the desire to make the Gospel more relevant to people and to culture today, some local Churches may insist on a certain aspect of dogma or on certain structures while other local Churches act differently. But it is necessary to remain faithful to Revelation, to the fundamental structure of the Church. It is the pope who watches over this unity.

"(c) A philosophical problem: The Church must take up a position with regard to the 'pluralistic' images of man taught by human sciences today."

Subcommissions were reported in continuing study of the theology of hope, the priesthood and moral theology.

With respect to moral theology, Msgr. Delhaye said the following points are being examined:

"(a) To what extent can the texts of the Old Testament . . . constitute a norm of behavior for Christians?

"(b) What is meant by evangelical law? How can the Sermon on the Mount, the parables, Pauline preaching, be expressed in directives for life?

"(c) How should the teaching and pastoral authority of the hierarchy be used to fix norms of conduct and also a minimum of Christian life, below which one would no longer belong among Christ's disciples?

"(d) How should the human sciences be used in Christian morality?"

COLLEGE OF CARDINALS

Cardinals are bishops chosen by the pope to serve as his principal assistants and advisers in the central administration of church affairs. Collectively, they form the Sacred College of Cardinals.

The college evolved gradually from synods of Roman clergy with whose assistance popes directed church affairs in the first 11 centuries. The first cardinals, in about the sixth century, were priests of the leading churches of Rome who were assigned liturgical, advisory and administrative duties with the Holy See, and the regional deacons of Rome.

For all cardinals except the Eastern patriarchs, membership in the college involves aggregation to the clergy of Rome. This aggregation is signified by the assignment to each cardinal, except the patriarchs, of a special or titular church in Rome.

History of the College

The Sacred College of Cardinals was not constituted in its present form and categories of membership until the 12th century, although before that time the pope had a body of advisers selected from among the bishops of dioceses neighboring Rome, priests and deacons of Rome. The college was given definite form in 1150, and in 1179 the selection of cardinals was reserved exclusively to the pope. Sixtus V fixed the number at 70, in 1586. John XXIII raised the number to 79 in 1959, to 85 in 1960 and to 87 in 1962. Paul VI increased membership to 118 in 1967 and to 134 (plus two *in petto*) in 1969.

In 1567 the title of cardinal was reserved to members of the college; previously it had been used by priests attached to parish churches of Rome and by the leading clergy of other notable churches. The Code of Canon Law promulgated in 1918 decreed that all cardinals must be priests. Previously there had been lay cardinals (e.g., Cardinal Giacomo Antonelli, d. 1876, Secretary of State to Pius IX). John XXIII provided in the motu proprio *Cum Gravissima* Apr. 15, 1962, that all cardinals would henceforth be bishops.

Pope Paul VI placed age limits on the functions of cardinals in the apostolic letter *Ingravescentem Aetatem,* dated Nov. 21, 1970, and effective as of Jan. 1, 1971. At 80, they cease to be members of curial departments and offices, and become ineligible to take part in papal elections. They retain membership in the College of Cardinals, however, with relevant rights and privileges.

Three Categories

The three categories of members of the college are cardinal bishops, cardinal priests and cardinal deacons.

Cardinal bishops include the six titular bishops of the suburban sees of Rome and Eastern Rite patriarchs.

First in rank are the titular bishops of the suburban sees, neighboring Rome: Ostia, Palestrina, Porto and Santa Rufina, Albano, Velletri, Frascati, Sabina and Poggio Mirteto. The dean of the college holds the title of the See of Ostia as well as his other suburban see.

The four major Eastern Rite patriarchs were made cardinal bishops by Paul VI in virtue of the motu proprio *Ad Purpuratorum Patrum* Feb. 11, 1965. (Two have died since that time.) Full recognition was given to their position as the heads of ancient liturgies and of sees of apostolic origin. Because of their patriarchal dignity and titles, which antedated the dignity and titles of cardinals, they were not aggregated to the Roman clergy and were not, like other cardinals, given title to Roman churches. The patriarchs were assigned rank among the cardinals in order of seniority, following the suburban titleholders.

Cardinal bishops, except the patriarchs, are engaged in full-time service in the central administration of church affairs in departments of the Roman Curia.

Cardinal priests, who were formerly in charge of leading churches in Rome, are bishops whose dioceses are outside Rome.

Cardinal deacons, who were formerly chosen according to regional divisions of Rome, are titular bishops assigned to full-time service in the Roman Curia.

The officers of the college are the dean and sub-dean, a chamberlain and a secretary. The dean and sub-dean are elected by the cardinal bishops, in accordance with a decree issued by Paul VI Feb. 26, 1965.

The dean of the college is Cardinal Amleto G. Cicognani.

Selection and Duties

Cardinals are selected by the pope and are inducted into the college in a three-step process. Their nomination is announced and approved at a meeting (secret consistory) attended only by the pope and cardinals who are already members of the college; word of their election and confirmation is then communicated to the cardinals designate by means of a document called a biglietto. They actually become cardinals on reception of the distinctive red biretta and ring (formerly sapphire, now gold). These presentations take place at a semi-public consistory, the first meeting of the college in which they take part, and at a public consistory during which they concelebrate Mass with the pope.

The cardinals elect the pope when the Holy See becomes vacant. They are major administrators of church affairs, serve in one or more departments of the Roman Curia, and enjoy a number of special rights and privileges. Their title, while symbolic of high honor, does not signify any extension of the powers of holy orders. They are called Princes of the Church.

A **cardinal in petto** is one whose selection has been made by the pope but whose name has not been disclosed; he has no title, rights or duties until such disclosure is made, at which time he takes precedence from the time of the secret selection.

BIOGRAPHIES OF CARDINALS

Biographies of the cardinals, as of Sept. 10, 1972, are given below in alphabetical order. For historical notes, order of seniority and geographical distribution of cardinals, see separate entries.

Alfrink, Bernard Jan: b. July 5, 1900, Nijkerk, Netherlands; ord. priest Aug. 15, 1924; professor of Sacred Scripture at Utrecht major seminary, 1933; consultor to Pontifical Biblical Commission, Rome, 1944; professor at Catholic University of Nijmegen, 1945; ord. titular archbishop of Tiana and coadjutor archbishop of Utrecht, July 17, 1951; archbishop of Utrecht, Oct. 31, 1955; cardinal Mar. 28, 1960; titular church, St. Joachim. Archbishop of Utrecht, military vicar for Netherlands, member of:
Congregations: Oriental Churches, Catholic Education, Evangelization of Peoples:
Commissions: Biblical Studies, Revision of Code of Canon Law.

Antoniutti, Ildebrando: b. Aug. 3, 1898, Nimis, Italy; ord. priest Dec. 5, 1920; served in Vatican diplomatic missions in China and Portugal, 1927-36; apostolic delegate to Albania, 1936-37; ord. titular archbishop of Synnada in Phrygia, June 29, 1936; charge d'affaires in Spain, 1937-38; apostolic delegate to Canada, 1938-53; nuncio to Spain, 1953-62; cardinal Mar. 19, 1962; titular church, St. Sebastian. Prefect of Sacred Congregation for Religious and Secular Institutes, member of:
Council for Public Affairs of Church:
Congregations: Doctrine of Faith, Oriental Churches, Bishops, Clergy, Catholic Education, Evangelization of Peoples;
Tribunal: Apostolic Signatura;
Commissions: Biblical Studies, Revision of Code of Canon Law.

Baggio, Sebastiano: b. May 16, 1913, Rosa, Italy; ord. priest Dec. 21, 1935; ord. titular archbishop of Ephesus, July 26, 1953; served in Vatican diplomatic corps, 1953-69; nuncio to Chile, apostolic delegate to Canada, nuncio to Brazil; cardinal Apr. 28, 1969; titular church, Guardian Angels, Archbishop of Cagliari, member of:
Council for Public Affairs of Church:
Congregations: Bishops, Divine Worship.

Barbieri, Antonio Maria, O.F.M. Cap.: b. Oct. 12, 1892), Montevideo, Uruguay; ord. priest Dec. 17, 1921; ord. titular archbishop of Macra and coadjutor archbishop of Montevideo, Nov. 8, 1936; founder of Catholic Action movement, major seminary in Uruguay; archbishop of Montevideo, Nov. 20, 1940; cardinal Dec. 15, 1958; titular church, St. Chrysogonus. Archbishop of Montevideo, member of:

Congregations: Clergy, Causes of Saints, Catholic Education.

Beltrami, Giuseppe: b. Jan. 17, 1889. Fossano, Italy; ord. priest Mar. 5, 1916; ord. titular archbishop of Damascus, Apr. 7, 1940; nuncio to Guatemala and El Salvador, 1940-45; nuncio to Colombia, 1945-49; nuncio to Lebanon, 1950-59; internuncio to Netherlands, 1959-67; cardinal June 26, 1967; titular church, St. Mary Liberatrice. Member of:
Congregation: Causes of Saints.

Bengsch, Alfred: b. Sept. 10, 1921, Berlin, Germany; called for military service while in seminary at Fulda, gravely wounded at Normandy and prisoner of Americans, 1944; resumed his studies after the war; ord. priest Apr. 2, 1950; member of faculty of seminaries at Erfurt and Neuzelle; ord. titular bishop of Tubia and auxiliary bishop of Berlin, June 11, 1959; bishop of Berlin, Aug. 16, 1961; received personal title of archbishop, Jan. 14, 1962; cardinal June 26, 1967; titular church, St. Philip Neri (in Eurosia). Archbishop of Berlin, member of:
Congregations: Oriental Churches, Divine Worship;
Secretariat: Christian Unity;
Commission: Revision of Code of Canon Law.

Bertoli, Paolo: b. Feb. 1, 1908, Poggio Garfagnana, Italy; ord. priest Aug. 15, 1930; ord. titular archbishop of Nicomedia May 11, 1952; served in Vatican diplomatic corps, 1952-69; apostolic delegate to Turkey, nuncio to Colombia, Lebanon and France; cardinal Apr. 28, 1969; deacon, St. Jerome of Charity. Prefect of Congregation for Causes of Saints, member of:
Council for Public Affairs of Church:
Congregations: Bishops, Oriental Churches, Divine Worship;
Commission: Revision of Code of Canon Law.

Bueno y Monreal, Jose Maria: b. Sept. 11, 1904, Zaragoza, Spain; ord. priest Mar. 19, 1927; ord. bishop of Jaca, Mar. 19, 1946; bishop of Vitoria, May 13, 1950; titular archbishop of Antioch in P sidia and coadjutor archbishop of Seville, Oct. 27, 1954; archbishop of Seville, Apr. 8, 1957; cardinal Dec. 15, 1958; titular church, Sts. Vitus, Modestus and Crescentia. Archbishop of Seville, member of:
Congregations: Religious and Secular Institutes, Causes of Saints.

Caggiano, Antonio: b. Jan. 30, 1889, Coronda, Argentina; ord. priest Mar. 23, 1912; general ecclesiastical counselor of Argentine Catholic Action, 1931; military vicar, 1933; ord. bishop of Rosario, Mar. 17, 1935; cardinal Feb. 18, 1946; titular church, St. Lawrence (in Panisperna). Archbishop of Buenos Aires, Aug. 15, 1959, military vicar of Argentina, member of:
Congregations: Oriental Churches, Clergy, Causes of Saints;

Commission: Revision of Code of Canon Law.

Carberry, John J.: b. July 31, 1904, Brooklyn, N. Y.; ord. priest July 28, 1929; ord. titular bishop of Elis and coadjutor bishop of Lafayette, Ind., July 25, 1956; bishop of Lafayette, Nov. 20, 1957; bishop of Columbus, Jan. 16, 1965; archbishop of St. Louis, Feb. 17, 1968; cardinal Apr. 28, 1969; titular church, St. John the Beptist (de Rossi). Archbishop of St. Louis, member of:

Congregations: Bishops, Evangelization of Peoples.

Carpino, Francesco: b. May 18, 1905, Palazzolo Acreide, Italy; ord. priest Aug. 14, 1927; ord. titular archbishop of Nicomedia and coadjutor archbishop of Monreale, Apr. 8, 1951; archbishop of Monreale, 1951-61; titular archbishop of Sardica, Jan. 19, 1961; assessor of Sacred Consistorial Congregation, 1961; pro-prefect of Sacred Congregation of the Council, Apr. 7, 1967; cardinal June 26, 1967; titular church, St. Mary Auxiliatrix; archbishop of Palermo, 1967-70. Former archbishop of Palermo, referendary of the Congregation of Bishops, 1970, and member of:

Congregations: Bishops, Clergy.

Casariego, Mario, C.R.S.: b. Feb. 13, 1909, Figueras de Castropol, Spain; ord. priest July 19, 1936; ord. titular bishop of Pudenziana and auxiliary bishop of Guatemala, Dec. 27, 1958; coadjutor archbishop of Guatemala, Sept. 22, 1963; archbishop of Guatemala, Dec. 1), 1964; cardinal Apr. 28, 1969; titular church, St. Mary in Aquira. Archbishop of Guatemala, member of:

Congregations: Bishops, Causes of Saints.

Cento, Fernando: b. Aug. 10, 1883, Pollenza. Italy; ord. priest Dec. 23, 1905; ord. bishop of Acireale, Sept. 3, 1922; titular archbishop of Seleucia Pieria, June 24, 1926; nuncio to Venezuela, 1926-36; nuncio to Peru, 1936-46; nuncio to Belgium and internuncio to Luxembourg, 1946-53; nuncio to Portugal, 1953-58; cardinal Dec. 15, 1958; entered order of cardinal bishops as titular bishop of Velletri, Apr. 23, 1965; major penitentiary, 1962-67. Member of:

Congregations: Religious and Secular Institutes, Evangelization of Peoples, Causes of Saints.

Cerejeira, Manuel Goncalves: b. Nov. 29, 1888, Lousado, Portugal; ord. priest Apr. 1, 1911; ord. titular archbishop of Mytilene and auxiliary archbishop of Lisbon, June 17, 1928; patriarch of Lisbon, 1929-71; cardinal Dec. 16, 1929; titular church, Sts. Marcellus and Peter. Former patriarch of Lisbon.

Cicognani, Amleto G.: b. Feb. 24, 1883, Brisighella, Italy; ord. priest Sept. 23, 1905; undersecretary of Sacred Consistorial Congregation, Dec. 16, 1922; assessor of Sacred Congregation for the Oriental Church, Feb. 16, 1928; secretary of Commission for Redaction of Oriental Canon Law, Dec. 2, 1929; apos-

tolic delegate to US, 1933-58; ord. titular archbishop of Laodicea of Phrygia, Apr. 23, 1933; during his 25 and one-half years as apostolic delegate, 10 ecclesiastical provinces and 32 new dioceses were erected in the US; cardinal Dec. 15, 1958; secretary of state, 1961-69; entered order of cardinal bishops as titular bishop of Frascati, May 23, 1962. Dean of the College of Cardinals, 1972, secretary of state emeritus, member of:

Council for Public Affairs of Church;

Congregations: Doctrine of Faith, Bishops, Clergy;

Commission: Revision of Code of Canon Law.

Cody, John P.: b. Dec. 24, 1907, St. Louis, Mo.; ord. priest Dec. 8, 1931, Rome, Italy; served in Rome, 1932-38; ord. titular bishop of Apollonia and auxiliary bishop of St. Louis, July 2, 1947; coadjutor bishop of St. Joseph, Mo., Jan. 27, 1954; apostolic administrator of St. Joseph, May 9, 1955; coadjutor bishop of Kansas City-St. Joseph, Aug. 29, 1956; titular archbishop of Bostra and coadjutor archbishop of New Orleans, Aug. 10, 1961; apostolic administrator of New Orleans, June 1, 1962; archbishop of New Orleans, Nov. 8, 1964; archbishop of Chicago, June 14, 1965; cardinal June 26, 1967; titular church, St. Cecilia. Archbishop of Chicago, member of:

Congregations: Clergy, Evangelization of Peoples, Divine Worship;

Office: Prefecture of Economic Affairs.

Colombo, Giovanni: b. Dec. 6, 1902, Caronno, Italy; ord. priest May 29, 1926; rector of Milan Seminary, 1953; ord. titular bishop of Filippopoli and auxiliary bishop of Milan, Dec. 7, 1960; archbishop of Milan, Aug. 10, 1963; cardinal Feb. 22, 1965; titular church, Sts. Sylvester and Martin (in Montibus). Archbishop of Milan, member of:

Congregations: Discipline of Sacraments, Catholic Education;

Commission: Revision of Code of Canon Law.

Concha, Luis: b. Nov. 7, 1891, Bogota, Colombia; ord. priest Oct. 28, 1916; ord. bishop of Manizales, Nov. 30, 1935; first archbishop of Manizales, May 10, 1954; archbishop of Bogota, 1959-72; cardinal Jan. 16, 1961; titular church, St. Mary (Nuova). Former archbishop of Bogota.

Confalonieri, Carlo: b. July 25, 1893, Seveso, Italy; ord. priest Mar. 18, 1916; private secretary to Pius XI for 17 years, to Pius XII for two years; ord. archbishop of L'Aquila, May 4, 1941; transferred to titular archbishopric of Nicopoli al Nesto, Feb. 22, 1950; cardinal Dec. 15, 1958; entered order of cardinal bishops as titular bishop of Frascati, Mar. 14, 1972. Archpriest of Patriarchal Liberian Basilica, prefect of the Sacred Congregation for Bishops, member of:

Council for Public Affairs of Church;

Congregations: Doctrine of Faith, Oriental

Churches, Clergy, Catholic Education, Evangelization of Peoples, Divine Worship, Causes of Saints;
Office: Administration of Patrimony of Apostolic See;
Commissions: Revision of Code of Canon Law, Latin America (President), Pastoral Care of Migrants and Other Travellers (President), Sanctuaries of Pompei and Loreto, Institute for Works of Religion.

Conway, William: b. Jan. 22, 1913, Belfast, Ireland; ord. priest June 20, 1937; ord. titular bishop of Neve and auxiliary bishop of Armagh, July 27, 1958; archbishop of Armagh and primate of all Ireland, Sept. 9, 1963; cardinal Feb. 22, 1965; titular church, St. Patrick. Archbishop of Armagh, member of:
Congregations: Bishops, Clergy, Evangelization of Peoples, Divine Worship;
Commission: Revision of Code of Canon Law.

Cooke, Terence J.: b. Mar. 1, 1921, New York, N. Y.; ord. priest Dec. 1, 1945; ord. titular bishop of Summa and auxiliary bishop of New York, Dec. 13, 1965; archbishop of New York, Mar. 2, 1968; military vicar for the US; cardinal Apr. 28, 1969; titular church, Sts. John and Paul. Archbishop of New York, member of:
Congregations: Bishops, Oriental Churches.

Cooray, Thomas B., O. M. I.: b. Dec. 28, 1901, Periyamulla Negombo, Ceylon; ord. priest June 23, 1929; ord. titular archbishop of Preslavo, Mar. 7, 1946; coadjutor archbishop of Colombo, Ceylon, 1946-47; succeded as archbishop of Colombo, July 26, 1947; cardinal Feb. 22, 1965; titular church, Sts. Nereus and Achilleus. Archbishop of Colombo, Ceylon, member of:
Congregations: Oriental Churches, Evangelization of Peoples;
Commission: Revision of Code of Canon Law.

Da Costa Nunes, Jose: b. Mar. 15, 1880, Azores; ord. priest July 26, 1903; ord. bishop Nov. 20, 1921; bishop of Macao, 1921-40; archbishop of Goa, primate of the East and patriarch of the East Indies, 1940-53; titular archbishop of Odessus with personal title of patriarch, Dec. 16, 1953; vice-camerlengo of the Holy Roman Church, 1953-62; cardinal Mar. 19, 1962; titular church, St. Prisca.

Danielou, Jean, S. J.: b. May 14, 1905, Neuilly-sur-Seine, France; ord. priest Aug. 20, 1938; joined theology faculty of Catholic Institute of Paris, 1943; dean of faculty there since 1962; ord. titular archbishop of Taormina, Apr. 19, 1969; cardinal Apr. 28, 1969; deacon, St. Saba. Member of:
Congregations: Religious and Secular Institutes, Catholic Education;
Secretariat: Non-Christians.

Darmojuwono, Justin: b. Nov. 2, 1914, Godean, Indonesia; ord. priest May 25, 1947; ord. archbishop of Semarang, Apr. 6, 1964;

cardinal June 26, 1967; titular church, Most Holy Names of Jesus and Mary. Archbishop of Semarang, member of:
Congregation: Evangelization of Peoples;
Secretariat: Non-Christians.

De Araujo Sales, Eugenio: b. Nov. 8, 1920, Acari, Brazil; ord. priest Nov. 21, 1943; ord. titular bishop of Tibica and auxiliary bishop of Natal, Aug. 15, 1954; archbishop of Sao Salvador, 1968-71; cardinal Apr. 28, 1969; titular church, St. Gregory VII. Archbishop of Rio de Janeiro (1971), member of:
Congregation: Clergy;
Commission: Social Communications.

Dearden, John F.: b. Oct. 15, 1907, Valley Falls, R. I.; ord. priest Dec. 8, 1932; ord. titular bishop of Sarepta and coadjutor bishop of Pittsburgh, May 18, 1948; bishop of Pittsburgh, Dec. 22, 1950; archbishop of Detroit, Dec. 18, 1958; first president of the National Conference of Catholic Bishops and the United States Catholic Conference, 1966-71; cardinal Apr. 28, 1969; titular church, St. Pius X (alla Balduina). Archbishop of Detroit, member of:
Congregations: Discipline of the Sacraments, Divine Worship;
Secretatiat: Non-Christians.

de Arriba y Castro, Benjamin: b. Apr. 8, 1886, Santa Maria de Penamayor, Spain; ord. priest July 14, 1912; ord. bishop of Mondonedo, June 16, 1935; bishop of Oviedo, Aug. 8, 1944; archbishop of Tarragona, 1949-70; cardinal Jan. 12, 1953; titular church, Sts. Vitalis, Valeria, Gervase and Protasius. Former archbishop of Tarragona, member of:
Congregations: Religious and Secular Institutes, Causes of Saints.

De Furstenberg, Maximilien: b. Oct. 23, 1904, Heerlen, Netherlands; ord. priest Aug. 9, 1931; ord. titular archbishop of Palto and apostolic delegate to Japan, Apr. 25, 1949; internuncio, 1952, when Japan established diplomatic relations with the Vatican; apostolic delegate to Australia, New Zealand and Oceania, Feb. 11, 1960; nuncio to Portugal, 1962-67; cardinal June 26, 1967; titular church, Most Sacred Heart of Jesus (a Castro Pretorio). Prefect of the Congregation for the Oriental Churches, member of:
Council for Public Affairs of Church;
Congregations: Bishops, Evangelization of Peoples;
Secretariat: Christian Unity;
Commissions: Revision of Code of Canon Law, Redaction of Oriental Code of Canon Law, Interpretation of Decrees of Vatican II, State of Vatican City, Institute for Works of Religion.

di Jorio, Alberto: b. July 18, 1884, Rome, Italy; ord. priest Apr. 18, 1908; regent of College of Cardinals, 1948; secretary of the 1958 conclave; cardinal Dec. 15, 1958; titular church, St. Pudentiana; ord. titular archbishop of Castra Nova, Apr. 19, 1962.

Doepfner, Julius: b. Aug. 26, 1913, Hausen, Germany; ord. priest Oct. 29, 1939; ord. bishop of Wuerzburg, Oct. 14, 1948; bishop of Berlin, Jan. 15, 1957; cardinal Dec. 15, 1958; titular church, St. Mary (della Scala). Archbishop of Munich and Freising (1961), member of:
Congregations: Oriental Churches, Clergy, Catholic Education, Evangelization of Peoples;
Commission: Revision of Code of Canon Law.

Duval, Leon-Etienne: b. Nov. 9, 1903, Chenex, France; ord. priest Dec. 18, 1926; ord. bishop of Constantine, Algeria, Feb. 11, 1947; archbishop of Algiers, Feb. 3, 1954; cardinal Feb. 22, 1965; titular church, St. Balbina. Archbishop of Algiers, member of:
Congregations: Discipline of Sacraments, Evangelization of Peoples;
Secretariat: Non-Christians;
Commissions: Revision of Code of Canon Law, Pontifical Council *Cor Unum.*

Enrique y Tarancon, Vicente: b. May 14, 1907, Burriana, Spain; ord. priest Nov. 1, 1929; ord. bishop of Solsona, Mar. 24, 1946; bishop of Oviedo, Apr. 12, 1964; archbishop of Toledo, 1969-71; cardinal Apr. 28, 1969; titular church, St. John Chrysostom (Montesacro). Archbishop of Madrid (1971), member of:
Congregations: Bishops, Divine Worship;
Commission: Revision of Code of Canon Law.

Felici, Pericle: b. Aug. 1, 1911, Segni, Italy; ord. priest Oct. 28, 1933; rector of Pontifical Roman Seminary for Legal Studies, 1938-48; judge of Roman Rota, 1947; served on antepreparatory commissions of the Second Vatican Council; ord. titular archbishop of Samosata, Oct. 28, 1960; secretary-general of the Second Vatican Council; accompanied Pope Paul VI on his trip to the UN, Oct. 4, 1965; cardinal June 26, 1967; deacon, St. Apollinare. Member of:
Council for Public Affairs of Church;
Congregations: Doctrine of Faith, Bishops, Discipline of Sacraments, Divine Worship, Causes of Saints;
Office: Administration of Patrimony of Holy See;
Commissions: Revision of Code of Canon Law (President), Interpretation of Decrees of Vatican II (President).

Feltin, Maurice: b. May 15, 1883, Delle, France; ord. priest July 3, 1909; ord. bishop of Troyes, Mar. 11, 1928; archbishop of Sens, Aug. 16, 1932; archbishop of Bordeaux, Dec. 16, 1935; archbishop of Paris, 1949-66; cardinal Jan. 12, 1953; titular church, St. Mary (della Pace). Former archbishop of Paris.

Ferretto, Giuseppe: b. Mar. 9, 1899, Rome, Italy; ord. priest Feb. 24, 1923; assessor of Consistorial Congregation, 1943-61; ord. titular archbishop of Sardica, Dec. 27, 1958; secretary of the College of Cardinals, 1959-61;

cardinal Jan. 16, 1961; entered order of cardinal bishops as bishop of Sabina and Poggio Mirteto, Mar. 26, 1961; titular bishop of Sabina and Poggio Mirteto, May 23, 1962. Major penitentiary, chamberlain of the College of Cardinals, member of:
Council for Public Affairs of Church;
Congregation: Bishops;
Commission: Revision of Code of Canon Law.

Flahiff, George B., C.S.B.: b. Oct. 26, 1905, Paris, Ont., Canada; ord. priest Aug. 17, 1930; professor of medieval history at the University of Toronto and Pontifical Institute of Medieval Studies in Toronto, 1934-54; superior general of Basilian Fathers, 1954; ord. archbishop of Winnipeg, May 31, 1961; president of Canadian Conference of Bishops, 1963-65; cardinal Apr. 28, 1969; titular church, St. Mary della Salute (Primavalle). Archbishop of Winnipeg, member of:
Congregations: Religious and Secular Institutes, Catholic Education.

Florit, Ermenegildo: b. July 5, 1901, Fagagna, Italy; ord. priest Apr. 11, 1925; taught Sacred Scripture at Lateran University from 1929; pro-rector of Lateran University and Institute of Civil and Canon Law, 1951-54; ord. titular archbishop of Hieropolis and coadjutor archbishop of Florence, Sept. 12, 1954; archbishop of Florence, Mar. 19, 1962; cardinal Feb. 22, 1965; titular church, Queen of the Apostles. Archbishop of Florence, member of:
Congregations: Catholic Education, Causes of Saints;
Commission: Revision of Code of Canon Law.

Forni, Efrem: b. Jan. 10, 1889, Milan, Italy; ord. priest July 6, 1913; served in Vatican diplomatic service in Portugal and France, 1921-37; ord. titular archbishop of Darnis, Feb. 20, 1938; nuncio to Ecuador, 1937-53; nuncio to Belgium, 1953-62; cardinal Mar. 19, 1962; titular church, Holy Cross in Jerusalem. Member of:
Council for Public Affairs of Church;
Congregations: Bishops, Clergy, Causes of Saints.

Frings, Josef: b. Feb. 6, 1887, Neuss, Germany; ord. priest Aug. 10, 1910; ord. archbishop June 21, 1942; archbishop of Cologne, 1942-69; cardinal Feb. 18, 1946; titular church, St. John (a Porta Latina). Former archbishop of Cologne, member of:
Congregations: Clergy, Religious and Secular Institutes, Evangelization of Peoples;
Commission: Revision of Code of Canon Law.

Garrone, Gabriel: b. Oct. 12, 1901, Aix-les-Bains, France; ord. priest Apr. 11, 1925; captain during World War II, cited for bravery, taken prisoner; rector of major seminary of Chambery, 1947; ord. titular archbishop of Lemno and coadjutor of Toulouse, June 24, 1947; archbishop of Toulouse, 1956-66; pro-

prefect of Congregation of Seminaries and Universities, Mar. 24, 1966; cardinal June 26, 1967; titular church, St. Sabina. Prefect of Congregation for Catholic Education, grand chancellor of the Pontifical Gregorian University, member of:
Congregations: Doctrine of Faith, Oriental Churches. Bishops, Evangelization of Peoples, Causes of Saints;
Commission: Revision of Code of Canon Law.

Gilroy, Norman Thomas: b. Jan. 22, 1896, Sydney, Australia; ord. priest Dec. 24, 1923; ord. bishop of Port Augusta, Mar. 17, 1935; titular archbishop of Cipsela and coadjutor archbishop of Sydney, July 1, 1937; archbishop of Sydney, 1940-71; cardinal Feb. 18, 1946; titular church, Four Crowned Martyrs. Member of:
Congregations: Oriental Churches, Evangelization of Peoples;
Commission: Revision of Code of Canon Law.

Gouyon, Paul: b. Oct. 24, 1910, Bordeaux, France; ord. priest Mar. 13, 1937; ord. bishop of Bayonne, Oct. 7, 1957; titular archbishop of Pessinonte and coadjutor archbishop of Rennes, Sept. 6, 1963; archbishop of Rennes, Sept. 4, 1964; cardinal Apr. 28, 1969; titular church, the Nativity (Via Gallia). Archbishop of Rennes, member of:
Secretariat: Non-Believers;
Commission: Social Communications.

Gracias, Valerian: b. Oct. 23, 1900, Karachi, Pakistan; ord. priest Oct. 3, 1926; ord. titular bishop of Thennesus and auxiliary bishop of Bombay, June 29, 1946; archbishop of Bombay, Dec. 1, 1950; cardinal Jan. 12, 1953; titular church, St. Mary (in Via Lata). Archbishop of Bombay, member of:
Congregations: Oriental Churches, Discipline of Sacraments, Divine Worship, Evangelization of Peoples;
Secretariat: Non-Christians;
Commission: Revision of Code of Canon Law.

Grano, Carlo: b. Oct. 14, 1887, Rome, Italy; ord. priest July 14, 1912; master of pontifical ceremonies for 26 years; ord. titular archbishop of Thessalonica, Dec. 27, 1958, by Pope John XXIII; nuncio to Italy, 1958-67; cardinal June 26, 1967; titular church, St. Marcellus. Member of:
Council for Public Affairs of Church;
Congregations: Bishops, Causes of Saints.

Gray, Gordon J.: b. Aug. 10, 1910, Edinburgh, Scotland; ord. priest June 15, 1935; ord. archbishop of Saint Andrews and Edinburgh, Sept. 21, 1951; chairman of International Committee for English in the Liturgy; cardinal Apr. 28, 1969; titular church, St. Clare. Archbishop of Saint Andrews and Edinburgh, member of:
Congregations: Evangelization of Peoples, Divine Worship:
Commission: Social Communications.

Guerri, Sergio: b. Dec. 25, 1905, Tarquinia, Italy; ord. priest Mar. 30, 1929; ord. titular archbishop of Trevi, Apr. 27, 1969; cardinal Apr. 28, 1969; deacon, Holy Name of Mary. Pro-president of Pontifical Commission for State of Vatican City, member of:
Congregations: Oriental Churches, Evangelization of Peoples:
Commission: Social Communications.

Heard, William T.: b. Feb. 24, 1884, Edinburgh, Scotland; convert 1910; ord. priest Mar. 30, 1918; parish priest in diocese of Southwark, England, 1921-27; judge of the Sacred Roman Rota, 1927-58; dean, 1958-59; cardinal Dec. 14, 1959; titular church, St. Theodore; ord. titular archbishop Feradi Maggiore, Apr. 19, 1962.

Heenan, John: b. Jan. 26, 1905, Ilford, England; ord. priest July 6, 1930; ord. bishop of Leeds, Mar. 12, 1951; archbishop of Liverpool, May 2, 1957; archbishop of Westminster, Sept. 2, 1963; cardinal Feb. 22, 1965; titular church, St. Sylvester (in Capite). Archbishop of Westminster, vice-president of Secretariat for Promoting Christian Unity, member of:
Congregation: Bishops;
Commission: Revision of Canon Law.

Hoeffner, Joseph: b. Dec. 24, 1906, Horhausen, Germany; ord. priest Oct. 30, 1932; ord. bishop of Munster, Sept. 14, 1962; titular archbishop of Aquileia and coadjutor archbishop of Cologne, Jan. 6, 1969; archbishop of Cologne, Feb. 24, 1969; cardinal Apr. 28, 1969; titular church, St. Andrew of the Valley. Archbishop of Cologne, member of:
Congregation: Catholic Education;
Secretariat: Non-Believers;
Office: Prefecture of Economic Affairs.

Jaeger, Lorenz: b. Sept. 23, 1892, Halle an der Saale, Germany; ord. priest Apr. 1, 1922; chaplain German army, 1939-41; active in ecumenical movement (Una Sancta): ord. archbishop of Paderborn, Oct. 19, 1941; cardinal Feb. 22, 1965; titular church, St. Leo I. Archbishop of Paderborn, member of:
Congregations: Clergy, Catholic Education;
Secretariat: Christian Unity;
Commission: Revision of Canon Law.

Journet, Charles: b. Jan. 26, 1891, Geneva, Switzerland; ord. priest July 15, 1917; professor of Dogmatic Theology at diocesan seminary at Fribourg, 1924; ord. titular archbishop of Fornos Minore, Feb. 20, 1965; cardinal Feb. 22, 1965; deacon, St. Mary (in Portico).

Kim, Stephan Sou Hwan: b. May 8, 1922, Tae Gu, Korea; ord. priest Oct. 27, 1947; ord. bishop of Masan, May 31, 1966; archbishop of Seoul, Apr. 9, 1968; cardinal Apr. 28, 1969; titular church, St. Felix of Cantalice (Centocelle). Archbishop of Seoul, member of:
Congregation: Evangelization of Peoples:
Secretariat: Non-Christians;
Commission: Interpretation of Decrees of Vatican II.

Koenig, Franz: b. Aug. 3, 1905, Rabenstein, Lower Austria; ord. priest Oct. 28, 1933; ord. titular bishop of Livias and coadjutor bishop of Sankt Poelten, Aug. 31, 1952; archbishop of Vienna, May 10, 1956; cardinal Dec. 15, 1958; titular church, St. Eusebius. Archbishop of Vienna, president of Secretariat for Non-Believers, member of:
Congregations: Doctrine of Faith, Bishops; Commissions: Biblical Studies, Revision of Code of Canon Law.

Krol, John J.: b. Oct. 26, 1910, Cleveland, Ohio; ord. priest Feb. 20, 1937; ord. titular bishop of Cadi and auxiliary bishop of Cleveland, Sept. 2, 1953; archbishop of Philadelphia, Feb. 11, 1961, installed Mar. 22, 1961; vice-president NCCB/USCC, 1966-72; cardinal June 26, 1967; titular church, St. Mary (della Merced) and St. Adrian Martyr. Archbishop of Philadelphia, president NCCB/USCC, 1972- , member of:
Congregations: Oriental Churches, Evangelization of Peoples:
Commissions: Revision of Code of Canon Law, Social Communications.

Landazuri Ricketts, Juan, O. F. M: b. Dec. 19, 1913, Arequipa, Peru; entered Franciscans, 1933; ord. priest Apr. 16, 1939; ord. titular archbishop of Roina and coadjutor archbishop of Lima, Aug. 24, 1952; archbishop of Lima, May 2, 1955; cardinal Mar. 19, 1962; titular church, St. Mary (in Aracoeli). Archbishop of Lima, member of:
Congregations: Discipline of Sacraments, Clergy, Causes of Saints, Religious and Secular Institutes.
Commission: Revision of Code of Canon Law.

Larraona, Arcadio, C. M. F.: b. Nov. 13, 1887, Oteiza de la Solana, Spain; made religious profession in Claretians, Dec. 8, 1903; ord. priest June 10, 1911; began teaching career as professor of Roman law at the Apollinare, Rome, 1918; undersecretary of Congregation of Religious, 1943, secretary, Nov. 11, 1950; founded practical school of the congregation, 1950; cardinal Dec. 14, 1959; grand penitentiary, 1961-62; ord. titular archbishop of Diocesarea di Isauria, Apr. 19, 1962; titular church, Sacred Heart of Mary.

Lefebvre, Joseph: b. Apr. 15, 1892, Tourcoing, France; ord. priest Dec. 17, 1921; ord. bishop of Troyes, Oct. 11, 1938; archbishop of Bourges, 1943-69; cardinal Mar. 28, 1960; titular church, St. John (dei Fiorentini). Former archbishop of Bourges.

Leger, Paul Emile, S.S.: b. Apr. 26, 1904, Valleyfield, Quebec, Canada; ord. priest May 25, 1929; rector Canadian College, Rome, 1947; ord. archbishop of Montreal, Apr. 26, 1950; cardinal Jan. 12, 1953; titular church, St. Mary (degli Angeli); resigned as archbishop of Montreal in 1967 to become missionary to lepers. Member of:
Congregations: Bishops, Discipline of Sacraments, Causes of Saints;

Commission: Revision of Code of Canon Law.

Lercaro, Giacomo: b. Oct. 28, 1891, Quinto al Mare, Italy; ord. priest July 25, 1914; ord. archbishop of Ravenna, Mar. 19, 1947; archbishop of Bologna, 1952-68; cardinal Jan. 12, 1953; titular church, St. Mary (in Traspontina). Former archbishop of Bologna.

Lienart, Achilles: b. Feb. 7, 1884, Lille, France; ord. priest June 29, 1907; French Army Chaplain in World War I; ord. bishop of Lille, Dec. 8, 1928 (retired 1968). cardinal June 30, 1930; titular church, St. Sixtus; prelate of Mission of France of Pontigny, 1954-64. Former bishop of Lille.

McCann, Owen: b. June 29, 1907, Woodstock, South Africa; ord. priest Dec. 21, 1935; ord. titular bishop of Stettorio and vicar apostolic of Cape Town, May 18, 1950; first archbishop of Cape Town, Jan. 11, 1951; opponent of apartheid policy; cardinal Feb. 22, 1965; titular church, St. Praxedes. Archbishop of Cape Town, member of:
Congregations: Evangelization of Peoples, Causes of Saints.

McGuigan, James Charles: b. Nov. 26, 1894, Hunter River, Canada; ord. priest May 26, 1918; chancellor and vicar general of archdiocese of Edmonton; rector of St. Joseph's Seminary, Edmonton; ord. archbishop of Regina, May 15, 1930; archbishop of Toronto, 1934-71; cardinal Feb. 18, 1946; titular church, St. Mary (del Popolo). Former archbishop of Toronto, member of:
Congregations: Bishops, Evangelization of Peoples.

McIntyre, James Francis: b. June 25, 1886, New York, N. Y.; ord. priest May 21, 1921; ord. titular bishop of Cirene and auxiliary bishop of New York, Jan 8, 1941; titular archbishop of Palto and coadjutor archbishop of New York, July 20, 1946; archbishop of Los Angeles, 1948-70; cardinal Jan. 12, 1953; titular church, St. Anastasia. Former archbishop of Los Angeles, member of:
Congregation: Bishops.

McKeefry, Peter Thomas: b. July 3, 1899, Greymouth, New Zealand; ord. priest Apr. 3, 1926; ord. titular archbishop of Derco, Oct. 19, 1947; coadjutor archbishop of Wellington, 1947-54; archbishop of Wellington, May 9, 1954; cardinal Apr. 28, 1969; titular church, Immaculate Conception (al Tiburtino). Archbishop of Wellington, member of:
Congregations: Clergy, Evangelization of Peoples.

Malula, Joseph: b. Dec. 12, 1917, Kinshasa, Zaire; ord. priest June 9, 1946; ord. titular bishop of Attanaso and auxiliary bishop of Kinshasa, Sept. 20, 1959; archbishop of Kinshasa. July 7, 1964; cardinal Apr. 28, 1969; titular church, the Protomartyrs (via Aurilio Antica). Archbishop of Kinshasa, member of:
Congregations: Evangelization of Peoples, Divine Worship;
Secretariat: Non-Christians.

Marella, Paolo: b. Jan. 25, 1895, Rome, Italy; ord. priest Feb. 23, 1918; aide in Congregation for Propagation of the Faith; on staff of apostolic delegation, Washington, D. C., 1923-33; ord. titular archbishop of Doclea, Oct. 29, 1933; apostolic delegate to Japan, 1933-48, to Australia, New Zealand and Oceania, 1948-53; nuncio to France, 1953-59; cardinal Dec. 14, 1959; entered order of cardinal bishops as titular bishop of Porto and Santa Rufina, Mar. 14, 1972. Archpriest of St. Peter's Basilica, president of Secretariat for Non-Christians, member of:
Council for Public Affairs of Church;
Congregations: Doctrine of Faith, Bishops, Evangelization of Peoples;
Tribunal: Apostolic Signatura;
Office: Administration of Patrimony of Apostolic See;
Commissions: Revision of Code of Canon Law, Sacred Art in Italy.

Martin, Joseph: b. Aug. 9. 1891, Orleans, France; ord. priest Dec. 18, 1920; military chaplain of French Army's 35th Division, 1939-40; ord. bishop of Le Puy-en-Velay, Apr. 2, 1940; archbishop of Rouen, 1948-68; cardinal Feb. 22, 1965; titular church, St. Teresa, Virgin. Former archbishop of Rouen.

Marty, Francois: b. May 16, 1904, Pachins, France; ord. priest June 28, 1930; ord. bishop of Saint-Flour, May 1, 1952; titular archbishop of Emesa and coadjutor archbishop of Rheims, Dec. 14, 1959; archbishop of Rheims, May 9, 1960; archbishop of Paris, Mar. 26, 1968; cardinal Apr. 28, 1969; titular church, St. Louis of France. Archbishop of Paris, member of:
Congregations: Oriental Churches, Clergy, Divine Worship;
Commission: Revision of Code of Canon Law.

Maurer, Jose Clemente, C.SS.R.: b. Mar. 13, 1900, Puttlingen, Germany; ord. priest Sept. 19, 1925; assigned to Bolivian missions, 1926; became a Bolivian citizen; ord. titular bishop of Cea and auxiliary bishop of La Paz, Apr. 16, 1950; archbishop of Sucre, Oct. 27, 1951; cardinal June 26, 1967; titular church, Most Holy Redeemer and St. Alphonsus. Archbishop of Sucre, member of:
Congregations: Religious and Secular Institutes, Catholic Education.

Meouchi, Paul Peter: b. Apr. 1, 1894, Djezzine, Lebanon; ord. priest Dec. 7, 1917; served in US Maronite parishes, 1920-34, became naturalized American citizen but relinquished it, 1934; appointed archbishop of Tyr of Maronites; ord. archbishop of Tyr of Maronites, Dec. 8, 1934; patriarch of Antioch of the Maronites, May 25, 1955; cardinal Feb. 22, 1965. Patriarch of Antioch for the Maronites, member of:
Congregation: Oriental Churches;
Commissions: Revision of Code of Canon Law, Redaction of Oriental Canon Law.

Mindszenty, Jozsef: b. Mar. 29, 1892, Csehimindszent, Hungary; ord. priest June 12, 1915; ord. bishop of Veszprem, Mar. 25, 1944; archbishop of Esztergom and primate of Hungary, Oct. 2, 1945; cardinal Feb. 18, 1946; titular church, St. Stephen (al Monte Celio). He was sentenced to life imprisonment by Communist Hungarian government Feb. 8, 1949; lived in refuge in US Embassy, Budapest, Nov. 1956-Oct. 1971. Archbishop of Esztergom (impeded), member of:
Congregations: Discipline of Sacraments, Catholic Education.

Miranda y Gomez, Miguel Dario: b. Dec. 19, 1895, Leon, Mexico; ord. priest Oct. 28, 1918; ord. bishop of Tulancingo, Dec. 8, 1937; titular archbishop of Selimbra and coadjutor archbishop of Mexico City, 1955; archbishop of Mexico City, June 28, 1956; president of the Latin American Bishops' Council (CELAM), 1960; cardinal Apr. 28, 1969; titular church, St. Mary of Guadalupe (Montemario). Archbishop of Mexico City, member of:
Congregation: Discipline of Sacraments;
Commission: Revision of Canon Law.

Motta, Carlos Carmelo de Vasconcellos: b. July 16, 1890, Bom Jesus do Amparos, Brazil; ord. priest June 29, 1918; ord. titular bishop of Algiza and auxiliary bishop of Diamantina, Oct. 30, 1932; archbishop of Sao Luis do Maranhao, Dec. 19, 1935; archbishop of Sao Paulo del Brasile, 1944-64; cardinal Feb. 18, 1946; titular church, St. Pancratius. Archbishop of Aparecida (1964).

Munoz Vega, Paolo, S. J.: b. May 23, 1903, Mira, Ecuador; ord. priest July 25, 1933; ord. titular bishop of Ceramo and auxiliary bishop of Quito, Mar. 19, 1964; archbishop of Quito, June 23, 1967; cardinal Apr. 28, 1969; titular church, St. Robert Bellarmine. Archbishop of Quito, member of:
Congregations: Religious and Secular Institutes, Catholic Education.

Nasalli Rocca di Corneliano, Mario: b. Aug. 12, 1903, Piacenza, Italy; ord. priest Apr. 9, 1927; ord. titular archbishop of Anzio, Apr. 20, 1969; cardinal Apr. 28, 1969; deacon, St. John the Baptist. Member of:
Congregations: Discipline of Sacraments, Causes of Saints;
Secretariat: Non-Believers.

O'Boyle, Patrick A.: b. July 18, 1896, Scranton, Pa.; ord. priest May 21, 1921; executive director of War Relief Services, NCWC, 1943; ord. archbishop of Washington, Jan. 14, 1948; cardinal June 26, 1967; titular church, St. Nicholas (in Carcere). Archbishop of Washington, D. C., member of:
Congregation: Evangelization of Peoples.

Oddi, Silvio: b. Nov. 14, 1910, Morfasso, Italy; ord. priest May 21, 1933; ord. titular archbishop of Mesembria, Sept. 27, 1953; served in Vatican diplomatic corps, 1953-69; apostolic delegate to Jerusalem, Palestine, Jordan and Cyprus, internuncio to the United

Arab Republic, and nuncio to Belgium and Luxembourg; cardinal Apr. 28, 1969; deacon, St. Agatha of the Goths, president of the Commission for Sanctuaries of Pompei and Loreto, member of:
Council for Public Affairs of Church;
Congregations: Bishops, Clergy, Oriental Churches, Causes of Saints.

Ottaviani, Alfredo: b. Oct. 29, 1890, Rome, Italy; ord. priest Mar. 18, 1916; undersecretary of Congregation for Extraordinary Ecclesiastical Affairs, 1928; substitute secretary of state, 1929; assessor of Sacred Congregation of the Holy Office, 1935-52; prefect of Congregation of Holy Office (now Doctrine of Faith), 1952-68; cardinal Jan. 12, 1953; ord. titular archbishop of Berrea, Apr. 19, 1962; titular church, St. Mary (in Dominica). Prefect emeritus of the Congregation for the Doctrine of the Faith, member of:
Council for Public Affairs of Church;
Congregations: Doctrine of Faith, Bishops;
Commission: Revision of Code of Canon Law.

Parecattil, Joseph: b. Apr. 1, 1912, Kidangoor, India; ord. priest Aug. 24, 1939; ord. titular bishop of Aretusa for Syrians and auxiliary bishop of Ernakulam, Nov. 30, 1953; archbishop of Ernakulam (Chaldean-Malabar Rite), July 20, 1956; vice-president of the Indian Bishops' Conference, 1966; appointed one of seven members of Pope Paul VI's advisory council for Eastern Rite churches, 1968; cardinal Apr. 28, 1969; titular church, Our Lady Queen of Peace. Archbishop of Ernakulam of the Chaldean-Malabar Rite, member of:
Congregation: Oriental Churches;
Commission: Redaction of Oriental Code of Canon Law.

Parente, Pietro: b. Feb. 16, 1891, Casalnuovo, Italy; ord. priest Mar. 18, 1916; director of Archiepiscopal Seminary at Naples, 1916-26; rector of Pontifical Urban College of Propagation of the Faith, 1934-38; Consultor of the Congregations of the Holy Office, Council, Propagation of the Faith, and Seminaries and Universities; ord. archbishop of Perugia, Oct. 23, 1955; titular archbishop of Tolemaide di Tebaide, Oct. 23, 1959; assessor of Congregation of Holy Office (now Doctrinal Congregation), 1959; cardinal June 26, 1967; titular church, St. Lawrence (in Lucina).

Paupini, Giuseppe: b. Feb. 25, 1907, Mondavio, Italy; ord. priest Mar. 19, 1930; ord. titular archbishop of Sebastopolis in Abasgia, Feb. 26, 1956; served in Vatican diplomatic corps, 1956-69; internuncio to Iran, 1956-57; nuncio to Guatemala and El Salvador, 1957-58, nuncio to Colombia, 1959-69; cardinal Apr. 28, 1969; deacon, All Saints Church. Member of:
Council for Public Affairs of Church;
Congregations: Bishops, Causes of Saints;
Commission: State of Vatican City.

Pellegrino, Michele: b. Apr. 25, 1903, Centallo, Italy; ord. priest Sept. 19, 1925; ord. archbishop of Turin, Oct. 17, 1965; cardinal June 26, 1967; titular church, Most Holy Name of Jesus. Archbishop of Turin, member of:
Congregations: Clergy, Divine Worship, Catholic Education.

Poma, Antonio: b. June 12, 1910, Villanterio, Italy; ord. priest Apr. 15, 1933; ord. titular bishop of Tagaste and auxiliary bishop of Mantova, Dec. 9, 1951; bishop of Mantova, Sept. 8, 1954; titular archbishop of Gerpiniano and coadjutor archbishop of Bologna, July 16, 1967; archbishop of Bologna, Feb. 12, 1968; cardinal Apr. 28, 1969; titular church, St. Luke (al Prenestino). Archbishop of Bologna, member of:
Congregations: Clergy, Catholic Education.

Quintero, Jose Humberto: b. Sept. 22, 1902, Mucuchies, Venezuela; ord. priest Aug. 22, 1926; ord. titular archbishop of Acrida and coadjutor archbishop of Merida, Dec. 6, 1953; archbishop of Caracas, Aug. 31, 1960; cardinal Jan. 16, 1961; titular church, Sts. Andrew and Gregory (al Monte Celio). Archbishop of Caracas, member of:
Congregations: Discipline of Sacraments, Catholic Education, Causes of Saints;
Secretariat: Christian Unity.

Rakotomalala, Jerome: b. July 15, 1914, Sainte Marie, Madagascar; ord. priest July 31, 1943; ord. archbishop of Tananarive, May 8, 1960; cardinal Apr. 28, 1969; titular church, St. Mary the Consoler (Casalbertone). Archbishop of Tananarive, member of;
Congregation: Evangelization of Peoples;
Secretariat: Non-Christians.

Renard, Alexandre C.: b. June 7, 1906, Avelin, France; ord. priest July 12, 1931; ord. bishop of Versailles, Oct. 19, 1953; archbishop of Lyons, May 28, 1967; cardinal June 26, 1967; titular church, St. Francis of Paola (ad Montes). Archbishop of Lyons, member of:
Congregations: Clergy, Religious and Secular Institutes.

Roberti, Francesco: b. July 7, 1889, Pergola, Italy; ord. priest Aug. 3, 1913; professor of Canon Law at Apollinare, 1918-38; held offices in several Roman Congregations; cardinal Dec. 15, 1958; ord. titular archbishop of Colonnata, Apr. 19, 1962; titular church, the Twelve Apostles; Prefect emeritus of Apostolic Signatura.

Rosales, Julio: b. Sept. 18, 1906, Calbayog, Philippines; ord. priest June 2, 1929; ord. bishop of Tagbilaran, Sept. 21, 1946; archbishop of Cebu, Dec. 17, 1949; cardinal Apr. 28, 1969; titular church, Sacred Heart of Jesus (a Vitinia). Archbishop of Cebu, member of:
Congregation: Clergy;
Secretariat: Non-Christians.

Rossi, Agnelo: b. May 4, 1913, Joaquim Egidio, Brazil; ord. priest Mar. 27, 1937; ord. bishop of Barra do Pirai, Apr. 15, 1956; archbishop of Ribeirao Preto, 1962-64; archbishop of Sao Paulo del Brazil, 1964-70; cardinal Feb. 22, 1965; titular church, Mother of God. Prefect of Congregation for Evangelization of Peoples, member of:

Council for Public Affairs of Church;

Congregations: Clergy, Doctrine of Faith, Causes of Saints, Religious and Secular Institutes, Catholic Education;

Secretariats: Christian Unity, Non-Christians;

Commissions: Revision of Code of Canon Law, Institute for Works of Religion.

Roy, Maurice: b. Jan. 25, 1905, Quebec, Canada; ord. priest June 12, 1927; chief of chaplains of Canadian Armed Forces during World War II; ord. bishop of Trois Rivieres, May 1, 1946; military vicar, June 8, 1946; archbishop of Quebec, June 2, 1947; primate of Canada, Jan. 25, 1956; cardinal Feb. 22, 1965; titular church, Our Lady of the Most Holy Sacrament and the Holy Canadian Martyrs. Archbishop of Quebec, primate of Canada, military vicar of Canada, member of:

Congregations: Clergy, Catholic Education;

Council of Laity (President), Commission on Justice and Peace (President);

Commission: Revision of Code of Canon Law.

Rugambwa, Laurean: b. July 12, 1912, Bukongo. Tanzania; ord. priest Dec. 12, 1943; ord. titular bishop of Febiano and vicar apostolic of Lower Kagera, Feb. 10, 1952; bishop of Rutabo, Mar. 25, 1953; cardinal Mar. 28, 1960; titular church, St. Francis (a Ripa); bishop of Bukavu, 1960-68. Archbishop of Dar-es-Salaam, 1968, member of:

Congregations: Divine Worship, Religious and Secular Institutes, Evangelization of Peoples; Causes of Saints;

Commission: Revision of Code of Canon Law.

Samore, Antonio: b. Dec. 4, 1905, Bardi, Italy; ord. priest June 10, 1928; served in apostolic nunciatures at Lithuania and Switzerland; worked in Vatican Secretariat of State during World War II; assigned to apostolic delegation in Washington, D.C., 1947; nuncio to Colombia, 1950; ord. titular archbishop of Tirnovo, Apr. 16, 1950; secretary of Congregation of Extraordinary Ecclesiastical Affairs, 1953; cardinal June 26, 1967; titular church, St. Mary (sopra Minerva). Prefect of Congregation for Discipline of Sacraments, member of:

Council for Public Affairs of Church;

Congregations: Oriental Churches, Bishops, Evangelization of Peoples, Divine Worship;

Tribunal: Apostolic Signatura;

Commission: Revision of Code of Canon Law.

Santos, Rufino I.: b. Aug. 26, 1908, Guagua, P. I.; ord. priest Oct. 25, 1931; imprisoned during Japanese occupation of Philippines, released by Americans, Feb. 5, 1945; vicar general of Manila, 1945; ord. titular bishop of Barca and auxiliary bishop of Manila, Oct. 24, 1947; archbishop of Manila, Feb. 10, 1953; cardinal Mar. 28, 1960; titular church, St. Mary (ai Monti). Archbishop of Manila, military vicar for the Philippines, member of:

Congregations: Religious and Secular Institutes, Evangelization of Peoples;

Commission: Revision of Code of Canon Law.

Scherer, Alfred Vicente: b. Feb. 5, 1903, Bom Principio, Brazil; ord. priest Apr. 3, 1926; ord. archbishop of Porto Alegre, Feb. 23, 1947; cardinal Apr. 28, 1969; titular church, Our Lady of LaSalette. Archbishop of Porto Alegre, Brazil, member of:

Congregations: Bishops, Evangelization of Peoples.

Seper, Franjo: b. Oct. 2, 1905, Osijek, Yugoslavia; ord. priest Oct. 26, 1930; secretary of Cardinal Stepinac, 1934-41; rector of Zagreb's major seminary, 1941-51; ord. titular archbishop of Filippopoli and coadjutor archbishop of Zagreb, Sept. 21, 1954; archbishop of Zagreb, 1960-69; cardinal Feb. 22, 1965; titular church, Sts. Peter and Paul (in Via Ostia). Prefect of Congregation for Doctrine of the Faith, member of:

Council for Public Affairs of Church;

Congregations: Bishops, Discipline of Sacraments, Clergy, Catholic Education;

Secretariat: Christian Unity;

Office: Administration of Patrimony of Holy See;

Commissions: Biblical (President), Theological (President), Revision of Code of Canon Law, Interpretation of Decrees of Vatican II.

Shehan, Lawrence J.: b. Dec. 18, 1898, Baltimore, Md.; ord. priest Dec. 23, 1922; ord. titular bishop of Lidda and auxiliary bishop of Baltimore and Washington, Dec. 12, 1945; bishop of Bridgeport, 1953-61; titular archbishop of Nicopolis ad Nestum and coadjutor archbishop of Baltimore, July 10, 1961; archbishop of Baltimore, Dec. 8, 1961; cardinal Feb. 22, 1965; titular church, St. Clement. Archbishop of Baltimore, president of the Permanent Committee for International Eucharistic Congresses, member of:

Congregations: Doctrine of Faith, Bishops;

Secretariat: Christian Unity;

Commission: Revision of Code of Canon Law.

Sidarouss, Stephanos I, C.M.: b. Feb. 22, 1904, Cairo, Egypt; ord. priest July 2, 1939; ord. titular bishop of Sais, Jan. 25, 1948; auxiliary to the patriarch of Alexandria for the Copts, 1948-58; patriarch of Alexandria, May 10, 1958; cardinal Feb. 22, 1965. Patriarch of Alexandria for the Copts, member of:

Congregation: Oriental Churches;

Commissions: Revision of Code of Canon

Law, Redaction of Code of Oriental Canon Law.

Silva Henriquez, Raul, S.D.B.: b. Aug. 27, 1907, Talca, Chile; ord. priest July 3, 1938; ord. bishop of Valparaiso, Nov. 29, 1959; archbishop of Santiago de Chile, Mar. 14, 1961; cardinal Mar. 19, 1962; titular church, St. Bernard (alle Terme). Archbishop of Santiago de Chile, member of:
Congregations: Clergy, Divine Worship, Catholic Education;
Commission: Revision of Code of Canon Law.

Siri, Giuseppe: b. May 20, 1906, Genoa, Italy; ord. priest Sept. 22, 1928; ord. titular bishop of Liviade and auxiliary bishop of Genoa, May 7, 1944; archbishop of Genoa, May 14, 1946; cardinal Jan. 12, 1953; titular church, St. Mary (della Vittoria). Archbishop of Genoa, member of:
Congregations: Discipline of Sacraments, Clergy, Catholic Education;
Commission: Revision of Code of Canon Law.

Slipyi or Slipyj, Josyf (Kobernyckyj-Dyckowskyj): b. Feb. 17, 1892, Zazdrist in the Ukraine; ord. priest Sept. 30, 1917; ord. titular archbishop of Serre, Dec. 22, 1939; coadjutor archbishop of Lwow for the Ukrainians, 1939-44; archbishop of Lwow, Nov. 1, 1944; imprisoned 1945-63 for unspecified crimes; released by Soviets and allowed to go to Rome in February, 1963; named major archbishop by Paul VI, 1963; cardinal Feb. 22, 1965; titular church, St. Athanasius. Archbishop of Lwow, (not permitted to exercise his office; he resides in Vatican City), primate of the Ukraine, member of:
Congregation: Oriental Churches;
Commissions: Revision of Code of Canon Law, Redaction of Code of Oriental Canon Law.

Staffa, Dino: b. Aug. 14, 1906, Santa Maria in Fabriago, Italy; ord. priest May 25, 1929; judge of Roman Rota, 1944; secretary of Congregation of Seminaries and Universities, 1958; ord. titular archbishop of Caesarea in Palestina, Oct. 28, 1960; cardinal June 26, 1967; titular church, Sacred Heart of Christ the King. Prefect of Apostolic Signatura, member of:
Congregations: Oriental Churches, Discipline of Sacraments;
Commission: Revision of Code of Canon Law.

Suenens, Leo Josef: b. July 16, 1904, Brussels, Belgium; ord. priest Sept. 4, 1927; ord. titular bishop of Isinda, Dec. 16, 1945; auxiliary bishop of Mechelen, 1945-61; archbishop of Mechelen-Brussels, 1961; cardinal Mar. 19, 1962; titular church, St. Peter in Chains. Archbishop of Mechelen-Brussels, military vicar for Belgium; member of:
Congregations: Catholic Education, Evangelization of Peoples, Causes of Saints;
Commission: Revision of Canon Law.

Tabera Araoz, Arturo, C.M.F.: b. Oct. 29, 1903, Barco de Avila, Spain; ord. priest Dec. 22, 1928; ord. titular bishop of Lirbe and apostolic administrator of Barbastro, May 5, 1946; bishop of Barbastro, Feb. 2, 1950; bishop of Albacete, May 13, 1950; archbishop of Pamplona, 1968-71; cardinal Apr. 28, 1969; titular church, St. Peter (in Montorio). Former archbishop of Pamplona, prefect of Sacred Congregation for Divine Worship (1971), member of:
Congregations: Religious and Secular Institutes, Causes of Saints, Discipline of Sacraments;
Tribunal: Apostolic Signatura;
Commission: Revision of Code of Canon Law.

Traglia, Luigi: b. Apr. 3, 1895, Albano Laziale, Italy; ord. priest Aug. 10, 1917; clerk of Congregation for Propagation of the Faith, 1927; judge of Roman Rota, 1936; ord. titular archbishop of Cesarea of Palestine and viceregent of Rome, Jan. 6, 1937; cardinal Mar. 28, 1960; entered order of cardinal bishops as titular bishop of Albano, Mar. 14, 1972. Chancellor of Holy Roman Church, member of:
Congregations: Doctrine of Faith, Oriental Churches, Bishops, Discipline of Sacraments, Evangelization of Peoples, Causes of Saints;
Tribunal: Apostolic Signatura;
Commission: State of Vatican City.

Ursi, Corrado: b. July 26, 1908, Andria, Italy; ord. priest July 25, 1931; vice-rector and later rector of the Pontifical Regional Seminary of Molfetta, 1931-51; ord. bishop of Nardo, Sept. 30, 1951; archbishop of Acerenza, Nov. 30, 1961; archbishop of Naples, May 23, 1966; cardinal June 26, 1967; titular church, St. Callistus. Archbishop of Naples, member of:
Congregations: Religious and Secular Institutes, Catholic Education.

Vagnozzi, Egidio: b. Feb. 2, 1906, Rome, Italy; ord. priest Dec. 22, 1928; served in US apostolic delegation; ord. titular archbishop of Mira, May 22, 1949; apostolic delegate to the Philippines, 1949; first nuncio to Philippines, 1951; apostolic delegate to the US, 1958-67; cardinal June 26, 1967; deacon, St. Joseph. President of Prefecture of Economic Affairs of Holy See, member of:
Council for Public Affairs of Church;
Congregations: Bishops, Oriental Churches;
Tribunal: Apostolic Signatura.

Villot, Jean: b. Oct. 11, 1905, Saint-Amant-Tallende, France; ord. priest Apr. 19, 1930; ord. titular bishop of Vinda and auxiliary bishop of Paris, Oct. 12, 1954; titular archbishop of Bosphorus and coadjutor archbishop of Lyons, Dec. 17, 1959; archbishop of Lyons, 1965-67; cardinal Feb. 22, 1965; titular church, Most Holy Trinity (in Monte Pincio). Secretary of State (1969), prefect of Council for Public Affairs of the Church, chamberlain of the Holy Roman Church, member of:

Congregations: Doctrine of Faith, Bishops, Catholic Education, Evangelization of Peoples, Causes of Saints;

Office: Administration of Patrimony of Holy See (President);

Commissions: Revision of Code of Canon Law, Interpretation of Decrees of Vatican II, Pontifical Council *Cor Unum* (President), Institute for Works of Religion, State of Vatican City (President).

Violardo, Giacomo: b. May 10, 1898, Govone, Italy; ord. priest June 29, 1923; ord. titular archbishop of Satafi, Mar. 19, 1966; secretary of Congregation for Discipline of the Sacraments; cardinal Apr. 28, 1969; deacon, St. Eustachius. Member of:

Congregations: Discipline of Sacraments, Oriental Churches;

Tribunal: Apostolic Signatura;

Office: Prefecture of Economic Affairs of Holy See;

Commission: Revision of Code of Canon Law, State of Vatican City.

Willebrands, Jan: b. Sept. 4, 1909, Bovenkarspel, Netherlands; ord. priest May 26, 1934; ord. titular bishop of Mauriana, June 28, 1964; secretary of Secretariat for Christian Unity, 1960-69; cardinal Apr. 28, 1969; deacon, Sts. Cosmas and Damian. President of Secretariat for Christian Unity (1969), member of:

Congregations: Doctrine of Faith, Discipline of Sacraments, Catholic Education, Evangelization of Peoples, Divine Worship;

Commission: Revision of Code of Canon Law.

Wojtyla, Karol: b. May 18, 1920, Wadowice, Poland; ord. priest Nov. 1, 1946; served on faculties of Catholic University of Lublin and University of Cracow; ord. titular bishop of Ombi and auxiliary bishop of Cracow, Sept. 28, 1958; archbishop of Cracow, Jan. 13, 1964; cardinal June 26, 1967; titular church, St. Caesarius (in Palatio). Archbishop of Cracow, member of:

Congregations: Oriental Churches, Clergy, Divine Worship.

Wright, John J.: b. July 18, 1909; Dorchester, Mass.; ord. priest Dec. 8, 1935; ord. titular bishop of Egee and auxiliary bishop of Boston, June 30, 1947; bishop of Worcester, Jan. 28, 1950; bishop of Pittsburgh, 1959-69; cardinal Apr. 28, 1969; titular church, Jesus the Divine Teacher. Prefect of Congregation for the Clergy (1969), member of:

Council for Public Affairs of Church;

Congregations: Doctrine of Faith, Bishops, Catholic Education, Evangelization of Peoples;

Commissions: Revision of Code of Canon Law, State of Vatican City, Sanctuaries of Pompei and Loreto.

Wyszynski, Stefan: b. Aug. 3, 1901, Zuzela, Poland; ord. priest Aug. 3, 1924; ord. bishop of Lublin, May 12, 1946; archbishop of Gniezno and Warsaw, Nov. 12, 1948; cardinal Jan. 12, 1953; titular church, St. Mary (in Trastavere). He was "deposed" by Polish government in fall of 1953, recognized, 1956. Archbishop of Gniezno and Warsaw, primate of Poland, member of:

Congregation: Clergy;

Commission: Revision of Canon Law.

Yu Pin, Paul: b. Apr. 13, 1901, Lan-si Sien, China; ord. priest Dec. 22, 1928; professor of Chinese literature and philosophy at Rome, 1929-36; returned to China, 1936; ord. titular bishop of Sozusa de Palestina and vicar apostolic of Nanking, Sept. 20, 1936; archbishop of Nanking, Apr. 11, 1946; cardinal Apr. 28, 1969; titular church, Jesus the Divine Worker. Archbishop of Nanking (in exile; residing in Taiwan), member of:

Congregations: Evangelization of Peoples, Catholic Education;

Secretariat: Non-Christians.

Zerba, Cesare: b. Apr. 15, 1892, Castelnuova Scrivia, Italy; ord. priest July 4, 1915; began Roman Curia service in 1924; undersecretary of Congregation of Sacramental Discipline, 1939; secretary, 1958-65; ord. titular archbishop of Colosse, Sept. 21, 1962; cardinal Feb. 22, 1965; titular church, Our Lady of the Sacred Heart (in Piazza Navona). Member of:

Office: Prefecture of Economic Affairs.

Zoungrana, Paul: b. Sept. 3, 1917, Ougadougou, Upper Volta; ord. priest May 2, 1942; ord. archbishop of Ougadougou at St. Peter's Basilica by John XXIII, May 8, 1960; cardinal Feb. 22, 1965; titular church, St. Camillus de Lellis. Archbishop of Ougadougou, member of:

Congregations: Religious and Secular Institutes, Evangelization of Peoples.

SENIORITY OF CARDINALS

Usually depends on order of elevation.

Information below includes the categories of cardinals and dates of consistories at which they were created. Two of these cardinals were named by Pius XI (consistories of Dec. 16, 1929, and June 30, 1930); 15 by Pius XII (consistories of Feb. 18, 1946, and Jan. 12, 1953); 26 by John XXIII (consistories of Dec. 15, 1958, Dec. 14, 1959, Mar. 28, 1960, Jan. 16, 1961, and Mar. 19, 1962); 73 by Paul VI (consistories of Feb. 22, 1965, June 26, 1967, and Apr. 28, 1969). (As of Sept. 10, 1972.)

Cardinal Bishops

Bishops of Suburban Sees:

1958 (Dec. 15): Fernando Cento, Amleto Cicognani, Carlo Confalonieri.

1959 (Dec. 14): Paolo Marella.

1960 (Mar. 28): Luigi Traglia.

1961 (Jan. 16): Giuseppe Ferretto.

Eastern Rite Patriarchs:

1965 (Feb. 22): Paul Peter Meouchi, Stephanos I Sidarouss, C.M.

Cardinal Priests

1929 (Dec. 16): Manuel Goncalves Cerejeira.

1930 (June 30): Achilles Lienart.

1946 (Feb. 18): James McGuigan, Carlos Carmelo de Vasconcellos Motta, Norman Gilroy, Joseph Frings, Jozsef Mindszenty, Antonio Caggiano.

1953 (Jan. 12): Maurice Feltin, Giuseppe Siri, James McIntyre, Giacomo Lercaro, Stefan Wyszynski, Benjamin de Arriba y Castro, Paul Emile Leger, S.S., Valerian Gracias, Alfredo Ottaviani.

1958 (Dec. 15): Antonio Maria Barbieri, Jose M. Bueno y Monreal, Franziskus Koenig, Julius Doepfner, Alberto di Jorio, Francesco Roberti.

1959 (Dec. 14): Arcadio Larraona, C.M.F., William Heard.

1960 (Mar. 28): Joseph Lefebvre, Bernard Jan Alfrink, Rufino Santos, Laurean Rugambwa.

1961 (Jan. 16): Jose Humberto Quintero, Luis Concha.

1962 (Mar. 19): Jose da Costa Nunes, Ildebrando Antoniutti, Efrem Forni, Juan Landazuri Ricketts, O.F.M., Raul Silva Henriquez, S.D.B., Leo Josef Suenens.

1965 (Feb. 22): Josyf Slipyi, Lorenz Jaeger, Thomas B. Cooray, Maurice Roy, Joseph M. Martin, Owen McCann, Leon-Etienne Duval, Ermenegildo Florit, Franjo Seper, John C. Heenan, Jean Villot, Paul Zoungrana, Lawrence J. Shehan, Cesare Zerba, Agnelo Rossi, Giovanni Colombo, William Conway.

1967 (June 26): Giuseppe Beltrami, Gabriel Garrone, Patrick O'Boyle, Maximilien de Furstenberg, Antonio Samore, Francesco Carpino, Jose Clemente Maurer, C.SS.R., Pietro Parente, Carlo Grano, Dino Staffa, John J. Krol, John P. Cody, Corrado Ursi, Alfred Bengsch, Justin Darmojuwono, Karol Wojtyla, Michele Pellegrino, Alexandre Renard.

1969 (Apr. 28): Paul Yu Pin, Alfredo Vicente Scherer, Julio Rosales, Gordon J. Gray, Peter T. McKeefry, Sebastiano Baggio, Miguel Dario Miranda y Gomez, Joseph Parecattil, John F. Dearden, Francois Marty;

Jerome Rakotomalala, George Flahiff, Paul Gouyon, Mario Casariego, Vicente Enrique y Tarancon, Joseph Malula, Pablo Muñoz Vega, S.J., Antonio Poma;

John J. Carberry, Terence J. Cooke, Stephan Sou Hwan Kim, Arturo Tabera Araoz, C.M.F., Eugenio de Araujo Sales, Joseph Hoeffner, John J. Wright.

Cardinal Deacons

1965 (Feb. 22): Charles Journet.

1967 (June 26): Egidio Vagnozzi, Pericle Felici.

1969 (Apr. 28): Paolo Bertoli, Silvio Oddi, Giuseppe Paupini, Giacomo Violardo, Jan Willebrands, Mario Nasalli Rocca di Corneliano, Sergio Guerri, Jean Danielou.

Ineligible To Vote

As of Sept. 10, 1972, 26 cardinals were ineligible to take part in a papal election in line with the apostolic letter *Ingravescentem Aetatem* effective Jan. 1, 1971, which limited the functions of cardinals after completion of their 80th year.

Cardinals affected were: Beltrami, Caggiano, Cento, Cerejeira, Cicognani, Concha, Da Costa Nunes, De Arriba y Castro, Di Jorio, Feltin, Forni, Frings, Grano, Heard, Journet, Larraona, Lefebvre, Lercaro, Lienart, McIntyre, Martin, Mindszenty, Motta, Ottaviani, Parente, Roberti, Slipyi, Zerba.

By the end of 1972, two more cardinals completed their 80th year: Barbieri, Oct. 12, and Jaeger, Sept. 23.

DISTRIBUTION OF CARDINALS

As of Sept. 10, 1972, there were 116 cardinals from 45 countries or areas. Listed below are areas, countries, number and last names.

Europe — 71

Italy (34): Antoniutti, Baggio, Beltrami, Bertoli Carpino, Cento, Cicognani, Colombo, Confalonieri, Di Jorio, Felici, Ferretto, Florit, Forni, Grano, Guerri, Lercaro, Marella, Nasalli Rocca di Corneliano, Oddi, Ottaviano, Parente, Paupini, Pellegrino, Poma, Roberti, Samore, Siri, Staffa, Traglia, Ursi, Vagnozzi, Violardo, Zerba.

France (10): Danielou, Feltin, Garrone, Gouyon, Lefebvre, Lienart, Martin, Marty, Renard, Villot.

Spain (5): Bueno y Monreal, De Arriba y Castro, Enrique y Tarancon, Larraona, Tabera Araoz, C.M.F.

Germany (5): Bengsch, Doepfner, Frings, Jaeger, Hoeffner.

Netherlands (3): Alfrink, De Furstenberg, Willebrands.

Poland (2): Wyszynski, Wojtyla.

Portugal (2): Da Costa Nunes (Azores), Goncalves Cerejeira.

Scotland (2): Heard, Gray.

One from each of the following countries: Austria, Koenig; Belgium, Suenens; England, Heenan; Hungary, Mindszenty; Ireland, Conway; Switzerland, Journet; Ukraine (now in USSR), Slipyi; Yugoslavia, Seper.

Asia — 9

India (2): Gracias, Parecattil.

Philippines (2): Santos, Rosales.

One from each of the following countries: Ceylon, Cooray; China, Yu Pin; Indonesia, Darmojuwono; Korea, Kim; Lebanon, Meouchi.

Oceania — 2

Australia, Gilroy; New Zealand, McKeefry.

Africa — 7

One from each of the following countries: Algeria, Duval; Egypt (United Arab Republic), Sidarouss; Malagasy Republic, Rakotomalala; South Africa, McCann; Tanzania, Rugambwa; Upper Volta, Zoungrana; Zaire, Malula.

North America — 14

United States (9): Carberry, Cody, Cooke, Dearden, Krol, McIntyre, O'Boyle, Shehan, Wright.

Canada (4): Flahiff, Leger, McGuigan, Roy.

Mexico (1): Miranda y Gomez.

Central and South America — 13

Brazil (4): De Araujo Sales, Motta, Rossi, Sherer.

One from each of the following countries: Argentina, Caggiano; Bolivia, Maurer; Chile, Silva Henriquez; Colombia, Concha; Ecuador, Munoz Vega, S.J.; Guatemala, Casariego (b. Spain); Peru, Landazuri Ricketts; Uruguay, Barbieri: Venezuela, Quintero.

Cardinals of US

As of June 19, 1972, US cardinals, years of elevation and sees:

James McIntyre, 1953, Los Angeles (retired 1970); Lawrence J. Shehan, 1965, Baltimore; Patrick A. O'Boyle, 1967, Washington; John J. Krol, 1967, Philadelphia; John P. Cody, 1967, Chicago; John F. Dearden, 1969, Detroit; John J. Carberry, 1969, St. Louis; Terence J. Cooke, 1969, New York; John J. Wright, 1969, prefect of the Congregation for the Clergy.

Deceased US cardinals, years of elevation, sees, years of birth and death:

John McCloskey, 1875, New York, 1810-1885; James Gibbons, 1886, Baltimore, 1834-1921; John Farley, 1911, New York, 1842-1918; William O'Connell, 1911, Boston, 1859-1944; Dennis Dougherty, 1921, Philadelphia, 1865-1951; Patrick Hayes, 1924, New York, 1867-1938; George Mundelein, 1924, Chicago, 1872-1939; John Glennon, 1946, St. Louis, 1862-1946; Edward Mooney, 1946, Detroit, 1882-1958;

Francis Spellman, 1946, New York, 1889-1967; Samuel Stritch, 1946, Chicago, 1887-1958; John O'Hara, C.S.C., 1958, Philadelphia, 1888-1960; Albert Meyer, 1959, Chicago, 1903-1965; Aloysius Muench, 1959, Fargo (and papal nuncio), 1889-1962; Joseph Ritter, 1961, St. Louis, 1892-1967; Francis Brennan, 1967, official of Roman Curia, 1894-1968; Richard Cushing, 1958, Boston, 1895-1970.

REPRESENTATIVES OF THE HOLY SEE

Papal representatives and their functions were the subject of a document entitled *Sollicitudo Omnium Ecclesiarum* which Pope Paul issued on his own initiative under the date of June 24, 1969.

Delegates and Nuncios

Papal representatives "receive from the Roman Pontiff the charge of representing him in a fixed way in the various nations or regions of the world.

"When their legation is only to local churches, they are known as apostolic delegates. When to this legation, of a religious and ecclesial nature, there is added diplomatic legation to states and governments, they receive the title of nuncio, pro-nuncio, and internuncio."

[An apostolic nuncio has the diplomatic rank of ambassador extraordinary and plenipotentiary. Traditionally, because the Vatican diplomatic service has the longest uninterrupted history in the world, a nuncio has precedence among diplomats in the country to which he is accredited and serves as dean of the diplomatic corps on state occasions. Since 1965 pro-nuncios, also of ambassadorial rank have been assigned to countries in which this prerogative is not recognized.]

(Other representatives, who are covered in the Almanac article, Vatican Representatives to International Organizations, are clerics and lay persons "who form . . . part of a pontifical mission attached to international organizations or take part in conferences and congresses." They are variously called delegates or observers.)

"The primary and specific purpose of the mission of a papal representative is to render ever closer and more operative the ties that bind the Apostolic See and the local churches.

"The ordinary function of a pontifical representative is to keep the Holy See regularly and objectively informed about the conditions of the ecclesial community to which he has been sent, and about what may affect the life of the Church and the good of souls.

"On the one hand, he makes known to the Holy See the thinking of the bishops, clergy, religious and faithful of the territory where he carries out his mandate, and forwards to Rome their proposals and their requests; on the other hand, he makes himself the interpreter, with those concerned, of the acts, documents, information and instructions emanating from the Holy See."

Service and Liaison

Representatives, while carrying out their general and special duties, are bound to respect the autonomy of local churches and bishops. Their service and liaison responsibilities include the following:

• **Nomination of Bishops:** To play a key role in compiling, with the advice of ecclesiastics and lay persons, and submitting lists of names of likely candidates to the Holy See with their own recommendations.

• **Bishops:** To aid and counsel local bishops without interfering in the affairs of their jurisdictions.

• **Episcopal Conferences:** To maintain close relations with them and to assist them in every possible way. (Papal representatives do not belong to these conferences.)

• **Religious Communities of Pontifical Rank:** To advise and assist major superiors for the purpose of promoting and consolidating conferences of men and women religious and to coordinate their apostolic activities.

• **Church-State Relations:** The thrust in this area is toward the development of sound relations with civil governments and collaboration in work for peace and the total good of the whole human family.

The mission of a papal representative begins with appointment and assignment by the pope and continues until termination of his mandate. He acts "under the guidance and according to the instructions of the cardinal secretary of state and prefect of the Council for the Public Affairs of the Church, to whom he is directly responsible for the execution of the mandate entrusted to him by the Supreme Pontiff." Normally, representatives are required to retire at the age of 75.

The Pope said clearly in the document that it was a response to demands made during the Second Vatican Council for clarification of the whole system of papal representation to local churches and governments throughout the world.

At the same time, but without any statement to that effect, the document appeared to be a response to criticism voiced in some quarters about the validity and desirability of this system. It was variously charged that the system interfered with administration in local churches; that it deprived local churches of reasonable independence; that it made the conduct of local church affairs dependent on the opinion of a foreigner in a country; that it violated the principle of subsidiarity; that it reflected an erroneous image of the pope as a would-be political sovereign. Refutation of all these charges was implicit in the broad introduction and specific articles of the document.

NUNCIOS AND DELEGATES

(Sources: *Annuario Pontificio, L'Osservatore Romano,* NC News Service.)

Data, as of June 30, 1972: country, rank of legation (corresponding to rank of legate unless otherwise noted), name of legate (archbishop unless otherwise noted) as available.

Africa, Central-West (Nigeria, Ghana): Lagos, Nigeria, Apostolic Delegation; Amelio Poggi.

Africa, North (Libya, Morocco): Algiers, Algeria, Apostolic Delegation; Sante Portalupi.

Africa, South (Botswana, Rhodesia, South Africa, Namibia, Swaziland): Pretoria, Apostolic Delegation; Alfredo Poledrino.

Africa, West (Guinea, Mali, Mauritania, Togo, Upper Volta): Dakar, Senegal, Apostolic Delegation; Giovanni Mariani.

Algeria: Lagos, Nuncciature, Sante Portalupi, Pro-Nuncio.

Argentina: Buenos Aires, Nunciature; Lino Zanini.

Australia, and Papua-New Guinea: North Sydney, Apostolic Delegation; Gino Paro.

Austria: Vienna, Nunciature; Opilio Rossi.

Belgium: Brussels, Nunciature; Igino Cardinale.

Bolivia: La Paz, Nunciature; Giovanni Gravelli.

Brazil: Rio de Janeiro, Nunciature; Umberto Mozzoni.

Burundi: Bujumbura, Nunciature; William Carew.

Cameroon: Yaounde, Nunciature; Jean Jadot, Pro-Nuncio.

Canada: Ottawa, Nunciature; Guido Del Mestri, Pro-Nuncio.

Central African Republic: Bangui, Nunciature; Mario Tagliaferri, Pro-Nuncio (also Apostolic Delegate to Chad and Congo-Brazzaville).

Chile: Santiago, Nunciature;Sotero Sanz Villalba.

China: Tapei (Taiwan), Nunciature; Edward Cassidy, Pro-Nuncio.

Colombia: Bogota, Nunciature; Angelo Palmas.

Costa Rica: San Jose, Nunciature; Angelo Pedroni.

Cuba: Havana Nunicature; Cesare Zacchi, Chargé d'Affaires.

Dahomey: Cotonou, Nunciature; Giovanni Mariani, Pro-Nuncio (resides in Dakar, Senegal).

Dominican Republic: Santo Domingo, Nunciature; Luciano Storero (also Apostolic Delegate to Puerto Rico).

Ecuador: Quito, Nunciature; Luigi Accogli.

Egypt: See United Arab Republic.

El Salvador: San Salvador, Nunciature; Girolamo Prigione.

Equatorial Guinea: Santa Isabel, Apostolic Delegation; Jean Jadot (resides in Yaounde, Cameroon).

Ethiopia: Addis Ababa, Nunciature; Maurice Perrin, Pro-Nuncio.

Finland: Helsinki, Nunciature; Josip Zabkar, Pro-Nuncio (resides in Copenhagen).

France: Paris, Nunciature; Egano Righi Lambertini.

Gabon Republic: Libreville, Nunciature; Jean Jadot, Pro-Nuncio (resides in Yaounde, Cameroon).

Germany: Bonn, Nunciature; Corrado Bafile.

Great Britain: London, Apostolic Delegation; Domenico Enrici (also Apostolic Delegate to Gibraltar).

Guatemala: Guatemala City, Nunciature; Girolamo Prigione.

Haiti: Port-au-Prince, Nunciature; Luigi Barbariti. (Apostolic Delegate also for region in Antilles Episcopal Conference.)

Honduras: Tegucigalpa, Nunciature; Lorenzo Antonetti.

India: New Delhi, Nunciature; John Gordon, Pro-Nuncio (also Apostolic Delegate to Burma).

Indonesia: Djakarta, Nunciature; Joseph Mees, Pro-Nuncio.

Iran: Teheran, Nunciature; Ernesto Gallina, Pro-Nuncio.

Iraq: Bagdad, Nunciature; Jean Rupp, Pro-Nuncio.

Ireland: Dublin, Nunciature; Gaetano Alibrandi.

Italy: Rome, Nunciature; Romolo Carboni.

Ivory Coast: Abidjan, Nunciature.

Japan: Tokyo, Nunciature; Bruno Wustenberg, Pro-Nuncio.

Jerusalem, Palestine, Jordan, Israel, Cyprus: Jerusalem, Apostolic Delegation; Pio Laghi.

Kenya: Nairobi, Nunciature; Pierluigi Sartorelli, Pro-Nuncio (also Apostolic Delegate to Seychelles Is.).

Korea: Seoul, Nunciature; Ippolito Rotoli, Pro-Nuncio.

Kuwait: Al Kuwait, Nunciature; Alfredo Bruniera, Pro-Nuncio (resides in Beirut, Lebanon).

Laos, Malaysia and Singapore: Bangkok, Apostolic Delegation; Giovanni Moretti (resides in Bangkok).

Lebanon: Beirut, Nunciature; Alfredo Bruniera.

Lesotho: Maseru, Nunciature; Alfredo Poledrino, Pro-Nuncio (resides in Pretoria, S. Africa).

Liberia: Monrovia, Nunciature; Francis Carroll, S.M.A., Pro-Nuncio (also Apostolic Delegate for Sierra Leone and Gambia).

Luxembourg: Nunciature; Igino Cardinale (resides in Brussels, Belgium).

Malagasy Republic: Tananarive, Nunciature; Michele Cecchini, Pro-Nuncio (also Apostolic Delegate to Reunion).

Malawi: Zomba, Nunciature; Luciano Angeloni, Pro-Nuncio (resides in Zambia).

Malta: La Valletta, Nunciature; Edoardo Pecoraio.

Mauritius: Port Louis, Nunciature; Michele Cecchini, Pro-Nuncio (resides in Tananarive, Malagasy Republic).

Mexico: Mexico City, Apostolic Delegation; Carlo Martini.

Netherlands: The Hague, Nunciature; Angelo Felici, Pro-Nuncio.

New Zealand and Pacific Islands: Wellington, Apostolic Delegation; Raymond Etteldorf.

Nicaragua: Managua, Nunciature; Lorenzo Antonetti.

Niger: Niamey, Nunciature; Giovanni Mariani, Pro-Nuncio (resides in Dakar, Senegal).

Pakistan Islamabad, Nunciature; Joseph Uhac, Pro-Nuncio.

Panama: Panama, Nunciature; Edoardo Rovida.

Paraguay: Asuncion, Nunciature; Antonio Innocenti.

Peru: Lima, Nunciature; Luigi Poggi.

Philippines: Manila, Nunciature; Carmine Rocco.

Portugal: Lisbon, Nunciature; Giuseppe Sensi.

Red Sea Region (Somalia, Afars and Issas, part of Arabian Peninsula): Khartoum, Apostolic Delegation; Ubaldo Calabresi.

Rwanda: Kigali, Nunciature; William Carew.

Scandinavia (Denmark, Sweden, Norway, Iceland): Copenhagen, Denmark, Apostolic Delegation; Josip Zabkar.

Senegal: Dakar, Nunciature; Giovanni Mariani, Pro-Nuncio.

Spain: Madrid, Nunciature; Luigi Dadaglio.

Sri Lanka: Colombo, Apostolic Delegation; Carlo Curis.

Sudan: Khartoum, Nunciature; Ubaldo Calabresi, Pro-Nuncio.

Switzerland: Bern, Nunciature; Ambrogio Marchioni.

Syria (Syrian Arab Republic): Damascus, Nunciature; Achille Glorieux, Pro-Nuncio.

Tanzania: Dar-es-Salaam, Nunciature; Franco Brambilla, Pro-Nuncio.

Thailand: Bangkok, Nunciature; Giovanni Moretti, Pro-Nuncio.

Tunisia: Tunis, Nunciature; Sante Portalupi, Pro-Nuncio (resides in Algiers, Algeria).

Turkey: Ankara, Nunciature; Salvatore Asta, Pro-Nuncio.

Uganda: Kampala, Nunciature; Luigi Bellotti, Pro-Nuncio.

United Arab Republic (Egypt): Cairo, Nunciature; Bruno Heim, Pro-Nuncio.

United States of America: Washington, D.C., Apostolic Delegation; Luigi Raimondi.

Uruguay: Montevideo, Nunciature; Augustine Sepinski, O.F.M.

Venezuela: Caracas, Nunciature; Antonio del Giudice.

Vietnam and Khmer Republic: Saigon, Apostolic Delegation; Henri Lemaitre.

Yugoslavia: Belgrade, Nunciature; Mario Cagna, Pro-Nuncio.

Zaire: Kinshasa-Kalina, Nunciature; Bruno Torpigliano.

Zambia: Lusaka, Nunciature; Luciano Angeloni, Pro-Nuncio.

Apostolic Delegate to US

The representative of the Pope to the Catholic Church in the United States is Archbishop Luigi Raimondi, apostolic delegate. He was born Oct. 25, 1912, at Lussito, Italy; was ordained to the priesthood June 6, 1936; was secretary of the apostolic nunciature in Guatemala (1938-1942), secretary and auditor of the apostolic delegation in the US (1942-1949), auditor of the apostolic internunciature in India (1949-1953); was appointed titular archbishop of Tarsus and papal nuncio to Haiti, Dec. 24, 1953; received episcopal consecration Jan. 31, 1954; was apostolic delegate to Mexico (1956-1967); was named apostolic delegate to the United States in 1967.

The US Apostolic Delegation was established Jan. 21, 1893. It is located at 3339 Massachusetts Ave. N.W., Washington, D.C. 20008.

Archbishop Raimondi's predecessors were Archbishops: Francesco Satolli (1893-1896), Sebastiano Martinelli, O.S.O. (1896-1902), Diomede Falconio, O.F.M. (1902-1911), Giovanni Bonzano (1911-1922), Pietro Fumasoni-Biondi (1922-1933), Amleto Cicognani (1933-1958), and Egidio Vagnozzi (1958-1967).

Amleto Cicognani, for 25 years apostolic delegate to the US, became a cardinal in 1958 and served as papal secretary of state from 1961 to 1969.

DIPLOMATS AT VATICAN

(Sources: *Annuario Pontificio, L'Osservatore Romano,* NC News Service. As of June 30, 1972.)

Algeria: Ambassador.

Argentina: Santiago de Estrada, Ambassador.

Austria: Hans Reichmann, Ambassador.

Belgium: Albert Hupperts, Ambassador.

Bolivia: Afredo Flores Suarez, Ambassador.

Brazil: Jose Jobim, Ambassador.

Burundi: Pierre Bigayimpunzi, Ambassador.

Cameroon: Ambassador.

Canada: John Everett Robbins, Ambassador.

Central African Republic: Ambassador.

Chile: Rene Rojas Galdames, Ambassador.

China (Taiwan): Chen Chih-mai Ambassador.

Colombia: Fernando Gomez Martinez, Ambassador.

Costa Rica: Ambassador.

Cuba: Luis Amado-Blanco, Ambassador.

Dahomey: Laurent Cyrille Faboumy, Ambassador.

Dominican Republic: Alvaro Lograno Battle, Ambassador.

Ecuador: Luis Antonio Penaherrera, Ambassador.

El Salvador: Alfonso Quinonez-Meza, Ambassador.

Ethiopia: Kidane Mariam Haile, Minister.

Finland: Jussi Makinen, Ambassador.

France: Rene Brouillet, Ambassador.

Gabon: Marcel Sandougnout, Ambassador.

Germany: Alexander Bökor, Ambassador.

Great Britain: Desmond John Chetwode Crawley, Minister.

Guatemala: Luis Valladares y Aycinena, Ambassador.

Haiti: Francois Guillaume, Ambassador.

Honduras: Carlos Lopez Contreras, Ambassador.

India: Arjun Singh, Ambassador.

Indonesia: Hussein Mutahar, Ambassador.

Iran: Mehdi Vakil, Ambassador.

Iraq: Hassan Mustafa Al-Nakib, Ambassador.

Ireland: Thomas V. Commins, Ambassador.

Italy: Gian Franco Pompei, Ambassador.

Ivory Coast: Joseph Amichia, Ambassador.

Japan: Hisaji Hattori, Ambassador.

Kenya: Ambassador.

Korea: Moon Bong Kang, Ambassador.

Kuwait: Ambassador.

Lebanon: Nagib Dahdah, Ambassador.

Lesotho: Ambassador.

Liberia: J. Dudley Lawrence, Ambassador.

Lithuania: Stasys Lozoraitis, Jr., first secretary.

Luxembourg: Emile Colling, Ambassador.

Malagasy Republic: Philibert Raondry, Ambassador.

Malawi: Bridger W. Katenga, Ambassador.

Malta: Ambassador.

Mauritius: Leckraz Teelock, Ambassador.

Monaco: Cesar Charles Solamito, Minister.

Netherlands: Baron Sweder Godfried van Voorst tot Voorst, Ambassador.

Nicaragua: Alejandro Arguello Montiel, Ambassador.

Niger: Ibra Kabo, Ambassador.

Order of Malta: Count Stanislaus Pecci, Minister.

Pakistan: H. N. Hossain, Ambassador.

Panama: Jose Calvo Velasquez, Ambassador.

Paraguay: Miguel T. Romero, Ambassador.

Peru: Jose Carlos Ferreyros Balta, Ambassador.

Philippines: Ambassador.

Poland: Casimir Papee (Gerent of the affairs of the Ambassadorship).

Portugal: Eduardo Brazao, Ambassador.

Rwanda: Ambassador.

San Marino: Don Giannandrea D'Ardia, Minister.

Senegal: Henry Rene Dodds, Ambassador.

Spain: Antonio Garrigues y Diaz-Canabate, Ambassador.

Sudan: Ambassador.

Syria (Arab Republic): Nach'at Al-Husseini, Ambassador.

Tanzania: Anthony Balthasar Nyakyi, Ambassador.

Thailand: Chatichal Choonhavan, Ambassador.

Tunisia: Tahar Belkhodja, Ambassador.
Turkey: Necdet Uran, Ambassador.
Uganda: John Patrick Barigye, Ambassador.
United Arab Republic (Egypt): Salal El Din Mohamed Wasfy, Ambassador.
Uruguay: Venancio Flores, Ambassador.
Venezuela: Francesco Romero Lobo, Ambassador.
Yugoslavia: Stane Kolman, Ambassador.
Zaire: Alphonse Sita, Ambassador.
Zambia: Amock Israel Phiri, Ambassador.

Diplomatic Actions: Among other diplomatic actions in 1972, the Vatican established relations with Bangladesh and ratified an agreement with Austria on school questions. Earlier agreements with the Austrian government on this matter had been signed Mar. 8, 1971, and July 9, 1962.

US — VATICAN RELATIONS

Official relations for trade and diplomatic purposes were maintained by the United States and the Papal States while the latter had the character of and acted like other sovereign powers in the international community.

Consular Relations

Consular relations developed in the wake of an announcement, made by the papal nuncio in Paris to the American mission there Dec. 15, 1784, that the Papal States had agreed to open several Mediterranean ports to US shipping.

US consular representation in the Papal States began with the appointment of John B. Sartori, a native of Rome, in June, 1797. Sartori's successors as consuls were:Felix Cicognani, also a Roman, and Americans George W. Greene, Nicholas Browne, William C. Sanders, Daniel LeRoy, Horatio V. Glentworth, W.J. Stillman, Edwin C. Cushman, David M. Armstrong.

Consular officials of the Papal States who served in the US were: Count Ferdinand Lucchesi, 1826 to 1829, who resided in Washington; John B. Sartori, 1829 to 1841, who resided in Trenton, N.J.; Daniel J. Desmond, 1841 to 1850, who resided in Philadelphia; Louis B. Binsse, 1850 to 1895, who resided in New York.

US recognition of the consul of the Papal States did not cease when the states were absorbed into the Kingdom of Italy in 1871, despite pressure from Baron Blanc, the Italian minister. Binsse held the title until his death Mar. 28, 1895. No one was appointed to succeed him.

Diplomatic Relations

The US Senate approved a recommendation, made by President James K. Polk in December, 1847, for the establishment of a diplomatic post in the Papal States. Jacob L. Martin, the first charge d'affaires, arrived in Rome Aug. 2, 1848, and presented his credentials to Pius IX Aug. 19. Martin, who died within a month, was succeeded by Lewis Cass, Jr. Cass became minister resident in 1854 and served in that capacity until his retirement in 1858.

John P. Stockton, who later became a US Senator from New Jersey, was minister resident from 1858 to 1861. Rufus King was named to succeed him but, instead, accepted a commission as a brigadier general in the Army. Alexander W. Randall of Wisconsin took the appointment. He was succeeded in August, 1862, by Richard M. Blatchford who served until the following year. King was again nominated minister resident and served in that capacity until 1867 when the ministry was ended because of objections from some quarters in the US and failure to appropriate funds for its continuation. J.C. Hooker, a secretary, remained in the Papal States until the end of March, 1868, closing the ministry and performing functions of courtesy.

The Taylor Mission

Late in 1939, President Franklin D. Roosevelt appointed Myron C. Taylor as his personal representative to Pius XII, with the rank but not the diplomatic status or prerogatives of ambassador. Mr. Taylor also served as the personal representative of President Harry S. Truman, until January, 1950.

President Truman, in October, 1951, nominated Gen. Mark W. Clark for the post of US ambassador to the State of Vatican City. General Clark, however, requested withdrawal of the nomination before it was forwarded to the Senate for approval. There was no action by the Senate on the nomination or on the question of establishing diplomatic relations with Vatican City.

The Lodge Appointment

President Richard M. Nixon named Henry Cabot Lodge to serve as his personal representative to the Vatican in June, 1970.

In announcing the appointment, White House Press Secretary Ronald Ziegler said the President had asked Mr. Lodge to make periodic visits to the Vatican "because he wishes to provide for greater continuity in the informal contacts which already have been taking place in the Administration and the Vatican since President Nixon took office. (The President) felt it was important to have the benefit of the Vatican's information and views on a continuing basis and to exchange views on a continuing basis. . . . Ambassador Lodge will be discussing any international or humanitarian subjects of interest and concern to the Vatican and the Pope and the President. . . . He will be conveying the views of the President and soliciting views on the subjects I have just mentioned."

It was made clear that Mr. Lodge would not have either diplomatic status or title.

VATICAN CITY

The State of Vatican City (Stato della Citta del Vaticano) is the territorial seat of the papacy. The smallest sovereign state in the world, it is situated within the city of Rome, embraces an area of 108.7 acres, and includes within its limits the Vatican Palace, museums, art galleries, gardens, libraries, radio station, post office, bank, astronomical observatory, offices, apartments, service facilities, St. Peter's Basilica, and neighboring buildings between the Basilica and Viale Vaticano.

The extraterritorial rights of Vatican City extend to more than 10 buildings in Rome, including the major basilicas and office buildings of various congregations of the Roman Curia, and to the **Villa of Castel Gandolfo** 15 miles southeast of the City of Rome. Castel Gandolfo is the summer residence of the Holy Father.

The government of Vatican City is in the hands of the reigning pope, who has full executive, legislative and judicial power. The administration of affairs, however, is handled by the Pontifical Commission for the State of Vatican City. The legal system is based on Canon Law; in cases where this code does not obtain, the laws of the City of Rome apply. The City is an absolutely neutral state and enjoys all the rights and privileges of a sovereign power. The Secretariat of State (Papal Secretariat) maintains diplomatic relations with other nations. The citizens of Vatican City, and they alone, owe allegiance to the pope as a temporal head of state.

Cardinals of the Roman Curia residing outside Vatican City enjoy the privileges of extraterritoriality.

The normal population is approximately 1,000. While the greater percentage is made up of priests and religious, there are several hundred lay persons living in Vatican City. They are housed in their own apartments in the City and are engaged in secretarial, domestic, trade and service occupations. About 3,000 persons are employed by the Vatican.

Services of honor and order are performed by the Swiss Guards, who have been charged with responsibility for the personal safety of popes since 1506. Additional police and ceremonial functions are under the supervision of a special office. These functions were formerly handled by the Papal Gendarmes, the Palatine Guard of Honor, and the Guard of Honor of the Pope (Pontifical Noble Guard) which Pope Paul disbanded Sept. 14, 1970.

The **Basilica of St. Peter,** built between 1506 and 1626, is the largest church in Christendom and the site of most papal ceremonies. The pope's own patriarchal basilica, however, is **St. John Lateran,** whose origins date back to 324.

St. Ann's is the parish church of Vatican City.

The **Vatican Library,** one of five in the City, has among its holdings 70,000 manuscripts, 770,000 printed books, and 7,500 incunabula.

The independent temporal power of the pope, which is limited to the confines of Vatican City and small areas outside, was for many centuries more extensive than it is now. As late as the nineteenth century, the pope ruled 16,000 square miles of Papal States across the middle of Italy, with a population of over 3,000,000. In 1870 forces of the Kingdom of Italy occupied these lands which, with the exception of the small areas surrounding the Vatican and Lateran in Rome and the Villa of Castel Gandolfo, became part of the Kingdom by the Italian law of May 13, 1871.

The **Roman Question,** occasioned by this seizure and the voluntary confinement of the pope to the limited papal lands, was finally settled with ratification of the Lateran Agreement on June 7, 1929, by the Italian government and Vatican City and provided a financial indemnity for the former Papal States, which became recognized as part of Italy. The Lateran Agreement became Article 7 of the Italian Constitution on Mar. 26, 1947.

Papal Flag

The Papal flag consists of two equal vertical stripes of yellow and white, charged with the insignia of the papacy on the white stripe — a triple crown or tiara over two crossed keys, one of gold and one of silver, tied with a red cord and two tassels. The divisions of the crown represent the teaching, sanctifying and ruling offices of the pope. The keys symbolize his jurisdictional authority.

The papal flag is a national flag inasmuch as it is the standard of the Supreme Pontiff as the sovereign of the state of Vatican City. It is also universally accepted by the faithful as a symbol of the supreme spiritual authority of the Holy Father.

In a Catholic church, the papal flag is displayed on a staff on the left side of the sanctuary (facing the congregation), and the American flag is displayed on the right.

Vatican Radio

The declared purpose of Vatican Radio Station HVJ is "that the voice of the Supreme Pastor may be heard throughout the world by means of the ether waves, for the glory of Christ and the salvation of souls." Designed by Guglielmo Marconi, the inventor of radio, and supervised by him until his death, the station was inaugurated by Pope Pius XI in 1931.

Vatican Radio operates on international wave lengths, transmits programs in more than 32 languages, and serves as a channel of communication between the Vatican, church officials and listeners in general in many parts of the world. The station broadcasts about

470 programs a week throughout the world.

The staff of 200 broadcasters and technicians includes 25 Jesuits and is directed by Father Giacomo Martegani, S.J. Headquarters are located in Vatican City. The transmitters are situated at Santa Maria di Galeria, a 200-acre site 16 miles from Rome.

The range of Vatican Radio programming was partially indicated in the spring, 1972, schedule of times (Greenwich Mean Time) and frequencies (kHz) of broadcasts to Africa, Oceania and Asia.

East Africa: 1000, weekdays (17,840 and 21,485); 1620, daily (11,705, 15,210 and 17,800).

Central-South Africa: 1050, weekdays; 1710, daily (frequencies as above).

West Africa: 1150, weekdays (17,840 and 21,485); 1935, daily (11,740 and 15,260).

Australia and New Zealand: 1125, daily (17,800 and 21,485); 2210, daily (7,235, 9,615 and 11,705).

China, in Chinese: 2230, Tues., Thurs., Sat. (7,235, 9,615 and 11,705).

India, in Hindi, Tamil, Malayam: 1505, weekdays (11,810, 15,330 and 17,885).

India, in English: 1515, weekdays (11,810, 15,330 and 17,885).

Japan, in Japanese: 2150, Mon., Wed., Fri. (7,235, 9,615 and 11,705).

Middle East, in Arabic: 1650, daily (11,705, 15,210 and 17,800).

Philippines, in English: 2230, Mon., Wed., Fri. (7,235, 9,615 and 11,705).

1972 Stamps

The Vatican Philatelic Office had four issues of stamps scheduled for 1972. Two of the four series were released by early summer.

• Series dedicated to Donato Bramante, architect: Issued Feb. 22 in three values: 25 lira, Bramante's design for the cupolo of St. Peter's Basilica; 90 lira, portrait of Bramante; 130 lira, a section of spiral stairs of the Belvedere of Innocent VIII in the Vatican.

• Series dedicated to Venice: Issued June 6 in six values with three subjects: 25 lira, 12th-13th century mosaic (original in the Basilica of St. Mark in the city) of an episode in the life of St. Mark; 50 lira, in four stamps, each depicting a portion of the map of Venice (when joined, form the map of the city as it was in 1581); 180 lira, painting, by designer Emidio Vangelli, of the front view of the Basilica of St. Mark.

• Series commemorating the fifth centenary of the death of Cardinal Giovanni Bessarione.

• Series commemorating the centenaries of the birth of Maestro Lorenzo Perosi and Don Luigi Orione.

Papal Audiences

General audiences are scheduled weekly, on Wednesday at noon.

In Vatican City, they are held in the Audience Hall on the south side of St. Peter's Basilica. The hall, which was opened in 1971, has a seating capacity of 6,800 and a total capacity of 12,000.

From about the middle of July to the middle of September, they are held in a smaller hall at Castel Gandolfo, where the pope spends a working vacation.

General audiences last from about 60 to 90 minutes, during which the pope gives a talk and his blessing. A résumé of the talk, which is usually in Italian, is given in several languages.

Arrangements for papal audiences are handled by an office of the Prefecture of the Apostolic Household.

American visitors can obtain passes for general audiences by applying to the Bishops' Office for United States Visitors to the Vatican, on the Via dell'Umilita in downtown Rome. The director of the office is Father John J. Bagley of Worcester, Mass.

Private and group audiences are reserved for dignitaries of various categories and for special occasions.

Publications

Acta Apostolicae Sedis: The only "official commentary" of the Holy See, was established in 1908 for the publication of activities of the Holy See, laws, decrees and acts of congregations and tribunals of the Roman Curia. The first edition was published in January, 1909.

St. Pius X made *AAS* an official organ in 1908. Laws promulgated for the Church ordinarily take effect three months after the date of their publication in this commentary.

The publication, mostly in Latin and Italian, is printed by the Vatican Polyglot Press.

The immediate predecessor of this organ was *Acta Sanctae Sedis*, founded in 1865 and given official status by the Congregation for the Propagation of the Faith in 1904.

Annuario Pontificio: The yearbook of the Holy See. It is edited by the Vatican Secretariat of State and is printed in Italian, with some portions in other languages, by the Vatican Polyglot Press. It covers the worldwide organization of the Church, lists members of the hierarchy, and includes a wide range of statistical information.

The publication of a statistical yearbook of the Holy See dates back to 1716, when a volume called *Notizie* appeared. Publication under the present title began in 1860, was suspended in 1870, and resumed again in 1872 under the title *Catholic Hierarchy*. This volume was printed privately at first, but has been issued by the Vatican Press since 1885. The title *Annuario Pontificio* was restored in 1912, and the yearbook was called an "official publication" until 1924.

L'Osservatore Romano: The daily newspaper of the Holy See. It began publication July 1, 1861, as an independent enterprise under the ownership and direction of four Catholic laymen headed by Marcantonio Pacelli, vice minister of the interior under Pope Pius IX and a grandfather of the late Pius XII. Leo XIII bought the publication in 1890, making it the "pope's" own newspaper.

The only official material in *L'Osservatore Romano* is that which appears under the heading, "Nostre Informazioni." This includes notices of appointments by the Holy See, the texts of papal encyclicals and addresses by the Holy Father and others, various types of documents, accounts of decisions and rulings of administrative bodies, and similar items. Additional material includes news and comment on developments in the Church and the world. Italian is the language most used.

The bulk of the contents of each edition is determined by a "well defined policy in line with the teaching and the attitudes of the Church . . . which the editorial staff follows with full and direct responsibility," according to Federico Alessandrini, Vatican press officer.

The editorial board is directed by Raimondo Manzini. A staff of about 15 reporters covers Rome news sources. A corps of correspondents provides foreign coverage.

A weekly roundup edition in English was inaugurated in 1968. Other weekly editions are printed in French, Spanish, Portuguese and German.

Vatican Press Office: The establishment of a single Vatican Press Office was announced Feb. 29, 1968, to replace service agencies formerly operated by *L'Osservatore Romano* and an office created for press coverage of the Second Vatican Council. Prof. Federico Alessandrini is the director.

Vatican Polyglot Press: The official printing plant of the Vatican.

The Vatican press was conceived by Marcellus II and Pius IV but was actually founded by Sixtus V on Apr. 27, 1587, to print the Vulgate and the writings of the Fathers of the Church and other authors. A Polyglot Press was established in 1626 by the Congregation for the Propagation of the Faith to serve the needs of the Oriental Church. St. Pius X merged both presses under this title.

The plant has facilities for the printing of a wide variety of material in about 30 languages.

Activities of the Holy See: An annual documentary volume covering the activities of the pope — his daily work, general and special audiences, discourses and messages on special occasions, visits outside the Vatican, missionary and charitable endeavors, meetings with diplomats, heads of state and others — and activities of the congregations, commissions, tribunals and offices of the Roman Curia.

Collection of Statistical Tables: Issued for the first time in 1972 by the Vatican Central Office for Statistics of the Church, containing 1969 and earlier statistics, tables and notes reflecting and status and mission of the Church throughout the world.

VATICAN REPRESENTATIVES

(Sources: *Annuario Pontifico*, NC News Service.)

The Vatican has representatives to a number of governmental and non-governmental organizations.

• **Governmental Organizations:** United Nations (Msgr. Alberto Giovannetti, permanent observer); UN Office in Geneva (Msgr. Silvio Luoni, permanent observer); International Atomic Energy Agency (Dr. Hermann Abs, Msgr. Orlano Quilici, delegates); UN Organization for Industrial Development (Msgr. Orlano Quilici, delegate); UN Food and Agriculture Organization (Most Rev. Agostino Ferrari-Toniolo, permanent observer); UN Educational, Scientific and Cultural Organization (Msgr. Luigi Conti, permanent observer);

Council of Europe (Abp. Igino Cardinale, special minister with function of permanent observer); International Institute for the Unification of Private Law (Prof. Pio Cipriotto, delegate); International Committee of Medicine and Pharmacy (Msgr. Victor Heylen); International Union of Official Organizations of Tourism (Rev. Giovanni Arrighi, O.P.); International Geographic Union (Prof. Gastone Imbrighi);

Universal Postal Union; International Telecommunications Union; International Council on Grain; International Union for the Protection of Literary and Artistic Works; International Union for the Protection of Industrial Property.

• **Non-Governmental Organizations:** International Committee of Historical Sciences (Msgr. Michele Maccarrone); International Committee of Paleography (Msgr. Jose Ruysschaert); International Committee of the History of Art (Dr. Deocletio Redig de Campos); International Committee of Anthropological and Ethnological Sciences;

International Committee for the Neutrality of Medicine (Rev. Michel Riquet, S.J., permanent observer); International Center of Study for the Preservation and Restoration of Cultural Goods (Dr. Deocletio Redig de Campos); International Institute of Administrative Sciences; International Technical Committee for Prevention and Extinction of Fires; World Medical Association.

AMERICAN CHURCH

The Church of Santa Susanna was established as the national church for Americans in Rome Feb. 28, 1922, and entrusted to the Paulist Fathers who have served there continuously since then except for several years during World War II. The golden jubilee was observed May 21, 1972.

Doctrine of the Catholic Church

Following are excerpts from the first two chapters of the *Dogmatic Constitution on the Church* promulgated by the Second Vatican Council. They describe the relation of the Catholic Church to the Kingdom of God, the nature and foundation of the Church, the People of God, the necessity of membership and participation in the Church for salvation.

Additional subjects in the constitution are treated in other Almanac entries.

I. MYSTERY OF THE CHURCH

". . . By her relationship with Christ, the Church is a kind of sacrament or sign of intimate union with God, and of the unity of all mankind . . ." (No. 1).

". . . He (the eternal Father) planned to assemble in the holy Church all those who would believe in Christ. Already from the beginning of the world the foreshadowing of the Church took place. She was prepared for in a remarkable way throughout the history of the people of Israel and by means of the Old Covenant. Established in the present era of time, the Church was made manifest by the outpouring of the Spirit. At the end of time she will achieve her glorious fulfillment. Then . . . all just men from the time of Adam, 'from Abel, the just one, to the last of the elect,' will be gathered together with the Father in the universal Church" (No. 2).

"When the work which the Father had given the Son to do on earth (cf. Jn. 17:4) was accomplished, the Holy Spirit was sent on the day of Pentecost in order that He might forever sanctify the Church, and thus all believers would have access to the Father through Christ in the one Spirit (cf. Eph. 2:18). . . .

"The Spirit dwells in the Church and in the hearts of the faithful as in a temple (cf. 1 Cor. 3:16; 6:19). . . . The Spirit guides the Church into the fullness of truth (cf. Jn. 16:13) and gives her a unity of fellowship and service. He furnishes and directs her with various gifts, both hierarchical and charismatic, and adorns her with the fruits of His grace (cf. Eph. 4:11-12; 1 Cor. 12:4; Gal. 5:22). By the power of the gospel He makes the Church grow, perpetually renews her, and leads her to perfect union with her Spouse. . . ." (No. 4).

Foundation of the Church

"The mystery of the holy Church is manifest in her very foundation, for the Lord Jesus inaugurated her by preaching the good news, that is, the coming of God's Kingdom, which, for centuries, had been promised in the Scriptures. . . . In Christ's word, in His works, and in His presence this kingdom reveals itself to men. . . .

"The miracles of Jesus also confirm that the kingdom has already arrived on earth. . . .

"Before all things, however, the kingdom is clearly visible in the very person of Christ, Son of God and Son of Man. . . .

"When Jesus rose up again after suffering death on the cross for mankind, He manifested that He had been appointed Lord, Messiah, and Priest forever (cf. Acts 2:36; Hb. 5:6; 7:17-21), and He poured out on His disciples the Spirit promised by the Father (cf. Acts 2:33). The Church, consequently, equipped with the gifts of her Founder and faithfully guarding His precepts . . . receives the mission to proclaim and to establish among all peoples the kingdom of Christ and of God. She becomes on earth the initial budding forth of that kingdom. While she slowly grows, the Church strains toward the consummation of the kingdom and, with all her strength, hopes and desires to be united in glory with her King" (No. 5).

Figures of the Church

"In the Old Testament the revelation of the kingdom had often been conveyed by figures of speech. In the same way the inner nature of the Church was now to be made known to us through various images. . . .

". . . The Church is a sheepfold . . . a flock . . . a tract of land to be cultivated, the field of God . . . His choice vineyard . . . the true Vine is Christ . . . the edifice of God . . . the house of God . . . the holy temple (whose members are) . . . living stones . . . this Holy City . . . a bride . . . 'our Mother' . . . the spotless spouse of the spotless lamb . . . and exile . . ." (No. 6).

"In the human nature which He united to Himself, the Son of God redeemed man and transformed him into a new creation (cf. Gal. 6:15; 2 Cor. 5:17) by overcoming death through His own death and resurrection. By communicating His Spirit to His brothers, called together from all peoples, Christ made them mystically into His own body.

"In that body, the life of Christ is poured into the believers, who, through the sacraments, are united in a hidden and real way to Christ who suffered and was glorified. Through baptism we are formed in the likeness of Christ. . . .

"Truly partaking of the body of the Lord in the breaking of the Eucharistic bread, we are taken up into communion with Him and with one another . . ." (No. 7).

One Body in Christ

"As all the members of the human body, though they are many, form one body, so also are the faithful in Christ (cf. 1 Cor. 12:12). Also, in the building up of Christ's body there is a flourishing variety of members and functions. There is only one Spirit who . . . distributes His different gifts for the welfare of the Church (cf. 1 Cor. 12:1-11). Among these gifts stands out the grace given to the Apostles. To their authority, the Spirit Himself subjected even those who were endowed with charisms (cf. 1 Cor. 14). . . .

"The head of this body is Christ . . ." (No. 7).

Mystical Body of Christ

"Christ, the one Mediator, established and ceaselessly sustains here on earth His holy Church, the community of faith, hope, and charity, as a visible structure. Through her He communicates truth and grace to all. But the society furnished with hierarchical agencies and the Mystical Body of Christ are not to be considered as two realities, nor are the visible assembly and the spiritual community, nor the earthly Church and the Church enriched with heavenly things. Rather they form one interlocked reality which is comprised of a divine and a human element. For this reason . . . this reality is compared to the mystery of the incarnate Word. Just as the assumed nature inseparably united to the divine Word serves Him as a living instrument of salvation, so, in a similar way, does the communal structure of the Church serve Christ's Spirit, who vivifies it by way of building up the body (cf. Eph. 4:16).

"This is the unique Church of Christ which in the Creed we avow as one, holy, catholic, and apostolic. After His Resurrection our Savior handed her over to Peter to be shepherded (Jn. 21:17), commissioning him and the other apostles to propagate and govern her (cf. Mt. 28:18, ff.). Her He erected for all ages as 'the pillar and mainstay of the truth' (1 Tm. 3:15). This Church, constituted and organized in the world as a society, subsists in the Catholic Church, which is governed by the successor of Peter and by the bishops in union with that successor, although many elements of sanctification and of truth can be found outside of her visible structure. These elements, however, as gifts properly belonging to the Church of Christ, possess an inner dynamism toward Catholic unity.

". . . the Church, embracing sinners in her bosom, is at the same time holy and always in need of being purified, and incessantly pursues the path of penance and renewal.

"The Church, 'like a pilgrim in a foreign land, presses forward . . .' announcing the cross and death of the Lord until He comes (cf. 1 Cor. 11:26) . . ." (No. 8).

II. THE PEOPLE OF GOD

"At all times and among every people, God has given welcome to whosoever fears Him and does what is right (cf. Acts 10:35). It has pleased God, however, to make men holy and save them not merely as individuals without any mutual bonds, but by making them into a single people, a people which acknowledges Him in truth and serves Him in holiness. He therefore chose the race of Israel as a people unto Himself. With it He set up a covenant. Step by step He taught this people by manifesting in its history both Himself and the decree of His will, and by making it holy unto Himself. All these things, however, were done by way of preparation and as a figure of that new and perfect covenant which was to be ratified in Christ. . . .

". . . Christ instituted this newcovenant, that is to say, the new testament, in His blood (cf. 1 Cor. 11:25), by calling together a people made up of Jew and Gentile, making them one, not according to the flesh but in the Spirit.

"This was to be the new People of God . . . reborn . . . through the Word of the living God (cf. 1 Pt. 1:23) . . . from water and the Holy Spirit (cf. Jn. 3:5-6) . . . 'a chosen race, a royal priesthood, a holy nation, a purchased people. . . . You who in times past were not a people, but are now the people of God' (1 Pt. 2:9-10).

"That messianic people has for its head Christ. . . . Its law is the new commandment to love as Christ loved us (cf. Jn. 13:34). Its goal is the kingdom of God, which has been begun by God Himself on earth, and which is to be further extended until it is brought to perfection by Him at the end of time. . . .

". . . This messianic people, although it does not actually include all men, and may more than once look like a small flock, is nonetheless a lasting and sure seed of unity, hope, and salvation for the whole human race. Established by Christ as a fellowship of life, charity, and truth, it is also used by Him as an instrument for the redemption of all, and is sent forth into the whole world as the light of the world and the salt of the earth (cf. Mt. 5:13-16).

"Israel according to the flesh . . . was already called the Church of God (2 Ezr. 13:1; cf. Nm. 20:4; Dt. 23:1, ff.). Likewise the new Israel . . . is also called the Church of Christ (cf. Mt. 16:18). For He has bought it for Himself with His blood (cf. Acts 20:28), has filled it with His Spirit, and provided it with those means which befit it as a visible and social unity. God has gathered together as one all those who in faith look upon Jesus as the author of salvation and the source of unity and peace, and has established them as the Church, that for each and all she may be the visible sacrament of this saving unity . . ." (No. 9)

Priesthood

". . . The baptized, by regeneration and the anointing of the Holy Spirit, are consecrated into . . . a holy priesthood . . .

(All members of the Church participate in the priesthood of Christ, through the common priesthood of the faithful. See Priesthood of the Laity.)

"Though they differ from one another in essence and not only in degree, the common priesthood of the faithful and the ministerial or hierarchical priesthood are nonetheless interrelated. Each of them in its own special way is a participation in the one priesthood of Christ . . ." (No. 10).

"It is through the sacraments and the exercise of the virtues that the sacred nature and organic structure of the priestly community is brought into operation . . ." (No. 11). (See Role of the Sacraments.)

Prophetic Office

"The holy People of God shares also in Christ's prophetic office. It spreads abroad a living witness to Him, especially by means of a life of faith and charity and by offering to God a sacrifice of praise. . . . The body of the faithful as a whole, anointed as they are by the Holy One (cf. Jn. 2:20;27), cannot err in matters of belief. Thanks to a supernatural sense of faith which characterizes the People as a whole, it manifests this unerring quality when, 'from the bishops down to the last member of the laity,' it shows universal agreement in matters of faith and morals.

". . . God's People accepts not the word of men but the very Word of God (cf. 1 Thes. 2:13). It clings without fail to the faith once delivered to the saints (cf. Jude 3), penetrates it more deeply by accurate insights, and applies it more thoroughly to life. All this it does under the lead of a sacred teaching authority to which it loyally defers.

"It is not only through the sacraments and Church ministries that the same Holy Spirit sanctifies and leads the People of God. . . . He distributes special graces among the faithful of every rank. By these gifts He makes them fit and ready to undertake the various tasks or offices advantageous for the renewal and upbuilding of the Church. . . . These charismatic gifts . . . are to be received with thanksgiving and consolation, for they are exceedingly suitable and useful for the needs of the Church.

". . . Judgment as to their genuineness and proper use belongs to those who preside over the Church, and to whose special competence it belongs . . . to test all things and hold fast to that which is good (cf. 1 Thes. 5:12; 19-21)" (No. 12).

All Are Called

"All men are called to belong to the new People of God. Wherefore this People, while remaining one and unique, is to be spread throughout the whole world and must exist in all ages, so that the purpose of God's will may be fulfilled. In the beginning God made human nature one. After His children were scattered, He decreed that they should at length be united again (cf. Jn. 11:52). It was for this reason that God sent His Son . . . that He might be Teacher, King, and Priest of all, the Head of the new and universal people of the sons of God. For this God finally sent His Son's Spirit as Lord and Lifegiver. He it is who, on behalf of the whole Church and each and every one of those who believe, is the principle of their coming together and remaining together in the teaching of the apostles and in fellowship, in the breaking of bread and in prayers (cf. Acts 2:42)" (No. 13).

One People of God

"It follows that among all the nations of earth there is but one People of God, which takes its citizens from every race, making them citizens of a kingdom which is of a heavenly and not an earthly nature. For all the faithful scattered throughout the world are in communion with each other in the Holy Spirit. . . . the Church or People of God . . . foster(s) and take(s) to herself, insofar as they are good, the ability, resources and customs of each people. Taking them to herself she purifies, strengthens, and ennobles them. . . . characteristic of universality which adorns the People of God is a gift from the Lord Himself. By reason of it, the Catholic Church strives energetically and constantly to bring all humanity with all its riches back to Christ its Head in the unity of His Spirit.

"In virtue of this catholicity each individual part of the Church contributes through its special gifts to the good of the other parts and of the whole Church. Thus through the common sharing of gifts . . . the whole and each of the parts receive increase. . . .

"All men are called to be part of this catholic unity of the People of God. . . . And there belong to it or are related to it in various ways, the Catholic faithful as well as all who believe in Christ, and indeed the whole of mankind. For all men are called to salvation by the grace of God" (No. 13).

The Catholic Church

"This sacred Synod turns its attention first to the Catholic faithful. Basing itself upon sacred Scripture and tradition, it teaches that the Church . . . is necessary for salvation. For Christ, made present to us in His Body, which is the Church, is the one Mediator and the unique Way of salvation. In explicit terms He Himself affirmed the necessity of faith and baptism (cf. Mk. 16:16; Jn. 3:5) and thereby affirmed also the necessity of the Church, for through baptism as through a door men enter the Church. Whosoever, therefore, knowing that the Catholic Church was made necessary by God through Jesus Christ, would refuse to enter her or to remain in her could not be saved.

"They are fully incorporated into the society of the Church who, possessing the Spirit of Christ, accept her entire system and all the means of salvation given to her, and through union with her visible structure are joined to Christ, who rules her through the Supreme Pontiff and the bishops. This joining is effected by the bonds of professed faith, of the sacraments, of ecclesiastical government, and of communion. He is not saved, however, who, though he is part of the body of the Church, does not persevere in charity. He remains indeed in the bosom of the Church, but . . . only in a 'bodily' manner and not 'in his heart.' . . .

"Catechumens who, moved by the Holy Spirit, seek with explicit intention to be incorporated into the Church are by that very intention joined to her. . . . Mother Church already embraces them as her own" (No. 14).

Other Christians, The Unbaptized

"The Church recognizes that in many ways she is linked with those who, being baptized, are honored with the name of Christian, though they do not profess the faith in its entirety or do not preserve unity of communion with the successor of Peter. . . .

" . . . We can say that in some real way they are joined with us in the Holy Spirit, for to them also He gives His gifts and graces, and is thereby operative among them with His sanctifying power . . ." (No. 15).

"Finally, those who have not yet received the gospel are related in various ways to the People of God. In the first place there is the people to whom the covenants and the promises were given and from whom Christ was born according to the flesh (cf. Rom. 9:4-5). On account of their fathers, this people remains most dear to God, for God does not repent of the gifts He makes nor of the calls He issues (cf. Rom. 11:28-29).

"But the plan of salvation also includes those who acknowledge the Creator. In the first place among these are the Moslems. . . . Nor is God Himself far distant from those who in shadows and images seek the unknown God. . . .

"Those also can attain to everlasting salvation who through no fault of their own do not know the gospel of Christ or His Church, yet sincerely seek God and, moved by grace, strive by their deeds to do His will as it is known to them through the dictates of conscience. Nor does divine Providence deny the help necessary for salvation to those who, without blame on their part, have not yet arrived at an explicit knowledge of God, but who strive to live a good life, thanks to His grace. Whatever goodness or truth is found among them is looked upon by the Church as a preparation for the Gospel. She regards such qualities as given by Him who enlightens all men so that they may finally have life . . ." (No. 16).

THE POPE, TEACHING AUTHORITY, COLLEGIALITY

The Roman Pontiff — the successor of St. Peter as the Vicar of Christ and head of the Church on earth — has full and supreme authority over the universal Church in matters pertaining to faith and morals (teaching authority), discipline and government (jurisdictional authority).

The primacy of the pope is real and supreme power. It is not merely a prerogative of honor — that is, of his being regarded as the first among equals. Neither does primacy imply that the pope is just the presiding officer of the collective body of bishops. The pope is the head of the Church.

Catholic belief in the primacy of the pope was stated in detail in the dogmatic constitution on the Church, *Pastor Aeternus,* approved in 1870 by the fourth session of the First Vatican Council. Some elaboration of the doctrine was made in the *Dogmatic Constitution on the Church* which was approved and promulgated by the Second Vatican Council Nov. 21, 1964. The entire body of teaching on the subject is based on Scripture and tradition and the centuries-long experience of the Church.

Infallibility

The essential points of doctrine concerning infallibility in the Church and the infallibility of the pope were stated by the Second Vatican Council in the *Dogmatic Constitution on the Church,* as follows:

"This infallibility with which the divine Redeemer willed his Church to be endowed in defining a doctrine of faith and morals extends as far as extends the deposit of divine revelation, which must be religiously guarded and faithfully expounded. This is the infallibility which the Roman Pontiff, the head of the college of bishops, enjoys in virtue of his office, when, as the supreme shepherd and teacher of all the faithful, who confirms his brethren in their faith (cf. Lk. 22:32), he proclaims by a definitive act some doctrine of faith or morals. Therefore his definitions, of themselves, and not from the consent of the Church, are justly styled irreformable, for they are pronounced with the assistance of the Holy Spirit, an assistance promised to him in blessed Peter. Therefore they need no approval of others, nor do they allow an appeal to any other judgment. For then the Roman Pontiff is not pronouncing judgment as a private person. Rather, as the supreme teacher of the universal Church, as one in whom the charism of the infallibility of the Church herself is individually present, he is expounding or defending a doctrine of Catholic faith.

"The infallibility promised to the Church resides also in the body of bishops when that body exercises supreme teaching authority with the successor of Peter. To the resultant definitions the assent of the Church can never be wanting, on account of the activity of that same Holy Spirit, whereby the whole flock of Christ is preserved and progresses in unity of faith.

"But when either the Roman Pontiff or the body of bishops together with him defines a judgment, they pronounce it in accord with revelation itself. All are obliged to maintain and be ruled by this revelation, which, as written or preserved by tradition, is transmitted in its entirety through the legitimate succession of bishops and especially through the care of the Roman Pontiff himself.

"Under the guiding light of the Spirit of truth, revelation is thus religiously preserved and faithfully expounded in the Church. The Roman Pontiff and the bishops, in view of their office and of the importance of the matter, strive painstakingly and by appropriate means to inquire properly into that revelation and to give apt expression to its contents. But they do not allow that there could be any new public revelation pertaining to the divine deposit of faith" (No. 25).

Authentic Teaching

The pope rarely speaks *ex cathedra* — that is, "from the chair" of St. Peter, for the purpose of making an infallible pronouncement. More often and in various ways he states authentic teaching in line with Scripture, tradition, the living experience of the Church, and the whole analogy of faith. Of such teaching, the Second Vatican Council said in its *Dogmatic Constitution on the Church* (No. 25):

". . . Religious submission of will and of mind must be shown in a special way to the authentic teaching authority of the Roman Pontiff, even when he is not speaking *ex cathedra*. That is, it must be shown in such a way that his supreme magisterium is acknowledged with reverence, the judgments made by him are sincerely adhered to, according to his manifest mind and will. His mind and will in the matter may be known chiefly either from the character of the documents, from his frequent repetition of the same doctrine, or from his manner of speaking."

With respect to bishops, the constitution said: "They are authentic teachers, that is, teachers endowed with the authority of Christ, who preach to the people committed to them the faith they must believe and put into practice. By the light of the Holy Spirit, they make that faith clear, bringing forth from the treasury of revelation new things and old (cf. Mt. 13:52), making faith bear fruit and vigilantly warding off any errors which threaten their flock (cf. Tm. 4:1-4).

"Bishops, teaching in communion with the Roman Pontiff, are to be respected by all as witnesses to divine and Catholic truth. In matters of faith and morals, the bishops speak in the name of Christ and the faithful are to accept their teaching and adhere to it with a religious assent of soul."

Magisterium—Teaching Authority

Responsibility for teaching doctrine and judging orthodoxy belongs to the official teaching authority of the Church

This authority is personalized in the pope, the successor of St. Peter as head of the Church, and in the bishops together and in union with the pope, as it was originally committed to Peter and to the whole college of Apostles under his leadership. They are the official teachers of the Church.

Others have auxiliary relationships with the magisterium: theologians, in the study and clarification of doctrine; teachers — priests, religious, lay persons — who cooperate with the pope and bishops in spreading knowledge of religious truth; the faithful, who by their sense of faith and personal witness contribute to the development of doctrine and the establishment of its relevance to life in the Church and the world.

The magisterium, Pope Paul noted in an address at a general audience Jan. 11, 1967, "is a subordinate and faithful echo and secure interpreter of the divine word." It does not reveal new truths, "nor is it superior to Sacred Scripture." Its competence extends to the limits of divine revelation manifested in Scripture and tradition and the living experience of the Church, with respect to matters of faith and morals and related subjects.

Official teaching in these areas is infallible when it is formally defined, for belief and acceptance by all members of the Church, by the pope, acting in the capacity of supreme shepherd of the flock of Christ; and when doctrine is proposed and taught with moral unanimity of bishops with the pope in a solemn collegial manner as in an ecumenical council, and/or in the ordinary course of events. Even when not infallibly defined, official teaching in the areas of faith and morals is authoritative and requires religious assent.

The teachings of the magisterium have been documented in creeds, formulas of faith, decrees and enactments of ecumenical and particular councils, various kinds of doctrinal statements, and other teaching instruments. They have also been incorporated into the liturgy, with the result that the law of prayer is said to be a law of belief.

Collegiality

The bishops of the Church, in union with the pope, have supreme teaching and pastoral authority over the whole Church in addition to the authority of office they have for their own dioceses.

This collegial authority is exercised in a solemn manner in an ecumenical council and can be exercised in other ways as well, "provided that the head of the college calls them to collegiate action, or at least so approves or freely accepts the united action of the dispersed bishops, that it is made a true collegiate act."

This doctrine is grounded on the fact that: "Just as, by the Lord's will, St. Peter and the other apostles constituted one apostolic college, so in a similar way the Roman Pontiff as the successor of Peter, and the bishops as the successors of the apostles are joined together."

Doctrine on collegiality was stated by the Second Vatican Council in the *Dogmatic Constitution on the Church* (Nos. 22 and 23).

REVELATION

Following are excerpts from the *Constitution on Revelation* promulgated by the Second Vatican Council. They describe the nature and process of divine revelation, inspiration and interpretation of Scripture, the Old and New Testaments, and the role of Scripture in the life of the Church.

I. Revelation Itself

". . . God chose to reveal Himself and to make known to us the hidden purpose of His will (cf. Eph. 1:9) by which through Christ, the Word made flesh, man has access to the Father in the Holy Spirit and comes to share in the divine nature (cf. Eph. 2:18; 2Pt. 1:4). Through this revelation, therefore, the invisible God (cf. Col. 1:15; 1 Tm. 1:17) . . . speaks to men as friends (cf. Ex. 33:11; Jn. 15:14-15) and lives among them (cf. Bar. 3:38) so that He may invite and take them into fellowship with Himself. This plan of revelation is realized by deeds and words having an inner unity: the deeds wrought by God in the history of salvation manifest and confirm the teaching and realities signified by the words, while the words proclaim the deeds and clarify the mystery contained in them. By this revelation then, the deepest truth about God and the salvation of man is made clear to us in Christ, who is the Mediator and at the same time the fullness of all revelation" (No. 2).

"God . . . from the start manifested Himself to our first parents. Then after their fall His promise of redemption aroused in them the hope of being saved (cf. Gn. 3:15), and from that time on He ceaselessly kept the human race in His care, in order to give eternal life to those who perseveringly do good in search of salvation (cf. Rom. 2:6-7). . . . He called Abraham in order to make of him a great nation (cf. Gn. 12:2). Through the patriarchs, and after them through Moses and the prophets, He taught this nation to acknowledge Himself as the one living and true God . . . and and to wait for the Savior promised by Him. In this manner He prepared the way for the gospel down through the centuries" (No. 3).

Revelation in Christ

"Then, after speaking in many places and varied ways through the prophets, God 'last of all in these days has spoken to us by His Son' (Hb. 1:1-2). . . . Jesus perfected revelation by fulfilling it through His whole work of making Himself present and manifesting Himself: through His words and deeds, His signs and wonders, but especially through His death and glorious resurrection from the dead and final sending of the Spirit of truth. Moreover, He confirmed with divine testimony what revelation proclaimed: that God is with us to free us from the darkness of sin and death, and to raise us up to life eternal.

"The Christian dispensation, therefore, as the new and definitive covenant, will never pass away, and we now await no further new public revelation before the glorious manifestation of our Lord Jesus Christ (cf. 1 Tm. 6:14; Ti. 2:13)" (No. 4).

II. Transmission of Revelation

". . . God has seen to it that what He had revealed for the salvation of all nations would abide perpetually in its full integrity and be handed on to all generations. Therefore Christ the Lord, in whom the full revelation of the supreme God is brought to completion (cf. 2 Cor. 1:20; 3:16; 4:6), commissioned the apostles to preach to all men that gospel which is the source of all saving truth and moral teaching, and thus to impart to them divine gifts. This gospel had been promised in former times through the prophets, and Christ Himself fulfilled it and promulgated it with His own lips. This commission was faithfully fulfilled by the apostles who, by their oral preaching, by example, and by ordinances, handed on what they had received from . . . Christ . . . or what they had learned through the prompting of the Holy Spirit. The commission was fulfilled, too, by those apostles and apostolic men who under the inspiration of the same Holy Spirit committed the message of salvation to writing" (No. 7).

Tradition

"But in order to keep the gospel forever whole and alive within the Church, the apostles left bishops as their successors, 'handing over their own teaching role' to them. This sacred tradition, therefore, and sacred Scripture of both the Old and the New Testament are like a mirror in which the pilgrim Church on earth looks at God . . ." (No. 7).

". . . The apostolic preaching, which is expressed in a special way in the inspired books, was to be preserved by a continuous succession of preachers until the end of time. Therefore the apostles, handing on what they themselves had received, warn the faithful to hold fast to the traditions which they have learned. . . . Now what was handed on by the apostles includes everything which contributes to the holiness of life, and the increase in faith of the People of God; and so the Church, in her teaching, life, and worship, perpetuates and hands on to all generations all that she herself is, all that she believes" (No. 8).

Development of Doctrine

"This tradition which comes from the apostles develops in the Church with the help of the Holy Spirit. For there is a growth in the understanding of the realities and the words which have been handed down. This happens through the contemplation and study made by believers . . . through the intimate understanding of spiritual things they experience, and through the preaching of those who have received through episcopal succession the sure gift of truth. For, as the centuries succeed one another, the Church constantly moves forward toward the fullness of divine truth until the words of God reach their complete fulfillment in her.

"The words of the holy Fathers witness to the living presence of this tradition, whose wealth is poured into the practice and life of the believing and praying Church. Through the same tradition the Church's full canon of the sacred books is known, and the sacred writings themselves are more profoundly understood and unceasingly made active in her; . . . and the Holy Spirit, through whom the living voice of the gospel resounds in the Church, and through her, in the world, leads unto all truth those who believe and makes the word of Christ dwell abundantly in them (cf. Col. 3:16)" (No. 8).

Tradition and Scripture

"Hence there exist a close connection and communication between sacred tradition and sacred Scripture. For both of them, flowing from the same divine wellspring, in a certain way merge into a unity and tend toward the same end. For sacred Scripture is the word of God inasmuch as it is consigned to writing under the inspiration of the divine Spirit. To the successors of the apostles, sacred tradition hands on in its full purity God's word, which was entrusted to the apostles by Christ the Lord and the Holy Spirit. Thus, led by the light of the Spirit of truth, these successors can in their preaching preserve this word of God faithfully, explain it, and make it more widely known. Consequently, it is not from sacred Scripture alone that the Church draws her certainty about everything which has been revealed. Therefore both sacred tradition and sacred Scripture are to be accepted and venerated with the same sense of devotion and reverence" (No. 9).

"Sacred tradition and sacred Scripture form one sacred deposit of the word of God, which is committed to the Church" (No. 10).

Teaching Authority of Church

"The task of authentically interpreting the word of God, whether written or handed on, has been entrusted exclusively to the living teaching office of the Church, whose authority is exercised in the name of Jesus Christ. This teaching office is not above the word of God, but serves it, teaching only what has been handed on . . . it draws from this one deposit of faith everything which it presents for belief as divinely revealed.

"It is clear, therefore, that sacred tradition, sacred Scripture, and the teaching authority of the Church . . . are so linked and joined together that one cannot stand without the others, and that all together and each in its own way under the action of the one Holy Spirit contribute effectively to the salvation of souls" (No. 10).

III. Inspiration, Interpretation

"Those . . . revealed realities . . . contained and presented in sacred Scripture have been committed to writing under the inspiration of the Holy Spirit. Holy Mother Church, relying on the belief of the apostles, holds that the books of both the Old and New Testament in their entirety, with all their parts, are sacred and canonical because, having been written under the inspiration of the Holy Spirit (cf. Jn. 20:31; 2 Tm. 3:16; 2 Pt. 1:19-21; 3:15-16) they have God as their author and have been handed on as such to the Church herself. In composing the sacred books, God chose men and while employed by Him they made use of their powers and abilities, so that with Him acting in them and through them, they, as true authors, consigned to writing everything and only those things which He wanted." (No. 11).

Inerrancy

"Therefore, since everything asserted by the inspired authors or sacred writers must be held to be asserted by the Holy Spirit, it follows that the books of Scripture must be acknowledged as teaching firmly, faithfully, and without error that truth which God wanted put into the sacred writings for the sake of our salvation. Therefore 'all Scripture is inspired by God and useful for teaching, for reproving, for correcting, for instruction in justice; that the man of God may be perfect, equipped for every good work' (2 Tm. 3:16-17)" (No. 11).

Literary Forms

"However, since God speaks in sacred Scripture through men in human fashion, the interpreter of sacred Scripture, in order to see clearly what God wanted to communicate to us, should carefully investigate what meaning the sacred writers really intended, and what God wanted to mainfest by means of their words.

". . . The interpreter must investigate what meaning the sacred writer intended to express and actually expressed in particular circumstances as he used contemporary literary forms in accordance with the situation of his own time and culture. For the correct understanding of what the sacred author wanted to assert, due attention must be paid to the customary and characteristic styles of perceiving, speaking, and narrating which prevailed at the time of the sacred writer, and to the customs men normally followed at that period in their everyday dealings with one another" (No. 12).

Analogy of Faith

". . . No less serious attention must be given to the content and unity of the whole of Scripture, if the meaning of the sacred texts is to be correctly brought to light. The living tradition of the whole Church must be taken into account along with the harmony which exists between elements of the faith. . . . all of what has been said about the way of interpreting Scripture is subject finally to the judgment of the Church, which carries out the divine commission and ministry of guarding and interpreting the word of God" (No. 12).

IV. The Old Testament

"In carefully planning and preparing the salvation of the whole human race, the God of supreme love, by a special dispensation, chose for Himself a people to whom He might entrust His promises. First He entered into a covenar: with Abraham (cf. Gn. 15:18) and, through Moses, with the people of Israel (cf. Ex. 24:8). To this people which He had acquired for Himself, He so manifested Himself through words and deeds as the one true and living God that Israel came to know by experience the ways of God with men. . . . The plan of salvation, foretold by the sacred authors, recounted and explained by them, is found as the true word of God in the books of the Old Testament: these books, therefore, written under divine inspiration, remain permanently valuable . . ." (No. 14).

Principal Purpose

"The principal purpose to which the plan of the Old Covenant was directed was to prepare for the coming both of Christ, the universal Redeemer, and of the messianic kingdom. . . . Now the books of the Old Testament, in accordance with the state of mankind before the time of salvation established by Christ, reveal to all men the knowledge of God and of man and the ways in which God . . . deals with men. These books . . . show us true divine pedagogy . . ." (No. 15).

". . . The books of the Old Testament with all their parts, caught up into the proclamation of the gospel, acquire and show forth their full meaning in the New Testament (cf. Mt. 5:17; Lk. 24:27; Rom. 16:25-26; 2 Cor. 3:14-16) and in turn shed light on it and explain it" (No. 16).

V. The New Testament

"The word of God . . . is set forth and shows its power in a most excellent way in the writings of the New Testament. For when the fullness of time arrived (cf. Gal. 4:4), the Word was made flesh and dwelt among us in the fullness of grace and truth (cf. Jn. 1:14). Christ established the Kingdom of God on earth, manifested His Father and Himself by deeds and words, and completed His work by His death, resurrection, and glorious ascension and by the sending of the Holy Spirit. Having been lifted up from the earth, He draws all men to Himself (cf. Jn. 12:32). . . . This mystery had not been manifested to other generations as it was now revealed to His holy apostles and prophets in the Holy Spirit (cf. Eph. 3:4-6), so that they might preach the Gospel, stir up faith in Jesus, Christ and Lord, and gather the Church together. To these realities, the writings of the New Testament stand as a perpetual and divine witness" (No. 17).

The Gospels and Other Writings

". . . The Gospels have a special preeminence . . . for they are the principal witness of the life and teaching of the incarnate Word, our Savior.

"The Church has always and everywhere held and continues to hold that the four Gospels are of apostolic origin. For what the apostles preached . . . afterwards they themselves and apostolic men, under the inspiration of the divine Spirit, handed on to us in writing: the foundation of faith, namely, the fourfold Gospel, according to Matthew, Mark, Luke, and John" (No. 18).

". . . The four Gospels, . . . whose historical character the Church unhesitatingly asserts, faithfully hand on what Jesus Christ, while living among men, really did and taught for their eternal salvation until the day He was taken up into heaven (see Acts 1:1-2). Indeed, after the ascension of the Lord the apostles handed on to their hearers what He had said and done. . . . The sacred authors wrote the four Gospels, selecting some things from the many which had been handed on by word of mouth or in writing, reducing some of them to a synthesis, explicating some things in view of the situation of their churches, and preserving the form of proclamation but always in such fashion that they told us the honest truth about Jesus. For their intention in writing was that . . . we might know 'the truth' concerning those matters about which we have been instructed (cf. Lk. 1:2-4)" (No. 19).

"Besides the four Gospels, the canon of the New Testament also contains the Epistles of St. Paul and other apostolic writings, composed under the inspiration of the Holy Spirit. In these writings . . . those matters which concern Christ the Lord are confirmed, His true teaching is more and more fully stated, the saving power of the divine work of Christ is preached, the story is told of the beginnings of the Church and her marvelous growth, and her glorious fulfillment is foretold" (No. 20).

VI. Scripture in Church Life

"The Church has always venerated the divine Scriptures just as she venerates the body of the Lord. . . . She has always regarded the Scriptures together with sacred tradition as the supreme rule of faith, and will ever do so. For, inspired by God and committed once and for all to writing, they impart the word of God Himself without change, and make the voice of the Holy Spirit resound in the words of the prophets and apostles. Therefore, like the Christian religion itself, all the preaching of the Church must be nourished and ruled by sacred Scripture . . ." (No. 21).

"Easy access to sacred Scripture should be provided for all the Christian faithful. That is why the Church from the very beginning accepted as her own that very ancient Greek translation of the Old Testament which is named after seventy men (the Septuagint); and she has always given a place of honor to other translations, Eastern and Latin, especially the one known as the Vulgate. But since the word of God should be available at all times, the Church with maternal concern sees to it that suitable and correct translations are made into different languages, especially from the original texts of the sacred books. And if, given the opportunity and the approval of Church authority, these translations are produced in cooperation with the separated brethren as well, all Christians will be able to use them" (No. 22).

Biblical Studies, Theology

The constitution encouraged the development and progress of biblical studies "under the watchful care of the sacred teaching office of the Church." (Such studies have made great progress in recent years.)

It noted also: "Sacred theology rests on the written word of God, together with sacred tradition, as its primary and perpetual foundation," and that "the study of the sacred page is, as it were, the soul of sacred theology" (Nos. 23, 24).

PONTIFICAL BIBLICAL COMMISSION

The Pontifical Biblical Commission, which has been instrumental in directing the course of Catholic biblical scholarship, was established by Leo XIII Oct. 30, 1902, with the apostolic letter, *Vigilantiae,* at a time when biblical studies were open to great promise as well as to the threat of Modernism.

The commission was ordered to promote biblical studies; to safeguard the correct interpretation of Scripture, in the pattern of the rule of faith and against the background of sound scholarship; to state positions which had to be held by Catholics on biblical questions; to indicate questions requiring further study and/or those which were open to the judgment of competent scholars. The commission was also authorized to set up standards for biblical studies and to grant degrees in Sacred Scripture.

The commission issued 23 decrees or decisions between 1905 and 1953; letters on the scientific study of the Bible (1941) and the Pentateuch (1948); instructions on teaching Scripture in seminaries (1950), biblical associations (1955), and the historical truth of the Gospels (1964).

Pope St. Pius X stated the authority of decisions of the commission in the letter *Illibatae,* which he issued June 29, 1910, on his own initiative:

"All are bound in conscience to submit to the decisions of the Pontifical Biblical Commission pertaining to doctrine, whether already issued or to be issued in the future, in the same way as to the decrees of the Sacred Congregations (of the Roman Curia) ap-proved by the Pontiff; nor can they avoid the stigma both of disobedience and temerity or be free from grave sin who by any spoken or written words impugn these decisions."

Decisions of the commission regarding points of doctrine are not infallible of themselves. They require religious assent, however, so long as there is no positive evidence that they are wrong. They do not close the door to continuing investigation and study.

The commission was reorganized July 8, 1971, in line with directives issued by Paul VI on his own initiative.

Fifteen new norms changed its structure from a virtually independent office of cardinals aided by lifetime consultors into a group of 20 biblical scholars with five-year terms (renewable) linked with the Congregation for the Doctrine of the Faith. Functionally, however, it remains the same.

The commission:

• receives questions and study topics referred to it by a variety of sources, from the pope to Catholic universities and biblical associations;

• is required to meet in plenary session at least once a year and to submit conclusions reached in such meetings to the pope and the Congregation for the Doctrine of the Faith;

• is under directive to promote relationships with non-Catholic as well as Catholic institutes of biblical studies;

• is to be consulted before any new norms on biblical matters are issued;

• retains its authorization to confer academic degrees in biblical studies.

THE BIBLE

The Catholic canon of the Old Testament consists of:
- The Pentateuch, the first five books: Genesis (Gn.), Exodus (Ex.), Leviticus (Lv.), Numbers (Nm.), Deuteronomy (Dt.).
- Historical Books: Joshua (Jos.), Judges (Jgs.), Ruth (Ru.), 1 and 2 Samuel (Sm.), 1 and 2 Kings (Kgs.), 1 and 2 Chronicles (Chr.), Ezra (Ezr.), Nehemiah (Neh.), Tobit (Tb.), Judith (Jdt.), Esther (Est.), 1 and 2 Maccabees (Mc.),
- Wisdom Books: Job (Jb.), Psalms (Ps.), Proverbs (Prv.), Ecclesiastes (Eccl.), Song of Songs (Song), Wisdom (Wis.), Sirach (Sir.).
- The Prophets: Isaiah (Is.), Jeremiah (Jer.), Lamentations (Lam.), Baruch (Bar.), Ezechiel (Ez.), Daniel (Dn.), Hosea (Hos.), Joel (Jl.), Amos (Am.), Obadiah (Ob.), Jonah (Jon.), Micah (Mi.), Nahum (Na.), Habakkuk (Hb.), Zephaniah (Zep.), Haggai (Hg.), Zechariah (Zec.), Malachi (Mal.).

The Catholic canon of the New Testament consists of:
- The Gospels of Matthew (Mt.), Mark (Mk.), Luke (Lk.), John (Jn.)
- The Acts of the Apostles (Acts).
- The Pauline Letters — Romans (Rom.), 1 and 2 Corinthians (Cor.), Galatians (Gal.), Ephesians (Eph.), Philippians (Phil.), Colossians (Col.), 1 and 2 Thessalonians (Thes.), 1 and 2 Timothy (Tm.), Titus (Ti.), Philemon (Phlm.), Hebrews (Heb.); the Catholic Letters — James (Jas.), 1 and 2 Peter (Pt.), 1, 2 and 3 John (Jn.), Jude (Jude).
- Revelation (Rv.).

Catholic and Other Canons

The Catholic canon of the Old Testament was determined by the tradition of the Church. It was firm by the fifth century, despite some questioning by scholars, and was stated by the African councils of Hippo in 393 and Carthage in 397 and 419, by Innocent I in 405, and by the Council of Florence in 1441. It was defined by the Council of Trent in the dogmatic decree, *De Canonicis Scripturis,* Apr. 8, 1546.

The Jews, although they generally accepted 22 or 24 books as sacred in the first century A.D., did not have a definite canon of sacred writings until late in the second or early in the third century. This canon was fixed by the consensus of rabbinical schools.

The canon of the Hebrew Masoretic Text, which is accepted by modern Jews, consists of 24 books, as follows:
- The Law: Genesis, Exodus, Leviticus, Numbers, Deuteronomy.
- The Prophets: earlier prophets — Joshua, Judges, Samuel, Kings; later prophets — Isaiah, Jeremiah, Ezekiel, and 12 others in one book (Hosea, Joel, Amos, Obadiah, Jonah, Micah, Nahum, Habakkuk, Zephaniah, Haggai, Zechariah, Malachi).

- The Writings: Psalms, Job, Proverbs, Ruth, Song of Songs, Ecclesiastes, Lamentations, Esther, Daniel, Ezra-Nehemiah, Chronicles.

This canon does not include a number of books in the Alexandrian collection of sacred writings — viz., 1 and 2 Maccabees, Tobit, Judith, Sirach, Wisdom, Baruch, and portions of Esther (10:4-12:34) and Daniel (chapters 13 and 14). These additional books and passages, contained in the Septuagint version of the Old Testament and called deuterocanonical, are in the Catholic canon.

These books and passages, called deuterocanonical in terminology coined by Sixtus of Siena (1520-1569), were under discussion for some time until questions about their canonicity were settled. Books admitted into the canon with little or no debate were called protocanonical. The canonical status of both categories of books is the same in the Catholic Bible.

The Protestant canon, in an arrangement of 39 books, is the same as the Hebrew canon.

The Old Testament canon has not been definitely settled by the Orthodox. Since the time of the Reformation, however, they have given some preference to the Protestant canon.

The New Testament canon was firm by the end of the fourth century. By the end of the second century all of the New Testament books were generally known and most of them were acknowledged as inspired. The Muratorian Fragment, dating from about 200, listed most of the books recognized in later decrees as canonical. Prior to the end of the fourth century, however, there were controversies over the inspired character of several books — viz., the Letter to the Hebrews, James, Jude, 2 Peter, 2 and 3 John, and Revelation. Controversy over these books ended in the fourth century, and the canon stated by the councils of Hippo and Carthage and reaffirmed by Innocent I in 405 was solemnly defined by the Council of Trent (1545-63).

Although Martin Luther eliminated the aforementioned books from his New Testament canon, they were reinstated by his followers by the year 1700. Anglicans and Calvinists always retained them.

The Greek and Russian Orthodox have the same New Testament canon as the Catholic Church. Some variations exist among other separated Eastern churches.

Languages of the Bible

Hebrew, Aramaic and Greek are the original languages of the Bible. Most of the Old Testament books were written in Hebrew. Portions of Daniel, Ezra, Jeremiah, Esther, and probably the books of Tobit and Judith were written in Aramaic. The Book of Wisdom, 2 Maccabees and all the books of the New Testament were written in Greek.

Manuscripts and Versions

The original writings of the inspired authors have been lost. The Bible has been transmitted through ancient copies called manuscripts and through translations or versions.

Authoritative Greek manuscripts include the Sinaitic and Vatican manuscripts of the fourth century and the Alexandrine and Parisian of the fifth century A. D.

The Septuagint and Vulgate translations are in a class by themselves.

The Septuagint version, a Greek translation of the Old Testament, was begun about 250 and completed about 100 B. C. The work of several Jewish translators at Alexandria, it differed from the Hebrew Bible in the arrangement of books and included several, later called deuterocanonical, which were not acknowledged as sacred by the community at Jerusalem.

The Vulgate was a Latin version of the Old and New Testaments produced from the original languages by St. Jerome from about 383 to 404. It became the most widely used Latin text for centuries and was regarded as basic long before the Council of Trent designated it as authentic and suitable for use in public reading, controversy, preaching and teaching. Because of its authoritative character, it became the basis for many translations into other languages.

Hebrew and Aramaic manuscripts of great antiquity and value have figured more significantly than before in recent scriptural work by Catholic scholars, especially since their use was strongly encouraged, if not mandated, in 1943 by Pius XII in the encyclical *Divino Afflante Spiritu.*

The English translation of the Bible in general use among Catholics until recent years was the *Douay-Rheims,* so called because of the places where it was prepared and published, the New Testament at Rheims in 1582 and the Old Testament at Douay in 1609. The translation was made from the Vulgate text. As revised and issued by Bishop Richard Challoner in 1749 and 1750, it became the standard Catholic English version for about 200 years.

A revision of the Challoner New Testament, made on the basis of the Vulgate text by scholars of the Catholic Biblical Association of America, was published in 1941 in the United States under the sponsorship of the Episcopal Committee of the Confraternity of Christian Doctrine.

New American Bible

A new translation of the entire Bible, the first ever made directly into English from the original languages under Catholic auspices, was projected in 1944 and completed in the fall of 1970 with publication of the *New American Bible.* The Episcopal Committee of the Confraternity of Christian Doctrine sponsored the NAB. The translators were members of the Catholic Biblical Association of America and several fellow scholars of other faiths. The typical edition was produced by St. Anthony Guild Press, Paterson, N. J.

Old Testament portions of the NAB were published in separate volumes before undergoing final revision and being bound in one cover. Genesis and Psalms were issued in 1948 and 1950; Genesis to Ruth, in 1952; Job to Sirach, in 1955; the Prophets, in 1961; Samuel to the Maccabees, in 1969. The new translation of the New Testament was issued for the first time in 1970.

Versions of the Bible approved for use in the Catholic liturgy are the *Douay-Rheims,* the *New American Bible, A New Translation from the Latin Vulgate* by Ronald A. Knox, the Catholic edition of the *Revised Standard Version,* and the *Jerusalem Bible.*

The *Jerusalem Bible* is an English translation of a French version based on the original languages. It was published by Doubleday & Co., Inc., which was also working toward completion of the *Anchor Bible.*

The Protestant counterpart of the *Douay-Rheims Bible* was the *King James Bible,* called the *Authorized Version* in England. Originally published in 1611, it was in general use for more than three centuries. Its modern revisions include the *English Revised Version,* published between 1881 and 1885; the *American Revised Version,* 1901, and revisions of the New Testament (1946) and the Old Testament (1952) published in 1957 in the United States as the *Revised Standard Version.*

The latest revision, a translation in the language of the present day made from Greek and Hebrew sources, is the *New English Bible,* published Mar. 16, 1970. Its New Testament portion was originally published in 1961.

Biblical Federation

In November, 1966, Pope Paul commissioned the Secretariat for Promoting Christian Unity to start work for the widest possible distribution of the Bible and to coordinate endeavors toward the production of Catholic-Protestant Bibles in all languages.

The World Catholic Federation for the Biblical Apostolate, established in 1969, sponsors a program designed to create greater awareness among Catholics of the Bible and its use in everyday life. Cardinal Franz Koenig, president of the federation since its inception, agreed to serve in the post for another six years at a four-day plenary meeting of 20 delegates from member organizations early in May, 1972. The meeting was held in Vienna.

The counterpart of the world federation in this country is the US Catholic Federation for the Biblical Apostolate, under the auspices of the National Conference of Catholic Bishops. Address: 1312 Massachusetts Ave. N. W., Washington, D. C. 20005.

APOCRYPHA

Apocrypha are books which have some resemblance to the canonical books in subject matter and title but which have not been recognized as canonical by the Church. They are characterized by a false claim to divine authority; extravagant accounts of events and miracles alleged to be supplemental revelation; material favoring heresy (especially in "New Testament" apocrypha); minimal, if any, historical value.

Among examples of this type of literature itemized by J. McKenzie, S.J., in *Dictionary of the Bible* are: *the Books of Adam and Eve, Martyrdom of Isaiah, Testament of the Patriarchs, Assumption of Moses, Sibylline Oracles; Gospel of James, Gospel of Thomas, Arabic Gospel of the Infancy, History of Joseph the Carpenter; Acts of John, Acts of Paul, Acts of Peter, Acts of Andrew,* and numerous epistles.

Books of this type are called pseudepigrapha by Protestants. They regard as apocrypha the books of the Catholic canon of Scripture which have been called deuterocanonical since the 16th century.

DEAD SEA SCROLLS

The Qumran Scrolls, popularly called the Dead Sea Scrolls, are a collection of manuscripts, all but one of them in Hebrew, found between 1947 and 1956 in caves in the Desert of Juda west of the Dead Sea.

Among the findings were a complete text of Isaiah dating from the second century, B.C., more or less extensive fragments of other Old Testament texts (including the deuterocanonical Tobit), and a commentary on Habakkuk. Until the discovery of these materials, the oldest known Hebrew manuscripts were from the 10th century, A.D.

Also found were messianic and apocalyptic texts, and other writings describing the beliefs and practices of the Essenes, a rigoristic Jewish sect.

The scrolls, dating from about the first century before and after Christ, are important sources of information about Hebrew literature, Jewish history during the period between the Old and New Testaments, and the history of Old Testament texts. They established the fact that the Hebrew text of the Old Testament was fixed before the beginning of the Christian era and have had definite effects in recent critical studies and translations of the Old Testament. Together with other scrolls found at Masada, they are still the subject of intensive study.

A theory was proposed in 1972 by Father Jose O'Callaghan, a Spanish papyrologist, that a scrap of one of the scrolls might be a fragment of St. Mark's Gospel dating from about the year 50. Father Pierre Benoit, O.P., discounted the hypothesis, stating that it was based on an erroneous analysis of a photocopy of the scrap in question.

BOOKS OF THE BIBLE

Old Testament
(Dates are before Christ.)

Pentateuch

The Pentateuch is the collective title of the first five books of the Bible. Substantially, they identify the Israelites as Yahweh's Chosen People, cover their history from Egypt to the threshold of the Promised Land, contain the Mosaic Law and Covenant, and disclose the promise of salvation to come. Principal themes concern the divine promise of salvation, Yahweh's fidelity, and the Covenant. Work on the composition of the Pentateuch was completed in the sixth century.

Genesis: The book of origins, according to its title in the Septuagint. In two parts, covers: religious prehistory, including accounts of the origin of the world and man, the original state of innocence and the fall, the promise of salvation, patriarchs before and after the Deluge, the Tower of Babel narrative, genealogies (first 11 chapters); the covenant with Abraham and patriarchal history from Abraham to Joseph (balance of the 50 chapters). Significant are the themes of Yahweh's universal sovereignty and mercy.

Exodus: Named with the Greek word for departure, is a religious epic which describes the oppression of the 12 tribes in Egypt and their departure, liberation or passover therefrom under the leadership of Moses; Yahweh's establishment of the Covenant with them, making them his Chosen People, through the mediation of Moses at Mt. Sinai; instructions concerning the tabernacle, the sanctuary and Ark of the Covenant; the institution of the priesthood. The book is significant because of its theology of liberation and redemption. In Christian interpretation, the Exodus is a figure of baptism.

Leviticus: Mainly legislative in theme and purpose, contains laws regarding sacrifices, ceremonies of ordination and the priesthood of Aaron, legal purity, the holiness code, atonement, the redemption of offerings, and other subjects. Summarily, Levitical laws provided directives for all aspects of religious observance and for the manner in which the Israelites were to conduct themselves with respect to Yahweh and each other. Leviticus was the liturgical handbook of the priesthood.

Numbers: Taking its name from censuses recounted at the beginning and near the end, is a continuation of Exodus. It combines narrative of the Israelites' desert pilgrimage from Sinai to the border of Canaan with laws related to and expansive of those in Leviticus.

Deuteronomy: The concluding book of the Pentateuch, recapitulates, in the form of a testament of Moses, the Law and much of the desert history of the Israelites; enjoins fidelity to the Law as the key to good or bad fortune for the people; gives an account of the commissioning of Joshua as the successor of Moses. Notable themes concern the election of Israel by Yahweh, observance of the Law, prohibitions against the worship of foreign gods, worship of and confidence in Yahweh, the power of Yahweh in nature. The Deuteronomic Code or motif, embodying all of these elements, was the norm for interpreting Israelite history.

Joshua, Judges, Ruth

Joshua: Records the fulfillment of Yahweh's promise to the Israelites in their conquest, occupation and division of Canaan under the leadership of Joshua. It also contains an account of the return of Transjordanian Israelites and of a renewal of the Covenant. It was redacted in final form probably in the sixth century or later.

Judges: Records the actions of charismatic leaders, called judges, of the tribes of Israel between the death of Joshua and the time of Samuel, and a crisis of idolatry among the people. The basic themes are sin and punishment, repentance and deliverance; its purpose was in line with the Dueteronomic motif, that the fortunes of the Israelites were related to their observance or non-observance of the Law and the Covenant. It was redacted in final form probably in the sixth century.

Ruth: Named for the Gentile (Moabite) woman who, through marriage with Boaz, became an Israelite and an ancestress of David (her son, Obed, became his grandfather). Themes are filial piety, faith and trust in Yahweh, the universality of messianic salvation. Dates ranging from c. 950 to the seventh century have been assigned to the origin of the book, whose author is unknown.

Historical Books

These books, while they contain a great deal of factual material, are unique in their preoccupation with interpreting it, in the Deuteronomic manner, in primary relation to the Covenant on which the nation of Israel was founded and in accordance with which community and personal life were judged.

The books are: Samuel 1 and 2, from the end of Judges (c. 1020) to the end of David's reign (c. 961); Kings 1 and 2, from the last days of David to the start of the Babylonian Exile and the destruction of the Temple (587); Chronicles 1 and 2, from the reign of Saul (c. 1020-1000) to the return of the people from the Exile (538); Ezra and Nehemiah, covering the reorganization of the Jewish community after the Exile (458-397); Maccabees 1 and 2, recounting the struggle against attempted suppression of Judaism (168-142).

Three of the books listed below — Tobit, Judith and Esther — are categorized as religious novels.

Samuel 1 and 2: A single work in concept and contents, containing episodic history of the last two Judges, Eli and Samuel, the establishment and rule of the monarchy under Saul and David, and the political consequences of David's rule. The royal messianic dynasty of David was the subject of Nathan's Oracle in 2 Sm. 7. They were edited in final form probably late in the seventh century or during the Exile.

Kings 1 and 2: Cover the last days of David and the career of Solomon, including the building of the Temple and the history of the kingdom during his reign; stories of the prophets Elija and Elisha; the history of the divided kingdom to the fall of Israel in the North (721) and the fall of Judah in the South (587), the destruction of Jerusalem and the Temple. They reflect the Deuteronomic motif in attributing the downfall of the people to corruption of belief and practice in public and private life. They were completed probably in the sixth century.

Chronicles 1 and 2: A collection of historical traditions interpreted in such a way as to present an ideal picture of one people governed by divine law and united in one Temple worship of the one true God. Contents include genealogical tables from Adam to David, the careers of David and Solomon, coverage of the kingdom of Judah to the Exile, and the decree of Cyrus permitting the return of the people and rebuilding of Jerusalem. Both are related to and were written about 400 by the same author, the Chronicler, who composed Ezra and Nehemiah.

Ezra and Nehemiah: A running account of the return of the people to their homeland after the Exile and of practical efforts, under the leadership of Ezra and Nehemiah, to restore and reorganize the religious and political community on the basis of Israelite traditions, divine worship and observance of the Law. Events of great significance were the building of the second Temple, the building of a wall around Jerusalem, and the proclamation of the Law by Ezra. This restored community was the start of Judaism. Both are related to and were written about 400 by the same author, the Chronicler, who composed Chronicles 1 and 2.

Tobit: Written in the literary form of a novel and having greater resemblance to wisdom than to historical literature, narrates the personal history of Tobit, a devout and charitable Jew in exile, and persons connected with him, viz., his son Tobiah, his kinsman Raguel, and Raguel's daughter Sarah. Its purpose was to teach people how to be good Jews. One of its principal themes is patience under trial, with trust in divine Providence which is symbolized by the presence and action of the angel Raphael. It was written about 200.

Judith: Recounts, in the literary form of a historical novel or romance, the preservation of the Israelites from conquest and ruin through the action of Judith. The essential themes are trust in God for deliverance from danger and emphasis on observance of the Law. It was written probably during the Maccabean period.

Esther: Relates, in the literary form of a historical novel or romance, the manner in which Jews in Persia were saved from annihilation through the central role played by Esther, the Jewish wife of Ahasuerus; a fact commemorated by the Jewish feast of Purim. Like Judith, it has trust in divine Providence as its theme and indicates that God's saving will is sometimes realized by persons acting in unlikely ways. Its origin and date are uncertain; it may have been written about 200 near the beginning of the period of strong Hellenistic influence on the Jews.

Maccabees 1 and 2: While related to some extent because of common subject matter, are quite different from each other.

The first book recounts the background and events of the 40-year (175-135) struggle for religious and political freedom led by Judas Maccabeus and his brothers against the Hellenist Seleucid kings and some Hellenophiles among the Jews. Victory was symbolized by the rededication of the Temple. Against the background of opposition between Jews and Gentiles, the author equated the survival of belief in the one true God with survival of the Jewish people, thus identifying religion with patriotism. It was written probably by a Palestinian Jew after 104.

The second book supplements the first to some extent, covering and giving a theological interpretation to events from 180 to 162. It explains the feast of the Dedication of the Temple, a key event in the survival of Judaism which is commemorated in the feast of Hanukkah; stresses the primacy of God's action in the struggle for survival; and indicates belief in an afterlife and the resurrection of the body. It was written probably by a Jew of Alexandria after 120.

Wisdom Books

With the exceptions of Psalms and the Song of Songs, the titles listed under this heading are called wisdom books because their purpose was to formulate the fruits of human experience in the context of meditation on sacred Scripture and to present them as an aid toward understanding the problems of life. Hebrew wisdom literature was distinctive from pagan literature of the same type, but it had limitations; these were overcome in the New Testament, which added the dimensions of the New Covenant to those of the Old. Solomon was regarded as the archtype of the wise man.

Job: A dramatic, didactic poem consisting mainly of several dialogues between Job and his friends concerning the mystery involved in the coexistence of the just God, evil, and the suffering of the just. It describes an innocent man's experience of suffering and conveys the truth that faith in and submission to God rather than complete understanding, which is impossible, make the experience bearable; also, that the justice of God cannot be defended by affirming that it is realized in this world. Of uncertain authorship, it was written probably between the fifth and third centuries.

Psalms: A collection of 150 religious songs or lyrics reflecting Israelite belief and piety dating from the time of the monarchy to the post-Exilic period, a span of well over 500 years. The psalms, which are a compendium of Old Testament theology, were used in the temple liturgy and were of several types suitable for the king, hymns, lamentations, expressions of confidence and thanksgiving, prophecy, historical meditation and reflection, and the statement of wisdom. About one-half of them are attributed to David; many, by unknown authors, date from the early post-Exilic period.

Proverbs: The oldest book of the wisdom type in the Bible, consisting of collections of sayings attributed to Solomon and other persons regarding a wide variety of subjects including wisdom and its nature, rules of conduct, duties with respect to one's neighbor, the conduct of daily affairs. It reveals many details of Jewish life. Its nucleus dates from the period before the Exile, but no definite date can be assigned for its final compilation.

Ecclesiastes: A treatise about many subjects whose unifying theme is the vanity of strictly human efforts and accomplishments with respect to the achievement of lasting happiness; the only things which are not vain are fear of the Lord and observance of his commandments. The pessimistic tone of the book is due to the absence of a concept of afterlife. It was written by an unknown author about 250.

Song of Songs: A collection of erotic lyrics reflecting various themes, including the celebration of fidelity and love between man and woman. According to one interpretation, the book is a parable of the love of Yahweh for Israel. It was written by an unknown author after the Exile.

Wisdom: Deals with many subjects including the reward of justice; praise of wisdom, a gift of Yahweh proceeding from belief in him and the practice of his Law; the part played by him in the history of his people, especially in their liberation from Egypt; the folly and shame of idolatry. Its contents are taken from the whole sacred literature of the Jews and represent a distillation of its wisdom based on the law, beliefs and traditions of Israel. Contains the first Old Testament affirmation of an afterlife with God. The last book of the Old Testament to be written, it was probably composed about 50 years before Christ by an unknown author to confirm the faith of the Jewish community in Alexandria.

Sirach: Resembling Proverbs, is a collection of sayings handed on by a grandfather to his grandson. It contains a variety of moral instruction and eulogies of patriarchs and other figures in Israelite history. Its moral maxims apply to individuals, the family and community, relations with God, friendship, education, wealth, the Law, divine worship. Its theme is that true wisdom consists in the Law. (It was formerly called Ecclesiasticus, the Church Book, because of its extensive use by the Church for moral instruction.) It was written in Hebrew between 200 and 175, during a period of strong Hellenistic influence, and was translated into Greek after 132.

The Prophets

These books and the prophecies they contain "express judgments of the people's moral conduct, on the basis of the Mosaic alliance between God and Israel. They teach sublime truths and lofty morals. They contain exhortations, threats, announcements of punishment, promises of deliverance. . . . In the affairs of men, their prime concern is the interests of God, especially in what pertains to the Chosen People through whom the Messiah is to come; hence their denunciations of idolatry and of that externalism in worship which exclude the interior spirit of religion. They are concerned also with the universal nature of the moral law, with personal responsibility, with the person and office of the Messiah, and with the conduct of foreign nations" (*The Holy Bible*, Prophetic Books, CCD Edition, 1961; Preface. There are four major (Isaiah, Jeremiah, Ezekiel, Daniel) and 12 minor prophets (distinguished by the length of books), Lamentations and Baruch. Earlier prophets, include Samuel, Gad, Nathan, Elijah and Elisha.

Before the Exile, prophets were the intermediaries through whom God communicated revelation to the people. Afterwards, prophecy lapsed and the written word of the Law served this purpose.

Isaiah: Named for the greatest of the prophets whose career spanned the reigns of three Hebrew kings from 742 to the beginning of the seventh century, in a period of moral breakdown in Judah and threats of invasion by foreign enemies. It is an anthology of poems and oracles credited to him and a number of followers deeply influenced by him. Of special importance are the prophecies concerning Immanuel (6 to 12), including the prophecy of the virgin birth (7:14). Chapters 40 to 55, called Deutero-Isaiah, are attributed to an anonymous poet toward the end of the Exile; this portion contains the Songs of the Servant. The concluding part of the book (56-66) contains oracles by later disciples. One of many themes in Isaiah concerned the saving mission of the remnant of Israel in the divine plan of salvation. It was edited in its present form by 180.

Jeremiah: Combines history, biography and prophecy in a setting of crisis caused by internal and external factors, viz., idolatry and general infidelity to the Law among the Israelites and external threats from the Assyrians, Egyptians and Babylonians. Jeremiah prophesied the promise of a new covenant as well as the destruction of Jerusalem and the Temple. His career began in 626 and ended some years after the beginning of the Exile. The book, the longest in the Bible, was edited in final form after the Exile.

Lamentations: A collection of five laments or elegies over the fall of Jerusalem and the fate of the people in Exile, written by an unknown eyewitness not long after 587. They convey the message that Yahweh struck the people because of their sins and reflect confidence in his love and power to restore his converted people.

Baruch: Against the background of the already begun Exile, it consists of an introduction and several parts: an exile's prayer of confession and petition for forgiveness and the restoration of Israel; a poem praising wisdom and the Law of Moses; a lament in which Jerusalem, personified, bewails the fate of her people and consoles them with the hope of blessings to come; and a polemic against idolatry. Although ascribed to Baruch, Jeremiah's secretary, it was written by several authors probably in the second century.

Ezekiel: Named for the priest-prophet who prophesied in Babylon from 593 to 571, during the first phase of the Exile. To prepare his fellow early exiles for the impending fall of Jerusalem, he reproached the Israelites for past sins and predicted woes to come upon them. After the destruction of the city, the burden of his message was hope and promise of restoration. Ezekiel had great influence on the religion of Israel after the Exile. The book, which contains the substance of his teaching, had a number of authors and editors.

Daniel: The protagonist is a fictional young Jew, taken early to Babylon where he lived until 537, who figured in a series of edifying stories. The stories, which originated from Israelite tradition, recount the trials and triumphs of Daniel and his three companions, and other episodes including those concerning Susannah, Bel, and the Dragon. The book is more apocalyptic than prophetic: it envisions Israel in glory to come and conveys the message that men of faith can resist temptation and overcome adversity. It states the prophetic themes of right conduct, divine control of men and events, and the final triumph of the kingdom. It was written by an unknown author in the 160's to give moral support to Jews during the persecutions of the Maccabean period.

Hosea: Consists of a prophetic parallel between Hosea's marriage and Yahweh's relations with his people. As the prophet was married to a faithless wife whom he would not give up, Yahweh was bound in Covenant with an idolatrous and unjust Israel whom he would not desert but would chastise for purification. Hosea belonged to the Northern Kingdom of Israel and began his career about the middle of the eighth century. He inaugurated the tradition of describing Yahweh's relation to Israel in terms of marriage.

Joel: Is apocalyptic and eschatological regarding divine judgment, the Day of the Lord, which is symbolized by a ravaging invasion of locusts, the judgment of the nations in the Valley of Josaphat, and the outpouring of the Spirit in the messianic era to come. Its message is that God will vindicate and save Israel, in view of the prayer and repentance of the people, and will punish their enemies. It was composed after the period of Nehemiah.

Amos: Consists of an indictment against foreign enemies of Israel; a strong denunciation of the people of Israel, whose infidelity, idolatry and injustice made them subject to divine judgment and punishment; and a messianic oracle regarding Israel's restoration. Amos prophesied in the Northern Kingdom of Israel, at Bethel, in the first half of the eighth century; chronologically, he was the first of the canonical prophets.

Obadiah: A 21-verse prophecy, the shortest and one of the sternest in the Bible, against the Edomites, invaders of southern Judah and enemies of those returning from the Exile to their homeland. It was redacted in final form no later than the end of the fourth century.

Jonah: A parable of divine mercy with the theme that Yahweh wills the salvation of all, not just a few, men who respond to his call. Its protagonist is a disobedient prophet; forced by circumstances beyond his control to preach penance among Gentiles, he is highly successful in his mission but baffled by the divine concern for those who do not belong to the Chosen People. It was written after the Exile.

Micah: Attacks the injustice and corruption of priests, false prophets, officials and people; announces judgment and punishment to come; foretells the restoration of Israel; refers to the saving remnant of Israel. Micah was a contemporary of Isaiah.

Nahum: Dating from about 613, concerns the destruction of Nineveh in 612 and the overthrow of the Assyrian Empire by the Babylonians.

Habakkuk: Dating from about 605-597, concerns sufferings to be inflicted by oppressors on the people of Judah because of their infidelity to the Lord. It also sounds a note of confidence in the Lord, the Savior, and declares that the just will not perish.

Zephaniah: Exercising his ministry in the second half of the seventh century, during a time of widespread idolatry, superstition and religious degradation, he prophesied impending judgment and punishment for Jerusalem and its people. He prophesied too that a holy remnant of the people (Anawim, mentioned also by Amos) would be spared. Zephaniah was a forerunner of Jeremiah.

Haggai: One of the first prophets after the Exile, Haggai in 520 encouraged the returning exiles to reestablish their community and to complete the second Temple (dedicated in 515), for which he envisioned greater glory, in a messianic sense, than that enjoyed by the original Temple of Solomon.

Zechariah: A contemporary of Haggai, he prophesied in the same vein. A second part of the book, called Deutero-Zechariah and composed by one or more unknown authors, relates a vision of the coming of the Prince of Peace, the Messiah of the Poor.

Malachi: Written by an anonymous author, presents a picture of life in the post-Exilic community between 516 and the initiation of reforms by Ezra and Nehemiah about 432. Blame for the troubles of the community is placed mainly on priests for failure to carry out ritual worship and to instruct the people in the proper manner; other factors were religious indifference and the influence of doubters who were scandalized at the prosperity of the wicked. The vision of a universal sacrifice to be offered to Yahweh (1:11) is interpreted in Christian theology as a prophecy of the sacrifice of the Mass.

OLD TESTAMENT DATES

c. 1800 — c. 1600: Period of the patriarchs (Abraham, Isaac, Jacob).

c. 1600: Israelites in Egypt.

c. 1250: Exodus of Israelites from Egypt.

c. 1210: Entrance of Israelites into Canaan.

c. 1210 — c. 1020: Period of the Judges.

c. 1020 — c. 1000: Reign of Saul, first king.

c. 1000 — c. 961: Reign of David.

c. 961 — 922: Reign of Solomon. Temple built during his reign.

922: Division of the Kingdom into Israel (North) and Judah (South).

721: Conquest of Israel by Assyrians.

587-538: Conquest of Judah by Babylonians.

587-538: Babylonian Captivity and Exile. Destruction of Jerusalem and the Temple, 587. Captivity ended with the return of exiles, following the decree of Cyrus permitting the rebuilding of Jerusalem.

515: Dedication of the Second Temple.

458-397: Restoration and reform of the Jewish religious and political community; building of the Jerusalem wall, 439. Leaders in the movement were Ezra and Nehemiah.

168-142: Period of the Maccabees; war against Syrians.

142: Independence granted to Jews by Demetrius II of Syria.

135-37: Period of the Hasmonean dynasty.

63: Beginning of Roman ruule.

37-4: Period of Herod the Great.

New Testament Books

Gospels

The term Gospel is derived from the Anglo-Saxon *god-spell* and the Greek *euangelion,* meaning good news, good tidings. In Christian use, it means the good news of salvation proclaimed by Christ and the Church, and handed on in written form in the Gospels of Matthew, Mark, Luke and John.

The initial proclamation of the coming of the kingdom of God was made by Jesus in and through his Person, teachings and actions, and especially through his Passion, death and resurrection. This proclamation became the center of Christian faith and the core of the oral Gospel tradition with which the Church spread the good news by apostolic preaching for some 30 years before it was committed to writing by the Evangelists.

According to an Instruction issued by the Pontifical Commission for Biblical Studies Apr. 21, 1964:

• The sacred writers selected from the material at their disposal (the oral Gospel tradition, some written collections of saying and deeds of Jesus, eyewitness accounts) those things which were particularly suitable to the various conditions (liturgical, catechetical, missionary) of the faithful and the aims they had in mind, and they narrated these things in such a way as to correspond with those circumstances and their aims.

• The life and teaching of Jesus were not simply reported in a biographical manner for the purpose of preserving their memory but were "preached" so as to offer the Church the basis of doctrine concerning faith and morals.

• In their works, the Evangelists presented the true sayings of Jesus and the events of his life in the light of the better understanding they had following their enlightenment by the Holy Spirit. They did not transform Christ into a "mythical" Person, nor did they distort his teaching.

Passion narratives are the core of all the Gospels, covering the suffering, death and resurrection of Jesus as central events in bringing about and establishing the New Covenant. Leading up to them are accounts of the mission of John the Baptizer and the ministry of Jesus, especially in Galilee and finally in Jerusalem before the Passion. The infancy of Jesus is covered by Luke and Matthew with narratives inspired by Old Testament citations appropriate to the birth of the Messiah.

Matthew, Mark and Luke, while different in various respects, have so many similarities that they are called Synoptic; their relationships are the subject of the Synoptic Problem.

Matthew: Written in the 70's or 80's for Jewish Christians, with clear reference to Jewish background and identification of Jesus as the divine Messiah, the fulfillment of the Old Testament. Distinctive are the use of Old Testament citations regarding the Person, activity and teaching of Jesus, and the presentation of doctrine in sermons and discourses. The canonical Matthew was written in Greek, with dependence on Mark.

Mark: The first of the Gospels, dating from about 65. Written for Gentile Christians, it is noted for the realism and wealth of concrete details with which it reveals Jesus as Son of God and Savior more by his actions and miracles than by his discourses. Theologically, it is less refined than the other gospels.

Luke: Written in the 70's or 80's for Gentile Christians. It is noted for the universality of its address, the insight it provides into the Christian way of life, the place it gives to women, the manner in which it emphasizes Jesus' friendship with sinners and compassion for the suffering.

John: Written sometime in the 90's, is the most sublime and theological of the Gospels, and is different from the Synoptics in plan and treatment. Combining accounts of signs with longer discourses and reflections, it progressively reveals the Person and mission of Jesus — as Word, Way, Truth, Life, Light — in line with the purpose, "to help you believe that Jesus is the Messiah, the Son of God, so that through this faith you may have life in his name" (Jn. 20:31). There are questions about the authorship but no doubt about the Johannine tradition behind the Gospel.

Acts of the Apostles

Acts of the Apostles: Written by Luke in the 70's or 80's as a supplement to his Gospel. It describes the origin and spread of Christian communities through the action of the Holy Spirit from the resurrection of Christ to the time of Paul's first Roman imprisonment.

Letters (Epistles)

These letters, the first documents of the New Testament, were written in response to existential needs of the early Christian communities for doctrinal and moral instruction, disciplinary action, practical advice, and exhortation to true Christian living.

Pauline Letters

These letters, which comprise approximately one-fourth of the New Testament, are primary and monumental sources of the development of Christian theology. Several of them may not have had Paul as their actual author, but evidence of the Pauline tradition behind them is strong. The letters to the Colossians, Philippians, Ephesians and Philemon have been called the "Captivity Letters" because of a tradition that they were written while Paul was under house arrest in Rome from 61 to 63.

Romans: Written in the late 50's from

Corinth on the central significance of Christ and faith in him for salvation, and the relationship of Christianity to Judaism; the condition of mankind without Christ; justification and the Christian life; duties of Christians.

Corinthians 1: Written near the beginning of 57 from Ephesus to counteract factionalism and disorders, it covers community dissensions, moral irregularities, marriage and celibacy, conduct at religious gatherings, the Eucharist, spiritual gifts (charisms) and their function in the Church, charity, the resurrection of the body.

Corinthians 2: Written later in the same year as 1 Cor., concerning Paul's defense of his apostolic life and ministry, and an appeal for a collection to aid poor Christians in Jerusalem.

Galatians: Written probably between 54 and 57 (perhaps earlier, according to some scholars) to counteract Judaizing opinions and efforts to undermine his authority, it asserts the divine origin of Paul's authority and doctrine, states that justification is not through Mosaic Law but through faith in Christ, insists on the practice of evangelical virtues, especially charity.

Ephesians: Written probably between 61 and 63, or perhaps in the 70's, mainly on the Church as the Mystical Body of Christ.

Philippians: Written between 61 and 63 primarily to thank the Philippians for their kindness to him while he was under house arrest in Rome.

Colossians: Written while he was under house arrest in Rome from 61 to 63 to counteract the influence of self-appointed teachers who were watering down doctrine concerning Christ. It includes two highly important Christological passages, a warning against false teachers, and an instruction on the ideal Christian life.

Thessalonians 1 and 2: Written within a short time of each other probably in 51 from Corinth, mainly on doctrine concerning the Parousia, the second coming of Christ.

Timothy 1 and 2, Titus: Written between 65 and 67, or perhaps in the 70's, giving pastoral counsels to Timothy and Titus who were in charge of churches in Ephesus and Crete, respectively. 1 Tm. emphasizes pastoral responsibility for preserving unity of doctrine; 2 Tm. describes Paul's imprisonment in Rome.

Philemon: A private letter written between 61 and 63 to a wealthy Colossian Concerning a slave, Onesimus, who had escaped from him; Paul appealed for kind treatment of the man.

Hebrews: Dating from some time between the mid-60's and the 80's, a complex theological treatise on Christology, the priesthood and sacrifice of Christ, the New Covenant, and the pattern for Christian living. Critical opinion is divided as to whether it was addressed to Judaeo or Gentile Christians.

Catholic Letters, Revelation

These seven letters have been called "catholic" because it was thought for some time, not altogether correctly, that they were not addressed to particular communities.

James: Written sometime between the mid-60's and the 80's (although datable before 62 according to some scholars) in the spirit of Hebrew wisdom literature and the moralism of Tobit. An exhortation to practical Christian living, it is also noteworthy for the doctrine it states on good works and its citation regarding anointing of the sick.

Peter 1 and 2: The first letter may have been written in the mid-60's; the second dates from 100 to 125. Addressed to Christians in Asia Minor, both are exhortations to perseverance in the life of faith despite trials and difficulties arising from pagan influences, isolation from other Christians, and false teaching.

John 1: Written sometime in the 90's and addressed to Asian churches, its message is that God is made known to us in the Son and that fellowship with the Father is attained by living in the light, justice and love of the Son.

John 2: Written sometime in the 90's and addressed to a church in Asia, it commends the people for standing firm in the faith and urges them to perseverance.

John 3: Written sometime in the 90's, it appears to represent an effort to settle a jurisdictional dispute in one of the churches.

Jude: Written sometime between the 70's and 90's, it is a brief treatise against erroneous teachings and practices opposed to law, authority and true Christian freedom.

Revelation: Written in the 90's along the lines of Johannine thought, it is a symbolic and apocalyptic treatment of things to come combined with warning but hope and assurance to the Church regarding the coming of the Lord in glory.

BIBLICAL AUTHORSHIP

Some books of the Bible were not written by the authors to whom they have been traditionally attributed; New Testament examples are the Gospels of Matthew and John, Hebrews, 1 and 2 Timothy, Titus, James, Jude.

This fact, which has never been the subject of dogmatic definition by the Church, does not militate against the canonicity of the books, since canonicity concerns the theological matter of inspiration rather than the historical question of human authorship.

Questions concerning authorship are explained in various ways: (1) according to an old custom whereby literary works of importance were sometimes attributed to famous persons so they would get a reading; (2) authorship, by a disciple or school of disciples, of works derived from the doctrine of a master; (3) authorship by persons writing in the spirit and tradition of a master.

GOSPEL PASSAGES

Discourses

The Sermon on the Mount is probably the best known of the many Gospel discourses.

Vindication of his authority (Jn. 2:18-22).

Spiritual rebirth, origin of his teaching, purpose of his coming, judgment on unbelievers; with Nicodemus (Jn. 3:1-21).

Of himself, his mission, everlasting life through him; with a Samaritan woman (Jn. 4:7-30).

Defense of his disciples for not fasting, for plucking corn on the Sabbath (Mt. 9:14-17, 12:1-8; Mk. 2:18-28; Lk. 5:33-39, 6:1-5).

Defense of himself for healing a man with a withered hand on the Sabbath (Mt. 12:9-13; Mk. 3:15; Lk. 6:6-10).

Sermon on the Mount (Mt. 5:1 to 7:29; Lk. 6:20-49).

Testimony concerning John the Baptist (Mt. 11:17-19; Lk. 7:24-35, 16:16).

Instructions for the apostolate (Mt. 10: 5-42; Mk. 6:8-13; Lk. 9:3-6, 10:1-12).

The bread of life (Jn. 6:22-72).

Defense of his claim to divinity (Jn. 5:19-47).

Defense of his disciples against Pharisees (Mt. 15:1-20; Mk. 7:1-23).

Promise of primacy to Peter (Mt. 16:13-20).

Predictions of the Passion and Resurrection (Mt. 16:21-23, 17:21-22, 20:17-19; Mk. 8:31-33, 9:29-31, 10:32-34; Lk. 9:22, 9:44-45, 18:31-34).

Doctrine of the cross (Mt. 16:24-28; Mk. 8:34-39; Lk. 9:23-27).

Scandal (Mt. 18:5-9; Mk. 9:41-49; Lk. 17:1-2).

Fraternal correction (Mt. 18:15-17, 21-22; Lk. 17:3-4).

Conversation with Martha and Mary (Lk. 10:38-42).

The adulteress (Jn. 8:3-11).

Efficacy of prayer (Mt. 7:7-11; Lk. 11:9-13).

Defense of his authority (Mt. 21:23-27; Mk. 11:27-33; Lk. 20:1-8).

Tribute to Caesar (Mt. 22:15-22; Mk. 12:13-17; Lk. 20:20-26).

The great commandment (Mt. 23:34-40; Mk. 12:28-34).

Destruction of Jerusalem and the Temple (Mt. 24:1-3, 15-22, 32-35; Mk. 13:1-20, 28-31; Lk. 21:5-6, 20-24, 29-33).

End of the world and coming of the Son of Man (Mt. 24:4-14, 23-31, 36-51 to 25:1-3; Mk. 13:21-27, 32-37; Lk. 21:7-19, 25-28, 34-36).

Last judgment (Mt. 25:31-46).

Discourses at the Last Supper (Mt. 26:20-29; Mk. 14:17-25; Lk. 22:14-38; Jn. 13:2 to 17:26).

Conferring of primacy on Peter (Jn. 21:15-17).

Commission of the Apostles to teach and baptize (Mt. 28:16-20; Mk. 16:15-18).

Parables

Essential to understanding a parable is identification of its points of reference.

The sower (Mt. 13:1-23; Mk. 4:1-20; Lk. 8:4-15).

The weeds (Mt. 13:24-30, 36-43).

The mustard seed (Mt. 13:31-32; Mk. 4:30-32; Lk. 13:18-19).

The leaven (Mt. 13:33; Lk. 12:20-21).

The treasure (Mt. 13:44).

The pearl (Mt. 13:45-46).

The net (Mt. 13:47-50).

The seed (Mk. 4:26-29).

The house built on rock (Mt. 7:24-27; Lk. 6:47-49).

The two debtors (Lk. 7:41-48).

The unmerciful servant (Mt. 18:21-35).

The good Samaritan (Lk. 10:25-37).

The importunate friend (Lk. 11:5-8).

The rich fool (Lk. 12:16-21).

A barren fig tree (Lk. 13:6-9).

The last seat (Lk. 14:7-11).

The lost sheep (Mt. 18:10-14; Lk. 15:1-7).

The lost coin (Lk. 15:8-10).

The prodigal son (Lk. 15:11-32).

The unjust steward (Lk. 16:1-13).

The rich man (Dives) and Lazarus (Lk. 16:19-31).

The godless judge (Lk. 18:1-8).

The Pharisee and the Publican (Lk. 18:9-14).

The laborers in the vineyard (Mt. 20:1-16).

The gold pieces (Lk. 19:11-27).

The two sons (Mt. 21:28-32).

The vine-dressers (Mt. 21:33-46; Mk. 12:1-12; Lk. 20:9-19).

The marriage feast (Mt. 22:1-10; Lk. 14:7-24).

The wedding garment (Mt. 22:11-14).

The great supper (Lk. 14:15-24).

The ten virgins (Mt. 25:1-13).

The talents (Mt. 25:14-30).

Similitudes and Allegories

"Physician, cure yourself" (Lk. 4:23).

The savor of salt (Mt. 5:13; Mk. 9:49; Lk. 14:34-35).

The lamp under a bushel basket (Mt. 5:14-15; Mk. 4:21; Lk. 8:16-18, 11:33-36).

The city on a mountain (Mt. 5:14).

The opponent (Mt. 5:25-26; Lk. 12:58-59).

The lamp of the body (Mt. 6:22-23; Lk. 11:33-36).

The two masters (Mt. 6:24; Lk. 16:13).

A son's request (Mt. 7:9-11; Lk. 11:11-13).

The tree and its fruit (Mt. 7:15-20, 12:33-37; Lk. 6:43-45).

The physician and the sick (Mt. 9:12-13; Mk. 2:17; Lk. 5:31-32).

The bridegroom and the wedding guests (Mt. 9:14-15; Mk. 2:18-20; Lk. 5:33-35).

A patch of raw cloth on an old garment (Mt. 9:16; Mk. 2:21; Lk. 5:36).

New wine in old wineskins (Mt. 9:17; Mk. 2:22; Lk. 5:37-38).

Secrets to be uncovered (Mt. 10:26-27; Mk. 4:22; Lk. 8:17, 12:2-3).

The servant not above the master (Mt. 10:24-25; Lk. 6:40).

The stubborn children (Mt. 11:16-19; Lk. 7:31-35).

The divided kingdom (Mt. 12:25-26; Mk. 3:23-26; Lk. 11:17-18).

The unclean spirit (Mt. 12:43-45; Lk. 11:24-26).

The wise scribe (Mt. 13:52).

The defilement of man (Mt. 15:10-20; Mk. 7:14-23).

Blind guides of blind men (Lk. 6:39; Mt. 15:14).

The children's bread (Mt. 15:26-27; Mk. 7:27-28).

Building a tower (Lk. 14:28-30).

Preparation for war (Lk. 14:31-33).

The watchful servants (Lk. 12:35-38; Mk. 13:34).

Faithful and unfaithful servants (Mt. 24:45-51; Lk. 12:42-48).

The unprofitable servant (Lk. 17:7-10).

The body and the eagles (Mt. 24:28; Lk. 17:37).

The thief (Mt. 24:43-44; Lk. 12:39-40).

The fig tree and the branches (Mt. 24:32-33; Mk. 13:28-29; Lk. 21:29-31).

The good Shepherd (Jn. 10:1-18).

The fine and the branches (Jn. 15:1-17).

Miracles

Changing of water into wine at the marriage feast (Jn. 2:1-11).

Cure of an official's son (Jn. 4:46-54).

Miraculous draft of fishes (Lk. 5:1-11).

The cure of a man possessed by the devil (Mk. 1:23-28; Lk, 4:33-37).

Cure of the fever of Peter's mother-in-law (Mt. 8:14-15; Mk. 1:29-31; Lk. 4:38-39).

Healing of many sick and diseased (Mt. 8:16-17; Mk. 1:32-34; Lk. 4:40-41).

Cure of a leper (Mt. 8:1-4; Mk. 1:40-45; Lk. 5:12-14).

Christ escapes from a mob (Lk. 4:28-30).

Cure of a paralytic (Mt. 9:1-8; Mk. 2:1-12; Lk. 5:18-26).

Cure of a sick man (Jn. 5:1-9).

Cure of a man with a withered hand (Mt. 12:9-13; Mk. 3:1-5; Lk. 6:6-10).

Healing of many sick and diseased (Lk. 6:18-19).

Cure of a centurion's servant (Mt. 8:5-13; Lk. 7:1-10).

Raising to life of a widow's son (Lk. 7:11-17).

Cure of a blind and dumb demoniac (Mt. 12:22-37).

Calming of a storm (Mt. 8:23-27; Mk. 4:36-40; Lk. 8:22-25).

Exorcism of unclean spirits (Mt. 8:28-34; Mk. 5:1-15; Lk. 8:26-35).

Cure of a woman with a hemorrhage (Mt. 9:20-22; Mk. 5:25-34; Lk. 8:43-48).

Raising to life of Jairus' daughter (Mt. 9:18-19, 23-26; Mk. 5:20-24, 35-43; Lk. 8:41-42, 49-56).

Cure of two blind men (Mt. 9:27-31).

Exorcism of a dumb demoniac (Mt. 9:32-34).

Feeding of over 5,000 with five loaves and two fishes (Mt. 14:13-21; Mk. 6:31-44; Lk. 9:12-17; Jn. 6:1-15).

Walking on the water (Mt. 14:22-33; Mk. 6:45-52; Jn. 6:16-21).

The exorcism of a Canaanite woman's daughter (Mt. 15:21-28; Mk. 7:24-30).

Cure of a deaf mute (Mk. 7:31-37).

Healing of many sick (Mt. 15:29-31).

Feeding of about 4,000 with seven loaves and a few fishes (Mt. 15:32-38; Mk. 8:1-9).

Cure of a blind man (Mk. 8:22-26).

Transfiguration (Mt. 17:1-9; Mk. 9:1-8; Lk. 9:28-36).

Exorcism of a possessed boy (Mt. 17:14-20; Mk. 9:13-28; Lk. 9:37-43).

Temple tax (Mt. 17:23-26).

Escape from his enemies (Jn. 8:59).

Cure of a man born blind (Jn. 9:1-41).

Exorcism of a possessed man (Lk. 11:14-26).

Cure of a crippled woman (Lk. 13:10-17).

Cure of a man afflicted with dropsy (Lk. 14:1-6).

Cure of 10 lepers (Lk. 17:12-19).

Raising of Lazarus to life (Jn. 11:1-44).

Cure of Bartimeus and another blind beggar (Mt. 20:29-34; Mk. 10:46-52; Lk. 18:35-43).

Withering of a barren fig tree (Mt. 21:18-19; Mk. 11:12-14).

Cure of many sick (Mt. 21:14).

Healing of a soldier's ear in the Garden (Mt. 26:51-52; Mk. 14:47; Lk. 22:49-51; Jn. 18:10-11).

Resurrection (Mt. 28:1-10; Mk. 16:1-14; Lk. 24:1-43; Jn. 20:1-20).

Miraculous draft of fishes after the Resurrection (Jn. 21:1-14).

The Ascension (Mk. 16:19; Lk. 24:50-51).

WORD OF GOD CONGRESS

Father John Burke, O.P., coordinator of the National Congress on the Word of God held in Washington Sept. 5 to 7, 1972, said after its conclusion that one of the great needs of the day "is not the art of preaching (but) the art of being a preacher." He announced the establishment of the Word of God Institute as a result of the congress.

Another participant in the congress, Archbishop John May, head of the Communications committee, US Catholic Conference, said: "The problem is to put the word of God into the word of the world. So often preaching is of another world . . . has no direct relation to people in the world who are trying to work out their lives. The communicator must certainly never dilute his preaching. But in every age the communicator has to give the word in the vernacular of the times."

INTERPRETATION OF THE BIBLE

According to the *Constitution on Revelation* issued by the Second Vatican Council, "the interpreter of Sacred Scripture, in order to see clearly what God wanted to communicate to us, should carefully investigate what meaning the sacred writers really intended, and what God wanted to manifest by means of their words" (No. 12).

Hermeneutics, Exegesis

This careful investigation proceeds in accordance with the rules of hermeneutics, the normative science of biblical interpretation and explanation. Hermeneutics in practice is called exegesis.

The principles of hermeneutics are derived from various disciplines and many factors which have to be considered in explaining the Bible and its parts. These include: the original languages and languages of translation of the sacred texts, through philology and linguistics; the quality of texts, through textual criticism; literary forms and genres, through literary and form criticism; cultural, historical, geographical and other conditions which influenced the writers, through related studies; facts and truths of salvation history; the truths and analogy of faith.

Distinctive to biblical hermeneutics, which differs in important respects from literary interpretation in general, is the premise that the Bible, though written by human authors, is the work of divine inspiration in which God reveals his plan for the salvation of men through historical events and persons, and especially through the Person and mission of Christ.

Textual, Form Criticism

Textual criticism is the study of biblical texts, which have been transmitted in copies several times removed from the original manuscripts, for the purpose of establishing the real state of the original texts. This purpose is served by comparison of existing copies; by application to the texts of the disciplines of philology and linguistics; by examination of related works of antiquity; by study of biblical citations in works of the Fathers of the Church and other authors; and by other means of literary study.

Since about 1920, the sayings of Christ have been a particular object of New Testament study, the purpose being to analyze the forms of expression used by the Evangelists in order to ascertain the words actually spoken by him.

Literary Criticism

Literary criticism aims to determine the origin and kinds of literary composition, called forms or genres, employed by the inspired authors. Such determinations are necessary for decision regarding the nature and purpose and, consequently, the meaning of biblical passages. Underlying these studies is the principle that the manner of writing was conditioned by the intention of the authors, the meaning they wanted to convey, and the then-contemporary literary style, mode or medium best adapted to carry their message — e.g., true history, quasi-historical narrative, poems, prayers, hymns, psalms, aphorisms, allegories, discourses. Understanding these media is necessary for the valid interpretation of their message.

Literal Sense

The key to all valid interpretation is the literal sense of biblical passages. Regarding this matter and the relevance to it of the studies and procedures described above, Pius XII wrote the following in the encyclical *Divino afflante Spiritu.*

"What the literal sense of a passage is, is not always as obvious in the speeches and writings of ancient authors of the East as it is in the works of our own time. For what they wished to express is not to be determined by the rules of grammar and philology alone nor solely by the context; the interpreter must, as it were, go back wholly in spirit to those remote centuries of the East and with the aid of history, archeology, ethnology, and other sciences accurately determine what modes of writing, so to speak, the authors of that ancient period would be likely to use and in fact did use. . . . In explaining the Sacred Scripture and in demonstrating and proving its immunity from all error (the Catholic interpreter) should make a prudent use of this means, determine to what extent the manner of expression or literary mode adopted by the sacred writer may lead to a correct and genuine interpretation; and let him be convinced that this part of his office cannot be neglected without serious detriment to Catholic exegesis."

The literal sense of the Bible is the meaning in the mind of and intended by the inspired writer of a book or passage of the Bible. This is determined by the application to texts of the rules of hermeneutics. It is not to be confused with word-for-word literalism.

Typical Sense

The typical sense is the meaning which a passage has not only in itself but also in reference to something else of which it is a type or foreshadowing. A clear example is the account of the Exodus of the Israelites: in its literal sense, it narrates the liberation of the Israelites from death and oppression in Egypt; in its typical sense, it foreshadowed the liberation of men from sin through the redemptive death and resurrection of Christ. The typical sense of this and other passages emerged in the working out of God's plan of salvation history. It did not have to be in the mind of the author of the original passage.

Accommodated Senses

Accommodated, allegorical and consequent senses are figurative and adaptive meanings given to books and passages of the Bible for moral and other purposes. Such interpretations involve the danger of stretching the literal sense beyond proper proportions. Hermeneutical principles require that interpretations like these respect the integrity of the literal sense of the passages in question.

In the Catholic view, the final word on questions of biblical interpretation belongs to the teaching authority of the Church. In other views, generally derived from basic principles stated by Martin Luther, John Calvin and other Reformers, the primacy belongs to individual judgment acting in response to the inner testimony of the Holy Spirit, the edifying nature of biblical subject matter, the sublimity and simplicity of the message of salvation, the intensity with which Christ is proclaimed.

Biblical Studies

The first center for biblical studies, in some strict sense of the term, was the School of Alexandria, founded in the latter half of the second century. It was noted for allegorical exegesis. Literal interpretation was a hallmark of the School of Antioch.

St. Jerome, who produced the Vulgate, and St. Augustine, author of numerous commentaries, were the most important figures in biblical studies during the patristic period. By the time of the latter's death, the Old and New Testament canons had been stabilized. For some centuries afterwards, there was little or no progress in scriptural studies, although collections were made of scriptural excerpts from the writings of the Fathers of the Church, and the systematic reading of Scripture became established as a feature of monastic life.

Advances were made in the 12th and 13th centuries with the introduction of new principles and methods of scriptural analysis stemming from renewed interest in Hebraic studies and the application of dialectics.

By the time of the Reformation, the Bible had become the first book set in movable type, and more than 100 vernacular editions were in use throughout Europe.

The Council of Trent

In the wake of the Reformation, the Council of Trent formally defined the Canon of the Bible; it also reasserted the authoritative role of tradition and the teaching authority of the Church as well as Scripture with respect to the rule of faith. In the heated atmosphere of the 16th and 17th centuries, the Bible was turned into a polemical weapon; Protestants used it to defend their doctrines, and Catholics countered with citations in support of the dogmas of the Church. One result of this state of affairs was a lack of substantial progress in biblical studies during the period.

Toward the end of the 17th century, Louis Cappel, a Protestant, introduced a methodology for textual criticism, and Richard Simon, a Catholic, inaugurated modern literary and historical criticism. Their work was poorly regarded, however, and went into eclipse until about the beginning of the 19th century. It was then taken over by men whose work threatened to destroy the credibility of not only the Bible but Christianity itself.

Rationalists, and later Modernists, denied the reality of the supernatural and doctrine concerning inspiration of the Bible, which they generally regarded as a strictly human production expressive of the religious sense and experience of mankind. In their hands, the tools of positive critical research became weapons for biblical subversion. The defensive Catholic reaction to their work had the temporary effect of alienating scholars of the Church from solid advances in archeology, philology, history, textual and literary criticism.

Catholic Developments

Major influences in bringing about a change in Catholic attitude toward use of these disciplines in biblical studies were two papal encyclicals and two institutes of special study, the Ecole Biblique, founded in Jerusalem in 1890, and the Pontifical Biblical Institute established in Rome in 1909. The encyclical *Providentissimus Deus,* issued by Leo XIII in 1893, marked an important breakthrough; in addition to defending the concept of divine inspiration and the formal inspiration of the Scriptures, it encouraged the study of allied and ancillary sciences and techniques for a more fruitful understanding of the sacred writings. The encyclical *Divino Afflante Spiritu,* 50 years later, gave encouragement for the use of various forms of criticism as tools of biblical research. The documents encouraged the work of scholars and stimulated wide communication of the fruits of their study.

Great changes in the climate and direction of biblical studies have occurred in recent years. One of them has been an increase in cooperative effort among Catholic, Protestant, Orthodox and Jewish scholars. Their common investigation of the Dead Sea Scrolls is well known. More recently productive was the collaboration in England of Catholics and Protestants in turning out a Catholic edition of the Revised Standard Version of the bible.

The development and results of biblical studies in this century have directly and significantly affected all phases of the contemporary renewal movement in the Church. Their influence on theology, liturgy, catechetics, and preaching indicate the importance of their function in the life of the Church.

APOSTLES AND EVANGELISTS

The Apostles were the men selected, trained and commissioned by Christ to preach the Gospel, to baptize, to establish, direct and care for his Church as servants of God and stewards of his mysteries. They were the first bishops of the Church.

St. Matthew's Gospel lists the Apostles in this order: Peter, Andrew, James the Greater, John, Philip, Bartholomew, Thomas, Matthew, James the Less, Jude, Simon and Judas Iscariot. Matthias was elected to fill the place of Judas. Paul became an Apostle by a special call from Christ. Barnabas was called an Apostle.

Two of the Evangelists, John and Matthew, were Apostles. The other two, Luke and Mark, were closely associated with the apostolic college.

Andrew: Born in Bethsaida, brother of Peter, disciple of John the Baptist, a fisherman, the first Apostle called; according to legend, preached the Gospel in Northern Greece, Epirus and Scythia, and was martyred at Patras about 70; in art, is represented with an x-shaped cross, called St. Andrew's Cross; feast, Nov. 30; is honored as the patron of Russia and Scotland.

Barnabas: Originally called Joseph but named Barnabas by the Apostles, among whom he is ranked because of his collaboration with Paul; a Jew of the Diaspora, born on Cyprus; a cousin of Mark and member of the Christian community at Jerusalem, influenced the Apostles to accept Paul, with whom he became a pioneer missionary outside Palestine and Syria, to Antioch, Cyprus and southern Asia Minor; legend says he was martyred on Cyprus during the Neronian persecution; feast, June 11.

Bartholomew (Nathaniel): A friend of Philip; according to various traditions, preached the Gospel in Ethiopia, India, Persia, and Armenia where he was martyred by being flayed and beheaded; in art, is depicted holding a knife, an instrument of his death; feast, Aug. 24 in the Roman Rite, Aug. 25 in the Byzantine Rite.

James the Greater: A Galilean, son of Zebedee, brother of John (with whom he was called a "son of thunder"), a fisherman; with Peter and John, witnessed the raising of Jairus' daughter to life, the transfiguration, the agony of Jesus in the Garden of Gethsemani; first of the Apostles to die, by the sword in 44 during the rule of Herod Agrippa; there is doubt about a journey legend says he made to Spain and also about the authenticity of relics said to be his at Santiago de Compostela; in art, is depicted carrying a pilgrim's bell; feast, July 25 in the Roman Rite, Apr. 30 in the Byzantine Rite.

James the Less: Son of Alphaeus, called "Less" because he was younger in age or shorter in stature than James the Greater; one

of the "catholic" epistles bears his name; was stoned to death in 62 or thrown from the top of the temple in Jerusalem and clubbed to death in 66; in art, is depicted with a club or heavy staff; feast, May 3 in the Roman Rite, Oct. 9 in the Byzantine Rite.

John: A Galilean, son of Zebedee, brother of James the Greater (with whom he was called a "son of thunder"), a fisherman, probably a disciple of John the Baptist, one of the Evangelists, called the "beloved disciple"; with Peter and James the Greater, witnessed the raising of Jairus' daughter to life, the transfiguration, the agony of Jesus in the Garden of Gethsemani; Mary was commended to his special care by Christ; the fourth Gospel, three "catholic" Epistles and Revelation bear his name; according to various accounts, lived at Ephesus in Asia Minor for some time and died a natural death about 100; in art, is represented by an eagle, symbolic of the sublimity of the contents of his Gospel; feast, Dec. 27 in the Roman Rite, May 8 in the Byzantine Rite.

Jude Thaddeus: One of the "catholic" epistles, the shortest, bears his name; various traditions say he preached the Gospel in Mesopotamia, Persia and elsewhere, and was martyred; in art, is depicted with a halberd, the instrument of his death; feast, Oct. 28 in the Roman Rite, June 19 in the Byzantine Rite.

Luke: A Greek convert to the Christian community, called "our most dear physician" by Paul, of whom he was a missionary companion; author of the third Gospel and Acts of the Apostles; the place — Achaia, Bithynia, Egypt — and circumstances of his death are not certain; in art, is depicted as a man, a writer, or an ox (because his Gospel starts at the scene of Temple sacrifice); feast, Oct. 18.

Mark: A cousin of Barnabas and member of the first Christian community at Jerusalem; a missionary companion of Paul and Barnabas, then of Peter; author of the Gospel which bears his name; according to legend, founded the Church at Alexandria, was bishop there and was martyred in the streets of the city; in art, is depicted with his Gospel and a winged lion, symbolic of the voice of John the Baptist crying in the wilderness, at the beginning of his Gospel; feast, Apr. 25.

Matthew: A Galilean, called Levi by Luke and John and the son of Alphaeus by Mark, a tax collector, one of the Evangelists; according to various accounts, preached the Gospel in Judea, Ethiopia, Persia and Parthia, and was martyred; in art, is depicted with a spear, the instrument of his death, and as a winged man in his role as Evangelist; feast, Sept. 21 in the Roman Rite, Nov. 16 in the Byzantine Rite.

Matthias: A disciple of Jesus whom the faithful 11 Apostles chose to replace Judas before the Resurrection; uncertain traditions report that he preached the Gospel in Palestine, Cappadocia or Ethiopia; in art, is represented with a cross and a halberd, the instruments of his death as a martyr; feast, May 14 in the Roman Rite, Aug. 9 in the Byzantine Rite.

Paul: Born at Tarsus, of the tribe of Benjamin, a Roman citizen; participated in the persecution of Christians until the time of his miraculous conversion on the way to Damascus; called by Christ, who revealed himself to him in a special way; became the Apostle of the Gentiles, among whom he did most of his preaching in the course of three major missionary journeys through areas north of Palestine, Cyprus, Asia Minor and Greece; 14 epistles bear his name; two years of imprisonment at Rome, following initial arrest in Jerusalem and confinement at Caesarea, ended with martyrdom, by beheading, outside the walls of the city in 64 or 67 during the Neronian persecution; in art, is depicted in various ways with St. Peter, with a sword, the instrument of his death, in the scene of his conversion; feasts, June 29, Jan. 25 (Roman Rite).

Peter: Simon, son of Jona, born in Bethsaida, brother of Andrew, a fisherman; called Cephas or Peter by Christ who made him the chief of the Apostles and head of the Church as his vicar; named first in the listings of Apostles in the Synoptic Gospels and the Acts of the Apostles; with James the Greater and John, witnessed the raising of Jairus' daughter to life, the transfiguration, the agony of Jesus in the Garden of Gethsemani; was the first to preach the Gospel in and around Jerusalem and was the leader of the first Christian community there; established a local Church in Antioch; presided over the Council of Jerusalem in 51; wrote two "catholic" epistles to the Christians in Asia Minor; established his see in Rome where he spent his last years and was martyred by crucifixion in 64 or 65 during the Neronian persecution; in art, is depicted carrying two keys, symbolic of his primacy in the Church; feasts, June 29, Feb. 22 (Roman Rite).

Philip: Born in Bethsaida; according to legend, preached the Gospel in Phrygia where he suffered martyrdom by crucifixion; feast, May 3 in the Roman Rite, Nov. 14 in the Byzantine Rite.

Simon: Called the Cananean or the Zealot; according to legend, preached in various places in the Near East and suffered martyrdom by being sawed in two; in art, is depicted with a saw, the instrument of his death, or a book, symbolic of his zeal for the Law; feast, Oct. 28 in the Roman Rite, May 10 in the Byzantine Rite.

Thomas (Didymus): Notable for his initial incredulity regarding the Resurrection and his subsequent forthright confession of the divinity of Christ risen from the dead; according to legend, preached the Gospel in places from the Caspian Sea to the Persian Gulf and eventually reached India where he was martyred near Madras; Thomas Christians trace their origin to him; in art, is depicted kneeling before the risen Christ, or with a carpenter's rule and square; feast, July 3 in the Roman Rite, Oct. 6 in the Byzantine Rite.

JUDAS

The Gospels record only a few facts about Judas, the Apostle who betrayed Christ.

The only non-Galilean among the Apostles, he was from Carioth, a town in southern Juda. He was keeper of the purse in the apostolic band. He was called a petty thief by John. He voiced dismay at the waste of money, which he said might have been spent for the poor, in connection with the anointing incident at Bethany. He took the initiative in arranging the betrayal of Christ. Afterwards, he confessed that he had betrayed an innocent man and cast into the Temple the money he had received for that action. Of his death, Matthew says that he hanged himself; the Acts of the Apostles states that he swelled up and burst open; both reports deal more with the meaning than the manner of his death — the misery of the death of a sinner.

The consensus of speculation over the reason why Judas acted as he did in betraying Christ focuses on disillusionment and unwillingness to accept the concept of a suffering Messiah and personal suffering of his own as an Apostle.

APOSTOLIC FATHERS, FATHERS, DOCTORS OF THE CHURCH

The writers listed below, were outstanding and authoritative witnesses to authentic Christian belief and practice, and played significant roles in giving them expression.

Apostolic Fathers

The Apostolic Fathers were Christian writers of the first and second centuries who are known or believed to have had personal relations with the Apostles, and whose writings echo genuine apostolic teaching.

Chief in importance are: St. Clement (d.c. 97), bishop of Rome and third successor of St. Peter in the papacy; St. Ignatius (50-c. 107), bishop of Antioch and second successor of St. Peter in that see, reputed to be a disciple of St. John; St. Polycarp (69-155), bishop of Smyrna and a disciple of St. John. The authors of the *Didache* and the *Epistle of Barnabas* are also numbered among the Apostolic Fathers.

Other early ecclesiastical writers included: St. Justin Martyr (100-165), of Asia Minor and Rome, a layman and apologist; St. Irenaeus (130-202), bishop of Lyons, who opposed Gnosticism; and St. Cyprian (210-258), bishop of Carthage, who opposed Novatianism.

Fathers and Doctors

The Fathers of the Church were theologians and writers of the first eight centuries who were outstanding for sanctity and learning. They were such authoritative witnesses to the belief and teaching of the Church that their unanimous acceptance of doctrines as divinely revealed has been regarded as evidence that such doctrines were so received by the Church in line with apostolic tradition and Sacred Scripture. Their unanimous rejection of doctrines branded them as heretical. Their writings, however, were not necessarily free of error in all respects.

The greatest of these Fathers were: Sts. Ambrose, Augustine, Jerome and Gregory the Great in the West; Sts. John Chrysostom, Basil the Great, Gregory of Nazianzen and Athanasius in the East.

The Doctors of the Church were ecclesiastical writers of eminent learning and sanctity who have been given this title because of the great advantage the Church has derived from their work. These writings, however, were not necessarily free of error in all respects.

Albert the Great, St. (c. 1200-1280): Born in Swabia, Germany; Dominican; bishop of Regensburg (1260-1262); wrote extensively on logic, natural sciences, ethics, metaphysics, Scripture, systematic theology; contributed to development of Scholasticism; teacher of St. Thomas Aquinas; canonized and proclaimed doctor, 1931; named patron of natural scientists, 1941; called Doctor Universalis, Doctor Expertus; feast, Nov. 15.

Alphonsus Liguori, St. (1696-1787): Born near Naples, Italy; bishop of Agatha of the Goths (1762-1775); founder of the Redemptorists; in addition to his principal work, *Theologiae Moralis* wrote on prayer, the spiritual life, and doctrinal subjects in response to controversy; canonized, 1839; proclaimed doctor, 1871; named patron of confessors and moralists, 1950; feast, Aug. 1.

Ambrose, St. (c. 340-397): Born in Treves, Germany; bishop of Milan (374-397); one of the strongest opponents of Arianism in the West; his homilies and other writings — on faith, the Holy Spirit, the Incarnation, the sacraments and other subjects — were pastoral and practical; influenced the development of a liturgy at Milan which was named for him; Father and Doctor of the Church; feast, Dec. 7.

Anselm, St. (1033-1109): Born in Aosta, Piedmont, Italy; Benedictine; archbishop of Canterbury (1093-1109); in addition to his principal work, *Cur Deus Homo,* on the atonement and reconciliation of man with God through Christ, wrote about the existence and attributes of God and defended the *Filioque* explanation of the procession of the Holy Spirit from the Father and the Son; canonized, 1494; proclaimed doctor, 1720; called Father of Scholasticism; feast, Apr. 21.

Anthony of Padua, St. (1195-1231): Born in Lisbon, Portugal; first theologian of the Franciscan Order; preacher; canonized, 1232; proclaimed doctor, 1946; called Evangelical Doctor; feast, June 13.

Athanasius, St. (c. 297-373): Born in Alexandria, Egypt; bishop of Alexandria (328-373); participant in the Council of Nicaea I while still a deacon; dominant opponent of Arians whose errors regarding Christ he refuted in *Apology against the Arians, Discourses against the Arians,* and other works; Father and Doctor of the Church; called Father of Orthodoxy; feast, May 2.

Augustine, St. (354-430): Born in Tagaste, North Africa; bishop of Hippo (395-430) after conversion from Manichaeism; works include the autobiographical and mystical *Confessions, City of God,* treatises on the Trinity, grace, passages of the Bible, and doctrines called into question and denied by Manichaeans, Pelagians and Donatists; had strong and lasting influence on Christian theology and philosophy; Father and Doctor of the Church; called Doctor of Grace; feast, Aug. 28.

Basil the Great, St. (c. 329-379): Born in Caesarea, Cappadocia, Asia Minor; bishop of Caesarea (370-379); wrote three books *Contra Eunomium* in refutation of Arian errors, a treatise on the Holy Spirit, many homilies, and several rules for monastic life, on which he had lasting influence; Father and Doctor of the Church; called Father of Monasticism in the East; feast, Jan. 2.

Bede the Venerable, St. (c. 673-735): Born in Northumberland, England; Benedictine; in addition to his principal work, *Ecclesiastical History of the English Nation* (covering the period 597-731), wrote scriptural commentaries; regarded as probably the most learned man in Western Europe of his time; called Father of English History; feast, May 25.

Bernard of Clairvaux, St. (c. 1090-1153): Born near Dijon, France; abbot; monastic reformer, called the second founder of the Cistercian Order; mystical theologian with great influence on devotional life; opponent of the rationalism brought forward by Abelard and others; canonized, 1174; proclaimed doctor, 1830; called Mellifluous Doctor because of his eloquence; feast, Aug. 20.

Bonaventure, St. (c. 1217-1274): Born near Viterbo, Italy; Franciscan; bishop of Albano (1273-1274); cardinal; wrote *Itinerarium Mentis in Deum, De Reductione Artium ad Theologiam, Breviloquium,* scriptural commentaries, additional mystical works affecting devotional life, and a life of St. Francis of Assisi; canonized, 1482; proclaimed doctor, 1588; called Seraphic Doctor; feast, July 15.

Catherine of Siena, St. (c. 1347-1380): Born in Siena, Italy; member of the Third Order of St. Dominic; mystic; authored a long series of letters, mainly concerning spiritual instruction and encouragement, to associates, and

Dialogue, a spiritual testament in four treatises; was active in support of a crusade against the Turks and efforts to end war between papal forces and the Florentine allies; had great influence in inducing Gregory XI to return himself and the Curia to Rome in 1376, to end the Avignon period of the papacy; canonized, 1461; proclaimed the second woman doctor, Oct. 4, 1970; feast, Apr. 29.

Cyril of Alexandria, St. (c. 376-444): Born in Egypt; bishop of Alexandria (412-444); wrote treatises on the Trinity, the Incarnation and other subjects, mostly in refutation of Nestorian errors; made key contributions to the development of Christology; presided at the Council of Ephesus, 431; proclaimed doctor, 1882; feast, June 27.

Cyril of Jerusalem, St. (c. 315-387): Bishop of Jerusalem (350-387); vigorous opponent of Arianism; principal work, *Catecheses,* a pre-baptismal explanation of the creed of Jerusalem; proclaimed doctor, 1882; feast, Mar. 18.

Ephraem, St. (c. 306-373): Born in Nisibis, Mesopotamia; counteracted the spread of Gnostic and Arian errors with poems and hymns of his own composition; wrote also on the Eucharist and Mary; proclaimed doctor, 1920; called Deacon of Edessa and Harp of the Holy Spirit; feast, June 9.

Francis de Sales, St. (1567-1622): Born in Savoy; bishop of Geneva (1602-1622); spiritual writer with strong influence on devotional life through treatises such as *Introduction to a Devout Life,* and *The Love of God;* canonized, 1665; proclaimed doctor, 1877; patron of Catholic writers and the Catholic press; feast, Jan. 24.

Gregory Nazianzen, St. (c. 330-c. 390): Born in Arianzus, Cappadocia, Asia Minor; bishop of Constantinople (381-390); vigorous opponent of Arianism; in addition to five theological discourses on the Nicene Creed and the Trinity for which he is best known, wrote letters and poetry; Father and Doctor of the Church; called the Christian Demosthenes because of his eloquence and, in the Eastern Church, The Theologian; feast, Jan. 2.

Gregory I, the Great, St. (c. 540-604): Born in Rome; pope (590-604): wrote many scriptural commentaries, a compendium of theology in the *Book of Morals* based on Job, *Dialogues* concerning the lives of saints, the immortality of the soul, death, purgatory, heaven and hell, and 14 books of letters; enforced papal supremacy and established the position of the pope vis-a-vis the emperor; worked for clerical and monastic reform and the observance of clerical celibacy; Father and Doctor of the Church; feast, Sept. 3.

Hilary of Poitiers, St. (c. 315-368): Born in Poitiers, France; bishop of Poitiers (c. 353-368); wrote *De Synodis,* with the Arian controversy in mind, and *De Trinitate,* the first lengthy study of the doctrine in Latin; introduced Eastern theology to the West; contributed to the development of hymnology; proclaimed doctor, 1851; called the Athanasius of the West because of his vigorous defense of the divinity of Christ against Arians; feast, Jan. 13.

Isidore of Seville, St. (c. 560-636): Born in Cartagena, Spain; bishop of Seville (c. 600-636); in addition to his principal work *Etymologiae,* an encyclopedia of the knowledge of his day, wrote on theological and historical subjects; regarded as the most learned man of his time; proclaimed doctor, 1722; feast, Apr. 4.

Jerome, St. (c. 343-420): Born in Stridon, Dalmatia; translated the Old Testament from Hebrew into Latin and revised the existing Latin translation of the New Testament to produce the Vulgate version of the Bible; wrote scriptural commentaries and treatises on matters of controversy; regarded as Father and Doctor of the Church from the eighth century; called Father of Biblical Science; feast, Sept. 30.

John Chrysostom, St. (c. 347-407): Born in Antioch, Asia Minor; archbishop of Constantinople (398-407); wrote homilies, scriptural commentaries and letters of wide influence in addition to a classical treatise on the priesthood; proclaimed doctor by the Council of Chalcedon, 451; called the greatest of the Greek Fathers; named patron of preachers, 1909; called golden-mouthed because of his eloquence; feast, Sept. 13.

John Damascene, St. (c. 675-c. 749): Born in Damascus, Syria; monk; wrote *Fountain of Wisdom,* a three-part work including a history of heresies and an exposition of the Christian faith, three *Discourses against the Iconoclasts,* homilies on Mary, biblical commentaries and treatises on moral subjects; proclaimed doctor, 1890; called golden speaker because of his eloquence; feast, Dec. 4.

John of the Cross, St. (1542-1591): Born in Old Castile, Spain; Carmelite; founder of Discalced Carmelites; one of the greatest mystical theologians, wrote *The Ascent of Mt. Carmel — The Dark Night, The Spiritual Canticle, The Living Flame of Love;* canonized, 1726; proclaimed doctor, 1926; called Doctor of Mystical Theology; feast, Dec. 14.

Lawrence of Brindisi, St. (1559-1619): Born in Brindisi, Italy; Franciscan (Capuchin); vigorous preacher of strong influence in the post-Reformation period; 15 tomes of collected works include scriptural commentaries, sermons, homilies and doctrinal writings; canonized, 1881; proclaimed doctor, 1959; feast, July 21.

Leo I, the Great, St. (c. 400-461): Born in Tuscany, Italy; pope (440-461); wrote the *Tome of Leo,* to explain doctrine concerning the two natures and one Person of Christ, against the background of the Nestorian and Monophysite heresies; other works included sermons, letters, and writings against the errors of Manichaeism and Pelagianism; was instrumental in dissuading Attila from sacking Rome in 452; proclaimed doctor, 1574; feast, Nov. 10.

Peter Canisius, St. (1521-1597): Born in Nijmegen, Holland; Jesuit; wrote popular expositions of the Catholic faith in several catechisms which were widely circulated in 20 editions in his lifetime alone; was one of the moving figures in the Counter-Reformation period, especially in southern and western Germany; canonized and proclaimed doctor, 1925; feast, Dec. 21.

Peter Chrysologus, St. (c. 400-450): Born in Imola, Italy; served as archbishop of Ravenna (c. 433-450); his sermons and writings, many of which were designed to counteract Monophysitism, were pastoral and practical; proclaimed doctor, 1729; feast, July 30.

Peter Damian, St. (1007-1072): Born in Ravenna, Italy; Benedictine; cardinal; his writings and sermons, many of which concerned ecclesiastical and clerical reform, were pastoral and practical; proclaimed doctor, 1828; feast, Feb. 21.

Robert Bellarmine, St. (1542-1621): Born in Tuscany, Italy; Jesuit; archbishop of Capua (1602-1605); wrote *Controversies,* a three-volume exposition of doctrine under attack during and after the Reformation, two catechisms and the spiritual work, *The Art of Dying* Well; was an authority on ecclesiology

and Church-state relations; canonized, 1930; proclaimed doctor, 1931; feast, Sept. 17.

Teresa of Avila, St. (1515-1582): Born in Avila, Spain; entered the Carmelite Order, 1535; in the early 1560's, initiated a primitive Carmelite, discalced-Alcantarine reform which greatly influenced men and women religious, especially in Spain; wrote extensively on spiritual and mystical subjects; principal works included her *Autobiography, Way of Perfection, The Interior Castle, Meditations on the Canticle, The Foundations, Visitation of the Disealced Nuns;* canonized, 1614; proclaimed first woman doctor, Sept. 27, 1970; feast, Oct. 15.

Thomas Aquinas, St. (1225-1274): Born near Naples, Italy; Dominican; teacher and writer on virtually the whole range of philosophy and theology; principal works were *Summa contra Gentiles,* a manual and systematic defense of Christian doctrine, and *Summa Theologiae,* a new (at that time) exposition of theology on philosophical principles; canonized, 1323; proclaimed doctor, 1567; called Doctor Communis, Doctor Angelicus, the Great Synthesizer because of the way in which he related faith and reason, theology and philosophy (especially that of Aristotle), and systematized the presentation of Christian doctrine; named patron of Catholic schools and education, 1880; feast, Jan. 28.

CREEDS

Creeds are formal and official statements of Christian doctrine. As summaries of the principal truths of faith, they are standards of orthodoxy and are useful for instructional purposes, for actual profession of the faith, and for expression of the faith in the liturgy.

The classical creeds are the Apostles' Creed and the Creed of Nicaea-Constantinople. Two others are the Athanasian Creed and the Creed of Pius IV.

Apostles' Creed

Text: I believe in God, the Father almighty, Creator of heaven and earth.

And in Jesus Christ, his only Son, our Lord; who was conceived by the Holy Spirit, born of the Virgin Mary, suffered under Pontius Pilate, was crucified, died, and was buried. He descended into hell; the third day he arose again from the dead; he ascended into heaven, sits at the right hand of God, the Father almighty; from thence he shall come to judge the living and the dead.

I believe in the Holy Spirit, the holy Catholic Church, the communion of saints, the forgiveness of sins, the resurrection of the body, and life everlasting. Amen.

Background: The Apostles' Creed reflects the teaching of the Apostles but is not of apostolic origin. It probably originated in the second century as a rudimentary formula of faith professed by catechumens before the reception of baptism. Baptismal creeds in

fourth-century use at Rome and elsewhere in the West closely resembled the present text, which was quoted in a handbook of Christian doctrine written between 710 and 724. This text was in wide use throughout the West by the ninth century. The Apostles' Creed is common to all Christian confessional churches in the West, but is not used in Eastern Churches.

Nicene Creed

The following translation of the Latin text of the creed was prepared by the International Committee on English in the Liturgy.

Text: We believe in one God, the Father, the Almighty, maker of heaven and earth, of all that is seen and unseen.

We believe in one Lord, Jesus Christ, the only Son of God, eternally begotten of the Father, God from God, Light from Light, true God from true God, begotten, not made, one in Being with the Father. Through him all things were made. For us men and for our salvation he came down from heaven: by the power of the Holy Spirit he was born of the Virgin Mary, and became man. For our sake he was crucified under Pontius Pilate; he suffered, died, and was buried. On the third day he rose again in fulfillment of the Scriptures; he ascended into heaven and is seated at the right hand of the Father. He will come again in glory to judge the living and the dead, and his kingdom will have no end.

We believe in the Holy Spirit, the Lord, the giver of life, who proceeds from the Father and the Son. With the Father and the Son he is worshiped and glorified. He has spoken through the prophets.

We believe in one holy catholic and apostolic Church. We acknowledge one baptism for the forgiveness of sins. We look for the resurrection of the dead, and the life of the world to come. Amen.

Background: The Nicene Creed (Creed of Nicaea-Constantinople) consists of elements of doctrine contained in an early baptismal creed of Jerusalem and enactments of the Council of Nicaea (325) and the Council of Constantinople (381). Its strong trinitarian content reflects the doctrinal errors, especially of Arianism, it served to counteract. Theologically, it is much more sophisticated than the Apostles' Creed. Since late in the fifth century, the Nicene Creed has been the only creed in liturgical use in the Eastern Churches. The Western Church adopted it for liturgical use by the end of the eighth century.

The Athanasian Creed

The Athanasian Creed, which has a unique structure, is a two-part summary of doctrine concerning the Trinity and the Incarnation-Redemption bracketed at the beginning and end with the statement that belief in the cited truths is necessary for salvation; it also contains a number of anathemas or condemnatory clauses regarding doctrinal errors. Although attributed to St. Athanasius, it was probably written after his death, between 381 and 428, and may have been authored by St. Ambrose. It is not accepted in the East; in the West, it has place in the liturgy of some other Christian churches as well as in the Roman-Rite Liturgy of the Hours and for the Solemnity of the Holy Trinity.

Creed of Pius IV

The Creed of Pius IV, also called the Profession of Faith of the Council of Trent, was promulgated in the bull *Injunctum Nobis,* Nov. 13, 1564. It is a summary of doctrine defined by the council concerning: Scripture and tradition, original sin and justification, the Mass and sacraments, veneration of the saints, indulgences, the primacy of the See of Rome. It was slightly modified in 1887 to include doctrinal formulations of the First Vatican Council.

REDDITIO OF CREED

The "giving back," by profession, of a baptismal creed by candidates for baptism to a bishop or his representative was one of the immediate preliminaries to reception of the sacrament at the conclusion of the catechumenate in the early church.

The interrogation concerning truths of faith in the present baptismal rite is reminiscent of this ancient practice.

CREED OF PEOPLE OF GOD

This Creed of the People of God was proclaimed by Paul VI at a Mass celebrated June 30, 1968, to mark the conclusion of the 1967-68 Year of Faith.

(This translation was circulated by NC News Service. Subheads have been added.)

Introduction

1. With this solemn liturgy we end the celebration of the nineteenth centenary of the martyrdom of the holy Apostles Peter and Paul, and thus close the Year of Faith. We dedicated it to the commemoration of the holy Apostles in order that we might give witness to our steadfast will to be faithful to the deposit of the faith which they transmitted to us, and that we might strengthen our desire to live by it in the historical circumstances in which the Church finds herself in her pilgrimage in the midst of the world.

2. We feel it our duty to give public thanks to all who responded to our invitation by bestowing on the Year of Faith a splendid completeness through the deepening of their personal adhesion to the Word of God, through the renewal in various communities of the profession of faith, and through the testimony of a Christian life. To our brothers in the episcopate especially, and to all the faithful of the holy Catholic Church, we express our appreciation and we grant our blessing.

Reasons for Profession

3. Likewise, we deem that we must fulfill the mandate entrusted by Christ to Peter, whose successor we are, the least in merit; namely, to confirm our brothers in the faith. With the awareness, certainly, of our human weakness, yet with all the strength impressed on our spirit by such a command, we shall accordingly make a profession of faith, pronounce a creed which, without being — strictly speaking — a dogmatic definition, repeats in substance, with some developments called for by the spiritual condition of our time, the Creed of Nicaea, the creed of the immortal tradition of the holy Church of God.

4. In making this profession, we are aware of the disquiet which agitates certain modern quarters with regard to the faith. They do not escape the influence of a world being profoundly changed, in which so many certainties are being disputed or discussed. We see even Catholics allowing themselves to be seized by a kind of passion for change and novelty. The Church, most assuredly, has always the duty to carry on the effort to study more deeply and to present in a manner ever better adapted to successive generations the unfathomable mysteries of God, rich for all in fruits of salvation. But, at the same time, the greatest care must be taken, while fulfilling the indispensable duty of research, to do no injury to the teachings of Christian doctrine;

for that would be to give rise, as is unfortunately seen in these days, to disturbance and perplexity in many faithful souls.

5. It is important in this respect to recall that, beyond scientifically verified phenomena, the intellect which God has given us reaches that which is, and not merely the subjective expression of the structures and development of consciousness: and, on the other hand, that the task of interpretation — of hermeneutics — is to try to understand and extricate, while respecting the word expressed, the sense conveyed by a text and not to recreate in some fashion this sense in accordance with arbitrary hypotheses.

Response to Expectations

6. But, above all, we place our unshakable confidence in the Holy Spirit, the soul of the Church, and in the theological faith upon which rests the life of the Mystical Body. We know that souls await the word of the Vicar of Christ, and we respond to that expectation with the instructions which we regularly give. But today we are given an opportunity to make a more solemn utterance.

7. On this day which is chosen to close the Year of Faith, on this feast of the Blessed Apostles Peter and Paul, we have wished to offer to the living God the homage of a profession of faith. And, as once at Caesarea Philippi the Apostle Peter spoke on behalf of the Twelve to make a true confession, beyond human opinions, of Christ as Son of the living God, so today his humble successor, Pastor of the Universal Church, raises his voice to give, on behalf of all the People of God, a firm witness to the divine truth entrusted to the Church to be announced to all nations.

Complete and Explicit

We have wished our profession of faith to be complete and explicit to a high degree, in order that it may respond in a fitting way to the need of light felt by so many faithful souls and by all those in the world, to whatever spiritual family they belong, who are in search of the truth.

To the glory of God Most Holy and of Our Lord Jesus Christ, trusting in the aid of the Blessed Virgin Mary and of the Holy Apostles Peter and Paul, for the profit and edification of the Church, in the name of all the pastors and all the faithful, we now pronounce this profession of faith, in full spiritual communion with you all, beloved brothers and sons.

Profession of Faith

8. We believe in one only God, Father, Son and Holy Spirit, Creator of things visible such as this world in which our transient life passes, of things invisible such as the pure spirits which are also called angels, and Creator in each man of his spiritual and immortal soul.

The Holy Trinity

9. We believe that this only God is absolutely one in his infinitely holy essence as also in all his perfections, in his omnipotence, his infinite knowledge, his providence, his will and his love. He is He Who Is, as he revealed to Moses; and he is Love, as the Apostle John teaches us; so that these two names, Being and Love, express ineffably the same divine reality of him who has wished to make himself known to us and who, "dwelling in light inaccessible" (1 Tm. 6:16), is in himself above every name, above every thing and above every created intellect. God alone can give us right and full knowledge of this reality by revealing himself as Father, Son and Holy Spirit, in whose eternal life we are by grace called to share, here below in the obscurity of faith and after death in eternal light. The mutual bonds which eternally constitute the Three Persons, who are each one and the same Divine Being, are the blessed inmost life of God Thrice Holy, infinitely beyond all that we can conceive in human measure. We give thanks, however, to the Divine Goodness that very many believers can testify with us before men to the unity of God, even though they know not the mystery of the Most Holy Trinity.

10. We believe, then, in the Father who eternally begets the Son; in the Son, the Word of God, who is eternally begotten; in the Holy Spirit, the uncreated Person who proceeds from the Father and the Son as their eternal love. Thus, in the Three Divine Persons, coeternal and coequal with each other, the life and beatitude of God perfectly One superabound and are consummated in the supreme excellence and glory proper to uncreated Being, and always "there should be venerated Unity in the Trinity and Trinity in the Unity."

God the Son

11. We believe in our Lord Jesus Christ, who is the Son of God. He is the Eternal Word, born of the Father before time began, and one in substance with the Father *(homoousios Patri)*, and through him all things were made. He was incarnate of the Virgin Mary by the power of the Holy Spirit, and was made man: equal therefore to the Father according to his divinity, and inferior to the Father according to his humanity, and himself one, not by some impossible confusion of his natures, but by the unity of his Person.

12. He dwelt among us, full of grace and truth. He proclaimed and established the kingdom of God and made us know in himself the Father. He gave us his new commandment to love one another as he loved us. He taught us the way of the Beatitudes of the Gospel: poverty in spirit, meekness, suffering borne with patience, thirst after justice, mercy, purity of heart, will for peace, persecu-

tion suffered for justice's sake. Under Pontius Pilate he suffered, the Lamb of God bearing in himself the sins of the world, and he died for us on the cross, saving us by his redeeming blood. He was buried, and, of his own power, rose the third day, raising us by his resurrection to that sharing in the divine life which is the life of grace. He ascended to heaven, and he will come again, this time in glory, to judge the living and the dead: each according to his merits — those who have responded to the love and piety of God going to eternal life, those who have refused them to the end going to the fire that is not extinguished.

And his kingdom will have no end.

God the Holy Spirit

13. We believe in the Holy Spirit, who is Lord and Giver of life, who is adored and glorified together with the Father and the Son. He spoke to us by the prophets; he was sent by Christ after his resurrection and his ascension to the Father; he illuminates, vivifies, proteccts and guides the Church; he purifies the Church's members if they do not shun his grace. His action, which penetrates to the inmost (depths) of the soul, enables man to respond to the call of Jesus: "Be perfect as your heavenly Father is perfect" (Mt. 5:48).

Mary

14. We believe that Mary is the Mother, who remained ever a Virgin, of the Incarnate Word, our God and Savior Jesus Christ, and that, by reason of this singular election, she was; in consideration of the merits of her Son, redeemed in a more eminent manner, preserved from all stain of original sin, and filled with the gift of grace more than all other creatures.

15. Joined by a close and indissoluble bond to the mysteries of the Incarnation and Redemption, the Blessed Virgin, the Immaculate, was at the end of her earthly life raised body and soul to heavenly glory and likened to her risen Son in anticipation of the future lot of all the just: and we believe that the Blessed Mother of God, the New Eve, Mother of the Church, continues in heaven her maternal role with regard to Christ's members, cooperating with the birth and growth of divine life in the souls of the redeemed.

Original Sin

16. We believe that in Adam all have sinned, which means that the original offense committed by him caused human nature, common to all men, to fall to a state in which it bears the consequences of that offense, and which is not the state in which it was at first in our first parents, established as they were in holiness and justice, and in which man knew neither evil nor death. It is human nature so fallen, stripped of the grace that clothed it, injured in its own natural powers and subjected to the dominion of death, that is transmitted to all men, and it is in this sense that every man is born in sin. We therefore hold, with the Council of Trent, that original sin is transmitted with human nature, "not by imitation, but by propagation," and that it is thus "proper to everyone."

17. We believe that our Lord Jesus Christ, by the Sacrifice of the Cross, redeemed us from original sin and all the personal sins committed by each one of us, so that, in accordance with the word of the Apostle, "where sin abounded, grace did more abound" (Rom. 5:20).

Baptism

18. We believe in one baptism instituted by our Lord Jesus Christ for the remission of sins. Baptism should be administered even to little children who have not yet been able to be guilty of any personal sin, in order that, born deprived of supernatural grace, they may be reborn "of water and the Holy Spirit" to the divine life in Christ Jesus.

The Church

19. We believe in one, holy, catholic, and apostolic Church, built by Jesus Christ on that rock which is Peter. She is the Mystical Body of Christ: at the same time a visible society instituted with hierarchical organs, and a spiritual community; the Church on earth, the pilgrim People of God here below, and the Church filled with heavenly blessings; the germ and the first fruits of the Kingdom of God through which the work and the sufferings of Redemption are continued throughout human history, and which looks for its perfect accomplishment beyond time in glory. In the course of time, the Lord Jesus forms his Church by means of the sacraments emanating from his plentitude. By these she makes her members participants in the mystery of the death and resurrection of Christ, in the grace of the Holy Spirit who gives her life and movement. She is therefore holy, though she has sinners in her bosom, because she herself has no other life but that of grace: it is by living by her life that her members are sanctified: it is by removing themselves from her life that they fall into sins and disorders that prevent the radiation of her sanctity. This is why she suffers and does penance for these offenses, of which she has the power to heal her children through the blood of Christ and the gift of the Holy Spirit.

Its Mission and Characteristics

20. Heiress of the divine promises and daughter of Abraham according to the Spirit, through that Israel whose Scriptures she lovingly guards and whose patriarchs and prophets she venerates; founded upon the Apostles and handing on faithfully from century to century their ever-living word and their

powers as pastors in the successor of Peter and the bishops in communion with him; perpetually assisted by the Holy Spirit: — she has the charge of guarding, teaching, explaining and spreading the truth which God revealed in a then-veiled manner by the prophets and fully by the Lord Jesus. We believe all that is contained in the Word of God written or handed down, and all that the Church proposes for belief as divinely revealed, whether by a solemn judgment or by the ordinary and universal magisterium. We believe in the infallibility enjoyed by the successor of Peter when he teaches *ex cathedra* as pastor and teacher of all the faithful, and which is assured also to the episcopal body when it exercises with him the supreme magisterium.

21. We believe that the Church founded by Jesus Christ and for which he prayed is indefectibly one in faith, worship and the bond of hierarchical communion. In the bosom of this Church, the rich variety of liturgical rites and the legitimate diversity of theological and spiritual heritages and special disciplines, far from injuring her unity, make it more manifest.

Hope for Unity

22. Recognizing also the existence, outside the organism of the Church of Christ, of numerous elements of truth and sanctification which belong to her as her own and tend to Catholic unity, and believing in the action of the Holy Spirit who stirs up in the heart of the disciples of Christ love of this unity, we entertain the hope that the Christians who are not yet in the full communion of the one only Church will one day be reunited in one Flock with one only Shepherd.

Necessity of Church for Salvation

23. We believe that the Church is necessary for salvation, because Christ, who is the sole Mediator and Way of salvation, renders himself present for us in his Body which is the Church. But the divine design of salvation embraces all men; and those who, without fault on their part, do not know the Gospel of Christ and his Church, but seek God sincerely, and under the influence of grace endeavor to do his will as recognized through the promptings of their conscience, they, in a number known only to God, can obtain salvation.

Eucharist—Sacrifice, Sacrament

24. We believe that the Mass, celebrated by the priest representing the Person of Christ by virtue of the power received through the sacrament of orders, and offered by him in the name of Christ and the members of his Mystical Body, is the Sacrifice of Calvary rendered sacramentally present on our altars. We believe that, as the bread and wine consecrated by the Lord at the Last Supper were changed into his Body and his Blood which

were to be offered for us on the cross, likewise the bread and wine consecrated by the priest are changed into the Body and Blood of Christ enthroned gloriously in heaven, and we believe that the mysterious presence of the Lord, under what continues to appear to our senses as before, is a true, real and substantial presence.

25. Christ cannot be thus present in this sacrament except by the change into His Body of the reality itself of the bread and the change into his Blood of the reality itself of the wine, leaving unchanged only the properties of the bread and wine which our senses perceive. This mysterious change is very appropriately called by the Church transubstantiation. Every theological explanation which seeks some understanding of this mystery must, in order to be in accord with Catholic faith, maintain that in the reality itself, independently of our mind, the bread and wine have ceased to exist after the consecration, so that it is the adorable Body and Blood of the Lord Jesus that from then on are really before us under the sacramental species of bread and wine, as the Lord willed it, in order to give himself to us as food and to associate us with the unity of his Mystical Body.

26. The unique and indivisible existence of the Lord glorious in heaven is not multiplied, but is rendered present by the sacrament in the many places on earth where Mass is celebrated. And this existence remains present, after the Sacrifice, in the Blessed Sacrament which is, in the tabernacle, the living heart of each of our churches. And it is our very sweet duty to honor and adore in the Blessed Host which our eyes see the Incarnate Word whom they cannot see, and who, without leaving heaven, is made present before us.

The Church and the World

27. We confess that the Kingdom of God begun here below in the Church of Christ is not of this world whose form is passing, and that its proper growth cannot be confounded with the progress of civilization, of science or of human technology, but that it consists in an ever more profound knowledge of the unfathomable riches of Christ, an ever stronger hope in eternal blessings, an ever more ardent response to the love of God, and an ever more generous bestowal of grace and holiness among men. But it is this same love which induces the Church to concern herself constantly about the true temporal welfare of men. Without ceasing to recall to her children that they have not here a lasting dwelling, she also urges them to contribute, each according to his vocation and his means, to the welfare of their earthly city, to promote justice, peace and brotherhood among men, to give their aid freely to their brothers, especially to the poorest and most unfortunate. The deep solicitude of the Church, the Spouse of Christ, for the needs of men, for their joys and hopes,

their griefs and efforts, is therefore nothing other than her great desire to be present to them, in order to illuminate them with the light of Christ and to gather them all in him, their only Savior. This solicitude can never mean that the Church conform herself to the things of this world, or that she lessen the ardor of her expectation of her Lord and of the eternal kingdom.

Last Things, Communion of Faithful

28. We believe in life eternal. We believe that the souls of all those who die in the grace of Christ, whether they must still be purified in purgatory, or whether from the moment they leave their bodies Jesus takes them to paradise as he did for the Good Thief, are the People of God in the eternity beyond death, which will be finally conquered on the day of the resurrection when these souls will be reunited united with their bodies.

MORAL OBLIGATIONS

The basic norm of Christian morality is life in Christ. This involves, among other things, the observance of the Ten Commandments, their fulfillment in the twofold law of love of God and neighbor, the implications of the Sermon on the Mount and the whole New Testament, and membership in the Church established by Christ.

The Ten Commandments

The Ten Commandments, the Decalogue, were given by God through Moses to his Chosen People for the guidance of their moral conduct in accord with the demands of the Covenant he established with them as a divine gift. Their observance was essential to participation in the Covenant and the order of salvation based on it.

In the traditional Catholic enumeration and according to Dt. 5:6-21, the Commandments are:

1. "I, the Lord, am your God . . . You shall not have other gods besides me. You shall not carve idols. . . ."
2. "You shall not take the name of the Lord, your God, in vain. . . ."
3. "Take care to keep holy the Sabbath day. . . ."
4. "Honor your father and your mother. . . ."
5. "You shall not kill."
6. "You shall not commit adultery."
7. "You shall not steal."
8. "You shall not bear dishonest witness against your neighbor."
9. "You shall not covet your neighbor's wife."
10. "You shall not desire your neighbor's house or field, nor his male or female slave, nor his ox or ass, nor anything that belongs to him" (summarily, his goods).

Another version of the Commandments, substantially the same, is given in Ex. 20:1-17.

29. We believe that the multitude of those gathered around Jesus and Mary in paradise forms the Church of heaven, where in eternal beatitude they see God as he is (1 Jn. 3:2), and where they also, in different degrees, are associated with the holy angels in the divine rule exercised by Christ in glory, interceding for us and helping our weakness by their brotherly care.

30. We believe in the communion of all the faithful of Christ, those who are pilgrims on earth, the dead who are attaining their purification, and the blessed in heaven, all together forming one Church; and we believe that in this communion the merciful love of God and his saints is ever listening to our prayers, as Jesus told us: "Ask and you will receive" (Lk. 10:9-10; Jn. 16:24). Thus it is with faith and in hope that we look forward to the resurrection of the dead, and the life of the world to come.

Blessed be God Thrice Holy. Amen.

The traditional enumeration of the Commandments in Protestant usage differs from the above. Thus: two commandments are made of the first, as above; the third and fourth are equivalent to the second and third, as above, and so on; and the 10th includes the ninth and 10th, as above.

Love of God and Neighbor

The first three of the commandments deal directly with man's relations with God, viz.: acknowledgment of one true God and the rejection of false gods and idols; honor due to God and his name; observance of the Sabbath as the Lord's day.

The rest cover interpersonal relationships, viz.: the obedience due to parents and, logically, to other persons in authority, and the obligations of parents to children and of persons in authority to those under their care; respect for life and physical integrity; fidelity in marriage, and chastity; justice and rights; truth; internal respect for faithfulness in marriage, chastity, and the goods of others.

Perfection in Christian Life

The moral obligations of the Ten Commandments are complemented by others flowing from the twofold law of love, the whole substance and pattern of Christ's teaching, and everything implied in full and active membership and participation in the community of salvation formed by Christ in his Church. Some of these matters are covered in other sections of the Almanac under appropriate headings.

Precepts of the Church

The precepts of the Church of Roman Rite oblige Catholics to:

1. Assist at Mass on Sundays and holy days of obligation. (Also, to desist from unnecessary servile work on these days.)

2. Fast and abstain on the days appointed. (The fasting obligation binds persons from the 21st until the 59th birthday; the days of fast are Ash Wednesday and Good Friday. The abstinence obligation binds from the 14th birthday on these days, and is recommended for all Fridays in Lent; it may be obligatory in some dioceses.) These regulations, which have been modified in recent years, are penitential in purpose but do not exhaust obligations of penance. Other ways of doing penance are left to personal option.

3. Confess their sins at least once a year.

4. Receive Holy Communion during the Easter time. (In the US, the Easter time extends from the First Sunday of Lent to Trinity Sunday.)

5. Contribute to the support of the Church.

6. Observe the laws of the Church concerning marriage.

SOCIAL DOCTRINE

Since the end of the last century, Catholic social doctrine has been formulated in a progressive manner in a number of authoritative documents. Outstanding examples are the encyclicals: *Rerum Novarum,* issued by Leo XIII in 1891; *Quadragesimo Anno,* by Pius XI in 1931; *Mater et Magistra* ("Christianity and Social Progress") and *Pacem in Terris* ("Peace on Earth"), by John XXIII in 1961 and 1963, respectively; and *Populorum Progressio* ("Development of Peoples"), by Paul VI in 1967. Pius XII, among other accomplishments of ideological importance in the social field, made a distinctive contribution with his formulation of a plan for world peace and order in Christmas messages from 1939 to 1941, and in other documents.

These documents represent the most serious attempts in modern times to systematize the social implications of the Gospel and the rest of divine revelation as well as the socially relevant writings of the Fathers and Doctors of the Church. Their contents are theological penetrations into social life, with particular reference to human rights, the needs of the poor and those in underdeveloped countries, and humane conditions of life, freedom, justice and peace. In some respects, they read like juridical documents; underneath, however, they are Gospel-oriented and pastoral in intention.

Nature of the Doctrine

Pope John, writing in *Christianity and Social Progress,* made the following statement about the nature and scope of the doctrine stated in the encyclicals in particular and related writings in general.

"What the Catholic Church teaches and declares regarding the social life and relationships of men is beyond question for all time valid.

"The cardinal point of this teaching is that individual men are necessarily the foundation, cause, and end of all social institutions . . . insofar as they are social by nature, and raised to an order of existence that transcends and subdues nature.

"Beginning with this very basic principle whereby the dignity of the human person is affirmed and defended, Holy Church — especially during the last century and with the assistance of learned priests and laymen, specialists in the field — has arrived at clear social teachings whereby the mutual relationships of men are ordered. Taking general norms into account, these principles are in accord with the nature of things and the changed conditions of man's social life, or with the special genius of our day. Moreover, these norms can be approved by all."

The Church In the World

Even more Gospel-oriented and pastoral in a distinctive way is the *Pastoral Constitution on the Church in the Modern World* promulgated by the Second Vatican Council in 1965.

Its purpose was to search out the signs of God's presence and meaning in and through the events of this time in human history. Accordingly, it dealt with the situation of men in present, circumstances of profound change, challenge and crisis on all levels of life.

The first part of the constitution developed the theme of the Church and man's calling, and focused attention on the dignity of the human person, the problem of atheism, the community of mankind, man's activity throughout the world, and the serving and saving role of the Church in the world. This portion of the document, it has been said, represents the first presentation by the Church in an official text of an organized Christian view of man and society.

The second part of the document considered several problems of special urgency: fostering the nobility of marriage and the family (see Marriage Doctrine), the proper development of culture, socio-economic life, the life of the political community, the fostering of peace (see Peace and War), and the promotion of a community of nations.

In conclusion, the constitution called·for action to implement doctrine regarding the role and work of the Church for the total good of mankind.

Following are a number of key excerpts from the ideological heart of the constitution.

One Human Family and Community: "God, who has fatherly concern for everyone, has willed that all men should constitute one family and treat one another in a spirit of brotherhood. . . .

"For this reason, love for God and neighbor is the first and greatest commandment. Sacred Scripture . . . teaches us that the love of God cannot be separated from love of neighbor. . . . To men growing daily more dependent on one another, and to a world becoming more unified every day, this truth proves (No. 24).

Human Person Is Central: "Man's social nature makes it evident that the progress of the human person and the advance of society itself hinge on each other. For the beginning, the subject and the goal of all social institutions is and must be the human person, which for its part and by its very nature stands completely in need of social life. This social life is not something added on to man. Hence, through his dealings with others, through reciprocal duties, and through fraternal dialogue he develops all his gifts and is able to rise to his destiny."

Influence of Social Circumstances: "But if by this social life the human person is greatly aided in responding to his destiny, even in its religious dimensions, it cannot be denied that men are often diverted from doing good and spurred toward evil by the social circumstances in which they live and are immersed from their birth. To be sure the disturbances which so frequently occur in the social order result in part from the natural tensions of economic, political, and social forms. But at a deeper level they flow from man's pride and selfishness, which contaminate even the social sphere. When the structure of affairs is flawed by the consequences of sin, man, already born with a bent toward evil, finds there new inducements to sin, which cannot be overcome without strenuous efforts and the assistance of grace" (No. 25).

"Every social group must take account of the needs and legitimate aspirations of other groups, and even of the general welfare of the entire human family."

Human Necessities: "At the same time however, there is a growing awareness of the exalted dignity proper to the human person, since he stands above all things, and his rights and duties are universal and inviolable. Therefore, there must be made available to all men everything necessary for leading a life truly human, such as food, clothing, and shelter; the right to choose a state of life freely and to found a family, the right to education, to employment, to a good reputation, to respect, to appropriate information, to activity in accord with the upright norm of one's own conscience, to protection of privacy and to rightful freedom in matters religious too.

"Hence, the social order and its development must unceasingly work to the benefit of the human person if the disposition of affairs is to be subordinate to the personal realm and not contrariwise, as the Lord indicated when He said that the Sabbath was made for man, and not man for the Sabbath" (as Pope John XXIII noted in *Mater et Magistra*).

Improvement of Social Order: "This social order requires constant improvement. It must be founded on truth, built on justice, and animated by love; in freedom it should grow every day toward a more humane balance. An improvement in attitudes and widespread changes in society will have to take place if these objectives are to be gained.

"God's Spirit, who with a marvelous providence directs the unfolding of time and renews the face of the earth, is not absent from this development. The ferment of the gospel, too, has aroused and continues to arouse in man's heart the irresistible requirements of his dignity" (No. 26).

Regard for Neighbor as Another Self: "Coming down to practical and particularly urgent consequences, this Council lays stress on reverence for man; everyone must consider his every neighbor without exception as another self, taking into account first of all his life and the means necessary to living it with dignity. . . .

"In our times a special obligation binds us to make ourselves the neighbor of absolutely every person, and of actively helping him when he comes across our path. . . ."

Inhuman Evils: ". . . Whatever is opposed to life itself, such as any type of murder, genocide, abortion, euthanasia, or willful self-destruction, whatever violates the integrity of the human person, such as mutilation, torments inflicted on body or mind, attempts to coerce the will itself; whatever insults human dignity, such as subhuman living conditions, arbitrary imprisonment, deportation, slavery, prostitution, the selling of women and children; as well as disgraceful working conditions, where men are treated as mere tools for profit, rather than as free and responsible persons; all these things and others of their like are infamies indeed. They poison human society, but they do more harm to those who practice them than those who suffer from the injury. Moreover, they are a supreme dishonor to the Creator" (No. 27).

Respect for Those Who Are Different: "Respect and love ought to be extended also to those who think or act differently than we do in social, political, and religious matters. In fact, the more deeply we come to understand their ways of thinking through such courtesy and love, the more easily will we be able to enter into dialogue with them."

Distinction between Error and Person in Error: "This love and good will, to be sure, must in no way render us indifferent to truth and goodness. Indeed love itself impels the disciples of Christ to speak the saving truth to all men. But it is necessary to distinguish between error, which always merits repudiation, and the person in error, who never loses the dignity of being a person, even when he is flawed by false or inadequate religious notions. God alone is the judge and searcher of hearts; for that reason He forbids us to make judgments about the internal guilt of anyone.

"The teaching of Christ even requires that we forgive injuries, and extends the law of love to include every enemy . . ." (No. 28).

Men Are Equal but Different: "Since all men possess a rational soul and are created in God's likeness, since they have the same nature and origin, have been redeemed by Christ, and enjoy the same divine calling and destiny, the basic equality of all must receive increasingly greater recognition.

"True, all men are not alike from the point of view of varying physical power and the diversity of intellectual and moral resources. Nevertheless, with respect to the fundamental rights of the person, every type of discrimination, whether social or cultural, whether based on sex, race, color, social condition, language, or religion, is to be overcome and eradicated as contrary to God's intent. . . ."

Humane Conditions for All: ". . . Although rightful differences exist between men, the equal dignity of persons demands that a more humane and just condition of life be brought about. For excessive economic and social differences between the members of the one human family and population groups cause scandal, and militate against social justice, equity, the dignity of the human person, as well as social and international peace.

"Human institutions, both private and public, must labor to minister to the dignity and purpose of man. At the same time let them put up a stubborn fight against any kind of slavery, whether social or political, and safeguard the basic rights of man under every political system. Indeed human institutions themselves must be accommodated by degrees to the highest of all realities, spiritual ones, even though, meanwhile, a long enough time will be required before they arrive at the desired goal" (No. 29).

"Profound and rapid changes make it particularly urgent that no one, ignoring the trend of events or drugged by laziness, content himself with a merely individualistic morality. It grows increasingly true that the obligations of justice and love are fulfilled only if each person, contributing to the common good, according to his own abilities and the needs of others, also promotes and assists the public and private institutions dedicated to bettering the conditions of human life."

Social Necessities Are Prime Duties: "Let everyone consider it his sacred obligation to count social necessities among the primary duties of modern man, and to pay heed to them. For the more unified the world becomes, the more plainly do the offices of men extend beyond particular groups and spread by degrees to the whole world. But this challenge cannot be met unless individual men and their associations cultivate in themselves the moral and social virtues, and promote them in society. Thus, with the needed help of divine grace, men who are truly new and artisans of a new humanity can be forthcoming" (No. 30).

"In order for individual men to discharge with greater exactness the obligations of their conscience toward themselves and the various groups to which they belong, they must be carefully educated to a higher degree of culture through the use of the immense resources available today to the human race. . . ."

Living Conditions and Freedom: ". . . A man can scarcely arrive at the needed sense of responsibility unless his living conditions allow him to become conscious of his dignity, and to rise to his destiny by spending himself for God and for others. But human freedom is often crippled when a man falls into extreme poverty, just as it withers when he indulges in too many of life's comforts and imprisons himself in a kind of splendid isolation. Freedom acquires new strength, by contrast, when a man consents to the unavoidable requirements of social life, takes on the manifold demands of human partnership, and commits himself to the service of the human community.

"Hence, the will to play one's role in common endeavors should be everywhere encouraged . . ." (No. 31).

Communitarian Character of Life: "God did not create man for life in isolation, but, for the formation of social unity. So also 'it has pleased God to make men holy and save them not merely as individuals, without any mutual bonds, but by making them into a single people, a people which acknowledges Him in truth and serves Him in holiness' *(Dogmatic Constitution on the Church,* No. 9). So from the beginning of salvation history He has chosen men not just as individuals but as members of a certain community. Revealing His mind to them, God called these chosen ones 'His people' (Ex. 3:7-12), and, furthermore, made a covenant with them on Sinai.

"This communitarian character is developed and consummated in the work of Jesus Christ. For the very Word made flesh willed to share in the human fellowship. He was present at the wedding of Cana, visited the house of Zacchaeus, ate with publicans and sinners. He revealed the love of the Father and the sublime vocation of man in terms of the most common of social realities and by making use of the speech and the imagery of plain everyday life. Willingly obeying the laws of His country, He sanctified those human ties, especially family ones, from which social relationships arise. He chose to lead the life proper to an artisan of His time and place.

"In His preaching He clearly taught the sons of God to treat one another as brothers. In His prayers He pleaded that all His disciples might be 'one.' Indeed, as the Redeemer of all, He offered Himself for all even to the point of death. . . . He commanded His apostles to preach to all peoples the gospel message so that the human race might become the Family of God, in which the fullness of the Law would be love."

The Community Founded by Christ: "As the first-born of many brethren and through the gift of His Spirit, He founded after His death and resurrection a new brotherly community composed of all those who receive Him in faith and in love. This he did through His Body, which is the Church. There everyone, as members one of the other, would render mutual service according to the different gifts bestowed on each.

"This solidarity must be constantly increased until that day on which it will be brought to perfection. Then, saved by grace, men will offer flawless glory to God as a family beloved of God and of Christ their Brother" (No. 32).

PEACE AND WAR

The following excerpts, stating principles and objectives of social doctrine concerning peace and war, are from the *Pastoral Constitution on the Church in the Modern World* (Nos. 77 to 82) promulgated by the Second Vatican Council.

Call to Peace: ". . . This Council fervently desires to summon Christians to cooperate with all men in making secure among themselves a peace based on justice and love, and in setting up agencies of peace. This Christians should do with the help of Christ, the Author of peace" (No. 77).

Conditions for Peace: "Peace is not merely the absence of war. Nor can it be reduced solely to the maintenance of a balance of power between enemies. Nor is it brought about by dictatorship. Instead, it is rightly and appropriately called 'an enterprise of justice' (Is. 32:7). Peace results from that harmony built into human society by its divine Founder, and actualized by men as they thirst after ever greater justice.

"The common good of men is in its basic sense determined by the eternal law. Still the concrete demands of this common good are constantly changing as time goes on. Hence peace is never attained once and for all, but must be built up ceaselessly. Moreover, since the human will is unsteady and wounded by sin, the achievement of peace requires that everyone constantly master his passions and that lawful authority keep vigilant.

"But such is not enough. This peace cannot be obtained on earth unless personal values are safeguarded and men freely and trustingly share with one another the riches of their inner spirits and their talents. A firm determination to respect other men and peoples and their dignity, as well as the studied practice of brotherhood, are absolutely necessary for the establishment of peace. Hence peace is likewise the fruit of love, which goes beyond what justice can provide."

Renunciation of Violence: ". . . We cannot fail to praise those who renounce the use of violence in the vindication of their rights and who resort to methods of defense which are otherwise available to weaker parties too, provided that this can be done without injury to the rights and duties of others or of the community itself . . ." (No. 78).

Mass Extermination: ". . . The Council wishes to recall first of all the permanent binding force of universal natural law and its all-embracing principles. Man's conscience itself gives ever more emphatic voice to these principles. Therefore, actions which deliberately conflict with these same principles, as well as orders commanding such actions, are criminal. Blind obedience cannot excuse those who yield to them. Among such must first be counted those actions designed for the methodical extermination of an entire people, nation, or ethnic minority. These actions must be vehemently condemned as horrendous crimes. The courage of those who openly and fearlessly resist men who issue such commands merits supreme commendation."

International Agreements: "On the subject of war, quite a large number of nations have subscribed to various international agreements aimed at making military activity and its consequences less inhuman. Such are conventions concerning the handling of wounded or captured soldiers, and various similar agreements. Agreements of this sort must be honored. They should be improved upon."

Conscientious Objectors: ". . . It seems right that laws make humane provisions for the case of those who for reasons of conscience refuse to bear arms, provided, however, that they accept some other form of service to the human community."

Legitimate Defense: "Certainly, war has not been rooted out of human affairs. As long as the danger of war remains and there is no competent and sufficiently powerful authority at the international level, governments cannot be denied the right to legitimate defense once every means of peaceful settlement has been exhausted. Therefore, government authorities and others who share public responsibility have the duty to protect the welfare of the people entrusted to their care and to conduct such grave matters soberly.

"But it is one thing to undertake military action for the just defense of the people, and something else again to seek the subjugation of other nations. Nor does the possession of war potential make every military or political use of it lawful. Neither does the mere fact that war has unhappily begun mean that all is fair between the warring parties."

Nature of Military Service: "Those who are pledged to the service of their country as members of its armed forces should regard themselves as agents of security and freedom on behalf of their people. As long as they fulfill this role properly, they are making a genuine contribution to the establishment of peace" (No. 79).

Total War Condemned: ". . . This most holy Synod makes its own the condemnations of total war already pronounced by recent Popes, and issues the following declaration:

"Any act of war aimed indiscriminately at the destruction of entire cities or of extensive areas along with their population is a crime against God and man himself. It merits unequivocal and unhesitating condemnation.

"The unique hazard of modern warfare consists in this: it provides those who possess modern scientific weapons with a kind of occasion for perpetrating just such abominations. Moreover, through a certain inexorable chain of events, it can urge men on to the most atrocious decisions. That such in fact may never happen in the future, the bishops of the whole world, in unity assembled, beg all men, especially government officials and military leaders, to give unremitting thought to the awesome responsibility which is theirs before God and the entire human race" (No. 80).

Retaliation and Deterrence: "Scientific weapons, to be sure, are not amassed solely for use in war. The defensive strength of any nation is considered to be dependent upon its capacity for immediate retaliation against an adversary. Hence this accumulation of arms, which increases each year, also serves, in a way heretofore unknown, as a deterrent to possible enemy attack. Many regard this state of affairs as the most effective way by which peace of a sort can be maintained between nations at the present time."

Arms Race: "Whatever be the case with this method of deterrence, men should be convinced that the arms race in which so many countries are engaged is not a safe way to preserve a steady peace. Nor is the so-called balance resulting from this race a sure and authentic peace. Rather than being eliminated thereby, the causes of war threaten to grow gradually stronger.

"While extravagant sums are being spent for the furnishing of ever new weapons, an adequate remedy cannot be provided for the multiple miseries afflicting the whole modern world. Disagreements between nations are not really and radically healed. On the contrary other parts of the world are infected with them. New approaches initiated by reformed attitudes must be adopted to remove this trap and to restore genuine peace by emancipating the world from its crushing anxiety.

"Therefore, it must be said again: the arms race is an utterly treacherous trap for humanity, and one which injures the poor to an intolerable degree. It is much to be feared that, if this race persists, it will eventually spawn all the lethal ruin whose path it is now making ready . . ." (No. 81).

Outlaw War: "It is our clear duty, then, to strain every muscle as we work for the time when all war can be completely outlawed by international consent. This goal undoubtedly requires the establishment of some universal public authority acknowledged as such by all, and endowed with effective power to safeguard, on the behalf of all, security, regard for justice, and respect for rights."

Multilateral and Controlled Disarmament: "But before this hoped-for authority can be set up, the highest existing international centers must devote themselves vigorously to the pursuit of better means for obtaining common security. Peace must be born of mutual trust between nations rather than imposed on them through fear of one another's weapons. Hence everyone must labor to put an end at last to the arms race, and to make a true beginning of disarmament, not indeed a unilateral disarmament, but one proceeding at an equal pace according to agreement, and backed up by authentic and workable safeguards.

"In the meantime, efforts which have already been made and are still under way to eliminate the danger of war are not to be underrated. On the contrary, support should be given to the good will of the very many leaders who work hard to do away with war, which they abominate. . . ."

Public Opinion: ". . . Men should take heed not to entrust themselves only to the efforts of others, while remaining careless about their own attitudes. For government officials, who must simultaneously guarantee the good of their own people and promote the universal good, depend on public opinion and feeling to the greatest possible extent. It does them no good to work at building peace so long as feelings of hostility, contempt, and distrust, as well as racial hatred and unbending ideologies, continue to divide men and place them in opposing camps.

"Hence arises a surpassing need for renewed education of attitudes and for new inspiration in the area of public opinion. Those who are dedicated to the work of education, particularly of the young, or who mold public opinion, should regard as their most weighty task the effort to instruct all in fresh sentiments of peace. Indeed, every one of us should have a change of heart as we regard the entire world and those tasks which we can perform . . . for the betterment of our race.

"But we should not let false hope deceive us. For enmities and hatred must be put away and firm, honest agreements concerning world peace reached in the future. Otherwise, for all its marvelous knowledge, humanity, which is already in the middlke of a grave crisis, will perhaps be brought to that mournful hour in which it will experience no peace other than the dreadful peace of death.

"But, while we say this, the Church of Christ takes her stand in the midst of the anxiety of this age, and does not cease to hope with the utmost confidence. She intends to propose to our age over and over again, in season and out of season, this apostolic message: 'Behold, now is the acceptable time' for a change of heart; 'behold, now is the day of salvation!' (cf. 2. Cor. 2:6)" (No. 82).

Liturgy

The nature and purpose of the liturgy, along with norms for its revision, were the subject matter of the *Constitution on the Sacred Liturgy* promulgated by the Second Vatican Council. The principles and guidelines stated in this document, the first issued by the Council, are summarized here and/or are incorporated in other Almanac entries on liturgical subjects.

Nature and Purpose of Liturgy

"It is through the liturgy, especially the divine Eucharistic Sacrifice, that 'the work of our redemption is exercised.' The liturgy is thus the outstanding means by which the faithful can express in their lives, and manifest to others, the mystery of Christ and the real nature of the true Church . . ." (No. 2).

"The liturgy is considered as an exercise of the priestly office of Jesus Christ. In the Liturgy the sanctification of man is manifested by signs perceptible to the senses, and is effected in a way which is proper to each of these signs; in the liturgy full public worship is performed by the Mystical Body of Jesus Christ, that is, by the Head and His members.

"From this it follows that every liturgical celebration, because it is an action of Christ the priest and of His Body the Church, is a sacred action surpassing all others. No other action of the Church can match its claim to efficacy, nor equal the degree of it" (No. 7).

"The liturgy is the summit toward which the activity of the Church is directed; at the same time it is the fountain from which all her power flows. For the goal of apostolic works is that all who are made sons of God by faith and baptism should come together to praise God in the midst of His Church, to take part in her sacrifice, and to eat the Lord's supper.

". . . From the liturgy, therefore, and especially from the Eucharist, as from a fountain, grace is channeled into us; and the sanctification of men in Christ and the glorification of God, to which all other activities of the Church are directed as toward their goal, are most powerfully achieved" (No. 10).

Full Participation

"Mother Church earnestly desires that all the faithful be led to that full, conscious, and active participation in liturgical celebrations which is demanded by the very nature of the liturgy. Such participation by the Christian people as 'a chosen race, a royal priesthood, a holy nation, a purchased people' (1 Pt. 2:9; cf. 2:4-5), is their right and duty by reason of their baptism.

"In the restoration and promotion of the sacred liturgy, this full and active participation by all the people is the aim to be considered before all else; for it is the primary and indispensable source from which the faithful are to derive the true Christian spirit . . ." (No. 14).

"In order that the Christian people may more securely derive an abundance of graces from the sacred liturgy, holy Mother Church desires to undertake with great care a general restoration of the liturgy itself. For the liturgy is made up of unchangeable elements divinely instituted, and elements subject to change. The latter not only may but ought to be changed with the passing of time if features have by chance crept in which are less harmonious with the intimate nature of the liturgy, or if existing elements have grown less functional.

"In this restoration, both texts and rites should be drawn up so that they express more clearly the holy things which they signify. Christian people, as far as possible, should be able to understand them with ease and to take part in them fully, actively, and as befits a community . . ." (No. 21).

Norms

Norms regarding the reforms concern the greater use of Scripture; emphasis on the importance of the sermon or homily on biblical and liturgical subjects; use of vernacular languages for prayers of the Mass and for administration of the sacraments; provision for adaptation of rites to cultural patterns.

Approval for reforms of various kinds — in liturgical texts, rites, etc — depends on the Holy See, regional conferences of bishops and individual bishops, according to provisions of law. No priest has authority to initiate reforms on his own. Reforms may not be introduced just for the sake of innovation, and any that are introduced in the light of present-day circumstances should embody sound tradition.

To assure the desired effect of liturgical reforms, training and instruction are necessary for the clergy, religious and the laity. The functions of diocesan and regional commissions for liturgy, music and art are to set standards and provide leadership for instruction and practical programs in their respective fields.

Most of the constitution's provisions regarding liturgical reforms have to do with the Roman Rite. The document clearly respects the equal dignity of all rites, leaving to the Eastern Churches control over their ancient liturgies.

For coverage of the **Mystery of the Eucharist,** see The Mass; **Other Sacraments,** see separate entry.

Sacramentals

Sacramentals, instituted by the Church, "are sacred signs which bear a resemblance to the sacraments: they signify effects, particularly of a spiritual kind, which are obtained through the Church's intercession. By them men are disposed to receive the chief effect of the sacraments, and various occasions in life are rendered holy" (No. 60).

"Thus, for well-disposed members of the faithful, the liturgy of the sacraments and sacramentals sanctifies almost every event in their lives; they are given access to the stream of divine grace which flows from the paschal mystery of the passion, death, and resurrection of Christ, the fountain from which all sacraments and sacramentals draw their power. There is hardly any proper use of material things which cannot thus be directed toward the sanctification of men and the praise of God" (No. 61). Some common sacramentals are priestly blessings, blessed palm, candles, holy water, medals, scapulars, prayers and ceremonies of the Roman Ritual.

Liturgy of the Hours

The Liturgy of the Hours (Divine Office) is the public prayer of the Church for praising God and sanctifying the day. Its daily celebration is required as a sacred obligation by men in holy orders and by men and women religious who have professed solemn vows. Its celebration by others is highly commended and is to be encouraged in the community of the faithful.

"By tradition going back to early Christian times, the Divine Office is arranged so that the whole course of the day and night is made holy by the praises of God. Therefore, when this wonderful song of praise is worthily rendered by priests and others who are deputed for this purpose by Church ordinance, or by the faithful praying together with the priest in an approved form, then it is truly the voice of the bride addressing her bridegroom; it is the very prayer which Christ Himself, together with His body, addresses to the Father" (No. 84).

"Hence all who perform this service are not only fulfilling a duty of the Church, but also are sharing in the greatest honor accorded to Christ's spouse, for by offering these praises to God they are standing before God's throne in the name of the Church their Mother" (No. 85).

The revised Liturgy of the Hours — its background, contents, scope and purposes — was described by Pope Paul in the apostolic constitution *Canticum Laudis,* dated Nov. 1, 1970. It consists of:

• Lauds and Vespers, the morning and evening prayers called "the hinges" of the Office;

• Matins, to be said at any time of the day, which retains the form of a nocturnal vigil service;

• Terce, Sext, None, any one of which may be chosen for prayer at an appropriate time of the day (9 a.m., 12 noon, 3 p.m.);

• Compline, a night prayer.

The hour of Prime was suppressed.

In the new Office, the hours are shorter than they had been, with greater textual variety, meditation aids, and provision for intervals of silence and meditation. The psalms are distributed over a four-week period instead of a week; some psalms, entirely or in part, are not included. Additional canticles from the Old and New Testaments are assigned for Lauds and Vespers, respectively. Additional scriptural texts have been added and variously arranged for greater internal unity, correspondence to readings at Mass, and relevance to events and themes of salvation history. Readings include some of the best material from the Fathers of the Church and other authors and improved selections on the lives of saints.

The book used for recitation of the Office is the **Breviary.**

Liturgical Year
(See Church Calendar.)

Sacred Music

"The musical tradition of the universal Church is a treasure of immeasurable value, greater even than that of any other art. The main reason for this pre-eminence is that, as sacred melody united to words, it forms a necessary or integral part of the solemn liturgy.

". . . Sacred music increases in holiness to the degree that it is intimately linked with liturgical action, winningly expresses prayerfulness, promotes solidarity, and enriches sacred rites with heightened solemnity. The Church indeed approves of all forms of true art, and admits them into divine worship when they show appropriate qualities" (No. 112).

The constitution decreed:

• Vernacular languages for the people's parts of the liturgy, as well as Latin, may be used.

• Participation in sacred song by the whole body of the faithful, and not just by choirs, is to be encouraged and brought about.

• Provisions should be made for proper musical training for clergy, religious and lay persons.

• While Gregorian Chant has a unique dignity and relationship to the Latin liturgy, other kinds of music are acceptable.

• Native musical traditions should be used, especially in mission areas.

• Various instruments compatible with the dignity of worship may be used.

Gregorian Chant: A form and style of chant called Gregorian was the basis and most highly regarded standard of liturgical music for centuries. It originated probably during the formative period of the Roman liturgy and developed in conjunction with Gallican and other forms of chant. Gregory the Great's connection with it is not clear, although it is known that he had great concern for and interest in church music. The earliest extant written versions of Gregorian chant date from the ninth century. A thousand years later, the Benedictines of Solesmes, France, initiated a revival of chant which gave impetus to the modern liturgical movement.

Sacred Art and Furnishings

"Very rightly the fine arts are considered to rank among the noblest expressions of human genius. This judgment applies especially to religious art and to its highest achievement, which is sacred art. By their very nature both of the latter are related to God's boundless beauty, for this is the reality which these human efforts are trying to express in some way. To the extent that these works aim exclusively at turning men's thoughts to God persuasively and devoutly, they are dedicated to God and to the cause of His greater honor and glory" (No. 122).

The objective of sacred art is "that all things set apart for use in divine worship should be truly worthy, becoming, and beautiful, signs and symbols of heavenly realities. . . . The Church has . . . always reserved to herself the right to pass judgment upon the arts, deciding which of the works of artists are in accordance with faith, piety, and cherished traditional laws, and thereby suited to sacred purposes.

". . . Sacred furnishings should worthily and beautifully serve the dignity of worship . . ." (No. 122).

According to the constitution:

• Contemporary art, as well as that of the past, shall "be given free scope in the Church, provided that it adorns the sacred buildings and holy rites with due honor and reverence . . ." (No. 123).

• Noble beauty, not sumptuous display, should be sought in art, sacred vestments and ornaments.

• "Let bishops carefully exclude from the house of god and from other sacred places those works of artists which are repugnant to faith, morals, and Christian piety, and which offend true religious sense either by their distortion of forms or by lack of artistic worth, by mediocrity or by pretense.

• "When churches are to be built, let great care be taken that they be suitable for the celebration of liturgical services and for the active participation of the faithful" (No. 124).

• "The practice of placing sacred images in churches so that they may be venerated by the faithful is to be firmly maintained. Nevertheless, their number should be moderate and their relative location should reflect right order. Otherwise they may create confusion among the Christian people and promote a faulty sense of devotion" (No. 125).

• Artists should be trained and inspired in the spirit and for the purposes of the liturgy.

• The norms of sacred art should be revised. "These laws refer especially to the worthy and well-planned construction of sacred buildings, the shape and construction of altars, the nobility, location, and security of the Eucharistic tabernacle, the suitability and dignity of the baptistery, the proper use of sacred images, embellishments, and vestments . . ." (No. 128).

RITES

A rite is the manner in which liturgical worship is carried out. It includes the forms and ceremonial observances of liturgical worship.

Different rites have evolved in the course of Church history, giving to liturgical worship forms and usages peculiar and proper to the nature of worship itself and to the culture of the faithful in various circumstances of time and place. Thus, there has been development since apostolic times in prayers and ceremonies of the Mass, the administration of the sacraments, requirements for celebration of the Divine Office. Practices within the patriarchates of Antioch, Rome, Alexandria and Constantinople were the principal sources of the rites in present use.

Eastern Rites, described elsewhere in the Almanac, are proper to Eastern Catholic Churches.

The **Roman** or **Latin Rite,** described in this section, prevails in the Western Church. It was derived from Roman practices and the use of Latin as an official language from the third century onward. Other rites in limited use in the Western Church have been the Ambrosian, the Mozarabic, the Lyonnais, the Braga, and rites peculiar to some religious orders like the Dominicans, Carmelites and Carthusians.

The revision of rites in progress since the Second Vatican Council is meant to renew them, not to eliminate the rites of particular churches or to reduce all rites to uniformity.

Pope Paul VI made this clear to the archbishop of Milan Apr. 11, 1970, when the prelate asked: "What are we to think of our Ambrosian Rite in these times of liturgical renewal?"

Behind the question were the conflicting views of some who advocated merging the Rite into the Roman Rite and of others who wanted to retain it without change, as a relic.

The Pope replied:

"Renewal, not levelling. The Ambrosian Rite can and must continue.

"Follow the norm: make adaptations without seeking uniformity. To seek uniformity would be to impoverish the Church, contrary to the letter and spirit of the Council. Make people love and understand the really characteristic elements of the Ambrosian Rite, which are capable of illuminating certain aspects of divine truth and of nourishing a fertile spirituality. The vitality of the Ambrosian Rite has been of great benefit in the past and will be of benefit also in the future, not just to the Diocese of Milan but also to the universal Church."

MASS, EUCHARISTIC SACRIFICE AND BANQUET

Declarations of Vatican II

The Second Vatican Council made the following declarations, among others, with respect to the Mass.

"At the Last Supper, on the night when He was betrayed, our Savior instituted the Eucharistic Sacrifice of His Body and Blood. He did this in order to perpetuate the sacrifice of the Cross throughout the centuries until He should come again, and so to entrust to His beloved spouse, the Church, a memorial of His death and resurrection: a sacrament of love, a sign of unity, a bond of charity, a paschal banquet in which Christ is consumed, the mind is filled with grace, and a pledge of future glory is given to us" (*Constitution on the Sacred Liturgy*, No. 47).

". . . As often as the sacrifice of the cross in which 'Christ, our passover, has been sacrificed' (1 Cor. 5:7) is celebrated on an altar, the work of our redemption is carried on. At the same time, in the sacrament of the Eucharistic bread the unity of all believers who form one body in Christ (cf. 1 Cor. 10:17) is both expressed and brought about. All men are called to this union with Christ . . ." (*Dogmatic Constitution on the Church*. No. 3).

". . . The ministerial priest, by the sacred power he enjoys, molds and rules the priestly people. Acting in the person of Christ, he brings about the Eucharistic Sacrifice, and offers it to God in the name of all the people. For their part, the faithful join in the offering of the Eucharist by virtue of their royal priesthood . . ." (*Ibid.*, No. 10).

Declarations of Trent

Among its decrees on the Holy Eucharist, the Council of Trent stated the following points of doctrine on the Mass.

1. There is in the Catholic Church a true Sacrifice, the Mass instituted by Jesus Christ. It is the Sacrifice of his Body and Blood, Soul and Divinity, Himself, under the appearances of bread and wine.

2. This Sacrifice is identical with the Sacrifice of the Cross, inasmuch as Christ is the Priest and Victim in both. A difference lies in the manner of offering, which was bloody upon the Cross and is bloodless on the altar.

3. The Mass is a propitiatory Sacrifice, atoning for sins of the living and dead for whom it is offered.

4. The efficacy of the Mass is derived from the Sacrifice of the Cross, whose super-abundant merits it applies to men.

5. Although the Mass is offered to God alone, it may be celebrated in honor and memory of the saints.

6. Christ instituted the Mass at the Last Supper.

7. Christ ordained the Apostles priests, giving them power and the command to consecrate his Body and Blood to perpetuate and renew the Sacrifice.

ORDER OF MASS

The Mass consists of two principal divisions called the **Liturgy of the Word**, which features the proclamation of the Word of God and the **Eucharistic Liturgy**, which focuses on the central act of sacrifice in the Consecration and on the Eucharistic Banquet in Holy Communion. (Formerly, these divisions were called, respectively, the **Mass of the Catechumens** and the **Mass of the Faithful**.) In addition to these principal divisions, there are ancillary introductory and concluding rites.

The following description covers the Mass as celebrated with participation by the people. This Order of the Mass was approved by Pope Paul VI in the apostolic constitution *Missale Missale Romanum* dated Apr. 3, 1969, and promulgated in a decree issued Apr. 6, 1969, by theCongregation for Divine Worship. The assigned effective date was Nov. 30, 1969.

Introductory Rites

Entrance: The introductory rites begin with the singing or recitation of the Introit or an equivalent entrance song while the priest approaches the altar, kisses it, and goes to the place where he will be seated. The Introit consists of one or more scriptural verses stating the theme of the mystery, season or feast commemorated in the Mass.

Greeting: The priest and people make the Sign of the Cross together. The priest then greets them in one of several alternative ways and they reply in a corresponding manner.

Introductory Remarks: At this point, the priest or another of the ministers may introduce the theme of the Mass.

Penitential Rite: The priest and people together acknowledge their sins as a preliminary step toward worthy celebration of the sacred mysteries. This rite includes a brief examination of conscience, a general confession of sin and plea for divine mercy in one of three ways, and a prayer of absolution by the priest. The *Kyrie, eleison* ("Lord, have mercy") is then said if it was not included in one of the foregoing pleas for divine mercy.

Glory to God: A doxology, a hymn of praise to God, sung or said on festive occasions.

Opening Prayer: A prayer of petition offered by the priest on behalf of the worshipping community.

I. Liturgy of the Word

Readings: The featured elements of this liturgy are readings of two or three passages from the Bible. If three readings are in order, the first is from the Old Testament, the second from the New Testament (Epistles, Acts,

Revelation), and the third from one of the Gospels; the final reading is always a selection from a Gospel. The first reading(s) is concluded with the formula, "This is the Word of the Lord," to which the people respond, "Thanks be to God." The Gospel reading is concluded with the formula, "This is the Gospel of the Lord," to which the people respond, "Praise to you, Lord Jesus Christ." Between the readings, psalm verses and a Gospel acclamation are sung or said.

Homily: Sermon on a scriptural or liturgical subject; ideally, it should be related to the liturgical service in progress.

Creed: The Nicene profession of faith, by priest and people, on certain occasions.

Prayer of the Faithful: Litany-type prayers of petition, with participation by the people. Called general intercessions, they concern needs of the Church, the salvation of the world, public authorities, persons in need, the local community.

II. Eucharistic Liturgy

Offertory Song: Scriptural verses related to the theme of the Mass, or a suitable hymn, sung or said while things are prepared at the altar for the Eucharistic Liturgy and while the offerings of bread and wine are brought to the altar.

Offertory Procession: Presentation to the priest of the gifts of bread and wine, principally, by participating members of the congregation.

Offering of the Gifts: Consists of the prayers and ceremonies with which the priest offers bread and wine as the elements of the sacrifice to take place during the Eucharistic Prayer and of the Lord's Supper to be shared in Holy Communion. If singing takes place during the offering, the priest can say the prayers and carry out the action silently; if there is no singing, he says the prayers aloud and the people, after each offering, respond with the words, "Blessed be God forever."

Washing of Hands: After offering the bread and wine, the priest cleanses his fingers with water in a brief ceremony of purification.

Pray, Brethren: Prayer that the sacrifice to take place will be acceptable to God. The first part of the prayer is said by the priest; the second, by the people.

Prayer over the Gifts: A prayer of petition offered by the priest on behalf of the worshipping community.

Eucharistic Prayer

Preface: A hymn of praise, introducing the Eucharistic Prayer or Canon, sung or said by the priest following directions of the people. The Order of the Mass contains a variety of prefaces, for use on different occasions.

Holy, Holy, Holy; Blessed Is He: Divine praises sung or said by the priest and people.

Canon: The Eucharistic Prayer of the Mass whose central portion is the Consecration,

when the essential act of sacrificial offering takes place with the changing of bread and wine into the Body and Blood of Christ. The prayers of the Canon, which are said by the celebrant only, commemorate principal mysteries of salvation history and include petitions for the Church, the living and dead, and remembrances of saints. There are four Eucharistic Prayers, for use on various occasions and at the option of the priest.

Doxology: A formula of divine praise sung or said by the priest while he holds aloft the chalice containing the consecrated wine in one hand and the paten containing the consecrated host in the other.

Communion Rite

Lord's Prayer: Sung or said by the priest and people.

Prayer for Deliverance from evil: Called an **embolism** because it is a development of the final petition of the Lord's Prayer; said by the priest. It concludes with a memorial of the return of the Lord to which the people respond, "For the kingdom, the power, and the glory are yours, now and forever."

Prayer for Peace: Said by the priest, with corresponding responses by the people. The priest can, in accord with local custom, bid the people to exchange a greeting of peace with each other.

Lamb of God: A prayer for divine mercy sung or said while the priest breaks the consecrated host and places a piece of it into the consecrated wine in the chalice.

Communion: The priest, after saying a preparatory prayer, administers Holy Communion to himself and then to the people, thus completing the sacrifice-banquet of the Mass. (This completion is realized even if the celebrant alone receives the Eucharist.) On giving the Eucharist to the people, the priest says, "The Body of Christ," to each recipient; the customary response is "Amen." If the Eucharist is administered under the forms of bread and wine, the priest says, "The Body and Blood of Christ."

Communion Song: Scriptural verses or a suitable hymn sung or said during the distribution of Holy Communion. After Holy Communion is received, some moments may be spent in silent meditation or in the chanting of a psalm or hymn of praise.

Prayer after Communion: A prayer of petition offered by the priest on behalf of the worshipping community.

Concluding Rite

Announcements: Brief announcements to the people are in order at this time.

Dismissal: Consists of a final greeting by the priest, a blessing, and a formula of dismissal. This rite is omitted if another liturgical action immediately follows the Mass; e.g., a procession, the blessing of the body during a funeral rite.

Some parts of the Mass are changeable with the liturgical season or feast, and are called the **proper** of the Mass. Other parts are said to be **common** because they always remain the same.

Additional Mass Notes

Catholics are seriously obliged to attend Mass in a worthy manner on Sundays and holy days of obligation. Failure to do so without a proportionately serious reason is gravely wrong.

It is the custom for priests to celebrate Mass daily whenever possible. To satisfy the needs of the faithful on Sundays and holy days of obligation, they are authorized to say Mass twice (**bination**) or even three times (**trination**). Bination is also permissible on weekdays. On Christmas and All Souls' Day every priest may say three Masses. Mass may be celebrated in the morning, afternoon or evening.

The **fruits of the Mass,** which in itself is of infinite value, are: **general,** for all the faithful; **special (ministerial),** for the intentions or persons specifically intended by the celebrant; **most special (personal),** for the celebrant himself. On Sundays and certain other days pastors are obliged to offer Mass for their parishioners. If a priest accepts a stipend or offering for a Mass, he is obliged in justice to apply the Mass for the designated intention. Mass may be applied for the living and the dead, or for any good intention.

Mass can be celebrated in several ways: e.g., with people present, without their presence (privately), with two or more priests as co-celebrants (concelebration), with greater or less solemnity.

Some of the various types of Masses are: **requiem,** for the dead (**Mass of the Resurrection,** for funerals; **month's mind** at monthly intervals of the day of death or burial; **anniversary,** at annual intervals of the day of death or burial), **nuptial,** for married couples, with or after the wedding ceremony; **votive,** to honor a Person of the Trinity, a saint, or for some special intention; **conventual,** the community Mass in houses of solemnly professed religious. A **red Mass** is a Votive Mass of the Holy Spirit, celebrated for members of the legal profession that they might exercise prudence and equity in their official capacities. **Gregorian Masses** are a series of 30 Masses celebrated on 30 consecutive days for a deceased person.

The only day of the year on which Mass is not celebrated is Good Friday. In its place, there is a **Solemn Liturgical Action.**

Places, Altars For Mass

The ordinary place for celebrating the Eucharist is a church or other sacred place, at a permanent or movable altar.

Outside of a sacred place, Mass may be celebrated in an appropriate place at a suitable table covered with a linen cloth and corporal. An **altar stone** containing the relics of saints, which was formerly prescribed, is not required by regulations in effect since the promulgation Apr. 6, 1969, of *Institutio Generalis Missalis Romani.*

A **permanent altar** should have a table of stone, be consecrated, and have enclosed within it relics of some saints.

A **movable altar** may be made of any solid and suitable material. If made of stone and consecrated, it should have enclosed within it relics of some saints; if blessed rather than consecrated, the enclosure of relics is not required.

LITURGICAL VESTMENTS

In the early years of the Church, vestments worn by the ministers at liturgical functions were the same as the garments in ordinary popular use. They became distinctive when their form was not altered to correspond with later variations in popular style. Liturgical vestments are symbolic of the sacred ministry and add appropriate decorum to divine worship.

Mass Vestments

Alb: A body-length tunic of white fabric; a vestment common to all ministers of divine worship.

Amice: A rectangular piece of white cloth worn about the neck, tucked into the collar and falling over the shoulders; worn under the alb.

Chasuble: Originally, a large mantle or cloak covering the body, it is the outer vestment of a priest celebrating Mass or carrying out other sacred actions connected with the Mass.

Cincture: A cord which serves the purpose of a belt, holding the alb close to the body.

Dalmatic: The outer vestment worn by a deacon in place of a chasuble.

Stole: A long, band-like vestment worn about the neck and falling to about the knees. (A stole is used for other functions also.)

Tunic: The outer vestment worn by a subdeacon in place of a chasuble.

The material, form and ornamentation of the aforementioned and other vestments are subject to variation and adaptation, according to norms and decisions of the Holy See and concerned conferences of bishops. The overriding norm is that they should be appropriate for use in divine worship. The customary ornamented vestments are the chasuble, dalmatic, stole and tunic.

The minimal vestments required for a priest celebrating Mass are the alb, stole and chasuble.

Liturgical Colors

The colors of outer vestments vary with liturgical seasons, feasts and other circumstances. The colors and their use are:

Green: For the season of the year.

Purple: For Advent and Lent; may also be used in Masses for the dead.

Red: For the Sunday of the Passion, the Wednesday of Holy Week, Good Friday, Pentecost; feasts of the Passion of Our Lord, the Apostles and Evangelists, martyrs.

Rose: May be used in place of purple on the Third Sunday of Advent (Gaudete Sunday) and the Fourth Sunday of Lent (Laetare Sunday).

White: For Christmastide and Eastertide; feasts and commemorations of Our Lord, except those of the Passion; feasts and commemorations of the Blessed Virgin Mary, angels, saints who are not martyrs, All Saints (Nov. 1), St. John the Baptist (June 24), St. John the Evangelist (Dec. 27), the Chair of St. Peter (Feb. 22), the Conversion of St. Paul (Jan. 25). White may generally be substituted for other colors, and can be used for the Mass of the Resurrection for the dead.

On more solemn occasions, better than ordinary vestments may be used, even though their color (e.g., gold) does not match the requirements of the day.

Considerable freedom is permitted in the choice of colors of vestments worn for votive Masses.

Other Vestments

Cappa Magna: Flowing vestment with a train, worn by bishops and cardinals.

Cassock: A full-length, close-fitting robe worn by priests and other clerics under liturgical vestments and in ordinary use; usually black for priests, purple for bishops and other prelates, red for cardinals, white for the pope. In place of a cassock, priests belonging to religious institutes wear the habit proper to their institute.

Cope: A mantle-like vestment open in front and fastened across the chest; worn by sacred ministers in processions and other ceremonies, as prescribed by appropriate directives.

Gremial: A rectangular veil of silk or linen placed over the knees of a bishop when he is seated during various episcopal ceremonies.

Habit: The ordinary garb of priests belonging to religious institutes, analogous to the cassock of diocesan priests; the form of habits varies from institute to institute.

Humeral Veil: A rectangular vestment worn about the shoulders by a deacon, subdeacon or priest in Eucharistic processions and for other prescribed liturgical ceremonies.

Mitre: A headdress worn at some liturgical functions by bishops, abbots and, in certain cases, other ecclesiastics.

Pallium: A circular band of white wool about two inches wide, with front and back pendants, marked with six crosses, worn about the neck by some major prelates. Symbolic of the fullness of the episcopal office, it is given by the pope on request to patriarchs,

primates, archbishops and, rarely, bishops. The pallium is made from the wool of lambs blessed by the pope on the feast of St. Agnes (Jan. 21).

Rochet: A knee-length, white linen-lace garment of prelates worn under outer vestments.

Surplice: A loose, flowing vestment of white fabric with wide sleeves. For some functions, it is interchangeable with an alb.

Zucchetto: A skullcap worn by bishops and other prelates.

SACRED VESSELS, LINENS

Vessels

Chalice and Paten: The principal sacred vessels required for the celebration of Mass are the **chalice** (cup) and **paten** (plate) in which wine and bread, respectively, are offered, consecrated and consumed. Both should be made of solid and noble material which is not easily breakable or corruptible. Gold coating is required of the interior parts of sacred vessels subject to rust. The cup of a chalice should be made of non-absorbent material.

Vessels for containing consecrated hosts (see below) can be made of material other than solid and noble metal — e. g., ivory, more durable woods — provided the substitute material is locally regarded as noble or rather precious and is suitable for sacred use.

Sacred vessels should be blessed or consecrated, according to prescribed requirements.

Vessels, in addition to the paten, for containing consecrated hosts are:

Ciborium: Used to hold hosts for distribution to the faithful and for reservation in the tabernacle.

Luna, Lunula, Lunette: A small receptacle which holds the sacred host in an upright position in the monstrance.

Monstrance, Ostensorium: A portable receptacle so made that the sacred host, when enclosed therein, may be clearly seen, as at Benediction or during extended exposition of the Blessed Sacrament.

Pyx: A watch-shaped vessel used in carrying the Eucharist to the sick.

Linens

Altar Cloth: A white cloth, usually of linen, covering the table of an altar. One cloth is sufficient. Three were used according to former requirements.

Burse: A square, stiff flat case, open at one end, in which the folded corporal is placed; the outside is covered with material of the same kind and color as the outer vestments of the celebrant.

Corporal: A square piece of white linen spread on the altar cloth, on which rest the vessels holding the Sacred Species — the consecrated host(s) and wine — during the Eucharistic Liturgy. The corporal is similarly used whenever the Blessed Sacrament is removed from the tabernacle; e. g., during Benediction the vessel containing the Blessed Sacrament rests on a corporal.

Finger Towel: A white rectangular napkin used by the priest to dry his fingers after cleansing them following the offering of gifts at Mass.

Pall: A square piece of stiff material, usually covered with linen, used to cover the chalice at Mass.

Purificator: A white rectangular napkin used for cleansing sacred vessels after the reception of Communion at Mass.

Veil: The chalice intended for use at Mass is covered with a veil made of the same material as the outer vestments of the celebrant.

THE CHURCH BUILDING

A church is a building set aside and dedicated for purposes of divine worship, the place of assembly for a worshiping community.

A Catholic church is the ordinary place in which the faithful assemble for participation in the Eucharistic Liturgy and other forms of divine worship.

In the early years of Christianity, the first places of assembly for the Eucharistic Liturgy were private homes (Acts 2:46; Rom. 16:5; 1 Cor. 16:5; Col. 4:15) and, sometimes, catacombs. Church building began in the latter half of the second century during lulls in persecution and became widespread after enactment of the Edict of Milan in 313, when it finally became possible for the Church to emerge completely from the underground. The oldest and basic norms regarding church buildings date from about that time.

The essential principle underlying all norms for church building was reformulated by the Second Vatican Council, as follows: "When churches are to be built, let great care be taken that they be suitable for the celebration of liturgical services and for the active participation of the faithful" *(Constitution on the Sacred Liturgy,* No. 124).

This principle was subsequently elaborated in detail by the Congregation for Divine Worship in a document entitled *Institutio Generalis Missalis Romani,* which was approved by Paul VI Apr. 3 and promulgated by a decree of the congregation dated Apr. 6, 1969. Coverage of the following items reflects the norms stated in Chapter V of this document.

Sanctuary: The part of the church where the altar of sacrifice is located, the place where the ministers of the liturgy lead the people in prayer, proclaim the word of God and celebrate the Eucharist. It is set off from the body of the church by a distinctive structural feature — e. g., elevation above the main floor — or by ornamentation. (The traditional **communion rail,** which has been removed in recent years in many churches, served this purpose of demarcation.) The customary location of the sanctuary is at the front of the church; it may, however, be centrally located.

Altar: The main altar of sacrifice and table of the Lord is the focal feature of the sanctuary and entire church. It stands by itself, so that the ministers can move about it freely, and is so situated that they face the people during the liturgical action. In addition to this main altar, there may also be others; in new churches, these are situated in side chapels or alcoves removed to some degree from the body of the church.

Adornment of the Altar: The altar table is covered with a suitable linen cloth. Required candelabra and a cross are placed upon or near the altar in plain sight of the people and are so arranged that they do not obscure their view of the liturgical action.

Seats of the Ministers: The seat of the celebrant, corresponding with his role as the presiding minister of the assembly, is best located behind the altar and facing the people; it is raised a bit above the level of the altar but must not have the appearance of a throne. The seats of other ministers are also located in the sanctuary.

Ambo, Pulpit: The stand at which scriptural lessons and psalm responses are read, the word of God preached, and the prayer of the faithful offered. It is so placed that the ministers can be easily seen and heard by the people.

Places for the People: Seats and kneeling benches (**pews**) and other accommodations for the people are so arranged that they can participate in the most appropriate way in the liturgical action and have freedom of movement for the reception of Holy Communion. Reserved seats are out of order.

Place for the Choir: Where it is located depends on the most suitable arrangement for maintaining the unity of the choir with the congregation and for providing its members maximum opportunity for carrying out their proper function and participating fully in the Mass.

Tabernacle: The best place for reserving the Blessed Sacrament is in a chapel suitable for the private devotion of the people. If this is not possible, reservation should be at a side altar or other appropriately adorned place. In either case, the Blessed Sacrament should be kept in a tabernacle, i. e., a safe-like, secure receptacle.

Statues: Images of the Lord, the Blessed Virgin Mary and the saints are legitimately proposed for the veneration of the faithful in churches. Their number and arrangement, however, should be ordered in such a way that they do not distract the people from the central celebration of the Eucharistic Liturgy. There should be only one statue of one and the same saint in a church.

General Adornment and Arrangement of

Churches: Churches should be so adorned and fitted out that they serve the direct requirements of divine worship and the needs and reasonable convenience of the people.

Other Items

Ambry: A box containing the holy oils, attached to the wall of the sanctuary in some churches.

Baptistery: The place for administering baptism. Some churches have baptisteries adjoining or near the entrance, a position symbolizing the fact that persons are initiated in the Church and incorporated in Christ through this sacrament. Contemporary liturgical practice favors placement of the baptistery near the sanctuary and altar, or the use of a portable font in the same position, to emphasize the relationship of baptism to the Eucharist, the celebration in sacrifice and banquet of the death and resurrection of Christ.

Candles: Used more for symbolical than illuminative purposes, they represent Christ, the light and life of grace, at liturgical functions. They are made of beeswax.

Confessional: A booth-like structure for the hearing of confessions, with separate compartments for the priest and penitents and a grating or screen between them. The use of confessionals became general in the Roman Rite after the Council of Trent.

Crucifix: A cross bearing the figure of the body of Christ, representative of the Sacrifice of the Cross.

Cruets: Vessels containing the wine and water used at Mass. They are placed on a credence table in the sanctuary.

Holy Water Fonts: Receptacles containing holy water, usually at church entrances, for the use of the faithful.

Sanctuary Lamp: A lamp which is kept burning continuously before a tabernacle in which the Blessed Sacrament is reserved, as a sign of the Real Presence of Christ.

LITURGICAL DEVELOPMENTS

The principal developments covered in this article are enactments of the Holy See and actions related to their implementation in the United States.

Modern Movement

Origins of the modern movement for renewal in the liturgy date back to the 19th century. The key contributing factor was a revival of liturgical and scriptural studies. Of special significance was the work of the Benedictine monks of Solesmes, France, who aroused great interest in the liturgy through the restoration of Gregorian Chant. St. Pius X approved their work in a motu proprio of 1903 and gave additional encouragement to liturgical study and development.

St. Pius X did more than any other single pope to promote early first Communion and the practice of frequent Communion, started the research behind a revised Breviary, and appointed a group to investigate possible revisions in the Mass.

The movement attracted some attention in the 1920's and 30's but made little progress.

Significant pioneering developments in the US during the 20's, however, were the establishment of the Liturgical Press, the beginning of publication of *Orate Fratres* (now *Worship*), and the inauguration of the League of the Divine Office by the Benedictines at St. John's Abbey, Collegeville, Minn. Later events of influence were the establishment of the Pius X School of Liturgical Music at Manhattanville College of the Sacred Heart and the organization of a summer school of liturgical music at Mary Manse College by the Gregorian Institute of America. The turning point toward real renewal was reached during and after World War II.

Pius XII gave it impetus and direction, principally through the background teaching in his encyclicals on the *Mystical Body* (1943), *Sacred Liturgy* (1947), and the *Discipline of Sacred Music* (1955), and by means of specific measures affecting the liturgy itself. His work was continued during the pontificates of John XXIII and Paul VI. The Second Vatican Council, in virtue of its *Constitution on the Sacred Liturgy,* inaugurated changes of the greatest significance.

Before and After Vatican II

The most significant liturgical changes made in the years immediately preceding the Second Vatican Council were the following:

(1) Revision of the Rites of Holy Week, for universal observance from 1956.

(2) Modification of the Eucharistic fast and permission for afternoon and evening Mass, in effect from 1953 and extended in 1957.

(3) The Dialogue Mass, introduced in 1958.

(4) Use of popular languages in administration of the sacraments.

(5) Calendar-missal-breviary reform, in effect from Jan. 1, 1961.

(6) Seven-step administration of baptism for adults, approved in 1962.

The *Constitution on the Sacred Liturgy* approved (2,174 to 4) and promulgated by the Second Vatican Council Dec. 4, 1963, marked the beginning of a profound renewal in the Church's corporate worship. Implementation of some of its measures was ordered by Paul VI Jan. 25, 1964, in the motu proprio *Sacram Liturgiam.* On Feb. 29, a special commission, the Consilium for Implementing the Constitution on the Sacred Liturgy, was formed to supervise the execution of the entire program of liturgical reform. Implementation of the program on local and regional levels was left to bishops acting through their own liturgical commissions and in concert with their fellow bishops in national conferences.

1964

Changes: Paul VI set Feb. 16 as the effective date for a number of actions with respect to: preliminary steps for the liturgical training of the clergy and laity; the establishment of diocesan commissions for the liturgy, music and art; the practice of preaching regularly on Sundays and holy days of obligation; revision of the marriage ceremony and imparting of the nuptial blessing at all weddings; changes in the Divine Office.

Churches, Mass: On Oct. 16, Paul VI approved changes affecting new churches, the ending of Mass (eliminating the last Gospel and following prayers), and the recitation aloud or the singing of some Mass prayers formerly said silently. The effective date of these changes was Mar. 7, 1965.

Rituals: Revised rituals for administration of the sacraments in popular languages were approved and passed into general use in many countries. By the end of the year popular languages were being used at Mass, in accord with principles stated in the Instruction, *Inter Oecumenici*, of Sept. 26.

Texts for Mass, Sacraments: In the United States, the bishops approved Apr. 2 English texts for Mass and the administration of the sacraments. These texts were ratified May 1 by the Pontifical Consilium for the Liturgy. On Sept. 14, the general use of English was authorized for administration of the sacraments. On Nov. 29, English was introduced in the celebration of Mass throughout the country. Permission was also granted for eliminating Psalm 42 at the beginning of Mass.

1965

Bishops' Secretariat: Early in 1965, the Secretariat of the US Bishops' Commission on the Liturgical Apostolate opened headquarters at 1312 Massachusetts Ave. N.W., Washington, D.C. 20005.

Holy Week: Additional revisions in the Holy Week liturgy, effective in 1965, introduced concelebration and placed new emphasis on commemorating the institution of the priesthood on Holy Thursday; they also modified Good Friday prayers for other Christians, Jews and other non-Christians.

1966

Home Masses: A number of bishops in this country granted permission for the celebration of Mass in private homes and other places.

Holy Communion: In October, the Sacred Congregation for the Discipline of the Sacraments authorized bishops to permit superiors of convents to distribute Holy Communion in the absence of priests, especially in missionary areas.

Folk Masses: Music for the new vernacular liturgy continued to present problems. Musical instruments were also a matter of debate.

Some bishops forbade the use of any instrument other than the organ, while others approved the use of stringed instruments and permitted "folk" Masses for young people.

1967

Several key documents were issued during the year by the Consilium for Implementing the Constitution on the Sacred Liturgy and the Sacred Congregation for Divine Worship. Among them were:

Music: An *Instruction on Music in the Liturgy*, dated Mar. 5 and effective as of May 14, which encouraged congregational singing during liturgical celebrations and attempted to clarify the role of choirs and trained singers. More significantly, the instruction indicated that a major development underway in the liturgy was a gradual erasure of the distinctive lines traditionally drawn between the sung liturgy and the spoken liturgy, between the high Mass and the low Mass.

Mass: An instruction entitled *Tres Abhinc Annos*, dated May 4 and effective as of June 29. Among other things, it simplified rubrical directives for the celebration of Mass, approved the practice of saying the canon aloud, altered the Communion and dismissal rites, permitted purple instead of black vestments in Masses for the dead, discontinued wearing of the maniple, and approved in principle the use of vernacular languages for the canon, ordination rites, and lessons of the Divine Office when read in choir. The document got its title from the fact that it was issued nearly three years after promulgation of the key liturgical instruction, *Inter Oecumenici*, Sept. 26, 1964.

Holy Eucharist: An instruction on *Worship of the Eucharistic Mystery*, issued by Pope Paul and dated May 25, which dealt with the Eucharist as the sacrifice-memorial-banquet of the death and Resurrection of Christ, and as a permanent sacrament.

English Canon: Several proposals agreed upon by members of the US Bishops' Commission on the Liturgical Apostolate in November, 1966, were implemented in 1967. The most important of these was introduction of the English canon on Oct. 22. Earlier authorization was obtained for use of a supplementary weekday lectionary containing alternate scriptural readings at Mass, with texts from any one of five translations — Confraternity of Christian Doctrine, Douay-Rheims-Challoner, Knox, Catholic edition of the Revised Standard Version, Jerusalem Bible.

Home Masses: On Feb. 16, the commission announced the formation of a new committee to direct liturgical experimentation. At the same time, it went on record in support of the celebration of Mass in private homes for sound pastoral reasons, and approved the use of contemporary music, as well as guitars and other suitable instruments, in the liturgy.

Experiments: Liturgical experimentation,

as well as the reluctance of some parties to put into effect the directives of the Second Vatican Council, was one of the subjects covered in a *Pastoral Statement on Liturgical Renewal* issued in May, 1967, by the National Conference of Catholic Bishops. The statement declared: "Liturgical experimentation has acquired several meanings. . . . If it means . . . privately initiated innovations, it must be disapproved. The Fathers of the council (Vatican II) had no intention whatever of encouraging experiments contrary to liturgical usage and discipline . . . . Unauthorized liturgical innovations are not genuine experiments at all. . . . They divert us from the educational work of renewal and from realizing the full potential of the present liturgy. Furthermore, this kind of unauthorized initiative is divisive of the Christian community."

The central part of the bishops' statement called for widened liturgical education and greater involvement by congregations in liturgical celebrations.

1968

US Practices: It was announced early in February that the Holy See had authorized several changes in liturgical usage in this country They were:

(1) Use of two additional texts of the Book of Psalms (of England's Grail Society and from the Jerusalem Bible), in addition to the text in the Confraternity of Christian Doctrine translation of the Bible.

(2) Omission of any reference to excommunication or other ecclesiastical censures in the formula for absolution in the sacrament of penance, "unless there be some indication that a censure was incurred" by the penitent.

(3) Substitution of an approved Eucharistic hymn at Benediction in place of the customary Latin hymn, *Tantum Ergo.*

(4) Variant use of traditional choral music even though the English texts were from earlier rather than contemporary translations.

(5) Use of musical instruments other than the organ in liturgical services, "provided they are played in a manner suitable to public worship."

The Consilium for Implementing the Constitution on the Sacred Liturgy turned down requests of the US bishops for permission to designate academic centers to supervise liturgical innovation, and to allow liturgical experimentation without prior examination by Rome.

New Canons: Long anticipated introduction of new canons, also called Eucharistic prayers or anaphoras, into the Mass was authorized by the Consilium for Implementing the Constitution on the Sacred Liturgy on May 23, 1968. The Latin texts of three such prayers were published June 14 along with permission for starting their use in approved vernacular versions on Aug. 15. The new canons, while different from each other and the customary Roman Canon, have the same basic structure.

The customary Roman Canon, which dates at least from the beginning of the fifth century and has remained substantially unchanged since the seventh century, is the first in the order of listing of the anaphoras. It can be used at any time, but is the one of choice for most Sundays, some special feasts like Easter and Pentecost, and for feasts of the Apostles and other saints who are commemorated in the canon. Any preface can be used with it.

The second Eucharistic prayer, the shortest and simplest of all, is best suited for use on weekdays and various special circumstances. It has a preface of its own, but others may be used with it. This anaphora bears a close resemblance to the one framed by St. Hippolytus about 215.

The third Eucharistic prayer is suitable for use on Sundays and feasts as an alternative to the Roman Canon. It can be used with any preface and has a special formula for remembrance of the dead.

The fourth Eucharistic prayer, the most sophisticated of them all, presents a broad synthesis of salvation history. Based on the Eastern tradition of Antioch, it is best suited for use at Masses attended by persons versed in Sacred Scripture. It has an unchangeable preface.

1969

New Order of Mass: In an apostolic constitution entitled *Missale Romanum* and dated Apr. 3, Paul VI authorized a new Order of the Mass and a thoroughly revised set of directive norms, to take the place of the Mass order prescribed by the Council of Trent.

The Mass changes were scheduled to go into effect Nov. 30, 1969. Because of publication delays, however, general implementation in this country did not take place until the spring of 1970.

Calendar Changes: Reorganization of the liturgical year and calendar was made public May 9, several months after Paul VI, on his own initiative, issued an enabling document on the subject. (The calendar is described in detail under its own title.)

Instructions, New Ritual: Additional documents of importance issued during the year were: an *Instruction on the Translation of Liturgical Texts,* by the Consilium for Implementing the Constitution on the Sacred Liturgy, Jan. 25; a new ritual for the sacrament of matrimony, Mar. 19; an instruction on reasons and norms for the celebration of Mass at special gatherings of the faithful, May 15; an instruction on the manner of administering Holy Communion, May 20; a new baptismal rite for infants, June 20. In response to demands of the Second Vatican Council, the Vatican Polyglot Press published in August a new Latin text of the Psalms to serve as the basis for translations to be used in the liturgy.

1970

Sunday Mass on Saturday: The Congregation for the Clergy, under date of Jan. 10, granted the request that the faithful, where bishops consider it pastorally necessary or useful, may satisfy the precept of participating in Mass in the late afternoon or evening hours of Saturdays and the days before holy days of obligation. The indult was granted for a period of five years.

Trination: The Congregation for the Sacraments, under date of Jan. 20, granted to all US bishops the authority to permit priests to celebrate Mass three times on Saturdays and days preceding holy days of obligation, on condition that the first and second Masses are celebrated for weddings and/or funerals and the third Mass is celebrated in the evening so that the precept (of participating in Mass) may be satisfied by the faithful. The indult was granted for a period of three years.

New Order of the Mass: The New Order of the Mass, authorized by Paul VI. Apr. 3, 1969, was introduced in most dioceses of the US on Palm Sunday, Mar. 22, or shortly thereafter.

New Lectionary: A new book of scriptural readings and psalm responsories for use at Mass was also introduced Mar. 22 throughout the US. Its texts were from the New American Bible, which was published later in the year.

The lectionary contains a three-year cycle of readings for Sundays and solemn feasts, a two-year weekday cycle, and a one-year cycle for the feasts of saints, in addition to readings for a great variety of Masses: for the common of saints, votive Masses, ritual Masses and Masses for various needs. There are also responsorial psalms to follow the first readings, and gospel or alleluia versicles to follow the second readings. The introductory material, summaries of readings, rubrics and refrains for the responsorial psalms were the work of the International Commission for English in the Liturgy.

Rites for Baptism and Marriage: New rites for the sacraments of baptism (for infants) and matrimony were introduced June 1 in this country. The baptismal rite, the first ever designed specifically for infants, emphasizes the actual life situation of the child and requires the parents to participate in the ceremony more actively than the sponsors. The marriage rite provides a great deal of flexibility and numerous options with respect to ceremonies, scriptural readings and prayers. Both rites are so devised as to be integral elements of ritual Masses for baptism and matrimony.

New Roman Missal: The Vatican Polyglot Press began distribution in June of the new *Roman Missal,* the first revision published in 400 years. Translations of the new and greatly expanded Latin missal were to be made on the authority of national or regional bishops' conferences.

The new missal is strictly a book of prayers and sacramental formulas and does not include the readings of the Mass, such as the Gospel and the Epistle.

The new missal supplies mostly new texts of introits, prefaces and other prayers of the Mass. The number of prefaces is four times greater than it had been. There are 10 commons (or sets of Mass prayers) of martyrs, two of doctors of the Church, and a dozen for saints or groups of saints of various kinds, such as religious, educators and mothers of families. There are Masses during which certain sacraments are administered and others for religious profession, the Church, the pope, priests, Christian unity, the evangelization of nations, persecuted Christians, and other intentions.

New Breviary: A provisional English version of the new Roman Breviary was published in July in England. Called *The Prayer of the Church*, it reflected the general plan of the revised breviary which was still awaiting publication.

Ordination Rites: Final approval was granted by the Holy See during the year for rites, introduced earlier on a trial basis, for the ordination of deacons, priests and bishops.

Instruction: A *Third Instruction on the Correct Application of the Constitution on the Sacred Liturgy* was issued by the Congregation for Divine Worship Sept. 3. The purpose of the document was to assist bishops in putting liturgical norms — especially those concerning the Mass — into full effect.

The document said: "Liturgical reform is not at all synonymous with so-called desacralization and is not intended as an occasion for what is called secularization. Thus, the liturgy must keep a dignified and sacred character.

"The effectiveness of liturgical actions does not consist in the continual search for newer rites or simpler forms, but in an ever deeper insight into the word of God and the mystery which is celebrated. The priest will assure the presence of God and His mystery in the celebration by following the rites of the Church rather than his own preferences."

The instruction, among other things: stated that no readings of any kind may be substituted for scriptural readings, and that official formulas of the Mass may not be altered; said that the Eucharistic prayer or canon is to be said by the priest alone; noted the Latin-Rite requirement of unleavened wheat bread for the host; provided that women, although they may not serve at the altar, may read scriptural lessons except the Gospel, say prayers of the faithful, make announcements and commentary, be musicians and leaders of song, and act as ushers at Mass; cautioned that experimentation, when necessary and useful, should be carried out in line with prescribed norms.

Liturgy of the Hours: Pope Paul VI described the background, contents, scope and purposes of the revised Divine Office in the apostolic constitution *Canticum Laudis* ("Song of Praise"), dated Nov. 1 and published several months later. (See separate entry.)

1971

New Books: The publication of three new liturgical books was reported early in January: a small Latin missal containing 30 separate Masses and prayers for various occasions; a Latin lectionary, first in a set of three, containing scriptural readings and responses for Advent, Pentecost, and eight other weeks of the year; simplified rites for the blessing of abbots and abbesses.

Holy Week and Funeral Rites: Cardinal John F. Dearden announced in January Vatican approval of English translations of the Holy Week liturgy, and of revised funeral services oriented to the resurrection theme for use beginning Nov. 1.

Holy Oils: The Congregation for Divine Worship issued a directive permitting the use of other oils — from plants, seeds or coconuts — instead of the traditional olive oil in administering some of the sacraments. The directive also provided that oils could be blessed at other times than at the usual Mass of Chrism on Holy Thursday, and authorized bishops' conferences to permit priests to bless oils in cases of necessity.

Laymen Distributing Holy Communion: Blanket permission for one year was given to US bishops in April to permit laymen to distribute Holy Communion under certain conditions of pastoral need.

Mass in Latin: According to a notice issued by the Congregation for Divine Worship June 1, 1971: (1) Bishops may permit the celebration of Mass in Latin for mixed-language groups. (2) Priests may celebrate Mass in Latin when people are not present. (3) When dates are set for mandatory use of new missal texts, in Latin or the vernacular, these texts must be used from then on, with exceptions covering older and some other priests.

Inter-Ritual Concelebration: The apostolic delegation in Washington, D.C., announced in June that it had received authorization to permit priests of Roman and Eastern rites to celebrate Mass together in the rite of the host church. It was understood that the inter-ritual concelebrations would always be "a manifestation of the unity of the Church and of communion among particular churches."

Religious Profession, Calendar: Approval was announced June 17 of new liturgical rites in English for the profession of vows by religious, and of a decision of the bishops to put the universal liturgical calendar into full effect in this country in 1972.

Confirmation: A new rite, *Ordo Confirmationis,* was issued by the Holy See Aug. 15 in conjunction with the apostolic constitution *Divinae Consortium Naturae;* its adoption was made mandatory as of Jan. 1, 1973. The essential formula of the sacrament was changed from the traditional (since the 12th century): "I sign you with the sign of the cross and confirm you with the chrism of salvation, in the name of the Father and of the Son and of the Holy Spirit," to: "N . . . , receive the seal of the Holy Spirit, the Gift of the Father." This form closely resembles the one used in the Byzantine Rite. The tap on the cheek, customary since the 13th century as a reminder of readiness to accept hardship in the practice of the faith, has no place in the revised rite. The age for reception of the sacrament was left to the discretion of bishops.

Minor Orders, Tonsure: US bishops were authorized by the Holy See to: (1) omit ordaining porters and exorcists, Oct. 5; (2) use revised rites for ordaining acolytes and lectors, and to use a service celebrating admission to the clerical state in place of the ceremony of tonsure which had previously served this purpose, Oct. 8.

1972

Christian Initiation: The Congregation for Divine Worship issued revised rites for the Christian initiation of adults, *Ordo Initiationis Christianae Adultorum,* Jan. 6. Authorization was given for immediate use of the Latin text and for the use of translations on approval. (See separate entry under Baptism.) This Ordo supplanted a seven-step ritual for the baptism of adults approved in 1962.

Lay Persons Giving Holy Communion: The Congregation for the Discipline of the Sacraments granted US bishops authority to permit:

(1) qualified persons to give Holy Communion to themselves, to distribute it to other members of the faithful, and bring it to the sick, in churches and public oratories, in the absence of an ordinary minister of Communion (priest, deacon) or if the latter is impeded by age, bad health, or pastoral ministry;

(2) lay superiors of religious communities or those who take their place to give Holy Communion to themselves and to distribute it to the members, the faithful who may be present, and the sick, in the oratory of the religious house and in the same circumstances;

(3) qualified persons to assist the celebrating priest in the administration of the Holy Eucharist during Mass in churches and public oratories, when a very lengthy distribution of Communion cannot otherwise be avoided.

The faculty, good for three years, was granted Jan. 18, two months before the expiration of an earlier one-year grant dated Mar. 9, 1971. It was given only for the spiritual good of the faithful.

Sacramentary: The US Bishops' Committee on the Liturgy announced plans early in the year to publish a sacramentary with liturgical texts, along with standard and provisional texts of some prayers and prefaces from the *Roman Missal,* for optional use on Sundays and other occasions.

Independence Day Mass: The Congregation for Divine Worship informed Cardinal John J. Krol that English Mass texts for "Independence Day and other civic observances," formally approved at the November, 1971, meeting of the National Conference of Catholic Bishops, had been confirmed by the Apostolic See for use in this country.

Holy Communion, Eucharistic Prayers: The Congregation for Divine Worship, meeting Mar. 7 to 11, discussed the formulation of a new rite for administering Holy Communion outside of Mass and set up a committee to study questions related to the adaptation and/or introduction of new Eucharistic Prayers in the liturgy of the Mass.

Decisions of Bishops: The National Conference of Catholic Bishops, meeting Apr. 11 to 13 in Atlanta, voted 146 to 30 in favor of a resolution to permit **minor adaptations** in the liturgy for a three-year experimental period, with a view toward eventual authorization of worthwhile variations. The measure envisioned culturally related additions, omissions and substitutions in rites for baptism, confirmation, marriage and funeral rites, and in the Mass. The bishops also voted, 140 to 40, to seek permission from the Holy See for more substantive changes. The resolutions were as follows.

(1) "That individual diocesan bishops, upon application to the Bishops' Committee on the Liturgy and under its supervision, be permitted to employ the adaptations indicated in . . . the liturgical books as falling within the competence of the episcopal conferences and that they be asked to submit, from experience over a period of three years in the case of each rite, the alternatives from which the NCCB will determine the national adaptations."

(2) "That a similar procedure be followed for more profound liturgical adaptations and for the development of a national ritual."

No action was taken with respect optional **in-hand reception of Holy Communion,** although 106 of 176 bishops polled informally favored the practice. Support for it was based on several reasons, including: its adoption in a number of countries; its adoption in some places and some circles in this country without authorization; the view that it does not lead to loss of reverence for the Eucharist; its optional character would not force reception of the sacrament in this manner. On the other hand, it was said that: lay persons do not want the practice; it involves the danger of profanation, especially among children; approval would validate a practice initiated

without authorization and would lead to requests for the approval of other practices started in a similar way. It was certain that the matter would come up for consideration again, after consultation with and probably a survey of lay persons.

The bishops, in a secret vote, decided not to call a halt to the practice of **first Communion without first confession,** but to let it continue for further experimentation and eventual evaluation and decision. It was reported at the time of the meeting that first Communion without first confession was more or less general practice in the parishes of 96 dioceses.

Ordo of the Sung Mass: In a decree dated June 24 and made public Aug. 24, the Congregation for Divine Worship issued a new *Ordo of the Sung Mass* — containing Gregorian chants for Masses sung in Latin — to replace the *Graduale Romanum.* The older Latin hymnbook was made obsolete by post-Vatican II changes in the liturgy.

Compliance with Regulations: Bishop Maurice Schexnayder of Lafayette (La.) called on priests, religious and lay persons to comply "conscientiously and faithfully" with regulations on divine worship, in a statement issued in May after discussions with diocesan consultors.

The discussions were prompted by reports that some irregularities had occurred in the celebration of Mass in the diocese.

Irregularities cited in the statement included: the use of table bread and wine for Mass; offering Mass without vestments; allowing ministers of other faiths to preach sermons at Mass; in-hand administration of Holy Communion and giving Communion to non-Catholics.

A diocesan spokesman said that Bishop Schexnayder and the consultors did not wish to condemn priests or to alarm Catholics by the statement. Their intentions he said, were to inform everyone that authority for changes in the liturgy belongs to the Holy See and the bishops, not to individual Catholics, priests or lay persons; that unauthorized actions in the celebration of Mass are particularly serious and that they, along with other liturgical abberations, were to cease.

The statement called for compliance with liturgical regulations approved by the Holy See and the bishops of this country. It emphasized that "liturgical services are not private functions, but are celebrations of the Church which is the 'sacrament of unity,' namely, a holy people united and organized under their bishops."

The document noted that recent changes in the liturgy provide for various options. "Other choices," however, "are without approval and are generally injurious to the unity of liturgical practice of the Church."

The forbidden irregularities were called "harmful to the unity and good order of the Church, and scandalous to the faithful."

Sacraments

The sacraments are actions of Christ and his Church which signify grace, cause it in the act of signifying it, and confer it upon persons properly disposed to receive it. They perpetuate the redemptive activity of Christ, making it present and effective. They infallibly communicate the fruit of that activity — namely, grace — to responsive persons with faith. Sacramental actions consist of the union of sensible signs (matter of the sacraments) with the words of the minister (form of the sacraments).

Christ instituted the sacraments: three of them — baptism, Holy Eucharist, penance — directly; the other four — confirmation, holy orders, anointing of the sick, matrimony — through the Church.

Christ is the principal priest or minister of every sacrament; human agents — an ordained priest, baptized persons contracting marriage with each other, any person conferring emergency baptism in a proper manner — are secondary ministers. Sacraments have efficacy from Christ, not from the personal dispositions of their human ministers.

Each sacrament confers sanctifying grace for the special purpose of the sacrament; this is, accordingly, called sacramental grace. It involves a right to actual graces corresponding to the purposes of the respective sacraments.

While sacraments infallibly produce the grace they signify, recipients benefit from them in proportion to their personal dispositions. One of these is the intention to receive sacraments as sacred signs of God's saving and grace-giving action. The state of grace is also necessary for fruitful reception of the Holy Eucharist, confirmation, matrimony, holy orders and anointing of the sick. Baptism is the sacrament in which grace is given in the first instance and original sin is remitted. Penance is the secondary sacrament of reconciliation, in which persons guilty of serious sin after baptism are reconciled with God and the Church, and in which persons already in the state of grace are strengthened in that state.

Role of Sacraments

The Second Vatican Council prefaced a description of the role of the sacraments with the following statement concerning participation by all the faithful in the priesthood of Christ and the exercise of that priesthood by receiving the sacraments (*Dogmatic Constitution on the Church*, Nos. 10 and 11).

". . . The baptized by regeneration and the anointing of the Holy Spirit, are consecrated into a spiritual house and a holy priesthood. Thus through all those works befitting Christian men they can offer spiritual sacrifice and proclaim the power of Him who

has called them out of darkness into His marvelous light (cf. 1 Pt. 2:4-10). . . ."

"Though they differ from one another in essence and not only in degree, the common priesthood of the faithful and the ministerial or hierarchical priesthood (of those ordained to holy orders) are nonetheless interrelated. Each of them in its own special way is a participation in the one priesthood of Christ. The ministerial priest, by the sacred power he enjoys, molds and rules the priestly people. Acting in the person of Christ, he brings about the Eucharistic Sacrifice, and offers it to God in the name of all the people. For their part, the faithful join in the offering of the Eucharist by virtue of their royal priesthood. They likewise exercise that priesthood by receiving the sacraments, by prayer and thanksgiving, by the witness of a holy life, and by self-denial and active charity."

"It is through the sacraments and the exercise of the virtues that the sacred nature and organic structure of the priestly community is brought into operation."

Baptism: "Incorporated into the Church through baptism, the faithful are consecrated by the baptismal character to the exercise of the cult of the Christian religion. Reborn as sons of God, they must confess before men the faith which they have received from God through the Church."

Confirmation: "Bound more intimately to the Church by the sacrament of confirmation, they are endowed by the Holy Spirit with special strength. Hence they are more strictly obliged to spread and defend the faith both by word and by deed as true witnesses of Christ."

Eucharist: "Taking part in the Eucharistic Sacrifice, which is the fount and apex of the whole Christian life, they offer the divine Victim to God, and offer themselves along with It. Thus, both by the act of oblation and through holy Communion, all perform their proper part in this liturgical service, not, indeed, all in the same way but each in that way which is appropriate to himself. Strengthened anew at the holy table by the Body of Christ, they manifest in a practical way that unity of God's People which is suitably signified and wondrously brought about by this most awesome sacrament."

Penance: "Those who approach the sacrament of penance obtain pardon from the mercy of God for offenses committed against Him. They are at the same time reconciled with the Church, which they have wounded by their sins, and which by charity, example, and prayer seeks their conversion."

Anointing of the Sick: "By the sacred anointing of the sick and the prayer of her priests, the whole Church commends those who are ill to the suffering and glorified Lord, asking that He may lighten their suffering and save them (cf. Jas. 5:14-16). She exhorts them, moreover, to contribute to the welfare of the whole People of God by associating themselves freely with the passion and death of Christ (cf. Rom. 8:17; Col. 1:24; 2 Tm. 2:11-12; 1 Pt. 4:13)."

Holy Orders: "Those of the faithful who are consecrated by holy orders are appointed to feed the Church in Christ's name with the Word and the grace of God."

Matrimony: "Christian spouses, in virtue of the sacrament of matrimony, signify and partake of the mystery of that unity and fruitful love which exists between Christ and His Church (cf. Eph. 5:32). The spouses thereby help each other to attain to holiness in their married life and by the rearing and education of their children. And so, in their state and way of life, they have their own special gift among the People of God (cf. 1 Cor. 7:7).

"For from the wedlock of Christians there comes the family, in which new citizens of human society are born. By the grace of the Holy Spirit received in baptism these are made children of God, thus perpetuating the People of God through the centuries. The family is, so to speak, the domestic Church. In it parents should, by their word and example, be the first preachers of the faith to their children. They should encourage them in the vocation which is proper to each of them, fostering with special care any religious vocation.

"Fortified by so many and such powerful means of salvation, all the faithful, whatever their condition or state, are called by the Lord, each in his own way, to that perfect holiness whereby the Father Himself is perfect."

Baptism

Baptism is the sacrament of spiritual regeneration by which a person is incorporated in Christ and made a member of His Mystical Body, given grace, and cleansed of original sin. Actual sins and the punishment due for them are remitted also if the person baptized was guilty of such sins (e.g., in the case of a person baptized after reaching the age of reason). The theological virtues of faith, hope and charity are given with grace. The sacrament confers a character on the soul and can be received only once. Baptism has been called a sacrament of the dead because its purpose is to confer sanctifying grace on persons who do not have it.

The matter is the pouring of water. The form is: "I baptize you in the name of the Father and of the Son and of the Holy Spirit."

The minister of solemn baptism is a priest or deacon, but in case of emergency anyone, including a non-Catholic, can validly baptize. The minister pours water on the forehead of the person being baptized and says the words of the form while the water is flowing. The water used in solemn baptism is blessed during the rite.

The Church recognizes as valid baptism by **immersion, aspersion** (sprinkling of the water), or **infusion** (pouring of the water). In the Western Church, i.e., Roman Rite, the method of infusion is prescribed. The Church recognizes as valid baptisms properly performed by non-Catholic ministers. The baptism of infants has always been considered valid and the general practice of infant baptism was well established by the fifth century. Baptism is conferred conditionally when there is doubt about the validity of a previous baptism or the dispositions of the person.

Baptism is necessary for salvation. If a person cannot receive the baptism of water described above, this can be supplied by baptism of blood (martyrdom suffered for the Catholic faith or some Christian virtue) or by baptism of desire (perfect contrition joined with at least the implicit intention of doing whatever God wills that men should do for salvation).

A sponsor is required for the person being baptized. (See Godparents, below).

A person must be validly baptized before he can receive any of the other sacraments.

Christian Initiation of Infants: Infants should be solemnly baptized as soon after birth as conveniently possible. In danger of death, anyone may baptize an infant. If the child survives, the ceremonies of solemn baptism should be supplied.

The sacrament is ordinarily conferred by a priest of the parents' parish.

Only Catholics, in their 14th year or older, may be **godparents** or sponsors. Only one is required. Two, one of each sex, are permitted. A non-Catholic cannot be a godparent for a Catholic child, but may serve as a witness to the baptism. A Catholic may not be a godparent for a child baptized in a non-Catholic religion, but may be a witness.

The role of godparents in baptismal ceremonies is secondary to the role of the parents. They serve as representatives of the community of faith and with the parents request baptism for the child and perform other ritual functions. Their function after baptism is to serve as proxies for the parents if the parents should be unable or fail to provide for the religious training of the child.

At baptism every child should be given a name with Christian significance, usually the name of a saint, to symbolize newness of life in Christ.

Christian Initiation of Adults: According to the *Ordo Initiationis Christianae Adultorum* ("Rite of the Christian Initiation of Adults") issued by the Congregation for Divine Worship under date of Jan. 6, 1972, adults are prepared for baptism and reception into the Church in several stages:

• An initial period of inquiry, instruction and evangelization.

• The catechumenate, a period of formal instruction and progressive formation in and familiarity with Christian life. It starts with a statement of purpose and includes a rite in which the catechumen is signed with the cross, blessings, exorcisms, and introduction into church for celebration of the word of God.

• Immediate preparation, called a period of purification and enlightenment, from the beginning of Lent to reception of the sacraments of initiation — baptism, confirmation, Holy Eucharist — at Easter. The period is marked by scrutinies, formal giving of the creed and the Lord's Prayer, the choice of a Christian name, and a final statement of intention.

• A final phase whose objective is greater familiarity with Christian life in the Church through observances of the Easter season and association with the community of the faithful.

The priest who baptizes a catechumen can, in the absence of a bishop, also administer the sacrament of confirmation.

A sponsor is required for the person being baptized.

The *Ordo* also provides a simple rite of initiation for adults in danger of death and for cases in which all stages of the initiation process are not necessary, and guidelines for: (1) the preparation of adults for the sacraments of confirmation and Holy Eucharist in cases where they have been baptized but have not received further formation in the Christian life; (2) for the formation and initiation of children of catechetical age.

The Church recognizes the right of anyone over the age of seven to request baptism and to receive the sacrament after completing a course of instruction and giving evidence of good will. Practically, in the case of minors in a non-Catholic family or environment, the Church accepts them when other circumstances favor their ability to practice the faith — e.g., well-disposed family situation, the presence of another or several Catholics in the family. Those who are not in such favorable circumstances are prudently advised to defer reception of the sacrament until they attain the maturity necessary for independent practice of the faith.

Reception of Baptized Christians: Procedure for the reception of already baptized Christians into full communion with the Catholic Church is distinguished from the catechumenate, since they have received some Christian formation. Instruction and formation are provided as necessary, however; and conditional baptism is administered if there is reasonable doubt about the validity of the person's previous baptism.

In the rite of reception, the person is invited to join the community of the Church in professing the Nicene Creed and is asked to state: "I believe and profess all that the holy Catholic Church believes, teaches, and proclaims as revealed by God." The priest places his hand on the head of the person, states the formula of admission to full communion, confirms (in the absence of a bishop), gives a sign of peace, and administers Holy Communion during a Eucharistic Liturgy.

Confirmation

Confirmation is the sacrament by which a baptized person, through anointing with chrism and the imposition of hands, is endowed with the gifts and special strength of the Holy Spirit for mature Christian living. The sacrament, which completes the Christian initiation begun with baptism, confers a character on the soul and can be received only once.

According to the apostolic constitution *Divinae Consortium Naturae* dated Aug. 15, 1971, in conjunction with the *Ordo Confirmationis* ("Rite of Confirmation"): "The sacrament of confirmation is conferred through the anointing with chrism on the forehead, which is done by the imposition of the hand (matter of the sacrament), and through the words: 'N . . . ., receive the seal of the Holy Spirit, the Gift of the Father'" (form of the sacrament).

The ordinary minister of confirmation in the Roman Rite is a bishop. Priests may be delegated for the purpose. A pastor can confirm a parishioner in danger of death, and a priest can confirm in ceremonies of Christian initiation.

Ideally, the sacrament is conferred during the Eucharistic Liturgy. Elements of the rite include renewal of the promises of baptism, which confirmation ratifies and completes, and the laying on of hands — by symbolic elevation over the heads of those being confirmed — by the confirming bishop and priests participating in the ceremony.

"The entire rite," according to the *Ordo;* "has a twofold meaning. The laying of hands upon the candidates, done by the bishop and the concelebrating priests, expresses the biblical gesture by which the gift of the Holy Spirit is invoked. . . . The anointing with chrism and the accompanying words clearly signify the effect of the Holy Spirit. Signed with the perfumed oil by the bishop's hand, the baptized person receives the indelible character, the seal of the Lord, together with the Spirit who is given and who conforms the person more perfectly to Christ and gives him the grace of spreading the Lord's presence among men."

A sponsor is required for the person being confirmed. This can be one of the baptismal sponsors or another person. Parents can serve as sponsors for their own children.

In the Roman Rite, it has been customary for children to receive confirmation within a reasonable time after first Communion and confession. There is a developing trend, however, to defer confirmation until later when its significance becomes more evident. In the Eastern Rites, confirmation is administered at the same time as baptism.

The Holy Eucharist

The Holy Eucharist is a sacrifice (see The Mass) and the sacrament in which Christ is present and is received under the appearances of bread and wine.

The matter is bread of wheat, unleavened in the Roman Rite and leavened in the Eastern Rites, and wine of grape. The form consists of the words of consecration said by the priest at Mass: "This is my body. . . . This is the cup of my blood" (according to the traditional usage of the Roman Rite).

Only a priest can consecrate bread and wine so they become the body and blood of Christ. After consecration, however, the Eucharist can be administered by deacons and, for various reasons, by religious and lay persons.

Priests celebrating Mass receive the Eucharist under the appearances of bread and wine. In the Roman Rite, others usually receive under the appearances of bread only, i.e., the consecrated host; in some circumstances, however, they may receive under the appearances of both bread and wine. In Eastern-Rite practice, the faithful generally receive a piece of consecrated leavened bread which has been dipped into consecrated wine.

Conditions for receiving the Eucharist, commonly called **Holy Communion,** are the state of grace, the right intention, and observance of the Eucharistic fast.

The faithful of Roman Rite are required by a precept of the Church to receive the Eucharist at least once a year, during the Easter time (in the US, from the First Sunday of Lent to Trinity Sunday, inclusive).

(See Eucharistic Fast, Mass, Transubstantiation, Viaticum.)

First Communion and Confession: Pastoral practices concerning first Communion and first confession have undergone some change in recent years.

• Increasing emphasis is placed on the responsibility and role of parents in preparing children for these sacraments and in determining when the children are ready to receive them in a worthy manner.

• In some places parents give the instructions formerly imparted in group classes, and children receive their first Communion with members of their families rather than in large peer groups.

• First confession is deferred until some time after the reception of first Communion, on the grounds that children are not considered capable of serious sin at the age of seven or eight, when Communion is generally received for the first time, and therefore prior reception of the sacrament of penance is not necessary. (See separate entry).

Penance

Penance is the sacrament instituted by Christ for the forgiveness of sins committed after baptism. Its primary purpose is the restoration to grace of persons in the state of mortal sin; its secondary object is to increase sanctifying grace for persons already in the state of grace.

The matter of the sacrament consists of the **acts of the penitent:** (1) contrition — sorrow for sin because of a supernatural motive; (2) confession — all previously unconfessed mortal sins must be confessed, venial sins may but must not of necessity be confessed; (3) satisfaction — the penitent must have the intention to perform the works of penance or satisfaction enjoined by the confessor. The form of the sacrament consists of the words of absolution: "I absolve you from your sins, in the name of the Father and of the Son and of the Holy Spirit."

The minister of the sacrament is an authorized priest — i.e., one who, besides having the power of orders to forgive sins, also has faculties of jurisdiction granted by a competent ecclesiastical superior and/or by Canon Law.

The sacrament is necessary, by the institution of Christ, for the forgiveness of serious sins committed after baptism. Perfect contrition can restore a person to the state of grace even before sacramental confession. This contrition implies the intention of confessing all mortal sins when possible; such confession should be made before any other sacrament is received.

A precept of the church obliges the faithful of Roman Rite guilty of serious sin to confess at least once a year.

The Church favors more frequent reception of the sacrament, not only for the forgiveness of serious sins but also for reasons of devotion when there are no serious sins to be confessed. Devotional confession — in which venial sins or previously forgiven sins are confessed — serves the purpose of confirming a person in penance and conversion to God, and confers an increase of sanctifying grace.

(See Absolution, Confession, Confessional, Confessor, Contrition, Faculties, Forgiveness of Sin, Power of the Keys, Seal of Confession, Sin.)

Penitential Celebrations: Communal penitential celebrations are designed to emphasize the social dimensions of Christian life, the community aspect and significance of sin and penance.

When the sacrament of penance is administered during such a celebration, private confession of sin is required. Absolution should be given on an individual basis, immediately following confession. Absolution given publicly — a less desirable practice in view of existing regulations — would have effect only for the persons who had confessed to the priest imparting the absolution. General absolution for persons not confessing as required is out of order and without effect, except in unusual circumstances (see Instruction on General Absolution).

Other observances, as on occasions when the sacrament is not administered, include common prayer, hymns and songs, scriptural and other readings, examination of conscience, general confession of guilt for sin and of sorrow therefor, acts of penance or reconciliation, and a form of absolution resembling the one in the penitential rite of the Mass.

Anointing of the Sick

This sacrament, promulgated by St. James the Apostle (Jas. 5:13-15), is for the spiritual and physical welfare of persons who are ill and in some danger of death from internal causes. By the anointing with blessed oil and the prayer of a priest, the sacrament confers on the person comforting grace; the remission of venial sins and inculpably unconfessed mortal sins, together with at least some of the temporal punishment due for sins; and, sometimes, results in an improved state of health.

The matter of this sacrament is the anointing with blessed oil (of the sick) of the eyes, ears, nose, mouth, hands and feet; in cases of necessity a single anointing, usually of the forehead, suffices. The form is: "By this holy anointing and his most loving mercy, may the Lord pardon you for any sins you have committed by sight, hearing, etc."

Anointing of the sick, formerly called extreme unction, may be received more than once, e.g., in new or continuing stages of serious illness. Ideally, the sacrament should be administered while the recipient is conscious and in conjunction with the sacraments of penance and the Eucharist. It may be administered conditionally even after apparent death.

The sacrament can be administered during a communal celebration in some circumstances, as in a home for the aged.

Matrimony

Coverage of the sacrament of matrimony is given in the articles, Marriage Doctrine of Vatican II, Marriage Laws of the Church, Mixed Marriage Guidelines.

Holy Orders

Holy orders is the sacrament by which spiritual power and grace are given to enable an ordained minister to consecrate the Eucharist, forgive sins, perform other pastoral and ecclesiastical functions, and form the community of the People of God. Holy orders confers a character on the soul and can be received only once. The minister of the sacrament is a bishop.

Holy orders, like matrimony but in a different way, is a social sacrament. As the Second Vatican Council declared in the *Dogmatic Constitution on the Church:*

"For the nurturing and constant growth of the People of God, Christ the Lord instituted in His Church a variety of ministries, which work for the good of the whole body. For those ministers who are endowed with sacred power are servants of their brethren, so that all who are of the People of God, and therefore enjoy a true Christian dignity, can work toward a common goal freely and in an orderly way, and arrive at salvation" (No. 18).

"With their helpers, the priests and deacons, bishops have . . . taken up the service of the community, presiding in place of God over the flock whose shepherds they are, as teachers of doctrine, priests of sacred worship, and officers of good order" (No. 20).

The fullness of the priesthood belongs to those who have received the order of **bishop.** Bishops, in hierarchical union with the pope and their fellow bishops, are the successors of the apostles as pastors of the Church: they have individual responsibility for the care of the local churches they serve and collegial responsibility for the care of the universal Church (see Collegiality). In the ordination or consecration of bishops, the essential form is the imposition of hands by the consecrator(s) and the assigned prayer in the preface of the rite of ordination.

A **priest** is an ordained minister with the power to celebrate Mass, administer the sacraments, preach and teach the word of God, impart blessings, and perform additional pastoral functions, according to the mandate of his ecclesiastical superior.

Concerning priests, the Second Vatican Council stated in the *Dogmatic Constitution on the Church* (No. 28):

". . . The divinely established ecclesiastical ministry is exercised on different levels by those who from antiquity have been called bishops, priests, and deacons. Although priests do not possess the highest degree of the priesthood, and although they are dependent on the bishops in the exercise of their power, they are nevertheless united with the bishops in sacerdotal dignity. By the power of the sacrament of orders, and in the image of Christ the eternal High Priest (Hb. 5:1-10; 7:24; 9:11-28), they are consecrated to preach the gospel, shepherd the faithful, and celebrate divine worship as true priests of the New Testament. . . .

"Priests, prudent cooperators with the episcopal order as well as its aides and instruments, are called to serve the People of God. They constitute one priesthood with their bishop, although that priesthood is comprised of different functions. . . ."

In the ordination of a priest of Roman Rite, the essential matter is the imposition of hands on the heads of those being ordained by the ordaining bishop. The essential form is the accompanying prayer in the preface of the ordination ceremony. Other elements in the rite are the presentation of the implements of sacrifice — the chalice containing wine and the paten containing a host — with accompanying prayers.

Regarding the order of **deacon**, the *Dogmatic Constitution on the Church* (No. 29) stated:

"At a lower level of the hierarchy are deacons, upon whom hands are imposed 'not unto the priesthood, but unto a ministry of service.' For strengthened by sacramental grace, in communion with the bishop and his group of priests, they serve the People of God in the ministry of the liturgy, of the word, and of charity. It is the duty of the deacon, to the extent that he has been authorized by competent authority, to administer baptism solemnly, to be custodian and dispenser of the Eucharist, to assist at and bless marriages in the name of the Church, to bring Viaticum to the dying, to read the sacred Scripture to the faithful, to instruct and exhort the people, to preside at the worship and prayer of the faithful, to administer sacramentals, and to officiate at funeral and burial services. (Deacons are) dedicated to duties of charity and administration. . . ."

". . . The diaconate can in the future be restored as a proper and permanent rank of the hierarchy. It pertains to the competent territorial bodies of bishops, of one kind or another, to decide, with the approval of the Supreme Pontiff, whether and where it is opportune for such deacons to be appointed for the care of souls. With the consent of the Roman Pontiff, this diaconate will be able to be conferred upon men of more mature age, even upon those living in the married state. It may also be conferred upon suitable young men. For them, however, the law of celibacy must remain intact" (No. 29).

The Apostles ordained the first seven deacons (Acts 6:1-6): Stephen, Philip, Prochorus, Nicanor, Timon, Parmenas, Nicholas.

Other Ministeries: The Church later assigned ministerial duties to men in several other orders, as:

Subdeacon, with specific duties in liturgical worship, especially at Mass. The order, whose first extant mention dates from about the middle of the third century, was regarded as minor until the 13th century; afterwards, it was called a major order in the West but not in the East.

Acolyte, to serve in minor capacities in liturgical worship; a function now performed by Mass servers.

Exorcist, to perform services of exorcism for expelling evil spirits; a function which came to be reserved to specially delegated priests.

Lector, to read scriptural and other passages during liturgical worship; a function now generally performed by lay persons

Porter, to guard the entrance to an assembly of Christians and to ward off undesirables who tried to gain admittance; an order of early origin and utility but of present insignificance.

Long after it became evident that these positions and functions had fallen into general disuse or did not require clerical ordination, the Holy See started a revision of the orders in 1971. By an indult of Oct. 5, the bishops of the United States were permitted to omit ordaining porters and exorcists. Another indult, dated three days later, permitted the use of revised rites for ordaining acolytes and lectors, and authorized the use of a service celebrating admission to the clerical state in place of the ceremony of tonsure which had previously served this purpose.

To complete the revision, Pope Paul VI abolished Sept. 14, 1972, the orders of porter, exorcist and subdeacon; decreed that laymen, as well as candidates for the diaconate and priesthood, can be installed (rather than ordained) in the ministries (rather than orders) of acolyte and lector; reconfirmed the suppression of tonsure and its replacement with a service of dedication to God and the Church; and stated that a man enters the clerical state on ordination to the diaconate.

There were no doctrinal obstacles to the Pope's action, because the abolished orders had been instituted by the Church for functional purposes and were not considered to be parts of the sacrament of holy orders.

PERMANENT DIACONATE

Authorization for restoration of the permanent diaconate in the Roman Rite — making it possible for men to become deacons without being required to become priests — was promulgated by Pope Paul VI June 27, 1967, in a document entitled *Sacrum Diaconatus Ordinem* ("Sacred Order of the Diaconate").

The Pope's action implemented the desire expressed by the Second Vatican Council for reestablishment of the diaconate as an independent order in its own right not only to supply ministers for carrying on the work of the Church but also to fill out the hierarchical structure of the Church of Roman Rite.

Permanent deacons have been traditional in the Eastern Church. The Western Church, however, which followed the practice of conferring the diaconate only as a sacred order preliminary to the priesthood, did not have them for centuries.

The Pope's document, issued on his own initiative, provided:

• Qualified unmarried men 25 years of age or older may be ordained permanent deacons. They cannot marry after ordination.

• Qualified married men 35 years of age or older may be ordained permanent deacons. The consent of the wife of a prospective deacon is required. A married deacon cannot remarry after the death of his wife.

• Preparation for the diaconate includes a two- or three-year course of study and formation.

• Candidates who are not religious must be affiliated with a diocese.

• Deacons will practice their ministry under the direction of a bishop and the priests with whom they will be associated. (For functions, see the description of deacon, under Holy Orders.)

Restoration of the permanent diaconate in the United States was approved by the Holy See in October, 1968. Shortly afterwards the US bishops established a committee of the same name, which was chaired by Bishop John S. Spence in 1972. The committee operates through a secretariat, of which Father William W. Philbin of Chicago is executive director. Its offices are located at 1312 Massachusetts Ave. N. W., Washington, D.C. 20005.

Present Status

Father Philbin, executive director of the bishops' secretariat, reported May 25, 1972, that 72 permanent deacons had been ordained since the start of the first training program in the US in 1968. Fifty-four of the deacons were white; 11, black; seven, Spanish-speaking. Forty dioceses had deacons ordained or candidates in training, and 25 more dioceses had training programs in various stages of preparation.

At the same time, a total of 599 candidates, representing 35 dioceses, were in training. Of these, 543 were married; 44, single; 12, widowers. Three hundred and 41 had completed college; 234, high school; 24, grade school. Four hundred and 66 were white; 90, Spanish-speaking; 43, black. Twenty were in the 20's; 220, in the 30's; 227, in the 40's; 110, in the 50's; 19, in the 60's; 3 in the 70's. All but five were in part-time programs, living with their families and continuing to support themselves by secular work. The same time-work-support pattern was generally anticipated after ordination.

One hundred ordinations to the permanent diaconate were scheduled in eight dioceses between the end of May and September, 1972: 38, the largest group, in Galveston-Houston, in five separate ceremonies (one entirely in Spanish); 19 in Baltimore, in individual ceremonies; 10 in Phoenix, May 29; eight in Des Moines, June 4; eight in San Antonio, individually in home parishes; nine in Washington, D.C.; seven in Detroit; one in Richmond.

In addition, eight deacons were scheduled for ordination in Hartford by the end of the year.

The 100 ordinations scheduled through the summer brought the number of permanent deacons at work in US dioceses to a total of 172. It was estimated that the number would rise to 300 by February, 1973.

Functions

Deacons have various functions, depending on the nature of their assignments. Liturgically, they can officiate at baptisms, and weddings, can preach and distribute Holy Communion. Some are engaged in religious education work. All are intended to carry out works of charity and pastoral service of one kind or another.

According to a report submitted to the April, 1972, meeting of the National Conference of Catholic Bishops:

"In general, the deacons, all but a few of whom are continuing their secular work, try to retain three dimensions of ministry — of liturgy, of the word, and of service in charity. But, depending on the individual deacon's abilities and preferences (some, for instance, are not authorized to preach), most deacons concentrate their energies on one particular field of service.

"Once the deacon has been ordained, a basic liturgical ministry of assisting at the Eucharist, administering baptism, witnessing marriages, leading prayer services, etc., has been easy to inaugurate in parish settings; a priest simply gives him orientation. This same simplicity of structure is to some extent true of the ministry of the word. The far more challenging and difficult ministries to develop have been those which extend services of charity to people somewhat removed from parish structures — alienated young people, prisoners, the sick in hospitals and rest homes, old people, and the poor. This creative work of developing new ministries is now engaging the energies of the new deacons."

Early Reservations

The growth of the permanent diaconate has dispelled a number of reservations expressed about it in some quarters.

One fear, according to Father Philbin, "was that it might inhibit the growth of the lay apostolate. But I think the more people thought about that the more they realized that, far from inhibiting the lay apostolate, it could actually promote it."

Another early objection was that the diaconate might threaten the traditional role of the priest, since a deacon can do nearly everything liturgical a priest can do except celebrate Mass, anoint the sick and hear confessions.

But most priests who felt this way at first have apparently come to see the deacon "as a bridge bringing lay people and priests together," Father Philbin observed. "They also realize that the deacon's role is broader than just his liturgical functions. The ministry of charitable service to individuals and the community is even more distinctive to the deacon."

In support of this view, he cited a finding from the four-year study of US priests which was sponsored by the National Conference of Catholic Bishops. The study showed that at least 80 per cent of bishops, religious superiors and priests — diocesan and religious — polled on the subject favored "introduction of the married diaconate whenever and however the local church chooses."

The show of support for the diaconate program meant that only a small minority of priests felt threatened by it, Father Philbin stated, "or their generous interest in the total apostolate must be the key factor — because they're for it."

The priest noted that "most people still haven't heard that much about the diaconate, except in dioceses which have programs." Knowledge of the restored ministry was increasing, however, especially since publication of a 1971 report by a study team of the Catholic Theological Society of America, which backgrounded the diaconate and supported its growth.

The National Conference of Catholic Bishops, meeting in April, 1972, approved a resolution to seek permission from the Holy See to lower the age, from 35 to 30, for the ordination of mature married men to the permanent diaconate. The permission was refused.

Training Programs

The first training centers for permanent deacons were located in Detroit and Orchard Lake, Mich.; Washington, D.C.; St. John's University, Collegeville, Minn.; Dubuque, Iowa, and Atlanta, Ga.

The Archdiocese of Chicago started the largest training program early in 1971 with 151 candidates. They included 43 Latins, 21 blacks, married and single men, with an age range of 26 to 70.

In Detroit, Cardinal John F. Dearden approved in March, 1971, a proposal to establish a training program for Latin-American candidates. The purpose of the program, it was stated, was to provide service to the Latin community by Hispanics who speak Spanish, identify with Latin culture and have the confidence of the community. According to Father Edward J. Baldwin, archdiocesan director of the diaconate program, the Latins consider the "lack of having their own people minister to them an ethnic problem, not a church problem. As such, they feel they can come up with a solution via their own diaconate program."

Efforts to enroll Spanish-speaking and black candidates in training programs have increased since 1971.

Training programs of spiritual, doctrinal and pastoral formation are generally based on *Permanent Deacons in the United States: Guidelines on Their Formation and Ministry,* published by the Bishops' Committee on the Permanent Diaconate in September, 1971.

Permanent diaconate training programs and their directors, as of July 31, 1972, were as follows. The listing is alphabetical by state; unless otherwise indicated, the diocese is the same as the city in the address.

Rev. R. William O'Brien, 400 E. Monroe, Phoenix, Ariz. 85004;

Rev. Henry F. Fawcett, 5961 Linda Vista Rd., San Diego, Calif. 92110;

Rev. Leo R. Horrigan, 938 Bannock St., P.O. Box 1620, Denver, Colo. 80201;

Rev. Joseph P. Donahue, 467 Bloomfield Ave., Bloomfield, Conn. 06002 (Hartford);

Rev. Robert Kearns, S.S.J., St. Joseph's Seminary, 1200 Varnum St. N. E., Washington, D.C. 20017 (and Richmond, Va.);

Rev. John D. Ring, 1307 S. Wabash, Chicago, Ill. 60605;

Mr. Kevin M. Ranaghan, Apostolic Institute, Inc., P. O. Box 14, Mishawaka, Ind. 46544 (Fort Wayne-South Bend);

Rev. Duane J. Weiland, P. O. Box 1816 - 2910 Grand Ave., Des Moines, Ia. 50306;

Mr. James Awalt, c/o 4418 Belvieu Ave., Baltimore, Md. 21215;

Rev. Edward J. Baldwin, 305 Michigan Ave., Detroit, Mich. 48226;

Rev. Michael A. Danner, 2001 Robinson Rd., Grand Rapids, Mich. 49506;

Rev. Anthony Kosnik, The Orchard Lake Seminary, Orchard Lake, Mich. 48034 (for several dioceses);

Rev. Kieran Nolan, O.S.B., St. John's University, Collegeville, Minn. 56321 (for several dioceses);

Rev. Msgr. Ernest J. Fiedler, 5141 Main St., Kansas City, Mo. 64112 (and Kansas City in Kansas);

Rev. Patrick McCaslin, 5316 N. 14th Ave., Omaha, Nebr. 68110;

Rev. Pius Winter, O.F.M., 415 East Green, Gallup, N.M. 87301;

Rev. Spencer Stopa, 3200 Canyon Rd., Los Alamos, N.M. 87544 (Santa Fe);

Rev. John H. O'Brien, Director of Spanish-Speaking Apostolate, 417 Sackett St., Brooklyn, N.Y. 11231;

Rev. Thomas P. Leonard, St. Joseph's Seminary, Seminary Ave., Dunwoodie, Yonkers, N.Y. 10704;

Rev. George E. Saladna, St. Paul Seminary, 2900 Noblestown Rd., Pittsburgh, Pa. 15205;

Rev. Thomas Duffy, 119 Broad St., Charleston, S.C. 29401.

Rev. Milam E. Kleas, 10726 Bessemer St., P. O. Box 34428, Houston, Tex. 77034;

Rev. Alton Rudolph, P.O. Box 13190, San Antonio, Tex. 78213;

The bishops of Puerto Rico reported in January, 1972, that they had started a training program for candidates — single and married men, and men religious — for the permanent diaconate.

In requesting Vatican approval of their program, the bishops stressed the shortage of priests in the four dioceses of the island (670 for 2.6 million Catholics), the need to free pastors from non-priestly functions, and opportunities in remote rural areas for the work of deacons.

MARRIAGE DOCTRINE

The following excerpts, stating key points of doctrine on marriage, are from the *Pastoral Constitution on the Church in the Modern World* (Nos. 48 to 51) promulgated by the Second Vatican Council.

Conjugal Covenant

"The intimate partnership of married life and love has been established by the Creator and qualified by His laws. It is rooted in the conjugal covenant of irrevocable personal consent. . . .

". . . God Himself is the author of matrimony, endowed as it is with various benefits and purposes. All of these have a very decisive bearing on the continuation of the human race, on the personal development and eternal destiny of the individual members of a family, and on the dignity, stability, peace, and prosperity of the family itself and of human society as a whole. By their very nature, the institution of matrimony itself and conjugal love are ordained for the procreation and education of children, and find in them their ultimate crown.

"Thus a man and a woman . . . render mutual help and service to each other through an intimate union of their persons and of their actions. Through this union they experience the meaning of their oneness and attain to it with growing perfection day by day. As a mutual gift of two persons, this intimate union, as well as the good of the children, imposes total fidelity on the spouses and argues for an unbreakable oneness between them" (No. 48).

Sacrament of Matrimony

"Christ the Lord abundantly blessed this many-faceted love. . . . The Savior of men and the Spouse of the Church comes into the lives of married Christians through the sacrament of matrimony. He abides with them thereafter so that, just as He loved the Church and handed Himself over on her behalf, the spouses may love each other with perpetual fidelity through mutual self-bestowal.

". . . Graced with the dignity and office of fatherhood and motherhood, parents will energetically acquit themselves of a duty which devolves primarily upon them, namely education, and especially religious education.

". . . The Christian family, which springs from marriage as a reflection of the loving covenant uniting Christ with the Church, and as a participation in that covenant, will manifest to all men the Savior's living presence in the world, and the genuine nature of the Church . . ." (No. 48).

Conjugal Love

"The biblical Word of God several times urges the betrothed and the married to nourish and develop their wedlock by pure conjugal love and undivided affection. . . .

"This love is an eminently human one since it is directed from one person to another through an affection of the will. It involves the good of the whole person. Therefore it can enrich the expressions of body and mind with a unique dignity, ennobling these expressions as special ingredients and signs of the friendship distinctive of marriage. This love the Lord has judged worthy of special gifts, healing, perfecting, and exalting gifts of grace and of charity.

"Such love, merging the human with the divine, leads the spouses to a free and mutual gift of themselves, a gift proving itself by gentle affection and by deed. Such love pervades the whole of their lives. Indeed, by its generous activity it grows better and grows greater. Therefore it far excels mere erotic inclination, which, selfishly pursued, soon enough fades wretchedly away.

"This love is uniquely expressed and perfected through the marital act. The actions within marriage by which the couple are united intimately and chastely are noble and worthy ones. Expressed in a manner which is truly human, these actions signify and promote that mutual self-giving by which spouses enrich each other with a joyful and a thankful will.

"Sealed by mutual faithfulness and hallowed above all by Christ's sacrament, this love remains steadfastly true in body and in mind, in bright days or dark. It will never be profaned by adultery or divorce. Firmly established by the Lord, the unity of marriage will radiate from the equal personal dignity of wife and husband, a dignity acknowledged by mutual and total love.

"The steady fulfillment of the duties of this Christian vocation demands notable virtue. For this reason, strengthened by grace for holiness of life, the couple will painstakingly cultivate and pray for constancy of love, largeheartedness, and the spirit of sacrifice . . ." (No. 49).

Fruitfulness of Marriage

"Marriage and conjugal love are by their nature ordained toward the begetting and educating of children. Children are really the supreme gift of marriage and contribute very substantially to the welfare of their parents. . . . God Himself . . . wished to share with man a certain special participation in His own creative work. Thus He blessed male and female, saying: 'Increase and multiply' (Gn. 1:28).

"Hence, while not making the other purposes of matrimony of less account, the true practice of conjugal love, and the whole meaning of the family life which results from it, have this aim: that the couple be ready with stout hearts to cooperate with the love of the

Creator and the Savior, who through them will enlarge and enrich His own family day by day.

"Parents should regard as their proper mission the task of transmitting human life and educating those to whom it has been transmitted. They should realize that they are thereby cooperators with the love of God the Creator, and are, so to speak, the interpreters of that love. Thus they will fulfill their task with human and Christian responsibility . . ." (No. 50).

Norms of Judgment

"They will thoughtfully take into account both their own welfare and that of their children, those already born and those which may be foreseen. For this accounting they will reckon with both the material and the spiritual conditions of the times as well as of their state in life. Finally, they will consult the interests of the family group, of temporal society, and of the Church herself.

"The parents themselves should ultimately make this judgment in the sight of God. But in their manner of acting, spouses should be aware that they cannot proceed arbitrarily. They must always be governed according to a conscience dutifully conformed to the divine law itself, and should be submissive toward the Church's teaching office, which authentically interprets that law in the light of the gospel. That divine law reveals and protects the integral meaning of conjugal love, and impels it toward a truly human fulfillment. . . .

"Marriage to be sure is not instituted solely for procreation. Rather, its very nature as an unbreakable compact between persons, and the welfare of the children, both demand that the mutual love of the spouses, too, be embodied in a rightly ordered manner, that it grow and ripen. Therefore, marriage persists as a whole manner and communion of life, and maintains its value and indissolubility, even when offspring are lacking — despite, rather often, the very intense desire of the couple" (No. 50).

Love and Life

"This Council realizes that certain modern conditions often keep couples from arranging their married lives harmoniously, and that they find themselves in circumstances where at least temporarily the size of their families should not be increased. As a result, the faithful exercise of love and the full intimacy of their lives are hard to maintain. But where the intimacy of married life is broken off, it is not rare for its faithfulness to be imperiled and its quality of fruitfulness ruined. For then the upbringing of the children and the courage to accept new ones are both endangered.

"To these problems there are those who presume to offer dishonorable solutions. Indeed, they do not recoil from the taking of life. But the Church issues the reminder that a true contradiction cannot exist between the divine laws pertaining to the transmission of life and those pertaining to the fostering of authentic conjugal love.

"For God, the Lord of Life, has conferred on men the surpassing ministry of safeguarding life — a ministry which must be fulfilled in a manner which is worthy of men. Therefore from the moment of its conception life must be guarded with the greatest care, while abortion and infanticide are unspeakable crimes. The sexual characteristics of man and the human faculty of reproduction wonderfully exceed the dispositions of lower forms of life. Hence the acts themselves which are proper to conjugal love and which are exercised in accord with genuine human dignity must be honored with great reverence" (No. 51).

Church Teaching

"Therefore when there is question of harmonizing conjugal love with the responsible transmission of life, the moral aspect of any procedure does not depend solely on the sincere intentions or on an evaluation of motives. It must be determined by objective standards. These, based on the nature of the human person and his acts, preserve the full sense of mutual self-giving and human procreation in the context of true love. Such a goal cannot be achieved unless the virtue of conjugal chastity is sincerely practiced. Relying on these principles, sons of the Church may not undertake methods of regulating procreation which are found blameworthy by the teaching authority of the Church in its unfolding of the divine law.

"Everyone should be persuaded that human life and the task of transmitting it are not realities bound up with this world alone. Hence they cannot be measured or perceived only in terms of it, but always have a bearing on the eternal destiny of men" (No. 51).

HUMANAE VITAE

Marriage doctrine and morality were the subjects of the encyclical *Humanae Vitae* ("Of Human Life") issued by Pope Paul July 29, 1968. Following are a number of key excerpts from the document, which was framed in the pattern of traditional teaching and statements by the Second Vatican Council.

". . . each and every marriage act ('quilibet matrimonii usus') must remain open to the transmission of life" (No. 11).

"Indeed, by its intimate structure, the conjugal act, while most closely uniting husband and wife, capacitates them for the generation of new lives, according to laws inscribed in the very being of man and of woman. By safeguarding both these essential aspects, the unitive and the procreative, the conjugal act preserves in its fullness the sense of true mutual love and its ordination toward man's most high calling to parenthood" (No. 12).

"It is, in fact, justly observed that a conjugal act imposed upon one's partner without regard for his or her condition and lawful desires is not a true act of love, and therefore denies an exigency of right moral order in the relationships between husband and wife. Hence, one who reflects well must also recognize that a reciprocal act of love which jeopardizes the responsibility to transmit life — which God the Creator, according to particular laws, inserted therein — is in contradiction with the design constitutive of marriage and with the will of the Author of life. To use this divine gift, destroying, even if only partially, its meaning and its purpose, is to contradict the nature both of man and of woman and of their most intimate relationship, and therefore it is to contradict also the plan of God and His will" (No. 13).

Forbidden Actions: ". . . the direct interruption of the generative process already begun, and, above all, directly willed and procured abortion, even if for therapeutic reasons, are to be absolutely excluded as licit means of regulating birth.

"Equally to be excluded . . . is direct sterilization, whether perpetual or temporary, whether of the man or of the woman. Similarly excluded is every action which, either in anticipation of the conjugal act, or in its accomplishment, or in the development of its natural consequences, proposes, whether as an end or as a means, to render procreation impossible.

Inadmissible Principles: "To justify conjugal acts made intentionally infecund, one cannot invoke as valid reasons the lesser evil, or the fact that such acts would constitute a whole together with the fecund acts already performed or to follow later and hence would share in one and the same moral goodness. In truth, if it is sometimes licit to tolerate a lesser evil in order to avoid a greater evil or to promote a greater good, it is not licit, even for the gravest reasons, to do evil so that good may follow therefrom; that is, to make into the object of a positive act of the will something which is intrinsically disorder, and hence unworthy of the human person, even when the intention is to safeguard or promote individual, family or social well-being.

"Consequently, it is an error to think that a conjugal act which is deliberately made infecund, and so is intrinsically dishonest, could be made honest and right by the ensemble of a fecund conjugal life" (No. 14).

Rhythm: "If, then, there are serious motives to space out births, which derive from the physical or psychological conditions of husband and wife, or from external conditions, the Church teaches that it is then licit to take into account the natural rhythms immanent in the generative functions, for the use of marriage in the infecund periods only, and in this way to regulate birth without offending "earlier stated principles (No. 16).

Authoritative Teaching: Pope Paul called the foregoing teaching authoritative, although not infallible. He left it open for further study. As a practical norm to be followed, however, he said it involved the binding force of religious assent.

With pastoral concern, the Pope said: "We do not at all intend to hide the sometimes serious difficulties inherent in the life of Christian married persons; for them, as for everyone else, 'the gate is narrow and the way is hard that leads to life.' But the hope of that life must illuminate their way, as with courage they strive to live with wisdom, justice and piety in this present time, knowing that the figure of this world passes away.

"Let married couples, then, face up to the efforts needed, supported by the faith and hope which 'do not disappoint . . . because God's love has been poured into our hearts through the Holy Spirit, who has been given to us.' Let them implore divine assistance by persevering prayer; above all, let them draw from the source of grace and charity in the Eucharist. And, if sin should still keep its hold over them, let them not be discouraged but rather have recourse with humble perseverance to the mercy of God, which is poured forth in the sacrament of penance" (No. 25).

Reactions: Exception was taken to the binding force of the encyclical — notably by the bishops of Belgium, Austria and France, and many theologians — for several reasons: rights of conscience; questions concerning the natural-law concept underlying the encyclical; the thesis of totality; the proposition that contraception may in some cases be the lesser of two evils. All agreed, however, that conscientious objection to the encyclical could not be taken without serious reasons and reflection.

Pope Paul, since publication of the encyclical, has not moved to alter its contents or to mitigate its binding force.

MARRIAGE LAWS

The Catholic Church, in line with the belief that it was established and commissioned by Christ to provide and administer the means of salvation to men, claims jurisdiction over its members in matters pertaining to marriage, which is a sacrament. The purpose of its laws in this area is to safeguard the validity and lawfulness of marriage.

Catholics are bound by all marriage laws of the Church. Non-Catholics, whether baptized or not, are not considered bound by these ecclesiastical laws except in cases of marriage with a Catholic. Certain natural laws, in the Catholic view, bind all men and women, irrespective of their religious beliefs; accordingly, marriage is prohibited before the time of puberty, without knowledge and free mutual consent, in the case of an already existing valid marriage bond, in the case of antecedent and perpetual impotence.

Formalities

These include, in addition to arrangements for the time and place of the marriage ceremony, doctrinal and moral instruction concerning marriage and the recording of data which verifies in documentary form the eligibility and freedom of the persons to marry. Records of this kind, which are confidential, are preserved in the archives of the church where the marriage takes place.

Premarital instructions are the subject matter of Pre-Cana Conferences.

Mixed Marriages

Pastoral experience, which the Catholic Church shares with other religious bodies, confirms the fact that marriages of persons of different beliefs involve special problems related to the continuing religious practice of the concerned persons and to the religious education and formation of their children.

Pastoral measures to minimize these problems include instruction of a non-Catholic party in essentials of the Catholic faith for purposes of understanding. Desirably, some instruction should also be given the Catholic party regarding his or her partner's beliefs.

The Catholic party to a mixed marriage is required to declare his (her) intention of continuing practice of the Catholic faith and to promise to do all in his power to share his faith with children born of the marriage by having them baptized and raised as Catholics. No declarations or promises are required of the non-Catholic party, but he (she) must be informed of the declaration and promise made by the Catholic.

Notice of the Catholic's declaration and promise is an essential part of the application made to a bishop for dispensation from the impediment of mixed religion or disparity of worship (see below).

Mixed marriages may take place with a Nuptial Mass.

A non-Catholic minister may not only attend a marriage but may also address, pray with and give his blessing to the couple following the marriage ceremony.

If a dispensation from the canonical form of marriage is granted by a bishop, a non-Catholic minister can officiate at a mixed marriage.

Banns

The banns are public announcements made in their parish churches, usually on three successive Sundays, of the names of persons who intend to marry. Persons who know of reasons in church law why a proposed marriage should not take place, are obliged to make them known to the pastor.

Marital Consent

The exchange of consent to the marriage contract, which is essential for valid marriage, must be rational, free, true and mutual.

Matrimonial consent can be invalidated by an essential defect, substantial error, the strong influence of force and fear, the presence of a condition or intention against the nature of marriage.

Form of Marriage

A Catholic is required, for validity and lawfulness, to contract marriage — with another Catholic or with a non-Catholic — in the presence of a competent priest or deacon and two witnesses.

There are two exceptions to this law. A Roman Rite Catholic (since Mar. 25, 1967) or an Eastern Rite Catholic (since Nov. 21, 1964) can contract marriage validly in the presence of a priest of a separated Eastern Rite Church, provided other requirements of law are complied with. With permission of the competent Roman-Rite or Eastern-Rite bishop, this form of marriage is lawful, as well as valid. (See Eastern Rite Laws, below.)

With these two exceptions, and aside from cases covered by special permission, the Church does not regard as valid any marriages involving Catholics which take place before non-Catholic ministers of religion or civil officials. (See Mixed Marriage Guidelines.)

An excommunication formerly in force against Catholics who celebrated marriage before a non-Catholic minister was abrogated in a decree issued by the Sacred Congregation for the Doctrine of the Faith on Mar. 18, 1966.

The ordinary place of marriage is the parish of the bride, of the Catholic party in case of a mixed marriage, or of an Eastern Rite groom.

Church law regarding the form of marriage does not affect non-Catholics in marriages among themselves. The Church recognizes as valid the marriages of non-Catholics before ministers of religion and civil officials, unless they are rendered null and void on other grounds.

Impediments

Impediments to marriage are factors which render a marriage unlawful or invalid.

Prohibitory Impediments, which make a marriage unlawful but do not affect validity:

• simple vows of virginity, perpetual chastity, celibacy, to enter a religious order or to receive sacred orders;

• difference of religion, which obtains when one party is a Catholic and the other is a baptized non-Catholic.

The impediment of legal relationship is not in force in the US.

Diriment Impediments, which make a marriage invalid as well as unlawful:

• age, which obtains before completion of the 14th year for a woman and the 16th year for a man;

• impotency, if it is antecedent to the marriage and permanent (this differs from sterility, which is not an impediment);

• the bond of an existing valid marriage;

• disparity of worship, which obtains when one party is a Catholic and the other party is unbaptized;

• sacred orders;

• religious profession of the solemn vow of chastity;

• abduction, which impedes the freedom of the person abducted;

• crime, variously involving elements of adultery, promise or attempt to marry, conspiracy to murder a husband or wife;

• blood relationship in the direct line (father-daughter, mother-son, etc.) and within the third degree of the collateral line (brother-sister, first and second cousins);

• affinity, or relationship resulting from a valid marriage, in any degree of the direct line and within the second degree of the collateral line;

• spiritual relationship arising through baptism — between a godchild and godparent, between the person baptized and the one who performed the baptism;

• public honesty, arising from an invalid marriage or from public or notorious concubinage; it renders either party incapable of marrying relatives of the other in the first and second degrees of the direct line.

Dispensations from Impediments: Persons hindered by impediments either may not or cannot marry unless they are dispensed therefrom in view of reasons recognized in canon law. Local bishops can dispense from the impediments most often encountered (e.g., difference of religion, disparity of worship) as well as others.

Decision regarding some dispensations is reserved to the Holy See.

Separation

A valid and consummated marriage of baptized persons cannot be dissolved by any human authority or any cause other than the death of one of the persons.

In other circumstances:

• 1. A valid but unconsummated marriage of baptized persons, or of a baptized and an unbaptized person, can be dissolved:

a. by the solemn religious profession of one of the persons, made with permission of the pope. In such a case, the bond is dissolved at the time of profession, and the other person is free to marry again;

b. by dispensation from the pope, requested for a grave reason by one or both of the persons. If the dispensation is granted, both persons are free to marry again.

Dispensations in these cases are granted for reasons connected with the spiritual welfare of the concerned persons.

• 2. A legitimate marriage, even consummated, of unbaptized persons can be dissolved in favor of one of them who subsequently receives the sacrament of baptism. This is the Pauline Privilege, so called because it was promulgated by St. Paul (1 Cor. 7:12-15) as a means of protecting the faith of converts. Requisites for granting the privilege are:

a. marriage prior to the baptism of either person;

b. reception of baptism by one person;

c. refusal of the unbaptized person to live in peace with the baptized person and without interfering with his or her freedom to practice the Christian faith. The privilege does not apply if the unbaptized person agrees to these conditions.

• 3. A legitimate and consummated marriage of a baptized and an unbaptized person can be dissolved by the pope in virtue of the Privilege of Faith, also called the Petrine Privilege.

Civil Divorce: Because of the unity and the indissolubility of marriage, the Church denies that civil divorce can break the bond of a valid marriage, whether the marriage involves two Catholics, a Catholic and a non-Catholic, or non-Catholics with each other.

In view of serious circumstances of marital distress, the Church permits an innocent and aggrieved party, whether wife or husband, to seek and obtain a civil divorce for the purpose of acquiring title and right to the civil effects of divorce, such as separate habitation and maintenance, and the custody of children. Permission for this kind of action should be obtained from proper church authority. The divorce, if obtained, does not break the bond of a valid marriage.

Under other circumstances — as would obtain if a marriage was invalid (see Decree of Nullity, below) — civil divorce is permitted for civil effects and as a civil ratification of the fact that the marriage bond really does not exist.

In the United States, according to a decree of the Third Plenary Council of Baltimore, the penalty of excommunication is automatically incurred by persons who attempt to contract marriage after having obtained a divorce from a valid marriage.

Decree of Nullity, sometimes improperly called an annulment. This is a decision by a competent church authority — e.g., a bishop, a diocesan marriage tribunal, the Sacred Roman Rota — that an apparently valid marriage was actually invalid from the beginning because of the unknown or concealed existence, from the beginning, of a diriment impediment, an essential defect in consent, radical incapability for marriage, or a condition placed by one or both of the parties against the very nature of marriage.

Eastern Rite Laws

Marriage laws of the Eastern Church differ in several respects from the legislation of the Roman Rite. The regulations in effect since

May 2, 1949, were contained in the motu proprio *Crebre Allatae* issued by Pius XII the previous February.

According to both the Roman Code of Canon Law and the Oriental Code, marriages between Roman Rite Catholics and Eastern Rite Catholics ordinarily take place in the rite of the groom and have canonical effects in that rite.

Regarding the form for the celebration of marriages between Eastern Catholics and baptized Eastern non-Catholics, the Second Vatican Council declared:

"By way of preventing invalid marriages between Eastern Catholics and baptized Eastern non-Catholics, and in the interests of the permanence and sanctity of marriage and of domestic harmony, this sacred Synod decrees that the canonical 'form' for the celebration of such marriages obliges only for lawfulness. For their validity, the presence of a sacred minister suffices, as long as the other requirements of law are honored" *(Decree on Eastern Catholic Churches,* No. 18).

Marriages taking place in this manner are lawful, as well as valid, with permission of a competent Eastern Rite bishop.

The Rota

The Sacred Roman Rota is the ordinary court of appeal for marriage, and some other cases, which are appealed to the Holy See from lower church courts. Appeals are made to the Rota if decisions by diocesan and archdiocesan courts fail to settle the matter in dispute.

MIXED MARRIAGES

Following are excerpts from a statement, *Implementation of the Apostolic Letter on Mixed Marriages,* approved by the National Conference of Catholic Bishops Nov. 16, 1970, and effective in the US since Jan. 1, 1971. The text of the statement was circulated by NC News Service. The text of the letter on which the statement was based, *Matrimonia Mixta,* was issued by Pope Paul VI Mar. 31, 1970; it appeared in the 1971 edition of the Almanac, pp. 278-81.

Aim of Church

Within marriage the Church seeks always to uphold the strength and stability of marital union and the family which flows from it.

As the Apostolic Letter observes, the "perfect union of mind and full communion of life" to which married couples aspire can be more readily achieved when both partners share the same Catholic belief and life. For this reason, the Church greatly desires that Catholics marry Catholics and generally discourages mixed marriages.

Yet, recognizing that mixed marriages do occur, the Church, upholding the principles of Divine Law, makes special arrangements for them. And, recognizing that these marriages do at times encounter special difficulties, the Church wishes to see that special help and support are extended to the couples concerned.

Pastoral Concern

The Apostolic Letter stresses the importance of individualized support for diverse situations. It recognizes that ". . . the canonical discipline on mixed marriages cannot be uniform and must be adapted . . ." and "the pastoral care to be given to the married people and children of marriage" must also be adapted "according to the distinct circumstances of the married couple and the differing degrees of their ecclesiastical communion." Consequently, pastors, in exercising their ministry in behalf of marriages that unite Catholics and others will do so with zealous concern and respect for the couples involved. They should have an active and positive regard for the holy state in which such couples are united.

In such marriages, the conscientious devotion of the Catholic to the Catholic Church is to be safeguarded, and the conscience of the other partner is to be respected. This is in keeping with the principle of religious liberty. (Cf. *Declaration on Religious Freedom.* (No. 30).

Values in Marriage

The sacred character of all valid marriages, including those which the Church does not consider as sacramental, is recognized.

The broad areas of agreement which unite Christians and Jews in their appreciation of the religious character of marriage should be kept significantly in mind. (Cf. *Joint Statement on Marriage and Family Life in the United States,* issued by the United States Catholic Conference, the National Council of the Churches of Christ, and the Synagogue Council of America, June 8, 1966.)

In this context, it should be clearly noted that, while Catholics are required to observe the Catholic form of marriage for validity, unless dispensed by their bishop, the Catholic Church recognizes the reality of marriages contracted validly among those who are not Christians and among those Christians separated from us.

Sacramental Marriage

In addition to the sacred character of all valid marriages, still more must be said of marriages between a Catholic and another baptized Christian. According to our Catholic tradition, we believe such marriages to be truly sacramental. The Apostolic Letter states that there exists between the persons united in them a special "communion of spiritual benefits." These spiritual bonds in which couples are united are grounded in the "true though imperfect, communion" which exists between the Catholic Church and all who believe in Christ and are properly baptized (cf. *Decree on Ecumenism.* No. 3). Along with us, such persons are honored by the title of Christian and are rightly regarded as brothers in the Lord. In marriages which unite Catholics and other baptized Christians, the couple should be encouraged to recognize in practical ways what they share together in the life of grace, in faith, hope and charity along with other interior gifts of the Holy Spirit, and that in service to the same Lord they await the salvation which He promised to those who would be His followers.

Difficulties

A number of the particular difficulties faced by Catholics and other Christians in mixed marriages result from the division among Christians. However successful these marriages may be, they do not erase the pain of that wider division. Yet this division need not weaken these marriages; and, given proper understanding, they may lead to a deep spiritual unity between the spouses.

Joint Pastoral Care

In order to aid these couples to come to this deep understanding of their married life together, when possible, their Catholic and other Christian pastors should jointly do all that they can to prepare them for marriage and to support them and their families with all the aids their ministry can provide.

The pastors of the different Christian communities can best bring the couple to a keen awareness of all that they have in common as Christians as well as to a proper appreciation of the gravity of the differences that yet remain between their churches.

In their homes, these couples should be encouraged in practical ways to develop a common life of prayer, calling upon the many elements of spirituality which they share as a common Christian heritage and expressing their own common faith in the Lord, together asking Him to help them grow in their love for each other, to bless their families with the graces they need, and to keep them always mindful of the needs of others. The example of parents united in prayer is especially important for the children whom God may give them. In regard to public worship together in each other's churches, pastors may explain to the couple the provisions made for this by the Holy See in the *Ecumenical Directory.*

Religious Education

Beyond this, parents have the right and the responsibility to provide for the religious education of their children. This right is clearly taught by Vatican II: "Since the family is a society in its own original right, it has the right freely to live its own domestic religious life under the guidance of parents. Parents, moreover, have the right to determine, in ac-

cordance with their own religious beliefs, the kind of religious education that their children are to receive" *(Declaration on Religious Freedom,* No. 5).

It is evident that in preparing for a mixed marriage, the couple will have to reach decisions and make specific choices in order to fulfill successfully the responsibility that is theirs toward their children in this respect. It is to be hoped for their own sake that in this matter the couple may reach a common mind.

If this issue is not resolved before marriage, the couple, as sad experience has shown, find a severe strain in their marital life that can subject them to well-meaning but tension-building pressures from relatives on both sides.

If this issue cannot be resolved, there is a serious question whether the couple should marry.

In reaching a concrete decision concerning the baptism and religious education of children, both partners should remember that neither thereby abdicates the fundamental responsibility of parents to see that their children are instilled with deep and abiding religious values.

In this the Catholic partner is seriously bound to act in accord with his faith which recognizes that: "This is the unique Church of Christ which in the Creed we avow as one, holy, catholic and apostolic. After His Resurrection our Savior handed her over to Peter to be shepherded (Jn. 21:17), commissioning him and the other apostles to propagate and govern her (cf. Mt. 28:18, ff.). Her He erected for all ages as 'the pillar and mainstay of the truth, (1 Tm. 3:15). This Church, constituted and organized in the world as a society, subsists in the Catholic Church, which is governed by the successor of Peter and by the bishops in union with that successor, although many elements of sanctification and of truth can be found outside of her visible structure. These elements, however, as gifts properly belonging to the Church of Christ, possess an inner dynamism toward Catholic unity" *(Dogmatic Constitution on the Church,* No. 8). This faith is the source of a serious obligation in conscience on the part of the Catholic, whose conscience in this regard must be respected.

Norms

Pastoral Responsibility: In every diocese, there shall be appropriate informational programs to explain both the reasons for restrictions upon mixed marriages and the positive spiritual values to be sought in such marriages when permitted. This is particularly important if the non-Catholic is a Christian believer and the unity of married and family life is ultimately based upon the baptism of both wife and husband. If possible, all such programs should be undertaken . . . in conjunction with non-Catholic authorities.

In addition to the customary marriage preparation programs, it is the serious duty of each one in the pastoral ministry, according to his own responsibility, office or assignment, to undertake:

(a) the spiritual and catechetical preparation, especially in regard to the "ends and essential properties of marriage (which) are not to be excluded by either party" (cf. *Matrimonia Mixta,* No. 6), on a direct and individual basis, of couples who seek to enter a mixed marriage, and

(b) continued concern and assistance to the wife and husband in mixed marriages and to their children, so that married and family life may be supported in unity, respect for conscience, and common spiritual benefit.

In the assistance which he gives in preparation for marriage between a Catholic and a non-Catholic, and his continued efforts to help all married couples and families, the priest should endeavor to be in contact and to cooperate with the minister or religious counselor of the non-Catholic.

Promise: The declaration and promise by the Catholic, necessary for dispensation from the impediment to a mixed marriage (either mixed religion or disparity of worship), shall be made in the following words or their substantial equivalent:

"I reaffirm my faith in Jesus Christ and, with God's help, intend to continue living that faith in the Catholic Church.

"I promise to do all in my power to share the faith I have received with our children by having them baptized and reared as Catholics."

The declaration and promise are made in the presence of a priest or deacon either orally or in writing as the Catholic prefers.

The form of the declaration and promise is not altered in the case of the marriage of a Catholic with another baptized Christian, but the priest should draw the attention of the Catholic to the communion of spiritual benefits in such a Christian marriage. The promise and declaration should be made in the light of the "certain, though imperfect, communion" of the non-Catholic with the Catholic Church because of his belief in Christ and baptism (cf. *Decree on Ecumenism,* No. 3).

Informing the Non-Catholic: At an opportune time before marriage, and preferably as part of the usual premarital instruction, the non-Catholic must be informed of the promises and of the responsibility of the Catholic. No precise manner or occasion of informing the non-Catholic is prescribed. It may be done by the priest, deacon or the Catholic party. No formal statement of the non-Catholic is required. But the mutual understanding of this question beforehand should prevent possible disharmony that might otherwise arise during married life.

The priest who submits the request for dispensation from the impediment to a mixed marriage shall certify that the declaration and promise have been made by the Catholic and that the non-Catholic has been informed of this requirement. This is done in the following or similar words:

"The required promise and declaration have been made by the Catholic in my presence. The non-Catholic has been informed of this requirement so that it is certain that he (she) is aware of the promise and obligation on the part of the Catholic."

The promise of the Catholic must be sincerely made, and is to be presumed to be sincerely made. If, however, the priest has reason to doubt the sincerity of the promise made by the Catholic, he may not recommend the request for the dispensation and should submit the matter to the local Ordinary.

Form, Ceremony of Marriage: Where there are serious difficulties in observing the Catholic canonical form in a mixed marriage, the local Ordinary of the Catholic party or of the place where the marriage is to occur may dispense the Catholic from the observance of the form for a just pastoral cause. An exhaustive list is impossible, but the following are the types of reasons: to achieve family harmony or to avoid family alienation, to obtain parental agreement to the marriage, to recognize the significant claims of relationship or special friendship with a non-Catholic minister, to permit the marriage in a church that has particular importance to the non-Catholic. If the Ordinary of the Catholic party grants a dispensation for a marriage which is to take place in another diocese, the Ordinary of that diocese should be informed beforehand.

Ordinarily this dispensation from the canonical form is granted in view of the proposed celebration of a religious marriage service. In some exceptional circumstances (e.g., certain Catholic-Jewish marriages) it may be necessary that the dispensation be granted so that a civil ceremony may be performed. In any case, a public form that is civilly recognized for the celebration of marriage is required.

It is not permitted to have two religious marriage services or to have a single service in which both the Catholic marriage ritual and a non-Catholic marriage ritual are celebrated jointly or successively (cf. *Matrimonia Mixta,* No. 13).

With the permission of the local Ordinary and the consent of the appropriate authority of the other church or community, a non-Catholic minister may be invited to participate in the Catholic marriage service by giving additional prayers, blessings, or words of greeting or exhortation. If the marriage is not part of the Eucharistic celebration, the minister may also be invited to read a lesson and/or to preach (cf. *Directory on Ecumenism* Part I, No. 56).

In the case where there has been a dispensation from the Catholic canonical form and the priest has been invited to participate in the non-Catholic marriage service, with the permission of the local Ordinary and the consent of the appropriate authority of the other church or communion, he may do so by giving additional prayers, blessings, or words of greeting and exhortation. If the marriage service is not part of the Lord's Supper or the principal liturgical service of the Word, the priest, if invited, may also read a lesson and/or preach (cf. *Ibid*).

"To the extent that Eucharistic sharing is not permitted by the general discipline of the Church, this is to be considered when plans are being made to have the mixed marriage at Mass or not.

Place of Marriage: The ordinary place of marriage is in the parish church or other sacred place. For serious reasons, the local Ordinary may permit the celebration of a mixed marriage, when there has been no dispensation from the canonical form and the Catholic marriage service is to be celebrated, outside a Catholic church or chapel, providing there is no scandal involved and proper delegation is granted (for example, where there is no Catholic church in the area, etc.).

If there has been a dispensation from canonical form, ordinarily the marriage service is celebrated in a non-Catholic church.

PROCEDURAL RULES

Pope Paul VI promulgated, June 11, 1971, a set of 13 rules designed to speed up the handling of cases in which the validity of marriage is questioned. Norms given in the document, which was issued by the Pope on his own initiative and became effective Oct.31, concern "the constitution of ecclesiastical tribunals and . . . the judicial process which will expedite the matrimonial process itself."

The norms do not affect the reasons for the validity or invalidity of marriages, but only the way in which cases of this kind are handled in church courts.

The norms provide:

• The court empowered to handle a case can be in a diocese where witnesses and evidence are most accessible. Formerly, the competent court was located in either the diocese where the marriage took place or where one of the parties had a residence.

• If three priests are not available to serve as judges, two priests and a layman can do so. For individual cases, a one-priest tribunal can be set up. These provisions, under the supervision of a national episcopal conference, will have the effect of increasing the number of tribunals for hearing cases. Women can serve as court notaries, or secretaries.

• Mandatory appeals are no longer necessary in all cases. First decisions for or against validity can simply be reviewed and ratified by a second court without a full-scale appeal process, provided there is no serious objec-

tion to ratification and no new evidence is brought forward.

• Bishops can issue a decree of nullity without trial when there is clear evidence of invalidity.

At the time the norms were issued, it was said that "they continue to guarantee the sanctity of the bond of marriage but provide for a speedy first trial and empower lower diocesan tribunals to rule against needless appeals which could drag on for years."

Twenty-three experimental norms in effect in the US since July, 1970, were broader in scope than those decreed by Pope Paul. Among other things, they provide for one-priest tribunals for specified periods of time instead of for individual cases; and for dispensation, granted by the National Conference of Catholic Bishops, from even the need for a review of first decisions regarding validity or invalidity of marriage. The US norms were drawn up by the Canon Law Society of America and approved by the NCCB and the Vatican. Their termination date was 1973.

Marriage Judgments

An article on the foregoing norms, appearing in the July 1, 1971, English edition of *L'Osservatore Romano*, noted: The judgments the Church "expresses with marriage sentences are of a spiritual nature, aimed at establishing the original nullity of marriage, at restoring spiritual order where disorder had been created owing to an invalid celebration" (of marriage).

"The Church does not . . . declare a validly contracted bond to be dissolved. . . . A bond that has never been contracted and is only apparently existent cannot be a source of sacramental grace for a Catholic until it is validated. . . . if, If, for objective reasons (of a serious type), she (the Church) makes modifications in the procedure that accompanies these processes (of investigating and judging cases), this in no way challenges the principle of the indissolubility of marriage or alters the structure or essence of the process." The process "aims at the spiritual good of the spouses."

Cases of Non-Consummation

Pope Paul VI promulgated May 31, 1972, norms designed to speed up the handling of cases involving questions about the validity of marriages entered legally but never consummated sexually. The regulations which went into effect July 1, granted local bishops powers previously reserved to the Holy See.

Accordingly local bishops can initiate procedures in cases of this type; testimony and documents are acceptable in any modern language and on tape; physical proof of non-consummation can be omitted if the bishop is satisfied with the statements of the parties and/or witnesses; the number of witnesses is left to the discretion of the bishop.

The Church Calendar

The calendar of the Roman Church consists of an arrangement throughout the year of a series of liturgical seasons and feasts of saints for purposes of divine worship.

The purposes of this calendar were outlined in the *Constitution on the Sacred Liturgy* (No. 102-105) promulgated by the Second Vatican Council.

"Within the cycle of a year . . . (the Church) unfolds the whole mystery of Christ, not only from His incarnation and birth until His ascension, but also as reflected in the day of Pentecost, and the expectation of a blessed, hoped-for return of the Lord.

"Recalling thus the mysteries of redemption, the Church opens to the faithful the riches of her Lord's powers and merits, so that these are in some way made present at all times, and the faithful are enabled to lay hold of them and become filled with saving grace" (No. 102).

"In celebrating this annual cycle of Christ's mysteries, holy Church honors with special love the Blessed Mary, Mother of God . . ." (No. 103).

"The Church has also included in the annual cycle days devoted to the memory of the martyrs and the other saints. . . . (who) sing God's perfect praise in heaven and offer prayers for us. By celebrating the passage of these saints from earth to heaven the Church proclaims the paschal mystery as achieved in the saints who have suffered and been glorified with Christ; she proposes them to the faithful as examples who draw all to the Father through Christ, and through their merits she pleads for God's favors" (No. 104).

". . . In the various seasons of the year and according to her traditional discipline, the Church completes the formation of the faithful by means of pious practices for soul and body, by instruction, prayer, and works of penance and mercy. . ." (No. 105).

THE REVISED CALENDAR

Pope Paul announced May 9, 1969, his approval of a reorganization of the liturgical year and calendar for the Roman Rite, in implementation of a directive from the Second Vatican Council in 1964. He made the announcement in a document issued on his own initiative and entitled *Paschalis Mysterii.*

The purpose of the action, the Pope said, was "no other . . . than to permit the faithful to communicate in a more intense way, through faith, hope and love, in 'the whole mystery of Christ which . . . unfolds within the cycle of a year.' "

The motu proprio was dated Feb. 14, 1969. The new calendar was promulgated a month later by a decree of the Congregation for Divine Worship and went into effect Jan. 1, 1970, with provisional modifications. Full implementation of all its parts was delayed in 1970 and 1971, pending the completion of work on related liturgical texts. The US bishops ordered the whole new calendar into effect for 1972.

The revised calendar, whose principal architect was Father Pierre Jounel, professor of liturgy at the Catholic University of Paris, involved some restructuring of the liturgical cycles and changes affecting the feasts of saints; some feasts were eliminated, as described below.

The Seasons

Advent: The liturgical year begins with the First Sunday of Advent, which introduces a season of four weeks or slightly less duration with the theme of expectation of the coming of Christ. During the first two weeks, the final coming of Christ as Lord and Judge at the end of the world is the focus of attention. From Dec. 17 to 24, the emphasis shifts to anticipation of the celebration of his Nativity on the feast of Christmas.

Advent has four Sundays. Since the 10th century, the first Sunday has marked the beginning of the liturgical year in the Western Church. In the Middle Ages, a kind of pre-Christmas fast was in vogue during the season.

Christmastide: Christmastide opens with the feast of the Nativity, Dec. 25, and lasts until the Sunday after Epiphany. The Holy Family is commemorated on the Sunday within the Christmas octave. Jan. 1 — formerly called the Octave Day of the Nativity and, before that, the feast of the Circumcision of Jesus — has the title of Solemnity of Mary the Mother of God. The Epiphany, scheduled for Jan. 6 in the universal calendar, is celebrated in the US on a Sunday between Jan. 2 and 8. The Baptism of the Lord, observed on the Sunday following Epiphany, marks the end of Christmastide.

The period between the end of Christmastide and the beginning of Lent belongs to the Season-through-the-Year. Of variable length, the pre-Lenten phase of this season includes what were formerly called the Sundays after Epiphany and the suppressed Sundays of Septuagesima, Sexagesima and Quinquagesima.

Lent: The penitential season of Lent begins on Ash Wednesday, which occurs between Feb. 4 and Mar. 11, depending on the date of Easter, and lasts until Easter. It has six Sundays and 40 weekdays. The climactic last week is called Holy Week. The last three days (Holy Thursday, Good Friday and Holy Saturday) are called the Paschal Triduum.
5 The origin of Lenten observances dates back to the fourth century or earlier.

Eastertide: Eastertide, whose theme is resurrection from sin to the life of grace, lasts for

50 days, from Easter to Pentecost. Easter, the first Sunday following the vernal equinox, occurs between Mar. 22 and Apr. 25. The terminal phase of Eastertide, between the feast of the Ascension of the Lord and Pentecost, stresses anticipation of the coming and action of the Holy Spirit.

Season-through-the-Year: The Season-through-the-Year includes not only the period between the end of Christmastide and the beginning of Lent, as noted above, but also all Sundays after Pentecost to the last Sunday of the liturgical year, which is celebrated as the feast of Christ the King. The number of Sundays before Lent and after Pentecost varies, depending on the date of the key feast of Easter. The overall purpose of the season is to elaborate the themes of salvation history.

The various liturgical seasons are characterized in part by the scriptural readings and Mass prayers assigned to each of them. During Advent, for example, the readings are messianic; during Eastertide, from the Acts of the Apostles, chronicling the Resurrection and the original proclamation of Christ by the Apostles, and from the Gospel of John; during Lent, baptismal and penitential passages. Mass prayers reflect the meaning and purpose of the various seasons.

Feasts of Saints

The feasts of saints are celebrated concurrently with the liturgical seasons and feasts of our Lord. Their purpose always has been to illustrate the paschal mysteries as reflected in the lives of saints, to honor them as heroes of holiness, and to appeal for their intercession. For various reasons, however, the number and variety of feasts distracted attention to some degree from the central mysteries of redemption and the universality of holiness in the Church. To remedy these defects, Pope Paul ordered a number of significant changes affecting the feasts of saints.

In line with revised regulations, some feasts were either abolished or relegated to observance in particular places by local option for one of two reasons: (1) serious doubt about historical justification for observance of the feasts; (2) lack of universal significance. More than 40 feasts were eliminated; 92 were made optional for particular places, e.g., the diocese or country in which a saint was martyred; more than 60 were ordered for observance throughout the Roman Rite.

Traditional feasts of our Lord have been retained, except for those of the Holy Name and the Precious Blood which were suppressed.

Most feasts of Blessed Mary the Virgin have been retained. Universal observance obtains for the feasts of the Assumption, Immaculate Conception, Birth, Annunciation (of Our Lord), Presentation of the Lord, Visitation, Our Lady of Sorrows, Our Lady of the Rosary, Presentation, Queenship. Local option governs celebration of the memorials of Our Lady of Lourdes, Our Lady of Mt. Carmel, Dedication of (the Basilica of) St. Mary Major, the Immaculate Heart.

St. Joseph, Husband of Mary, is honored universally on Mar. 19 and by local option on another date (feast of St. Joseph the Worker, which may be observed May 1).

The archangels — Michael, Raphael and Gabriel — are honored with a common feast, Sept. 29, instead of with three separate feasts as before. The feast of the Guardian Angels, Oct. 2, stands.

The traditional feasts of the Apostles and Evangelists have been retained, with several date changes. Sts. Peter and Paul, who are honored with a common feast June 29, each have an additional feast on Feb. 22 (Chair of St. Peter) and Jan. 25 (Conversion of St. Paul).

Other saints, as noted above, are honored on universal and optional feasts throughout the year.

The universality of holiness in the Church is reflected in the distribution of feasts among saints of different periods and locations. Sixty-four saints are of the first 10 centuries, 79 of the last 10 centuries. Most represented are the fourth century (25 saints), the 12th (12), the 16th (17), and the 17th (17). Geographically, there are 126 feasts of European saints, 14 of Asians, eight of Africans, four of Americans, and one of a saint of Oceania.

The feast of a saint, as a general rule, is observed on the day of his death *(dies natalis,* day of birth to glory with God in heaven). Exceptions to this rule include the feasts of St. John the Baptist, who is honored on the day of his birth; Sts. Basil the Great and Gregory Nazianzen, and the brother Saints, Cyril and Methodius, who are commemorated in joint feasts.

Application of this general rule in the revised calendar resulted in date changes of some feasts.

Sundays and Feast Days

Sunday is the original Christian feast day because of the unusually significant events of salvation history which took place and are commemorated on the first day of the week — viz., the Resurrection of Christ, the key event of his life and the fundamental fact of Christianity; and the descent of the Holy Spirit upon the Apostles on Pentecost, the birthday of the Church. The transfer of observance of the Lord's Day from the Sabbath to Sunday was made in apostolic times. The Mass and Liturgy of the Hours (Divine Office) of each Sunday reflect the themes and set the tones of the various liturgical seasons.

Categories of feasts according to dignity and manner of observance are: solemnity (highest, corresponding to former first-class feasts); feast (corresponding to former second-class feasts); memorial (corresponding to former third-class feasts); optional memorial (observable by local choice). Feasts of the first three categories are observed universally in the Roman Rite.

Fixed feasts are those which are regularly celebrated on the same calendar day each year.

Movable feasts are those which are not observed on the same calendar day each year. Examples of these are Easter (the first Sunday after the first full moon following the vernal equinox), Ascension (40 days after Easter), Pentecost (50 days after Easter), Trinity Sunday (first after Pentecost), Christ the King (last Sunday of the liturgical year).

Holy Days of Obligation

Holy days of obligation are special feasts on which Catholics who have reached the age of reason are seriously obliged, as on Sundays, to assist at Mass and to avoid unnecessary servile work. Serious reasons excuse from the observance of either or both of these obligations.

By enactment of the Third Plenary Council of Baltimore, and with the approval of the Holy See, the holy days of obligation observed in the United States are: Christmas, the Nativity of Jesus, Dec. 25; Solemnity of Mary the Mother of God, Jan. 1; Ascension of the Lord, May 31, 1973; Assumption of Blessed Mary the Virgin, Aug. 15; All Saints' Day, Nov. 1; Immaculate Conception of Blessed Mary the Virgin, Dec. 8.

In addition to these, there are four other holy days of obligation prescribed in the general law of the Church which are not so observed in the US: Epiphany; St. Joseph, Mar. 19; Corpus Christi; Sts. Peter and Paul, June 29.

Ferial, Ember, Rogation Days

Ferial days are weekdays on which no proper feast or vigil is celebrated in the Mass or Liturgy of the Hours (Divine Office). On such days, the Mass may be that of the preceding Sunday, which expresses the liturgical spirit of the season, an optional memorial, a votive Mass, or a Mass for the dead. Ferial days of Advent and Lent are in a special category of their own.

Aside from feast-day considerations, Monday through Friday are called ferial days, and are consecutively numbered from two to six. The first day of the week is Sunday or the Lord's Day, and the seventh is called the Sabbath.

Ember days originated at Rome about the fifth century, probably as Christian replacements for seasonal festivals of agrarian cults. They were observances of penance, thanksgiving, and petition for divine blessing on the various seasons; they also were occasions for special prayer for clergy to be ordained. These days were observed four times a year:

on the Wednesday, Friday and Saturday following the Third Sunday of Advent, the First Sunday of Lent, Pentecost, and the third Sunday of September. In line with the calendar reform of 1969, decision with respect to the observance of ember days rests with the National Conference of Catholic Bishops.

Rogation days originated in France about the fifth century. They were penitential in character and also occasions of prayer for a bountiful harvest and protection against evil. Minor days of rogation were observed on the three days before the feast of the Ascension; Apr. 25 was a day of major rogation. In line with the calendar reform of 1969, decision with respect to the observance of rogation days rests with the National Conference of Catholic Bishops.

Days of Abstinence and Fast

The apostolic constitution *Paenitemini,* in effect since Feb. 23, 1966, authorized the substitution of other works of penance for the customary and common observances of abstinence and fast on various days of the year.

In this country, in line with provisions of the constitution and an order of the bishops of the United States which went into effect on Nov. 27, 1966, Ash Wednesday and Good Friday are the only days of strict abstinence and fast. For maintenance of the practice of penance, abstinence is recommended on the other Fridays of Lent.

The obligation to abstain from meat binds Catholics 14 years of age and older. The obligation to fast, limiting oneself to one full meal and two lighter meals in the course of a day, binds Catholics from the ages of 21 to 59.

Eliminated Feasts

The following feasts were eliminated from the revised calendar.

January: Telesphorus, 5; Hyginus, 6; Marius, Martha, Audifax, Abacus, 19; Agnes (a duplicated feast), 28.

February: Dorothy, 6; Faustinus and Jovita, 15.

March: Lucius, 4; 40 Holy Martyrs, 10.

April: Anicetus, 17; Soter and Cajus, 22; Cletus and Marcellinus, 26.

May: Domitilla, 12; Boniface of Tarsus, 14; Urban I, 25; Eleutherius, 26; Felix I, 30.

June: Basilidis, Cyrinus, Nabor and Nazarius, 12; Modestus and Crescentia, 15.

July: Seven Holy Brothers, 10; Pius I, 11; Alexius, 17; Symphorosa and her Seven Sons, 18; Margaret of Antioch, 20; Victor I, 28; Innocent I, 28.

August: Hippolytus (a duplicated feast), 22; Zephyrinus, 26.

September: 12 Holy Brothers, 1; Lucy (a duplicated feast), 16; Geminianus, 16; Companions of St. Januarius, 19; Eustace and Companions, 20; Linus, 23; Thecla, 23; Cyprianus and Justina, 26.

October: Placid and Companions, 5; Sergius, 8; Ursula and Companions, 21; Evaristus, 26.

November: Tryphon, Respicius and Nympha, 10; Catherine of Alexandria, 25.

December: Barbara, 4.

Commenting on the elimination of these feasts, *L'Osservatore Della Domenica,* the Vatican City weekly, said: "Generally, the removal of a name from the calendar does not mean passing judgment on the nonexistence (of a saint) or lack of holiness. Many (saints) have been removed (from the calendar) because all that remains certain about them is their name, and this would say too little to the faithful in comparison with many others. Other feasts were removed because they lacked universal significance.

BYZANTINE CALENDAR

The Byzantine-Rite calendar has many distinctive features of its own, although it shares common elements with the Roman-Rite calendar—e.g., general purpose, commemoration of the mysteries of faith and of the saints, identical dates for some feasts. Among the distinctive things are the following.

The liturgical year begins on Sept. 1, the **Day of Indiction,** in contrast with the Latin or Roman start on the First Sunday of Advent late in November or early in December. The Advent season begins on Dec. 10.

Cycles of the Year

As in the Roman usage, the dating of feasts follows the Gregorian Calendar. Formerly, until well into this century, the Julian Calendar was used. (The Julian Calendar, which is now about 13 days late, is still used by some Eastern-Rite Churches.)

The year has several cycles, which include proper seasons, the feasts of saints, and series of New Testament readings. All of these elements of worship are contained in liturgical books of the rite.

The ecclesiastical calendar, called the **Menologion,** explains the nature of feasts, other observances and matters pertaining to the liturgy for each day of the year. In some cases, its contents include the lives of saints and the history and meaning of feasts.

The Divine Liturgy (Mass) and Divine Office for the proper of the saints, fixed feasts, and the Christmas season are contained in the **Menaion.** The **Triodion** covers the pre-Lenten season of preparation for Easter; Lent begins two days before the Ash Wednesday observance of the Roman Rite. The **Pentecostarion** contains the liturgical services from Easter to the Sunday of All Saints, the first after Pentecost. The **Evangelion** and **Apostolos** are books in which the Gospels, and Acts of the Apostles and the Epistles, respectively, are arranged according to the order of their reading in the Divine Liturgy and Divine Office throughout the year.

The cyclic progression of liturgical music throughout the year, in successive and repetitive periods of eight weeks, is governed by the **Oktoechos,** the Book of Eight Tones.

Sunday Names

Many Sundays are named after the subject of the Gospel read in the Mass of the day or after the name of a feast falling on the day — e.g., Sunday of the Publican and Pharisee, of the Prodigal Son, of the Samaritan Woman, of St. Thomas the Apostle, of the Fore-Fathers (Old Testament Patriarchs). Other Sundays are named in the same manner as in the Roman calendar — e.g., numbered Sundays of Lent and after Pentecost.

Holy Days, Abstinence, Fast

The calendar lists about 28 holy days. Many of the major holy days coincide with those of the Roman calendar, but the feast of the Immaculate Conception is observed on Dec. 9 instead of Dec. 8, and the feast of All Saints falls on the Sunday after Pentecost rather than on Nov. 1. Instead of a single All Souls' Day, there are five All Souls' Saturdays.

According to regulations in effect in the Byzantine-Rite (Ruthenian) Dioceses of Passaic and Pittsburgh, holy days are obligatory, solemn and simple, and attendance at the Divine Liturgy is required on five obligatory days — the feasts of the Epiphany, the Ascension, Sts. Peter and Paul, the Assumption of the Blessed Virgin Mary, and Christmas. Although attendance at the liturgy is not obligatory on 15 solemn and seven simple holy days, it is recommended.

In the Byzantine-Rite (Ukrainian) Archeparchy of Philadelphia and its suffragan sees of St. Nicholas (Chicago) and Stamford, the obligatory feasts are the Circumcision, Epiphany, Annunciation, Easter, Ascension, Pentecost, Dormition (Assumption of Mary), Immaculate Conception and Christmas.

Lent

The first day of Lent — the Monday before Ash Wednesday of the Roman Rite — and Good Friday are days of strict abstinence for persons between the ages of 21 and 59. No meat, eggs, or dairy products may be eaten on these days.

All persons over the age of 14 must abstain from meat on Fridays during Lent, Holy Saturday, and the vigils of the feasts of Christmas and Epiphany; abstinence is urged, but is not obligatory, on Wednesdays of Lent. The abstinence obligation is not in force on certain "free" or "privileged" Fridays.

Synaxis

An observance without a counterpart in the Roman calendar is the synaxis. This is a commemoration, on the day following a feast, of persons involved with the occasion for the feast — e.g., Sept. 9, the day following the feast of the Nativity of the Blessed Virgin Mary, is the Synaxis of Joachim and Anna, her parents.

Holy Week

In the Byzantine Rite, Lent is liturgically concluded with the Saturday of Lazarus, the day before Palm Sunday, which commemorates the raising of Lazarus from the dead.

On the following Monday, Tuesday and Wednesday, the Liturgy of the Presanctified is prescribed.

On Holy Thursday, the Liturgy of St. Basil the Great is celebrated together with Vespers.

Good Friday, except when the feast of the Annunciation coincides with it, is the only day of the year on which the Divine Liturgy is not celebrated.

On Holy Saturday, the Liturgy of St. Basil the Great is celebrated along with Vespers.

CALENDAR NOTES

Scriptural Readings

The texts of scriptural readings for Mass on Sundays, holy days and some other days are indicated under the respective dates. The second (B) cycle of readings in the Lectionary is prescribed for the 1973 liturgical year; the third (C) cycle is prescribed from the first Sunday of Advent (Dec. 2) on.

Sunday Mass on Saturday

In recent years many bishops in the United States have introduced Sunday Mass-on-Saturday in their dioceses by authorizing fulfillment of the Sunday Mass obligation through attendance at Mass late in the afternoon or in the evening of the preceding Saturday. Reasons for the action are pastoral, including: a shortage of priests in some areas to celebrate a sufficient number of Masses on Sunday; inadequate facilities, as in vacation resorts, for large congregations attending a limited number of Masses on Sunday; the reasonable convenience of the faithful. The holy day Mass obligation can be fulfilled in a similar manner, where authorized.

Holiday Masses, Holy Days

Liturgical experiments in recent years have led to the development of votive Masses for national holidays, like those introduced in the US for Thanksgiving Day in 1969 and July 4 in 1972. This development is in line with a custom whereby "from the earliest times the Church has crowned many non-Christian feasts with Christian fulfillment by instituting its own liturgical festivals" to coincide with them.

Labor Day, in lieu of a special votive Mass, may be observed with celebration of the Mass of St. Joseph the Worker.

The text of a Mass for Thanksgiving Day — approved by the Congregation for Divine Worship and published by the US Bishops' Committee on the Liturgy — was introduced in the United States in 1969.

The Mass includes prayers appropriate to the spirit of the day and provides for the presentation of gifts of food, clothing and other necessities, to be given to the poor, in a gesture which "will serve as a reminder to the faithful of our obligation to share the goods of our stewardship."

Developments like the evolution of Masses for Independence Day, Labor Day, Thanksgiving Day and other occasions of national significance in this country are in line with the traditions of liturgical growth.

One factor which makes changes of this kind appear novel is lack of historical perspective. Another is the fixation of liturgical practices in patterns which have not changed for centuries.

Monthly Prayer Intentions

Mission intentions recommended by Pope Paul to the prayers of the faithful in 1973 are as follows.

JANUARY: That missionary vocations may increase in number in the Christian West.

FEBRUARY: That the peoples of the Third World may seek in Christ the fundamental inspiration for realizing their own progress and for establishing international cooperation.

MARCH: That the advancement of the people of Asia may be firmly rooted in authentic religious values.

APRIL: That the youth of Asia may be made fully conscious of their responsibility and seek in the Gospel the solution of serious problems.

MAY: That among the Chinese, Christian values may be received with greater trust and be esteemed more highly.

JUNE: That fruitful dialogue may be established in Burma between the Christian religion and Buddhism.

JULY: That the various religious groups in Southern Asia may work together with good will and cooperation.

AUGUST: That Christian amity and helpful action may be fostered toward the peoples who live isolated in Oceania.

SEPTEMBER: That the number of priests in Africa may increase.

OCTOBER: That in the newly developed churches the transfer of duties and responsibilities from the missionaries to the local clergy may proceed in a truly fraternal spirit.

NOVEMBER: That among the many peoples of Africa the pluralism of tribes or ethnic groups may not become an impediment but a positive gain for spiritual, social and community progress.

DECEMBER: That the indigenous peoples of Latin America may be fully integrated into civil society and make progress along spiritual and social lines.

JANUARY 1973

1 — **Mon. Solemnity of Mary, Mother of God. Holy day of obligation.** (Nm. 6:22-27; Gal. 4:4-7; Lk. 2:16-21.)
2 — Tues. Sts. Basil the Great and Gregory Nazianzen, bishops-doctors; memorial.
3 — Wed. Weekday.
4 — Thurs. Bl. Elizabeth Ann Seton; memorial (in US).
5 — Fri. Bl. John Neumann, bishop; memorial (in US).
6 — Sat. Weekday.
7 — **Sun. Epiphany of Our Lord** (in US); solemnity. (Is. 60:1-6; Eph. 3:2-3a, 5-6; Mt. 2:1-12.) [St. Raymond of Pennafort, priest; optional memorial.]
8 — Mon. Weekday.
9 — Tues. Weekday.
10 — Wed. Weekday.
11 — Thurs. Weekday.
12 — Fri. Weekday.
13 — Sat. Weekday. St. Hilary, bishop-doctor; optional memorial.
14 — **Second Sunday of the Year.** (1 Sm. 3b-10, 19; 1 Cor. 6:13c-15a, 17-20; Jn. 1:35-42.)
15 — Mon. Weekday.
16 — Tues. Weekday.
17 — Wed. St. Anthony, abbot; memorial.
18 — Thurs. Weekday.
19 — Fri. Weekday.
20 — Sat. Weekday. St. Fabian, pope, or St. Sebastian, soldier, martyrs; optional memorials.
21 — **Third Sunday of the Year.** (Jon. 3:1-5, 10; 1 Cor. 7:29-31; Mk. 1:14-20.) [St. Agnes, virgin-martyr; memorial.]
22 — Mon. Weekday. St. Vincent, deacon-martyr; optional memorial.
23 — Tues. Weekday.
24 — Wed. St. Francis de Sales, bishop-doctor; memorial.
25 — Thurs. Conversion of St. Paul, apostle; feast.
26 — Fri. Sts. Timothy and Titus, bishops; memorial.
27 — Sat. Weekday. St. Angela Merici, virgin; optional memorial.
28 — **Fourth Sunday of the Year.** (Dt. 18:15-20; 1 Cor. 7:32-35; Mk. 1:21-28.) [St. Thomas Aquinas, priest-doctor; memorial.]
29 — Mon. Weekday.
30 — Tues. Weekday.
31 — Wed. St. John Bosco, priest; memorial.

Key observances of the month are the Solemnity of Mary, Jan. 1, the feast of the Epiphany, Jan. 6, and the Week of Prayer for Christian Unity, Jan. 18 to 25.

Although the latter does not have liturgical status, it is significant as an exercise of the spiritual ecumenism which has been called the very "soul of ecumenism." Interfaith prayer services are held in many places.

FEBRUARY 1973

1 — Thurs. Weekday.
2 — Fri. Presentation of the Lord; feast.
3 — Sat. Weekday. St. Blaise, bishop-martyr, or St. Ansgar, bishop; optional memorials.
4 — **Fifth Sunday of the Year.** (Jb. 7:1-4, 6-7; 1 Cor. 9:16-19, 22-23; Mk. 1:29-39.)
5 — Mon. St. Agatha, virgin-martyr; memorial.
6 — Tues. Sts. Paul Miki and companions, martys; memorial.
7 — Wed. Weekday.
8 — Thurs. Weekday. St. Jerome Emilian; optional memorial.
9 — Fri. Weekday.
10 — Sat. St. Scholastica, virgin; memorial.
11 — **Sixth Sunday of the Year.** (Lv. 13:1-2, 45-46; 1 Cor. 10:31 to 11:1; Mk. 1:40-45.) [Our Lady of Lourdes; optional memorial.]
12 — Mon. Weekday.
13 — Tues. Weekday.
14 — Wed. Sts. Cyril, monk, and Methodius, bishop; memorial.
15 — Thurs. Weekday.
16 — Fri. Weekday.
17 — Sat. Weekday. Seven Holy Founders of the Servites; optional memorial.
18 — **Seventh Sunday of the Year.** (Is. 43:18-19, 21-22, 24b-25; 2 Cor. 1:18-22; Mk. 2:1-12.)
19 — Mon. Weekday.
20 — Tues. Weekday.
21 — Wed. Weekday. St. Peter Damian, bishop-doctor; optional memorial.
22 — Thurs. Chair of St. Peter, apostle; feast.
23 — Fri. St. Polycarp, bishop-martyr; memorial.
24 — Sat. Weekday.
25 — **Eighth Sunday of the Year.** (Hos. 2:16b, 17b, 21-22; 2 Cor. 3:1b-6; Mk. 2:18-22.)
26 — Mon. Weekday.
27 — Tues. Weekday.
28 — Wed. Weekday.

Pope Paul's recommendation of prayer during the month for the peoples of the Third World envisions Christ as the fundamental inspiration of their own and others' efforts for the development of their countries. Imparting and fostering this inspiration is the primary purpose of evangelization, which is related to works for human development.

In line with a practice of long standing, the blessing of throats is generally conferred on the feast of St. Blaise, Feb. 3. According to legend, he was instrumental in saving a boy from death by choking. The formula of the blessing is: "Through the intercession of St. Blaise, bishop and martyr, may the Lord free you from ills of the throat and from every other evil. In the name of the Father and of the Son and of the Holy Spirit."

MARCH 1973

1 — Thurs. Weekday.
2 — Fri. Weekday.
3 — Sat. Weekday.
4 — **Ninth Sunday of the Year.** (Dt. 5:12-15; 2 Cor. 4:6-11; Mk. 2:23 to 3:6.) [St. Casimir; optional memorial.]
5 — Mon. Weekday.
6 — Tues. Weekday.
7 — Ash Wednesday. Beginning of Lent. Fast and abstinence. [Sts. Perpetua and Felicitas, martyrs; memorial.]
8 — Thurs. Weekday of Lent. [St. John of God, religious; optional memorial.]
9 — Fri. Weekday of Lent. [St. Frances of Rome, religious; optional memorial.]
10 — Sat. Weekday of Lent.
11 — **First Sunday of Lent.** (Gn. 9:8-15; 1 Pt. 3:18-22; Mk. 1:12-15.)
12 — Mon. Weekday of Lent.
13 — Tues. Weekday of Lent.
14 — Wed. Weekday of Lent.
15 — Thurs. Weekday of Lent.
16 — Fri. Weekday of Lent.
17 — Sat. Weekday of Lent. [St. Patrick, bishop; optional memorial.]
18 — **Second Sunday of Lent.** (Gn. 22:1-2, 9a, 10-13, 15-18; Rom. 8:31b-34; Mk. 9:2-10.) [St. Cyril of Jerusalem, bishop-doctor; optional memorial.]
19 — Mon. St. Joseph; solemnity.
20 — Tues. Weekday of Lent.
21 — Wed. Weekday of Lent.
22 — Thurs. Weekday of Lent.
23 — Fri. Weekday of Lent. [St. Turibius, bishop; optional memorial.]
24 — Sat. Annunciation of the Lord (transferred from Mar. 25); solemnity.
25 — **Third Sunday of Lent.** (Ex. 20:1-17; 1 Cor. 1:22-25; Jn. 2:13-25.)
26 — Mon. Weekday of Lent.
27 — Tues. Weekday of Lent.
28 — Wed. Weekday of Lent.
29 — Thurs. Weekday of Lent.
30 — Fri. Weekday of Lent.
31 — Sat. Weekday of Lent.

The purpose and spirit of Lent, which begins on Ash Wednesday, Mar. 7, is penance, in reparation for sin and as a means of increasing conversion to God and life in Christ. The negative aspect of penance involves self-discipline and self-deprivation; the positive aspect is growth in the likeness of Christ.

The only works of penance imposed by present regulations of the Church are abstinence from meat by everyone over the age of 14 on Ash Wednesday and Good Friday, and fasting on the same days by everyone between the ages of 21 and 59. Abstinence is recommended, and may be ordered by local bishops, on all Fridays of Lent.

Additional works of penance, at one's option, are also necessary.

APRIL 1973

1 — **Fourth Sunday of Lent.** (2 Chr. 36:14-16, 19-23; Eph. 2:4-10; Jn. 3:14-21.)
2 — Mon. Weekday of Lent. [St. Francis of Paola, hermit; optionnal memorial.]
3 — Tues. Weekday of Lent.
4 — Wed. Weekday of Lent. [St. Isidore of Seville, bishop-doctor; optional memorial.]
5 — Thurs. Weekday of Lent. [St. Vincent Ferrer, priest; optional memorial.]
6 — Fri. Weekday of Lent.
7 — Sat. Weekday of Lent. [St. John Baptist de la Salle, priest; memorial]
8 — **Fifth Sunday of Lent.** (Jer. 31:31-34; Heb. 5:7-9; Jn. 12:20-33.)
9 — Mon. Weekday of Lent.
10 — Tues. Weekday of Lent.
11 — Wed. Weekday of Lent. [St. Stanislaus, bishopp-martyr; optional memorial.]
12 — Thurs. Weekday of Lent.
13 — Fri. Weekday of Lent. [St. Martin I, pope-martyr; optional memorial.]
14 — Sat. Weekday of Lent.
15 — **Sunday of the Passion.** (Procession — Mk. 11:1-10 or Jn. 12:12-16. Mass — Is. 50:4-7; Phil. 2:6-11; Mk. 14:1 to 15:47.)
16 — Monday of Holy Week.
17 — Tuesday of Holy Week.
18 — Wednesday of Holy Week.
19 — Thursday of Holy Week. Holy Thursday. The Paschal Triduum begins with the evening Mass of the Supper of the Lord.
20 — Friday of the Passion of the Lord. Good Friday. Fast and abstinence.
21 — Holy Saturday. The Easter Vigil. [St. Anselm, bishop-doctor; optional memorial.]
22 — **Easter Sunday; solemnity.** (Acts 10:34a, 37-43; Col. 3:1-4 or 1 Cor. 5:6b-8; Jn. 20:1-9 or Mt. 28:1-10.)
23 — Easter Monday. [St. George, martyr; optional memorial.]
24 — Easter Tuesday. [St. Fidelis of Sigmaringen, priest-martyr; optional memorial.]
25 — Easter Wednesday. [St. Mark, evangelist; feast.]
26 — Easter Thursday.
27 — Easter Friday.
28 — Easter Saturday. [St. Peter Chanel, priest-martyr; optional memorial.]
29 — **Second Sunday of Easter.** (Acts 4:32-35; 1 Jn. 5:1-6; Jn. 20:19-31.) [St. Catherine of Siena, virgin-doctor; memorial.]
30 — Mon. Weekday. [St. Pius V, pope; optional memorial.]

The climax of the liturgical year is reached during Holy Week, Apr. 15 to 21, and Easter, when the Church recapitulates and makes effectively present again the central paschal mysteries of the suffering, death and resurrection of Christ.

MAY 1973

1 — Tues. Weekday, St. Joseph, Worker; optional memorial.
2 — Wed. St. Athanasius, bishop-doctor; memorial.
3 — Thurs. Sts. Philip and James, apostles; feast.
4 — Fri. Weekday.
5 — Sat. Weekday.
6 — **Third Sunday of Easter.** (Acts. 3:13-15, 17-19; 1 Jn. 2:1-5a; Lk. 24:35-48.)
7 — Mon. Weekday.
8 — Tues. Weekday.
9 — Wed. Weekday.
10 — Thurs. Weekday.
11 — Fri. Weedkay.
12 — Sat. Weekday. Sts. Nereus and Archileus, martyrs, or St. Pancras, martyr; optional memorials.
13 — **Fourth Sunday of Easter** (Acts. 4:8-12; 1 Jn. 3:1-2; Jn. 10:11-18.)
14 — Mon. St. Matthias, apostle; feast.
15 — Tues. Weekday. St. Isidore the Farmer (in US); optional memorial.
16 — Wed. Weekday.
17 — Thurs. Weekday.
18 — Fri. Weekday. St. John I, pope-martyr; optional memorial.
19 — Sat. Weekday.
20 — **Fifth Sunday of Easter.** (Acts 9:26-31; 1 Jn. 3:18-24; Jn. 15:1-8.) [St. Bernardine of Siena, priest; optional memorial.]
21 — Mon. Weekday.
22 — Tues. Weekday.
23 — Wed. Weekday.
24 — Thurs. Weekday.
25 — Fri. Weekday. St. Bede the Venerable, priest-doctor, St. Gregory VII, pope, or St. Mary Magdalene of Pazzi, virgin; optional memorials.
26 — Sat. St. Philip Neri, priest; memorial.
27 — **Sixth Sunday of Easter** (Acts. 10:25-26, 34-35, 44-48; 1 Jn. 4:7-10; Jn. 15:9-17.) [St. Augustine of Canterbury, bishop; optional memorial.]
28 — Mon. Weekday.
29 — Tues. Weekday.
30 — Wed. Weekday.
31 — **Thurs. Ascension of the Lord; solemnity. Holy day of obligation.** (Acts 1:1-11; Eph. 1:17-23; Mk. 16:15-20.) [Visitation of Blessed Mary the Virgin; feast.]

The customary dedication of the month of May is to Mary. Recitation of the Rosary daily during the month has been recommended by all popes from Leo XIII to Paul VI.

The Church received its explicit missionary mandate from Christ when he ordered the Apostles to go forth into the whole world and teach all nations and baptize men in the name of the Father and of the Son and of the Holy Spirit. All members of the Church share in some way in this missionary vocation.

JUNE 1973

1 — Fri. St. Justin, martyr; memorial.
2 — Sat Weekday. St. Marcellinus and Peter, martyrs; optional memorial.
3 — **Seventh Sunday of Easter.** (Acts 1:15-17, 20a, 20c-26; 1 Jn. 4:11-16; Jn. 17:11b-19.) [Sts. Charles Lwanga and companions, martyrs; memorial.]
4 — Mon. Weekday.
5 — Tues. St. Boniface, bishop-martyr; memorial.
6 — Wed. Weekday. St. Norbert, bishop; optional memorial.
7 — Thurs. Weekday.
8 — Fri. Weekday.
9 — Sat. Weekday. St. Ephraem, deacon-doctor; optional memorial.
10 — **Sun. Penecost; solemnity.** (Acts 2:1-11; 1 Cor. 12:3b-7, 12-13; Jn. 20:19-23.)
11 — Mon. (Tenth Week of the Year). St. Barnabas, apostle; memorial.
12 — Tues. Weekday.
13 — Wed. St. Anthony of Padua, priest-doctor; memorial.
14 — Thurs. Weekday.
15 — Fri. Weekday.
16 — Sat. Weekday.
17 — **Sun. Holy Trinity; solemnity.** (Dt. 4:32-34, 39-40; Rom. 8:14-17; Mt. 28:16-20.)
18 — Mon. (Eleventh Week of the Year). Weekday.
19 — Tues. Weekday. St. Romuald, abbot; optional memorial.
20 — Wed. Weekday.
21 — Thurs. St. Aloysius Gonzaga, religious; memorial.
22 — Fri. Weekday. St. Paulinus of Nola, bishop, or Sts. John Fisher, bishop-martyr, and Thomas More, martyr; optional memorials.
23 — Sat. Birth of St. John the Baptist (transferred from June 24); solemnity.
24 — **Sun. Corpus Christi; solemnity.** (Ex. 24:3-8; Heb. 9:11-15; Mk. 14:12-16, 22-26.)
25 — Mon. (Twelfth Week of the Year). Weekday.
26 — Tues. Weekday.
27 — Wed. Weekday. St. Cyril of Alexandria, bishop-doctor; optional memorial.
28 — Thurs. St. Irenaeus, bishop-martyr; memorial.
29 — Fri. Sacred Heart of Jesus; solemnity. (Hos. 11:1, 3-4, 8c-9; Eph. 3:8-12, 14-19; Jn. 19:31-37.)
30 — Sat. Weekday. Immaculate Heart of Mary or First Martyrs of the Roman Church; optional memorials.

Pentecost, June 10, marks the beginning of the Church and the Solemnity of Corpus Christi, June 24, focuses attention on the Eucharist as the wellspring and apex of its whole life. In between is the Solemnity of the Holy Trinity, recalling the deepest mystery of the Christian faith.

JULY 1973

1 — **Sun. Sts. Peter and Paul, apostles, solemnity** (transferred from June 29), (Acts. 12:1-11; 2 Tim. 4:6-8, 17-18; Mt. 16:13-19.)

2 — Mon. (Thirteenth Week of the Year). Weekday.

3 — Tues. St. Thomas, apostle; feast.

4 — Wed. Weekday. St. Elizabeth of Portugal; optional memorial.

5 — Thurs. Weekday. St. Anthony Mary Zaccaria, priest; optional memorial.

6 — Fri. Weekday. St. Maria Goretti, virgin-martyr; optional memorial.

7 — Sat. Weekday.

8 — **Fourteenth Sunday of the Year.** (Ez. 2:2-5; 2 Cor. 12:7-10; Mk. 6:1-6.)

9 — Mon. Weekday.

10 — Tues. Weekday.

11 — Wed. St. Benedict, abbot; memorial.

12 — Thurs. Weekday.

13 — Fri. Weekday. St. Henry; optional memorial.

14 — Sat. Weekday. St. Camillus de Lellis, priest; optional memorial.

15 — **Fifteenth Sunday of the Year.** (Am. 7:12-15; Eph. 1:3-24; Mk. 6:7-13.) [St. Bonaventure, bishop-doctor; memorial.]

16 — Mon. Weekday. Our Lady of Mt. Carmel; optional memorial.

17 — Tues. Weekday.

18 — Wed. Weekday.

19 — Thurs. Weekday.

20 — Fri. Weekday.

21 — Sat. Weekday. St. Lawrence of Brindisi, priest-doctor; optional memorial.

22 — **Sixteenth Sunday of the Year.** (Jer. 23:1-6; Eph. 2:13-18; Mk. 6:30-34.) [St. Mary Magdalene; memorial.]

23 — Mon. Weekday. St. Bridget of Sweden, religious; optional memorial.

24 — Tues. Weekday.

25 — Wed. St. James, the Greater, apostle; feast.

26 — Thurs. St. Joachim and Anne, parents of Mary; memorial.

27 — Fri. Weekday.

28 — Sat. Weekday.

29 — **Seventeenth Sunday of the Year.** (2 Kgs. 4:42-44; Eph. 4:1-6; Jn. 6:1-15.) [St. Martha; memorial.]

30 — Mon. Weekday. St. Peter Chrysologus, bishop-doctor; optional memorial.

31 — Tues. St. Ignatius Loyola, priest; memorial.

Celebrations were held in 1972 in southeastern India to mark the 19th centenary of the death of St. Thomas the Apostle who, according to centuries-old legend, preached the Gospel there and was martyred near Madras. Christians of the area call themselves "Thomas Christians."

A votive Mass for Independence Day has been authorized for use in the US July 4.

AUGUST 1973

1 — Wed. St. Alphonsus Liguori, bishop-doctor; memorial.

2 — Thurs. Weekday. St. Eusebius of Vercelli, bishop; optional memorial.

3 — Fri. Weekday.

4 — Sat. St. John M. Vianney (Cure of Ars), priest; memorial.

5 — **Eighteenth Sunday of the Year.** (Ex. 16:2-4, 12-15; Eph. 4:17, 20-24; Jn. 6:24-35.) [Dedication of Basilica of St. Mary Major; optional memorial.]

6 — Mon. Transfiguration of the Lord; feast.

7 — Tues. Weekday. Sts. Sixtus II, pope and companions, martyrs, or St. Cajetan, priest; optional memorials.

8 — Wed. St. Dominic, priest; memorial.

9 — Thurs. Weekday.

10 — Fri. St. Lawrence, deacon-martyr; feast.

11 — Sat. St. Clare, virgin; memorial.

12 — **Nineteenth Sunday of the Year.** (1 Kgs. 19:4-8; Eph. 4:30 to 5:2; Jn. 6:41-51.)

13 — Mon. Weekday. St. Pontianus, pope, and Hippolytus, martyrs; optional memorial.

14 — Tues. Weekday.

15 — **Wed. Assumption of Blessed Mary the Virgin; solemnity. Holy day of obligation.** (Rv. 11:19a; 12:1-6a, 10ab; 1 Cor. 15:20-26; Lk. 1:39-56.)

16 — Thurs. Weekday. St. Stephen of Hungary; optional memorial.

17 — Fri. Weekday.

18 — Sat. Weekday.

19 — **Twentieth Sunday of the Year.** (Prv. 9:1-6; Eph. 5:15-20; Jn. 6:51-58.) [St. John Eudes, priest; optional memorial.]

20 — Mon. St. Bernard of Clairvaux, abbot-doctor; memorial.

21 — Tues. St. Pius X, pope; memorial.

22 — Wed. Queenship of Blessed Mary the Virgin; memorial.

23 — Thurs. Weekday. St. Rose of Lima, virgin; optional memorial.

24 — Fri. St. Bartholomew, apostle; feast.

25 — Sat. Weekday. St. Louis or St. Joseph Calasanctius, priest; optional memorials.

26 — **Twenty-First Sunday of the Year.** (Jos. 24:1-2a, 15-17, 18b; Eph. 5:21-32; Jn. 6:60-69.)

27 — Mon. St. Monica; memorial.

28 — Tues. St. Augustine, bishop-doctor; memorial.

29 — Wed. Passion of St. John the Baptist; memorial.

30 — Thurs. Weekday.

31 — Fri. Weekday.

The Eastern Rite title of the Solemnity of the Assumption of Mary is the Dormition of Mary. The dogma of the Assumption, formally stating traditional belief, was proclaimed by Pope Pius XII Nov. 1, 1950.

SEPTEMBER 1973

1 — Sat. Weekday.
2 — **Twenty-Second Sunday of the Year.** (Dt. 4:1-2, 6-8; Jas. 1:17-18, 21b-22, 27; Mk. 7:1-8, 14-15, 21-23.)
3 — Mon. St. Gregory the Great, pope-doctor; memorial.
4 — Tues. Weekday.
5 — Wed. Weekday.
6 — Thurs. Weekday.
7 — Fri. Weekday.
8 — Sat. Birth of Blessed Mary the Virgin; feast.
9 — **Twenty-Third Sunday of the Year.** (Is. 35:4-7a; Jas. 2:1-5; Mk. 7:31-37.) [St. Peter Claver, priest; memorial in US.]
10 — Mon. Weekday.
11 — Tues. Weekday.
12 — Wed. Weekday.
13 — Thurs. St. John Chrysostom, bishop-doctor; memorial.
14 — Fri. Triumph of the Cross; feast.
15 — Sat. Our Lady of Sorrows; memorial.
16 — **Twenty-Fourth Sunday of the Year.** (Is. 50:5-9a; Jas. 2:14-18; Mk. 8:27-35.) [Sts. Cornelius, pope, and Cyprian, bishop martyrs; memorial.]
17 — Mon. Weekday. St. Robert Bellarmine, bishop-doctor; optional memorial.
18 — Tues. Weekday.
19 — Wed. Weekday. St. Januarius, bishop-martyr; optional memorial.
20 — Thurs. Weekday.
21 — Fri. St. Matthew, apostle-evangelist; feast.
22 — Sat. Weekday.
23 — **Twenty-Fifth Sunday of the Year.** (Wis. 2:12, 17-20; Jas. 3:16 to 4:3; Mk. 9:30-37.)
24 — Mon. Weekday.
25 — Tues. Weekday.
26 — Wed. Weekday. St. Cosmas and Damian, martyrs; optional memorial.
27 — Thurs. St. Vincent de Paul, priest; memorial.
28 — Fri. Weekday. St. Wenceslaus, martyr; optional memorial.
29 — Sat. Sts. Michael, Gabriel and Raphael, archangels; feast.
30 — **Twenty-Sixth Sunday of the Year.** (Nm. 11:25-29; Jas. 5:1-6; Mk. 9:38-43, 45, 47-48.) [St. Jerome, priest-doctor; memorial.]

Increase in the number of African priests, the prayer intention recommended by Pope Paul for this month, will make possible greater self-support, self-direction and Africanization of the Church on that continent. Indigenization of this kind — forming the native Christian community and enabling it to carry on with its own personnel and resources — is the objective of work by "foreign" missionaries. Considerable progress has been made in recent years in setting up local hierachies with native bishops and priests.

OCTOBER 1973

1 — Mon. St. Therese of the Child Jesus, virgin; memorial.
2 — Tues. Guardian Angels; memorial.
3 — Wed. Weekday.
4 — Thurs. St. Francis of Assisi; memorial.
5 — Fri. Weekday.
6 — Sat. Weekday. St. Bruno, priest; optional memorial.
7 — Twenty-Seventh Sunday of the Year. (Gn. 2:18-24; Heb. 2:9-11; Mk. 10:2-16.) [Our Lady of the Rosary; memorial.]
8 — Mon. Weekday.
9 — Tues. Weekday. Sts. Denis, bishop, and companions, martyrs, or St. John Leonard, priest; optional memorials.
10 — Wed. Weekday.
11 — Thurs. Weekday.
12 — Fri. Weekday.
13 — Sat. Weekday.
14 — **Twenty-Eighth Sunday of the Year.** (Wis. 7:7-11; Heb. 4:12-13; Mk. 10:17-30.) [St. Callistus I, pope-martyr; optional memorial.]
15 — Mon. St. Teresa of Avila, virgin-doctor; memorial.
16 — Tues. Weekday. St. Hedwig, religious, or St. Margaret Mary Alacoque, virgin; optional memorials.
17 — Wed. St. Ignatius of Antioch, bishop-doctor; memorial.
18 — Thurs. St. Luke, evangelist; feast.
19 — Fri. Sts. Isaac Jogues, John de Brebeuf, priests, and companions, martyrs; memorial (in US). Weekday. St. Paul of the Cross; optional memorial.
20 — Sat. Weekday.
21 — **Twenty-Ninth Sunday of the year.** (Is. 53:10-11; Heb. 4:14-16; Mk. 10:3545.)
22 — Mon. Weekday.
23 — Tues. Weekday. St. John Capistran, priest; optional memorial.
24 — Wed. Weekday. St. Anthony MMARY Claret, bishop; optional memorial.
25 — Thurs. Weekday.
26 — Fri. Weekday.
27 — Sat. Weekday.
28 — **Thirtieth Sunday of the Year.** (Jer. 31:7-9; Heb. 5:1-6; Mk. 10:46-52.) [Sts. Simon and Jude, apostles; feast.]
29 — Mon. Weekday.
30 — Tues. Weekday.
31 — Wed. Weekday.

October has long been known as the month of the Rosary. The memorial commemorating the Rosary, Oct. 7, is not observed this year because it is outranked by a Sunday.

St. Francis of Assisi, whose memorial is observed Oct. 4, has been suggested several times in recent years as a patron of environmentalists because of his love for all creatures of God and his sense of environmental stewardship.

NOVEMBER 1973

1 — **Thurs. All Saints; solemnity, Holy day of obligation.** (Rv. 7:2-4, 9-14; 1 Jn. 3:1-3; Mt. 5:1-12a.)

2 — Fri. Commemoration of All the Faithful Departed (All Souls' Day).

3 — Sat. Weekday, St. Martin de Porres, religious; optional memorial.

4 — **Thirty-First Sunday of the Year.** (Dt. 6:2-6; Heb. 7:23-28; Mk. 12:28b-34.) [St. Charles Borromeo, bishop; memorial.]

5 — Mon. Weekday.

6 — Tues. Weekday.

7 — Wed. Weekday.

8 — Thurs. Weekday.

9 — Fri. Dedication of Lateran Basilica; feast.

10 — Sat. St. Leo the Great, pope-doctor; memorial.

11 — **Thirty-Second Sunday of the Year.** (1 Kgs. 17:10-16; Heb. 9:24-28; Mk. 12:38-44.) [St. Martin of Tours, bishop; memorial.]

12 — Mon. St. Josaphat, bishop-martyr; memorial.

13 — Tues. St. Frances X. Cabrini, virgin; memorial (in US).

14 — Wed. Weekday.

15 — Thurs. Weekday. St. Albert the Great, bishop-doctor; optional memorial.

16 — Fri. Weekday. St. Margaret of Scotland or St. Gertrude, virgin; optional memorials.

17 — Sat. St. Elizabeth of Hungary, religious; memorial.

18 — **Thirty-Third Sunday of the Year.** (Dn. 12:1-3; Heb. 10:11-14, 18: Mk. 13:24-32.) [Dedication of Basilicas of St. Peter and Paul; optional memorial.]

19 — Mon. Weekday.

20 — Tues. Weekday.

21 — Wed. Presentation of Blessed Mary the Virgin; memorial.

22 — Thurs. St. Cecilia. virgin-martyr; memorial. Thanksgiving Day Votive Mass (in US).

23 — Fri. Weekday. St. Clement I, pope-martyr, or St. Columban, abbot; optional memorials.

24 — Sat. Weekday.

25 — **Sun. Christ the King; solemnity.** (Dn. 7:13-14; Rv. 1:5-8; Jn. 18:33b-37.)

26 — Mon. (Thirty-Fourth and Last Week of the Year). Weekday.

27 — Tues. Weekday.

28 — Wed. Weekday.

29 — Thurs. Weekday.

30 — Fri. St. Andrew, apostle; feast.

Devotion practice makes November the Month of the Holy Souls.

The first and only US Citizen-Saint to date is Mother Frances X. Cabrini, whose memorial is observed Nov. 13.

DECEMBER 1973

1 — Sat. Weekday.

2 — **First Sunday of Advent.** (Jer. 33:14-16; 1 Thes. 3:12 to 4:2; Lk. 21:25-28, 34-36.)

3 — Mon. St. Francis Xavier, priest; memorial.

4 — Tues. Weekday. St. John Damascene, priest-doctor; optional memorial.

5 — Wed. Weekday.

6 — Thurs. Weekday. St. Nicholas, bishop; optional memorial.

7 — Fri. St. Ambrose, bishop-doctor; memorial.

8 — **Sat. Immaculate Conception of Blessed Mary the Virgin; solemnity. Holy day of obligation;** (Gn. 3:9-15, 20; Eph. 1:3-6, 11-12; Lk. 1:26-38.)

9 — **Second Sunday of Advent.** (Bar. 5:1-9; Phil. 1:4-6, 8-11; Lk. 3:1-6.)

10 — Mon. Weekday.

11 — Tues. Weekday. St. Damasus I, pope; optional memorial.

12 — Wed. Our Lady of Guadalupe; memorial (in US). Weekday. St. Jane Frances de Chantal, religious; optional memorial.

13 — Thurs. St. Lucy, virgin-martyr; memorial.

14 — Fri. St. John of the Cross, priest-doctor; memorial.

15 — Sat. Weekday.

16 — **Third Sunday of Advent.** (Zep. 3:14-18a; Phil. 4:4-7; Lk. 3:10-18.)

17 — Mon. Weekday of Advent.

18 — Tues. Weekday of Advent.

19 — Wed. Weekday of Advent.

20 — Thurs. Weekday of Advent.

21 — Fri. Weekday of Advent. [St. Peter Canisius, priest-doctor; optional memorial.]

22 — Sat. Weekday of Advent.

23 — **Fourth Sunday of Advent.** (Mi. 5:1-4a; Heb. 10:5-10; Lk. 1:39-45.) [St. John Kanty, priest; optional memorial.]

24 — Mon. Weekday of Advent.

25 — **Tues. Christmas. Birth of the Lord; solemnity. Holy day of obligation.** (Midnight — Is. 9:1-6; Ti. 2:11-14; Lk. 2:1-14. Dawn — Is. 62:11-12; Ti. 3:4-7; Lk. 2:15-20. During the day — Is. 57:7-10; Heb. 1:1-6; Jn. 1:1-18.)

26 — Wed. St. Stephen, first martyr; feast.

27 — Thurs. St. John, apostle-evangelist; feast.

28 — Fri. Holy Innocents, martyrs; feast.

29 — Sat. Fifth Day of Christmas Octave. St. Thomas Becket, bishop-martyr; optional memorial.

30 — **Sun. Holy Family; feast.** (Sir. 3:2-6, 12-14; Col. 3:12-21; Lk. 2:41-52.)

31 — Mon. Seventh Day of Christmas Octave. St. Sylvester I, pope; optional memorial.

The Blessed Virgin Mary is the patroness of the United States.

TABLE OF MOVABLE FEASTS

Year	Ash Wednesday	Easter	Ascension	Pentecost	Week	Ends	Week	Begins	First Sunday of Advent
					Before Lent		After Pent.		
1973	Mar. 7	Apr. 22	May 31	June 10	9	Mar. 6	10	June 11	Dec. 2
1974	Feb. 27	Apr. 14	May 23	June 2	7	Feb. 26	9	June 3	Dec. 1
1975	Feb. 12	Mar. 30	May 8	May 18	5	Feb. 11	7	May 19	Nov. 30
1976	Mar. 3	Apr. 18	May 27	June 6	8	Mar. 2	10	June 7	Nov. 28
1977	Feb. 23	Apr. 10	May 19	May 29	7	Feb. 22	9	May 30	Nov. 27
1978	Feb. 8	Mar. 26	May 4	May 14	5	Feb. 7	6	May 15	Dec. 3
1979	Feb. 28	Apr. 15	May 24	June 3	8	Feb. 27	9	June 4	Dec. 2
1980	Feb. 20	Apr. 6	May 15	May 25	6	Feb. 19	8	May 26	Nov. 30
1981	Mar. 4	Apr. 19	May 28	June 7	8	Mar. 3	10	June 8	Nov. 29
1982	Feb. 24	Apr. 11	May 20	May 30	7	Feb. 23	9	May 31	Nov. 28
1983	Feb. 16	Apr. 3	May 12	May 22	6	Feb. 15	8	May 23	Nov. 27
1984	Mar. 7	Apr. 22	May 31	June 10	9	Mar. 6	10	June 11	Dec. 2
1985	Feb. 20	Apr. 7	May 16	May 26	6	Feb. 19	8	May 27	Dec. 1
1986	Feb. 12	Mar. 30	May 8	May 18	5	Feb. 11	7	May 19	Nov. 30
1987	Mar. 4	Apr. 19	May 28	June 7	9	Mar. 3	10	June 8	Nov. 29
1988	Feb. 17	Apr. 3	May 12	May 22	6	Feb. 16	8	May 23	Nov. 27
1989	Feb. 8	Mar. 26	May 4	May 14	5	Feb. 7	6	May 15	Dec. 3
1990	Feb. 28	Apr. 15	May 24	June 3	8	Feb. 27	9	June 4	Dec. 2
1991	Feb. 13	Mar. 31	May 9	May 19	5	Feb. 12	7	May 20	Dec. 1
1992	Mar. 4	Apr. 19	May 28	June 7	9	Mar. 3	10	June 8	Nov. 29
1993	Feb.24	Apr. 11	May 20	May 30	7	Feb. 23	9	May 31	Nov. 28
1994	Feb. 16	Apr. 3	May 12	May 22	6	Feb. 15	8	May 23	Nov. 27
1995	Mar. 1	Apr. 16	May 25	June 4	8	Feb. 28	9	June 5	Dec. 3
1996	Feb. 21	Apr. 7	May 16	May 26	7	Feb. 20	8	May 27	Dec. 1
1997	Feb. 12	Mar. 30	May 8	May 18	5	Feb. 11	7	May 19	Nov. 30
1998	Feb. 25	Apr. 12	May 21	May 31	7	Feb. 24	9	June 1	Nov. 29
1999	Feb. 17	Apr. 4	May 13	May 23	6	Feb. 16	8	May 24	Nov. 28
2000	Mar. 8	Apr. 23	June 1	June 11	9	Mar. 7	10	June 12	Dec. 3

Weeks of Season-through-Year

+ Season through Year

Weeks between the end of Christmastide and the beginning of Lent, and from the day after Pentecost to the last Sunday of the liturgical year, belong to the Season-through-the-Year. The table indicates the number and terminal date of the week ending the first part, and the number and starting date of the week beginning the second part, of this season. In some years, as in 1974, a week of this season is eliminated because of calendar conditions.

Date of Easter

The Second Vatican Council's *Constitution on the Sacred Liturgy* said there would be no objection "if the feast of Easter were assigned to a particular Sunday of the Gregorian calendar, provided that those whom it may concern especially the brethren who are not in communion with the Apostolic See, give their assent." Agreement has not yet been reached, although the late Ecumenical Patriarch Athenagoras I proposed that Easter be celebrated each year on the second Sunday of April. Calendar expert Father Pierre Jounel made this comment on the subject: "There is no change in the new liturgical calendar concerning fixing the date of Easter. . . . It seems there is no way of arriving at a universal agreement on this point for many years, especially until the general council of the Orthodox Church puts the problem on its agenda."

HOLY DAYS AND OTHER FEASTS

The following list includes the six holy days of obligation observed in the United States and additional observances of devotional and historical significance. The dignity or rank of observances is indicated by the terms: **solemnity** (highest in rank, the equivalent of former first class feasts); **feast** (equivalent to former second class feasts); **memorial** (equivalent to former third class feasts, for universal observance); **optional memorial** (for celebration by choice).

All Saints, Nov. 1, holy day of obligation, solemnity. Commemorates all the blessed in heaven, and is intended particularly to honor the blessed who have no special feasts. The background of the feast dates to the fourth century when groups of martyrs, and later other saints, were honored on a common day in various places. In 609 or 610, the Pantheon, a pagan temple at Rome, was consecrated as a Christian church for the honor of Our Lady and the martyrs (later all saints). In 835, Gregory IV fixed Nov. 1 as the date of observance.

All Souls, Commemoration of the Faithful Departed, Nov. 2 (transferable to Nov. 3). The dead were prayed for from the earliest day of Christianity. By the sixth century it was customary in Benedictine monasteries to hold a commemoration of deceased members of the order at Pentecost. A common commemoration of all the faithful departed on the day after All Saints was instituted in 998 by St. Odilo, of the Abbey of Cluny, and an observance of this kind was generally adopted throughout the Church. In 1915, Benedict XV granted priests throughout the world permission to celebrate three Masses for this commemoration. He also granted a special indulgence for the occasion.

Annunciation of the Lord (formerly, Annunciation of the Blessed Virgin Mary), Mar. 25, solemnity. A feast of the Incarnation which commemorates the announcement by the Archangel Gabriel to the Virgin Mary that she was to become the Mother of Christ (Lk. 1:26-38), and the miraculous conception of Christ by her. The feast was instituted about 430 in the East. The Roman observance dates from the seventh century, when celebration was said to be universal.

Ascension of the Lord, movable observance held 40 days after Easter, holy day of obligation, solemnity. Commemorates the Ascension of Christ into heaven 40 days after his Resurrection from the dead (Mk. 16:19; Lk. 24:51; Acts 1:2). The feast recalls the completion of Christ's mission on earth for the salvation of men and his entry into heaven with glorified human nature. The Ascension is a pledge of the final glorification of all who achieve salvation. Documentary evidence of the feast dates from early in the fifth century, but it was observed long before that time in connection with Pentecost and Easter.

Ash Wednesday, movable observance, six and one-half weeks before Easter. It was set as the first day of Lent by St. Gregory the Great (590-604) with the extension of an earlier and shorter penitential season to a total period including 40 weekdays of fasting before Easter. Ashes, symbolic of penance, are blessed and distributed among the faithful during the day. They are used to mark the forehead with the Sign of the Cross, with the reminder: "Remember, man, that you are dust, and unto dust you shall return," or: "Repent, and believe the Good News."

Assumption Aug. 15, holy day of obligation, solemnity. Commemorates the taking into heaven of Mary, soul and body, at the end of her life on earth, a truth of faith that was proclaimed a dogma by Pius XII on Nov. 1, 1950. One of the oldest and most solemn feasts of Mary, it has a history dating back to at least the seventh century when its celebration was already established at Jerusalem and Rome.

Baptism of the Lord, movable, celebrated on the Sunday after Epiphany, feast. Recalls the baptism of Christ by John the Baptist (Mk. 1:9-11), an event associated with the liturgy of the Epiphany. This baptism was the occasion for Christ's manifestation of Himself at the beginning of his public life.

Birth of Mary, Sept. 8, feast. This is a very old feast which originated in the East and found place in the Roman liturgy in the seventh century.

Candlemas Day, Feb. 2. See Presentation of the Lord.

Chair of Peter, Feb. 22, feast. Commemorates establishment of the see of Antioch by Peter. The feast, which has been in the Roman calendar since 336, is a liturgical expression of belief in the episcopacy and hierarchy of the Church.

Christmas, Birth of Our Lord Jesus Christ, Dec. 25, holy day of obligation, solemnity. Commemorates the birth of Christ (Lk. 2:1-20). This event was originally commemorated in the East on the feast of Epiphany or Theophany. The Christmas feast itself originated in the West; by 354 it was certainly kept on Dec. 25. This date may have been set for the observance to offset pagan ceremonies held at about the same time to commemorate the birth of the sun at the winter solstice. Priests may celebrate three Masses on Christmas Day. Christmastide begins with this feast and continues until the Sunday after Epiphany.

Christ the King, movable, celebrated on the last Sunday of the liturgical year, solemnity. Commemorates the royal prerogatives of Christ and is equivalent to a declaration of his rights to the homage, service and fidelity of men in all phases of individual and social life. Pius XI instituted the feast Dec. 11, 1925.

Corpus Christi, movable observance held in the US on the Sunday following Trinity Sunday, solemnity. Commemorates the institution of the Holy Eucharist (Mt. 26:26-28). The feast originated at Liege in 1246 and was extended throughout the Church in the West by Urban IV in 1264. St. Thomas Aquinas composed the Office for the feast.

Dedication of St. John Lateran, Nov. 9, feast. Commemorates the first public consecration of a church, that of the Basilica of the Most Holy Savior by Pope St. Sylvester Nov. 9, 324. The church, as well as the Lateran Palace, was the gift of Emperor Constantine. Since the 12th century it has been known as St. John Lateran, in honor of John the Baptist after whom the adjoining baptistery was named. It was rebuilt by Innocent X (1644-55), reconsecrated by Benedict XIII in 1726, and enlarged by Leo XIII (1878-1903). This basilica is regarded as the church of highest dignity in Rome and throughout the Roman Rite.

Dedication of St. Mary Major, Aug. 5, optional memorial. Commemorates the rebuilding and dedication by Sixtus III (432-40) of a church in honor of Blessed Mary the Virgin. This is the Basilica of St. Mary Major on the Esquiline Hill in Rome. An earlier building was erected during the pontificate of Liberius (352-66); according to legend, it was located on a site covered by a miraculous fall of snow seen by a nobleman favored with a vision of Mary.

Easter, movable celebration held on the first Sunday after the full moon following the vernal equinox (between Mar. 22 and Apr. 25), solemnity with an octave. Commemorates the Resurrection of Christ from the dead (Mk. 16:1-7). The observance of this mystery, kept since the first days of the Church, extends throughout the Easter season which lasts until the feast of Pentecost, a period of 50 days. Every Sunday in the year is regarded as a "little" Easter. The date of Easter determines the dates of movable feasts, such as Ascension and Pentecost, and the number of Sundays after Epiphany and Pentecost.

Easter Vigil (Holy Saturday), day before Easter. Ceremonies are all related to the Resurrection and renewal-in-grace theme of Easter: blessing of the new fire and Paschal Candle, reading of prophecies, blessing of water and the baptismal font, the baptism of converts and renewal of baptismal vows by the faithful, the Litany of the Saints, and the celebration of Mass. The vigil ceremonies are held after sundown, preferably at a time that makes possible the celebration of Mass at midnight.

Epiphany of Our Lord, Jan. 6 or (in the US) a Sunday between Jan. 2 and 8, solemnity. Commemorates the manifestations of the divinity of Christ. It is one of the oldest Christian feasts, with an Eastern origin traceable to the beginning of the third century and antedating the Western feast of Christmas. Originally, it commemorated the manifestations of Christ's divinity — or Theophany — in his birth, the homage of the Magi, and baptism by John the Baptist. Later, the first two of these commemorations were transferred to Christmas when the Eastern Church adopted that feast between 380 and 430. The central feature of the Eastern observance now is the manifestation or declaration of Christ's divinity in his baptism and at the beginning of his public life. The Epiphany was adopted by the Western Church during the same period in which the Eastern Church accepted Christmas. In the Roman Rite, commemoration is made in the Mass of the homage of the wise men from the East (Mt. 2:1-12).

Good Friday, the Friday before Easter, privileged feria of Holy Week. Liturgical elements of the observance are commemoration of the Passion and Death of Christ in the reading of the Passion (according to John), special prayers for the Church and people of all ranks, the veneration of the Cross, and a Communion service. The Solemn Liturgical Action takes place between noon and 9 p.m. This is the only day in the year on which the Eucharistic Liturgy is not celebrated in the Roman Rite.

Guardian Angels, Oct. 2, memorial. Commemorates the angels who protect men from spiritual and physical dangers and assist them in doing good. A feast in their honor celebrated in Spain in the 16th century was extended to the whole Church by Paul V in 1608. In 1670, Clement X set Oct. 2 as the date of observance. Earlier, guardian angels were honored liturgically in conjunction with the feast of St. Michael.

Holy Family, movable observance on the Sunday after Christmas, feast. Commemorates the Holy Family of Jesus, Mary and Joseph as the model of domestic society, holiness and virtue. The devotional background of the feast was very strong in the 17th century. In the 18th century, in prayers composed for a special Mass, a Canadian bishop likened the Christian family to the Holy Family, Leo XIII consecrated families to the Holy Family. In 1921, Benedict XV extended the Divine Office and Mass of the feast to the whole Church.

Holy Innocents, Dec. 28, feast. Commemorates the infants who suffered death at the hands of Herod's soldiers seeking to kill the child Jesus (Mt. 2:13-18). A feast in their honor has been observed since the fifth century.

Holy Thursday, the Thursday before Easter, privileged feria of Holy Week. Commemorates the institution of the Holy Eucharist (which is later celebrated on the special feast of Corpus Christi) and other events of the Last Supper. Ceremonies include the celebration of a principal Mass between 4 and

9 p.m., the washing of feet in imitation of the act of Christ who washed the feet of the Apostles at the Last Supper, the stripping of the altar at the conclusion of Mass. There is also a procession of the Blessed Sacrament to a special place of reposition where It is reserved for veneration by the faithful until the Solemn Liturgical Action on Good Friday. At a special Mass of Chrism, bishops bless oils (of catechumens, chrism, of the sick) for use during the year.

Immaculate Conception, Dec. 8, holy day of obligation, solemnity. Commemorates the fact that Mary, in view of her calling to be the Mother of Christ and in virtue of his merits, was preserved from the first moment of her conception from original sin and was filled with grace from the very beginning of her life. She was the only person so preserved from original sin. The present form of the feast dates from Dec. 8, 1854, when Pius IX defined the dogma of the Immaculate Conception. An earlier feast of the Conception, which testified to long-existing belief in this truth, was observed in the East by the eighth century, in Ireland in the ninth, and subsequently in European countries. In 1846, Mary was proclaimed patroness of the US under this title.

Immaculate Heart of Mary, Saturday following the second Sunday after Pentecost, optional memorial. On May 4, 1944, Pius XII ordered this feast observed throughout the Church in order to obtain Mary's intercession for "peace among nations, freedom for the Church, the conversion of sinners, the love of purity and the practice of virtue." Two years earlier, he consecrated the entire human race to Mary under this title. Devotion to Mary under the title of her Most Pure Heart originated during the Middle Ages. It was given great impetus in the 17th century by the preaching of St. John Eudes, who was the first to celebrate a Mass and Divine Office of Mary under this title. A feast, celebrated in various places and on different dates, was authorized in 1799.

Joachim and Ann, July 26, memorial. Commemorates the parents of Mary. A joint feast, celebrated Sept. 9, originated in the East near the end of the sixth century. Devotion to Ann, introduced in the eighth century at Rome, became widespread in Europe in the 14th century; her feast was extended throughout the Latin Church in 1584. A feast of Joachim was introduced in the West in the 15th century.

John the Baptist, Birth, June 24, solemnity. The precursor of Christ, whose cousin he was, was commemorated universally in the liturgy by the fourth century. He is the only saint, except the Blessed Virgin Mary, whose birthday is observed as a feast. Another feast, on Aug. 29, commemorates his passion and death at the order of Herod (Mk. 6:14-29).

Joseph, Mar. 19, solemnity. Joseph is honored as the husband of the Blessed Virgin Mary, the patron and protector of the universal Church and workman. Devotion to him already existed in the eighth century in the East, and in the 11th in the West. Various feasts were celebrated before the 15th century when Mar. 19 was fixed for his commemoration; this feast was extended to the whole Church in 1621 by Gregory XV. In 1955, Pius XII instituted the feast of St. Joseph the Workman for observance May 1; this feast, which may be celebrated by local option, supplanted the Solemnity or Patronage of St. Joseph formerly observed on the third Wednesday after Easter. St. Joseph was proclaimed protector and patron of the universal Church in 1870 by Pius IX.

Michael, Gabriel and Raphael, Archangels, Sept. 29, feast. A feast bearing the title of Dedication of St. Michael the Archangel formerly commemorated on this date the consecration in 530 of a church near Rome in honor of Michael, the first angel given a liturgical feast. For a while, this feast was combined with a commemoration of the Guardian Angels. The separate feasts of Gabriel (Mar. 24) and Raphael (Oct. 24) were suppressed by the calendar reform of 1969 and this joint feast of the three archangels was instituted.

Octave of Christmas, Jan. 1. See Solemnity of Mary, Mother of God.

Our Lady of Sorrows, Sept. 15, memorial. Recalls the sorrows experienced by Mary in her association with Christ: the prophecy of Simeon (Lk. 2:34-35), the flight into Egypt (Mt. 2:13-21), the three-day separation from Jesus (Lk. 2:41-50), and four incidents connected with the Passion: her meeting with Christ on the way to Calvary, the crucifixion, the removal of Christ's body from the cross, and his burial (Mt. 27:31-61; Mk. 15:20-47; Lk. 23:26-56; Jn. 19:17-42). A Mass and Divine Office of the feast were celebrated by the Servites, especially, in the 17th century, and in 1817 Pius VII extended the observance to the whole Church.

Our Lady of the Rosary, Oct. 7, memorial. Commemorates the Virgin Mary through recall of the mysteries of the Rosary which recapitulate events in her life and the life of Christ. The feast was instituted to commemorate a Christian victory over invading Mohammedan forces at Lepanto on Oct. 7, 1571, and was extended throughout the Church by Clement XI in 1716.

Passion (Palm) Sunday, the Sunday before Easter. Recalls the triumphal entry of Christ into Jerusalem at the beginning of the last week of his life (Mt. 21:1-9). A procession and other ceremonies commemorating this event were held in Jerusalem from very early Christian times and were adopted in Rome by the ninth century, when the blessing of palm for the occasion was introduced. Full liturgical observance includes the blessing of palm and a procession before the principal Mass of the day. The Passion, by Matthew, Mark or Luke, is read during the Mass.

Pentecost, also called **Whitsunday,** movable celebration held 50 days after Easter, solemnity. Commemorates the descent of the Holy Spirit upon the Apostles, the preaching of Peter and the other Apostles to Jews in Jerusalem, the baptism and aggregation of some 3,000 persons to the Christian community (Acts 2:1-41). It is regarded as the birthday of the Catholic Church. The original observance of the feast antedated the earliest extant documentary evidence from the third century.

Peter and Paul, June 29, solemnity. Commemorates the dual martyrdom of Peter by crucifixion and Paul by beheading during the Neronian persecution. This joint commemoration of the two greatest Apostles dates at least from 258 at Rome.

Presentation of the Lord (formerly called Purification of the Blessed Virgin Mary, also Candlemas), Feb. 2, feast. Commemorates the presentation of Jesus in the Temple — according to prescriptions of Mosaic Law (Lv. 12:2-8; Ex. 13:2; Lk. 2:22-32) — and the purification of Mary 40 days after his birth. In the East, where the feast antedated fourth century testimony regarding its existence, it was observed primarily as a feast of Our Lord; in the West, where it was adopted later, it was regarded more as a feast of Mary until the calendar reform of 1969. Its date was set for Feb. 2 after the celebration of Christmas was fixed for Dec. 25, late in the fourth century. The blessing of candles, probably in commemoration of Christ who was the Light to enlighten the Gentiles, became common about the 11th century and gave the feast the secondary name of Candlemas.

Queenship of Mary, Aug. 22, memorial. Commemorates the high dignity of Mary as Queen of heaven, angels and men. Universal observance of the memorial was ordered by Pius XII in the encyclical *Ad Caeli Reginam* Oct. 11, 1954, near the close of a Marian Year observed in connection with the centenary of the proclamation of the dogma of the Immaculate Conception and four years after the proclamation of the dogma of the Assumption. The original date of the memorial was May 31.

Resurrection. See Easter.

Sacred Heart of Jesus, movable observance held on the Friday after Corpus Christi, solemnity. The object of the devotion is the divine Person of Christ, whose heart is the symbol of his love for men — for whom he accomplished the work of Redemption. The Mass and Office now used on the feast were prescribed by Pius XI in 1929. Devotion to the Sacred Heart was introduced into the liturgy in the 17th century through the efforts of St. John Eudes who composed an Office and Mass for the feast. It was furthered as the result of the revelations of St. Margaret Mary

Alacoque after 1675 and by the work of Claude de la Colombiere, S.J. In 1765, Clement XIII approved a Mass and Office for the feast, and in 1856 Pius IX extended the observance throughout the Roman Rite.

Solemnity of Mary, Mother of God, Jan. 1, holy day of obligation, solemnity. The calendar reform of 1969, in accord with Eastern tradition, reinstated the Marian character of this commemoration on the octave day of Christmas. The former feast of the Circumcision, dating at least from the first half of the sixth century, marked the initiation of Jesus (Lk. 02:21) in Judaism and by analogy focused attention on the initiation of persons in the Christian religion and their incorporation in Christ through baptism. The feast of the Solemnity supplants the former feast of the Maternity of Mary observed on Oct. 11.

Transfiguration of the Lord, Aug. 6, feast. Commemorates the revelation of his divinity by Christ to Peter, James and John on Mt. Tabor (Mt. 17:1-9). The feast, which is very old, was extended throughout the universal Church in 1457 by Callistus III.

Trinity, Most Holy, movable observance held on the Sunday after Pentecost, solemnity. Commemorates the most sublime mystery of the Christian faith, i.e., that there are Three Divine Persons — Father, Son and Holy Spirit — in one God (Mt. 28:18-20). A votive Mass of the Most Holy Trinity dates from the seventh century; an Office was composed in the 10th century; and in 1334, John XXII extended the feast to the universal Church.

Triumph of the Cross, Sept. 14, feast. Commemorates the finding of the cross on which Christ was crucified, in 326 through the efforts of St. Helena, mother of Constantine; the consecration of the Basilica of the Holy Sepulchre nearly 10 years later: and the recovery in 628 or 629 by Emperor Heraclius of a major portion of the cross which had been removed by the Persians from its place of veneration at Jerusalem. The feast originated in Jerusalem and spread through the East before being adopted in the West. General adoption followed the building at Rome of the Basilica of the Holy Cross "in Jerusalem," so called because it was the place of enshrinement of a major portion of the cross of crucifixion.

Visitation, May 31, feast. Commemorates Mary's visit to her cousin Elizabeth after the Annunciation and before the birth of John the Baptist, the precursor of Christ (Lk. 1:39-47). The feast had a medieval origin and was observed in the Franciscan Order before being extended throughout the Church by Urban VI in 1389. It is one of the feasts of the Incarnation and is notable for its recall of the Magnificat, one of the few New Testament canticles, which acknowledges the unique gifts of God to Mary because of her role in the redemptive work of Christ. The canticle is recited at Vespers in the Liturgy of the Hours.

SAINTS

Biographical sketches of additional saints are under other Almanac titles. See Index.

An asterisk with a feast date indicates that a memorial or feast is observed according to the revised Roman-Rite calendar.

Adjutor, St. (d. 1131): Norman knight; fought in First Crusade; monk-recluse after his return; legendary accounts of incidents on journey to Crusade probably account for his patronage of yachtsmen; Apr. 30.

Agatha, St. (d. c. 250): Sicilian virgin-martyr; her intercession credited in Sicily with stopping eruptions of Mt. Etna; patron of nurses; Feb. 5*.

Agnes, St. (d. c. 304): Roman virgin-martyr; martyred at age of 10 or 12; patron of young girls; Jan. 21*.

Aloysius Gonzaga, St. (1568-1591): Italian Jesuit; died while nursing plague-stricken; canonized 1726; patron of youth; June 21*.

Amand, St. (d. c. 676): Apostle of Belgium; b. France; established monasteries throughout Belgium; Feb. 6.

Andre Grasset de Saint Sauveur, Bl. (1758-1792): Canadian priest; martyred in France, Sept. 2, 1792, during the Revolution; one of a group called the Martyrs of Paris who were beatified in 1926.

Andrew Corsini, St. (1302-1373): Italian Carmelite; bishop of Fiesoli; mediator between quarrelsome Italian states; canonized 1629; Feb. 4.

Andrew Fournet, St. (1752-1834): French priest; co-founder with St. Jeanne Elizabeth des Anges of the Congregation of Daughters of the Cross; canonized 1933; May 13.

Angela Merici, St. (1474-1540): Italian nun; foundress of Institute of St. Urusla, 1535, the first teaching order of nuns in the Church; canonized 1807; Jan. 27*.

Anne Mary Javouhey, Bl. (1779-1851): French virgin; foundress of Institute of St. Joseph of Cluny, 1812; beatified 1950; July 15.

Ansgar, St. (801-865): Bishop, Benedictine monk; b. near Amiens; missionary in Denmark, Sweden, Norway and Northern Germany; apostle of Denmark; Feb. 3*.

Anthony Abbot, St. (c. 251-c. 354): Egyptian hermit; patriarch of all monks; established communities for hermits which became models for monastic life, especially in the East; friend and supporter of St. Athanasius in the latter's struggle with the Arians; Jan. 17*.

Anthony Mary Claret, St. (1807-1870): Spanish priest; founder of Missionary Sons of the Immaculate Heart of Mary (Claretians), 1849; archbishop of Santiago, Cuba, 1851-57; canonized 1950; Oct. 24*.

Anthony Mary Zaccaria, St. (1502-1539): Italian priest; founder of Barnabites (Clerks Regular of St. Paul), 1530; canonized 1897; July 5*.

Apollonia, St. (d. 249): Deaconess of Alexandria; martyred during persecution of Decius; her patronage of dentists probably rests on tradition that her teeth were broken by pincers by her persecutors; Feb. 9.

Augustine of Canterbury, St. (d. 604 or 605): Italian missionary; apostle of the English; sent by Pope Gregory I with 40 monks to evangelize England; arrived there 597; first archbishop of Canterbury; May 27*.

Benedict of Nursia, St. (c. 4480-547): Abbot; founder of monasticism in Western Europe; established monastery at Monte Cassino; proclaimed patron of Europe by Paul VI in 1964; July 11*.

Benedict the Black (il Moro), St. (1526-1589): Sicilian Franciscan; born a slave; joined Franciscans as lay brother; appointed guardian and novice master; canonized 1807; Apr. 4.

Bernadette Soubirous, St. (1844-1879): French peasant girl favored with series of visions of Blessed Birgin Mary at Lourdes (see Lourdes Apparitions); joined Institute of Sisters of NotreDame at Nevers, 1866; canonized 1933; Apr. 16.

Bernard of Menthon, St. (d. 1081): Italian priest; founded Alpine hospices near the two passes named for him; patron of mountaineers; May 28.

Bernardine of Siena, St. (1380-1444): Italian Franciscan; noted preacher and missioner; spread of devotion to Holy Name is attributed to him; represented in art holding to his breast the monogram IHS; canonized 1450; May 20*.

Blaise, St. (d. c. 316): Armenian bishop; martyr; the blessing of throats on his feast day derives from tradition that he miraculously saved the life of a boy who had half-swallowed a fish bone; Feb. 3*.

Boniface (Winfrid), St. (d. 754): English Benedictine; bishop, martyr; apostle of Germany; established monastery at Fulda which became center of German missionary work; archbishop of Mainz; martyred near Dukkum in Holland; June 5*.

Brendan, St. (c. 489-583): Irish abbot; founded monasteries; his patronage of sailors probably rests on tradition that he made a seven-year voyage in search of a fabled paradise; called Brendan the Navigator; May 16.

Bridget (Brigid), St. (c. 450-525): Irish nun; founded nunnery at Kildare, the first erected on Irish soil; patron, with Sts. Patrick and Columba, of Ireland; Feb. 1.

Bridget (Birgitta), St. (c. 1303-1373): Swedish mystic; widow; foundress of Order of Our Savior (Brigittines); canonized 1391; wrote *Revelationes*, accounts of her visions; patroness of Sweden; July 23*.

Bruno, St. (1030-1101): German monk; founded Carthusians, 1084, in France; Oct. 6*.

Cabrini, Mother: See Index.

Cajetan of Thiene, St. (1480-1547): Italian lawyer; religious reformer; a founder of Oratory of Divine Love, forerunner of the Theatines; canonized 1671; Aug. 7*.

Callistus I, St. (d. 222): Pope, 217-222; martyr; condemned Sabellianism and other heresies; advocated a policy of mercy towards repentant sinners; Oct. 14*.

Camillus de Lellis, St. (1550-1614): Italian priest; founder of Camillians (Ministers of the Sick); canonized 1746; patron of the sick and of nurses; July 14*.

Casimir, St. (1458-1484): Polish prince; grand duke of Lithuania; noted for his piety; buried at cathedral in Vilna, Lithuania; canonized 1521; patron of Poland and Lithuania; Mar. 4*.

Cassian, St. (d. 298): Roman martyr; an official court stenographer who declared himself a Christian; patron of stenographers; Dec. 3.

Catherine Laboure, St. (1806-1876): French nun; favored with series of visions; first Miraculous Medal (see Index) struck as the result of one of the visions; canonized 1947; Dec. 31.

Catherine of Bologna, St. (1413-1463): Italian Poor Clare; mystic, writer, artist; canonized 1712; patron of artists; Mar. 9.

Cecilia, St. (2nd-3rd century): Roman virgin-martyr; traditional patron of musicians; Nov. 22*.

Charles Borromeo, St. (1538-1584): Italian cardinal; nephew of Pope Pius IV; cardinal bishop of Milan; influential figure in Church reform in Italy; promoted education of clergy; canonized 1610; Nov. 4*.

Charles Lwanga and Companions, Sts. (d. 1886 and 1887): Martyrs of Uganda; pages of King Mwanga of Uganda; Charles Lwanga and 12 companions were martyred near Rubaga, June 3, 1886; the other nine were martyred between May 26, 1886, and Jan. 27, 1887; canonized 1964; first martyrs of black Africa; June 3*.

Christopher, St. (3rd cent.): Early Christian martyr inscribed in Roman calendar about 1550; feast relegated to particular calendars because of legendary nature of accounts of his life; traditional patron of travelers; July 25.

Clare, St. (1194-1253): Foundress of Poor Clares; b. at Assisi; later joined in religious life by her sisters Agnes and Beatrice, and her mother Ortolana; canonized 1255; patroness of television; Aug. 11*.

Clement I, St. (d. c. 100): Pope, 88-97; third successor of St. Peter; wrote important letter to Church in Corinth settling disputes there; venerated as a martyr; Nov. 23*.

Columba, St. (521-597): Irish monk; founded monasteries in Ireland; missionary in Scotland; established monastery at Iona which became the center for conversion of Picts, Scots, and Northern English; Scotland's most famous saint; June 9.

Columbanus, St. (545-615): Irish monk; scholar; founded monasteries in England and Brittany (famous abbey of Leuxil); forced into exile because of his criticism of Frankish court; spent last years in northern Italy where he founded abbey at Bobbio; Nov. 23*.

Contardo Ferrini, Bl. (1859-1902): Italian Franciscan tertiary; model of the Catholic professor; beatified 1947; patron of universities; Oct. 17.

Cornelius, St. (d. 253): Pope, 251-253; promoted a policy of mercy with respect to readmission of repentant Christians who had fallen away during the persecution of Decius *(lapsi);* banished from Rome during persecution of Gallus; regarded as a martyr; Sept. 16 (with Cyprian)*.

Cosmas and Damian, Sts. (d. c. 303): Arabian twin brothers; physicians who were martyred during Diocletian persecution; patrons of physicians; Sept. 26*.

Crispin and Crispinian, Sts. (3rd cent.): Early Christian martyrs; said to have met their deaths in Gaul; patrons of shoemakers, a trade they pursued; Oct. 25.

Cyprian, St. (d. 258): Early ecclesiastical writer; b. Africa; bishop of Carthage, 249-258; supported Pope St. Cornelius concerning the readmission of Christians who had apostasized in time of persecution; erred in his teaching that baptism administered by heretics and schismatics was invalid; wrote *De Unitate;* Sept. 16 (with St. Cornelius).*

Cyril and Methodius, Sts.: Greek missionaries; brothers venerated as apostles of the Slavs; Cyril (d. 869) and Methodius (d. 885) began their missionary work in Moravia in 863; developed a Slavonic alphabet, and eventually their use of the vernacular in the liturgy was approved; Feb. 14*.

Damasus I, St. (d. 384): Pope, 366-384; opposed Arians and Apollinarians; commissioned St. Jerome to work on Bible translation; developed Roman liturgy; Dec. 11*.

Damian, St.: See Cosmas and Damian, Sts.

David, St. (5th-6th cent.): Welsh monk; founded monastery at Menevia; patron saint of Wales; Mar. 1.

Dismas, St. (1st cent.): Name given to repentant thief (Good Thief) to whom Jesus promised salvation; regarded as patron of prisoners; Mar. 25.

Dominic, St. (Dominic de Guzman) (1170-1221): Spanish priest; founder of Dominican Order (Friars Preachers), 1215; preached against the Albigensian heresy; a contemporary of St. Francis of Assisi; canonized 1234; Aug. 8*.

Dominic Savio, St. (1842-1857): Italian youth; pupil of St. John Bosco; died before his 15th birthday; canonized 1954; patron of choir boys; Mar. 9.

Dunstan, St. (c. 910-988): English monk; archbishop of Canterbury; initiated reforms in religious life; royal counselor to several kings; considered one of greatest Anglo-Saxon saints; patron of armorers, goldsmiths, locksmiths, jewelers; May 17.

Dymphna, St. (dates uncertain): Nothing certain known of her life; presumably she was an Irish maiden whose relics were discovered at Gheel near Antwerp, Belgium, in the 13th century; since that time many cases of mental illness and epilepsy have been cured at her shrine; patron of those suffering from mental illness; May 15.

Edmund Campion, St. (1540-1581): English Jesuit; convert 1573; martyred at Tyburn; canonized 1970, one of the Forty English and Welsh Martyrs; Dec. 1.

Elizabeth Bayley Seton, Bl. (1774-1821): American foundress; convert, 1905; founded Sisters of Charity in the US; beatified 1963, the first American-born blessed; Jan. 4 (US)*.

Elizabeth of Hungary, St. (1207-1231): Queen; became Franciscan tertiary after death of her husband in 1227; devoted life to poor and destitute; a patron of the Third Order of St. Francis; Nov. 17*.

Elizabeth of Portugal, St. (1271-1336): Queen of Portugal; b. Spain; retired to Poor Clare convent as a tertiary after the death of her husband; July 4*.

Erasmus, St. (d. 303): Life surrounded by legend; martyred during Diocletian persecution; patron of sailors; June 2.

Ethelbert, St.(552-676): King of Kent; baptized by St. Augustine 597; issued legal code; furthered spread of Christianity; Feb. 24.

Euphrasia Pelletier, St. (1796-1868): French nun; founded Sisters of the Good Shepherd at Angers, 1829; canonized 1940; Apr. 24.

Eusebius Vercelli, St. (283-370): Italian bishop; exiled from his see for a time because of his opposition to Arianism; considered a martyr because of sufferings he endured; Aug. 2*.

Fabian, St. (d. 250): Pope, 236-250; martyred under Decius; Jan. 20*.

Felicitas, St. See Perpetua and Felicitas, Sts.

Felix of Valois, St. (1127-1212): French hermit; co-founder with St. John of Matha of Trinitarians for the ransom of captives from Moors; Nov. 20.

Ferdinand III, St. (1198-1252): King of Castile and Leon; waged successful crusade against Mohammedans in Spain; founded university at Salamanca; canonized 1671; May 30.

Fiacre, St. (d. c. 670): Irish hermit; patron of gardeners; Aug. 30.

Fidelis of Sigmaringen, St. (Mark Rey) (1577-1622): German Capuchin; lawyer before he joined the Capuchins; missionary to Swiss Protestants; stabbed to death by peasants who were told he was agent of Austrian emperor; Apr. 24*.

Frances of Rome, St. (1384-1440): Italian model for housewives and widows; happily married for 40 years; after death of her hus-band in 1436 joined community of Benedictine Oblates she had founded; canonized 1608; patron of motorists; Mar. 9*.

Frances Xavier Cabrini, St. (Mother Cabrini) (1850-1917): American foundress; b. Italy; foundress of Missionary Sisters of the Sacred Heart, 1877; settled in the US 1889; became an American citizen at Seattle 1909; worked among Italian immigrants; canonized 1946, the first American citizen so honored; Nov. 13 (US)*.

Francis Borgia, St. (1510-1572): Spanish Jesuit; joined Jesuits after death of his wife in 1546; became General of the Order, 1565; Oct. 10.

Francis of Assisi, St. (Giovanni di Bernardone) (1182-1226): Founder of the Franciscans, 1209; received stigmata 1224; canonized 1228; one of best known and best loved saints; patron of Catholic Action and of Italy; Oct. 4*.

Francis of Paula, St. (1416-1507): Italian hermit; founder of Minim Friars; Apr. 2*.

Francis Xavier, St. (1506-1552): Spanish Jesuit; missionary to Far East; canonized 1602; patron of foreign missions; considered one of greatest Christian missionaries; Dec. 3*.

Gabriel of the Sorrowful Mother, St. (Francis Possenti) (1838-1862): Italian Passionist; died while a scholastic; canonized 1920; Feb. 27.

Genesius, St. (d. c. 300): Roman actor; according to legend, was converted while performing a burlesque of Christian baptism and was subsequently martyred; patron of actors.

Genevieve, St. (422-500): French nun; a patroness and protectress of Paris; events of her life not authenticated; Jan. 3.

George, St. (d. c. 300): Martyr, probably during Diocletian persecution in Palestine; all other incidents of his life, including story of the dragon, are legendary; patron of England; Apr. 23*.

Gerard Majella, St. (1725-1755): Italian Redemptorist lay brother; noted for supernatural occurrences in his life including bilocation and reading of consciences; canonized 1904; patron of mothers; Oct. 16.

Gertrude, St. (1256-1302): German mystic writer; helped spread devotion to the Sacred Heart; Nov. 16*.

Gregory VII (Hildebrand), St. (1020?-1085): Pope, 1075-1085; Benedictine monk; adviser to several popes; as pope, strengthened interior life of Church and fought against lay investiture; driven from Rome by Henry IV; died in exile; May 25*.

Gregory the Illuminator, St. (257-332): Martyr; bishop; apostle and patron saint of Armenia; helped free Armenia from the Persians; Sept. 30.

Hedwig, St. (1174-1243): Moravian noblewoman; married duke of Silesia, head of Polish royal family; fostered religious life in country; canonized 1266; Oct. 16*.

Helen, St. (250-330): Empress; mother of Constantine the Great; associated with discovery of the True Cross; Aug. 18.

Henry, St. (972-1024): Bavarian emperor; cooperated with Benediction abbeys in restoration of ecclesiastical and social discipline; canonized 1146; July 13*.

Hippolytus, St. (d. c. 236): Roman priest; opposed Pope St. Callistus I in his teaching about the readmission of Christians who had apostasized during time of persecution; elected antipope; reconciled before his martyrdom; important ecclesiastical writer; Aug. 13*.

Hubert, St. (d. 727): Bishop; his patronage of hunters is based on legend that he was converted while hunting; Nov. 3.

Hugh of Cluny (the Great), St. (1024-1109): Abbot of Benedictine foundation at Cluny; supported popes in efforts to reform ecclesiastical abuses; canonized 1120; Apr. 29.

Ignatius of Antioch, St. (d. c. 107): Early ecclesiastical writer; martyr; bishop of Antioch in Syria for 40 years; Oct. 17*.

Ignatius of Loyola, St. (1491-1556): Spanish soldier; renounced military career after recovering from wounds received at siege of Pampeluna (Pamplona) in 1521; founded society of Jesus (Jesuits), 1534, at Paris; canonized 1622; author *The Book of Spiritual Exercises;* July 31*.

Isidore the Farmer, St. (d. 1170): Spanish layman; farmer; canonized 1622; patron of farmers; Oct. 25 (US)*.

Jane Frances de Chantal, St. (1572-1641): French widow; foundress, under guidance of St. Francis de Sales, of Order of the Visitation; canonized 1767; Dec. 12*.

Januarius (Gennaro), St. (d. 304): Bishop of Benevento; martyred during Diocletian persecution; fame rests on liquefaction of some of his blood preserved in a phial at Naples, an unexplained phenomenon which has occurred regularly about 18 times each year for over 400 years; Sept. 19*.

Jerome Aemilian, St. (1481-1537): Venetian priest; founded Somascan Fathers, 1532, for care of orphans; canonized 1767; patron of orphans and abandoned children; Feb. 8*.

Joan of Arc, St. (1412-1431): Fench heroine, called The Maid of Orleans, La Pucelle; led French army against English invaders; captured by Burgundians, turned over to ecclesiastical court on charge of heresy, found guilty and burned at the stake; her innocence was declared in 1456; canonized 1920; patroness of France; May 30.

John I, St. (d. 526): Pope, 523-526; martyr; May 18*.

John Baptist de la Salle, St. (1651-1719): French priest; founder of Brothers of the Christian Schools, 1680; canonized 1900; Apr. 7*.

John Berchmans, St. (1599-1621): Belgian Jesuit scholastic; patron of Mass servers; canonized 1888; Aug. 13.

John Bosco, St. (1815-1888): Italian priest; founded Salesians, 1864, for education of boys and the Daughters of Mary Auxiliatrix for education of girls; canonized 1934; Jan. 31*.

John Capistran, St. (1386-1456): Italian Franciscan; preacher; papal diplomat; canonized 1690; Oct. 23*.

John Eudes, St. (1601-1680): French priest; founder of Sisters of Our Lady of Charity of Refuge, 1642, and Congregation of Jesus-Mary (Eudists), 1643; canonized 1925; Aug. 19*.

John Fisher, St. (1469-1535): English prelate; theologian; martyr; bishop of Rochester, cardinal; refused to recognize validity of Henry VIII's marriage to Anne Boleyn; upheld supremacy of the pope; beheaded for refusing to acknowledge Henry as head of the Church; canonized 1935; June 22 (with St. Thomas More)*.

John Kanty (Cantius), St. (1395-1473): Polish theologian; canonized 1767; Dec. 23*.

John Leonardi, St. (1550-1609): Italian priest; worked among prisoners and the sick; founded Clerics Regular of the Mother of God; canonized 1938; Oct. 9*.

John Nepomucene, St. (1345-1393): Bohemian priest; regarded as a martyr; canonized 1729; patron of Czechoslovakia; May 16.

John Nepomucene Neumann, Bl. (1811-1860): American prelate; b. Bohemia; ordained in New York 1836; missionary among Germans near Niagara Falls before joining Redemptorists, 1840; bishop of Philadelphia, 1852; first bishop in US to prescribe Forty Hours devotion in his diocese; beatified 1963; Jan. 5 (US)*.

John of God, St. (1495-1550): Portuguese founder; his work among the sick poor led to foundation of Brothers Hospitallers of St. John of God, 1540, in Spain; canonized 1690; patron of sick, hospitals, nurses; Mar. 8*.

John Vianney (Cure of Ars), St. (1786-1859): French parish priest; noted confessor; spent 16 to 18 hours a day in confessional; canonized 1925; patron of parish priests; Aug. 4*.

Josaphat Kuncevyc, St. (1584-1623): Basilian monk; b. Poland; archbishop of Polotsk, Lithuania; worked for reunion of separated Easterners; martyred by mob of schismatics; canonized 1867; Nov. 12*.

Joseph Benedict Cottolengo, St. (1786-1842): Italian priest; established Little Houses of Divine Providence (Piccolo Casa) for care of orphans, sick; canonized 1934; Apr. 30.

Joseph Cafasso, St. (1811-1860): Italian priest; renowned confessor; promoted devotion to Blessed Sacrament; canonized 1947; June 22.

Joseph Calasanctius, St. (1556-1648): Spanish priest; founder of Piarists (Order of Pious Schools); canonized 1767; Aug. 25*.

Joseph of Cupertino, St. (1603-1663): Italian Franciscan; noted for remarkable incidents of levitation; canonized 1767; Sept. 18.

Justin Martyr, St. (100-165): Early ecclesiastical writer; *Apologies for the Christian Religion, Dialog with the Jew Tryphon;* martyred at Rome; June 1*.

Ladislaus, Saint (1040-1095): King of Hungary; supported Pope Gregory VII against Henry IV; canonized 1192; June 27.

Lawrence, St. (d. 258): Widely venerated martyr who suffered death, according to a long-standing but unverifiable legend, by being roasted alive on a gridiron; Aug. 10*.

Leonard of Port Maurice, St. (1676-1751): Italian Franciscan; ascetical writer; preached missions throughout Italy; canonized 1867; patron of parish missions; Nov. 26.

Louis, IX, St. (1215-1270): King of France, 1226-1270; participated in Sixth Crusade; patron of Third Order of St. Francis; canonized 1297; Aug. 25*.

Louis de Montfort, St. (1673-1716): French priest; founder of Sisters of Divine Wisdom, 1703, and Missionaries of Company of Mary, 1715; wrote *True Devotion to the Blessed Virgin;* canonized 1947; Apr. 28.

Louise de Marillac, St. (1591-1660): French foundress, with St. Vincent de Paul, of the Sisters of Charity; canonized 1934; Mar. 15.

Lucy, St. (d.304): Sicilian maiden; martyred during Diocletian persecution; one of most widely venerated early virgin-martyrs; patron of Syracuse, Sicily; invoked by those suffering from eye diseases (based on legend that she offered her eyes to a suitor who admired them); Dec. 13*.

Marcellinus and Peter, Sts. (d.c. 304): Early Roman martyrs; June 2*.

Margaret Clitherow, St. (1556-1586): English martyr; convert shortly after her marriage; one of Forty Martyrs of England and Wales; canonized 1970.

Margaret Mary Alacoque, St. (1647-1690): French nun; spread devotion to Sacred Heart in accordance with revelations made to her in 1675 (see Sacred Heart); canonized 1920; Oct. 16*.

Margaret of Scotland, St. (1050-1093): Queen of Scotland; noted for solicitude for the poor and promotion of justice; canonized 1251; Nov. 16*.

Maria Goretti, St. (1890-1902): Italian virgin-martyr; a model of purity; canonized 1950; July 6*.

Mariana Paredes of Jesus, St. (1618-1645): South American recluse; Lily of Quito; canonized, 1950; May 26.

Martha, St. (1st cent.): Sister of Lazarus and Mary of Bethany; Gospel accounts record her concern for homely details; patron of cooks; July 29*.

Martin I, St. (d. 655): Pope, 649; banished from Rome by emperor because of his condemnation of Monothelites; considered a martyr; Apr. 13*.

Martin of Tours, St. (316-397): Bishop of Tours; opposed Arianism and Priscillianism; pioneer of Western monasticism, before St. Benedict; Nov. 11*.

Mary Magdalen, St. (1st cent.): Gospels record her as devoted follower of Christ to whom he appeared after the Resurrection; her identification with Mary of Bethany (sister of Martha and Lazarus) and the woman sinner (Lk 7:36-50) has been questioned; July 22*.

Mary Magdalen de Pazzi, St. (1566-1607): Italian Carmelite nun; recipient of mystical experiences; canonized 1669; May 25*.

Maximilian Kolbe, Bl. (1894-1941): Polish Conventual Franciscan; prisoner at Auschwitz who heroically offered his life in place of a fellow prisoner; beatified 1971.

Methodius, St.: See Index.

Monica, St. (332-387): Mother of St. Augustine; model of a patient mother; her feast is observed in the Roman calendar the day before her son's; Aug. 27*.

Nereus and Achilleus, Sts. (d. c. 100): Early Christian martyrs; soldiers who, according to legend, were baptized by St. Peter; May 12*.

Nicholas of Myra, St. (4th cent.): Bishop of Myra in Asia Minor; one of most popular saints in both East and West; most of the incidents of his life are based on legend; patron of Russia; Dec. 6*.

Nicholas of Tolentino, St. (1245-1365): Italian hermit; famed preacher; canonized 1446; Sept. 10.

Norbert, St. (1080-1134): German bishop; founder of Norbertines or Premonstratensians, 1120; promoted reform of the clergy, devotion to Blessed Sacrament; canonized 1582; June 6*.

Odilia, St. (d. c. 72): Benedictine abbess; according to legend she was born blind, abandoned by her family and adopted by a convent where her sight was miraculously restored; patron of blind; Dec. 13.

Oliver Plunkett, Bl. (1629-1681): Irish martyr; theologian; archbishop of Armagh and primate of Ireland; beatified 1920.

Pancratius, St. (d. c. 304): Roman martyr; May 12*.

Paschal Baylon, St. (1540-1592): Spanish Franciscan lay brother; spent life as doorkeeper in various Franciscan friaries; defended doctrine of Real Presence in Blessed Sacrament; canonized 1690; patron of all Eucharistic confraternities and congresses, 1897; May 17.

Patrick, St. (389-461): Famous missionary of Ireland; began missionary work in Ireland about 432; organized the Church there and established it on a lasting foundation; patron of Ireland, with Sts. Bridget and Columba; Mar. 17*.

Paul Miki and Companions, Sts. (d. 1597): Martyrs of Japan; Paul Miki, Jesuit, and twenty-five other priests and laymen were martyred at Nagasaki; canonized 1862, the first canonized martyrs of the Far East; Feb. 6*.

Paul of the Cross, St. (1694-1775): Italian religious; founder of the Passionists; canonized 1867; Oct. 19*.

Paulinus of Nola, St. (d. 451): Bishop of Nola (Spain); writer; June 22*.

Peregrine, St. (1260-1347): Italian Servite; invoked against cancer (he was miraculously cured of cancer of the foot after a vision); canonized 1726; May 1.

Perpetua and Felicitas, Sts. (d. 203): Marytrs; Mar. 7*.

Peter Chanel, St. (1803-1841): French Marist; missionary to Oceania, where he was martyred; canonized 1954; Apr. 28*.

Peter Gonzalez, St. (1190-1246): Spanish Dominican; worked among sailors; court chaplain and confessor of King St. Ferdinand of Castile; patron of sailors; Apr. 14.

Peter of Alcantara, St. (1499-1562): Spanish Franciscan; mystic; initiated Franciscan reform; confessor of St. Teresa of Avila; canonized 1669; Oct. 19.

Philip Neri, St. (1515-1595): Italian religious; founded Congregation of the Oratory; considered a second apostle of Rome because of his mission activities there; canonized 1622; May 26*.

Philip of Jesus, St. (1571-1597): Mexican Franciscan; martyred at Nagasaki, Japan; canonized 1862; patron of Mexico City; Feb. 6*.

Pius V, St. (1504-1572): Pope, 1566-1572; enforced decrees of Council of Trent; organized expedition against Turks resulting in victory at Lepanto; canonized 1712; Apr. 30*.

Polycarp, St. (2nd cent.): Bishop of Smyrna; ecclesiastical writer; martyr; Feb. 23*.

Pontian, St. (d. c. 235): Pope, 230-235; exiled to Sardinia by the emperor; regarded as a martyr; Aug. 13 (with Hippolytus)*.

Raymond Nonnatus, St. (d. 1240): Spanish Mercedarian; cardinal; devoted his life to ransoming captives from the Moors; Aug. 31.

Raymond Pennafort, St. (1175-1275): Spanish Dominican; confessor of Gregory IX; systematized and codified canon law, in effect until 1917; master general of Dominicans, 1238; canonized 1601; Jan. 7*.

Robert Southwell, St. (1561-1595): English Jesuit; poet; martyred at Tyburn; canonized 1970, one of the Forty English and Welsh Martyrs.

Roch, St. (1350-1379): French layman; pilgrim; devoted life to care of plague-stricken; widely venerated; invoked against pestilence; Aug. 17.

Romuald, St. (951-1027): Italian monk; founded Camaldolese Benedictines; June 19*.

Rose of Lima, St. (1586-1617): Peruvian Dominican tertiary; first native-born saint of the New World; canonized 1671; Aug. 23*.

Scholastica, St. (d. c. 559): Sister of St. Benedict; regarded as first nun of the Benedictine Order; Feb. 10*.

Sebastian, St. (3rd cent.): Roman martyr; traditionally pictured as a handsome youth; martyred by being pierced with arrows; patron of athletes; Jan. 20*.

Seven Holy Founders of the Servants of Mary (Buonfiglio Monaldo, Alexis Falconieri, Benedict dell'Antello, Bartholomew Amidei, Ricovero Uguccione, Gerardino Sostegni, John Buonagiunta Monetti): Florentine youths who founded Servites, 1233, in obedience to a vision; canonized 1888; Feb. 17*.

Sixtus II and Companions, Sts. (d. 258): Sixtus, pope 257-258, and four deacons, martyrs; Aug. 7*.

Stanislaus, St. (1030-1079): Polish bishop; martyr; canonized 1253; Apr. 11*.

Stephen, St. (d. c. 33): First Christian martyr; chosen by the Apostles as the first of the seven deacons; stoned to death; Dec. 26*.

Stephen, St. (975-1038): King; apostle of Hungary; welded Magyars into national unity; canonized 1087; Aug. 16*.

Sylvester I. St. (d. 335): Pope 314-335; first ecumenical council held at Nicaea during his pontificate; Dec. 31*.

Tarcisius, St. (d. 3rd cent.): Early martyr; according to tradition, was martyred while carrying the Blessed Sacrament to some Christians in prison; patron of first communicants; Aug. 15.

Therese Couderc, St. (1805-1885): French religious; foundress of the Religious of Our Lady of the Retreat in the Cenacle, 1827; canonized 1970; Sept. 26.

Therese of Lisieux, St. (1873-1897): French Carmelite nun; b. Therese Martin; allowed to enter Carmel at 15, died nine years later of tuberculosis; her "little way" of spiritual perfection became widely known through her spiritual autobiography; despite her obscure life, became one of the most popular saints; canonized 1925; patron of foreign missions; Oct. 1*.

Thomas a Becket, St. (1118-1170): English martyr; archbishop of Canterbury; chancellor under Henry II; murdered for upholding rights of the Church; canonized 1173; Dec. 29*.

Thomas More, St. (1478-1535): English martyr; statesman, chancellor under Henry VIII; author of *Utopia*; opposed Henry's divorce, refused to renounce authority of the papacy; beheaded; canonized 1935; June 22 (with St. John Fisher)*.

Timothy, St. (d. c. 97): Bishop of Ephesus; disciple and companion of St. Paul; martyr; Jan. 26*.

Titus, St. (d. c. 96): Bishop; companion of St. Paul; recipient of one of Paul's epistles; Jan. 26*.

Valentine, St. (d. 269); Priest physician; martyred at Rome; legendary patron of lovers; Feb. 14.

Vincent, St. (d. 304): Spanish deacon; martyr; Jan. 22*.

Vincent de Paul, St. (1581?-1660): French priest; founder of Congregation of the Mission (Vincentians, Lazarists) and co-founder of Sisters of Charity; declared patron of all charitable organizations and works by Leo XIII; canonized 1737; Sept. 27*.

Vincent Ferrer, St. (1350-1418): Spanish Dominican; famed preacher; Apr. 5*.

Wenceslaus, St. (d. 935): Duke of Bohemia; martyr; patron of Bohemia; Sept. 28*.

Zita, St. (1218-1278): Italian maid; noted for charity to poor; patron of domestics.

SAINTS—PATRONS AND INTERCESSORS

A patron is a saint who is venerated as a special intercessor before God. Most patrons have been so designated as the result of popular devotion and long-standing custom. In many cases, the fact of existing patronal devotion is clear despite historical obscurity regarding its origin. The Church has made official designation of relatively few patrons; in such cases, the dates of designation are given in the list below. The theological background of the patronage of saints includes the dogmas of the Mystical Body of Christ and the Communion of Saints.

Listed below are patron saints of occupations and professions, and saints whose intercession is sought for special needs.

Accountants: St. Matthew.
Actors: St. Genesius.
Advertisers: St. Bernardine of Siena (May 20, 1960).
Alpinists: St. Bernard of Menthon (Aug. 20, 1923).
Altar boys: St. John Berchmans.
Anesthetists: St. Rene Goupil.
Archers: St. Sebastian.
Architects: St. Thomas, Apostle.
Armorers: St. Dunstan.
Art: St. Catherine of Bologna.
Artists: St. Luke, St. Catherine of Bologna.
Astronomers: St. Dominic.
Athletes: St. Sebastian.
Authors: St. Francis de Sales.
Aviators: Our Lady of Loreto (1920), St. Therese of Lisieux, St. Joseph of Cupertino.
Bakers: St. Elizabeth of Hungary, St. Nicholas.
Bankers: St. Matthew.
Barbers: Sts. Cosmas and Damian, St. Louis.
Barren women: St. Anthony of Padua, St. Felicitas.
Basket-makers: St. Anthony, Abbot.
Blacksmiths: St. Dunstan.
Blind: St. Odilia, St. Raphael.
Blood banks: St. Januarius.
Bodily ills: Our Lady of Lourdes.
Bookbinders: St. Peter Celestine.
Bookkeepers: St. Matthew.
Booksellers: St. John of God.
Boy Scouts: St. George.
Brewers: St. Augustine of Hippo, St. Luke, St. Nicholas of Myra.
Bricklayers: St. Stephen.
Brides: St. Nicholas of Myra.
Brush makers: St. Anthony, Abbot.
Builders: St. Vincent Ferrer.
Butchers: St. Anthony, Abbot, St. Hadrian, St. Luke.
Cab drivers: St. Fiacre.

Cabinetmakers: St. Anne.
Cancer patients: St. Peregrine.
Canonists: St. Raymond of Pennafort.
Carpenters: St. Joseph.
Catechists: St. Viator, St. Charles Borromeo, St. Robert Bellarmine.
Catholic Action: St. Francis of Assisi (1916).
Chandlers: St. Ambrose, St. Bernard of Clairvaux.
Charitable societies: St. Vincent de Paul (May 12, 1885).
Children: St. Nicolas of Myra.
Children of Mary: St. Agnes, St. Maria Goretti.
Choir boys: St. Dominic Savio (June 8, 1956), Holy Innocents.
Church: St. Joseph (Dec. 8, 1870).
Clerics: St. Gabriel of the Sorrowful Mother.
Comedians: St. Vitus.
Communications personnel: St. Bernardine.
Confessors: St. Alphonsus Liguori (Apr. 26, 1950), St. John Nepomucene.
Convulsive children: St. Scholastica.
Cooks: St. Lawrence, St. Martha.
Coopers: St. Nicholas of Myra.
Coppersmiths: St. Maurus.
Dairy workers: St. Brigid.
Deaf: St. Francis de Sales.
Dentists: St. Apollonia.
Desperate situations: St. Gregory of Neocaesarea, St. Jude Thaddeus.
Dietitians (in hospitals): St. Martha.
Dyers: Sts. Maurice and Lydia.
Dying: St. Joseph.
Ecologists: St. Francis of Assisi.
Editors: St. John Bosco.
Emigrants: St. Frances Xavier Cabrini, (Sept. 8, 1950).
Epilepsy: St. Vitus.
Engineers: St. Ferdinand III.
Eucharistic congresses and societies: St. Paschal Baylon (Nov. 28, 1897).
Expectant mothers: St. Raymund Nonnatus, St. Gerard Majella.
Eye diseases: St. Lucy.
Falsely accused: St. Raymund Nonnatus.
Farmers: St. George, St. Isidore.
Farriers: St. John Baptist.
Firemen: St. Florian.
Fire prevention: St. Catherine of Siena.
First communicants: St. Tarcisius.
Fishermen: St. Andrew.
Florists: St. Therese of Lisieux.
Forest workers: St. John Gualbert.
Foundlings: Holy Innocents.
Fullers: St. Anastasius, St. James the Less.

Funeral directors: St. Joseph of Arimathea, St. Dismas.

Gardeners: St. Adelard, St. Tryphon, St. Fiacre, St. Phocas.

Glassworkers: St. Luke.

Goldsmiths: St. Dunstan, St. Anastasius.

Gravediggers: St. Anthony, Abbot.

Greetings: St. Valentine.

Grocers: St. Michael.

Hairdressers: St. Martin de Porres.

Happy meetings: St. Raphael.

Hatters: St. Severus of Ravenna, St. James the Less.

Haymakers: Sts. Gervase and Protase.

Headache sufferers: St. Teresa of Avila.

Heart patients: St. John of God.

Hospital administrators: St. Basil the Great, St. Frances X. Cabrini.

Hospitals: St. Camillus de Lellis and St. John of God (June 22, 1886), St. Jude Thaddeus.

Housewives: St. Anne.

Hunters: St. Hubert, St. Eustachius.

Infantrymen: St. Maurice.

Innkeepers: St. Amand, St. Martha.

Invalids: St. Roch.

Jewelers: St. Eligius, St. Dunstan.

Journalists: St. Francis de Sales (Apr. 26, 1923).

Jurists: St. John Capistran.

Laborers: St. Isidore, St. James, St. John Bosco.

Lawyers: St. Ivo, St. Genesius, St. Thomas More.

Learning: St. Ambrose.

Librarians: St. Jerome.

Lighthouse keepers: St. Venerius.

Locksmiths: St. Dunstan.

Maids: St. Zita.

Marble workers: St. Clement I.

Mariners: St. Michael, St. Nicholas of Tolentino.

Medical record librarians: St. Raymond of Pennafort.

Medical social workers: St. John Regis.

Medical technicians: St. Albert the Great.

Mentally ill: St. Dympha.

Merchants: St. Francis of Assisi, St. Nicholas of Myra.

Messengers: St. Gabriel.

Metal workers: St. Eligius.

Millers: St. Arnulph, St. Victor.

Missions, Foreign: St. Francis Xavier (Mar. 25, 1904), St. Therese of Lisieux (Dec. 14, 1927).

Missions, Negro: St. Peter Claver (1896, Leo XIII), St. Benedict the Black.

Missions, Parish: St. Leonard of Port Maurice (Mar. 17, 1923).

Mothers: St. Monica.

Motorcyclists: Our Lady of Grace.

Motorists: St. Christopher, St. Frances of Rome.

Mountaineers: St. Bernard of Menthon.

Musicians: St. Gregory the Great, St. Cecilia, St. Dunstan.

Nail makers: St. Cloud.

Notaries: St. Luke, St. Mark.

Nurses: St. Camillus de Lellis and St. John of God (1930, Pius XI), St. Agatha, St. Raphael.

Nursing and nursing service: St. Elizabeth of Hungary, St. Catherine of Siena.

Orators: St. John Chrysostom (July 8, 1908).

Organ builders: St. Cecilia.

Orphans: St. Jerome Aemilian.

Painters: St. Luke.

Paratroopers: St. Michael.

Pawnbrokers: St. Nicholas.

Pharmacists: Sts. Cosmas and Damian, St. James the Greater.

Pharmacists (in hospitals): St. Gemma Galgani.

Philosophers: St. Justin.

Physicians: St. Pantaleon, Sts. Cosmas and Damian, St. Luke, St. Raphael.

Pilgrims: St. James.

Plasterers: St. Bartholomew.

Poets: St. David, St. Cecilia.

Poison sufferers: St. Benedict.

Policemen: St. Michael.

Poor: St. Lawrence, St. Anthony of Padua.

Poor souls: St. Nicholas of Tolentino.

Porters: St. Christopher.

Possessed: St. Bruno, St. Denis.

Postal employees: St. Gabriel.

Priests: St. Jean-Baptiste Vianney (Apr. 23, 1929).

Printers: St. John of God, St. Augustine of Hippo, St. Genesius.

Prisoners: St. Dismas, St. Joseph Cafasso.

Protector of crops: St. Ansovinus.

Public relations: St. Bernardine of Siena (May 20, 1960).

Public relations (of hospitals): St. Paul, Apostle.

Radiologists: St. Michael (Jan. 15, 1941).

Radio workers: St. Gabriel.

Retreats: St. Ignatius Loyola (July 25, 1922).

Rheumatism: St. James the Greater.

Saddlers: Sts. Crispin and Crispinian.

Sailors: St. Cuthbert, St. Brendan, St. Eulalia, St. Christopher, St. Peter Gonzales, St. Erasmus, St. Nicholas.

Scholars: St. Brigid.

Schools, Catholic: St. Thomas Aquinas (Aug. 4, 1880), St. Joseph Calasanctius (Aug. 13, 1948).

Scientists: St. Albert (Aug. 13, 1948).

Sculptors: St. Claude.

Seamen: St. Francis of Paolo.

Searchers for lost articles: St. Anthony of Padua.

Secretaries: St. Genesius.

Seminarians: St. Charles Borromeo.

Servants: St. Martha, St. Zita.

Shoemakers: Sts. Crispin and Crispinian.

Sick: St. Michael, St. John of God and St. Camillus de Lellis (June 22, 1886).

Silversmiths: St. Andronicus.

Singers: St. Gregory, St. Cecilia.
Skaters: St. Lidwina.
Skiers: St. Bernard.
Social workers: St. Louise de Marillac (Feb. 12, 1960).
Soldiers: St. Hadrian, St. George, St. Ignatius, St. Sebastian, St. Martin of Tours, St. Joan of Arc.
Speleologists: St. Benedict.
Stenographers: St. Genesius, St. Cassian.
Stonecutters: St. Clement.
Stonemasons: St. Stephen.
Students: St. Thomas Aquinas.
Surgeons: Sts. Cosmas and Damian, St. Luke.
Swordsmiths: St. Maurice.
Tailors: St. Homobonus.
Tanners: Sts. Crispin and Crispinian, St. Simon.
Tax collectors: St. Matthew.
Teachers: St. Gregory the Great, St. John Baptist de la Salle (May 15, 1950).
Telecommunications workers: St. Gabriel (Jan. 12, 1951).
Telegraph/telephone workers: St. Gabriel.
Television: St. Clare of Assisi (Feb. 14, 1958).
Television workers: St. Gabriel.
Tertiaries (Franciscan): St. Louis of France, St. Elizabeth of Hungary.
Theologians: St. Augustine, St. Alphonsus Liguori.
Throat sufferers: St. Blaise.
Travelers: St. Anthony of Padua, St. Nicholas of Myra, St. Christopher, St. Raphael.
Travel hostesses: St. Bona (Mar. 2, 1962).
Universities: Blessed Contardo Ferrini.
Vocations: St. Alphonsus.
Watchmen: St. Peter of Alcantara.
Weavers: St. Paul the Hermit, St. Anastasius the Fuller, St. Anastasia.
Wine merchants: St. Amand.
Women in labor: St. Anne.
Women's Army Corps: St. Genevieve.
Workingmen: St. Joseph.
Writers: St. Francis de Sales (Apr. 26, 1923), St. Lucy.
Yachtsmen: St. Adjutor.
Young girls: St. Agnes.
Youth: St. Aloysius Gonzaga (1729, Benedict XIII; 1926, Pius XI), St. John Berchmans, St. Gabriel Possenti.

Patrons of Places

Alsace: St. Odile.
Americas: Our Lady of Guadalupe; St. Rose of Lima.
Argentina: Our Lady of Lujan.
Armenia: St. Gregory Illuminator.
Asia Minor: St. John, Evangelist.
Australia: Our Lady Help of Christians.
Belgium: St. Joseph.
Bohemia: Sts. Wenceslaus, Ludmilla.
Borneo: St. Francis Xavier.
Brazil: Nossa Senhora de Aparecida, Immaculate Conception; St. Peter of Alcantara.

Canada: St. Joseph; St. Anne.
Ceylon (Sri Lanka): St. Lawrence.
Chile: St. James; Our Lady of Mt. Carmel.
China: St. Joseph.
Colombia: St. Peter Claver; St. Louis Bertran.
Corsica: Immaculate Conception.
Czechoslovakia: St. Wenceslaus; St. John Nepomucene; St. Procopius.
Denmark: St. Ansgar; St. Canute.
Dominican Republic: Our Lady of High Grace; St. Dominic.
East Indies: St. Thomas, Apostle.
Ecuador: Sacred Heart.
England: St. George.
Europe: St. Benedict.
Finland: St. Henry.
France: Our Lady of the Assumption; St. Joan of Arc; St. Therese.
Germany: Sts. Boniface, Michael.
Greece: St. Nicholas; St. Andrew.
Holland: St. Willibrord.
Hungary: Blessed Virgin, "Great Lady of Hungary"; St. Stephen, King.
India: Our Lady of Assumption.
Ireland: Sts. Patrick, Brigid and Columba.
Italy: St. Francis of Assisi; St. Catherine of Siena.
Japan: St. Peter Baptist.
Lesotho: Immaculate Heart of Mary.
Lithuania: St. Casimir, Bl. Cunegunda.
Malta: St. Paul; Our Lady of the Assumption.
Mexico: Our Lady of Guadalupe.
Monaco: St. Devota.
Moravia: Sts. Cyril and Methodius.
New Zealand: Our Lady Help of Christians.
Norway: St. Olaf.
Paraguay: Our Lady of Assumption.
Peru: St. Joseph.
Philippines: Sacred Heart of Mary.
Poland: St. Casimir; Bl. Cunegunda; St. Stanislaus of Cracow; Our Lady of Czestochowa.
Portugal: Immaculate Conception; St. Francis Borgia; St. Anthony of Padua; St. Vincent; St. George.
Republic of South Africa: Our Lady of Assumption.
Russia: St. Andrew; St. Nicholas of Myra; St. Therese of Lisieux.
Scandinavia: St. Ansgar.
Scotland: St. Andrew; St. Columba.
Silesia: St. Hedwig.
Slovakia: Our Lady of Sorrows.
South America: St. Rose of Lima.
Spain: St. James; St. Teresa.
Sweden: St. Bridget; St. Eric.
United States: Immaculate Conception. The bishops of this country proclaimed Mary, under this title, patroness of the US in 1846.
Uruguay: Our Lady of Lujan.
Wales: St. David.
West Indies: St. Gertrude.

Apostles of Places

Alps: St. Bernard of Menthon.
Andalusia (Spain): St. John of Avila.
Antioch: St. Barnabas.
Armenia: St. Gregory the Illuminator; St. Bartholomew.
Austria: St. Severine.
Bavaria: St. Killian.
Brazil: Jose Anchieta.
California: Junipero Serra.
Carinthia (Yugoslavia): St. Vigil.
Colombia: St. Louis Bertran.
Corsica: St. Alexander Sauli.
Crete: St. Titus.
Cyprus: St. Barnabas.
Denmark: St. Ansgar.
England: St. Augustine of Canterbury; St. Gregory the Great.
Ethiopia: St. Frumentius.
Finland: St. Henry.
Florence: St. Andrew Corsini.
France: St. Remigius; St. Martin of Tours; St. Denis.
Friesland (Germany): St. Suitbert; St. Willibrord.
Gaul: St. Irenaeus.
Gentiles: St. Paul.
Georgia (Russia): St. Nino.
Germany: St. Boniface; St. Peter Canisius.
Gothland (Sweden): St. Sigfrid.
Guelderland (Holland): St. Plechelm.
Highlanders (Scotland): St. Columba.
Hungarians (Magyars): St. Stephen, King; St. Gerard; Bl. Astricus.
India: St. Thomas, Apostle.
Indies: St. Francis Xavier.
Ireland: St. Patrick.
Iroquois: Francois Picquit.
Italy: St. Bernardine of Siena.
Japan: St. Francis Xavier.
Malta: St. Paul.
Mexico: The twelve Apostles of Mexico (Franciscans), headed by Fra. Martin de Valencia.
Negro Slaves: St. Peter Claver.
Netherlands: St. Willibrord.
Northumbria (Britain): St. Aidan.
Norway: St. Olaf.
Ottawas (Indians): Fr. Claude Allouez.
Persia: St. Maruthas.
Poland: St. Hyacinth.
Portugal: St. Christian.
Prussia (Slavs): St. Adalbert; St. Bruno of Querfurt.
Rome: St. Philip Neri.
Rumania: St. Nicetas.
Ruthenia: St. Bruno.
Sardinia: St. Ephesus.
Saxony: St. Willihad.
Scandinavia (North): St. Ansgar.
Scotland: St. Palladius.
Slavs: Sts. Cyril and Methodius, St. Adalbert.
Spain: St. James; Sts. Euphrasius and Felix.
Sweden: St. Ansgar.
Switzerland: St. Andeol.
Tournai (Belgium): St. Eligius, St. Piaton.

Emblems of Saints

St. Agatha: Tongs, veil.
St. Agnes: Lamb.
St. Ambrose: Bees, dove, ox, pen.
St. Andrew: Transverse cross.
St. Anne, Mother of the Blessed Virgin: A door.
St. Anthony, Abbot: Bell, hog.
St. Anthony of Padua: Infant Jesus, bread, book, lily.
St. Augustine of Hippo: Dove, child, shell, pen.
St. Barnabas: Stones, ax, lance.
St. Bartholomew: Knife, flayed and holding his skin.
St. Benedict: Broken cup, raven, bell, crozier, bush.
St. Bernard of Clairvaux: Pen, bees, instruments of Passion.
St. Bernardine of Siena: tablet or sun inscribed with IHS.
St. Blaise: Wax, taper, iron comb.
St. Bonaventure: Communion, ciborium, cardinal's hat.
St. Boniface: Oak, ax, book, fox, scourge, fountain, raven, sword.
St. Bridget of Sweden: Book, pilgrim's staff.
St. Bridget of Kildare: Cross, flame over her head, candle.
St. Catherine of Ricci: Ring, crown, crucifix.
St. Catherine of Siena: Stigmata, cross, ring, lily.
St. Cecilia: Organ.
St. Charles Borromeo: Communion, coat of arms with word "Humilitas."
St. Christopher: Giant, torrent, tree, Child Jesus on his shoulders.
St. Clare of Assisi: Monstrance.
Sts. Cosmas and Damian: A phial, box of ointment.
St. Cyril of Alexandria: Blessed Virgin holding the Child Jesus, pen.
St. Cyril of Jerusalem: Purse, book.
St. Dominic: Rosary, star.
St. Edmund the Martyr: Arrow, sword.
St. Elizabeth of Hungary: Alms, flowers, bread, the poor, a pitcher.
St. Francis of Assisi: Deer, wolf, birds, fish, skull, the Stigmata.
St. Francis Xavier: Crucifix, bell, vessel, Negro.
St. Genevieve: Bread, keys, herd, candle.
St. George: Dragon.
St. Gertrude: Crown, taper, lily.
Sts. Gervasius and Protasius: Scourge, club, sword.
St. Gregory I (the Great): Tiara, crosier, dove.
St. Helena: Cross.
St. Hilary: Stick, pen, child.

St. Ignatius Loyola: Communion, chasuble, book, appraition of Our Lord.

St. Isidore: Bees, pen.

St. James the Greater: Pilgrim's staff, shell, key, sword.

St. James the Greater: Pilgrim's staff, shell, key, sword.

St. James the Less: Square rule, halberd, club.

St. Jerome: Lion.

St. John Berchmans: Rule of St. Ignatius, cross, rosary.

St. John Chrysostom: Bees, dove, pen.

St. John of God: Alms, a heart, crown of thorns.

St. John the Baptist: Lamb, head cut off on platter, skin of an animal.

St. John the Evangelist: Eagle, chalice, kettle, armor.

St. Josaphat Kuncevyc: Chalice, crown, winged deacon.

St. Joseph, Spouse of the Blessed Virgin; Infant Jesus, lily, rod, plane, carpenter's square.

St. Jude: Sword, square rule, club.

St. Justin Martyr: Ax, sword.

St. Lawrence: Cross, book of the Gospels, gridiron.

St. Leander of Seville: A pen.

St. Liborius: Pebbles, peacock.

St. Longinus: In arms at foot of the cross.

St. Louis IX of France: Crown of thorns, nails.

St. Lucy: Cord, eyes.

St. Luke: Ox, book, brush, palette.

St. Mark: Lion, book.

St. Martha: Holy water sprinkler, dragon.

St. Mary Magdalene: Alabaster box of ointment.

St. Mathias: Lance.

St. Matilda: Purse, alms.

St. Matthew: Winged man, purse, lance.

St. Maurus: Scales, spade, crutch.

St. Meinrad: Two ravens.

St. Michael: Scales, banner, sword, dragon.

St. Monica: Girdle, tears.

St. Nicholas: Three purses or balls, anchor or boat, child.

St. Patrick: Cross, harp, serpent, baptismal font, demons, shamrock.

St. Paul: Sword, book or scroll.

St. Peter: Keys, boat, cock.

St. Philip, Apostle: Column.

St. Philip Neri: Altar, chasuble, vial.

St. Roch: Angel, dog, bread.

St. Rose of Lima: Crown of thorns, anchor, city.

St. Sebastian: Arrows, crown.

Sts. Sergius and Bacchus: Military garb, palm.

St. Simon: Saw, cross.

St. Simon Stock: Scapular.

St. Teresa of Avila: Heart, arrow, book.

St. Therese of Lisieux: Roses entwining a crucifix.

St. Thomas, Apostle: Lance, ax.

St. Thomas Aquinas: Chalice, monstrance, dove, ox, person trampled under foot.

St. Vincent: Gridiron, boat.

St. Vincent de Paul: Children.

St. Vincent Ferrer: Pulpit, cardinal's hat, trumpet, captives.

THE MOTHER OF JESUS IN CATHOLIC UNDERSTANDING

(This article was written for the Catholic Almanac by the Rev. Eamon R. Carroll, O. Carm., professor in the School of Sacred Theology, Catholic University of America, and lecturer on Mariology.)

Current Catholic understanding about the Virgin Mary, Mother of Jesus, is based on the place the Second Vatican Council gave to the mystery of Mary. The key statements are found in the *Constitution on the Sacred Liturgy* and in the final chapter of the *Dogmatic Constitution on the Church.*

Considering the liturgy and the way in which the Church unfolds the whole mystery of Christ's life in the course of a year — so that the events of redemption are "in some way made present at all times" — the council said: "In celebrating this annual cycle of Christ's mysteries, holy Church honors with special love the Blessed Mary, Mother of God, who is joined by an inseparable bond to the saving work of her Son. In Mary the Church holds up and admires the most excellent fruit of the redemption; in Mary the Church joyfully contemplates, as in a spotless model, that which the Church herself wholly desires and aspires to be" (*Constitution on the Sacred Liturgy,* No. 103).

In linking respect for Mary to the liturgical celebration of the mystery of Christ in the Church, the council joined doctrine and devotion. The *Dogmatic Constitution on the Church* took a similar approach, with a follow-through from the place of Mary in the communion of saints in the seventh chapter to treatment in the eighth chapter of "The Blessed Virgin Mary, Mother of God, in the Mystery of Christ and the Church." The seventh chapter recalls Mary's place with the risen Christ, as in the eucharistic prayer: "In union with the whole Church we honor Mary, the ever-virgin Mother of Jesus Christ our Lord and God." The eighth chapter opens and closes with the same liturgical theme, on Mary's place among God's friends, and appeals also to the Church, "knowing Mary's role by experience" (*Ibid.,* No. 52) and "contemplating Mary's hidden holiness (*Ibid.,* No. 64), in support of "the singular cult of Mary that has always existed in the Church" (*Ibid.,* No. 66).

Mary in the Bible

Recent studies by Protestants and Catholics have traced in the Bible a theological portrait of the Mother of Jesus which emphasizes her faith-commitment to God's will and her

Son's saving work. Differences in Catholic and Protestant interpretations of the sense in which Mary is joined to the saving work of Jesus underlie different views regarding Mary as a type of the Church.

Not only the stories of the birth and childhood of Jesus in Matthew and Luke but also John's Gospel illustrate the meaning of Mary with respect to Christ and to the Church. In her "pilgrimage of faith," her earthly association with Jesus "even to the cross," Mary was "a type of the Church — in the order of faith, charity and perfect union with Christ" (*Dogmatic Constitution on the Church*, Nos. 58, 63).

The opening chapters of Matthew and Luke are complex reflections on Jesus as Messiah and Redeemer, permeated with the sense of fulfillment of the Old Testament. When the Evangelists composed the Gospels, they worked backwards, beginning with the death and resurrection, then taking up the public life, beginning with Jesus' baptism by John the Baptist, and finally adding the stories of his infancy and childhood — the better to bring out the meaning of the Redeemer's mission. The light of the Easter faith shines with particular strength on these opening chapters, the last to be written down.

In harmony with the Gospel sense of fulfillment, the council referred to Mary as "the exalted daughter of Zion in whom the times are fulfilled, after the long waiting for the promise, and the new economy inaugurated when the Son of God takes on human nature from her in order to free men from sin by the mysteries of His flesh" (*Dogmatic Constitution on the Church*, No. 55). Daughter of Zion in the Old Testament meant the people of Israel. Daughter of her people, Mary of Nazareth fulfills all the longings of Israel for the coming of the Messiah. "She stands out among the Lord's lowly and poor who confidently look for salvation from Him and receive it" (*Ibid.*, No. 55).

Virgin Birth of Christ

Matthew and Luke state the fact of the "virgin birth," that Mary conceived Jesus without a human father — a truth that has formed part of the faith from the earliest creeds to the present teaching and preaching of the Church, in East and West alike.

In her religious and cultural world, it is not likely Mary had previously resolved to remain a virgin; the Old Testament regarded being unmarried as a calamity and childlessness as a disgrace. Mary's question, "How shall this be because I know not man" (Lk. 1:34), is regarded as the inspired reflection of the early Church on the virginal conception of Jesus, comparable to Matthew's account of Joseph's dream-vision (Mt. 1:20). Mary and Joseph accepted as God's will the virginal conception, as unprecedented event that put them both totally at the service of Jesus.

The Gospel offers a comparison between the faith of Abraham — whose son, Isaac, was born of the aged Sara — and Mary's faith in God's power to bring forth the Messiah from her virginal womb. God accomplishes salvation independently of the will of the flesh and of the will of man (Jn. 1:13), though not without a free and loving, if certainly wondering too, acceptance by the humble handmaid of the Lord. God shows his favor when and as he chooses, whether in the barren Sara or in the Virgin Mary, "because nothing shall be impossible with God" (Lk. 1:37 and Gn. 18:14). Jews and Christians honor Abraham as "our father in faith." On Gospel evidence, Mary is "mother in faith, mother of believers."

Mary at Cana and Calvary

John's Gospel pictures Mary at Cana and Calvary, the beginning and end of her Son's public life. In both incidents Jesus addresses her as "woman"; both scenes refer to the "hour" of Jesus' glorification at his death.

Mary's presence at Cana has deeper overtones than her sensitivity to the need for more wine. Jesus' reply to his Mother is an invitation to deepen her faith, to look beyond the failing wine to his messianic career about to begin. The change of water into wine symbolizes the benefits the Savior brings; the marriage feast looks to the "hour" in which the Bridegroom, Christ, will lay down his life in love for his Bride, the Church. Mary is present as the "daughter of Zion" greeting the messianic Bridegroom; she is model of the Church, new People of God, spotless Bride of Christ.

On Calvary Mary stands "by the cross of Jesus," and John records the words of the dying Jesus as he sees her there together with the beloved disciple: "Woman, behold your son. . . . Behold your mother" (Jn. 19:26-27). It is certain that more is meant here than simply our Lord's providing for his Mother's care. The word, "woman," finds an explanation in the Savior's farewell discourse at the Last Supper. To strengthen his followers, Jesus recalled an example from the Bible: "A woman about to give birth has sorrow because her hour has come. But when she has brought forth the child, she no longer remembers the anguish for her joy that a man is born into the world" (Jn. 16:21). Israel's longing for the messianic age was sometimes compared to labor pains. The daughter of Zion had been promised a progeny that would include all races, all nations. The words of Jesus announce the fulfillment of that promise, for Mary on Calvary symbolizes the "woman" who is mother Church, new Israel, new People of God, mother of all, Jew and Gentile.

About Mary's later life, the Scriptures are silent. The last time she appears is in the Acts of the Apostles, at the heart of the band of Apostles praying for the coming of the Holy

Spirit at Pentecost. At the overshadowing of the Spirit at the Annunciation, Mary awaited the birth of Jesus; now she awaits again the coming of the Spirit and the birth of Jesus in His Church. (*Dogmatic Constitution on the Church*, No. 59; *Decree on the Missionary Activity of the Church*, No. 4)

Understanding and Veneration

The process of understanding the mystery of dmary that began in Gospel times has continued in the Church. This is true also of Christian veneration for the Mother of Jesus, shown already in the words of the Magnificat — "All generations shall call me blessed," (Lk. 1:48) — and in the incident from Jesus' public life when the praise of an enthusiastic woman from the crowd is repeated on a deeper level by Jesus himself, "Still happier those who hear the word of God and keep it" (Lk. 11:28). For Luke, no one heard the word of God more perfectly than the Mother of Jesus, as in Elizabeth's praise of Mary's faith: "Of all women you are the most blessed . . . blessed is she who believed that the promise made her by the Lord would be fulfilled" (Lk. 1:42- 45).

The New Eve

The oldest title for Mary after the Gospel is "new Eve." Christian authors as early as the mid-second century compared Mary, the obedient virgin who heard the angel's word, to the first Eve, who heeded the evil angel and disobeyed God. The axiom, "Death through Eve, life through Mary," was coined by the time of St. Jerome.

By the fourth century, Christians were holding that Mary remained a virgin all her life. The Gospels speak of "brethren" of Jesus, but leave their identity undecided — whether they were blood brothers and sisters or cousins. Christian experience of the faith solved the question not by scientific study of the Scriptures but by a contemplative awareness that Mary's commitment to Jesus was lifelong in this virginal sense also.

What is at stake here is an early example of "development of doctrine," and Protestant and Catholic positions still differ strongly on the legitimacy of such a "traditional" interpretation, where the Scriptures are not clear or are even silent.

Two Dogmas

Two other Roman Catholic beliefs about Mary encounter the same Protestant objection of the seeming silence of the Scriptures: the Immaculate Conception (Mary's freedom from original sin) and the Assumption (Mary's being one with the risen Christ in the fullness of her being, body as well as soul). Both doctrines have been solemnly proclaimed as revealed truth in dogmatic definitions, by Pius IX in 1854 and by Pius XII in 1950.

Mother of God

In early Christian times it was usually the need to defend the mystery of Jesus Christ and of Christian life that called forth from the Church clarifications about the Mother of Jesus. In the fourth century the Christian sense of Mary as model of a life of consecrated virginity led to the understanding that she remained always a virgin. At Ephesus in 431, the third ecumenical council defined the title, "Bearer of God" *(Theotokos)* as revealed truth, precisely to defend the truth that the Son of Mary is actually the Son of God, for Jesus is the God-man. To this day, "Mother of God" remains a title that protects the central truth of the Incarnation, even though some Western Christians find difficulty in the popular use of "Mother of God" for Mary in Catholic and Eastern Orthodox traditions. They fear the conciliar title is not well understood by many who use it, that sometimes it is almost pagan in meaning.

Mother in Order of Grace

As Christianity developed, people turned to Mary as a model of holy response to Christ, as the perfect believer in Jesus. The sense of communion between Mary in heaven and the brethren of her Son on earth grew stronger also. This is what is meant by the "intercession of Mary in the communion of saints" — a mysterious bond between those who are already with the risen Christ and their earthly brothers and sisters still on pilgrimage. Mary's association with Jesus on earth continues now with the risen Lord in a further stage beyond the limitations of the present world. As early as St. Augustine (d. 430), Mary was regarded as the "Mother of the members of Christ" — that is, the members of his Body, which is the Church; for, more than anyone else, she cooperated by her love and faith in the birth of the faithful in the Church, fulfilling the advice of Jesus, "Anyone who does the will of God, that person is my brother and sister and mother" (Mk. 3:35).

In this sense Mary has become "our Mother in the order of grace" *(Dogmatic Constitution on the Church*, No. 61), with a maternity not limited to her life of faith and union with Jesus on earth, but with a "saving role" that continues even "to the eternal fulfillment of the elect" *(Ibid.,* No. 62). "Inseparably joined to the saving work of Christ," is the way the *Constitution on the Sacred Liturgy* states this. What Catholics call Mary's "mediation of grace" is her continuing involvement in God's saving plan.

Early Christian authors, like St. Ambrose in the fourth century, expressed the view that Mary was a model to the Church, that her virginal maternity was reflected in the Church's spiritual maternity of the brethren of Christ. In the Middle Ages the likenesses between

Mary and the Church were further explored. As the French Cistercian, Blessed Guerric of Igney (d. 1157), put it: "Like the Church of which she is a figure, Mary is Mother of all those who are born to life." Medieval devotion shifted the emphasis from admiration of the holiness of the Mother of God to confidence in her role as all-powerful intercessor, Queen and Mother. Doctrine and devotion to Mary were in accord with the strong sense of community between the Church on earth and the Church triumphant in heaven.

At times devotion to Mary and other saints took bizarre forms, and there were many abuses. When the Reformation took place, calling upon the saints, even St. Mary, for help was rejected by the Reformers as taking away from the unique mediatorship of Christ. Ever since that time, Christians of the West have differed in their understanding of this aspect of the communion of saints.

Ecumenical Considerations

The dogmas of the Immaculate Conception and the Assumption, which remain formidable ecumenical difficulties, are now viewed less as "special privileges," personal and private to Mary, than as saving events that happened to her for the sake of Christ and his Church.

Mary was the child of two human parents, but kept free from original sin. This initial holiness, called the Immaculate Conception, was entirely God's gift to her and is a sign of the love Christ has for his Bride, the Church, which — even though composed of sinners — is "holy Church."

Mary's Assumption means that she is one with the risen Christ in body and soul, that is, in the fullness of her personality. The meaning for the Church is that the Mother of Jesus is "a sign of sure hope and comfort for the pilgrim People of God," showing forth the fullest meaning of being redeemed. Here again Mary is the "spotless image" of the Church responding in joy to the invitation of Christ, himself the "first-fruits from the dead" and the glorious Bridegroom inviting his Church to join him at the Father's right hand. The Church has answered her Lord's invitation in one of her daughters — Mary assumed into heaven — who is "the image and beginning of the Church as she is to be perfected in the world to come" *(Dogmatic Constitution on the Church*, No. 68).

Approach of Vatican II

The Second Vatican Council was highly senstive to the views and feelings of other Christians when it spoke about the Mother of Jesus. Only once, for example, did it use the difficult term, "Mediatrix," which it explained as strengtheninng rather than lessening confidence in Christ, the one Mediator. More significantly, its biblical approach to Mary, with a strong accent on her pilgrimage of faith, is in accord with the pattern of Protestant theology.

Catholics and Protestants, in spite of a common faith in the Trinity and in Christ, are still divided about several main doctrinal issues. In connection with them, the council noted the necessity of remembering "that in Catholic teaching there exists an order or 'hierarchy,' of truths, since they vary in their relationship to the foundation of the Christian faith." *(Decree on Ecumenism,* No. 11). The council also listed these truths is this order: the meaning of redemption, the mystery and ministry of the Church, and the role of Mary in the work of salvation *(Ibid.,* No. 20).

Present indications are that the mystery of Mary in the setting of the larger mystery of Christ and the Church will occupy increasing attention from Catholics, Protestants and Orthodox listening to one another in the Spirit of Jesus — the same Spirit who inspired Mary's prophecy: "All generations shall call me blessed, because he who is mighty has done great things for me" (Lk. 1:48-49).

APPARITIONS OF THE BLESSED VIRGIN MARY

Only eight of the best known apparitions of the Blessed Virgin Mary are described briefly below.

The sites of the following apparitions have become shrines and centers of pilgrimage. Miracles of the moral and physical orders have been reported as occurring at these places and/or in connection with related practices of prayer and penance.

Banneux, near Liege, Belgium: Mary appeared eight times between Jan. 15 and Mar. 2, 1933, to an 11-year-old peasant girl, Mariette Beco, in a garden behind the family cottage in Banneux, near Liege. She called herself the Virgin of the Poor, and has since been venerated as Our Lady of the Poor, the Sick, and the Indifferent. A small chapel was built by a spring near the site of the apparitions and was blessed Aug. 15, 1933. Approval of devotion to Our Lady of Banneux was given in 1949 by Bishop Louis J. Kerkhofs of Liege, and a statue of that title was solemnly crowned in 1956.

Over 100 sanctuaries throughout the world are dedicated to the honor of Our Lady of Banneux.

The **International Union of Prayer,** for devotion to the Virgin of the Poor, has approximately two million members.

Beauraing, Belgium: Mary appeared 33 times between Nov. 29, 1932, and Jan. 3, 1933, to five children in the garden of a convent school in Beauraing. A chapel, which became a pilgrimage center, was erected on the spot. Reserved approval of devotion to Our Lady of Beauraing was given Feb. 2, 1943, and final approbation July 2, 1949, by Bishop Charue of Namur.

The **Marian Union of Beauraing,** a prayer association for the conversion of sinners, has thousands of members throughout the world (see Pro Maria Committee).

Fatima, Portugal: Mary appeared six times between May 13 and Oct. 13, 1917, to three children in a field called Cova da Iria near Fatima, north of Lisbon. She recommended frequent recitation of the Rosary; urged works of mortification for the conversion of sinners; called for devotion to herself under the title of her Immaculate Heart; asked that the people of Russia be consecrated to her under this title, and that the faithful make a Communion of reparation on the first Saturday of each month.

The apparitions were declared worthy of belief in October, 1930, after a seven-year canonical investigation, and devotion to Our Lady of Fatima was authorized under the title of Our Lady of the Rosary. In October, 1942, Pius XII consecrated the world to Mary under the title of her Immaculate Heart. Ten years later, in the first apostolic letter addressed directly to the peoples of Russia, he consecrated them in a special manner to Mary.

Fatima, with its sanctuary and basilica, ranks with Lourdes as the greatest of modern Marian shrines.

(See First Saturday Devotion.)

Guadalupe, Mexico: Mary appeared four times in 1531 to an Indian, Juan Diego, on Tepeyac hill outside of Mexico City, and instructed him to tell Bishop Zumarraga of her wish that a church be built there. The bishop complied with the request about two years later after being convinced of the genuineness of the apparition by the evidence of a miraculously painted life-size figure of the Virgin on the mantle of the Indian. The mantle bearing the picture has been preserved and is enshrined in the Basilica of Our Lady of Guadalupe, which has a long history as a center of devotion and pilgrimage in Mexico. The shrine church, originally dedicated in 1709 and subsequently enlarged, has the title of basilica.

Benedict XIV, in a decree issued in 1754, authorized a Mass and Office under the title of Our Lady of Guadalupe for celebration on Dec. 12, and named Mary the patroness of New Spain. Our Lady of Guadalupe was designated patroness of Latin America by St. Pius X in 1910 and patroness of the Americas by Pius XII in 1945.

Knock, Ireland: An apparition of Mary, along with the figures of St. Joseph and St. John the Apostle, was witnessed by at least 15 persons in the evening of Aug. 21, 1879, near the parish church of Knock, County Mayo. A commission appointed by the Bishop of Tuam to investigate the matter reported that testimony confirming the apparition was "trustworthy and satisfactory."

La Salette, France: Mary appeared as a sorrowing and weeping figure Sept. 19, 1846, to two peasant children, Melanie Matthieu, 15, and Maximin Giraud, 11, at La Salette in southern France. The message she confided to them, regarding the necessity of penance, was communicated to Pius IX in 1851 and has since been known at the "secret" of La Salette. Bishop de Bruillard of Grenoble declared in 1851 that the apparition was credible, and devotion to Mary under the title of Our Lady of La Salette was authorized. The devotion has been confirmed by popes since the time of Pius IX, and a Mass and Office with this title were authorized in 1942. The shrine church was given the title of minor basilica in 1879.

Lourdes, France: Mary, identifying herself as the Immaculate Conception, appeared 18 times between Feb. 11 and July 16, 1858, to 14-year-old Bernadette Soubirous at the grotto of Massabielle near Lourdes in southern France. Her message concerned the necessity of prayer and penance for the conversion of men. Mary's request that a chapel be built at the grotto and spring was fulfilled in 1862 after four years of rigid examination established the credibility of the apparitions. Devotion under the title of Our Lady of Lourdes was authorized later, and a Feb. 11 feast commemorating the apparitions was instituted by Leo XIII. St. Pius X extended this feast throughout the Church in 1907.

The Church of Notre Dame was made a basilica in 1870, and the Church of the Rosary was built later. The underground Church of St. Pius X, consecrated Mar. 25, 1958, is the second largest church in the world, with a capacity of 20,000 persons.

Our Lady of the Miraculous Medal, France: Mary appeared three times in 1830 to Catherine Laboure in the chapel of the motherhouse of the Daughters of Charity of St. Vincent de Paul, Rue de Bac, Paris. She commissioned Catherine to have made the medal of the Immaculate Conception, now known as the Miraculous Medal, and to spread devotion to her under this title. In 1832, the medal was struck according to the model revealed to Catherine.

Secret of Fatima

Sister Lucy, a Carmelite nun and one of the trio of shepherd children to whom Mary appeared, wrote a three-part account of an apparition which occurred July 13, 1917. The first part concerned a vision of hell. The second dealt with the conversion of the peoples of Russia through devotion to Mary under the title of her Immaculate Heart. The third part was the so-called "secret" which, it was said, was not to be opened until 1960 or the death of Sister Lucy, whichever came first. Presumably, the "secret" was a prophecy of dire events. To date, it has not been disclosed. Church officials have decried morbid concern about it.

Eastern Catholic Churches

The Eastern Catholic Churches are those which are organized under the major patriarchates of Alexandria, Antioch and Jerusalem (Constantinople, formerly), and the minor patriarchates of Babylon (Iraq) and Cilicia (Turkey).

Origin

The Church had its beginnings in Palestine, whence it spread to other regions of the world. As it spread, certain cities or jurisdictions became key centers of Christian life and missionary endeavor—notably, Jerusalem, Alexandria, Antioch and Constantinople in the East, and Rome in the West — with the result that their practices became diffused throughout their spheres of influence. Various rites originated from these practices which although rooted in the essentials of Christian faith, were different in significant respects because of their relationships to particular cultural patterns.

Patriarchal Jurisdictions

The main lines of Eastern Church organization and liturgy had been drawn long before the Roman Empire was definitely separated into Eastern and Western divisions about 395. It was originally co-extensive with the boundaries of the Eastern Empire. Its jurisdictions were those of the patriarchates of Alexandria and Antioch (recognized) as such by the Council of Nicaea in 325), and of Jerusalem and Constantinople (given similar recognition by the Council of Chalcedon in 451). These were the major parent bodies of the Eastern Rite Church which for centuries were identifiable only with limited numbers of nationality and language groups in Eastern Europe, the Middle East and parts of Asia and Africa. Their members are now scattered throughout the world.

Vatican II Decree

The Second Vatican Council, in its *Decree on Eastern Catholic Churches,* stated the following points.

"That Church, Holy and Catholic, which is the Mystical Body of Christ, is made up of the faithful who are organically united in the Holy Spirit through the same faith, the same sacraments, and the same government and who, combining into various groups held together by a hierarchy, form separate Churches or rites. . . . It is the mind of the Catholic Church that each individual Church or rite retain its traditions whole and entire, while adjusting its way of life to the various needs of time and place" (No. 2).

"Such individual Churches, whether of the East or of the West, although they differ somewhat among themselves in what are called rites (that is, in liturgy, ecclesiastical discipline, and spiritual heritage) are, never-theless, equally entrusted to the pastoral guidance of the Roman Pontiff, the divinely appointed successor of St. Peter in supreme government over the universal Church. They are consequently of equal dignity, so that none of them is superior to the others by reason of rite" (No. 3).

Eastern Heritage: "Each and every Catholic, as also the baptized . . . of every non-Catholic Church or community who enters into the fullness of Catholic communion, should everywhere retain his proper rite, cherish it, and observe it to the best of his ability . . ." . . ." (No. 4).

". . . The Churches of the East, as much as those of the West, fully enjoy the right, and are in duty bound, to rule themselves. Each should do so according to its proper and individual procedures . . ." (No. 5).

"All Eastern rite members should know and be convinced that they can and should always preserve their lawful liturgical rites and their established way of life, and that these should not be altered except by way of an appropriate and organic development . . ." . . ." (No. 6)

Patriarchs: "The institution of the patriarchate has existed in the Church from the earliest times and was recognized by the first ecumenical Synods.

"By the name Eastern Patriarch is meant the bishop who has jurisdiction over all bishops (including metropolitans), clergy, and people of his own territory or rite, in accordance with the norms of law and without prejudice to the primacy of the Roman Pontiff . . ." (No. 7).

"Though some of the patriarchates of the Eastern Churches are of later origin than others, all are equal in patriarchal dignity. Still the honorary and lawfully established order of precedence among them is to be preserved" (No. 8).

"In keeping with the most ancient tradition of the Church, the Patriarchs of the Eastern Churches are to be accorded exceptional respect, since each presides over his patriarchate as father and head.

"This sacred Synod, therefore, decrees that their rights and privileges should be re-established in accord with the ancient traditions of each Church and the decrees of the ecumenical Synods.

"The rights and privileges in question are those which flourished when East and West were in union, though they should be somewhat adapted to modern conditions.

"The Patriarchs with their synods constitute the superior authority for all affairs of the patriarchate, including the right to establish new eparchies and to nominate bishops of their rite within the territorial bounds_ of the patriarchate, without prejudice to the inalienable right of the Roman Pontiff to intervene in individual cases" (No. 8).

"What has been said of Patriarchs applies as well, under the norm of law, to major archbishops, who preside over the whole of some individual Church or rite" (No. 10).

Sacraments: "This sacred Ecumenical Synod endorses and lauds the ancient discipline of the sacraments existing in the Eastern Churches, as also the practices connected with their celebration and administration . . ." (No. 12).

"With respect to the minister of holy chrism (confirmation), let that practice be fully restored which existed among Easterners in most ancient times. Priests, therefore, can validly confer this sacrament, provided they use chrism blessed by a Patriarch or bishop" (No. 13).

"In conjunction with baptism or otherwise, all Eastern-Rite priests can confer this sacrament validly on all the faithful of any rite, including the Latin; licitly, however, only if the regulations of both common and particular law are observed. Priests of the Latin rite, to the extent of the faculties they enjoy for administering this sacrament, can confer it also on the faithful of Eastern Churches, without prejudice to rite. They do so licitly if the regulations of both common and particular law are observed" (No. 14).

"The faithful are bound on Sundays and feast days to attend the divine liturgy or, according to the regulations or custom of their own rite, the celebration of the Divine Praises. That the faithful may be able to satisfy their obligation more easily, it is decreed that this obligation can be fulfilled from the Vespers of the vigil to the end of the Sunday or the feast day . . ." (No. 15).

"Because of the everyday intermingling of the communicants of diverse Eastern Churches in the same Eastern region or territory, the faculty for hearing confession, duly and unrestrictedly granted by his proper bishop to a priest of any rite, is applicable to the entire territory of the grantor, also to the places and the faithful belonging to any other rite in the same territory, unless an Ordinary of the place explicitly decides otherwise with respect to the places pertaining to his rite" (No. 16).

". . . This sacred Synod ardently desires that where it has fallen into disuse the office of the permanent diaconate be restored. The legislative authority of each individual church should decide about the subdiaconate and the minor orders . . ." (No. 17).

"By way of preventing invalid marriages between Eastern Catholics and baptized Eastern non-Catholics, and in the interests of the permanence and sanctity of marriage and of domestic harmony, this sacred Synod decrees that the canonical 'form' for the celebration of such marriages obliges only for lawfulness. For their validity, the presence of a sacred minister suffices, as long as the other requirements of law are honored" (No. 18).

Worship: "Henceforth, it will be the exclusive right of an ecumenical Synod or the Apostolic See to establish, transfer, or suppress feast days common to all the Eastern Churches. To establish, transfer, or suppress feast days for any of the individual Churches is within the competence not only of the Apostolic See but also of a patriarchal or archiepiscopal synod, provided due consideration is given to the entire region and to other individual Churches" (No. 19).

"Until such time as all Christians desirably concur on a fixed day for the celebration of Easter, and with a view meantime to promoting unity among the Christians of a given area or nation, it is left to the Patriarchs or supreme authorities of a place to reach a unanimous agreement, after ascertaining the views of all concerned, on a single Sunday for the observance of Easter" (No. 20).

"With respect to rules concerning sacred seasons, individual faithful dwelling outside the area or territory of their own rite may conform completely to the established custom of the place where they live. When members of a family belong to different rites, they are all permitted to observe sacred seasons according to the rules of any one of these rites" (No. 21).

"From ancient times the Divine Praises have been held in high esteem among all Eastern Churches. Eastern clerics and religious should celebrate these Praises as the laws and customs of their own traditions require. To the extent they can, the faithful too should follow the example of their forbears by assisting devoutly at the Divine Praises" (No. 22).

RITES AND FAITHFUL OF EASTERN CHURCHES

(Principal source of statistics: *Annuario Pontificio.* The statistics are for Eastern-Rite jurisdictions only, and do not include Eastern-Rite Catholics under the jurisdiction of Roman-Rite bishops. Some of the figures reported are only approximate. Some of the jurisdictions listed may be inactive because of government suppression.)

The Byzantine, Alexandrian, Antiochene, Armenian and Chaldean are the five principal rites used in their entirety or in modified form

by the various Eastern churches. The number of Eastern Catholics throughout the world is approximately 11 million.

Alexandrian Rite

Called the Liturgy of St. Mark, the Alexandrian Rite was modified by the Copts and Melkites, and contains elements of the Byzantine Rite of St. Basil and the liturgies of Sts. Mark, Cyril and Gregory of Nazianzen. The liturgy is substantially that of the Coptic

Church, which is divided into two branches — the Coptic or Egyptian, and the Ethiopian or Abyssinian.

The faithful of this rite are:

COPTS: Returned to Catholic unity about 1741; situated in Egypt, the Near East; liturgical languages are Coptic, Arabic. Jurisdictions (located in Egypt): patriarchate of Alexandria, three dioceses; 100,000.

ETHIOPIANS: Returned to Catholic unity in 1846: situated in Ethiopia, Eritrea, Jerusalem, Somalia; liturgical language is Geez. Jurisdictions (located in Ethiopia): one archdiocese, two dioceses; 75,432.

Antiochene Rite

This is the source of more derived rites than any of the other parent rites. Its origin can be traced to the Eighth Book of the *Apostolic Constitutions* and to the Liturgy of St. James of Jerusalem, which ultimately spread throughout the whole patriarchate and displaced older forms based on the *Apostolic Constitutions.*

The faithful of this rite are:

MALANKARESE: Returned to Catholic unity in 1930; situated in India; liturgical languages are Syrian, Malayalam. Jurisdictions (located in India): one archdiocese, one diocese; 194,153.

MARONITES: United to the Holy See since the time of their founder, St. Maron; have no counterparts among the separated Eastern Christians: situated throughout the world: liturgical languages are Syriac, Arabic. Jurisdictions (located in Lebanon, Cyprus, Egypt, Syria, US, Brazil): patriarchate of Antioch, one metropolitan, 12 archdioceses and dioceses, one apostolic administration; 1,068,368. Where no special jurisdictions exist, they are under jurisdiction of local Roman-Rite bishops.

SYRIANS: Returned to Catholic unity in 1781; situated in Asia, Africa, the Americas, Australia; liturgical languages are Syriac, Arabic. Jurisdictions (located in Lebanon, Iraq, Egypt, Syria and Turkey): eight archdioceses and dioceses; 96,120.

Armenian Rite

Substantially, although using a different language, this is the Greek Liturgy of St. Basil; it is considered an older form of the Byzantine Rite, and incorporates some modifications from the Antiochene Rite.

The faithful of this rite are:

ARMENIANS: exclusively: Returned to Catholic unity during the time of the Crusades; situated in the Near East, Europe, Africa, the Americas, Australasia: liturgical language is Classical Armenian. Jurisdictions (located in Lebanon, Iran, Iraq, Egypt, Syria, Turkey, Poland, France, Greece, Rumania): patriarchate of Cilicia, 22 archdioceses and dioceses, one exarchate, two ordinariates.

Byzantine Rite

Based on the Rite of St. James of Jerusalem and the churches of Antioch, and reformed by Sts. Basil and John Chrysostom, the Byzantine Rite is proper to the Church of Constantinople. (The city was called Byzantium before Constantine changed its name; the modern name is Istanbul.) It is now used by the majority of Eastern Catholics and by the Eastern Orthodox Church (which is not in union with Rome). It is, after the Roman, the most widely used rite.

The faithful of this rite are:

ALBANIANS: Returned to Catholic unity about 1628; situated in Albania; liturgical language is Albanian. Jurisdiction (located in Albania): one apostolic administration.

BULGARIANS: Returned to Catholic unity about 1861; situated in Bulgaria; liturgical language is Old Slavonic. Jurisdiction (located in Bulgaria): one apostolic exarchate.

BYELORUSSIANS, also known as WHITE RUSSIANS: Returned to Catholic unity in the 17th century; situated in Europe, the Americas, Australia; liturgical language is Old Slavonic. They have an apostolic visitor residing at Rome.

GEORGIANS: Returned to Catholic unity in 1861; situated in Georgia (Southern Russia), France; liturgical language is Georgian. They have an apostolic administrator.

GREEKS: Returned to Catholic unity in 1829; situated in Greece, Asia Minor, Europe; liturgical language is Greek. Jurisdictions (located in Greece and Turkey): two exarchates; 3,134.

HUNGARIANS: Descendants of Ruthenians who returned to Catholic unity in 1646; situated in Hungary, the rest of Europe, the Americas; liturgical languages are Greek, Hungarian, English. Jurisdictions (located in Hungary): one diocese and one exarchate; 269,100.

ITALO-ALBANIANS: Have never been separated from Rome; situated in Italy, Sicily, the Americas; liturgical languages are Greek, Italo-Albanian. Jurisdictions (located in Italy): two dioceses, one abbacy; 69,080.

MELKITES: Returned to Catholic unity during the time of the Crusades, but definitive reunion did not take place until early in the 18th century; situated in the Middle East, Asia, Africa, Europe, the Americas, Australia; liturgical languages are Greek, Arabic, English, Portuguese, Spanish. Jurisdictions (located in Syria, Lebanon, Jordan, Israel, US, Brazil): patriarchate of Antioch (also has jurisdiction over Melkites in Egypt, Sudan, Jerusalem and Iraq), 15 archdioceses and dioceses, one exarchate; approximately 1,000,000.

ROMANIANS: Returned to Catholic unity in 1697; situated in Rumania, the rest of Europe, the Americas; liturgical language is Modern Romanian. Jurisdictions (located in

Rumania): one archdiocese, four dioceses. They have an apostolic visitor in the US.

RUSSIANS: Returned to Catholic unity about 1905; situated in Europe, the Americas, Australia, China; liturgical language is Old Slavonic. Jurisdictions (located in Russia and China): two exarchates.

RUTHENIANS, or CARPATHO-RUS-SIANS (Rusins): Returned to Catholic unity in the Union of Brest-Litovek, 1596, and the Union of Uzhorod, Apr. 24, 1646; situated in Hungary, Czechoslovakia, elsewhere in Europe, the Americas, Australia; liturgical languages are Old Slavonic, English. Jurisdictions (located in Russia and the US): one archdiocese, three dioceses.

SLOVAKS: Jurisdiction (located in Czechoslovakia): one diocese (also has jurisdiction over Ruthenians, Ukrainians and Hungarians of country).

TURKS: Jurisdiction (located in Turkey): one apostolic exarchate.

UKRAINIANS, or GALICIAN RUTH-ENIANS: returned to Catholic unity about 1595; situated in Europe, the Americas, Australasia; liturgical languages are Old Slavonic and Ukrainian. Jurisdictions (located in Russian Galicia, Poland, the US, Canada, England, Australia, Guam, France, Brazil, Argentina): three archdioceses, eight dioceses, six apostolic exarchates; 4,607,924 (some figures date from 1943).

YUGOSLAVS, SERBS and CROATIANS: Returned to Catholic unity in 1611; situated in Yugoslavia, the Americas; liturgical language is Old Slavonic. Jurisdiction (located in Yugoslavia): one diocese (which also has jurisdiction over all Byzantine-Rite faithful in Yugoslavia); 62,000. They are under the jurisdiction of Ruthenian bishops elsewhere.

Chaldean Rite

This rite, listed as separate and distinct by the Sacred Congregation for the Oriental Churches, was derived from the Antiochene Rite.

The faithful of this rite are:

CHALDEANS: Descendants of the Nestorians, returned to Catholic unity in 1692; situated throughout the Middle East, in Europe, Africa, the Americas; liturgical languages are Syriac, Arabic. Jurisdictions (located in Iraq, Iran, Lebanon, Syria, Turkey): patriarchate of Babylonia, 18 archdioceses and dioceses; 259,991. There are patriarchal vicars for Jordan and Egypt.

SYRO-MALABARESE: Descended from the St. Thomas Christians of India; normal relations with Rome were established in 1599; situated mostly in the Malabar region of India; they use a Westernized and *Latinized form of the Chaldean Rite in Syriac and Malayalam. Jurisdictions (located in India): two archdioceses, five dioceses, six exarchates; 2,160,958.

EASTERN JURISDICTIONS

For centuries Eastern-Rite Catholics were identifiable with a limited number of nationality and language groups in certain countries of the Middle East, Eastern Europe, Asia and Africa. The persecution of religion in the Soviet Union since 1917 and in Iron Curtain countries since World War II, however — in addition to decimating and destroying the Church in those places—has resulted in the emigration of many Eastern-Rite Catholics from their homelands. This forced emigration, together with voluntary emigration, has led to the spread of Eastern Rites and their faithful to many other countries.

Europe

(Ukrainian faithful of the Byzantine Rite in Europe lack a hierarchy but have an apostolic visitor, Archbishop Miroslav Maruzyn.)

ALBANIA: Byzantine Rite, apostolic administration.

AUSTRIA: Byzantine Rite, ordinariate.

BULGARIA: Byzantine Rite (Bulgarians), apostolic exarchate.

CZECHOSLOVAKIA: Byzantine Rite (Slovakians and other Byzantine-Rite Catholics), eparchy.

ENGLAND: Byzantine Rite (Ukrainians), apostolic exarchate.

FRANCE: Byzantine Rite (Ukrainians), apostolic exarchate.

Armenian Rite, apostolic exarchate.

Ordinariate for all other Eastern-Rite Catholics.

GERMANY: Byzantine Rite (Ukrainians), apostolic exarchate.

GREECE: Byzantine Rite, apostolic exarchate.

Armenian Rite, ordinariate.

HUNGARY: Byzantine Rite (Hungarians), eparchy, apostolic exarchate.

ITALY: Byzantine Rite (Italo-Albanians), two eparchies, one abbacy.

POLAND: Byzantine Rite (Ukrainians), apostolic exarchate.

Armenian Rite, archeparchy.

Ordinariate for all other Eastern-Rite Catholics.

RUMANIA: Byzantine Rite (Romanians), metropolitan, four eparchies.

Armenian Rite, ordinariate.

RUSSIA: Byzantine Rite (Russians), apostolic exarchate; (Ruthenians), eparchy; (Ukrainians), major archeparchy, two eparchies.

YUGOSLAVIA: Byzantine Rite (Yugoslav and other Byzantine-Rite Catholics), eparchy.

Asia

CHINA: Byzantine Rite (Russians), apostolic exarchate.

CYPRUS: Antiochene Rite (Maronites), archeparchy.

INDIA: Antiochene Rite (Malankarese), metropolitan see, eparchy.

Chaldean Rite (Syro-Malabarese), two metropolitan sees, five eparchies, six apostolic exarchates.

IRAN: Chaldean Rite (Chaldeans), two metropolitan sees, two archeparchies.

Armenian Rite, eparchy.

IRAQ: Antiochene Rite (Syrians), two archeparchies.

Byzantine Rite (Melkites), patriarchal vicar.

Chaldean Rite (Chaldeans), patriarchate, metropolitan see, nine archeparchies and eparchies.

Armenian Rite, archeparchy.

ISRAEL (includes Jerusalem): Antiochene Rite (Syrians), patriarchal vicar.

Byzantine Rite (Melkites), patriarchate, archeparchy.

Chaldean Rite (Chaldeans), patriarchal vicar.

Armenian Rite, patriarchal vicar.

JORDAN: Byzantine Rite (Melkites), archeparchy.

LEBANON: Antiochene Rite (Maronites), patriarchate, one metropolitan see, six archeparchies and eparchies; (Syrians), patriarchate.

Byzantine Rite (Melkites), seven metropolitan and archeparchal sees.

Chaldean Rite (Chaldeans), eparchy.

Armenian Rite, patriarchate, eparchy.

SYRIAN ARAB REPUBLIC: Antiochene Rite (Maronites), one archeparchy, one eparchy, one apostolic administration; (Syrians), four archeparchies.

Byzantine Rite (Melkites), patriarchate, five metropolitan sees, one archeparchy.

Chaldean Rite (Chaldeans), eparchy.

Armenian Rite, archeparchy, eparchy, patriarchal vicariate.

TURKEY (Europe and Asia): Antiochene Rite (Syrians), one eparchy.

Byzantine Rite, apostolic exarchate.

Chaldean Rite (Chaldeans), one archeparchy, one eparchy.

Armenian Rite, 15 archeparchies and eparchies.

Oceania

AUSTRALIA: Byzantine Rite (Ukrainians), apostolic exarchate.

Africa

EGYPTIAN ARAB REPUBLIC: Alexandrian Rite (Copts), patriarchate, three eparchies.

Antiochene Rite (Maronites), eparchy; (Syrians), eparchy.

Byzantine Rite (Melkites), patriarchal vicar.

Chaldean Rite (Chaldeans), patriarchal vicar.

Armenian Rite, eparchy.

ETHIOPIA: Alexandrian Rite (Ethiopians), metropolitan see, two eparchies.

SUDAN: Byzantine Rite (Melkites), patriarchal vicar.

North America

CANADA: Byzantine Rite (Ukrainians), one metropolitan, three eparchies; (Slovaks), apostolic visitor.

UNITED STATES: Antiochene Rite (Maronites), eparchy. ·

Byzantine Rite (Ukrainians), one metropolitan see, two eparchies; (Ruthenians), one metropolitan see, two eparchies; (Melkites), apostolic exarchate.

Other Eastern-Rite Catholics are under the jurisdiction of local Roman-Rite bishops. (See Eastern-Rite Catholics in the United States.)

South America

ARGENTINA: Byzantine Rite (Ukrainians), apostolic exarchate.

Ordinariate for all other Eastern-Rite Catholics.

BRAZIL: Antiochene Rite (Maronites), eparchy.

Byzantine Rite (Melkites), eparchy; (Ukrainians), eparchy.

SYNODS, ASSEMBLIES

These assemblies are collegial bodies which have pastoral authority over members of the Eastern Rite Churches.

Patriarchal Synods: Maronites: Cardinal Paul Pierre Meouchi, patriarch of Antioch of the Maronites.

Melkites: Maximos V Hakim, patriarch of Antioch of the Melkites.

Chaldeans: Paul II Cheikho, patriarch of Babylonia of the Chaldeans.

Copts: Cardinal Stephanos I Sidarouss, C.M., patriarch of Alexandria of the Copts.

Syrians: Ignace Antoine Hayek, patriarch of Antioch of the Syrians.

Armenians: Ignace Pierre XVI Batanian, patriarch of Cilicia of the Armenians.

Assemblies: Assembly of Ordinaries of the United Arab Republic: Cardinal Stephanos I Sidarouss, C.M., patriarch of Alexandria of the Copts.

Assembly of Catholic Patriarchs and Bishops of Lebanon: Cardinal Paul Pierre Meouchi, patriarch of Antioch of the Maronites.

Assembly of Ordinaries of the Syrian Arab Republic: Maximos V Hakim, patriarch of Antioch of the Melkites.

Conference of the Ukrainian Catholic Hierarchy (Feb. 9, 1962): Archbishop Maxim Hermaniuk, Winnipeg.

Malabarese Episcopal Conference: Cardinal Joseph Parecattil, Ernakulam.

Of the collegial bodies listed above, the patriarchal synods have the most authority. In addition to other prerogatives, they have the right to elect bishops and regulate discipline for their respective rites.

EASTERN RITES IN US

Byzantine Rite

Ukrainians: There are approximately 285,000 in three jurisdictions in the US: the metropolitan see of Philadelphia (1924, metropolitan 1958) and the suffragan sees of Stamford, Conn. (1956), and St. Nicholas of Chicago (1961).

Ruthenians: There are approximately 278,000 in three jurisdictions in the US: the metropolitan see of Munhall (formerly Pittsburgh, est. 1924; metropolitan and transferred to Munhall, 1969) and the suffragan sees of Passaic, N.J. (1963), and Parma, Ohio (1969). Hungarian and Croatian Byzantine Catholics in the US are also under the jurisdiction of Ruthenian-Rite bishops.

Melkites: There are 55,000 in the US under the jurisdiction of the exarchate established in 1965, with headquarters at Boston, Mass.

Romanians: There are 17 Romanian Catholic Byzantine Rite parishes in the US, each under the jurisdiction of the Roman-Rite bishop of the territory in which it is located: Cleveland diocese (3 parishes), Detroit (2), Erie (2), Gary (2), Pittsburgh (1), Rockford (2), Trenton (2), and Youngstown (3). No separate statistics are available. The Association of Romanian Catholics of America (see index) was established in 1948 to preserve the identity of Romanian Catholics within the general framework of the Catholic Church in America. It has petitioned the Holy See for a bishop of the rite in the US.

Byelorussians: Have one parish in the US — Christ the Redeemer, Chicago, Ill. — and are under the jurisdiction of the local Roman-Rite bishop.

Russians: Have parishes in California (St. Andrew, El Segundo, and Our Lady of Fatima Center, San Francisco) Illinois (Annunciation Reunion Center, Chicago); Massachusetts (Our Lady of Kazan, Boston); New York (St. Michael's Chapel, Pope John XXIII Reunion Center); and Oregon (Our Lady of Tychvin Chapel, Portland). They are under the jurisdiction of local Roman-Rite bishops.

Antiochene Rite

There are approximately 152,407 Maronites in the US under the jurisdiction of the eparchy of St. Maron of Detroit (established as an exarchate, 1966; eparchy, 1972).

Armenian Rite

Have parishes in California (Queen of Martyrs, Los Angeles); Massachusetts (Holy Cross, Cambridge); Michigan (St. Vartan, Detroit); New Jersey (Sacred Heart, Paterson); New York (Armenian Catholic Community, 343 W. 25th St., New York, N.Y. 10001); and Pennsylvania (St. Mark, Philadelphia). They are under the jurisdiction of local Roman-Rite bishops.

Chaldean Rite

Have parishes in California (St. Thomas the Apostle, Turlock); Illinois (St. Ephram, Chicago); and Michigan (Mother of God, Detroit). They are under the jurisdiction of local Roman-Rite bishops.

BYZANTINE DIVINE LITURGY

The Divine Liturgy in all rites is based on the consecration of bread and wine by the narration-reactualization of the actions of Christ at the Last Supper. Aside from this fundamental usage, there are differences between the Roman (Latin) Rite and Eastern Rites, and among the Eastern Rites themselves. Following is a general description of the Byzantine Divine Liturgy which is in widest use in the Eastern-Rite Churches.

In the Byzantine, as in all Eastern Rites, the bread and wine are prepared at the start of the Liturgy. The priest does this in a little niche or at a table on the gospel side of the sanctuary. Taking a round loaf of leavened bread stamped with religious symbols, he cuts out a square host and other particles while reciting verses expressing the symbolism of the action. When the bread and wine are ready, he says a prayer of offering and incenses the oblations, the altar, the icons and the people.

At the altar a litany for all classes of people is sung by the priest. The congregation answers, "Lord, have mercy."

The Little Entrance comes next. In procession, the priest leaves the sanctuary carrying the Book of the Gospels, and then returns. He sings prayers especially selected for the day and the feast. These are followed by the solemn singing of the prayer, "Holy God, Holy Mighty One, Holy Immortal One."

The Epistle follows. The Gospel is sung or read by the priest facing the people at the middle door of the sanctuary.

An interruption after the Liturgy of the Catechumens, formerly an instructional period for those learning the faith, is clearly marked. Catechumens, if present, are dismissed with a prayer. Following this are a prayer and litany for the faithful.

The Great Entrance or solemn Offertory Procession then takes place. The priest first says a long silent prayer for himself, in preparation for the great act to come. Again he incenses the oblations, the altar, the icons and people. He goes to the table on the gospel side for the veil-covered paten and chalice. When he arrives back at the sanctuary door, he announces the intention of the Mass in the prayer: "May the Lord God remember all of you in his kingdom, now and forever."

After another litany, the congregation recites the Nicene Creed.

Consecration

The most solemn portion of the sacrifice is introduced by the preface, which is very much like the preface of the Roman Rite. At the beginning of the last phrase, the priest raises his voice to introduce the singing of the Sanctus. During the singing he reads the introduction to the words of consecration.

The words of consecration are sung aloud, and the people sing "Amen" to both consecrations. As the priest raises the Sacred Species in solemn offering, he sings: "Thine of Thine Own we offer unto Thee in behalf of all and for all."

A prayer to the Holy Spirit is followed by the commemorations, in which special mention is made of the all-holy, most blessed and glorious Lady, the Mother of God and ever-Virgin Mary. The dead are remembered and then the living, who comprise the hierarchy, the whole Catholic world, the pope and numerous classes of persons.

A final litany for spiritual gifts precedes the Our Father. The Sacred Body and Blood are elevated with the words, "Holy Things for the Holy." The Host is then broken and commingled with the Precious Blood. The Priest recites preparatory prayers for Holy Communion, consumes the Sacred Species, and distributes Holy Communion to the people under the forms of both bread and wine. During this time a communion verse is sung by the choir or congregation.

The Liturgy closes quickly after this. The consecrated Species of bread and wine are removed to the side table to be consumed later by the priest. A prayer of thanksgiving is recited, a prayer for all the people is said in front of the icon of Christ, a blessing is invoked upon all, and the people are dismissed.

VESTMENTS, APPURTENANCES

Sticharion: A long white garment of linen or silk with wide sleeves and decorated with embroidery; formerly the vestment for clerics in minor orders, acolytes, lectors, chanters, and subdeacons; symbolic of purity.

Epitrachelion: A stole with ends sewn together, having a loop through which the head is passed; its several crosses symbolize priestly duties.

Zone: A narrow clasped belt made of the same material as the epitrachelion; symbolic of the wisdom of the priest, his strength against enemies of the Church and his willingness to perform holy duties.

Epimanikia: Ornamental cuffs; the right cuff symbolizing strength, the left, patience and good will.

Phelonion: An ample cape, long in the back and sides and cut away in front; symbolic of the higher gifts of the Holy Spirit.

Antimension: A silk or linen cloth laid on the altar for the Liturgy; it may be decorated with a picture of the burial of Christ and the instruments of his passion; the relics of martyrs are sewn into the front border.

Eileton: A linen cloth which corresponds to the Roman-Rite corporal.

Poterion: A chalice or cup which holds the wine and Precious Blood.

Diskos: A shallow plate, which may be elevated on a small stand, corresponding to the Roman-Rite paten.

Asteriskos: Made of two curved bands of gold or silver which cross each other to form a double arch; a star depends from the junction, which forms a cross; it is placed over the diskos holding the consecrated bread and is covered with a veil.

Veils: Three are used, one to cover the poterion, the second to cover the diskos, and the third to cover both.

Spoon: Used in administering Holy Communion by intinction; consecrated leavened bread is dipped into consecrated wine and spooned onto the tongue of the communicant.

Lance: A metal knife used for cutting up the bread to be consecrated during the Liturgy.

BYZANTINE FEATURES

Art: Named for the empire in which it developed, Byzantine art is a unique blend of imperial Roman and classic Hellenic culture with Christian inspiration. The art of the Greek Middle Ages, it reached a peak of development in the 10th or 11th century. Characteristic of its products, particularly in mosaic and painting, are majesty, dignity, refinement and grace. Its sacred paintings, called icons, are reverenced highly in all Eastern Rites.

Church Building: The classical model of Byzantine church architecture is the Church of the Holy Wisdom (Hagia Sophia), built in Constantinople in the first half of the sixth century and still standing. The square structure, extended in some cases in the form of a cross, is topped by a distinctive onion-shaped dome and surmounted by a triple-bar cross. The altar is at the eastern end of building, where the wall bellies out to form an apse. The altar and sanctuary are separated from the body of the church by a fixed or movable screen, the iconostas, to which icons or sacred pictures are attached (see below).

Clergy: The Byzantine Rite has married as well as celibate priests. In places other than the US, where married candidates have not been accepted for ordination since about 1929, men already married can be ordained to the diaconate and priesthood and can continue in marriage after ordination. Celibate deacons and priests cannot marry after ordination; neither can a married priest remarry after the death of his wife. Bishops must be unmarried.

Iconostas: A large screen decorated with sacred pictures or icons which separates the sanctuary from the nave of a church; its equivalent in the roman Rite, for thus separating the sanctuary from the nave, is an altar rail.

An iconostas has three doors through which the sacred ministers enter the sanctuary during the Divine Liturgy: smaller (north and south) Deacons' Doors and a large central Royal Door.

The Deacons' Doors usually feature the icons of Sts. Gabriel and Michael; the Royal Door, the icons of the Evangelists — Matthew, Mark, Luke and John. To the right and left of the Royal Door are the icons of Christ the Teacher and of the Blessed Virgin Mary with the Infant Jesus. To the extreme right and left are the icons of the patron of the church and St. John the Baptist (or St. Nicholas of Myra).

Immediately above the Royal Door is a picture of the Last Supper. To the right are six icons depicting the major feasts of Christ, and to the left are six icons portraying the major feasts of the Blessed Virgin Mary. Above the picture of the Last Supper is a large icon of Christ the King.

Some icon screens also have pictures of the 12 Apostles and the major Old Testament prophets surmounted by a crucifixion scene.

Liturgical Language: In line with Eastern tradition, Byzantine practice has favored the use of the language of the people in the liturgy. Two great advocates of the practice were Sts. Cyril and Methodius, apostles of the Slavs, who devised the Cyrillic alphabet and pioneered the adoption of Slavonic in the liturgy.

Sacraments: Baptism is administered by immersion, and confirmation is conferred at the same time. The Eucharist is administered by intinction, i.e., by giving the communicant a piece of consecrated leavened bread which has been dipped into the consecrated wine. When giving absolution in the sacrament of penance, the priest holds his stole over the head of the penitent. Distinctive marriage ceremonies include the crowning of the bride and groom. Ceremonies for anointing the sick closely resemble those of the Roman Rite. Holy orders are conferred by a bishop.

Sign of the Cross: Eastern-Rite Catholics have a distinctive way of making it (see enttry in the Glossary). The sign of the cross in conjunction with a deep bow, instead of a genuflection, expresses reverence for the presence of Christ in the Blessed Sacrament.

THE UKRAINIAN PATRIARCHATE QUESTION

Two 1972 developments connected with questions about the proposed establishment of a patriarchate for the Ukrainian Rite were the first meeting, June 4 to 8 in Rome, of what was called the permanent synod of the Ukrainian Rite, and the observance of a special "Day of Autonomy" by Ukrainian Catholics in the US on Feb. 20.

Bishops' Meeting

The only things reported about the meeting were the names of the participants; the fact that they worked on a constitution for the Ukrainian Church that was proposed by Cardinal Josyf Slipyi, major archbishop and titular head of the rite; and the additional fact that Cardinal Jean Villot, papal secretary of state, objected to the meeting.

The synod, inaugurated in November, 1971, did not have canonical status.

Participants in the meeting, in addition to the Cardinal, were: Archbishop Ambrose Senyshyn of Philadelphia; Bishop Vasil Velechkovsky, former administrator of the Diocese of Lvov who was released earlier in the year after spending three years in prison in the Soviet Union; Bishop Ivan Prasko, apostolic exarch of Australia; Archbishop Ivan Buchko, former apostolic visitor for Ukrainians in Western Europe; Archbishop Andrew Sapelak, apostolic exarch of Argentina; Archbishop Maxim Hermaniuk of Winnipeg.

The principal purposes of the "Day of Autonomy" celebrated by Ukrainian Catholics in this country on Feb. 20 were to confirm resolutions framed at the 1971 synod of

Ukrainian bishops in Rome and to emphasize their strivings for self-determination under a patriarchal system, similar to other Eastern Rites of the Church.

1971 Developments

Agitation for the establishment of a patriarchate peaked in the spring and summer of 1971, some 20 months after Cardinal Slipyi and 17 other Ukrainian bishops petitioned Pope Paul for patriarchal status for their rite and nearly a year and a half after they were told by the prefect of the Congregation for Oriental Churches that their request had been turned down.

In Canada, some members of the rite protested against Cardinal Slipyi's failure to visit the country to participate in several functions, principally the national congress of the Ukrainian Catholic Council in July. They claimed he was prevented from making the visit by the intervention of officials of the Eastern Rite congregation.

The same charge was raised in the US where several hundred demonstrators, also objecting to the Cardinal's absence, disrupted ordination ceremonies for two auxiliary bishops — John Stock and Basil H. Losten — May 25 in Philadelphia. They took exception as well to what they called bypassing of the Cardinal in the appointment of the new bishops.

In June, 900 persons attending a New York convention of the Society for the Promotion of a Patriarchal System for the Ukrainian Catholic Church protested against what they called "the intrusion by the Congregation for the Eastern Rite Churches into the internal affairs of the Ukrainian Catholic Church."

Fear over the possible results of extremist agitation — sparked, according to some observers, by the strong nationalism of recent immigrants and evident in intemperate charges made by the Society for the Promotion of a Patriarchal System for the Ukrainian Catholic Church — appeared to have been the reason why the prelate went along with a Vatican advisory against visiting the US and Canada.

Cardinal Slipyi's View

Cardinal Slipyi told the Canadian Catholic Council in a taped address that the establishment of a patriarchate is indeed "the central point of our present national strivings." He said, however, that "it would be folly in the present state of friction and misunderstanding to fall into schism."

The Cardinal stated further: "We have lived through difficult moments which have touched to the depths our Church and our people. But we must learn from this experience not only to avoid further disruptions of God's plans but also to prevent others from repeating them. We must judiciously proceed to our ultimate goal, the erection of our patriarchate. Our common concerted action within the Church and our community must be enlightened by the sincere and fervent prayer of all, united in action. This is the first and most effective means."

The "difficult moments" mentioned by the prelate included 18 years of imprisonment which began a year before Soviet authorities absorbed the Ukrainian Church into the Russian Orthodox Church in 1946 and continued until January, 1963. Toward the end of that year he was named major archbishop of the Ukrainian Rite. Exiled from his see city of Lvov, he resides in Rome.

Proponents of patriarchal status and the synodal system for the Ukrainian Rite Church quoted the Second Vatican Council in support of their position. According to the *Decree on Eastern Catholic Churches* (Nos. 9, 10):

"The patriarchs with their synods constitute the superior authority for all affairs of the patriarchate, including the right to establish new eparchies (dioceses) and to nominate bishops of their title within the territorial bounds of the patriarchate, without prejudice to the inalienable right of the Pontiff to intervene in individual cases.

"What has been said of patriarchs applies as well, under the norm of law, to major archbishops who preside over the whole of some individual church or rite."

Pope's View

Pope Paul turned down the patriarch request of the Ukrainian Church with the Apostolic Slipyi under date of July 7. He said: "There are canonical, historical, spiritual and pastoral reasons which, unfortunately, do not at present allow us to satisfy the wishes of the Catholic Ukrainian hierarchy."

Under existing conditions, a Ukrainian patriarch could not carry out his office in his home territory, where the Church is outlawed and from which Cardinal Slipyi was himself in exile. Historically, the Ukrainian Rite never had a patriarch.

Pastorally, the Pope observed: "We must . . . carefully consider the possible consequences for Ukrainian Catholics who, still compelled to silence because of fidelity to their faith, live in regions where at present the lawfulness of the Ukrainian Church is not recognized. . . . Would the burden borne by these outstandingly faithful Christians not be made heavier still if a new patriarchate were publicly created in foreign lands and were openly to assume their rights and their hopes but could not share their fate and lighten that fate by its presence?"

Disagreement

Cardinal Slipyi did not agree with the Pope's reasons for not setting up a patriarchate, nor with what he considered Vatican reticence concerning the plight of Catholics in the Ukraine.

In an address to the 26th session of the third assembly of the Synod of Bishops in the fall of 1971, he said: "Because of diplomatic negotiations, Ukrainian Catholics, who have suffered so much as martyrs and confessors, are pushed aside as inconvenient witnesses of past evils. We have become an obstacle for church diplomacy.

" 'Cardinal Slipyi does nothing for his Church,' it is being said. But what can we do? The Vatican has interceded for Latin Catholics, but has kept silent about our six million Ukrainian faithful who are suffering for their faith."

His complaints were the first public reference made by him to conditions in the Ukraine since his release by Soviet authorities in 1963.

Vatican sources said the Cardinal's long silence indicated that Pope Paul had asked him to refrain from commenting on the situation in order to ease negotiations with the USSR and other Communist regimes.

Pastoral Letter

In support of their plea for a patriarchate, 16 Ukrainian Catholic bishops convened their fifth archiepiscopal synod Oct. 30 to Nov. 5, 1971, in Rome and issued a joint pastoral letter which recalled the Brest-Litovsk Union of the Ukrainian Church with the Apostolic See in 1596.

Their letter said that the Union "constituted the restoration of the original Christianity in the lands of the Ukraine. . . . Our

Church found itself again at the sumptuous spring-well of Christ's Church sprouting from Peter's Rock, yet retaining all the grandeur and beauty of our own Ukrainian Rite and order. The Union was not only meant to become a basis for the establishment of a Ukrainian patriarchate within Christ's Church, but it was intended to serve as a center of Eastern Catholicism for the entire Slavic East."

The letter called on all Ukrainian Catholics to a renewal in the spirit of faith and trust in God, and to continued work in unity and love for the benefit of their souls under the leadership of their Major Archbishop, Cardinal Slipyi. It assured them that the denial of a patriarchate was merely temporary and urged them to press for the elevation of the Cardinal to a patriarchate.

The bishops protested strongly against conditions of repression affecting all religious communities in the Ukraine and appealed to the Church and governments for action to end religious discrimination and persecution there.

Ukrainian Holy Days

As of Jan. 1, 1972, the obligatory holy days for Catholics of the Ukrainian Archdiocese of Philadelphia were: the Circumcision, Epiphany, the Annunciation, Easter, the Ascension, Pentecost, the Dormition (Assumption) of Mary, the Immaculate Conception, Christmas, and all Sundays.

The number of obligatory feasts was reduced "in an attempt to make the Ukrainian Catholic Church more meaningful and accessible," according to Archbishop Ambrose Senyshyn. "New social and economic conditions, work and life-styles of the faithful and . . . dispensations already in force" dictated the need for change, he said.

The shortened list was in line with regulations of the Ukrainian Archiepiscopal Synod and had the approval of the Holy See.

Melkite Convention

A request for permission to have married priests, the establishment of a diocesan pastoral council and a reaffirmation of traditional beliefs were the principal items of business conducted by clergy and lay delegates at the 13th annual convention of Melkite-Rite Catholics in July, 1972.

• Delegates voted to ask the Vatican to reverse a 1929 directive against the ordination of married men belonging to the rite in this country. The resolution pointed out that married men are regularly ordained in the rite in other countries, in line with an Eastern tradition which one delegate said "goes back almost to apostolic times." At the same time, it was clearly stated in the resolution that members of the rite have the "highest esteem" for

the celibate priesthood and their unmarried priests.

• The delegates, who included elected lay persons for the first time, formed a pastoral council for the 25-parish diocese of some 50,000 members headquartered in Boston. Council members included six elected and two appointed lay persons, three elected and two appointed priests, and officials of the diocese (exarchate).

In connection with this council, the delegates resolved: "We . . . subscribe to the establishment and effective implementation of a diocesan pastoral council for the sake of the work of evangelization, and deem the council to be most fit and advisable, for only through the close collaboration of clergy and people will our Church grow and blossom on this continent."

• The convention "willingly and gratefully" reaffirmed traditional beliefs concerning the divinity of Christ, the Trinity and Mary, by endorsing the declaration on these subjects issued by the Congregation for the Doctrine of the Faith in February, 1972. (See separate entry for text of the declaration.)

Maronite Diocese

St. Maron's Diocese of Detroit-USA was formally established June 4, 1972, with ceremonies which included the installation of the first Bishop, Francis M. Zayek, by Archbishop Luigi Raimondi, apostolic delegate to the United States. Creation of the diocese, to serve some 150,000 Maronites in more than 40 parishes in the Midwest, New England and along the Atlantic coast, was announced by Pope Paul Mar. 25.

Ninety per cent of nearly two million Maronite Catholics are of Lebanese descent.

Romanians Want Bishop

Delegates attending the annual convention of the Association of Romanian Catholics in America late in June, 1972, voted unanimously to ask "competent church authorities (for) a bishop of our own whose presence among us might provide the source of identity and cohesiveness which could preserve us as a Church." The resolution said that this request was "in complete accord with the thinking of the (Second Vatican) Council Fathers as expressed in the *Decree on Eastern Catholic Churches.*"

At the time of the convention, Romanian (Byzantine-Rite) Catholics had no bishop of their own in this country and were under the supervision of Roman-Rite bishops in about eight dioceses. Several months after the convention, the Holy See appointed an apostolic visitor for them.

In other actions, the Aurora (Ill.) convention condemned abortion and euthanasia "as a vicious gospel insidiously attacking the most sacred of all human rights: the right to life itself."

SEPARATED EASTERN CHURCHES

Orthodox

Orthodox Churches, the largest and most widespread of the separated Eastern Churches, have much in common with their Eastern Catholic counterparts, including many matters of faith and morals, general discipline, valid orders and sacraments, and liturgy. One important difference is their acceptance of only the first seven ecumenical councils. Another is their rejection of any single supreme head of the Church. They do not acknowledge and hold communion with the pope.

Like their Catholic counterparts, Orthodox Churches are organized in jurisdictions under patriarchs. The patriarchs are the heads of approximately 15 autocephalic and several other autonomous jurisdictions organized along lines of nationality and/or language.

The Ecumenical Patriarch of Constantinople, Dimitrios I, has the primacy of honor among his equal patriarchs but his actual jurisdiction is limited to his own patriarchate. As the spiritual head of worldwide Orthodoxy, he keeps the book of the Holy Canons of the Autocephalous Churches, in which recognized Orthodox Churches are registered, and has the right to call Pan-Orthodox assemblies.

The definitive Orthodox break with Rome dates from 1054.

Top-level relations between the Churches have improved in recent years through the efforts of former Ecumenical Patriarch Athenagoras I, John XXIII and Paul VI. Pope Paul met with the Patriarch three times before the latter's death in 1972. The most significant action of both spiritual leaders was their mutual nullification of excommunications imposed by the two Churches on each other in 1054.

The largest Orthodox body in the western hemisphere is the Greek Orthodox Archdiocese of North and South America headed by Archbishop Iakovos, with an estimated membership of some 1.5 million. The second largest is the Orthodox Church of America, with approximately 850,000 members; it was given independent status by the Patriarchate of Moscow May 18, 1970, against the will of Athenagoras I who refused to register it in the book of the Holy Canons of Autocephalous Churches. An additional 650,000 or more Orthodox belong to smaller national and language jurisdictions.

Heads of Orthodox jurisdictions in this hemisphere hold membership in the Standing Conference of Canonical Orthodox Bishops in the Americas.

Jurisdictions

The principal jurisdictions of the Greek, Russian and other Orthodox Churches are as follows.

Greek: Patriarchate of Constantinople, with jurisdiction in Turkey, Crete, the Dodecanese, Western Europe, the Americas, Australia; Dimitrios I is Ecumenical Patriarch.

Patriarchate of Alexandria, with jurisdiction in Egypt and the rest of Africa; there is also a native African Orthodox Church in Kenya and Uganda.

Patriarchate of Antioch (Melkites or Syrian Orthodox), with jurisdiction in Syria, Lebanon, Iraq, Australasia, the Americas; Syrian or Arabic, in place of Greek, is the liturgical language.

Patriarchate of Jerusalem, with jurisdiction in Israel and Jordan.

Churches of Greece, Cyprus and Sinai are autocephalic but maintain relations with their fellow Orthodox.

Russia: Patriarchate of Moscow with jurisdiction centered in the Soviet Union.

Other: Patriarchate of Serbia, with jurisdiction in Yugoslavia, Western Europe, the Americas, Australasia.

Patriarchates of Rumania and Bulgaria.

Katholikate of Georgia, the Soviet Union.

Byelorussians and Ukrainian Byzantines.

Churches of Albania, China, Czechoslovakia, Estonia, Finland, Hungary, Japan, Latvia, Lithuania, Poland.

Other minor communities in various places; e.g., Korea, the US, Carpatho-Russia.

The Division of Archives and Statistics of the Eastern Orthodox World Foundation reported a 1970 estimate of more than 200 million Orthodox Church members throughout the world. Other sources estimate the total to be approximately 125 million.

Nestorians, Monophysites

Unlike the majority of Eastern Christian Churches, several bodies do not acknowledge all of the first seven ecumenical councils. Nestorians acknowledge only the first two councils; they do not accept the doctrinal definition of the Council of Ephesus concerning Mary as the Mother of God. Monophysite Armenians, Syrians, Copts, Ethiopians and Jacobites acknowledge only the first three councils; they do not accept the doctrinal definition of the Council of Chalcedon concerning the two natures in Christ.

The Armenian Church has communicants in the Soviet Union, the Middle and Far East, the Americas.

The Coptic Church has communicants in Egypt and elsewhere.

The Ethiopian or Abyssinian Church has communicants in Africa, the Middle East, the Americas, India.

The Jacobite Church (West Syrians) has communicants in the Middle East, the Americas, India.

Nestorians (Assyrians) are scattered throughout the world.

It is estimated that there are approximately

10 million or more members of these other Eastern Churches throughout the world. For various reasons, a more accurate determination is not possible.

Conference of Orthodox Bishops

Archbishop Iakovos, primate of the Greek Orthodox Archdiocese of North and South America was reelected unanimously, in December, 1971, chairman of the Standing Conference of Canonical Orthodox Bishops in the Americas. He was also chosen to head a reconstituted ecumenical commission.

Other conference officers elected were: Bishop John Martin of the Carpatho-Russian Orthodox Greek Catholic Church, vice chairman; Father Robert G. Stephanopoulos, executive secretary; Bishop Andrey of the Ukrainian Orthodox Church, treasurer.

The conference continued to be bothered by tensions resulting from a decision of the Russian Orthodox Greek Catholic Church in America to claim and get administrative independence from the Moscow patriarchate, against the wishes of the Orthodox Ecumenical Patriarch, Athenagoras I. On becoming autocephalic in April, 1970, the Church took the name Orthodox Church in America. The tensions were not eased by failure of the conference to elect an officer from the ranks of OCA clergy.

Orthodox Patriarchs

Dimitrios I: Metropolitan Archbishop Dimitrios (Papadopoulos), 58, was elected Ecumenical Patriarch by the Holy Synod of the Orthodox Church July 16, 1972, and was enthroned the following day in St. George's Church, Istanbul. He was the 269th successor to St. Andrew as Archbishop of Constantinople.

Dimitrios was born in 1914 in Istanbul. After early schooling in Therapia, he started theological studies at the age of 17, at the now closed patriarchal island seminary and monastery of Halka. He was ordained to the diaconate in 1937 and to the priesthood in 1942; was chaplain to the Greek Orthodox community in Teheran from 1945 to 1950; taught Greek and theology; was ordained a bishop in 1964. He became Metropolitan Archbishop of Imbros and Tenedos, Turkish islands near the entrance to the Dardanelles, Feb. 15, 1972.

At the time of his election, the junior Metropolitan of the patriarchate had the reputation of a pastoral man and a moderately progressive theologian. His candidacy, one of three approved by the Turkish government, had been favored by Metropolitan Meliton of Chalcedon, influential dean of the Holy Synod, who had been ruled out of the running by the government.

As Patriarch, Dimitrios is the spiritual leader of Orthodox Christians throughout the world and holds the first place of honor, but not of jurisdiction, among his fellow bishops. His direct administration is over the Church of Istanbul and a number of Orthodox dioceses in North and South America, Western Europe, and Pacific territories.

Pope Paul congratulated Dimitrios I on his election and restated in a special message the pledge of the Roman Catholic Church to seek unity with Eastern Orthodoxy. He told the Patriarch that he would "always find the Bishop of Rome to be an affectionate brother" and one who wished to take further steps toward "the day, so strongly desired by your great predecessor, when our fully recovered unity shall be sealed."

The Pope was represented at the Patriarch's installation by Archbishop Salvatore Asta, pro-nuncio to Turkey, and the Rev. Pierre Duprey, undersecretary of the Vatican Secretariat for Christian Unity.

Shenuda III: Bishop Shenuda (Nazeer Gayed), 48, was chosen the 117th successor to St. Mark as Patriarch of the Coptic Orthodox Church and Pope of Alexandria Oct. 31, 1971. He was crowned Pope Shenuda III Nov. 14.

The Patriarch, a graduate of Cairo University, served with Egyptian forces in the war with Israel in 1948. After resigning his reserve-officer commission, he spent several years in the early '50s as a hermit in the Surian Monastery in the Western Desert. Before being selected to head the Coptic Church, he was a religious educator and secretary to his predecessor, Kyrollos.

PATRIARCH ATHENAGORAS I

Greek Orthodox Ecumenical Patriarch Athenagoras I, 86, the spiritual leader of worldwide Orthodoxy and an advocate of cordial relations with other churches, died of kidney failure July 6, 1972, in the Balikli Greek Orthodox hospital in Istanbul.

Son of the physician of the village of Vassilikon in the Province of Epirus, he began studies for the priesthood at the age of 18 at the Holy Trinity Theological Seminary on the island of Halki. He was ordained a deacon in 1910, at which time he changed his given name, Aristokles Spirou, to Athenagoras ("One who speaks in Athens"). He then spent a year at the monastery of Mt. Athos and was ordained to the priesthood in 1911.

He was secretary to the archbishop of Athens for several years after World War I. He was ordained bishop of Corfu in 1922 and served in that see for eight years before being designated Archbishop and Metropolitan of the Greek Orthodox Archdiocese of North and South America in 1930. He was installed in 1931 and held this office until he was elected archbishop of Constantinople and Ecumenical Patriarch by a 17-member synod in 1948.

As head of the Orthodox Church in the western hemisphere, he conducted a wide-ranging pastoral tour of the churches of his archdiocese; made efforts to ease relations between rival factions; and established a seminary for the training of priests, to avoid unnecessary importation of priests from Greece. He became an American citizen in 1938.

Ten years later he was elected Patriarch and spiritual leader of some 125 million Orthodox throughout the world. From the start, his patriarchate had an ecumenical thrust; it eventually became effective in the improvement of relations with other Christian Churches, despite the opposition of some of his fellow bishops. He led the Orthodox Church into the World Council of Churches late in the 40's. He won the approval of his colleagues for ecumenical overtures to the Roman Catholic Church, which resulted in three meetings with Pope Paul VI in 1964 and 1967, the mutual nullification of excommunications imposed by the two Churches against each other in 1054, and a whole new climate in relations between Catholics and Orthodox.

In his own Church, Athenagoras sought to ease internal controversies arising from nationalistic and other causes, but he was not always successful. One case in point concerned the action of the Moscow patriarchate in granting autonomy to the (Russian) Orthodox Church of America in 1970. Athenagoras refused to recognize it as canonical and declined to register OCA in the book of the Holy Canons of the Autocephalous Churches.

Like Pope John XXIII, who died before the end of the Second Vatican Council he had convoked, Athenagoras died in the midst of unfinished business—a series of Pan-Orthodox assemblies pointing in the direction of a Great Orthodox Council, the first in more than 1,000 years. He left this legacy of preparation to his successor, Dimitrios I.

Athenagoras also left him a legacy of uneasy relations with the Turkish government.

EASTERN ECUMENISM

The Second Vatican Council, in the *Decree on Eastern Catholic Churches,* pointed out the special role they have to play "in promoting the unity *of all Christians, particularly Easterners." The document also stated in part:*

"The Eastern Churches in communion with the Apostolic See of Rome have a special role to play in promoting the unity of all Christians, particularly Easterners, according to the principles of this sacred Synod's *Decree on Ecumenism* first of all by prayer, then by the example of their lives, by religious fidelity to ancient Eastern traditions, by greater mutual knowledge, by collaboration, and by a brotherly regard for objects and attitudes" (No. 24).

"If any separated Eastern Christian should, under the guidance of grace of the Holy Spirit, join himself to Catholic unity, no more should be required of him than what a simple profession of the Catholic faith demands. A valid priesthood is preserved among Eastern clerics. Hence, upon joining themselves to the unity of the Catholic Church, Eastern clerics are permitted to exercise the orders they possess, in accordance with the regulations established by the competent authority" (No. 25).

"Divine Law forbids any common worship (*communicatio in sacris*) which would damage the unity of the Church, or involve formal acceptance of falsehood or the danger of deviation in the faith, of scandal, or of indifferentism. At the same time, pastoral experience clearly shows that with respect to our Eastern brethren there should and can be taken into consideration various circumstances affecting individuals, wherein the unity of the Church is not jeopardized nor are intolerable risks involved, but in which salvation itself and the spiritual profit of souls are urgently at issue.

"Hence, in view of special circumstances of time, place, and personage, the Catholic Church has often adopted and now adopts a milder policy, offering to all the means of salvation and an example of charity among Christians through participation in the sacraments and in other sacred functions and objects. With these considerations in mind, and 'lest because of the harshness of our judgment we prove an obstacle to those seeking salvation,' and in order to promote closer union with the Eastern Churches separated from us, this sacred Synod lays down the following policy:

"In view of the principles recalled above, Eastern Christians who are separated in good faith from the Catholic Church, if they ask of their own accord and have the right dispositions, may be granted the sacraments of penance, the Eucharist, and the anointing of the sick. Furthermore, Catholics may ask for these same sacraments from those non-Catholic ministers whose Churches possess valid sacraments, as often as necessity or a genuine spiritual benefit recommends such a course of action, and when access to a Catholic priest is physically or morally impossible" (Nos. 26, 27).

"Again, in view of these very same principles, Catholics may for a just cause join with their separated Eastern brethren in sacred functions, things, and places" (No. 28).

"This more lenient policy with regard to common worship involving Catholics and their brethren of the separated Eastern Churches is entrusted to the care and execution of the local Ordinaries so that, by taking counsel among themselves and, if circumstances warrant, after consultation also with the Ordinaries of the separated Churches, they may govern relations between Christians by timely and effective rules and regulations" (No. 29).

Men, Doctrines, Churches of the Reformation

Some of the leading figures, doctrines and churches of the Reformation are covered below. A companion article covers Major Protestant Churches in the United States.

John Wycliff (c. 1320-1384): English priest and scholar who advanced one of the leading Reformation ideas nearly 200 years before Martin Luther — that the Bible alone is the sufficient rule of faith — but had only an indirect influence on the 16th century Reformers. Supporting belief in an inward and practical religion, he denied the divinely commissioned authority of the pope and bishops of the Church; he also denied the Real Presence of Christ in the Holy Eucharist, and wrote against the sacrament of penance and the doctrine of indulgences. Nearly 20 of his propositions were condemned by Gregory XI in 1377; his writings were proscribed more extensively by the Council of Constance in 1415. His influence was strongest in Bohemia and Central Europe.

John Hus (c. 1369-1415): A Bohemian priest and preacher of reform who authored 30 propositions condemned by the Council of Constance. Excommunicated in 1411 or 1412, he was burned at the stake in 1415. His principal errors concerned the nature of the Church and the origin of papal authority. He spread some of the ideas of Wycliff but did not subscribe to his views regarding faith alone as the condition for justification and salvation, the sole sufficiency of Scripture as the rule of faith, the Real Presence of Christ in the Eucharist, and the sacramental system. In 1457 some of his followers founded the Church of the Brotherhood which later became known as the United Brethren or Moravian Church and is considered the earliest independent Protestant body.

Martin Luther (1483-1546): An Augustinian friar, the key figure in the Reformation. In 1517, as a special indulgence was being preached in Germany, and in view of needed reforms within the Church, he published at Wittenberg 95 theses concerning matters of Catholic belief and practice. Leo X condemned 41 statements from Luther's writings in 1520. Luther, refusing to recant, was excommunicated the following year. His teachings strongly influenced subsequent Lutheran theology, although the norm of Lutheran doctrine is not Luther's teaching alone but the Book of Concord (1580), which consists of the three Catholic creeds, plus seven particular symbols or confessions of faith, of which only three are by Luther.

Luther's doctrine included the following:

The sin of Adam, which corrupted human nature radically (but not substantially), has affected every aspect of man's being. Although God holds man responsible for his moral actions, unregenerated man cannot by his innate powers, without the help of divine grace, make himself acceptable to God. Justification, understood as the forgiveness of sins, is by grace for Christ's sake through faith. Faith involves not merely intellectual assent but an act of confidence by the will. Good works are indispensably necessary concomitants of faith, but do not merit salvation. Of the sacraments, Luther retained baptism, penance and the Holy Communion as effective vehicles of the grace of the Holy Spirit; he held that in the Holy Communion the consecrated bread and wine are the Body and Blood of Christ. The rule of faith is the divine revelation in the Sacred Scriptures. He rejected purgatory, indulgences and the invocation of the saints, and held that prayers for the dead have no efficacy.

Lutheran tenets not in agreement with Catholic doctrine were condemned by the Council of Trent.

Anabaptism: Originated in Saxony in the first quarter of the 16th century and spread rapidly through southern Germany. Its doctrine included several key Lutheran tenets but was not regarded with favor by Luther, Calvin or Zwingli. Anabaptists believed that baptism is for adults only and that infant baptism is invalid. Their doctrine of the Inner Light, concerning the direct influence of the Holy Spirit on the believer, implied rejection of Catholic doctrine concerning the sacraments and the nature of the Church. Eighteen articles of faith were formulated in 1632 in Holland. Mennonites are Anabaptists.

Ulrich Zwingli (1484-1531): A priest who triggered the Reformation in Switzerland with a series of New Testament lectures in 1519, later disputations and by other actions. He held the Gospel to be the only basis of truth; rejected the Mass (which he suppressed in 1525 at Zurich), penance and other sacraments; denied papal primacy and doctrine concerning purgatory and the invocation of saints; rejected celibacy, monasticism and many traditional practices of piety. His symbolic view of the Eucharist, which was at odds with Catholic doctrine, caused an irreconcilable controversy with Luther and his followers. Zwingli was killed in a battle between the forces of Protestant and Catholic cantons in Switzerland.

John Calvin (1509-1564): French leader of the Reformation in Switzerland, whose key tenet was absolute predestination of some persons to heaven and others to hell. He rejected Catholic doctrine in 1533 after becoming convinced of a personal mission to reform the Church. In 1536 he published the first edition of *Institutes of the Christian Religion*, a systematic exposition of his doctrine which became the classic textbook of Reformed — as distinguished from Lutheran — theology. To Luther's principal theses — regarding Scripture as the sole rule of faith, the radical corruption of human nature, and justification by faith alone — he added absolute predestination, certitude of salvation for the elect, and the incapability of the elect to lose grace. His Eucharistic theory, which failed to mediate the Zwingli-Luther controversy, was at odds with Catholic doctrine. From 1555 until his death Calvin was the virtual dictator of Geneva, the capital of the non-Lutheran Reformation in Europe.

Arminianism: A modification of the rigid predestinationism of Calvin, set forth by Jacob Arminius (1560-1609) and formally stated in the *Remonstrance* of 1610. Arminianism influenced some Calvinist bodies.

Unitarianism: A 16th century doctrine which rejected the Trinity and the divinity of Christ in favor of a uni-personal God. It claimed scriptural support for a long time but became generally rationalistic with respect to "revealed" doctrine as well as in ethics and its world-view. One of its principal early proponents was Faustus Socinus (1539-1604), a leader of the Polish Brethren.

A variety of communions developed in England in the Reformation and post-Reformation periods.

Anglican Communion: This communion, which regards itself as the same apostolic Church as that which was established by early Christians in England, derived not from Reformation influences but from the renunciation of papal jurisdiction by Henry VIII (1491-1547). His Act of Supremacy in 1534 called Christ's Church an assembly of local churches subject to the prince, who was vested with fullness of authority and jurisdiction. In spite of Henry's denial of papal authority, this Act did not reject substantially other principal articles of faith. Notable changes, proposed and adopted for the reformation of the church, took place in the subsequent reigns of James VI and Elizabeth, with respect to such matters as Scripture as the rule of faith, the sacraments, the nature of the Mass, and the constitution of the hierarchy.

The Anglican Communion is called Episcopal because its prelates have the title and function of bishops. (See Anglican Orders.)

Puritans: Extremists who sought church reform along Calvinist lines in severe simplicity. (Use of the term was generally discontinued after 1660.)

Presbyterians: Basically Calvinistic, called Presbyterian because church polity centers around assemblies of presbyters or elders. John Knox (c. 1513-1572) established the church in Scotland.

Congregationalists: Evangelical in spirit and seeking a return to forms of the primitive church, they uphold individual freedom in religious matters, do not require the acceptance of a creed as a condition for communion, and regard each congregation as autonomous. Robert Browne influenced the beginnings of Congregationalism.

Quakers: Their key belief is in internal divine illumination, the inner light of the living Christ, as the only source of truth and inspiration. George Fox (1624-1691) was one of their leaders in England. Called the Society of Friends, the Quakers are noted for their pacifism.

Baptists: So called because of their doctrine concerning baptism. They reject infant baptism and consider only baptism by immersion as valid. Leaders in the formation of the church were John Smyth (d. 1612) in England and Roger Williams (d. 1683) in America.

Methodists: A group who broke away from the Anglican Communion under the leadership of John Wesley (1703-1791), although some Anglican beliefs were retained. Doctrines include the witness of the Spirit to the individual and personal assurance of salvation. Wesleyan Methodists do not subscribe to some of the more rigid Calvinistic tenets held by other Methodists.

Universalism: A product of 18th-century liberal Protestantism in England. The doctrine is not Trinitarian and includes a tenet that all men will ultimately be saved.

MAJOR PROTESTANT CHURCHES IN THE UNITED STATES

There are more than 250 Protestant church bodies in the United States.

The majority of US Protestants belong to the following denominations: Baptist, Methodist, Lutheran, Presbyterian, Protestant Episcopal, the United Church of Christ, the Christian Church (Disciples of Christ), Holiness Sects.

Baptist Churches
(Courtesy of Dr. Frank A. Sharp, Department of Public Interpretation, American Baptist Churches in the U.S.A.)

Baptist churches, comprising the largest of all American Protestant denominations, were first established by John Smyth near the beginning of the 17th century in England. The first Baptist church in America was founded at Providence by Roger Williams in 1639.

Largest of the nearly 30 Baptist bodies in the US are:

The Southern Baptist Convention, 460 James Robertson Parkway, Nashville, Tenn. 37219, with 11.3 million members;

The National Baptist Convention, U.S.A., Inc., 915 Spain St., Baton Rouge, La. 70802, with 6.4 million members;

The National Baptist Convention of America, 1724 Jefferson St., Jacksonville, Fla. 32206, with 2.6 million members.

The American Baptist Churches in the U.S.A., Valley Forge, Pa. 19481, with 1.3 million members.

The total number of US Baptists is more than 27 million.

Proper to Baptists is their doctrine on baptism. Called an "ordinance of Christ" rather than a sacrament, baptism by immersion is a sign that one has experienced and decided in favor of the salvation offered by Christ. It is administered only to persons who are capable of the experience of faith, which is the sole criterion of salvation and which involves the obligation to a life of virtue. Baptism is not administered to infants.

Baptists do not have a formal creed but generally subscribe to two professions of faith formulated in 1689 and 1832 and are in general agreement with classical Protestant theology regarding Scripture as the sole rule of faith, original sin, justification through faith in Christ, and the nature of the Church. Their local churches are autonomous.

Worship services differ in form from one congregation to another. Usual elements are the reading of Scripture, a sermon, hymns, vocal and silent prayer. The Lord's Supper, called an "ordinance of Christ," is celebrated at various intervals.

Methodist Churches

(Courtesy of the Librarian, Commission on Archives and History, and Dr. A. Walz, Statistician.)

Methodism derived from the teaching of John Wesley, an Anglican minister who experienced a new conversion to Christ in 1738. The first self-supporting Methodist congregation was established in London two years later. By the end of the 18th century Methodism was strongly rooted in America.

Methodists, with approximately 14 million members, comprise the second largest Protestant denomination in the US. The United Methodist Church, formed in a merger of the Methodist Church and the Evangelical United Brethren Church in 1968, is the largest of more than 20 bodies, with 10.5 million members; its principal agencies are located in New York, Evanston, Ill., Nashville, Tenn., Washington, D.C., Dayton, O., and Lake Junaluska, N.C. The second largest body, with some 1.5 million communicants, is the African Methodist Episcopal Church; its headquarters are located at 1724 Villa Place, Nashville, Tenn.

Methodism, although it has a base in Calvinistic theology, rejects absolute predestination and maintains that Christ offers grace freely to all men, not just to a select elite. Wesley's distinctive doctrine was the "witness of the Spirit" to the individual soul and personal assurance of salvation. He also emphasized the central themes of conversion and holiness. Methodists are in general agreement with classical Protestant theology regarding

Scripture as the sole rule of faith, original sin, justification through faith in Christ, the nature of the Church, and the sacraments of baptism and the Lord's Supper. Church polity is structured along episcopal, presbyterian and congregational lines. Congregations are free to choose various forms of worship services, which generally follow those in the Book of Common Prayer. Elements of a typical service are readings from Scripture, a sermon, prayers and hymns.

Lutheran Churches

(Courtesy of Division of Public Relations, Lutheran Council in the USA, 315 Park Ave., South, New York, N.Y. 10010.)

The actual origin of Lutheranism is generally traced to Oct. 31, 1517, when Martin Luther published a list of 95 theses and tacked them to the door of the church at Wittenberg. This act signaled the beginning of the Reformation in Germany. While the Lutheran Reformers did not intend to establish a new denomination, the subsequent excommunication of Luther and his followers completed the shattering of Western religious unity. The separate institutional existence of the Lutheran Church was necessitated in 1530 when, at the Diet of Augsburg, the Holy Roman Emperor, Charles V, rejected the Augsburg Confession of the Lutherans.

During the 17th century, Lutheranism came to this hemisphere chiefly from its strongholds in Northern and Central Europe. Its membership increased greatly as a result of the immigrations of the 19th century. Lutherans now form the third largest Protestant denomination in the United States, with more than 9.2 million members.

The three largest Lutheran bodies in the US are:

The Lutheran Church in America, 231 Madison Ave., New York, N.Y. 10016, with 3.2 million members. This body was formed June 28, 1962, by consolidation of the American Evangelical Lutheran Church, the Augustana Evangelical Lutheran Church, the Finnish Evangelical Lutheran Church, and the United Lutheran Church in America.

The Lutheran Church-Missouri Synod, 210 N. Broadway, St. Louis, Mo., with 2.8 million members. This body was formed in 1847.

The American Lutheran Church, 422 S. 5th St., Minneapolis, Minn., with 2.5 million members. This body was formed in April, 1960, by a merger of the American Lutheran Church, the Evangelical Lutheran Church, and the United Evangelical Lutheran Church.

These three bodies participate in the Lutheran Council in the U.S.A., a cooperative agency for theological studies and Christian service in missions, welfare, education and related fields. The LC/USA, formed in 1966, is headquartered in New York City.

The normative statement of Lutheran beliefs is found in the *Book of Concord* (1580).

All the major Lutheran bodies in this country subscribe to this collection of symbolical documents, which consists of the three ancient Creeds (Apostles', Nicene and Athanasian), the *Augsburg Confession* (1530), the *Apology of the Augsburg Confession* (1531), the *Smalcald Articles* (1536-1538), the *Treatise on the Authority and Primacy of the Pope* (1537), the *Large and Small Catechisms* (1529), and the *Formula of Concord* (1577), plus the Preface to the *Book of Concord.*

That we "receive forgiveness of sins and become righteous before God by grace, for Christ's sake, through faith," is the central article of faith in the Lutheran confessions. Lutherans believe in two sacraments, baptism and the Holy Eucharist, both of which are visible means of grace. Baptism is necessary for salvation (*Augsburg Confession,* II and IX), and through it a person is born again to newness of life. In the Holy Eucharist, the consecrated bread and wine are the Body and the Blood of Christ (*Smalcald Article* 3, Part Two, VI). The sacraments are "signs and testimonies of God's will toward us for the purpose of awakening and strengthening our faith" (*Augsburg Confession,* XIII). Although private confession is not obligatory, it is regarded as highly beneficial (*Apology,* XIII, 4). The formula reads: "According to the command of our Lord Jesus Christ, I forgive you all your sins in the name of the Father and of the Son and of the Holy Ghost" (*Small Catechism,* V. 28). Through the rite of confirmation, which is not regarded as a sacrament, children and baptized converts are admitted to adult membership in the Lutheran Church.

In the United States, church polity is largely congregation-centered, although national bodies, synods and conferences exercise differing degrees of influence and control over member congregations.

Although forms of worship and ceremonial are not wholly uniform, the commonly followed order of the service consists of Introit, Kyrie, Gloria, collect, (Old Testament lesson), epistle, gospel, creed, sermon, offertory, Great Intercession, preface and Sanctus, consecration, Pax Agnus, distribution of Holy Communion, post communion, Benedicamus and blessing, with interspersed hymns. When Holy Communion is not celebrated, a blessing after the Great Intercession ends the service. Matins and Vespers are used occasionally. The historic vestments are worn to a varying extent. Lutherans follow the church year. Music has always occupied a prominent place in Lutheran liturgical worship and successive generations have built up a rich tradition of church music and hymnody.

Presbyterian Churches

Presbyterians are so called because of their type of church government, by presbyters or elders.

Presbyterianism was founded by John Knox about the middle of the 16th century in Scotland, and by others in Switzerland, France, Holland and other countries, on theological positions laid down by John Calvin. Its doctrine generally includes a modification of the absolute predestination characteristic of rigid Calvinism.

Presbyterianism spread widely in this country in the latter part of the 18th century and afterwards. Presently, it has approximately 4.5 million communicants in nine bodies. The largest of these are:

The United Presbyterian Church in the U.S.A., Witherspoon Building, Philadelphia, Pa. 19107, with 3 million members. This body was formed May 28, 1958, by a merger of the Presbyterian Church in the U.S.A and the United Presbyterian Church of North America.

The Presbyterian Church in the United States, 341 Ponce de Leon Boulevard N.E., Atlanta, Ga. 30308, with about 950,000 members.

In Presbyterian doctrine, baptism and the Lord's Supper, viewed as seals of the covenant of grace, are regarded as sacraments. Baptism, which is not necessary for salvation, is conferred on infants and adults. The Lord's Supper is celebrated as a memorial of the Sacrifice of Christ.

The Church is twofold, being invisible and also visible; it consists of all of the elect and all those Christians who are united in Christ as their immediate head.

Presbyterians are in general agreement with classical Protestant theology regarding Scripture as the sole rule of faith, original sin, and justification through faith in Christ.

Presbyterian churches are organized according to elements of episcopalism and congregationalism. Elders are chosen to govern the congregations, but on higher levels there are presbyteries, synods and a general assembly with various degrees of authority over local bodies.

Worship services, simple and dignified, include sermons, prayer, reading of the Scriptures and hymns. The Lord's Supper is celebrated at intervals.

Doctrinal developments of the previous several years reached a high point in May, 1967, when the General Assembly of the United Presbyterian Church voted approval of a new, contemporary confession of faith to supplement the historic Westminster Confession. The new confession emphasizes the commitment of the Church and its members to reconcilatory and apostolic works in society.

Protestant Episcopal Church

(Courtesy of Charles M. Guilbert, Executive Officer of the General Convention and Custodian of the Standard Book of Common Prayer.)

The Protestant Episcopal Church, also officially known as the Episcopal Church, regards itself as the same apostolic church as that which was established by early Christians in England. It was established in this country during the Revolutionary period. Its constitution and Prayer Book were adopted at a general convention held in 1789. It has approximately 3.6 million members.

Offices of the US executive council are located at 815 Second Ave., New York, N.Y. 10017.

This church, which belongs to the Anglican Communion, subscribes to the branch theory of the Church of Christ, holding that it consists of the Church of Rome, the Eastern Orthodox Church, and the Anglican Communion, and that the heads of these churches are of equal rank in authority.

There is considerable variety in Protestant Episcopal beliefs and practices. Official statements of belief and practice are found in the Apostles' Creed, the Nicene Creed and the Book of Common Prayer, but interpretation is not uniform. Scripture has primary importance with respect to the rule of faith, and some authority is attached to tradition.

All seven sacraments, veneration of the saints, and a great many other Catholic teachings are accepted by some Episcopalians but contested by others.

An episcopal system of church government prevails, but clergymen of lower rank and lay persons also have an active voice in ecclesiastical affairs. The levels of government are the general convention, the executive council, territorial provinces and dioceses, and local parishes. At the parish level, the congregation has the right to select its own rector or pastor.

Liturgical worship is according to the Book of Common Prayer or authorized experimental forms, but ceremonial practices correspond with the doctrinal positions of the various congregations and range from a ceremony similar to the Roman Mass to services of a less elaborate character.

United Church of Christ

(Courtesy of Dorothea H. Lindsey, Associate Director, Office of Communication, United Church of Christ.)

The 1,960,608-member United Church of Christ was formed in 1957 by a union of the Congregational Christian and the Evangelical and Reformed Churches. The former was originally established by the Pilgrims and the Puritans of the Massachusetts Bay Colony, while the latter was founded in Pennsylvania in the early 1700's by settlers from Central Europe. The denomination has 6,727 congregations throughout the United States.

Its headquarters are located at 297 Park Ave. South, New York, N.Y. 10010.

Its statement of faith recognizes Jesus Christ as "our crucified and risen Lord (who) shared our common lot, conquering sin and death and reconciling the world to himself." It believes in the life after death, and the fact

that God "judges men and nations by his righteous will declared through prophets and apostles."

The United Church further believes that Christ calls its members to share in his baptism "and eat at his table, to join him in his passion and victory." Ideally, according to its Lord's Day Service, Communion is to be celebrated weekly. Like other Calvinistic bodies, it believes that Christ is spiritually present in the sacrament.

The United Church is governed along congregational lines, and each local church is autonomous. However, the pronouncements of its biennial general synod are taken with great seriousness by congregations. Between synods, a 42-member executive council oversees the work of the church.

Christian Church (Disciples of Christ)

(Courtesy of Robert L. Friedly, Executive Director, Office of Communication.)

The Christian Church (Disciples of Christ) originated early in the 1800's from two movements against rigid denominationalism led by Presbyterians Thomas and Alexander Campbell in western Pennsylvania and Barton W. Stone in Kentucky. The two movements developed separately for about 25 years before being merged in 1832.

The church, which identifies itself with the Protestant mainstream, now has approximately 1.4 million members in the US and Canada. The greatest concentration of members in the US is located roughly along the old frontier line, in an arc sweeping from Ohio and Kentucky through the Midwest and down into Oklahoma and Texas.

The general offices of the church are located at 222 South Downey Ave., Box 1986, Indianapolis, Ind. 46206.

The church's persistent concern for Christian unity is based on a conviction expressed in a basic document, *Declaration and Address,* dating from its founding. The document states: "The church of Christ upon earth is essentially, intentionally and constitutionally one."

The Disciples have no official doctrine or dogma. Their worship practices vary widely from more common informal services to what could almost be described as "high church" services. Membership is granted after a simple statement of belief in Jesus Christ and baptism by immersion; many congregations admit un-immersed transfers from other denominations. The Lord's Supper, generally called Communion, is always open to Christians of all persuasions. Laymen routinely preside over the Lord's Supper, which is celebrated each Sunday; they often preach and perform other pastoral functions as well. Distinction between ordained and non-ordained members is blurred somewhat because of the Disciples' emphasis on all members of the church as ministers.

The Christian Church is oriented to congregational government, and has a unique structure in which three levels of polity (general, regional and congregational) operate as equals rather than in a pyramid of authority. At the national or international level, it is governed by a general assembly which has voting representation direct from congregations as well as from 38 regions and a number of general units. It also has a 222-member general board, at least half of whose membership consists of lay persons, and a 40-member administrative committee. The chief employed official of the church is the general minister and president.

The Holiness Sects

Perfectionist and Pentecostal churches and sects have a total membership of some two million persons in the US.

These groups do not form a denomination in the strict sense of the term, since they are separate and have their own particular characteristics. Classification under a common heading is possible, however, because they all share the same general spirit and spring from a common origin. John Wesley's teaching on justification is the doctrinal thread common to all of these churches — personal holiness, realized in the life of each individual, is the key to a full Christian life. Hence the name, "Holiness Movement." Its origin is traceable to the revival movement of the 19th century.

The Perfectionist branch of this large group includes such foundations as the Church of the Nazarene, the Church of God (Anderson, Ind.), and the Pilgrim Holiness Church. On the Pentecostal side are the Assemblies of God, the numerous Churches of God, and many bodies with the word Pentecostal in their titles. There are also many other very small cults which are similar in spirit to the larger churches.

Among the fundamental Christian doctrines maintained by Holiness believers are those of the Trinity and the divinity of Christ. They accept baptism. Classical Protestantism is reflected in their beliefs regarding the effect of original sin on human nature, the nature of justification, principles of biblical interpretation, and the rejection of tradition.

Some tenets are limited to the Pentecostal and Perfectionist bodies, such as beliefs in the imminent coming of Christ for the second time and a second baptism of the Holy Spirit in which holiness is acquired. There are many different opinions regarding the nature of this holiness.

The Pentecostals hold that justification and holiness are essentially related to the events that accompanied the descent of the Holy Spirit upon the Apostles at Pentecost. Hence, speaking i tongues and other related phenomena are significant. The Perfectionist and Pentecostal churches and sects are generally organized in a congregational manner.

WORLD RELIGIOUS POPULATION

(Source: *Britannica Book of the Year, 1972.*)

Christians: 985,363,400 (North and Central America, 224,880,000; South America, 168,258,000; Europe, 407,717,700; Asia, 76,468,000; Africa, 100,692,600; Oceania, 7,347,100).

Roman Catholics: 566,771,600 (North and Central America, 128,705,000; South America, 164,527,500; Europe, 190,488,000; Asia, 46,106,000; Africa, 35,178,000; Oceania, 1,767,100). See Index, Catholic World Statistics, for Catholic population figures reported by the Vatican's Central Statistics Office.

Eastern Orthodox: 123,877,000 (North and Central America, 3,900,000; South America, 50,000; Europe, 92,927,800; Asia, 1,920,000; Africa, 25,000,000; Oceania, 80,000).

Protestants: 294,714,300 (North and Central America, 92,275,000; South America, 3,680,500; Europe, 124,302,200; Asia, 28,442,000; Africa, 40,514,600; Oceania, 5,500,000).

Jewish: 14,490,500 (North and Central America, 6,160,000; South America, 784,000; Europe, 4,390,500; Asia, 2,766,000; Africa, 310,000; Oceania, 80,000).

Muslim: 471,338,700 (North and Central America, 168,000; South America, 400,000; Europe, 24,347,200; Asia, 331,114,500; Africa, 114,784,000; Oceania, 525,000).

Zoroastrian: 125,000 (Asia).

Shinto: 60,130,000 (North and Central America, 30,000; South America, 100,000; Asia, 60,000,000).

Confucian: 304,595,000 (North and Central America, 95,000; South America, 100,000; Europe, 50,000; Asia, 304,300,000; Oceania, 50,000).

Buddhist: 301,436,000 (North and Central America, 200,000; South America, 160,000; Europe, 18,000; Asia, 301,058,000).

Hindu: 472,358,000 (North and Central America, 55,000; South America, 700,000; Europe, 180,000; Asia, 469,988,500; Africa, 1,060,000; Oceania, 375,000).

Total Religious Population: 2,661,120,100 (North and Central America, 231,603,000; South America, 170,520,000; Europe, 436,703,400; Asia, 1,597,070,000; Africa, 216,846,600; Oceania, 8,377,100).

Total Population of World: 3,552,000,000 (North and Central America, 314,000,000; South America, 186,000,000; Europe, 700,000,000; Asia, 1,988,000,000; Africa, 345,000,000; Oceania, 18,900,000).

Ecumenism

The modern ecumenical movement, which started about 1910 among Protestants and led to formation of the World Council of Churches in 1948, developed outside the mainstream of Catholic interest for many years. It has now become for Catholics as well one of the great religious facts of our time.

The magna charta of ecumenism for Catholics is a complex of several documents which include, in the first place, the *Decree on Ecumenism* promulgated by the Second Vatican Council Nov. 21, 1964. Other enactments underlying and expanding this decree are the *Dogmatic Constitution on the Church, the Decree on Eastern Catholic Churches,* and the *Pastoral Constitution on the Church in the Modern World.*

VATICAN II DECREE

The following excerpts from the *Decree on Ecumenism* cover the broad theological background and principles and indicate the thrust of the Church's commitment to ecumenism.

". . . Men who believe in Christ and have been properly baptized are brought into a certain, though imperfect, communion with the Catholic Church. Undoubtedly, the differences that exist in varying degrees between them and the Catholic Church — whether in doctrine and sometimes in discipline, or concerning the structure of the Church — do indeed create many and sometimes serious obstacles to full ecclesiastical communion. These the ecumenical movement is striving to overcome . . ." (No. 3).

Elements Common to Christians

"Moreover some, even very many, of the most significant elements or endowments which together go to build up and give life to the Church herself can exist outside the visible boundaries of the Catholic Church: the written word of God; the life of grace; faith, hope, and charity, along with other interior gifts of the Holy Spirit and visible elements. All of these, which come from Christ and lead back to Him, belong by right to the one Church of Christ" (No. 3).

[In a later passage, the decree singled out a number of elements which the Catholic Church and other churches have in common but not in complete agreement: confession of Christ as Lord and God and as mediator between God and man; belief in the Trinity; reverence for Scripture as the revealed word of God; baptism and the Lord's Supper; Christian life and worship; faith in action; concern with moral questions.]

"The brethren divided from us also carry out many of the sacred actions of the Christian religion. Undoubtedly, in ways that vary according to the condition of each Church or Community, these actions can truly engender a life of grace, and can be rightly described as capable of providing access to the community of salvation.

"It follows that these separated Churches and Communities, though we believe they suffer from defects already mentioned, have by no means been deprived of significance and importance in the mystery of salvation. For the Spirit of Christ has not refrained from using them as means of salvation which derive their efficacy from the very fullness of grace and truth entrusted to the Catholic Church" (No. 3).

Unity Lacking

"Nevertheless, our separated brethren, whether considered as individuals or as Communities and Churches, are not blessed with that unity which Jesus Christ wished to bestow on all those whom He has regenerated and vivified into one body and newness of life — that unity which the holy Scriptures and the revered tradition of the Church proclaim. For it is through Christ's Catholic Church alone, which is the all-embracing means of salvation, that the fullness of the means of salvation can be obtained. It was to the apostolic college alone, of which Peter is the head, that we believe our Lord entrusted all the blessings of the New Covenant, in order to establish on earth the one Body of Christ into which all those should be fully incorporated who already belong in any way to God's People . . ." (No. 3).

What the Movement Involves

"Today, in many parts of the world, under the inspiring grace of the Holy Spirit, multiple efforts are being expended through prayer, word, and action to attain that fullness of unity which Jesus Christ desires. This sacred Synod, therefore, exhorts all the Catholic faithful to recognize the signs of the times and to participate skillfully in the work of ecumenism.

"The 'ecumenical movement' means those activities and enterprises which, according to various needs of the Church and opportune occasions, are started and organized for the fostering of unity among Christians. These are:

• "First, every effort to eliminate words, judgments, and actions which do not respond to the condition of separated brethren with truth and fairness and so make mutual relations between them more difficult.

• "Then, 'dialogue' between competent experts from different Churches and Communities (scholarly ecumenism). . . .

• "In addition, these Communions cooperate more closely in whatever projects a Christian conscience demands for the common good (social ecumenism).

• "They also come together for common prayer, where this is permitted (spiritual ecumenism).

• "Finally, all are led to examine their own faithfulness to Christ's will for the Church and, wherever necessary, undertake with vigor the task of renewal and reform.

". . . It is evident that the work of preparing and reconciling those individuals who wish for full Catholic communion is of its nature distinct from ecumenical action. But there is no opposition between the two, since both proceed from the wondrous providence of God" (No. 4).

Primary Duty of Catholics

"In ecumenical work, Catholics must assuredly be concerned for their separated brethren, praying for them, keeping them informed about the Church, making the first approaches towards them. But their primary duty is to make an honest and careful appraisal of whatever needs to be renewed and achieved in the Catholic household itself, in order that its life may bear witness more loyally and luminously to the teachings and ordinances which have been handed down from Christ through the apostles.

". . . Every Catholic must . . . aim at Christian perfection (cf. Jas. 1:4; Rom. 12:1-2) and, each according to his station, play his part so that the Church . . . may daily be more purified and renewed, against the day when Christ will present her to Himself in all her glory, without spot or wrinkle (cf. Eph. 5:27).

". . . Catholics must joyfully acknowledge and esteem the truly Christian endowments from our common heritage which are to be found among our separated brethren. . . .

"Nor should we forget that whatever is wrought by the grace of the Holy Spirit in the hearts of our separated brethren can contribute to our own edification. Whatever is truly Christian never conflicts with the genuine interests of the faith; indeed, it can always result in a more ample realization of the very mystery of Christ and the Church . . ." (No. 4).

Participation in Worship

Norms concerning participation by Catholics in the worship of other Christian Churches were sketched in this conciliar decree and elaborated in a number of other documents such as: the *Decree on Eastern Catholic Churches,* promulgated by the Second Vatican Council in 1964; *Interim Guidelines for Prayer in Common,* issued June 18, 1965, by the US Bishops' Committee for Ecumenical and Inter-Religious Affairs; a *Directory on Ecumenism,* published in 1967 by the Vatican Secretariat for Promoting Christian Unity; additional communications from the US Bishops' Committee, and numerous sets of guidelines issued locally by and for dioceses throughout the US.

The norms encourage common prayer services for Christian unity and other intentions. Beyond that, they draw a distinction between separated churches of the Reformation tradition and separated Eastern churches, in view of doctrine and practice the Catholic Church has in common with the latter concerning the apostolic succession of bishops, holy orders, liturgy, and other credal matters.

Full participation by Catholics in official Protestant liturgies is prohibited, because it implies profession of the faith expressed in the liturgy. Intercommunion is generally forbidden. Otherwise, however: A Catholic may stand as a witness, but not as a sponsor, in baptism, and as a witness in the marriage of separated Christians. Similarly, a Protestant may stand as a witness, but not as a sponsor, in a Catholic baptism, and as a witness in the marriage of Catholics.

Separated Eastern Churches

The principal norms regarding liturgical participation with separated Eastern Christians are included under Eastern Ecumenism.

ECUMENICAL AGENCIES

Vatican Secretariat

The top-level agency for Catholic ecumenical efforts is the Vatican Secretariat for Promoting Christian Unity, which originated in 1960 as a preparatory commission for the Second Vatican Council. Its purposes are to provide guidance and, where necessary, coordination for ecumenical endeavor by Catholics, and to establish and maintain relations with representatives of other Christian Churches for ecumenical dialogue and action.

The secretariat, first under the direction of Cardinal Augustin Bea, S. J., and now of Cardinal Jan Willebrands, has established firm working relations with a number of representative agencies of other churches, principally the World Council of Churches and the Lutheran World Federation; has joined the Anglican Communion and the Orthodox in dialogue; and is carrying forward with the World Alliance of Reformed Churches (a Presbyterian alliance) studies regarding the possibilities of future dialogue. In the past several years, staff members and representatives of the secretariat have been involved in one way or another in nearly every significant ecumenical enterprise and meeting held throughout the world, including the Fourth General Assembly of the World Council of Churches and the Tenth Lambeth Conference in 1968.

While the secretariat and its counterparts in other churches have focused primary attention on theological and other related problems of Christian unity, they have also begun, and in increasing measure, to emphasize the responsibilities of the churches for greater unity of witness and effort in areas of humanitarian need.

Bishops' Committee

The US Bishops' Committee for Ecumenical and Interreligious Affairs was established by the American hierarchy in 1964. Its purposes are to maintain relationships with other Christian churches and other religious communities at the national level, to advise and assist dioceses in developing and applying ecumenical policies, and to maintain liaison with corresponding Vatican offices — the Secretariats for Christian Unity, Non-Christian Religions, and Non-Believers.

This standing committee of the National Conference of Catholic Bishops is chaired by Bishop Charles H. Helmsing of Kansas City-St. Joseph. Operationally, the committee is assisted by secretariats headed by the Rev. John F. Hotchkin, secretary for Christian Unity, and the Rev. Edward H. Flannery, secretary for Catholic-Jewish Relations.

The committee co-sponsors several national consultations with other churches and confessional families. These bring together on a regular basis Catholic representatives and their counterparts from the American Baptist Convention, the Christian Church (Disciples of Christ), the Episcopal Church, the Lutheran World Federation (US Committee), the United Methodist Church, the Orthodox Churches, and the Alliance of Reformed Churches (North American area). Reports of consultations conducted under committee auspices are published periodically and are available through the Publications Office of the US Catholic Conference. (See Ecumenical Dialogues.)

The committee has also facilitated regional meetings in conjunction with the Home Mission Board of the Southern Baptist Convention.

The committee relates with the National Council of Churches of Christ, and is sponsoring a joint study committee investigating the possibility of Roman Catholic membership in that body.

Through the Secretariat for Catholic-Jewish Relations, the committee is in contact with several national Jewish agencies and bodies. Issues of mutual interest and shared concern are reviewed for the purpose of furthering deeper understanding between the Catholic and Jewish communities.

Offices of the committee are located at 1312 Massachusetts Ave. N. W., Washington, D. C. 20005.

World Council

The World Council of Churches is a fellowship of churches which acknowledge "Jesus Christ as Lord and Savior." It is a permanent organization providing constituent members — in 1972, 252 churches with some 450 million communicants in 90 countries — with opportunities for meeting, consultation and cooperative action with respect to doctrine, worship, practice, social mission, evangelism and missionary work, and other matters of mutual concern.

The WCC was formally established Aug. 23, 1948, in Amsterdam with ratification of a constitution by 138 communions. This action merged two previously existing movements — Life and Work (social mission), Faith and Order (doctrine) — which had initiated practical steps toward founding a fellowship of Christian churches at meetings held in Oxford, Edinburgh and Utrecht in 1937 and 1938. A third movement for cooperative missionary work, which originated about 1910 and, remotely, led to formation of the WCC, was incorporated into the council in 1971 under the title of the International Missionary Council (World Mission and Evangelism).

Three additional general assemblies of the council have been held since the charter meeting of 1948, in Evanston, Ill. (1954), New Delhi, India (1961), and Uppsala, Sweden (1968).

Between assemblies, the council operates through a central committee which meets every 12 or 18 months, and an executive committee which meets every six months.

The council continues the work of the International Missionary Council, the Commission on Faith and Order, and the Commission on Church and Society. The structure of the council has three program units: Faith and Witness, Justice and Service, Education and Communication.

Liaison between the council and the Vatican has been maintained since 1966 through a joint working group. Roman Catholic membership in the WCC is a question officially on the agenda of this body. The Joint Commission on Society, Development and Peace (SODEPAX) is an agency of the council and the Pontifical Commission for Justice and Peace. Roman Catholics serve individually as full members of the Commission on Faith and Order and in various capacities on other program committees of the council.

WCC headquarters are located in Geneva, Switzerland. The United States Conference for the World Council of Churches at 475 Riverside Drive, New York, N. Y. 10027, provides liaison between the US churches and Geneva. The WCC also maintains fraternal relations with regional, national and local councils of churches throughout the world.

The Rev. Philippe A. Potter, a Methodist from the Island of Dominica, West Indies, was elected secretary general of the WCC in August, 1972. The Rev. Dr. Eugene L. Smith is executive secretary of the US Conference.

WCC presidents are: Mrs. Dr. Kiyoko Takeda Cho (Japan), His Holiness German (Yugoslavia), Rev. Dr. Hanns Lilje (Germany), Rev. Dr. Ernest A. Payne (United Kingdom), Rev. Dr. John Coventry Smith (USA), Rt. Rev. A. H. Zulu (South Africa).

National Council

The National Council of The Churches of Christ in the USA, the largest ecumenical organization in the United States, is a cooperative federation of 33 Protestant, Orthodox and Anglican church bodies having about 42 million members.

The NCC, established by the churches in 1950, was structured through the merger of 12 separate cooperative agencies. Presently, through four main program divisions, the NCC carries on work in behalf of member churches in home and overseas missions, Christian education and communications, disaster relief and rehabilitation, family life, religious broadcast and film-making, regional and local ecumenism, and other areas.

The NCC is governed by a general board of approximately 260 representatives appointed by the constituent churches which meets three times a year. The highest governing body is the general assembly of approximately 850 members, which meets triennially and elects new officers for a three-year period. The most recent general assembly was held Dec. 3 to 8, 1972, in Dallas.

The NCC's annual budget approximates $16 million, about 60 percent of which is devoted to compassionate ministries of aid and relief to victims of disasters and endemic poverty in lands overseas. The work of the NCC is financially supported for the most part by the member churches and their boards and agencies.

Dr. Cynthia C. (Mrs. Theodore O.) Wedel was elected to a three-year term as president in 1969. The chief executive officer is Dr. R. H. Edwin Espy, general secretary.

NCC headquarters are located at 475 Riverside Drive, New York, N. Y. 10027.

Consultation

The Consultation on Church Union was inaugurated in 1962 for the purpose of formulating and putting into effect a plan of union for Christian churches in the United States. The original participants in the Consultation were the Methodist Church, the Protestant Episcopal Church, the United Presbyterian Church and the United Church of Christ.

At the ninth annual meeting of the Consultation, held in March, 1970, in St. Louis, 90 delegates unanimously approved for study by member churches a plan for the eventual formation of a single, 25-million-member Church of Christ Uniting. The delegates represented: the Protestant Episcopal Church, the United Methodist Church, the United Church of Christ, the United Presbyterian Church in the USA, the Presbyterian Church in the US, the Christian Church (Disciples of Christ), the Christian Methodist Episcopal Church, the African Episcopal Church, and the African Methodist Episcopal Zion Church.

The United Presbyterian Church, one of the original participants, withdrew from the Consultation in May, 1972.

Dr. George G. Beazley, Jr., of Indianapolis, a representative of the Christian Church, is chairman of the Consultation. The executive secretary is Dr. Paul A. Crow, Jr.

Offices are located at 228 Alexandria Ave., Princeton, N.J. 08540.

ECUMENICAL DIALOGUES

(Source: Secretariat for Ecumenical and Interreligious Affairs, National Conference of Catholic Bishops.)

Following is a list of principal consultations, from Mar. 16, 1965, involving representatives of the US Catholic Bishops' Committee for Ecumenical and Interreligious Affairs and representatives of other Christian Churches, with names of the churches, places and dates of meetings, and the subject matter of discussions.

Baptist Convention, American (Division of Cooperative Christianity): (1) De Witt, Mich., Apr. 3, 1967 — American Baptist and Roman Catholic dialogue; a Baptist view of areas of theological agreement. (2) Green Lake, Wis., Apr. 29, 1968 — Baptism and confirmation; Christian freedom and ecclesiastical authority. (3) Schiller Park, Ill., Apr. 28, 1969 — Nature and communication of grace; Christian freedom and ecclesiastical authority; baptism and confirmation.

(4) Atchison, Kan., Apr. 17, 1970 — Role of the Church, resume of years past and the future; Roman Catholic-American Baptist dialogues; observations concerning bilateral ecumenical conversations and the future course of American Baptist-Roman Catholic conversations.

(5) Detroit, Mich., Apr. 23 to 24, 1971 — Theological perspective on clergy and lay issues and relations; theology of the local church; growth in understanding. (6) Liberty, Mo., Apr. 14 to 15, 1972 — Relationships between Church and State.

Baptists, Southern (Ecumenical Institute, Wake Forest University): (1) Winston-Salem, N. C., May 8, 1969 — Impact of biblical criticism on Roman Catholicism and contemporary Christianity in general; holy use of the world; creeds and the Faith; liturgy and spontaneity in worship; retreat, revival and monasticism; world view of ecumenism.

(2) St. Benedict, La., Feb. 4, 1970 — Liturgy and spontaneity in worship; perspectives on Baptist views on Scripture and tradition; the priesthood of all Christians; authority of the Old Testament; Baptist concepts of the Church; retreat, revival and monasticism. (3) Louisville, Ky., May 13, 1970 — The priesthood of all Christians; the ecumenical tide — a pastoral perspective; the enduring meaning of the Old Testament; retreat, revival and monasticism.

(4) Daytona Beach, Fla., Feb. 1 to 3, 1971

— Issues and answers, prepared by the Interfaith Witness Department of the Southern Baptist Convention. (5) Houston, Tex., Oct. 16 to 18, 1972 — Second regional conference planned in conjunction with the Interfaith Witness Department.

Christian Church, Disciples of Christ (Council on Christian Unity): (1) Indianapolis, Ind., Mar. 16, 1967 — A look at Disciples for Catholics. (2) Kansas City, Mo., Sept. 25, 1967 — Roman Catholic view of the nature of unity being sought; opportunities in the contemporary ecumenical movement. (3) St. Louis, Mo., Apr. 29, 1968 — Eucharistic sharing.

(4) Washington, D. C., Oct. 16, 1968 — Disciple of Christ inquiry regarding the sacramentality of marriage; pastoral reflections on mixed marriage. (5) New York, N. Y., Apr. 25, 1969 — Recognition and reconciliation of ministries; theological presuppositions concerning ministry among the Disciples; role of the priest in the Catholic community.

(6) Columbus, O., Nov. 3 to 5, 1970 — The parish concept in a plan of union (Consultation on Church Union); directions emerging in Catholic parish life. (7) New York, N.Y., June 8 to 10, 1971 — Disciples' theology of baptism; meaning of baptism as liberation, incorporation, empowerment.

(8) Indianapolis, Ind., Mar. 8 to 10, 1972 — Ministry of healing and reconciliation as practiced in the two communities. (9) Madison, Wis., June 26 to 28, 1972 — Review and summary of five years of dialogue; planning for future themes.

Episcopal (The Anglican-Roman Catholic Consultation, Joint Commission on Ecumenical Relations): (1) Washington, D.C., June 22, 1965 — Preliminary discussions. (2) Kansas City, Mo., Feb. 2, 1966 — Eucharist as source or expression of community; Eucharist as sign and cause of unity, and the Church as a Eucharistic fellowship.

(3) Providence, R.I., Oct. 10, 1966 — Function of the minister in Eucharistic celebration; minister of the Eucharist. (4) Milwaukee, Wis., May 2, 1967 — Eucharist. (5) Jackson, Miss., Jan. 5, 1968 — Various aspects of the ministerial priesthood and the priesthood of the faithful in Eucharistic celebration; the priest's place and function in the Church's mission of service; the laity in Episcopal Church government.

(6) Liberty, Mo., Dec. 2, 1968 — Directions of the ecumenical movement; episcopal symbol of unity in the Christian community; collegiality; Citizens for Educational Freedom; a layman's view of jurisdictional and cultural factors in division; Church and society in contemporary America.

(7) Boynton Beach, Fla., Dec. 8, 1969 — All in each place; toward the reconciliation of the Roman Catholic Church and Churches of the Anglican Communion; an approach to designing a Roman Catholic-Episcopal parish; preparation of joint statement on the meeting. (8) Green Bay, Wis., June 17, 1970 — Is the (COCU — Consultation on Church Union) plan of union truly Catholic, with special reference to the priest and the episcopacy?; Anglican-Roman Catholic dialogue — achievement and prognostication.

(9) St. Benedict, La., Jan. 26 to 29, 1971 — The primacy of jurisdiction of the Roman Pontiff according to the First Vatican Council; the teaching of the Second Vatican Council concerning the hierarchy of truths; analysis of the ground of "Church Elements: An Ecclesiological Investigation."

(10) Liberty, Mo., June 20 to 23, 1971 — Gift of infallibility; sharing in the teaching authority of the Church; official view of episcopacy in the Episcopal Church in the USA; symposium on Hans Kung's *Infallibility? An Inquiry*; dogma as an ecumenical problem; Revelation and statement in Anglicanism; revised working paper on theological truth, propositions and Christian unity; reflections on the teaching ministry of the Church.

(11) New York, N.Y., Jan 20 to 24, 1972 — Theological truth, propositions and Christian unity; the Protestant Episcopal Church's view of authority, tradition and the Bible; a comment on the Windsor "Statement of Eucharistic Agreement" issued by the International Anglican-Roman Catholic Consultation.

(12) Cincinnati, O., June 12 to 15, 1972 — The notion of *typos* and *typoi* as applied to the forms of the Christian Church; correspondences and differences in the Anglican and Roman Catholic understanding and exercise of teaching authority.

Lutheran, U.S.A. (National Committee of the Lutheran World Federation): (1) Baltimore, Md., Mar. 16, 1965 — Exploratory discussion. (2) Baltimore, Md., July 6, 1965 — Nicene Creed as dogma of the Church. (3) Chicago, Ill., Feb. 10, 1966 — Baptism, in the context of the New Testament; Lutheran understanding; teaching of the Council of Trent.

(4) Washington, D.C., Sept. 22, 1966 — Eucharist as sacrifice, in traditional and contemporary Catholic and Lutheran contexts. (5) New York, N.Y., Apr 7, 1967 — Propitiation and five presentations on various aspects of the Eucharist. (6) St. Louis, Mo.. Sept. 29, 1967 — Eucharist. (7) New York, Mar. 8, 1968 — Intercommunion, with respect to Catholic discipline, Lutheran practice, and theological reflections.

(8) Williamsburg, Va., Sept. 27, 1968 — Ministry; the competent minister of the Eucharist; scriptural foundations of diakonia (ministry of service). (9) San Francisco, Calif., Feb. 21, 1969 — Apostolic succession in the patristic era and in a contemporary view; Lutheran view of the validity of Lutheran orders; Christian priesthood in the light of documents of the Second Vatican Council.

(10) Baltimore, Md., Sept. 26, 1969 — The

minister of the Eucharist, according to the Council of Trent; the use of "Church" as applied to Protestant denominations in the documents of Vatican II; Lutheran doctrine of the ministry — Catholic and Reformed; the ordained minister and layman in Lutheranism. (11) St. George, Bermuda, Feb. 19, 1970 — Preparation of joint statement on the ministry.

(12) New York, N.Y., May, 1970. (13) Chicago, Ill., Oct. 30 to Nov. 1, 1970. (14) Miami, Fla., Feb. 19 to 22, 1971 — Peter and the New Testament; the papacy in the late patristic era, Middle Ages, Renaissance; text of the *Dogmatic Constitution on the Church* (Vatican II) with respect to the papacy and infallibility.

(15) Seabury, Conn., Sept. 24 to 27, 1971 — An investigation of the concept of divine right *(jus divinum);* teaching of the First Vatican Council on primacy and infallibility; a Lutheran understanding of what papal primacy in the Church might mean.

(16) New Orleans, La., Feb. 18 to 21, 1972 — Further discussion of the concept of divine right; ecumenical projections concerning the Petrine office; teaching authority in the Lutheran Church. (17) Minneapolis, Minn., Sept. 22 to 25, 1972 — Further investigation of the Petrine function; councils and conciliarism.

Methodist (United Methodist Church): (1) Chicago, Ill., June 28, 1966 — Methodists and Roman Catholics: comments for Catholic-Methodist conversation. (2) Chicago, Ill., Dec. 18, 1966 — Salvation, faith and good works; Catholic Church and faith. (3) Lake Junaluska, N. C., June 28, 1967 — Roman Catholic position regarding the Spirit in the Church; mission of the Holy Spirit, in the light of the Second Vatican Council's *Dogmatic Constitution on the Church* and the writings of John Wesley.

(4) New York, N.Y., Dec. 17, 1967 — Three generations of Church-State argumentation. (5) San Antonio, Tex., Sept. 30, 1968 — Shared convictions about education. (6) Delaware, O., Oct. 9, 1969 — Major Methodist ecumenical documents; an appraisal of some documents of Vatican II; racial confrontation in Roman Catholicism, Methodism and the National Council of Churches. (7) Chicago, Ill., Jan. 30, 1970 — Review and planning.

(8) Washington, D. C., Dec. 16, 1970 — Completion of a statement of shared convictions about education. Task force meetings during 1971. (9) Cincinnati, O., Feb. 25 to 26, 1972 — Ministry in the United Methodist Church and the spirituality of the ordained ministry; problems of ministry. (10) Dec. 13 to 14, 1972 — Further dialogue on the spirituality of the ministry.

Orthodox (Standing Conference of Canonical Orthodox Bishops of America): Sept. 9, 1965 — Preliminary discussions. (1) New York, N. Y., Sept. 29, 1966 — Consultation led to appointment of task forces to investigate differences in theological methods, questions of sacramental sharing, possible cooperation in theological education and the formation of seminarians. (2) Worcester, Mass., May 5, 1967 — Theological diversity and unity; intercommunion; common witness in theological education. (3) Maryknoll, N. Y., Dec. 7, 1968 — Eucharist and Church; indissolubility of marriage; Cooperation in theological education.

(4) Worcester, Mass., Dec. 12, 1969 — Orthodox and Catholic views of the Eucharist and membership in the Church; an agreed statement on the Eucharist. (5) New York, N.Y., May 19, 1970 — New Order of the Mass; membership of schismatics and heretics in the ancient Church; current legislation of the Catholic Church and current practices of the Greek Orthodox Church concerning common worship; current legislation of the Catholic Church concerning mixed marriages; Orthodox view of mixed marriages; an agreed statement on mixed marriages.

(6) Brookline, Mass., Dec. 4, 1970 — Ministers, doctrine and practice of matrimony in Eastern and Western traditions. (7) Barlin Acres, Mass., Nov. 3 to 4, 1971 — Ethical issues relating to marriage; revision of an agreed statement on mixed marriages; the primacy of Rome as seen by the Eastern Church.

Presbyterian Reformed (The Roman Catholic-Presbyterian Consultation Group, North American Council of the World Alliance of Reformed Churches): (1) Washington, D.C., July 27, 1965 — Exploratory discussions. (2) Philadelphia, Pa., Nov. 26, 1965 — Role of the Holy Spirit in renewal and reform of the Church. (3) New York, May 12, 1966 — Roman Catholic view of Scripture and tradition; apostolic and ecclesiastical tradition.

(4) Chicago, Ill., Oct. 27, 1966 — Development of doctrine; dialogue, a program of peace, prayer and study for Roman Catholics and Protestants. (5) Collegeville, Minn., Apr. 26, 1967 — Order and ministry in the Reformed tradition; validity of orders; changes in mixed marriage. (6) Lancaster, Pa., Oct. 26, 1967 — Work was begun on a joint statement on ministry. (7) Bristow, Va., May 9, 1968 — Structures and ministries. (8) Allen Park, Mich., Oct. 24, 1968 — Marriage. (9) Charleston, S.C., May 21, 1969 — Validation of ministries and ministry; theological view of marriage.

(10) Macatawa, Mich., Oct. 30, 1969 — Apostles and apostolic succession in the patristic era; report concerning office; divorce and remarriage as understood in the United Presbyterian Church in the USA; the Church and second marriage; recommendations for changes regarding inter-Christian marriages. (11) Morristown, N.J., May 13, 1970 — Joint statements on ministry in the Church and women in Church and society.

(12) Princeton, N.J., Oct. 29 to 30, 1970 — Episcopal/presbyter polity; episcopacy. (13) Columbus, O., May 13 to 15, 1971 — Ministry in the Church; man-woman relationships; the future of the Church. (14) Richmond, Va., Oct. 28 to 30, 1971 — Reports finalized on women in the Church and ministry in the Church. (15) Oct. 26 to 29, 1972 — The shape of the unity we seek.

QUESTIONS IN ECUMENISM

Doldrums?

Against a background of criticism that ecumenism was in the doldrums after the high point of the Second Vatican Council and developments immediately thereafter, Pope Paul maintained that "it is not true that the cause of ecumenism has now come to a stop."

Pope's View

In an address to a gathering in St. Peter's Square Jan. 23, 1972, he said that perhaps a type of "superficial ecumenism" or one that tries to resolve the problems of Christianity merely by fusing religious beliefs has slowed because it "neglects its (ecumenism's) real demands of true faith and effective communion." Ecumenism "founded on sincere study and common prayer," however, continues to make progress, he declared.

The Holy Father stated that the ecumenical movement has filled Christians "with great visions and great hopes." These are "not dreams," he added, but "graces which we implore from God. . . .'"

Progress

Evidence of ecumenical progress in 1971 was cited by Cardinal Jan Willebrands, president of the Secretariat for Promoting Christian Unity, in a radio broadcast during the 1972 Week of Prayer for Christian Unity.

Items concerning the Eastern Churches were:

• letters exchanged between Pope Paul and Orthodox Patriarch Athenagoras which stressed the need for the growth of a truly brotherly attitude in both communities toward the day that they might "communicate together with the same chalice of the Lord";

• the Cardinal's visit to the Patriarch and presentation to him of a 700-page volume of 285 documents exchanged by the Vatican and the patriarchate in the previous 12 years;

• official visits of the Cardinal and other Catholic prelates with Orthodox leaders of Greece and Crete, and with Rumanian and Syrian Orthodox patriarchs.

Items concerning other Christian Churches included:

• the completion of studies by a Catholic-Lutheran commission on "The Gospel and the Church";

• an initial series of conversations on the international level with Methodists concerning problems of Christian spirituality, the Eucharist, matrimony and the Christian family;

• conversations with the World Reform Alliance on "The Presence of Christ in the Church and in the World";

• the agreement reached by Roman Catholic and Anglican discussants on the Eucharist, which was published Dec. 31, 1971 (see Index for text).

The Cardinal's broadcast report, which was limited to developments on the international level, did not cover ecumenical events in various countries.

Other Views

Thirty cardinals and bishops attending a plenary session of the Unity Secretariat Feb. 8 to 16, 1972, agreed that ecumenism's golden dawn had vanished but denied the truth of rumors that ecumenism was dead. Instead, they said it had entered the phase of patient, plodding effort to seek the unity Christ wants for His Church.

Dr. Eugene Carson Blake, general secretary of the World Council of Churches, insisted at a New York news conference in June, 1972, that "the ecumenical movement is not going backward; on that I am quite clear. In the past 10 years the ecumenical movement has produced relationships and results that nobody could have predicted."

WCC Membership?

A joint meeting of 24 representatives of the Catholic Church and the World Council of Churches announced June 2, 1972, that the Vatican would not be applying for membership in the WCC in the near future. The announcement added: "It is not realistic at present to attempt to set a date by which one must arrive at an answer to the question: Should the Catholic Church apply for membership?"

It was announced at the same time that the Vatican Secretariat for Promoting Christian Unity was preparing a study on regional and local levels of cooperation between the two bodies.

Dr. Eugene Carson Blake, general secretary of the WCC, told a New York news conference shortly afterwards that the Vatican's decision did not reflect a slackening commitment to ecumenism by the Catholic Church.

Under Study

Dr. Blake recalled that, when Pope Paul addressed the headquarters staff of the WCC in 1969 in Geneva, he said the question of Catholic membership in the council needed study.

"We have done the study and it did not seem adequate" to the Vatican, he commented, but added: "I am assured by the ecumenists in the Vatican that it is not basically a decision against the World Council of Churches."

CATHOLIC-JEWISH RELATIONS

The Second Vatican Council, in addition to the *Decree on Ecumenism* concerning the movement for unity among Christians, stated the mind of the Church on a similar matter in a *Declaration on the Relationship of the Church to Non-Christian Religions*. This document, as the following excerpts indicate, backgrounds the reasons and directions of the Church's regard for the Jews. (Other portions of the document, not cited here, refer to Hindus, Buddhists and Moslems.)

Spiritual Bond

"As this sacred Synod searches into the mystery of the Church, it recalls the spiritual bond linking the people of the New Covenant with Abraham's stock.

"For the Church of Christ acknowledges that, according to the mystery of God's saving design, the beginnings of her faith and her election are already found among the patriarchs, Moses, and the prophets. She professes that all who believe in Christ, Abraham's sons according to faith (cf. Gal. 3:7), are included in the same patriarch's call, and likewise that the salvation of the Church was mystically foreshadowed by the Chosen People's exodus from the land of bondage.

"The Church, therefore, cannot forget that she received the revelation of the Old Testament through the people with whom God in His inexpressible mercy deigned to establish the Ancient Covenant. Nor can she forget that she draws sustenance from the root of that good olive tree onto which have been grafted the wild olive branches of the Gentiles (cf. Rom.11:17-24). Indeed, the Church believes that by His cross Christ, our Peace, reconciled Jew and Gentile, making them both one in Himself (cf. Eph. 2:14-16).

". . . The Jews still remain most dear to God because of their fathers, for He does not repent of the gifts He makes nor of the calls He issues (cf. Rom. 11:28-29). In company with the prophets and the same Apostle (Paul), the Church awaits that day, known to God alone, on which all peoples will address the Lord in a single voice and 'serve him with one accord' (Zeph. 3:9; Cf. Is. 66:23; Ps. 65:4; Rom. 11:11-32).

"Since the spiritual patrimony common to Christians and Jews is thus so great, this sacred Synod wishes to foster and recommend that mutual understanding and respect which is the fruit above all of biblical and theological studies, and of brotherly dialogues.

No Anti-Semitism

"True, authorities of the Jews and those who followed their lead pressed for the death of Christ (cf. Jn. 19:6); still, what happened in His passion cannot be blamed upon all the Jews then living, without distinction, nor upon the Jews of today. Although the Church is the new People of God, the Jews should not be presented as repudiated or cursed by God, as if such views followed from the holy Scriptures. All should take pains, then, lest in catechetical instruction and in the preaching of God's Word they teach anything out of harmony with the truth of the gospel and the spirit of Christ.

"The Church repudiates all persecutions against any man. Moreover, mindful of her common patrimony with the Jews, and motivated by the gospel's spiritual love and by no political considerations, she deplores the hatred, persecutions, and displays of anti-Semitism directed against the Jews at any time and from any source. . . ." (4).

". . . The Church rejects, as foreign to the mind of Christ, any discrimination against men or harassment of them because of their race, color, condition of life, or religion. . . ." (No. 5).

Bishops' Secretariat

The American hierarchy's first move toward implementation of the Vatican II *Declaration on the Relationship of the Church to Non-Christian Religions* was to establish, in 1965, a Subcommission for Catholic-Jewish Relations in the framework of its Commission for Ecumenical and Interreligious Affairs. This subcommission was reconstituted and given the title of secretariat in September, 1967. Its moderator is Bishop Francis J. Mugavero of Brooklyn. The executive director is Father Edward Flannery. The Secretariat for Catholic-Jewish Relations is located at 1312 Massachusetts Ave. N.W., Washington, D.C. 20005.

According to the key norm of a set of guidelines issued by the secretariat Mar. 16, 1967: "The general aim of all Catholic-Jewish meetings (and relations) is to increase our understanding both of Judaism and the Catholic faith, to eliminate sources of tension and misunderstanding, to initiate dialogue or conversations on different levels, to multiply intergroup meetings between Catholics and Jews, and to promote cooperative social action."

Developments in recent years, in the view of Rabbi Marc H. Tanenbaum, director of interreligious affairs of the American Jewish Committee, have reflected a growing commitment by Christian leaders "to lay a foundation for constructive relations between Christians and Jews in this country."

Even so, progress toward better Christian-Jewish relations appears to be greater on the theological and scholarly levels than among local church organizations and synagogue communities. There are indications that some strides forward are being made there as well, however, in mutual discussion programs, temple visits by Catholics, interest in the rituals and observances of Judaism, and the involvement of Catholics and Jews in social action projects.

Relations Improving

Rabbi Marc H. Tanenbaum reported evidence of steadily improving Jewish-Christian relations at the five-day 66th annual meeting of the American Jewish Committee early in May, 1972, in New York City.

The evidence emerged from an analysis of statements from a variety of Catholic and other sources. Among the findings, as reported in *The New York Times,* were:

• "A growing and positive shift in Christian sentiment about Israel, 'including a balanced perspective on the rights of Palestinians and the future of a unified Jerusalem, in which Christian churches are beginning to see their role as one of promoting reconciliation rather than polarization.' "

• "Recognition of Judaism as a source of 'fundamental truth' to its adherents and a repudiation of the use of interfaith dialogues for purposes of conversion."

• "Widespread sensitivity to the plight of Soviet Jews and recognition of the fact that their struggle for justice is 'inextricably linked to the denial of human rights to Christians and various national communities in the Soviet Union.' "

JUDAISM

Judaism is the religion of the Old Testament and of contemporary Jews. Divinely revealed and with a patriarchal background (Abraham, Isaac, Jacob), it originated with the Mosaic Covenant, was identified with the Israelites, and achieved distinctive form and character as the religion of The Law from this Covenant and reforms initiated by Ezra and Nehemiah after the Babylonian Exile.

Judaism does not have a formal creed but its principal points of belief are clear. Basic is belief in one transcendent God who reveals himself through The Law, the prophets, the life of his people and events of history. The fatherhood of God involves the brotherhood of men. Religious faith and practice are equated with just living according to The Law. Moral conviction and practice are regarded as more important than precise doctrinal formulation and profession. Formal worship, whose principal act was sacrifice from Canaanite times to 70 A. D., is by prayer, reading and meditating upon the sacred writings, and observance of the Sabbath and festivals.

Judaism has messianic expectations of the complete fulfillment of the Covenant, the coming of God's kingdom, the ingathering of his people, final judgment and retribution for all men. Views differ regarding the manner in which these expectations will be realized—through a person, the community of God's people, an evolution of historical events, an eschatological act of God himself. Individual salvation expectations also differ, depending on views about the nature of immortality, punishment and reward, and related matters.

The sacred books are the 24 books of the Masoretic Hebrew Text of The Law, the Prophets and the Writings (see The Bible). Together, they contain the basic instruction or norms for just living. In some contexts, the term Law or Torah refers only to the Pentateuch (Genesis, Exodus, Leviticus, Numbers, Deuteronomy); in others, it denotes all the sacred books and/or the whole complex of written and oral tradition.

Also of great authority are two Talmuds which were composed in Palestine and Babylon in the fourth and fifth centuries A.D., respectively. They consist of the Mishna, a compilation of oral laws, and the Gemara, a collection of rabbinical commentary on the Mishna. Midrash are collections of scriptural comments and moral counsels.

Priests were the principal official ministers during the period of sacrificial and temple worship. Rabbis were, and continue to be, teachers and leaders of prayer. The synagogue is the place of community worship. The family and home are focal points of many aspects of Jewish worship and practice.

Of the various categories of Jews, Orthodox are the most conservative in adherence to strict religious traditions. Others — Reformed, Conservative, Reconstructionist — are liberal in comparison with the Orthodox. They favor greater or less modification of religious practices in accommodation to contemporary culture and living conditions.

Principal events in Jewish life include the circumcision of males, according to prescriptions of the Covenant; the bar mitzvah which marks the coming-of-age of boys in Judaism at the age of 13; marriage; and observance of the Sabbath and festivals.

Sabbath and Festivals

Observances of the Sabbath and festivals begin at sundown of the previous calendar day and continue until the following sundown.

Sabbath: Saturday, the weekly day of rest prescribed in the Decalogue.

Booths (Tabernacles): A seven-to-nine-day festival in the month of Tishri (Sept.-Oct.), marked by some Jews with Covenant-renewal and reading of The Law. It originated as an agricultural feast at the end of the harvest and got its name from the temporary shelters used by workers in the fields.

Hanukkah (The Festival of Lights, the Feast of Consecration and of the Maccabees): Commemorates the dedication of the new altar in the Temple at Jerusalem by Judas Maccabeus in 165 B.C. The eight-day festival, during which candles in an eight-branch candelabra are lighted in succession, one each day, occurs near the winter solstice, close to Christmas time.

Passover: A seven-day festival commemorating the liberation of the Israelites from Egypt. The narrative of the Exodus, the Haggadah, is read at ceremonial Seder meals on the first and second days of the festival, which begins on the 14th day of Nisan (Mar.-Apr.).

Pentecost (Feast of Weeks): Observed 50 days after Passover. Some Jews regard it as commemorative of the anniversary of the revelation of The Law to Moses.

Purim: A joyous festival observed on the 14th day of Adar (Feb.-Mar.), commemorating the rescue of the Israelites from massacre by the Persians through the intervention of Esther. The festival is preceded by a day of fasting. A gift- and alms-giving custom became associated with it in medieval times.

Rosh Hashana (Feast of the Trumpets, New Year): Observed on the first day of Tishri (Sept.-Oct.), the festival focuses attention on the day of judgment and is marked with meditation on the ways of life and the ways of death. It is second in importance only to the most solemn observance of Yom Kippur, which is celebrated 10 days later.

Yom Kippur (Day of Atonement): The highest holy day, observed with strict fasting. It occurs 10 days after Rosh Hashana.

ISLAM

Islam is the religion of Mohammed and his followers, called Moslems, Muslims, Mohammedans. Islam, meaning submission to God, originated with Mohammed (570-632), an Arabian, who taught that he had received divine revelation and was the last and greatest of the prophets.

Moslems believe in one God. There were six great prophets—Adam, Noah, Abraham, Moses, Jesus and Mohammed—and Mohammed was the greatest. The creed states: "There is no God but Allah and Mohammed is the prophet of Allah."

The principal duties of Moslems are to: profess the faith by daily recitation of the creed; pray five times a day facing in the direction of the holy city of Mecca; give alms; fast daily from dawn to dusk during the month of Ramadan; make a pilgrimage to Mecca once if possible.

Moslems believe in a final judgment, heaven and hell. Polygamy is practiced. Some dietary regulations are in effect. The weekly day of worship is Friday, and the principal service is at noon in a mosque. Moslems do not have an ordained ministry. The general themes of their prayer are adoration and thanksgiving.

The basis of Islamic belief is the Koran, the created word of God revealed to Mohammed by the angel Gabriel over a period of 20 years. The contents of this sacred book are complemented by the Sunna, a collection of sacred traditions, and reinforced by Ijma, the consensus of Moslems which guarantees them against error in matters of belief and practice. There are several sects of Moslems.

Conciliar Statement

The attitude of the Church toward Islam was stated as follows in the Second Vatican Council's *Declaration on the Relationship of the Church to Non-Christian Religions* (No. 3).

"Upon the Moslems, too, the Church looks with esteem. They adore one God, living and enduring, merciful and all-powerful, Maker of heaven and earth and Speaker to men. They strive to submit wholeheartedly even to His inscrutable decrees, just as did Abraham, with whom the Islamic faith is pleased to associate itself. Though they do not acknowledge Jesus as God, they revere Him as a prophet. They also honor Mary, His virgin mother; at times they call on her, too, with devotion. In addition they await the day of judgment when God will give each man his due after raising him up. Consequently, they prize the moral life, and give worship to God especially through prayer, almsgiving and fasting.

"Although in the course of the centuries many quarrels and hostilities have arisen between Christians and Moslems, this most sacred Synod urges all to forget the past and to strive sincerely for mutual understanding. On behalf of all mankind, let them make common cause of safeguarding and fostering social justice, moral values, peace and freedom."

Dialogue

The purposes of Catholic-Moslem dialogue, which has been rather sketchy, were the subject of joint agreement between Cardinal Paul Marella, president of the Vatican Secretariat for Non-Christians, and a delegation of the Supreme Council of Islamic Affairs, at a Vatican meeting Dec. 16 to .20, 1970.

Their objectives, as stated in a communique, were to:

• hold regular consultations on Moslem-Christian relations, social, cultural and spiritual questions;

• maintain contact through appointed officers and in other ways;

• do everything possible to develop good relations between Christians and Moslems, in order to strengthen the fraternity existing among believers who share respect for all religious values and faith in God;

• continue efforts for justice and peace in the world.

Representatives of the secretariat and the council denounced every type of discrimination in national and international life. They also expressed hope for the success of efforts to establish peace with justice and honor in the Middle East.

NON-REVEALED RELIGIONS

Hinduism: The traditional religion of India with origins dating to about 5,000 B.C. Its history is complex, including original Vedic Hinduism, with a sacred literature (Veda) of hymns, incantations and other elements, and with numerous nature gods; Brahmanism, with emphasis on ceremonialism and its power over the gods; philosophical speculation, reflected in the Upanishads, with development of ideas concerning Karma, reincarnation, Brahman, and the manner of achieving salvation; the cults of Vishnu, Shiva and other deities; reforms in Hinduism and in relation to Islam and Christianity.

The principal tenets of Hinduism are open to various interpretations. Karma is the law of the deed, of sowing and reaping, of retribution. It determines the progress of a person toward liberation from the cycle of rebirths necessary for salvation. Liberation is accomplished in stages, through successive reincarnations which indicate the previous as well as the existing state of a person. The means of liberation are the practice of ceremonialism and asceticism; faith in, devotion to and worship of the gods Vishnu and Shiva in their several incarnations; and/or knowledge attained through disciplined meditation called Yoga. Salvation, according to philosophical Hinduism, consists in absorption in Brahman, the neuter world-soul. Vishnu, the sun-god, and Shiva, the destroyer or generative force of the universe, are the principal popular deities. Ancient belief in nature gods (pantheism) is reflected in sacred respect for some animals. The concept of reincarnation underlies the caste system in Indian society.

There are many sects in Hinduism, which does not have a definite creed. It lends itself easily to syncretism or amalgamation with other beliefs, as evidenced in the 15th century Sikh movement which adopted the monotheism and militancy of Islam. Hindu rituals are various and elaborate, with respect to foods, festivals, pilgrimages, marriage and other life-events.

Buddhism: Originated in the sixth century B.C. in reaction to formalism, pantheism and other trends in Hinduism. The Buddha, the Enlightened One, was Sidartha Gautama, an Indian prince, who sought to explain human suffering and evil and to find a middle way between the extremes of austerity and sensuality.

The four noble truths of Buddhism are: (1) existence involves suffering or pain; (2) suffering comes from craving: (3) craving can be overcome; (4) the way to overcome craving is to follow the "noble eightfold path" of right views, right intention, right speech, right action, right livelihood, right effort, right mindfulness and right concentration.

Karma, the deed-principle of judgment and retribution, and reincarnation are elements of Buddhism. The ultimate objective of life is Nirvana — the absorption of a person in the absolute — which ends the cycles of rebirth.

Buddhism is essentially atheistic and more of a moral philosophy and ethical system than a religion. It has a cultic element in veneration for Buddha. Monasteries, temples and shrines are places of contemplation and ritualistic observance. There are several categories of Buddhist monks and nuns.

Buddhism has many sects. Mahayana Buddhism, with an elaborate ideology, is strong in China, Korea and Japan. Hinayana Buddhism is common in Southeast Asia. Zen Buddhism is highly contemplative. Lamaism in Tibet is a combination of Buddhism and local demonolatry.

Confucianism: An ethical system based on the teachings of Confucius (c. 551-479 B.C.). It is oriented toward the moral perfection of individuals and society, the attainment of the harmony of individual and social life with the harmony of the universe, through conduct governed by the relationships of humanity, justice, ritual and courtesy, wisdom, and fidelity. Originally and basically humanistic. Confucianism was eventually mingled with elements of Chinese religion. It exerted a strong influence on national life in China from 125 to the beginning of the 20th century, despite some periods of decline.

Taoism: Originated in China several centuries before the Christian era and became a fully developed religious system by the fifth century A.D. As a religion of mystery, it developed extreme polytheism, with the Jade Emperor as the highest deity; sought blessings and long life by means of alchemy; fostered superstition and witchcraft; took on organizational and other aspects of Buddhism, with several categories of priests and nuns; exerted strong ethical influence on the lower classes; split into many sects; adopted features from other religions; became the starting point of many secret societies. One of its key tenets — that the way of nature is the guide to human conduct — resulted in a form of quietism opposed to the social concern of Confucianism.

Shinto: The way of the gods, the sum total of the cultic beliefs and practices of the ancestral religion of Japan which originated from nature and ancestor worship. Shinto is pantheistic and has many objects of devotion, the highest being the Ruler of Heaven; is practiced with detailed rituals in public shrines, which are cultic centers; has strong social influence. Sectarian Shinto has about 13 recognized sects and many offshoots. Shinto, with principal concern for this-worldly blessing, has ben affected by Buddhist and Confucian influences.

Eastern cults — with their mysticism and associated disciplines and practices — have recurrent periods of vogue in the West.

Glossary

A

Abbess: The female superior of a monastic community of nuns; e.g., Benedictines, Poor Clares, some others. Elected by members of the community, an abbess has general authority over her community but no sacramental jurisdiction. Earlist evidence of use of the title, a feminine derivative of the Aramaic *abba* (father), dates from early in the sixth century.

Abbey: See Monastery.

Abbot: The male superior of a monastic community of men religious; e.g., Benedictines, Cistercians, some others. Elected by members of the community, an abbot has ordinary jurisdiction and general authority over his community. He has some episcopal privileges. The title derives from the Aramaic *abba* (father); first given to the spiritual fathers and guides of hermits in Egypt in the fourth century, it was appropriated in the Rule of St. Benedict to the heads of abbeys and monasteries. Eastern-Rite equivalents of an abbot are a *hegumen* and an *archimandrite*.

A regular abbot is the head of an abbey or monastery. An abbot general or archabbot is the head of a congregation consisting of several monasteries. An abbot primate is the head of the modern Benedictine Confederation. A few regular abbots have jurisdiction over the residents and institutions of a district *(abbacy)* which does not belong to any diocese; jurisdiction of this kind is similar to that of a bishop in his diocese. The only abbot of this kind in the US is the abbot of Belmont Abbey, N.C.

Abjuration: Renunciation of apostasy, heresy or schism by a solemn oath.

Ablution: A term derived from Latin, meaning washing or cleansing, and referring to the cleansing of the hands of a priest celebrating Mass, after the offering of gifts; and to the cleansing of the chalice with water and wine after Communion.

Abortion: The expulsion of a nonviable human fetus from the womb of the mother, with moral implications stemming from the humanity of the fetus from the moment of conception and its consequent right to life.

Accidental expulsion, as in cases of miscarriage, is without moral fault.

Direct abortion, in which a fetus is intentionally removed from the womb, constitutes a direct attack on an innocent human being a violation of the Fifth Commandment. It is punished in church law by the penalty of excommunication, which is automatically incurred by all baptized persons involved; i.e., the consenting mother and necessary physical and/or moral cooperators. Direct abortion is not justifiable for any reason, e.g.: therapeutic, for the physical and/or psychological welfare of the mother; preventive, to avoid the birth of a defective or unwanted child; social, in the interests of family and/or community.

Indirect abortion, which occurs when a fetus is expelled during medical or other treatment of the mother for a reason other than procuring expulsion, is permissible under the principle of double effect for a proportionately serious reason; e.g., when a medical or surgical procedure is necessary to save the life of the mother.

Absolution: The act by which an authorized priest, acting as the agent of Christ and minister of the Church, grants forgiveness of sins in the sacrament of penance. The essential formula of absolution is: "I absolve you from your sins; in the name of the Father, and of the Son, and of the Holy Spirit. Amen."

Priests receive the power to absolve in virtue of their ordination and the right to exercise this power in virtue of faculties of jurisdiction given them by their bishop, their religious superior, or by canon law. The faculties of jurisdiction can be limited or restricted regarding certain sins and penalties or censures.

In cases of necessity, and also in cases of the absence of their own confessors, Eastern and Roman Rite Catholics may ask for and receive sacramental absolution from a priest of a separated Eastern Church. Separated Eastern Christians may similarly ask for and receive sacramental absolution from an Eastern or Roman Rite priest.

Any priest can absolve a person in danger of death; in the absence of a properly qualified priest, this includes a priest who is under the penalty of excommunication or suspension.

Absolution, General: (1) Sacramental absolution given without confession of sin, when confession is impossible. Persons so absolved are required to confess, in their next confession, the mortal sins from which they were so absolved.

(2) A blessing of the Church to which a plenary indulgence is attached, given at the hour of death, and at stated times to members of religious institutes and third orders.

Accessory to Another's Sin: One who culpably assists another in the performance of an evil action. This may be done by counsel, command, provocation, consent, praise, flattery, concealment, participation, silence, defense of the evil done.

Adoration: The highest act and purpose of religious worship, which is directed in love and reverence to God alone in acknowledgment of his infinite perfection and goodness, and of his total dominion over creatures. Adoration, which is also called *latria*, consists of internal and external elements, private and social prayer, liturgical acts and ceremonies, and especially sacrifice.

Adultery: (1) Sexual intercourse between a married person and another to whom one is not married; a violation of the obligations of chastity and justice. The Sixth Commandment prohibition against adultery is also regarded as a prohibition against all external sins of a sexual nature.

(2) Any sin of impurity (thought, desire, word, action) involving a married person who is not one's husband or wife has the nature of adultery.

Adventists: Members of several Christian sects whose doctrines are dominated by belief in a more or less imminent second advent or coming of Christ upon earth for a glorious 1,000-year reign of righteousness. This reign, following victory by the forces of good over evil in a final Battle of Armageddon, will begin with the resurrection of the chosen and will end with the resurrection of all other men and the annihilation of the wicked. Thereafter, the just will live forever in a renewed heaven and earth. A sleep of the soul takes place between the time of death and the day of judgment. There is no hell. The Bible, in fundamentalist interpretation, is regarded as the only rule of faith and practice.

About six sects have developed in the course of the Adventist movement which originated with William Miller (1782-1849) in the United States. Miller, on the basis of calculations made from the Book of Daniel, predicted that the second advent of Christ would occur between 1843 and 1844. After the prophecy went unfulfilled, divisions occurred in the movement and the Seventh Day Adventists, whose actual formation dates from 1860, emerged as the largest single body. The observance of Saturday instead of Sunday as the Lord's Day dates from 1844.

Advent Wreath: A wreath of laurel, spruce, or similar foliage with four candles which are lighted successively in the weeks of Advent to symbolize the approaching celebration of the birth of Christ, the Light of the World, at Christmas. The wreath originated among German Protestants.

Agape: A Greek word, meaning love, love feast, designating the meal of fellowship eaten at some gatherings of early Christians. Although held in some places in connection with the Mass, the agape was not part of the Mass, nor was it of universal institution and observance. Legislation against it was passed by the Council of Carthage (397) and other councils because of abuses. It was infrequently observed by the fifth century and disappeared altogether between the sixth and eighth centuries. In recent years, a limited revival has taken place in the course of the liturgical and ecumenical movements.

Age of Reason: (1) The time of life when one begins to distinguish between right and wrong, to understand an obligation and take on moral responsibility; seven years of age is the presumption in church law.

(2) Historically, the 18th century period of Enlightenment in England and France, the age of the Encyclopedists and Deists. According to a basic thesis of the Enlightenment, human experience and reason are the only sources of certain knowledge of truth; consequently, faith and revelation are discounted as valid sources of knowledge, and the reality of supernatural truth is called into doubt and/or denied.

Aggiornamento: An Italian word having the general meaning of bringing up to date, renewal, revitalization, descriptive of the processes of spiritual renewal and institutional reform and change in the Church; fostered by the Second Vatican Council.

Agnosticism: A theory which holds that man cannot have certain knowledge of immaterial reality, especially the existence of God and things pertaining to him. Immanuel Kant, one of the philosophical fathers of agnosticism, stood for the position that God, as well as the human soul, is unknowable on speculative grounds; nevertheless, he found practical imperatives for acknowledging God's existence, a view shared by many agnostics. The First Vatican Council declared that the existence of God and some of his attributes can be known with certainty by human reason, even without divine revelation. The word agnosticism was first used, in the sense given here, by T. H. Huxley in 1869.

Agnus Dei: A Latin phrase, meaning Lamb of God.

(1) A title given to Christ, the Lamb (victim) of the Sacrifice of the New Law (on Calvary and in Mass).

(2) A prayer said at Mass before the reception of Holy Communion.

(3) A sacramental. It is a round paschal-candle fragment blessed by the pope. On one side it bears the impression of a lamb, symbolic of Christ. On the reverse side, there may be any one of a number of impressions; e.g., the figure of a saint, the name and coat of arms of the reigning pope. The *agnus dei* may have originated at Rome in the fifth century. The first definite mention of it dates from about 820.

Alleluia: An exclamation of joy derived from Hebrew, All hail to him who is, praise God. It is used in the liturgy and other prayer on joyful occasions during the church year.

Allocution: A formal type of papal address, as distinguished from an ordinary sermon or statement of views.

Alms: An act, gift or service of compassion, motivated by love of God and neighbor, for the help of persons in need; an obligation of charity, which is measurable by the ability of one person to give assistance and by the degree of another's need. Almsgiving, along with prayer and fasting, is regarded as a work of penance as well as an exercise of charity. (See Corporal and Spiritual Works of Mercy.)

Alpha and Omega: The first and last letters of the Greek alphabet, used to symbolize the eternity of God (Rv. 1:8) and the divinity and eternity of Christ, the beginning and end of all things (Rv. 21:6; 22:13). Use of the letters as a monogram of Christ originated in the fourth century or earlier.

Amen: A Hebrew word meaning truly, it is true. In the Gospels, Christ used the word to add a note of authority to his statements. In other New Testament writings, as in Hebrew usage, it was the concluding word to doxologies. As the concluding word of prayers, it expresses assent to and acceptance of God's will.

Anathema: A Greek word with the root meaning of cursed or separated and the adapted meaning of excommunication, used in church documents, especially the canons of ecumenical councils, for the condemnation of heretical doctrines and of practices opposed to proper discipline.

Anchorite: A kind of hermit living in complete isolation and devoting himself exclusively to exercises of religion and severe penance according to a rule and way of life of his own devising. In early Christian times, anchorites were the forerunners of the monastic life. The closest contemporary approach to the life of an anchorite is that of Carthusian and Camaldolese hermits.

Angels: Purely spiritual beings with intelligence and free will, whose name indicates their mission as ministers of God and ministering spirits to men. They were created before the creation of the visible universe; the devil and bad angels, who were created good, fell from glory through their own fault. In addition to these essentials of defined doctrine, it is held that angels are personal beings; they can intercede for men; fallen angels were banished from God's glory in heaven to hell; bad angels can tempt men to commit sin. The doctrine of guardian angels, although not explicitly defined as a matter of faith, is rooted in long-standing tradition. No authoritative declaration has ever been issued regarding choirs or various categories of angels: according to theorists, there are nine choirs, consisting of seraphim, cherubim, thrones, dominations, principalities, powers, virtues, archangels and angels. In line with scriptural usage, only three angels can be named—Michael, Raphael and Gabriel.

Angelus: A devotion which commemorates the Incarnation of Christ. It consists of three versicles, three Hail Marys and a special prayer, and recalls the announcement to Mary by the Archangel Gabriel that she was chosen to be the Mother of Christ, her acceptance of the divine will, and the Incarnation (Lk. 1:26-38). The Angelus is recited at 6 a.m., noon and 6 p.m. The practice of reciting the Hail Mary in honor of the Incarnation was introduced by the Franciscans in 1263. The *Regina Caeli,* commemorating the joy of Mary at Christ's Resurrection, replaces the Angelus during the Easter season.

Anger: Passionate displeasure arising from some kind of offense suffered at the hands of another person, frustration or other cause, combined with a tendency to strike back at the cause of the displeasure; a violation of the Fifth Commandment and one of the capital sins if the displeasure is out of proportion to the cause and/or if the retaliation is unjust.

Anglican Orders: Holy orders conferred according to the rite of the Anglican (Episcopal) Church, which Leo XIII declared null and void in the bull *Apostolicae Curae,* Sept. 13, 1896. The orders were declared null because they were conferred according to a rite that was considered substantially defective in form and intent, and because of a break in apostolic succession that occurred when Matthew Parker became head of the Anglican hierarchy in 1559.

In making his declaration, Pope Leo cited earlier arguments against validity made by Julius III in 1553 and 1554 and by Paul IV in 1555. He also noted related directives requiring absolute ordination, according to the Catholic ritual, of convert ministers who had been ordained according to the Anglican Ordinal.

Antichrist: The man of sin, the lawless and wicked antagonist of Christ and the work of God; a mysterious figure of prophecy mentioned in the New Testament. Supported by Satan, submitting to no moral restraints, and armed with tremendous power, Antichrist will set himself up in opposition to God, work false miracles, persecute the People of God, and employ unimaginable means to lead men into error and evil during a period of widespread defection from the Christian faith before the end of time; he will be overcome by Christ. Catholic thinkers have regarded Antichrist as a person, a caricature of Christ, who will lead a final violent struggle against God and His people; they have also applied the title to personal and impersonal forces in history hostile to God and the Church. Official teaching has said little about Antichrist. In 1318, it labeled as partly heretical, senseless, and fanciful the assertions made by the Fraticelli about his coming; in 1415, the Council of Constance condemned the Wycliff thesis that excommunications made by the pope and other prelates were the actions of Antichrist.

Antiphon: (1) A short verse or text, generally from Scripture, recited in the Liturgy of the Hours before and after psalms and canticles.

(2) Any verse sung or recited by one part of a choir or congregation in response to the other part, as in antiphonal or alternate chanting.

Apologetics: The science and art of building and presenting the case for, accounting for, explaining, defending, justifying the reasonableness of the Christian faith, by a wide variety of means including facts of experience, history, science, philosophy. The constant objective of apologetics is preparation for response to God in faith; its ways and means, however, are subject to change in accordance with the various needs of people and different sets of circumstances.

Apostasy: (1) The total and obstinate rejection or abandonment of the Christian faith by a baptized person who continues to call himself a Christian. External manifestation of this rejection constitutes the crime of apostasy, and the person, called an *apostate,* automatically incurs a penalty of excommunication.

(2) Apostasy from orders is the unlawful withdrawal from or rejection of the obligations of the clerical state by a man who has received major orders. The canonical penalty for such apostasy is excommunication.

(3) Apostasy from the religious life occurs when a religious with perpetual vows unlawfully leaves the community with the intention of not returning, or actually remains outside the community for 30 days without permission. The canonical penalty for such apostasy is excommunication.

Apostolate: The ministry or work of an apostle. In Catholic usage, the word is an umbrella-like term covering all kinds and areas of work and endeavor for the service of God and the Church and the good of people. Thus, the apostolate of bishops is to carry on the mission of the Apostles as pastors of the People of God: of priests, to carry out the sacramental and pastoral ministry for which they are ordained; of religious, to follow and do the work of Christ in conformity with the evangelical counsels and their rule of life; of lay persons, as individuals and/or in groups, to give witness to Christ and build up the kingdom of God through practice of their faith, professional competence and the performance of good works in the concrete circumstances of daily life. Apostolic works are not limited to those done within the Church or by specifically Catholic groups, although some apostolates are officially assigned to certain persons or groups and are under the direction of church authorities. Apostolate derives from the commitment and obligation of baptism, confirmation, holy orders, matrimony, the duties of one's state in life, etc.

Archangel: An angel who carries out special missions for God in his dealings with men. Three of them are named in the Bible: Michael, leader of the angelic host and protector of the synagogue; Raphael, guide of Tobiah and healer of his father, who is regarded as the patron of travelers; Gabriel, called the angel of the Incarnation because of his announcement to Mary that she was to be the Mother of Christ.

Archdiocese: An ecclesiastical jurisdiction headed by an archbishop. An archdiocese is usually a metropolitan see, i.e., the principal one of a group of dioceses comprising a province; the other dioceses in the province are suffragan sees.

Archives: Documentary records, and the place where they are kept, of the spiritual and temporal government and affairs of the Church, a diocese, church agencies like the departments of the Roman Curia, bodies like religious institutes, and individual parishes. The collection, cataloguing, preserving, and use of these records are governed by norms stated in canon law and particular regulations. The strictest secrecy is always in effect for confidential records concerning matters of conscience, and documents of this kind are destroyed as soon as circumstances permit.

Archpriest: For some time, before and during the Middle Ages, a priest who took the place of a bishop at liturgical worship. In Europe, the term is sometimes used as an honorary title. It is also an honorary title in Eastern-Rite Churches.

Asceticism: The practice of self-discipline. In the spiritual life, asceticism — by personal prayer, meditation, self-denial, works of mortification, and outgoing interpersonal works — is motivated by love of God and contributes to growth in holiness.

Ashes: Religious significance has been associated with their use as symbolic of penance since Old Testament times. Thus, ashes of palm blessed on the previous Sunday of the Passion are placed on the foreheads of the faithful on Ash Wednesday to remind them to do works of penance, especially during the season of Lent, and that they are dust and unto dust will return. Ashes are a sacramental.

Aspergillum: A vessel or device used for sprinkling holy water. The ordinary type is a metallic rod with a bulbous tip which absorbs the water and discharges it at the motion of the user's hand.

Aspersory: A portable metallic vessel, similar to a pail, for carrying holy water.

Aspiration: Short exclamatory prayer; e.g., My Jesus, mercy.

Atheism: Denial of the existence of God, finding expression in a system of thought (speculative atheism) or a manner of acting (practical atheism) as though there were no God.

The Second Vatican Council, in its *Pastoral Constitution on the Church in the Modern World* (Nos. 19 to 21), noted that a profession of atheism may represent an explicit denial of God, the rejection of a wrong notion of God, an affirmation of man rather than of God, an extreme protest against evil. It said that such a profession might result from acceptance of such propositions as: there is no absolute truth; man can assert nothing, absolutely nothing, about God; everything can be explained by scientific reasoning alone; the whole question of God is devoid of meaning.

The constitution also cited two opinions of

influence in atheistic thought. One of them regards recognition of dependence on God as incompatible with human freedom and independence. The other views belief in God and religion as a kind of opiate which sedates man on earth, reconciling him to the acceptance of suffering, injustice, shortcomings, etc., because of hope for greater things after death, and thereby hindering him from seeking and working for improvement and change for the better here and now.

All of these views, in one way or another, have been involved in the No-God and Death-of-God schools of thought in recent and remote history.

Atonement: The redemptive activity of Christ, who reconciled man with God through his Incarnation and entire life, and especially by his suffering and Resurrection. The word also applies to prayer and good works by which men join themselves with and take part in Christ's work of reconciliation and reparation for sin.

Attributes of God: Perfections of God. God possesses—and is—all the perfections of being, without limitation. Because he is infinite, all of these perfections are one, perfectly united in him. Man, however, because of the limited power of understanding, views these perfections separately, as distinct characteristics—even though they are not actually distinct in God. God is: almighty, eternal, holy, immortal, immense, immutable, incomprehensible, ineffable, infinite, invisible, just, loving, merciful, most high, most wise, omnipotent, omniscient, omnipresent, patient, perfect, provident, supreme, true.

Avarice (Covetousness): A disorderly and unreasonable attachment to and desire for material things; called a capital sin because it involves preoccupation with material things to the neglect of spiritual goods and obligations of justice and charity.

Ave Maria: See Hail Mary.

B

Baldachino: A canopy over an altar.

Beatification: A preliminary step toward canonization of a saint. It begins with an investigation of the candidate's life, writings and heroic practice of virtue, and the certification of at least two miracles worked by God through his intercession. If the findings of the investigation so indicate, the pope decrees that the Servant of God may be called *Blessed* and may be honored locally or in a limited way in the liturgy. Additional procedures lead to canonization (see separate entry).

Beatific Vision: The intuitive, immediate and direct vision and experience of God enjoyed in the light of glory by all the blessed in heaven. The vision is a supernatural mystery.

Beatitude: A literary form of the Old and New Testaments in which blessings are promised to persons for various reasons. Beatitudes are mentioned 26 times in the Psalms, and in other books of the Old Testament. The best known beatitudes — identifying blessedness with participation in the kingdom of God and his righteousness, and descriptive of the qualities of Christian perfection — are those recounted in Mt. 5:3-11 and Lk. 6:20-22.

In Matthew's account, the beatitudes are:

"How blest are the poor in spirit: the reign of God is theirs.

"Blest too are the sorrowing; they shall be consoled.

"(Blest are the lowly; they shall inherit the land.)

"Blest are they who hunger and thirst for holiness; they shall have their fill.

"Blest are they who show mercy; mercy shall be theirs.

"Blest are the single-hearted for they shall see God.

"Blest too are the peacemakers; they shall be called sons of God.

"Blest are those persecuted for holiness' sake; the reign of God is theirs.

"Blest are you when they insult you and persecute you and utter every kind of slander against you because of me."

In Luke's account, the beatitudes are:

"Blest are you poor; the reign of God is yours.

"Blest are you who hunger; you shall be filled.

"Blest are you who are weeping; you shall laugh.

"Blest shall you be when men hate you, when they ostracize you and insult you and proscribe your name as evil because of the Son of Man."

Benediction of the Blessed Sacrament: A short exposition of the Eucharist for adoration by and blessing of the faithful. Devotional practices include the singing of Eucharistic and other hymns, and recitation of the Divine Praises. Benediction, in its present form, dates from about the 15th century and is a form of liturgical worship.

Benedictus: The canticle or hymn uttered by Zechariah at the circumcision of St. John the Baptist (Lk. 1:68-79). It is an expression of praise and thanks to God for sending John as a precursor of the Messiah. The *Benedictus* is recited in the Liturgy of the Hours as part of Lauds.

Bible Service: A devotion consisting essentially of common prayer of a biblical or liturgical character, several readings from Scripture, and a homily on the texts.

Biglietto: A papal document of notification of appointment to the cardinalate.

Biretta: A stiff, square hat with three ridges on top worn by clerics in church and on other occasions.

Blasphemy: Any expression of insult or contempt with respect to God, principally, and to holy persons and things, secondarily; a violation of the honor due to God in the context of the First and Second Commandments.

Blasphemy of the Spirit: Deliberate resistance to the Holy Spirit, called the unforgivable sin (Mt. 12:31) because it makes his saving action impossible. Thus, the only unforgivable sin is the one for which a person will not seek pardon from God.

Blessing: Invocation of God's favor, by official ministers of the Church or by private individuals. Blessings are recounted in the Old and New Testaments, and are common in the Christian tradition. The Church, through its ordained ministers (bishops and priests, especially), invokes divine favor in liturgical blessings; e.g., of the people at Mass, of the gifts to be consecrated at Mass, of persons and things on various occasions. Sacramentals — such as crucifixes, crosses, rosaries, scapulars, medals — are blessed by ministers of the Church for the invocation of God's favor on those who use them in the proper manner. Many types of blessings are listed in the *Roman Ritual*. Private blessings, as well as those of an official kind, are efficacious. Blessings are imparted with the Sign of the Cross and appropriate prayer.

Boat: A small vessel used to hold incense which is to be placed in the censer.

Brief, Apostolic: A papal letter, less formal than a bull, signed for the pope by a secretary and impressed with the seal of the Fisherman's Ring. Simple apostolic letters of this kind are issued for beatifications and with respect to other matters.

Bull, Apostolic: The most solemn form of papal document, beginning with the name and title of the pope (e.g., Paul VI, Servant of the Servants of God), dealing with an important subject, and having attached to it either a leaden seal called a bulla or a red ink imprint of the device on the seal. Bulls are known as apostolic letters with the seal. The seal, on one side, has representations of the heads of Sts. Peter and Paul; on the other side, the name of the reigning pope. Bulls are issued to confer the titles of bishops and cardinals, to promulgate canonizations, and for other purposes. A collection of bulls is called a *bullarium*.

Burial, Ecclesiastical: Interment with church rites and in consecrated ground. Catechumens as well as baptized Catholics have a right to ecclesiastical burial. A non-Catholic partner in a mixed marriage may be buried in a Catholic cemetery with the Catholic partner.

C

Calumny: Harming the name and good reputation of a person by lies; a violation of obligations of justice and truth. Restitution is due for calumny.

Calvary: A knoll about 15 feet high just outside the western wall of Jerusalem where Christ was crucified, so called from the Latin *calvaria* (skull) which described its shape.

Canon: A Greek word meaning rule, norm, standard, measure.

(1) The word designates the Canon of Sacred Scripture, which is the list of books recognized by the Church as inspired by the Holy Spirit.

(2) In the sense of regulating norms, the word designates the body or corpus of Canon Law enacted and promulgated by ecclesiastical authority for the orderly administration and government of the Church. The Code of Canon Law now in force in the Roman Church has been in effect since 1918. It consists of 2,414 canons which are divided into five books covering general rules, ecclesiastical persons, sacred things, trials, crimes and punishments. The code is now under review for the purpose of revision. Eastern-Rite Churches have their own canon law.

(3) The term also designates the four Canons or Eucharistic Prayers of the Mass, the core of the liturgy.

(4) Certain dignitaries of the Church have the title of Canon, and some religious are known as Canons.

Canonization: An infallible declaration by the pope that a person, who died as a martyr and/or practiced Christian virtue to a heroic degree, is now in heaven and is worthy of honor and imitation by all the faithful. Such a declaration is preceded by the process of beatification and another detailed investigation concerning the person's reputation for holiness, his writings, and (except in the case of martyrs) miracles ascribed to his intercession after his death. Miracles are not required for martyrs. The pope can dispense from some of the formalities ordinarily required in canonization procedures (equivalent canonization), as Pope John XXIII did in the canonization of St. Gregory Barbarigo on May 26, 1960. A saint is worthy of honor in liturgical worship throughout the universal Church.

From its earliest years the Church has venerated saints. Public official honor always required the approval of the bishop of the place. Martyrs were the first to be honored. St. Martin of Tours, who died in 397, was the first non-martyr venerated as a saint. The first official canonization by a pope for the universal Church was that of St. Ulrich by John XV in 993. Alexander III reserved the process of canonization to the Holy See in 1171. In 1588 Sixtus V established the Sacred Congregation of Rites for the principal purpose of handling causes for beatification and canonization: this function is now the work of the Congregation for the Causes of Saints. The present procedure is outlined in canons 1999-2141 of the Code of Canon Law and in a 1969 enactment by Paul VI.

The essential portion of a canonization decree states:

"For the honor of the holy and undivided Trinity; for the exaltation of the Catholic faith and the increase of Christian life; with the authority of our Lord Jesus Christ, of the blessed Apostles Peter and Paul, and with our own authority; after mature deliberation and with the divine assistance, often implored; with the counsel of many of our brothers.

"We decree and define that (name) is a saint and we inscribe him (her) in the Catalogue of Saints, stating that he (she) shall be venerated in the universal Church with pious devotion.

"In the name of the Father and of the Son and of the Holy Spirit. Amen."

The official listing of saints and blessed is contained in the *Roman Martyrology* and related decrees issued after its last publication. Butler's unofficial *Lives of the Saints* (1956) contains 2,565 entries.

The Church regards all persons in heaven as saints, not just those who have been officially canonized.

(See Beatification, Saints, Canonizations by Leo XIII and His Successors.)

Canticle: A scriptural chant or prayer differing from the psalms. Those of the canticles prescribed for use in the Liturgy of the Hours are: the *Magnificat* (Lk. 1:46-55), the *Benedictus* (1:68-79), and the *Nunc Dimittis* (Lk. 2:29-32).

Capital Punishment: Punishment for crime by means of the death penalty. The political community, which has authority to provide for the common good, has the right to defend itself and its members against unjust aggression and may in extreme cases punish with the death penalty persons found guilty before the law of serious crimes against individuals and a just social order. Such punishment is essentially vindictive. Its value as a crime-deterrent is a matter of perennial debate. The prudential judgment as to whether or not there should be capital punishment belongs to the civic community.

Capital Sins: Moral faults which, if habitual, give rise to many more sins. They are: pride, covetousness, lust, anger, gluttony, envy, sloth.

The opposite virtues are: humility, liberality, chastity, meekness, temperance, brotherly love, diligence.

Cardinal Virtues: The four principal moral virtues are prudence, justice, temperance and fortitude.

Cassock: A full-length, close-fitting robe worn by priests and other clerics; usually black for priests, purple for bishops and other prelates, red for cardinals, white for the pope. It is made of various fabrics; e.g., silk, wool, broadcloth, synthetics. Its form, with modifications, dates from the 11th century. In place of a cassock, men religious wear the habit proper to their institute.

Catacombs: Underground Christian cemeteries in various cities of the Roman Empire and Italy, especially in the vicinity of Rome; the burial sites of many martyrs and other Christians. Developed from aboveground cemeteries, their passageways, burial niches and assembly rooms were dug out of tuffa, a soft clay which hardened into rock-like consistency on drying. The earliest ones date from the third century; in the fourth, they became the scene of memorial services as the veneration of martyrs increased in popularity; in the seventh and eighth centuries, they were plundered by the Lombards and other invaders. The relics of many martyrs were removed to safer places in the ninth century; afterwards, the catacombs fell into neglect and oblivion until interest in them revived in the 16th century. The catacombs have been excavated extensively, yielding considerable information about early Christian symbolism and art, dating from the third century on, and other aspects of Christian life and practice.

Catafalque: A small structure like a bier, used at services for the dead in the absence of the corpse.

Catechism: A summary of Christian doctrine in question and answer form, used for purposes of instruction.

Catechumen: A person preparing, in a program of instruction and spiritual formation, for baptism and reception into the Church.

Cathedra: A Greek word for chair, designating the chair or seat of a bishop in the principal church of his diocese, which is therefore called a cathedral (see separate entry).

Cathedraticum: The tax paid to a bishop by all churches and benefices subject to him for the support of episcopal administration and for works of charity.

Catholic: A Greek word, meaning universal, first used in the title Catholic Church in a letter written by St. Ignatius of Antioch about 107 to the Christians of Smyrna.

Celebret: A Latin word, meaning Let him celebrate, the name of a document issued by a bishop or other superior stating that a priest is in good standing and therefore should be given opportunity to celebrate Mass or perform other priestly functions.

Celibacy: The unmarried state of life, required in the Roman or Latin Church of candidates for holy orders and of men already ordained to holy orders, for the practice of perfect chastity and total dedication to the service of people in the ministry of the Church. Celibacy is enjoined as a condition for ordination by church discipline and law, not by dogmatic necessity.

In the Roman Church, a consensus in favor of celibacy developed in the early centuries while the clergy included both celibates and men who had been married once. The first local legislation on the subject was enacted by a local council held in Elvira, Spain, about 306; it forbade bishops, priests, deacons and other ministers to have wives. Similar enactments were passed by other local councils from that time on, and by the 12th century particular laws regarded marriage by clerics in major orders to be not only unlawful but also null and void. The latter view was translated by the Second Lateran Council in 1139 into what seems to be the first written universal law making holy orders an invalidating impediment to marriage. In 1563 the Council of Trent ruled definitely on the matter and established the discipline still in force in the Roman Church.

Some exceptions to this discipline have been made in recent years. Several married Protestant ministers who became converts and were subsequently ordained to the priesthood have been permitted to continue in marriage. Married men over the age of 35 can be ordained to the permanent diaconate.

In recent years, considerable agitation has developed in favor of optional rather than mandatory celibacy for priests.

Eastern Church discipline on celibacy differs from that of the Roman Church. In line with legislation enacted by the Synod of Trullo in 692 and still in force, candidates for holy orders may marry before becoming deacons and may continue in marriage thereafter, but marriage after ordination is forbidden. Eastern-Rite bishops in the US, however, do not ordain married candidates for the priesthood. Eastern-Rite bishops are unmarried.

Cenacle: The room in Jerusalem where Christ ate the Last Supper with his Apostles.

Censer: A metal vessel with a perforated cover and suspended by chains, in which incense is burned. It is used at some Masses, Benediction of the Blessed Sacrament and other liturgical functions.

Censorship of Books: An exercise of vigilance by the Church for safeguarding authentic religious teaching.

Censorship procedure requires that books and other works dealing with matters of faith and morals and related subjects be cleared for doctrinal orthodoxy before publication. This is accomplished by having the works reviewed by officials called censors.

Permission to publish works of a religious character, together with the apparatus of reviewing them beforehand, generally falls under the authority of the bishop of the place where the writer lives or where the works are published.

Clearance for publication is usually indicated by the terms *Nihil obstat* (Nothing stands in the way) issued by the censor and *Imprimatur* (Let it be printed) authorized by the bishop. The occasional equivalent of these formal terms is the statement, Printed with ecclesiastical approval. The clearing of works for publication does not necessarily imply approval of an author's viewpoint or his manner of handling a subject.

Censures: Spiritual penalties inflicted by the Church on baptized persons for committing certain serious sins, which are classified as crimes in canon law, and for being or re-

maining obstinate therein. Excommunication, suspension and interdict have been the censures in force since the time of Innocent III (1214). Their intended purposes are to deter persons from committing sins which, more seriously and openly than others, threaten the common good of the Church and its members; to punish and correct offenders; and to provide for the making of reparation for harm done to the community of the Church. Censures may be incurred automatically (*ipso facto*) on the commission of certain offenses for which fixed penalties have been laid down in church law (*latae sententiae*); or they may be inflicted by sentence of a judge (*ferendae sententiae*). Obstinacy in crime—also called contumacy, disregard of a penalty, defiance of church authority — is presumed by law in the commission of crimes for which automatic censures are decreed. The presence and degree of contumacy in other cases, for which judicial sentence is required, is subject to determination by a judge. Absolution can be obtained from any censure, provided the person repents and desists from obstinacy. Absolution may be reserved to the pope, the bishop of a place, or the major superior of an exempt clerical religious institute. In danger of death, any priest can absolve from all censures; in other cases, faculties to absolve from reserved censures can be exercised by competent authorities or given to other priests.

Ceremonies, Master of: One who directs the proceedings of a rite or ceremony during the function.

Chamberlain: (1) The Chamberlain of the Holy Roman Church is a cardinal who administers the property and revenues of the Holy See. On the death of the pope he becomes head of the College of Cardinals and summons and directs the conclave until a new pope is elected.

(2) The Chamberlain of the Sacred College of Cardinals has charge of the property and revenues of the College and keeps the record of business transacted in consistories.

(3) The Chamberlain of the Roman Clergy is the president of the secular clergy of Rome.

Chancellor: Notary of a diocese, who draws up written documents in the government of the diocese; takes care of, arranges and indexes diocesan archives, records of dispensations and ecclesiastical trials.

Chancery (1) A branch of church administration that handles written documents used in the government of a diocese.

(2) The administrative office of a diocese, a bishop's office.

Chapel: A building or part of another building used for divine worship; a portion of a church set aside for the celebration of Mass or for some special devotion.

Chaplain: A priest appointed for the pastoral service of any division of the armed forces, religious communities, institutions, various groups of the faithful.

Chaplet: A term, meaning little crown, applied to a rosary or, more commonly, to a small string of beads used for devotional purposes; e.g., the Infant of Prague chaplet.

Chapter: A general meeting of delegates of religious orders for elections and the handling of other important affairs of their communities.

Charisms: Gifts or graces given by God to men for the good of others and the Church. Examples are special gifts for apostolic work, prophecy, healing, discernment of spirits, the life of evangelical poverty, here-and-now witness to faith in various circumstances of life.

The Second Vatican Council made the following statement about charisms in the *Dogmatic Constitution on the Church* (No. 12):

"It is not only through the sacraments and Church ministries that the same Holy Spirit sanctifies and leads the People of God and enriches it with virtues. Allotting His gifts 'to everyone according as he will' (1 Cor. 12:11), He distributes special graces among the faithful of every rank. By these gifts He makes them fit and ready to undertake the various tasks or offices advantageous for the renewal and upbuilding of the Church, according to the words of the Apostle: 'The manifestation of the Spirit is given to everyone for profit' (1 Cor. 12:7). These charismatic gifts, whether they be the most outstanding or the more simple and widely diffused, are to be received with thanksgiving and consolation, for they are exceedingly suitable and useful for the needs of the Church.

"Still, extraordinary gifts are not to be rashly sought after, nor are the fruits of apostolic labor to be presumptuously expected from them. In any case, judgment as to their genuineness and proper use belongs to those who preside over the Church, and to whose special competence it belongs, not indeed to extinguish the Spirit, but to test all things and hold fast to that which is good" (cf. 1 Thes. 5:12; 19-21).

Charity: Love of God above all things for his own sake, and love of one's neighbor as oneself because and as an expression of one's love for God; the greatest of the three theological virtues. The term is sometimes also used to designate sanctifying grace.

Chastity: Properly ordered behavior with respect to sex. In marriage, the exercise of the procreative power is integrated with the norms and purposes of marriage. Outside of marriage, the rule is self-denial of the voluntary exercise and enjoyment of the procreative faculty in thought, word or action.

The vow of chastity, which reinforces the virtue of chastity with the virtue of religion, is an evangelical counsel and one of the three vows professed by religious.

Chirograph or Autograph Letter: A letter written by a pope himself, in his own handwriting.

Christ: The title of Jesus, derived from the Greek translation *Christos* of the Hebrew term *Messiah,* meaning the Anointed of God, the Savior and Deliverer of his people. Christian use of the title is a confession of belief that Jesus is the Savior.

Christianity: The sum total of things related to belief in Christ — the Christian religion, Christian churches, Christians themselves, society based on and expressive of Christian beliefs, culture reflecting Christian values.

Christians: The name first applied about the year 43 to followers of Christ at Antioch, the capital of Syria. It was used by the pagans as a contemptuous term. The word applies to persons who profess belief in the divinity and teachings of Christ and who give witness to him in life.

Christian Science: A religious doctrine consisting of Mary Baker Eddy's interpretation and formulation of the actions and teachings of Christ. Its basic tenets reflect Mrs. Eddy's ideas regarding the reality of spirit and its control and domination of what is not spirit. The basic statement of the doctrine is contained in *Science and Health, with Key to the Scriptures,* which she first published in 1875, nine years after being saved from death and healed on reading the New Testament.

Mary Baker Eddy (1821-1910) established the church in 1879, and in 1892 founded at Boston the First Church of Christ, Scientist, of which all other Christian Science churches are branches. The individual churches are self-governing and self-supporting under the general supervision of a board of directors. Services consist of readings of portions of Scripture and *Science and Health.* One of the church's publications, *The Christian Science Monitor,* has a worldwide reputation as a journal of news and opinion.

Church: (1) See several entries under Church, Catholic. The universal Church is the Church spread throughout the world. The local Church is the Church in a particular locality; e.g., a diocese. Inasmuch as the members of the Church are on earth, in purgatory, or in glory in heaven, the Church is called militant, suffering, or triumphant.

(2) In general, any religious body.

(3) Place of divine worship.

Churching: A rite of thanksgiving in which a blessing is given to women after childbirth. The rite is reminiscent of the Old Testament ceremony of purification (Lv. 12:2-8).

Circumcision: A ceremonial practice symbolic of initiation and participation in the covenant between God and Abraham.

Circumincession: The indwelling of each divine Person of the Holy Trinity in the others.

Clergy: Men ordained to holy orders and assigned to pastoral and other ministries for the service of the people and the Church.

(1) Diocesan or secular clergy are committed to pastoral ministry in parishes and in other capacities in a local church (diocese)

under the direction of their bishop, to whom they are bound by a promise of obedience.

(2) Regular clergy belong to religious institutes (orders, congregations, societies) and are so called because they observe the rule (*regula,* in Latin) of their respective institutes. They are committed to the ways of life and apostolates of their institutes. In ordinary pastoral ministry, they are under the direction of local bishops as well as their own superiors.

Clericalism: A term generally used in a derogatory sense to mean action, influence and interference by the Church and the clergy in matters with which they allegedly should not be concerned. Anticlericalism is a reaction of antipathy, hostility, distrust and opposition to the Church and clergy arising from real and/or alleged faults of the clergy, overextension of the role of the laity, or for other reasons.

Cloister: The enclosure of a convent or monastery, which members of the community may not leave or outsiders enter without due permission. Enclosure is of two kinds: papal, in monasteries of religious with solemn vows; episcopal, in the houses of other religious.

Code: A digest of rules or regulations, such as the Code of Canon Law.

Collegiality: The bishops of the Church, in union with and subordinate to the pope — who has full, supreme and universal power over the Church which he can always exercise independently — have supreme teaching and pastoral authority over the whole Church. In addition to their proper authority of office for the good of the faithful in their respective dioceses or other jurisdictions, the bishops have authority to act for the good of the universal Church. This collegial authority is exercised in a solemn manner in an ecumenical council and can also be exercised in other ways sanctioned by the pope. Doctrine on collegiality was set forth by the Second Vatican Council in the *Dogmatic Constitution on the Church.* (See separate entry.)

By extension, the concept of collegiality is applied to other forms of participation and co-responsibility by members of a community.

Commissariat of the Holy Land: A special jurisdiction within the Order of Friars Minor, whose main purposes are the collecting of alms for support of the Holy Places in Palestine and staffing of the Holy Places and missions in the Middle East with priests and brothers. There are 69 such commissariats in 33 countries. One of them has headquarters at Mt. St. Sepulchre, Washington, D.C. Franciscans have had custody of the Holy Places since 1342.

Communion of Faithful, Saints: The communion of all the People of God — on earth, in heavenly glory, in purgatory — with Christ and each other in faith, grace, prayer and good works.

Concelebration: The liturgical act in which several priests, led by one member of the group, offer Mass together, all consecrating the bread and wine. Concelebration has always been common in churches of Eastern Rite. In the Roman Rite, it was long restricted, taking place only at the ordination of bishops and the ordination of priests. The *Constitution on the Sacred Liturgy* issued by the Second Vatican Council set new norms for concelebration.

Concordat: A Church-state treaty with the force of law concerning matters of mutual concern — e.g., rights of the Church, appointment of bishops, arrangement of ecclesiastical jurisdictions, marriage laws, education. Approximately 150 agreements of this kind have been negotiated since the Concordat of Worms in 1122.

Concupiscence: Any tendency of the sensitive appetite. The term is most frequently used in reference to desires and tendencies for sinful sense pleasure.

Confession: Sacramental confession is the act by which a person tells or confesses his sins to a priest who is authorized to give absolution in the sacrament of penance.

Confessor: (1) A male saint who lived a life of eminent sanctity and heroic virtue, but who did not suffer martyrdom for his faith. The first confessor honored as a saint was Martin of Tours.

(2) A priest who administers the sacrament of penance.

Confraternity: An association whose members practice a particular form of religious devotion and/or are engaged in some kind of apostolic work. When a confraternity reaches the stage where affiliations similar to itself are formed and adopt its rules, it takes the name of archconfraternity.

Conscience: Practical judgment concerning the moral goodness or sinfulness of an action. In the Catholic view, this judgment is made by reference of the action, its attendant circumstances and the intentions of the person to the requirements of divine law as expressed in the Ten Commandments, the summary law of love for God and neighbor, the life and teaching of Christ, and the authoritative teaching and practice of the Church with respect to the total demands of divine Revelation.

A person is obliged: (1) to obey a certain and correct conscience; (2) to obey a certain conscience even if it is inculpably erroneous; (3) not to obey, but to correct, a conscience known to be erroneous or lax; (4) to rectify a scrupulous conscience by following the advice of a confessor and by other measures; (5) to resolve doubts of conscience before acting.

It is legitimate to act for solid and probable reasons when a question of moral responsibility admits of argument (see Probabilism). It is also legitimate to resolve doubts in difficult cases by having recourse to a reflex principle (e.g., by following the manner of acting of a well-informed and well-intentioned group of persons in similar circumstances).

Conscience, Examination of: Self-examination to determine one's spiritual state before God, especially regarding one's sins and faults. It is recommended as a regular practice and is practically necessary in preparing for the sacrament of penance. The *particular examen* is a regular examination to assist in overcoming specific faults and imperfections.

Consecration of a Church: See Dedication of a Church.

Consistory: An assembly of cardinals presided over by the pope. Consistories are secret (pope and cardinals only), semi-public (plus other prelates), and public (plus other attendants).

Constitution: (1) An apostolic or papal constitution is a document in which a pope enacts and promulgates law.

(2) A formal and solemn document issued by an ecumenical council on a doctrinal or pastoral subject, with binding force in the whole Church; e.g., the four constitutions issued by the Second Vatican Council on the Church, liturgy, Revelation, and the Church in the modern world.

(3) The constitutions of religious orders spell out details of and norms drawn from the various rules for the guidance and direction of the life and work of members of each institute.

Consubstantiation: A theory which holds that the Body and Blood of Christ coexist with the substance of bread and wine in the Holy Eucharist. This theory, also called *impanation,* is incompatible with the doctrine of transubstantiation.

Contraception: Anything done to prevent sexual intercourse from resulting in conception. Direct contraception is against the order of nature. Indirect contraception — as a secondary effect of medical treatment or other action having a necessary, good, non-contraceptive purpose — is permissible under the principle of double effect.

Contrition: Sorrow for sin coupled with a purpose of amendment. Contrition arising from a supernatural motive is necessary for the forgiveness of sin.

(1) Perfect contrition is sorrow for sin arising from the motive of pure love of God. Perfect contrition, which implies the intention of doing all God wants done for the forgiveness of sin, is sufficient for the forgiveness of serious sin and the remission of all temporal punishment due for sin. (The intention to receive the sacrament of penance is implicit — even if unrealized, as in the case of some persons — in perfect contrition.)

(2) Imperfect contrition or attrition is sorrow arising from a quasi-selfish supernatural motive; e.g., the fear of losing heaven, suffering the pains of hell, etc. Imperfect contrition

is sufficient for the forgiveness of serious sin when joined with absolution in confession, and sufficient for the forgiveness of venial sin even outside of confession.

Contumely: Personal insult, reviling a person in his presence by accusation of moral faults, by refusal of recognition or due respect; a violation of obligations of justice and charity.

Corporal Works of Mercy: Feeding the hungry, giving drink to the thirsty, clothing the naked, visiting the imprisoned, sheltering the homeless, visiting the sick, burying the dead.

Councils: Bodies representative of various categories of members of the Church which participate with bishops and other church authorities in making decisions and carrying out action programs for the good of the Church and the accomplishment of its mission to its own members and society in general. Examples are priests' senates or councils, councils of religious and lay persons, parish councils, diocesan pastoral councils.

Councils, Plenary: National councils or councils of the bishops of several ecclesiastical provinces, assembled under the presidency of a papal legate to take action related to the life and mission of the Church in the area under their jurisdiction. The membership of such councils is fixed by canon law; their decrees, when approved by the Holy See, are binding in the territory (see Index, Three Plenary Counccils of Baltimore).

Councils, Provincial: Meetings of the bishops of a province. The metropolitan, or ranking archbishop, of an ecclesiastical province convenes and presides over such councils in a manner prescribed by canon law to take action related to the life and mission of the Church in the province. Acts and decrees must be approved by the Holy See before being promulgated. Provincial councils should be held at least once every 20 years.

Counsels, Evangelical: Gospel counsels of perfection, especially voluntary poverty, perfect chastity and obedience, which were recommended by Christ to those who would devote themselves exclusively and completely to the immediate service of God. Religious bind themselves by public vows to observe these counsels in a life of total consecration to God and service to people through various kinds of apostolic works.

Counter-Reformation: The period of approximately 100 years following the Council of Trent, which witnessed a reform within the Church to stimulate genuine Catholic life and to counteract effects of the Reformation.

Covenant: A bond of relationship between parties pledged to each other. God-initiated covenants in the Old Testament included those with Abraham, Noah, Moses, Levi, David. The Mosaic (Sinai) covenant made Israel God's Chosen People on terms of fidelity to true faith, true worship, and righteous conduct according to the Decalogue. The New Testament covenant, prefigured in the Old Testament, is the bond men have with God through Christ. All men are called to be parties to this perfect and everlasting covenant, which was mediated and ratified by Christ.

Creation: The production by God of something out of nothing. The biblical account of creation is contained in the first two chapters of Genesis.

Creator: God, the supreme, self-existing Being, the absolute and infinite First Cause of all things.

Creature: Everything in the realm of being is a creature, except God.

Cremation: The reduction of a human corpse to ashes by means of fire. Cremation is not in line with Catholic tradition and practice, even though it is not opposed to any article of faith. It can be permitted for serious reasons. The general practice, however, was forbidden in a decree issued May 19, 1886, by the Sacred Congregation of the Holy Office.

This ruling was incorporated in the Code of Canon Law (Canons 1203, 1240), which generally banned the practice of cremation, forbade following orders for cremation, and deprived of the last rites and ecclesiastical burial those who directed that their bodies be cremated and did not retract the directions.

The principal reason behind the prohibition against cremation was the fact that, historically, the practice had represented an attempt to deny the doctrine of the resurrection of the body. It also appeared to be a form of violence against the body which, as the temple of the Holy Spirit during life, should be treated with reverence.

The Congregation for the Doctrine of the Faith, under date of May 8, 1963, circulated among bishops an instruction which upheld the traditional practices of Christian burial but modified anti-cremation legislation. Cremation may be permitted for serious reasons, of a private as well as public nature, provided it does not involve any contempt of the Church or of religion, or any attempt to deny, question, or belittle the doctrine of the resurrection of the body. The person may receive the last rites and be given ecclesiastical burial. A priest may say prayers for the deceased at the crematorium, but full liturgical ceremonies may not take place there.

Crib: A devotional representation of the birth of Jesus. The custom of erecting cribs is generally attributed to St. Francis of Assisi who in 1223 obtained from Pope Honorius III permission to use a crib and figures of the Christ Child, Mary, St. Joseph, and others, to represent the mystery of the Nativity.

Crosier: The bishop's staff, symbolic of his pastoral office, responsibility and authority.

Crypt: An underground or partly underground chamber; e.g., the lower part of a church used for worship and/or burial.

Cura Animarum: A Latin phrase, meaning care of souls, designating the pastoral ministry and responsibility of bishops and priests.

Curia: The personnel and offices through which (1) the pope administers the affairs of the universal Church, the *Roman Curia* (see separate entry), or (2) a bishop the affairs of a diocese, *diocesan curia*. The principal officials of a diocesan curia are the vicar general of the diocese, the chancellor, officials of the diocesan tribunal or court, examiners, consultors, auditors, notaries.

Custos: A religious superior who presides over a number of convents collectively called a custody. In some religious institutes, a custos may be the deputy of a higher superior.

D

Dean: (1) A priest with supervisory responsibility over a section of a diocese known as a deanery. The post-Vatican II counterpart of a dean is an episcopal vicar.

(2) The senior or ranking member of a group.

Dean of the Sacred College: The president of the College of Cardinals (the ranking cardinal bishop). He is elected by the cardinals holding title to the suburban sees of Rome.

Decision: A judgment or pronouncement on a cause or suit, given by a church tribunal or official with judicial authority. A decision has the force of law for concerned parties.

Declaration: (1) An ecclesiastical document which presents an interpretation of an existing law.

(2) A position paper on a specific subject; e.g., the three declarations issued by the Second Vatican Council on religious freedom, non-Christian religions, and Christian education.

Decree: An edict or ordinance issued by a pope and/or by an ecumenical council, with binding force in the whole Church; by a department of the Roman Curia, with binding force for concerned parties; by a territorial body of bishops, with binding force for persons in the area; by individual bishops, with binding force for concerned parties until revocation or the death of the bishop.

The nine decrees issued by the Second Vatican Council were combinations of doctrinal and pastoral statements with executive orders for action and movement toward renewal and reform in the Church.

Dedication of a Church: The ceremony whereby a church is solemnly set apart for the worship of God. The custom of dedicating churches had an antecedent in Old Testament ceremonies for the dedication of the Temple, as in the times of Solomon and the Maccabees. The earliest extant record of the dedication of a Christian church dates from early in the fourth century, when it was done simply by the celebration of Mass. Other ceremonies developed later. A church can be dedicated by a simple blessing or a solemn consecration. The rite of consecration is performed by a bishop.

Definitors: Members of the governing council of a religious order, each one having a decisive vote equal to the vote of the general or provincial superior.

Deism: A system of natural religion which acknowledges the existence of God but regards him as so transcendent and remote from man and the universe that divine revelation and the supernatural order of things are irrelevant and unacceptable. It developed from rationalistic principles in England in the 17th and 18th centuries, and had Voltaire, Rousseau and the Encyclopedists among its advocates in France.

Despair: Abandonment of hope for salvation arising from the conviction that God will not provide the necessary means for attaining it, that following God's way of life for salvation is impossible, or that one's sins are unforgivable; a serious sin against the Holy Spirit and the theological virtues of hope and faith, involving distrust in the mercy and goodness of God and a denial of the truths that God wills the salvation of all men and provides sufficient grace for it. Real despair is distinguished from unreasonable fear with respect to the difficulties of attaining salvation, from morbid anxiety over the demands of divine justice, and from feelings of despair.

Detachment: Control of affection for creatures by two principles: (1) supreme love and devotion belong to God; (2) love and service of creatures should be an expression of love for God.

Detraction: Revelation of true but hidden faults of a person without sufficient and justifying reason; a violation of requirements of justice and charity, involving the obligation to make restitution when this is possible without doing more harm to the good name of the offended party. In some cases, e.g., to prevent evil, secret faults may and should be disclosed.

Devil: (1) Lucifer, Satan, chief of the fallen angels who sinned and were banished from heaven. Still possessing angelic powers, he can cause such diabolical phenomena as possession and obsession, and can tempt men to sin.

(2) Any fallen angel.

Devil's Advocate: See Promoter of the Faith.

Devotion: (1) Religious fervor, piety; dedication.

(2) The consolation experienced at times during prayer; a reverent manner of praying.

Devotions: Pious practices of members of the Church include not only participation in various acts of the liturgy but also in other acts of worship generally called popular or private devotions. Concerning these, the Second Vatican Council said in the *Constitution on the Sacred Liturgy* (No. 13): "Popular devotions of the Christian people are warmly commended, provided they accord with the laws and norms of the Church. Such is especially the case with devotions called for by the Apostolic See. Devotions proper to the individual churches also have a special dignity. . . . These devotions should be so drawn up that they harmonize with the liturgical seasons, accord with the sacred liturgy, are in some fashion derived from it, and lead the people to it, since the liturgy by its very nature far surpasses any of them."

Devotions of a liturgical type are Benediction of the Blessed Sacrament, recitation of the Little Office of the Blessed Virgin Mary or of Vespers and Compline. Examples of paraliturgical devotion are a Bible Service or Vigil, and the Angelus, Rosary and Stations of the Cross, which have a strong scriptural basis.

Dies Irae: The opening Latin words, Day of Wrath, of a hymn for Requiem Masses, written in the 13th century by the Franciscan Thomas of Celano.

Diocese: A fully organized ecclesiastical jurisdiction under the pastoral direction of a bishop as local ordinary.

Discalced: Of Latin derivation and meaning without shoes, the word is applied to religious orders or congregations whose members go barefoot or wear sandals.

Disciple: A term used sometimes in reference to the Apostles but more often to a larger number of followers (70 or 72) of Christ mentioned in Lk. 10:1.

Disciplina Arcani: A Latin phrase, meaning discipline of the secret and referring to a practice of the early Church, especially during the Roman persecutions, to: (1) conceal Christian truths from those who, it was feared, would misinterpret, ridicule and profane the teachings, and persecute Christians for believing them; (2) instruct catechumens in a gradual manner, withholding the teaching of certain doctrines until the catechumens proved themselves of good faith and sufficient understanding.

Dispensation: The relaxation of a law in a particular case. Laws made for the common good sometimes work undue hardship in particular cases. In such cases, where sufficient reasons are present, dispensations may be granted by proper authorities. Bishops, religious superiors and others may dispense from certain laws; the pope can dispense from all ecclesiastical laws. No one has authority to dispense from obligations of the divine law.

Divination: Attempting to foretell future or hidden things by means of things like dreams, necromancy, spiritism, examination of entrails, astrology, augury, omens, palmistry, drawing straws, dice, cards, etc. Practices like these attribute to creatural things a power which belongs to God alone and are violations of the First Commandment.

Divine Praises: Fourteen praises recited or sung at Benediction of the Blessed Sacrament in reparation for sins of sacrilege, blasphemy and profanity. Some of these praises date from the end of the 18th century.

Blessed be God.

Blessed be his holy Name.

Blessed be Jesus Christ, true God and true Man.

Blessed be the Name of Jesus.

Blessed be his most Sacred Heart.

Blessed be his most Precious Blood.

Blessed be Jesus in the most holy Sacrament of the Altar.

Blessed be the Holy Spirit, the Paraclete.

Blessed be the great Mother of God, Mary most holy.

Blessed be her holy and Immaculate Conception.

Blessed be her glorious Assumption.

Blessed be the name of Mary, Virgin and Mother.

Blessed be St. Joseph, her most chaste Spouse.

Blessed be God in his Angels and in his Saints.

Double Effect Principle: Actions sometimes have two effects closely related to each other, one good and the other bad, and a difficult moral question can arise: Is it permissible to place an action from which two such results follow? It is permissible to place the action, if: the action is good in itself and is directly productive of the good effect; the circumstances are good; the intention of the person is good; the reason for placing the action is proportionately serious to the seriousness of the indirect bad effect. For example: Is it morally permissible for a pregnant woman to undergo medical or surgical treatment for a pathological condition if the indirect and secondary effect of the treatment will be the loss of the child? The reply is affirmative, for these reasons: The action, i.e., the treatment, is good in itself, cannot be deferred until a later time without very serious consequences, and is ordered directly to the cure of critically grave pathology. By means of the treatment, the woman intends to save her life, which she has a right to do. The loss of the child is not directly sought as a means for the cure of the mother but results indirectly and in a secondary manner from the placing of the action, i.e., the treatment, which is good in itself.

The double effect principle does not support the principle that the end justifies the means.

Doxology: (1) The lesser doxology, or ascription of glory to the Trinity, is the Glory be to the Father. The first part dates back to the third or fourth century, and came from the form of baptism. The concluding words, As it was in the beginning, etc., are of later origin.

(2) The greater doxology, Glory to God in the highest, begins with the words of angelic praise at the birth of Christ recounted in the Infancy Narrative (Lk. 2:14). It is often recited at Mass. Of early Eastern origin, it is found in the *Apostolic Constitutions* in a form much like the present.

Dulia: A Greek term meaning the veneration or homage, different in nature and degree from that given to God, paid to the saints. It includes honoring the saints and seeking their intercession with God.

Duty: A moral obligation deriving from the binding force of law, the exigencies of one's state in life, and other sources.

E

Easter Controversy: A three-phase controversy over the time for the celebration of Easter.

Some early Christians in the Near East, called Quartodecimans, favored the observance of Easter on the 14th day of Nisan, the spring month of the Hebrew calendar, whenever it occurred. Against this practice, Pope St. Victor I, about 190, ordered a Sunday observance of the feast.

The Council of Nicaea, in line with usages of the Church at Rome and Alexandria, decreed in 325 that Easter should be observed on the first Sunday following the first full moon of spring.

Uniformity of practice in the West was not achieved until several centuries later, when the British Isles, in delayed compliance with measures enacted by the Synod of Whitby in 664, accepted the Roman date of observance.

Unrelated to the controversy is the fact that some Eastern Christians, in accordance with traditional calendar practices, celebrate Easter at a different time than the Roman and Eastern-Rite churches.

Easter Duty: The serious obligation binding Catholics of Roman Rite, by a precept of the Church, to receive Holy Communion during the Easter time; in the US, from the first Sunday of Lent to Trinity Sunday.

Easter Water: Holy water blessed with special ceremonies and distributed on the Easter Vigil; used during Easter Week for blessing the faithful and homes.

Ecclesiology: Study of the nature, constitution, members, mission, functions, etc., of the Church.

Ecstasy: An extraordinary state of mystical experience in which a person is so absorbed in God that the activity of the exterior senses is suspended.

Ecumenism: The movement of Christians and their churches toward the unity willed by Christ. The Second Vatican Council called the movement "those activities and enterprises which, according to various needs of the Church and opportune occasions, are started and organized for the fostering of unity among Christians" (*Decree on Ecumenism,* No. 4). Spiritual ecumenism, i.e., mutual prayer for unity, is the heart of the movement. The movement also involves scholarly and pew-level efforts for the development of mutual understanding and better interfaith relations in general, and collaboration by the churches and their members in the social area.

Elevation: The raising of the host after consecration at Mass for adoration by the faithful. The custom was introduced in the Diocese of Paris about the close of the 12th century to offset an erroneous teaching of the time which held that transubstantiation of the bread did not take place until after the consecration of the wine in the chalice. The elevation of the chalice following the consecration of the wine was introduced in the 15th century.

End Justifies the Means: An unacceptable ethical principle which states that evil means may be used to produce good effects.

Envy: Sadness over another's good fortune because it is considered a loss to oneself or a detraction from one's own excellence; one of the seven capital sins, a violation of the obligations of charity.

Epikeia: A Greek word meaning reasonableness and designating a moral theory and practice, a mild interpretation of the mind of a legislator who is prudently considered not to wish positive law to bind in certain circumstances. Use of the principle is justified in practice when the lawgiver himself cannot be appealed to and when it can be prudently assumed that in particular cases, e.g., because of special hardship, he would not wish the law to be applied in a strict manner. Epikeia may not be applied with respect to acts that are intrinsically wrong or those covered by laws which automatically make them invalid.

Episcopate: (1) The office, dignity and sacramental powers bestowed upon a bishop at his ordination.

(2) The body of bishops collectively.

Equivocation: (1) The use of words, phrases, or gestures having more than one meaning in order to conceal information which a questioner has no strict right to know. It is permissible to equivocate (have a broad mental reservation) in some circumstances.

(2) A lie, i.e., a statement of untruth. Lying is intrinsically wrong. A lie told in joking, evident as such, is not wrong.

Eschatology: Doctrine concerning the last things: death, judgment, heaven and hell, and the final state of perfection of the People and Kingdom of God at the end of time.

Eternity: The interminable, perfect possession of life in its totality without beginning or end; an attribute of God, who has no past or future but always is. Man's existence has a beginning but no end and is, accordingly, called immortal.

Ethics: Moral philosophy, the science of the morality of human acts deriving from natural law, the natural end of man, and the powers of human reason. It includes all the spheres of human activity — personal, social, economic, political, etc. Ethics is distinct from but can be related to moral theology, whose primary principles are drawn from divine Revelation.

Eucharistic Congresses: Public demonstrations of faith in the Holy Eucharist. Combining liturgical services, other public ceremonies, subsidiary meetings, different kinds of instructional and inspirational elements, they are unified by central themes and serve to increase understanding of and devotion to Christ in the Eucharist, and to relate this liturgy of worship and witness to life.

International congresses are planned and held under the auspices of a permanent committee for international Eucharistic congresses. Participants include clergy, religious and lay persons from many countries, and representatives of national and international Catholic organizations. Popes have usually been represented by legates, but Paul VI attended two congresses personally, the 38th at Bombay and the 39th at Bogota.

Forty international congresses were held from 1881 to 1973:

Lille (1881), Avignon (1882), Liege (1883), Freiburg (1885), Toulouse (1886), Paris (1888), Antwerp (1890), Jerusalem (1893), Rheims (1894), Paray-le-Monial (1897), Brussels (1898), Lourdes (1899), Angers (1901), Namur (1902), Angouleme (1904), Rome (1905), Tournai (1906), Metz (1907), London (1908), Cologne (1909), Montreal (1910), Madrid (1911), Vienna (1912), Malta (1913), Lourdes (1914), Rome (1922), Amsterdam (1924), Chicago (1926), Sydney (1928), Carthage (1930), Dublin (1932), Buenos Aires (1934), Manila (1937), Budapest (1938), Barcelona (1952), Rio de Janeiro (1955), Munich, Germany (1960), Bombay, India (1964), Bogota, Colombia (1968), Melbourne, Australia (1973).

Eugenics: The science of heredity and environment for the physical and mental improvement of offspring. Extreme eugenics is untenable in practice because it advocates immoral means, such as compulsory breeding of the select, sterilization of persons said to be unfit, abortion, and unacceptable methods of birth regulation.

Euthanasia: Mercy killing, the direct causing of death by painless means for the purpose of ending human suffering. Euthanasia is murder and is totally illicit, for the natural law forbids the direct taking of one's own life or that of an innocent person.

The use of drugs to relieve suffering in serious cases, even when this results in a shortening of life as an indirect and secondary effect, is permissible under conditions of the double effect principle. It is also permissible for a seriously ill person to refuse to follow — or for other responsible persons to refuse to permit — extraordinary medical procedures even though the refusal might entail shortening of life.

Evolution: Scientific theory concerning the development of the physical universe from unorganized matter (inorganic evolution) and, especially, the development of existing forms of vegetable, animal and human life from earlier and more primitive organisms (organic evolution). Various ideas about evolution were advanced for some centuries before scientific evidence in support of the main-line theory of organic evolution, which has several formulations, was discovered and verified in the second half of the 19th century and afterwards. This evidence — from the findings of comparative anatomy and other sciences — confirmed evolution within species and cleared the way to further investigation of questions regarding the processes of its accomplishment. While a number of such questions remain open with respect to human evolution, a point of doctrine not open to question is the immediate creation of the human soul by God.

For some time, theologians regarded the theory with hostility, considering it to be in opposition to the account of creation in the early chapters of Genesis and subversive of belief in such doctrines as creation, the early state of man in grace, and the fall of man from grace. This state of affairs and the tension it generated led to considerable controversy regarding an alleged conflict between religion and science. Gradually, however, the tension was diminished with the development of biblical studies from the latter part of the 19th century onwards, with clarification of the distinctive features of religious truth and scientific truth, and with the refinement of evolutionary concepts.

So far as the Genesis account of creation is concerned, the Catholic view is that the writer(s) did not write as a scientist but as the communicator of religious truth in a manner adapted to the understanding of the people of his time. He used anthropomorphic language, the figure of days and other literary devices to state the salvation truths of creation, the fall of man from grace, and the promise of redemption. It was beyond the competency and purpose of the writer(s) to describe creation and related events in a scientific manner.

Excommunication: A penalty or censure by which a baptized person is excluded from the communion of the faithful, for committing and remaining obstinate in certain sins specified in canon law and technically called crimes. As by baptism a person is made a member of the Church in which there is a communication of spiritual goods, so by excommunication he is deprived of the same spiritual goods until he repents and receives absolution. Even though excommunicated, a person is still responsible for the normal obligations of a Catholic.

Existentialism: A philosophy with radical concern for the problems of individual existence and identity viewed in particular here-and-now patterns of thought which presuppose irrationality and absurdity in human life and the whole universe. It is preoccupied with questions about freedom, moral decision and responsibility against a background of denial of objective truth and universal norms of conduct; is characterized by prevailing anguish, dread, fear, pessimism, despair; is generally atheistic, although its modern originator, Soren Kierkegaard (d. 1855), and Gabriel Marcel attempted to give it a Christian orientation. Pius XII called it "the new erroneous philosophy which, opposing itself to idealism, immanentism and pragmatism, has assumed the name of existentialism, since it concerns itself only with the existence of individual things and neglects all consideration of their immutable essences" (Encyclical *Humani Generis*, Aug. 12, 1950).

Exorcism: (1) Driving out evil spirits; a rite in which evil spirits are charged and commanded on the authority of God and with the prayer of the Church to depart from a person or to cease causing harm to a person suffering from diabolical possession or obsession. The sacramental is officially administered by a priest delegated for the purpose by the bishop of the place. Elements of the rite include the Litany of Saints; recitation of the Our Father, one or more creeds, and other prayers; specific prayers of exorcism; the reading of Gospel passages, and use of the Sign of the Cross. Private exorcism for the liberation of a person from the strong influence of evil spirits, through prayer and the use of sacramentals like holy water, can be done by anyone.

(2) Exorcisms which do not imply the conditions of either diabolical possession or obsession form part of the ceremony of baptism, and are also included in formulas for various blessings; e.g., of water.

F

Faculties: Grants of jurisdiction, or authority, granted by the law of the Church or superiors (pope, bishop, religious superior) for exercise of the powers of holy orders; e.g., priests are given faculties to hear confessions, officiate at weddings; bishops are given faculties to grant dispensations, etc.

Faith: In religion, faith has several aspects. Catholic doctrine calls faith the assent of the mind to truths revealed by God, the assent being made with the help of grace and by command of the will on account of the authority and trustworthiness of God revealing. The term faith also refers to the truths that are believed (content of faith) and to the way in which a person, in response to Christ, gives witness to and expresses his belief in daily life (living faith).

All of these elements, and more, are included in the following statement:

" 'The obedience of faith' (Rom. 16:26; cf. 1:5; 2 Cor. 10:5-6) must be given to God who reveals, an obedience by which man entrusts his whole self freely to God, offering 'the full submission of intellect and will to God who reveals' (First Vatican Council, *Dogmatic Constitution on the Catholic Faith*, Chap. 3), and freely assenting to the truth revealed by Him. If this faith is to be shown, the grace of God and the interior help of the Holy Spirit must precede and assist, moving the heart and turning it to God, opening the eyes of the mind, and giving 'joy and ease to everyone in assenting to the truth and believing it' " (Second Council of Orange, Canon 7) (Second Vatican Council, *Constitution on Revelation*, No. 5).

Faith is necessary for salvation.

Faith, Rule of: The norm or standard of religious belief. The Catholic doctrine is that belief must be professed in the divinely revealed truths in the Bible and tradition as interpreted and proposed by the infallible teaching authority of the Church.

Faithful: Members of the Church, so called because of their profession and commitment to its common faith.

Fast, Eucharistic: Eating and the drinking of any liquids except water are prohibited for one hour before the reception of Holy Communion. Water never breaks the Eucharistic fast, which is prescribed for reasons of reverence and preparation.

Those who are ill, even though not confined to bed, may take nonalcoholic beverages and liquid or solid medicine before Holy Communion without any time limit.

Father: A title of priests, who are regarded as spiritual fathers because they are the ordinary ministers of baptism, by which persons are born to supernatural life, and because of their pastoral service to people.

Fear: A mental state caused by the apprehension of present or future danger. Grave fear does not necessarily remove moral responsibility for an act, but may lessen it. Grave fear may invalidate marriage if it seriously impedes freedom of consent.

First Friday: A devotion consisting of the reception of Holy Communion on the first Friday of nine consecutive months in honor of the Sacred Heart of Jesus and in reparation for sin. (See Sacred Heart, Promises.)

First Saturday: A devotion tracing its origin to the apparitions of the Blessed Virgin Mary at Fatima in 1917. Those practicing the devotion go to confession and, on the first Saturday of five consecutive months, receive Holy Communion, recite five decades of the Rosary, and meditate on the mysteries for 15 minutes.

Fisherman's Ring: A signet ring engraved with the image of St. Peter fishing from a boat, and encircled with the name of the reigning pope. It is not worn by the pope. It is used to seal briefs, and is destroyed after each pope's death.

Forgiveness of Sin: Catholics believe that sins are forgiven by God through the media-tion of Christ in view of the repentance of the sinner and by means of the sacrament of penance. (See Penance.)

Fortitude: Courage to face dangers or hardships for the sake of what is good; one of the four cardinal virtues and one of the seven gifts of the Holy Spirit.

Fortune Telling: Attempting to predict the future or the occult by means of cards, palm reading, etc.; a form of divination, prohibited by the First Commandment.

Forum: The sphere in which ecclesiastical authority or jurisdiction is exercised.

(1) External: Authority is exercised in the external forum to deal with matters affecting the public welfare of the Church and its members. Those who have such authority because of their office (e.g., diocesan bishops) are called ordinaries.

(2) Internal: Authority is exercised in the internal forum to deal with matters affecting the private spiritual good of individuals. The sacramental forum is the sphere in which the sacrament of penance is administered; other exercises of jurisdiction in the internal forum take place in the non-secramental forum.

Franciscan Crown: A seven-decade rosary used to commemorate the seven Joys of the Blessed Virgin: the Annunciation, the Visitation, the Nativity of Our Lord, the Adoration of the Magi, the Finding of the Child Jesus in the Temple, the Apparition of the Risen Christ to his Mother, the Assumption and Coronation of the Blessed Virgin. Introduced in 1422, the Crown originally consisted only of seven Our Fathers and 70 Hail Marys. Two Hail Marys were added to complete the number 72 (thought to be the number of years of Mary's life), and one Our Father, Hail Mary and Glory be to the Father are said for the intention of the pope.

Freedom, Religious: The Second Vatican Council declared that the right to religious freedom in civil society "means that all men are to be immune from coercion on the part of individuals or of social groups and of any human power, in such wise that in matters religious no one is to be forced to act in a manner contrary to his own beliefs. Nor is anyone to be restrained from acting in accordance with his own beliefs, whether privately or publicly, whether alone or in association with others, within due limits" of requirements for the common good. The foundation of this right in civil society is the "very dignity of the human person" (*Declaration on Religious Freedom*, No. 2).

The conciliar statement did not deal with the subject of freedom within the Church. It noted the responsibility of the faithful "careful to attend to the sacred and certain doctrine of the Church" (No. 14).

Freemasons: A fraternal order which originated in London in 1717 with the formation of the first Grand Lodge of Freemasons, From England, the order spread to Europe and elsewhere. Its original deistic and non-denominational ideology was transformed in Latin countries into a compound of atheism, anticlericalism and irreligion. Since 1877, Grand Orient Freemasonry has been denied recognition by the Scottish and York Rites because of its failure to require belief in God and the immortality of the soul as a condition of membership. In some places, Freemasonry has been regarded as subversive of the state; in Catholic quarters, it has been considered hostile to the Church and its doctrine. In the United States, Freemasonry is generally known as a fraternal and philanthropic order.

Catholics have been forbidden to join the Freemasons, under penalty of excommunication, for serious pastoral reasons. Eight different popes in 17 different pronouncements, and at least six different local councils, condemned Freemasonry. The first condemnation was made by Clement XII in 1738. Eastern Orthodox and many Protestant bodies have also opposed the order.

Present relations between the Catholic Church and Freemasonry in the United States are marked by greater cordiality and mutual understanding than in the past, but the prohibition against Catholic membership still stands.

Free Will: The faculty or capability of making a reasonable choice among several alternatives. Freedom of will underlies the possibility and fact of moral responsibility.

Friar: Term applied to members of mendicant orders to distinguish them from members of monastic orders. (See Mendicants.)

Fruits of the Holy Spirit: Charity, joy, peace, patience, benignity, goodness, longanimity, mildness, faith, modesty, continence, chastity.

G

Gambling: The backing of an issue with a sum of money or other valuables, which is permissible if the object is honest, if the two parties have the free disposal of their stakes, without prejudice to the rights of others, if the terms are thoroughly understood by both parties, and if the outcome is not known beforehand. Gambling often falls into disrepute and may be forbidden by civil law, as well as by divine law, because of cheating, fraud and other accompanying evils.

Gehenna: Greek form of a Jewish name, *Gehinnom*, for a valley near Jerusalem, the site of Moloch worship; used as a synonym for hell.

Genuflection: Bending of the knee, a natural sign of adoration or reverence, as when persons genuflect with the right knee in passing before the tabernacle to acknowledge the Eucharistic presence of Christ. In the Eastern Rites, a deep bow is customary instead of a genuflection.

Gethsemani: A Hebrew word meaning oil press, designating the place on the Mount of Olives where Christ prayed and suffered in agony the night before he died.

Gifts of the Holy Spirit: Supernatural habits disposing a person to respond promptly to the inspiration of grace; promised by Christ and communicated through the Holy Spirit, especially in the sacrament of confirmation. They are: wisdom, understanding, counsel, fortitude, knowledge, piety, fear of the Lord.

Gluttony: An unreasonable appetite for food and drink; one of the seven capital sins.

God: The infinitely perfect Supreme Being, uncaused and absolutely self-sufficient, eternal, the Creator and final end of all things. The one God subsists in three equal Persons, the Father and the Son and the Holy Spirit. God, although transcendent and distinct from the universe, is present and active in the world in realization of his plan for the salvation of men, principally through Revelation, the operations of the Holy Spirit, the life and ministry of Christ, and the continuation of Christ's ministry in the Church.

The existence of God is an article of faith, clearly communicated in divine Revelation. Even without this Revelation, however, the Church teaches, in a declaration by the First Vatican Council, that men can acquire certain knowledge of the existence of God and some of his attributes. This can be done on the bases of principles of reason and reflection on human experience.

Non-revealed arguments or demonstrations for the existence of God have been developed from the principle of causality; the contingency of man and the universe; the existence of design, change and movement in the universe; human awareness of moral responsibility; widespread human testimony to the existence of God.

Grace: A free gift of God to men (and angels), grace is a created sharing or participation in the life of God. It is given to men through the merits of Christ and is communicated by the Holy Spirit. It is necessary for salvation. The principal means of grace are the sacraments (especially the Eucharist), prayer and good works.

Sanctifying or habitual grace makes men holy and pleasing to God, adopted children of God, members of Christ, temples of the Holy Spirit, heirs of heaven capable of supernaturally meritorious acts. With grace, God gives men the supernatural virtues and gifts of the Holy Spirit. The sacraments of baptism and penance were instituted to give grace to those who do not have it; the other sacraments, to increase it in those already in the state of grace. The means for growth in holiness, or the increase of grace, are prayer, the sacraments, and good works. Sanctifying grace is lost by the commission of serious sin.

Each sacrament confers sanctifying grace for the special purpose of the sacrament; in this context, grace is called sacramental grace.

Actual grace is a supernatural help of God which enlightens and strengthens a person to do good and to avoid evil. It is not a permanent quality, like sanctifying grace. It is necessary for the performance of supernatural acts. It can be resisted and refused. Persons in the state of serious sin are given actual grace to lead them to repentance.

Grace at Meals: Prayers said before meals, asking a blessing of God, and after meals, giving thanks to God.

Gremial: A rectangular veil of silk or linen placed over the knees of a bishop when he is seated during various pontifical ceremonies.

H

Habit: (1) A disposition to do things easily, given with grace (and therefore supernatural) and/or acquired by repetition of similar acts.

(2) The garb worn by religious.

Hagiography: Writings or documents about saints and other holy persons.

Hail Mary: A prayer addressed to the Blessed Virgin Mary; also called the *Ave Maria* (Latin equivalent of Hail Mary) and the Angelic Salutation. In three parts, it consists of the words addressed to Mary by the Archangel Gabriel on the occasion of the Annunciation, in the Infancy Narrative (Hail full of grace, the Lord is with you, blessed are you among women.); the words addressed to Mary by her cousin Elizabeth on the occasion of the Visitation (Blessed is the fruit of your womb.); a concluding petition (Holy Mary, Mother of God, pray for us sinners now and at the hour of our death. Amen.). The first two salutations were joined in Eastern Rite formulas by the sixth century, and were similarly used at Rome in the seventh century. Insertion of the name of Jesus at the conclusion of the salutations was probably made by Urban IV about 1262. The present form of the petition was incorporated into the breviary in 1514.

Heaven: The state of those who, having achieved salvation, are in glory with God and enjoy the beatific vision.

The phrase, kingdom of heaven, refers to the order or kingdom of God, grace, salvation.

Hell: The state of punishment of the damned — i.e., those who die in mortal sin, in a condition of self-alienation from God and of opposition to the divine plan of salvation. The punishment of hell begins immediately after death and lasts forever.

Hermit: See Anchorite.

Heroic Act of Charity: The completely unselfish offering to God of one's good works and merits for the benefit of the souls in purgatory rather than for oneself. Thus, a person may offer to God for the souls in purgatory all the good works he performs during life, all the indulgences he gains, and all the prayers and indulgences that will be offered for him after his death. The act is revocable at will, and is not a vow. Its actual ratification depends on the will of God.

Heterodoxy: False doctrine, teaching or belief; a departure from truth.

Holy See: (1) The diocese of the pope, Rome.

(2) The pope himself and/or the various officials and bodies of the Church's central administration at Vatican City — the Roman Curia — which act in the name and by authority of the pope.

Holy Spirit: God the Holy Spirit, third Person of the Holy Trinity, who proceeds from the Father and the Son and with whom he is equal in every respect; inspirer of the prophets and writers of sacred Scripture; promised by Christ to the Apostles as their advocate and strengthener; appeared in the form of a dove at the baptism of Christ and as tongues of fire at his descent upon the Apostles; soul of the Church and guarantor, by his abiding presence and action, of truth in doctrine; communicator of grace to men, for which reason he is called the sanctifier.

Holy Water: Water blessed by the Church and used as a sacramental, a practice which originated in apostolic times.

Holy Year: A year during which the pope grants the Jubilee Indulgence to all the faithful who fulfill the prescribed conditions (confession, Communion, visits and prayer for the intentions of the pope in the basilicas of St. Peter, St. John Lateran, St. Paul, St. Mary Major). The Holy Year has been proclaimed every 25 years since 1450.

This year of special grace and prayer, which begins and ends with the opening and closing of the holy doors in the major basilicas of Rome on consecutive Christmas Eves, has a historical precedent in the year of jubilee prescribed by God in the Old Testament (Lv. 25:10-15).

Hope: One of the three theological virtues, by which one firmly trusts that God wills his salvation and will give him the means to attain it.

Hosanna: A Hebrew word, meaning O Lord, save, we pray.

Host, The Sacred: The bread under whose appearances Christ is and remains present in a unique manner after the consecration which takes place during Mass. (See Transubstantiation.)

Humility: A virtue which induces a person to evaluate himself at his true worth, to recognize his dependence on God, and to give glory to God for the good he has and can do.

Hyperdulia: The special veneration accorded the Blessed Virgin Mary because of her unique role in the mystery of Redemption, her exceptional gifts of grace from God, and her pre-eminence among the saints. Hyperdulia is not adoration; only God is adored.

Hypnosis: A mental state resembling sleep, induced by suggestion, in which the subject does the bidding of the hypnotist. Hypnotism is permissible under certain conditions: the existence of a serious reason, e.g., for anesthetic or therapeutic purposes, and the competence and integrity of the hypnotist. Hypnotism may not be practiced for the sake of amusement. Experiments indicate that, contrary to popular opinion, hypnotized subjects may be induced to perform immoral acts which, normally, they would not do.

Hypostatic Union: The union of the human and divine natures in the one divine Person of Christ.

I

Icons: Byzantine-style paintings or representations of Christ, the Blessed Virgin and other saints, venerated in the Eastern Churches where they take the place of statues.

Idolatry: Worship of any but the true God; a violation of the First Commandment.

IHS: In Greek, the first three letters of the name of Jesus — Iota, Eta, Sigma.

Immortality: The survival and continuing existence of the human soul after death.

Immunity of the Clergy: Exemption of clerics from military duty and civil service.

Impurity: Unlawful indulgence in sexual pleasure. (See Chastity.)

Incardination: The affiliation of a priest to his diocese. Every secular priest must belong to a certain diocese. Similarly, every priest of a religious community must belong to some jurisdiction of his community; this affiliation, however, is not called incardination.

Incarnation: (1) The coming-into-flesh or taking of human nature by the Second Person of the Trinity. He became human as the Son of Mary, being miraculously conceived by the power of the Holy Spirit, without ceasing to be divine. His divine Person hypostatically unites his divine and human natures.

(2) The supernatural mystery coextensive with Christ from the moment of his human conception and continuing through his life on earth; his sufferings and death; his resurrection from the dead and ascension to glory with the Father; his sending, with the Father, of the Holy Spirit upon the Apostles and the Church; and his unending mediation with the Father for the salvation of men.

Incense: A granulated substance which, when burnt, emits an aromatic smoke. It symbolizes the zeal with which the faithful should be consumed, the good odor of Christian virtue, the ascent of prayer to God.

Incest: Sexual intercourse with relatives by blood or marriage; a sin of impurity and also a grave violation of the natural reverence due to relatives. Other sins of impurity (desire, etc.) concerning relatives have the nature of incest.

Index of Prohibited Books: A list of books which Catholics were formerly forbidden to read, possess or sell, under penalty of excommunication. The books were banned by the Holy See after publication because their treatment of matters of faith and morals and related subjects were judged to be erroneous or serious occasions of doctrinal error. Some books were listed in the Index by name; others were covered under general norms. The Congregation for the Doctrine of the Faith declared June 14, 1966, that the Index and its related penalties of excommunication no longer had the force of law in the Church. Persons are still obliged, however, to take normal precautions against occasions of doctrinal error.

The first *Roman Index of Prohibited Books,* which served the same purposes as earlier lists, was published in 1559 by the Holy Office at the order of Paul IV. The Council of Trent, with the approval of the same pope, authorized another Index in 1564. Seven years later, St. Pius V set up a special Congregation for the Reform of the Index and Correction of Books, and gave it universal jurisdiction. In the course of time, many additions and modifications affecting the Index were made. In 1897, Leo XIII issued complete legislation on the subject, and in 1917 Benedict XV turned over to the Congregation of the Holy Office the function of censoring publications in accordance with the provisions of canon law.

Indifferentism: A theory that any one religion is as true and good — or false — as any other religion, and that it makes no difference, objectively, what religion one professes, if any. The theory is completely subjective, finding its justification entirely in personal choice without reference to or respect for objective validity. It is also self-contradictory, since it regards as equally acceptable — or unacceptable — the beliefs of all religions, which in fact are not only not all the same but are in some cases opposed to each other.

Indulgence: According to *The Doctrine and Practice of Indulgences,* an apostolic constitution issued by Paul VI Jan. 1, 1967, an indulgence is the remission before God of the temporal punishment due for sins already forgiven as far as their guilt is concerned, which a follower of Christ — with the proper dispositions and under certain determined conditions — acquires through the intervention of the Church. The Church grants indulgences in accordance with doctrine concerning the superabundant merits of Christ and the saints, the Power of the Keys, and the sharing of spiritual goods in the Communion of Saints.

An indulgence is partial or plenary, depending on whether it does away with either part or all of the temporal punishment due for sin. Both types of indulgences can always be applied to the dead by way of suffrage; the actual disposition of indulgences applied to the dead rests with God.

(1) Partial indulgence: Properly disposed faithful who perform an action to which a partial indulgence is attached obtain, in addition to the remission of temporal punishment

acquired by the action itself, an equal remission of punishment through the intervention of the Church. (This grant was formerly designated in terms of days and years.) The proper dispositions for gaining a partial indulgence are sorrow for sin and freedom from serious sin, performance of the required good work, and the intention (which can be general or immediate) to gain the indulgence.

In addition to customary prayers and other good works to which partial indulgences are attached, the *Enchiridion Indulgentiarum* published in 1968 included general grants of partial indulgences to the faithful who: (a) with some kind of prayer, raise their minds to God with humble confidence while carrying out their duties and bearing the difficulties of everyday life; (b) motivated by the spirit of faith and compassion, give of themselves or their goods for the service of persons in need; (c) in a spirit of penance, spontaneously refrain from the enjoyment of things which are lawful and pleasing to them.

(2) Plenary indulgence: To gain a plenary indulgence, it is necessary for a person to be free of all attachment to sin, to perform the work to which the indulgence is attached, and to fulfill the three conditions of sacramental confession, Eucharistic Communion, and prayer for the intention of the pope. The three conditions may be fulfilled several days before or after the performance of the prescribed work, but it is fitting that Communion be received and prayers for the intentions of the pope be offered on the same day the work is performed. The condition of praying for the pope's intention is fully satisfied by praying one Our Father and one Hail Mary, and sometimes the Creed, but persons are free to choose other prayers.

Four of the several devotional practices for which a plenary indulgence is granted are: (a) adoration of the Blessed Sacrament for at least one-half hour; (b) devout reading of sacred Scripture for at least one-half hour; (c) the Way of the Cross; (d) recitation of the Marian Rosary in a church or public oratory or in a family group, a religious community or pious association. Only one plenary indulgence can be gained in a single day.

Indult: A favor or privilege granted by competent ecclesiastical authority, giving permission to do something not allowed by the common law of the Church.

Infant Jesus of Prague: An 18-inch-high wooden statue of the Child Jesus which has figured in a form of devotion to the Holy Childhood and Kingship of Christ since the 17th century. Of uncertain origin, the statue was presented by Princess Polixena to the Carmelites of Our Lady of Victory Church, Prague, in 1628.

Infused Virtues: The theological virtues of faith, hope, and charity; principles or capabilities of supernatural action, they are given with sanctifying grace by God rather than acquired by repeated acts of a person. They can be increased by practice; they are lost by contrary acts. Natural-acquired moral virtues, like the cardinal virtues of prudence, justice, temperance, and fortitude, can be considered infused in a person whose state of grace gives them supernatural orientation.

Inquisition: A tribunal for dealing with heretics, authorized by Gregory IX in 1231 to search them out, hear and judge them, sentence them to various forms of punishment, and in some cases to hand them over to civil authorities for punishment. The Inquisition was a creature of its time when crimes against faith, which threatened the good of the Christian community, were regarded also as crimes against the state, and when heretical doctrines of such extremists as the Cathari and Albigensians threatened the very fabric of society. The institution, which was responsible for many excesses, was most active in the second half of the 13th century.

Inquisition, Spanish: An institution peculiar to Spain and the colonies in Spanish America. In 1478, at the urging of King Ferdinand, Pope Sixtus IV approved the establishment of the Inquisition for trying charges of heresy brought against Jewish (Marranos) and Moorish (Moriscos) converts. It acquired jurisdiction over other cases as well, however, and fell into disrepute because of irregularities in its functions, cruelty in its sentences, and the manner in which it served the interests of the Spanish crown more than the accused persons and the good of the Church. Protests by the Holy See failed to curb excesses of the Inquisition, which lingered in Spanish history until early in the 19th century.

I N R I: The first letters of words in the Latin inscription atop the cross on which Christ was crucified: (I)esus (N)azaraenus, (R)ex (J)udaeorum — Jesus of Nazareth, King of the Jews.

Insemination, Artificial: The implanting of human semen by some means other than consummation of natural marital intercourse. In view of the principle that procreation should result only from marital intercourse, donor insemination is not permissible. The use of legitimate artificial means to further the fruitfulness of marital intercourse is permissible.

In Sin: The condition of a person called spiritually dead because he does not possess sanctifying grace, the principle of supernatural life, action and merit. Such grace can be regained through repentance.

Instruction: A document containing doctrinal explanations, directive norms, rules, recommendations, admonitions, issued by the pope, a department of the Roman Curia or other competent authority in the Church. To the extent that they so prescribe, instructions have the force of law.

Intercommunion: The common celebration and reception of the Eucharist by members of different Christian churches; a pivotal issue in ecumenical theory and practice. Catholic participation and intercommunion in the Eucharistic liturgy of another church without a valid priesthood and with a variant Eucharistic belief is out of order. Intercommunion is acceptable to some Protestant churches and unacceptable to others.

Interdict: An ecclesiastical penalty imposed on persons and places for certain violations of church law. If the interdict is personal, the interdicted persons may not take part in certain liturgical services, administer or receive certain sacraments. If the interdict is local, persons may not take part in certain liturgical services, administer or receive certain sacraments in the interdicted places.

Interdict is different from excommunication, and does not involve exclusion of a person from the community of the faithful.

Interregnum: The period of time between the death of one pope and the election of his successor. Another term applied to the period is *Sede vacante,* meaning the See (of Rome) being vacant.

Interregnum procedures follow norms contained in two apostolic constitutions: *Vacantis Apostolicae Sedis,* issued by Pius XII Dec. 8, 1945, and *Summi Pontificis Electione,* issued by John XXIII Sept. 5, 1962.

The main concerns during an interregnum are things connected with the death and burial of the pope, the election of his successor, and the maintenance of ordinary routine for the proper functioning of the Roman Curia.

The chamberlain of the Holy Roman Church takes over the ordinary administration of most Roman affairs. He — or the dean of the College of Cardinals prior to a chamberlain's election by the cardinals — certifies the death of the pope; orders the destruction of the Fisherman's Ring and other personal seals of the pope; and sets in motion the procedures for notifying the world about the pope's death, for funeral preparations, and for summoning the cardinals to a conclave for the election of a new pontiff.

The vicar of Rome exercises ordinary jurisdiction over the diocese.

The congregations, offices and tribunals of the Roman Curia retain ordinary jurisdiction for routine affairs but may not initiate new business during the interregnum.

The secretary of the College of Cardinals replaces the secretary of state and maintains the secretariat in a status quo.

The deceased pope is buried in St. Peter's Basilica within four or five days, following the usual customs for public viewing of the body and the offering of a solemn Mass. Nine consecutive daily Masses are offered for the repose of the pontiff, and the mourning period lasts about 10 days.

The conclave for the election of a new pope begins no later than 18 days after the death of his predecessor. On the election of the new pope, the interregnum comes to an end. (See Papal Election.)

Intinction: A method of administering Holy Communion under the dual appearances of bread and wine, in which the consecrated host is dipped in the consecrated wine before being given to the communicant. The administering of Holy Communion in this manner, which has been traditional in Eastern-Rite liturgies, was authorized in the Roman Rite for various occasions by the *Constitution on the Sacred Liturgy* promulgated by the Second Vatican Council.

Irenicism: Peace-seeking, conciliation, as opposed to polemics; an important element in ecumenism, provided it furthers pursuit of the Christian unity willed by Christ without degenerating into a peace-at-any-price disregard for religious truth.

Irregularity: An impediment to the lawful reception or exercise of holy orders. The Church instituted irregularities — which include apostasy, heresy, homicide, attempted suicide — out of reverence for the dignity of the sacraments.

Itinerarium: Prayers for a spiritually profitable journey.

J

Jansenism: Opinions developed and proposed by Cornelius Jansenius (1585-1638). He held that: human nature was radically and intrinsically corrupted by original sin; efficacious grace infallibly determines the will to do good; some men are predestined to heaven and others to hell; Christ died only for those predestined to heaven. Jansenism also advocated an extremely rigorous code of morals and asceticism. The errors were proscribed by Urban VIII in 1642, by Innocent X in 1653, by Clement XI in 1713, and by other popes. Despite these condemnations, the rigoristic spirit of Jansenism lingered for a long time afterwards, particularly in France.

Jehovah's Witnesses: The Witnesses, together with the Watchtower and Bible Tract Society, trace their beginnings to a Bible class organized by Charles Taze Russell in 1872 at Allegheny, Pa. They take their name from a passage in Isaiah (43:12): " 'You are my witnesses,' says Jehovah." They are generally fundamentalist and revivalist with respect to the Bible, and believe that Christ is God's Son but is inferior to God. They place great emphasis on the Battle of Armageddon (as a decisive confrontation of good and evil) that is depicted vividly in Revelation, believing that God will then destroy the existing system of things and that, with the establishment of Jehovah's Kingdom, a small band of 144,000 spiritual sons of God will go to heaven, rule with Christ, and share in some way their happiness with some others.

Each Witness is considered by the society

to be an ordained minister charged with the duty of spreading the message of Jehovah, which is accomplished through publications, house-to-house visitations, and other methods. The Witnesses refuse to salute the flag of any nation, regarding this as a form of idolatry, or to sanction blood transfusions even for the saving of life. There are approximately one million Witnesses in more than 22,000 congregations in some 80 countries. The freedom and activities of Witnesses are restricted in some places.

Jesus: The name of Jesus, meaning Savior in Christian usage, derived from the Aramaic and Hebrew *Yeshua* and *Joshua,* meaning *Yahweh* is salvation.

Joys of the Blessed Virgin Mary, Seven: (See Franciscan Crown.)

Judgment: (1) Last or final judgment: Final judgment by Christ, at the end of the world and the general resurrection.

(2) Particular judgment: The judgment that takes place immediately after a person's death, followed by entrance into heaven, hell or purgatory.

Juniorate: The name of some houses of study and formation for candidates or younger members of a religious community.

Jurisdiction: Right, power, authority to rule. Jurisdiction in the Church is of divine institution; has pastoral service for its purpose; includes legislative, judicial and executive authority; can be exercised only by persons with the power of orders.

(1) Ordinary jurisdiction is attached to ecclesiastical offices by law; the officeholders, called ordinaries, have authority over those who are subject to them.

(2) Delegated jurisdiction is that which is granted to persons rather than attached to offices. Its extent depends on the terms of the delegation.

Justice: One of the four cardinal virtues by which a person gives to others what is due to them as a matter of right. (See Cardinal Virtues.)

Justification: The act by which God makes a person just, and the consequent change in the spiritual status of a person, from sin to grace; the remission of sin and the infusion of sanctifying grace through the merits of Christ and the action of the Holy Spirit.

K

Kerygma: Proclaiming the word of God, in the manner of the Apostles, as here and now effective for salvation. This method of preaching or instruction, centered on Christ and geared to the facts and themes of salvation history, is designed to dispose people to faith in Christ and/or to intensify the experience and practice of that faith in those who have it.

Keys, Power of the: Spiritual authority and jurisdiction in the Church, symbolized by the keys of the kingdom of heaven. Christ prom-

ised the keys to St. Peter, as head-to-be of the Church (Mt. 16:19), and commissioned him with full pastoral responsibility to feed his lambs and sheep (Jn. 21:15-17), The pope, as the successor of St. Peter, has this power in a primary and supreme manner. The bishops of the Church also have the power, in union with and subordinate to the pope. Priests share in it through holy orders and the delegation of authority.

Examples of the application of the Power of the Keys are the exercise of teaching and pastoral authority by the pope and bishops, the absolving of sins in the sacrament of penance, the granting of indulgences, the imposing of spiritual penalties on persons who commit certain serious sins.

L

Laicization: (1) The process by which a man ordained to holy orders is relieved of the obligations of orders and the ministry and is returned to the status of a lay person. Applications by diocesan clergy are filed with their bishop and forwarded for processing to the congregation of the Roman Curia authorized to grant the indult of laicization.

(2) The process by which a religious is relieved of the obligations of vows and membership in his or her institute. Applications are filed with the proper religious superior and forwarded for processing to the Congregation for Religious which is authorized to grant the appropriate indult.

Languages of the Church: The first language in church use, for divine worship and the conduct of ecclesiastical affairs, was Aramaic, the language of the first Christians in and around Jerusalem. As the Church spread westward, Greek was adopted and prevailed until the third century when it was supplanted by Latin for official use in the West.

According to traditions established very early in churches of the Eastern Rites, many different languages were adopted for use in divine worship and for the conduct of ecclesiastical affairs. The practice was, and still is, to use the vernacular or a language closely related to the common tongue of the people.

In the Western Church, Latin prevailed as the general official language until the promulgation on Dec. 4, 1963, of the *Constitution on the Sacred Liturgy* by the second session of the Second Vatican Council. Since that time, vernacular languages have come into use in the Mass, administration of the sacraments, and the Liturgy of the Hours. The change was introduced in order to make the prayers and ceremonies of divine worship more informative and meaningful to all. Latin, however, remains the official language for administrative and procedural matters.

Law: An ordinance or rule governing the activity of things.

(1) Natural law: Moral norms corresponding to man's nature by which he orders

his conduct toward God, neighbor, society and himself. This law, which is rooted in human nature, is of divine origin, can be known by the use of reason, and binds all men having the use of reason. The Ten Commandments are declarations and amplifications of natural law. The primary precepts of natural law, to do good and to avoid evil, are universally recognized, despite differences with respect to understanding and application resulting from different philosophies of good and evil.

(2) Divine positive law: That which has been revealed by God. Among its essentials are the twin precepts of love of God and love of neighbor, and the Ten Commandments.

(3) Ecclesiastical law: That which is established by the Church for the spiritual welfare of the faithful and the orderly conduct of ecclesiastical affairs. (See Canon Law.)

(4) Civil law: That which is established by a socio-political community for the common good.

Lector: A reader of scriptural passages and other selections at Mass and other services of worship.

Legitimation: Removal of the status of illegitimacy; e.g., by marriage of the parents.

Liberalism: A multiphased trend of thought and movement favoring liberty, independence and progress in moral, intellectual, religious, social, economic and political life. Traceable to the Renaissance, it developed through the Enlightenment, the rationalism of the 19th century, and modernist- and existentialist-related theories of the 20th century. Evaluations of various kinds of liberalism depend on the validity of their underlying principles. Extremist positions — regarding subjectivism, libertinarianism, naturalist denials of the supernatural, and the alienation of individuals and society from God and the Church were condemned by Gregory XVI in the 1830's, Pius IX in 1864, Leo XIII in 1899, and St. Pius X in 1907. There is, however, nothing objectionable about forms of liberalism patterned according to sound principles of Christian doctrine.

Life in Outer Space: Whether rational life exists on other bodies in the universe besides earth, is a question for scientific investigation to settle. The possibility can be granted, without prejudice to the body of revealed truth.

Limbo: The limbo of the fathers was the state of rest and natural happiness after death enjoyed by the just of pre-Christian times until they were admitted to heaven following the Ascension of Christ. Belief in this matter is stated in the Apostles' Creed. The existence of a limbo for unbaptized persons of infant status — a state of rest and natural happiness — has never been formally defined.

Litany: A prayer in the form of responsive petition; e.g., St. Joseph, pray for us, etc. There are seven litanies approved for liturgical use: Litanies of Loreto (Litany of the Blessed Mother), the Holy Name, All Saints, the Sacred Heart, the Precious Blood, St. Joseph, Litany for the Dying. Others may be used privately.

Little Office of the Blessed Virgin Mary: A shortened version of a Liturgy of the Hours honoring the Blessed Virgin. It dates from about the middle of the eighth century.

Liturgical Languages: (See Languages of the Church.)

Loreto, House of: A Marian shrine in Loreto, Italy, consisting of the home of the Holy Family which, according to an old tradition, was transported in a miraculous manner from Nazareth to Dalmatia and finally to Loreto between 1291 and 1294. Investigations conducted shortly after the appearance of the structure in Loreto revealed that its dimensions matched those of the house of the Holy Family missing from its place of enshrinement in a basilica at Nazareth. Among the many popes who regarded it with high honor was John XXIII, who went there on pilgrimage Oct. 4, 1962. The house of the Holy Family is enshrined in the Basilica of Our Lady.

Lust: A disorderly desire for sexual pleasure; one of the seven capital sins.

M

Magi: In the Infancy Narrative of St. Matthew's Gospel (2:1-12), three wise men from the East whose visit and homage to the Child Jesus at Bethlehem indicated Christ's manifestation of himself to non-Jewish people. The narrative teaches the universality of salvation. The traditional names of the Magi are Caspar, Melchior and Balthasar.

Magnificat: The canticle or hymn uttered by the Virgin Mary after she was greeted by her cousin Elizabeth on the occasion of the Visitation (Lk. 1:46-55). It is an expression of praise, thanksgiving and acknowledgement of the great blessings given by God to Mary, the Mother of the Second Person of the Blessed Trinity made Man.

Martyr: A Greek word, meaning witness, denoting one who voluntarily suffered death for the faith or some Christian virtue.

Martyrology: A catalogue of martyrs and other saints, arranged according to the calendar. The *Roman Martyrology* contains the official list of saints venerated by the Church. Additions to the list are made in beatification and canonization decrees of the Congregation for the Causes of Saints. The Martyrology is being revised to conform with other liturgical books.

Mass for the People: On Sundays and certain feasts throughout the year pastors are required to offer Mass for the faithful committed to their care. If they cannot offer the Mass on these days, they must do so at a later date or provide that another priest offer the Mass.

Master of Novices: The person in charge of the training and formation of candidates for a religious institute during novitiate.

Materialism: Theory which holds that matter is the only reality, and everything in existence is merely a manifestation of matter; there is no such thing as spirit, and the supernatural does not exist. Materialism is incompatible with Christian doctrine.

Meditation: Mental, as distinguished from vocal, prayer, in which thought, affections, and resolutions of the will predominate. There is a meditative element to all forms of prayer, which always involves the raising of the heart and mind to God.

Mendicants: A term derived from Latin and meaning beggars, applied to members of religious orders without property rights; the members, accordingly, worked or begged for their support. The original mendicants were Franciscans and Dominicans in the early 13th century; later, the Carmelites, Augustinians, Servites and others were given the mendicant title and privileges, with respect to exemption from episcopal jurisdiction and wide faculties for preaching and administering the sacrament of penance. The practice of begging is limited at the present time, although it is still allowed with the permission of competent superiors and bishops. Mendicants are supported by free will offerings and income received for spiritual services and other work.

Mercy, Divine: The love and goodness of God, manifested particularly in a time of need.

Merit: In religion, the right to a supernatural reward for good works freely done for a supernatural motive by a person in the state of and with the assistance of grace. The right to such reward is from God, who binds himself to give it. Accordingly, good works, as described above, are meritorious for salvation.

Metempsychosis: Theory of the passage or migration of the human soul after death from one body to another for the purpose of purification from guilt. The theory denies the unity of the soul and human personality, and the doctrine of individual moral responsibility.

Millennium: A thousand-year reign of Christ and the just upon earth before the end of the world. This belief of the Millenarians, Chiliasts, and some sects of modern times is based on an erroneous interpretation of Rv. 20.

Miracles: Observable events or effects in the physical or moral order of things, with reference to salvation, which cannot be explained by the ordinary operation of laws of nature and which, therefore, are attributed to the direct action of God. They make known, in an unusual way, the concern and intervention of God in human affairs for the salvation of men. The most striking examples are the miracles worked by Christ. Numbering about 35, they included his own Resurrection; the raising of three persons to life (Lazarus, the daughter of Jairus, the son of the widow of Naim); the healing of blind, leprous and other persons; nature miracles; and prophecies, or miracles of the intellectual order.

The foregoing notion of miracles, which is based on the concept of a fixed order of nature, was not known by the writers of Sacred Scripture. In the Old Testament, particularly, they called some things miraculous which, according to the definition in contemporary use, may or may not have been miracles. Essentially, however, the occurrences so designated were regarded as exceptional manifestations of God's care and concern for the salvation of his people. The miracles of Christ were miracles in the full sense of the term.

The Church believes it is reasonable to accept miracles as manifestations of divine power for purposes of salvation. God, who created the laws of nature, is their master; hence, without disturbing the ordinary course of things, he can — and has in the course of history before and after Christ — occasionally set aside these laws and has also produced effects beyond their power of operation. The Church does not call miraculous anything which does not admit of easy explanation; on the contrary, miracles are admitted only when the events have a bearing on the order of grace and every possible natural explanation has been tried and found wanting.

(The transubstantiation — i.e., the conversion of the whole substance of bread and wine, their sensible appearances alone remaining, into the Body and Blood of Christ in the act of Consecration at Mass — is not an observable event. Traditionally, however, it has been called a miracle.)

Missal: A liturgical book of Roman Rite which contains the prayers, readings and ceremonial directions for the celebration of Mass. In line with liturgical developments, the contents of the *Roman Missal* have been incorporated in separate books — the lectionary (readings, scriptural responsories, etc.) and sacramentary (Mass prayers and ceremonial directives).

Missiology: Study of the missionary nature, constitution and activity of the Church in all aspects: theological reasons for missionary activity, laws and instructions of the Holy See, history of the missions, social and cultural background, methods, norms for carrying on missionary work.

Mission: (1) Strictly, it means being sent to perform a certain work, such as the mission of Christ to redeem mankind, the mission of the Apostles and the Church and its members to perpetuate the prophetic, priestly and royal mission of Christ.

(2) A place where: the Gospel has not been proclaimed; the Church has not been firmly established; the Church, although established, is weak.

(3) An ecclesiastical territory with the simplest kind of canonical organization, under the jurisdiction of the Congregation for the Evangelization of Peoples.

(4) A church or chapel without a resident priest.

(5) A special course of sermons and spiritual exercises conducted in parishes for the purpose of renewing and deepening the spiritual life of the faithful and for the conversion of lapsed Catholics.

Mitre: A headdress worn during some functions by bishops, abbots, and, in certain cases, by other ecclesiastics.

Modernism: The "synthesis of all heresies," which appeared near the beginning of the 20th century. It undermines the objective validity of religious beliefs and practices which, it contends, are products of the subconscious developed by mankind under the stimulus of a religious sense. It holds that the existence of a personal God cannot be demonstrated, the Bible is not inspired, Christ is not divine, nor did he establish the Church or institute the sacraments. A special danger lies in modernism, which is still influential, because it uses Catholic terms with perverted meanings. St. Pius X condemned 65 propositions of modernism in 1907 in the decree *Lamentabili* and issued the encyclical *Pascendi* to explain and analyze its errors.

Monastery: The dwelling place, as well as the community thereof, of monks belonging to the Benedictine and Benedictine-related orders like the Cistercians and Carthusians; also, the Augustinians and Canons Regular. Distinctive of monasteries are: their separation from the world; the papal enclosure or strict cloister; the permanence or stability of attachment characteristic of their members; autonomous government in accordance with a monastic rule, like that of St. Benedict in the West or of St. Basil in the East; the special dedication of its members to the community celebration of the liturgy as well as to work that is suitable to the surrounding area and the needs of its people. Monastic superiors of men have such titles as abbot and prior; of women, abbess and prioress. In most essentials, an abbey is the same as a monastery.

Monk: A member of a monastic order — e.g., the Benedictines, the Benedictine-related Cistercians and Carthusians, and the Basilians, who bind themselves by religious profession to stable attachment to a monastery, the contemplative life and the work of their community. In popular use, the title is wrongly applied to many men religious who really are not monks.

Monotheism: Belief in and worship of one God.

Morality: Conformity or difformity of behavior to standards of right conduct. (See Commandments of God, Precepts of the Church, Conscience, Law.)

Moral Re-Armament: The title, since 1938, of a movement initiated by Frank Buchman, a Lutheran minister with wide experience in evangelistic preaching and work in the US and abroad; also called Buchmanism, after him, and the Oxford Group Movement, because of the membership of Oxford University students in the First Christian Century Fellowship organized by Buchman in England in the late 1920's. MRA aspires to reform the world through propagation of and witness to the four absolutes of honesty, disinterestedness, purity and love.

Mormons: Members of the Church of Jesus Christ of Latter-Day Saints. The church was established by Joseph Smith (1805-1844) at Fayette, N.Y., three years after he said he had received from an angel golden tablets containing the *Book of the Prophet Mormon.* This book, the Bible, *Doctrine and Covenants,* and *The Pearl of Great Price,* are the basic doctrinal texts of the church. Characteristic of the Mormons are strong belief in the revelations of their leaders, among whom was Brigham Young; a strong community of religious-secular concern; a dual secular and spiritual priesthood, and vigorous missionary activity. The headquarters of the church are located at Salt Lake City, Utah, where the Mormons first settled in 1847.

Mortification: Acts of self-discipline, including prayer, hardship, austerities and penances undertaken for the sake of progress in virtue.

Motu Proprio: A Latin phrase designating a document issued by a pope on his own initiative. Documents of this kind often concern administrative matters.

Mysteries of Faith: Supernatural truths whose existence cannot be known without revelation by God and whose intrinsic truth, while not contrary to reason, can never be wholly understood even after revelation. These mysteries are above reason, not against reason. Among them are the divine mysteries of the Trinity, Incarnation and Eucharist.

Some mysteries — e.g., concerning God's attributes — can be known by reason without revelation, although they cannot be fully understood.

N

Necromancy: Supposed communication with the dead; a form of divination.

Non-Expedit: A Latin expression. It is not expedient (fitting, proper), used to state a prohibition or refusal of permission.

Novena: A term designating public or private devotional practices over a period of nine consecutive days; or, by extension, over a period of nine weeks, in which one day a week is set aside for the devotions.

Novice: A person preparing, in a formal period of trial and formation called the *novitiate,* for membership in a religious institute. The novitiate lasts more than a year and ends with the profession of temporary vows or other temporary commitment to the religious life. Current norms require a total 12-month period of seclusion for novices; to this is added other periods of time spent in apostolic work for the sake of experience. A novice, while acquiring experience of the religious life, is not bound by the obligations of professed members of the institute, is free to leave at any time, and may be discharged at the discretion of competent superiors. The immediate superior of a novice is a master or mistress of novices.

Nun (1) Strictly, a member of a religious order of women with solemn vows (moniales).

(2) In general, all women religious, even those in simple vows who are more properly called sisters.

Nunc Dimittis: The canticle or hymn of Simeon when he saw Christ at the Temple on the occasion of his presentation (Lk. 2:29-32). It is an expression of joy and thanksgiving for the blessing of having lived to see the Messiah. It is one of the canticles prescribed in the Liturgy of the Hours.

O

Oath: Calling upon God to witness the truth of a statement. Violating an oath, e.g., by perjury in court, or taking an oath without sufficient reason, is a violation of the honor due to God.

Obedience: Submission to one in authority. General obligations of obedience fall under the Fourth Commandment. The vow of obedience professed by religious is one of the evangelical counsels.

Obsession, Diabolical: The extraordinary state of one who is seriously molested by evil spirits in an external manner. Obsession is more than just temptation.

Occultism: Practices involving ceremonies, rituals, chants, incantations, other cult-related activities intended to affect the course of nature, the lives of practitioners and others, through esoteric powers of magic, diabolical or other forces; one of many forms of superstition.

Octave: A period of eight days given over to the celebration of a major feast such as Easter.

Oils, Holy: The oils consecrated by bishops on Holy Thursday or another suitable day, and by priests under certain conditions for use in certain sacraments and consecrations.

(1) The oil of catechumens (olive or other vegetable oil), used at baptism and the ordination of priests.

(2) Chrism (olive or other vegetable oil mixed with balm), used at baptism, in confirmation, at the consecration of a bishop, in the consecration of churches, altars, altarstones, chalices, patens, and in the blessing of bells.

(3) Oil of the sick (olive or other vegetable oil), used in anointing the sick.

Old Catholics: Several sects, including (1) the Church of Utrecht which severed relations with Rome in 1724; (2) the National Polish Church in the US, which had its origin near the end of the 19th century; (3) the Yu-goslav Old Catholic Church; (4) especially, a denomination founded by German priests and lay persons who broke away from union with Rome following the First Vatican Council in 1870. The doctrinal reason for the break was strong objection to the dogma of papal infallibility.

The formation of this Old Catholic Church began in 1870 at a public meeting held in Nuremberg under the leadership of A. Dollinger; four years later, episcopal succession was established with the valid consecration of a German bishop by a prelate of the Church of Utrecht. Old Catholics accept the first seven ecumenical councils and doctrine formulated before 1054, but reject communion with the pope and a number of Roman Catholic doctrines and practices. Since 1932, they have had full intercommunion with the Anglican Church. The Roman Church recognizes the validity of Old Catholic orders and other sacraments.

Oratory: A chapel.

Ordinariate: An ecclesiastical jurisdiction for special purposes and people. Examples are the military ordinariate of the US, for service personnel, and Eastern-Rite ordinariates in places where Eastern-Rite dioceses do not exist.

Ordinary: One who has the jurisdiction of an office: the pope, diocesan bishops, vicars general, prelates of missionary territories, vicars apostolic, prefects apostolic, vicars capitular during the vacancy of a see, superiors general, abbots primate and other major superiors of men religious.

Ordination: The consecration of sacred ministers for divine worship and the service of men in things pertaining to God. The power of ordination comes from Christ and the Church, and must be conferred by a minister capable of communicating it.

Organ Transplants: The transplanting of organs from one person to another is permissible for serious reasons provided it is done with the consent of the concerned parties and does not result in the death or essential mutilation of the donor.

Original Sin: The sin of Adam (Gn. 2:8—3:24), personal to him and passed on to all men as a state of privation of grace. Despite this privation and the related wounding of human nature and weakening of natural powers, original sin leaves unchanged all that man himself is by nature. The scriptural basis of the doctrine was stated especially by St. Paul in 1 Cor. 15:21, ff., and Romans 5:12-21. Original sin is remitted by baptism and incorporation in Christ, through whom grace is given to persons.

O Salutaris Hostia: The first three Latin words, O Saving Victim, of a Benediction hymn.

Oxford Movement: A movement in the Church of England from 1833 to about 1845 which had for its objective a threefold defense of the church as a divine institution, the apostolic succession of its bishops, and the Book of Common Prayer as the rule of faith. The movement took its name from Oxford University and involved a number of intellectuals who authored a series of influential *Tracts for Our Times*. Some of its leading figures — e.g., F. W. Faber, John Henry Newman and Henry Edward Manning — became converts to the Catholic Church. In the Church of England, the movement affected the liturgy, historical and theological scholarship, the status of the ministry, and other areas of ecclesiastical life.

P

Paganism: A term referring to non-revealed religions, i.e., religions other than Christianity, Judaism and Mohammedanism.

Pallium: A circular band of white wool, about two inches wide, worn about the neck by certain major prelates. A papal vestment symbolic of the office of bishop, it is given upon request to patriarchs, primates, archbishops and, rarely, to bishops. The pallium is made from the wool of lambs blessed by the pope on the feast of St. Agnes and is marked with six black crosses.

Palms: Blessed palms are a sacramental. They are blessed and distributed on the Sunday of the Passion in commemoration of the triumphant entrance of Christ into Jerusalem. Ashes of the burnt palms are used on Ash Wednesday.

Pange Lingua: First Latin words, Sing, my tongue, of a hymn in honor of the Holy Eucharist, used particularly on Holy Thursday and in Eucharistic processions.

Pantheism: Theory that all things are part of God, divine, in the sense that God realizes himself as the ultimate reality of matter or spirit through being and/or becoming all things that have been, are, and will be. The theory leads to hopeless confusion of the Creator and the created realm of being, identifies evil with good, and involves many inherent contradictions.

Papal Election: The Roman Pontiff is elected by the cardinals in secret conclave, being chosen by a two-thirds majority vote (if the number present and voting is exactly divisible by three) or by a two-thirds, plus one, majority (if the number is not exactly divisible by three). This procedure, a modification of former voting methods, was decreed by John XXIII in the apostolic letter *Summi Pontificis Electio*, Sept. 5, 1962.

The conclave, which is held in a sealed-off area of the Vatican Palace, may begin on the 15th day after the death of a pope and must begin no later than the 18th day. Cardinals under the age of 80 are eligible to attend and vote.

Voting takes place in the Sistine Chapel where four secret ballots are cast each day, two in the morning and two in the afternoon.

Voting continues until one of the candidates receives the required majority.

The candidate so elected is asked by the dean of the College of Cardinals whether he accepts the office of the papacy. He becomes pope immediately on giving an affirmative reply. The subsequent coronation is only a ceremonial recognition of the fact that he is the pope. In a ceremony called *adoratio*, the cardinals signify their obedience to the new pontiff in the Sistine Chapel before public announcement of his name is made from the main balcony of the Vatican. The fact of election is first signaled to the outside world by means of white smoke.

The pope is elected for life. If he should resign, which he may do, a new pope is elected. Any male Catholic may be elected, even one who is not a priest. If a layman were elected and accepted the office, he would be ordained as a priest and bishop. If a priest were chosen he would be ordained as a bishop.

Paraclete: A title of the Holy Spirit meaning, in Greek, Advocate, Consoler.

Parental Duties: All duties related to the obligation of parents to provide for the welfare of their children. These obligations fall under the Fourth Commandment.

Parish: A community of the faithful served by a pastor charged with responsibility for providing them with full pastoral service. Most parishes are territorial, embracing all of the faithful in a certain area of a diocese: some are personal or national, for certain classes of people, without strict regard for their places of residence.

Parousia: The coming, or saving presence, of Christ which will mark the completion of salvation history and the coming to perfection of God's kingdom at the end of the world.

Paschal Candle: A large candle, symbolic of the risen Christ, blessed and lighted on the Easter Vigil and placed at the Gospel side of the altar until Ascension Day. It is ornamented with five large grains of incense, representing the wounds of Christ, inserted in the form of a cross; the Greek letters Alpha and Omega, symbolizing Christ the beginning and end of all things, at the top and bottom of the shaft of the cross; and the figures of the current year of salvation in the quadrants formed by the cross.

Paschal Precept: The church law requiring the faithful to receive Holy Communion during the Easter time.

Passion of Christ: Sufferings of Christ, recorded in the four Gospels.

Pastor: An ordained minister charged with responsibility for the doctrinal, sacramental and related service of people committed to his care; e.g., a bishop for the people in his diocese, a priest for the people of his parish.

Pater Noster: The initial Latin words, Our Father, of the Lord's Prayer.

Peace, Sign of: A gesture of greeting —

e.g., a handshake — exchanged by the ministers and participants at Mass.

Pectoral Cross: A cross worn on a chain about the neck and over the breast by bishops and abbots as a mark of their office.

Penance or Penitence: (1) The spiritual change or conversion of mind and heart by which a person turns away from sin, and all that it implies, toward God, through a personal renewal under the influence of the Holy spirit. In the apostolic constitution *Paenitemini,* Pope Paul VI called it "a religious, personal act which has as its aim love and surrender to God." Penance involves sorrow and contrition for sin, together with other internal and external acts of atonement. It serves the purposes of reestablishing in one's life the order of God's love and commandments, and of making satisfaction to God for sin. A divine precept states the necessity of penance for salvation: "Unless you do penance, you shall all likewise perish" . . . "Be converted and believe in the Gospel."

In the penitential discipline of the Church, the various works of penance have been classified under the headings of prayer (interior), fasting and almsgiving (exterior). The Church has established minimum requirements for the common and social observance of the divine precept by Catholics — e.g., by requiring them to fast and/or abstain on certain days of the year. These observances, however, do not exhaust all the demands of the divine precept, whose fulfillment is a matter of personal responsibility; nor do they have any real value unless they proceed from the internal spirit and purpose of penance.

Related to works of penance for sins actually committed are works of mortification. The purpose of the latter is to develop — through prayer, fasting, renunciations and similar actions — self-control and detachment from things which could otherwise become occasions of sin.

(2) Penance is a virtue disposing a person to turn to God in sorrow for sin and to carry out works of amendment and atonement.

(3) The sacrament of penance and sacramental penance.

Perjury: Taking a false oath, lying under oath, a violation of the honor due to God.

Persecution, Religious: A campaign waged against a church or other religious body by persons and governments intent on its destruction. The best known campaigns of this type against the Christian Church were the Roman persecutions which occurred intermittently from about 54 to the promulgation of the Edict of Milan in 313, The most extensive persecutions took place during the reigns of Nero, the first major Roman persecutor, Domitian, Trajan, Marcus Aurelius, and Diocletian. Besides the Roman persecutions, the Catholic Church has been subject to many others, including those of the 20th century in Communist-controlled countries.

Peter's Pence: A collection made each year among Catholics for the maintenance of the pope and his works of charity. It was originally a tax of a penny on each house, and was collected on St. Peter's day, whence the name. It originated in England in the eighth century.

Petition: One of the four purposes of prayer. In prayers of petition, persons ask of God the blessings they and others need, in accordance with his will.

Pharisees: Influential class among the Jews, referred to in the Gospels, noted for their self-righteousness, legalism, strict interpretation of the Law, acceptance of the traditions of the elders as well as the Law of Moses, and beliefs regarding angels and spirits, the resurrection of the dead and judgment. Most of them were laymen, and they were closely allied with the Scribes; their opposite numbers were the Sadducees. The Pharisaic and rabbinical traditions had a lasting influence on Judaism following the destruction of Jerusalem in 70 A.D.

Pilgrimage: A journey to a sacred place or shrine undertaken as an act of devotion or penance.

Pious Fund: Property and money originally accumulated by the Jesuits to finance their missionary work in Lower California. When the Jesuits were expelled from the territory in 1767, the fund was appropriated by the Spanish Crown and used to support Dominican and Franciscan missionary work in Upper and Lower California. In 1842 the Mexican government took over administration of the fund, incorporated most of the revenue into the national treasury, and agreed to pay the Church interest of six per cent a year on the capital so incorporated. From 1848 to 1967 the fund was the subject of lengthy negotiations between the US and Mexican governments because of the latter's failure to make payments as agreed. A lump-sum settlement was made in 1967 with payment by Mexico to the US government of more than $700,000, to be turned over to the Archdiocese of San Francisco.

Polytheism: Belief in and worship of many gods or divinities, especially prevalent in pre-Christian religions.

Poor Box: Alms-box; found in churches from the earliest days of Christianity.

Pope Joan: Alleged name of a woman falsely said to have been pope from 855-858, the years of the reign of Benedict III. The myth was not heard of before the 13th century.

Portiuncula: (1) Meaning little portion (of land), the Portiuncula was the chapel of Our Lady of the Angels near Assisi, Italy, which the Benedictines gave to St. Francis early in the 13th century. He repaired the chapel and made it the first church of the Franciscan Order. It is now enshrined in the Basilica of St. Mary of the Angels in Assisi.

(2) The Portiuncula Indulgence, or Pardon of Assisi, was authorized by Honorius III.

Originally, it could be gained for the souls in purgatory only in the chapel of Our Lady of the Angels; by later concessions, it could be gained also in other Franciscan and parish churches. According to legislation now in force, the Portiuncula Indulgence can be gained once on the day of Aug. 2, or on the following Sunday with permission of the bishop of the place. The conditions are, in addition to freedom from attachment to sin: reception of the sacraments of penance and the Eucharist on or near the day; a visit to a parish church on the day, during which the Our Father and Creed are offered for the intentions of the pope.

Possession, Diabolical: The extraordinary state of a person who is tormented from within by evil spirits who exercise strong influence over his powers of mind and body.

Postulant: One of several names used to designate a candidate for membership in a religious institute during the period before novitiate.

Poverty: (1) The quality or state of being poor, in actual destitution and need, or being poor in spirit. In the latter sense, poverty means the state of mind and disposition of persons who regard material things in proper perspective as gifts of God for the support of life and its reasonable enrichment, and for the service of others in need. It means freedom from unreasonable attachment to material things as ends in themselves, even though they may be possessed in small or large measure.

(2) One of the evangelical counsels professed by religious as a vow. It involves the voluntary renunciation of rights of ownership and of independent use and disposal of material goods (solemn vow); or, the right of independent use and disposal, but not of the radical right of ownership (simple vow). Religious institutes provide their members with necessary and useful goods and services from common resources. The manner in which goods are received and/or handled by religious is determined by poverty of spirit and the rule and constitutions of their institute. Practice of the vow of poverty is undergoing some change in the contemporary renewal in religious life.

Pragmatism: Theory that the truth of ideas, concepts and values depends on their utility or capacity to serve a useful purpose rather than on their conformity with objective standards; also called utilitarianism.

Prayer: The raising of the mind and heart to God in adoration, thanksgiving, reparation and petition. Prayer, which is always mental because it involves thought and love of God, may be vocal, meditative, private and personal, social, and official. The official prayer of the Church as a worshipping community is called the liturgy.

Precepts: Commands or orders given to individuals or communities in particular cases;

they establish law for concerned parties. Preceptive documents are issued by the pope, departments of the Roman Curia and other competent authority in the Church.

Presence of God: A devotional practice of increasing one's awareness of the presence and action of God in daily life.

Presumption: A violation of the theological virtue of hope, by which a person striving for salvation either relies too much on his own capabilities or expects God to do things which he cannot do, in keeping with his divine attributes, or does not will to do, according to his divine plan. Presumption is the opposite of despair.

Preternatural Gifts: Exceptional gifts, beyond the exigencies and powers of human nature, enjoyed by Adam in the state of original justice: immunity from suffering and death, superior knowledge, integrity or perfect control of the passions. These gifts were lost as the result of original sin; their loss, however, implied no impairment of the integrity of human nature.

Pride: Unreasonable self-esteem; one of the seven capital sins.

Prie-Dieu: A French phrase, meaning pray God, designating a kneeler or bench suitable for kneeling while at prayer.

Priesthood of the Laity: Lay persons share in the priesthood of Christ in virtue of the sacraments of baptism and confirmation. They are not only joined with Christ for a life of union with him but are also deputed by him for participation in his mission, now carried on by the Church, of worship, teaching, witness and apostolic works. St. Peter called Christians "a royal priesthood" (1 Pt. 2:9) in this connection. St. Thomas Aquinas declared: "The sacramental characters (of baptism and confirmation) are nothing else than certain sharings of the priesthood of Christ, derived from Christ himself."

The priesthood of the laity differs from the official ministerial priesthood of ordained priests and bishops — who have the power of holy orders for celebrating the Eucharist, administering the other sacraments, and providing pastoral care. The ministerial priesthood, by divine commission, serves the universal priesthood. (See Role of Sacraments.)

Primary Option: The life-choice of a person for or against God which shapes the basic orientation of moral conduct.

Prior: A superior or an assistant to an abbot in a monastery.

Privilege: A favor, an exemption from the obligation of a law. Privileges of various kinds, with respect to ecclesiastical laws, are granted by the pope, departments of the Roman Curia and other competent authority in the Church.

Probabilism: A moral system for use in cases of conscience which involve the obligation of doubtful laws. There is a general principle that a doubtful law does not bind. Probabilism, therefore, teaches that it is permissible to follow an opinion favoring liberty, provided the opinion is certainly and solidly probable. Probabilism may not be invoked when there is question of: a certain law or the certain obligation of a law; the certain right of another party; the validity of an action; something which is necessary for salvation.

Pro-Cathedral: A church used as a cathedral.

Promoter of the Faith: An official of the Congregation for the Causes of Saints, whose role in beatification and canonization procedures is to establish beyond reasonable doubt the validity of evidence regarding the holiness of prospective saints and miracles attributed to their intercession.

Prophecies of St. Malachy: These so-called prophecies, listing the designations of 102 popes and 10 antipopes, bear the name they have because they have been falsely attributed to St. Malachy, bishop of Armagh, who died in 1148. Actually, they are forgeries by an unknown author and came to light only in the last decade of the 16th century.

The first 75 prophecies cover the 65 popes and 10 antipopes from Celestine II (1143-1144) to Gregory XIV (1590-91), and are exact with respect to names, coats of arms, birthplaces, and other identifying characteristics. This portion of the work, far from being prophetic, is the result of historical knowledge or hindsight. The 37 designations following that of Gregory are vague, fanciful, and subject to wide interpretation. According to the prophecies, Paul VI, the Flower of Flowers, will have only four successors before the end of the world.

Prophecy: (1) The communication of divine revelation by inspired intermediaries, called prophets between God and his people. Old Testament prophecy was unique in its origin and because of its ethical and religious content, which included disclosure of the saving will of Yahweh for the people, moral censures and warnings of divine punishment because of sin and violations of the Law and Covenant, in the form of promises, admonitions, reproaches and threats. Although Moses and other earlier figures are called prophets, the period of prophecy is generally dated from the early years of the monarchy to about 100 years after the Babylonian Exile. From that time on the written Law and its interpreters supplanted the prophets as guides of the people. Old Testament prophets are cited in the New Testament, with awareness that God spoke through them and that some of their oracles were fulfilled in Christ. John the Baptist is the outstanding prophetic figure in the New Testament. Christ never claimed the title of prophet for himself, although some people thought he was one. There were prophets in the early Church, and St. Paul mentioned the charism of prophecy in 1 Cor. 14:1-5. Prophecy disappeared after New Testament times.

Revelation is classified as the prophetic book of the New Testament.

(2) In contemporary non-scriptural usage, the term is applied to the witness given by persons to the relevance of their beliefs in everyday life and action.

Province: (1) A territory comprising one archdiocese called the metropolitan see and one or more dioceses called suffragan sees. The head of the archdiocese, an archbishop, has metropolitan jurisdiction over the province.

(2) A division of a religious order under the jurisdiction of a provincial superior.

Prudence: Practical wisdom and judgment regarding the choice and use of the best ways and means of doing good; one of the four cardinal virtues.

Punishment Due for Sin: The punishment which is a consequence of sin. It is of two kinds:

(1) Eternal punishment is the punishment of hell, to which one becomes subject by the commission of mortal sin. Such punishment is remitted when mortal sin is forgiven.

(2) Temporal punishment is a consequence of venial sin and/or forgiven mortal sin; it is not everlasting and may be remitted in this life by means of penance. Temporal punishment unremitted during this life is remitted by suffering in purgatory.

Purgatory: The state or condition in which those who have died in the state of grace suffer for a time before they are admitted to the glory and happiness of heaven. In this state and period of passive suffering, they are purified of unrepented venial sins, satisfy the demands of divine justice for temporal punishment due for sins, and are thus converted to a state of worthiness of the beatific vision.

R

Racism: A theory which holds that any one or several of the different races of the human family are inherently superior or inferior to any one or several of the others. The teaching denies the essential unity of the human race, the equality and dignity of all men because of their common possession of the same human nature, and the participation of all men in the divine plan of redemption. It is radically opposed to the virtue of justice and the precept of love of neighbor. Differences of superiority and inferiority which do exist are the result of accidental factors operating in a wide variety of circumstances, and are in no way due to essential defects in any one or several of the branches of the one human race. The theory of racism, together with practices related to it, is incompatible with Christian doctrine.

Rash Judgment: Attributing faults to another without sufficient reason; a violation of the obligations of justice and charity.

Rationalism: A theory which makes the mind the measure and arbiter of all things, including religious truth. A product of the

Enlightenment, it rejects the supernatural, divine revelation, and authoritative teaching by any church.

Recollection: Meditation, attitude of concentration or awareness of spiritual matters and things pertaining to salvation and the accomplishment of God's will.

Relativism: Theory which holds that all truth, including religious truth, is relative, i.e., not absolute, certain or unchanging; a product of agnosticism, indifferentism, and an unwarranted extension of the notion of truth in positive science. Relativism is based on the tenet that certain knowledge of any and all truth is impossible. Therefore, no religion, philosophy or science can be said to possess the real truth; consequently, all religions, philosophies and sciences may be considered to have as much or as little of truth as any of the others.

Relics: The physical remains and effects of saints, which are considered worthy of veneration inasmuch as they are representative of persons in glory with God. First class relics are parts of the bodies of saints, and instruments of their penance and death; second class relics are objects which had some contact with their persons. Catholic doctrine proscribes the view that relics are not worthy of veneration. In line with norms laid down by the Council of Trent and subsequent enactments, discipline concerning relics is subject to control by the Congregation for the Causes of Saints.

Religion: The adoration and service of God as expressed in divine worship and in daily life. Religion is concerned with all of the relations existing between God and man, and between man and man because of the central significance of God. Objectively considered, religion consists of a body of truth which is believed, a code of morality for the guidance of conduct, and a form of divine worship. Subjectively, it is man's total response, theoretically and practically, to the demands of faith; it is living faith, personal engagement, self-commitment to God. Thus, by creed, code and cult, a person orders and directs his life in reference to God and, through what the love and service of God implies, to his fellow men and all things.

Reliquary: A vessel for the preservation and exposition of a relic; sometimes made like a small monstrance.

Reparation: The making of amends to God for sin committed; one of the four ends of prayer and the purpose of penance.

Rescript: A written reply by an ecclesiastical superior regarding a question or request; its provisions bind concerned parties only. Papal dispensations are issued in the form of rescripts.

Reserved Case: A sin or censure, absolution from which is reserved to religious superiors, bishops, the pope, or confessors having special faculties. Reservations are made because of the serious nature and social effects of certain sins and censures.

Restitution: An act of reparation for an injury done to another. The injury may be caused by retaining what belongs to another or by damaging either the property or reputation of another. The intention of making restitution, usually in kind, is required as a condition for the forgiveness of sins of injustice, even though actual restitution is not possible.

Ring: In the Church a ring is worn as part of the insignia of bishops, abbots, et al.; by nuns or sisters to denote their consecration to God and the Church. The wedding ring symbolizes the love and union of husband and wife.

Ritual: A book of prayers and ceremonies used in the administration of the sacraments and other ceremonial functions. In the Roman Rite, the standard book of this kind is the Roman Ritual. Numerous revisions have been made in recent years in line with liturgical changes — e.g., in the rites of baptism — since the Second Vatican Council.

Rogito: The official notarial act or document testifying to the burial of a pope.

Rosary: A form of mental and vocal prayer centered on mysteries or events in the lives of Jesus and Mary. Its essential elements are meditation on the mysteries and the recitation of a number of decades of Hail Marys, each beginning with the Lord's Prayer. Introductory prayers may include the Apostles' Creed, an initial Our Father, three Hail Marys and a Glory be to the Father; each decade is customarily concluded with a Glory be to the Father; at the end, it is customary to say the Hail, Holy Queen and a prayer from the liturgy for the feast of the Blessed Virgin Mary of the Rosary.

The **Mysteries of the Rosary,** which are the subject of meditation, are: (1) Joyful — the Annunciation to Mary that she was to be the Mother of Christ, her visit to Elizabeth, the birth of Jesus, the presentation of Jesus in the Temple, the finding of Jesus in the Temple. (2) Sorrowful — Christ's agony in the Garden of Gethsemani, scourging at the pillar, crowning with thorns, carrying of the Cross to Calvary, and crucifixion. (3) Glorious — the Resurrection and Ascension of Christ, the descent of the Holy Spirit upon the Apostles, Mary's Assumption into heaven and her crowning as Queen of angels and men.

The complete Rosary, called the Dominican Rosary, consists of 15 decades. In customary practice, only five decades are usually said at one time. Rosary beads are used to aid in counting the prayers without distraction.

The Rosary originated through the coalescence of popular devotions to Jesus and Mary from the 12th century onward. Its present form dates from about the 15th century. Carthusians contributed greatly toward its development; Dominicans have been its greatest promoters.

S

Sabbath: The seventh day of the week, observed by Jews and Sabbatarians as the day for rest and religious observance.

Sacramentary: One of the first liturgical books, containing the celebrant's part of the Mass and rites for administration of the sacraments. The earliest book of this kind, the Leonine Sacramentary, dates from the middle or end of the sixth century.

The sacramentary, incorporating most of the contents of the *Roman Missal*, was reintroduced in the Roman Rite following the promulgation of the *Constitution on the Sacred Liturgy* by the Second Vatican Council.

Sacrarium: A basin with a drain leading directly into the ground; standard equipment of a sacristy.

Sacred Heart, Enthronement: An acknowledgment of the sovereignty of Jesus Christ over the Christian family, expressed by the installation of an image or picture of the Sacred Heart in a place of honor in the home, accompanied by an act of consecration.

Sacred Heart, Promises: Twelve promises to persons having devotion to the Sacred Heart of Jesus, which were communicated by Christ to St. Margaret Mary Alacoque in a private revelation in 1675: (1) I will give them all the graces necessary in their state in life. (2) I will establish peace in their homes. (3) I will comfort them in all their afflictions. (4) I will be their secure refuge during life and, above all, in death. (5) I will bestow abundant blessing upon all their undertakings. (6) Sinners shall find in my Heart the source and the infinite ocean of mercy. (7) By devotion to my Heart tepid souls shall grow fervent. (8) Fervent souls shall quickly mount to high perfection. (9) I will bless every place where a picture of my Heart shall be set up and honored. (10) I will give to priests the gift of touching the most hardened hearts. (11) Those who promote this devotion shall have their names written in my Heart, never to be blotted out. (12) I will grant the grace of final penitence to those who communicate (receive Holy Communion) on the first Friday of nine consecutive months.

Sacrilege: Violation of and irreverence toward a person, place or thing that is sacred because of public dedication to God; a sin against the virtue of religion. Personal sacrilege is violence of some kind against a cleric or religious, or a violation of chastity with a cleric or religious. Local sacrilege is the desecration of sacred places. Real sacrilege is irreverence with respect to sacred things, such as the sacraments and sacred vessels.

Sacristy: A utility room where vestments, church furnishings and sacred vessels are kept and where the clergy vest for sacred functions.

Sadducees: The predominantly priestly party among the Jews in the time of Christ, noted for extreme conservatism, acceptance only of the Law of Moses, and rejection of the traditions of the elders. Their opposite numbers were the Pharisees.

Saints, Cult of: The veneration, called dulia, of holy persons who have died and are in glory with God in heaven; it includes honoring them and petitioning them for their intercession with God. Liturgical veneration is given only to saints officially recognized by the Church; private veneration may be given to anyone thought to be in heaven. The veneration of saints is essentially different from the adoration given to God alone; by its very nature, however, it terminates in the worship of God.

According to the Second Vatican Council's *Dogmatic Constitution on the Church* (No. 50): "It is supremely fitting . . . that we love those friends and fellow heirs of Jesus Christ, who are also our brothers and extraordinary benefactors, that we render due thanks to God for them and 'suppliantly invoke them and have recourse to their prayers, their power and help in obtaining benefits from God through His Son, Jesus Christ, our Lord, who is our sole Redeemer and Savior.' For by its very nature every genuine testimony of love which we show to those in heaven tends toward and terminates in Christ, who is the 'crown of all saints.' Through Him it tends toward and terminates in God, who is wonderful in His saints and is magnified in them."

Salvation: The liberation of men from sin and its effects, reconciliation with God in and through Christ, the attainment of union with God forever in the glory of heaven as the supreme purpose of life and as the God-given reward for fulfillment of his will on earth. Salvation-in-process begins and continues in this life through union with Christ in faith professed and in action; its final term is union with God and the whole community of the saved in the ultimate perfection of God's kingdom. The Church teaches that: God wills the salvation of all men; men are saved in and through Christ; membership in the Church established by Christ, known and understood as the community of salvation, is necessary for salvation; men with this knowledge and understanding who deliberately reject this Church, cannot be saved. In the context of Catholic belief, the Catholic Church is the Church founded by Christ. (See below, Salvation outside the Church.)

Salvation History: The facts and the record of God's relations with men, in the past, present and future, for the purpose of leading them to live in accordance with his will for the eventual attainment after death of salvation, or everlasting happiness with him in heaven.

The essentials of salvation history are: God's love for all men and will for their salvation; his intervention and action in the world to express this love and bring about their salvation; the revelation he made of himself and the covenant he established with the Israelites in the Old Testament; the perfecting of this revelation and the new covenant of grace through Christ in the New Testament; the continuing action-for-salvation carried on in and through the Mystical Body of Christ, the Church; the communication of saving grace to men through the merits of Christ and the operations of the Holy Spirit in the here-and-now circumstances of daily life and with the cooperation of men themselves.

Salvation outside the Church: The Second Vatican Council covered this subject summarily in the following manner: "Those also can attain to everlasting salvation who through no fault of their own do not know the gospel of Christ or His Church, yet sincerely seek God and, moved by grace, strive by their deeds to do His will as it is known to them through the dictates of conscience. Nor does divine Providence deny the help necessary for salvation to those who, without blame on their part, have not yet arrived at an explicit knowledge of God, but who strive to live a good life, thanks to His grace. Whatever good or truth is found among them is looked upon by the Church as a preparation for the gospel. She regards such qualities as given by Him who enlightens all men so that they may finally have life" *(Dogmatic Constitution on the Church,* No. 16).

Satanism: Worship of the devil, a blasphemous inversion of the order of worship which is due to God alone.

Scandal: Conduct which is the occasion of sin to another person.

Scapular: (1) A part of the habit of some religious orders like the Benedictines and Dominicans; a nearly shoulder-wide strip of cloth worn over the tunic and reaching almost to the feet in front and behind. Originally a kind of apron, it came to symbolize the cross and yoke of Christ.

(2) Scapulars worn by lay persons as a sign of association with religious orders and for devotional purposes are an adaptation of monastic scapulars. Approved by the Church as sacramentals, they consist of two small squares of woolen cloth joined by strings and are worn about the neck. They are given for wearing in a ceremony of investiture or enrollment. There are nearly 20 scapulars for devotional use: the five principal ones are generally understood to include those of Our Lady of Mt. Carmel (the brown Carmelite Scapular), the Holy Trinity, Our Lady of the Seven Dolors, the Passion, the Immaculate Conception.

Scapular Medal: A medallion with a representation of the Sacred Heart on one side and of the Blessed Virgin Mary on the other. Authorized by St. Pius X in 1910, it may be worn or carried in place of a scapular by persons already invested with a scapular.

Scapular Promise: According to a legend of the Carmelite Order, the Blessed Virgin Mary appeared to St. Simon Stock in 1251 at Cambridge and declared that wearers of the brown Carmelite Scapular would be saved from hell and taken to heaven by her on the first Saturday after death. The validity of the legend has never been the subject of official decision by the Church. Essentially, it expresses belief in the intercession of Mary and the efficacy of sacramentals in the context of truly Christian life.

Schism: Derived from a Greek word meaning separation, the term designates formal and obstinate refusal by a baptized person, called a *schismatic,* to be in communion with the pope and the Church. The canonical penalty is excommunication. One of the most disastrous schisms in history resulted in the definitive separation of the Church in the East from union with Rome about 1054.

Scholasticism: The term usually applied to the Catholic theology and philosophy which developed in the Middle Ages.

Scribes: Hebrew intellectuals noted for their knowledge of the Law of Moses, influential from the time of the Exile to about 70 A.D. Many of them were Pharisees. They were the antecedents of rabbis and their traditions, as well as those of the Pharisees, had a lasting influence on Judaism following the destruction of Jerusalem in 70 A.D.

Scruple: A morbid, unreasonable fear and anxiety that one's actions are sinful when they are not, or more seriously sinful than they actually are. Compulsive scrupulosity is quite different from the transient scrupulosity of persons of tender or highly sensitive conscience, or of persons with faulty moral judgment.

Seal of Confession: The obligation of secrecy which must be observed regarding knowledge of things learned in connection with the confession of sin in the sacrament of penance. The seal covers matters whose revelation would make the sacrament burdensome. Confessors are prohibited, under penalty of excommunication, from making any direct revelation of confessional matter; this prohibition holds, outside of confession, even with respect to the person who made the confession unless the person releases the priest from the obligation. Persons other than confessors are obliged to maintain secrecy, but not under penalty of excommunication. General, non-specific discussion of confessional matter does not violate the seal.

Secularism: A school of thought, a spirit and manner of action which ignores and/or repudiates the validity or influence of supernatural religion with respect to individual and social life. In describing secularism in their annual statement in 1947, the bishops of the United States said in part: " . . . There are many men — and their number is daily increasing — who in practice live their lives without recognizing that this is God's world.

For the most part they do not deny God. On formal occasions they may even mention his name. Not all of them would subscribe to the statement that all moral values derive from merely human conventions. But they fail to bring an awareness of their responsibility to God into their thought and action as individuals and members of society. This, in essence, is what we mean by secularism."

See: Another name for diocese or archdiocese.

Seminary: A house of study and formation for men, called seminarians, preparing for the priesthood. Traditional seminaries date from the Council of Trent in the middle of the 16th century; before that time, candidates for the priesthood were variously trained in monastic schools, universities under church auspices, and in less formal ways. At the present time, seminaries are undergoing considerable change for the improvement of academic and formation programs and procedures.

Sermon on the Mount: A compilation of sayings of Our Lord in the form of an extended discourse in Matthew's Gospel (5:1 to 7:27) and, in a shorter discourse, in Luke (6:17-49). The passage in Matthew, called the "Constitution of the New Law," summarizes the living spirit of believers in Christ and members of the kingdom of God. Beginning with the Beatitudes and including the Lord's Prayer, it covers the perfect justice of the New Law, the fulfillment of the Old Law in the New Law of Christ, and the integrity of internal attitude and external conduct with respect to love of God and neighbor, justice, chastity, truth, trust and confidence in God.

Servile Work: Work that is mainly physical and done for the sake of material purposes, in distinction from so-called liberal and artistic work which, although involving physical effort, is of a mental and intellectual nature. Commonly classified as servile are such works as farming, manufacturing, commercial operations, mining, etc. Liberal works are those like studying, teaching, designing, writing, typing, etc. The classification of work as servile or otherwise depends in part on custom and cultural interpretation. The reception of pay for work has nothing to do with its classification. Servile work is prohibited on Sundays and holy days of obligation unless there is sound reason for it.

Seven Last Words of Christ: Words of Christ on the Cross. (1) "Father, forgive them; for they do not know what they are doing." (2) To the penitent thief: "I assure you: today you will be with me in Paradise." (3) To Mary and his Apostle John: "Woman, there is your son . . . There is your mother." (4) "My God, my God, why have you forsaken me?" (5) "I am thirsty." (6) "Now it is finished." (7) "Father, into your hands I commend my spirit."

Shrine, Crowned: A shrine approved by the Holy See as a place of pilgrimage. The approval permits public devotion at the shrine and implies that at least one miracle has resulted from devotion at the shrine. Among the best known crowned shrines are those of the Virgin Mary at Lourdes and Fatima.

Shroud of Turin: A strip of brownish linen cloth, 14 feet, three inches in length and three feet, seven inches in width, bearing the front and back imprint of a human body. A tradition dating from the seventh century, which has not been verified beyond doubt, claims that the shroud is the fine linen in which the body of Christ was wrapped for burial. The early history of the shroud is obscure. It was enshrined at Lirey, France, in 1354 and was transferred in 1578 to Turin, Italy, where it has been kept in the cathedral down to the present time. Scientific investigation, which began in 1898, seems to indicate that the markings on the shroud are those of a human body.

Sick Calls: When a person is confined at home by illness or other cause and is unable to go to church for reception of the sacraments, a parish priest should be informed and arrangements made for him to visit the person at home. Such visitations are common in pastoral practice, both for special needs and for providing persons with regular opportunities for receiving the sacraments.

Prepared for the visit should be: a conveniently placed table covered with a white cloth; on it should be a crucifix, two lighted candles, a glass with water, a spoon and napkin.

The priest, carrying the Blessed Sacrament, should be escorted to and from the sick person by someone carrying a lighted candle. Members of the household should be present when the sick person receives Holy Communion and/or anointing of the sick.

Sign of the Cross: A sign, ceremonial gesture or movement in the form of a cross by which a person confesses faith in the Holy Trinity and Christ, and intercedes for the blessing of himself, other persons, and things. In Roman-Rite practice, a person making the sign touches the fingers of the right hand to his forehead, below the breast, left shoulder and right shoulder while saying: "In the name of the Father, and of the Son, and of the Holy Spirit." The sign is also made with the thumb on the forehead, the lips, and the breast. For the blessing of persons and objects, a large sign of the cross is made by movement of the right hand. In Eastern-Rite practice, the sign is made with the thumb and first two fingers of the right hand joined together and touching the forehead, below the breast, the right shoulder and the left shoulder; the formula generally used is the doxology, "O Holy God, O Holy Strong One, O Immortal One." The Eastern manner of making the sign was general until the first half of the 13th century; by the 17th century, Western practice involved the whole right hand and the reversal of direction from shoulder to shoulder.

Signs of the Times: Contemporary events, trends and features in culture and society, the needs and aspirations of people, all the factors that form the context in and through which the Church has to carry on its saving mission. The Second Vatican Council spoke on numerous occasions about these signs and the relationship between them and a kind of manifestation of God's will, positive or negative, and about subjecting them to judgment and action corresponding to the demands of divine revelation through Scripture, Christ, and the experience, tradition and teaching authority of the Church.

Simony: The deliberate intention and act of selling and/or buying spiritual goods or material things so connected with the spiritual that they cannot be separated therefrom; a violation of the virtue of religion, and a sacrilege, because it wrongfully puts a material price on spiritual things, which cannot be either sold or bought. In church law, actual sale or purchase is subject to censure in some cases. The term is derived from the name of Simon Magus, who attempted to buy from Sts. Peter and John the power to confirm people in the Holy Spirit (Acts 8:4-24).

Sin: (1) Actual sin is rejection of God manifested by free and deliberate violation of his law by thought, word or action. (a) Mortal sin — involving serious matter, sufficient reflection and full consent — results in total alienation from God, making a person dead to sanctifying grace, incapable of performing meritorious supernatural acts and subject to everlasting punishment. (b) Venial sin — involving less serious matter, reflection and consent — does not have such serious consequences.

(2) Original sin is the sin of Adam, with consequences for all men. (See separate entries.)

Sins against the Holy Spirit: Despair of salvation, presumption of God's mercy, impugning the known truths of faith, envy at another's spiritual good, obstinacy in sin, final impenitence. Those guilty of such sins stubbornly resist the influence of grace and, as long as they do so, cannot be forgiven.

Sins, Occasions of: Circumstances (persons, places, things, etc.) which easily lead to sin. There is an obligation to avoid voluntary proximate occasions of sin, and to take precautions against the dangers of unavoidable occasions.

Sins That Cry to Heaven for Vengeance: Willful murder, sins against nature, oppression of the poor, widows and orphans, defrauding laborers of their wages.

Sister: Any woman religious, in popular speech; strictly, the title applies only to women religious belonging to institutes whose members never professed solemn vows. Most of the institutes whose members are properly called sisters were established during and since the 19th century. Women religious with solemn vows, or belonging to institutes whose members formerly professed solemn vows, are properly called nuns.

Sisterhood: A generic term referring to the whole institution of the life of women religious in the Church, or to a particular institute of women religious.

Situation Ethics: A subjective, individualistic ethical theory which denies the binding force of ethical principles as universal laws and preceptive norms of moral conduct, and proposes that morality is determined only by situational conditions and considerations and the intention of the person. In an instruction issued on the subject in May, 1956, the Congregation for the Holy Office said:

"It ignores the principles of objective ethics. This 'New Morality,' it is claimed, is not only the equal of objective morality, but is superior to it.

"The authors who follow this system state that the ultimate determining norm for activity is not the objective order as determined by the natural law and known with certainty from this law. It is instead some internal judgment and illumination of the mind of every individual by which the mind comes to know what is to be done in a concrete situation.

"This ultimate decision of man is, therefore, not the application of the objective law to a particular case after the particular circumstances of a 'situation' have been considered and weighed according to the rules of prudence, as the more important authors of objective ethics teach; but it is, according to them, immediate, internal illumination and judgment.

"With regard to its objective truth and correctness, this judgment, at least in many things, is not ultimately measured, is not to be measured or is not measurable by any objective norm found outside man and independent of his subjective persuasion, but it is fully sufficient in itself. . . .

"Much that is stated in this system of 'Situation Ethics' is contrary to the truth of reality and to the dictate of sound reason. It gives evidence of relativism and modernism, and deviates far from the Catholic teaching handed down through the ages."

Slander: Attributing to a person faults which he does not have; a violation of the obligations of justice and charity, for which restitution is due.

Sloth: One of the seven capital sins; spiritual laziness, involving distaste and disgust for spiritual things; spiritual boredom, which saps the vigor of spiritual life. Physical laziness is a counterpart of spiritual sloth.

Sorcery: A kind of black magic in which evil is invoked by means of diabolical intervention; a violation of the virtue of religion.

Soteriology: The division of theology which treats of the mission and work of Christ as Redeemer.

Species, Sacred: The appearances of bread

and wine (color, taste, smell, etc.) which remain after the substance has been changed at the Consecration of the Mass into the Body and Blood of Christ. (See Transubstantiation.)

Spiritism: Attempts to communicate with spirits and departed souls by means of seances, table tapping, ouija boards, and other methods; a violation of the virtue of religion. Spiritualistic practices are noted for fakery.

Spiritual Works of Mercy: Works of spiritual assistance, motivated by love of God and neighbor, to persons in need: counseling the doubtful, instructing the ignorant, admonishing sinners, comforting the afflicted, forgiving offenses, bearing wrongs patiently, praying for the living and the dead.

Stational Churches, Days: Churches, especially in Rome, where the clergy and lay people were accustomed to gather with their bishop on certain days for the celebration of the liturgy. The 25 early titular or parish churches of Rome, plus other churches, each had their turn as the site of divine worship in practices which may have started in the third century. The observances were rather well developed toward the latter part of the fourth century, and by the fifth they included a Mass concelebrated by the pope and attendant priests. On some occasions, the stational liturgy was preceded by a procession from another church called a collecta. There were 42 Roman stational churches in the eighth century, and 89 stational services were scheduled annually in connection with the liturgical seasons. Stational observances fell into disuse toward the end of the Middle Ages. Some revival was begun by John XXIII in 1959 and continued by Paul VI.

Stations of the Cross: A series of meditations on the sufferings of Christ: his condemnation to death and taking up of the Cross; the first fall on the way to Calvary; meeting his Mother; being assisted by Simon of Cyrene, and by Veronica who wiped his face; the second fall; meeting the women of Jerusalem; the third fall; being stripped and nailed to the Cross; his death; the removal of his body from the Cross and his burial. Depictions of these scenes are mounted in most churches, chapels and in some other places, beneath small crosses.

A person making the Way of the Cross passes before these Stations, or stopping points, pausing at each for meditation. If the Stations are made by a group of people, only the leader has to pass from Station to Station. Prayer for the intentions of the pope is required for gaining the indulgence granted for the Stations.

5 Those unable to make the Stations in the ordinary manner, because they are impeded from visiting a church or other place where the Stations are, can still practice the devotion by meditating on the sufferings of Christ;

Praying the Our Father, Hail Mary and Glory for each Station and five times in commemoration of the wounds of Christ; and praying for the intentions of the pope. This practice has involved a Stations Crucifix.

A recent development in this devotion is toward greater awareness of the relation of the Passion to the Resurrection-Ascension; this trend, in some circles, has led to the erection of a 15th—unofficial—station. The concept amounts to an extension of the whole customary thrust of the devotion.

The Stations originated, remotely, from the practice of Holy Land pilgrims who visited the actual scenes of incidents in the Passion of Christ. Representations elsewhere of at least some of these scenes were known as early as the fifth century. Later, the Stations evolved in connection with and as a consequence of strong devotion to the Passion in the 12th and 13th centuries. Franciscans, who were given custody of the Holy Places in 1342, promoted the devotion widely; one of them, St. Leonard of Port Maurice, became known as the greatest preacher of the Way of the Cross in the 18th century. The general features of the devotion were fixed by Clement XII in 1731.

Statutes: Virtually the same as decrees (see separate entry), they almost always designate laws of a particular council or synod rather than pontifical laws.

Stigmata: Marks of the wounds suffered by Christ in his crucifixion, in hands and feet by nails, and side by the piercing of a lance. Some persons, called stigmatists, have been reported as recipients or sufferers of marks like these. The Church, however, has never issued any infallible declaration about their possession by anyone, even in the case of St. Francis of Assisi whose stigmata seem to be the best substantiated and may be commemorated in the Roman-Rite liturgy. Ninety percent of some 300 reputed stigmatists have been women. Judgment regarding the presence, significance, and manner of causation of stigmata would depend, among other things, on irrefutable experimental evidence.

Stipend, Mass: An offering given to a priest for applying the fruits of the Mass according to the intention of the donor. The offering is a contribution to the support of the priest. The disposition of the fruits of the sacrifice, in line with doctrine concerning the Mass in particular and prayer in general, is subject to the will of God. In the early Christian centuries, when Mass was not offered for the intentions of particular persons, the participants made offerings of bread and wine for the sacrifice and their own Holy Communion, and of other things useful for the support of the clergy and the poor. Some offerings may have been made as early as the fourth century for the celebration of Mass for particular intentions, and there are indications of the existence of this practice from the sixth century when private Masses began to be offered. The earliest certain proof of stipend practice, however, dates from the eighth century. By the 11th century, along with private Mass, it was established custom.

Stole Fee: An offering given on certain occasions; e.g., at a baptism, wedding, funeral, for the support of the clergy who administer the sacraments and perform other sacred rites.

Stoup: A vessel used to contain holy water.

Suffragan See: Any diocese, except the archdiocese, within a province.

Suicide: The taking of one's own life; a violation of God's dominion over human life. Ecclesiastical burial is denied to persons who deliberately commit suicide while in full possession of their faculties; it is permitted in cases of doubt.

Supererogation: Good and virtuous actions which go beyond the obligations of duty and the requirements enjoined by God's law as necessary for salvation. Examples of these works are the profession and observance of the evangelical counsels of poverty, chastity, and obedience, and efforts to practice charity to the highest degree.

Supernatural: Above the natural; that which exceeds and is not due or owed to the essence, exigencies, requirements, powers and merits of created nature. While man has no claim on supernatural things and does not need them in order to exist and act on a natural level, he does need them in order to exist and act in the higher order or economy of grace established by God for his salvation.

God has freely given to man certain things which are beyond the powers and rights of his human nature. Examples of the supernatural are: grace, a kind of participation by man in the divine life, by which man becomes capable of performing acts meritorious for salvation; divine revelation by which God manifests himself to man and makes known truth that is inaccessible to human reason alone; faith, by which man believes divine truth because of the authority of God who reveals it through Sacred Scripture and tradition and the teaching of his Church.

Superstition: A violation of the virtue of religion, by which God is worshipped in an unworthy manner or creatures are given honor which belongs to God alone. False, vain, or futile worship involves elements which are incompatible with the honor and respect due to God, such as error, deception, and bizarre practices. Examples are: false and exaggerated devotions, chain prayers and allegedly unfailing prayers, the mixing of unbecoming practices in worship. The second kind of superstition attributes to persons and things powers and honor which belong to God alone. Examples are: idolatry, divination, magic, spiritism, necromancy.

Suspension: A penalty by which a cleric is forbidden to exercise some or all of his powers of orders and jurisdiction, or to accept the financial support of his benefices.

Swearing: Taking an oath; calling upon God to witness the truth of a statement; a legitimate thing to do for serious reasons and under proper circumstances, as in a court of law. To swear without sufficient reason is to dishonor God's name; to swear falsely in a court of law is perjury.

Swedenborgianism: A doctrine developed in and from the writings of Emmanuel Swedenborg (1688-1772), who claimed that during a number of visions he had in 1745 Christ taught him the spiritual sense of Sacred Scripture and commissioned him to communicate it to others. He held that, just as Christianity succeeded Judaism, so his teaching supplemented Christianity. He rejected belief in the Trinity, original sin, the Resurrection, and all the sacraments except baptism and the Eucharist. His followers are members of the Church of the New Jerusalem or of the New Church.

Syllabus, The: (1) When not qualified, the term refers to the list of 80 errors accompanying Pope Pius IX's encyclical *Quanta Cura,* issued in 1864.

(2) The *Syllabus* of St. Pius X in the decree *Lamentabili,* issued by the Holy Office July 4, 1907, condemning 65 heretical propositions of modernism. This schedule of errors was followed shortly by that pope's encyclical *Pascendi,* the principal ecclesiastical document against modernism, issued Sept. 8, 1907.

Synod, Diocesan: Meeting of representative persons of a diocese — priests, religious, lay persons — with the bishop, called by him for the purpose of considering and taking action on matters affecting the life and mission of the Church in the diocese. Persons taking part in a synod have consultative status; the bishop alone is the legislator, with power to authorize synodal decrees. According to canon law, every diocese should have a synod every 10 years.

T

Te Deum: The opening Latin words, Thee, God, of a hymn of praise and thanksgiving prescribed for use in the Office of Readings (Matins of the Liturgy of the Hours) on many Sundays, solemnities and feasts.

Temperance: Moderation, one of the four cardinal virtues.

Temptation: Any enticement to sin, from any source: the strivings of one's own faculties, the action of the devil, other persons, circumstances of life, etc. Temptation itself is not sin. Temptation can be avoided and overcome with the use of prudence and the help of grace.

Thanksgiving: An expression of gratitude to God for his goodness and the blessings he grants; one of the four ends of prayer.

Theism: A philosophy which admits the existence of God and the possibility of divine revelation; it is generally monotheistic and acknowledges God as transcendent and also active in the world. Because it is a philosophy rather than a system of theology derived from revelation, it does not include specifically Christian doctrines, like those concerning the Trinity, the Incarnation and Redemption.

Theological Virtues: The virtues which have God for their direct object: faith, or belief in God's infallible teaching; hope, or confidence in divine assistance; charity, or love of God. They are given to a person with grace in the first instance, through baptism and incorporation in Christ.

Theology: Knowledge of God and religion, deriving from and based on the data of divine Revelation, organized and systematized according to some kind of scientific method. It involves systematic study and presentation of the truths of divine Revelation in Sacred Scripture, tradition, and Church teaching.

The Second Vatican Council made the following declaration about theology and its relation to divine Revelation: "Sacred theology rests on the written word of God, together with sacred tradition, as its primary and perpetual foundation. By scrutinizing in the light of faith all truth stored up in the mystery of Christ, theology is most powerfully strengthened and constantly rejuvenated by that word. For the sacred Scriptures contain the word of God and, since they are inspired, really are the word of God; and so the study of the sacred page is, as it were, the soul of sacred theology" *(Constitution on Revelation.* No. 24).

Theology has been divided under various subject headings. Some of the major fields have been: dogma, moral, pastoral, ascetics (the practice of virtue and means of attaining holiness and perfection), mysticism (higher states of religious experience). Other subject headings include ecumenism (Christian unity, interfaith relations), ecclesiology (the nature and constitution of the Church), Mariology (doctrine concerning the Blessed Virgin Mary), the sacraments, etc.

Tithing: Contribution of a portion of one's income, originally one-tenth, for purposes of religion and charity. The practice is mentioned 46 times in the Bible. In early Christian times, tithing was adopted in continuance of Old Testament practices of the Jewish people, and the earliest positive church legislation on the subject was enacted in 567. Catholics are bound in conscience to contribute to the support of their church, but the manner in which they do so is not fixed by law. Tithing, which amounts to a pledged contribution of a portion of one's income, has aroused new attention in recent years in the United States.

Titular Sees: Dioceses where the Church once flourished but which later were overrun by pagans or Moslems and now exist only in name or title. Bishops without a territorial or residential diocese of their own; e.g., auxiliary bishops, are given titular sees.

Transfinalization, Transignification: Terms coined to express the sign value of consecrated bread and wine with respect to the presence and action of Christ in the Eucharistic sacrifice and the spiritually vivifying purpose of the Eucharistic banquet in Holy Communion. The theory behind the terms has strong undertones of existential and "sign" philosophy, and has been criticized for its openness to interpretations at variance with the doctrine of transubstantiation and the abiding presence of Christ under the appearances of bread and wine after the sacrifice of the Mass and Communion have been completed. The terms, if used as substitutes for transubstantiation, are unacceptable; if they presuppose transubstantiation, they are acceptable as clarifications of its meaning.

Transubstantiation; "The way Christ is made present in this sacrament (Holy Eucharist) is none other than by the change of the whole substance of the bread into his Body, and of the whole substance of the wine into his Blood (in the Consecration at Mass) . . . this unique and wonderful change the Catholic Church rightly calls transubstantiation" (encyclical *Mysterium Fidei* of Paul VI, Sept. 3, 1965). The first official use of the term was made by the Fourth Council of the Lateran in 1215. Authoritative teaching on the subject was issued by the Council of Trent.

Treasury of the Church: The superabundant merits of Christ and the saints from which the Church draws to confer spiritual benefits, such as indulgences.

Triduum: A three-day series of public or private devotions.

U-Z

Usury: Excessive interest charged for the loan and use of money; a violation of justice.

Veronica: A word resulting from the combination of a Latin word for true, *vera,* and a Greek word for image, *eikon,* designating a likeness of the face of Christ or the name of a woman said to have given him a cloth on which he caused an imprint of his face to appear. The veneration at Rome of a likeness depicted on cloth dates from about the end of the 10th century; it figured in a popular devotion during the Middle Ages, and in the Holy Face devotion practiced since the 19th century. A faint, undiscernible likeness said to be of this kind is preserved in St. Peter's Basilica. The origin of the likeness is uncertain, and the identity of the woman is unknown. Before the 14th century, there were no known artistic representations of an incident concerning a woman who wiped the face of Christ with a piece of cloth while He was carrying the Cross to Calvary.

Viaticum: Holy Communion given to those in danger of death. The word, derived from Latin, means provision for a journey through death to life hereafter.

Vicar General: A prelate appointed by a bishop to help him, as a deputy, in the administration of his diocese. Because of his office, he has the same jurisdictional authority as the bishop except in cases reserved to the bishop by himself or by church law.

Virginity: Observance of perpetual sexual abstinence. The state of virginity, which is embraced for the love of God by religious with a public vow or by others with a private vow, was singled out for high praise by Christ (Mt. 19:10-12) and has always been so regarded by the Church. In the encyclical *Sacra Virginitas,* Pius XII stated: "Holy virginity and that perfect chastity which is consecrated to the service of God is without doubt among the most perfect treasures which the founder of the Church has left in heritage to the society which he established."

Paul VI approved in 1970 a rite in which women can consecrate their virginity "to Christ and their brethren" without becoming members of a religious institute. The *Ordo Consecrationis Virginum,* a revision of a rite promulgated by Clement VII in 1596, is traceable to the Roman liturgy of about 500.

Virtue: A habit or established capability for performing good actions. Virtues are *natural* (acquired and increased by repeating good acts) and/or *supernatural* (given with grace by God).

Vocation: A call to a way of life. Generally, the term applies to the common call of all men, from God, to holiness and salvation. Specifically, it refers to particular states of life, each called a vocation, in which response is made to this universal call; viz., marriage, the religious life and/or priesthood, the single state freely chosen or accepted for the accomplishment of God's will. The term also applies to the various occupations in which persons make a living. The Church supports the freedom of each individual in choosing a particular vocation, and reserves the right to pass on the acceptability of candidates for the priesthood and religious life. Signs or indicators of particular vocations are many, including a person's talents and interests, circumstances and obligations, invitations of grace and willingness to respond thereto.

Vow: A promise made to God with sufficient knowledge and freedom, which has as its object a moral good that is possible and better than its voluntary omission. A person who professes a vow binds himself by the virtue of religion to fulfill his promise. The best known examples of vows are those of poverty, chastity and obedience professed by religious (see Evangelical Counsels, individual entries).

Public vows are made before a competent person, acting as an agent of the Church, who accepts the profession in the name of the Church, thereby giving public recognition to the person's dedication and consecration to God and divine worship. Vows of this kind are either solemn, rendering all contrary acts invalid as well as unlawful; or simple, rendering contrary acts unlawful. Solemn vows are for life; simple vows are for a definite period of time or for life. Vows professed without public recognition by the Church are called private vows. The Church, which has authority to accept and give public recognition to vows, also has authority to dispense persons from their obligations for serious reasons.

Week of Prayer for Christian Unity: Eight days of prayer, from Jan. 18 to 25, for the union of all men in the Church established by Christ. On the initiative of Father Paul James Francis, S.A., of Graymoor, N.Y., it originated in 1908 as the Chair of Unity Octave. In recent years, its observance on an interfaith basis has increased greatly.

Witness, Christian: Practical testimony or evidence given by Christians of their faith in all circumstances of life — by prayer and general conduct, through good example and good works, etc.; being and acting in accordance with Christian belief; actual practice of the Christian faith.

Zucchetto: A skullcap worn by bishops and other prelates.

Apparitions Denied

Garabandal: Claims of Vatican support for alleged apparitions of the Blessed Virgin Mary to four young girls at Garabandal, Spain, were denied May 10, 1969, by the Congregation for the Doctrine of the Faith. The congregation, stating that investigation and decision on the matter rested with authorities in the Diocese of Santander, said that it stood by the "official note" authorized by Bishop Vicente Puchol Montiz Aug. 17, 1965. The note said there had been no apparitions of the Blessed Virgin, St. Michael the Archangel or other saints. (It had been reported that the first of several appearances occurred June 18, 1961.) It also said that there was no message of private revelation. (One was reported Oct. 18, 1961.) Summarily, the note stated that all reported incidents were explainable on a natural basis.

Necedah: Reporting in February, 1971, a special commission of the La Crosse diocese agreed with the conclusions of a 1950-1955 investigation that alleged revelations and visions of a woman in Necedah, Wis., were not of supernatural origin. The events were connected with the local Shrine of the Queen of the Holy Rosary, Mediatrix of Peace. The commission recommended that religious worship at the shrine be prohibited.

The authenticity of religious devotion and experience is behind the Church's concern over apparitions and similiar phenomena. To approve of them without adequate investigation and ruling out natural means of explanation would be to foster superstitution. The Church admits the credibility of apparitions only with the support of evidence of supernatural origin.

Biographies of Catholics

(In addition to the biographical entries below, others are listed in the Index.)

A

Abelard, Peter (1079-1142); French philosopher, theologian; contributed to scholastic method although he had nominalistic tendencies.

Achillini, Alessandro (1463-1512): Italian physicist, astronomer; inaugurated reaction against Ptolemaic astronomy.

Adam, Karl (1876-1966): German theologian, writer; *Spirit of Catholicism.*

Adenauer, Konrad (1876-1967): German statesman; chancellor of West Germany, 1949-63.

Africanus, Sextus Julius (3rd cent.): Christian historian; wrote history of world from creation to 221 A.D.

Agreda, Mary of (1602-1665): Spanish Poor Clare, mystical writer; *Mystical City of God and the Divine History of the Virgin Mother of God.*

Alan of Walsingham (died 1364): English monk, architect.

Alarcon, Pedro Antonio de (1833-1891): Spanish writer, statesman.

Albert or Albrecht (died 1229): Founder and first bishop of Riga, apostle of Livonia.

Albornoz, Gil Alvarez Carillo de (1310-1367): Spanish cardinal, general, statesman; negotiated return of the papal states, 1354; his *Egidian Constitutions* for them prevailed until 1816; archbishop of Toledo.

Alcuin, Albinus (735-804): English scholar; abbot of Tours; educator among Franks.

Alexander of Hales (1180-1245): English theologian, philosopher; first Franciscan teacher at Paris; called Doctor Irrefragabilis.

Alfred the Great (849-899): First Saxon king of England; noted for wise laws, spread of religion and learning.

Allen, Frances (1784-1819) American religious; daughter of Ethan Allen; convert, 1807; professed vows in community of Hospital Sisters at Hotel-Dieu, Montreal, 1810.

Allers, Rudolf (1883-1963): Austrian-born psychologist; d. Maryland; taught at Catholic University of America, 1938-48, and Georgetown University, 1948-63.

Allori, Alessandro (1535-1607) and his son **Cristofano** (1577-1621): Italian painters, Florentine school.

Amiot, Jean Marie (1718-1793): French Jesuit, missionary to China, author.

Ammen, Daniel (1820-1898): American naval officer in Civil War; author.

Ampere, Andre Marie (1775-1836): French physicist; pioneer in electrodynamics; term ampere named for him.

Anderson, William H. (1799-1875): American mathematician and astronomer; on US expedition to Dead Sea, 1848; convert, 1849.

Angelico, Fra (Giovanni da Fiesole) (1387-1455): Italian Dominican painter of religious subjects.

Anglin, Timothy (1822-1896): Canadian journalist and legislator. Father of **Margaret Mary Anglin** (1876-1958): actress, Laetare medalist.

Animuccia, Giovanni (1500?-1571): Italian composer of sacred music.

Apponyi, Albert, Count (1846-1933): Hungarian statesman, parliamentary leader for 40 years; head of Hungary's peace delegation in Paris, 1920.

Argenlieu, Georges Thierry d' (1889-1964): French admiral, Carmelite priest; naval officer in World War I; entered Carmelites, 1920, and ordained priest (Father Louis of the Trinity); recalled to active duty during World War II, fought with Free French; governor general of Indo-China after the war; returned to monastery, 1947.

Arnold, Thomas (1823-1900): English educator; convert, 1856.

Avery, Martha (Moore) (1851-1929): American Socialist, political economist, author; convert, 1903; a founder of the Catholic Truth Guild, 1917.

B

Bacon, Roger (1214-1294): English Franciscan, philosopher, experimental scientist; considered optical and astronomical laws, possibilities of scientific invention, gunpowder.

Baegert, Johann Jacob (1717-1777): Jesuit missionary, ethnographer; author of works on Lower California.

Balboa, Vasco Nunez de (1475-1517): Spanish adventurer; discovered Pacific Ocean, 1513.

Baldwin, Charles Sears (1867-1935): American educator, author; convert, 1934.

Baldwin, Geoffrey P. (1892-1951): American military officer in World Wars I and II; convert, 1937; chief of CARE in Italy.

Banim, John (1798-1842) and **Michael** (1796-1874): First national novelists of Ireland; John called the Scott of Ireland.

Barber, Virgil (1787-1847): American Jesuit; prominent New England Episcopal minister before his conversion, 1816, with his wife and five children; all eventually entered religious life; ordained 1822; established first Catholic church and school in New Hampshire at Claremont. His father **Daniel** (1756-1834) was also an Episcopal minister before he followed the rest of his family into the Church in 1818; wrote *Catholic Worships and Piety Explained.*

Barbour, John (1316?-1395): Scottish poet, author of the Epic *Brus.*

Baring, Maurice (1874-1945): English poet, novelist, critic, author of works on Russia; convert, 1909.

Barry, John (1745-1803): American naval officer, b. Ireland; naval hero in Revolution.

Bartholomeus Anglicus (13th cent.): English Franciscan, author of a medieval encyclopedia of science.

Bartolommeo, Fra (1475-1517): Florentine Dominican, religious painter.

Bayley, James Roofevelt (1814-1877): American prelate; convert, 1842; ordained priest, 1844; bishop of Newark, N. J. 1853-72; archbishop of Baltimore 1872-77.

Bayma, Joseph (1816-1892): Italian Jesuit, mathematician, scientist; author of *Molecular Mechanics.*

Bazin, Rene (1853-1932): French novelist, biographer, travel writer; member of French Academy.

Bea, Augustin (1881-1968): German Jesuit, cardinal, Biblical scholar, leader in Christian reunion movement.

Beardsley, Aubrey Vincent (1872-1898): British illustrator; convert, 1895.

Beaton (Bethune), David (1494-1546): Scottish prelate, statesman; cardinal archbishop of St. Andrews; chancellor of Scotland; opposed efforts of Henry VIII to separate Scotland from loyalty to Holy See.

Beauregard, Pierre (1818-1893): American Confederate general; graduate of West Point; superintendent of West Point for five days; resigned to serve with Confederate Army.

Beccaria, Giovanni Battista (1716-1781): Italian physicist; early researcher in electricity.

Becquerel, Antoine Cesar (1788-1878): French physicist, electrochemist; invented the constant cell, a differential galvanometer, an electric thermometer.

Becquerel, Antoine Henri (1852-1908): French physicist; discoverer of radioactivity in uranium; shared 1903 Nobel Prize in physics with the Curies.

Beethoven, Ludwig van (1770-1827): German composer; works include symphonies, concertos and sonatas.

Behaim, Martin (1459-1507): German geographer; constructed a terrestrial globe, 1492.

Bellini, Gentile (1429-1507) and **Giovanni** (1430-1516): Venetian painters.

Belloc, Hilaire (1870-1953): English journalist, essayist, poet, novelist, historian, biographer, critic, apologist.

Benson, Robert Hugh (1871-1914): English author of historical fiction, other works; Anglican clergyman before conversion, 1903; ordained to priesthood, 1904.

Benson, William Shepherd (1855-1932): American naval officer; first chief of naval operations, 1915-19; convert.

Bentley, John Francis (1839-1902): English architect; promoted Gothic revival in England; designed Cathedral of Westminster.

Berengario da Carpi, Jacopo (1470-1530): Italian anatomist; a founder of modern science of anatomy.

Bernanos, Georges (1888-1948): French journalist, novelist; works concerned principally with struggle of the soul against evil.

Bernard, Claude (1813-1878): French physiologist; studied the glycogenic function of the liver, sympathetic nervous system.

Bernini, Giovanni Lorenzo (1598-1680): Italian sculptor; architect of St. Peter's.

Bertrand, Louis (1866-1941): French novelist, biographer.

Beschi, Costanzo Giuseppi (1680-1746): Italian Jesuit missionary; famous for linguistic and literary work in the Tamil language.

Besse, Jean Martial Leon (1861-1920): Benedictine monk, historian.

Bianchini, Francesco (1662-1729): Italian astronomer; secretary, under Clement XI, of papal commission for calendar reform.

Bickerstaffe-Drew, Francis (1858-1928): English author (under pseudonym of **John Ayscough**); convert, priest.

Bielski, Marcin (1495-1575): Polish historian, poet.

Bienville, Sieur de (1680-1768); French explorer, governor of Lousiana colony.

Biggs, Richard Keys (1886-1962): American concert organist, composer, choir master; convert.

Billuart, Charles Rene (1685-1757): Belgian Dominican theologian, preacher, controversialist.

Binet, Jacques Philippe Marie (1786-1856): French mathematician, astronomer; Binet's theorem.

Biondo, Flavio (1388-1463): Italian historian, archaeologist.

Biot, Jean Baptiste (1774-1862): French physicist; studied polarization of light; Biot's law.

Blondel, Maurice (1861-1949): French philosopher; works include *L'Action, La Pensée.*

Bloy, Leon (1846-1917): French writer, social reformer.

Boccaccio, Giovanni (1313-1375): Italian author; known as father of Italian prose; *Decameron.*

Boethius, Anicius Manlius (480?-524?): Roman statesman and philosopher; author of *The Consolation of Philosophy.*

Boileau-Despreaux, Nicolas (1636-1711): French poet, satirist, critic.

Bolland, Jomn van (1596-1665): Flemish Jesuit; editor of *Acta Sanctorum,* continued by Boglandists.

Bolzano, Bernard (1781-1848): Bohemian mathematician; formulated theory of functions.

Bona, Giovanni (1609-1674): Italian cardinal, author of liturgical encyclopedia.

Bonaparte, Charles J. (1851-1921): American cabinet official; secretary of navy 1905-06; attorney general, 1906-09.

Bordone, Paris (1500-1571): Venetian painter, pupil of Titian.

Borrus, Christopher (1583-1632): Oceanic geographer.

Boscovich, Ruggiero Giuseppe (1711-1787); Italian Jesuit, astronomer, physicist; offered a molecular theory of matter.

Bosio, Antonio (1575-1629): Italian archaeologist, called Columbus of the Catacombs.

Bossuet, Jacques Benigne (1627-1704): French pulpit orator.

Botticelli, Sandro (1444-1510): Florentine painter.

Bourdaloue, Louis (1632-1704): French Jesuit, pulpit orator.

Bourgeois, Louis (1819-1878): French archaeologist; presented and developed problem of the eoliths, 1863.

Bracton, Henry de (died 1268): English jurist; author of treatise *On the Laws and Customs of England.*

Braille, Louis (1809-1852): Blind French teacher of the blind; inventor of Braille system of raised-point printing.

Bramante, Donato (1444-1514): Italian architect; made plan for reconstruction of St. Peter's.

Branly, Edouard (1846-1940): French physicist; discovered coherer, making wireless telegraphy possible.

Brennan, Francis J. (1894-1968): American cardinal, Roman Curia official; ordained priest, 1920; professor at St. Charles Seminary, Overbrook, Pa., 1920-40; judge, 1940-59, and dean, 1959-67, of the Sacred Roman Rota; ord. bishop June 25, 1967; cardinal, June 26, 1967.

Brentano, Klemens (1778-1842): German poet; rejoined Catholic Church, 1818; recorded revelations of Anne Catherine Emmerich.

Breuil, Henri (1877-1961): French priest, archaeologist; authority on prehistoric art.

Broun, Heywood Campbell (1888-1939): American journalist, author; convert, 1939.

Browne, Charles Farrar (pseud. Artemus Ward) (1834-1867): American humorist, journalist, lecturer.

Brownson, Orestes Augustus (1803-1876): American scholar, essayist, philosopher, controversialist; was successively a Presbyterian, Universalist minister and Unitarian minister before his conversion, 1844.

Bruckner, Anton (1824-1896): Austrian composer and organist.

Brumidi, Constantini (1805-1880): American painter, b. Italy; became naturalized citizen; noted for his frescoes in Capitol at Washington, D.C.

Brunelleschi, Filippo (1377-1466): Italian architect; called founder of Renaissance architecture; established theory of perspective.

Brunetiere, Ferdinand (1849-1906): French critic, editor, professor of literature; convert.

Buck, Edward Eugene (Gene) (1885-1957): American popular song lyricist, producer; president of American Society of Composers, Authors and Publishers (ASCAP), 1924-41.

Bullitt, William C. (1891-1967): American diplomat; first ambassador to Russia; convert shortly before his death.

Burke, John (1859-1937): American jurist, politician; governor of North Dakota, 1907-21; treasurer of US, 1913-21; judge, 1924, and later chief justice of North Dakota supreme court. Represents North Dakota in Statuary Hall.

Burke, Thomas Nicholas (1830-1882): Irish Dominican preacher.

Burnand, Sir Francis Crowley (1836-1917): English playwright; editor of *Punch* (1880-1906), and English *Catholic Who's Who;* convert, 1857.

Burnett, Peter Hardemann (1807-1895): American jurist, politician; judge of Oregon supreme court, first governor of California, member of California supreme court; convert, 1846.

Butler, Alban (1711-1773): English author; *Lives of the Saints.*

Butler, Pierce (1866-1939): American attorney, jurist; associate Justice US Supreme Court, 1923-39.

Byrd, William (1540?-1623): English organist, composer; founder of English Madrigal School.

C

Cabeza de Vaca, Alvar Nunez (1490-1557): Spanish explorer; colonial governor in Paraguay.

Cabot, John (1450-1498): Italian navigator; discovered mainland of North America, June 24, 1497.

Cabral, Pedro Alvarez de (1460-1526): Portuguese navigator; discovered Brazil, which he named Vera Cruz.

Caedmon (died 670): First great English Christian poet; lay brother at monastery in Whitby.

Caius (Kees, Keys, Kay, Key), John (1510-1573): English physician; one of first to introduce publicly the practice of dissection into England, 1573.

Cajetan, Tommaso De Vio (1469-1534): Italian cardinal, philosopher, theologian.

Caldani, Leopold Marco Antonio (1725-1813): Italian anatomist, physiologist; furthered anatomical studies on function of spinal cord.

Calderon de La Barca, Pedro (1600-1681): Spanish priest, dramatist; author of over 200 works.

Calvert, Cecil (1605-1675): English proprietor; second Lord Baltimore; responsible for enactment of religious toleration in Maryland colony.

Calvert, George (1580-1632): English proprietor; first Lord Baltimore; held important posts under James I; was granted territory of Baltimore colony but died before grant of charter; convert, 1625.

Camel (Kamel), George Joseph (1661-1706): Moravian Jesuit missionary, botanist; studied plants and natural history of Philippines.

Camoes, Luiz Vaz de (1524-1580): Portuguese poet, dramatist.

Campbell, James (1812-1893): American jurist, cabinet official; US postmaster general, 1853-57.

Cano, Melchior (1509-1560): Spanish Dominican, theologian; called father of fundamental theology.

Canova, Antonio (1757-1822): Italian sculptor of the modern classic school.

Canute (II) the Great (994?-1035): King of Denmark, England, Norway.

Cardano, Girolamo (1501-1576): Italian physician, mathematician; solved cubic equation named after him.

Cardijn, Joseph (1882-1967): Belgian cardinal, founder of the Young Christian Workers; cardinal, 1965.

Carey, Mathew (1760-1839): American publisher, economist and author, b. Ireland; first extensive US Catholic publisher.

Carnoy, Jean Baptiste (1836-1899): Belgian priest, founder of the science of cytology.

Carpini, Giovanni de Piano (c. 1180-1252): Italian Franciscan, companion of St. Francis; missionary in Germany; papal envoy to Great Khan of the Mongols, 1246; wrote *Liber Tartarorum* recounting in detail the life and customs of the Mongols.

Carrel, Alexis (1873-1944): French surgeon, biologist; developed surgical techniques, experimented on transplantation of organs; author; member Pontifical Academy of Sciences; Nobel Prize for physiology and medicine, 1912.

Carroll, Charles (1737-1832): American statesman; member of Continental Congress, 1776-78; signer of Declaration of Independence; member Maryland Congress and first US Senate, 1789-92. Represents Maryland in Statuary Hall.

Carroll, Daniel (1730-1796): American patriot; brother of Archbishop John Carroll; delegate to Continental Congress, 1780-84, Constitutional Convention, 1787; congressman from Maryland, 1789-91.

Carroll, John (1735-1815): American prelate; ordained priest, 1761; first bishop of the hierarchy of the US (bishop, 1789-1808, and archbishop, 1808-15 of Baltimore); also apostolic administrator of Louisiana and Two Floridas, 1805-15; founder of Georgetown University, 1791.

Carson, Christopher (Kit) (1809-1868): American trapper, scout, Indian agent.

Cartier, Jacques (1491-c. 1557): French explorer of coasts of Labrador and Newfoundland; ascended the St. Lawrence to Montreal.

Caruso, Enrico (1873-1921): Italian operatic tenor.

Cassini, Jean Dominique (1625-1712): French astronomer; first director of Paris observatory; made important discoveries regarding Saturn, parallax of sun.

Cassiodorus, Flavius Aurelius (c. 490-c. 580): Roman statesman, writer, founder of monasteries.

Castelli, Benedetto (c. 1572-1644): Italian Benedictine, mathematician, physicist; authority on hydraulics.

Cauchy, Augustin Louis (1789-1857): French mathematician; did research in calculus, developed wave theory in optics.

Cavalieri, Francesco Bonaventura (1598-1647): Italian religious, mathematician; originated method of indivisibles; forerunner of integral calculus.

Caxton, William (1422-1491): First English printer.

Cellini, Benvenuto (1500-1571): Italian sculptor; worker in gold and bronze.

Cervantes Saavedra, Miguel de (1547-1616): Spanish novelist; *Don Quixote.*

Cesalpino, Andrea (1519-1603): Italian botanist, physician; important contributor to work on plant morphology, physiology; anticipated Linnaean system of classification.

Cezanne, Paul (1839-1906): French painter; a leader of postimpressionism.

Challoner, Richard (1691-1781): English bishop; re-edited Douay Bible.

Champlain, Samuel de (1567-1635): French explorer; Father of New France, founder of Quebec; discovered Lake Champlain.

Champollion, Jean Francois (1790-1832): French Egyptologist; discovered through the Rosetta Stone a system for deciphering hieroglyphics.

Chandler, Joseph Ripley (1792-1880): American journalist, congressman; Grand Master of Free Masons before conversion, 1849; US minister to Naples during administration of Buchanan; US congressman from Pennsylvania, 1849-55.

Charlemagne (742-814): King of the Franks, Emperor of the West, founder of Holy Roman Empire; promoted spread of Christianity, learning; defender of the papacy.

Charles Martel (c. 689-741): Duke of Austrasia, son of Pepin; halted Saracen advance on western Europe at Battle of Tours (732), and thereafter was called Martel *(The Hammer);* grandfather of Charlemagne.

Chateaubriand, Francois Rene de (1768-1848): French author; influential in history of Romantic Movement.

Chaucer, Geoffrey (1340-1400): Father of English poetry; *Canterbury Tales.*

Chauliac, Guy de (1300-1370): French surgeon; gave authoritative description of bubonic plague, Black Death of 14th century.

Chavez, Dennis (1888-1962): American legislator; member New Mexico State legislature, 1920-30; US congressman, 1931-35; US senator, 1935-62. Represents New Mexico in Statuary Hall.

Cherubini, Maria Luigi (1760-1842): Italian composer of ecclesiastical and operatic works.

Chesterton, Gilbert K. (1874-1936); English essayist, poet, novelist, biographer, journalist; Prince of Paradox; convert, 1922.

Chevereul, Michel Eugene (1786-1889): French chemist; did research in animal fats; discovered margarine, oleine, stearine.

Cimabue, Giovanni (Cenni di Pepo) (1240-1302): Florentine painter; religious subjects.

Claudel, Paul (1868-1955): French author, diplomat; elected to French Academy, 1946.

Clavius, Christopher (1537-1612): Jesuit astronomer, mathematician; introduced decimal point.

Clerke, Agnes Mary (1842-1907): Irish astronomer.

Coady, Moses Michael (1882-1959): Canadian priest, educator; organizer of cooperatives among Canadian fishermen, known as Antigonish movement.

Corbo, Bernabe (1582-1657): Spanish Jesuit, naturalist; author of *History of the New World*, on Latin America.

Cody, Col. William F. (Buffalo Bill) (1846-1917: American Pony Express rider, army guide and scout, hunter, Indian fighter; entered Church just before death.

Collins, Michael (1890-1922): Irish revolutionary leader and soldier.

Colombo, Matteo Realdo (1516-1559): Italian anatomist; discovered pulmonary circulation.

Columbus, Christopher (1451-1506): Genoese explorer; discovered the Americas in 1492.

Connell, Francis J. (1888-1967): American Redemptorist priest, moral theologian, author.

Connelly, Mother Cornelia (1809-1879): American-born foundress; married to Pierce Connelly, an Episcopalian minister; her conversion, 1835, was followed three months later by her husband's; granted permanent separation by Rome and entered convent so her husband could become a priest; sent to England at request of Cardinal Wiseman and founded Society of the Holy Child Jesus, 1846; her husband renounced the priesthood, 1849; his legal attempt to force her to return to married life was unsuccessful.

Constantine the Great (c. 280-337): Roman emperor; granted liberty of worship to Christians by Edict of Milan, 313; established Constantinople as capital of the Eastern Empire.

Copernicus, Nicolaus (1473-1543): Polish astronomer; founder of modern astronomy, taught the revolution of planets around the sun and the rotation of the earth on its axis.

Coppee, Francois (1842-1908): French poet, dramatist, novelist; member of French Academy, 1884.

Cordoba, Francisco Fernandez de (d. 1518?): Spanish explorer; discovered Yucatan, 1517.

Corneille, Pierre (1606-1684): French dramatist; great influence on French tragedy, *Le Cid*.

Corot, Jean Baptiste Camille (1796-1875): French landscape artist.

Correggio, Antonio Allegri (1494-1534): Lombard painter; noted for mastery of light and shade; religious subjects.

Cortez, Hernando (1485-1547): Spanish explorer, soldier; conquered Mexico.

Cory, Herbert Ellsworth (1883-1947): American educator, social scientist, author; convert, 1933.

Coulomb, Charles Augustine (1736-1806): French physicist; investigated electricity and magnetism; stated coulomb's law; the coulomb named for him.

Couperin, Francois (1668-1733): French composer; first great composer for the harpsichord.

Cousin, Jean (1490-1560), and his son **Jean** (1522-1590): French painters, workers in stained glass.

Crashaw, Richard (1613-1649): English poet of metaphysical school; convert, 1646.

Crawford, Francis Marion (1854-1909): American novelist, b. Italy; convert, 1880.

Credi, Lorenz di (1459-1537): Florentine painter; religious subjects.

Creighton, John (1831-1907) and his brother **Edward** (1802-1874): American philanthropists; benefactors of Creighton University; in 1861 took part in laying first telegraph line linking California to rest of the nation.

Cushing, Richard J. (1895-1970): American cardinal; ordained priest, 1921; auxiliary bishop of Boston, 1939-44; archbishop of Boston, 1944-70; cardinal, 1958; founded Missionary Society of St. James the Apostle to recruit diocesan priests for Latin American missions; promoted charitable works especially among exceptional children.

D

Dablon, Claude (1619-1697): French Jesuit missionary in America; superior of Canadian missions.

Daly, Thomas A. (1871-1948): American journalist and poet.

Damien, Father (Joseph de Veuster) (1840-1889): Belgian missionary; joined Picpus Fathers, 1860; from 1873 to his death, devoted his life to caring for lepers on Molokai, in Hawaiian Islands; contracted the disease three years before his death. Represents Hawaii in National Statuary Hall.

Daniel-Rops, Henri (pseud. of Henri Jules Petiot) (1901-1965): French writer on Church history and other subjects; member of French Academy.

Dante Alighieri (1265-1321): Florentine poet; *Divina Commedia, Vita Nuova, De Monarchia.*

Daumer, Georg Friedrich (1800-1875): German writer; anti-Christian works until conversion, 1858; author of *Meine Konversion.*

Davenport, Sir William (1606-1668): English poet and dramatist.

Dawson, Christopher (1889-1970): English author and scholar; convert from Anglicanism, 1914; principal themes of his works are cultural history and the philosophy of religion.

DeGaulle, Charles Andre Joseph Marie (1890-1970): French general, statesman; leader of French forces in World War II; interim president of France, 1945-46; president of Fifth Republic, 1959-69.

Delacroix, Ferdinand Victor Eugene (1799-1863: French painter: romantic school.

Delaroche, Paul (1797-1856): French painter, of the Eclectic school; portrait and historical subjects.

DeRossi, Giovanni Battista (1822-1894): Italian archaeologist; aroused interest in Christian antiquities.

Descartes, Rene (1596-1650): French scientists and philosopher; founder of analytic geometry.

De Soto, Hernando (1500-1542): Spanish explorer; discovered lower course of Mississippi River, 1541.

De Vaux, Roland (1903-1971): French Dominican; biblical archeologist and exegete; head of Ecole Biblique, Jerusalem; headed international team of scholars who edited Dead Sea Scrolls.

Devlin, Joseph (1872-1934): Irish politician.

Dias, Bartholomew (1450-1500): Portuguese navigator; discovered Cape of Good Hope, 1488.

Dimnet, Ernest (1869-1954): French priest, lecturer, writer.

Dior, Christian (1905-1957): French fashion designer.

Divisch, Wenceslaus (religious name, **Procopius**) (1698-1765): Moravian Premonstratensian monk; erected a lightning rod in 1754, before Franklin's work was known.

Dolci, Carlo (1616-1686): Florentine painter; religious and portrait subjects.

Donatello or **Donato di Niccolo di Betto Bardi** (1386-1466): Italian sculptor; called the founder of modern sculpture.

Dongon, Thomas (1634-1715): Colonial governor of New York, 1682-88; b. Ireland.

Donizetti, Gaetano (1797-1848): Italian operatic composer.

Dooley, Thomas A. (1927-1961): American physician; co-founder of MEDICO, organized to establish medical services in underdeveloped countries; author.

Doria, Andrea (1468-1560): Genoese admiral, statesman; Father of Peace, Liberator of Genoa.

Drexel, Mary Katherine (1858-1955): American missionary; foundress of Sisters of the Blessed Sacrament for Indians and Colored People, 1891.

Drum, Hugh A. (1879-1951): American army officer in World Wars I and II.

Dryden, John (1631-1700): English poet, playwright; poet laureate, 1670; convert, 1686.

Duffy, Sir Charles Gavan (1816-1903): Irish nationalist, political leader in Australia after he emigrated there (1856), author.

Dulong, Pierre Louis (1785-1838): French chemist, physicist; author with Petit of formula determining the specific heat of solids.

Dumas, Jean Baptiste (1800-1884); French chemist; did important research on vapor densities.

Dunne, Peter Finley (1867-1936): American humorist, journalist; creator of Irish philosophical character "Mr. Dooley."

Duns Scotus, John (1256-1308): Scottish scholastic theologian; Franciscan; advanced best theological arguments for doctrine of the Immaculate Conception; known as Doctor Subtilis.

Durer, Albrecht (1471-1528): German painter of Renaissance school, engraver, wood-cut artist; called the inventor of etching.

Durkin, Martin P. (1894-1955): American union leader, cabinet official; secretary of labor, 1953.

Dutton, Ira (Brother Joseph) (1843-1931): American missionary; convert, 1883; assisted Father Damien in work among lepers at Molokai, served there for 42 years, beginning in 1886.

Dwight, Thomas (1843-1911): American surgeon, anatomist; taught anatomy at Harvard and Maine medical schools; convert, 1855.

E

Eck, Johann (1486-1543): German theologian; outstanding opponent of Luther.

Eckhel, Joseph Hilarius (1737-1798): Austrian Jesuit; founder of the scientific numismatics of classical antiquity.

Eichendorff, Joseph von (1788-1857): German lyric poet, novelist, critic.

Elgar, Edward (1857-1934): English composer. *Pomp and Circumstance.*

Emmerich, Anne Catherine (1774-1824): German Augustinian nun, mystic; her visions were recorded by the poet Klemens Brentano.

Endlicher, Stephen (1804-1849): Hungarian botanist, linguist; elaborated a system of classifying plants.

England, John (1786-1842): American prelate, b. Ireland, bishop of Charleston, S. C., 1820-42; founded *United States Catholic Miscellany,* the first US Catholic weekly newspaper; opponent of trusteeism.

Epee, Charles Michel de L' (1712-1789): French priest; developed a sign alphabet for deaf and dumb.

Erasmus, Desiderius (1466-1536): Dutch scholar, Renaissance leader.

Estaing, Jean Baptiste d' (1729-1794): French naval commander; aided Americans during Revolution.

Eustachius, Bartolommeo (1524-1574): Italian anatomist; Eustachian tube, valve, named for him.

Ewing, J. Franklin (1905-1968): American Jesuit priest, anthropologist, missiologist, author.

Ewing, Thomas (1789-1871): American lawyer; US senator from Ohio, 1831-37, 1850-51; secretary of the treasury, 1841; secretary of the interior, 1849-50; convert, 1871.

Eyck, Hubert Van (1366-1426) and his brother **Jan** (1370-1440): Painters, founders of Flemish school; developed process of oil painting; religious and portrait subjects.

F

Faber, Frederick William (1814-1863): British author of spiritual works, hymns; convert, 1845; priest.

Fabre, Jean Henri (1823-1915): French entomologist and author.

Fabricius, Hieronymus (Fabricius ab Aquapendente) (1537-1619): Italian anatomist, surgeon; described valvular system of the veins; teacher of Harvey.

Fallopio, Gabriello (1523-1562): Italian anatomist; discovered Fallopian tubes.

Farley, John (1842-1918): American cardinal, b. Ireland; came to US 1864; ordained priest, 1870; vicar general, 1891, auxiliary, 1895, and archbishop, 1902-18, of New York; cardinal, 1911.

Faye, Herve Auguste Etienne Albans (1814-1902): French astronomer; discovered comet named for him; invented zenithal collimator.

Fenelon, Francois de Salignac de la Mothe (1651-1715): French prelate, writer; archbishop of Cambrai.

Ferrari, Ludovico (1522-1565): Italian mathematician; discovered method of resolving equations of the fourth degree.

Fink, Francis A. (1907-1971): American editor, publisher; associated with Our Sunday Visitor from 1930 until his death; president of the Catholic Press Association, 1950-52; recipient of CPA Award in 1971 for his contribution to the Catholic press in the US and Canada.

Fischer, Max (1893-1954): European and American journalist, b. Germany; teacher, author; convert, while a student.

Fitzgibbon, Catherine (Sister Irene) (1823-1896): American religious, b. England; joined Sisters of Charity, 1850; founder and director of Foundling Hospital in New York City, 1869.

FitzSimons, Thomas (1741-1811): American merchant and congressman, b. Ireland; signer of the Constitution; member of first Congress of US.

Fizeau, Armand Hippolyte Louis (1819-1896): French physicist; experimentally determined velocity of light.

Flanagan, Edward Joseph (1886-1948): American priest, b. Ireland; founder of Boys' Town, Nebraska, 1917.

Floyd, John P. (1807-1863): American politician, cabinet official, military leader; governor of Virginia, 1850-53; secretary of war, 1857-61; brigadier general of Confederate Army, 1861; convert, about 1852.

Foch, Ferdinand (1851-1929): French soldier; supreme commander of Allied forces, 1918; led 1918 offensive to victory.

Ford, Francis X. (1892-1952): American Maryknoll missioner; sent to China, 1918; bishop of Kaying, 1935; imprisoned by communists in 1950; he died as a result of his treatment.

Fortunatus of Brescia (1701-1754); Italian Franciscan, pioneer morphologist.

Fortunatus, Venantius Honorius Clementianus (530-610): Latin poet; bishop of Poitiers; wrote the hymn *Vexilla Regis.*

Foster, John G. (1823-1874): American army officer; served with Union army in Civil War; convert, 1861.

Foucauld, Charles Eugene de (1858-1916): French hermit; army officer and explorer in Africa before joining Trappists, 1890; set up hermitage in Sahara among Moslem tribes; killed by desert tribesmen revolting against French; produced studies of Tuareg language and literature.

Foucault, Jean Bernard Leon (1819-1868): French physicist; experimented on light and heat; invented gyroscope, 1852; discovered Foucault electric current.

Fowler, Gene (1891-1960): American journalist, playwright, author.

Francis of Vitoria (1480-1546): Spanish Dominican, theologian; a founder of international law.

Franck, Cesar Auguste (1822-1890): Belgian-French composer; pioneer of modern French instrumental school.

Frassen, Claudius (1620-1711): French Franciscan theologian; author of *Scotus Academicus,* a presentation of the theology of Duns Scotus.

Fraunhofer, Joseph von (1787-1826): Bavarian physicist, optician; discovered Fraunhofer lines; initiated spectrum analysis, the basis of spectrography.

Frechette, Louis Honore (1839-1908): Canadian journalist, poet, prose writer.

Freppel, Charles Emile (1827-1891): French prelate, pulpit orator; bishop of Angers; leader of clerical party; founder of Catholic University of the West (Angers), 1875.

Fresnel, Augustin Jean (1788-1827): French physicist; contributor to science of optics, wave theory of light; introduced compound lenses for lighthouse use.

Froissart, Jean (1337-1410): French historian.

Frontenac, Louis de Buade, Count (1620-1698): French soldier, colonial governor of New France; encouraged explorations of Joliet, La Salle, others.

G

Gagarin, Ivan Sergeevich (1814-1882): Russian diplomat, writer; convert, 1843; joined Jesuits.

Galilei, Galileo (1564-1642): Italian astronomer, physicist; discovered moon shines with reflected light, observed milky way, four satellites of Jupiter, phases of Venus, sunspots; discovered laws of projectiles, principles of virtual velocities, gave exposition of principles of flotation. Summoned before Inquisition on two occasions for his defense of the Copernican system, an action which at the time was considered irreconcilable with implications of Christian faith.

Galvani, Luigi (1737-1798): Italian physician, physicist; experimented to determine electrical forces involved in muscular movements; founder of galvanism.

Gama, Vasco da (1469?-1524): Portuguese explorer; discovered new sea route to India.

Garcia, Moreno Gabriel (1821-1875): Ecuadorian journalist, patriot, president of Ecuador; assassinated.

Garrigou-Lagrange, Reginald (1877-1964): French Dominican theologian, philosopher, author of works in all fields of theology; teacher at the University of St. Thomas (Angelicum), Rome, 1909-58; consultor to congregations of the Roman Curia.

Gasquet, Francis Aidan (1846-1929): English Benedictine, cardinal; head of commission for revision of the Vulgate; historian.

Gassendi, Pierre (1592-1655): French philosopher, called Bacon of France; advocate of empirical method.

Gaston, William (1778-1844): American jurist; first student at Georgetown University; North Carolina congressman, judge, member of North Carolina supreme court; responsible for repeal of law which disenfranchised Catholics in his native state, 1835.

Gay-Lussac, Joseph Louis (1778-1850): French chemist, physicist; conducted important research on gases; improved methods of organic analysis.

Geoffrey of Monmouth (1100-1154): English bishop, chronicler; influential in development of national romance in English literature.

Ghiberti, Lorenzo di Cione di Ser Buonaccorso (1378-1455): Florentine painter, sculptor, goldsmith.

Ghirlandajo, Domenico (Domenico de Tommaso Bigordi) (1449-1498): Florentine painter, mosaic and fresco artist; teacher of Michelangelo.

Gibbons, Floyd (1887-1939): American journalist, war correspondent.

Gibbons, James (1834-1921): American cardinal; ordained priest, 1861; vicar apostolic of North Carolina, 1868-72; bishop of Richmond, 1872-77; archbishop of Baltimore 1877-1921; cardinal, 1886; patriot, controversialist, writer; Apostolic Delegate to Third Plenary Council of Baltimore; championed rights of labor.

Gibson, Hugh S. (1883-1954): American diplomat; minister to Poland, ambassador to Belgium, 1927-33, 1937-38, and Brazil; director, Intergovernmental Committee for European Migration; convert, 1938.

Gigli, Beniamino (1890-1957): Italian operatic tenor.

Gill, Eric (1882-1940): English sculptor, engraver, author; convert, 1913.

Gillis, James Martin (1876-1957): American Paulist priest, author, editor, radio orator; editor of the *Catholic World* for 26 years.

Gilmore, Patrick (1829-1892): American bandmaster and composer, b. Ireland.

Giocondo de Verona (1433-1515): Franciscan architect, engineer, antiquarian; architect of St. Peter's.

Gioja, Flavio (14th c.): Italian mariner; contributed to improvement of compass.

Giorgione, Giorgio (1478-1511): Painter of Venetian school.

Giotto di Bondone (1276-1337): Florentine painter, architect, sculptor, fresco artist.

Glennon, John (1862-1946): American cardinal, b. Ireland; ordained priest, 1884; coadjutor bishop of Kansas City, Mo., 1896-1903; archbishop of St. Louis, 1903-46; cardinal, 1946; one of founders of the National Catholic War Council.

Gluck, Christoph Willibald (1714-1787): German operatic composer.

Gobban, Saer (560-645): Irish ecclesiastical architect.

Godfrey of Bouillon (1061-1100): French crusader, duke of Lower Lorraine; elected ruler of Jerusalem after its capture in 1099; defender of the Holy Sepulchre.

Goldstein, David (1870-1958): American apologist, b. England; convert, 1905; pioneer of street preaching and Catholic Evidence Guild work; organized the Catholic Truth Guild of Boston, 1917; author.

Goodyear, William Henry (1846-1923): American author, museum curator in New York and Brooklyn, historian; convert, 1880.

Gordon, Andrew (1712-1751): Scottish Benedictine monk; first to use a cylinder of glass to produce frictional electricity; invented electrical chimes.

Gorres, Joseph von (1776-1848): German journalist, literateur.

Gounod, Charles Francois (1818-1893): French composer of operatic and Church music.

Gower, John (1325-1408): English poet.

Goya y Lucientes, Francisco Jose de (1746-1828): Spanish painter, etcher, lithographer; greatest painter of Spanish national customs.

Greco, El (Kyriakos Theotokopoulos) (1548-1614 or 1625): Greek-born painter of Castillian school.

Gregory of Valencia (1550-1603): Spanish Jesuit, moral theologian; works on usury and lawful rates of interest.

Grijalva, Juan de (1489-1527): Spanish explorer; completed exploration of Yucatan, discovering Mexico.

Grimaldi, Francesco Maria (1618-1663): Italian Jesuit, physicist; discovered diffraction of light.

Guardini, Romano (1885-1968): German priest (b. Italy), theologian, philosopher, author; *The Lord.*

Guido d'Arezzo (995-1050): Benedictine monk, musical theorist; reformer of musical notation.

Guilday, Peter (1884-1947): American priest; leading authority on Church history in US, founder of *Catholic Historical Review.*

Guiney, Louise Imogen (1861-1920): American poet and essayist.

Gurian, Waldemar (1902-1954): American educator and author, b. Russia; convert from Judaism.

Gutenberg, Johann (1400-1468): German printer, inventor of printing from movable type; first to print the Bible, 1452.

H

Haldeman, Samuel Stehman (Felix Aqo, pseud.) (1812-1880): American educator, author; convert, 1843; founder of National Academy of Sciences.

Hannegan, Robert E. (1903-1949): American cabinet official, politician; US postmaster general, 1945-47.

Hardee, William J. (1817-1873): American Confederate general; graduate West Point, 1838; author of *Rifle and Light Infantry Tactics,* used as army textbook at that time.

Harland, Henry (1861-1905): American novelist; used pseudonym **Sidney Luska** in earlier works; convert, 1897.

Harris, Joel Chandler (1848-1908): American journalist, author; creator of Uncle Remus; convert two weeks before his death.

Hassard, John Rose Greene (1836-1888): American journalist, author; convert, 1851; first editor of the *Catholic World.*

Hauy, Rene Just (1743-1822): French priest, mineralogist; a founder of the science of crystallography.

Hawks, Edward F. (1878-1955): American priest, author, b. South Wales; Anglican clergyman before conversion, 1908; ordained priest, 1911.

Haydn, Franz Joseph (1732-1809): Austrian composer; earliest master of symphony and quartet; composer of Austrian national anthem.

Hayes, Carlton J. H. (1882-1964): American historian, educator, diplomat, author; *Political and Social History of Modern Europe;* convert, 1904.

Hayes, Patrick J. (1867-1938): American cardinal; ordained priest, 1892; auxiliary of New York, 1914; ordinary of the armed forces, 1917; archbishop of New York, 1919-38; cardinal, 1924; one of founders of National Catholic Welfare Council.

Healy, George (1813-1894): American portrait painter.

Hebert, Louis Philippe (1850-1917): Canadian sculptor; member of Royal Canadian Academy, 1883.

Hecker, Isaac Thomas (1819-1888): American priest, founder of the Congregation of St. Paul (Paulists); convert, 1844; joined Redemptorists and ordained priest, 1849; founded Paulists 1858 with several companions; first superior, 1858-88; founder of the *Catholic World.*

Heis, Eduard (1806-1877): German astronomer; first ascertained the point of departure of meteors; drew chart of 5,421 stars, with first authentic map of milky way.

Helmont, Jan Baptista van (1577-1644): Flemish physician, chemist; introduced chemical methods in biological studies; introduced word "gas" to designate aeriform fluids.

Hengler, Lawrence (1806-1858): German priest; inventor of horizontal pendulum used in seismographs.

Hennepin, Louis (1640-1701): Belgian Franciscan, explorer; first European to see, describe and depict Niagara Falls; explored Great Lakes region, upper Mississippi.

Henry the Navigator (1394-1460): Portuguese prince; discovered Azores, Madeira, Cape Verde Islands; traced African coast as far as Sierra Leone.

Herdtrich, Christian Wolfgang (1625-1684): Austrian Jesuit missionary; probably wrote first Chinese-Latin dictionary; made Confucius known to Europeans.

Herrera, Francisco de, the Elder (1576-1656): Spanish painter; a founder of the National School of Spain.

Heude, Pierre (1836-1902): French Jesuit missionary, zoologist; authority on land mollusks of China.

Hewit, Augustine Francis (1820-1897); American priest; Congregationalist, Episcopalian minister before conversion, 1846; ordained priest, 1847; assisted Isaac Hecker in founding Paulists.

Heywood, John (1497-1580): English poet, dramatist.

Hill, John Austin (Speakman) (1779-1828): American Dominican, b. England; after conversion joined Dominicans and was ordained priest at Rome; missionary in Ohio.

Holbein, Hans, the Younger (1497-1543): German portrait and historical painter; woodcut artist.

Holland, John Philip (1840-1914): American inventor, b. Ireland; settled at Paterson, N.J.; inventor of first practical submarine.

Hopkins, Gerard Manley (1844-1889): English Jesuit, poet; convert, 1866.

Horner, William Edmonds (1793-1853): American surgeon, anatomist, author; convert, 1839; discovered tensor tarsi, now called Horner's muscle, 1824.

Hubbard, Bernard R. (1889-1962): American Jesuit explorer; called The Glacier Priest; convert, joined Jesuits, 1908; Alaskan explorer; head of Santa Clara Univ. department of geology.

Hugh of St. Victor (1096-1141): Theologian, philosopher, mystic; a founder of scholasticism.

Hughes, John J. (1797-1864): American prelate, b. Ireland; arrived US, 1817; ordained priest, 1826; coadjutor (1837), bishop

(1842) and first archbishop (1850-64) of New York; vigorous defender of Catholicism against Know-Nothings and Native Americans; abolished trusteeism; established Catholic school system in his archdiocese; laid cornerstone of St. Patrick's Cathedral (1858).

Hunton, George K. (1888-1967): American lawyer, editor; pioneer in Catholic field for interracial justice.

Hunyady, Janos (1387-1456): Hungarian defender of Christendom against the Turks; assisted at crucial defense of Belgrade, 1456.

Huysmans, Joris Karl (1848-1907): French novelist; convert 1895; Benedictine Oblate.

I

Ingres, Jean (1780-1867): Leading French classical painter; historical subjects.

Innocent III (1161-1216): Pope, 1198-1216; encouraged fourth crusade, promoted efforts against the Albigensians; convoked and presided at the Fourth Lateran Council, 1215; strenuously asserted supremacy of the Church over the State.

Ireland, John (1838-1918): American prelate, b. Ireland; arrived US, 1849; ordained priest, 1861; chaplain in Union army, 1862-63; bishop (1884) and first archbishop (1888-1918) of St. Paul; helped found Catholic University of America (1889); outspoken opponent of national churches.

Ives, Levi Silliman (1797-1867): American Episcopal bishop; convert, 1852; founder of New York Catholic Protectory.

J

Jacopone da Todi (1230-1306): Italian Franciscan poet; *Stabat Mater.*

Jaricot, Pauline (1799-1862): French charitable worker; founded Society for the Propagation of the Faith, 1822, to raise funds for foreign missions.

Jimenez, Juan Ramon (1881-1958): Spanish lyric poet; awarded Nobel Prize for literature, 1956.

John of Austria, Don (1547-1578): Spanish general; commander of fleet that defeated Turks at Lepanto, 1571.

Joliet, Louis (1645-1700): French Canadian explorer of Mississippi with Marquette, 1673.

Jones, Inigo (1573-1652): English architect; designer of stage sets for Ben Jonson and others; introduced Palladian type of architecture in England.

Jorgensen, Johannes (1866-1956): Danish writer; convert, 1896; author of *St. Francis of Assisi.*

Judge, Thomas A. (1868-1933): American priest; founder of Missionary Servants of the Most Blessed Trinity (sisters), 1927, and the Missionary Servants of the Most Holy Trinity (priests and brothers).

Jugan, Jeanne (1792-1879): French foundress; established Little Sisters of the Poor, 1839, to care for aged poor.

Jussieu, Bernard de (1699-1777): French botanist; introduced a natural system for classification of plants.

Justinian I (483-565): Eastern Roman emperor; issued *Corpus Juris Civilis,* code of Roman law.

K

Katona, Stephen (1732-1811): Hungarian Jesuit, historian; author of 40-volume history of Hungary.

Kaye-Smith, Sheila (1887-1956): English author; convert 1929.

Kelly, William (1811-1888): American ironmaster; invented converter for the making of steel; now known as Bessemer's process after Englishman who patented a similar process.

Kenna, John E. (1848-1893): American legislator; private in Confederate Army; US congressman, 1876-80; US senator, 1883-93. Represents West Virginia in Statuary Hall.

Kennedy, John F. (1917-1963): Thirty-fifth president of the United States and first Catholic to hold that office; elected to Congress, 1946, 1948, 1950; to the Senate, 1952, 1958; to the presidency of the US, 1960; assassinated Nov. 22, 1963, at Dallas, Tex.; author; *Why England Slept, Profiles in Courage.*

Kennedy, Joseph P. (1888-1969): American businessman, diplomat; father of John and Robert Kennedy.

Kennedy, Robert F. (1925-1968): American politician, brother of President John F. Kennedy; cabinet official; attorney with justice department, 1951-52; US attorney general, 1961-65; US senator from New York, 1965-68: assassinated while campaigning for Democratic presidential nomination.

Keyes, Edward Lawrence (1843-1924): American physician; convert.

Keyes, Frances Parkinson (1885-1970): American author of popular novels and other works; wrote more than 50 books; convert, 1939.

Kilmer, Alfred Joyce (1886-1918): American poet; convert, 1913, with his wife; killed in action in World War I; works include *Trees and Other Poems.* His wife **Aline Murray Kilmer** (1888-1941): Lecturer, poet; wrote several books of collected verse.

Kir, Felix-Adrien (1876-1968): French priest, politician; mayor of Dijon from 1940.

Kircher, Athanasius (1601-1680): German Jesuit, archaeologist; inventor of magic lantern; stated germ theory of disease.

Knox, Ronald A. (1888-1957): English priest, author; convert, ordained, 1919; translated Vulgate Bible into English.

Kodaly, Zoltan (1882-1967): Hungarian composer; authority on folk music.

Konarski, Stanislaus (1700-1773): Polishh priest, educator, author; influential in development of modern Polish literature.

Kosciusko, Tadeusz (1746-1817): Polish patriot; served in Continental Army in American Revolution; headed Polish rebellion, 1794, became dictator; died in Switzerland.

Kreisler, Fritz (1873-1962): American violinist and composer, b. Austria; became US citizen, 1943; convert, 1947.

L

La Bruyere, Jean de (1645-1696): French critic and moralist.

Lacordaire, Jean Baptiste Henri (1802-1861): French Dominican, pulpit orator; member of French Academy.

Laennec, Rene Theophile Hyacinthe (1781-1826): French physician; introduced auscultation, invented stethoscope.

La Farge, John (1835-1910): American artist and author.

La Farge, John (1880-1963): American Jesuit priest, son of artist John La Farge; scholar, author, editor of *America*, 1944-1948; leader in interracial work, a founder and director of the Catholic Interracial Council of New York City, and of the National Catholic Rural Life Conference; author of *The Manner Is Ordinary*, *The Catholic Viewpoint on Race Relations*, *An American Amen*.

La Fontaine, Jean de (1621-1695): French poet, known as a fabulist.

Lainez, Diego (1512-1565): Spanish theologian; second general of the Society of Jesus; made important contribution to work of Council of Trent.

Lamarck, Jean Baptiste de Monet, Chevalier de (1744-1829): French botanist, zoologist; originator of evolutionary theory called Lamarckism; divided animals into vertebrates and invertebrates.

Langton, Stephen (d. 1228): English prelate, cardinal archbishop of Canterbury; led English barons against King John; first of the subscribing witnesses to the Magna Charta.

Laplace, Pierre Simon (1749-1827): French astronomer, mathematician; proposed the nebular hypothesis.

LaSalle, Rene Robert Cavelier, Sieur de (1643-1687): French explorer; discovered Ohio River, explored Mississippi River valley.

Lasso, Orlando di (1532-1594): Belgian composer of over 2,000 works.

Lathrop, Rose Hawthorne (Mother Alphonsa) (1851-1926): American foundress, author; daughter of Nathaniel Hawthorne; convert, 1891, with her husband, **George Parsons Lathrop** (1851-1898): founded Dominican Congregation of St. Rose of Lima (Servants of Relief for Incurable Cancer) after her husband's death; established home at Hawthorne, N.Y.

Latreille, Pierre Andre (1762-1833): French entomologist; classified insects and crustaceans.

Laurier, Sir Wilfrid (1841-1919): Canadian statesman; prime minister, 1896-1911.

Lavigerie, Charles Martial Allemand (1825-1892): French prelate; archbishop of Algiers, 1867; cardinal, 1882; leader in abolition of slavery; founded White Fathers, 1874, for mission work in Africa.

Lavoisier, Antoine Laurent (1743-1794): French chemist; called father of modern chemistry.

Le Fort, Gertrud von (1876-1971): German poet and novelist; convert, 1925; works include *The Veil of Veronica* and *The Song on the Scaffold*, which was the source for the opera *Dialogue of the Carmelites*.

Lehar, Ferenc or **Franz** (1870-1948): Hungarian composer of operettas, orchestral works.

Lemaitre, Jules (1853-1914): French writer, literary and dramatic critic.

Lemcke, Henry (1796-1882): American Benedictine, b. Germany; Lutheran preacher; convert, 1824; ordained priest, 1826; came to US as missionary, 1834; instrumental in bringing first Benedictines to the US; joined Benedictines, 1852.

L'Enfant, Pierre Charles (1754-1825): French engineer; drew up plans for national capital, Washington, D.C.

Leo XIII (1810-1903): Pope, 1878-1903; scholar, statesman, Latinist; author of many encyclicals (see Index).

Leverrier, Urbain Jean Joseph (1811-1877): French astronomer; calculated presence of Neptune; founded the International Meteorological Institute.

Linacre, Thomas (1460-1524): English physician, humanist; assisted in founding of College of Physicians.

Lingard, John (1771-1851): English priest, author of historical works on England.

Linton, Moses L. (1808-1878): American physician; convert, 1844; president of first US Conference of St. Vincent de Paul Society, 1845; organized first medical monthly in US, *The St. Louis Medical and Surgical Journal*, 1848.

Lippi, Fra Filippo (1406-1469): Florentine painter; religious subjects.

Liszt, Franz von (1811-1886): Hungarian piano virtuoso, composer.

Locke, Jesse A. (1859-1952): American educator; Protestant Episcopal minister; convert, 1893.

Lombard, Peter (1100-1160): Italian theologian; bishop of Paris; author of *Sententiarum Libri Quatuor*, a synthesis of theology which exerted wide influence.

Longstreet, James (1821-1904): American army officer; graduate of West Point; resigned commission to serve with Confederate forces; convert, 1877.

Lord, Daniel (1888-1955): American Jesuit; popular writer; associated with editorial staff of *Queen's Work* from 1913 until his death; wrote hundreds of pamphlets; his books include *Played by Ear*, his autobiography.

Lorraine, Claude de (1600-1682): French painter; landscape subjects.

Louis the Great (1326-1382): King of Hungary, 1342-1382, and Poland, 1370-1382.

Loviner, John Forest (1896-1970): American Franciscan priest; founder and director of St.

Anthony's Guild; publisher of catechetical materials for the Confraternity of Christian Doctrine; key figure in production of the *New American Bible*.

Lugo, John de (1583-1660): Spanish Jesuit, cardinal, theologian.

M

Mabillon, Jean (1632-1707): French Benedictine, father of science of paleography; author of *Acta Sanctorum Ordinis S. Benedicti.*

McCarran, Patrick A. (1876-1954): American jurist, legislator; chief justice Nevada supreme court, 1917-18; US senator, 1932-54; sponsored Internal Security (McCarran) Act, 1950; co-sponsor of McCarran-Walter Immigration and Nationality Act, 1952. Represents Nevada in Statuary Hall.

McCarthy, Joseph R. (1908-1957): American politician; senator from Wisconsin, 1946 until his death; controversial investigator of Communism in US.

McClellan, William Hildrup (1874-1951): American educator, author; Episcopalian minister; convert, 1908; ordained Jesuit priest, 1918.

McCloskey, John (1810-1885): First American cardinal; ordained priest, 1834; coadjutor bishop of New York 1844-47; first bishop of Albany, 1847-64; archbishop of New York, 1864-65; cardinal, 1875.

McCormick, Anne O'Hare (1882-1954): American journalist, b. England of American parents; awarded Pulitzer prize (1937) for European correspondence.

McGivney, Michael Joseph (1852-1890): American priest; founder of Knights of Columbus, 1882.

McGranery, James P. (1895-1963): American congressman, cabinet official; US attorney general, 1952-53.

McGrath, J. Howard (1903-1966): American politician, cabinet official; governor of Rhode Island, 1940-46; US senator, 1946; US attorney general, 1949-52.

McKay, Claude (1890-1948): American Negro poet and novelist, b. Jamaica, B.W.I.; came to US, 1912; author of *A Long Way from Home* (1937), his autobiography; convert, 1944.

McKenna, Joseph (1843-1926): American jurist, cabinet official; US congressman from California, 1885-92; US circuit judge, 1892-97; US attorney general 1897-98; associate justice US Supreme Court, 1898-1925.

McLoughlin, John (1784-1857): Pioneer settler of Oregon, b. Canada; fur trader, physician; called Father of Oregon; formally received into Church, 1842 (he had been baptized but not raised a Catholic). Represents Oregon in Statuary Hall.

MacMahon, Marie Edme Patrice Maurice de (1808-1893): Marshal of France, 1859, and president, 1873-1897; military leader in Crimean War, Franco-Prussian War, other campaigns.

McQuaid, Bernard J. (1823-1909): American prelate; ordained priest, 1848; helped found Seton Hall College; chaplain in Civil War; first bishop of Rochester, N.Y., 1868-1909; voted against papal infallibility at Vatican I; promoter of Catholic schools.

Madeleva, Sister M. (Mary Evaline Wolf) (1887-1964): American educator, poet; joined Holy Cross Sisters, 1908.

Magellan, Ferdinand (1480-1521): Portuguese navigator; led expedition which first circumnavigated globe; discovered Strait of Magellan, Ladrones, Philippines where he was slain.

Magsaysay, Ramon (1907-1957): Philippine statesman; crushed the Communist (Huk) Rebellion in 1948-53; third president of the Philippine Republic.

Mahler, Gustav (1880-1911): Bohemian composer and conductor; convert, Feb. 23, 1897.

Malherbe, Francois de (1555-1628): French poet; influenced exact usage of language.

Mallinckrodt, Hermann von (1821-1874): German leader of Center Party against Kulturkampf.

Mallory, Stephen Russell (1813-1873): American Confederate political leader, b. Trinidad; US senator from Florida, 1851-1861; resigned when Florida seceded; naval secretary of the Confederacy.

Malory, Sir Thomas (d. 1470): English author of the *Morte d'Arthur.*

Malpighi, Marcello (1628-1694): Italian anatomist; called father of microscopic anatomy.

Malus, Etienne Louis (1775-1812): French engineer, physicist; discovered polarization of light, invented polariscope.

Mangan, James C. (1803-1849): Irish poet.

Manning, Henry Edward (1808-1892): English cardinal, author; convert, 1851.

Mansard, Nicolas Francois (1598-1666): French architect.

Mantegna, Andrea (1431-1506): Italian painter, muralist, engraver; leader of Paduan school.

Manutius, Aldus (1450-1515): Italian scholar, printer, publisher; founded Aldine press.

Manzoni, Alessandro (1785-1873): Italian poet, novelist; *I Promessi Sposi.*

Marconi, Guglielmo (1874-1937): Italian engineer, inventor; outstanding contributor to development of wireless telegraphy, radio; Nobel Prize for physics, 1909.

Mariotte, Edme (1620-1684): French physicist; researcher in hydrodynamics.

Martini, Giambattista (1706-1784): Italian Franciscan, composer of Church music, theorist and teacher.

Masaccio, Tommaso (1401-1428): Italian painter; fresco artist of Florentine school; influenced advance to Renaissance painting; called father of modern art.

Massillon, Jean Baptiste (1663-1742): French preacher; bishop of Clermont.

Matthias Corvinus (Hunyady) (1440-1490): One of Hungary's greatest kings, 1458-1490; repelled Turks, fought against Bohemians, Frederick III; patron of arts, literature; introduced Golden Age in Hungary; founded library.

Mauriac, Francois (1885-1970): French writer; awarded Nobel Prize for literature, 1952; works include the novels *The Desert of Love, The Viper's Triangle.*

Mauro, Fra (d. c. 1459): Italian Camaldolese monk, cosmographer; Fra Mauro Highlands, named for him by 17th century astronomers, was the landing site of Apollo 14.

Maxmilian I, the Great (1573-1651): Duke and elector of Bavaria; opposed Protestant cause; founded Catholic League, 1609.

Mazarin, Jules (1602-1661): French cardinal, statesman; prime minister of France under Louis XIII and Louis XIV; concluded Thirty Years' War by the Treaty of Westphalia; strengthened France as a European power.

Meagher, Thomas F. (1823-1867): American politician and soldier, b. Ireland; came to US, 1852; joined Union forces in Civil War; became Brigadier general of Irish Brigade organized by him; territorial secretary of Montana, 1865.

Mendel, Gregor Johann (1822-1884): Austrian Augustinian monk, botanist; formulated Mendelian laws of heredity.

Mercier, Desire Joseph (1851-1926): Belgian prelate, philosopher; cardinal archbishop of Malines; promoter of neo-scholastic philosophy; leader against demands of German invaders in 1914; restored Louvain University after World War I; in 1924 began Malines Conversations, an attempt to unify the Anglican and Roman churches.

Mersenne, Marin (1588-1648): French mathematician.

Merton, Thomas (Father M. Louis) (1915-1968): American Trappist priest and author, b. France; convert, 1939; works include *The Seven Storey Mountain,* his autobiography, *Waters of Siloe, Conjectures of a Guilty Bystander,* articles and others works on a wide variety of subjects.

Mestrovic, Ivan (1883-1962): Yugoslav sculptor; religious and mythological subjects, Slav folklore, portrait busts; works include *Pieta* at Notre Dame Univ., where he was a professor from 1955-62.

Metternich, Klemens Wenzel, Nepomuk Lothar von (1773-1859): Austrian statesman and diplomat.

Meynell, Alice Thompson (1847-1922): English poet, essayist, leader in Catholic literary revival in England; convert. Her husband, **Wilfrid Meynell** (1852-1948): Journalist, publisher, biographer; he and his wife discovered Francis Thompson; convert.

Mezzofanti, Giuseppe (1774-1849): Italian cardinal, linguist, custodian-in-chief of Vatican Library.

Michelangelo, Buonarroti (1474-1564): Italian architect, sculptor, painter, poet; outstanding figure of the Renaissance.

Mikolajczyk, Stanislaus (1901-1967): Polish politician; leader of Polish Peasant party in exile; settled in US, 1947.

Miller, Nathan L. (1868-1953): American politician; governor of New York; convert shortly before death.

Millet, Jean Francois (1814-1875): French painter; landscape and religious subjects.

Minton, Sherman (1890-1965): American jurist; US senator, 1935-40; associate justice US Supreme Court, 1949-56; convert, 1961.

Mistral, Gabriela (pen name of **Lucila Godoy de Alcayaga**) (1889-1957): Chilean poet; Nobel Prize for literature, 1945.

Mitchell, James P. (1902-1964): American cabinet official; labor relations expert; US secretary of labor, 1953-61.

Mitchell, John (1870-1919): American labor leader; president of United Mine Workers; convert, 1907.

Mohler, Johann Adam (1796-1838): German theologian.

Mohr, Josef (1792-1848): Austrian priest, poet; *Silent Night.*

Molina, Luis de (1535-1600): Spanish Jesuit, theologian; author of *Concordia,* expounding a system for the reconciliation of grace and free will, called Molinism.

Mondino (dim. for Raimondo) dei Luicci (1275-c. 1327): Italian anatomist.

Monge, Gaspard (1746-1818): French mathematician; called founder of descriptive geometry.

Montcalm, Marquis Louis Joseph de (1712-1759): French marshal, military commander in Canada; fatally wounded in Battle of Quebec.

Montessori, Maria (1870-1952): Italian physician, educator; originator of Montessori method for education of children.

Monteux, Pierre (1875-1964): American conductor, b. France; US citizen, 1942; led most of the world's greatest orchestras.

Moon, Parker Thomas (1892-1936): American historian, educator, author, editor; convert, 1914.

Moore, Thomas (1779-1852): National lyricist of Ireland.

Moore, Thomas Verner (1877-1969): American priest, psychiatrist, educator, author; joined Carthusians in 1947 — had earlier been a Paulist and Benedictine.

Morgagni, Giovanni Battista (1682-1771): Italian physician; founder of anatomical pathology.

Morley, Sylvanus Griswold (1883-1948): American archeologist; converted before his death.

Moylan, Stephen (1734-1811); American patriot, b. Ireland; immigrated to US 1768; joined Continental Army, 1775; aide-de-camp and secretary to General Washington, 1776; leader of cavalry division.

Mozart, J. C. Wolfgang Amadeus (1756-1791): Austrian composer of more than 600 works in a wide range of forms.

Muench, Aloysius J. (1889-1962): American cardinal; ordained priest, 1913; bishop of Fargo, 1935-59; apostolic visitator and liaison representative between US military government and German hierarchy, 1946; nuncio to Germany, 1951-59; cardinal, 1959.

Muller, Johann (1436-1476): German mathematician, astronomer; assisted in calendar reform.

Muller, Johannes Peter (1801-1858): German physiologist, comparative anatomist.

Murillo, Bartolome Esteban (1617-1682): Spanish artist of the Andalusian school; master of color contrast; religious subjects.

Murphy, Frank (1890-1949): American jurist, cabinet official; mayor of Detroit, 1930-33; US high commissioner to the Philippines, 1935-36; governor of Michigan, 1936-38; US attorney general 1939-40; associate justice of US Supreme Court, 1940-49.

Murphy, John Benjamin (1857-1916): American surgeon; inventor of Murphy button; Laetare Medalist, 1902.

Murray, John C. (1904-1967): American Jesuit priest, educator, theologian, ecumenist, international expert on Church-State relations, author.

Murray, Philip (1886-1952): American labor leader, b. Scotland.

N

Nathan, George Jean (1882-1958): American dramatic critic, editor, author; founder with H. L. Mencken of *The American Mercury*; convert, 1957.

Nelaton, Auguste (1807-1873): French surgeon; inventor of Nelaton probe.

Newman, John Henry (1801-1890): English cardinal, theologian; leader of Oxford Movement; convert, 1845; ordained to priesthood, 1847; founded Oratorians in England; master of prose style; author of historical and apologetical works, poems, novels.

Nicholas of Lyra (1270-1340): Franciscan biblical scholar.

Nieuland, Julius Arthur (1878-1936): American priest of Congregation of Holy Cross, b. Belgium; chemist, botanist; Notre Dame scientist, contributed to invention of Lewisite gas, production of synthetic rubber.

Niza, Marcos de (d. 1558): Franciscan missionary, explored parts of Arizona and New Mexico, 1539; accompanied Coronado's expedition.

Nobili, Leopoldo (1784-1835): Italian physicist, inventor of the thermopile.

Noll, John F. (1875-1956): American prelate, author, editor; ordained priest, 1898; bishop of Fort Wayne, Ind., 1925-56; founder and editor of weekly newspaper *Our Sunday Visitor*, 1912; wrote *Father Smith Instructs Jackson*, other books and pamphlets.

Nollet, Jean-Antoine (1700-1770): French priest, physicist; researcher in electricity; invented an electroscope.

Noyes, Alfred (1880-1958): English poet; convert, 1927.

O

O'Callahan, Joseph (1906-1964): American Jesuit priest; Navy chaplain in World War II; awarded the Congressional Medal of Honor, for action aboard the carrier Franklin on Mar. 19, 1945.

Ocampo, Sebastian (1466-1521): Spanish explorer; circumnavigated Cuba, proved its insular character.

O'Connell, Daniel (1775-1847): Irish statesman, nationalist leader; known as the Liberator; responsible for Catholic emancipation, 1829.

O'Connor, (Mary) Flannery (1925-1964): American novelist and short-story writer.

O'Dwyer, Joseph (1841-1898): American physician; developed method of aiding breathing to prevent asphyxia in diphtheria.

Oertel, Abraham (1527-1598): Flemish geographer; publisher of an atlas.

O'Hara, Edwin Vincent (1881-1956): American prelate; ordained priest, 1905; bishop of Great Falls, Mont. 1930-39; bishop of Kansas City, Mo., 1939-56; title of archbishop, 1954; leader in catechetical work in the US; founder of National Catholic Rural Life Conference.

O'Higgins, Bernardo (1778-1842): Chilean soldier, statesman; Liberator of Chile.

Olaf (II) Haraldsson, Saint (995-1030): King of Norway, 1016-1028; attempted conversion of his country; killed in battle; patron of Norway; canonized, 1164.

Orellana, Francisco de (1500-1546): Spanish navigator, explored the Amazon River.

Origen (185-254): Theologian and writer, head of catechetical schools at Alexandria, Caesarea; author of biblical, theological works.

Orosius, Paul (380?-?): Spanish priest; author of book of universal history.

Oursler, Fulton (1893-1952): American author, editor, lecturer; convert 1943; works include *The Greatest Story Ever Told* and *The Greatest Book Ever Written*.

Ozanam, Frederic (1813-1853): French historian; a founder of St. Vincent de Paul Society. (See Index.)

Ozanam, Jacques (1640-1717): French mathematician.

P

Pacioli, Luca (1450?-1520?): Italian Franciscan, mathematician; author of first description of double-entry bookkeeping.

Paderewski, Ignace (1860-1941): Polish pianist, conductor, composer; first premier of Poland after World War I.

Palestrina, Giovanni Pierluigi da (1526-1594): Italian composer of Church music in medieval moods; noted for polyphonic style.

Palladio, Andrea (1518-1580): Italian architect; controlling influence of 17th-century architecture called Palladian.

Palmer, Gretta (1905-1953): American journalist, author; convert, 1946.

Papini, Giovanni (1881-1956): Italian writer; convert, 1918; author of *Life of Christ*.

Pare, Ambroise (1517-1590): French surgeon; called father of modern surgery; introduced artery ligature.

Paris, Bruno Paulin Gaston (1839-1903): French philologist, author.

Parsch, Pius (1884-1954): Austrian Augustinian, theologian, Scripture scholar, liturgist.

Parsons, Wilfrid (1887-1958): American Jesuit priest, editor, author, educator; editor-in-chief of *America*, 1925-36.

Pascal, Blaise (1623-1662): French philosopher, scientist; demonstrated that a column of air has weight; author of *Pensees*.

Pasteur, Louis (1822-1895): French chemist; developed a vaccine against hydrophobia; founded Pasteur Institute; father of bacteriology.

Pastor, Ludwig von (1854-1928): German historian; *The History of the Popes from the Beginning of the Middle Ages*.

Patmore, Coventry (1823-1896): English poet; convert, 1864.

Pazmany, Peter (1570-1637): Hungarian Jesuit, cardinal; leader of Counter Reformation; translated Bible into Hungarian; called founder of modern Hungarian literature.

Peguy, Charles Pierre (1873-1914): French poet and writer; outstanding Catholic defender of Dreyfus; founded the journal *Cahiers de la Quinzaine*; works include *The Mystery of the Charity of Joan of Arc* and religious meditations.

Pelouze, Theophile Jules (1807-1867): French chemist; developed production of guncotton, nitrocellulose.

Pepin the Short (714-768): King of the Franks, son of Charles Martel, father of Charlemagne; first Frank crowned with religious ceremonies; defeated Lombards and restored central Italy to the Holy See.

Perosi, Lorenzo (1872-1956): Italian priest, composer.

Perugino, Il (Pietro Vannucci) (1446-1523): Italian painter; leader of Umbrian school; teacher of Raphael; religious subjects.

Petau (Petavius), Denys (1583-1652): French Jesuit, theologian; called father of the history of dogma.

Petrarch (Francesco Petrarca) (1304-1374): Italian poet.

Piazzi Giuseppe (1746-1826): Italian monk, astronomer; discovered Ceres, first known asteroid.

Picard, Jean (1620-1682): French astronomer; accurately measured degree of a meridian.

Pinturicchio, Bernardino di Betto di Biagio (1454-1513): Italian painter of the Umbrian school; historical and religious subjects.

Pio, Padre (Francesco Forgione) (1887-1968): Italian Capuchin priest; reputed stigmatist.

Pire, Dominique Georges (1910-1969): Belgian priest; awarded Nobel Peace Prize in 1958 for work for displaced persons.

Pisano, Andrea (1270-1348) and his son **Nino** (1315-1368); Italian sculptors.

Pisano, Nicolo (1225-1278): Italian sculptor; works among greatest of Romanesque style. His son, **Giovanni** (1240-1320): Sculptor, architect.

Pitra, Jean Baptiste Francois (1812-1889): French Benedictine, cardinal, scholar.

Pizarro, Francisco (1470-1541): Spanish explorer, conqueror of Peru.

Plumier, Charles (1646-1704): French botanical explorer of Antilles, Central America.

Pole, Reginald (1500-1558): English prelate, cardinal archbishop of Canterbury; opposed divorce of Henry VIII; papal legate, participant in Council of Trent.

Polo, Marco (1245-1324): Early traveler to China, b. Venice; *Book of Marco Polo*.

Ponce de Leon (1460-1521): Spanish explorer; discovered Florida.

Pope, Alexander (1688-1744): English poet; master of the rimed couplet.

Pouget Jean Francois Albert du, Marquis de Nadaillac (1817-1904): French authority on cave drawings.

Poussin, Nicolas (1594-1665): French painter; historical and landscape subjects.

Price, Thomas Frederick (1860-1919): American missionary; co-founder with Bishop Walsh of the Catholic Foreign Mission Society of America (Maryknoll Fathers); called the Tar Heel Apostle.

Pro, Miguel (1891-1927): Mexican Jesuit; fled Mexico during 1914 Revolution; returned to Mexico, 1926, after his ordination in Belgium; arrested, 1927, and shot to death by police in Mexico City.

Prohaszka, Ottokar (1858-1927): Hungarian bishop; preacher, author.

Provancher, Leon Abel (1820-1892): Canadian priest, naturalist; called father of natural history in Canada.

Puccini, Giacomo (1858-1924): Italian operatic composer.

Pugin, Augustus Welby Northmore (1812-1852): English architect.

Pulaski, Casimir (1748-1779): Polish patriot, fought in American Revolution; called Father of the American Cavalry; fatally wounded at Savannah.

Puvis de Chavannes, Pierre (1824-1898): French muralist.

Q

Quinlan, Thomas (1896-1970): Irish Columban missionary bishop; served in China, 1920-34; prefect apostolic of Chun Cheon, Korea, 1934; interned by Japanese during World War II; imprisoned by North Koreans, 1950-53.

Quinones, Francis (1482-1540): Spanish Franciscan, cardinal, liturgist; worked on revision of breviary.

R

Racine, Jean Baptiste (1639-1699): French dramatic poet.

Rameau, Jean-Philippe (1683-1764): French organist, music theorist, operatic composer.

Randall, James Ryder (1839-1908): American journalist, poet, song writer; *Maryland, My Maryland.*

Raphael, Santi (1483-1520): Italian painter of religious, portrait, other subjects; architect of St. Peter's; among greatest of Renaissance painters.

Reeve, Arthur Benjamin (1882-1936): American educator, author; convert, 1926.

Regnault, Henri Victor (1810-1878): French chemist, physicist; authority in thermometry.

Reiffenstuel, Anaclete (Johann Georg) (1641-1703): German Franciscan, theologian, canonist.

Reinhold, Hans (1897-1968): American pioneer in liturgical movement, b. Germany; came to US, 1936; naturalized citizen.

Reni, Guido (1575-1642): Italian painter of the Eclectic school; religious and other subjects.

Repplier, Agnes (1858-1950): American author, essayist.

Reymont, Wladislaw (1867-1925): Polish novelist; awarded Nobel Prize for literature in 1924 for *The Peasants.*

Ribera, Jose (1588-1652): Spanish painter of Neapolitan school, etcher; religious subjects.

Ricci, Mateo (1552-1610): Italian Jesuit missionary in India and China; introduced Christianity in China; author.

Riccioli, Giovanni Battista (1598-1671): Italian Jesuit, astronomer; introduced some lunar nomenclature in use today.

Richelieu, Armand Jean du Plessis, Duc de (1585-1642): French cardinal, statesman; founder of the French Academy, 1634.

Ritter, Joseph E. (1892-1967): American cardinal; ordained priest, 1917; auxiliary bishop, 1933, bishop, 1934, and first archbishop, 1944, of Indianapolis; archbishop of St. Louis, 1946-67; cardinal, 1961; ordered desegregation of St. Louis archdiocesan schools, 1957; was outspoken US progressive bishop at Vatican II; first Mass in vernacular in US offered in his diocese.

Robbia, Luca della (1400-1482): Florentine sculptor; developed a glaze for terra cotta ware (Robbia work).

Robinson, William Callyhan (1834-1911): American jurist, author; Episcopalian minister; convert, 1863.

Rochambeau, Jean Baptiste Donatien de Vimeur, Conte de (1725-1807): French soldier; led French forces sent to aid Americans in Revolution.

Rockne, Knute Kenneth (1888-1931): American football player and coach, b. Norway; immigrated to US, 1893; football coach at Notre Dame University, 1918-31; convert, 1925.

Rodzinski, Artur (1894-1958): American symphony conductor, b. Yugoslavia; became US citizen, 1933.

Rosecrans, William Starke (1819-1898): American army officer; graduate of West Point; army commmander during the Civil War; Federal official; convert, 1845.

Rossini, Gioacchino Antonio (1792-1868): Italian operatic composer and innovator in orchestration.

Roualt, Georges (1871-1958): French painter of modern school; convert.

Rubens, Peter Paul (1577-1640): Flemish painter; great colorist, landscape, portrait, historical, religious subjects.

Rubruck, William (1220-1293): French Franciscan missionary and traveler in the East, especially China.

Ruth, George Herman (Babe) (1894-1948): American baseball player and record holder; convert, 1906.

Ruysbroeck, John, Bl. (1293-1381): Flemish mystical theologian; beatified, 1908.

Ryan, Abram J. (1838-1886): American priest, poet; called Poet of the Confederacy.

S

San Gallo, Giuliano Giamberti da (1445-1516); his brother, **Antonio da San Gallo, the Elder** (1455-1534); their nephew, **Antonio da San Gallo, the Younger** (1483-1546): Italian architects.

San Martin, Jose de (1778-1850): South American soldier, statesman; defeated Spanish in Argentina, established independence of Chile, proclaimed independence and called Protector of Peru.

Santorini, Giovanni Domenico (1681-1737): Italian physician, anatomist; discovered emissary veins leading out of sinuses, risory muscles, fissures in external ear.

Sarbiewki, Mathias Casimir (1595-1640): Polish Jesuit, called the Horace of Poland.

Sarto, Andrea del (1486-1531): Florentine painter; great colorist, master of light and shade; religious subjects.

Savage, (Charles) Courtenay (1890-1946): American playwright, author; convert, 1937.

Scanderbeg (George Castriota) (c. 1403-1468): Albanian national hero; leader in Albanian independence movement against Turks.

Scarlatti, Alessandro (1659-1725): Italian operatic composer; called founder of modern opera.

Scheiner, Christoph (1579-1650): German Jesuit, astronomer; made independent discovery of sun spots; invented a pantograph.

Schlegel, Friedrich von (1772-1829): German Romantic poet, essayist, novelist; convert, 1803.

Schmid, Christoph von (1768-1854): German educator, pioneer writer of children's books.

Schmidt, Wilhelm (1868-1954): German Divine Word priest, ethnologist and historian of religions: *dthe Origin of the Idea of God.*

Schubert, Franz Peter (1797-1828): Austrian composer of symphonic and other orchestral works.

Schuman, Robert (1886-1963): French statesman; leader of the Popular Republican Party; Premier of France twice (Nov., 1947-July, 1948; Aug. 31-Sept. 9, 1948); major figure in post-World War II efforts at European unity; author of Schuman Plan for pooling French and German coal and steel production, a forerunner of the Common Market.

Schuyler, Philippa (1932-1967): American pianist, news correspondent.

Searle, George Mary (1839-1918): American priest and astronomer, b. England of American parents; came to US, 1840; convert, 1866; joined Paulists, 1868; ordained, 1871; director of Vatican Observatory, 1898.

Schwann, Theodor (1810-1882): German anatomist, physiologist; founder of cell theory.

Schwarz, Berthold (13th or 14th c.): German Franciscan; called inventor of gunpowder.

Secchi, Angelo (1818-1878): Italian Jesuit, astronomer; professor at Georgetown University; did spectroscopic work on sun, stars, classification of stars; invented meteorograph.

Segura y Saenz, Pedro (1880-1957): Spanish cardinal, primate of Spain; outspoken critic of Nazism, Fascism and Franco regime.

Seidl, Johann Gabriel (1804-1875): Austrian journalist, poet; author of words for Austrian national anthem.

Semmelweis, Ignaz Philipp (1818-1865): Hungarian physician; pioneer of antiseptic treatment in obstetrics.

Semmes, Raphael (1809-1877): American naval officer, lawyer; commander in US Navy; resigned, 1861, to enter Confederate Navy; commanded the Sumter and the Alabama, commerce destroyers.

Sienkiewicz, Henryk (1846-1916): Polish novelist; awarded Nobel Prize for literature in 1905.

Shea, Sir Ambrose (1815-1905): Canadian political leader; member of House of Assembly of Newfoundland; governor of the Bahamas.

Shea, John Dawson Gilmary (1824-1892): American historian, author; *History of the Catholic Church in the United States.*

Sheridan, Philip H. (1831-1888): American army officer; graduate of West Point; general cavalry commander during the Civil War.

Shevchenko, Taras (1814-1861): Ukrainian poet, nationalist; founder of the Society of Sts. Cyril and Methodius for Ukrainian independence.

Shields, James (1806-1879): American soldier and statesman, b. Ireland; arrived US, 1823, settled in Kaskaskia, Ill.; army officer, politician; general in Mexican War; governor of Oregon Territory, 1849; US senator from Illinois, 1849-55, from Minnesota, 1858-59; moved to California, 1859; brigadier general in Civil War, resigned commission, 1863; moved to Missouri; US senator from Missouri, 1879. Represents Illinois in Statuary Hall.

Shipman, Andrew Jackson (1857-1915): American lawyer, author; convert, 1876; authority on Church law.

Sitwell, Edith (1887-1964): English poet, critic, novelist; convert, 1955.

Skinner, Henrietta Channing Dana (1857-1928): American author; convert, 1878.

Smith, Alfred Emanuel (1873-1944): American politician; governor of New York; Democratic presidential candidate, 1928, the first Catholic ever nominated.

Smith, Ignatius (1886-1957): American Dominican priest, orator, teacher, retreat master.

Smith, Matthew (1891-1960): American editor; founder of Register chain of newspapers.

Sobieski, John III (1624-1696): Polish king, soldier; rescued Vienna from Turks, caused their expulsion from Poland and Hungary.

Spalding, John Lancaster (1840-1916): American prelate; nephew of Martin Spalding, below; author of books on religion, philosophy and social issues; advocate of Catholic parochial school system; served on President Roosevelt's Anthracite Coal Strike Commission, 1902; first bishop of Peoria, 1876-1908, when he resigned because of ill health.

Spalding, Martin J. (1810-1872): American prelate; bishop of Louisville, 1848-64; archbishop of Baltimore, 1864-72; author of numerous books; helped establish American College of Louvain; advocate of a North American College in Rome and an American Catholic university.

Spallanzani, Lazzaro (1729-1799): Italian naturalist; experimenter on digestion, other functions; disproved theory of spontaneous generation.

Spearman, Frank Hamilton (1859-1937): American author; convert, 1884; Laetare Medalist, 1935.

Spellman, Francis J. (1889-1967): American cardinal; ordained priest, 1916; served in papal secretariat of state, 1925-32; auxiliary of Boston, 1932; archbishop of New York, 1939-67; cardinal, 1946; military vicar of US; author.

Starr, Eliza Allen (1824-1901): American educator; convert, 1856; first woman Laetare Medalist, 1885.

Stensen, Niels (Steno, Nicolous) (1638-1687): Danish bishop, anatomist; discovered excretory duct of parotid glands, convert, 1667.

Stoddard, Charles Warren (1843-1909): American journalist, poet, author; convert, 1867.

Stoddard, John Lawson (1850-1931): American author, lecturer; convert, 1922.

Stone, James Kent (Fr. Fidelis, C.P.) (1840-1921): American missionary priest, author; Episcopalian minister, 1866; convert, 1869; ordained priest, 1872.

Storer, Horatio Robinson (1830-1922): American physician, medical professor, author; convert, 1897.

Stoss, Veit (1440-1533): German sculptor; master wood-carver.

Stradivari, Antonio (1644-1737): Italian violin maker.

Stritch, Samuel (1887-1958): American cardinal; ordained priest, 1910; bishop of Toledo, 1921-30; archbishop of Milwaukee, 1930-39; archbishop of Chicago, 1939-58; cardinal, 1946; first American appointed to the Roman Curia, died before he could take up his post as pro-prefect of the Sacred Congregation for the Propagation of the Faith.

Sturzo, Luigi (1871-1959): Italian priest-statesman.

Suarez, Francisco (1548-1617): Spanish Jesuit, theologian; considered a founder of international law; author of many works; *Doctor Eximius.*

T

Tabb, John Banister (1845-1909): American poet, served in Confederate navy, convert, 1872; ordained priest, 1884.

Taggart, Marion Ames (1866-1945): American author, convert, 1880.

Takamine, Jokichi (1854-1922): Japanese-American chemist; developed Takadiastase, isolated adrenalin; convert.

Talbot, Matthew (1856-1925): Irish layman noted for his sanctity; a reformed alcoholic, is considered a model for those with this condition; his cause for beatification is under consideration.

Taney, Roger Brooke (1777-1864): American jurist, cabinet official; US attorney general, 1831-33; secretary of the treasury, 1833-34; chief justice US Supreme Court, 1936-64; associated with the Dred Scott decision, 1857.

Tasso, Torquato (1544-1595): Italian poet.

Teilhard de Chardin, Pierre (1881-1955): French Jesuit; paleontologist and explorer.

Tekakwitha, Kateri (1656-1680): American Indian maiden; Lily of the Mohawks; instructed by Jesuit missionaries and baptized at age of 20; her cause for beatification is under consideration.

Thayer, John (1755-1815): American priest; Protestant chaplain during Revolutionary War; convert, 1783; first native New England priest; missionary in Kentucky; author.

Thomas, Charles Louis Ambrose (1811-1896): Alsatian composer of operatic and other works.

Thomas a Kempis (1380-1471): Dutch Augustinian, considered author of the *Imitation of Christ.*

Thomas of Celano (1200-1255): Italian Franciscan; biographer of St. Francis of Assisi.

Thompson, Francis (1859-1907): English poet; *The Hound of Heaven.*

Tieffentaller, Joseph (1710-1785): Jesuit missionary, geographer.

Tintoretto, Jacopo Robusti (1518-1594): Italian painter of Venetian school; religious and portrait subjects.

Titian or **Tiziano Vecelli** (1477-1576): Italian painter, greatest of the Venetian school; frescoes in wide range of subjects; portraits.

Tobin, Maurice J. (1901-1953): American politician, cabinet official; mayor of Boston, 1937, 1941; governor of Massachusetts, 1944; US secretary of labor, 1949-53.

Tocqueville, Alexis Charles de (1805-1859): French writer, statesman; *La Democritie en Amerique.*

Torricelli, Evangelista (1608-1647): Italian mathematician, physicist; improved telescope, invented barometer.

Toscanelli, Paolo dal Pozzo (1397-1482): Italian physician, geographer; probably aided Columbus.

Toscanini, Arturo (1867-1957): Italian operatic and symphony conductor.

Tulasne, Louis Rene (1815-1885): French botanist; called founder of modern mycology.

U

Undset, Sigrid (1882-1949): Norwegian novelist; Nobel Prize for literature, 1928; *Kristen Lavransdatter;* convert, 1924.

V

Valentine, Basil (born 1394): Benedictine monk; founder of analytical chemistry.

Vandyke (Van Dyck), Sir Anthony (1599-1641): Flemish associate of Rubens, English court painter; religious and portrait subjects.

Vasari, Giorgio (1511-1574): Italian painter, architect; founder of modern art history and criticism.

Vasquez, Gabriel (1551-1604): Spanish Jesuit, theologian.

Vega, Lope Felix de (Vega) Carpio (1562-1635): Spanish priest, dramatic poet; founder of Spanish national drama.

Velasquez, Diego Rodriguez de Silva y (1599-1660): Spanish painter; master of naturalism; historical, portrait, religious and other subjects.

Verdi, Giuseppe (1813-1901): Italian composer of operatic and other works.

Verne, Jules (1828-1905): French writer; scientific fiction.

Vernier, Pierre (1580-1637): French mathematician; formulated vernier scale for accurate linear and angular magnitude.

Veronese, Paolo (1528-1588): Italian painter of Venetian school; Painter of Pageants; religious frescoes and paintings.

Verrazano, Giovanni da (1485-1528): Italian navigator; explored coast of North America for Francis I of France; claimed by his countrymen to be discoverer of Hudson River.

Verrocchio, Andrea del (1435-1488): Florentine sculptor and painter of Tuscan school.

Vesalius, Andreas (1514-1564): Belgian anatomist founder of modern anatomy.

Vespucci, Amerigo (1451-1512): Italian navigator; called discoverer of mainland of America, named after him.

Vico, Francesco de (1805-1848): Italian Jesuit, astronomer; discovered six comets.

Viete (Vieta), Francois, Seigneur de La Bigottiere (1540-1603): French mathematician; founder of modern algebra, which he applied to geometry and trigonometry.

Vignola, Giacomo Barozzi da (1507-1573): Italian architect; architectural theorist.

Vincent of Beauvais (1190-1264): French Dominican; author of comprehensive scientific encyclopedia.

Vinci, Leonardo da (1452-1519): Florentine painter, sculptor, architect, engineer, scientist; paintings, mainly of religious subjects; founder of science of hydraulics, researcher in meteorology, anatomy, mathematics.

Vladimir, Saint (956-1015): First Christian ruler of Russia.

Volta, Alessandro, Count (1754-1827): Italian physicist; early researcher in electricity; the volt named for him.

Vorosmarty, Michael (1800-1855): Hungarian poet; his lyric poem "Szozat" became a national anthem.

W

Wagner, Robert F. (1877-1953): American public official and judge, b. Nastatten Hessen, Germany; US senator, 1926-49; sponsor of Wagner National Labor Relations Act; convert, 1946.

Waldseemuller, Martin (1470-1518): German cartographer; made first modern atlas; first to use the name America.

Walker, Frank C. (1886-1959): American politician, cabinet official; US postmaster general, 1940-45.

Walsh, James Joseph (1865-1942): American physician, author; *The Thirteenth, the Greatest of Centuries.*

Walsh, William Thomas (1891-1949): American historian.

Walworth, Clarence Augustus (1820-1900): American priest; convert, 1845; ordained, 1848; assisted Isaac Hecker in founding the Paulists, whom he left because of illness; author.

Warren, Leonard (1911-1960): American opera star; convert from Judaism 1942; baritone of Metropolitan Opera.

Wattson, Lewis Thomas (Father James Francis Paul) (1863-1940): American founder; as Episcopalian presbyter, founded Friars of the Atonement, 1899; inaugurated Chair of Unity Octave, 1908; founded St. Christopher's Inn, Garrison, N.Y.; convert with members of his community, 1909; ordained priest, 1910.

Waugh, Evelyn (1903-1966): English writer; convert, 1930.

Weber, Karl Maria von (1786-1826): German composer of operatic and other works; a founder of German opera.

Weigel, Gustave (1900-1964): American Jesuit priest, theologian, author; pioneer in Catholic-Protestant dialogue; consultor of the Vatican Secretariat for Promoting Christian Unity.

White, Edward Douglass (1845-1921): American jurist; US senator, 1891-94; associate justice US Supreme Court, 1894-1910; chief justice, 1910-21; wrote decisions for more than 700 of the 4,000 cases decided during his time on the Court. Represents Louisiana in Statuary Hall.

White, Helen C. (1896-1967): American educator, author.

Wilde, Oscar (1856-1900): Irish poet; dramatist; reconciled to the Church before his death in France.

William of Ockham (Occam) (1300-1349): English Franciscan; philosopher, logician, author of the philosophical axiom, "Beings must not be multiplied without necessity."

William the Conqueror (1027-1087): Duke or Normandy; invaded England, 1066, defeated Harold at Hastings, crowned King of England.

Williams, Michael (1877-1950): American journalist and author, b. Halifax, Nova Scotia; founded *Commonweal*, 1924.

Winckelmann, Johann Joachim (1717-1768): German art historian, classical archaeologist; convert, 1754.

Windle, Sir Bertram (1858-1929): English scientist; author of works (at Toronto University) intended to explain relations between scientific progress and Church teaching.

Windthorst, Ludwig (1812-1891): German statesman, leader of Center Party.

Wiseman, Nicholas Patrick (1802-1865): English cardinal, archbishop of Westminster; influenced Catholic revival, encouraged Oxford Movement.

Wynne, Robert J. (1851-1922): American cabinet official; US postmaster general, 1904-05.

X-Z

Ximenez (Jimenez) de Cisneros, Francisco (1437-1517): Spanish Franciscan, cardinal, statesman.

Yoshida, Shigeru (1878-1967): Japanese statesman; prime minister of Japan, 1946-54; convert shortly before his death.

Zrinyi, Nicholas, Count (1620-1664): Hungarian general, poet; author of first Hungarian epic, *The Fall of Szigets.*

Zurbaran, Francisco de (1598-1664): Spanish painter; religious and monastic portrait subjects.

MISSIONARIES TO THE AMERICAS

Allouez, Claude Jean (1622-1689): French Jesuit; missionary in Canada and midwestern US; preached to 20 different tribes of Indians and baptized over 10,000; vicar general of Northwest.

Altham, John (1589-1640): English Jesuit; missionary among Indians in Maryland.

Anchieta, Jose (1534-1597): Portuguese Jesuit; missionary in Brazil; writer.

Andreis, Felix de (1778-1820): Italian Vincentian; missionary and educator in western US.

Aparicio, Bl. Sebastian (1502-1600): Franciscan brother, born Spain; settled in Mexico, c. 1533; worked as road builder and farmer before becoming Franciscan at about the age of 70; beatified, 1787.

Badin, Stephen T. (1768-1853): French missioner; came to US, 1792, when Sulpician seminary in Paris was closed; ordained, 1793, Baltimore, the first priest ordained in US; missionary in Kentucky, Ohio and Michigan; bought land on which Notre Dame University now stands; buried on its campus.

Baraga, Frederic (1797-1868): Slovenian missionary bishop in US; studied at Ljubljana and Vienna, ordained, 1823; came to US, 1830; missionary to Indians of Upper Michigan; first bishop of Marquette, 1857-1868; wrote Chippewa grammar, dictionary, prayer book and other works.

Bertran, St. Louis (1526-1581): Spanish Dominican; missionary in Colombia and Caribbean, 1562-69; canonized, 1671.

Bourgeoys, Bl. Marguerite (1620-1700): French foundress, missionary; settled in Canada, 1653; founded Congregation of Notre Dame de Montreal, 1658; beatified, 1950.

Brebeuf, St. John de (1593-1649): French Jesuit; missionary among Huron Indians in Canada; martyred by Iroquois, Mar. 16, 1649; canonized, 1930; one of Jesuit North American martyrs.

Cancer de Barbastro, Louis (1500-1549): Spanish Dominican; began missionary work in Middle America, 1533; killed at Tampa Bay, Fla.

Castillo, Bl. John de (1596-1628): Spanish Jesuit; worked in Paraguay Indian mission settlements (reductions); martyred; beatified, 1934.

Catala, Magin (1761-1830): Spanish Franciscan; worked in California mission of Santa Clara for 36 years.

Chabanel, St. Noel (1613-1649): French Jesuit; missionary among Huron Indians in Canada; murdered by renegade Huron, Dec. 8, 1649; canonized, 1930; one of Jesuit North American martyrs.

Chaumonot, Pierre Joseph (1611-1693): French Jesuit; missionary among Indians in Canada.

Claver, St. Peter (1581-1654): Spanish Jesuit; missionary among Negroes of South America and West Indies; canonized, 1888; patron of Catholic missions among Negroes.

Daniel, St. Anthony (1601-1648): French Jesuit; missionary among Huron Indians in Canada; martyred by Iroquois, July 4, 1648; canonized, 1930; one of Jesuit North American martyrs.

De Smet, Pierre Jean (1801-1873): Belgian-born Jesuit; missionary among Indians of northwestern US; served as intermediary between Indians and US government; wrote on Indian culture.

Duchesne, Bl. Rose Philippine (1769-1852): French nun; educator and missionary in the US; established first convent of the Society of the Sacred Heart in the US, at St. Charles, Mo. (later Florissant); founded schools for girls; did missionary work among Indians; beatified, 1940.

Farmer, Ferdinand (family name, Steinmeyer) (1720-1786): German Jesuit; missionary in Philadelphia, where he died; one of the first missionaries in New Jersey.

Flaget, Benedict J. (1763-1850): French Sulpician bishop; came to US, 1792; missionary and educator in US; first bishop of Bardstown, Ky. (now Louisville), 1810-32; 1833-50.

Gallitzin, Demetrius (1770-1840): Russian prince, born The Hague; convert, 1787; ordained priest at Baltimore, 1795; frontier missionary, known as Father Smith; Gallitzin, Pa., named for him.

Garnier, St. Charles (c. 1606-1649): French Jesuit; missionary among Hurons in Canada; martyred by Iroquois, Dec. 7, 1649; canonized, 1930; one of Jesuit North American martyrs.

Gibault, Pierre (1737-1804): Canadian missionary in Illinois and Indiana; aided in securing states of Ohio, Indiana, Illinois, Michigan and Wisconsin for the Americans during Revolution.

Gonzalez, Bl. Roch (1576-1628): Paraguayan Jesuit; worked in Paraguay Indian mission settlements (reductions); martyred; beatified, 1934.

Goupil, St. Rene (1607-1642): French Jesuit brother; missionary companion of St. Isaac Jogues among the Hurons; martyred, Sept. 29, 1642; canonized, 1930; one of Jesuit North American martyrs.

Gravier, Jacques (1651-1708): French Jesuit; missionary among Indians of Canada and midwestern US.

Jogues, St. Isaac (1607-1646): French Jesuit; missionary among Indians in Canada; martyred near present site of Auriesville, N.Y., by Mohawks, Oct. 18, 1646; canonized, 1930; one of Jesuit North American martyrs.

Kino, Eusebio (1645-1711): Italian Jesuit; missionary and explorer in US; arrived Southwest, 1681; established 25 Indian missions, took part in 14 exploring expeditions in northern Mexico, Arizona and southern California; helped develop livestock raising and farming in the area. He was selected in 1965 to represent Arizona in Statuary Hall.

Lalande, St. John (d. 1646): French Jesuit brother; martyred by Mohawks at Auriesville, N. Y., Oct. 19, 1646; canonized, 1930; one of Jesuit North American martyrs.

Lalemant, St. Gabriel (1610-1649): French Jesuit; missionary among the Hurons in Canada; martyred by the Iroquois, Mar. 17, 1649; canonized, 1930; one of Jesuit North American martyrs.

Lamy, Jean Baptiste (1814-1888): French prelate; came to US, 1839; missionary in Ohio and Kentucky; bishop in Southwest from 1850; first bishop (later archbishop) of Santa Fe, 1850-1885. He was nominated in 1951 to represent New Mexico in Statuary Hall.

Las Casas, Bartolome (1474-1566): Spanish Dominican; missionary in Haiti, Jamaica and Venezuela; reformer of abuses against Indians and Negroes; bishop of Chalapas, Mexico, 1544-47; historian.

Manogue, Patrick (1831-1895): Missionary bishop in US, b. Ireland; migrated to US; miner in California; studied for priesthood at St. Mary's of the Lake, Chicago, and St. Sulpice, Paris; ordained, 1861; missionary among Indians of California and Nevada; coadjutor bishop, 1881-84, and bishop, 1884-86, of Grass Valley; first bishop of Sacramento, 1886-1895, when see was transferred there.

Margil, Antonio (1657-1726): Spanish Franciscan; missionary in Middle America; apostle of Guatemala; established missions in Texas.

Marie de l'Incarnation, Ven. (1599-1672): French Ursuline nun; arrived in Canada, 1639; first superior of Ursulines in Quebec; missionary to Indians; writer.

Marquette, Jacques (1637-1675): French Jesuit; missionary and explorer in America; sent to New France, 1666; began missionary work among Ottawa Indians on Lake Superior, 1668; accompanied Joliet down the Mississippi to mouth of the Arkansas, 1673, and returned to Lake Michigan by way of Illinois River; made a second trip over the same route; his diary and map are of historical significance. He was selected in 1895 to represent Wisconsin in Statuary Hall.

Massias, Bl. John de (1585-1645): Dominican brother, a native of Spain; entered Dominican Friary at Lima, Peru, 1622; served as doorkeeper until his death; beatified, 1837.

Mazzuchelli, Samuel C. (1806-1864): Italian Dominican; missionary in midwestern US; called Builder of the West; writer.

Membre, Zenobius (1645-1687): French Franciscan; missionary among Indians of Illinois; accompanied LaSalle expedition down the Mississippi (1681-1682) and Louisiana colonizing expedition (1684) which landed in Texas; murdered by Indians.

Mogrovejo, St. Toribio Alfonso de (1538-1606): Spanish archbishop of Lima, Peru, c. 1580-1606; canonized 1726.

Nerinckx, Charles (1761-1824): Belgian priest; missionary in Kentucky; founded Sisters of Loretto at the Foot of the Cross.

Nobrega, Manoel (1517-1570): Portuguese Jesuit; leader of first Jesuit missionaries to Brazil, 1549.

Padilla, Juan de (d. 1542): Spanish Franciscan; missionary among Indians of Mexico and southwestern US; killed by Indians in Kansas; protomartyr of the US.

Palou, Francisco (c. 1722-1789): Spanish Franciscan; accompanied Junipero Serra to Mexico, 1749; founded Mission Dolores in San Francisco; wrote history of the Franciscans in California.

Peter of Ghent (d. 1572): Belgian Franciscan brother; missionary in Mexico for 49 years.

Porres, St. Martin de (1569-1639): Peruvian Dominican oblate; his father was a Spanish soldier and his mother a Negro freedwoman from Panama; called wonder worker of Peru; beatified, 1837; canonized, 1962.

Quiroga, Vasco de (1470-1565): Spanish missionary in Mexico; founded hospitals; bishop of Michoacan, 1537.

Ravalli, Antonio (1811-1884): Italian Jesuit; missionary in farwestern US, mostly Montana, for 40 years.

Raymbaut, Charles (1602-1643): French Jesuit; missionary among Indians of Canada and northern US.

Richard, Gabriel (1767-1832): French Sulpician; missionary in Illinois and Michigan; a founder of University of Michigan; elected delegate to Congress from Michigan, 1823; first priest to hold seat in the House of Representatives.

Rodriguez, Bl. Alonso (1598-1628): Spanish Jesuit; missionary in Paraguay; martyred; beatified, 1934.

Rosati, Joseph (1789-1843): Italian Vincentian; missionary bishop in US (vicar apostolic of Mississippi and Alabama, 1822; coadjutor of Louisiana and the Two Floridas, 1823-26; administrator of New Orleans, 1826-29; first bishop of St. Louis, 1826-1843).

Sahagun, Bernardino de (c. 1500-1590): Spanish Franciscan; missionary in Mexico for over 60 years; expert on Aztec archaeology.

Seelos, Francis X. (1819-1867): Redemptorist missionary, born Bavaria; ordained, 1844, at Baltimore; missionary in Pittsburgh and New Orleans.

Serra, Junipero (1713-1784): Spanish Franciscan, b. Majorca; missionary in America; arrived Mexico, 1749, where he did missionary work for 20 years; began work in Upper California in 1769 and established nine of the 21 Franciscan missions along the Pacific coast; baptized some 6,000 Indians and confirmed almost 5,000; a cultural pioneer of California. Represents California in Statuary Hall.

Seghers, Charles J. (1839-1886): Belgian missionary bishop in North America; Apostle of Alaska; archbishop of Oregon City (now Portland), 1880-1884; murdered by berserk companion while on missionary journey.

Solanus, St. Francis (1549-1610): Spanish Franciscan; missionary in Paraguay, Argentina and Peru; Wonder Worker of the New World; canonized, 1726.

Sorin, Edward F. (1814-1893): French priest; member of Congregation of Holy Cross; sent to US in 1841; founder and first president of the University of Notre Dame; missionary in Indiana and Michigan.

Todadilla, Anthony de (1704-1746): Spanish Capuchin; missionary to Indians of Venezuela; killed by Motilones.

Twelve Apostles of Mexico (early 16th century): Franciscan priests; arrived in Mexico, 1524: Fathers Martin de Valencia (leader), Francisco de Soto, Martin de la Coruna, Juan Suares, Antonio de Ciudad Rodrigo, Toribio de Benevente, Garcia de Cisneros, Luis de Fuensalida, Juan de Ribas, Francisco Ximenes; Brothers Andres de Coroboda, Juan de Palos.

Valdivia, Luis de (1561-1641): Spanish Jesuit; defender of Indians in Peru and Chile.

Vasques de Espinosa, Antonio (early 17th century); Spanish Carmelite; missionary and explorer in Mexico, Panama and western coast of South America.

Vieira, Antonio (1608-1687): Portuguese Jesuit; preacher; missionary in Peru and Chile; protector of Indians against exploitation by slave owners and traders; considered foremost prose writer of 17th-century Portugal.

White, Andrew (1579-1656): English Jesuit; missionary among Indians in Maryland.

Wimmer, Boniface (1809-1887): German Benedictine; missionary among German immigrants in the US.

Youville, Bl. Marie Marguerite d' (1701-1771): Canadian widow; foundress of Sisters of Charity (Grey Nuns), 1738, at Montreal: beatified, 1959.

Zumarraga, Juan de (1468-1548): Spanish Franciscan; missionary; first bishop of Mexico; introduced first printing press in New World, published first book in America, a catechism for Aztec Indians; extended missions in Mexico and Central America; vigorous opponent of exploitation of Indians; approved of devotions at Guadalupe; leading figure in early church history in Mexico.

FRANCISCAN MISSIONS OF UPPER CALIFORNIA

The 21 Franciscan missions of Upper California were established during the 54-year period from 1769 to 1822. Located along the old El Camino Real, or King's Highway, they extended from San Diego to San Francisco and were the centers of Indian civilization, Christianity and industry in the early history of the state.

Fray Junipero Serra was the great pioneer of the missions of Upper California. He and his successor as superior of the work, Fray Fermin Lasuen, each directed the establishment of nine missions. One hundred and 46 priests of the Order of Friars Minor, most of them Spaniards, labored in the region from 1769 to 1845; 67 of them died at their posts, two as martyrs. The regular time of mission service was 10 years.

The missions were secularized by the Mexican government in the 1830's but were subsequently restored to the Church by the US government. They are now variously used as the sites of parish churches, a university, houses of study and museums.

The names of the missions and the order of their establishment were as follows:

San Diego de Alcala, San Carlos Borromeo (El Carmelo), San Antonio de Padua, San Gabriel Arcangel, San Luis Obispo de Tolosa, San Francisco de Asis (Dolores), San Juan Capistrano;

Santa Clara de Asis, San Buenaventura, Santa Barbara, La Purisima Concepcion de Maria Santisima, Santa Cruz, Nuestra Senora de la Soledad, San Jose de Guadalupe;

San Juan Bautista, San Miguel Arcangel, San Fernando Rey de Espana, San Luis Rey de Francia, Santa Ines, San Rafael Arcangel, San Francisco Solano de Sonoma (Sonoma).

MARQUETTE SITE

Michigan State University archeologists reported in August, 1972, that they had discovered the site where Father Jacques Marquette was buried by Huron Indians in the 17th century.

The diggers also said they had found a portion of the Huron village located next to Father Marquette's mission near present-day St. Ignace, Mich.

"We have enough evidence now to warrant planning major restoration work at and near the Marquette mission site," said Dr. Lyle M. Stone, director of the university's surveys and diggings.

The MSU team reported it had found artifacts near the cellar in which the Jesuit missionary was buried that indicated the existence of a large Huron Indian village near St. Ignace.

The artifacts, they said, included remains of two walls, Indian pottery, flint chippings, arrowheads, and a trash pit full of fish bones.

The cellar in which Father Marquette had been buried originally was discovered by Father Edward Jacker in 1877. He had learned that the body had been moved to the St. Ignace location in 1677 from present-day Ludington where the missionary died in 1675. Sometime after Father Jacker's discovery, the location of the site was again lost. This was the site located by the MSU team.

The Church in Countries Throughout the World

(Principal source for statistics: *Annuario Pontificio, 1972.* Other sources are noted in the text. See Index for additional entries on 1972 events in various countries.)

Abbreviations code: archd., — archdiocese; dioc. — diocese; ap. ex. — apostolic exarchate; prel. — prelature; abb. — abbacy; v.a. — vicariate apostolic; p.a. — prefecture apostolic; a.a. — apostolic administration; card. — cardinal; abp., — archbishop; nat. — native; bp. — bishop; priests (dioc. — diocesan or secular priests; rel. — those belonging to religious orders); sem. — seminarians; p.d. — permanent deacons; m. rel. — men religious (include brothers and priests belonging to religious orders); w. rel. — women religious; sch. — schools; inst. — charitable institutes; Caths. — Catholic population; tot. pop. — total population.

Afars and Issas (formerly French Somaliland): French territory in east Africa, on the Gulf of Aden; capital, Djibouti. Christianity in the area, formerly part of Ethiopia, antedated but was overcome by the Arab invasion of 1200. Modern evangelization, begun in the latter part of the 19th century, had meager results. The hierarchy was established in 1955. The territory has an apostolic delegate (to the Red Sea Region).

Dioc., 1; bp., 1; parishes, 5; priests, 9 (2 dioc.; 7 rel.); sem., 3; m. rel., 21; w. rel., 34; sch., 1; inst., 17; Caths., 11,000; tot. pop., 125,000.

Afghanistan: Constitutional monarchy in south-central Asia; capital, Kabul. Christianity antedated Moslem conquest in the seventh century but was overcome by it. All inhabitants are subject to the law of Islam. Christian missionaries are prohibited. The few Catholics in the country are foreign embassy and technical personnel. Population (UN est., 1970), 17,125,000.

Albania: Communist people's republic in the Balkans, bordering the Adriatic Sea; capital, Tirana. Christianity was introduced before the middle of the fourth century. The Byzantine Church became Orthodox following the schism of 1054. The Orthodox Church now existing is under government control. The Latin (Roman) Church, which prevailed in the north, has been practically wiped out by persecution since 1945, with the expulsion of Italian missionaries; a number of death and prison sentences and other repressive measures against bishops, priests, religious and lay persons; the closing of Catholic schools and a seminary; the cutting of lines of communication with the Holy See. In 1967, the government proclaimed itself the first atheist state in the world.

Archd., 2; dioc., 3; abb., 1; a.a. 1; bp., 3. No statistics are available. The Catholic population was estimated at 143,500 in 1969 by the CSMC "World Mission Map"; tot. pop. (1970 est.), 2,100,000.

Algeria: Republic in northwest Africa: capital, Algiers. Christianity, introduced at an early date, succumbed to Vandal devastation in the fifth century and Moslem conquest in 709, but survived for centuries in small communities into the 12th century. Missionary work was unsuccessful except in service to traders, military personnel and captives along the coast. Church organization was established after the French gained control of the territory in the 1830's. A large number of Catholics were among the estimated million Europeans who left the country after it secured independence from France July 5, 1962. Islam is the state religion. Algeria maintains diplomatic relations with Vatican City.

Archd., 1; dioc., 3; card., 1; bp., 4; parishes, 106; priests, 379 (179 dioc.; 200 rel.); sem., 4; p.d., 1; m. rel., 253; w. rel., 1,209; sch., 415; inst., 61; Caths., 71,350; tot. pop., 13,808,201.

Andorra: Autonomous principality in the Pyrenees, under the rule of co-princes — the French head of state and the bishop of Urgel, Spain; capital, Andorra la Vella. Christianity was introduced at an early date. Catholicism is the state religion. The principality is under the ecclesiastical jurisdiction of the Spanish diocese of Urgel.

Total pop., (1971), 20,551 (almost entirely Catholic).

Angola: Portuguese territory in west Africa; capital, Luanda. Evangelization by Catholic missionaries, dating from about 1570, reached high points in the 17th and 18th centuries.

Archd., 1; dioc., 7; abp., 1; bp., 8 (1 nat.); parishes, 131; priests, 534 (210 dioc., 324 rel.); sem., 190; m. rel., 467; w. rel., 778; sch., 1,233; inst., 216; Caths., 2,362,640; tot. pop., 5,485,948.

Arabian Peninsula: Includes Saudi Arabia, Peoples Republic of Yemen, Yemen Arab Republic, Oman, Bahrein, Qatar, Union of Arab Emirates. Christianity, introduced in various parts of the peninsula in early Christian centuries, succumbed to Islam in the seventh century. The native population is entirely Moslem. The only Christians are foreigners. The peninsula has an apostolic delegate (to the Red Sea Region).

V.a., 1; parishes 13; priests, 15 (1 dioc., 14 rel.); m. rel., 14; w. rel., 33; sch., 14; inst., 1; Caths., 6,873; tot. pop., 12,534,200. (Statistics are for the vicariate apostolic of Arabia which includes most of the Arabian Peninsula; the vicariate is located in Aden, Peoples Republic of Yemen.)

Argentina: Republic in southeast South America, bordering on the Atlantic; capital, Buenos Aires. Priests were with the Magellan exploration party and the first Mass in the country was celebrated Apr. 1, 1519. Missionary work began in the 1530's, diocesan organization in the late 1540's and effective evangelization about 1570. Independence from Spain was proclaimed in 1816. Since its establishment in the country, the Church has been influenced by Spanish cultural and institutional forces, antagonistic liberalism, government interference and opposition; the latter reached a climax during the regime of Juan Peron (1946-1955). Catholicism is the state religion. Argentina maintains diplomatic relations with Vatican City.

Archd., 12; dioc., 39; prel., 2; ap. ex., 1; ord., 1; card., 1; abp., 12; bp., 50; parishes, 1,828; priests, 5,279 (2,480 dioc., 2,799 rel.); sem., 357; p.d., 2; m. rel., 4,086; w. rel., 12,749; sch., 2,151; inst., 526; Caths., 21,853,000; tot. pop., 24,275,000.

Australia: Commonwealth, member of the British Commonwealth, island continent southeast of Asia; capital, Canberra. The first Catholics in the country were Irish under penal sentence, 1795-1804; the first public Mass was celebrated May 15, 1803. Official organization of the Church dates from 1820. Australia has an apostolic delegate.

Archd., 7; dioc., 19; abb., 1; mission "sui juris," 1; ap. ex., 1; card., 1; abp., 8; bp., 25; parishes, 1,263; priests, 3,798 (2,392 dioc., 1,406 rel.); sem., 508; p.d., 2; m. rel., 4,225; w. rel., 13,450; sch., 2,206; inst., 310; Caths., 3,008,449; tot. pop., 12,833,669.

Austria: Republic in central Europe; capital, Vienna. Christianity was introduced by the end of the third century, strengthened considerably by conversion of the Bavarians from about 600, and firmly established in the second half of the eighth century. Catholicism survived and grew stronger as the principal religion in the country in the post-Reformation period, but suffered from Josephinism in the 18th century. Although liberated from much government harassment in the aftermath of the Revolution of 1848, it came under pressure again some 20 years later in the Kulturkampf. During this time the Church became involved with a developing social movement. The Church faced strong opposition from Socialists after World War I and suffered persecution from 1938 to 1945 during the Nazi regime. Some Church-state matters are regulated by a concordat originally concluded in 1934. Austria maintains diplomatic relations with Vatican City.

Archd., 2; dioc., 7; card., 1; abp., 2; bp., 12; parishes, 2,965; priests, 6,297 (3,821 dioc., 2,476 rel.); sem., 462; p.d., 17; m. rel., 3,718; w. rel., 13,724; sch., 312; inst., 584; Caths., 6,792,237; tot. pop., 7,559,848.

Azores: North Atlantic island group 750 miles west of Portugal, of which it is part. Christianity was introduced in the second quarter of the 15th century.

Bahamas: Colony in the British Commonwealth, consisting of several hundred small islands southeast of Florida and north of Cuba; capital, Nassau. On Oct. 12, 1492, Columbus landed on one of these islands, where the first Mass was celebrated in the New World. Organization of the Catholic Church in the Bahamas dates from about the middle of the 19th century.

Dioc., 1; bp., 1; parishes, 26; priests, 58 (22 dioc., 36 rel.); sem., 3; m. rel., 42; w. rel., 83; sch., 18; inst., 7; Caths., 33,220; tot. pop., 168,838.

Balearic Islands: Spanish province consisting of an island group in the western Mediterranean. Statistics are included in those for Spain.

Bahrein: See Arabian Peninsula.

Bangladesh: Formerly the eastern portion of Pakistan. Officially constituted as a separate nation Dec. 16, 1971; capital, Dacca. Islam is the principal religion; freedom of religion is granted. There were Jesuit, Dominican and Augustinian missionaries in the area in the 16th century. A vicariate apostolic (of Bengali) was established in 1834; the hierarchy was erected in 1950.

Archd., 1; dioc., 3; abp., 1 (nat.); bp., 3 (nat.); parishes, 57; priests, 128 (35 dioc., 93 rel.); sem., 21; m. rel., 160; w. rel., 347; sch., 221; inst., 76; Caths., 115,171; tot. pop., 61,981,378.

Barbados: Parliamentary democracy in the British Commonwealth (independent since 1966), easternmost of the Caribbean islands; capital, Bridgetown. About 70 per cent of the people are Anglicans. Statistics are included in those for West Indies.

Belgium: Constitutional monarchy in northwestern Europe; capital, Brussels. Christianity was introduced about the first quarter of the fourth century and major evangelization was completed about 730. During the rest of the medieval period the Church had firm diocesan and parochial organization, generally vigorous monastic life, and influential monastic and cathedral schools. Lutherans and Calvinists made some gains during the Reformation period but there was a strong Catholic restoration in the first half of the 17th century, when the country was under Spanish rule. Jansenism disturbed the Church from about 1640 into the 18th century. Josephinism, imposed by an Austrian regime, hampered the Church late in the same century. Repressive and persecutory measures were enforced during the Napoleonic conquest. Freedom came with separation of Church and state in the wake of the Revolution of 1830, which ended the reign of William I. Thereafter, the Church encountered serious problems with philosophical liberalism and political socialism. Catholics have long been engaged in strong educational, social and political movements. Except for one five-year period (1880-1884), Belgium has maintained diplomatic relations with Vatican City since 1835.

Archd., 1; dioc., 7; card., 1; bp., 13; parishes, 3,921; priests, 12,257 (9,546 dioc., 2,711 rel.); sem., 615; p.d., 22; m. rel., 4,148; w. rel., 22,887; sch., 5,974; inst., 1,343; Caths., 8,901,000; tot. pop., 9,658,558.

Bermuda: British colony, consisting of 360 islands (20 of them inhabited) nearly 600 miles east of Cape Hatteras; capital, Hamilton. Catholics were not permitted until about 1800. Occasional pastoral care was provided the few Catholics there by visiting priests during the 19th century. Early in the 1900's priests from Halifax began serving the area. A prefecture apostolic was set up in 1953. The first bishop assumed jurisdiction in 1956. The only Catholic school in Bermuda was the first to admit black students, in 1961.

Dioc., 1; bp., 1; parishes, 6; priests, 11 (2 dioc., 9 rel.); w. rel., 16; Caths., 8,500; tot. pop., 53,000. (Figures are from the Caribbean Catholic Directory.)

Bhutan: Constitutional monarchy in the Himalayas, northeast of India; capital, Thimpu. Most of the population are Buddhists. Ecclesiastical jurisdiction is under the archdiocese of Shillong-Gauhati, India.

Bolivia: Republic in central South America; capital, Sucre; seat of government, La Paz. Catholicism, the official religion, was introduced in the 1530's and the first bishopric was established in 1552. Effective evangelization among the Indians, slow to start, reached high points in the middle of the 18th and the beginning of the 19th centuries and was resumed about 1840. Independence from Spain was proclaimed in 1825, at the end of a campaign that started in 1809. The republic inherited the Spanish right of nominating candidates for bishoprics. Church-state relations are regulated by a 1951 concordat with the Holy See, and Bolivia maintains diplomatic relations with Vatican City.

Archd., 2; dioc., 5; prel., 3; v.a., 6; card., 1; abp., 1; bp., 18; parishes, 815; priests, 859 (257 dioc., 602 rel.); sem., 33; m. rel., 839; w. rel., 1,388; sch., 388; inst., 180; Caths., 4,148,603; tot. pop., 4,750,656.

Botswana: Republic (independent since 1966) in southern Africa, member of the British Commonwealth; capital, Gaborone. Botswana has an apostolic delegate (to South Africa).

Dioc., 1; bp., 1; priests, 24 (2 dioc., 22 rel.); sem., 1; m. rel., 24; w. rel., 33; sch., 11; inst., 2; Caths., 19,317; tot. pop. (UN est., 1970), 648,000.

Brazil: Republic in northeast South America, capital, Brasilia. One of several priests with the discovery party celebrated the first Mass in the country Apr. 26, 1500. Evangelization began some years later and the first diocese was erected in 1551. During the colonial period, which lasted until 1882, evangelization made some notable progress—especially in the Amazon region between 1680 and 1750—but was seriously hindered by govern-

ment policy and the attitude of colonists regarding Amazon Indians the missionaries tried to protect from exploitation and slavery. The Jesuits were suppressed in 1782 and other missionaries expelled as well. Liberal anti-Church influence grew in strength. The government gave minimal support but exercised maximum control over the Church. After the proclamation of independence from Portugal in 1822 and throughout the regency, government control was tightened and the Church suffered greatly from dissident actions of ecclesiastical brotherhoods, Masonic anticlericalism and general decline in religious life. Church and state were separated by the constitution of 1891, proclaimed two years after the end of the empire. The Church carried into the 20th century a load of inherited liabilities and problems amid increasingly difficult political economic and social conditions affecting the majority of the population. A number of bishops, priests, religious and lay persons have been active in movements for social and religious reform. Brazil maintains diplomatic relations with Vatican City.

Archd., 32; dioc., 132; prel., 41; abb., 2; card., 4; abp., 33; bp., 198; parishes, 5,636; priests, 12,534 (5,528 dioc., 7,006 rel.); sem., 1,046; p.d., 41; m. rel., 10,327; w. rel., 37,038; sch., 3,918; inst., 3,359; Caths. (est.), 84,300,000; tot. pop., 93,700,000.

Brunei: State under British protection, on the northern coast of Borneo; capital, Brunei. Statistics are included in those for Malaysia.

Bulgaria: People's republic in southeastern Europe on the eastern part of the Balkan peninsula; capital, Sofia. Christianity was introduced before 343 but disappeared with the migration of Slavs into the territory. The baptism of Boris I about 865 ushered in a new period of Christianity which soon became involved in switches of loyalty between Constantinople and Rome. Through it all the Byzantine, and later Orthodox, element remained stronger and survived under the rule of Ottoman Turks into the 19th century. The few modern Latin Catholics in the country are traceable to 17th century converts from heresy. The Byzantines are products of a reunion movement of the 19th century. In 1947 the constitution of the new republic decreed the separation of Church and state. Catholic schools and institutions were abolished and foreign religious banished in 1948. A year later the apostolic delegate was expelled. Bishop Eugene Bosilkoff was condemned to death (his fate is still unknown) and Ivan Romanoff, the vicar apostolic of Plovdiv, died in prison in 1952. Roman and Bulgarian Rite vicars apostolic were permitted to attend the Second Vatican Council from 1962 to 1965. All church activity is under surveillance and/or control by the government, which professes to be atheistic. Pastoral and related activities are strictly limited. Most of the population is Orthodox.

Dioc., 1; v.a., 1; ap. ex., 1; bp., 3; parishes, 44; priests, 52 (16 dioc., 36 rel.); sem., 1; m. rel., 4; Cath., 65,0000; tot. pop., 8,436,000.

Burma: Union of Burma, a republic in southeast Asia, on the Bay of Bengal; capital, Rangoon. Christianity was introduced about 1500. Small-scale evangelization had limited results from the middle of the 16th century until the 1850's when effective organization of the Church began. The hierarchy was established in 1955. Buddhism was declared the state religion in 1961, although all other religions are respected. In 1965, church schools were nationalized. In 1966, all foreign missionaries who had entered the country after 1948 for the first time were forced to leave when the government refused to renew their work permits. Despite these setbacks, the Church has shown some progress in recent years. Burma has an apostolic delegate (pronuncio to India).

Archd., 2; dioc., 6; abp., 2 (nat.); bp., 7 (3 nat.); parishes, 140; priests, 167 (132 dioc., 35 rel.); sem., 83; m. rel., 103; w. rel., 471; sch., 165 (nationalized in 1966); inst., 102; Caths., 260,940; tot. pop. (UN est., 1970), 27,584,000.

Burundi: Republic since 1966, near the equator in east-central Africa; capital, Bjumbura. The first permanent Catholic mission station was established late in the 19th century. Large numbers of persons were received into the Church following the ordination of the first Burundi priests in 1925. The first native bishop was appointed in 1959. Most education takes place in schools under Catholic auspices. Burundi maintains diplomatic relations with Vatican City.

Archd., 1; dioc., 4; abp., 1 (nat.); bp., 4 (3 nat.); parishes, 169; priests, 434 (157 dioc., 277 rel.); sem., 55; m. rel., 420; w. rel., 601; sch., 677; inst., 46; Caths., 1,925,447; tot. pop., 4,380,000.

Cambodia: See Khmer Republic.

Cameroon: Republic in west Africa, bordering on the Gulf of Guinea; capital, Yaounde. Effective evangelization began in the 1890's, although Catholics had been in the country long before that time. In the 40-year period from 1920 to 1960, the number of Catholics increased from 60,000 to 700,000. The first native priests were ordained in 1935. Twenty years later the first native bishops were ordained and the hierarchy established. In 1971 Bishop Albert Ndongmo of Nkongsamba was sentenced to death after being convicted of plotting to overthrow the government; the sentence was later commuted to life imprisonment. Cameroon maintains diplomatic relations with Vatican City.

Archd., 1; dioc., 10; p.a., 2; abp., 1 (nat.); bp., 13 (6 nat.); parishes, 202; priests, 733 (256 dioc., 477 rel.); sem., 100; p.d., 7; m. rel., 784; w. rel., 965; sch., 1,131; inst., 150; Caths., 1,305,065; tot. pop. (UN est., 1970), 5,836,000.

Canada: Independent federation in the British Commonwealth, comprising the northern half of North America; capital, Ottawa. (See The Church in Canada.)

Archd., 18; dioc., 49; abb., 1; card., 4; abp., 16; bp., 52; parishes, 4,284; priests, 12,580 (8,290 dioc., 4,290 rel.); sem., 873; p.d., 7; m. rel., 9,113; w. rel., 45,724; sch., 1,576; inst., 495; Caths., 9,093,264; tot. pop., 20,470,311.

Canary Islands: Two Spanish provinces, consisting of seven islands, off the northwest coast of Africa. Evangelization began about 1400. Almost all of the one million inhabitants are Catholics. Statistics are included in those for Spain.

Cape Verde Islands: Portuguese overseas territory, consisting of 14 islands 300 miles west of Senegal. Evangelization began some years before establishment of the first diocese in the islands in 1532.

Dioc., 1; bp., 1; parishes, 30; priests, 50 (14 dioc., 36 rel.); sem., 16; m. rel., 39; w. rel., 36; sch., 67; inst., 4; Caths., 250,916; tot. pop., 260,000.

Caroline and Marshall Islands: US trust territory in the southwest Pacific. Effective evangelization began in the late 1880's.

V.a., 1; bp., 1; priests, 36 (1 dioc., 35 rel.); sem., 4; m. rel., 45; w. rel., 44; Caths., 34,987; tot. pop., 96,000.

Central African Republic: Republic (independent since 1960) in central Africa; capital, Bangui. Effective evangelization dates from 1894. The region was organized as a mission territory in 1909. The first native priest was ordained in 1938. The hierarchy was organized in 1955. The Central African Republic maintains diplomatic relations with Vatican City.

Archd., 1; dioc., 4; abp., 1 (nat.); bp., 3; parishes, 80; priests, 215 (33 dioc., 182 rel.); sem., 25; m. rel., 244; w. rel., 294; sch., 60; inst., 33; Caths., 291,944; tot. pop., 2,000,000.

Ceuta: Spanish possession (city) on the northern tip of Africa, south of Gibraltar. Statistics are included in those for Spain.

Ceylon: See Sri Lanka, Republic of.

Chad: Republic (independent since 1960) in north-central Africa, member of the French Community; capital, Fort Lamy. Evangelization began in 1929, leading to firm organization in 1947 and establishment of the hierarchy in 1955. Chad has an apostolic delegate (pro-nuncio, Central African Republic).

Archd., 1; dioc., 3; abp., 1; bp., 3; parishes, 80; priests, 157 (25 dioc., 132 rel.); sem., 6; m. rel., 176; w. rel., 183; sch., 64; inst., 27; Caths., 174,308; tot. pop., 4,000,000.

Chile: Republic on the southwestern coast of South America; capital, Santiago. Priests were with the Spanish conquistadores on their entrance into the territory early in the 16th century. The first parish was established in 1547 and the first bishopric in 1561. Overall organization of the Church took place later in the century. By 1650 most of the peaceful Indians in the central and northern areas were evangelized. Missionary work was more difficult in the southern region. Church activity was hampered during the campaign for independence, 1810 to 1818, and through the first years of the new government, to 1830. Later gains were made, into this century, but hindering factors were shortages of native clergy and religious and attempts by the government to control church administration through the patronage system in force while the country was under Spanish control. Separation of Church and state were decreed in the constitution of 1925. Chile maintains diplomatic relations with Vatican City.

Archd., 5; dioc., 14; prel., 3; v.a., 2; card., 1; abp., 4; bp., 21; parishes, 742; priests, 2,377 (988 dioc., 1,389 rel.); sem., 125; p.d., 11; m. rel., 1,999; w. rel., 5,821; sch., 917; inst., 247; Caths., 8,519,881; tot. pop., 9,728,907.

China *(This article concerns mainland China which has been under Communist control since 1949):* People's Republic in eastern part of Asia; capital, Peking. Christianity was introduced by Nestorians who had some influence on part of the area from 635 to 845 and again from the 11th century until 1368. John of Monte Corvino started a Franciscan mission in 1294; he was ordained an archbishop about 1307. Missionary activity involving more priests increased for a while thereafter but the Franciscan mission ended in 1368. The Jesuit Matteo Ricci initiated a remarkable period of activity in the 1580's. By 1700 the number of Catholics was reported to be 300,000. The Chinese Rites controversy, concerning the adaptation of rituals and other matters to Chinese traditions and practices, ran throughout the 17th century, ending in a negative decision by mission authorities in Rome. Bl. Francis de Capillas, the protomartyr of China, was killed in 1648. Persecution, a feature of Chinese history as recurrent as changes in dynasties, occurred several times in the 18th century and resulted in the departure of most missionaries from the country. The Chinese door swung open again in the 1840's and progress in evangelization increased with an extension of legal and social tolerance. At the turn of the 20th century, however, the Boxer Rebellion took one or the other kind of toll among an estimated 30,000 victims. Missionary work in the 1900's reached a new high in every respect before the disaster of persecution initiated by Communists before and especially since they established the republic in 1949. The Reds began a savage persecution as soon as they came into power. Among its results were the expulsion of over 5,000 foreign missionaries, 510 of whom were American priests, brothers and nuns; the arrest, imprisonment and harassment of all members of the native religious, clergy and hierarchy; the forced closing of 3,932 schools, 216 hospitals, 781 dispensaries, 254 orphanages, 29 printing presses and 55 periodicals; denial of the free exercise of religion to all the faithful; the detention of hundreds of priests, religious and lay persons in jail and their employment in slave labor; the proscription of the Legion of Mary and other Catholic Action groups for "counter-revolutionary activities" and "crimes against the new China"; complete outlawing of missionary work and pastoral activity. The government formally established a Patriotic Association of Chinese Catholics in July, 1957. Relatively few priests and lay persons joined the organization, which was condemned by Pius XII in 1958. The government formed the nucleus of what it hoped might become the hierarchy of a schismatic Chinese church by "electing" 26 bishops and having them consecrated validly but illicitly between Apr. 13, 1958, and Nov. 15, 1959, without the permission or approval of the Holy See. By Jan. 21, 1962, a total of 42 bishops were consecrated in this manner. In March, 1960, Bishop James E. Walsh, M.M., the last American missionary in China, was sentenced and placed in custody for a period of 20 years. He was released in the summer of 1970.

Archd., 20; dioc., 93; p.a., 29. No Catholic statistics are available. In 1949 there were between 3,500,000-4,000,000 Catholics, about .7 per cent of the total population; the 1969 "CSMC World Mission Map" estimated 3,200,000 Catholics, .5 per cent of the population. The latter figure is only an estimate; there is no way of knowing the actual situation. Tot. pop. (1971 est.), 750,000,000.

Colombia: Republic in northwest South America, with Atlantic and Pacific borders; capital, Bogota. Evangelization began in 1508. The first two dioceses were established in 1534. Vigorous development of the Church was reported by the middle of the 17th century despite obstacles posed by the multiplicity of Indian languages, government interference through patronage rights and otherwise, rivalry among religious orders and the small number of native priests among the predominantly Spanish clergy. Some persecution, including the confiscation of property, followed in the wake of the proclamation of independence from Spain in 1819. The Church was affected in many ways by the political and civil unrest of the nation through the 19th century and into the 20th. Various aspects of Church-state relations are regulated by concordats formulated in 1887 and 1892. There is some measure of annual support given the Church by the government. Colombia maintains diplomatic relations with Vatican City.

Archd., 9; dioc., 29; prel., 2; v.a., 9; p.a., 6; card., 1; abp., 9; bp., 48; parishes, 1,857; priests, 5,114 (3,058 dioc., 2,056 rel.); sem., 871; m. rel., 3,105; w. rel., 17,164; sch., 1,858; inst., 990; Caths. (est.), 20,397,000; tot. pop., 21,790,000.

Congo Republic: Republic in west central Africa, member of the French Community; capital, Brazzaville. Small-scale missionary work with little effect preceded modern evangelization dating from the 1880's. The work of the Church has been affected by political instability, Communist influence, tribalism and hostility to foreigners. The hierarchy was established in 1955. Congo has an apostolic delegate (pronuncio, Central African Republic).

Archd., 1; dioc., 2; abp., 1 (nat.); bp., 1; parishes, 69; priests, 162 (41 dioc., 121 rel.); sem., 15; m. rel., 143; w. rel., 84; inst., 8; Caths., 414,837; tot. pop., 915,000.

Cook Islands: Self-governing territory of New Zealand, an archipelago of small islands in Oceania. Evangelization by Protestant missionaries started in 1821, resulting in a predominantly Protestant population. The first Catholic missionary work began in 1894. The hierarchy was established in 1966.

Dioc., 1; parishes, 11; priests, 12 (1 dioc., 11 rel.); m. rel., 11; w. rel., 8; sch., 2; Caths., 2,723; tot. pop., 19,247.

Costa Rica: Republic in Central America; capital, San Jose. Evangelization began about 1520 and proceeded by degrees to real development and organization of the Church in the 17th and 18th centuries. The republic became independent in 1838. Twelve years later church jurisdiction also became independent with the establishment of a bishopric in the present capital. Costa Rica maintains diplomatic relations with Vatican City.

Archd., 1; dioc., 3; v.a., 1; abp., 1; bp., 5; parishes, 142; priests, 368 (243 dioc., 125 rel.); sem., 69; m. rel., 184; w. rel., 869; sch., 75; inst., 28; Caths., 1,636,681; tot. pop., 1,800,000.

Cuba: Republic under Communist dictatorship, south of Florida; capital, Havana. Effective evangelization began about 1514, leading eventually to the predominance of Catholicism on the island. Native vocations to the priesthood and religious life were unusually numerous in the 18th century but declined in the 19th. The island became independent of Spain in 1902 following the Spanish-American War. Fidel Castro took control of the government Jan. 1, 1959. In 1961, after Cuba was officially declared a socialist state, the University of Villanueva was closed, 350 Catholic schools were nationalized and 136 priests expelled. A greater number of foreign priests and religious had already left the country. Freedom of worship and religious instruction are limited to church premises and no social action is permitted the Church, which survives under surveillance. Cuba maintains diplomatic relations with Vatican City.

Archd., 2; dioc., 4; abp., 2; bp., 6; parishes, 228; priests, 193 (80 dioc., 113 rel.); sem., 58; m. rel., 149; w. rel., 227; inst., 8; Caths., 6,327,028; tot. pop., 8,547,326.

Cyprus: Republic in the eastern Mediterranean; capital, Nicosia. Christianity was preached on the island in apostolic times and has a continuous history from the fourth century. Latin and Eastern rites were established but the latter prevailed and became Orthodox after the schism of 1054. Roman and Orthodox Christians have suffered under many governments, particularly during the period of Turkish dominion from late in the 16th to late in the 19th centuries, and from differences between the 80 per cent Greek majority and the Turkish minority. About 80 per cent of the population are Orthodox. Cyprus has an apostolic delegate. Maronite Rite Catholics are under the jurisdiction of the diocese of Cyprus (of the Maronites), whose bishop resides in Lebanon. Roman Rite Catholics are under the jurisdiction of the Roman Rite patriarch of Jerusalem.

There are approximately 6,700 Catholics; total population, 640,000.

Czechoslovakia: Federal socialist republic (since 1969) in Central Europe, consisting of the Czech Socialist Republic, capital Prague; and the Slovak Socialist Republic, capital Bratislava. The republics have local autonomy but are subordinate to the Federal Assembly at Prague made up of representatives from both regions. The Czech and Slovak regions of the country have separate religious and cultural backgrounds. Christianity was introduced in Slovakia in the 8th century by Irish and German missionaries and the area was under the jurisdiction of German bishops. In 863, at the invitation of the Slovak ruler Rastislav who wanted to preserve the cultural and liturgical heritage of the people, Sts. Cyril and Methodius began pastoral and missionary work in the region, ministering to the people in their own language. The saints introduced Old Slovak (Old Church Slavonic) into the liturgy and did so much to evangelize the territory that they are venerated as the apostles of Slovakia. A diocese established at Nitra in 880 had a continuous history except for a century ending in 1024. The Church in Slovakia was severely tested by the Reformation and political upheavals. After World War I, when it became part of the Republic of Czechoslovakia, it was 75 per cent Catholic. In the Czech lands, the martyrdom of Prince Wenceslaus in 929 triggered the spread of Christianity. Prague has had a continuous history as a diocese since 973. A parish system was organized about the 13th century in Bohemia and Moravia, the land of the Czechs. Mendicant orders strengthened relations with the Latin Rite in the 13th century. In the next century the teachings of John Hus in Bohemia brought trouble to the Church in the forms of schism and heresy, and initiated a series of religious wars which continued for decades following his death at the stake in 1415. Church property was confiscated, monastic communities were scattered and even murdered, ecclesiastical organization was shattered, and so many of the faithful joined the Bohemian Brethren that Catholics became a minority. The Reformation, with the way prepared by the Hussites and cleared by other factors, affected the Church seriously. A Counter Reformation got underway in the 1560's and led to a gradual restoration through the thickets of Josephinism, the Enlightenment, liberalism and troubled politics. In 1920, two years after the establishment of the Republic of Czechoslovakia, the schismatic Czechoslovak Church was proclaimed at Prague, resulting in numerous defections from the Catholic Church in the Czech region. In Ruthenia, 112,000 became Russian Orthodox between 1918 and 1930. Vigorous persecution of the church began in Slovakia before the end of World War II when Communists mounted a 1944 offensive against bishops, priests and religious. In 1945, church schools were nationalized, youth organizations were disbanded, the Catholic press was curtailed, the training of students for the priesthood was seriously impeded. Msgr. Josef Tiso, president of the Slovak Republic, was tried for "treason" in December, 1947, and was executed the following April. Between 1945 and 1949 approximately 10 per cent of the Slovak population spent some time in jail or a concentration camp. Persecution began later in the Czech part of the country, following the accession of the Gottwald regime to power early in 1948. Hospitals, schools and property were nationalized and Catholic organizations were liquidated. A puppet organization was formed in 1949 to infiltrate the Church and implement an unsuccessful plan for establishing a schismatic church. In the same year Archbishop Josef Beran of Prague was placed under house arrest and began 14 years of surveillance. (He left the country in 1965, was made a cardinal, and died in 1969 in Rome.) A number of theatrical trials of bishops and priests were staged in 1950. All houses of religious were taken over between Mar., 1950, and the end of 1951. An Eastern Rite diocese, Presov, in Slovakia, was dissolved in 1950 and pressure was applied on the clergy and faithful to join the Orthodox Church. Diplomatic relations with Vatican City were terminated in 1950. About 3,000 priests were deprived of liberty in 1951 and attempts were made to force "peace priests" on the people. In 1958 it was reported that 450 to 500 priests were in jail; an undisclosed number of religious and Byzantine Rite priests had been deported; two bishops released from prison in 1956 were under house arrest; one bishop was imprisoned at Leopoldov and two at the Mirov reformatory. In Bohemia, Moravia and Silesia, five of six dioceses were without ruling bishops; one archbishop and two bishops were active but subject to "supervision"; most of the clergy refused to join the "peace priests." In 1962 only three bishops were permitted to attend the first session of the Second Vatican Council. From January to October, 1968, Church-state relations improved to some ex-

tent under the Dubcek regime: a number of bishops were reinstated; some 3,000 priests were engaged in the pastoral ministry, although 1,500 were still barred from priestly work; the "peace priests" organization was disbanded; the Eastern Rite Church, with 147 parishes, was reestablished. In 1969, an end was ordered to rehabilitation trials for priests and religious, but no wholesale restoration of priests and religious to their proper ways of life and work was in prospect. In 1972 the government ordered the removal of nuns from visible but limited apostolates to farms and mental hospitals where they would be out of sight.

Archd., 2; dioc., 10; a.a., 2; bp., 6; parishes, 4,291; priests, 4,247 (3,685 dioc., 562 rel.); sem., 556; m. rel., 616; w. rel., 4,933; sch., 1; inst., 10; Caths. (est.), 10,000,000; tot. pop. (UN est., 1970), 14,467,000.

Dahomey: Republic in west Africa, bordering on the Atlantic; member of the French Community; capitals, Cotonou, Porto Novo. Missionary work was very limited from the 16th to the 18th centuries. Effective evangelization dates from 1894. The hierarchy was established in 1955. The majority of Christians are Catholics. Dahomey maintains diplomatic relations with Vatican City.

Archd., 1; dioc., 5; abp., 1 (nat.); bp., 5 (2 nat.); parishes, 76; priests, 177 (82 dioc., 95 rel.); sem., 27; m. rel., 108; w. rel., 303; sch., 204; inst., 31; Caths., 384,985; tot. pop., 2,643,000.

Danzig (Gdansk): Baltic seaport at the mouth of the Vistula River; incorporated into Poland after World War II. The diocese, has a Christian history dating from the 10th century.

Dioc., 1; bp., 1; parishes, 61; priests, 243 (135 dioc., 108 rel.); sem., 53; m. rel., 124; w. rel., 213; Caths., 507,000; tot. pop., 531,780.

Denmark, including the Faroe Islands and Greenland: Constitutional monarchy in northwestern Europe, north of West Germany; capital, Copenhagen. Christianity was introduced in the ninth century and the first diocese for the area was established in 831. Intensive evangelization and full-scale organization of the Church occurred from the second half of the 10th century and ushered in a period of great development and influence in the 12th and 13th centuries. Decline followed, resulting in almost total loss to the Church during the Reformation when Lutheranism became the national religion. Catholics were considered foreigners until religious freedom was legally assured in 1849. Modern development of the Church dates from the second half of the 19th century. About 95 per cent of the population are Evangelical Lutherans. Denmark has an apostolic delegate (to Scandinavia).

Dioc., 1; bp., 1; parishes, 41; priests, 123 (35 dioc., 88 rel.); sem., 4; m. rel., 89; sch., 27; inst., 40; Caths., 25,897; tot. pop., 4,844,319.

Dominican Republic: Caribbean republic on the eastern two-thirds of the island of Hispaniola, bordering on Haiti; capital, Santo Domingo. Evangelization began shortly after discovery by Columbus in 1492 and church organization, the first in America, was established by 1510. Catholicism is the state religion. The Dominican Republic maintains diplomatic relations with Vatican City.

Archd., 1; dioc., 4; abp., 2; bp., 4; parishes, 189; priests, 458 (109 dioc., 349 rel.); sem., 46; p.d., 3; m. rel., 476; w. rel., 1,228; sch., 167; inst., 32; Caths., 3,721,146; tot. pop., 4,034,877.

Ecuador: Republic on the west coast of South America; capital, Quito. Evangelization began in the 1530's. The first diocese was established in 1545. A synod, probably the first in America, was held in 1570's. Multiphased missionary work, spreading from the coastal and mountain regions into the Amazon, made the Church highly influential during the colonial period. The Church was practically enslaved by the constitution enacted in 1824, two years after Ecuador, as part of Colombia, gained independence from Spain. Some change for the better took place later in the century, but from 1891 until the 1930's the Church labored under serious liabilities imposed by liberal governments. The concordat of 1866 was violated; foreign missionaries were barred from the country for some time; the property of religious orders was confiscated; education was taken over by the state; traditional state support was refused; legal standing was denied; attempts to control church offices were made through insistence on rights of patronage. A period of harmony and independence for the Church began after agreement was reached on Church-state relations in 1937. Ecuador maintains diplomatic relations with Vatican City.

Archd., 3; dioc., 10; prel., 1; v.a., 5; p.a., 3; card., 1; abp., 2; bp., 18; parishes, 516; priests, 1,431 (625 dioc., 866 rel.); sem., 175; p.d., 1; m. rel., 1,224; w. rel., 3,027; sch., 666; inst., 201; Caths., 5,689,000; tot. pop., 6,093,798.

El Salvador: Republic in Central America; capital, San Salvador. Evangelization affecting the whole territory followed Spanish occupation in the 1520's. The country was administered by the captaincy general from Spain was declared and it was annexed to Mexico. El Salvador joined the Central American Federation in 1825, decreed its own independence in 1841 and became a republic formally in 1856. El Salvador maintains diplomatic relations with Vatican City.

Archd., 1; dioc., 4; abp., 1; bp., 6; parishes, 209; priests, 435 (222 dioc., 213 rel.); sem., 72; m. rel., 278; w. rel., 687; sch., 279; inst., 41; Caths., 3,239,641; tot. pop., 3,540,753.

England: Center of the United Kingdom of Great Britain (England, Scotland, Wales) and Northern Ireland, off the northwestern coast of Europe; capital, London. The arrival of St. Augustine of Canterbury and a band of monks in 597 marked the beginning of evangelization. Real organization of the Church took place some years after the Synod of Whitby, held in 663. Heavy losses were sustained in the wake of the Danish invasion in the 780's, but recovery starting from the time of Alfred the Great and dating especially from the middle of the 10th century led to Christianization of the whole country and close Church-state relations. The Norman Conquest of 1066 opened the Church in England to European influence. The 13th century was climactic, but decline had already set in by 1300 when the country had an all-time high of 17,000 religious. In the 14th century, John Wycliff presaged the Protestant Reformation. Henry VIII, failing in 1529 to gain annulment of his marriage to Catherine of Aragon, refused to acknowledge papal authority over the Church in England, had himself proclaimed its head, suppressed all houses of religious, and persecuted persons — Sts. Thomas More and John Fisher, among others — for not subscribing to the Oath of Supremacy and Act of Succession. He held the line on other-than-papal doctrine, however, until his death in 1547. Doctrinal aberrations were introduced during the reign of Edward VI (1547-53), through the Order of Communion, two books of Common Prayer, and the Articles of the Established Church. Mary Tudor's attempted Catholic restoration (1553-58) was a disaster, resulting in the deaths of more than 300 Protestants. Elizabeth (1558-1603) firmed up the Established Church with formation of a hierarchy, legal enactments and multi-phased persecution. One hundred and 11 priests and 62 lay persons were among the casualties of persecution during the underground Catholic revival which followed the return to England of missionary priests from France and The Lowlands. Several periods of comparative toleration ensued after Elizabeth's death. The first of several apostolic vicariates was established in 1685; this form of church government was maintained until the restoration of the hierarchy and diocesan organization in 1850. The revolution of 1688 and subsequent developments to about 1781 subjected Catholics to a wide variety of penal laws and disabilities in religious, civic and social life. The situation began to improve in 1791, and from 1801 Parliament frequently considered proposals for the repeal of penal laws against Catholics. The Act of Emancipation restored citizenship rights to Catholics in 1829. Restrictions remained in force for some time afterwards, however, on public religious worship and activity. The hierarchy was restored in 1850. Since then the Catholic Church, existing side by side with the Established Churches of England and Scotland, has followed a general pattern of growth and development. England has an apostolic delegate.

Archd., 4; dioc., 13; ap. ex., 1; card., 1; abp., 3; bp., 29; parishes, 2,237; priests, 6,056 (4,250 dioc., 1,806 rel.); sem., 697; m. rel., 2,488; w. rel., 10,945; sch., 2,231; inst., 281; Caths., 3,991,231; tot. pop., 46,253,000.

Equatorial Guinea: Republic on the west coast of Africa, consisting of Rio Muni on the mainland and the islands of Fernando Po and Annobon in the Gulf of Guinea: capital, Santa Isabel. Evangelization began in 1841.

Dioc., 2; bp., 2; parishes, 57; priests, 41 (17 dioc., 24 rel.); sem., 27; m. rel., 29; w. rel., 40; sch., 13; inst., 4; Caths., 229,212; tot. pop. (1970 est.), 300,000.

Ethiopia (Abyssinia): Constitutional monarchy in northeast Africa; capital, Addis Ababa. The country was evangelized by missionaries from Egypt in the fourth century and had a bishop by about 340. Following the lead of its parent body, the Egyptian (Coptic) Church, the Church in the area succumbed to the Monophysite heresy in the sixth century. Catholic influence was negligible for centuries. An ordinariate for the Ethiopian Rite was established in Eritrea in 1930. An apostolic delegation was set up in Addis Ababa in 1937 and several jurisdictions were organized, some under the Congregation for the Oriental Churches and others under the Congregation for the Evangelization of Peoples. Most of the Catholics in the country are in the former Italian colony of Eritrea. Ethiopia maintains diplomatic relations with Vatican City.

Archd., 1; dioc., 2; v.a., 3; p.a., 2; abp., 1; bp., 7; parishes, 28; priests, 350 (61 dioc., 289 rel.); sem., 60; m. rel., 429; w rel., 956; sch., 180; inst., 98; Caths., 188,632; tot. pop., 25,000,000.

Falkland Islands: British colony off the southern tip of South America.

P.a., 1; parishes, 2; priests, 2 (rel.); m. rel., 3; Caths., 330; tot. pop., 2,100.

Fiji: Independent member of the British Commonwealth, 100 inhabited islands in the southwest Pacific; capital, Suva. Marist missionaries began work in 1844 after Methodism had been firmly established. A prefecture apostolic was organized in 1863. The hierarchy was established in 1966.

Archd., 1; abp., 1; parishes, 35; priests, 78 (10 dioc., 68 rel.); sem., 4; m. rel., 116; w. rel., 243; sch., 44; inst., 3; Caths., 42,618; tot. pop., 530,000.

Finland: Republic in northern Europe; capital, Helsinki. Swedes evangelized the country in the 12th century. The Reformation swept the country, resulting in the prohibition of Catholicism in 1595, general reorganization of ecclesiastical life and affairs, and dominance of the Evangelical Lutheran Church. Catholics were given religious liberty in 1781 but missionaries and conversions were forbidden by law. The first Finnish priest since the Reformation was ordained in 1903 in Paris. A vicariate apostolic for Finland was erected in 1920. A law on religious liberty, enacted in 1923, banned the foundation of monasteries. Finland maintains diplomatic relations with Vatican City.

Dioc., 1; bp., 1; parishes, 5; priests, 22 (5 dioc., 17 rel.); m. rel., 12; w. rel., 39; sch., 2; Caths., 2,809; tot. pop., 4,602,000.

France: Republic in western Europe; capital, Paris. Christianity was known around Lyons by the middle of the second century. By 250 there were 30 bishoprics. The hierarchy reached a fair degree of organization by the end of the fourth century. Vandals and Franks subsequently invaded the territory and caused barbarian turmoil and doctrinal problems because of their Arianism. The Frankish nation was converted following the baptism of Clovis about 496. Christianization was complete by some time in the seventh century. From then on the Church, its leaders and people, figured in virtually every important development — religious, cultural, political and social — through the periods of the Carolingians, feudalism, the Middle Ages and monarchies to the end of the 18th century. The great university of Paris became one of the intellectual centers of the 13th century. Churchmen and secular rulers were involved with developments surrounding the Avignon residence of the popes and curia from 1309 until near the end of the 14th century and with the disastrous Western Schism that followed. Strong currents of Gallicanism and conciliarism ran through ecclesiastical and secular circles in France; the former was an ideology and movement to restrict papal control of the Church in the country, the latter sought to make the pope subservient to a general council. Calvinism invaded the country about the middle of the 16th century and won a strong body of converts. Jansenism with its rigorous spirit and other aberrations appeared in the next century, to be followed by the highly influential Enlightenment. The Revolution which started in 1789 and was succeeded by the Napoleonic period completely changed the status of the Church, taking a toll of numbers by persecution and defection and disenfranchising the Church in practically every way. Throughout the 19th century the Church was caught up in the whirl of imperial and republican developments and made the victim of official hostility, popular indifference and liberal opposition. In this century, the Church has struggled with problems involving the heritage of the Revolution and its aftermath, the alienation of intellectuals, liberalism, the estrangement of the working classes because of the Church's former identification with the ruling class, and the massive needs of contemporary society. France maintains diplomatic relations with Vatican City.

Archd., 18; dioc., 73; prel., 1; ap. ex., 2; ord., 1; card., 10; abp., 15; bp., 98; parishes, 36,162; priests, 46,068 (37,997 dioc., 8,071 rel.); sem., 2,682; m. rel., 13,821; w. rel.,

95,066; sch., 9,825; inst., 2,105; Caths. (est.), 44,500,000; tot. pop., 50,775,000.

Gabon: Republic on the west coast of Equatorial Africa, member of the French Community; capital, Libreville. Sporadic missionary effort took place before 1881 when effective evangelization began. The hierarchy was established in 1955. Gabon maintains diplomatic relations with Vatican City.

Archd., 1; dioc., 2; abp., 1; bp., 2 (1 nat.); parishes, 51; priests, 114 (43 dioc., 71 rel.); sem., 3; m. rel., 121; w. rel., 155; sch., 253; inst., 42; Caths., 267,148; tot. pop., 500,000.

Gambia, The: Republic (1970) on the northwestern coast of Africa, smallest state in Africa, member of the British Commonwealth; capital, Bathurst. The country was under the jurisdiction of a vicariate apostolic until 1931. The hierarchy was established in 1957. The Gambia has a papal representative (the pro-nuncio to Liberia).

Dioc., 1; bp., 1; parishes, 10; priests, 17 (rel.); m. rel., 19; w. rel., 16; sch., 63; inst., 3; Caths., 8,061; tot. pop., 357,000.

Germany: Country in northern Europe partitioned in 1949 into the Communist German Democratic Republic in the East (capital, East Berlin) and the German Federal Republic in the West (capital, Bonn). Christianity was introduced in the third century, if not earlier. Trier, which became a center for missionary activity, had a bishop by 400. Visigoth invaders introduced Arianism in the fifth century but were converted in the seventh century by the East Franks, Celtic and other missionaries. St. Boniface, the apostle of Germany, established real ecclesiastical organization in the eighth century. The Church had great influence during the Carolingian period. Bishops from that time onward began to act in dual roles as pastors and rulers, a state of affairs which led inevitably to confusion and conflict in Church-state relations and perplexing problems of investiture. The Church developed strength and vitality through the Middle Ages but succumbed to abuses which antedated and prepared the ground for the Reformation. Luther's actions from 1517 made Germany a confessional battleground. Religious strife continued until conclusion of the Peace of Westphalia at the end of the Thirty Years' War in 1648. Nearly a century earlier the Peace of Augsburg (1555) had been designed, without success, to assure a degree of tranquillity by recognizing the legitimacy of different religious confessions in different states, depending on the decisions of princes. The implicit principle that princes should control the churches emerged in practice into the absolutism and Josephinism of subsequent years. St. Peter Canisius and his fellow Jesuits spearheaded a Counter Reformation in the second half of the 16th century. Before the end of the century, however, 70 per cent of the population of north and central Germany were Lutheran. Calvinism also had established a strong presence. The Church gained internal strength in a defensive position. Through much of the 19th century, however, its influence was eclipsed by Protestant intellectuals and other influences. It suffered some impoverishment also as a result of shifting boundaries and the secularization of property shortly after 1800. It came under direct attack in the Kulturkampf of the 1870's but helped to generate the opposition which resulted in a dampening of the campaign of Bismarck against it. Despite action by Catholics on the social front and other developments, discrimination against the Church spilled over into the 20th century and lasted beyond World War I. Catholics in politics struggled with others to pull the country through numerous postwar crises. The dissolution of the Center Party, agreed to by the bishops in 1933 without awareness of the ultimate consequences, contributed negatively to the rise of Hitler to supreme power. Church officials protested the Nazi anti-Church and anti-Semitic actions, but to no avail. After World War II Christian leadership had much to do with the recovery of Western Germany. East Germany, gone Communist under Russian auspices, initiated a program of control and repression of the Church in 1948 and 1949. With no prospect of success for measures designed to split bishops, priests, religious and lay persons, the regime has concentrated most of its attention on mind control, especially of the younger generation, by the elimination of religious schools, curtailment of freedom for religious instruction and formation, severe restriction of the religious press, and the substitution since the mid-50's of youth initiation and Communist ceremonies for the rites of baptism, confirmation, marriage, and funerals. Bishops are generally forbidden to travel outside the Republic. The number of priests is decreasing, partly because of reduced seminary enrollments ordered by the government since 1958.

Archd., 5; dioc., 18; ap. ex., 1; card. 5; abp., 2; bp., 51; parishes, 11,546; priests, 25,669 (19,366 dioc., 6,303 rel.); sem., 2,542; p.d., 79; m. rel., 11,337; w. rel., 74,919; sch., 909; inst., 10,187. Catholics number 30,839,824; they constitute approximately 46 per cent of the West German population of 61,682,000 (UN est., 1970) and 10 per cent of the East German population of 17,259,000 (UN est., 1970).

Ghana: Republic on the western coast of Africa, bordering on the Gulf of Guinea, member of the British Commonwealth; capital, Accra. Priests visited the country in 1482, 11 years after discovery by the Portuguese, but missionary effort — hindered by the slave trade and other factors — was slight until 1880 when systematic evangelization began. A prefecture apostolic was set up in 1943. The hierarchy was established in 1950. Ghana has an apostolic delegate.

Archd., 1; dioc., 7; abp., 1 (nat.); bp., 7 (4 nat.); parishes, 128; priests, 316 (93 dioc., 223 rel.); sem., 83; p.d., 1; m. rel., 360; w. rel., 313; sch., 1,760; inst., 50; Caths., 1,041,366; tot. pop. (UN est., 1970), 9,030,000.

Gibraltar: British colony on the tip of the Spanish Peninsula on the Mediterranean. Evangelization took place after the Moors were driven out near the end of the 15th century. The Church was hindered by the British who acquired the colony in 1713. Most of the Catholics were, and are, Spanish and Italian immigrants and their descendants. A vicariate apostolic was organized in 1817. The diocese was erected in 1910.

Dioc., 1; bp., 1; parishes, 2; priests, 9 (dioc.); sem., 1; m. rel., 10; w. rel., 22; sch., 3; inst., 1; Caths., 19,133; tot. pop., 28,000.

Gilbert Islands: British colony in the southwest Pacific in Oceania, consisting of 16 coral atolls including the Gilbert and Ellice Islands. French Missionaries of the Sacred Heart began work in the islands in 1888. A vicariate for the islands was organized in 1897. The hierarchy was established in 1966.

Dioc., 1; bp., 1; parishes, 18; priests, 23 (3 dioc., 20 rel.); m. rel., 30; w. rel., 42; sch., 115; Caths., 25,352; tot. pop., 59,000.

Greece, including Crete: Kingdom in southeastern Europe on the Balkan Peninsula; capital, Athens. St. Paul preached the Gospel at Athens and Corinth on his second missionary journey and visited the country again on his third tour. Other Apostles may have passed through also. Two bishops from Greece attended the First Council of Nicaea. After the division of the Roman Empire, the Church remained Eastern in rite and later broke ties with Rome as a result of the schism of 1054. A Latin-Rite jurisdiction was set up during the period of the Latin Empire of Constantinople, 1204-1261, but crumbled afterwards. Unity efforts of the Council of Florence had poor results. The country now has Greek Catholic and Latin jurisdictions. The Greek Orthodox Church is predominant.

Archd., 3; dioc., 4; v.a., 1; ap. ex., 1; ord., 1; abp., 3; bp., 2; parishes, 37; priests, 112 (66 dioc., 46 rel.); sem., 18; m. rel., 99; w. rel., 181; sch., 30; inst., 14; Caths., 45,688; tot. pop. (1971 census), 8,736,367.

Greenland: Danish island province northeast of North America; capital, Godthaab. Catholicism was introduced about 1000. The first diocese was established in 1124 and a line of bishops was dated from then until 1537. The first known churches in the western hemisphere, dating from about the 11th century, were on Greenland; the remains of 19 have been unearthed. The departure of Scandinavians and spread of the Reformation reduced the Church to nothing. The Moravian Brethren evangelized the Eskimos from the 1720's to 1901. By 1930 the Danish Church — Evangelical Lutheran — was in full possession. Since 1930 priests have been in Greenland, which is part of the Copenhagen diocese. There are about 50 Catholics in the area.

Guadeloupe and Martinique: French overseas departments in the Leeward Islands of the West Indies; capitals, Basse-Terre (Guadeloupe) and Fort-de-France (Martinique). Catholicism was introduced in the islands in the 16th century. The hierarchy was established in 1967.

Archd., 1; dioc., 1; abp., 1; bp., 2; parishes, 92; priests, 227 (101 dioc., 126 rel.); sem., 13; m. rel., 171; w. rel., 490; sch., 30; inst., 22; Caths., 620,000; tot. pop., 669,000.

Guam: US territory in the southwest Pacific; capital, Agana. The first Mass was offered in the Mariana Islands in 1521. The islands were evangelized by the Jesuits, from 1668, and other missionaries. The first native Micronesian bishop was ordained in 1970.

Dioc., 1; bp., 1; parishes, 25; priests, 54 (22 dioc., 32 rel.); sem., 6; m. rel., 41; w. rel., 186; sch., 15; inst., 1; Caths., 83,941; tot. pop., 104,083.

Guatemala: Republic in Central America; capital, Guatemala City. Evangelization dates from the beginning of Spanish occupation in 1524. The first diocese, for all Central American territories administered by the captaincy general of Guatemala, was established in 1534. The country became independent in 1839, following annexation to Mexico in 1821, secession in 1823 and membership in the Central American Federation from 1825. In 1870, a government installed by a liberal revolution repudiated the concordat of 1853 and took active measures against the Church. Separation of Church and state was decreed; religious orders were suppressed and their property seized; priests and religious were exiled; schools were secularized. Full freedom was subsequently granted. Guatemala maintains diplomatic relations with Vatican City.

Archd., 1; dioc., 8; prel., 2; a.a., 2; card., 1; bp., 15; parishes, 296; priests, 603 (185 dioc.; 418 rel.); sem., 57; p.d., 1; m. rel., 614; w. rel., 777; sch., 213; inst., 125; Caths. (est.), 4,500,000; tot. pop., 5,183,000.

Guiana, French: French overseas department on the northeast coast of South America; capital, Cayenne. Catholicism was introduced in the 17th century. The Cayenne diocese was established in 1956.

Dioc., 1; bp., 1; parishes, 21; priests, 28 (7 dioc., 21 rel.); sem., 2; m. rel., 22; w. rel., 94; sch., 12; inst., 18; Caths., 42,062; tot. pop. (1971 est.), 51,000.

Guinea: Republic on the west coast of Africa; capital, Conakry. Occasional missionary work followed exploration by the Portuguese about the middle of the 15th century; organized effort dates from 1877. The hierarchy was established in 1955. Following independence from France in 1958, Catholic schools were nationalized, youth organizations banned and missionaries restricted. Foreign missionaries were expelled in 1967. In 1971

Archbishop Tchidimbo of Conakry was sentenced to life imprisonment on a charge of conspiring to overthrow the government. Guinea has an apostolic delegate (to West Africa).

Archd., 1; dioc., 1; p.a., 1; abp., 1 (nat., imprisoned 1971); bp. 1 (living in Switzerland); parishes, 12; priests, 13 (11 dioc., 2 rel.); sem., 9; m. rel., 3; w. rel., 12; inst., 1; Caths., 36,235; tot. pop., 3,993,000.

Guinea, Portuguese: Portuguese territory on the west coast of Africa; capital, Bissau. Catholicism was introduced in the second half of the 15th century but limited missionary work, hampered by the slave trade, had meager results. Missionary work in this century dates from 1933. A prefecture apostolic was established in 1955.

P.a., 1; parishes, 13; priests, 31 (rel.); m. rel., 44; w. rel., 30; sch., 82; inst., 22; Caths., 30,491; tot. pop., 560,000.

Guyana: Republic on the northern coast of South America; capital, Georgetown. In 1899 the Catholic Church and other churches were given equal status with the Church of England and the Church of Scotland, which had sole rights up to that time. Most of the Catholics are Portuguese. The Georgetown diocese was established in 1956, 10 years before Guyana became independent of England. The first native bishop was appointed in 1971.

Dioc., 1; bp., 2 (1 nat.); parishes, 24; priests, 71 (6 dioc., 65 rel.); sem., 11; m. rel., 71; w. rel., 75; sch., 60; inst., 8; Caths., 107,000; tot. pop. (UN est., 1970), 783,500.

Haiti: Caribbean republic on the western third of Hispaniola adjacent to the Dominican Republic; capital, Port-au-Prince. Evangelization followed discovery by Columbus in 1492. Capuchins and Jesuits did most of the missionary work in the 18th century. From 1804, when independence was declared, until 1860, the country was in schism. Relations were regularized by a concordat concluded in 1860, when an archdiocese and four dioceses were established. Factors hindering the development of the Church have been a shortage of native clergy, inadequate religious instruction and the prevalence of voodoo. Political upheavals in the 1960's had serious effects on the Church. Haiti maintains diplomatic relations with Vatican City.

Archd., 1; dioc., 6; abp., 1; bp., 9; parishes, 189; priiests, 395 (231 dioc., 164 rel.); sem., 41; m. rel., 348; w. rel., 796; sch., 280; inst., 88; Caths., 4,240,700; tot. pop., 4,901,000.

Honduras: Republic in Central America; capital, Tegucigalpa. Evangelization preceded establishment of the first diocese in the 16th century. Under Spanish rule and after independence from 1823, the Church held a favored position until 1880 when equal legal status was given to all religions. Honduras maintains diplomatic relations with Vatican City.

Archd., 1; dioc., 3; prel., 2; abp., 1; bp., 6;
parishes, 110; priests, 234 (61 dioc., 173 rel.); sem., 22; m. rel., 200; w. rel., 421; sch., 54; inst., 27; Caths., 2,412,601; tot. pop., 2,582,000.

Honduras, British: Crown colony in Central America; capital, Belize. Its history has points in common with the history of Guatemala, where evangelization began in the 16th century.

Dioc., 1; bp., 1; parishes, 12; priests, 36 (10 dioc., 26 rel.); sem., 3; m. rel., 34; w. rel., 114; sch., 111; inst., 1; Caths., 75,679; tot. pop., 119,645.

Hong Kong: British crown colony at the mouth of the Canton River, adjacent to the southeast Chinese province of Kwangtung. A prefecture apostolic was established in 1841. Members of the Pontifical Institute for Foreign Missions began work there in 1858. The Hong Kong diocese was erected in 1946.

Dioc., 1; bp., 2; parishes, 29; priests, 351 (68 dioc., 283 rel.); sem., 36; m. rel., 435; w. rel., 798; sch., 262; inst., 70; Caths., 247,961; tot. pop., 4,100,000.

Hungary: People's republic in east central Europe; capital, Budapest. The early origins of Christianity in the country, whose territory was subject to a great deal of change, is not known. Magyars accepted Christianity about the end of the 10th century. St. Stephen I (d. 1038) promoted its spread and helped to organize some of its historical dioceses. Bishops early became influential in politics as well as in the Church. For centuries the country served as a buffer for the Christian West against barbarians from the East, notably the Mongols in the 13th century. Religious orders, whose foundations started from the 1130's, provided the most effective missionaries, pastors and teachers. Outstanding for years were the Franciscans and Dominicans; the Jesuits were noted for their work in the Counter-Reformation from the second half of the 16th century onwards. Hussites and Waldensians prepared the way for the Reformation which struck at almost the same time as the Turks. The Reformation made considerable progress after 1526, resulting in the conversion of large numbers to Lutheranism and Calvinism by the end of the century. Most of them or their descendants returned to the Church later, but many Magyars remained staunch Calvinists. Turks repressed the churches, Protestant as well as Catholic, during a reign of 150 years but they managed to survive. Domination of the Church was one of the objectives of government policy during the reigns of Maria Theresa and Joseph II in the second half of the 18th century; their Josephinism affected Church-state relations until the first World War. More than 100,000 Eastern Rite schismatics were reunited with Rome about the turn of the 18th century. Secularization increased in the second half of the 19th century, which also witnessed the birth of many new Catholic organizations and movements to influence life in the nation and the Church. Catholics were involved in the social chaos and anti-religious atmosphere of the years following World War I, struggling with their compatriots for religious as well as political survival. After World War II Communist strength, which had manifested itself with less intensity earlier in the century, was great long before it forced the legally elected president out of office in 1947 and imposed a Soviet type of constitution on the country in 1949. The campaign against the Church started with the disbanding of Catholic organizations in 1946. In 1948, "Caritas," the Catholic charitable organization, was taken over and all Catholic schools, colleges and institutions were suppressed. Interference in church administration and attempts to split the bishops preceded the arrest of Cardinal Mindszenty on Dec. 26, 1948, and his sentence to life imprisonment in 1949. (He was free for a few days during the unsuccessful uprising of 1956. He then took up residence at the US Embassy in Budapest where he remained until September, 1971, when he was permitted to leave the country. In 1972, he was residing in Vienna.) In 1950, religious orders and congregations were suppressed and 10,000 religious were interned. At least 30 priests and monks were assassinated, jailed or deported. About 4,000 priests and religious were confined in jail or concentration camps. The government sponsored a national "Progressive Catholic" church and captive organizations for priests and "Catholic Action," which attracted only a small minority. Signs were clear in 1965 and 1966 that a 1964 agreement with the Holy See regarding episcopal appointments had settled nothing. Six bishops were appointed by the Holy See and some other posts were filled, but none of the prelates were free from government surveillance and harassment. Four new bishops were appointed by the Holy See in January and ordained in Budapest in February, 1969; three elderly prelates resigned their sees. Shortly thereafter, peace priests complained that the "too Roman" new bishops would not deal with them. In 1972 the government accepted the appointment of five new bishops.

Archd., 3; dioc., 9; abb., 1; ap. ex., 1; card., 1; abp., 2; bp., 14; parishes, 2,074; priests, 3,699 (3,531 dioc., 168 rel.); sem., 290; m. rel., 202; w. rel., 57; sch., 6; inst., 6; Caths., 6,241,645; tot. pop. (UN est., 1970), 10,331,000.

Iceland: Island republic between Norway and Greenland; capital, Reykjavik. Irish hermits were there in the eighth century. Missionaries subsequently evangelized the island and Christianity was officially accepted about 1000. The first bishop was ordained in 1056. The Black Death had dire effects and spiritual decline set in during the 15th century. Lutheranism was introduced from Denmark between 1537 and 1552 and made the official

religion. Some Catholic missionary work was done in the 19th century. Religious freedom was granted to the few Catholics in 1874. A vicariate was erected in 1929. Iceland has an apostolic delegate (to Scandinavia).

Dioc., 1; bp., 1; parishes, 2; priests, 8 (2 dioc., 6 rel.); m. rel., 6; w. rel., 57; sch., 1; inst., 3; Caths., 1,081; tot. pop., 204,344.

India: Republic on the subcontinent of south central Asia, member of the British Commonwealth; capital, New Delhi. Longstanding tradition credits the Apostle Thomas with the introduction of Christianity in the Kerala area. Evangelization followed the establishment of Portuguese posts and the conquest of Goa in 1510. Jesuits, Franciscans, Dominicans, Augustinians and members of other religious orders figured in the early missionary history. An archdiocese for Goa, with two suffragan sees, was set up in 1558. Five provincial councils were held between 1567 and 1606. The number of Catholics in 1572 was estimated to be 280,000. This figure rose to 800,000 in 1700 and declined to 500,000 in 1800. Missionaries had some difficulties with the British East India Co. which exercised virtual government control from 1757 to 1858. They also had trouble because of a conflict that developed between policies of the Portuguese government, which pressed its rights of patronage in episcopal and clerical appointments, and the Congregation for the Propagation of the Faith, which sought greater freedom of action in the same appointments. This struggle eventuated in the schism of Goa between 1838 and 1857. In 1886, when the number of Catholics was estimated to be one million, the hierarchy for India and Ceylon was restored. Jesuits contributed greatly to the development of Catholic education from the second half of the 19th century. A large percentage of the Catholic population, mostly from the lower castes, is located around Goa and Kerala and farther south. The country is predominantly Hindu. India maintains diplomatic relations with Vatican City.

Patriarchate, 1 (titular, of East Indies); archd., 18; dioc., 60; p.a., 3; ap. ex., 6; card., 2; abp., 15; bp., 65; parishes, 3,239; priests, 9,440 (5,883 dioc., 3,557 rel.); sem., 2,208; p.d., 12; m. rel., 7,719; w. rel., 33,910; sch., 7,899; inst., 2,219; Caths., 8,832,335; tot. pop. (1971 census est.) 547,000,000.

Indonesia: Republic southeast of Asia, consisting of some 3,000 islands including Kalimantan (Borneo), Celebes, Java, the Lesser Sundas, Moluccas, Sumatra, Timor and Irian Barat (western part of New Guinea); capital, Djakarta. Evangelization by the Portuguese began about 1511. St. Francis Xavier, greatest of the modern missionaries, spent some 14 months in the area. Christianity was strongly rooted in some parts of the islands by 1600. Islam's rise to dominance began at this time. The Dutch East Indies Co., which gained effective control in the 17th century, banned evangelization by Catholic missionaries for some time but Dutch secular and religious priests managed to resume the work. A vicariate of Batavia for all the Dutch East Indies was set up in 1841. About 90 per cent of the population is Moslem. The hierarchy was established in 1961. Indonesia maintains diplomatic relations with Vatican City.

Archd., 7; dioc., 24; p.a., 2; card., 1 (nat.); abp., 7 (2 nat.); bp., 21 (1 nat.); parishes, 353; priests, 1,427 (117 dioc., 1,310 rel.); sem., 202; m. rel., 2,421; w. rel., 3,630; sch., 4,003; inst., 582; Caths., 2,337,645; tot. pop. (UN, 1970), 121,209,000.

Iran: Constitutional monarchy in southwestern Asia, between the Caspian Sea and the Persian Gulf; capital, Teheran. Some of the earliest Christian communities were established in this area outside the (then) Roman Empire. They suffered persecution in the fourth century and were then cut off from the outside world. Nestorianism was generally professed in the late fifth century. Islam became dominant after 640. Some later missionary work was attempted but without success. Religious liberty was granted in 1834, but Catholics were the victims of a massacre in 1918. Islam is the religion of perhaps 98 per cent of the population. In 1964 the country had 100,000 Monophysites, the largest group of Christians, and some 20,000 Nestorians. Catholics belong to the Latin, Armenian and Chaldean rites. Iran (Persia until 1935) maintains diplomatic relations with Vatican City.

Archd., 4; dioc., 2; abp., 2; bp., 1; parishes, 20; priests, 46 (6 dioc., 40 rel.); sem., 1; m. rel., 52; w. rel., 54; sch., 27; inst., 8; Caths. (approx.), 30,000; tot. pop. (UN est., 1970), 28,682,000.

Iraq: Republic in southwestern Asia, between Iran and Saudi Arabia; capital, Baghdad. Some of the earliest Christian communities were established in the area, whose history resembles that of Iran. Catholics belong to the Armenian, Chaldean, Latin and Syrian rites; Chaldeans are most numerous. Islam is the religion of some 90 per cent of the population. Iraq maintains diplomatic relations with Vatican City.

Patriarchate, 1 (titular, Babylonia for the Chaldeans); archd., 8; dioc., 5; mission "sui juris," 1; patriarch, 1; abp., 7; bp., 4; parishes, 119; priests, 157 (128 dioc., 29 rel.); sem., 44; m. rel., 53; w. rel., 203; Caths., 257,662; tot. pop. (UN est., 1970), 9,440,000.

Ireland: Republic in the British Isles; capital, Dublin. St. Patrick, who is venerated as the apostle of Ireland, evangelized parts of the island for some years after the middle of the fifth century. Conversion of the island was not accomplished, however, until the seventh century or later. Celtic monks were the principal missionaries. The Church was organized along monastic lines at first, but a movement developed in the 11th century for the establishment of jurisdiction along episcopal lines. By that time many Roman usages had been adopted. The Church gathered strength during the period from the Norman Conquest of England to the reign of Henry VIII despite a wide variety of rivalries, wars and other disturbances. Henry introduced an age of repression of the faith which continued for many years under several of his successors. The Irish suffered from proscription of the Catholic faith, economic and social disabilities, subjection to absentee landlords and a plantation system designed to keep them from owning property, and actual persecution which took an uncertain toll of lives up until about 1714. Most of those living in the northern part of Ireland became Anglican and Presbyterian in the 1600's but the south remained strong in faith. Some penal laws remained in force until emancipation in 1829. Nearly 100 years later Ireland was divided by two enactments which made Northern Ireland, consisting of six counties, part of the United Kindgom (1920) and gave dominion status to the Irish Free State, made up of the other 26 counties (1922). This state (Eire, in Gaelic) was proclaimed the Republic of Ireland in 1949. The Catholic Church enjoys privileged status but religious freedom is guaranteed for all. Ireland maintains diplomatic relations with Vatican City.

Archd., 4; dioc., 22; card., 1; abp., 3; bp., 24; parishes, 1,190; priests, 5,624 (3,649 dioc., 1,975 rel.); sem., 672; m. rel., 5,342; w. rel., 14,335; sch., 4,377; inst., 235 (preceding figures include Northern Ireland); Caths., 2,750,000; tot. pop., 2,944,000.

Ireland, Northern: Part of the United Kingdom, it consists of six of the nine counties of Ulster in the northeast corner of Ireland; capital, Belfast. History is given under Ireland, above. For 1972 developments, see Index.

Caths. (approx.), 504,000; · tot. pop., 1,524,000 (other statistics are included in Ireland).

Israel: Parliamentary democracy in the Middle East, at the eastern end of the Mediterranean; capitals, Jerusalem and Tel Aviv (diplomatic). Israel was the birthplace of Christianity, the site of the first Christian communities. Some persecution was suffered in the early Christian era and again during the several hundred years of Roman control. Moslems conquered the territory in the seventh century and, except for the period of the Kingdom of Jerusalem established by Crusaders, remained in control most of the time up until World War I. The Church survived in the area, sometimes just barely, but it did not prosper greatly or show any notable increase in numbers. The British took over the protectorate of the area after World War I. Partition into Israel for the Jews and Palestine for the Arabs was approved by the United Nations in 1947. War broke out a year later with the proclamation of the Republic of

Israel. The Israelis won the war and 50 percent more territory than they had originally been ceded. War broke out again for six days in June, 1967, resulting in a Middle East crisis that shows no signs of early settlement. Caught in the middle of the conflict are hundreds of thousands of dispossessed Palestinian refugees. Judaism is the faith professed by about 85 percent of the inhabitants; approximately one-third of them are considered observants. Most of the Arab minority are Moslems. The Acre archdiocese for Melkites is situated in Israel. Maronites are subject to the bishop of Tyr, Lebanon. Latins are under the jurisdiction of the Roman patriarchate of Jerusalem. Israel has an apostolic delegate.

Caths. (1969), 43,864; tot. pop. (1971 est.), 3,000,000.

Italy: Republic in southern Europe; capital, Rome. A Christian community was formed early at Rome, probably by the middle of the first century. St. Peter established his see there. He and St. Paul suffered death for the faith there in the 60's. The early Christians were persecuted at various times there, as in other parts of the empire, but the Church developed in numbers and influence, gradually spreading out from towns and cities in the center and south to rural areas and the north. Organization, in the process of formation in the second century, developed greatly between the fifth and eighth centuries. By the latter date the Church had already come to grips with serious problems, including doctrinal and disciplinary disputes that threatened the unity of faith, barbarian invasions, and the need for the pope and bishops to take over civil responsibilities because of imperial default. The Church has been at the center of life on the peninsula throughout the centuries. It emerged from underground in 313, with the Edict of Milan, and rose to a position of prestige and lasting influence. It educated and converted the barbarians, preserved culture through the early Middle Ages and passed it on to later times, suffered periods of decline and gained strength through recurring reforms, engaged in military combat for political reasons and intellectual combat for the preservation and development of doctrine, saw and patronized the development of the arts, experienced all human strengths and weaknesses in its members, knew triumph and the humiliation of failure. For long centuries, from the fourth to the 19th, the Church was a temporal as well as spiritual power. This temporal aspect complicated its history in Italy. Since the 1870's, however, when the Papal States were annexed by the Kingdom of Italy, the history became simpler — but remained complicated — as the Church, shorn of temporal power, began to find new freedom for the fulfillment of its spiritual mission. Italy maintains diplomatic relations with Vatican City.

Patriarchate 1; archd., 53; dioc., over 200;

prel., 4; abb., 9; card., 34 (as of Aug. 30, 1972); abp., 49; bp., 219; parishes, 27,117; priests, 63,498 (42,007 dioc., 21,491 rel.); sem., 6,580; p.d., 20; m. rel., 31,384; w. rel., 151,050; sch., 4,924; inst., 4,432; Caths. (1969) 53,025,212; tot. pop., 53,700,000.

Ivory Coast: Republic in western Africa, member of the French Community; capital, Abidjan. The Holy Ghost Fathers began systematic evangelization in 1895. The first native priests from the area were ordained in 1934. The hierarchy was set up in 1955. Ivory Coast maintains diplomatic relations with Vatican City.

Archd., 1; dioc., 7; abp., 1 (nat.); bp., 8 (3 nat.); parishes, 120; priests, 363 (91 dioc., 272 rel.); sem., 38; m. rel., 355; w. rel., 366; sch., 493; inst., 55; Caths., 501,262; tot. pop., 4,400,000.

Jamaica: Parliamentary democracy in the West Indies, member of the British Commonwealth; capital, Kingston. Franciscans and Dominicans evangelized the island from about 1512 until 1655. Missionary work was interrupted after the English took possession but was resumed by Jesuits about the turn of the 19th century. A vicariate apostolic was organized in 1837. The hierarchy was established in 1967.

Archd., 1; dioc., 1; abp., 1; bp., 1; parishes, 16; priests, 120 (22 dioc., 98 rel.); sem., 8; m. rel., 110; w. rel., 248; sch., 68; inst., 8; Caths., 158,000; tot. pop. (UN est., 1970), 2,000,000.

Japan: Constitutional monarchy in the northwest Pacific; capital, Tokyo. Jesuits began evangelization in the middle of the 16th century and about 300,000 converts, most of them in Kyushu, were reported at the end of the century. The Nagasaki Martyrs were victims of persecution in 1597. Another persecution took some 4,000 lives between 1614 and 1651. Missionaries, banned for two centuries, returned about the middle of the 19th century and found Christian communities still surviving in Nagasaki and other places in Kyushu. A vicariate was organized in 1846. The hierarchy was established in 1891. Religious freedom was guaranteed in 1889. Japan maintains diplomatic relations with Vatican City.

Archd., 3; dioc., 12; p.a., 1; abp., 3; bp., 14; parishes, 677; priests, 19,926 (447 dioc., 1,479 rel.); sem., 140; m. rel., 2,015; w. rel., 6,474; sch., 378; inst., 239; Caths., 357,478; tot. pop., 105,000,000 (most figures are from Fides).

Jerusalem: The entire city, site of the first Christian community, has been under Israeli control since the Israeli-Arab war of June, 1967. There are two patriarchates in the city, Melkite and Latin. Jerusalem has an apostolic delegate.

Jordan: Hashemite kingdom in the Middle East; capital, Amman. Christianity there dates from apostolic times. Survival of the faith was threatened many times under the rule of Moslems from 636 and Ottoman Turks from 1517 to 1918, and in the Islamic

Emirate of Trans-Jordan from 1918 to 1949. Since the creation of Israel, some 500,000 Palestinian refugees, some of them Christians, have been in Jordan. Islam is the state religion but religious freedom is guaranteed for all. Jordan has an apostolic delegate.

The statistics which follow are for the Melkite-Rite Catholics of the Archdiocese of Petra and Philadelphia in Jordan. Separate statistics are not available for the Latin (Roman)-Rite Catholics under the jurisdiction of the Latin patriarchate of Jerusalem.

Archd., 1; abp., 1; parishes, 36; priests, 20 (16 dioc., 4 rel.); sem., 3; m. rel., 4; w. rel., 25; sch., 20; inst., 3; Caths., 16,000 (statistics are for Archdiocese of Petra and Philadelphia for the Melkites; tot. pop. (UN est., 1970), 2,320,000.

Kashmir and Jammu: Statistics included in India.

Kenya: Republic in eastern Africa bordering on the Indian Ocean, member of the British Commonwealth; capital, Nairobi. Systematic evangelization by the Holy Ghost Fathers began in 1892, nearly 40 years after the start of work by Protestant missionaries. The hierarchy was established in 1953. Kenya maintains diplomatic relations with Vatican City.

Archd., 1; dioc., 10; p.a., 2; abp., 1 (nat.); bp., 9 (4 nat.); parishes, 173; priests, 634 (114 dioc., 520 rel.); sem., 149; m. rel., 683; w. rel., 1,223; sch., 1,686; inst., 607; Caths., 1,628,102; tot. pop., 11,000,000.

Khmer Republic (Cambodia): Republic (Oct. 9, 1970) in southeast Asia, bordering on the Gulf of Siam, Thailand, Laos and Vietnam; capital Phnompenh. Evangelization dating from the second half of the 16th century had limited results, more among Vietnamese than Khmers. Several thousand Catholics of Vietnamese origin were forced to flee in 1970. Buddhism is the state religion. Khmer has an apostolic delegate.

V.a., 1; p.a., 2; bp., 1; parishes, 6; priests, 44 (24 dioc., 20 rel.); sem., 1; m. rel., 24; w. rel., 91; Caths., 21,057; tot. pop., 6,600,000.

Korea: Peninsula in eastern Asia, east of China, divided into the (Communist) Democratic People's Republic in the North, formed May 1, 1948, with Pyongyang as its capital; and the Republic of Korea in the South, with Seoul as the capital. Some Catholics may have been in Korea before it became a "hermit kingdom" toward the end of the 16th century and closed its borders to foreigners. The real introduction to Catholicism came through lay converts in the last quarter of the 18th century. A priest arriving in the country in 1794 found 4,000 Catholics there who had never seen a priest. A vicariate was erected in 1831 but was not manned for several years thereafter. There were 15,000 Catholics by 1857. Four persecutions in the 19th century took a terrible toll; several thousands died in the last one, 1866-69. Freedom of religion was

granted in 1883 when Korea opened its borders. Progress was made thereafter. The hierarchy was established in 1962. Since the war of 1950-1953, there have been no signs of Catholic life in the North, which has been blanketed by a news blackout. The South maintains diplomatic relations with Vatican City.

North Korea: Dioc., 2; abb., 1; bp., 1; Caths. (1969), 100,000; tot. pop. (UN est., 1970), 13,980,000.

South Korea: Archd., 3; dioc., 10; p.a., 1; card., 1; abp., 1; bp., 10; parishes, 416; priests, 908 (587 dioc., 321 rel.); sem., 579; m. rel., 535; w. rel., 2,232; sch., 88; inst., 111; Caths., 793,267; tot. pop. (UN est., 1970), 31,793,000.

Kuwait: Constitutional monarchy (sultanate or sheikdom) in southwest Asia bordering on the Persian Gulf. Remote Christian origins probably date to apostolic times. Islam is the predominant and official religion. Kuwait maintains diplomatic relations with Vatican City.

V.a., 1; parishes, 4; priests, 12 (6 dioc., 6 rel.); m. rel., 6; w. rel., 31; Caths., 17,200; tot. pop., 733,196.

Laos: Constitutional monarchy in southeast Asia, surrounded by China, Vietnam, Khmer Republic, Thailand and Burma; capitals, Vientiane (administrative) and Luang Prabang (royal). Systematic evangelization by French missionaries started about 1881; earlier efforts ended in 1688. A vicariate apostolic was organized in 1899 when there were 8,000 Catholics and 2,000 catechumens in the country. Buddhism is the state religion. Laos has an apostolic delegate.

V.a., 4; bp., 4; priests, 111 (14 dioc., 97 rel.); sem., 3; m. rel., 112; w. rel., 168; sch., 54; inst., 45; Caths., 27,736; tot. pop. (UN est., 1970), 2,982,000.

Lebanon: Republic in the Middle East, north of Israel; capital, Beirut. Christianity, introduced in apostolic times, was firmly established by the end of the fourth century and has remained so despite heavy Moslem influence since early in the seventh century. The country is the center of the Maronite Rite. Lebanon maintains diplomatic relations with Vatican City.

There are 16 ecclesiastical jurisdictions in Lebanon serving the following rites: Armenian (1 diocese); Chaldean (1 diocese); Roman (1 vicariate apostolic); Maronite (3 archdioceses and 3 dioceses); Melkite (3 archdioceses, 5 dioceses); the Syrians are served by a patriarchal vicar. The patriarchs of Antioch of the Syrians and Antioch of the Maronites reside in Lebanon.

Caths. (1969), 812,717; tot. pop. (UN est., 1970), 2,790,000.

Lesotho: Constitutional monarchy, an enclave in the southeastern part of the Republic of South Africa; capital, Maseru. Oblates of Mary Immaculate, the first Catholic missionaries in the area, started evangelization in

1862. A prefecture apostolic was organized in 1894. The hierarchy was established in 1951. Lesotho maintains diplomatic relations with Vatican City.

Archd., 1; dioc., 2; abp., 1 (nat.), bp., 2 (1 nat.); parishes, 44; priests, 147 (18 dioc., 129 rel.); sem., 11; m. rel., 239; w. rel., 705; sch., 486; inst., 63; Caths., 422,021; tot. pop. (UN est., 1970), 1,040,000.

Liberia: Republic in western Africa, bordering on the Atlantic; capital, Monrovia. Missionary work and influence, dating interruptedly from the 16th century, were slight before the Society of African Missions undertook evangelization in 1906. Liberia maintains diplomatic relations with Vatican City.

V.a., 2; abp., 1; bp., 1; parishes, 13; priests, 44 (6 dioc., 38 rel.); sem., 3; m. rel., 57; w. rel., 71; sch., 41; inst., 12; Caths., 21,545; tot. pop. (UN est., 1970), 1,170,000.

Libya: Arab republic in northern Africa, on the Mediterranean between the United Arab Republic (Egypt) and Tunisia; capitals are Tripoli and Benghasi. Christianity was probably preached in the area at an early date but was overcome by the spread of Islam from the 630's. Islamization was complete by 1067 and there has been no Christian influence since then. The Catholics in the country belong to the foreign colony. Islam is the state religion. Libya has an apostolic delegate (to North Africa).

V.a., 3; p.a., 1; bp., 2; parishes, 23; priests, 42 (rel.); m. rel., 68; w. rel., 159; sch., 15; inst., 25; Caths., 41,579; tot. pop., 1,726,000.

Liechtenstein: Constitutional monarchy in central Europe, in the Alps and on the Rhine between Switzerland and Austria; capital, Vaduz. Christianity in the country dates from the fourth century; the area has been under the jurisdiction of Chur, Switzerland, since about that time. The Reformation had hardly any influence in the country. Catholicism is the state religion but religious freedom for all is guaranteed by law. Pop., 21,000.

Luxembourg: Constitutional monarchy in western Europe, between Belgium, Germany and France; capital, Luxembourg. Christianity, introduced in the fifth and sixth centuries, was firmly established by the end of the eighth century. A full-scale parish system was in existence in the ninth century. Monastic influence was strong until the Reformation, which had minimal influence in the country. The Church experienced some adverse influence from the currents of the French Revolution. Luxembourg maintains diplomatic relations with Vatican City.

Dioc., 1; bp., 1; parishes, 274; priests, 526 (429 dioc., 97 rel.); sem., 18; m. rel., 126; w. rel., 1,634; sch., 23; inst., 69; Caths., 319,000 (1969); tot. pop., (UN est., 1970), 340,000.

Macao: Portuguese province in southeast Asia across the Pearl River estuary from Hong Kong. Christianity was introduced by the Jesuits in 1557. Diocese was established in 1576. Macao served as a base for missionary work in Japan and China.

Dioc., 1; bp., 1; parishes, 8; priests, 80 (45 dioc., 35 rel.); sem., 17; m. rel., 49; w. rel., 224; sch., 87; inst., 19; Caths., 26,371; tot. pop., 260,000.

Madeira Islands: Portuguese province, an archipelago 340 miles west of the northwestern coast of Africa; capital, Funchal. Catholicism has had a continuous history since the first half of the 15th century. Statistics are included in those for Portugal.

Malagasy Republic (Madagascar and adjoining islands): Member of the French Community, off the eastern coast of Africa; capital, Tananarive. Missionary efforts were generally fruitless from early in the 16th century until the Jesuits were permitted to start open evangelization about 1845. A prefecture apostolic was set up in 1850 and a vicariate apostolic in the north was placed in charge of the Holy Ghost Fathers in 1898. There were 100,000 Catholics by 1900. The first native bishop was ordained in 1936. The hierarchy was established in 1955. The Malagasy Republic maintains diplomatic relations with Vatican City.

Archd., 3; dioc., 14; card., 1 (nat.); abp., 2 (1 nat.); bp., 13 (2 nat.); parishes, 122; priests, 733 (127 dioc., 606 rel.); sem., 80; m. rel., 998; w. rel., 1,643; sch., 1,998; inst., 104; Caths., 1,543,904; tot. pop., 6,826,000.

Malawi: Republic in the interior of eastern Africa, member of the British Commonwealth; capital, Zomba. Missionary work, begun by Jesuits in the late 16th and early 17th centuries, was generally ineffective until the end of the 19th century. The White Fathers arrived in 1889 and later were joined by others. A vicariate was set up in 1897. The hierarchy was established in 1959. Malawi maintains diplomatic relations with Vatican City.

Archd., 1; dioc., 5; p.a., 1; abp., 1 (nat.); bp., 5 (1 nat.); parishes, 93; priests, 311 (66 dioc., 245 rel.); sem., 50; m. rel., 345; w. rel., 476; sch., 789; inst., 84; Caths., 860,376; tot. pop. (UN est., 1970), 4,530,000.

Malaysia: Parliamentary democracy in southeastern Asia, member of the British Commonwealth, federation of former states of Malaya, North Borneo or Sabah, and Sarawak; capital, Juala Lumpur. Christianity, introduced by Portuguese colonists about 1511, was confined almost exclusively to Malacca until late in the 18th century.

The effectiveness of evangelization increased from then on because of the recruitment and training of native clergy. Singapore (see separate entry), founded in 1819, became a center for missionary work. Seventeen thousand Catholics were in the Malacca diocese in 1888. Effective evangelization in North Borneo and Sarawak began in the second half of the 19th century. Malaysia has an apostolic delegate.

Dioc., 2; v.a., 3; bp., 6; parishes, 160; priests, 245 (133 dioc., 112 rel.); sem., 32; p.d., 1; m. rel., 286; w. rel., 570; sch., 297; inst., 43; Caths., 268,072; tot. pop. (UN est., 1970), 10,790,000.

Maldives: Republic, an archipelago 400 miles southwest of India and Ceylon; capital, Male. No serious attempt was ever made to evangelize the area, which is completely Moslem.

Tot. pop. (UN est., 1969), 108,000.

Mali: Republic, inland in western Africa; capital, Bamako. Catholicism was introduced late in the second half of the 19th century. Missionary work made little progress in the midst of the predominantly Moslem population. A vicariate was set up in 1921. The hierarchy was established in 1955. Mali has an apostolic delegate (to West Africa).

Archd., 1; dioc., 5; abp., 1; bp., 5; parishes, 27; priests, 165 (20 dioc., 145 rel.); sem., 8; m. rel., 170; w. rel., 170; sch., 65; inst., 41; Caths., 40,803; tot. pop., 5,000,000.

Malta: Parliamentary democracy, member of the British Commonwealth, 58 miles south of Sicily; capital, Valletta. Early catacombs and inscriptions are evidence of the early introduction of Christianity. St. Paul was shipwrecked on Malta in 60. Saracens controlled the island(s) from 870 to 1090, a period of difficulty for the Church. The line of bishops extends from 1090 to the present. Malta maintains diplomatic relations with Vatican City.

Archd., 1; dioc., 1; abp., 1; bp., 4; parishes, 71; priests, 1,068 (560 dioc., 508 rel.); sem., 129; m. rel., 593; w. rel., 1,649; sch., 81; inst., 30; Caths., 310,222; tot. pop., 324,000.

Mauritania: Islamic republic on the northwest coast of Africa; capital, Nouakchott. With few exceptions, the Catholics in the country are members of the foreign colony.

Dioc., 1; bp., 1; priests, 9 (1 dioc., 8 rel.); m. rel., 8; w. rel., 12; sch., 2; inst., 7; Caths. (1969), 5,483; tot. pop., 1,140,000.

Mauritius: Self-governing island state, member of the British Commonwealth, 500 miles east of the Malagasy Republic; capital, Port Louis. Catholicism was introduced by Vincentians in 1722. Port Louis, made a vicariate in 1819, was a jumping-off point for missionaries to Australia, Madagascar and South Africa. Mauritius maintains diplomatic relations with Vatican City.

Dioc., 1; bp., 1; parishes, 36; priests, 93 (53 dioc., 40 rel.); sem., 12; m. rel., 68; w. rel., 285; sch., 72; inst., 13; Caths., 273,000; tot. pop. 819,200.

Melilla: Spanish possession in northern Africa. Statistics are included in those for Spain.

Mexico (United States of Mexico): Republic in Middle America. Christianity was introduced early in the 16th century. Mexico City, made a diocese in 1530, became the missionary and cultural center of the whole country. Missionary work, started in 1524 and forwarded principally by Franciscans, Dominicans, Augustinians and Jesuits, resulted in the baptism of all persons in the central plateau by the end of the century. Progress there and in the rest of the country continued in the following century but tapered off and went into decline in the 18th century, for a variety of reasons ranging from diminishing government support to relaxations of Church discipline. The wars of independence, 1810-21, in which some Catholics participated, created serious problems of adjustment for the Church. Social problems, political unrest and government opposition climaxed in the constitution of 1917 which practically outlawed the Church. Persecution took serious tolls of life and kept the Church underground, under Calles, 1924-1928, again in 1931, and under Cardenas in 1934. President Camacho, 1940-1946, ended persecution and instituted a more lenient policy. The Church, however, still labors under legal and practical disabilities. Mexico has an apostolic delegate.

Archd., 11; dioc., 49; prel., 5; v.a., 1; p.a., 1; abp., 11; bp., 58; parishes, 2,901; priests, 8,899 (6,348 dioc., 2,551 rel.); sem., 2,858; p.d., 4; m. rel., 4,151; w. rel., 21,633; sch., 2,436; inst., 590; Caths., 43,353,845; tot. pop., 48,313,438.

Monaco: Constitutional monarchy, an enclave on the Mediterranean coast of France near the Italian border; capital, Monaco-Ville. Christianity was introduced before 1000. Catholicism is the official religion but freedom is guaranteed for all. Monaco maintains diplomatic relations with Vatican City.

Dioc., 1; parishes, 4; priests, 32; (15 dioc., 17 rel.); sem., 2; m. rel., 51; w. rel., 104; sch., 8; inst., 4; Caths., 20,148; tot. pop., 23,035.

Mongolian Peoples' Republic: Republic in north central Asia; capital Ulan Bator. Christianity was introduced by Nestorians. Some Franciscans were in the country in the 13th and 14th centuries, en route to China. Limited evangelization efforts from the 18th century had little success among the Mongols in Outer Mongolia, where Buddhism has predominated for hundreds of years. No Christians were known to be there in 1953. There may be a few Catholics in Inner Mongolia. No foreign missionaries have been in the country since 1953.

Morocco: Constitutional monarchy in northwest Africa with Atlantic and Mediterranean coastlines; capital, Rabat. Christianity was known in the area by the end of the third century. Bishops from Morocco attended a council at Carthage in 484. Catholic life survived under Visigoth and, from 700, Arab rule; later it became subject to influence from the Spanish, Portuguese and French. Islam is the state religion. The hierarchy was established in 1955. Morocco has an apostolic delegate (to North Africa).

Archd., 2; abp., 2; parishes, 55; priests, 187 (57 dioc., 130 rel.); rel., 171; w. rel., 670; sch.,

60; inst., 14; Caths., 137,950; tot. pop., 15,500,000.

Mozambique: Portuguese overseas province in southeast Africa, bordering on the Indian Ocean; capital, Laurenco Marques. Christianity was introduced by Portuguese Jesuits about the middle of the 16th century. Evangelization continued from then until the 18th century when it went into decline largely because of the Portuguese government's expulsion of the Jesuits. Conditions worsened in the 1830's, improved after 1881, but deteriorated again during the anticlerical period from 1910 to 1925. Conditions have been normal since Portugal concluded a new concordat with the Holy See in 1940, the year the hierarchy was established. The White Fathers withdrew their missionaries in 1971.

Archd., 1; dioc., 8; abp., 1; bp., 8; parishes, 128; priests, 630 (89 dioc., 541 rel.); sem., 138; p.d., 1; m. rel., 768; w. rel., 1,235; sch., 4,013; inst., 222; Caths., 1,538,744; tot. pop., 7,702,000.

Namibia (South West Africa): Territory in South Africa in dispute between the Republic of South Africa and the United Nations; capital, Windhoek. The area shares the history of the Republic of South Africa. Namibia (formerly South West Africa) has an apostolic delegate (to South Africa).

V.a., 2; bp., 2; parishes, 32; priests, 82 (2 dioc., 80 rel.); sem., 5; m. rel., 138; w. rel., 326; sch., 165; inst., 93; Caths., 109,473; tot. pop., 661,144.

Nepal: Constitutional monarchy, the only Hindu kingdom in the world, in central Asia south of the Himalayas between India and Tibet; capital, Katmandu. Little is known of the country before the 15th century. Some Jesuits passed through from 1628 and some sections were evangelized in the 18th century, with minimal results, before the country was closed to foreigners. Conversions from Hinduism, the state religion, are not recognized in law. Christian missionary work is not allowed. Any Catholics in the country have been under the jurisdiction of the Patna diocese, India, since 1919.

Tot. pop., 11,000,000.

Netherlands: Kingdom in northwest Europe; capital, Amsterdam (seat of the government, The Hague). Evangelization, begun about the turn of the sixth century by Irish, Anglo-Saxon and Frankish missionaries, resulted in Christianization of the country by 800 and subsequent strong influence on The Lowlands. Invasion by French Calvinists in 1572 brought serious losses to the Catholic Church and made the Reformed Church dominant. Catholics suffered a practical persecution of official repression and social handicap in the 17th century. The schism of Utrecht occurred in 1724. Only one-third of the population was Catholic in 1726. The Church had only a skeleton organization from 1702 to 1853, when the hierarchy was reestablished. Despite this upturn, cultural isolation was the experience of Catholics until about 1914. From then on new vigor came into the life of the Church, and a whole new climate of interfaith relations began to develop. Before and since the Second Vatican Council, the vigor and variety of thought and practice in the Dutch Church have moved it to the vanguard position of "progressive" renewal. The Netherlands maintains diplomatic relations with Vatican City.

Archd., 1; dioc., 6; card., 3; bp., 6; parishes, 1,836; priests, 7,430 (3,564 dioc., 3,866 rel.); sem., 403; m. rel., 8,095; w. rel., 5,869; sch., 3; inst., 57; Caths., 5,299,264; tot. pop., 13,068,088.

Netherlands Antilles: Autonomous part of the Kingdom of The Netherlands, two groups of islands in the Caribbean off the northern coast of Venezuela (Windward) and 500 miles to the northeast (Leeward); capital, Willemstad on Curacao. Christianity was introduced in the 16th century.

Dioc., 1; bp., 1; parishes, 30; priests, 127 (65 dioc., 62 rel.); sem., 4; m. rel., 179; w. rel., 298; sch., 290; inst., 18; Caths., 180,000; tot. pop., 220,000.

New Caledonia: French territory consisting of several islands in Oceania east of Queensland, Australia; capital, Noumea. Catholicism was introduced in 1843, nine years after Protestant missionaries began evangelization. A vicariate was organized in 1847. The hierarchy was established in 1966.

Archd., 1; abp., 2; parishes, 33; priests, 53 (8 dioc., 45 rel.); sem., 4; m. rel., 138; w. rel., 243; sch., 103; inst., 1; Caths., 63,000; tot. pop., 98,000.

New Hebrides: Islands in the southwest Pacific, about 500 miles west of Fiji, under joint British-French administration; capital, Vila. Effective, though slow, evangelization by Catholic missionaries began about 1887. A vicariate apostolic was set up in 1904. The hierarchy was established in 1966.

Dioc., 1; bp., 1; parishes, 16; priests, 26 (3 dioc., 23 rel.); sem., 3; m. rel., 25; w. rel., 79; sch., 27; inst., 15; Caths., 13,230; tot. pop., 84,000.

New Zealand: Dominion in the British Commonwealth, a group of islands in Oceania 1,200 miles southeast of Australia; capital, Wellington. Protestant missionaries were the first evangelizers. On North Island, Catholic missionaries started work before the establishment of two dioceses in 1848; their work among the Maoris was not organized until about 1881. On South Island, whose first resident priest arrived in 1840, a diocese was established in 1869. These three jurisdictions were joined in a province in 1896. The Marists were the outstanding Catholic missionaries in the area. New Zealand has an apostolic delegate.

Archd., 1; dioc., 3; card., 1; bp., 3; parishes, 282; priests, 838 (505 dioc., 333 rel.); sem., 99;

m. rel., 748; w. rel., 2,543; sch., 334; inst., 41; Caths., 434,133; tot. pop., (1970 govt. est.), 2,857,000.

Nicaragua: Republic in Central America: capital, Managua. Evangelization began shortly after the Spanish conquest about 1524 and eight years later the first bishop took over jurisdiction of the Church in the country. Jesuits were leaders in missionary work during the colonial period, which lasted until the 1820's. Evangelization endeavor increased after establishment of the republic in 1838. In this century it was extended to the Atlantic coastal area where Protestant missionaries had begun work about the middle of the 1900's. Nicaragua maintains diplomatic relations with Vatican City.

Archd., 1; dioc., 4; prel., 1; v.a., 1; abp., 1; bp., 5; parishes, 144; priests, 307 (121 dioc., 186 rel.); sem., 31; m. rel., 230; w. rel., 497; sch., 384; inst., 46; Caths., 1,767,722; tot. pop., 2,000,000.

Niger: Republic in west central Africa; capital, Niamey. The first mission was set up in 1831. A prefecture apostolic was organized in 1942 and the first diocese was established in 1961. The country is predominantly Moslem. Niger maintains diplomatic relations with Vatican City.

Dioc., 1; bp., 1; parishes, 7; priests, 25 (6 dioc., 18 rel.); sem., 1; m. rel., 34; w. rel., 68; sch., 19; inst., 12; Caths., 12,500; tot. pop., 4,010,000.

Nigeria: Republic in western Africa; capital, Lagos. The Portuguese introduced Catholicism in the coastal region in the 15th century. Capuchins did some evangelization in the 17th century but systematic missionary work did not get underway along the coast untiliabout 1840. A vicariate for this area was organized in 1870. A prefecture was set up in 1911 for missions in the northern part of the country where Islam was strongly intrenched. From 1967, when Biafra seceded, until early in 1970 the country was torn by civil war. The hierarchy was established in 1950. Nigeria has an apostolic delegate (to Central-West Africa).

Archd., 3; dioc., 20; p.a., 2; abp., 3 (2 nat.), bp., 25 (13 nat.); parishes, 220; priests, 783 (286 dioc., 497 rel.); sem., 482; p.d., 4; m. rel., 669; w. rel., 708; sch., 2,141; inst., 343; Caths., 3,288,188; tot. pop. (UN est., 1970), 66,174,000.

Norway: Constitutional monarchy in northern Europe, the western part of the Scandinavian peninsula; capital, Oslo. Evangelization begun in the ninth century by missionaries from England and Ireland put the Church on a firm footing about the turn of the 11th century. The first diocese was set up in 1153 and development of the Church progressed until the Black Death in 1349 inflicted losses from which it never recovered. Lutheranism, introduced from outside in 1537 and furthered cautiously, gained general acceptance by about 1600 and was made the state religion. Legal and other measures crippled the Church, forcing priests to flee the country and completely disrupting normal activity. Changes for the better came in the 19th century, with the granting of religious liberty in 1845 and the repeal of many legal disabilities in 1897. Norway was administered as a single apostolic vicariate from 1892 to 1932, when it was divided into three jurisdictions under the supervision of the Congregation for the Propagation of the Faith, Norway has an apostolic delegate (to Scandinavia).

Dioc., 1; v.a., 2; bp., 3; parishes, 27; priests, 65; sem., 2; m. rel., 47; w. rel., 470; sch., 3; inst., 21; Caths., 10,000; tot. pop., c. 3,950,000 (figures provided by the Bishop of Oslo).

Oman: See Arabian Peninsula.

Pakistan: Islamic republic in southwestern Asia, member of the British Commonwealth; capital, Islamabad. (Formerly included East Pakistan which became the independent nation of Bangladesh in 1971.) Islam, firmly established in the eighth century, is the state religion. Christian evangelization of the native population began about the middle of the 19th century, years after earlier scattered attempts. The hierarchy was established in 1950. Pakistan maintains diplomatic relations with Vatican City.

Archd., 1; dioc., 5; abp., 1; bp., 6; parishes, 38; priests, 240 (66 dioc., 174 rel.); sem., 47; m. rel., 250; w. rel., 556; sch., 215; inst., 99; Caths., 336,990; tot. pop., 45,000,000.

Panama: Republic in Central America; capital, Panama City. Catholicism was introduced by Franciscan missionaries and evangelization started in 1514. The Panama diocese, oldest in the Americas, was set up at the same time. The Catholic Church has favored status and state aid for missions, charities and parochial schools, but religious freedom is guaranteed to all religions. Panama maintains diplomatic relations with Vatican City.

Archd., 1; dioc., 3; prel., 1; v.a., 1; abp., 1; bp., 6; parishes, 100; priests, 253 (79 dioc., 174 rel.); sem., 21; m. rel., 211; w. rel., 304; sch., 40; inst., 17; Caths., 1,303,000; tot. pop., 1,460,000.

Panama Canal Zone: Under control of the United States, which was given Canal rights following Panamanian independence from Colombia in 1903. Catholic statistics are included in those reported for Panama, above.

Papua-New Guinea: Consists of the eastern half of the southwestern Pacific island of New Guinea and the Northern Solomon Islands, under Australian administration; capital, Lae. (For statistics on the Indonesian portion of New Guinea, see Indonesia.) Marists began evangelization about 1844 but were handicapped by many factors, including "spheres of influence" laid out for Catholic and Protestant missionaries. A prefecture apostolic was set up in 1896 and placed in charge of the Divine Word Missionaries. The territory suffered greatly during World War II. Hierarchy was established for New Guinea and adjacent islands in 1966. The area has an apostolic delegate.

Archd., 3; dioc., 13; abp., 3; bp., 12; parishes, 243; priests, 859 (354 dioc., 505 rel.); sem., 38; p.d., 1; m. rel., 836; w. rel., 976; sch., 1,143; inst., 382; Caths., 655,000; tot. pop., 2,600,000.

Paraguay: Republic in central South America; capital, Asuncion. Catholicism was introduced in 1542, evangelization began almost immediately. A diocese erected in 1547 was occupied for the first time in 1556. On many occasions thereafter dioceses in the country were left unoccupied because of political and other reasons. Jesuits who came into the country after 1609 devised the reductions system for evangelizing the Indians, teaching them agriculture, husbandry, trades and other useful arts, and giving them experience in property use and community life. The reductions were communes of Indians only, under the direction of the missionaries. About 50 of them were established in southern Brazil, Uruguay and northeastern Argentina as well as in Paraguay. They had an average population of three to four thousand. At their peak, some 30 reductions had a population of 100,000. Political officials regarded the reductions with disfavor because they did not control them and feared that the Indians trained in them might foment revolt and upset the established colonial system under Spanish control. The reductions lasted until about 1768 when their Jesuit founders and directors were expelled from Latin America. Church-state relations following independence from Spain in 1811 were tense as often as not because of government efforts to control the Church through continued exercise of Spanish patronage rights and by other means. The Church as well as the whole country suffered a great deal during the War of the Triple Alliance from 1865-70. After that time, the Church had the same kind of experience in Paraguay as in the rest of Latin America with forces of liberalism, anticlericalism, massive educational needs, poverty, a shortage of priests and other personnel. Most recently church leaders have been challenging the government to initiate long-needed economic and social reforms. Paraguay maintains diplomatic relations with Vatican City.

Archd., 1; dioc., 4; prel., 3; v.a., 2; abp., 1; bp., 9; parishes, 194; priests, 480 (191 dioc., 289 rel.); sem., 57; m. rel., 440; w. rel., 749; sch., 339; inst., 109; Caths., 2,231,936; tot. pop., 2,300,000.

Peru: Republic on the western coast of South America; capital, Lima. An effective diocese became operational in 1537, five years after the Spanish conquest. Evangelization, already underway, developed for some time after 1570 but deteriorated before the end of the colonial period in the 1820's. The first native-born saint of the new world was a Peruvian, Rose of Lima, a Dominican tertiary who died in 1617 and was canonozed in 1671. In the new republic founded after the wars of independence the Church experienced problems of adjustment and many of the difficulties that cropped up in other South American countries: government efforts to control it through continuation of the patronage rights of the Spanish crown; suppression of houses of religious and expropriation of church property; religious indifference and outright hostility. The Church was given special status but was not made the established religion. Peru maintains diplomatic relations with Vatican City.

Archd., 7; dioc., 12; prel., 14; v.a., 8; card., 1; abp., 6; bp., 38; parishes, 923; priests, 2,211 (800 dioc., 1,411 rel.); sem., 202; p.d., 6; m. rel., 1,873; w. rel., 4,243; sch., 791; inst., 234; Caths., 12,505,923; tot. pop., 13,750,000.

Philippine Islands: Republic, an archipelago of 7,000 islands off the southeast coast of Asia; capital, Quezon City. Systematic evangelization was begun in 1564 and resulted in firm establishment of the Church by the 19th century. During the period of Spanish rule, which lasted from the discovery of the islands by Magellan in 1521 to 1898, the Church experienced difficulties with the patronage system under which the Spanish crown tried to control ecclesiastical affairs through episcopal and other appointments. This system ended in 1898 when the United States gained possession of the islands and instituted a policy of separation of Church and state. Anticlericalism flared late in the 19th century. The Aglipayan schism, an attempt to set up a nationalist church, occurred a few years later, in 1902. The republic maintains diplomatic relations with Vatican City.

Archd., 9; dioc., 28; prel., 12; v.a., 4; card., 2; abp., 9; bp., 54; parishes, 1,712; priests, 4,427 (2,115 dioc., 2,312 rel.); sem., 1,850; m. rel., 3,345; w. rel., 6,542; sch., 1,692; inst., 358; Caths., 29,710,000; tot. pop. (UN est., 1970), 38,493,000.

Poland: People's republic in eastern Europe; capital, Warsaw. The first traces of Christianity date from the second half of the ninth century. Its spread was accelerated by the union of the Slavs in the 10th century. The first bishopric was set up in 968. The Gniezno archdiocese, with suffragan sees and a mandate to evangelize the borderlands as well as Poland, was established in 1000. Steady growth continued thereafter, with religious orders and their schools playing a major role. Some tensions with the Orthodox were experienced. The Reformation, supported mainly by city dwellers and the upper classes, peaked from about the middle of the 16th century, resulting in numerous conversions to Lutheranism, the Reformed Church and the Bohemian Brethren. A successful Counter-

Reformation, with the Jesuits in a position of leadership, was completed by about 1632. The movement served a nationalist as well as religious purpose; in restoring religious unity to a large degree, it united the country against potential invaders, the Swedes, Russians and Turks. The Counter-Reformation had bad side effects, leading to the repression of Protestants long after it was over and to prejudice against Orthodox who returned to allegiance with Rome in 1596 and later. The Church, in the same manner as the entire country, was adversely affected by the partitions of the 18th and 19th centuries. Russification hurt the Orthodox who had reunited with Rome and the Latins who were in the majority. Germans extended their Kulturkampf to the area they controlled. The Austrians exhibited some degree of tolerance. In the republic established after World War I the Church reorganized itself, continued to serve as a vital force in national life, and enjoyed generally harmonious relations with the state. Progressive growth was strong until 1939 when disaster struck in the form of invasion by German and Russian forces and six years of war. In 1945, seven years before the adoption of a Soviet-type of constitution, the Communist-controlled government initiated a policy that included a constant program of atheistic propaganda; a strong campaign against the hierarchy and clergy; the imprisonment in 1948 of 700 priests and even more religious; rigid limitation of the activities of religious; censorship and curtailment of the Catholic press and Catholic Action; interference with church administration and appointments of the clergy; the "deposition" of Cardinal Wyszynski in 1953 and the imprisonment of other members of the hierarchy; the suppression of "Caritas," the Catholic charitable organization; promotion of "Progressive Catholic" activities and a small minority of "patriotic priests." Establishment of the Gomulka regime, the freeing of Cardinal Wyszynski in October, 1956, and the signing of an agreement two months later by bishops and state officials, led to some improvement of conditions. The underlying fact, however, was that the regime conceded to Catholics only so much as was necessary to secure support of the government as a more tolerable evil than the harsh and real threat of a Russian-imposed puppet government like that in Hungary. This has been the controlling principle in Church-state relations. Auxiliary Bishop Ladislaw Rubin of Warsaw sketched the general state of affairs in March, 1968. He said that there was no sign that the government had any intention of releasing its oppressive grip on the Church. As evidence of the "climate of asphyxiation" in the country he cited: persistent questioning of priests by officials concerning their activities; the prohibition against Catholic schools, hospitals and charitable works; the financial burden of a 60 per

cent tax on church income. Cardinal Wyszynski denounced "enforced atheism" in a Lenten pastoral in the same year. In May, 1969, the bishops drafted a list of grievances against the government which, they said, were "only some examples of difficulties which demonstrated the situation of the Church in our homeland." The grievances were: refusal of permits to build new churches and establish new parishes; refusal of permission "for the organization of new religion classes"; pressure on Catholics who attend religious ceremonies; censorship and the lack of an independent Catholic daily newspaper; lack of representation in public life; restriction of "freedom to conduct normal pastoral work" in the western portion of the country. There was some improvement in Church-state relations in 1971-72.

Archd., 9; dioc., 22; ap. ex., 1; card., 2; abp., 1; bp., 56; parishes, 8,155; priests, 18,247 (14,587 dioc., 3,660 rel.); sem., 3,280; m. rel., 4,903; w. rel., 17,370; sch., 28; inst., 238; Caths., 30,903,000; tot. pop., (UN est., 1970), 32,807,000.

Polynesia, French: French possession in the southern Pacific, including Tahiti and the Marquesas Islands; capital, Papeete. The first phase of evangelization in the Marquesas Islands, begun in 1838, resulted in 216 baptisms in 10 years. A vicariate was organized in 1848 but real progress was not made until after the baptism of native rulers in 1853. Persecution caused missionaries to leave the islands several times. By the 1960's, more than 95 per cent of the population was Catholic. Isolated attempts to evangelize Tahiti were made in the 17th and 18th centuries. Two Picpus Fathers began missionary work in 1831. A vicariate was organized in 1848. By 1908, despite the hindrances of Protestant opposition, disease and other factors, the Church had firm roots.

Archd., 1; dioc., 1; abp., 2; bp., 1; parishes, 84; priests, 44 (9 dioc., 35 rel.); sem., 2; m. rel., 65; w. rel., 59; sch., 21; inst., 1; Caths., 35,020; tot. pop., 119,075.

Portugal: Republic in the western part of the Iberian peninsula; capital, Lisbon. Christianity was introduced before the fourth century. From the fifth century to early in the eighth century the Church experienced difficulties from the physical invasion of barbarians and the intellectual invasion of doctrinal errors in the forms of Arianism, Priscillianism and Pelagianism. The Church survived under the rule of Arabs from about 711 and of the Moors until 1249. Ecclesiastical life was fairly vigorous from 1080 to 1185, and monastic influence became strong. A decline set in about 1450. Several decades later Portugal became the jumping-off place for many missionaries to newly discovered colonies. The Reformation had little effect in the country. Beginning about 1750, Pombal, minister of foreign affairs and prime minister, mounted a frontal attack on the Jesuits whom he succeeded in expelling from Portugal and the colonies. His anti-Jesuit campaign successful Pombal also attempted, and succeeded to some extent, in controlling the Church in Portugal until his fall from power about 1777. Liberal revolutionaries with anti-Church policies made the 19th century a difficult one for the Church. Similar policies prevailed in Church-state relations in this century until the accession of Salazar to power in 1928. In 1940 he concluded a concordat with the Holy See which regularized Church-state relations but still left the Church in a subservient condition. The prevailing spirit of church authorities in Portugal remains rather conservative. In 1971 several priests were tried for subversion for speaking out against colonialism and for taking part in guerrilla activities in Angola. Portugal maintains diplomatic relations with Vatican City.

Patriarchate, 1; archd., 2; dioc., 14; card., 2; abp., 2; bp., 14; parishes, 4,307; priests, 5,176 (4,281 dioc., 895 rel.); sem., 644; m. rel., 1,842; w. rel., 5,705; sch., 361; inst., 589; Caths., 9,148,000, tot. pop. (UN est., 1970), 9,630,000.

Puerto Rico: A US commonwealth, the smallest of the Greater Antilles, 885 miles southeast of the southern coast of Florida; capital, San Juan. Following its discovery by Columbus in 1493, the island was evangelized by Spanish missionaries and remained under Spanish ecclesiastical as well as political control until 1898 when it became a possession of the United States. The original diocese, San Juan, was erected in 1511. The present hierarchy was established in 1960.

Archd., 1; dioc., 3; abp., 1; bp., 4; parishes, 226; priests, 566 (211 dioc., 355 rel.); sem., 49; m. rel., 576; w. rel., 1,214; sch., 215; inst., 79; Caths., 2,588,000; tot. pop., 3,243,000 (population figures are from The Official Catholic Directory, 1972).

Reunion: French overseas department, 450 miles east of Madagascar; capital, Saint-Denis. Catholicism was introduced in 1667 and some intermittent missionary work was done through the rest of the century. A prefecture apostolic was organized in 1712. Vincentians began work there in 1817 and were joined later by Holy Ghost Fathers. Reunion has an apostolic delegate.

Dioc., 1; bp., 1; parishes, 64; priests, 118 (57 dioc., 61 rel.); sem., 16; m. rel., 114; w. rel., 499; sch., 36; inst., 28; Caths., 419,321; tot. pop., 451,247.

Rhodes: Greek island in the Aegean Sea, 112 miles from the southwestern coast of Asia Minor. A diocese was established about the end of the third century. A bishop from Rhodes attended the Council of Nicaea in 325. Most of the Christians followed the Eastern Churches into schism in the 11th century and became Orthodox. Turks controlled the island from 1522 to 1912. The small Catholic population, for whom a diocese existed from 1328 to 1546, lived in crossfire between Turks and Orthodox. After 1719 Franciscans provided pastoral care for the Catholics, for whom an archdiocese was erected in 1928.

Archd., 1; parishes, 2; priests, 3 (rel.); m. rel., 3; sch., 5; Caths., 350.

Rhodesia: Self-governing state in south central Africa; capital, Salisbury. Earlier unsuccessful missionary ventures preceded the introduction of Catholicism in 1879. Missionaries began to make progress after 1893. The hierarchy was established in 1955. In 1969, four years after the government of Ian Smith made a unilateral declaration of independence from England, a new constitution was enacted for the purpose of assuring continued white supremacy over the black majority. Catholic and Protestant prelates in the country have protested rigorously against the constitution and related enactments as opposed to human rights of the blacks and restrictive of the Church's freedom to carry out its pastoral, educational and social service functions. Rhodesia has an apostolic delegate (to South Africa).

Archd., 1; dioc., 4; abp., 1; bp., 4; parishes, 85; priests, 380 (36 dioc., 344 rel.); sem., 69; m. rel., 498; w. rel., 1,029; sch., 474; inst., 169; Caths., 500,140; tot. pop., 5,125,023.

Rumania: Socialist republic in southeastern Europe; capital, Bucharest. Latin Christianity, introduced in the third century, all but disappeared during the barbarian invasions. The Byzantine Rite was introduced by the Bulgars about the beginning of the eighth century and established firm roots. It eventually became Orthodox, but a large number of its adherents returned later to union with Rome. Attempts to reintroduce the Latin Rite on any large scale have been unsuccessful. Communists took over the government following World War II, forced the abdication of Michael I in 1947, and enacted a Soviet type of constitution in 1952. By that time a campaign against religion was already in progress. In 1948 the government denounced a concordat concluded in 1929, nationalized all schools and passed a law on religions which resulted in the disorganization of Church administration. The 1.5 million-member Rumanian Byzantine Rite Church, by government decree, was incorporated into the Rumanian Orthodox Church, and the Orthodox bishops then seized the cathedrals of Roman Catholic bishops. Five of the six Latin Rite bishops were immediately disposed of by the government, and the last was sentenced to 18 years' imprisonment in 1951, when a great many arrests of priests and laymen were made. Religious orders were suppressed in 1949. Since 1948 more than 50 priests have been executed and 200 have died in prison. One hundred priests were reported in prison at the end of 1958. Some change for the better in Church-state relations was reported after the middle of the summer of 1964, although restrictions were still in effect.

About 1,200 priests were engaged in parish work in August, 1965.

Archd., 2; dioc., 8; ord., 1; bp., 2; Caths. (1969), 1,140,000; tot. pop. (UN est., 1970), 20,233,000.

Rwanda: Republic in east central Africa; capital, Kigali. Catholicism was introduced about the turn of the 20th century. The hierarchy was established in 1959. Rwanda maintains diplomatic relations with Vatican City.

Archd., 1; dioc., 4; abp., 1; bp., 4 (nat.); parishes, 124; priests, 390 (225 dioc., 165 rel.); sem., 119; m. rel., 419; w. rel., 762; sch., 1,140; inst., 74; Caths., 1,398,840; tot. pop., 3,800,000.

St. Pierre and Miquelon: French overseas territory, islands near the southwest coast of Newfoundland. Catholicism was introduced about 1689.

V.a., 1; bp., 1; priests, 7 (2 dioc., 5 rel.); m. rel., 6; w. rel., 17; sch., 5; inst., 2; Caths., 5,380; tot. pop., 5,430.

Samoa: Includes the independent state of Western Samoa, American Samoa, and the New Zealand dependency of Tokelau in the southwestern Pacific. Catholic missionary work began in 1845. Most of the missions now in operation were established by 1870 when the Catholic population numbered about 5,000. Additional progress was made in missionary work from 1896. The first Samoan priest was ordained in 1892. The hierarchy was established in 1966.

Dioc., 1; bp., 1; parishes, 21; priests, 32 (5 dioc., 27 rel.); sem., 8; m. rel., 47; w. rel., 105; sch., 29; Caths., 36,798; tot. pop., 174,866.

San Marino: Republic, a 24-square-mile enclave in northeastern Italy; capital, San Marino. The date of initial evangelization is not known, but a diocese was established by the end of the third century. San Marino maintains diplomatic relations with Vatican City.

Population (entirely Catholic), 19,000.

Sao Tome and Principe: Portuguese overseas territory, islands off the western coast of Africa in the Gulf of Guinea. Evangelization was begun by the Portuguese who discovered the islands in 1471-72. The Sao Tome diocese was established in 1534.

Dioc., 1; bp., 1; parishes, 10; priests, 15 (rel.); m. rel., 17; w. rel., 18; sch., 5; inst., 3; Caths., 59,572; tot. pop., 66,000.

Saudi Arabia: See Arabian Peninsula.

Scotland: Part of the United Kingdom, in the northern British Isles; capital, Edinburgh. Christianity was introduced by the early years of the fifth century. The arrival of St. Columba and his monks in 563 inaugurated a new era of evangelization which reached into remote areas by the end of the sixth century. He was extremely influential in determining the character of the Celtic Church, which was tribal, monastic, and in union with Rome. Considerable disruption of church activity resulted from Scandinavian invasions in the late eighth and ninth centuries. By 1153 the Scottish Church took a turn away from its insularity and was drawn into closer contact with the European community. Anglo-Saxon religious and political relations, complicated by rivalries between princes and ecclesiastical superiors, were not always the happiest. Religious orders expanded greatly in the 12th century. From shortly after the Norman Conquest of England to 1560 the Church suffered adverse effects from the Hundred Years' War, the Black Death, the Western Schism and other developments. In 1560 parliament abrogated papal supremacy over the Church in Scotland and committed the country to Protestantism in 1567. The Catholic Church was proscribed, to remain that way for more than 200 years, and the hierarchy was disbanded. Defections made the Church a minority religion from that time on. Presbyterian church government was ratified in 1690. Priests launched the Scottish Mission in 1653, incorporating themselves as a mission body under a prefect apostolic and working underground to serve the faithful in much the same way their confreres did in England. About 100 heather priests, trained in cladestine places in the heather country, were ordained by the early 19th century. Catholics got some relief from legal disabilities in 1793 and more later. Many left the country about that time. Some of their numbers were filled subsequently by immigrants from Ireland. The hierarchy was restored in 1878. Scotland, though predominantly Protestant, has a better record for tolerance than Northern Ireland.

Archd., 2; dioc., 6; card., 2; abp., 1; bp., 9; parishes, 446; priests, 1,222 (963 dioc., 259 rel.); sem., 131; m. rel., 472; w. rel., 1,325; sch., 150; inst., 41; Caths., 817,097; tot. pop., 5,068,845.

Senegal: Republic, member of the French Community, in western Africa; capital, Dakar. The country had its first contact with Catholicism through the Portuguese some time after 1460. Some incidental missionary work was done by Jesuits and Capuchins in the 16th and 17th centuries. A vicariate for the area was placed in charge of the Holy Ghost Fathers in 1779. More effective evangelization efforts was accomplished after the Senegambia vicariate was organized in 1863. The hierarchy was established in 1955. Senegal maintains diplomatic relations with Vatican City.

Archd., 1; dioc., 4; p.a., 1; abp., 1 (nat.); bp. 4 (nat.); parishes, 37; priests, 201 (48 dioc., 153 rel.); sem., 19; m. rel., 274; w. rel., 460; sch., 238; inst., 67; Caths., 164,145; tot. pop. (UN est., 1970), 3,930,000.

Seychelles Islands: British colony in the Indian Ocean 970 miles east of Kenya; capital, Victoria on Mahe. Catholicism was introduced in the 18th century. A vicariate apostolic was organized in 1852. All education in the islands was conducted under Catholic auspices until 1954. The colony has an apostolic delegate (pro-nuncio to Kenya).

Dioc., 1; bp., 1; parishes, 17; priests, 28 (5 dioc., 23 rel.); sem., 3; m. rel., 39; w. rel., 64; sch., 32; inst., 4; Caths., 49,473; tot. pop., 53,000.

Siberia: Republic in the USSR, in northern Asia.

Dioc., 1; v.a. 1.

Sierra Leone: Republic, member of the British Commonwealth, on the western coast of Africa; capital, Freetown. Catholicism was introduced in 1858. Members of the African Missions Society, the first Catholic missionaries in the area, were joined by Holy Ghost Fathers in 1864. Protestant missionaries were active in the area before their Catholic counterparts. Educational work had a major part in Catholic endeavor. The hierarchy was established in 1950. Sierra Leone has an apostolic delegate (the pro-nuncio to Liberia).

Archd., 1; dioc., 2; abp., 1; bp., 2 (1 nat.); parishes, 20; priests, 81 (2 dioc., 79 rel.); m. rel., 95; w. rel., 63; sch., 397; inst., 28; Caths., 42,820; tot. pop., 2,512,000.

Sikkim: Protectorate of India in the Himalayas south of Tibet; capital, Gangtok. Some evangelization took place after 1848. Buddhism is the state religion. The territory is under the jurisdiction of the diocese of Darjeeling, India.

Tot. pop., 191,000.

Singapore: Independent island republic off the southern tip of the Malay Peninsula; member of the British Commonwealth. Christianity was introduced in the area by Portuguese colonists about 1511. Singapore was founded in 1819; the first parish church was built in 1846. The archbishop of the Malacca-Singapore metropolitan see resides in Singapore. Singapore has an apostolic delegate.

Archd., 1 (Malacca-Singapore which includes part of Malaysia); abp., 1; parishes, 27; priests, 93 (85 dioc., 8 rel.); Caths., c. 80,000; tot. pop. (1971 census), 2,075,000 (figures are from Fides).

Solomon Islands: British protectorate in Oceania; capital, Honiara, on Guadalcanal. Evangelization of the Southern Solomons, begun earlier but interrupted because of violence against them, was resumed by the Marists in 1898. A vicariate apostolic was organized in 1912. A similar jurisdiction was set up for the Western Solomons in 1959. World War II caused a great deal of damage to mission installations. Catholic statistics for the Northern Solomons, where Catholic missionary work started in 1899 and a vicariate was set up in 1930, are included in those reported for New Guinea.

Dioc., 2; bp., 2; parishes, 45; priests, 45 (5 dioc., 40 rel.); sem., 1; m. rel., 64; w. rel., 127; inst., 24; Caths., 32,569; tot. pop., 160,000.

Somalia: Republic on the eastern coast of Africa; capital, Mogadishu. The country has been Moslem for centuries. Pastoral activity has been confined to immigrants. Somalia has an apostolic delegate (to the Red Sea Region).

V.a., 1; bp., 1; priests, 18 (rel.); m. rel., 26; w. rel., 94; sch., 23; inst., 29; Caths., 2,623; tot. pop., 3,000,000.

Somaliland, French: See Afars and Issas.

South Africa: Republic in the southern part of Africa; capitals, Capetown (legislative) and Pretoria (administrative). Christianity was introduced by the Portuguese who discovered the Cape of Good Hope in 1498. Boers, who founded Cape Town in 1652, expelled Catholics from the region. There was no Catholic missionary activity from that time until the 19th century. After a period of British opposition, a bishop established residence in 1837 and evangelization got underway thereafter among the Bantus and white immigrants. In recent years church authorities have strongly protested the white supremacy policy of apartheid which seriously infringes the human rights of the native blacks and impedes the Church from carrying out its pastoral, educational and social service functions. The hierarchy was established in 1951. South Africa has an apostolic delegate.

Archd., 4; dioc., 16; abb., 1; p.a., 5; card., 1; abp., 3; bp., 17; parishes, 307; priests, 1,206 (302 dioc., 904 rel.); sem., 92; p.d., 2; m. rel., 1,471; w. rel., 4,760; sch., 931; inst., 297; Caths., 1,447,115; tot. pop. (1970 govt. est.), 21,314,000.

South West Africa: See Namibia.

Spain: Nominal monarchy on the Iberian peninsula in southwestern Europe; capital, Madrid. Christians were on the peninsula by 200; some of them suffered martyrdom during persecutions of the third century. A council held in Elvira about 304/6 enacted the first legislation on clerical celibacy in the West. Vandals invaded the peninsula in the fifth century, bringing with them an Arian brand of Christianity which they retained until their conversion following the baptism of their king Reccared, in 589. One of the significant developments of the seventh century was the establishment of Toledo as the primatial see. The Visigoth kingdom lasted to the time of the Arab invasion, 711-14. The Church survived under Moslem rule but experienced some doctrinal and disciplinary irregularities as well as harassment. Reconquest of most of the peninsula was accomplished by 1248; unification was achieved during the reign of Ferdinand and Isabella. The discoveries of Columbus and other explorers ushered in an era of colonial expansion in which Spain became one of the greatest mission-sending countries in history. In 1492, in repetition of anti-Semitic actions of 694, the expulsion of unbaptized Jews was decreed, leading to mass baptisms but a questionable number of real conversions in 1502. (The Jewish minority numbered about 165,000.) Activity by the Inquisition followed. Spain was not seriously affected by the Reformation. Ecclesiastical decline set in about 1650. Anti-Church actions authorized by a constitution enacted in 1812 resulted in the suppression of religious and other encroachments on the leaders, people and goods of the Church. Political, religious and cultural turmoil recurred during the 19th century and into the 20th. A revolutionary republic was proclaimed in 1931, triggering a series of developments which led to civil war from 1936 to 1939. During the conflict, which pitted leftist Loyalists against the forces of Francisco Franco, 6,632 priests and religious and unknown number of lay persons perished in addition to thousands of victims of combat. One-man, one-party rule, established after the civil war, has come underpressure recently for liberalization of its conservative stance and policy with respect to personal liberties and social and economic reforms. Generallyy conservative church leaders have come under the same pressure from some of their colleagues, priests and lay persons. The Catholic Church is the state religion, but the constitution provides for general religious freedom. Spain maintains diplomatic relations with Vatican City.

Archd., 14; dioc., 50; prel., 1; card., 5; abp., 12; bp., 63 parishes, 20,647; priests, 35,061 (24,453 dioc., 10,608 rel.); sem., 3,521; p.d., 1; m. rel., 20,923; w. rel., 83,266; sch., 6,499; inst., 1,383; Caths., 32,397,015; tot. pop., 34,000,000.

Spanish North Africa: Includes the cities of Ceuta and Melilla on the northern coast of Africa, which are considered part of metropolitan Spain.

Spanish Sahara: Spanish province on the northwestern coast of Africa. Islam is the religion of non-Europeans. A prefecture apostolic was set up in 1954 for the European Catholics there.

P.a., 1; parishes, 5; priests, 11 (rel); m. rel., 13; w. rel., 31; Caths., 22,511; tot. pop., 70,000 (figures are for the area covered by the prefecture apostolic of Spanish Sahara).

Sri Lanka (formerly Ceylon): Independent socialist republic, island southeast of India; capital, Colombo. Effective evangelization began in 1543 and made great progress by the middle of the 17th century. The Church was seriously hampered during the Dutch period from about 1650 to 1795. Anti-Catholic laws were repealed by the British in 1806. The hierarchy was established in 1886. Leftist governments and other factors have worked against the Church since the country became independent in 1948. The high percentage of indigenous clergy and religious has been of great advantage to the Church. Sri Lanka has an apostolic delegate.

Archd., 1; dioc., 5; card., 1 (nat.), bp., 10 (9 nat.); parishes, 252; priests, 5994 (307 dioc.,

287 rel.); sem., 149; m. rel., 730; w. rel., 2,403; sch., 41; inst., 98; Caths., 941,842; tot. pop., 12,747,000.

Sudan: Republic in northeastern Africa, the largest country on the continent; capital, Khartoum. Christianity was introduced from Egypt and gained acceptance in the sixth century. Under Arab rule, it was eliminated in the northern region. No Christians were in the country in 1600. Evangelization attempts begun in the 19th century in the south yielded hard-won results. By 1931 there were nearly 40,000 Catholics there, and considerable progress was made by missionaries after that time. In 1957, a year after the republic was established, Catholic schools were nationalized. An act restrictive of religious freedom went into effect in 1962, resulting in the harassment and expulsion of foreign missionaries. By 1964 all but a few Sudanese missionaries had been forced out of the southern region. The northern area, where Islam predominates, is impervious to Christian influence. Late in 1971 some missionaries were allowed to return to work in the South. Southern Sudan was granted regional autonomy within a unified country in March, 1972, thus ending often bitter fighting between the North and South dating back to 1955. Sudan maintains diplomatic relations with Vatican City.

V.a., 5; p.a., 2; bp., 2; parishes, 3; priests, 105 (43 dioc., 62 rel.); sem., 67; m. rel., 104; w. rel., 209; sch., 22; inst., 4; Caths., 433,930; tot. pop., 15,000,000.

Surinam (Dutch Guiana): Autonomous part of the Kingdom of The Netherlands, in northern South America; capital, Paramaribo, Catholicism was introduced in 1683. Evangelization began in 1817.

Dioc., 1; bp., 1; parishes, 9; priests, 56 (4 dioc., 52 rel.); sem., 2; m. rel., 90; w. rel., 145; sch., 31; inst., 22; Caths., 80,000; tot. pop. (1970 est.); 403,000.

Swaziland: Constitutional monarchy in southern Africa, almost totally surrounded by the Republic of South Africa; capital, Mbabane. Missionary work was entrusted to the Servites in 1913. A prefecture apostolic was organized in 1923. The hierarchy was established in 1951. Swaziland has an apostolic delegate (to South Africa).

Dioc., 1; bp., 1; parishes, 10; priests, 34 (2 dioc., 32 rel.); sem., 1; m. rel., 46; w. rel., 120; sch., 63; inst., 11; Caths., 37,102; tot. pop., 410,000.

Sweden: Kingdom in northwestern Europe; capital, Stockholm. Christianity was introduced by St. Ansgar, a Frankish monk, in 829/30. The Church became well established in the 12th century and was a major influence at the end of the Middle Ages. Political and other factors favored the introduction and spread of the Lutheran Church which became the state religion in 1560. The Augsburg Confession of 1530 was accepted by the government; all relations with Rome, in the country since the 12th century, were severed; monasteries were suppressed; the very presence of Catholics in the country was forbidden in 1617. A decree of tolerance for foreign Catholics was issued about 1781. Two years later a vicariate apostolic was organized for the country. In 1873 Swedes were given the legal right to leave the Lutheran Church and join another Christian church. (Membership in the Lutheran Church is presumed by law unless notice is given of membership in another church.) In 1923 there were only 11 priests and five churches in the country. Since 1952 Catholics have enjoyed almost complete religious freedom. The hierarchy was reestablished in 1953. Hindrances to growth of the Church are the strongly entrenched established church, limited resources, a clergy shortage and the size of the country. Sweden has an apostolic delegate (to Scandinavia). Its Catholic bishop is an American, John E. Taylor, O.M.I.

Dioc., 1; bp., 1; parishes, 24; priests, 93 (28 dioc., 65 rel.); sem., 2; m. rel., 72; w. rel., 239; sch., 2; inst., 16; Caths., 55,108; tot. pop. (1970 govt. est.); 8,093,000.

Switzerland: Republic in central Europe; capital, Bern. Christianity was introduced in the fourth century or earlier and was established on a firm footing before the barbarian invasions of the sixth century. Constance, established as a diocese in the seventh century, was a stronghold of the faith against the pagan Alamanni, in particular, who were not converted until some time in the ninth century. During this period of struggle with the barbarians, a number of monasteries of great influence were established. The Reformation in Switzerland was triggered by Zwingli in 1519 and furthered by him at Zurich until his death in battle against the Catholic cantons in 1531. Calvin set in motion the forces that made Geneva the international capital of the Reformation and transformed it into a theocracy. Catholics mobilized a Counter-Reformation in 1570, six years after Calvin's death. Struggle between Protestant and Catholic cantons was a fact of Swiss life for several hundred years. The Helvetic Constitution enacted at the turn of the 19th century embodied anti-Catholic measures and consequences, among them the dissolution of 130 monasteries. The Church was reorganized later in the century to meet the threats of liberalism, radicalism and the Kulturkampf. In the process, the Church, even though on the defensive, gained the strength and cohesion that characterizes it to the present time. The five dioceses in the country are immediately subject to the Holy See. There is a papal nuncio to Switzerland, but Switzerland does not have a diplomatic officer accredited to Vatican City.

Dioc., 6; abb., 2; card., 1; bp., 7; parishes, 1,561; priests, 4,037 (2,938 dioc., 1,099 rel.); sem., 303; m. rel., 1,327; w. rel., 9,062; sch.,

57; inst., 156; Caths., 2,860,215; tot. pop., 6,188,704.

Syria: Arab republic in southwest Asia; capital, Damascus. Christian communities were formed in apostolic times. It is believed that St. Peter established a see at Antioch before going to Rome. Damascus became a center of influence. The area was the place of great men and great events in the early history of the Church. Monasticism developed there in the fourth century. So did the Monophysite and Monothelite heresies to which portions of the Church succumbed. Byzantine Syrians who remained in communion with Rome were given the name Melkites. Christians of various persuasions — Jacobites, Orthodox and Melkites — were subject to various degrees of harassment from the Arabs who took over in 638 and from the Ottoman Turks who isolated the country and remained in control from 1516 to the end of World War II. Syria maintains diplomatic relations with Vatican City.

There are 19 ecclesiastical jurisdictions in Syria serving the following rites: Armenian (1 archdiocese, 2 dioceses); Roman (1 vicariate apostolic); Maronite (1 patriarchate, whose patriarch resides in Lebanon, 2 archdioceses and 1 apostolic administration); Melkite (1 patriarchate, 5 archdioceses); Syrian (1 patriarchate, whose patriarch resides in Lebanon, 4 archdioceses). Catholics (1969), 141,380; tot. pop. (1970 est.), 6,100,000.

Taiwan (Formosa): Location of the Nationalist Government of the Republic of China, an island 100 miles off the southern coast of mainland China; capital, Taipei. Attempts to introduce Christianity in the 17th century were unsuccessful. Evangelization in the 19th century resulted in some 1,300 converts in 1895. Missionary endeavor was hampered by the Japanese who occupied the island following the Sino-Japanese war of 1894-95. Nine thousand Catholics were reported in 1938. Great progress was made in missionary endeavor among the Chinese who emigrated to the island following the Communist take-over of the mainland in 1949. The hierarchy was established in 1952. Nationalist China maintains diplomatic relations with Vatican City.

Archd., 1; dioc., 6; abp., 1; bp., 6; parishes, 407; priests, 768 (216 dioc., 552 rel.); sem., 55; m. rel., 667; w. rel., 874; sch., 99; inst., 119; Caths., 304,116; tot. pop., 14,523,746.

Tanzania: Republic (consisting of former Tanganyika on the eastern coast of Africa and former Zanzibar, an island group off the eastern coast); capital, Dar es Salaam. The first Catholic mission in the former Tanganyikan portion of the republic was manned by Holy Ghost Fathers in 1868. The hierarchy was established there in 1953. Zanzibar was the landing place of Augustinians with the Portuguese in 1499. Some evangelization was attempted between then and 1698 when the Arabs expelled all priests from the territory. There was no Catholic missionary activity from then until the 1860's. The Holy Ghost Fathers arrived in 1863. and were entrusted with the mission in 1872. Zanzibar was important as a point of departure for missionaries to Tanganyika, Kenya and other places in East Africa. A vicariate for Zanzibar was set up in 1906. Tanzania maintains diplomatic relations with Vatican City.

Archd., 2; dioc., 20; prel., 1; p.a., 1; a.a., 1; card., 1 (nat.); abp., 1 (nat.); bp., 20 (15 nat.); parishes, 462; priests, 1,302 (472 dioc., 830 rel.); sem., 343; m. rel., 1,135; w. rel., 2,445; sch., 178; inst., 292; Caths., 2,576,745; tot. pop. (1970 est.), 13,300,000.

Thailand: Constitutional monarchy in southeastern Asia; capital, Bangkok. The first Christians in the region were Portuguese traders who arrived early in the 16th century. A number of missionaries began arriving in 1554 but pastoral care was confined mostly to the Portuguese until the 1660's. Evangelization of the natives got underway from about that time. A seminary was organized in 1665, a vicariate was set up four years later, and a point of departure was established for missionaries to Tonkin, Cochin China and China. Persecution and death for some of the missionaries ended evangelization efforts in 1688. It was resumed, however, and made progress from 1824 onwards. In 1881 missionaries were sent from Siam to neighboring Laos. The hierarchy was established in 1965. Thailand maintains diplomatic relations with Vatican City.

Archd., 2; dioc., 8; abp., 2 (nat.); bp., 7 (2 nat.); parishes, 105; priests, 262 (115 dioc., 147 rel.); sem., 75; m. rel., 335; w. rel., 1,074; sch., 282; inst., 33; Caths., 150,276; tot. pop. (1970 census), 35,550,105.

Tibet: Autonomous region of China in eastern Asia, north of the Himalayas; capital, Lhasa. Christian contact and evangelization attempts have been almost fruitless. Some 1,200 Catholics were reported in Tibet about 1950. Syrians visited the area in the seventh century and evangelization attempts were made by Jesuits, 1624-35 and later, Capuchins, 1707-45, and others afterwards. They all met resistance and some met death. Missionaries do not have access to the country.

Tot. pop., 2,000,000.

Timor, Portuguese: Overseas province in the Malay archipelago; capital, Dili. A Dominican was the first priest in the territory about 1561. Twenty other Dominicans arrived in 1641 and began intensive evangelization. Some of the missionaries exercised civil as well as ecclesiastical authority until early in the 18th century. Anticlerical influences in the Portuguese government forced the missionaries out in 1834. Some improvement in Church-state relations preceded their return in 1874, but in 1910 they were expelled again and the activity of secular priests was restrict-

ed. The Catholic population numbered about 19,000 in 1930. Japanese occupation during World War II had an adverse effect on the missions. Dili was made a diocese in 1940.

Dioc., 1; bp., 1; parishes, 3; priests, 44 (32 dioc., 12 rel); sem., 21; m. rel., 18; w. rel., 48; sch., 44; inst., 4; Caths., 170,999; tot. pop. 628,842.

Togo: Republic on the western coast of Africa; capital, Lome. The first Catholic missionaries in the area, where slave raiders operated for nearly 200 years, were members of the African Missions Society who arrived in 1563. They were followed by Divine Word Missionaries in 1914, when a prefecture apostolic was organized. At that time the Catholic population numbered about 19,000. The African Missionaries returned after their German predecessors were deported following World War I. The first native priest was ordained in 1922. The hierarchy was established in 1955. Togo has an apostolic delegate (to West Africa).

Archd., 1; dioc., 3; abp., 1 (nat.); bp., 3 (2 nat.); parishes, 105; priests, 130 (54 dioc., 76 rel.); sem., 37; m. rel., 90; w. rel., 257; sch., 310; inst., 21; Caths., 411,090; tot. pop., 1,900,000.

Tonga: Polynesian monarchy in the southwestern Pacific, consisting of about 150 islands, member of the British Commonwealth; capital Nuku'alofa. Marists started missionary work in 1842, some years after Protestants had begun evangelization. By 1880 the Catholic population numbered about 1,700. A vicariate was organized in 1937. The hierarchy was established in 1966.

Dioc., 1; bp., 1 (nat.); parishes, 13; priests, 5 (4 dioc., 1 rel.); sem., 6; m. rel., 9; w. rel., 63; sch., 18; inst., 1; Caths., 15,417; tot. pop., 82,429.

Trinidad and Tobago: Independent nation, consisting of two islands in the Caribbean, member of the British Commonwealth; capital, Port-of-Spain. The first Catholic church in Trinidad was built in 1591, years after several missionary ventures had been launched and a number of missionaries killed. Capuchins were there from 1618 until about 1802. Missionary work continued after the British gained control early in the 19th century. Cordial relations have existed between the Church and state, both of which have manifested their desire for the development of native clergy.

Archd., 1; abp., 1; parishes, 60; priests, 139 (23 dioc., 116 rel.); sem., 7; m. rel., 153; w. rel., 281; sch., 160; inst., 19; Caths., 361,455; tot. pop., 1,048,254.

Tunisia: Republic on the northern coast of Africa; capital, Tunis. There were few Christians in the territory until the 19th century. A prefecture apostolic was organized in 1843 and the Carthage archdiocese was established in 1884. The Catholic population in 1892 consisted of most of the approximately 50,000

Europeans in the country. When Tunis became a republic in 1956, most of the Europeans left the country. The Holy See and the Tunisian government concluded an agreement in 1964 which changed the Carthage archdiocese into a prelacy and handed over some ecclesiastical property to the republic. A considerable number of Moslem students are in Catholic schools, but the number of Moslem converts to the Church has been small. Tunisia maintains diplomatic relations with Vatican City.

Prel., 1; bp., 1; parishes, 23; priests, 79 (35 dioc., 44 rel.); m. rel., 67; w. rel., 359; sch., 42; inst., 5; Caths., 35,090; tot. pop., 5,190,000.

Turkey: Republic in Asia Minor and southeastern Europe, capital, Ankara. Christian communities were established in apostolic times, as attested in the Acts of the Apostles, some of the Epistles of St. Paul, and Revelation. The territory was the scene of heresies and ecumenical councils, the place of residence of Fathers of the Church, the area in which ecclesiastical organization reached the dimensions of more than 450 sees in the middle of the seventh century. The region remained generally Byzantine except for the period of the Latin occupation of Constantinople from 1204 to 1261, but was conquered by the Ottoman Turks in 1453 and remained under their domination until establishment of the republic in 1923. Christians, always a minority, numbered more Orthodox than Latins; they were all under some restriction during the Ottoman period. They suffered persecution in the 19th and 20th centuries, the Armenians being the most numerous victims. Turkey is overwhelmingly Moslem. Catholics are tolerated to a degree. Turkey maintains diplomatic relations with Vatican City.

Patriarchate, 1 (the patriarch resides in Lebanon); archd., 4 (2 Armenian rite, 1 Chaldean, 1 Roman); dioc., 14 (12 Armenian, 1 Chaldean, 1 Syrian); v.a., 1 (Roman); missions "sui juris," 2 (Roman); (most of the dioceses are inactive; Caths. (1969), 26,539; tot. pop., (UN est., 1970), 35,230,000.

Uganda: Republic in eastern Africa, member of the British Commonwealth; capital, Kampala. The White Fathers were the first Catholic missionaries, starting in 1879. Persecution broke out from 1885 to 1887, taking a toll of 22 Catholic martyrs, who were canonized in 1964, and a number of Anglican victims. (Pope Paul honored all those who died for the faith during a visit to Kampala in 1969.) By 1888, there were more than 8,000 Catholics. Evangelization was resumed in 1894, after being interrupted by war, and proceeded thereafter. The first native African bishop was ordained in 1939. The hierarchy was established in 1953. Uganda maintains diplomatic relations with Vatican City.

Archd., 1; dioc., 11 abp., 1 (nat.); bp., 12 (8 nat.); parishes, 626; priests, 858 (340 dioc., 518 rel.); sem., 198; m. rel., 852; w. rel., 1,794; sch., 1,331; inst., 105; Caths., 3,121,996; tot. pop., 9,587,790.

Union of Soviet Socialist Republics: Union of 15 Soviet Socialist Republics in northern Eurasia, from the Baltic Sea to the Pacific; Russian capital, Moscow. The Orthodox Church has been predominant in Russian history. It developed from the Byzantine Church before 1064. Some of its members subsequently established communion with Rome as the result of reunion movements but most of them remained Orthodox. The government has always retained some kind of general or particular control of this church. Latins, always a minority, had a little more freedom. From the beginning of the Communist government in 1917, all churches of whatever kind — including Jews and Moslems — became the targets of official campaigns designed to negate their influence on society and/or to eliminate them entirely. An accurate assessment of the situation of the Catholic Church in Russia is difficult to make. Its dimensions, however, can be gauged from the findings of a team of research specialists made public by the Judiciary Committee of the US House of Representatives in 1964. It was reported: "The fate of the Catholic Church in the USSR and countries occupied by the Russians from 1917 to 1959 shows the following: (a) the number killed: 55 bishops; 12,800 priests and monks; 2.5 million Catholic believers; (b) imprisoned or deported: 199 bishops; 32,000 priests and 10 million believers; (c) 15,700 priests were forced to abandon their priesthood and accept other jobs; and (d) a large number of seminaries and religious communities were dissolved; 1,600 monasteries were nationalized, 31,779 churches were closed. 400 newspapers were prohibited, and all Catholic organizations were dissolved." Several Latin Rite churches are open; e.g., in Moscow, Leningrad, Odessa and Tiflis. An American chaplain is stationed in Moscow to serve Catholics at the US embassy there. Recent reports indicate that, despite repression and attempts at Russification, the strongholds of Catholicism in the USSR are Lithuania (incorporated in the USSR in 1940, together with Estonia and Latvia) and the Ukraine.

Archd., 4 (1 in Russia, 2 in Lithuania, 1 in Latvia); dioc., 10 (4 in Russia, 4 in Lithuania, 1 in Latvia, 1 in the Ukraine); bp., 8 (7 in Lithuania, 1 in Latvia; 3 are impeded, there is no indication that the others are permitted to exercise their office); tot. pop., (Kremlin census, 1970), 241,748,000.

United Arab Republic (Egypt): Republic in northeastern Africa, bordering on the Mediterranean; capital, Cairo. Alexandria was the influential hub of a Christian community established by the end of the second century; it became a patriarchate and the center of the Coptic Church, and had great influence on the spread of Christianity in various parts of

Africa; Monasticism developed from desert communities of hermits in the third and four centuries. Arianism was first preached in Egypt in the 320's. In the fifth century, the Coptic church went Monophysite through failure to accept doctrine formulated by the Council of Chalcedon in 451 with respect to the two natures of Christ. The country was thoroughly Arabized after 640 and was under the rule of Ottoman Turks from 1517 to 1798. English influence was strong during the 19th century. A monarchy established in 1922 lasted about 30 years, ending with the proclamation of a republic in 1953-54. By that time Egypt had become the leader of pan-Arabism against Israel. It waged two unsuccessful wars against Israel in 1948-49 and 1967. Between 1958 and 1961 it was allied with Syria and Yemen, in the United Arab Republic. Islam, the religion of some 90 percent of the population, is the state religion. Egypt maintains diplomatic relations with Vatican City.

Patriarchate, 2 (Alexandria for the Copts and the Melkites); dioc., 6; v.a., 3; card., 1; bp., 8; parishes, 212; priests, 338 (146 dioc., 192 rel.); sem., 39; m. rel., 271; w. rel., 1,372; sch., 189; inst., 114; Caths. (1969), 165,072; tot. pop. (UN est., 1969), 32,501,000.

United States: See Catholic History in the United States, Statistics of the Church in the United States.

Upper Volta: Republic inland in western Africa; capital, Ouagadougou. White Fathers started the first missions in 1900 and 1901. White Sisters began work in 1911. A minor and a major seminary were established in 1926 and 1942, respectively. The first native bishop in modern times from West Africa was ordained in 1956 and the first cardinal created in 1965. The hierarchy was established in 1955. Upper Volta has an apostolic delegate (to West Africa).

Archd., 1; dioc., 8; card., 1 (nat.); bp., 8 (5 nat.); parishes, 90; priests, 368 (94 dioc., 274 rel.); sem., 68; m. rel., 448; w. rel., 569; sch., 49; inst., 44; Caths., 283,073; tot. pop., 5,372,614.

Uruguay: Republic (called the Eastern Republic of Uruguay) on the southeast coast of South America; capital, Montevideo. The Spanish established a settlement in 1624 and evangelization followed. Missionaries followed the reduction pattern to reach the Indians, form them in the faith and train them in agriculture, husbandry, other useful arts, and the experience of managing property and living in community. Montevideo was made a diocese in 1878. The constitution of 1830 made Catholicism the religion of the state and subsidized some of its activities, principally the missions to the Indians. Separation of Church and state was provided for in the constitution of 1917. Uruguay maintains diplomatic relations with Vatican City.

Archd., 1; dioc., 9; card., 1; abp., 1; bp., 10; parishes, 211; priests, 601 (199 dioc., 402 rel.);
sem., 55; p.d., 4; m. rel., 664; w. rel., 1,068; sch., 337; inst., 61; Caths., 2,492,922; tot. pop., 2,885,948.

Vatican City: See separate entry.

Venezuela: Republic in northern South America; capital, Caracas. Evangelization began in 1513-14 and involved members of a number of religious orders who worked in assigned territories, developing missions into pueblos or towns and villages of Indian converts. Nearly 350 towns originated as missions. Fifty-four missionaries met death by violence from the start of missionary work until 1817. Missionary work was seriously hindered during the wars of independence in the second decade of the 19th century and continued in decline through the rest of the century as dictator followed dictator in a period of political turbulence. Restoration of the missions got underway in 1922. The first diocese was established in 1531. Most of the bishops have been native Venezuelans. The first diocesan synod was held in 1574. Church-state relations are regulated by an agreement concluded with the Holy See in 1964. Venezuela maintains diplomatic relations with Vatican City.

Archd., 5; dioc., 16; prel., 1; v.a., 4; card., 1; abp., 5; bp., 25; parishes, 852; priests, 1,986; (852 dioc., 1,134 rel.); sem., 154; m. rel., 1,503; w. rel., 4,032; sch., 533; inst., 141; Caths., 9,500,000; tot. pop. (UN est., 1970), 10,400,000.

Vietnam: Country in southeastern Asia partitioned in 1954 into the Democratic Peoples' Republic of Vietnam in the North (capital, Hanoi) and the Republic of Vietnam in the South (capital, Saigon). Catholicism was introduced in 1533 but missionary work was intermittent until 1615 when Jesuits arrived to stay. One hundred thousand Catholics were reported in 1639. Two vicariates were organized in 1659. A seminary was set up in 1666 and two native priests were ordained two years later. A congregation of native women religious formed in 1670 is still active. Severe persecution broke out in 1698, three times in the 18th century, and again in the 19th. Between 100,000 and 300,000 persons suffered in some way from persecution during the 50 years before 1883 when the French moved in to secure religious liberty for the Catholics. Most of the 117 beatified Martyrs of Vietnam were killed during this 50-year period. After the French were forced out of Vietnam in 1954, the country was partitioned at the 17th parallel. The North went Communist and the Viet Cong, joined by North Vietnamese regular army troops in 1964, fought to gain control of the South. In 1954 there were approximately 1,114,000 Catholics in the North and 480,000 in the South. More than 650,000 fled to the South to avoid the government repression that has since silenced the Church in the North. In the South, the Church has continued to grow and develop despite the war. The hierarchy was established in 1960. Vietnam has an apostolic delegate.

North Vietnam: Archd., 1; dioc., 9; bp., 10; parishes, 626; priests, 315 (311 dioc., 4, rel.); sem., 119; m. rel., 9; w. rel., 293; inst., 40; Caths., 799,845 (some figures date from 1963); tot. pop. (UN est., 1970), 21,150,000.

South Vietnam: Archd., 2; dioc., 12; abp., 2; bp., 13; parishes, 688; priests, 1,706 (1,348 dioc., 358 rel.); sem., 786; m. rel., 1,497; w. rel., 5,942; sch., 1,265; inst., 446; Caths., 1,827,030; tot. pop. (UN est., 1970), 18,130,000.

Virgin Islands: Organized unincorporated US territory, about 34 miles east of Puerto Rico; capital, Charlotte Amalie on St. Thomas (one of the three principal islands). The islands were discovered by Columbus in 1493 and named for St. Ursula and her virgin companions. Missionaries began evangelization in the 16th century. A church on St. Croix dates from about 1660; another, on St. Thomas, from 1774. The Baltimore archdiocese had jurisdiction over the islands from 1804 to 1820 when it was passed on to the first of several places in the Caribbean area. Some trouble arose over a pastoral appointment in the 19th century, resulting in a small schism. The Redemptorists took over pastoral care in 1858; normal conditions have prevailed since.

Prel., 1; bp., 1; parishes, 6; priests, 16 (1 dioc., 15 rel.); m. rel., 17; w. rel., 26; sch., 5; Caths., 19,883; tot. pop., 70,000.

Wales: Part of the United Kingdom, on the western part of the island of Great Britain. Celtic missionaries completed evangelization by the end of the sixth century, the climax of what has been called the age of saints. Welsh Christianity received its distinctive Celtic character at this time. Some conflict developed when attempts were made — and proved successful later — to place the Welsh Church under the jurisdiction of Canterbury; the Welsh opted for direct contact with Rome. The Church made progress despite the depredations of Norsemen in the eighth and ninth centuries. Norman infiltration occurred near the middle of the 12th century, resulting in a century-long effort to establish territorial dioceses and parishes to replace the Celtic organizational plan of monastic centers and satellite churches. The Western Schism produced split views and allegiances. Actions of Henry VIII in breaking away from Rome had serious repercussions. Proscription and penal laws crippled the Church, resulted in heavy defections and touched off a 150-year period of repression in which more than 91 persons died for the faith. Methodism prevailed by 1750. Modern Catholicism came to Wales with Irish immigrants in the 19th century, when the number of Welsh Catholics was negligible. Catholic emancipation was granted in 1829. The hierarchy was restored in 1850.

Archd., 1; dioc., 1; abp., 1; bp., 3; parishes, 169; priests, 365 (196 dioc., 169 rel.); sem., 22; m. rel., 190; w. rel., 794; sch., 85; inst., 50; Caths., 140,167; tot. pop., 2,740,959.

Wallis and Futuna Islands: French territory in the southwestern Pacific. Marists, who began evangelizing the islands in 1836-7, were the first Catholic missionaries. The entire populations of the two islands were baptized by the end of 1842 (Wallis) and 1843 (Futuna). The first missionary to the latter island was killed in 1841; he was the first martyr of the Pacific. Most of the priests on the islands are native Polynesians. The hierarchy was established in 1966.

Dioc., 1; bp., 1; parishes, 5; priests, 16 (6 dioc., 10 rel.); sem., 8; m. rel., 14; w. rel., 70; sch., 7; Caths., 8,362; tot. pop., 9,900.

West Indies: (St. Lucia, Grenada, St. Vincent, Dominica, Antigua, St. Kitts-Nevis-Anguilla.)

Dioc., 5; bp., 5; parishes, 76; priests, 113 (15 dioc., 98 rel.); sem., 12; m. rel., 142; w. rel., 232; sch., 139; inst., 10; Caths., 262,761. Figures, from AP, are for dioceses of Castries (St. Lucia), Roseau (Dominica), St. George's (Grenada), Bridgetown-Kingston (Bardados-St. Vincent) and St. John's (Antigua).

Yemen: Arab republic in southwestern Arabia; capital, Sana. Christians perished in the first quarter of the sixth century. Moslems have been in control since the seventh century. The state religion is Islam.

Tot. pop., 5,000,000.

Yemen, Peoples Democratic Republic of: Republic in the southern part of the Arabian peninsula; capitals, Aden and Medinat as-Shaab. No Christian community has existed there since the Moslem conquest of the seventh century. See Arabian Peninsula.

Yugoslavia: Socialist republic in southeastern Europe; capital, Belgrade. Christianity was introduced from the seventh to ninth centuries in the regions which were combined to form the nation after World War I. Since these regions straddled the original line of demarcation for the Western and Eastern Empires (and churches), and since the Reformation had little lasting effect, the Christians are nearly all either Roman Catholics or Byzantines (some in communion with Rome, the majority Orthodox). Yugoslavia was proclaimed a Socialist republic in 1945. Repression of religion became government policy. Between May, 1945, and December, 1950, persecution took the following toll: almost two-thirds of 22 dioceses lost their bishops; about 348 priests were killed; 200 priests were under arrest and in prison; 12 of 18 seminaries were closed; the Catholic press was confiscated; religious instruction was suppressed in all schools; 300 religious houses and institutions were confiscated, and nuns and other religious driven out; all Church property was expropriated; the ministry of priests was severely restricted and subject to government interference; many thousands of the faithful shared the fate of priests and religious in death, imprisonment and slave labor. Cardinal Stepinac arrested in 1946 and the symbol of the Church under persecution in Yugoslavia, died Feb. 10, 1960. In an agreement signed June 25, 1966, the government recognized the Holy See's spiritual jurisdiction over the Church in the country and guaranteed to bishops the possibility of maintaining contact with Rome in ecclesiastical and religious matters. The Holy See confirmed the principle that the activity of ecclesiastics, in the exercise of priestly functions, must take place within the religious and ecclesiastical sphere, and that abuse of these functions for political ends would be illegal. Less than two months after the agreement was signed, a group of exiled Croatian priests issued a statement in which they accused the Yugoslav government of failing to abide by it. According to others, an improvement was noticeable. Yugoslavia maintains diplomatic relations with Vatican City.

Archd., 8; dioc., 13; a.a., 1; card., 1; abp., 9; bp., 16; parishes, 2,404; priests, 3,309 (2,296 dioc., 1,013 rel.); sem., 974; m. rel., 2,229; w. rel., 6,235; sch., 6; inst., 5; Caths., 6,675,852; tot. pop. (UN est., 1970), 20,530,000.

Zaire (formerly the Congo): Republic in south central Africa; capital, Kinshasa. Christianity was introduced in 1484 and evangelization began about 1490. The first native bishop in black Africa was ordained in 1518. Subsequent missionary work was hindered by faulty methods of instruction and formation,

inroads of the slave trade, wars among the tribes, and Portuguese policy based on the patronage system and having all the trappings of anti-clericalism in the 18th and 19th centuries. Modern evangelization started in the second half of the 19th century. The hierarchy was established in 1959. In the civil disorders which followed independence in 1960, some missions and other church installations were abandoned, thousands of people reverted to tribal religions and many priests and religious were killed. Zaire maintains diplomatic relations with Vatican City.

Archd., 6; dioc., 42; card., 1 (nat.); abp., 5 (4 nat.); bp., 45 (29 nat.); parishes, 727; priests, 2,711 (609 dioc., 2,102 rel.); sem., 429; m. rel., 3,254; w. rel., 4,145; sch., 6,827; inst., 956; Caths., 8,925,077; tot. pop. (1970 govt. est.), 21,637,000.

Zambia: Republic in central Africa; capital, Lusaka. Portuguese priests did some evangelizing in the 16th and 17th centuries but no results of their work remained in the 19th century. Jesuits began work in the south in the 1880's and White Fathers in the north and east in 1895. Evangelization of the western region began for the first time in 1831. The number of Catholics doubled in the 20 years following World War II. Zambia maintains diplomatic relations with Vatican City.

Archd., 2; dioc., 6; p.a., 1; abp., 2 (nat.), bp., 6 (3 nat.); parishes, 140; priests, 443 (63 dioc., 380 rel.); sem., 22; p.d., 2; m. rel. (brothers), 187; w. rel., 600; sch., 642; inst., 88; Caths., 817,720; tot. pop., 4,154,459 (most of the figures are from Fides).

CATHOLIC WORLD STATISTICS

(Principal source: *Annuario Pontificio, 1972.*)

Patriarchates: 11 (Asia, 7; Africa, 2; Europe, 2).

Archdioceses: 480 (Asia, 124; Oceania, 14; Africa, 47; Europe, 144; South America, 77; North and Middle America, 74).

Dioceses: 1,716 (Asia, 326; Oceania, 44; Africa, 260; Europe, 529; South America, 273; North and Middle America, 284).

Prelatures: 102 (Asia, 12; Africa, 2; Europe, 6; South America, 70; North and Middle America, 12).

Abbacies: 22 (Asia, 1; Oceania, 1; Africa, 2; Europe, 14; South America, 2; North and Middle America, 2).

Vicariates Apostolic: 82 (Asia, 17; Oceania, 1; Africa, 19; Europe, 4; South America, 36; North and Middle America, 5).

Prefectures Apostolic: 72 (Asia, 38; Africa, 23; South America, 10; North and Middle America, 1).

Apostolic Administrations, 10 (Asia, 1; Africa, 1; Europe, 6; North and Middle America, 2).

Missions "Sui Juris": 5 (Asia, 4; Oceania, 1).

Apostolic Exarchates, Ordinariates: 25 (Asia, 7; Oceania, 1; Europe, 14; South America, 2; North and Middle America, 1).

Cardinals: 116 (Asia, 9; Oceania, 2; Africa, 7; Europe, 71; South America, 12; North and Middle America, 15). Figures as of Sept. 15, 1972.

Patriarchs: 10 (Asia, 7; Africa, 1; Europe, 2). Two of the patriarchs are cardinals.

Archbishops: 380 (Asia, 66; Oceania, 16; Africa, 42; Europe, 106; South America, 74; North and Middle America, 76). Figures are for residential and coadjutor archbishops.

Bishops, 2,137 (Asia, 249; Oceania, 50; Africa, 287; Europe, 661; South America, 439; North and Middle America, 451). Figures are for residential, coadjutor and auxiliary bishops.

Priests, Total: 416,960 (Asia, 25,182; Oceania, 5,917; Africa, 17,120; Europe, 250,578; South America, 33,089; North and Middle America, 85,074).

Priests, Diocesan: 271,926 (Asia, 12,984; Oceania, 3,328; Africa, 5,004; Europe, 182,445; South America, 14,995; North and Middle America, 53,170).

Priests, Religious: 145,034 (Asia, 12,198; Oceania, 2,589; Africa, 12,116; Europe,

68,133; South America, 18,094; North and Middle America, 31,904).

Seminarians: 65,313 (Asia, 6,696; Oceania, 691; Africa, 3,123; Europe, 24,503; South America, 3,090; North and Middle America, 27,210).

Permanent Deacons: 424: (Asia, 13; Oceania, 3; Africa, 17; Europe, 139; South America, 65; North and Middle America, 187).

Men Religious: 238,109 (Asia, 22,517; Oceania, 6,414; Africa, 18,237; Europe, 114,269; South America, 26,246; North and Middle America, 50,426). Figures include priest and non-priest members of religious institutes.

Women Religious: 879,939 (Asia, 71,880; Oceania, 18,238; Africa, 33,707; Europe, 445,383; South America, 87,593; North and Middle America, 223,138).

Catholic Population: 633,000,000 (17.8 per cent of total world population): Asia, 47,600,000 (2.3 per cent); Oceania, 4,400,000 (23.2 per cent); Africa, 38,100,000 (11 per cent); Europe, 266,600,000 (38.3 per cent); South America, 157,650,000 (85.2 per cent); North and Middle America, 118,650,000 (37.7 per cent).

Population figures are estimates as of Dec. 31, 1969, and include persons baptized as Catholics. They are from the compilation of statistical tables published in 1971 by the Central Statistics Office of the Church.

The actual Catholic population based on questionnaires returned to the Central Statistics Office amounted to 605,918,000; an additional 27,000,000 baptized Catholics were estimated for countries from which no accurate information could be obtained (China, North Korea, Mongolia, Siberia, North Vietnam, Albania, East Germany, USSR), bringing the estimated total as of Dec. 31, 1969, to the 633,000,000 noted above.

Totals from the *Annuario Pontificio, 1972,* amounted to more than 645,000,000 baptized Catholics.

Despite the differences in total Catholic population figures, the Catholic population was still between 17 and 18 per cent of the general population.

COMMUNISM

The substantive principles of modern Communism, a theory and system of economics and social organization, were stated about the middle of the 19th century by Karl Marx, author of *The Communist Manisfesto* and, with Friedrich Engels, *Das Kapital.*

The elements of Communist ideology include: radical materialism; dialectical determinism; the inevitability of class struggle, which is to be furthered, for the ultimate establishment of a worldwide classless society; common ownership of productive and other goods; the subordination of all persons and institutions to the dictatorship of the collectivity; denial of the rights, dignity and liberty

of persons; militant atheism and hostility to religion; utilitarian morality.

Communism in theory and practice has been the subject of many papal documents and statements. Pius IX condemned it in 1846. Leo XIII dealt with it at length in the encyclicals *Quod Apostolici Muneris* in 1878 and *Rerum Novarum* in 1891. Pius XI wrote on the same subject in the encyclicals *Quadragesimo Anno* in 1931 and *Divini Redemptoris* in 1937.

Pius XII, besides writing and speaking about Communism on many occasions, authorized the June 13, 1949, decree of the Congregation of the Holy Office which contained these as well as other provisions: Catholics are forbidden to join the Communist Party; Catholics who knowingly and willingly profess the doctrines of Communism, or defend its principles, or spread its errors are automatically excommunicated. Catholics who join the Communist Party under the force of hard circumstances (as in Iron Curtain countries, for the sake of work needed to support their families) but do not subscribe to its ideology, are not excommunicated.

John XXIII condemned the errors of Communism as intrinsically evil. In the encyclical *Peace on Earth,* however, without going soft on Communism, he sanctioned prudent and cautious efforts to work with Communists for the solution of social and economic problems.

Virtually all of the papal documents on Communism set forth Christian social teachings and urge action for the establishment of a just social order which should be its own best defense against Communism.

CHURCH IN CUBA

Father Jose M. Gonzales Ruiz, after attending a Christian student congress in Cuba, said in August, 1972, that the Church there "has withdrawn into a shell."

The Spanish theologian, who was well known for his radical views on the Church and social reform, also said he had seen some positive gains under the Marxist regime in Cuba. "Socialism in Cuba is nonsectarian," but somehow it shows constant nostalgia for traditional Christian values," he declared.

In his opinion, the Church in Cuba "has folded itself inward, with unity and discipline prevailing over any possible moves for renewal."

In the rest of Latin America, and in Spain, he added, "the Second Vatican Council has provoked the dynamics of conflict, thus pushing for renewal and self-evaluation. The Church in Cuba has no conflict experience within (itself). It is running the risk of becoming frozen in history."

The work of the Church there, Father Ruiz said, "must be to bring the Gospel to that 'new man' the (Castro) revolution has created, a new man whose values offer tremendous coincidences with those of the Christian."

EPISCOPAL CONFERENCES

(Principal source: *Annuario Pontificio.)*

Episcopal conferences, organized and operating under general norms and particular statutes approved by the Holy See, are official bodies in and through which the bishops of a given country or territory act together as pastors of the Church.

Listed are countries with conferences, dates when statutes were approved where available, names and sees of presidents (archbishops unless otherwise noted).

AFRICA, North (Feb. 27, 1967): Cardinal Leon-Etienne Duval, Algiers.

AFRICA, South (Apr. 28, 1970): Cardinal Owen McCann, Cape Town.

ANGOLA and SAO TOME (Apr. 15, 1967); Manuel Nunes Gabriel, Luanda.

ANTILLES (Dec. 10, 1957): Samuel E. Carter, Kingston in Jamaica.

ARAB COUNTRIES: Latin Bishops (Mar. 31, 1967): Patriarch Giacomo Beltritti, Jerusalem.

ARGENTINA (Jan. 14, 1967): Adolfo Servando Tortolo, Parana.

AUSTRALIA (Apr. 3, 1971): James Darcy Freeman, Sydney.

AUSTRIA (Dec. 20, 1969): Cardinal Franz Koenig, Vienna.

BANGLADESH: See Pakistan.

BELGIUM: (Aug. 21, 1971): Cardinal Leo Suenens, Mechelen-Brussels.

BOLIVIA (Aug. 8, 1966): Cardinal Jose Clemente Maurer, Sucre.

BRAZIL (Jan. 23, 1971): Bishop Alois Lorscheider, Santo Angelo.

BULGARIA: Bishop Metodio Dimitrow Stratiew, apostolic exarch, Sofia.

BURMA (Feb. 10, 1967): Gabriel Thohey, Rangoon.

CAMEROON: Jean Zoa, Yaounde.

CANADA (Jan. 23, 1955): Bishop William E. Power, Antigonish.

CENTRAL AFRICAN REPUBLIC: Joachym N'Dayen, Bangui.

CEYLON: See Sri Lanka, Republic of.

CHAD: Paul Dalmais, Fort Lamy.

CHILE (June 13, 1970): Cardinal Raul Silva, Santiago.

CHINA (Feb. 10, 1967): Cardinal Paul Yu Pin, Nanking.

COLOMBIA (Apr. 2, 1966): Anibal Munoz Duque, coadjutor, Bogota.

CONGO: Emile Biayenda, Brazzaville.

COSTA RICA (Oct. 6, 1967): Bishop Roman Arrieta Villalobos, Tileran.

CUBA (Aug. 26, 1967): Francisco Ricardo Oves Fernandez, San Cristobal de Havana.

CZECHOSLOVAKIA: Bishop Stepan Trochta, Litomerice.

DAHOMEY: President. . . .

DOMINICAN REPUBLIC (Oct. 6, 1967): Octavio Beras Rojas, Santo Domingo.

ECUADOR (Mar. 3, 1967): Cardinal Pablo Munoz Vega, Quito.

EL SALVADOR (June 15, 1968): Bishop Benjamin Barrera y Reyes, Santa Ana.

ETHIOPIA (Dec. 15, 1966): Asrate M. Yemmeru, Addis Ababa.

FRANCE (Nov. 21, 1966): Cardinal Francois Marty, Paris.

GABON: Fernand Anguile, Libreville.

GAMBIA: See Liberia, Sierra Leone and Gambia.

GERMANY (Dec. 10, 1966): Cardinal Julius Doepfner, Munich and Freising. Additional conferences for West Germany and Bavaria, of which Cardinal Doepfner is president; and for Berlin, of which Cardinal Alfred Bengsch, Berlin, is president.

GHANA: J. K. Amissah, Cape Coast.

GREAT BRITAIN (June 15, 1968): Cardinal John Heenan, Westminster (England and Wales); Cardinal Gordon J. Gray, St. Andrews and Edinburgh (Scotland).

GREECE (Apr. 17, 1967): Antonio Varhalitis, Corfu, Zante and Cefalonia.

GUATEMALA (May 21, 1966): Bishop Humberto Lara Mejia, Santa Cruz del Quiche.

GUINEA: Raymond-Marie Tchidimbo, Conakry.

HAITI (Mar. 29, 1967): Bishop Jean Jacques Claudius Agenor, Les Cayes.

HONDURAS (Mar. 23, 1967): Hector Santos y Hernandez, Tegucigalpa.

HUNGARY (May 3, 1969): Jozsef Ijjas, Kalocsa.

INDIA (Apr. 29, 1967): Cardinal Joseph Parecattil, Ernakulam.

INDONESIA (Oct. 13, 1967): Cardinal Justin Darmojuwona, Semarang.

IRELAND (Aug. 9, 1969): Cardinal William Conway, Armagh.

ITALY (May 8, 1971): Cardinal Antonio Poma, Bologna.

IVORY COAST: Bernard Yago, Abidjan.

JAPAN (Jan. 28, 1967): Paul Yoshigoro Taguchi, Osaka.

KENYA (Jan. 18, 1969): Maurice Otunga, Nairobi (Seychelles Islands included in this conference).

KOREA (Dec. 4, 1967): Cardinal Stephan Sou Hwan Kim, Seoul.

LAOS and CAMBODIA (Apr. 23, 1971): Bishop Etienne Loosdregt, vicar apostolic, Vientiane.

LATVIA: Bishop Julian Vaivods, apostolic administrator, Riga and Liepaja.

LESOTHO (established 1972; statutes to be submitted to Rome); Alphonsus Morapeli, O.M.I., Maseru.

LIBERIA, SIERRA LEONE and GAMBIA (interterritorial episcopal conference): Thomas J. Brosnahan, Freetown and Bo.

LITHUANIA: Bishop Joseph Matulaitis-Labukas, apostolic administrator, Kaunas and Vilkaviskis.

MALAGASY REPUBLIC (June 18,

1969): Albert J. Tsiahoana, Diego-Suarez.

MALAWI (Oct. 1, 1969): James Ciona, Blantyre.

MALAYSIA and SINGAPORE (Dec. 14, 1967): Bishop Anthony D. Galvin, vicar apostolic, Miri.

MALI: Luc Auguste Sangare, Bamako.

MALTA (July 3, 1971): President, . . .

MEXICO (Jan. 7, 1967): Ernesto Corripio Ahumada, Antequera.

MOZAMBIQUE (Apr. 20, 1967): Francesco Nunes Teixeira, Quelimone.

NETHERLANDS (Nov. 21, 1967): Cardinal Bernard Alfrink, Utrecht.

NEW ZEALAND (Jan. 21, 1968): Cardinal Peter McKeefry, Wellington.

NICARAGUA (Apr. 8, 1967): Miguel Obando Bravo, Managua.

NIGERIA: President, . . .

PACIFIC (Mar. 25, 1971): Pierre Martin, Noumea.

PAKISTAN: Theotonius A. Ganguly, Dacca. (Bangladesh gained independence early in 1972.)

PANAMA (Aug. 26, 1967): Bishop Jose Maria Carrizo Villareal, Chitre.

PAPUA-NEW GUINE and SOLOMON ISLANDS)dec. 6, 1966): Bishop Leo Arkfeld, Wewak.

PARAGUAY (Nov. 7, 1966): Bishop Ramon Bogarin Argana, San Juan Bautista.

PERU (Dec. 15, 1967): Cardinal Juan Landazuri Ricketts, O.F.M., Lima.

PHILIPPINE ISLANDS (Dec. 12, 1967): Teopista Alberto J. Valderramo, Caceres.

POLAND (Mar. 15, 1969): Cardinal Stefan Wyszynski, Gniezno and Warsaw.

PORTUGAL (July 10, 1967): Cardinal Manuel Goncalves Cerejeira, former patriarch of Lisbon.

PUERTO RICO (June 19, 1971): Luis Aponte Martinez, San Juan.

RHODESIA (Oct. 1, 1969): Bishop Donal Raymond Lamont, Umtali.

RUMANIA: Bishop Aaron Marton, Alba Julia.

RWANDA-BURUNDI (May 5, 1969): Andre Makarakiza, Kitega.

SCANDINAVIA (Apr. 30, 1969): Bishop John E. Taylor, Stockholm.

SENGAL-MAURITANIA: Hyacinthe Thiandoum, Dakar.

SIERRA LEONE: See Liberia, Sierra Leone and Gambia.

SPAIN (May 14, 1966): Cardinal Vicente Enrique y Tarancon, Madrid (ad interim).

SRI LANKA, REPUBLIC OF (CEYLON))apr. 24, 1970): Cardinal Thomas Cooray, Colombo.

SUDAN (July 15, 1971): Bishop Ireneus Wien Dud, vicar apostolic, Wau.

SWITZERLAND (Dec. 12, 1967): Bishop Francois Nestor Adam, Sion.

TANZANIA (Sept. 29, 1969): Bishop James Sangu, Mbeya.

THAILAND (Mar. 28, 1969): Joseph Khiamsun Nittayo, Bangkok.

TOGO: Robert Dosseh Anyron, Lome.

UGANDA: (Sept. 29, 1969): Emmanuel Nsubuga, Kampala.

UNITED STATES OF AMERICA (Dec. 19, 1970): Cardinal John Krol, Philadelphia.

UPPER VOLTA and NIGER: Cardinal Paul Zoungrana, Ouagadougou.

URUGUAY: (Aug. 29, 1966): Carolos Parteli, coadjutor and apostolic administrator, Montevideo.

VENEZUELA (Mar. 23, 1967): Cardinal Humberto Quintero, Caracas.

VIETNAM (Feb. 24, 1967): Paul Nguyen van Binh, Saigon.

YUGOSLAVIA (May 27, 1967): Franjo Kuharic, Zagreb.

ZAIRE (Feb. 7, 1969): Bishop Leon Lesambo, Inongo.

ZAMBIA (Dec. 20, 1966): Bishop James Corboy, Monze.

Territorial Conferences

Territorial as well as national episcopal conferences have been established in some places. Some conferences of this kind are still in the planning stage.

Africa: Association of Member Episcopal Conferences in Eastern Africa (AMECEA): Represents Uganda, Kenya, Tanzania, Zambia and Malawi; Cardinal Laurean Rugambwa, Dar es Salaam, Tanzania, president.

Symposium of Episcopal Conferences of Africa and Madagascar (Malagasy Republic) (SECAM): Cardinal Paul Zoungrana, Ouagadougou, Upper Volta, president.

Plenary Council of Bishops of West Africa: Abp. Bernard Yago, Abidjan, Ivory Coast.

Association of Episcopal Conferences of Central Africa and Cameroon: Abp. Paul Dalmais, Fort Lamy, Chad, president.

Asia: Federation of Asian Bishops' Conferences (FABC): Represents 13 Asian episcopal conferences (excluding the Middle East); approved by Asian Bishops' Conference in the Philippines in 1970. A secretariat with headquarters in Hong Kong coordinates and implements decisions made by the conference.

Europe: Council of European Bishops' Conferences: Abp. Roger Etchegaray, Marseilles, France, president.

Central and South America: Latin American Bishops' Conference (Consejo Episcopal LatinoAmericano, CELAM): Established in 1956; statutes approved experimentally Nov. 27, 1969. Represents 22 Latin American national bishops' conferences. Abp. Avelar Brandao Vilela, Sao Salvador da Bahia, Brazil, president. Address of the secretariat: Apartado Aereo 5278, Bogota, D.E., Colombia.

Episcopal Secretariat of Central America and Panama: Statutes approved experimentally Sept. 26, 1970. Bishop Luis Manresa Formosa, Quezaltenago, president.

The Catholic Church in Canada

The first date in the remote background of the Catholic history of Canada was July 7, 1534, when a priest in the exploration company of Jacques Cartier celebrated Mass on the Gaspe Peninsula.

Successful colonization and the significant beginnings of the Catholic history of the country date from the foundation of Quebec in 1608 by Samuel Champlain and French settlers. Montreal was established in 1642.

The earliest missionaries were Franciscan Recollects and Jesuits who arrived in 1615 and 1625, respectively. They provided some pastoral care for the settlers but worked mainly among the 100,000 Indians — Algonquins and Huron-Iroquois — in the interior and in the Lake Ontario region. Eight Jesuits, the North American Martyrs, were killed in the 1640's. Sulpician Fathers, who arrived in Canada late in the 1640's, played a part in the great missionary period which ended about 1700.

Kateri Tekakwitha, Lily of the Mohawks, the first North American Indian candidate for canonization, died in 1680.

The communities of women religious with the longest histories in Canada are the Canonesses of St. Augustine, since 1637; the Ursulines, since 1639; and the Hospitallers of St. Joseph, since 1642. Communities of Canadian origin are the Congregation of Notre Dame, founded by Marguerite Bourgeoys in 1658, and the Grey Nuns, formed by Mother d'Youville in 1738.

Start of Church Organization

Ecclesiastical organization began with the appointment of Francois Montmorency de Laval as vicar apostolic of New France in 1658 — 26 years after France canceled England's claim to possession of the country. In 1674, Quebec became the first diocese in the territory.

In 1713, the French Canadian population numbered 18,000. In the same year, the Treaty of Utrecht ceded Acadia, Newfoundland and the Hudson Bay Territory to England. The Acadians were scattered among the American Colonies in 1755.

The English acquired possession of Canada and its 70,000 French-speaking inhabitants in virtue of the Treaty of Paris in 1763. Anglo-French and Anglican-Catholic differences and tensions developed. The pro-British government at first refused to recognize the titles of church officials, hindered the clergy in their work and tried to install a non-Catholic educational system. Laws were passed which guaranteed religious liberties to Catholics (Quebec Act of 1774, Constitutional Act of 1791, legislation approved by Queen Victoria in 1851), but it took some time before actual respect for these liberties matched the legal enactments. The initial moderation of government antipathy toward the Church was caused partly by the loyalty of Catholics to the Crown during the American Revolution and the War of 1812.

Growth

The 15 years following the passage in 1840 of the Act of Union, which joined Upper and Lower Canada, were significant. New communities of men and women religious joined those already in the country. The Oblates of Mary Immaculate, missionaries par excellence in Canada, advanced the penetration of the West which had been started in 1818 by Abbe Provencher. New jurisdictions were established, and Quebec became a metropolitan see in 1844. The first Council of Quebec was held in 1851. The established Catholic school system enjoyed a period of growth.

Laval University was inaugurated in 1854 and canoically established in 1876.

Archbishop Taschereau of Quebec was named Canada's first cardinal in 1886.

The apostolic delegation to Canada was set up in 1899. It became a nunciature in 1970, with the establishment of diplomatic relations with the Vatican.

Early in this century, Canada had eight ecclesiastical provinces, 23 dioceses, three vicariates apostolic, 3,500 priests, 2.4 million Catholics, about 30 communities of men religious, and 70 or more communities of women religious. The Church in Canada was phased out of mission status and removed from the jurisdiction of the Congregation for the Propagation of the Faith in 1908.

The greatest concentration of Catholics is in the eastern portion of the country. In the northern and western portions, outside metropolitan centers, there are some of the most difficult parish and mission areas in the world. Bilingual (English-French) differences in the general population are reflected in the Church; for example, in the parallel structures of the Canadian Catholic Conference, which was established in 1943. Quebec is the center of French cultural influence. Many language groups are represented among Catholics, who include about 216,000 members of Eastern Rite in a metropolitan see and three eparchies.

Education, a past source of friction between the Church and the government, is administered by the civil provinces in a variety of arrangements authorized by the Canadian Constitution. Denominational schools have tax support in one way in Quebec and Newfoundland, and in another way in Alberta, Ontario and Saskatchewan. Several provinces provide tax support only for public schools, making private financing necessary for separate church-related schools.

ECCLESIASTICAL JURISDICTIONS OF CANADA

Provinces

Names of ecclesiastical provinces and metropolitan sees in bold face: suffragan sees in parentheses. The Winnipeg archdiocese (Latin) is not a metropolitan see.

Edmonton (Calgary, St. Paul).

Grouard-McLennan (Mackenzie-Ft. Smith, Prince George, Whitehorse).

Halifax (Antigonish, Charlottetown, Yarmouth).

Keewatin-LePas (Churchill-Hudson Bay, Labrador-Schefferville, Moosonee).

Kingston (Alexandria, Peterborough, Sault Ste. Marie).

Moncton (Bathurst, Edmundston, St. John).

Montreal (Joliette, St. Jean-de-Quebec, St. Jerome, Valleyfield).

Ottawa (Hearst, Hull, Mont-Laurier, Pembroke, Timmins).

Quebec (Amos, Chicoutimi, Ste.-Anne-de-la-Pocatiere, Trois Rivieres).

Regina (Gravelbourg, Prince Albert, Saskatoon, Abbey of St. Peter).

Rimouski (Gaspe, Hauterive).

St. Boniface (no suffragans).

St. John's (Grand Falls, St. George).

Sherbrooke (Nicolet, St. Hyacinthe).

Toronto (Hamilton, London, St. Catharines, Thunder Bay).

Vancouver (Kamloops, Nelson, Victoria).

Winnipeg — Ukrainian (Edmonton, Saskatoon, Toronto).

Archdioceses, Archbishops

Edmonton, Alta. (St. Albert, 1871; archdiocese, transferred Edmonton, 1912): Anthony Jordan, O.M.I., archbishop, 1964.

Grouard-McLennan, Alta. (v. a. Athabaska-Mackenzie, 1862; Grouard, 1927; archdiocese Grouard-McLennan, 1967); Henri Routhier, O. M. I., archbishop, 1967.

Halifax, N. S. (1842; archdiocese, 1852): James M. Hayes, archbishop, 1967.

Keewatin-Le Pas, Man. (v. a., 1910; archdiocese, 1967): Paul Dumouchel, O. M. I., archbishop, 1967.

Kingston, Ont. (1826; archdiocese, 1889): Joseph L. Wilhelm, archbishop, 1966.

Moncton, N. B. (1936): Norbert Robichaud, archbishop, 1942.

Montreal, Que. (1836; archdiocese, 1886): Paul Gregoire, archbishop, 1968. Lawrence P. Whelan, Leo Blais, Valerien Belanger, Andre Cimichella, O. S. M., Leonard Crowley, auxiliaries.

Ottawa, Ont. (1847; archdiocese, 1886): Joseph Aurele Plourde, archbishop, 1967.

Quebec, Que. (v. a., 1658; diocese, 1674; archdiocese, 1819; metropolitan, 1844; primatial see, 1956): Cardinal Maurice Roy, archbishop, 1947. Lionel Audet, Laurent Noel, auxiliaries.

Regina, Sask. (1910; archdiocese, 1915): Michael C. O'Neill, archbishop, 1948.

Rimouski, Que. (1867; archdiocese, 1946): Louis Levesque, archbishop, 1967.

St. Boniface, Man. (1847; archdiocese, 1871): Maurice Baudoux, archbishop, 1955. Antoine Hacault, auxiliary.

St. John's, Nfld. (p. a., 1784; v. a., 1796; diocese, 1847; archdiocese, 1904): Patrick J. Skinner, C. J. M., archbishop, 1951.

Sherbrooke, Que. (1874; archdiocese, 1951); J.-M. Fortier, archbishop, 1968.

Toronto, Ont. (1841; archdiocese, 1870): Philip F. Pocock, archbishop, 1971. Francis V. Allen, Thomas Fulton, auxiliaries.

Vancouver, B. C. (v. a. British Columbia, 1863; diocese New Westminster, 1890; archdiocese Vancouver, 1908): James F. Carney, archbishop, 1969.

Winnipeg, Man. (1915): Cardinal George B. Flahiff, C. S. B., archbishop, 1961.

Winnipeg, Man. (Ukrainian Byzantine Rite) (Ordinariate of Canada, 1912; ap. ex. Central Canada, 1948; ap. ex. Manitoba, 1951; archdiocese Winnipeg, 1956): Maxim Hermaniuk, C. Ss. R., archbishop, 1956.

Dioceses, Bishops

Alexandria, Ont. (1890): Adolph Proulx, bishop, 1967.

Amos, Que. (1938): Gaston Hains, bishop, 1968.

Antigonish, N. S. (Arichat, 1844; transferred, 1886): William E. Power, bishop, 1960.

Bathurst, N. B. (Chatham, 1860; transferred, 1938): Edgar Godin, bishop, 1969.

Calgary, Alta. (1912): Paul J. O'Byrne, bishop, 1968.

Charlottetown, P. E. I. (1829): Francis J. Spence, bishop, 1970.

Chicoutimi, Que. (1878): Marius Pare, bishop, 1961.

Churchill-Hudson Bay, Man. (p.,a., 1925; v. a. Hudson Bay, 1931; diocese Churchill, 1967; Churchill-Hudson Bay, 1968): Omer Robidoux, O. M. I., bishop, 1970.

Edmonton, Alta. (Ukrainian Byzantine Rite) (ap. 2x., 1948; diocese, 1956): Neil Nicholas Savaryn, O. S. B. M., bishop, 1948.

Edmundston, N. B. (1944): Fernand Lacroix, C. J. M., bishop, 1970.

Gaspe, Que. (1922): Gilles Ouellet, P. M. E., bishop, 1968.

Grand Falls, Nfld. (Harbour Grace, 1856; present title, 1964): John M. O'Neill, bishop, 1940.

Gravelbourg, Sask. (1930): Aime Decosse, bishop, 1954.

Hamilton, Ont. (1856): Joseph F. Ryan, bishop, 1937. Paul F. Reding, auxiliary.

Hauterive, Que. (p. a., 1882; v. a., 1905; diocese Gulf of St. Lawrence, 1945; name changed, 1960): Gerard Couturier, 1957.

Hearst, Ont. (p. a., 1918; v. a., 1920; diocese, 1938).

Hull, Que. (1963): Paul Emile Charbonneau, bishop, 1963.

Joliette, Que. (1904): Rene Audet, bishop, 1968.

Kamloops, B. C. (1945): Michael A. Harrington, bishop, 1952.

Labrador-Schefferville (v. a. Labrador, 1945; diocese, 1967); Henri Legare, O. M. I., bishop, 1967.

London, Ont. (1885; transferred Sandwich, 1859; London, 1869): G. Emmett Carter, bishop, 1964.

Mackenzie-Fort Smith, N. W. T. (v. a. Mackenzie, 1901; diocese Mackenzie-Fort Smith, 1967): Paul Piché, O. M. I., bishop, 1967.

Mont-Laurier, Que. (1913): Andre Ouellette, bishop, 1965.

Moosonee, Ont. (v. a. James Bay, 1938; diocese Moosonee, 1967): Jules Leguerrier, O. M. I., bishop, 1967.

Nelson, B. C. (1936): Wilfred Emmett Doyle, bishop, 1958.

Nicolet, Que. (1885): Joseph A. Martin, bishop, 1950.

Pembroke, Ont. (v. a., 1882; diocese, 1898): Joseph R. Windle, bishop, 1971.

Peterborough, Ont. (1882): Francis A. Marrocco, bishop, 1968.

Prince Albert, Sask. (v. a., 1890; diocese, 1907): Laurent Morin, bishop, 1959.

Prince George, B. C. (p. a., 1908; v. a. Yukon and Prince Rupert, 1944; diocese Prince George, 1967): J. Fergus O'Grady, O. M. I., bishop, 1967.

Sainte-Anne-de-la-Pocatiere, Que. (1951): C.-H. Levesque, bishop, 1968.

St. Catharines, Ont. (1958): Thomas J. McCarthy, bishop, 1958.

St. George's, Nfld. (p. a., 1870; v. a., 1890; diocese, 1904): Richard T. McGrath, bishop, 1970.

St. Hyacinthe, Que. (1852): Albert Sanschagrin, O. M. I., bishop, 1967.

Saint-Jean-de-Quebec, (1933): Gerard Marie Coderre, bishop, 1955.

St. Jerome, Que. (1951): Bernard Hubert, bishop, 1971.

Saint John, N. B. (1842): Joseph N. MacNeil, bishop, 1969.

St. Paul in Alberta (1948): Raymond Roy, bishop, 1972.

Saskatoon, Sask. (1933): James P. Mahoney, bishop, 1967.

Saskatoon, Sask. (Ukrainian Byzantine Rite) (ap. ex., 1951; diocese, 1956): Andrew J. Roborecki, bishop, 1951.

Sault Ste. Marie, Ont. (1904): Alexander Carter, bishop, 1958. Roger Despatie, auxiliary.

Thunder Bay, Ont. (Ft. William, 1952; transferred, 1970): Norman J. Gallagher, bishop, 1970.

Timmins, Ont. (v. a. Temiskaming, 1908; diocese Haileybury, 1915; present title, 1938): Jacques Landriault, bishop, 1971.

Toronto, Ont. (Ukrainian Byzantine Rite) (ap. ex., 1948; diocese, 1956): Isidore Borecky, bishop, 1948. Michael Rusnak, C. Ss. R., auxiliary.

Trois-Rivieres, Que. (1852): Georges-Leon Pelletier, bishop, 1947.

Valleyfield, Que. (1892): Guy Belanger, bishop, 1969.

Victoria, B. C. (diocese Vancouver Is., 1846; archdiocese, 1903; diocese Victoria, 1908): Remi J. De Roo, bishop, 1962.

Whitehorse, Y. T. (v.a., 1944; diocese 1967): Hubert P. O'Connor, O. M. I., bishop, 1971.

Yarmouth, N. S. (1953): Austin Emile Burke, bishop, 1968.

Military Vicariate of Canada (1951): Cardinal Maurice Roy, military vicar.

Abbacy of St. Peter, Muenster, Sask. (1921): Jerome Weber, O. S. B. (blessed, 1960).

BIOGRAPHIES OF CANADIAN BISHOPS

Allen, Francis V.: b. June 25, 1909, Toronto, Ont.; ord. priest June 10, 1933; ord. titular bishop of Avensa and auxiliary bishop of Toronto, Oct. 7, 1954.

Audet, Lionel: b. May 22, 1908, Ste. Marie de Beauce, Que.; ord. priest July 8, 1934; ord. titular bishop of Tibari and auxiliary bishop of Quebec, May 1, 1952.

Audet, Rene: b. Jan. 18, 1920, Montreal, Que.; ord. priest May 30, 1948; ord. titular bishop of Chonochora and auxiliary bishop of Ottawa, July 31, 1963; bishop of Joliette, Jan. 3, 1968.

Baudoux, Maurice: b. July 10, 1902, Louviere, Belgium; ord. priest July 17, 1929; ord. bishop of St. Paul in Alberta, Oct. 28, 1948; titular archbishop of Preslavus and coadjutor archbishop of St. Boniface, Mar. 4, 1952; archbishop of St. Boniface, Sept. 14, 1955.

Belanger, Guy: b. Jan. 24, 1928, Valleyfield,

Que.; ord. priest May 19, 1951; ord. bishop of Valleyfield, Nov. 23, 1969.

Belanger, Valerien: b. Apr. 6, 1902, Valleyfield, Que.; ord. priest May 29, 1926; ord titular bishop of Cyrene and auxiliary bishop of Montreal, May 11, 1956.

Blais, Leo: b. Apr. 28, 1904, Dollar Bay, Mich.; ord. priest June 14, 1930; ord. bishop of Prince Albert, Aug. 28, 1952; titular bishop of Geron and auxiliary bishop of Montreal, Feb. 28, 1959.

Borecky, Isidore: b. Oct. 1, 1911, Ostrovec, Ukraine; ord. priest July 17, 1938; ord. titular bishop of Amathus in Cypro and exarch of Toronto, May 27, 1948; bishop of Toronto (Ukrainians), Nov. 3, 1956.

Brodeur, Rosario L.: b. Oct. 30, 1889, Acton Vale, Que.; ord. priest June 17, 1916; ord. titular bishop of Mideo and coadjutor bishop of Alexandria, June 30, 1941; bishop of Alexandria, July 10, 1941; retired Oct. 15, 1966.

Burke, Austin Emile: b. Jan. 22, 1922, Sluice Point, N.S.; ord. priest Mar. 25, 1950; ord. bishop of Yarmouth, May 14, 1968.

Cabana, Georges: b. Oct. 22, 1894, Notre Dame de Granby, Que; ord. priest July 28, 1918; ord. titular archbishop of Anchialo and coadjutor archbishop of St. Boniface, June 30, 1941; coadjutor archbishop of Sherbrooke, Jan. 20, 1952; archbishop of Sherbrooke, May 28, 1952; retired 1968.

Carney, James F.: b. June 28, 1915, Vancouver, B.C.; ord. priest Mar. 21, 1942; ord. titular bishop of Obori and auxiliary bishop of Vancouver, Feb. 11, 1966; archbishop of Vancouver, Jan. 8, 1969.

Carter, Alexander: b. Apr. 16, 1909, Montreal, Que; ord. priest June 6, 1936; ord. titular bishop of Sita and coadjutor bishop of Sault Ste. Marie, Feb. 2, 1957; bishop of Sault Ste. Marie, Nov. 22, 1958.

Carter, G. Emmett: b. Mar. 1, 1912, Montreal, Que; ord. priest May 22, 1937; ord. titular bishop of Altiburo and auxiliary bishop of London, Ont., Feb. 2, 1962; bishop of London, Feb. 17, 1964, installed Mar. 12, 1964.

Caza, Percival: b. Aug. 13, 1896, Saint-Anicet, Que; ord. priest June 29, 1922; ord. titular bishop of Albule and auxiliary of Valleyfield, Oct. 19, 1948; coadjutor bishop of Valleyfield, 1955; bishop of Valleyfield, Sept. 22, 1966; retired Mar. 18, 1969.

Charbonneau, Paul E.: b. May 4, 1922, Ste. Therese de Blainville, Que; ord. priest May 31, 1947; ord. titular bishop of Thapsus and auxiliary bishop of Ottawa, Jan. 18, 1961; first bishop of Hull, May 21, 1963.

Cimichella, Andre, O.S.M.: b. Feb. 21, 1921, Grotte Santo Stefano, Italy; ord. priest May 26, 1945; ord. titular bishop of Quiza and auxiliary of Montreal, July 16, 1964.

Coderre, Gerard Marie: b. Dec. 19, 1904, St. Jacques de Montcalm, Que; ord. priest May 30, 1931; ord. titular bishop of Aegae and coadjutor bishop of St.-Jean-de-Quebec, Sept. 12, 1951; bishop of St.-Jean-de-Quebec, Feb. 3, 1955.

Couturier, Gerard: b. Jan. 12, 1913, St. Louis du Ha Ha, Que; ord. priest Mar. 25, 1938; ord. bishop of Hauterive, Feb. 28, 1957.

Crowley, Leonard: b. Dec. 28, 1921, Montreal, Que; ord. priest May 31, 1947; ord. titular bishop of Mons and auxiliary bishop of Montreal, Mar. 24, 1971.

Decosse, Aime: b. June 21, 1903, Somerset, Man.; ord. priest July 4, 1926; ord. bishop of Gravelbourg, Jan. 20, 1954.

De Roo, Remi J.: b. Feb. 24, 1924, Swan Lake, Man.; ord. priest June 8, 1950; ord. bishop of Victoria, Dec. 14, 1962.

Desmarais, Joseph A.: b. Oct. 31, 1891, Upton, Que; ord. priest July 25, 1914; ord. titular bishop of Ruspe and auxiliary bishop of St. Hyacinthe, Apr. 22, 1931; bishop of

Amos, June 20, 1939; retired Oct. 31, 1968.

Despatie, Roger A.: b. Apr. 12, 1927, Sudbury, Ont.; ord. priest Apr. 12, 1952; ord. titular bishop of Usinaza and auxiliary bishop of Sault Ste. Marie, June 28, 1968.

Desrochers, Bruno: b. Apr. 17, 1910, St. Loui de Lotbiniere, Que; ord. priest June 30, 1934; ord. first bishop of Sainte-Anne-de-la Pocatiere, Sept. 21, 1951; resigned May 24, 1970; vicar general of Sainte-Anne-de-la-Pocatiere.

Douville, Arthur: b. July 22, 1894, St. Casimir de Portneuf, Que; ord. priest May 25, 1919; ord. titular bishop of Vita and auxiliary bishop of St. Hyacinthe, Jan. 29, 1940; coadjutor bishop of St. Hyacinthe, Mar. 21, 1942; bishop of St. Hyacinthe, Nov. 27, 1942; retired June 13, 1967.

Doyle, Wilfrid E.: b. Feb. 18, 1913, Calgary, Alta.; ord. priest June 5, 1938; ord. bishop of Nelson, Dec. 3, 1958.

Dumouchel, Paul, O.M.I.: b. Sept. 19, 1911, St. Boniface, Man.; ord. priest June 24, 1936; ord. titular bishop of Sufes and vicar apostolic of Keewatin, May 24, 1955; archbishop of Keewatin-Le Pas, July 13, 1967.

Flahiff, George F.: (See Cardinals Biographies.)

Fortier, Jean-Marie: b. July 1, 1920, Quebec, Que; ord. priest June 16, 1944; ord. titular bishop of Pomaria and auxiliary bishop of Ste. Anne-de-la-Pocatiere, Jan. 23, 1961; bishop of Gaspe, Jan. 19, 1965; archbishop of Sherbrooke, Apr. 20, 1968.

Frenette, Emilien: b. May 6, 1905, Montreal, Que; ord. priest May 30, 1930; ord. bishop of St. Jerome, Sept. 12, 1951; retired June 11, 1971.

Fulton, Thomas B.: b. Jan. 13, 1918, St. Catharines, Ont.; ord. priest June 7, 1941; ord. titular bishop of Cursola and auxiliary bishop of Toronto, Jan. 6, 1969.

Gagnon, Edouard, P.S.S.: b. Jan. 15, 1918, Port Daniel, Que; ord. priest Aug. 15, 1940; ord. bishop of St. Paul in Alberta, Mar. 25, 1969; app. rector of Canadian College in Rome, 1972.

Gallagher, Norman J.: b. May 24, 1917, Coatbridge, Scotland; ord. priest Mar. 29, 1941; ord. titular bishop of Adrasus and auxiliary bishop of Montreal, Sept. 12, 1963; bishop of Thunder Bay, April 22, 1970.

Godin, Edgar: b. May 31, 1911, Neguac, N.B.; ord. priest June 15, 1941; ord. bishop of Bathurst, July 25, 1969.

Gregoire, Paul: b. Oct. 24, 1911, Verdun, Que; ord. priest May 22, 1937; ord. titular bishop of Curubis and auxiliary bishop of Montreal, Dec. 27, 1961; archbishop of Montreal, Apr. 20, 1968.

Hacault, Antoine: b. Jan. 17, 1926, Bruxelles, Man.; ord. priest May 20, 1951; ord. titular bishop of Media and auxiliary bishop of St. Boniface, Sept. 8, 1964.

Hains, Gaston: b. Sept. 10, 1921, Drummondville, Que; ord. priest June 15, 1946;

ord. titular bishop of Belesansa and auxiliary bishop of St. Hyacinthe, Oct. 18, 1964; coadjutor bishop of Amos, 1967; bishop of Amos, Oct. 31, 1968.

Harrington, Michael A.: b. Sept. 15, 1900, Killaloe, Ont.; ord. priest May 29, 1926; ord. bishop of Kamloops, Nov. 20, 1952.

Hayes, James M.: b. May 27, 1924, Halifax, N.S.; ord. priest June 15, 1947; ord. titular bishop of Reperi and apostolic administrator of Halifax, Apr. 20, 1965; archbishop of Halifax, June 22, 1967.

Hermaniuk, Maxim, C.SS.R.: b. Oct. 30, 1911, Nove Selo, Ukraine; ord. priest Sept. 4, 1938; ord. titular bishop of Sinna and exarch of Manitoba (Ukrainians), June 29, 1951; archbishop of Winnipeg (Ukrainians), Nov. 3, 1956.

Hubert, Bernard: b. June 1, 1929, Beloeil, Que.; ord. priest May 30, 1953; ord. bishop of St. Jerome, Sept. 12, 1971.

Jennings, Edward Q.: b. Oct. 4, 1896, Saint John, N.B.; ord. priest Dec. 27, 1925; ord. titular bishop of Sala and auxiliary bishop of Vancouver, June 11, 1941; bishop of Kamloops, Feb. 22, 1946; bishop of Fort William (now Thunder Bay), May 14, 1962; resigned Sept. 18, 1969.

Johnson, Martin M.: b. Mar. 18, 1899, Toronto; ord. priest June 14, 1924; ord. first bishop of Nelson, Sept. 29, 1936; titular archbishop of Cio and coadjutor archbishop of Vancouver, Nov. 27, 1954; archbishop of Vancouver, Mar. 11, 1964; retired 1969.

Jordan, Anthony, O.M.I.: b. Nov. 10, 1901, Broxburn, Scotland; ord. priest June 23, 1929; ord. titular bishop of Vada and vicar apostolic of Prince Rupert, B.C., Sept. 8, 1945; titular archbishop of Silyum and coadjutor archbishop of Edmonton, Apr. 17, 1955; archbishop of Edmonton, Aug. 11, 1964.

LaBrie, Napoleon-Alexandre, C.J.M.: b. Aug. 5, 1893, Godbout, Que.; ord. priest Apr. 15, 1922; ord. titular bishop of Limata and vicar apostolic of Gulf of St. Lawrence, July 17, 1938; first bishop of Gulf of St. Lawrence (now Hauterive), Dec. 2, 1945; retired Dec. 1, 1956.

Lacroix, Fernand, C.J.M.: b. Oct. 16, 1919, Quebec; ord. priest Feb. 10, 1946; ord. bishop of Edmundston, Oct. 20, 1970.

Lacroix, Marc, O.M.I.: b. Apr. 25, 1906, Saint Simon-de-Bsgot, Que.; ord. priest May 21, 1933; ord. titular bishop of Roso and vicar apostolic of Hudson Bay, Feb. 22, 1943; bishop of Churchill-Hudson Bay, July 13, 1967; retired Oct. 25, 1968.

Landriault, Jacques: b. Sept. 23, 1921, Alfred, Ont.; ord. priest Feb. 9, 1947; ord. titular bishop of Cadi and auxiliary bishop of Alexandria, July 25, 1962; bishop of Hearst, May 27, 1964; app. bishop of Timmins, Mar. 30, 1971.

Landry, Georges: b. Dec. 3, 1895, Pomquet, N.S.; ord. priest June 24, 1921; ord. bishop of Hearst, May 1, 1946; retired Jan. 14, 1952.

Le Blanc, Camille A.: b. Aug. 25, 1898, Neguac, N.B.; ord. priest Apr. 5, 1924; ord. bishop of Bathurst, Sept. 8, 1942; retired Jan. 8, 1969.

Legare, Henri, O.M.I.: b. Feb. 20, 1918, Willow Bunch, Sask.; ord. priest June 29, 1943; ord. first bishop of Labrador-Schefferville, Sept. 9, 1967.

Leguerrier, Jules, O.M.I.: b. Feb. 18, 1915, Clarence Creek, Ont.; ord. priest June 19, 1943; ord. titular bishop of Bavagaliana and vicar apostolic of James Bay, June 29, 1964; first bishop of Moosonee, July 13, 1967.

Levesque, Charles Henri: b. Dec. 29, 1921, St. Andre de Kamouraska, Que.; ord. priest June 13, 1948; ord. titular bishop of Guzabeta and auxiliary bishop of Ste.-Anne-de-la-Pocatiere, Dec. 27, 1965; bishop of Ste.-Anne-de-la-Pocatiere, Aug. 17, 1968.

Levesque, Louis: b. May 27, 1908, Amqui, Que.; ord. priest June 26, 1932; ord. bishop of Hearst, Aug. 15, 1952; titular archbishop of Egnatia and coadjutor archbishop of Rimouski, Apr. 13, 1964; archbishop of Rimouski, Feb. 25, 1967.

Lussier, Philippe, C.SS.R.: b. Oct. 3, 1911, Weedon, Que.; ord. priest Sept. 18, 1937; ord. bishop of St. Paul in Alberta, Aug. 17, 1952; retired Aug. 17, 1968.

McCarthy, Thomas J.: b. Oct. 4, 1905, Goderich, Ont.; ord. priest May 25, 1929; ord. bishop of Nelson, Aug. 1, 1955; bishop of St. Catharines, Nov. 9, 1958.

MacEachern, Malcolm A.: b. Oct. 5, 1901, Broad Cove Chapel, N.S.; ord. priest June 11, 1927; ord. bishop of Charlottetown, Jan. 18, 1955; retired Feb. 24, 1970.

McGrath, Richard T.: b. June 17, 1912, Oderin, Placentia Bay, Nfld.; ord. priest June 24, 1936; ord. bishop of St. George's, Nfld., July 22, 1970.

McGuigan, James Charles: (Cardinals, Biographies.)

MacNeil, Joseph N.: b. Apr. 15, 1924, Sydney, N.S.; ord. priest May 23, 1948; ord. bishop of St. John, N.B., June 24, 1969.

Mahoney, James P.: b. Dec. 7, 1927, Saskatoon, Sask.; ord. priest June 7, 1952; ord. bishop of Saskatoon Dec. 13, 1967.

Marrocco, Francis A.: b. June 20, 1913, Peterborough, Ont.; ord. priest June 12, 1938; ord. titular bishop of Limne and auxiliary bishop of Toronto, Feb. 22, 1956; bishop of Peterborough, June 10, 1968.

Martin, Joseph A.: b. Oct. 4, 1913, Southbridge, Mass.; ord. priest May 18, 1939; ord. titular bishop of Bassiana and coadjutor bishop of Nicolet, Oct. 7, 1950; bishop of Nicolet, Nov. 8, 1950.

Melancon, Georges: b. Apr. 7, 1886, Saint-Guillaume d'Upton, Que.; ord. priest Sept. 12, 1909; ord. bishop of Chicoutimi, July 23, 1940; retired Feb. 18, 1961.

Morin, Laurent: b. Feb. 14, 1908, Montreal, Que.; ord. priest May 24, 1934; ord. titular bishop of Arsamosata and auxiliary bishop of Montreal, Oct. 30, 1955; bishop of Prince Albert, Feb. 28, 1959.

Mulvihill, James P., O.M.I.: b. Oct. 15, 1905, Old Chelsea, Ont.; ord. priest, June 24, 1937; ord. titular bishop of Caput Cilla and vicar apostolic of Whitehorse, Jan. 25, 1966; bishop of Whitehorse, July 13, 1967; retired Oct. 15, 1971.

Nelligan, Charles L.: b. Aug. 20, 1894, Tignish, P.E.I.; ord. priest June 7, 1925; ord. bishop of Pembroke, Oct. 28, 1937; retired May 19, 1945.

Noel, Laurent: b. Mar. 19, 1920, Saint-Just-de-Bretenieres, Que.; ord. priest June 16, 1944; ord. titular bishop of Agathopolis and auxiliary bishop of Quebec, Aug. 29, 1963.

O'Connor, Hubert P., O.M.I.: b. Feb. 17, 1928, Huntington, Que.; ord. priest June 5, 1954; ord. bishop of Whitehorse, Dec. 8, 1971.

O'Byrne, Paul J.: b. Dec. 21, 1922, Calgary, Alta.; ord. priest Feb. 21, 1948; ord. bishop of Calgary, Aug. 22, 1968.

O'Grady, John Fergus, O.M.I.: b. July 27, 1908, Macton, Ont.; ord. priest June 29, 1934; ord. titular bishop of Aspendus and vicar apostolic of Prince Rupert, Mar. 7, 1956; first bishop of Prince George, July 13, 1967.

O'Neill, John M.: b. Oct. 26, 1903, Harbor Grace, Nfld.; ord. priest Apr. 24, 1927; ord. bishop of Grand Falls, July 7, 1940.

O'Neill, Michael C.: b. Feb. 15, 1898, Kemptville, Ont.; ord. priest Dec. 21, 1927; ord. archbishop of Regina, Apr. 14, 1948.

O'Reilly, Michael: b. Feb. 13, 1894, Mullabrack, Ireland; ord. priest June 17, 1917; ord. bishop of St. George's, Sept. 9, 1941; retired Dec. 22, 1969.

Ouellet, Gilles, P.M.E.: b. Aug. 14, 1922 Bromptonville, Que.; ord. priest June 30, 1946; ord. bishop of Gaspe, Nov. 23, 1968.

Ouellette, Andre: b. Feb. 4, 1913, Salem, Mass.; ord. priest June 11, 1938; ord. titular bishop of Carre and auxiliary bishop of Mont-Laurier, Feb. 25, 1957; bishop of Mont-Laurier, Mar. 27, 1965.

Pare, Marius: b. May 22, 1903, Montmagny, Que.; ord. priest July 3, 1927; ord. titular bishop of Aegae and auxiliary bishop of Chicoutimi, May 1, 1956; bishop of Chicoutimi, Feb. 18, 1961.

Parent, Charles Eugene: b. Apr. 22, 1902, Notre Dame-de-Neiges-de-Trois-Pistoles, Que.; ord. priest Mar. 7, 1925; ord. titular bishop of Diana and auxiliary bishop of Rimouski, May 24, 1944; app. archbishop of Rimouski, Mar. 2, 1951; retired Feb. 25, 1967.

Pelletier, George Leon: b. Aug. 19, 1904, Saint-Epiphane, Que.; ord. priest July 24, 1931; ord. titular bishop of Hephaestus and auxiliary bishop of Quebec, Feb. 24, 1943; bishop of Trois Rivieres, July 26, 1947.

Piche, Paul, O.M.I.: b. Sept. 14, 1909, Gravelbourg, Sask.; ord. priest Dec. 23, 1934;

ord. titular bishop of Orcistus and vicar apostolic of Mackenzie, June 11, 1959; first bishop of Mackenzie-Fort Smith, July 13, 1967.

Plourde, Joseph Aurele: b. Jan. 12, 1915, St. Francois de Madawaska, N.B.; ord. priest May 7, 1944; ord. titular bishop of Lapda and auxiliary bishop of Alexandria, Aug. 24, 1964; archbishop of Ottawa, Jan. 12, 1967.

Pocock, Philip: b. July 2, 1906, St. Thomas, Ont.; ord. priest June 14, 1930; ord. bishop of Saskatoon, June 29, 1944; titular archbishop of Aprus and coadjutor archbishop of Winnipeg, Aug. 6, 1951; archbishop of Winnipeg, Jan. 14, 1952; titular archbishop of Isauropolis and coadjutor archbishop of Toronto, Feb. Feb. 18, 1961; archbishop of Toronto, Mar. 30, 1971.

Power, William E.: b. Sept. 27, 1915; Montreal, Que.; ord. priest June 7, 1941; ord. bishop of Antigonish, July 20, 1960; president Canadian Catholic Conference, 1971-73.

Proulx, Adolph E.: b. Dec. 12, 1927, Hanmer, Ont., Canada; ord. priest Apr. 17, 1954; ord. titular bishop of Missua and auxiliary bishop of Sault Ste. Marie, Feb. 24, 1965; bishop of Alexandria, Apr. 28, 1967.

Reding, Paul F.: b. Feb. 14, 1925, Hamilton, Ont.; ord. priest June 3, 1950; ord. titular bishop of Liberalia and auxiliary bishop of Hamilton, Sept. 14, 1966.

Robichaud, Norbert: b. Apr. 1, 1905, St. Charles, N.B.; ord. priest May 1, 1931; ord. archbishop of Moncton, Sept. 8, 1942.

Robidoux, Omer, O.M.L.: b. Dec. 19, 1913; ord. priest June 29, 1939; ord bishop of Churchill-Hudson Bay, May 21, 1970.

Roborecki, Andrew: b. Dec. 12, 1910, in western Ukraine; arrived Winnipeg, Man., 1912; ord. priest July 18, 1934; ord. titular bishop of Tanais and auxiliary bishop of Ukrainian Catholic Diocese of Central Canada, May 27, 1948; exarch of Saskatechewan, 1951; bishop of Saskatoon, (Ukrainians), Nov. 3, 1956.

Routhier, Henri, O.M.I.: b. Feb. 28, 1900, Pincher Creek, Alta.; ord. priest Sept. 7, 1924; ord. titular bishop of Naissus and coadjutor vicar apostolic of Grouard, Sept. 8, 1945; vicar apostolic of Grouard, 1953; archbishop of Grouard-McLennan, July 13, 1967.

Roy, Maurice: (Cardinals, Biographies.)

Roy, Raymond: b. May 3, 1919, Fisher Branch, Man.; ord. priest May 31, 1947; ord. bishop of St. Paul in Alberta, July 18, 1972.

Rusnak, Michele: b. Aug. 21, 1921, Beaverdale, Pa.; ord. priest July 3, 1949; ord. titular bishop of Tzernicus and auxiliary bishop of Toronto eparchy and apostolic visitor to Slovak Catholics of Byzantine rite in Canada, Jan. 2, 1965.

Ryan, Joseph F.: b. Mar. 1, 1897, Dundas, Ont.; ord. priest May 21, 1921; ord. bishop of Hamilton, Oct. 19, 1937.

Sanschagrin, Albert, O.M.I.: b. Aug. 5, 1911, Saint-Tite, Que.; ord. priest May 24, 1936; ord. titular bishop of Bagi and coadjutor bishop of Amos Sept. 14, 1957; bishop of Saint-Hyacinthe, June 23, 1967.

Savaryn, Nile Nicholas, O.S.B.M.: b. May 19, 1905, Stary Sambir, Ukraine; ord. priest Aug. 23, 1931; ord. titular bishop of Jos and auxiliary bishop of the Catholic Ukrainian diocese in Canada, July 1, 1943; bishop of apostolic exarchate for western Canada, 1948; bishop of Edmonton (Ukrainians), Nov. 3, 1956.

Skinner, Patrick J., C.J.M.: b. Mar. 9, 1904, St. John's, Nfld.; ord. priest May 30, 1929; ord. titular bishop of Zenobia and auxiliary bishop of St. John's, Mar. 17, 1950; archbishop of St. John's, Mar. 23, 1951.

Smith, William J.: b. Jan. 2, 1897, Greenfield, Ont.; ord. priest June 16, 1927; ord. bishop of Pembroke, July 25, 1945; retired Feb. 17, 1971.

Spence, Francis J.: b. June 3, 1926, Perth, Ont.; ord. priest, Apr. 16, 1950; ord. titular bishop of Nova and auxiliary bishop of the military vicariate, June 15, 1967; bishop of Charlottetown, Aug. 15, 1970.

Tessier, Maxime: b. Oct. 9, 1906, St. Sebas-

tien, Que.; ord. priest June 14, 1930; ord. titular bishop of Christopolis and auxiliary bishop of Ottawa, Aug. 2, 1951; coadjutor bishop of Timmins, 1953; bishop of Timmins, May 8, 1955; retired Mar. 24, 1971.

Webster, Benjamin I.: b. Mar. 7, 1898, Spofforth, Eng.; ord. priest May 26, 1923; ord. titular bishop of Paphos and auxiliary bishop of Toronto, Nov. 21, 1946; bishop of Peterborough, Apr. 21, 1954; retired 1968.

Whelan, Lawrence P.: b. Oct. 16, 1899, Montreal, Que.; ord. priest Dec. 19, 1925; ord. titular bishop of Opus and auxiliary bishop of Montreal, Aug. 15, 1941.

Wilhelm, Joseph L.: b. Nov. 16, 1909, Walkerton, Ont.; ord. priest June 9, 1934; ord. titular bishop of Saccaea and auxiliary bishop of Calgary, Aug. 22, 1963; archbishop of Kingston, Dec. 14, 1966.

Windle, Joseph R.: b. Aug. 28, 1917, Ashdad, Ont.; ord. priest May 16, 1943; ord. titular bishop of Uzita and auxiliary bishop of Ottawa, Jan. 18, 1961; coadjutor bishop of Pembroke, 1969; bishop of Pembroke, Feb. 15, 1971.

CANADIAN CATHOLIC CONFERENCE

The Canadian Catholic Conference was established Oct. 12, 1943, as a permanent voluntary association of the bishops of Canada, was given official approval by the Holy See in 1948, and acquired the status of an episcopal conference after the Second Vatican Council.

The CCC acts in two ways: (1) as a strictly ecclesiastical body through which the bishops act together with pastoral authority and responsibility for the Church throughout the country; (2) as an operational secretariat through which the bishops act on a wider scale for the good of the Church and society.

At the top of the CCC organizational table are the president, an executive committee, an administrative board and a plenary assembly. The membership consists of all the bishops of Canada.

Departments and Offices

The CCC has four departments with 25 offices: (I) Doctrine and Faith Department with six offices — theology (French and English), liturgy (French and English), religious education (French and English), (II) Social Life Department with five offices — social action (French), social action/family life (English), Social Communications (French and English), health and welfare (French); (III) Internal Relations Department with six offices — clergy (French), clergy, seminaries, education, vocations (English), religious (French and English), lay apostolate (French and English); (IV) Missions and Ecumenism Department with eight offices — apostolic and missionary assistance (French and English), missions, Latin America (French and English), ecumenism (French and English), non-believers (French).

The general secretariat consists of general secretaries and assistants, and directors of public relations.

Administrative services, under a general director, are for purchasing, archives and library, accounting, editions, printing and expedition, personnel and publications.

Advisory councils, with a mixed membership of lay persons, religious, priests and bishops, are the National Council on Liturgy, the National Council on Fiscal Affairs, the Canadian Catholic Education Council, and the National Missionary Council.

Operations

Meetings for the transaction of business are held twice a year by the plenary assembly, every second month except July and August by the executive committee, and twice a year by the central commission.

The CCC has agencies and services operating in Ottawa, Toronto and Montreal.

All constituent organs of the CCC have French and English counterparts.

Bishop William E. Power of Antigonish is president of the CCC; Archbishop Jean-Marie Fortier of Sherbrooke is vice president.

Headquarters are located at 90 Parent Ave., Ottawa, 2, Canada.

ORGANIZATIONS

The Catholic Church Extension Society of Canada supports home missions. Address: 67 Bond St., Toronto 205, Ontario.

The Oblate Indian-Eskimo Council of Canada, 238 Argyle St., Ottawa.

The Canadian Catholic Women's League, with a membership of more than 100,000. Address: 890 St. James St., Winnipeg, Man.

MEETING OF CCC

"Justice in Canada" was the theme of the semiannual assembly of the Canadian Catholic Conference Apr. 7 to 21, 1972, in Ottawa.

Following is a summary of the assembly's actions.

Eskimos and Indians: Under the heading of "A Cry of Conscience," the conference addressed itself to the plight of Indians and Eskimos confronted with problems of poverty, urbanization and secularization. The bishops also announced plans to develop distinctive liturgical ceremonies and catechetical programs appropriate to the cultures of the country's 144,000 Catholic Indians and Eskimos.

Guaranteed Income: The conference called for greater sharing and equalization of income. "The riches of Canada are unequally shared. This inequality, which keeps so many people poor, is a social sin. We invite Canadians to accept the social goal of an equitable distribution of income. We also call for acceptance of the principle that each Canadian should be assured that level of income necessary for decent human living and full participation in society."

Behind the appeal for a guaranteed income were reports of several recent studies, one of which showed that 25 per cent of all Canadians were living in poverty, that unequal distribution of income had not changed for two decades, and that the top 20 per cent of the population was receiving about 40 per cent of the national income.

A theological working paper on the subject noted: "The affluent Canadian has come to accept as a matter of course that the government 'invisibly' supports him. But he refuses to get used to any subsidy given the 'unproductive' poor. Yet it is not so much the initiative of the affluent as the social fabric which accounts for their own affluence. Indeed, most of us are not so much 'contributors'; rather we were born winners, brought up to be winners; society is geared to proffer us its best. In this context the call to share rather than to grow economically is a call to shift our perceptions of the world. It is a call to put social policy ahead of economic policy."

Mass attendance: In view of diminishing church attendance, the bishops reaffirmed the obligation of participation in the Mass on Sundays, or Saturdays where authorized.

Ministries: Many bishops felt that new and diverse ministries should be developed and shaped in response to pastoral needs and conditions in the country, according to Bishop Paul O'Byrne of Calgary, Alta. Bishop Augustin E. Burke of Yarmouth, Nova Scotia, said "it is not impossible" that the bishops, seeing vast missionary areas of Canada going without priests, might request permission from Pope Paul or ordain married men as an "urgent need."

Pastoral Implications of Political Choices: In a statement with this title, the conference cited the necessity for Christians to discern the options and commitments necessary to improve the social, political and economic order of things. The statement also said that the role of the Church in this connection is one of "presence" and "service of the People of God," whatever their political persuasions might be.

The conference took no stand on the issue of "autodetermination" in the Province of Quebec.

Program for Social Justice: The bishops drafted a progress report which called on Canadian Catholics to join in a "continuing examination of social conscience," and offered an 11-point proposal for furthering "witness to the Gospel's radical ethic of solidarity, simplicity and sharing." Among the points were the following.

"Most of us — bishops, priests, religious and laity — are challenged to practice more voluntary penance, such as greater restraint in the use of goods, and more generous sharing in the spirit of stewardship, even to the point of sacrificing what many people think is their due." The statement called for corresponding *changes in life styles.*

"It is increasingly evident that changes in living modes depend on a *change of attitudes.* Such an awakening of conscience — 'conscientization' — demands a renewed emphasis of social education, one which is adapted to each time and place. This social formation should emphasize meaningful liturgy, a social catechesis, special school programs, animation in small groups, and community involvement."

"The *rights of church personnel* . . . be reviewed periodically so as to ensure that they receive just incomes, fair working conditions, and security on retirement."

"Ways in which neighboring *dioceses might share* specialized personnel and resources need to be explored."

"In the interests of fraternal *accountability,* the conference recommends financial openness throughout the Canadian Church."

"Social usefulness should be a major consideration in making *investments.'*

"Catholic groups should seek more ways to respond without paternalism to the expectations of the unorganized *poor.* We should collaborate with them so that their voices may be heard as they work out their own liberation."

"We commend *local credit unions and cooperatives* as effective examples of organized self-help."

"We reaffirm support of the *Canadian Coalition for Development* (of churches and other organizations), while emphasizing the need for similar coalitions of churches and other voluntary groups at community levels."

"*Social justice* in the Church, in Canada, and in the world will remain a major and constant concern of this conference.''

CATHOLIC POPULATION STATISTICS OF CANADA

(Source: *Annuario Pontificio*, 1972 and 1971 editions.)

Archdioceses are indicated by an asterisk. For dioceses marked +, see Canadian Dioceses with Interprovincial Lines.

Canada's 10 civil provinces and two territories are divided into 17 ecclesiastical provinces consisting of 17 metropolitan sees (archdioceses) and 50 suffragan sees (49 dioceses and one abbacy); there is also one archdiocese immediately subject to the Holy See. (See listing of Ecclesiastical Provinces elsewhere in this section.)

This table presents a regional breakdown of Catholic statistics. In some cases, the totals are approximate because diocesan boundaries fall within several civil provinces.

Civil Province / Dioceses	Dioc.	Priests Rel.	Tot.	Sems.	Men Rel.	Wom. Rel.	Parishes	Cath. Pop.	Tot. Pop.
Newfoundland	127	39	166	22	134	645	87	178,209	541,210
*St. John's	57	13	70	7	75	402	39	85,940	155,210
Grand Falls	39	—	39	5	14	95	28	34,131	250,000
St. George's	30	1	31	10	12	118	20	39,396	92,000
Labrador-Schefferville+	1	25	26	—	33	30	—	18,742	44,000
Prince Edward Island									
Charlottetown	82	3	85	6	3	284	46	44,584	108,000
Nova Scotia	331	71	402	29	91	1,293	167	255,045	763,644
*Halifax	100	47	147	23	49	508	50	100,000	400,000
Antigonish	200	6	206	6	22	689	92	123,931	239,153
Yarmouth	31	18	49	—	20	96	25	31,114	124,491
New Brunswick	325	178	503	24	304	1,341	191	284,756	603,414
*Moncton	81	89	170	1	135	336	47	70,721	137,648
Bathurst	93	33	126	21	78	429	55	98,104	121,422
Edmundston	61	38	99	1	69	301	38	49,194	64,344
St. John	90	18	108	1	22	275	51	66,737	280,000
Quebec	4,994	3,203	8,197	552	7,593	31,315	1,771	4,903,616	5,793,657
*Montreal	856	1,400	2,256	121	2,627	10,112	257	1,600,000	2,300,000
*Quebec	1,020	599	1,619	129	1,596	6,860	271	777,215	784,113
*Rimouski	295	54	349	14	175	1,210	120	167,981	168,679
*Sherbrooke	363	171	534	20	232	1,920	133	179,252	207,559
Amos	87	32	119	1	75	431	76	94,877	97,000
Chicoutimi	321	141	462	107	364	1,297	95	254,661	256,174
Gaspe	111	16	127	5	25	488	61	102,560	113,063
Hauterive	65	37	102	—	60	326	41	86,000	90,000
Hull	109	85	194	8	125	471	55	133,029	154,019
Joliette	172	66	238	12	210	824	54	115,081	118,189
Mont-Laurier	95	46	141	2	79	356	55	67,451	69,044
Nicolet	257	38	295	59	287	1,186	85	154,426	156,002
St. Anne-de-la-Pocatiere	195	10	205	11	41	600	53	90,155	90,393
Saint Hyacinthe	298	98	396	18	480	1,807	106	254,441	270,116
St. Jean de Quebec	199	104	303	19	313	844	86	300,822	349,800
St. Jerome	115	131	246	6	270	435	63	165,764	172,085
Trois-Riviers	298	114	412	18	456	1,632	98	234,159	238,250
Valleyfield	138	61	199	2	178	516	62	125,742	159,171
Ontario	1,485	1,315	2,800	152	2,268	6,266	971	1,986,449	7,793,068
*Kingston	75	17	92	9	21	310	53	53,607	250,000
*Ottawa	181	320	501	8	722	1,600	100	203,700	662,700
*Toronto	304	407	711	32	748	602	169	650,000	3,275,000
Alexandria	55	10	65	6	16	225	32	55,000	78,200
Hamilton	142	150	292	23	208	644	106	218,287	1,042,626
Hearst	34	10	44	2	16	92	31	32,012	48,004
London	244	128	372	28	176	1,034	143	276,175	1,038,345
Moosonee+	—	15	15	—	34	22	—	3,000	14,000
Pembroke+	92	4	96	10	6	335	52	54,154	117,394
Peterborough	59	4	63	6	7	207	33	36,424	262,000
St. Catharines	56	49	105	7	56	142	47	93,893	319,612
Sault Ste. Marie	133	110	243	16	116	550	98	160,000	342,000
Thunder Bay	29	42	71	1	48	141	39	55,000	200,000
Timmins+	81	49	130	4	94	362	68	95,197	143,187

Civil Province Dioceses	Priests Dioc.	Priests Rel.	Priests Tot.	Sems.	Men Rel.	Wom. Rel.	Par- ishes	Cath. Pop.	Tot. Pop.
Manitoba	**155**	**252**	**407**	**21**	**335**	**1,233**	**200**	**195,601**	**989,604**
*Keewatin-LePas+	—	51	51	—	79	148	33	23,000	62,300
*St. Boniface	92	75	167	17	117	664	76	71,629	300,000
*Winnipeg	63	103	166	4	110	410	75	97,500	612,956
Churchill-Hudson Bay+	—	23	23	—	29	11	16	3,472	14,348
Saskatchewan	**210**	**189**	**399**	**24**	**253**	**1,166**	**247**	**207,625**	**913,702**
*Regina	98	65	163	12	85	350	99	97,148	435,000
Gravelbourg	26	17	43	1	21	182	27	16,006	78,702
Prince Albert	50	52	102	3	73	315·	53	41,322	185,000
Saskatoon	36	43	79	8	51	234	42	40,249	195,000
St. Peter Muenster (abbacy)	—	12	12	—	23	85	26	12,900	20,000
Alberta	**235**	**237**	**472**	**18**	**307**	**1,207**	**229**	**306,564**	**1,540,698**
*Edmonton	116	106	222	5	145	738	88	136,000	776,045
*Grouard-McLennan	6	57	63	—	69	124	28	30,064	88,344
Calgary	84	65	149	7	84	200	69	112,000	580,000
St. Paul	29	9	38	6	9	145	44	28,500	96,309
British Columbia	**159**	**161**	**320**	**11**	**220**	**735**	**184**	**269,457**	**1,838,042**
*Vancouver	82	90	172	7	120	408	69	150,000	1,023,960
Kamloops	13	2	15	—	7	45	13	19,000	135,000
Nelson	35	18	53	1	19	55	32	33,937	188,432
Prince George	2	26	28	3	42	46	18	33,520	135,031
Victoria	27	25	52	—	32	181	52	33,000	355,619
Yukon Territory Whitehorse+	—	22	22	1	27	22	5	5,912	17,000
Northwest Territories+ Mackenzie- Fort Smith	—	47	47	—	79	102	29	18,466	36,072
Byzantine Rite **Ukrainians**	**187**	**81**	**268**	**13**	**126**	**157**	**157**	**436,985**	**—**
*Winnipeg	44	13	57	2	16	25	40	60,000	—
Edmonton	42	22	64	1	44	35	41	51,985	—
Saskatoon	28	15	43	1	20	40	8	270,000	—
Toronto	73	31	104	9	46	57	68	55,000	—
TOTALS	**8,290**	**5,798**	**14,088**	**873**	**11,740**	**45,766**	**4,284**	**9,093,269**	**20,937,311**

Dioceses With Interprovincial Lines

The following dioceses, indicated by + in the table, have interprovincial lines.

Labrador-Schefferville includes the Labrador region of Newfoundland and the northern part of Quebec province.

Moosonee, Ont., includes part of Quebec province.

Pembroke, Ont., includes one county of Quebec province.

Timmins, Ont., includes part of Quebec province.

Keewatin-Le Pas includes part of Manitoba and Saskatchewan provinces.

Churchill-Hudson Bay includes part of Northwest Territories.

Whitehorse, Y.T., includes part of British Columbia.

Northwest Territories totals do not include an area within the boundaries of the Churchill-Hudson Bay diocese.

CANADIAN CATHOLIC PUBLICATIONS

(Sources: *Catholic Press Directory,* Canadian Catholic Conference.)

Newspapers

British Columbia Catholic, The, w; 150 Robson St., Vancouver 3, B.C.; 7,913.

Catholic Register, The, w; 67 Bond St., Toronto, Ont.; 57,600.

Monitor, The, m; P.O. Box 986, St. John's, Nfld.; 8,500.

New Freeman, The, w; Box 609, St. John, N.B.

Our Sunday Visitor (national) w: 1301 Wellington Crescent, Winnipeg, Man.; 24,144.

Prairie Messenger, w; St. Peter's Press, Muenster, Sask.; SOK 2 YO; 8,056.

Teviskes, Ziburiai, (Lithuanian), w; 941 Dundas St. W., Toronto 3, Ont.; 5,560.

Western Catholic Reporter, w; 9537-76th Ave., Edmonton, Alta.; 23,090.

Magazines

Annals of Good St. Anne de Beaupre, m; Basilica of St. Anne, Que.; 77,300.

Annals of the Holy Childhood, q; 15 Wellington St., St. Catharines, Ont.; 65,000.

Apostolat, bm; Richelieu, Que., Oblates of Mary Immaculate; 42,000.

Canadian Catholic Institutions, bm; 27 Carlton St., Toronto 2, Ont.; 5,209.

Canadian League, The, 6 times a year; 77 MacLaren St., Ottawa, Ont. KzP OK5; 111,000.

Centre News, q; 830 Bathurst St., Toronto, Ont.; 2,200.

Christian Communications, 6 times a year; 223 Main St., Ottawa 1, Ont.; 2,500.

Companion of St. Francis and St. Anthony, m; 15 Chestnut Park Rd., Toronto, Ont.; Conventual Franciscan Fathers; 11,396.

Field At Home, q; 10 Montcrest Blvd., Toronto 279, Ont.; 3,117.

Logos, (Ukrainian, English and French), q; 165 Catherine St., Yorkton, Sask.; 380.

Magazine Actualite, m; 2120 Sherbrooke St. E., Montreal 133, Que.; 97,027.

Maintenant, m; 2715 Ch. Cote St., Catherine, Montreal, Que.

Martyrs' Shrine Message, q; R. R. No. 1, Midland, Ont.; 4,000.

Messager de Saint Antoine, m; Lac-Bouchette, Roberval, Que.

Messenger of the Sacred Heart, m; 68 Broadview Ave., Toronto 250, Ont.; 18,000.

Missions Etrangeres, m; 58 Rue Desnoyers, Laval, Que.; 76,000.

Oblate Missions, bm; 17 Graham Ave., Ottawa KISB6, Ont.; 6,800.

Oratory, 10 times a year; Ch. Reine - Maries, Montreal 247, Que.; 9,344.

Our Family, m; P. O. Box 249, Battleford, Sask.; Oblates of Mary Immaculate; 4,265.

Our Lady of the Atonement Annals, q; P.O. Box 370, Smokey Lake, Alta.; 900.

Redeemer's Voice, m; 165 Catherine St., Yorkton, Sask.; 1,750.

Regard de Foi, 6 times a year; 5875 Est. rue Sherbrooke, Montreal, Que.; 15,114.

Relations, m; 8100 Blvd., Saint-Laurent, Montreal 351, Que.; Jesuit Fathers.

Restoration, m; Combermere, P.O. Ont., Canada; Madonna House; 6,333.

Scarboro Mission Magazine, m; 2685 Kingston Rd., Scarboro, Ont.; 50,000.

CANADIAN SHRINES

Our Lady of the Cape (Cap de la Madeleine), Queen of the Most Holy Rosary: The Three Rivers, Quebec, parish church, built of fieldstone in 1714 and considered the oldest stone church on the North American continent preserved in its original state, was rededicated June 22, 1888, as a shrine of the Queen of the Most Holy Rosary. Thereafter, the site increased in importance as a pilgrimage and devotional center, and in 1904 St. Pius X decreed the crowning of a statue of the Blessed Virgin which had been donated 50 years earlier to commemorate the dogma of the Immaculate Conceptionl In 1909, the First Plenary Council of Quebec declared the church a shrine of national pilgrimage. In 1964, the church at the shrine was given the status and title of minor basilica.

St. Anne de Beaupre: The devotional history of this shrine in Quebec, which has been called the "Lourdes of the New World," began with the reported cure of a cripple, Louis Grimont, on Mar. 16, 1658, the starting date of construction work on a small chapel of St. Anne. The original building was successively enlarged and replaced by a stone church which was given the rank of minor basilica in 1888. The present structure, a Romanesque-Gothic basilica, houses the shrine proper in its north transept. The centers of attraction are an eight-foot-high oaken statue and the great relic of St. Anne, a portion of her forearm.

St. Joseph's Oratory: The massive oratory basilica standing on the western side of Mount Royal and overlooking the city of Montreal had its origin in a primitive chapel erected there by Brother Andre, C.S.C., in 1904. Eleven years later, a large crypt was built to accommodate an increasing number of pilgrims, and in 1924 construction work was begun on the large church. A belfry, housing a 60-bell carillon and standing on the site of the original chapel, was dedicated May 15, 1955, as the first major event of the jubilee year observed after the oratory was given the rank of minor basilica.

Martyrs' Shrine: A shrine commemorating several of the Jesuit Martyrs of North America who were killed between 1642 and 1649 in the Ontario and northern New York area is located on the former site of old Forte Sainte Marie. Before its location was fixed near Midland, Ont., in 1925, a small chapel had been erected in 1907 at old Mission St. Ignace to mark the martyrdom of Fathers Jean de Brebeuf and Gabriel Lalemant. This sanctuary has a US counterpart in the Shrine of the North American Martyrs near Auriesville, N.Y., under the care of the Jesuits.

Others

Other shrines and historic churches in Canada include the following.

In Quebec City: the Basilica of Notre Dame, dating from 1650, once the cathedral of a diocese stretching from Canada to Mexico; Notre Dame des Victoires, on the waterfront, dedicated in 1690; the Ursuline Convent, built in 1720, on du Parloir St.

In Montreal: Notre Dame Church, patterned after the famous basilica of the same name in Paris, constructed in 1829; the Shrine of Mary, Queen of All Hearts.

Near Montreal: the Chapel of Mother d'Youville, foundress of the Grey Nuns; Notre Dame de Lourdes, at Rigaud.

CONFERENCE OF RELIGIOUS

The Canadian Religious Conference is a union of major superiors of men and women in Canada. Father Albert Dumont, O.P., is the executive director. Offices are located at 324 Laurier Ave. E., Ottawa, Canada.

The Catholic Church in the United States

The starting point of the mainstream of Catholic history in the United States was Baltimore at the end of the Revolutionary War, although before that time Catholic explorers had traversed much of the country and missionaries had done considerable work among the Indians in the Southeast, Northeast and Southwest.

Beginning of Organization

Father John Carroll's appointment as superior of the American missions on June 9, 1784, was the first step toward organization of the Church in this country.

At that time, according to a report he made to Rome in 1785, there were approximately 25,000 Catholics in the general population of four million. Many of them had been in the Colonies for several generations. Among them were such outstanding figures as Charles Carroll, a member of the Continental Congress and signer of the Declaration of Independence; Thomas FitzSimons of Philadelphia and Oliver Pollock, the Virginia agent, who raised funds for the militia; Commander John Barry, father of the American Navy, and numerous high-ranking army officers. For the most part, however, Catholics were an unknown minority laboring under legal and social handicaps.

Father Carroll, the brother of Charles Carroll, was named the first American bishop in 1789 and placed in charge of the Diocese of Baltimore, whose boundaries were coextensive with those of the United States. He was consecrated in England Aug. 15, 1790, and installed in his see the following Dec. 12.

Ten years later, Father Leonard Neale became his coadjutor and the first bishop ordained in the United States. Bishop Carroll became an archbishop in 1808 when Baltimore was designated a metropolitan see and the new dioceses of Boston, New York, Philadelphia and Bardstown were established. These jurisdictions were later subdivided, and by 1840 there were, in addition to Baltimore, 15 dioceses, 500 priests and 663,000 Catholics in the general population of 17 million.

Priests and First Seminaries

The number of the 24 original priests was gradually augmented with the arrival of others from France, after the Civil Constitution on the Clergy went into effect there, and other countries. Among the earliest arrivals were several Sulpicians who established the first seminary in the US, St. Mary's, Baltimore, in 1791. By 1815, 30 alumni of the school had been ordained to the priesthood. By that time, two additional seminaries were in operation: Mt. St. Mary's, established in 1809 at Emmitsburg, Md., and St. Thomas, founded two years later, at Bardstown, Ky.

These and similar institutions founded later played key roles in the development and growth of the American clergy.

Early Schools

Early educational enterprises included the establishment in 1791 of a school at Georgetown which later became the first Catholic university in the US; the opening of a secondary school for girls, conducted by Visitation nuns, in 1792 at Georgetown; and the start of a similar school in the first decade of the 19th century at Emmitsburg, Md., by Blessed Elizabeth Ann Seton and the Sisters of Charity of St. Joseph, the first religious community of American foundation.

By the 1840's, which saw the beginnings of the present public school system, more than 200 Catholic elementary schools, half of them west of the Alleghenies, were in operation. From this start, the Church subsequently built the greatest private system of education in the world.

Trusteeism

The initial lack of organization in ecclesiastical affairs, nationalistic feeling among Catholics and the independent action of some priests were factors involved in several early crises.

In Philadelphia, some German Catholics withdrew from one parish in 1789 and founded one of their own, Holy Trinity, which they maintained until 1802. Controversy over the affair reached the point of schism in 1796. Philadelphia was also the scene of the Hogan Schism, which developed in the 1820's when Father William Hogan, with the aid of lay trustees, seized control of St. Mary's Cathedral. His movement, for churches and parishes controlled by other than canonical procedures and run in extra-legal ways, was nullified by a decision of the Pennsylvania Supreme Court in 1822.

Similar troubles seriously disturbed the peace of the Church in other places, principally New York, Baltimore, Buffalo, Charleston and New Orleans.

Dangers arising from the exploitation of lay control were gradually diminished with the extension and enforcement of canonical procedures and with changes in civil law about the middle of the century.

Bigotry

Bigotry against Catholics waxed and waned during the 19th century and into the 20th. The first major campaign of this kind, which developed in the wake of the panic of 1819 and lasted for about 25 years, was mounted in 1830 when the number of Catholic immigrants began to increase to a noticeable degree. Nativist anti-Catholicism generated a great deal of violence, represented by climaxes in loss of life and property in Charlestown, Mass., in 1834, and in Philadelphia 10 years later. Later bigotry was fomented by the Know-Nothings, in the 1850's; the Ku Klux Klan, from 1866; the American Protective Association, from 1887; and the Guardians of Liberty. Perhaps the last eruption of overt anti-Catholicism occurred during the campaign of Alfred E. Smith for the presidency in 1928. Observers feel the issue was laid to rest in the political area with the election of John F. Kennedy to the presidency in 1960.

Growth and Immigration

Between 1830 and 1900, the combined factors of natural increase, immigration and conversion raised the Catholic population to 12 million. A large percentage of the growth figure represented immigrants: some 2.7 million, largely from Ireland, Germany and France, between 1830 and 1880; and another 1.25 million during the 80's when eastern and southern Europeans came in increasing numbers. By the 1860's the Catholic Church, with most of its members concentrated in urban areas, was one of the largest religious bodies in the country.

The efforts of progressive bishops to hasten the acculturation of Catholic immigrants occasioned a number of controversies, which generally centered around questions concerning national or foreign-language parishes. One of them, called Cahenslyism, arose from complaints that German Catholic immigrants were not being given adequate pastoral care.

Immigration continued after the turn of the century, but its impact was more easily cushioned through the application of lessons learned earlier in dealing with problems of nationality and language.

Councils of Baltimore

The bishops of the growing US dioceses met at Baltimore for seven provincial councils between 1829 and 1849.

In 1846, they proclaimed the Blessed Virgin Mary patroness of the United States under the title of the Immaculate Conception, eight years before the dogma was proclaimed.

After the establishment of the Archdiocese of Oregon City in 1846 and the elevation to metropolitan status of St. Louis, New Orleans, Cincinnati and New York, the first of the three plenary councils of Baltimore was held.

The first plenary assembly was convoked on May 9, 1852, with Archbishop Francis P. Kenrick of Baltimore as papal legate. The bishops drew up regulations concerning parochial life, matters of church ritual and ceremonies, the administration of church funds and the teaching of Christian doctrine.

The second plenary council, meeting from Oct. 7 to 21, 1866, under the presidency of Archbishop Martin J. Spalding, formulated a condemnation of several current doctrinal errors and established norms affecting the organization of dioceses, the education and conduct of the clergy, the management of ecclesiastical property, parochial duties and general education.

Archbishop (later Cardinal) James Gibbons called into session the third plenary council which lasted from Nov. 9 to Dec. 7, 1884. Among highly significant results of actions taken by this assembly were the preparation of the line of Baltimore catechisms which became a basic means of religious instruction in this country; legislation which fixed the pattern of Catholic education by requiring the building of elementary schools in all parishes; the establishment of the Catholic University of America in Washington, D.C., in 1889; and the determination of six holy days of obligation for observance in this country.

The enactments of the three plenary councils have had the force of particular law for the Church in the United States.

The Holy See established the Apostolic Delegation at Washington, D.C., on Jan. 24, 1893.

Slavery and Negroes

In the Civil War period, as before, Catholics reflected attitudes of the general population with respect to the issue of slavery. Some supported it, some opposed it, but none were prominent in the Abolition Movement. Gregory XVI had condemned the slave trade in 1839, but no contemporary pope or American bishop published an official document on slavery itself. The issue did not split Catholics in schism as it did Baptists, Methodists and Presbyterians.

Catholics fought on both sides in the Civil War. Five hundred members of 20 or more sisterhoods served the wounded of both sides.

One hundred thousand of the four million slaves emancipated in 1863 were Catholics; the highest concentrations were in Louisiana, about 60,000, and Maryland, 16,000. Three years later, their pastoral care was one of the subjects covered in nine decrees issued by the Second Plenary Council of Baltimore. The measures had little practical effect with respect to integration of the total Catholic community, predicated as they were on the proposition that individual bishops should handle questions regarding segregation in churches and related matters as best they could in the pattern of local customs.

Long entrenched segregation practices continued in force through the rest of the 19th century and well into the 20th. The first effective efforts to alter them were initiated by Cardinal Joseph Ritter of St. Louis in 1947, Cardinal Patrick (then Archbishop) O'Boyle of Washington in 1948, and Bishop Vincent Waters of Raleigh in 1953.

Friend of Labor

The Church became known during the 19th century as a friend and ally of labor in seeking justice for the working man. Cardinal Gibbons journeyed to Rome in 1887, for example, to defend and prevent a condemnation of the Knights of Labor by Leo XIII. The encyclical *Rerum Novarum* was hailed by many American bishops as a confirmation, if not vindication, of their own theories. Catholics have always formed a large percentage of union membership, and some have served unions in positions of leadership.

The American Heresy

Near the end of the century some controversy developed over what was characterized as Americanism or the phantom heresy. It was alleged that Americans were discounting the importance of contemplative virtues, exalting the practical virtues, and watering down the purity of Catholic doctrine for the sake of facilitating convert work.

The French translation of Father Walter Elliott's *Life of Isaac Hecker,* which fired the controversy, was one of many factors that led to the issuance of Leo XIII's *Testem Benevolentiae* in January, 1899, in an attempt to end the matter. It was the first time the orthodoxy of the Church in the US was called into question.

Schism

In the 1890's, serious friction developed between Poles and Irish in Scranton, Buffalo and Chicago, resulting in schism and the establishment of the Polish National Church. A central figure in the affair was Father Francis Hodur, who was exxcommunicated by Bishop William O'Hara of Scranton in 1898. Nine years later, his ordination by the Old Catholic Archbishop of Utrecht gave the new church its first bishop.

Another schism of the period led to formation of the American Carpatho-Russian Orthodox Greek Catholic Church.

Coming of Age

In 1900, there were 12 million Catholics in the total US population of 76 million, 82 dioceses in 14 provinces, and 12,000 priests and members of about 40 communities of men religious. Many sisterhoods, most of them of European origin and some of American foundation, were engaged in Catholic educational and hospital work, of which they have always been the main support.

The Church in the United States was removed from mission status with promulgation of the apostolic constitution *Sapienti Consilio* by Pope St. Pius X on June 29, 1908.

Before that time, and even into the early 20's, the Church in this country received financial assistance from mission-aid societies in France, Bavaria and Austria. Already, however, it was making increasing contributions of its own. At the present time, it is the heaviest national contributor to the worldwide Society for the Propagation of the Faith.

American foreign missionary personnel increased from 14 or less in 1906 to 9,655 (4,009 priests, 869 brothers, 208 scholastics, 4,150 sisters, 419 lay persons), by Jan. 1, 1968. The first missionary seminary in the US was in operation at Techny, Ill., in 1909, under the auspices of the Society of the Divine Word. Maryknoll, the first American missionary society, was established in 1911 and sent its first priests to China in 1918. Despite these contributions, the Church in the US has not matched the missionary commitment of some other nations.

Bishops' Conference

A highly important apparatus for mobilizing the Church's resources was established in 1917 under the title of the National Catholic War Council. Its name was changed to National Catholic Welfare Conference several years later, but its objectives remained the same: to serve as an advisory and coordinating agency of the American bishops for advancing works of the Church in fields of social significance and impact — education, communications, immigration, social action, legislation, youth and lay organizations.

The forward thrust of the bishops' social thinking was evidenced in a program of social reconstruction they recommended in 1919. By 1945, all but one of their twelve points had been enacted into legislation.

The NCWC was renamed the United States Catholic Conference (USCC) in November, 1966, when the hierarchy also organized itself as a territorial conference with pastoral-juridical authority under the title, National Conference of Catholic Bishops. The USCC is carrying on the functions of the former NCWC.

Pastoral Concerns

The potential for growth of the Church in this country by immigration was sharply reduced but not entirely curtailed after 1921 with the passage of restrictive Federal legislation. As a result, the Catholic population became more stabilized and, to a certain extent and for many reasons, began to acquire an identity of its own.

Some increase-from-outside has taken place in the past 40 years, however; from Canada, from central and eastern European countries, and from Puerto Rico and Latin American countries since World War II. This influx, while not as great as that of the 19th century and early 20th, has enriched the Church here with a sizable body of Eastern-Rite Catholics for whom eight ecclesiastical jurisdictions were established between 1924 and 1969. It has also created a challenge for pastoral care of the Spanish-speaking.

The Church continues to grapple with serious pastoral problems in rural areas, where nearly 650 counties are no-priest land. The National Catholic Rural Life Conference was established in 1922 in an attempt to make the Catholic presence felt on the land, and the Glenmary Society since its foundation in 1939 has devoted itself to this single apostolate. Religious communities and diocesan priests are similarly engaged.

Other challenges lie in the cities and suburbs where 75 percent of the Catholic population lives. Conditions peculiar to each segment of the metropolitan area have developed in recent years as the flight to the suburbs has not only altered some traditional aspects of parish life but has also, in combination with many other factors, left behind a complex of special problems in the inner city.

Phenomena of Change

The Church in the US is presently in a stage of transition from a relatively stable and long established order of life and action to a new order of things. Some of the phenomena of this period are:

• differences in trends and emphasis in theology, and in interpretation and implementation of directives of the Second Vatican Council, resulting in situations of conflict;

• the changing spiritual formation, professional education, style of life and ministry of priests, which are altering influential patterns of pastoral and specialized service;

• vocations to the priesthood and religious life, which are generally in decline;

• departures from the priesthood and religious life which, while small percentage-wise, are numerous enough to be a matter of serious concern;

• exercise of authority along the lines of collegiality and subsidiarity;

• structure and administration, marked by a trend toward greater participation in the life and work of the Church by its members on all levels, from the parish on up;

• alienation from the Church, leading some persons into the catacombs of an underground church;

• education, undergoing crisis and change in Catholic schools and seeking new ways of reaching out to the young not in Catholic schools and to adults;

• social witness in ministry to the world, which is being shaped by the form of contemporary needs — e.g., race relations, poverty, the peace movement, the Third World.

• ecumenism, involving the Church in interfaith relations from the level of scholarly discussion to collaboration in the social field.

BACKGROUND DATES IN US CATHOLIC CHRONOLOGY

Dates in this section refer mostly to earlier "firsts" and developments in the background of Catholic history in the United States. For other dates, see various sections of the Almanac.

Alabama

1540: Priests crossed the territory with De Soto's expedition.

1560: Five Dominicans in charge of mission at Santa Cruz des Nanipacna.

1682: La Salle claimed territory for France.

1704: Jesuits established first parish church at Fort Louis de la Mobile.

1722: Mobile, formerly under the Quebec diocese, became part of a vicariate apostolic with Florida. Capuchins, Carmelites and Jesuits working there.

1829: Mobile-Birmingham diocese established; made two separate dioceses, 1969.

1830: Spring Hill College, Mobile, established.

1834: Visitation Nuns established an academy at Summerville.

Alaska

1779: Mass celebrated for first time on shore of Port Santa Cruz on lower Bucareli Bay on May 13 by Franciscan John Riobo.

1868: Alaska placed under jurisdiction of Vancouver Island.

1878: Father John Althoff became first resident missionary.

1886: Archbishop Charles J. Seghers, "Apostle of Alaska," murdered by a guide;

had surveyed southern and northwest Alaska in 1873 and 1877, respectively.

Sisters of St. Anne first nuns in Alaska.

1894: Alaska made prefecture apostolic.

1901: Jesuits reorganized their missions, established a church at Nome.

1905: Sisters of Providence opened hospital at Nome.

1916: Alaska made vicariate apostolic.

1917: In first ordination in territory, Rev. G. Edgar Gallant raised to priesthood.

1951: Juneau diocese established.

1962: Fairbanks diocese established.

1966: Anchorage archdiocese established.

Arizona

1539: Franciscan Marcos de Niza explored the state.

1540: Franciscans Juan de Padilla, Juan de la Cruz and Marcos de Niza accompanied Coronado expedition through the territory.

1629: Spanish Franciscans began work among Moqui Indians.

1632: Franciscan Martin de Arvide killed by Indians.

1680: Franciscans Jose de Espeleta, Augustin de Santa Maria, Jose de Figueroa and Jose de Trujillo killed in Pueblo Revolt.

1700: Jesuit Eusebio Kino established mission at San Xavier del Bac, near Tucson.

1767: Jesuits expelled; Franciscans took over 10 missions.

1828: Spanish missionaries expelled by Mexican government.

1863: Jesuits returned to San Xavier.
1869: Sisters of Loretto arrived to conduct schools at Bisbee and Douglas.
1897: Tucson diocese established.
1969: Phoenix diocese established.

Arkansas

1541: Priests accompanied De Soto expedition through the territory.
1673: Marquette visited Indians in east.
1686: Henri de Tonti established trading post, first white settlement in territory.
1702: Fr. Nicholas Foucault working among Indians.
1805: Bishop Carroll of Baltimore appointed Administrator Apostolic of Arkansas.
1838: Sisters of Loretto opened first Catholic school.
1843: Little Rock diocese established. There were about 700 Catholics in state, two churches, one priest.
1853: Sisters of Mercy founded St. Mary's Convent at Fort Smith.

California

1542: Cabrillo discovered Upper (Alta) California; name of priest accompanying expedition unknown.
1602: On Nov. 12 Carmelite Andres de la Ascencion offered first recorded Mass in California on shore of San Diego Bay.
1697: Missionary work in Lower and Upper Californias entrusted to Jesuits.
1767: Jesuits expelled from territory. Spanish Crown confiscated their property, including the Pious Fund for Missions. Upper California missions entrusted to Franciscans.
1769: Franciscan Junipero Serra began establishment of Franciscan missions in California, near present San Diego. (See Franciscan Missions of Upper California.)
1775: Franciscan Luis Jayme killed by Indians at San Diego Mission.
1779: Diocese of Sonora, Mexico, which included Upper California, established.
1781: On Sept. 4 an expedition from San Gabriel Mission founded present city of Los Angeles — Pueblo "de Nuestra Senora la Reina de Los Angeles."
Franciscans Francisco Hermenegildo Garces, Juan Antonio Barreneche, Juan Marcello Diaz and Jose Matias Moreno killed by Indians.
1812: Franciscan Andres Quintana killed at Santa Cruz Mission.
1822: Interference and aggression toward missions initiated by Mexican government.
Dedication on Dec. 8 of Old Plaza Church, "Assistant Mission of Our Lady of the Angels," oldest church in Los Angeles.
1833: Missions secularized, finally confiscated.
1840: Pope Gregory XVI established Diocese of Both Californias.
1846: Peter H. Burnett, first governor of California, received into Catholic Church.

1848: Upper California ceded to the United States.
1850: Monterey diocese erected; title changed to Monterey-Los Angeles, 1859; and to Los Angeles, 1922.
1851: University of Santa Clara chartered.
1852: Lower California detached from Monterey diocese.
1853: San Francisco archdiocese established.
1855: US returned confiscated California missions to Church.
1863: Sisters of Notre Dame de Namur opened women's College of Notre Dame at Belmont.
1868: Grass Valley diocese established; transferred to Sacramento in 1886.
1922: Monterey-Fresno diocese established; became separate dioceses, 1967.
1934: Sesquicentennial of Serra's death observed; Serra Year officially declared by Legislature and Aug. 24 observed as Serra Day.
1936: Los Angeles made archdiocese. San Diego diocese established.
1952: Law exempting non-profit, religious-sponsored elementary and secondary schools from taxation upheld in referendum, Nov. 4.
1953: Archbishop James Francis McIntyre of Los Angeles made cardinal by Pius XII.
1962: Oakland, Santa Rosa and Stockton dioceses established.

Colorado

1858: First parish in Colorado established.
1864: Sisters of Loretto at the Foot of the Cross, first nuns in the state, established academy at Denver.
1868: Vicariate Apostolic of Colorado and Utah established.
1887: Denver diocese established.
1888: Regis College founded.
1951: Denver made archdiocese.
Pueblo diocese established.

Connecticut

1651: Probably first priest to enter state was Jesuit Gabriel Druillettes; ambassador of Governor of Canada, he participated in a New England Colonial Council at New Haven.
1755: Catholic Acadians, expelled from Nova Scotia, settled in the state.
1791: Rev. John Thayer, first missionary to visit state's Catholics on regular basis, offered Mass at home of Noah Webster.
1808: Connecticut became part of Boston diocese.
1818: Religious freedom established by new Constitution, although the Congregational Church remained, in practice, the state church.
1828: Father Bernard O'Cavanaugh became first resident priest in state.
1829: First Catholic church in state established at Hartford.
Catholic Press of Hartford established.

1843: Hartford diocese established.
1882: Knights of Columbus founded by Father Michael J. McGivney.
1942: Fairfield University founded.
1953: Norwich and Bridgeport dioceses established. Hartford made archdiocese.
1956: Byzantine Rite Exarchate of Stamford established; made eparchy, 1958.

Delaware

1730: Mount Cuba, New Castle County, the scene of Catholic services.
1750: Jesuit mission at Apoquiniminck administered from Maryland.
1772: First permanent parish established at Coffee Run.
1792: French Catholics from Santo Domingo settled near Wilmington.
1816: St. Peter's Church, later the Cathedral of the diocese, erected at Wilmington.
1830: Daughters of Charity opened school and orphanage at Wilmington.
1868: Wilmington diocese established.
1869: Visitation Nuns established residence in Wilmington.

District of Columbia

1641: Jesuit Andrew White evangelized Anacosta Indians.
1774: Father John Carroll ministered to Catholics.
1789: Georgetown, first Catholic college in US, established.
1791: Pierre Charles L'Enfant designed the Federal City of Washington. His plans were not fully implemented until the early 1900's.
1792: James Hoban designed the White House.
1794: Father Anthony Caffrey began St. Patrick's Church, first parish church in the new Federal City.
1801: Poor Clares opened school for girls in Georgetown; first school established by nuns in US.
1802: First mayor of Washington, appointed by President Jefferson, was Judge Robert Brent.
1889: Catholic University of America founded.
1893: Apostolic Delegation established with Archbishop Francesco Satolli as the first delegate.
1919: National Catholic Welfare Conference (now the United States Catholic Conference) organized by American hierarchy to succeed National Catholic War Council.
1920: Cornerstone of National Shrine of Immaculate Conception laid.
1939: Washington made archdiocese of equal rank with Baltimore, under direction of same archbishop.
1947: Washington archdiocese received its own archbishop, was separated from Baltimore.
1967: Archbishop Patrick A. O'Boyle of Washington made cardinal by Pope Paul VI.

Florida

1513: Ponce de Leon discovered Florida.
1521: Missionaries accompanying Ponce de Leon and other explorers probably said first Masses within present limits of US.
1528: Franciscans landed on western shore.
1539: Twelve missionaries landed with De Soto at Tampa Bay.
1549: Dominican Luis Cancer de Barbastro and two companions slain by Indians near Tampa Bay.
1565: City of St. Augustine, oldest in US, founded by Pedro Menendez de Aviles, who was accompanied by four secular priests.
America's oldest mission, Nombre de Dios, was established.
Father Martin Francisco Lopez de Mendoza Grajales became the first parish priest of St. Augustine, where the first parish in the US was established.
1572: St. Francis Borgia, General of the Society, withdrew Jesuits from Florida.
1606: Bishop Juan de las Cabeyas de Altamirano, O.P., conducted the first episcopal visitation in the US.
1620: The chapel of Nombre de Dios was dedicated to Nuestra Senora de la Leche y Buen Parto (Our Nursing Mother of the Happy Delivery); oldest shrine to the Blessed Mother in the US.
1704: Destruction of Florida's northern missions by English and Indian troops led by Governor James Moore of South Carolina. Franciscans Juan de Parga, Dominic Criodo, Tiburcio de Osorio, Augustine Ponze de Leon, Marcos Delgado and two Indians, Anthony Enixa and Amador Cuipa Feliciano were slain by the invaders.
1735: Bishop Francis Martinez de Tejadu Diaz de Velasco, Auxiliary of Santiago, was the first bishop to take up residence in US, at St. Augustine.
1793: Florida and Louisiana were included in Diocese of New Orleans.
1857: Eastern Florida made a vicariate apostolic.
1870: St. Augustine diocese established.
1917: Convent Inspection Bill passed; repealed 1935.
1958: Miami diocese established.
1968: Miami made metropolitan see; Orlando and St. Petersburg dioceses established.

Georgia

1540: First priests to enter were chaplains with De Soto. They celebrated first Mass within territory of 13 original colonies.
1566: Pedro Martinez, first Jesuit martyr of the New World, was slain by Indians on Cumberland Island.
1569: Jesuit mission was opened at Guale Island by Father Antonio Sedeno.
1572: Jesuits withdrawn from area.
1595: Five Franciscans assigned to Province of Guale.

1597: Five Franciscan missionaries killed in coastal missions.

1606: Bishop Altamirano, O.P., conducted visitation of the Georgia area.

1612: First Franciscan province in US erected under title of Santa Elena; it included Georgia, South Carolina and Florida.

1655: Franciscans had nine flourishing missions among Indians.

1702: Spanish missions ended as result of English conquest.

1796: Augustinian Father Le Mercier was first post-colonial missionary to Georgia.

1798: Catholics granted right of refuge.

1800: First church erected in Savannah on lot given by City Council.

1810: First church erected in Augusta on lot given by State Legislature.

1850: Savannah diocese established; became Savannah-Atlanta, 1937; divided into two separate sees, 1956.

1962: Atlanta made metropolitan see.

Hawaii

1825: Pope Leo XII entrusted missionary efforts in Islands to Sacred Heart Fathers.

1827: The first Catholic missionaries arrived — Fathers Alexis Bachelot, Abraham Armand and Patrick Short, along with three lay brothers. After three years of persecution, the priests were forcibly exiled.

1836: Father Arsenius Walsh, SS. CC., a British subject, was allowed to remain in Islands but was not permitted to proselytize or conduct missions.

1839: Hawaiian government signed treaty with France granting Catholics freedom of worship and same privileges as Protestants.

1844: Vicariate Apostolic of Sandwich Islands (Hawaii) erected.

1873: Father Damien de Vuester of the Sacred Heart Fathers arrived in Molokai and spent the remainder of his life working among lepers.

1941: Honolulu diocese established, made a suffragan of San Francisco.

Idaho

1840: Jesuit Pierre de Smet preached to the Flathead and Pend d'Oreille Indians; probably offered first Mass in state.

1842: Jesuit Nicholas Point opened a mission among Coeur d'Alene Indians near Maries.

1863: Secular priests sent from Oregon City to administer to incoming miners.

1867: Sisters of Holy Names of Jesus and Mary opened first Catholic school at Idaho City.

1868: Idaho made a vicariate apostolic.

1870: First church in Boise established.

Church lost most of its missions among Indians of Northwest Territory when Commission on Indian Affairs appointed Protestant missionaries to take over.

1893: Boise diocese established.

Illinois

1673: Jesuit Jacques Marquette, accompanying Joliet, preached to Indians.

1674: Pere Marquette set up a cabin for saying Mass in what later became City of Chicago.

1675: Pere Marquette established Mission of the Immaculate Conception among Kaskaskia Indians.

1679: La Salle brought with him Franciscans Louis Hennepin, Gabriel de la Ribourde, and Zenobius Membre.

1680: Father Ribourde was killed by Kickapoo Indians.

1689: Jesuit Claude Allouez died after 32 years of missionary activity among Indians of Midwest; he had evangelized 100,000 Indians of 20 different tribes and baptized 10,000. Jesuit Jacques Gravier succeeded Allouez as vicar general of Illinois.

1730: Father Gaston, a diocesan priest, was killed at the Cahokia Mission.

1763: British conquest of the territory resulted in banishment of Jesuits.

1778: Father Pierre Gibault championed Colonial cause in the Revolution and aided greatly in securing states of Ohio, Indiana, Illinois, Michigan and Wisconsin for Americans.

1827: The present St. Patrick's Parish at Ruma, oldest English-speaking Catholic congregation in state, was founded.

1833: Visitation Nuns established residence in Kaskaskia.

1843: Chicago diocese established.

1853: Quincy diocese established; transferred to Alton, 1857; Springfield, 1923.

1860: Quincy College founded.

1877: Peoria diocese established.

1880: Chicago made archdiocese.

1887: Belleville diocese established.

1908: Rockford diocese established.

First American Missionary Congress held in Chicago.

1924: Archbishop Mundelein of Chicago made cardinal by Pope Pius XI.

1926: The 28th International Eucharistic Congress, first held in US, convened in Chicago.

1946: Blessed Frances Xavier Cabrini, former resident of Chicago, was canonized; first US citizen raised to dignity of altar.

Archbishop Samuel A. Stritch of Chicago made cardinal by Pope Pius XII.

1948: Joliet diocese established.

1958: Cardinal Stritch appointed Pro-Prefect of the Sacred Congregation for the Propagation of the Faith — the first US-born prelate to be named to the Roman Curia.

1959: Archbishop Albert G. Meyer of Chicago made cardinal by Pope John XXIII.

1961: Eparchy of St. Nicholas of the Ukrainians established at Chicago.

1967: Archbishop John P. Cody of Chicago made cardinal by Pope Paul VI.

Indiana

1679: Recollects Louis Hennepin and Gabriel de la Ribourde entered state.

1686: Land near present Notre Dame University at South Bend given by French government to Jesuits for mission.

1732: Church of St. Francis Xavier founded at Vincennes.

1778: Father Gibault aided George Rogers Clark in campaign against British in conquest of Northwest Territory.

1793: First school in Indiana built at Vincennes by Father John Francis Rivet.

1834: Vincennes diocese, later Indianapolis, established.

1840: Sisters of Providence founded St. Mary-of-the-Woods College for women.

1842: University of Notre Dame founded by Holy Cross Fathers.

1843: Immigration of German farmers to Indiana swelled Catholic population.

1853: First Benedictine community established in state at St. Meinrad.

1857: Fort Wayne diocese established; changed to Fort Wayne-South Bend, 1960.

1944: Indianapolis made archdiocese. Lafayette and Evansville dioceses established.

1957: Gary diocese established.

Iowa

1673: A Peoria village on Mississippi was visited by Pere Marquette.

1679: Fathers Louis Hennepin and Gabriel de la Ribourde visited Indian villages.

1836: First permanent church, St. Raphael's, founded at Dubuque by Dominican Samuel Mazzuchelli.

1837: Dubuque diocese established.

1838: St. Joseph's Mission founded at Council Bluffs by Jesuit Father De Smet.

1843: Sisters of Charity of the Blessed Virgin Mary were first Sisterhood in state.

Sisters of Charity opened Clarke College, Dubuque.

1844: Brothers of St. Joseph opened academy for boys at Dubuque.

1850: First Trappist Monastery in state, Our Lady of New Melleray, was begun.

1881: Davenport diocese established.

1882: St. Ambrose College, Davenport, established.

1893: Dubuque made archdiocese.

1902: Sioux City diocese established.

1911: Des Moines diocese established.

Kansas

1542: Franciscan Juan de Padilla, first martyr of the United States, was killed in central Kansas.

1858: St. Benedict's College founded.

1863: Sisters of Charity opened orphanage at Leavenworth, and St. John's Hospital in following year.

1877: Leavenworth diocese established; transferred to Kansas City in 1947.

1887: Dioceses of Concordia (transferred to Salina in 1944) and Wichita established.

1888: Oblate Sisters of Providence opened an orphanage for Negro boys at Leavenworth, first west of Mississippi.

1951: Dodge City diocese established.

1952: Kansas City made archdiocese.

Kentucky

1775: First settlers in Kentucky were Catholics.

1787: Father Charles Francis Whelan, first resident priest, ministered to settlers of Bardstown.

1806: Dominican Fathers built Priory of St. Rose, later founded St. Thomas Aquinas College.

1808: Bardstown diocese established; transferred to Louisville, 1840.

1811: Rev. Guy L. Chabrat became first priest ordained west of the Allegheny Mountains.

1812: Sisters of Loretto founded, first religious community in US without foreign affiliation.

Sisters of Charity of Nazareth founded, the second native community of women founded in the West.

1814: Nazareth College for women established.

1816: Cornerstone of St. Joseph's Cathedral, Bardstown, laid; called "The Cathedral in the Wilderness."

1817: St. Thomas Seminary founded.

1830: Hon. Benjamin J. Webb founded *Catholic Advocate* first Catholic weekly in Kentucky.

1847: Trappist monks took up residence in Gethsemani.

1849: Cornerstone of Cathedral of the Assumption laid at Louisville.

1852: Know-Nothing troubles in state.

1853: Covington diocese established.

1937: Louisville made archdiocese. Owensboro diocese established.

1956: State Court of Appeals upheld right of Catholic Sisters to teach in state's public schools even though they wear religious habits.

Louisiana

1682: La Salle's expedition, accompanied by two priests, completed discoveries of De Soto at mouth of Mississippi. La Salle named territory Louisiana.

1699: French Catholics founded colony of Louisiana.

First recorded Mass offered Mar. 3, by Franciscan Father Anastase Douay.

1706: Father John Francis Buisson de St. Cosme was killed near Donaldsonville.

1717: Franciscan Anthony Margil established first Indian mission school of San Miguel de Linares.

1718: City of New Orleans founded by Jean Baptiste Le Moyne de Bienville.

1720: First resident priest in New Orleans was the French Recollect Prothais Boyer.

1725: Capuchin Fathers opened school for boys.

1727: Ursuline Nuns founded convent in New Orleans, oldest convent in what is now US; they conducted a school, hospital and orphan asylum.

1793: New Orleans diocese established.

1850: New Orleans made archdiocese.

1853: Natchitoches diocese established; transferred to Alexandria in 1910.

1892: Sisters of Holy Family, a Negro congregation, established at New Orleans.

1912: Loyola University of South established.

1918: Lafayette diocese established.

1925: Xavier University established in New Orleans.

1961: Baton Rouge diocese established.

1962: Catholic schools on all levels desegregated in New Orleans archdiocese.

Maine

1604: First Mass in territory celebrated by Father Nicholas Aubry, accompanying De Monts' expedition which was authorized by King of France to begin colonizing region.

605: Colony founded on St. Croix Island; two secular priests served as chaplains.

1613: Four Jesuits attempted to establish permanent French settlement near mouth of Kennebec River.

1619: French Franciscans began work among settlers and Indians; driven out by English in 1628.

1630: New England made a prefecture apostolic in charge of French Capuchins.

1633: Capuchin Fathers founded missions on Penobscot River.

1646: Jesuits established Assumption Mission on Kennebec River.

1688: Church of St. Anne, oldest in New England, built at Oldtown.

1704: English soldiers destroyed French missions.

1724: English forces again attacked French settlements, killed Jesuit Sebastian Rale.

1853: Portland diocese established.

1854: Know-Nothing uprising resulted in burning of church in Bath.

1856: Anti-Catholic feeling continued; church at Ellsworth burned.

1864: Sisters of Congregation of Notre Dame from Montreal opened academy at Portland.

1875: James A. Healy, first bishop of Negro blood consecrated in US, became second Bishop of Portland.

Maryland

1634: Maryland established by Lord Calvert. Two Jesuits among first colonists.

First Mass offered on Island of St. Clement in Lower Potomac by Jesuit Father Andrew White.

St. Mary's founded by English and Irish Catholics.

1641: St. Ignatius Parish founded by Jesuits of Chapel Point, near Fort Tobacco.

1649: Religious Toleration Act passed by Maryland Assembly. It was repealed in 1654 by Puritan-controlled government.

1651: Cecil Calvert, second Lord Baltimore, gave Jesuits 10,000 acres for use as Indian mission.

1658: Lord Baltimore restored Toleration Act.

1672: Franciscans came to Maryland under leadership of Father Massius Massey.

1688: Maryland became royal colony as a result of the Revolution in England; Anglican Church became the official religion (1692); Toleration Act repealed; Catholics disenfranchised and persecuted until 1776.

1784: Father John Carroll made prefect apostolic for territory of the new Republic.

1789: Baltimore became first diocese established in US, with John Carroll as first Bishop.

1790: Carmelite Nuns founded convent at Port Tobacco, the first in the English-speaking Colonies.

1791: First Synod of Baltimore held.

St. Mary's Seminary, first seminary in US, established.

1793: Rev. Stephen T. Badin first priest ordained by Bishop Carroll.

1800: Jesuit Leonard Neale became first Bishop consecrated in present limits of US.

1806: Cornerstone of Assumption Cathedral, Baltimore, was laid.

1808: Baltimore made archdiocese.

1809: St. Joseph's College, first women's college in US, founded.

1811: Sisters of Charity of Emmitsburg approved by Bishop Carroll; first native American Sisterhood.

1821: Assumption Cathedral, Baltimore, formally opened.

1829: Oblate Sisters of Charity, a Negro congregation, established at Baltimore.

First Provincial Council of Baltimore held; six others followed, in 1833, 1837, 1840, 1843, 1846 and 1849.

1836: Roger B. Taney appointed Chief Justice of Supreme Court by President Jackson.

1852: First of the three Plenary Councils of Baltimore convened. Subsequent Councils were held in 1866 and 1884.

1855: German Catholic Central Verein founded.

1886: Archbishop Gibbons of Baltimore made cardinal by Pope Leo XIII.

1965: Archbishop Shehan of Baltimore made cardinal by Pope Paul VI.

Massachusetts

1630: New England made a prefecture apostolic in charge of French Capuchins.

1647: Massachusetts Bay Company enacted an anti-priest law.

1732: Although Catholics were not legally admitted to colony, a few Irish families were in Boston; a priest was reported working among them.

1755-56: Acadians landing in Boston were denied services of a Catholic priest.

1775: General Washington discouraged Guy Fawkes Day procession in which pope was carried in effigy, and expressed surprise that there were men in his army "so void of common sense as to insult the religious feelings of the Canadians with whom friendship and an alliance are being sought."

1780: The Massachusetts State Constitution granted religious liberty, but required a religious test to hold public office and provided for tax to support Protestant teachers of piety, religion and morality.

1788: First public Mass said in Boston on Nov. 2 by Abbe de la Poterie, first resident priest.

1803: Church of Holy Cross erected in Boston with financial aid given by Protestants headed by John Adams.

1808: Boston diocese established.

1831: Irish Catholic immigration increased.

1832: St. Vincent's Orphan Asylum, oldest charitable institution in Boston opened by Sisters of Mercy.

1834: Ursuline Convent in Charlestown burned by a Nationalist mob.

1843: Holy Cross College founded.

1855: Catholic militia companies disbanded; nunneries' inspection bill passed.

1859: St. Mary's, first parochial school in Boston, opened.

1860: Portuguese Catholics from Azores settled in New Bedford.

1870: Springfield diocese established.

1875: Boston made archdiocese.

1904: Fall River diocese established.

1911: Archbishop O'Connell of Boston made cardinal by Pope Pius X.

1950: Worcester diocese established.

1958: Archbishop Richard J. Cushing of Boston made cardinal by Pope John XXIII.

1966: Apostolic Exarchate for Melkites in the US established, with headquarters in Boston.

Michigan

1641: Jesuits Isaac Jogues and Charles Raymbaut preached to Chippewas; named Sault Sainte Marie rapids.

1660: Jesuit Rene Menard opened first regular mission in Lake Superior region.

1668: Pere Marquette founded Sainte Marie Mission at Sault-Sainte Marie.

1671: Pere Marquette founded St. Ignace Mission at Michilimackinac.

1701: Fort Pontchartrain founded on present site of Detroit and placed in command of Antoine de la Mothe Cadillac. The Chapel of Sainte-Anne-de-Detroit founded.

1706: Franciscan Father Delhalle killed by Indians at Detroit.

1823: Father Gabriel Richard elected delegate to Congress from Michigan territory; he was the first priest chosen for the House of Representatives.

1833: Father Frederic Baraga celebrated first Mass in present Grand Rapids. Detroit diocese established, embracing whole Northwest Territory.

1843: "Western Catholic Register" founded at Detroit.

1845: St. Vincent's Hospital, Detroit opened by Sisters of Charity.

1848: Cathedral of Sts. Peter and Paul, Detroit, consecrated.

1853: Vicariate Apostolic of Upper Michigan established.

1857: Sault Ste. Marie diocese established; later transferred to Marquette.

1877: University of Detroit founded.

1882: Grand Rapids diocese established.

1897: Nazareth College for women founded.

1937: Detroit made archdiocese. Lansing diocese established.

1938: Saginaw diocese established.

1946: Archbishop Edward Mooney of Detroit created Cardinal by Pope Pius XII.

1949: Opening of St. John's Theological (major) Seminary at Plymouth; this was first seminary in US serving an entire ecclesiastical province (Detroit).

1966: Apostolic Exarchate for Maronites in US established, with headquarters in Detroit; made an eparchy in 1972.

1969: Archbishop John Dearden of Detroit made cardinal by Pope Paul VI.

1971: Gaylord and Kalamazoo dioceses established.

Minnesota

1680: Falls of St. Anthony discovered by Franciscan Louis Hennepin.

1727: First chapel, St. Michael the Archangel, erected near town of Frontenac and placed in charge of French Jesuits.

1732: Fort Charles built; Jesuits ministered to settlers.

1736: Jesuit Jean Pierre Aulneau killed by Indians.

1739: Swiss Catholics from Canada settled near Fort Snelling; Bishop Loras of Dubuque, accompanied by Father Pellamourgues, visited the Fort and administered sacraments.

1841: Father Lucian Galtier built Church of St. Paul, thus forming nucleus of modern city of same name.

1850: St. Paul diocese established.

1851: Sisters of St. Joseph arrived in state.

1857: University of St. John founded.

1888: St. Paul made archdiocese; name changed to St. Paul-Minneapolis in 1966.

1889: Duluth, St. Cloud and Winona dioceses established.

1909: Crookston diocese established.

1958: New Ulm diocese established.

Mississippi

1540: Chaplains with De Soto expedition entered territory.

1682: Franciscans Zenobius Membre and Anastase Douay preached to Taensa and Natchez Indians. Father Membre offered first recorded Mass in the state on Mar. 29, Easter Sunday.

1698: Priests of Quebec Seminary founded missions near Natchez and Fort Adams.

1702: Father Nicholas Foucault murdered by Indians near Fort Adams.

1721: Missions practically abandoned, with only Father Juif working among Yazoos.

1725: Jesuit Mathurin de Petit carried on mission work in northern Mississippi.

1729: Indians tomahawked Jesuit Paul du Poisson near Fort Rosalie; Father Jean Souel shot by Yazoos.

1736: Jesuit Antoine Senat burned at stake by Chickasaws.

1822: Vicariate Apostolic of Mississippi and Alabama established.

1825: Mississippi made a separate vicariate apostolic.

1837: Natchez diocese established (later changed to Natchez-Jackson).

1848: Sisters of Charity opened orphan asylum and school in Natchez.

Missouri

1700: Jesuit Gabriel Marest established a mission among Kaskaskia Indians near St. Louis.

1734: French Catholic miners and traders settled Old Mines and Sainte Genevieve.

1750: Jesuits visited French settlers.

1762: Mission established at St. Charles.

1767: Carondelet mission established.

1770: First church founded at St. Louis.

1811: Jesuits established Indian mission school at Florissant.

1818: Bishop Dubourg arrived at St. Louis, with Vincentians Joseph Rosati and Felix de Andreis. St. Louis University, the diocesan (Kenrick) seminary and the Vincentian Seminary in Perryville trace their origins to them.

1826: St. Louis diocese established.

1828: Sisters of Charity opened first hospital west of the Mississippi, at St. Louis.

1832: "The Shepherd of the Valley," first Catholic paper west of the Mississippi, established.

1845: First conference of Society of St. Vincent de Paul in US founded at St. Louis.

1847: St. Louis made archdiocese.

1865: A Test Oath Law passed by State Legislature (called Drake Convention) to crush Catholicism in Missouri. Law declared unconstitutional by Supreme Court in 1866.

1867: College of St. Teresa for women founded at Kansas City.

1868: St. Joseph diocese established.

1880: Kansas City diocese established.

1946: Archbishop John J. Glennon of St. Louis made cardinal by Pope Pius XII.

1956: Kansas City and St. Joseph dioceses combined into one see. Jefferson City and Springfield-Cape Girardeau dioceses established.

1961: Archbishop Joseph E. Ritter of St. Louis made cardinal by Pope John XXIII.

1969: Archbishop John J. Carberry of St. Louis made cardinal by Pope Paul VI.

Montana

1743: Pierre and Francois Verendrye, accompanied by Jesuit Father Coquart, may have explored territory.

1833: Indian missions handed over to care of Jesuits by Second Provincial Council of Baltimore.

1840: Jesuit Pierre De Smet began missionary work among Flathead and Pend d'Oreille Indians.

1841: St. Mary's Mission established by Father De Smet and two companions on the Bitter Root River in present Stevensville.

1845: Jesuit Antonio Ravalli placed in charge of St. Mary's Mission; Ravalli County named in his honor.

1859: Fathers Point and Hoecken established St. Peter's Mission near the Great Falls.

1869: Sisters of Charity founded a hospital, school and orphanage in Helena.

1877: Vicariate Apostolic of Montana established.

1884: Helena diocese established.

1904: Great Falls diocese established.

1910: Carroll College founded.

1935: Rev. Joseph M. Gilmore became first Montana priest elevated to hierarchy.

Nebraska

1541: Coronado expedition, accompanied by Franciscan Juan de Padilla, reached the Platte River.

1673: Pere Marquette visited Nebraska Indians.

1720: Franciscan Juan Miguel killed by Indians near Columbus.

1855: Father J. F. Tracy administered Catholic settlement of St. Patrick and to Catholics in Omaha.

1856: Land was donated by Governor Alfred Cumming for a church in Omaha.

1857: Nebraska vicariate apostolic established.

1878: Creighton University established.

1881: Poor Clares, first contemplative group in state, arrived in Omaha.

Duchesne College established.

1885: Omaha diocese established.

1887: Lincoln diocese established.

1912: Kearney diocese established; name changed to Grand Island, 1917.

1917: Father Flanagan founded Boy's Town for homeless boys, an institution which gained national and international recognition in subsequent years.

1945: Omaha made archdiocese.

Nevada

1774: Franciscan missionaries passed through Nevada on way to California missions.

1860: First parish, serving Genoa, Carson City and Virginia City, established.

1862: Rev. Patrick Manogue appointed pastor of Virginia City. He established a school for boys and girls, an orphanage and hospital.

1871: Church erected at Reno.

1931: Reno diocese established.

New Hampshire

1630: Territory made part of a prefecture apostolic embracing all of New England.

1784: State Constitution included a religious test which barred Catholics from public office; local support was provided for public Protestant teachers of religion.

1818: The Barber family of Claremont was visited by their son Virgil (converted to Catholicism in 1816) accompanied by Father Charles Ffrench, O.P. The visit led to the conversion of the entire Barber family.

1823: Father Virgil Barber, minister who became a Jesuit priest, built first Catholic church and school at Claremont.

1830: Church of St. Aloysius erected at Dover.

1853: New Hampshire made part of the Portland diocese.

1858: Sisters of Mercy began to teach school at St. Anne's, Manchester.

1877: Catholics obtained full civil liberty and rights.

1884: Manchester diocese established.

1893: St. Anselm's College founded; St. Anselm's Abbey canonically erected.

1937: Francis P. Murphy became first Catholic governor of New Hampshire.

New Jersey

1668: William Douglass of Bergen was refused a seat in General Assembly because he was a Catholic.

1672: Fathers Harvey and Gage visited Catholics in Woodbridge and Elizabethtown.

1701: Tolerance granted to all but "papists."

1744: Jesuit Theodore Schneider of Pennsylvania visited German Catholics of New Jersey.

1762: Fathers Ferdinand Farmer and Robert Harding working among Catholics in state.

1776: State Constitution tacitly excluded Catholics from office.

1799: Foundation of first Catholic school in state, St. John's at Trenton.

1803: First parish in northern New Jersey founded at Echo Lake.

1814: First church in Trenton erected.

1844: Catholics obtained full civil liberty and rights.

1853: Newark diocese established.

1856: Seton Hall University established.

1881: Trenton diocese established.

1937: Newark made archdiocese. Paterson and Camden dioceses established.

1947: US Supreme Court ruled on N. J. bus case, permitting children attending non-public schools to ride on buses and be given other health services provided for those in public schools.

1957: Seton Hall College of Medicine and Dentistry established: the first medical school in state; it was run by Seton Hall until 1965.

1963: Byzantine Eparchy of Passaic established.

New Mexico

1539: Territory explored by Franciscan Marcos de Niza.

1544: Franciscans Juan de la Cruz and Louis de Ubeda, lay brother, killed by Indians.

1581: Franciscans Augustin Rodriguez, Juan de Santa Maria and Francisco Lopez named the region "New Mexico"; they later died at hands of Indians.

1598: Juan de Onate founded a colony at Chamita, where first chapel in state was built.

1609: Santa Fe founded, future headquarters for missions of New Mexico.

1631: Franciscan Pedro de Miranda was killed by Indians.

1632: Franciscan Francisco Letrado was killed by Indians.

1672: Franciscan Pedro de Avila y Ayala was killed by Indians.

1675: Franciscan Alonso Gil de Avila was killed by Indians.

1680: Indians massacred 21 missionaries; missions destroyed.

1684: Franciscan Manuel Beltran was killed by Indians.

1692: Missions restored.

1696: Indians rebelled, massacred five more missionaries.

1850: Jean Baptiste Lamy appointed head of newly established Vicariate Apostolic of New Mexico.

1852: Sisters of Loretto arrived in Santa Fe.

1853: Santa Fe diocese established.

1859: Christian Brothers arrived, established first school for boys in New Mexico (later St. Michael's College).

1865: Sisters of Charity started first orphanage and hospital in Santa Fe. It was closed in 1966.

1875: Santa Fe made archdiocese.

1939: Gallup diocese established.

New York

1524: Giovanni de Verrazano was first white man to enter New York Bay.

1627: Franciscan Joseph d'Aillon discovered oil at Seneca Springs, near Cuba, N. Y.

1642: Jesuits Isaac Jogues and Rene Goupil

were mutilated by Mohawks; Rene Goupil was killed by them shortly afterwards. Dutch Calvinists rescued Father Jogues.

1646: Jesuits Isaac Jogues and John Lalande were martyred by Iroquois at Ossernenon, now Auriesville.

1654: The Onondagas were visited by Jesuits from Canada.

1655: First permanent mission established near Syracuse.

1656: Church of St. Mary erected near Lake Onondaga.

Catherine Tekakwitha, "Lily of the Mohawks," was born at Ossernenon, now Auriesville (d. in Canada, 1680).

1658: Indian uprisings destroyed missions among Cayugas, Senecas and Oneidas.

1664: English took New Amsterdam and replaced French priests with their own missionaries.

Duke of York ordered religious freedom in Province of New York.

1667: Missions were restored under protection of Garaconthie, Onondaga chief.

1678: Franciscan Louis Hennepin, first white man to view Niagara Falls, celebrated Mass there.

1682: Thomas Dongan appointed governor by Duke of York.

1683: English Jesuits came to New York, later opened a school.

1700: Although Assembly enacted a bill calling for religious toleration of all Christians in 1683, other penal laws were now enforced against Catholics; all priests were ordered out of the province.

1709: Jesuit missions were abandoned.

1741: Because of an alleged popish plot to burn city of New York, four whites were hanged and 11 Negroes burned at stake.

1777: A rejected amendment of the State Constitution stated that Catholics ought not to hold lands or participate in civil rights unless they swore that no pope or priests may absolve them from allegiance to the state.

1785: Cornerstone was laid for St. Peter's Church, New York City, first permanent structure of Catholic worship in state.

Trusteeism began to cause trouble at New York.

1806: State Test Oath repealed.

1808: New York diocese established.

1828: New York State Legislature enacted a law upholding sanctity of seal of confession.

1834: First native New Yorker to become a secular priest, Rev. John McCloskey, was ordained.

1841: Fordham University and Manhattanville College established.

1847: Albany and Buffalo dioceses established.

1850: New York made archdiocese.

1853: Brooklyn diocese established.

1856: Present St. Bonaventure University and Christ the King Seminary founded at Allegany.

1858: Cornerstone of St. Patrick's Cathedral, New York City, was laid.

1868: Rochester diocese established.

1872: Ogdensburg diocese established.

1875: Archbishop John McCloskey of New York made first American cardinal by Pope Pius IX.

1878: Franciscan Sisters of Allegany were first native American community to send members to foreign missions.

1880: William R. Grace was first Catholic mayor of New York City.

1886: Syracuse diocese established.

1911: Archbishop John M. Farley of New York made cardinal by Pope Pius X.

Catholic Foreign Mission Society of America (Maryknoll) opened a seminary for foreign missions, the first of its kind in US. The Maryknollers were also unique as the first US-established foreign mission society.

1917: Military Ordinariate established with headquarters at New York.

1919: Alfred E. Smith became first elected Catholic governor.

1924: Archbishop Patrick Hayes of New York made cardinal by Pope Pius XI.

1930: Jesuit Martyrs of New York and Canada were canonized on June 29.

1946: Archbishop Francis J. Spellman of New York made Cardinal by Pope Pius XII.

1957: Rockville Centre diocese established.

1969: Archbishop Terence Cooke of New York made cardinal by Pope Paul VI.

North Carolina

1526: The Ayllon expedition attempted to establish a settlement on Carolina coast.

1540: De Soto expedition, accompanied by chaplains, entered state.

1776: State Constitution denied office to "those who denied the truths of the Protestant religion."

1805: The few Catholics in state were served by visiting missionaries.

1821: Bishop John England celebrated Mass in the ballroom of the home of William Gaston at New Bern, marking the start of organization of the first parish, St. Paul's, in the state.

1835: William Gaston, State Supreme Court Justice, succeeded in having repealed the article denying religious freedom.

1852: First Catholic church erected in Charlotte.

1868: North Carolina vicariate apostolic established.

Catholics obtained full civil liberty and rights.

1874: Sisters of Mercy arrived, opened an academy, several schools, hospitals and an orphanage.

1878: Belmont Abbey College founded.

1910: Mary Help of Christians Abbey Nullius established at Belmont.

1924: Raleigh diocese established.

North Dakota

1742: Pierre and Francois Verendrye, accompanied by Jesuit Father Coquart explored territory.

1818: Canadian priests ministered to Catholics in area.

1839: Jesuit Father De Smet made first of five trips among Mandan and Gros Ventre Indians.

1848: Father George Belcourt, first American resident priest in territory, reestablished Pembena Mission.

1874: Grey Nuns invited to conduct a school at Fort Totten.

1889: Fargo diocese established.

1893: Benedictines founded St. Gall Monastery at Devil's Lake. (It became an abbey in 1903.)

1909: Bismarck diocese established.

1959: Archbishop Aloysius J. Muench, Bishop of Fargo, made cardinal by Pope John XXIII.

Ohio

1749: Jesuits in expedition of Celeron de Bienville preached to Indians.

First religious services were held within present limits of Ohio. Jesuits Joseph de Bonnecamp and Peter Potier celebrated Mass at mouth of Little Miami River and in vicinity of Sandusky Bay, respectively.

1751: First Catholic settlement founded among Huron Indians near Sandusky by Father de la Richardie.

1790: Benedictine Pierre Didier ministered to French immigrants.

1812: Bishop Flaget of Bardstown visited and baptized Catholics of Lancaster and Somerset Counties.

1818: Dominican Father Fenwich built St. Joseph's Church and established first Dominican convent in Ohio.

1821: Cincinnati diocese established.

1831: Xavier University founded.

1843: Seven members of Congregation of Most Precious Blood arrived in Cincinnati from France.

1845: Cornerstone laid for St. Peter's Cathedral, Cincinnati; this was first cathedral west of Alleghenies.

1847: Cleveland diocese established.

1850: Cincinnati made archdiocese.

Marianists opened St. Mary's Institute, now University of Dayton.

1865: Sisters of Charity opened hospital in Cleveland, first institution of its kind in city.

1868: Columbus diocese established.

1871: Ursuline College for women opened at Cleveland.

1910: Toledo diocese established.

1935: Archbishop John T. McNicholas, O.P., founded the Institutum Divi Thomae in Cincinnati for fundamental research in natural sciences.

1943: Youngstown diocese established.

1944: Steubenville diocese established.

1969: Byzantine Rite Eparchy of Parma established.

Oklahoma

1540: De Soto expedition, accompanied by chaplains, explored territory.

1541: Coronado expedition, accompanied by Franciscan Juan de Padilla, explored state.

1630: Spanish Franciscan Juan de Salas labored among Indians.

1700: Scattered Catholic families were visited by priests from Kansas and Arkansas.

1874: First Catholic church built by Father Smyth at Atoka.

1876: Prefecture Apostolic of Indian Territory established with Benedictine Isidore Robot as its head.

1886: First Catholic day school for Choctaw and white children opened by Sisters of Mercy at Kribs.

1891: Vicariate Apostolic of Oklahoma and Indian Territory established.

1905: Oklahoma diocese established; title changed to Oklahoma City and Tulsa, 1930.

1917: Benedictine Heights College for women founded.

Carmelite Sisters of St. Theresa of the Infant Jesus were founded at Oklahoma City.

Oregon

1603: Vizcaino explored northern Oregon coast.

1774: Franciscan missionaries accompanied Juan Perez on his expedition to coast, and Heceta a year later.

1811: Catholic Canadian trappers and traders with John J. Astor expedition founded first American settlement — Astoria.

1834: Indian missions in Northwest entrusted to Jesuits by Holy See.

1838: Abbe Blanchet appointed vicar general to Bishop of Quebec with jurisdiction over area which included Oregon Territory.

1839: First church in Pacific Northwest, under patronage of St. Paul the Apostle, was blessed at Champoig.

1842: Dr. John McLoughlin, "Father of Oregon," was received into the Church.

1843: Oregon vicariate apostolic established.

St. Joseph's College for boys opened.

1844: Jesuit Pierre de Smet established Mission of St. Francis Xavier near St. Paul.

Sisters of Notre Dame de Namur, first to enter Oregon, opened an academy for girls.

1846: Vicariate made an ecclesiastical province with Bishop Blanchet as first Archbishop of Oregon City (now Portland).

Walla Walla diocese established; suppressed in 1853.

First priest was ordained in Oregon.

1848: First Provincial Council of Oregon.

1865: Rev. H. H. Spalding, a Protestant missionary, published the Whitman Myth to hinder work of Catholic missionaries.

1874: Catholic Indian Mission Bureau established.

1875: St. Vincent's Hospital, first in state, opened at Portland.

1903: Baker diocese established.

1922: Anti-private school bill sponsored by Scottish Rite Masons was passed by popular vote, 115,506 to 103,685.

1925: US Supreme Court declared Oregon anti-private school bill unconstitutional.

1953: First Trappist monastery on West Coast established in Willamette Valley north of Lafayette.

Pennsylvania

1673: Priests from Maryland ministered to Catholics in the Colony.

1682: Religious toleration was extended to members of all faiths.

1720: Jesuit Joseph Greaton became first resident missionary of Philadelphia.

1734: St. Joseph's Church, first Catholic church in Philadelphia, was opened.

1741: Jesuit Fathers Schneider and Wappeler ministered to German immigrants.

1782: St. Mary's Parochial School opened at Philadelphia.

1788: Holy Trinity Church, Philadelphia, was incorporated; first exclusively national church organized in US.

1797: Augustinian Matthew Carr founded St. Augustine parish, Philadelphia.

1799: Prince Demetrius Gallitzin (Father Augustine Smith) built church in western Pennsylvania, at Loretto.

1808: Philadelphia diocese established.

1814: St. Joseph's Orphanage was opened at Philadelphia; first Catholic institution for children in US.

1842: University of Villanova founded by Augustinians.

1843: Pittsburgh diocese established.

1844: Thirteen persons killed, two churches and a school burned in Know-Nothing riots at Philadelphia.

1846: First Benedictine Abbey in New World founded near Latrobe by Father Boniface Wimmer.

1853: Erie diocese established.

1868: Scranton and Harrisburg dioceses established.

1871: Chestnut Hill College, first for women in state, founded.

1875: Philadelphia made archdiocese.

1901: Altoona-Johnstown diocese established.

1913: Byzantine Rite Apostolic Exarchate of Philadelphia established; became metropolitan see, 1958.

1921: Archbishop Dennis Dougherty made cardinal by Pope Benedict XV.

1924: Byzantine Rite Apostolic Exarchate of Pittsburgh established; made an eparchy in 1963; raised to metropolitan status and transferred to Munhall, 1969.

1951: Greensburg diocese established.

1958: Archbishop John O'Hara, C.S.C., of Philadelphia made cardinal by Pope John.

1961: Allentown diocese established.

1967: Archbishop John J. Krol of Philadelphia made cardinal by Pope Paul VI.

1969: Bishop John J. Wright of Pittsburgh made cardinal by Pope Paul VI and transferred to Curia post.

Rhode Island

1663: Colonial Charter granted freedom of conscience.

1719: Laws denied Catholics the right to hold public office.

1829: St. Mary's Church, Pawtucket, was first Catholic church in state.

1837: Parochial schools inaugurated in state.

First Catholic church in Providence was built.

1851: Sisters of Mercy began work in Rhode Island.

1872: Providence diocese established.

1900: Trappists took up residence in state.

1917: Providence College founded.

South Carolina

1569: Jesuit Juan Rogel was the first resident priest in the territory.

1573: First Franciscans arrived in southeastern section.

1606: Bishop Altamirano conducted visitation of area.

1655: Franciscans had two missions among Indians; later destroyed by English.

1697: Religious liberty granted to all except "papists."

1790: Catholics given right to vote.

1820: Charleston diocese established.

1822: Bishop England founded "U.S. Catholic Miscellany," first Catholic paper of a strictly religious nature in US.

1830: Sisters of Our Lady of Mercy, first in state, took up residence at Charleston.

1847: Cornerstone of Cathedral of St. John the Baptist, Charleston, was laid.

1861: Cathedral and many institutions destroyed in Charleston fire.

South Dakota

1842: Father Augustine Ravoux began ministrations to French and Indians at Fort Pierre, Vermilion and Prairie du Chien; printed devotional book in Sioux language the following year.

1867: Parish organized among the French at Jefferson.

1878: Benedictines opened school for Sioux children at Fort Yates.

1889: Sioux Falls diocese established.

1902: Lead diocese established; transferred to Rapid City, 1930.

1950: Mount Marty College for women founded.

1952: Blue Cloud Abbey, first Benedictine foundation in state, was dedicated.

Tennessee

1541: Cross planted in shore of Mississippi by De Soto; accompanying the expedition were Fathers John de Gallegos and Louis De Soto.

1682: Franciscan Fathers Membre and Douay accompanied La Salle to present site of Memphis; may have offered the first Masses in the territory.

1800: Catholics were served by priests from Bardstown, Ky.

1822: Non-Catholics assisted in building church in Nashville.

1837: Nashville diocese established.

1843: Sisters of Charity opened a school for girls in Nashville.

1921: Sisters of St. Dominic opened Siena College for women at Memphis.

1940: Christian Brothers College founded at Memphis.

1970: Memphis diocese established.

Texas

1541: Missionaries with De Soto and Coronado entered territory.

1553: Dominicans Diego de la Cruz, Hernando Mendez, Juan Ferrer, Brother Juan de Mina killed by Indians.

1675: Bosque-Larios missionary expedition entered region; Father Juan Larios offered first recorded Mass.

1689: Four Franciscans founded first Mission, San Francisco de los Tejas.

1703: Mission San Francisco de Solano founded on Rio Grande.

1717: Franciscan Antonio Margil founded six missions in northeast.

1721: Franciscan Brother Jose Pita killed by Indians at Carnezeria.

1728: Site of San Antonio settled.

1738: Construction of San Fernando Cathedral at San Antonio.

1744: Mission of San Francisco de Solano rebuilt as the Alamo.

1750: Franciscan Francisco Xavier was killed by Indians; so were Jose Ganzabal in 1752, and Alonzo Ferrares and Jose San Esteban in 1758.

1793: Mexico secularized missions.

1825: Government of Texas secularized all Indian missions.

1830: Irish priests ministered to settlements of Refugio and San Patricio.

1841: Vicariate of Texas established.

1847: Ursuline Sisters established their first academy in territory at Galveston.
Galveston diocese established.

1852: Oblate Fathers and Franciscans arrived in Galveston to care for new influx of German Catholics.
St. Mary's College founded at San Antonio.

1854: Know-Nothing Party began to stir up hatred against Catholics.

1858: Texas Legislature passed law entitling all schools granting free scholarships and meeting state requirements to share in school fund.

1874: San Antonio diocese established.

1881: St. Edward's College founded: became first chartered college in state in 1889.
Sisters of Charity founded Incarnate Word College at San Antonio.

1890: Dallas-Ft. Worth, 1953; made two separate dioceses, 1969.

1912: Corpus Christi diocese established.

1914: El Paso diocese established.

1926: San Antonio made archdiocese. Amarillo diocese established.

1947: Austin diocese established.

1961: San Angelo diocese established.

1965: Brownsville diocese established.

1966: Beaumont diocese established.

Utah

1776: Franciscans Silvestre de Escalante and Atanasio Dominguez reached Utah (Salt) Lake; first white men known to enter the territory.

1858: Jesuit Father De Smet accompanied General Harney as chaplain on expedition sent to settle troubles between Mormons and US Government.

1866: On June 29 Father Edward Kelly offered first Mass in Salt Lake City in Mormon Assembly Hall.

1886: Utah vicariate apostolic established.

1891: Salt Lake City diocese established.

1926: College of St. Mary-of-the-Wasatch for women was founded.

Vermont

1609: Champlain expedition passed through territory.

1666: Captain La Motte built fort and shrine of St. Anne on Isle La Motte; Sulpician Father Dollier de Casson celebrated first Mass.

1668: Bishop Laval of Quebec administered confirmation in region; this was the first area in northeastern US to receive an episcopal visit.

1710: Jesuits ministered to Indians near Lake Champlain.

1793: Discriminatory measures against Catholics were repealed.

1830: Father Jeremiah O'Callaghan became first resident priest in state.

1853: Burlington diocese established.

1854: Sisters of Charity arrived to conduct St. Joseph's Orphanage at Burlington.

1904: St. Michael's College founded.

1951: First Carthusian foundation in America established at Whitingham.

Virginia

1526: Dominican Antonio de Montesinos offered first Mass on Virginia soil.

1561: Dominicans visited the coast.

1571: Father John Baptist de Segura and seven Jesuit companions killed by Indians.

1642: Priests outlawed and Catholics denied right to vote.

1689: Capuchin Christopher Plunket was captured and exiled to a coastal island where he died in 1697.

1776: Religious freedom granted.

1791: Father Jean Dubois arrived at Richmond with letters from Lafayette. The House of Delegates was placed at his disposal for celebration of Mass.

1796: A church was built at Alexandria.

1820: Richmond diocese established.

1822: Trusteeism created serious problems in diocese; Bishop Kelly resigned the see.

1848: Sisters of Charity opened an orphan asylum at Norfolk.

1866: School Sisters of Notre Dame and Sisters of Charity opened academies for girls at Richmond.

Washington

1775: Spaniards explored the region.

1838: Fathers Blanchet and Demers, "Apostles of the Northwest," were sent to territory by Archbishop of Quebec.

1840: Log church for Indians was built on Whidby Island, Puget Sound.

1843: Vicariate Apostolic of Oregon, including Washington, was established.

1844: Mission of St. Paul founded at Colville.

Six Sisters of Notre Dame de Namur began work in area.

1850: Nesqually diocese established; transferred to Seattle, 1907.

1856: Sisters of Charity established first permanent school and hospital in Northwest at Fort Vancouver.

1887: Gonzaga University founded.

1913: Spokane diocese established.

1951: Seattle made archdiocese. Yakima diocese established.

West Virginia

1749: Father Joseph de Bonnecamps, accompanying the Bienville expedition, may have offered first Mass in the territory.

1821: First Catholic church in Wheeling.

1838: Sisters of Charity founded school at Martinsburg.

1848: Visitation Nuns established academy for girls at Mt. de Chantal.

1850: Wheeling diocese established.

Wheeling Hospital incorporated, the oldest Catholic charitable institution in territory.

1955: Wheeling College establsshed.

Wisconsin

1661: Jesuit Rene Menard, first known missionary in the territory, was killed or lost in the Black River district.

1665: Jesuit Claude Allouez founded Mission of the Holy Ghost at La Pointe Chegoimegon, now Bayfield; this was first permanent mission in region.

1673: Father Marquette and Louis Joliet traveled from Green Bay down the Wisconsin and Mississippi rivers.

1762: Suppression of Jesuits in French Colonies closed many missions for 30 years.

1843: Milwaukee diocese established.

1853: St. John's Cathedral, Milwaukee, was built.

1864: Marquette University established.

1868: Green Bay and La Crosse dioceses established.

1875: Milwaukee made archdiocese.

1905: Superior diocese established.

1946: Madison diocese established.

Wyoming

1840: Jesuit Pierre de Smet offered first Mass near Green River.

1851: Father De Smet held peace conference with Indians near Fort Laramie.

1867: Father William Kelly, first resident priest, arrived in Cheyenne and built first church a year later.

1873: Father Eugene Cusson became first resident pastor in Laramie.

1875: Sisters of Charity of Leavenworth opened school and orphanage at Laramie.

1884: Jesuits took over pastoral care of Shoshone and Arapaho Indians.

1887: Cheyenne diocese established.

1949: Weston Memorial Hospital opened near Newcastle.

Catholics in Presidents' Cabinets

(For biographical data on some of these entries, see Index.)

Roger B. Taney, Attorney General 1831-33, Secretary of Treasury 1833-34; app. by Andrew Jackson.

James Campbell, Postmaster General 1853-57; app. by Franklin Pierce.

John B. Floyd, Secretary of War 1857-61; app. by James Buchanan.

Joseph McKenna, Attorney General 1897-98; app. by William McKinley.

Robert J. Wynne, Postmaster General 1904-05; app. by Theodore Roosevelt.

Charles Bonaparte, Secretary of Navy 1905-06, Attorney General 1906-09; app. by Theodore Roosevelt.

James A. Farley, Postmaster General 1933-40; app. by Franklin D. Roosevelt.

Frank Murphy, Attorney General 1939-40; app. by Franklin D. Roosevelt.

Frank C. Walker, Postmaster General 1940-45; app. by Franklin D. Roosevelt.

Robert E. Hannegan, Postmaster General 1945-47; app. by Harry S. Truman.

J. Howard McGrath, Attorney General 1949-52; app. by Harry S. Truman.

Maurice J. Tobin, Secretary of Labor; 1949-53; app. by Harry S. Truman.

James P. McGranery, Attorney General 1952-53; app. by Harry S. Truman.

Martin P. Durkin, Secretary of Labor 1953; app. by Dwight D. Eisenhower.

James P. Mitchell, Secretary of Labor 1953-61; app. by Dwight D. Eisenhower.

Robert F. Kennedy, Attorney General 1961-65; app. by John F. Kennedy, reapp. by Lyndon B. Johnson.

Anthony Celebrezze, Secretary of Health, Education and Welfare 1962-65; app. by John F. Kennedy, reapp. by Lyndon B. Johnson.

John S. Gronouski, Postmaster General 1963-65; app. by John F. Kennedy, reapp. by Lyndon B. Johnson.

John T. Connor, Secretary of Commerce 1965-67; app. by Lyndon B. Johnson.

Lawrence O'Brien, Postmaster General 1965-68; app. by Lyndon B. Johnson.

Walter J. Hickel, Secretary of Interior 1969-71; app. by Richard M. Nixon.

John A. Volpe, Secretary of Transportation 1969-; app. by Richard M. Nixon.

Maurice H. Stans, Secretary of Commerce, 1969-71; app. by Richard M. Nixon.

Men who became Catholics after leaving Cabinet posts: Thomas Ewing, Secretary of Treasury under William A. Harrison, and Secretary of Interior under Zachary Taylor; Luke E. Wright, Secretary of War under Theodore Roosevelt; Albert B. Fall, Secretary of Interior under Warren G. Harding.

Catholic Justices of the Supreme Court

(For biographical data on some of these entries, see Index.)

Roger B. Taney, Chief Justice 1836-64; app. by Andrew Jackson.

Edward D. White, Associate Justice 1894-1910, app. by Grover Cleveland; Chief Justice 1910-21, app. by William H. Taft.

Joseph McKenna, Associate Justice 1898-1925; app. by William McKinley.

Pierce Butler, Associate Justice 1923-39; app. by Warren G. Harding.

Frank Murphy, Associate Justice 1940-49; app. by Franklin D. Roosevelt.

William Brennan, Associate Justice 1956-; app. by Dwight D. Eisenhower.

Sherman Minton, Associate Justice from 1949 to 1956, became a Catholic several years before his death in 1965.

Catholics Represented In National Statuary Hall

(For biographies, see Index.)

Statues of 12 Catholics deemed worthy of national commemoration by the donating states are among 90 enshrined in National Statuary Hall and other places in the US Capitol. The Hall, formerly the chamber of the House of Representatives, was erected by Act of Congress July 2, 1864.

Donating states, names and years of placement are listed. An asterisk indicates placement of a statue in the Hall itself.

Arizona: Rev. Eusebio Kino, S. J., missionary, 1965.

California: Rev. Junipero Serra, O. F. M.* missionary, 1931.

Hawaii: Father Damien, 1969.

Illinois: Gen. James Shields, statesman, 1893.

Louisiana: Edward D. White, Justive of the U.S. Supreme Court (1894-1921), 1955.

Maryland: Charles Carroll,* statesman, 1901.

Nevada: Patrick A. McCarran,* statesman, 1960.

New Mexico: Dennis Chavez, statesman, 1966. (Archbishop Jean B. Lamy, pioneer prelate of Santa Fe, was nominated for Hall honor in 1951.)

North Dakota: John Burke,* US treasurer, 1963.

Oregon: Dr. John McLoughlin, pioneer, 1953.

West Virginia: John E. Kenna, statesman, 1901.

Wisconsin: Rev. Jacques Marquette, S. J., missionary, explorer, 1895.

CHURCH-STATE DECISIONS OF THE SUPREME COURT

(Among sources of this listing of US Supreme Court decisions was *The Supreme Court on Church and State,* Joseph Tussman, editor; Oxford University Press, New York, 1962.)

Terrett v. Taylor, 9 Cranch 43 (1815): The Court declared unconstitutional an act of the Virginia Legislature which denied property rights to Protestant Episcopal churches in the state. Religious corporations, like other corporations, have rights to their property.

Vidal v. Girard's Executors, 2 Howard 205 (1844): The Court upheld the will of Stephen Girard, which barred ministers of any religion from serving as faculty members or visitors in a school he established for orphans.

Watson v. Jones, 13 Wallace 679 (1872): The Court declared that a member of a religious organization may not appeal to secular

courts against a decision made by a church tribunal within the area of its competence.

Reynolds v. United States, 98 US 145 (1879): The Court declared, in reference to the Mormon practice of polygamy, that one may not knowingly violate by external practices the law of the land on religious grounds, since such conduct would make the professed doctrines of belief superior to federal or state law. One must keep the external practice of religion within the framework of laws enacted for the common welfare. This was the first decision rendered on the Free Exercise Clause of the First Amendment.

Davis v. Beason, 133 US 333 (1890): The Court upheld the denial of the right of Mormons to vote in Idaho if they refused to sign a registration oath stating that they were not bigamists or polygamists and would not encourage or preach bigamy or polygamy.

Church of Latter-Day Saints v. United States, 136 US 1 (1890): The Court upheld an Act of Congress which annulled the charter of the Corporation of the Church of Jesus Christ of Latter-Day Saints, and declared "forfeited to the government all its real estate except a small portion used exclusively for public worship" (Tussman, *op. cit.,* p. 33). The Court held that the Corporation continually used its power to violate US laws prohibiting polygamy.

Church of the Holy Trinity v. United States, 143 US 226 (1892): The Court declared it is not "a misdemeanor for a church of this country to contract for the services of a Christian minister residing in another nation" (from the text of the decision).

Bradfield v. Roberts, 175 US 291 (1899): The Court denied that an appropriation of government funds for an institution (Providence Hospital, Washington, D.C.) run by Roman Catholic sisters violated the No Establishment Clause of the First Amendment.

Pierce v. Society of Sisters, 268 US 510 (1925): The Court denied that a state can require children to attend public schools only. The Court held that the liberty of the Constitution forbids standardization by such compulsion, and that the parochial schools involved had claims to protection under the Fourteenth Amendment.

Cochran v. Board of Education, 281 US 370 (1930): The Court upheld a Louisiana statute providing textbooks at public expense for children attending public or parochial schools. The Court held that the children and state were beneficiaries of the appropriations, with incidental secondary benefit going to the schools.

United States v. MacIntosh, 283 US 605 (1931): The Court denied that anyone can place allegiance to the will of God above his allegiance to the government, since such a person could make his own interpretation of God's will the decisive test as to whether he would or would not obey the nation's law. The Court stated that the nation, which has a duty to survive, can require citizens to bear arms in its defense.

Hamilton v. Regents of University of California, 293 US 245 (1934): The Court rejected a "claim to exemption from R.O.T.C. based on conscientious objection to war" (Tussman *op. cit.,* p. 64.) If such an exemption were allowed, the liberties of the objector might be extended to the point of refusal to pay taxes in furtherance of a war or any other end condemned by his conscience. This would be an undue exaltation of the right of private judgment.

Cantwell v. Connecticut, 310 US 296 (1940): The Court declared that the right to religious freedom is violated by a statute requiring a person to secure a permit from a government official before soliciting money for alleged re-

ligious purposes from someone not of his or her sect. Such a practice would constitute censorship of religion.

Minersville School District v. Gobitis, 310 US 586 (1940): The Court upheld the right of a state to require the salute to the national flag from school children, even from those who refused to do so for sincere religious reasons.

Jones v. City of Opelika, 316 US 584 (1942): The court upheld licensing ordinances in three municipalities against "the claim by Jehovah's Witnesses that they interfere with the free exercise of religion" (Tussman, *op. cit.,* p. 91).

Murdock v. Commonwealth of Pennsylvania, 319 US 105 (1943): In a reversal of the decision handed down in Jones v. City of Opelika, the Court declared the licensing unconstitutional since it violated a freedom guaranteed under the First Amendment. The selling of religious literature by traveling preachers does not make evangelism the equivalent of a commercial enterprise taxable by the State.

Jones v. City of Opelika, 316 US 584 105 (1943): The Court declared that the Constitution denies a city the right to control the expression of men's minds and denies also the right of men to win others to their views through a program of taxes levied against such activity.

Douglas v. City of Jeannette, 319 US 157 (1943): The Court again upheld the proselytizing rights of Jehovah's Witnesses, ruling unconstitutional the action of any public authority in regulating or taxing such activity.

West Virginia State Board of Education v. Barnette, 319 US 624 (1943): In a reversal of the decision handed down in Minersville School District v. Gobitis, the Court declared unconstitutional a state statute requiring of all children a salute to the national flag and a pledge of allegiance which a child may consider contrary to sincere religious beliefs.

Prince v. Commonwealth of Massachusetts, 321 US 158 (1944): The Court upheld a "child-labor regulation against the claim that it prevents a child from performing her religious duty" (Tussman, *op. cit.,* p. 170). The Court asserted a general principle that the state has a wide range of power for limiting parental freedom and authority in things affecting the child's welfare.

United States v. Ballard, 322 US 78 (1944): The Court upheld the general principle that "the truth of religious claims is not for secular authority to determine" (Tussman, *op. cit.,* p. 181).

In Re Summers, 325 US 561 (1945): The Court upheld "the denial, to an otherwise qualified applicant, of admission to the bar on the basis of the applicant's religiously motivated 'conscientious scruples against participation in war' " (Tussman, *op. cit.,* p. 192). The petitioner was barred because he could not in good faith take the prescribed oath to support the Constitution of Illinois which required service in the state militia in times of necessity.

Girouard v. United States, 328 US 61 (1946): In a ruling related to that handed down in United States v. MacIntosh, the Court affirmed the opinion that the refusal of an alien to bear arms does not deny him citizenship.

Everson v. Board of Education, 330 US 1 (1947): The Court upheld the constitutionality of a New Jersey statute authorizing free school bus transportation for parochial as well as public school students. The Court expressed the opinion that the benefits of public welfare legislation, included under such bus transportation, do not run contrary to the concept of separation of Church and State.

McCollum v. Board of Education, 333 US 203 (1948): the Court declared unconstitutional a program for releasing children, with parental consent, from public school classes so they could receive religious instruction on public school premises from representatives of their own faiths.

Zorach v. Clauson, 343 US 306 (1952): The Court upheld the constitutionality of a New York statute permitting, on a voluntary basis, the release during school time of students from public school classes for religious instruction given off public school premises.

Kedroff v. St. Nicholas Cathedral, 344 US 94 (1952): The Court ruled against an action of New York in taking "control of St. Nicholas Cathedral away from the Moscow hierarchy" (Tussman, *op. cit.,* p. 292), on the ground that the controversy involved a matter of church government.

Fowler v. Rhode Island, 345 US 67 (1953): The Court upheld the right of a Jehovah's Witness to preach in a public park against a city ordinance which forbade such preaching. The Court held that the ordinance, as construed and applied, discriminated against the Witness and therefore amounted to preferment by the state of other religious groups.

Torcaso v. Watkins, 367 US 488 (1961): the Court declared unconstitutional a Maryland requirement that one must make a declaration of belief in the existence of God as part of the oath of office for notaries public.

McGowan v. Maryland, 81 Sp Ct 1101; **Two Guys from Harrison v. McGinley,** 81 Sp Ct 1135; **Gallagher v. Crown Kosher Super Market,** 81 Sp Ct 1128; **Braunfield v. Brown,** 81 Sp Ct 1144 (1961): The Court ruled that Sunday closing laws do not violate the No Establishment of Religion Clause of the First Amendment, even though the laws were religious in their inception and still have some religious overtones. The Court held that, "as presently written and administered, most of them, at least, are of a secular rather than of a religious character, and that presently they bear

no relationship to establishment of religion as those words are used in the Constitution of the United States."

Engel v. Vitale, 370 US 42 (1962): The Court declared that the voluntary recitation in public schools of a prayer composed by the New York State Board of Regents is unconstitutional on the ground that it violates the No Establishment of Religion Clause of the First Amendment.

Abington Township School District v. Schempp and **Murray v. Curlett,** 83 Sp Ct 1560 (1963): The Court ruled that Bible reading and recitation of the Lord's Prayer in public schools, with voluntary participation by students, are unconstitutional on the ground that they violate the No Establishment of Religion Clause of the First Amendment.

Sherbert v. Verner, 83 A Sp Ct 1790 (1963): The Court ruled that individuals of any religious faith may not, because of their faith or lack of it, be deprived of the benefits of public welfare legislation.

Chamberlin v. Dade County, 83 Sp Ct 1864 (1964): The Court reversed a decision of the Florida Supreme Court concerning the constitutionality of prayer and devotional Bible reading in public schools during the school day, as sanctioned by a state statute which specifically related the practices to a sound public purpose.

Board of Education v. Allen, No. 660 (1968): The Court declared constitutional the New York school book loan law which requires local school boards to purchase books with state funds and lend them to parochial and private school students.

Flast v. Cohen, No. 416 (1968): The Court held that individual taxpayers can bring suits to challenge federal expenditures on grounds that they violate the principle of separation of Church and State even though generally taxpayers cannot challenge federal expenditures in court.

Walz v. Tax Commission of New York (1970): The Court upheld the constitutionality of a New York statute exempting church-owned property from taxation.

Earle v. DiCenso, Robinson v. DiCenso, Lemon v. Kurtzman, Tilton v. Richardson (1971): In Earle v. DiCenso and Robinson v. DiCenso, the Court ruled unconstitutional a 1969 Rhode Island statute which provided salary supplements to teachers of secular subjects in parochial schools; in Lemon v. Kurtzman, the Court ruled unconstitutional a 1968 Pennsylvania statute which authorized the state to purchase services for the teaching of secular subjects in nonpublic schools. The principal argument against constitutionality in these cases was that the statutes and programs at issue entailed excessive entanglement of government with religion. In Tilton v. Richardson, the Court held that this argument did not apply to a prohibitive degree with respect to federal grants, under the Higher Education Facilities Act of 1963, for the construction of facilities for nonreligious purposes by four church-related institutions of higher learning, three of which were Catholic, in Connecticut.

Amish Decision (1972): In a case appealed on behalf of Yoder, Miller and Yutzy, the Court ruled that Amish parents were exempt from a Wisconsin statute requiring them to send their children to school until the age of 16. The Court said in its decision that secondary schooling exposed Amish children to attitudes, goals and values contrary to their beliefs, and substantially hindered "the religious development of the Amish child and his integration into the way of life of the Amish faith-community at the crucial adolescent state of development."

THE WALL OF SEPARATION

Thomas Jefferson, in a letter written to the Danbury (Conn.) Baptist Association Jan. 1, 1802, coined the metaphor, "a wall of separation between Church and State," to express a theory concerning interpretation of the religion clauses of the First Amendment: "Congress shall make no law respecting an establishment of religion or prohibiting the free exercise thereof."

The metaphor was cited for the first time in judicial proceedings in 1879, in the opinion by Chief Justice Waite in Reynolds v. United States. It did not, however, figure substantially in the decision.

Accepted as Rule

In 1947 the wall of separation gained acceptance as a constitutional rule, in the decision handed down in Everson v. Board of Education. Associate Justice Black, in describing the principles involved in the No Establishment Clause, wrote:

"Neither a state nor the Federal Government can set up a church. Neither can pass laws which aid one religion, aid all religions, or prefer one religion over another. Neither can force nor influence a person to go to or to remain away from church against his will or force him to profess a belief or disbelief in any religion. No person can be punished for entertaining or professing religious beliefs or disbeliefs, for church attendance or non-attendance. No tax in any amount, large or small, can be levied to support any religious activities or institutions, whatever they may be called, or whatever form they may adopt to teach or practice religion. Neither a state nor the Federal Government can, openly or secretly, participate in the affairs of any religious organizations or groups and vice versa. In the words of Jefferson, the clause against establishment of religion by law was intended to erect 'a wall of separation between Church and State.' "

Mr. Black's associates agreed with his statement of principles, which were framed without reference to the Freedom of Exercise Clause. They disagreed, however, with respect to application of the principles, as the split decision in the case indicated. Five members of the Court held that the benefits of public welfare legislation — in this case, free bus transportation to school for parochial as well as public school students — did not run contrary to the concept of separation of Church and State embodied in the First Amendment.

Different Opinions

Inside and outside the legal profession, opinion is divided concerning the wall of separation and the balance of the religion clauses of the First Amendment.

The view of absolute separationists, carried to the extreme, would make government the adversary of religion. The bishops of the United States, following the McCollum decision in 1948, said that the wall metaphor had become for some persons the "shibboleth of doctrinaire secularism."

Proponents of governmental neutrality toward religion are of the opinion that such neutrality should not be so interpreted as to prohibit incidental aid to religious institutions providing secular services.

In the realm of practice, federal and state legislatures have enacted measures involving incidental benefits to religious bodies. Examples of such measures are the tax exemption of church property; provision of bus rides, book loans and lunch programs to students in church-related as well as public schools; military chaplaincies; loans to church-related hospitals; the financing of studies by military veterans at church-related colleges under GI bills of rights.

CHURCH TAX EXEMPTION

The exemption of church-owned property was ruled constitutional by the US Supreme Court May 4, 1970, in the case of Walz v. The Tax Commission of New York.

Suit in the case was brought by Frederick Walz, who purchased in June, 1967, a 22-by-29-foot plot of ground in Staten Island valued at $100 and taxable at $5.24 a year. Shortly after making the purchase, Walz instituted a suit in New York State, contending that the exemption of church property from taxation authorized by state law increased his own tax rate and forced him indirectly to support churches in violation of his constitutional right to freedom of religion under the First Amendment. Three New York courts dismissed the suit, which had been instituted by mail. The Supreme Court, judging that it had probable jurisdiction, then took the case.

In a 7-1 decision affecting Church-state relations in every state in the nation, the Court upheld the New York law under challenge.

For and Against

Chief Justice Warren E. Burger, who wrote the majority opinion, said that Congress from its earliest days had viewed the religion clauses of the Constitution as authorizing statutory real estate tax exemption to religious bodies. He declared: "Nothing in this national attitude toward religious tolerance and two centuries of uninterrupted freedom from taxation has given the remotest sign of leading to an established church or religion, and on the contrary it has operated affirmatively to help guarantee the free exercise of all forms of religious beliefs."

Justice William O. Douglas wrote in dissent that the involvement of government in religion as typified in tax exemption may seem inconsequential but: "It is, I fear, a long step down the establishment path. . . . Perhaps I have been misinformed. But, as I read the Constitution and the philosophy, I gathered that independence was the price of liberty."

Burger rejected Douglas' "establishment" fears. If tax exemption is the first step toward establishment, he said, "the second step has been long in coming."

The basic issue centered on the following question: Is there a contradiction between federal constitutional provisions against the establishment of religion, or the use of public funds for religious purposes, and state statutes exempting church property from taxation?

In the Walz' decision, the Supreme Court ruled that there is no contradiction.

Legal Background

The US Constitution makes no reference to tax exemption.

There was no discussion of the issue in the Constitutional Convention nor in debates on the Bill of Rights.

In the Colonial and post-Revolutionary years, some churches had established status and were state-supported. This state of affairs changed with enactment of the First Amendment, which laid down no-establishment as the federal norm. This norm was adopted by the states which, however, exempted churches from tax liabilities.

No establishment, no hindrance, was the early American view of Church-state relationships.

This view, reflected in custom law, was not generally formulated in statute law until the second half of the 19th century, although specific tax exemption was provided for churches in Maryland in 1798, in Virginia in 1800, and in North Carolina in 1806.

The first major challenge to church property exemption was initiated by the Liberal League in the 1870's. It reached the point that President Grant included the recommendation in a State of the Union address in 1875, stating that church property should bear its own proportion of taxes. The plea fell on deaf ears in Congress, but there was some support for the idea at state levels. The exemption, however, continued to survive various challenges.

At the present time, 36 state constitutions contain either mandatory or permissive provisions for exemption. Statues provide for exemption in all other states.

There has been considerable litigation challenging this special exemption, but most of it focused on whether a particular property satisfied statutory requirements. Few cases before Walz focused on the strictly constitutional question, whether directly under the First Amendment or indirectly under the Fourteenth Amendment.

Unrelated Income

Taxation of the unrelated business income of churches is a different matter. In a joint statement on this subject issued in May, 1969, the US Catholic Conference and the National Council of Churches said they favored "elimination of the specific exemption of churches from taxation on income from regularly conducted commercial business activities which are unrelated to their exempt functions."

The two groups prefaced the statement with the observation:

"Under existing law many types of orgainzations are granted exemption from the income tax. Certain exempt organizations, including charitable, educational and some religious organizations, labor unions, business leagues, etc., are nevertheless subjected to tax upon their incomes from any unrelated business; and rents derived from debt-financed property (under leases for periods in excess of five years) are included in unrelated business taxable income.

"The tax upon unrelated business taxable income does not apply to churches, or conventions or associations of churches. "Such exemption makes available to churches a potential advantage over tax-paying organizations engaged in commercial business activities."

Objections

Objectors to the tax exempt status of churches feel that churches should share, through taxation, in the cost of the ordinary benefits of public services they enjoy, and/or that the amount of "aid" enjoyed through exemption should be proportionate to the amount of social good they do.

According to one opinion, exemption is said to weaken the independence of churches from the political system which benefits them by exemption.

In another view, exemption is said to involve the government in decisions regarding what is and what is not religion.

US Catholic Jurisdictions, Hierarchy, Statistics

The organizational structure of the Catholic Church in the United States consists of 31 provinces comprising as many archdioceses (metropolitan sees), 132 suffragan sees (129 dioceses, 2 exarchates, 1 prelacy), the US Military Ordinariate, and one jurisdiction immediately subject to the Holy See — the Abbacy of Mary Help of Christians, Belmont, N. C. With the exception of the abbacy, each of these jurisdictions is under the direction of an archbishop or bishop, called an ordinary, who has apostolic responsibility and authority for the pastoral service of the people in his care.

The structure includes the territorial episcopal conference known as the National Conference of Catholic Bishops. In and through this body, which is strictly ecclesiastical and has defined juridical authority, the bishops exercise their collegiate pastorate over the Church in the entire country (see Index).

Related to the NCCB is the United States Catholic Conference, a civil corporation and operational secretariat through which the bishops, in cooperation with other members of the Church, act on a wider-than-ecclesiastical scale for the good of the Church and society in the United States (see Index).

The representative of the Holy See to the Church in this country is the Apostolic Delegate, Archbishop Luigi Raimondi (see Index).

ECCLESIASTICAL PROVINCES

(Sources: *The Official Catholic Directory, 1972;* NC News Service.)

The 31 ecclesiastical provinces bear the names of archdioceses, i.e., of metropolitan sees.

Anchorage: Archdiocese of Anchorage and suffragan sees of Fairbanks, Juneau. Geographical area: Alaska.

Atlanta: Archdiocese of Atlanta (Ga.) and suffragan sees of Savannah (Ga.), Charlotte and Raleigh (N.C.), Charleston (S.C.). Geographical area: Georgia, North Carolina (except Belmont Abbacy), South Carolina.

Baltimore: Archdiocese of Baltimore (Md.) and suffragan sees of Wilmington (Del.), Richmond (Va.), Wheeling (W. Va.). Geographical area: Maryland (except five counties), Delaware, Virginia, West Virginia.

Boston: Archdiocese of Boston (Mass.) and suffragan sees of Fall River, Springfield and Worcester (Mass.), Portland (Me.), Manchester (N.H.), Burlington (Vt.). Geographical area: Massachusetts, Maine, New Hampshire, Vermont.

Chicago: Archdiocese of Chicago and suffragan sees of Belleville, Joliet, Peoria, Rockford, Springfield. Geographical area: Illinois.

Cincinnati: Archdiocese of Cincinnati and suffragan sees of Cleveland, Columbus, Steubenville, Toledo, Youngstown. Geographical area: Ohio.

Denver: Archdiocese of Denver (Colo.) and suffragan sees of Pueblo (Colo.), Cheyenne (Wyo.). Geographical area: Colorado, Wyoming.

Detroit: Archdiocese of Detroit and suffragan sees of Gaylord, Grand Rapids, Kalamazoo, Lansing, Marquette, Saginaw. Geographical area: Michigan.

Dubuque: Archdiocese of Dubuque and suffragan sees of Davenport, Des Moines, Sioux City. Geographical area: Iowa.

Hartford: Archdiocese of Hartford (Conn.) and suffragan sees of Bridgeport and Norwich (Conn.), Providence (R.I.). Geographical area: Connecticut, Rhode Island.

Indianapolis: Archdiocese of Indianapolis and suffragan sees of Evansville, Fort Wayne-South Bend, Gary, Lafayette. Geographical area: Indiana.

Kansas City (Kans.): Archdiocese of Kansas City and suffragan sees of Dodge City, Salina, Wichita. Geographical area: Kansas.

Los Angeles: Archdiocese of Los Angeles and suffragan sees of Fresno, Monterey, San Diego. Geographical area: Southern California.

Louisville: Archdiocese of Louisville (Ky.) and suffragan sees of Covington and Owensboro (Ky.), Memphis and Nashville (Tenn.). Geographical area: Kentucky, Tennessee.

Miami: Archdiocese of Miami and suffragan sees of Orlando, St. Augustine, St. Petersburg. Geographical area: Florida.

Milwaukee: Archdiocese of Milwaukee and suffragan sees of Green Bay, La Crosse, Madison, Superior. Geographical area: Wisconsin.

Munhall (Byzantine Rite): Metropolitan See of Munhall, Pa. and Eparchies of Passaic (N.J.), Parma (Ohio).

Newark: Archdiocese of Newark and suffragan sees of Camden, Paterson, Trenton. Geographical area: New Jersey.

New Orleans: Archdiocese of New Orleans (La.) and suffragan sees of Alexandria, Baton Rouge and Lafayette (La.), Birmingham and Mobile (Ala.), Little Rock (Ark.), Natchez-Jackson (Miss.). Geographical area: Louisiana, Alabama, Arkansas, Mississippi.

New York: Archdiocese of New York and suffragan sees of Albany, Brooklyn, Buffalo, Ogdensburg, Rochester, Rockville Centre, Syracuse. Geographical area: New York.

Omaha: Archdiocese of Omaha and suffragan sees of Grand Island, Lincoln. Geographical area: Nebraska.

Philadelphia: Archdiocese of Philadelphia and suffragan sees of Allentown, Altoona-Johnstown, Erie, Greensburg, Harrisburg, Pittsburgh, Scranton. Geographical area: Pennsylvania.

Philadelphia (Byzantine Rite): Metropolitan See of Philadelphia (Byzantine Rite) and Eparchies of St. Nicholas of the Ukrainians in Chicago and Stamford, Conn. The jurisdiction extends to all Ukrainian Catholics in the US from the ecclesiastical province of Galicia in the Ukraine.

Portland: Archdiocese of Portland (Ore.) and suffragan sees of Baker (Ore.), Boise (Ida.), Great Falls and Helena (Mont.). Geographical area: Oregon, Idaho, Montana.

St. Louis: Archdiocese of St. Louis and suffragan sees of Jefferson City, Kansas City-St. Joseph, Springfield-Cape Girardeau. Geographical area: Missouri.

St. Paul and Minneapolis: Archdiocese of St. Paul and Minneapolis (Minn.) and suffragan sees of Crookston, Duluth, New Ulm, St. Cloud and Winona (Minn.), Bismarck and Fargo (N.D.), Rapid City and Sioux Falls (S.D.). Geographical area: Minnesota, North Dakota, South Dakota.

San Antonio: Archdiocese of San Antonio (Tex.) and suffragan sees of Amarillo, Austin, Beaumont, Brownsville, Corpus Christi, Dallas, Fort Worth, Galveston-Houston and San Angelo (Tex.), Oklahoma City and Tulsa (Okla.). Geographical area: Texas (except the Diocese of El Paso), Oklahoma.

San Francisco: Archdiocese of San Francisco (Calif.) and suffragan sees of Oakland, Sacramento, Santa Rosa and Stockton (Calif.), Agaña (Guam), Honolulu (H.I.), Reno (Nev.), Salt Lake City (Utah). Geographical area: Northern California, Nevada, Utah, Hawaii, Guam.

Santa Fe: Archdiocese of Santa Fe (N.M.) and suffragan sees of Gallup (N.M.), Phoenix and Tucson (Ariz.), El Paso (Tex.). Geographical area: New Mexico, Arizona, Diocese of El Paso.

Seattle: Archdiocese of Seattle and suffragan sees of Spokane, Yakima. Geographical area: Washington.

Washington: Archdiocese of Washington, D.C., and suffragan see of Prelacy of Virgin Islands. Geographical area: District of Columbia, five counties of Maryland, Virgin Islands.

ARCHDIOCESES, DIOCESES, ARCHBISHOPS, BISHOPS

(Sources: *The Official Catholic Directory, 1972:* NC News Service.)

Archdioceses are indicated by an asterisk.

Albany, N.Y. (1847): Edwin B. Broderick, bishop, 1969. Edward J. Maginn, auxiliary.

Former bishops: John McCloskey, 1847-64; John J. Conroy, 1865-77; Francis McNeirny, 1877-94; Thomas M. Burke, 1894-1915; Thomas F. Cusack, 1915-18; Edmund F. Gibbons, 1919-54; William A. Scully, 1954-69.

Alexandria, La. (1853): Charles P. Greco, bishop, 1946.

Established at Natchitoches, transferred, 1910.

Former bishops: Augustus M. Martin, 1853-75; Francis X. Leray, 1877-79, administrator, 1879-83; Anthony Durier, 1885-1904; Cornelius Van de Ven, 1904-32; D. F. Desmond, 1933-45.

Allentown, Pa. (1961): Joseph McShea, bishop, 1961.

Altoona-Johnstown, Pa. (1901): James J. Hogan, bishop, 1966.

Established as Altoona, name changed, 1957.

Former bishops: Eugene A. Garvey, 1901-20; John J. McCort, 1920-36; Richard T. Guilfoyle, 1936-57; Howard J. Carroll, 1958-60; J. Carroll McCormick, 1960-66.

Amarillo, Tex. (1926): Lawrence M. DeFalco, bishop, 1963.

Former bishops; Rudolph A. Gerken, 1927-33; Robert E. Lucey, 1934-41; Laurence J. Fitzsimons, 1941-58; John L. Morkovsky, 1958-63.

Anchorage,* Alaska (1966): Joseph T. Ryan, archbishop, 1966.

Atlanta,* Ga. (1956; archdiocese, 1962): Thomas A. Donnellan, archbishop, 1968.

Former ordinaries: Francis E. Hyland, 1956-61; Paul J. Hallinan, first archbishop, 1962-68.

Austin, Tex. (1947): Vincent M. Harris, bishop, 1971.

Former bishop: Louis J. Reicher, 1947-71.

Baker, Ore. (1903): Thomas J. Connolly, bishop, 1971.

Established as Baker City, name changed, 1952.

Former bishops: Charles J. O'Reilly, 1903-18; Joseph F. McGrath, 1919-50; Francis P. Leipzig, 1950-71.

Baltimore,* Md. (1789; archdiocese, 1808): Cardinal Lawrence J. Shehan, archbishop, 1961. T. Austin Murphy, F. Joseph Gossman, auxiliaries.

Former ordinaries: John Carroll, 1789-1815, first archbishop; Leonard Neale, 1815-17; Ambrose Marechal, S.S., 1817-28; James Whitfield, 1828-34; Samuel Eccleston, S.S., 1834-51; Francis P. Kenrick, 1851-63; Martin J. Spalding, 1864-72; James R. Bayley, 1872-77; Cardinal James Gibbons, 1877-1921; Michael J. Curley, 1921-47; Francis P. Keough, 1947-61.

Baton Rouge, La. (1961): Robert E. Tracy, bishop, 1961.

Beaumont, Tex. (1966): Warren L. Boudreaux, bishop, 1971.

Former bishop: Vincent M. Harris, 1966-71.

Belleville, Ill. (1887): Albert R. Zuroweste, bishop, 1948.

Former bishops: John Janssen, 1888-1913; Henry Althoff, 1914-47.

Birmingham, Ala. (1969): Joseph G. Vath, bishop, 1969.

Bismarck, N. Dak. (1909): Hilary B. Hacker, bishop, 1957.

Former bishops: Vincent Wehrle, O.S.B., 1910-39; Vincent J. Ryan, 1940-51; Lambert A. Hoch, 1952-56.

Boise, Ida. (1893): Sylvester Treinen, bishop, 1962.

Former bishops: Alphonse J. Glorieux, 1893-1917; Daniel M. Gorman, 1918-27; Edward J. Kelly, 1928-56; James J. Byrne, 1956-62.

Boston,* Mass. (1808; archdiocese, 1875): Humberto S. Medeiros, archbishop, 1970. Jeremiah F. Minihan, Thomas J. Riley, Joseph M. Maguire, Lawrence J. Riley, auxiliaries.

Former ordinaries: John L. de Cheverus, 1810-23; Benedict J. Fenwick, S.J., 1825-46; John B. Fitzpatrick, 1846-66; John J. Williams, 1866-1907, first archbishop; Cardinal William O'Connell, 1907-44; Cardinal Richard Cushing, 1944-70.

Bridgeport, Conn. (1953): Walter W. Curtis, bishop, 1961.

Former bishop: Lawrence J. Shehan, 1953-61.

Brooklyn, N.Y. (1853): Francis J. Mugavero, bishop, 1968. John J. Boardman, Charles R. Mulrooney, Joseph P. Denning, auxiliaries.

Former bishops: John Loughlin, 1853-91; Charles E. McDonnell, 1892-1921; Thomas E. Molloy, 1921-56; Bryan J. McEntegart, 1957-68.

Brownsville, Tex. (1965): John J. Fitzpatrick, bishop, 1971.

Former bishops: Adolph Marx, 1965; Humberto S. Medeiros, 1966-70.

Buffalo, N.Y. (1847): Pius A. Benincasa, Bernard J. McLaughlin, auxiliaries.

Former bishops: John Timon, C.M., 1847-67; Stephen V. Ryan, C.M., 1868-96; James E. Quigley, 1897-1903; Charles H. Colton, 1903-15; Dennis J. Dougherty, 1915-18; William Turner, 1919-36; John A. Duffy, 1937-44; John F. O'Hara, C.S.C., 1945-51; Joseph A. Burke, 1952-62; James McNulty, 1963-72.

Burlington, Vt. (1853): John A. Marshall, b shop, 1972.

Former bishops: Louis De Goesbriand, 1853-99; John S. Michaud, 1899-1908; Joseph J. Rice, 1910-38; Matthew F. Brady, 1938-44; Edward F. Ryan, 1945-56; Robert F. Joyce, 1957-71.

Camden, N.J. (1937): George H. Guilfoyle, bishop, 1968. James L. Schad, auxiliary.

Former bishops: Bartholomew J. Eustace, 1938-56; Justin J. McCarthy, 1957-59; Celestine J. Damiano, 1960-67.

Charleston, S.C. (1820): Ernest L. Unterkoefler, bishop, 1964.

Former bishops: John England, 1820-42; Ignatius A. Reynolds, 1844-45; Patrick N. Lynch, 1858-82; Henry P. Northrop, 1883-1916; William T. Russell, 1917-27; Emmet M. Walsh, 1927-49; John J. Russell, 1950-58; Paul J. Hallinan, 1958-62; Francis F. Reh, 1962-64.

Charlotte, N.C. (1971): Michael J. Begley, bishop, 1972.

Cheyenne, Wyo. (1887): Hubert M. Newell, bishop, 1951.

Former bishops: Maurice F. Burke, 1887-93; Thomas M. Lenihan, 1897-1901; James J. Keane, 1902-11; Patrick A. McGovern, 1912-51.

Chicago,* Ill. (1843; archdiocese, 1880): Cardinal John Cody, archbishop, 1965; Thomas J. Grady, William E. McManus, Alfred L. Abramowicz, Michael R. Dempsey, Nevin Hayes, O. Carm., auxiliaries.

Former ordinaries: William Quarter, 1844-48; James O. Van de Velde, S.J., 1849-53; Anthony O'Regan, 1854-58; James Duggan, 1859-70; Thomas P. Foley, administrator, 1870-79; Patrick A. Feehan, 1880-1902, first archbishop; James E. Quigley, 1903-15; Cardinal George Mundelein, 1915-39; Cardinal Samuel Stritch, 1939-58; Cardinal Albert Meyer, 1958-65.

Cincinnati,* Ohio (1821; archdiocese, 1850): Vacant. Nicholas Elko, auxiliary.

Former ordinaries: Edward D. Fenwick, O.P., 1822-32; John B. Purcell, 1833-83, first archbishop; William H. Elder, 1883-1904; Henry Moeller, 1904-1925; John T. McNicholas, O.P., 1925-50; Karl J. Alter, 1950-69; Paul F. Leibold, 1969-72.

Cleveland, Ohio (1847): Clarence G. Issenmann, mann, bishop, 1966. William M. Cosgrove, auxiliary.

Former bishops: L. Amadeus Rappe, 1847-70; Richard Gilmour, 1872-91; Ignatius F. Horstmann, 1892-1908; John P. Farrelly, 1909-21; 1909-21; Joseph Schrembs, 1921-45; Edward F. Hoban, 1945-66. Hoban, 1945-66.

Columbus, Ohio (1868): Clarence E. Elwell, bishop, 1968. Edward G. Hettinger, auxiliary.

Former bishops: Sylvester H. Rosecrans, 1868-78; John A. Watterson, 1880-99; Henry Moeller, 1900-03; James J. Hartley, 1904-44; Michael J. Ready, 1944-57; Clarence Issenmann, 1957-64; John J. Carberry, 1965-68.

Corpus Christi, Tex. (1912): Thomas J. Drury, bishop, 1965.

Former bishops: Paul J. Nussbaum, C.P., 1913-20; Emmanuel B. Ledvina, 1921-49; Mariano S. Garriga, 1949-65.

Covington, Ky. (1853): Richard Ackerman, C.S.Sp., bishop, 1960.

Former bishops: George A. Carrell, S.J., 1853-68; Augustus M. Toebbe, 1870-84; Camillus P. Maes, 1885-1914; Ferdinand Brossart, 1916-23; Francis W. Howard, 1923-44; William T. Mulloy, 1945-59.

Crookston, Minn. (1909): Kenneth J. Povish, bishop, 1970.

Former bishops: Timothy Corbett, 1910-38; John H. Peschges, 1938-44; Francis J. Schenk, 1945-60; Laurence A. Glenn, 1960-70.

Dallas, Tex. (1890): Thomas Tschoepe, bishop, 1969.

Former bishops: Thomas F. Brennan,

1891-92; Edward J. Dunne, 1893-1910; Joseph P. Lynch, 1911-54; Thomas K. Gorman, 1954-69.

Davenport, Ia. (1881): Gerald F. O'Keefe, bishop, 1966.

Former bishops: John McMullen, 1881-83; Henry Cosgrove, 1884-1906; James Davis, 1906-26; Henry P. Rohlman, 1927-44; Ralph L. Hayes, 1944-66.

Denver,* Colo. (1887; archdiocese, 1941): James V. Casey, archbishop, 1967. George R. Evans, auxiliary.

Former ordinaries: Joseph P. Machebeuf, 1887-89; Nicholas C. Matz, 1889-1917; J. Henry Tihen, 1917-31; Urban J. Vehr, 1931-67, first archbishop.

Des Moines, Ia. (1911): Maurice J. Dingman, bishop, 1968.

Former bishops: Austin Dowling, 1912-19; Thomas W. Drumm, 1919-33; Gerald T. Bergen, 1934-48; Edward C. Daly, O.P., 1948-64; George J. Biskup, 1965-67.

Detroit,* Mich. (1833; archdiocese, 1937): Cardinal John F. Dearden, archbishop, 1958. Thomas J. Gumbleton, Walter J. Schoenherr, auxiliaries.

Former ordinaries: Frederic Rese, 1833-71; Peter P. Lefevere, administrator, 1841-69; Caspar H. Borgess, 1871-88; John S. Foley, 1888-1918; Michael J. Gallagher, 1918-37; Cardinal Edward Mooney, 1937-58, first archbishop.

Dodge City, Kans. (1951): Marion F. Forst, bishop, 1960.

Former bishop: John B. Franz, 1951-59.

Dubuque,* Iowa (1837; archdiocese, 1893): James J. Byrne, archbishop, 1962. Francis J. Dunn, auxiliary.

Former ordinaries: Mathias Loras, 1837-58; Clement Smyth, O.C.S.O., 1858-65; John Hennessy, 1866-1900, first archbishop; John J. Keane, 1900-11; James J. Keane, 1911-29; Francis J. Beckman, 1930-46; Henry P. Rohlman, 1946-54; Leo Binz, 1954-61.

Duluth, Minn. (1889): Paul F. Anderson, bishop, 1969.

Former bishops: James McGolrick, 1889-1918; John T. McNicholas, O.P., 1918-25; Thomas A. Welch, 1926-59; Francis J. Schenk, 1960-69.

El Paso, Tex. (1914): Sidney M. Metzger, bishop, 1942.

Former bishop: Anthony J. Schuler, S.J., 1915-42.

Erie, Pa. (1853): Alfred M. Watson, bishop, 1969.

Former bishops: Michael O'Connor, 1853-54; Josue M. Young, 1854-66; Tobias Mullen, 1868-99; John E. Fitzmaurice, 1899-1920; John M. Gannon, 1920-66; John F. Whealon, 1966-69.

Evansville, Ind. (1944): Francis Raymond Shea, bishop, 1969.

Former bishops: Henry J. Grimmelsman, 1944-65; Paul F. Leibold, 1966-69.

Fairbanks, Alaska (1962): Robert L. Whe-

lan, S.J., bishop, 1968.

Former bishop: Francis D. Gleeson, S.J., 1948-68.

Fall River, Mass. (1904): Daniel A. Cronin, bishop, 1970. James J. Gerrard, auxiliary.

Former bishops: William Stang, 1904-07; Daniel F. Feehan, 1907-34; James E. Cassidy, 1934-51; James L. Connolly, 1951-70.

Fargo, N. Dak. (1889): Justin A. Driscoll, bishop, 1970.

Established at Jamestown, transferred, 1897.

Former bishops: John Shanley, 1889-1909; James O'Reilly, 1910-34; Aloysius J. Muench, 1935-59; Leo F. Dworschak, 1960-70.

Fort Wayne-South Bend, Ind. (1857): Leo A. Pursley, bishop, 1957. Joseph R. Crowley, auxiliary.

Established as Fort Wayne, name changed, 1960.

Former bishops: John H. Luers, 1858-71; Joseph Dwenger, C.Pp. S., 1872-93; Joseph Rademacher, 1893-1900; Herman J. Alerding, 1900-24; John F. Noll, 1925-56.

Fort Worth, Tex. (1969): John J. Cassata, bishop, 1969.

Fresno, Calif. (1967): Hugh A. Donohoe, bishop, 1969.

Former bishop: Timothy Manning, 1967-69.

Gallup, N. Mex. (1939): Jerome J. Hastrich, bishop, 1969.

Former bishop: Bernard T. Espelage, O.F.M., 1940-69.

Galveston-Houston, Tex. (1847): Wendelin J. Nold, bishop, 1950. John L. Morkovsky, coadjutor, apostolic administrator.

Established as Galveston, name changed, 1959.

Former bishops: John M. Odin, C.M., 1847-61; Claude M. Dubuis, 1862-92; Nicholas A. Gallagher, 1892-1918; Christopher E. Byrne, 1918-50.

Gary, Ind. (1957): Andrew G. Grutka, bishop, 1957.

Gaylord, Mich. (1971): Edmund C. Szoka, bishop, 1971.

Grand Island, Neb. (1912): John J. Sullivan, bishop, 1972.

Established at Kearney, transferred, 1917.

Former bishops: James A. Duffy, 1913-31; Stanislaus V. Bona, 1932-44; Edward J. Hunkeler, 1945-51; John L. Paschang, 1951-72.

Grand Rapids, Mich. (1882): Joseph Breitenbeck, bishop, 1969. Joseph C. McKinney, auxiliary.

Former bishops: Henry J. Richter, 1883-1916; Michael J. Gallagher, 1916-18; Edward D. Kelly, 1919-26; Joseph G. Pinten, 1926-40; Joseph C. Plagens, 1941-43; Francis J. Haas, 1943-53; Allen J. Babcock, 1954-69.

Great Falls, Mont. (1904): Eldon B. Schuster, bishop, 1968.

Former bishops: Mathias C. Lenihan, 1904-30; Edwin V. O'Hara, 1930-39; William J. Condon, 1939-67.

Green Bay, Wis. (1868): Aloysius J. Wycislo, bishop, 1968. John B. Grellinger, Mark Schmitt, auxiliaries.

Former bishops: Joseph Melcher, 1868-73; Francis X. Krautbauer, 1875-85; Frederick X. Katzer, 1886-91; Sebastian G. Messmer, 1892-1903; Joseph J. Fox, 1904-14; Paul P. Rhode, 1915-45; Stanislaus V. Bona, 1945-67.

Greensburg, Pa. (1951): William G. Connare, bishop, 1960.

Former bishop: Hugh L. Lamb, 1951-59.

Harrisburg, Pa. (1868): Joseph T. Daley, bishop, 1971.

Former bishops: Jeremiah F. Shanahan, 1868-86; Thomas McGovern, 1888-98; John W. Shanahan, 1899-1916; Philip R. McDevitt, 1916-35; George L. Leech, 1935-71.

Hartford,* Conn. (1843; archdiocese, 1953): John F. Whealon, archbishop, 1969. John F. Hackett, Joseph F. Donnelly, auxiliaries.

Former ordinaries: William Tyler, 1844-49; Bernard O'Reilly, 1850-56; F. P. Mac-Farland, 1858-74; Thomas Galberry, O.S.A., 1876-78; Lawrence S. McMahon, 1879-93; Michael Tierney, 1894-1908; John J. Nilan, 1910-34; Maurice F. McAuliffe, 1934-44; Henry J. O'Brien, 1945-68, first archbishop.

Helena, Mont. (1884): Raymond Hunthausen, bishop, 1962.

Former bishops: John B. Brondel, 1884-1903; John P. Carroll, 1904-25; George J. Finnigan, C.S.C., 1927-32; Ralph L. Hayes, 1933-35; Joseph M. Gilmore, 1936-62.

Honolulu, H.I. (1941); John J. Scanlan, bishop, 1968.

Former bishop: James J. Sweeney, 1941-68.

Indianapolis,* Ind. (1834; archdiocese, 1944); George J. Biskup, archbishop, 1970. Established at Vincennes, transferred, 1898.

Former ordinaries: Simon G. Bruté, 1834-39; Celestine de la Hailandiere, 1839-47; John S. Bazin, 1847-48; Maurice de St. Palais, 1849-77; Francis S. Chatard, 1878-1918; Joseph Chartrand, 1918-33; Joseph E. Ritter, 1934-46, first archbishop; Paul C. Schulte, 1946-70.

Jefferson City, Mo. (1956): Michael F. McAuliffe, bishop, 1969.

Former bishop: Joseph Marling, C.Pp.S., 1956-59.

Joliet, Ill. (1948): Romeo Blanchette, bishop, 1966. Raymond J. Vonesh, auxiliary.

Former bishop: Martin D. McNamara, 1949-66.

Juneau, Alaska (1951): Francis T. Hurley, bishop, 1971.

Former bishops: Dermot O'Flanagan, 1951-68; Joseph T. Ryan, administrator, 1968-71.

Kalamazoo, Mich. (1971): Paul V. Donovan, bishop, 1971.

Kansas City,* Kans. (1877; archdiocese, 1952): Ignatius J. Strecker, archbishop, 1969.

Established as vicariate apostolic, 1850, became Diocese of Leavenworth, 1877, transferred to Kansas City 1947.

Former ordinaries: J. B. Miege, vicar apostolic, 1851-74; Louis M. Fink, O.S.B., vicar apostolic, 1874-77, first bishop, 1877-1904; Thomas F. Lillis, 1904-10; John Ward, 1910-29; Francis Johannes, 1929-37; Paul C. Schulte, 1937-46; George J. Donnelly, 1946-50; Edward Hunkeler, 1951-69, first archbishop.

Kansas City-St. Joseph, Mo. (Kansas City, 1880; St. Joseph, 1868; united 1956): Charles H. Helmsing, bishop, 1962. Joseph V. Sullivan, auxiliary.

Former bishops (Kansas City): John J. Hogan, 1880-1913; Thomas F. Lillis, 1913-38; Edwin V. O'Hara, 1939-56; John P. Cody, 1956-61.

Former bishops (St. Joseph): John J. Hogan, 1868-80, administrator, 1880-93; Maurice F. Burke, 1893-1923; Francis Gilfillan, 1923-33; Charles H. Le Blond, 1933-56.

La Crosse, Wis. (1868): Frederick W. Freking, bishop, 1965.

Former bishops: Michael Heiss, 1868-80; Kilian C. Flasch, 1881-91; James Schwebach, 1892-1921; Alexander J. McGavick, 1921-48; John P. Treacy, 1948-64.

Lafayette, Ind. (1944): Raymond J. Gallagher, bishop, 1965.

Former bishops: John G. Bennett, 1944-57; John J. Carberry, 1957-65.

Lafayette, La. (1918): Maurice Schexnayder, bishop, 1956.

Former bishop: Jules B. Jeanmard, 1918-56.

Lansing, Mich. (1937): Alexander Zaleski, bishop, 1965. James Sullivan, auxiliary.

Former bishop: Joseph H. Albers, 1937-65.

Lincoln, Neb. (1887): Glennon P. Flavin, bishop, 1967.

Former bishops: Thomas Bonacum, 1887-1911; J. Henry Tihen, 1911-17; Charles J. O'Reilly, 1918-23; Francis J. Beckman, 1924-30; Louis B. Kucera, 1930-57; James V. Casey, 1957-67.

Little Rock, Ark. (1843): Andrew J. McDonald, bishop, 1972. Lawrence P. Graves auxiliary.

Former bishops: Andrew Byrne, 1844-62; Edward Fitzgerald, 1867-1907; John Morris, 1907-46; Albert L. Fletcher, 1946-72.

Los Angeles,* Calif. (1840; archdiocese, 1936): Timothy Manning, archbishop, 1970. John J. Ward, William R. Johnson, Juan A. Arzube, auxiliaries.

Former ordinaries: Francisco Garcia Diego y Moreno, O.F.M., 1840-46; Joseph S. Alemany, O.P., 1850-53; Thaddeus Amat, C.M., 1854-78; Francis Mora, 1878-96; George T. Montgomery, 1896-1903; Thomas J. Conaty, 1903-15; John J. Cantwell, 1917-47, first archbishop; Cardinal James McIntyre, 1948-70.

Louisville,* Ky. (1808; archdiocese, 1937): Thomas J. McDonough, archbishop, 1967. Charles G. Maloney, auxiliary.

Established at Bardstown, transferred, 1841.

Former ordinaries: Benedict J. Flaget, S.S. 1810-32; John B. David, S.S., 1832-33; Benedict J. Flaget, S.S., 1833-50; Martin J. Spalding, 1850-64; Peter J. Lavialle, 1865-67; William G. McCloskey, 1868-1909; Denis O'Donaghue, 1910-24; John A. Floersh, 1924-67, first archbishop.

Madison, Wis. (1946): Cletus F. O'Donnell, bishop, 1967.

Former bishop: William P. O'Connor, 1946-67.

Manchester, N.H. (1884): Ernest J. Primeau, bishop, 1960.

Former bishops: Denis M. Bradley, 1884-1903; John B. Delany, 1904-06; George A. Guertin, 1907-32; John B. Peterson, 1932-44; Matthew F. Brady, 1944-59.

Marquette, Mich. (1857): Charles A. Salatka, bishop, 1968.

Former bishops: Frederic Baraga, 1857-68; Ignatius Mrak, 1869-78; John Vertin, 1879-99; Frederick Eis, 1899-1922; Paul J. Nussbaum, C. P., 1922-35; Joseph C. Plagens, 1935-40; Francis Magner, 1941-47; Thomas L. Noa, 1947-68.

Memphis, Tenn. (1970): Carroll T. Dozier, bishop, 1971.

Miami,* Fla. (1958; archdiocese, 1968): Coleman F. Carroll, bishop, 1958, first archbishop, 1968. Rene H. Gracida, auxiliary.

Milwaukee,* Wis. (1843; archdiocese, 1875): William E. Cousins, archbishop, 1959. Leo J. Brust, auxiliary.

Former ordinaries: John M. Henni, 1844-81, first archbishop; Michael Heiss, 1881-90; Frederick X. Katzer, 1891-1903; Sebastian G. Messmer, 1903-30; Samuel A. Stritch, 1930-39; Moses E. Kiley, 1940-53; Albert G. Meyer, 1953-58.

Mobile, Ala. (1829): John L. May, bishop, 1969.

Former bishops: Michael Portier, 1829-59; John Quinlan, 1859-83; Dominic Manucy, 1884; Jeremiah O'Sullivan, 1885-96; Edward P. Allen, 1897-1926; Thomas J. Toolen, 1927-69.

Monterey in California (1967): Harry A. Clinch, bishop, 1967.

Formerly Monterey-Fresno, 1922.

Former bishops (Monterey-Fresno): John J. Cantwell, administrator, 1922-24; John B. MacGinley, first bishop, 1924-32; Philip G. Sher, 1933-53; Aloysius J. Willinger, 1953-67.

Munhall,* Pa. (Byzantine Rite) (1924; metropolitan, 1969): Stephen J. Kocisko, metropolitan, 1968.

Former ordinaries: Basil Takach 1924-48; Daniel Ivancho, 1948-54; Nicholas T. Elko, 1955-67.

Nashville, Tenn. (1837): Joseph A. Durick, bishop, 1969.

Former bishops: Richard P. Miles, O.P., 1838-60; James Whelan, O.P., 1860-64; Patrick A. Feehan, 1865-80; Joseph Rade-

macher, 1883-93; Thomas S. Byrne, 1894-1923; Alphonse J. Smith, 1924-35; William L. Adrian, 1936-69.

Natchez-Jackson, Miss. (1837): Joseph B. Brunini, bishop, 1968.

Former bishops: John J. Chanche, S.S., 1841-52; James Van de Velde, S.J., 1853-55; William H. Elder, 1857-80; Francis A. Janssens, 1881-88; Thomas Heslin, 1889-1911; John E. Gunn, S.M., 1911-24; Richard O. Gerow, 1924-67.

Newark, N.J. (1853; archdiocese, 1937): Thomas A. Boland, archbishop, 1953, Martin Stanton, John J. Dougherty, Joseph A. Costello, auxiliaries.

Former ordinaries: James R. Bayley, 1853-72; Michael A. Corrigan, 1873-80; Winand M. Wigger, 1881-1901; John J. O'Connor, 1901-27; Thomas J. Walsh, 1928-52, first archbishop.

New Orleans, La. (1793; archdiocese, 1850): Philip M. Hannan, archbishop, 1965. L. Abel Caillouet, Harold R. Perry, S. V. D., auxiliaries.

Former ordinaries: Luis Penalver y Cardenas, 1793-1801; John Carroll, administrator, 1809-15; W. Louis Dubourg, S.S., 1815-25; Joseph Rosati, C.M., administrator, 1826-29; Leo De Neckere, C.M., 1829-33; Anthony Blanc, 1835-60, first archbishop; Jean Marie Odin, C.M., 1861-70; Napoleon J. Perche, 1870-83; Francis X. Leray, 1883-87; Francis A. Janssens, 1888-97; Placide L. Chapelle, 1897-1905; James H. Blenk, S.M., 1906-17; John W. Shaw, 1918-34; Joseph F. Rummel, 1935-64; John P. Cody, 1964-65.

New Ulm, Minn. (1957): Alphonse J. Schladweiler, bishop, 1958.

New York,* N.Y. (1808; archdiocese, 1850): Cardinal Terence J. Cooke, archbishop, 1968. John J. Maguire, coadjutor archbishop, 1965. Edward V. Dargin, Joseph M. Pernicone, John M. Fearns, Edward E. Swanstrom, Patrick V. Ahern, Edward D. Head, auxiliaries.

Former ordinaries: Richard L. Concanen, O.P., 1808-10; John Connolly, O.P., 1814-25; John Dubois, S.S., 1826-42; John J. Hughes, 1842-64, first archbishop; Cardinal John McCloskey, 1864-85; Michael A. Corrigan, 1885-1902; Cardinal John Farley, 1902-18; Cardinal Patrick Hayes, 1919-38; Cardinal Francis Spellman, 1939-67.

Norwich, Conn. (1953): Vincent J. Hines, bishop, 1960.

Former bishop: Bernard J. Flanagan, 1953-59.

Oakland, Calif. (1962): Floyd L. Begin, bishop, 1962.

Ogdensburg, N. Y. (1872): Stanislaus Brzana, bishop, 1968.

Former bishops: Edgar P. Wadhams, 1872-91; Henry Gabriels, 1892-1921; Joseph H. Conroy, 1921-39; Francis J. Monaghan, 1939-42; Bryan J. McEntegart, 1943-53; Walter P. Kellenberg, 1954-57; James J. Navagh, 1957-63; Leo R. Smith, 1963; Thomas A. Donnellan, 1964-68.

Oklahoma City and Tulsa, Okla. (1905): John R. Quinn, 1971.

Former bishops: Theophile Meerschaert, 1905-24; Francis C. Kelley, 1924-48; Eugene J. McGuinness, 1948-57; Victor J. Reed, 1958-71.

Omaha,* Nebr. (1885; archdiocese, 1945): Daniel E. Sheehan, archbishop, 1969.

Former ordinaries: James O'Gorman, O.C.S.O., 1859-74, vicar apostolic; James O'Connor, vicar apostolic, 1876-85, first bishop, 1885-90; Richard Scannell, 1891-1916; Jeremiah J. Harty, 1916-27; Francis Beckman, administrator, 1926-28; Joseph F. Rummel, 1928-35; James H. Ryan, 1935-47, first archbishop; Gerald T. Bergan, 1948-69.

Orlando, Fla. (1968): William Borders, bishop, 1968.

Owensboro, Ky. (1937): Henry J. Soenneker, bishop, 1961.

Former bishop: Francis R. Cotton, 1938-60.

Parma, Ohio (Byzantine Rite) (1969): Emil Mihalik, eparch, 1969.

Passaic, N.J. (Byzantine Rite) (1963): Michael J. Dudick, eparch, 1968.

Former bishop: Stephen Kocisko, 1963-68.

Paterson, N. J. (1937): Lawrence B. Casey, bishop, 1966.

Former bishops: Thomas H. McLaughlin, 1937-47; Thomas A. Boland, 1947-52; James A. McNulty, 1953-63; James J. Navagh, 1963-65.

Peoria, Ill. (1877): Edward W. O'Rourke, bishop, 1971.

Former bishops: John L. Spalding, 1877-1908; Edmund M. Dunne, 1909-29; Joseph H. Schlarman, 1930-51; William E. Cousins, 1952-58; John B. Franz, 1959-71.

Philadelphia,* Pa. (1808; archdiocese, 1875): Cardinal John Krol, archbishop, 1961. Gerald V. McDevitt, John J. Graham, Martin Lohmuller, Thomas J. Welsh, auxiliaries.

Former ordinaries: Michael Egan, O. F. M., 1810-14; Henry Conwell, 1820-42; Francis P. Kenrick, 1842-51; John N. Neumann, C.SS.R., 1852-60; James F. Wood, 1860-83, first archbishop; Patrick J. Ryan, 1884-1911; Edmond F. Prendergast, 1911-18; Cardinal Dennis Dougherty, 1918-51; Cardinal John O'Hara, C.S.C., 1951-60.

Philadelphia,* Pa. (Byzantine Rite) (1924; metropolitan, 1958): Ambrose Senyshyn, O.S.B.M., metropolitan, 1961. Basil Losten, auxiliary.

Former ordinaries: Stephen Ortynsky, O.S.B.M., 1907-16; Constantine Bohachevsky, 1924-61.

Phoenix, Ariz. (1969): Edward A. McCarthy, bishop, 1969.

Pittsburgh, Pa. (1843): Vincent M. Leonard, bishop, 1969. John B. McDowell, Anthony G. Bosco, auxiliaries.

Former bishops: Michael O'Connor, 1843-

53, 1854-60; Michael Domenec, C.M., 1860-76; J. Tuigg, 1876-89; Richard Phelan, 1889-1904; J. F. Regis Canevin, 1904-20; Hugh C. Boyle, 1921-50; John F. Dearden, 1950-58; John J. Wright, 1959-69.

Portland, Me. (1853): Peter L. Gerety, bishop, 1969. Edward C. O'Leary, auxiliary.

Former bishops: David W. Bacon, 1855-74; James A. Healy, 1875-1900; William H. O'Connell, 1901-06; Louis S. Walsh, 1906-24; John G. Murray, 1925-31; Joseph E. McCarthy, 1932-55; Daniel J. Feeney, 1955-69.

Portland,* Ore. (1846): Robert J. Dwyer, archbishop, 1966.

Established as Oregon City, name changed, 1928.

Former ordinaries: Francis N. Blanchet, 1846-80 vicar apostolic, first archbishop; Charles J. Seghers, 1880-84; William H. Gross, C.SS.R., 1885-98; Alexander Christie, 1899-1925; Edward D. Howard, 1926-66.

Providence, R. I. (1872): Louis E. Gelineau, bishop, 1972.

Former bishops: Thomas F. Hendricken, 1872-86; Matthew Harkins, 1887-1921; William A. Hickey, 1921-33; Francis P. Keough, 1934-47; Russell J. McVinney, 1948-71.

Pueblo, Colo. (1941): Charles A. Buswell, bishop, 1959.

Former bishop: Joseph C. Willging, 1942-59.

Raleigh, N. C. (1924): Vincent S. Waters, bishop, 1945. George E. Lynch, auxiliary.

Former bishops: William J. Hafey, 1925-37; Eugene J. McGuinness, 1937-44.

Rapid City, S. Dak. (1902): Harold J. Dimmerling, bishop, 1969.

Established at Lead, transferred, 1920.

Former bishops: John Stariha, 1902-09; Joseph F. Busch, 1910-15; John J. Lawler, 1916-48; William T. McCarty, C.SS.R., 1948-69.

Reno, Nev. (1931): Joseph Green, bishop, 1967.

Former bishops: Thomas K. Gorman, 1931-52; Robert J. Dwyer, 1952-66.

Richmond, Va. (1820): John J. Russell, bishop, 1958. J. Louis Flaherty, Walter F. Sullivan, auxiliaries.

Former bishops: Patrick Kelly, 1820-22; Richard V. Whelan, 1841-50; John McGill, 1850-72; James Gibbons, 1872-77; John J. Keane, 1878-88; Augustine Van de Vyver, 1889-1911; Denis J. O'Connell, 1912-26; Andrew J. Brennan, 1926-45; Peter L. Ireton, 1945-58.

Rochester, N. Y. (1868): Joseph L. Hogan, bishop, 1969. Dennis W. Hickey, John E. McCafferty, auxiliaries.

Former bishops: Bernard J. McQuaid, 1868-1909; Thomas F. Hickey, 1909-28; John F. O'Hern, 1929-33; Edward F. Mooney, 1933-37; James E. Kearney, 1937-66; Fulton J. Sheen, 1966-69.

Rockford, Ill. (1908): Arthur J. O'Neill, bishop, 1968.

Former bishops: Peter J. Muldoon, 1908-

27; Edward F. Hoban, 1928-42; John J. Boylan, 1943-53; Raymond P. Hillinger, 1953-56; Loras T. Lane, 1956-68.

Rockville Centre, N. Y. (1957): Walter P. Kellenberg, bishop, 1957. Vincent J. Baldwin, John R. McGann, auxiliaries.

Sacramento, Calif. (1886): Alden J. Bell, bishop, 1962.

Former bishops: Patrick Manogue, 1886-95; Thomas Grace, 1896-1921; Patrick J. Keane, 1922-28; Robert J. Armstrong, 1929-57; Joseph T. McGucken, 1957-62.

Saginaw, Mich. (1938): Francis F. Reh, bishop, 1969.

Former bishops: William F. Murphy, 1938-50; Stephen S. Woznicki, 1950-68.

St. Augustine, Fla. (1870): Paul F. Tanner, bishop, 1968.

Former bishops: Augustin Verot, S.S., 1870-76; John Moore, 1877-1901; William J. Kenny, 1902-13; Michael J. Curley, 1914-21; Patrick J. Barry, 1922-40; Joseph P. Hurley, 1940-67.

St. Cloud, Minn. (1889): George H. Speltz, bishop, 1968.

Former bishops: Otto Zardetti, 1889-94; Martin Marty, O.S.B., 1895-96; James Trobec, 1897-1914; Joseph F. Busch, 1915-53; Peter Bartholome, 1953-68.

St. Louis,* Mo. (1826; archdiocese, 1847): Cardinal John J. Carberry, archbishop, 1968. George J. Gottwald, Joseph A. McNicholas, Charles A. Koester, Edward T. O'Meara, auxiliaries.

Former ordinaries: Joseph Rosati, C.M., 1827-43; Peter R. Kenrick, 1843-95, first archbishop; John J. Kain, 1895-1903; Cardinal John Glennon, 1903-46; Cardinal Joseph Ritter, 1946-67.

St. Maron of Detroit (Maronite Rite) (1966; eparchy, 1972): Francis Zayek, exarch, 1966, first eparch, 1972.

St. Nicholas in Chicago (Byzantine Rite Eparchy of St. Nicholas of the Ukrainians) (1961): Jaroslav Gabro, eparch, 1961.

St. Paul and Minneapolis,* Minn. (1850; archdiocese, 1888): Leo Binz, archbishop, 1962. Leo C. Byrne, coadjutor archbishop, 1967. Leonard P. Cowley, Raymond A. Lucker, John R. Roach, auxiliaries.

Former ordinaries: Joseph Cretin, 1851-57; Thomas L. Grace, O.P., 1859-84; John Ireland, 1884-1918, first archbishop; Austin Dowling, 1919-30; John G. Murray, 1931-56; William O. Brady, 1956-61.

St. Petersburg, Fla. (1968): Charles McLaughlin, bishop, 1968.

Salina, Kans. (1887): Cyril J. Vogel, bishop, 1965.

Established at Concordia, transferred, 1944.

Former bishops: Richard Scannell, 1887-91; John J. Hennessy, administrator, 1891-98; John F. Cunningham, 1898-1919; Francis J. Tief, 1921-38; Frank A. Thill, 1938-57; Frederick W. Freking, 1957-64.

Salt Lake City, Utah (1891): J. Lennox Federal, bishop, 1960.

Former bishops: Lawrence Scanlan, 1891-1915; Joseph S. Glass, C.M., 1915-26; John J. Mitty, 1926-32; James E. Kearney, 1932-37; Duane G. Hunt, 1937-60.

San Angelo, Tex. (1961): Stephen A. Leven, bishop, 1969.

Former bishops: Thomas J. Drury, 1962-65; Thomas Tschoepe, 1966-69.

San Antonio,* Tex. (1874; archdiocese, 1926): Francis Furey, archbishop, 1969. Patrick Flores, auxiliary.

Former ordinaries: Anthony D. Pellicer, 1874-80; John C. Neraz, 1881-94; John A. Forest, 1895-1911; John W. Shaw, 1911-18; Arthur Jerome Drossaerts, 1918-40, first archbishop; Robert E. Lucey, 1941-69.

San Diego, Calif. (1936): Leo T. Maher, bishop, 1969. John R. Quinn, auxiliary.

Former bishops: Charles F. Buddy, 1936-66; Francis J. Furey, 1966-69.

San Francisco,* Calif. (1853): Joseph T. McGucken, archbishop, 1962. William J. McDonald, Norman F. McFarland, auxiliaries.

Former ordinaries: Joseph S. Alemany, O.P., 1853-84; Patrick W. Riordan, 1884-1914; Edward J. Hanna, 1915-35; John Mitty, 1935-61.

Santa Fe,* N. Mex. (1850; archdiocese, 1875): James P. Davis, archbishop, 1964.

Former ordinaries: John B. Lamy, 1850-85, first archbishop; John B. Salpointe, 1885-94; Placide L. Chapelle, 1894-97; Peter Bourgade, 1899-1908; John B. Pitaval, 1909-18; Albert T. Daeger, O.F.M., 1919-32; Rudolph A. Gerken, 1933-43; Edwin V. Byrne, 1943-63.

Santa Rosa, Calif. (1962): Mark J. Hurley, bishop, 1969.

Former bishop: Leo T. Maher, 1962-69.

Savannah, Ga. (1850): Gerard L. Frey, bishop, 1967.

Former bishops: Francis X. Gartland, 1850-54; John Barry, 1857-59; Augustin Verot, S.S., 1861-70; Ignatius Persico, O.F.M. Cap., 1870-72; William H. Gross, C.SS.R., 1873-85; Thomas A. Becker, 1886-99; Benjamin J. Keiley, 1900-22; Michael Keyes, S.M., 1922-35; Gerald P. O'Hara, 1935-59; Thomas J. McDonough, 1960-67.

Scranton, Pa. (1868): J. Carroll McCormick, bishop, 1966. Henry T. Klonowski, auxiliary.

Former bishops: William O'Hara, 1868-99; Michael J. Hoban, 1899-1926; Thomas C. O'Reilly, 1928-38; William J. Hafey, 1938-54; Jerome D. Hannan, 1954-65.

Seattle,* Wash. (1850; archdiocese, 1951): Thomas A. Connolly, archbishop, 1950. Thomas E. Gill, auxiliary.

Established as Nesqually, name changed, 1907.

Former ordinaries; Augustin M. Blanchet, 1850-79; Aegidius Junger, 1879-95; Edward J. O'Dea, 1896-1932; Gerald Shaughnessy, S.M., 1933-50.

Sioux City, Ia. (1902): Frank Greteman, bishop, 1970.
Former bishops: Philip J. Garrigan, 1902-19; Edmond Heelan, 1919-48; Joseph M. Mueller, 1948-70.
Sioux Falls, S. Dak. (1889): Lambert A. Hoch, bishop, 1956.
Former bishops: Martin Marty, O.S.B., 1889-94; Thomas O'Gorman, 1896-1921; Bernard J. Mahoney, 1922-39; William O. Brady, 1939-56.
Spokane, Wash. (1913): Bernard J. Topel, bishop, 1955.
Former bishops: Augustine F. Schinner, 1914-25; Charles D. White, 1927-55.
Springfield-Cape Girardeau, Mo. (1956): William Baum, bishop, 1970.
Former bishops: Charles Helmsing, 1956-62; Ignatius J. Strecker, 1962-69.
Springfield, Ill. (1853): William A. O'Connor, bishop, 1949.
Former bishops: Henry D. Juncker, 1857-68; Peter J. Baltes, 1870-86; James Ryan, 1888-1923; James A. Griffin, 1924-48.
Springfield, Mass. (1870): Christopher J. Weldon, bishop, 1950.
Former bishops: Patrick T. O'Reilly, 1870-92; Thomas D. Beaven, 1892-1920; Thomas M. O'Leary, 1921-49.
Stamford, Conn. (Byzantine Rite) (1956): Joseph M. Schmondiuk, eparch, 1961.
Former eparch, Ambrose Senyshyn, O.S.B.M., 1956-61.
Steubenville, Ohio (1944): John K. Mussio, bishop, 1945.
Stockton, Calif. (1962): Merlin J. Guilfoyle, bishop, 1969.
Former bishopL Hugh A. Donohoe, 1962-69.
Superior, Wis. (1905): George A. Hammes, bishop, 1960.
Former bishops: Augustine F. Schinner, 1905-13; Joseph M. Koudelka, 1913-21; Joseph G. Pinten, 1922-26; Theodore M. Reverman, 1926-41; William P. O'Connor, 1942-46; Albert G. Meyer, 1946-53; Joseph Annabring, 1954-59.
Syracuse, N. Y. (1886): David F. Cunningham, bishop, 1970. Francis J. Harrison, auxiliary.
Former bishops: Patrick A. Ludden, 1887-1912; John Grimes, 1912-22; Daniel J. Curley, 1923-32; John A. Duffy, 1933-37; Walter A. Foery, 1937-70.
Toledo, Ohio (1910): John A. Donovan, bishop, 1967.
Former bishops: Joseph Schrembs, 1911-21; Samuel A. Stritch, 1921-30; Karl J. Alter, 1931-50; George J. Rehring, 1950-67.
Trenton, N. J. (1881): George W. Ahr, bishop, 1950; John C. Reiss, auxiliary.
Former bishops: Michael J. O'Farrell, 1881-94; James A. McFaul, 1894-1917; Thomas J. Walsh, 1918-28; John J. McMahon, 1928-32; Moses E. Kiley, 1934-40; William A. Griffin, 1940-50.

Tucson, Ariz. (1897): Francis J. Green, bishop, 1960.
Former bishops: Peter Bourgade, 1897-99; Henry Granjon, 1900-22; Daniel J. Gercke, 1923-60.
Washington,* D.C. (1939); Cardinal Patrick O'Boyle, archbishop, 1948. John S. Spence, E. J. Herrmann, auxiliaries.
Former ordinary: Michael J. Curley, 1939-47.
Wheeling, W. Va. (1850): Joseph H. Hodges, bishop, 1962.
Former bishops: Richard V. Whelan, 1850-74; John J. Kain, 1875-93; Patrick J. Donahue, 1894-1922; John J. Swint, 1922-62.
Wichita, Kans. (1887): David M. Maloney, bishop, 1967.
Former bishops: John J. Hennessy, 1888-1920; Augustus J. Schwertner, 1921-39; Christian H. Winkelmann, 1940-46; Mark K. Carroll, 1947-67.
Wilmington, Del. (1868): Thomas Mardaga, bishop, 1968.
Former bishops: Thomas A. Becker, 1868-86; Alfred A. Curtis, 1886-96; John J. Monaghan, 1897-1925; Edmond Fitzmaurice, 1925-60; Michael Hyle, 1960-67.
Winona, Minn. (1889): Loras J. Watters, bishop, 1969.
Former bishops: Joseph B. Cotter, 1889-1909; Patrick R. Heffron, 1910-27; Francis M. Kelly, 1928-49; Edward A. Fitzgerald, 1949-69.
Worcester, Mass. (1950): Bernard J. Flanagan, bishop, 1959. Timothy J. Harrington, auxiliary.
Former bishop: John J. Wright, 1950-59.
Yakima, Wash. (1951): Cornelius M. Power, bishop, 1969.
Former bishop: Joseph P. Dougherty, 1951-69.
Youngstown, Ohio (1943): James W. Malone, bishop, 1968.
Former bishops: James A. McFadden, 1943-52; Emmet M. Walsh, 1952-68.
Apostolic Exarchate for Melkites (1966): Archbishop Joseph Tawil, exarch, 1969.
Former exarch: Justin Najmy, 1966-68.
Military Ordinariate (1917): Cardinal Terence J. Cooke, military vicar, 1968. Philip J. Furlong, William Moran, military delegates.
Former military vicars: Cardinal Patrick Hayes, 1917-38; Cardinal Francis Spellman, 1939-67.
Abbacy of Belmont, N. C. (1910): Edmund F. McCaffrey, O.S.B., abbot, 1970.
Former abbots: Leo M. Haid, O.S.B., 1910-24; Vincent G. Taylor. O.S.B., 1925-59; Walter A. Coggin, O.S.B., 1960-70.

Military Ordinariate

The Military Ordinariate or Vicariate, is the diocese which serves members of the armed forces of the United States wherever they are. It has jurisdiction over: military and

Veterans Administration hospital chaplains; personnel of the armed forces and members of their families and dependents habitually living with them; members of the Coast Guard, National Guard, Air National Guard and Civil Air Patrol when on active duty; persons living on military installations and/or attached to military offices or VA facilities.

The ordinariate was canonically established on a permanent basis by a decree of the Sacred Consistorial Congregation dated Sept. 8, 1957. Cardinal Terence J. Cooke, Archbishop of New York, is Military Vicar. Offices of the ordinariate are located at 30 East 51st St., New York, N.Y. 10022.

MISSIONARY BISHOPS

Africa

Nigeria: Sokoto (diocese), Michael J. Dempsey, O.P.

Rhodesia: Bulawayo (diocese), Adolph G. Schmitt, C.M.M.

South Africa: De Aar (diocese), Joseph A. De Palma, S.C.J.

Keimos (diocese), John Minder, O.S.F.S.

Kimberley (diocese), John Bokenfohr, O.M.I.

Southwest Africa: Keetmanshoop (vicariate apostolic), Edward F. Schlotterback, O.S.F.S.

Tanzania: Arusha (diocese), Dennis V. Durning, C. S.Sp.

Musoma (diocese), John Rudin, M.M.

Nachingwea (diocese), Bernard R. Cotey, S.D.S.

Shinyanga (diocese), Edward A. McGurkin, M.M.

Uganda: Fort Portal (diocese), Vincent McCauley, C.S.C.

Asia

Burma: Prome (diocese), Thomas A. Newman, M.S.

Ceylon: Trincomalee-Batticaloa (diocese), Ignatius T. Glennie, S.J.

China: Chowtsun (diocese), Henry A. Pinger, O.F.M. Expelled.

Wuchow (diocese), Frederick A. Donaghy, M.M. Expelled.

India: Bhagalpur (diocese), Urban McGarry, T.O.R.

Patna (diocese), Augustine F. Wildermuth, S.J.

Indonesia: Agats (diocese), Alphonse A. Sowada, O.S.C.

Israel: Acre (archdiocese, Melkite Rite), Joseph Raya.

Korea: Inchon (diocese), William J. McNaughton, M.M.

Kwang Ju (archdiocese), James E. Michaels, S.S.C., auxiliary.

Cheju-Do (prefecture), Harold W. Henry, S.S.C., ap. admin.

Lebanon: Beirut (vicariate apostolic for Latin Rite), Eustace J. Smith, O. F. M.

Pakistan: Multan (diocese), Ernest B. Boland, O. P.

Philippine Islands: Marbel (prelacy), Reginald Arliss, C. P.

Tagum (prelacy), Joseph W. Regan, M. M.

Taiwan: Taichung (diocese), William F. Kupfer, M. M.

Thailand: Udon Thani (diocese), Clarence J. Duhart, C. SS. R.

Turkey: Izmir (archdiocese), John H. Boccella, T. O. R.

Central America, West Indies

Bahamas: Nassau (diocese), Paul L. Hagarty, O. S. B.

Dominican Republic: San Juan de la Maguana (diocese), Thomas F. Reilly, C. SS. R.

Guatemala: Guatemala (archdiocese), Richard J. Ham, M. M., auxiliary.

Huehuetenango (diocese), Hugo Gerbermann, M. M.

Honduras: Comayagua (diocese), Bernardino Mazzarella, O. F. M.

Olancho (prelacy), Nicholas D'Antonio Salza, O.F.M.

Honduras, British: Belize (diocese), Robert L. Hodapp, S. J.

Nicaragua: Bluefields (vicariate apostolic), Salvator Schlaefer, O. F. M. Cap.

Puerto Rico: Arecibo (diocese), Alfred Mendez, C. S. C.

Virgin Islands: (prelacy), Edward Harper, C. SS. R.

Europe

Sweden: Stockholm (diocese), John E. Taylor, O. M. I.

Oceania

Caroline and Marshall Islands: (vicariate apostolic), Martin J. Neylon, S. J.

Fiji Islands: Suva (archdiocese), George H. Pearce, S. M.

New Guinea: Goroko (diocese), John E. Cohill, S. V. D.

Kavieng (diocese), Alfred M. Stemper, M. S. C.

Madang (archdiocese), Adolph A. Noser, S. V. D.

Mendi (diocese), Firmin Schmidt, O. F. M. Cap.

Mount Hagen (diocese), George Bernarding, S. V. D.

Wewak (diocese), Leo Arkfeld, S. V. D.

Solomon Islands: Bougainville (diocese), Leo Lemay, S. M.

South America

Bolivia: Coroico (prelacy), Thomas R. Manning, O. F. M.

La Paz (archdiocese), Andrew B. Schierhoff, auxiliary.

Santa Cruz (diocese), Charles A. Brown, M. M., auxiliary.

Brazil: Abaete do Tocantina (prelacy), Angelo Frosi, S. X.

Belem do Para (archdiocese), Jude Prost, O. F. M., auxiliary.

Borba (prelacy), Adrian J. M. Veigle, T. O. R.

Coari (prelacy), Robert E. Anglim, C. SS. R.

Cristalandia (prelacy), James A. Schuck, O. F. M.

Jatai (diocese), Benedict D. Coscia, O. F. M. Mathias Schmidt, O. S. B., auxiliary.

Juazeiro (diocese), Thomas W. Murphy, C. SS. R.

Paranagua (diocese), Bernard Nolker, C. SS. R.

Santarem (prelacy), James C. Ryan, O. F. M.

Paraguay: Coronel Oviedo (prelacy), Jerome Pechillo, T. O. R.

Peru: Chimbote (prelacy), James E. Burke, O. P.

Chulucanas (prelacy), John C. McNabb, O. S. A.

Juli (prelacy), E. L. Fedders, M.M.

US STATISTICAL SUMMARY

(Principal source: *The Official Catholic Directory, 1972.* Comparisons are with figures reported in the previous edition.)

Catholic Population: 48,390,990; 23.3 per cent of total population; increase, 176,261.

Jurisdictions: 31 archdioceses; 131 dioceses (including Guam); 1 exarchate; 1 prelacy; 1 abbacy; the military ordinariate.

Cardinals: 9 (7 head archiepiscopal sees; 1 is an official of the Roman Curia; 1 is retired).

Archbishops: 53 (30 residential archbishops, including 7 cardinals; 3 coadjutors or auxiliaries; 13 retired, including 1 cardinal; 7 serving outside the US).

Bishops: 320 (221 residential and titular bishops; 37 retired; 62 serving outside the US).

Abbots: 53.

Priests: 57,421; decrease, 740. Includes: diocesan or secular priests, 36,727 (decrease, 293); religious order priests, 20,694 (decrease, 447).

Brothers: 9,740; decrease, 416.

Sisters, 146,914; decrease, 6,731.

Seminarians: 22,963; decrease, 2,747. Includes: diocesan seminarians, 13,554 (decrease, 1,433); religious, 9,409 (decrease, 1,314).

Infant Baptisms: 1,054,933; decrease, 33,530.

Converts: 79,012; decrease, 5,522. Lowest number since 1940, when the total was 76,705.

Marriages: 416,924; decrease, 9,385.

Deaths: 407,956; decrease, 9,823.

Parishes: 18,259; increase, 15.

Seminaries, Diocesan: 106; decrease, 4.

Religious Seminaries, Novitiates, Scholasticates: 326; decrease, 14.

Colleges and Universities: 273; decrease, 10. Students, 428,853; increase, 2,648.

High Schools: 1,815; decrease, 139. Students, 961,996; decrease, 53,717.

Elementary Schools: 9,206; decrease, 400. Students, 3,105,417; decrease, 308,193.

Teachers, 188,527; decrease, 11,911. Includes: priests, 8,700 (decrease, 1,104); scholastics, 625 (increase, 120); brothers, 4,302 (decrease, 612); sisters, 70,664 (decrease, 7,707); lay teachers, 104,236 (decrease, 2,608). Lay teachers are 55 per cent of the total.

Public School Students in Religious Instruction Programs: 5,579,060; increase, 94,562. Includes: high school students, 1,327,331 (increase, 24,299); elementary school students, 4,251,729 (increase, 70,263).

Hospitals: 836; decrease, 35. Patients, 23,240,723; increase, 722,944.

Nurses' Schools: 201; decrease, 19. Student Nurses: 21,987; decrease, 447.

Homes for Invalids and Aged: 432; increase, 12. Guest facilities: 43,277; increase, 1,442.

Orphanages: 206; children, 16,468.

Children in Foster Homes: 19,908.

Action Groups

Lay Mission-Helpers Association (1955): It trains and assigns men and women for work in overseas apostolates for periods of three years. In 1971, 52 members were in overseas assignments and eight in home missions. Overseas assignments included a wide variety of work in Cameroons, Ghana, Kenya, Malawi, New Guinea, Republic of South Africa, Rhodesia, Sierra Leone, Tanzania and West Irian. Affiliated is the Mission Doctors Association, which recruits, prepares and sends Catholic physicians and dentists, and their families, to mission hospitals and clinics throughout the world for tours of three years. The Rev. Msgr. Lawrence O'Leary is director of both associations. Headquarters: 1531 West Ninth St., Los Angeles, Calif. 90015.

Legion of Mary (1921): Founded at Dublin, its purposes are exclusively spiritual, viz., the sanctification of its members and service to others. It is one of the largest lay organizations in the Church. US address for information: The Legion of Mary, St. Louis Regional Senatus, Box 1313, St. Louis, Mo. 63188. The supreme governing body has offices at De Montfort House, Dublin 7, Ireland.

Marianist Mission Institute (1962): For mission-bound Christians and missionaries on furlough, provides five weeks (late June to late July) of orientation and acculturation in missiology, anthropology, social action in the Third World, group action, mission catechetics, mission health, American government, credit unions, cooperatives. The director is Rev. Philip Hoelle, S.M., University of Dayton, Box 158, Dayton, O. 45409.

CATHOLIC POPULATION OF THE UNITED STATES

(Source: *The Official Catholic Directory, 1972.* Figures are as of Jan. 1, 1972.)
Archdioceses are indicated by an asterisk. For dioceses marked +, see Dioceses with Interstate Lines.

Section, State Diocese	Dioc.	Priests Rel.	Total	Bros.	Srs.	Parishes	Missions	Catholics
NEW ENGLAND	4,533	2,379	6,912	857	15,650	1,672	232	5,654,952
Maine, Portland	252	93	345	41	1,129	140	58	271,428
New Hampshire, Manchester	311	106	417	83	1,166	126	39	263,233
Vermont, Burlington	193	63	256	20	498	103	41	144,239
Massachusetts	2,438	1,517	3,955	403	8,555	780	52	3,049,671
*Boston	1,589	984	2,573	203	5,664	401	20	2,018,034
Fall River	237	195	432	45	828	112	16	305,000
Springfield	296	142	438	30	1,073	136	13	383,052
Worcester	316	196	512	125	990	131	3	343,585
Rhode Island, Providence	379	224	603	144	1,555	154	11	600,595
Connecticut	960	376	1,336	166	2,747	369	31	1,325,786
*Hartford	580	170	750	94	1,629	217	7	806,902
Bridgeport	234	141	375	31	733	82	7	322,500
Norwich+	146	65	211	41	385	70	17	196,384
MIDDLE ATLANTIC	010,023	4,379	14,402	2,864	42,224	3,868	446	13,237,080
New York	4,872	2,090	6,962	1,965	20,846	1,706	211	6,512,662
*New York	1,201	947	2,148	1,010	7,729	406	57	1,800,000
Albany	426	28	454	125	1,881	211	37	424,219
Brooklyn	1,088	286	1,374	487	3,388	229	--	1,487,360
Buffalo	698	510	1,208	97	2,877	282	14	931,623
Ogdensburg	208	41	249	34	506	122	40	171,536
Rochester	380	118	498	58	1,238	160	29	316,790
Rockville Centre	472	47	519	105	2,257	127	11	969,611
Syracuse	399	113	512	49	970	169	23	411,523
New Jersey	1,904	865	2,769	393	6,581	672	50	3,061,109
*Newark	859	468	1,327	255	2,919	253	3	1,703,356
Camden	400	58	458	19	754	123	10	319,984
Paterson	255	246	501	66	1,279	102	9	308,042
Trenton	390	93	483	53	1,629	194	28	729,727
Pennsylvania	3,247	1,424	4,671	506	14,797	1,490	185	3,663,309
*Philadelphia	1,051	655	1,706	271	6,407	316	13	1,359,012
Allentown	308	111	419	42	1,085	151	25	256,443
Altoona-Johnstown	170	82	252	28	499	120	16	147,069
Erie	285	55	340	13	952	126	--	213,286
Greensburg	187	106	293	18	475	116	29	220,043
Harrisburg	188	59	247	21	998	102	18	190,252
Pittsburgh	601	262	863	100	3,030	320	23	921,148
Scranton	457	94	551	13	1,351	239	61	356,056
SOUTH ATLANTIC	2,123	2,097	4,220	758	7,469	1,099	309	2,414,961
Delaware, Wilmington+	123	79	202	30	412	53	23	115,036
Maryland, *Baltimore+	396	423	819	132	2,455	143	15	416,622
District of Columbia								
*Washington+	384	769	1,153	378	781	123	5	387,220
Virginia, Richmond+	188	162	350	29	800	120	25	249,453
West Virginia, Wheeling	135	66	201	15	552	100	72	96,621
North Carolina	113	94	207	11	386	108	46	69,999
Belmont Abbey	2	46	48	10	--	1	--	571
Charlotte	47	21	68	1	233	50	24	34,208
Raleigh	64	27	91	--	153	57	22	35,220
South Carolina, Charleston	83	57	140	29	254	65	30	46,752
Georgia	144	125	269	33	373	78	49	95,302
*Atlanta	69	86	155	25	159	36	21	59,452

Section, State Diocese	Priests Dioc.	Priests Rel.	Total	Bros.	Srs.	Par- ishes	Mis- sions	Catholics
Savannah	75	39	114	8	214	42	28	35,850
Florida	**557**	**322**	**879**	**101**	**1,456**	**309**	**44**	**937,956**
*Miami	294	158	452	65	761	115	7	569,543
Orlando	83	23	106	--	175	54	4	136,957
St. Augustine	85	28	113	--	163	70	19	76,828
St. Petersburg	95	113	208	36	357	70	14	154,628
EAST NORTH CENTRAL	**8,318**	**4,607**	**12,925**	**2,249**	**38,609**	**4,119**	**498**	**10,390,462**
Ohio	**2,061**	**981**	**3,042**	**595**	**8,584**	**932**	**51**	**2,284,276**
*Cincinnati	464	388	852	328	2,451	259	--	529,220
Cleveland	647	267	914	168	2,984	236	5	879,771
Columbus	237	102	339	4	842	105	--	178,000
Steubenville	171	24	195	20	237	73	21	55,600
Toledo	283	117	400	17	1,439	142	21	328,977
Youngstown	259	83	342	58	631	117	4	312,708
Indiana	**778**	**649**	**1,427**	**357**	**4,446**	**462**	**38**	**718,369**
*Indianapolis	266	170	436	89	2,342	164	19	209,412
Evansville	128	20	148	11	615	74	6	85,074
Ft. Wayne-South Bend	128	319	447	200	868	81	7	155,624
Gary	142	90	232	42	415	87	1	184,876
Lafayette	114	50	164	15	206	56	5	83,383
Illinois	**2,201**	**1,561**	**3,762**	**714**	**12,005**	**1,101**	**125**	**3,536,801**
*Chicago	1,169	1,006	2,175	458	8,067	452	6	2,496,300
Belleville	177	52	229	36	605	130	18	115,250
Joliet	198	195	393	125	1,028	109	10	322,000
Peoria	267	115	382	19	833	170	47	214,968
Rockford	181	95	276	29	470	97	8	205,609
Springfield	209	98	307	47	1,002	143	36	182,674
Michigan	**1,614**	**613**	**2,227**	**211**	**5,715**	**788**	**132**	**2,358,397**
*Detroit	861	436	1,297	159	3,600	327	5	1,619,081
Gaylord	63	14	77	2	130	58	24	66,000
Grand Rapids	167	43	210	--	712	81	19	147,672
Kalamazoo	59	21	80	16	311	45	18	83,416
Lansing	162	51	213	30	482	83	7	184,309
Marquette	146	20	166	2	231	92	44	100,359
Saginaw	156	28	184	2	249	102	15	157,560
Wisconsin	**1,664**	**803**	**2,467**	**372**	**7,859**	**836**	**152**	**1,492,619**
*Milwaukee	687	508	1,195	227	4,082	265	20	696,090
Green Bay	341	179	520	96	1,167	193	33	317,102
La Crosse	315	44	359	33	1,055	178	21	200,023
Madison	212	42	254	16	826	112	24	195,132
Superior	109	30	139	--	729	88	54	84,272
EAST SOUTH CENTRAL	**974**	**422**	**1,396**	**350**	**4,143**	**580**	**179**	**608,109**
Kentucky	**550**	**159**	**709**	**160**	**2,959**	**279**	**52**	**344,773**
*Louisville	277	129	406	139	1,253	124	22	192,861
Covington	197	18	215	16	1,123	83	30	103,500
Owensboro	76	12	88	5	583	72	--	48,412
Tennessee	**131**	**38**	**169**	**88**	**224**	**73**	**28**	**92,564**
Memphis	50	20	70	62	175	27	9	39,006
Nashville	81	18	99	26	49	46	19	53,558
Alabama	**154**	**154**	**308**	**41**	**602**	**123**	**51**	**86,218**
Birmingham	71	64	135	19	276	57	29	41,202
Mobile	83	90	173	22	326	66	22	45,016
Mississippi, Natchez-Jackson	**139**	**71**	**210**	**61**	**358**	**105**	**48**	**84,554**
WEST NORTH CENTRAL	**4,410**	**1,950**	**6,360**	**613**	**17,028**	**2,803**	**550**	**3,223,456**
Minnesota	**1,109**	**387**	**1,496**	**190**	**4,815**	**718**	**117**	**1,013,280**
*St. Paul and Minneapolis	444	154	598	73	1,673	218	8	541,958

Section, State Diocese	Dioc.	Priests Rel.	Total	Bros.	Srs.	Parishes	Missions	Catholics
Minnesota								
Crookston	53	23	76	3	320	51	31	38,591
Duluth	108	35	143	2	311	86	34	99,318
New Ulm	126	1	127	-	195	86	10	69,673
St. Cloud	182	155	337	80	1,420	146	34	145,347
Winona	196	19	215	32	896	131	--	118,393
Iowa	**994**	**121**	**1,115**	**96**	**2,942**	**554**	**59**	**525,744**
*Dubuque	429	83	512	89	1,721	201	34	230,215
Davenport	212	23	235	6	540	119	--	108,365
Des Moines	137	5	142	-	253	93	3	80,786
Sioux City	216	10	226	1	428	141	22	106,378
Missouri	**950**	**803**	**1,753**	**155**	**4,128**	**484**	**83**	**751,027**
*St. Louis	552	543	1,095	95	2,926	248	9	517,870
Jefferson City	146	12	158	8	243	83	29	66,000
Kansas City-St. Joseph	173	220	393	43	748	94	14	126,695
Springfield-Cape Girardeau	79	28	107	9	211	59	31	40,462
North Dakota	**246**	**91**	**337**	**27**	**849**	**199**	**98**	**171,826**
Bismarck	96	63	159	19	393	83	43	72,968
Fargo	150	28	178	8	456	116	55	98,858
South Dakota	**200**	**119**	**319**	**42**	**620**	**177**	**88**	**135,673**
Rapid City	54	54	108	12	104	51	48	36,000
Sioux Falls	146	65	211	30	516	126	40	99,673
Nebraska	**455**	**196**	**651**	**62**	**1,512**	**331**	**55**	**310,170**
*Omaha	234	173	407	48	1,103	139	21	199,045
Grand Island	85	2	87	--	178	56	34	51,169
Lincoln	136	21	157	14	231	136	--	59,956
Kansas	**456**	**233**	**689**	**41**	**2,162**	**340**	**50**	**315,736**
*Kansas City	136	150	286	25	964	96	22	138,350
Dodge City	68	7	75	1	208	49	12	33,408
Salina	90	45	135	5	462	99	--	55,776
Wichita	162	31	193	10	528	96	16	88,202
WEST SOUTH CENTRAL	**1,935**	**1,643**	**3,578**	**682**	**7,329**	**1,446**	**691**	**3,486,334**
Arkansas, Little Rock	**113**	**68**	**181**	**54**	**606**	**79**	**39**	**55,025**
Louisiana	**649**	**582**	**1,231**	**256**	**2,410**	**465**	**182**	**1,280,717**
*New Orleans	243	362	605	178	1,500	163	22	666,702
Alexandria	128	56	184	15	282	86	59	73,451
Baton Rouge	84	65	149	26	207	65	27	145,529
Lafayette	194	99	293	37	421	151	74	395,035
Oklahoma, Oklahoma City-Tulsa	**193**	**71**	**264**	**26**	**563**	**122**	**69**	**116,608**
Texas	**980**	**922**	**1,902**	**346**	**4,313**	**780**	**401**	**2,033,984**
*San Antonio	193	223	416	188	1,705	152	73	533,382
Amarillo	75	20	95	--	120	56	27	64,571
Austin	96	63	159	52	180	81	30	138,221
Beaumont	48	33	81	2	142	33	28	91,200
Brownsville	24	85	109	16	183	57	45	264,186
Corpus Christi	76	73	149	18	328	72	45	180,060
Dallas	94	107	201	17	432	52	14	111,984
El Paso+	115	70	185	23	374	71	61	200,664
Fort Worth	58	35	93	16	200	47	22	67,076
Galveston-Houston	156	187	343	14	597	117	19	320,300
San Angelo	45	26	71	--	52	42	37	62,340
MOUNTAIN	**1,089**	**719**	**1,808**	**302**	**3,390**	**729**	**718**	**1,505,695**
Montana	**235**	**60**	**295**	**16**	**444**	**129**	**121**	**138,416**
Great Falls	100	41	141	5	272	72	74	67,916
Helena	135	19	154	11	172	57	47	70,500
Idaho, Boise	**90**	**22**	**112**	**2**	**201**	**66**	**36**	**59,117**
Wyoming, Cheyenne+	**65**	**6**	**71**	**2**	**100**	**39**	**30**	**45,000**
Colorado	**269**	**236**	**505**	**47**	**1,095**	**177**	**103**	**403,981**
*Denver	173	167	340	34	864	117	45	298,784

Section, State Diocese	Priests Dioc.	Rel.	Total	Bros.	Srs.	Par- ishes	Mis- sions	Catholics
Colorado								
Pueblo	96	69	165	13	231	60	58	105,197
New Mexico	**159**	**148**	**307**	**170**	**551**	**133**	**321**	**335,712**
*Santa Fe	138	95	233	151	415	90	280	267,231
Gallup	21	53	74	19	136	43	41	68,481
Arizona	**164**	**175**	**339**	**32**	**714**	**111**	**79**	**385,888**
Phoenix	81	111	192	22	330	57	24	211,131
Tucson	83	64	147	10	384	54	55	174,757
Utah, Salt Lake City	**51**	**34**	**85**	**19**	**147**	**36**	**12**	**50,581**
Nevada, Reno	**56**	**38**	**94**	**14**	**138**	**38**	**16**	**87,000**
PACIFIC	**2,795**	**2,406**	**5,201**	**1,051**	**10,556**	**1,488**	**454**	**5,145,041**
Washington	377	302	679	45	1,380	221	75	458,826
*Seattle	208	194	402	36	799	126	38	336,475
Spokane	96	102	198	8	519	57	30	71,967
Yakima	73	6	79	1	62	38	7	50,384
Oregon	250	135	385	83	1,149	150	62	211,879
*Portland	201	129	330	83	1,043	119	33	188,061
Baker	49	6	55	--	106	31	29	23,818
California	2,095	1,792	3,887	823	7,575	1,004	235	4,210,300
*Los Angeles	676	728	1,404	334	3,168	324	37	1,791,932
*San Francisco	341	511	852	156	1,636	151	11	827,950
Fresno	120	47	167	21	251	84	47	268,145
Monterey	79	38	117	33	220	43	15	95,000
Oakland	147	213	360	162	775	82	4	331,700
Sacramento	199	74	273	56	408	89	45	226,028
San Diego	390	112	502	22	829	164	29	512,412
Santa Rosa	90	24	114	32	186	36	31	64,169
Stockton	53	45	98	7	102	31	16	92,964
Alaska	35	55	90	11	65	47	35	47,536
*Anchorage	19	17	36	4	25	16	9	30,588
Fairbanks	6	33	39	7	28	24	20	13,241
Juneau	10	5	15	--	12	7	6	3,707
Hawaii, Honolulu	38	122	160	89	387	66	47	216,500
EASTERN RITES	**527**	**92**	**619**	**24**	**516**	**455**	**27**	**734,900**
*Philadelphia	124	10	134	--	152	101	8	167,085
*Munhall	81	12	93	5	166	77	--	150,000
St. Nicholas of Chicago	37	10	47	--	21	28	11	29,893
Parma	53	5	58	-	51	46	-	27,847
Passaic	87	7	94	3	50	79	4	99,968
Stamford	68	25	93	16	71	57	--	87,700
St. Maron of Detroit	55	--	55	--	5	43	1	152,407
Melkite Exarchate	22	23	45	--	--	24	3	20,000
MILITARY ORDINARIATE	--	--	--	--	--	--	--	**1,990,000**
TOTALS 1972	**36,727**	**20,694**	**57,421**	**9,740**	**146,914**	**18,259**	**4,195**	**48,390,990**
Totals 1971	**37,020**	**21,141**	**58,161**	**10,156**	**153,645**	**18,244**	**4,121**	**48,214,729**
Totals 1962	**33,774**	**21,807**	**55,581**	**11,502**	**173,351**	**17,156**	**4,735**	**42,882,166**

Largest Archdioceses and Dioceses: According to *The Official Catholic Directory, 1972,* the ecclesiastical jurisdictions with the largest number of Catholics were:

Chicago, with 2,496,300, representing 42.49 percent of the general population of the area;
Boston, with 2,018,034 (50.28 percent);
New York, with 1,800,00 (35.29 percent);
Los Angeles, with 1,791,932 (19.44 per-

cent);
Los Angeles, with 1,791,932 (19.44 percent);
Newark, with 1,703,356 (55.05 percent);
Detroit, with 1,619,081 (33.33 percent);
Brooklyn, with 1,487,360 (31.95 percent);
Philadelphia, with 1,359,012 (34.54 percent).

Areas with the smallest percentages of Catholics were East South Central (4.88 percent), and South Atlantic (7.75 percent).

PERCENTAGE OF CATHOLICS IN US POPULATION

(Source: *The Official Catholic Directory, 1972.* Figures are as of Jan. 1, 1972.)
Archdioceses are indicated by an asterisk. For dioceses marked +, see Dioceses with Interstate Lines.

Section State Diocese	Cath. Pop.	Total Pop.	Cath. Pct.
NEW ENGLAND	5,654,952	12,115,331	46.68
Maine, Portland	271,428	993,663	27.32
New Hampshire,			
Manchester	263,233	754,013	34.91
Vermont, Burlington	144,239	453,000	31.84
Massachusetts	3,049,671	5,954,467	51.22
*Boston	2,018,034	4,013,394	50.28
Fall River	305,000	516,290	59.08
Springfield	383,052	791,643	48.39
Worcester	343,585	633,140	54.27
Rhode Island,			
Providence	600,595	949,723	63.24
Connecticut	1,325,786	3,010,465	44.04
*Hartford	806,902	1,705,776	47.30
Bridgeport	322,500	800,500	40.29
Norwich+	196,384	504,189	38.95
MIDDLE ATLANTIC	13,237,08	37,738,104	35.08
New York	6,512,662	18,587,150	35.04
*New York	1,800,000	5,100,000	35.29
Albany	424,219	1,472,684	28.81
Johnstown	1,487,360	4,655,000	31.95
Buffalo	931,623	1,758,355	52.98
Ogdensburg	171,536	374,854	45.76
Rochester	316,790	1,433,972	22.09
Rockville Centre	969,611	2,583,728	37.53
Syracuse	411,523	1,208,557	34.05
New Jersey	3,061,109	7,299,402	41.94
*Newark	1,703,356	3,093,922	55.05
Camden	319,984	1,029,100	31.09
Paterson	308,042	957,163	32.18
Trenton	729,727	2,219,217	32.88
Pennsylvania	3,663,309	11,851,552	30.91
*Philadelphia	1,359,012	3,901,000	34.84
Allentown	256,443	976,716	26.25
Altoona-			
Johnstown	147,069	627,403	23.44
Erie	213,286	874,471	24.39
Greensburg	220,043	691,749	31.81
Harrisburg	190,252	1,540,000	12.35
Pittsburgh	921,148	2,327,771	39.57
Scranton	356,056	912,442	39.02
SOUTH ATLANTIC	2,414,961	31,302,620	7.71
Delaware			
Wilmington+	115,036	850,979	13.52
Maryland			
*Baltimore+	416,622	2,372,270	17.56
District of Columbia			
*Washington+	387,220	2,036,782	19.01
Virginia			
Richmond+	249,453	4,648,494	5.37
W. Virginia, Wheeling	96,621	2,093,583	4.62

Section State Diocese	Cath. Pop.	Total Pop.	Cath. Pct.
North Carolina	69,999	5,197,065	1.35
Belmont Abbey	571	628	90.92
Charlotte	34,208	2,716,044	1.26
Raleigh	35,220	2,480,393	1.42
South Carolina			
Charleston	46,752	2,590,516	1.80
Georgia	95,302	4,410,300	2.16
*Atlanta	59,452	2,710,300	2.19
Savannah	35,850	1,700,000	2.11
Florida	937,956	7,102,631	13.21
*Miami	569,543	2,669,322	21.34
Orlando	136,957	1,360,727	10.06
St. Augustine	76,828	1,554,881	4.94
St. Petersburg	154,628	1,517,701	10.19
EAST NORTH CENTRAL	10,390.46	40,526,080	25.64
Ohio	2,284,276	10,696,760	21.35
*Cincinnati	529,220	2,670,727	19.82
Cleveland	879,771	3,004,834	29.28
Columbus	178,000	1,786,746	9.96
Steubenville	55,600	545,060	10.20
Toledo	328,977	1,443,318	22.79
Youngstown	312,708	1,246,075	25.09
Indiana	718,369	5,117,254	14.04
*Indianapolis	209,412	2,022,366	10.35
Evansville	85,074	421,000	20.21
Ft. Wayne-			
South Bend	155,624	929,019	16.75
Gary	184,876	757,989	24.39
Lafayette	83,383	986,880	8.45
Illinois	3,536,801	11,083,145	31.91
*Chicago	2,496,300	5,875,007	42.49
Belleville	115,250	807,682	14.27
Joliet	322,000	940,079	34.25
Peoria	214,968	1,434,248	14.99
Rockford	205,609	934,938	21.99
Springfield	182,674	1,091,191	16.74
Michigan	2,358,397	9,199,426	25.64
*Detroit	1,619,081	4,857,242	33.33
Gaylord	66,000	288,556	22.87
Grand Rapids	147,672	890,408	16.58
Kalamazoo	83,416	796,912	10.47
Lansing	184,309	1,426,878	12.92
Marquette	100,359	304,347	32.97
Saginaw	157,560	635,083	24.81
Wisconsin	1,492,619	4,429,495	33.70
*Milwaukee	696,000	2,006,317	34.69
Green Bay	317,102	728,512	43.53
La Crosse	200,023	667,849	29.95
Madison	195,132	718,082	27.17
Superior	84,272	308,735	27.30
EAST SOUTH CENTRAL	608,109	12,473,335	4.88

Section State Diocese	Cath. Pop.	Total Pop.	Cath. Pct.
Kentucky	344,773	3,221,249	10.70
*Louisville	192,861	1,201,974	16.05
Covington	103,500	1,341,506	7.72
Owensboro	48,412	677,769	7.14
Tennessee	92,564	3,662,168	2.53
Memphis	39,006	1,178,168	3.31
Nashville	53,558	2,484,000	2.16
Alabama	86,218	3,373,006	2.56
Birmingham	41,202	2,143,875	1.92
Mobile	45,016	1,229,131	3.66
Mississippi			
Natchez-Jackson	84,554	2,216,912	3.81
WEST NORTH CENTRAL	**3,223,456**	**16,246,470**	**19.84**
Minnesota	1,013,280	3,769,929	26.88
*St. Paul and Minneapolis	541,958	2,017,225	26.87
Crookston	38,591	215,227	17.93
Duluth	99,318	392,188	25.32
New Ulm	69,673	279,054	24.97
St. Cloud	145,347	349,853	41.55
Winona	118,393	516,382	22.93
Iowa	525,744	2,781,456	18.90
*Dubuque	230,215	956,078	24.08
Davenport	108,365	687,310	15.77
Des Moines	80,786	625,185	12.92
Sioux City	106,378	512,883	20.74
Missouri	751,027	4,696,904	15.99
*St. Louis	517,870	1,921,000	26.96
Jefferson City	66,000	670,860	9.84
Kansas City- St. Joseph	126,695	1,271,375	9.97
Springfield- Cape Girardeau	40,462	833,669	4.85
North Dakota	171,826	617,760	27.81
Bismarck	72,968	244,777	29.81
Fargo	98,858	372,983	26.50
South Dakota	135,673	661,326	20.52
Rapid City	36,000	180,000	20.00
Sioux Falls	99,673	481,326	20.71
Nebraska	310,170	1,493,195	20.77
*Omaha	199,045	711,156	27.99
Grand Island	51,169	289,721	17.66
Lincoln	59,956	492,318	12.18
Kansas	315,736	2,225,900	14.18
*Kansas City	138,350	882,028	15.69
Dodge City	33,408	191,072	17.48
Salina	55,776	330,979	16.85
Wichita	88,202	821,821	10.73
WEST SOUTH CENTRAL	**3,486,335**	**19,640,241**	**17.75**
Arkansas, Little Rock	55,025	1,923,295	28.61
Louisiana	1,280,717	3,707,511	34.54
*New Orleans	666,702	1,365,005	48.84
Alexandria	73,451	1,083,132	6.78
Baton Rouge	145,529	572,607	25.42
Lafayette	395,035	686,767	57.52

Section State Diocese	Cath. Pop.	Total Pop.	Cath. Pct.
Oklahoma, Oklahoma Citý Tulsa	116,608	2,500,312	4.66
Texas	2,033,984	11,509,123	17.67
*San Antonio	533,382	1,250,000	42.67
Amarillo	64,571	703,723	9.18
Austin	138,221	938,115	14.73
Beaumont	91,200	586,598	15.55
Brownsville	264,186	347,168	76.10
Corpus Christi	180,060	555,894	32.39
Dallas	111,984	2,297,400	4.87
El Paso+	200,664	654,213	30.67
Fort Worth	67,076	1,284,800	5.22
Galveston-Houston	320,300	2,334,251	13.72
San Angelo	62,340	556,961	11.19
MOUNTAIN	**1,505,695**	**8,141,233**	**18.49**
Montana	138,416	681,021	20.32
Great Falls	67,916	351,858	19.30
Helena	70,500	329,163	21.42
Idaho, Boise	59,117	716,000	8.26
Wyoming, Cheyenne+	45,000	330,000	13.64
Colorado	403,981	2,201,985	18.35
*Denver	298,784	1,805,277	16.55
Pueblo	105,197	396,708	26.52
New Mexico	335,712	937,000	35.83
*Santa Fe	267,231	700,000	38.18
Gallup+	68,481	237,000	28.89
Arizona	385,888	1,696,489	22.75
Phoenix	211,131	1,079,509	19.56
Tucson	174,757	616,980	28.32
Utah, Salt Lake City	50,581	1,090,000	4.64
Nevada, Reno	87,000	488,738	17.80
PACIFIC	**5,145,041**	**26,891,491**	**19.13**
Washington	458,826	3,431,231	13.37
*Seattle	336,475	2,613,300	12.88
Spokane	71,967	479,327	15.01
Yakima	50,384	338,604	14.88
Oregon	211,879	2,203,606	9.62
*Portland	188,061	1,931,306	9.74
Baker	23,818	272,300	8.75
California	4,210,300	20,188,983	20.85
*Los Angeles	1,791,932	9,216,669	19.44
*San Francisco	827,950	2,542,655	32.56
Fresno	268,145	1,172,808	22.86
Monterey	95,000	484,363	19.61
Oakland	331,700	1,658,650	20.00
Sacramento	226,028	1,502,200	15.05
San Diego	512,412	2,629,405	19.49
Santa Rosa	64,169	458,059	14.01
Stockton	92,964	524,324	17.73
Alaska	47,536	297,758	15.96
*Anchorage	30,588	160,000	19.12
Fairbanks	13,241	92,758	14.27
Juneau	3,707	45,000	8.24
Hawaii, Honolulu	**216,500**	**769,913**	**28.12**
TOTALS 1972	**48,390,99**	**208,056,000**	**23.26**

INFANT BAPTISMS AND CONVERTS IN THE US

(Source: *The Official Catholic Directory, 1972.* Figures are as of Jan. 1, 1972.)
Archdioceses are indicated by an asterisk. For dioceses marked +, see Dioceses with Inter-state Lines.

Section / State / Diocese	Infant Baptisms	Converts
NEW ENGLAND	**102,045**	**2,709**
Maine, Portland	5,922	444
New Hampshire		
Manchester	6,173	189
Vermont, Burlington	3,528	229
Massachusetts	50,906	938
*Boston	30,840	508
Fall River	6,289	104
Springfield	7,325	190
Worcester	6,452	136
Rhode Island		
Providence	9,804	290
Connecticut	25,712	619
*Hartford	16,122	362
Bridgeport	6,018	142
Norwich+	3,572	115
MIDDLE ATLANTIC	**282,537**	**13,999**
New York	153,715	7,231
*New York	48,750	4,000
Albany	9,291	372
Brooklyn	37,341	600
Buffalo	13,563	609
Ogdensburg	3,908	240
Rochester	8,682	634
Rockville Centre	22,575	319
Syracuse	9,605	457
New Jersey	56,308	1,837
*Newark	24,586	719
Camden	7,923	411
Paterson	7,812	199
Trenton	15,987	508
Pennsylvania	72,514	4,931
*Philadelphia	28,025	2,025
Allentown	6,036	349
Altoona-Johnstown	2,964	296
Erie	4,465	409
Greensburg	3,485	330
Harrisburg	4,027	397
Pittsburgh	17,047	809
Scranton	6,465	316
SOUTH ATLANTIC	**55,621**	**6,508**
Delaware, Wilmington+	2,823	153
Maryland, *Baltimore+	9,802	905
District of Columbia		
*Washington+	9,727	1,123
Virginia, Richmond+	6,792	802
West Virginia, Wheeling+	1,958	469
North Carolina	2,110	364
Belmont Abbey	32	5
Charlotte	877	183
Raleigh	1,201	176
South Carolina, Charleston	1,318	299
Georgia	2,712	570
*Atlanta	1,622	325
Savannah	1,090	245
Florida	18,379	1,823
*Miami	10,752	606
Orlando	2,307	385
St. Augustine	2,101	395
St. Petersburg	3,219	437
EAST NORTH CENTRAL	**210,217**	**19,899**
Ohio	46,996	5,307
*Cincinnati	10,021	1,128
Cleveland	17.795	1,486
Columbus	4,247	793
Steubenville	1,308	384
Toledo	7,838	917
Youngstown	5,787	599
Indiana	15,894	2,287
*Indianapolis	4,885	809
Evansville	1,823	229
Ft. Wayne-S. Bend	3,385	481
Gary	3,881	389
Lafayette	1,920	379
Illinois	67,301	5,324
*Chicago	45,467	2,623
Belleville	2,431	392
Joliet	6,648	421
Peoria	4,831	792
Rockford	4,449	452
Springfield	3,475	644
Michigan	48,342	4,434
*Detroit	29,504	1,975
Gaylord	1,688	204
Grand Rapids	3,619	564
Kalamazoo	1,943	368
Lansing	5.073	699
Marquette	2,162	191
Saginaw	4,353	433
Wisconsin	31,684	2,547
*Milwaukee	14,760	1,002
Green Bay	6,709	405
La Crosse	4,566	474
Madison	3,799	492
Superior	1,850	174
EAST SOUTH CENTRAL	**13,632**	**2,824**
Kentucky	7,342	890
*Louisville	4,168	451
Covington	2,093	244
Owensboro	1,081	195
Tennessee	2,133	857
Memphis	918	301
Nashville	1,215	556

Section State Diocese	Infant Baptisms	Converts
Alabama	2,091	679
Birmingham	927	313
Mobile	1,164	366
Mississippi		
Natchez-Jackson	2,066	398
WEST NORTH CENTRAL	**74,364**	**9,760**
Minnesota	24,715	2,278
*St. Paul and Minneapolis	13,852	1,093
Crookston	942	99
Duluth	2,345	228
New Ulm	1,536	149
St. Cloud	3,210	289
Winona	2,830	420
Iowa	12,363	1,706
*Dubuque	5,193	581
Davenport	2,729	349
Des Moines	2,043	407
Sioux City	2,398	369
Missouri	15,557	2,378
*St. Louis	10,251	1,237
Jefferson City	1,523	346
Kansas City-St. Joseph	2,968	577
Springfield-Cape Girardeau	815	218
North Dakota	3,862	419
Bismarck	1,694	167
Fargo	2,168	252
South Dakota	3,449	479
Rapid City	1,212	179
Sioux Falls	2,237	300
Nebraska	7,083	1,187
*Omaha	4,456	662
Grand Island	1,237	213
Lincoln	1,390	312
Kansas	7,335	1,313
*Kansas City	3,142	502
Dodge City	748	125
Salina	1,358	238
Wichita	2,087	448
WEST SOUTH CENTRAL	**103,404**	**5,823**
Arkansas, Little Rock	1,190	280
Louisiana	28,123	1,600
*New Orleans	12,934	619
Alexandria	1,765	313
Baton Rouge	3,859	318
Lafayette	9,565	350
Oklahoma		
Oklahoma City-Tulsa	2,833	636
Texas	71,258	3,307
*San Antonio	15,423	408
Amarillo	2,943	176
Austin	3,121	342
Beaumont	1,806	266
Brownsville	9,238	83
Corpus Christi	8,473	149
Dallas	4,433	425
El Paso+	10,592	122
Fort Worth	2,256	272
Galveston-Houston	10,556	953
San Angelo	2,417	111
MOUNTAIN	**40,797**	**3,573**
Montana	3,185	330
Great Falls	1,640	179
Helena	1,545	151
Idaho, Boise	1,869	406
Wyoming, Cheyenne+	1,314	164
Colorado	10,341	947
*Denver	7,487	799
Pueblo	2,854	148
New Mexico	9,178	836
*Santa Fe	7,807	238
Gallup+	1,371	598
Arizona	11,699	537
Phoenix	6,526	317
Tucson	5,173	220
Utah, Salt Lake City	1,561	198
Nevada, Reno	1,650	155
PACIFIC	**140,001**	**10,507**
Washington	9,855	1,500
*Seattle	6,819	1,001
Spokane	1,685	306
Yakima	1,351	193
Oregon	5,028	849
*Portland	4,432	738
Baker	596	111
California	118,509	7,782
*Los Angeles	61,570	2,757
*San Francisco	15,003	1,555
Fresno	8,390	347
Monterey	2,663	156
Oakland	7,889	1,232
Sacramento	5,107	482
San Diego	13,527	823
Santa Rosa	1,697	220
Stockton	2,663	210
Alaska	855	103
*Anchorage	449	77
Fairbanks	297	18
Juneau	109	8
Hawaii, Honolulu	5,754	273
EASTERN RITES	**5,295**	**402**
*Philadelphia	962	48
*Munhall	1,400	200
St. Nicholas of Chicago	349	31
Parma	554	39
Passaic	787	33
Stamford	399	10
St. Maron of Detroit	438	16
Melkite Exarchate	406	25
MILITARY ORDINARIATE	**27,020**	**3,008**
TOTALS 1972	**1,054,933**	**79,012**

CATHEDRALS IN THE UNITED STATES

A cathedral is the principal church in a diocese, the one in which the bishop has his seat *(cathedra)*. He is the actual rector, although many functions of the church, which usually serves a parish, are the responsibility of a priest serving as the administrator. Because of the dignity of a cathedral, the date of its dedication and its patronal feast are observed throughout a diocese.

The pope's cathedral, the Basilica of St. John Lateran, is the highest-ranking church in the world.

(Archdioceses are indicated by asterisk.)

Albany, N.Y.: Immaculate Conception.
Alexandria, La.: St. Francis Xavier.
Allentown, Pa.: St. Catherine of Siena.
Altoona-Johnstown, Pa.: Blessed Sacrament (Altoona); St. John Gualbert (Johnstown Co-Cathedral).
Amarillo, Tex.: Sacred Heart.
Anchorage,* Alaska: Holy Family.
Atlanta,* Ga.: Christ the King.
Austin, Tex.: St. Mary.
Baker, Ore.: St. Francis de Sales.
Baltimore,* Md.: Mary Our Queen; Basilica of the Assumption of the Blessed Virgin Mary (Co-Cathedral).
Baton Rouge, La.: St. Joseph.
Beaumont, Tex.: St. Anthony.
Belleville, Ill.: St. Peter.
Belmont Abbey, N.C.: Mary Help of Christians.
Birmingham, Ala.: St. Paul.
Bismarck, N.D.: Holy Spirit.
Boise, Ida.: St. John the Evangelist.
Boston,* Mass.: Holy Cross.
Bridgeport, Conn.: St. Augustine.
Brooklyn, N.Y.: St. James (Pro-Cathedral).
Brownsville, Tex.: Immaculate Conception.
Buffalo, N.Y.: St. Joseph.
Burlington, Vt.: Immaculate Conception (destroyed by fire in 1972).
Camden, N.J.: Immaculate Conception.
Charleston, S.C.: St. John the Baptist.
Charlotte, N.C.: St. Patrick.
Cheyenne, Wyo.: St. Mary.
Chicago, Ill.: Holy Name.
Cincinnati,* Ohio: St. Peter in Chains.
Cleveland, Ohio: St. John the Evangelist.
Columbus, Ohio: St. Joseph.
Corpus Christi, Tex.: Corpus Christi.
Covington, Ky.: Basilica of the Assumption.
Crookston, Minn.: Immaculate Conception.
Dallas, Tex.: Sacred Heart.
Davenport, Ia.: Sacred Heart.
Denver,* Colo.: Immaculate Conception.
Des Moines, Ia.: St. Ambrose.
Detroit,* Mich.: Blessed Sacrament.
Dodge City, Kans.: Sacred Heart.
Dubuque,* Ia.: St. Raphael.
Duluth, Minn.: Holy Rosary.
El Paso, Tex.: St. Patrick.
Erie, Pa.: St. Peter.

Evansville, Ind.: Most Holy Trinity (Pro-Cathedral).
Fairbanks, Alaska: Sacred Heart.
Fall River, Mass.: St. Mary of the Assumption.
Fargo, N.D.: St. Mary.
Fort Wayne-S. Bend, Ind.: Immaculate Conception (Fort Wayne); St. Matthew (South Bend Co-Cathedral).
Fort Worth, Tex.: St. Patrick.
Fresno, Calif.: St. John.
Gallup, N.M.: Sacred Heart.
Galveston-Houston, Tex.: St. Mary (Galveston); Sacred Heart (Houston Co-Cathedral).
Gary, Ind.: Holy Angels.
Gaylord, Mich.: St. Mary.
Grand Island, Nebr.: Nativity of Blessed Virgin Mary.
Grand Rapids, Mich.: St. Andrew.
Great Falls, Mont.: St. Ann.
Green Bay, Wis.: St. Francis Xavier.
Greensburg, Pa.: Blessed Sacrament.
Harrisburg, Pa.: St. Patrick.
Hartford,* Conn.: St. Joseph.
Helena, Mont.: St. Helena.
Honolulu, H.I.: Our Lady of Peace.
Indianapolis,* Ind.: Sts. Peter and Paul.
Jefferson City, Mo.: St. Joseph.
Joliet, Ill.: St. Raymond.
Juneau, Alaska: Nativity of the Blessed Virgin Mary.
Kalamazoo, Mich.: St. Augustine.
Kansas City,* Kans.: St. Peter the Apostle.
Kansas City-St. Joseph, Mo.: Immaculate Conception (Kansas City); St. Joseph (St. Joseph Co-Cathedral).
La Crosse, Wis.: St. Joseph.
Lafayette, Ind.: St. Mary.
Lafayette, La.: St. John the Evangelist.
Lansing, Mich.: St. Mary.
Lincoln, Nebr.: Cathedral of the Risen Christ.
Little Rock, Ark.: St. Andrew.
Los Angeles,* Calif.: St. Vibiana.
Louisville,* Ky.: Assumption.
Madison, Wis.: St. Raphael.
Manchester, N.H.: St. Joseph.
Marquette, Mich.: St. Peter.
Memphis, Tenn.: Immaculate Conception.
Miami,* Fla.: St. Mary.
Milwaukee,* Wis.: St. John.
Mobile, Ala.: Immaculate Conception (Minor Basilica).
Monterey, Calif.: San Carlos Borromeo.
Munhall,* Pa. (Greek Rite): St. John the Baptist.
Nashville, Tenn.: Incarnation.
Natchez-Jackson, Miss.: Our Lady of Sorrows (Natchez); St. Peter (Jackson Co-Cathedral).
Newark,* N.J.: Sacred Heart.
New Orleans,* La.: Cathedral (Basilica) of St. Louis.

New Ulm, Minn.: Holy Trinity.
New York,* N.Y.: St. Patrick.
Norwich, Conn.: St. Patricl.
Oakland, Calif.: St. Francis de Sales.
Ogdensburg, N.Y.: St. Mary.
Oklahoma City and Tulsa, Okla.: Our Lady of Perpetual Help (Oklahoma City); Holy Family (Tulsa Co-Cathedral).
Omaha,* Nebr.: St. Cecilia.
Orlando, Fla.: St. Charles Borromeo.
Owensboro, Ky.: St. Stephen.
Parma, Ohio (Greek Rite): St. John the Baptist.
Passaic, N.J. (Greek Rite): St. Michael.
Paterson, N.J.: St. John the Baptist.
Peoria, Ill.: St. Mary.
Philadelphia,* Pa.: Sts. Peter and Paul.
Philadelphia,* Pa. (Byzantine Rite): Immaculate Conception.
Phoenix, Ariz.: Sts. Simon and Jude.
Pittsburgh, Pa.: St. Paul.
Portland, Me.: Immaculate Conception.
Portland,* Ore.: Immaculate Conception.
Providence, R.I.: Sts. Peter and Paul.
Pueblo, Colo.: Sacred Heart.
Raleigh, N.C.: Sacred Heart.
Rapid City, S.D.: Our Lady of Perpetual Help.
Reno, Nev.: St. Thomas Aquinas.
Richmond, Va.: Sacred Heart.
Rochester, N.Y.: Sacred Heart.
Rockford, Ill.: St. Peter.
Rockville Centre, N.Y.: St. Agnes.
Sacramento, Calif.: Blessed Sacrament.
Saginaw, Mich.: St. Mary.
St. Augustine, Fla.: St. Augustine.
St. Cloud, Minn.: St. Mary.
St. Louis,* Mo.: St. Louis.
St. Maron of Detroit (Maronite Rite): St. Maron.
St. Nicholas in Chicago (Ukrainian Rite): St. Nicholas.
St. Paul and Minneapolis,* Minn.: St. Paul (St. Paul); Basilica of St. Mary (Minneapolis Co-Cathedral).
St. Petersburg, Fla.: St. Jude the Apostle.
Salina, Kans.: Sacred Heart.
Salt Lake City, Utah: The Madeleine.
San Angelo, Tex.: Sacred Heart.
San Antonio,* Tex.: San Fernando.
San Diego, Calif.: St. Joseph.
San Francisco,* Calif.: St. Mary (Assumption).
Santa Fe,* N.M.: San Francisco de Asis.
Santa Rosa, Calif.: St. Eugene.
Savannah, Ga.: St. John the Baptist.
Scranton, Pa.: St. Peter.
Seattle,* Wash.: St. James.
Sioux City, Ia.: Epiphany.
Sioux Falls, S.D.: St. Joseph.
Spokane, Wash.: Our Lady of Lourdes.
Springfield, Ill.:Immaculate Conception.
Springfield, Mass.: St. Michael.
Springfield-Cape Girardeau, Mo.: St. Agnes (Springfield): St. Mary (Cape Girardeau Co-Cathedral).

Stamford, Conn. (Byzantine): St. Vladimir (Pro-Cathedral).
Steubenville, Ohio: Holy Name.
Stockton, Calif: St. Mary of the Annunciation.
Superior, Wis.: Christ the King.
Syracuse, N.Y.: Immaculate Conception.
Toledo, Ohio: Blessed Virgin Mary of the Holy Rosary.
Trenton, N.J.: St. Mary.
Tucson, Ariz.: St. Augustine.
Washington,* D.C.: St. Matthew.
Wheeling, W. Va.: St. Joseph.
Wichita, Kans.: Immaculate Conception.
Wilmington, Del.: St. Peter.
Winona, Minn.: Sacred Heart.
Worcester, Mass.: St. Paul.
Yakima, Wash.: St. Paul.
Youngstown, Ohio: St. Columba.
Apostolic Exarchate of the Melkites: Our Lady of the Annunciation (Boston, Mass.).

BASILICAS IN US, CANADA

Basilica is a title assigned to certain churches because of their antiquity, dignity, historical importance or significance as centers of worship. Major basilicas have the papal altar and holy door, which is opened at the beginning of a Jubilee Year; minor basilicas enjoy certain ceremonial privileges.

Among the major basilicas are the patriarchal basilicas of St. John Lateran, St. Peter, St. Paul Outside the Walls and St. Mary Major in Rome; St. Francis and St. Mary of the Angels in Assisi, Italy.

The patriarchal basilica of St. Lawrence, Rome, is a minor basilica.

The dates in the listings below indicate when the churches were designated as basilicas.

Minor Basilicas In US

Alabama: Mobile, Cathedral of the Immaculate Conception (Mar. 10, 1962).
California: San Francisco, Mission Dolores (Feb. 8, 1952); Carmel, Old Mission of San Carlos (Feb. 5, 1960).
Illinois: Chicago, Our Lady of Sorrows (May 4, 1956), Queen of All Saints (Mar. 26, 1962).
Indiana: Vincennes, Old Cathedral (Mar. 14, 1970).
Iowa: Dyersville, St. Francis Xavier (May 11, 1956).
Kentucky: Trappist, Our Lady of Gethsemani (May 3, 1949); Covington, Cathedral of Assumption (Dec. 8, 1953).
Louisiana: New Orleans, St. Louis King of France (Dec. 9, 1964).
Maryland: Baltimore, Assumption of the Blessed Virgin Mary (Sept. 1, 1937).
Massachusetts: Roxbury, Perpetual Help ("Mission Church") (Sept. 8, 1954).
Minnesota: Minneapolis. St. Mary (Feb. 1, 1926).
Missouri: Conception, Basilica of Immacu-

late Conception (Sept. 14, 1940); St. Louis, St. Louis King of France (Jan. 27, 1961).

New York: Brooklyn, Our Lady of Perpetual Help (Sept. 5, 1969); Buffalo, St. Adalbert's (Aug. 11, 1907); Lackawanna, Our Lady of Victory (1926).

Ohio: Carey, Shrine of Our Lady of Consolation (Oct. 21, 1971).

Pennsylvania: Latrobe, St. Vincent Basilica, Benedictine Archabbey (Aug. 22, 1955); Conewago, Basilica of the Sacred Heart (June 30, 1962).

Wisconsin: Milwaukee, St. Josaphat (Mar. 10, 1929).

Minor Basilicas In Canada

Manitoba: St. Boniface, Cathedral Basilica of St. Boniface (June 10, 1949).

Newfoundland: St. John's, Cathedral Basilica of St. John the Baptist.

Nova Scotia: Halifax, St. Mary's Basilica (June 14, 1950).

Ontario: Ottawa, Basilica of Notre Dame; London, St. Peter's Cathedral (Dec. 13, 1961).

Prince Edward Island: Charlottetown, Basilica of St. Dunstan.

Quebec: Sherbrooke, Cathedral Basilica of St. Michael (July 31, 1959). Montreal, Cathedral Basilica of St. James the Greater; St. Joseph of Mount Royal. Cap-de-la-Madeleine,

Basilica of Our Lady of the Cape (Aug. 15, 1964). Quebec, Basilica of Notre Dame; St. Anne de Beaupre, Basilica of St. Anne.

Dioceses With Interstate Lines

Diocesan lines usually fall within a single state and in some cases include a whole state. The following dioceses are exceptions.

Norwich, Conn., includes Fisher's Island, N.Y.

Wilmington, Del., includes nine counties of Maryland and two of Virginia.

Baltimore, includes all of Maryland except nine counties under the jurisdiction of Wilmington and five under Washington.

Washington, D.C., includes five counties of Maryland.

Richmond includes all of Virginia except two counties under the jurisdiction of Wilmington and 18 under Wheeling; Richmond also includes eight counties of West Virginia.

Wheeling includes all of West Virginia except eight counties under the jurisdiction of Richmond; it also includes 18 counties of Virginia.

El Paso, Tex., includes seven counties of New Mexico.

Gallup, N.M., has jurisdiction over several counties of Arizona.

Cheyenne, Wyo., includes all of Yellowstone National Park.

CHANCERY OFFICES OF US ARCHDIOCESES AND DIOCESES

A chancery office, under this or another title, is the central administrative office of an archdiocese or diocese.

(Archdioceses are indicated by asterisk.)

Albany, N.Y.: 465 State St., Box 6045, Quail Station. 12206.

Alexandria, La.: 2315 Texas Ave., P. O. Box 5665. 71301.

Allentown, Pa.: 1729 Turner St. 18104.

Altoona-Johnstown, Pa.: Logan Blvd., Holidaysburg Pa. 16648.

Amarillo, Tex.: 1800 N. Spring St., P. O. Box 5644. 79107.

Anchorage,* Alaska: 811 Sixth Ave., P. O. Box 2239. 99501.

Atlanta,* Ga.: 756 W. Peachtree St. N.W. 30308.

Austin, Tex.: N. Congress and 16th, P. O. Box 13327. Capitol Sta. 78711.

Baker, Ore.: Baker and First Sts., P. O. Box 826, 97814.

Baltimore,* Md.: 320 Cathedral St. 21201.

Baton Rouge, La.: P. O. Box 2028. 70821.

Beaumont, Tex.: 703 Archie St., P. O. Box 3948. 7704

Belleville, Ill.: 222 S. Third St., Box 546. 62221.

Belmont Abbey, N.C.: Belmont, N.C., 28012.

Birmingham, Ala.: P. O. Box 2086. 35201.

Bismarck, N.D.: 420 Raymond St., Box 1575. 58501.

Boise, Ida.: Box 769, 420 Idaho St. 83701.

Boston,* Mass.: 2121 Commonwealth Ave., Brighton, Mass. 02135.

Bridgeport, Conn.: 250 Waldemere Ave. 06604.

Brooklyn, N.Y.: 75 Greene Ave. 11238.

Brownsville, Tex.: P. O. Box 2279, 1910 E. Elizabeth St. 78520.

Buffalo, N.Y.: 35 Lincoln Parkway. 14222.

Burlington, Vt.: 52 Williams St. 05401.

Camden, N.J.: 1845 Haddon Ave., P. O. Box 709, 01801.

Charleston, S.C.: 119 Broad St. P. O. Box 818. 29402.

Charlotte, N.C.: P. O. Box 4502 Charlotte-town Sta. 28204.

Cheyenne, Wyo.: Box 426. 82001.

Chicago,* Ill.: 211 E. Chicago Ave. 60611.

Cincinnati,* O.: 29 E. 8th St. 45202.

Cleveland, O.: 350 Chancery Bldg., Cathedral Sq., 1027 Superior Ave. 44114.

Columbus, O.: 198 E. Broad St. 43215.

Corpus Christi, Tex.: 620 Lipan St. 78401.

Covington, Ky.: 1140 Madison Ave., P. O. Box 192. 41012.

Crookston, Minn.: 1200 Memorial Dr., P. O. Box 610. 56716.

Dallas, Tex.: 3915 Lemmon Ave., P. O. Box 19507. 75219.

Davenport, Ia.: 811 Kahl Bldg., 3rd and Ripley Sts. 52801.

Denver,* Colo.: 934 Bannock St. 80204.

Des Moines, Ia.: 2910 Grand Ave., P. O. Box 1816. 50306.

Detroit,* Mich.: 1234 Washington Blvd. 48226.

Dodge City, Kans.: 910 Central Ave., P. O. Box 849. 67801.

Dubuque,* Ia.: 1229 Mt. Loretta Ave. 52001.

Duluth, Minn.: 215 W. 4th St. 55806.

El Paso, Tex.: 1012 N. Mesa St. 79902.

Erie, Pa.: 205 W. 9th St. 16501.

Evansville, Ind.: 219 N. W. Third St. 47708.

Fairbanks, Alaska: 1316 Peger Rd. 99701.

Fall River, Mass.: 362 Highland Ave., Box 30. 02722.

Fargo, N. D.: 504 Black Bldg., Box 1750. 58102.

Fort Wayne-South Bend, Ind.: P. O. Box 390, Fort Wayne. 46801.

Fort Worth, Tex.: 1206 Throckmorton St. 76102.

Fresno, Calif.: P. O. Box 1668, 1550 N. Fresno St. 93717.

Gallup, N. Mex.: 406 W. Aztec St., P. O. Box 1338. 87301.

Galveston-Houston, Tex.: 1700 San Jacinto St., Houston. 77002.

Gary, Ind.: 668 Pierce St., P. O. Box 474. 46401.

Gaylord, Mich.: M-32 West, P. O. Box 700. 49735.

Grand Island, Nebr.: 607 W. Division St., P. O. Box 996. 68801.

Grand Rapids, Mich.: 265 Sheldon Ave. S. E. 49502.

Great Falls, Mont.: 725 Third Ave. N., P. O. Box 1399. 59403.

Green Bay, Wis.: Box 66. 54305.

Greensburg, Pa.: 723 E. Pittsburgh St. 15601.

Harrisburg, Pa.: 111 State St. P. O. Box 2153. 17105.

Hartford,* Conn.: 134 Farmington Ave. 06105.

Helena, Mont.: 612 Harrison Ave., P. O. Box 1729. 59601.

Honolulu, H. I.: 1184 Bishop St. 96813.

Indianapolis,* Ind.: 1350 N. Pennsylvania St. 46206.

Jefferson City, Mo.: 605 Clark Ave. P. O. Box 417. 65101.

Joliet, Ill.: 425 Summit St. 60435.

Juneau, Alaska: 329 5th St. 99801.

Kalamazoo, Mich.: 215 N. Westnedge. 49005.

Kansas City,* Kans.: 2220 Central Ave., P. O. Box 2328. 66110.

Kansas City-St. Joseph, Mo.: P. O. Box 1037, Kansas City. 64141.

La Crosse, Wis.: 421 Main St. 54601.

Lafayette in Indiana: 610 Lingle Ave. 47902.

Lafayette, La.: P. O. Drawer 3387. 70501.

Lansing, Mich.: 300 W. Ottawa. 48933. 3400 Sheridan Blvd., P. O. Box 80328. 68501.

Little Rock, Ark.: 2415 N. Tyler St. 72207.

Los Angeles,* Calif.: 1531 W. 9th St. 90015.

Louisville,* Ky.: 212 E. College St., P. O. Box 1073. 40201.

Madison, Wis.: 15 E. Wilson St. 53701.

Manchester, N. H.: 153 Ash St. 03105.

Marquette, Mich.: 444 S. Fourth St., P. O. Box 550. 49855.

Memphis, Tenn.: 1325 Jefferson Ave., 38104.

Miami,* Fla.: 6301 Biscayne Blvd. 33138.

Milwaukee,* Wis.: 345 N. 95th St. 53226.

Mobile, Ala.: 400 Government St., P. O. Box 1966. 36601.

Monterey, Calif.: 580 Fremont Blvd. 93940.

Munhall,* Pa. (Greek Rite), 54 Riverview Ave., Pittsburgh. 15214.

Nashville, Tenn.: 421 Charlotte Ave. 37219.

Natchez-Jackson, Miss.: 237 E. Amite St., P. O. Box 2248, Jackson. 39205.

Newark,* N. J.: 31 Mulberry St. 07102.

New Orleans,* La.: 7887 Walmsley Ave. 70125.

New Ulm, Minn.: Chancery Drive. 56073.

New York,* N. Y.: 451 Madison Ave. 10022.

Norwich, Conn.: 201 Broadway, P. O. Box 587. 06360.

Oakland, Calif.: 2900 Lakeshore Ave. 94610.

Ogdensburg, N. Y.: 622 Washington St. 13669.

Oklahoma City and Tulsa, Okla.: 1521 N. Hudson, Oklahoma City. 73103.

Omaha,* Nebr.: 100 N. 62nd St. 68132.

Orlando, Fla.: P. O. Box 3069. 32802.

Owensboro, Ky.: c/o Chancellor's Residence, 4003 Frederica St. 42301.

Parma, Ohio (Greek Rite): 1900 Carlton Rd. 44134.

Passaic, N. J. (Byxantine Rits): 101 Market St. 07055.

Paterson, N. J.: 24 De Grasse St. 07505.

Peoria, Ill.: 607 N. E. Madison Ave. 61603.

Philadelphia,* Pa.: 222 N. 17th St. 19103.

Philadelphia,* Pa. (Ukrainian Rite): 815 N. Franklin St. 19123.

Phoenix, Ariz.: 400 E. Monroe St. 85004.

Pittsburgh, Pa.: 111 Blvd. of the Allies. 15222.

Portland, Me.: 510 Ocean Ave., Woodfords P. O. Box H. 04103.

Portland in Oregon*: 2838 E. Burnside St. 97207.

Providence, R. I.: Cathedral Sq. 02903.

Pueblo, Colo.: 1426 Grand Ave. 81003.

Raleigh, N. C.: P. O. Box 1949. 27602.

Rapid City, S. D.: 520 Cathedral Dr., P. O. Box 752. 57701.

Reno, Nev.: 515 Court St. 89501. P. O. Box 1211, 89504.

Richmond, Va.: 807 Cathedral Pl. 23220.

Rochester, N. Y.: 50 Chestnut St. 14604. P. O. Box 2G. 23203.

Rockford, Ill.: 1245 N. Court St. 61101.

Rockville Centre, N.Y.: 253 Sunrise Highway. 11570.

Sacramento, Calif.: 1119 K St., P. O. Box 1706. 95808.

Saginaw, Mich.: 2555 Wieneke Rd. 48603.

St. Augustine, Fla.: Suite 1648, Gulf Life Tower, Jacksonville, Fla. 32207.

St. Cloud, Minn.: P. O. Box 1248. 56301.

St. Louis,* Mo.: 4445 Lindell Blvd. 63108.

St. Maron of Detroit, Mich.: 11470 Kercheval, P. O. Box 3307, Jefferson Sta., Detroit, Mich. 48214.

St. Nicholas in Chicago (Ukrainian Rite): 2245 W. Rice St. 60622.

St. Paul and Minneapolis,* Minn.: 226 Summit Ave., St. Paul. 55102.

St. Petersburg, Fla.: 5201 Central Ave. 33710. P. O. Box 13109. 33733.

Salina, Kans.: 421 Country Club Rd., P. O. Box 999. 67401.

Salt Lake City, Utah: 333 E. S. Temple. 84111.

San Angelo, Tex.: 116 S. Oakes. Box 1829. 76901.

San Antonio,* Tex.: 9123 Lorene Lane, P. O. Box 13190. 78284.

San Diego, Calif.: Alcala Park. 92110.

San Francisco,* Calif.: 445 Church St. 94114.

Santa Fe,* N. Mex.: 202 Morningside Dr. S. E. Albuquerque. 87108.

Santa Rosa, Calif.: 398 10th St., P. O. Box 1499. 95403.

Savannah, Ga.: 225 Abercorn St., P. O. Box 8789. 31402.

Scranton, Pa.: 300 Wyoming Ave. 18503.

Seattle,* Wash.: 907 Terry Ave. 98104.

Sioux City, Ia.: P. O. Box 1530. 51102.

Sioux Falls, S.D.: 423 N. Duluth Ave. 57104.

Spokane, Wash.: 1023 W. Riverside Ave. 99201.

Springfield-Cape Girardeau, Mo.: 410 Landers Bldg., Springfield. 65806.

Springfield in Illinois: 524 E. Lawrence Ave. 62705.

Springfield, Mass.: 76 Elliot St. 01105. P. O. Box 1730. 01101.

Stamford, Conn. (Ukrainian Rite): 161 Glenbrook Rd. 06902.

Steubenville, Ohio: 422 Washington St., P. O. Box 969. 43952.

Stockton, Calif.: 1105 N. Lincoln St. 95203. P. O. Box 4237. 95204.

Superior, Wis.: 1201 Hughitt Ave. 54880.

Syracuse, N.Y.: 240 E. Onondaga St., 13202.

Toledo, Ohio: 2544 Parkwood Ave. 43610.

Trenton, N.J.: 701 Lawrenceville Rd. 08638.

Tucson, Ariz.: 192 S. Stone Ave., Box 31, 85702.

Washington,* D.C.: 1721 Rhode Island Ave. N. W. 20036.

Wheeling, W. Va.: 1300 Byron St. 26003.

Wichita, Kans.: 424 N. Broadway. 67202.

Wilmington, Del.: P. O. Box 2030. 19899.

Winona, Minn.: 275 Harriet St. 55987.

Worcester, Mass.: 49 Elm St. 01609.

Yakima, Wash.: 228 Liberty Bldg., P.O. Box 901. 98901.

Youngstown, Ohio: 144 W. Wood St. 44503.

Apostolic Exarchate of the Melkites: 19 Dartmouth St., W. Newton, Mass. 02165.

NATIONAL CATHOLIC CONFERENCES

The two conferences described below are related in membership and directive control but distinct in nature, purpose and function.

The National Conference of Catholic Bishops (NCCB) is a strictly ecclesiastical body in and through which the bishops of the United States act together, officially and with authority as pastors of the Church. It is the sponsoring organization of the United States Catholic Conference.

The United States Catholic Conference (USCC) is a civil corporation and operational secretariat in and through which the bishops, together with other members of the Church, act on a wider scale for the good of the Church and society. It is sponsored by the National Conference of Catholic Bishops.

The principal officers of both conferences are: Cardinal John J. Krol, president; Archbishop Leo C. Byrne, vice president; Archbishop John Maguire, treasurer; Bishop Joseph L. Bernardin, general secretary.

Cardinal Krol, elected in November, 1971, succeeded Cardinal John F. Dearden of Detroit as president.

Headquarters of both conferences are located at 1312 Massachusetts Ave. N. W., Washington, D. C. 20005.

NCCB

The National Conference of Catholic Bishops, established by action of the US hierarchy Nov. 14, 1966, is a strictly ecclesiastical body with defined juridical authority over the Church in this country. It was set up with the approval of the Holy See and in line with directives from the Second Vatican Council. Its constitution was formally ratified during the November, 1967, meeting of the US hierarchy.

The NCCB is the successor to the Annual Meeting of the Bishops of the United States, whose pastoral character was originally approved by Pope Benedict XV Apr. 10, 1919.

The address of the Conference is 1312 Massachusetts Ave. N. W., Washington, D. C. 20005.

Pastoral Council

The conference, one of many similar territorial conferences, envisioned in the conciliar *Decree on the Pastoral Office of Bishops in the Church* (No. 38), is "a council in which the bishops of a given nation or territory (in this case, the United States) jointly exercise their pastoral office to promote the greater good which the Church offers mankind, especially through the forms and methods of the apostolate fittingly adapted to the circumstances of the age."

Its decisions, "provided they have been approved legitimately and by the votes of at least two-thirds of the prelates who have a deliberative vote in the conference, and have been recognized by the Apostolic See, are to have juridically binding force only in those cases prescribed by the common law or determined by a special mandate of the Apostolic See, given either spontaneously or in response to a petition of the conference itself."

All bishops who serve or have served the Church in the US, its territories and possessions, have full membership and voting rights in the NCCB.

Officers, Committees

The conference operates through a number of bishops' committees with functions in specific areas of work and concern. Their basic assignments are to prepare materials on the basis of which the bishops, assembled as a conference, make decisions, and to put suitable action plans into effect.

The principal officers are: Cardinal John J. Krol, president; Archbishop Leo C. Byrne, vice president; Archbishop John J. Maguire, treasurer; Bishop Joseph L. Bernardin, general secretary.

These officers, with several other bishops, hold positions on executive-level committees — Executive Committee, the Committee on Budget and Finance, the committee on Personnel and Administrative Services, and the Committee on Research, Plans and Programs. They also, with other bishops, serve on the NCCB Administrative Committee.

The standing committees and their chairmen (Archbishops and Bishops) are as follows.

Arbitration, David F. Cunningham.

Boundaries of Dioceses and Provinces, John J. Krol.

Canonical Affairs, Francis F. Reh.

Church in Latin America, Humberto S. Medeiros.

Doctrine, John F. Whealon.

Ecumenical and Interreligious Affairs, Charles H. Helmsing.

Liaison with Priests, Religious and Laity, Thomas J. McDonough.

Liturgy, Charles W. Malone.

Men Religious, Cletus F. O'Donnell.

Missions, Glennon P. Flavin.

Nomination of Bishops (inoperative), John J. Krol.

North American College, Louvain, Stephen A. Leven.

North American College, Rome, Cardinal Terence Cooke.

Pastoral Research and Practices, John R. Quinn.

Permanent Diaconate, John S. Spence.

Priestly Formation, Thomas J. Grady.

Vocations, Raymond J. Vonesh.

Welfare Emergency Relief, Cardinal John J. Krol.

Women Religious, James J. Hogan.

Ad hoc committees and their chairmen are as follows.

Crusade against Poverty, Francis J. Mugavero.

Diocesan Financial Statements, Cardinal Terence Cooke.

Liaison with National Office for Black Catholics, Peter L. Gerety.

Farm Labor, Joseph F. Donnelly.

Lay Apostolate, Francis J. Furey.

Priestly Life and Ministry, Cardinal Krol.

Nominations to Conference Offices (chair not filled).

Women in the Church and in Society, Leo C. Byrne.

Priestly Life and Ministry, Philip M. Hannan.

Migrants, Seamen and Travellers, Robert E. Tracy.

USCC

The United States Catholic Conference, Inc. (USCC), is the operational secretariat and service agency of the National Conference of Catholic Bishops for carrying out the civic-religious work of the Church in this country. It is a civil corporation related to the NCCB in membership and directive control but distinct from it in purpose and function.

The address of the Conference is 1312 Massachusetts Ave. N.W., Washington, D.C. 20005.

Service Secretariat

The USCC, as of Jan. 1, 1967, took over the general organization and operations of the former National Catholic Welfare Conference, Inc., whose origins dated back to the National Catholic War Council of 1917. The council underwent some change after World War I and was established on a permanent basis Sept. 24, 1919, as the National Catholic Welfare Council to serve as a central agency for organizing and coordinating the efforts of US Catholics in carrying out the social mission of the Church in this country. In 1923, its name was changed to National Catholic Welfare Conference, Inc., and clarification was made of its nature as a service agency of the bishops and the Church rather than as a conference of bishops with real juridical authority in ecclesiastical affairs.

The Official Catholic Directory states that the USCC assists "the bishops in their service to the Church in this country by uniting the people of God where voluntary collective action on a broad interdiocesan level is needed. The USCC provides an organizational structure and the resources needed to insure coordination, cooperation, and assistance in the public, educational and social concerns of the Church at the national or interdiocesan level."

Officers, Departments

The principal officers of the USCC are Cardinal John J. Krol, president; Archbishop Leo C. Byrne, vice president; Archbishop John J. Maguire, treasurer; Bishop Joseph L. Bernardin, general secretary. These officers, with several other bishops, hold positions on executive-level committees — the Executive Committee; the Committee on Research, Plans and Programs; the Committee on Budget and Finance; the Committee on Personnel and Administrative Services. They also, with 21 other bishops, serve on the Administrative Board.

The Executive Committee, organized in 1969, is authorized to handle matters of urgency between meetings of the Administrative Board and the general conference, to coordinate items for the agenda of general meetings, and to speak in the name of the USCC.

The major departments and their chairmen (Archbishops and Bishops) are: Communications, John L. May; Education, William A. McManus; Health Affairs, Edward D. Head; Social Development, Raymond J. Gallagher. Each department is supervised by a committee composed of an equal number of episcopal and non-episcopal members, including lay persons.

A National Advisory Council of bishops, priests, men and women religious, lay men and women advises the Administrative Board on overall plans and operations of the USCC.

The administrative general secretariat, in addition to other duties, supervises staff-service offices of Finance and Administration, General Counsel, Government Liaison, and Research, Plans and Programs.

USCC bureaus and offices are divisions under the departments, as follows:

• **Communications:** National Catholic Office for Information, National Catholic Office for Film and Broadcasting, NC News Service, Creative Services.

• **Education:** Elementary and Secondary Education, Higher Education, Religious Education CCD (includes Adult Education, in reorganization authorized in April, 1972), Youth Activities.

• **Health Affairs:** Chaplains' Services, Drug Education.

• **Social Development:** Family Life, Rural Life, Spanish-Speaking, Urban Life. Includes the former International Affairs Department (Latin America, Migration and Refugees Services, World Justice and Peace), in reorganization plan authorized in April, 1972.

• **Campaign for Human Development,** for anti-poverty programs.

• **Related Organizations:** National Conference of Catholic Laity, National Catholic Community Service.

Most of the 35 organizations and associations affiliated with the USCC are covered in separate Almanac entries.

MEETINGS OF THE CONFERENCE OF BISHOPS

Nov. 15 to 19, 1971

The meeting, held in Washington, was attended by more than 250 members of the US hierarchy. It marked the end of the presidency of Cardinal John F. Dearden, who had headed the organization through the five years following its establishment as a national conference under norms laid down by the Second Vatican Council. He was succeeded, for a three-year term, by Cardinal John J. Krol.

The following were major items of business.

Budget: Approval was voted for a budget of $9,839,836; the sum of $10,740,274 had been sought. About one-third of the amount ($3,398,836) was allocated for staff operations of the NCCB and the USCC. Diocesan assessments for support of the two organizations amounted to $2,450,000.

No funds were allocated to the National Office for Black Catholics, which still had $120,000 of $150,000 granted earlier in the year.

Ended were allocations of $100,000 for the Montezuma Seminary and $39,400 for PADRES.

Reduced allocations went to the National Catholic Office for Film and Broadcasting, from $142,098 to $87,320; the Division of Migration and Refugee Services, USCC, from $593,177 to $519,672; the Division for the Spanish-Speaking, USCC, from $25,000 to $19,419 (it was getting $200,000 from other sources).

Environment: Endorsed a statement on environmental problems and related issues, with the hope of issuing another one at a future date.

Ethical Directives: Approved, 232 to 7, with two abstentions, a set of "Ethical and Religious Directives for Catholic Health Facilities" (see Index for text).

Financial Reporting: Received a report that a series of seminars on diocesan accounting and financial reporting procedures would start about the middle of January, 1972. Fifty-two dioceses were said to have shown interest in such seminars by the end of October.

Liturgy: Withheld approval of special-group liturgies until adequate Mass texts and directives become available.

Missions: Adopted a statement, released Dec. 10, on the Missions and missionary obligations of all Catholics.

Open Meetings: Voted, 144 to 106, with three abstentions, to open future conference meetings to the press. (The proposal had been brought up twice before, in November, 1970, and April, 1971.) In a related vote, the conference approved, 169 to 76, attendance by 20 to 25 observers.

Parental Rights: Approved and published a "Statement on Parental Rights and the Free Exercise of Religion," stating the case for tax aid to parents for education of their children in church-related schools (see Index for text).

Pastoral Council: Endorsed the target date of 1976 for establishment of a National Pastoral Council. Pending that development, matters which would eventually come under the aegis of the council would be handled by the Advisory Committee of the USCC.

Priestly Life and Ministry: Appointed Msgr. Colin A. MacDonald of Manchester, N.H., executive director of a new secretariat in charge of carrying out recommendations indicated in the bishops' study of priestly life and ministry.

Pulpit Exchanges: Voted down, 152 to 81, with one abstention, a resolution to ask the Holy See for restudy of a general prohibition against pulpit exchanges by priests and ministers at full liturgical celebrations such as Mass and Protestant Eucharistic services. (Permission for this can be, and is, given by bishops in particular cases; the proposal called for general permission. Pulpit exchange is no problem in less formal prayer services.)

Spiritual Directors: Endorsed establishment of a National Conference of Spiritual Directors of candidates for the priesthood. (There were some 300 such directors across the country.)

Vietnam War: Approved, with a nearly unanimous voice vote, a resolution on US involvement in Southeast Asia, stating: "It is our firm conviction . . . that the speedy ending of this war is a moral imperative of the highest priority." The resolution also asked for amnesty for conscientious objectors (see Index for text).

Apr. 11 to 13, 1972

Two hundred and thirty-seven bishops attended the meeting in Savannah. It was the first meeting of the NCCB ever opened to the press and observers.

The following were major items of business.

Black Catholics: Commended a fund-raising effort to be undertaken later in the year by the National Office for Black Catholics.

Education: Received a progress report on a proposed pastoral letter on Catholic education.

First Confession: Voted in executive session not to ban First Communion before First Confession but to let it continue for purposes of experimentation and decision at a future date. It was reported that the practice was in use in 96 of about 120 dioceses which responded to a survey. More than half of the parishes in 53 dioceses delayed the reception of the sacrament of penance for some time after the reception of First Communion.

Justice: Adopted without dissent a proposal that the Department of Social Action collaborate with the USCC's international affairs office on plans for a nationwide conference on justice keyed to the US bicentennial in 1976.

Liturgical Changes: Voted, 146 to 30, to authorize minor changes in the Mass and administration of the sacraments provided for in liturgical enactments of the Holy See, for an experimental period of three years. Examples of the changes were said to be moving the Greeting of Peace to an earlier part of Mass, omission of anointing with chrism at baptism, changes in the colors and types of liturgical vestments.

Approved, 140 to 40, a similar experimental procedure for "more profound liturgical adaptations and for the development of a national ritual," subject to decision by the Holy See.

Took no action with respect to in-hand reception of Holy Communion in view of a survey indicating that less than two-thirds of the bishops favored the practice. A survey of lay persons on the subject was suggested.

National Catechetical Directory: Adopted a program for development of a National Catechetical Directory by the spring of 1974 at a projected cost of $93,280. It was agreed that wide consultation should take place — of lay persons, religious educators, religious, priests and bishops — before compilation of the directory.

Permanent Deacons: Voted, 182 to 44, to ask the Holy See for permission to ordain 30-year-old married men to the permanent diaconate. (The required age was 35). The assembly also received a report on permanent diaconate programs in operation in the US (see Permanent Diaconate).

Population Growth: Took sharp exception to the three-part report published in March by the Congressional Commission on Population Growth and the American Future, and adopted unanimously a counter-statement entitled "Population and the American Future — A Response" (see Index for text).

Priesthood Study: Disagreed over publication of a theological study of the priesthood headed by Father Carl J. Armbruster, S.J., because of alleged conflict between it and views stated at the 1971 assembly of the Synod of Bishops (concerning celibacy, for one thing). Decision to publish or not to publish was reserved to the administrative committee. Agreement had already been reached for publication of psychological and sociological portions of the overall study.

Reorganization and Budget of USCC: Approved reorganization of the US Catholic Conference and new budgeting to save about $1 million in annual operating expenses. The reorganization plan consolidated Adult Education and Religious Education/CCD into a single division, merged the International Affairs and Social Development departments, and phased out the Division for UN Affairs.

Spring Meetings: Voted to substitute 12 regional meetings for the general meeting in the spring, thus making the November meeting the only general one of the year.

Women: Received a committee report which stated that questions concerning their rights to equality in the Church, including the possibility of ordination to the priesthood, were under study.

State Catholic Conferences

These conferences are agencies of bishops and dioceses in the various states. Their general purposes are to develop and sponsor cooperative programs designed to cope with pastoral and common-welfare needs, and to represent the dioceses before governmental bodies, the public, and in private sectors. Their membership consists of representatives from the dioceses in the states — bishops, clergy and lay persons in various capacities.

The **National Association of State Catholic Conferences** maintains liaison with the general secretariat of the US Catholic Conference. Theodore N. Staudt of Ohio is president.

California Catholic Conference, 926 J St., Suite 1100, Sacramento, Calif. 95814; exec. dir., Msgr. John S. Cummins.

Colorado Catholic Conference, 310 Symes Building, Denver, Colo. 80202; exec. dir., Ronald Hayes.

Connecticut Catholic Conference, 134 Farmington Ave., Hartford, Conn. 06105; exec. dir., William Wholean.

Florida Catholic Conference, P.O. Box 1571, Tallahassee, Fla. 32302; exec. dir., Thomas A. Horkan.

Illinois Catholic Conference, 25 W. Chicago Ave., Chicago, Ill. 60610; dir., Rev. Thomas B. McDonough.

Indiana Catholic Conference, Room 543, Illinois Building, Illinois and Market Sts., Indianapolis, Ind. 46204; exec. sec., John J. Christy.

Iowa Catholic Conference, 918 Insurance Exchange Building, Des Moines, Iowa 50309; exec. dir., Timothy McCarthy.

Kansas Catholic Conference, Room 702, Commercial National Bank Building, 601 Minnesota Ave., Kansas City, Kan. 66101; exec. dir., Vincent W. DeCoursey.

Kentucky Catholic Conference, 605 Bank of Commerce Building, Lexington, Ky. 40507; exec. dir. and general counsel, Donald P. Moloney.

Louisiana Catholic Conference, P.O. Box 2108, Baton Rouge, La. 70821; exec. dir., John J. Kennedy.

Maryland Catholic Conference, 1100 One Charles Center, Baltimore, Md. 21201; exec. dir., Joseph G. Finnerty.

Massachusetts Catholic Conference, 60 School St., Boston, Mass. 02107; exec. dir., Joseph J. Reilly.

Michigan Catholic Conference, P.O. Box 157, 505 N. Capitol Ave., Lansing, Mich. 48901; exec. dir., Thomas M. Bergeson.

Minnesota Catholic Conference, 145 University Ave., W., St. Paul, Minn. 55103; exec. dir., John F. Markert.

Missouri Catholic Conference, 1204 E. Elm St., P.O. Box 1022, Jefferson City, Mo. 65101; exec. dir., Anthony F. Hiesberger.

Montana Catholic Conference, P.O. Box 404, Helena, Mont. 59601; exec. dir., John Frankino.

Nebraska Catholic Conference, 521 S. 14th St., Room 301, Lincoln, Nebr. 68508; exec. dir., Paul V. O'Hara.

New Jersey Catholic Conference, 495 W. State St., Trenton, N.J. 08618; exec. dir., Edward J. Leadem.

New York State Catholic Committee, 11 N. Pearl St., Albany, N.Y. 12207; exec. secy., Charles J. Tobin, Jr.

North Dakota Catholic Conference, 304 Ave. A. West, Bismarck, N. Dak. 58501; exec. dir., Edwin C. Becker.

Ohio, Catholic Conference of, 22 South Young St., Columbus, Ohio 43125; exec. dir., Theodore N. Staudt.

Pennsylvania Catholic Conference, 509 Second St., Harrisburg, Pa. 17105; exec. dir., Howard J. Fetterhoff.

Texas Catholic Conference, 702 Commodore Perry Building, Austin, Tex. 78701; exec. dir., Callan Graham.

Washington Catholic Conference, 301 Security Building, Olympia, Wash. 98501; exec. dir., Francis J. Walker.

Wisconsin Catholic Conference, 16 N. Carroll St., Room 314, Madison, Wis. 53703; exec. dir., Charles M. Phillips.

State Catholic conferences developed as logical local-level counterparts of the United States Catholic Conference, with appropriate organizations and programs.

Other Conferences

International Organizations: The Union of Superiors General (Men), which was established in 1957, had its statutes approved by the Congregation for Religious and Secular Institutes in 1967, and has Pedro Arrupe, S.J., as president; the International Union of Superiors General (Women), which was established in 1965, had its statutes approved in 1967, and has M. Mary Linscatts, of the Sisters of Our Lady of Namur, as president.

Regional Organization: The Latin American Confederation of Religious, which was established in 1959, had its statutes approved in 1967, and has Manuel Edwards, SS.CC., as president.

Other Conferences: National conferences of superiors of religious, generally separate for men and women, have been established in 17 countries in Europe, 14 in North and Central America, 10 in South America, 17 in Africa, and 18 in Asia and Australia.

Biographies of American Bishops

(Sources: Almanac survey, *The Official Catholic Directory*, NC News Service.)

A

Abramowicz, Alfred L.: b. Jan. 27, 1919, Chicago, Ill.; educ. St. Mary of the Lake Seminary (Mundelein, Ill.), Gregorian Univ. (Rome); ord. priest May 1, 1943; ord. titular bishop of Paestum and auxiliary bishop of Chicago, June 13, 1968.

Ackerman, Richard Henry, C.S.Sp.: b. Aug. 30, 1903, Pittsburgh, Pa.; educ. Duquesne Univ. (Pittsburgh, Pa.), St. Mary's Scholasticate (Norwalk, Conn.), Univ. of Fribourg (Switzerland); ord. priest Aug. 28, 1926; ord. titular bishop of Lares and auxiliary bishop of San Diego, May 22, 1956; app. bishop of Covington, Apr. 4, 1960.

Ahern, Patrick V.: b. Mar. 8, 1919, New York, N.Y.; educ. Manhattan College and Cathedral College (New York City), St. Joseph's Seminary (Yonkers, N. Y.), St. Louis Univ. (St. Louis, Mo.), Notre Dame Univ. (Notre Dame, Ind.); ord. priest Jan. 27, 1945; ord. titular bishop of Naiera and auxiliary bishop of New York, Mar. 19, 1970.

Ahr, George William: b. June 23, 1904, Newark, N.J.; educ. St. Vincent College (Latrobe, Pa.), Seton Hall College (S. Orange, N.J.), North American College (Rome); ord. priest July 29, 1928; ord. bishop of Trenton, Mar. 20, 1950.

Alter, Karl Joseph: b. Aug. 18, 1885, Toledo, O.; educ. St. John's Univ. (Toledo, O.), St. Mary's Seminary (Cleveland, O.); ord. priest June 4, 1910; ord. bishop of Toledo, June 17, 1931; app. archbishop of Cincinnati, June 14, 1950; resigned 1969.

Anderson, Paul F.: b. Apr. 20, 1917, Roslindale, Mass.; educ. Boston College (Chestnut Hill, Mass.), St. John's Seminary (Brighton, Mass.); ord. priest Jan. 6, 1943; ord. titular bishop of Polignando and coadjutor bishop of Duluth, Oct. 17, 1968; bishop of Duluth, Apr. 30, 1969.

Anglim, Robert, C.SS.R.: b. Mar. 4, 1922, Lombard, Ill.; ord. priest Jan. 6, 1948; ord. titular bishop of Gaguari and prelate of Coari, Brazil, June 2, 1966.

Arkfeld, Leo, S.V.D.: b. Feb. 4, 1912, Butte, Nebr.; educ. Divine Word Seminary (Techny, Ill.), Sacred Heart College (Girard, Pa.); ord. priest Aug. 15, 1943; ord. titular bishop of Bucellus and vicar apostolic of Central New Guinea, Nov. 30, 1948; name of vicariate changed to Wewak, May 15, 1952; first bishop of Wewak, Nov. 15, 1966.

Arliss, Reginald, C.P.: b. Sept. 8, 1906, East Orange, N.J.; educ. Immaculate Conception Seminary (Jamaica, N.Y.) and other Passionist houses of study; ord. priest Apr. 28, 1934; missionary in China for 16 years, expelled 1951; missionary in Philippines; rector of the Pontifical Philippine College Seminary in Rome, 1961-69; ord. titular bishop of Cerbali and prelate of Marbel, Philippines, Jan. 30, 1970.

Arzube, Juan: b. June 1, 1918, Guayaquil, Ecuador; educ. Rensselaer Polytechnic Institute (Troy, N.Y.), St. John's Seminary (Camarillo, Calif.); ord. priest 1954; app. titular bishop of Civitate and auxiliary bishop of Los Angeles, Feb. 19, 1971.

B

Baldwin, Vincent J.: b. July 13, 1907, Brooklyn, N.Y.; educ. Cathedral College (Brooklyn, N.Y.), Institute of Philosophy (Huntington, N.Y.), Capranica College (Rome); ord. priest July 26, 1931, Rome; ord. titular bishop of Bencenna and auxiliary bishop of Rockville Centre, July 26, 1962; app. episcopal vicar, Nov. 3, 1971.

Bartholome, Peter William: b. Apr. 2, 1893, Bellechester, Minn.; educ. Campion College (Prairie du Chien, Wis.), St. Paul Seminary (St. Paul, Minn.), Apollinare (Rome); ord. priest June 12, 1917; ord. titular bishop of Lete and coadjutor bishop of St. Cloud, Mar. 3, 1942; bishop of St. Cloud, May 31, 1953; resigned 1968; assigned the titular see of Tanaramusa.

Baum, William W.: b. Nov. 21, 1926, Dallas, Tex.; educ. Kenrick Seminary (St. Louis, Mo.), Angelicum (Rome); ord. priest May 12, 1951; executive director of NCCB commission on ecumenical affairs, 1964-67; appointed member of joint working group of the World Council of Churches and Vatican Secretariat for Promoting Christian Unity, 1965; ord. bishop of Springfield-Cape Girardeau, Apr. 6, 1970.

Begin, Floyd L.: b. Feb. 5, 1902, Cleveland, O.; educ. St. John's Cathedral College (Cleveland, O.), North American College and Apollinare (Rome); ord. priest July 31, 1927; ord. titular bishop of Sala and auxiliary bishop of Cleveland, May 1, 1947; app. first bishop of Oakland, Feb. 21, 1962.

Begley, Michael J.: b. Mar. 12, 1909, Mattineague, Mass.; educ. Mt. St. Mary Seminary (Emmitsburg, Md.); ord. priest May 26, 1934; ord. first bishop of Charlotte, N.C., Jan. 12, 1972.

Bell, Alden J.: b. July 11, 1904, Peterborough, Ont., Canada; educ. St. Joseph's College (Mountain View, Calif.), St. Patrick's Seminary (Menlo Park, Calif.), Catholic Univ. (Washington, D.C.); ord. priest May 14, 1932; ord. titular bishop of Rhodopolis and auxiliary bishop of Los Angeles, June 4, 1956; app. bishop of Sacramento, Mar. 30, 1962.

Benincasa, Pius A.: b. July 8, 1913, Niagara Falls, N.Y.; educ. Propaganda Univ. and Lateran Univ. (Rome); ord. priest Mar. 27,

1937; served in Vatican Secretariat of State, 1954-64; ord. titular bishop of Buruni and auxiliary bishop of Buffalo, June 29, 1964.

Bernardin, Joseph L.: b. Apr. 2, 1928, Columbia, S.C.; educ. St. Mary's Seminary (Baltimore, Md.), Catholic Univ. (Washington, D.C.); ord. priest Apr. 26, 1952; ord. titular bishop of Lugura and auxiliary bishop of Atlanta, Apr. 26, 1966; app. general secretary of the USCC and NCCB, 1968.

Bernarding, George, S.V.D.: b. Feb. 15, 1912, Carrick, Pa.; educ. Divine Word Seminary (Girard, Pa.); ord. priest Aug. 13, 1939; ord. titular bishop of Belabitene and first vicar apostolic of Mount Hagen, New Guinea, Apr. 21, 1960; first bishop of Mount Hagen, Nov. 15, 1966.

Binz, Leo: b. Oct. 31, 1900, Stockton, Ill.; educ. Loras College (Dubuque, Ia.), St. Mary's Seminary (Baltimore, Md.), Sulpician Seminary (Washington, D.C., North American College, Propaganda Univ., Gregorian Univ. (Rome); ord. priest Mar. 15, 1924; ord. titular bishop of Pinara and coadjutor bishop and apostolic administrator of Winona, Dec. 21, 1942; app. titular archbishop of Silyum and coadjutor archbishop of Dubuque, Oct. 15, 1949; app. assistant at the papal throne, June 11, 1954; archbishop of Dubuque, Dec. 2, 1954; app. archbishop of St. Paul, Dec. 16, 1961, installed Feb. 28, 1962; title changed to St. Paul and Minneapolis, 1966.

Biskup, George J.: b. Aug. 23, 1911, Cedar Rapids, Ia.; educ. Loras College (Dubuque, Ia.) North American College (Rome), State Univ. of Iowa (Iowa City, Ia); ord. priest Mar. 19, 1937; ord. titular bishop of Hemeria and auxiliary bishop of Dubuque, Apr. 24, 1957; app. bishop of Des Moines, Jan. 30, 1965; app. titular archbishop of Tamalluma and coadjutor of Indianapolis, July 26, 1967; archbishop of Indianapolis, Jan. 14, 1970.

Blanchette, Romeo: b. Jan. 6, 1913, St. George, Ill.; educ. St. Mary of the Lake Seminary (Mundelein, Ill.), Gregorian Univ. (Rome); ord. priest Apr. 3, 1937; vicar general of Joliet, 1950-66; ord. titular bishop of Maxita and auxiliary of Joliet, Apr. 3, 1965; app. bishop of Joliet, July 19, 1966, installed Aug. 31, 1966.

Boardman, John J.: b. Nov. 7, 1894, Brooklyn N. Y.; educ. St. John's College (Brooklyn, N. Y.), St. John's Seminary (Brooklyn, N.Y.); ord. priest May 21, 1921; ord. titular bishop of Gunela and auxiliary bishop of Brooklyn, June 11, 1952; named assistant at the papal throne; treasurer of the Society for the Propagation of the Faith.

Boccella, John H., T. O. R.: b. June 25, 1912, Castelfranci, Italy; came to US at the age of two; educ. St. Francis College and Seminary (Loretto, Pa.), Angelicum Univ. (Rome), Catholic Univ. (Washington, D. C.); ord. priest Mar. 29, 1941; provincial of Third Order Regular in US, 1945-47; minister general of Third Order Regular, 1947-68; ord.

archbishop of Izmir, Turkey, Apr. 17, 1968.

Bokenfohr, John, O.M.I.: b. Jan. 28, 1903, West Point, Nebr.; ord. priest July 11, 1927; ord. bishop of Kimberley, S. Africa, May 3, 1963.

Boland, Ernest B., O.P.: b. July 10, 1925, Providence, R. I.; educ. Providence College (Rhode Island), Dominican Houses of Study (Somerset, Ohio; Washington, D. C.); ord. priest June 9, 1955; ord. bishop of Multan, Pakistan, July 25, 1966.

Boland, Thomas A.: b. Feb. 17, 1896, Orange, N.J.; educ. Seton Hall College (South Orange, N.J.), North American College (Rome), Fordham Univ. (New York City); ord. priest Dec. 23, 1922; ord. titular bishop of Irina and auxiliary bishop of Newark, July 25, 1940; app. bishop of Paterson, June 21, 1947; app. archbishop of Newark, Nov. 15, 1952, installed Jan. 14, 1953.

Borders, William D.: b. Oct. 9, 1913, Washington, Ind.; educ. St. Meinrad Seminary (St. Meinrad, Ind.), Notre Dame Seminary (New Orleans, La.), Notre Dame Univ. (Notre Dame, Ind.); ord. priest May 18, 1940; ord. first bishop of Orlando, June 14, 1968.

Bosco, Anthony G.: b. Aug. 1, 1927, New Castle, Pa.; educ. St. Vincent Seminary (Latrobe, Pa.), Lateran Univ. (Rome); ord. priest June 7, 1952; ord. titular bishop of Labicum and auxiliary Pittsburgh, June 30, 1970.

Boudreaux, Warren L.: b. Jan. 25, 1918, Berwick, La.; educ. St. Joseph's Seminary (St. Benedict, La.), St. Sulpice Seminary (Paris, France), Notre Dame Seminary (New Orleans, La.), Catholic Univ. (Washington, D. C.); ord. priest May 30, 1942; ord. titular bishop of Calynda and auxiliary bishop of Lafayette, La., July 25, 1962; app. bishop of Beaumont, June 5, 1971.

Breitenbeck, Joseph M.: b. Aug. 3, 1914, Detroit, Mich.; educ. University of Detroit, Sacred Heart Seminary (Detroit, Mich.), North American College and Lateran Univ. (Rome), Catholic Univ. (Washington, D.C.); ord. priest May 30, 1942; ord. titular bishop of Tepelta and auxiliary bishop of Detroit, Dec. 20, 1965; app. bishop of Grand Rapids, Oct. 15, 1969, installed Dec. 2, 1969.

Brizgys, Vincas: b. Nov. 10, 1903, Plynial, Lithuania; ord. priest June 5, 1927; ord. titular bishop of Bosano and auxiliary bishop of Kaunas, Lithuania, May 10, 1940; taken into custody and deported to Germany, 1944; liberated, 1945; US citizen, 1958.

Broderick, Edwin B.: b. Jan. 16, 1917, New York, N. Y.; educ. Cathedral College (New York City), St. Joseph's Seminary (Yonkers, N. Y.), Fordham Univ. (New York City); ord. priest May 30, 1942; ord. titular bishop of Tizica and auxiliary of New York, Apr. 21, 1967; bishop of Albany May 10, 1969.

Brown, Charles, A., M.M.: b. Aug. 20, 1919, New York, N. Y.; educ. Cathedral College (New York City), Maryknoll Seminary (Maryknoll, N. Y.); ord. priest June 9, 1946;

ord. titular bishop of Vallis and auxiliary bishop of Santa Cruz, Bolivia, Mar. 27, 1957.

Brunini, Joseph B.: b. July 24, 1909, Vicksburg, Miss.; educ. Georgetown Univ. (Washington, D. C.), North American College (Rome), Catholic Univ. (Washington, D.C.); ord. priest Dec. 5, 1933; ord. titular bishop of Axomis and auxiliary bishop of Natchez-Jackson, Jan. 29, 1957; apostolic administrator of Natchez-Jackson, 1966; bishop of Natchez-Jackson, 1967.

Brust, Leo J.: b. Jan. 7, 1916, St. Francis, Wis.; educ. St. Francis Seminary (Milwaukee, Wis.), Canisianum (Innsbruck, Austria), Catholic Univ. (Washington, D. C.); ord. priest May 30, 1942; ord. titular bishop of Suelli and auxiliary bishop of Milwaukee, Oct. 16, 1969.

Brzana, Stanislaus J.: b. July 1, 1917, Buffalo, N.Y.; educ. Christ the King Seminary (St. Bonaventure, N.Y.), Gregorian Univ. (Rome); ord. priest June 7, 1941; ord, titular bishop of Cufruta and auxiliary bishop of Buffalo, June 29, 1964; bishop of Ogdensburg, Oct. 22, 1968.

Burke, James C., O.P.: b. Nov. 30, 1926, Wilkes-Barre, Pa.; educ. King's College (Wilkes-Barre, Pa.), Providence College (R.I.): ord. priest June 8, 1956; ord. titular bishop of Lamiggiga and prelate of Chimbote, Peru, May 25, 1967.

Buswell, Charles A.: b. Oct. 15, 1913, Homestead, Okla.; educ. St. Louis Preparatory Seminary (St. Louis, Mo.), Kenrick Seminary (Webster Groves, Mo.), American College, Univ. of Louvain (Belgium); ord. priest July 9, 1939; ord. bishop of Pueblo, Sept. 30, 1959.

Byrne, James J.: b. July 28, 1908, St. Paul, Minn.; educ. Nazareth Hall Preparatory Seminary and St. Paul Seminary (St. Paul, Minn.), Univ. of Minnesota (Minneapolis, Minn.); Louvain Univ. (Belgium); ord. priest June 3, 1933; ord. titular bishop of Etenna and auxiliary bishop of St. Paul, July 2, 1947; app. bishop of Boise, June 16, 1956; app. archbishop of Dubuque, Mar. 19, 1962, installed May 8, 1962.

Byrne, Leo Christopher: b. Mar. 19, 1908, St. Louis, Mo.: educ. Kenrick Seminary (St. Louis, Mo.); ord. priest June 10, 1933; ord. titular bishop of Sabadia and auxiliary bishop of St. Louis, June 29, 1954; installed as coadjutor bishop of Wichita, April 25, 1961; apostolic administrator of Wichita, 1963; app. titular archbishop of Plestra and coadjutor of St. Paul and Minneapolis, Aug. 2, 1967; elected vice-president of NCCB/USCC, Nov. 18, 1971.

C

Caillouet, L. Abel.: b. Aug. 2, 1900, Thibodaux, La.; educ. St. Joseph's Preparatory Seminary (St. Benedict, La.), St. Mary's Seminary (Baltimore, Md.), North American College (Rome); ord. priest Mar. 7, 1925; ord. titular bishop of Setea and auxiliary bishop of New Orleans, Oct. 28, 1947.

Carberry, John J.: (See Cardinals, Biographies.)

Carroll, Coleman Francis: b. Feb. 9, 1905, Pittsburgh, Pa.; educ. Duquesne Univ. (Pittsburgh, Pa.), St. Vincent Seminary (Latrobe, Pa.), Catholic Univ. (Washington, D.C.); ord. priest June 15, 1930; ord. titular bishop of Pitanae and auxiliary bishop of Pittsburgh, Nov. 10, 1953; app. first bishop of Miami, installed Oct. 7, 1958; became first archbishop, 1968.

Carroll, Mark K.: b. Nov. 19, 1896, St. Louis, Mo.; educ. St. Louis Preparatory Seminary and St. Louis Theological Seminary (St. Louis, Mo.); ord. priest June 10, 1922; ord. bishop of Wichita, Apr. 23, 1947; retired, 1963, but retained title; resigned, 1967.

Casey, James V.: b. Sept. 22, 1914, Osage, Ia.; educ. Loras College (Dubuque, Ia.), North American College (Rome), Catholic Univ. (Washington, D.C.); ord. priest Dec. 8, 1939; ord. titular bishop of Citium and auxiliary bishop of Lincoln, Apr. 24, 1957; bishop of Lincoln, June 14, 1957; app. archbishop of Denver, Feb. 22, 1967, installed May 17, 1967.

Casey, Lawrence B.: b. Sept. 6, 1905, Rochester, N.Y.; educ. St. Bernard's Seminary (Rochester, N.Y.); ord. priest June 7, 1930; ord. titular bishop of Cea and auxiliary bishop of Rochester, May 5, 1953; app. bishop of Paterson, installed May 12, 1966.

Cassata, John J.: b. Nov. 8, 1908, Galveston, Tex.; educ. St. Mary's Seminary (La Porte, Tex.), North American College, Urbana Univ. and Gregorian Univ. (Rome); ord. priest Dec. 8, 1932; ord. titular bishop of Bida and auxiliary bishop of Dallas-Fort Worth, June 5, 1968; app. bishop of Fort Worth, Aug. 27, 1969, installed Oct. 21, 1969.

Clinch, Harry A.: b. Oct. 27, 1908, San Anselmo, Calif.; educ. St. Joseph's College (Mountain View, Calif.), St. Patrick's Seminary (Menlo Park, Calif.); ord. priest June 6, 1936; ord. titular bishop of Badiae and auxiliary bishop of Monterey-Fresno, Feb. 27, 1957; app. first bishop of Monterey in California, installed Dec. 14, 1967.

Cody, John P.: (See Cardinals, Biographies.)

Cohill, John Edward, S.V.D.: b. Dec. 13, 1907, Elizabeth, N.J.; educ. Divine Word Seminary (Techny, Ill.); ord. priest Mar. 20, 1936; ord. first bishop of Goroko, New Guinea, Mar. 11, 1967.

Collins, Thomas Patrick, M.M.: b. Jan. 13, 1915, San Francisco, Calif.; educ. Maryknoll Seminary (Maryknoll, N.Y.); ord. priest June 21, 1942; ord. titular bishop of Sufetula and vicar apostolic of Pando, Bolivia, Mar. 7, 1961; retired 1968.

Comber, John W., M.M.: b. Mar. 12, 1906, Lawrence, Mass.; educ. St. John's Preparatory College (Danvers, Mass.), Boston College (Boston, Mass.), Maryknoll Seminary (Maryknoll, N.Y.); ord. priest Feb. 1, 1931; superior general of Maryknoll, 1956-66; ord. titular bishop of Foratiana, Apr. 9, 1959.

Connare, William G.: b. Dec. 11, 1911, Pittsburgh, Pa.; educ. Duquesne Univ. (Pittsburgh, Pa.), St. Vincent Seminary (Latrobe, Pa.); ord. priest June 14, 1936; ord. bishop of Greensburg, May 4, 1960.

Connolly, James L.: b. Nov. 15, 1894, Fall River, Mass.; educ. St. Charles College (Catonsville, Md.), St. Mary's Seminary (Baltimore, Md.), Catholic Univ. (Washington, D.C.), Louvain Univ. (Belgium); ord. priest Dec. 21, 1923; rector of St. Paul (Minn.) minor seminary 1940-43, major seminary 1943-45; ord. titular bishop of Mylasa and coadjutor of Fall River, May 24, 1945; bishop of Fall River, May 17, 1951; resigned Oct. 30, 1970.

Connolly, Thomas Arthur: b. Oct. 5, 1899, San Francisco, Calif.; educ. St. Patrick's Seminary (Menlo Park, Calif.), Catholic Univ. (Washington, D.C.); ord. priest June 11, 1926; ord. titular bishop of Sila and auxiliary bishop of San Francisco, Aug. 24, 1939; app. coadjutor bishop of Seattle, Feb. 28, 1948; succeeded as bishop of Seattle, May 18, 1950; first archbishop of Seattle, June 23, 1951.

Connolly, Thomas J.: b. July 18, 1922, Tonopah, Nev.; educ. St. Patrick's Seminary (Menlo Park, Calif.), Catholic Univ. (Washington, D.C.), Lateran Univ. (Rome); ord. priest Apr. 8, 1947; ord. bishop of Baker, June 30, 1971.

Cooke, Terence J.: (See Cardinals, Biographies.)

Coscia, Benedict Dominic, O.F.M.: b. Aug. 10, 1922, Brooklyn, N.Y.; educ. St. Francis College (Brooklyn, N.Y.), Holy Name College (Washington, D.C.); ord. priest June 11, 1949; ord. bishop of Jatai, Brazil, Sept. 21, 1961.

Cosgrove, William M.: b. Nov. 26, 1916, Canton, Ohio; educ. John Carroll Univ. (Cleveland, O.); ord. priest Dec. 18, 1943; ord. titular bishop of Trisipa and auxiliary bishop of Cleveland, Sept. 3, 1968.

Costello, Joseph A.: b. May 9, 1915, Newark, N.J.; educ. Seton Hall Univ. (S. Orange, N.J.), Immaculate Conception Seminary (Darlington, N.J.); ord. priest June 7, 1941; ord. titular bishop of Choma and auxiliary bishop of Newark, Jan. 24, 1963.

Cotey, Bernard R., S.D.S.: b. June 15, 1921, Milwaukee, Wis.; educ. Divine Savior Seminary (Lanham, Md.), Marquette Univ. (Milwaukee, Wis.); ord. priest June 7, 1949; ord. first bishop of Nachingwea, Tanzania, Oct. 20, 1963.

Cousins, William E.: b. Aug. 20, 1902, Chicago, Ill.; educ. Quigley Seminary (Chicago, Ill.), St. Mary of the Lake Seminary (Mundelein, Ill.); ord. priest Apr. 23, 1927; ord. titular bishop of Forma and auxiliary bishop of Chicago, Mar. 7, 1949; app. bishop of Peoria,

May 21, 1952; archbishop of Milwaukee, Jan. 27, 1959.

Cowley, Leonard P.: b. Feb. 3, 1913, St. Paul, Minn.; educ. Nazareth Hall Seminary and St. Paul Seminary (St. Paul, Minn.); ord. priest June 4, 1938; ord. titular bishop of Pertusa and auxiliary bishop of St. Paul, Jan. 29, 1958; title changed to St. Paul and Minneapolis, 1966.

Cronin, Daniel A.: b. Nov. 14, 1927, Newton, Mass.; educ. St. John's Seminary (Boston, Mass.), North American College and Gregorian Univ. (Rome); ord. priest Dec. 20, 1952; attaché apostolic nunciature (Addis Ababa), 1957-61; served in papal Secretariat of State, 1961-68; ord. titular bishop of Egnatia and auxiliary bishop of Boston, Sept. 12, 1968; bishop of Fall River, Dec. 16, 1970.

Crowley, Joseph R.: b. Jan. 12, 1915, Fort Wayne, Ind.; educ. St. Mary's College (St. Mary, Ky.), St. Meinrad Seminary (St. Meinrad, Ind.); served in US Air Force, 1942-46; ord. priest May 1, 1953; editor of *Our Sunday Visitor* 1958-67; ord. titular bishop of Maraguis and auxiliary bishop of Fort Wayne-South Bend, Aug. 24, 1971; named vicar general and diocesan director of religious education, Feb. 1, 1972.

Cunningham, David F.: b. Dec. 3, 1900, Walkerville, Mont.; educ. St. Michael's College (Toronto, Canada), St. Bernard's Seminary (Rochester, N.Y.), Catholic Univ. (Washington, D.C.); ord. priest June 12, 1926; ord. titular bishop of Lampsacus and auxiliary bishop of Syracuse, June 8, 1950; app. coadjutor bishop of Syracuse with right of succession, 1967; bishop of Syracuse, Aug. 4, 1970.

Curtis, Walter W.: b. May 3, 1913, Jersey City, N.J.; educ. Fordham Univ. (New York City), Seton Hall Univ. (South Orange, N.J.), Immaculate Conception Seminary (Darlington, N.J.), North American College and Gregorian Univ. (Rome), Catholic Univ. (Washington, D.C.); ord. priest Dec. 8, 1937; ord. titular bishop of Bisica and auxiliary bishop of Newark, Sept. 24, 1957; app. bishop of Bridgeport, 1961, installed Nov. 21, 1961.

D

Daley, Joseph T.: b. Dec. 21, 1915, Connerton, Pa.; educ. St. Charles Borromeo Seminary (Philadelphia, Pa.); ord. priest June 7, 1941; ord. titular bishop of Barca and auxiliary bishop of Harrisburg, Pa., Jan. 7, 1964; coadjutor bishop of Harrisburg, Aug. 2, 1967; bishop of Harrisburg, Oct. 19, 1971.

Danglmayr, Augustine: b. Dec. 11, 1898, Muenster, Tex.; educ. Subiaco College (Arkansas), St. Mary's Seminary (La Porte, Tex.), Kenrick Seminary (St. Louis, Mo.); ord. priest June 10, 1922; ord. titular bishop of Olba, Oct. 7, 1942; auxiliary bishop of Dallas-Ft. Worth, 1942-69.

D'Antonio Salza, Nicholas, O.F.M.: b. July 10, 1916, Rochester, N.Y.; educ. St. Anthony's Friary (Catskill, N.Y.); ord. priest June 7, 1942; ord. titular bishop of Giufi Salaria and prelate of Olancho, Honduras, July 25, 1966.

Dargin, Edward Vincent: b. Apr. 25, 1898, New York, N.Y.; educ. Fordham Univ. (New York City), St. Joseph Seminary (Dunwoodie, N.Y.), Catholic Univ. (Washington, D.C.); ord. priest Sept. 23, 1922; ord. titular bishop of Amphipolis and auxiliary bishop of New York, Oct. 5, 1953; app. episcopal vicar, 1966.

Davis, James Peter: b. June 9, 1904, Houghton, Mich.; educ. St. Joseph's College (Mountain View, Calif.), St. Patrick's Seminary (Menlo Park, Calif.); ord. priest May 19, 1929; ord. bishop of San Juan, Puerto Rico, Oct. 6, 1943; app. first archbishop of San Juan, July 30, 1960; app. archbishop of Santa Fe, installed Feb. 25, 1964.

Dearden, John Francis: (See Cardinals, Biographies.)

De Falco, Lawrence M.: b. Aug. 25, 1915, McKeesport, Pa.; educ. St. Vincent's College (Latrobe, Pa.), St. John's Seminary (Little Rock, Ark.), Gregorian Univ. (Rome); ord. priest June 11, 1942; ord. bishop of Amarillo, May 30, 1963.

Deksnys, Anthony L.: b. May 9, 1906, Buteniskis, Lithuania; educ. Metropolitan Seminary and Theological and Philosophical Faculty at Vytautas the Great Univ. (all at Kaunas, Lithuania), Univ. of Fribourg (Switzerland); ord. priest May 30, 1931; served in US parishes at Mt. Carmel, Pa., and East St. Louis, Ill.; ord. titular bishop of Lavellum, June 15, 1969; assigned to pastoral work among Lithuanians in Western Europe.

Dempsey, Michael J., O.P.: b. Feb. 22, 1912, Providence, R.I.; entered Order of Preachers (Dominicans), Chicago province, 1935; ord. priest June 11, 1942; ord. bishop of Sokoto, Nigeria, Aug. 15, 1967.

Dempsey, Michael R.: b. Sept. 10, 1918, Chicago, Ill.; educ. St. Mary of the Lake Seminary (Mundelein, Ill.); ord. priest May 1, 1943; ord. titular bishop of Truentum and auxiliary bishop of Chicago, June 13, 1968; first national director of US Bishops' Campaign for Human Development, 1970.

Denning, Joseph P.: b. Jan. 4, 1907, Flushing, L. I.; educ. Cathedral College (Brooklyn, N. Y.), Immaculate Conception Seminary (Huntington, L. I.), St. Mary's Seminary (Baltimore, Md.); ord. priest May 21, 1932; ord. titular bishop of Mallus and auxiliary bishop of Brooklyn, Apr. 22, 1959.

De Palma, Joseph A., S.C.J.: b. Sept. 4, 1913, Walton, N. Y.; ord. priest May 20, 1944; superior general of Congregation of Priests of the Sacred Heart, 1959-67; ord. first bishop of De Aar, South Africa, July 19, 1967.

Dimmerling, Harold J.: b. Sept. 23, 1914, Braddock, Pa.; educ. St. Fidelis Preparatory Seminary (Herman, Pa.), St. Charles Semi-

nary (Columbus, O.), St. Francis Seminary (Loretto, Pa.); ord. priest May 2, 1940; ord. bishop of Rapid City, Oct. 30, 1969.

Dingman, Maurice J.: b. Jan. 20, 1914, St. Paul, Ia.; educ. St. Ambrose College (Davenport, Ia.), North American College and Gregorian Univ. (Rome), Catholic Univ. (Washington, D. C.); ord. priest Dec. 8, 1939; ord. bishop of Des Moines, June 19, 1968.

Donaghy, Frederick Anthony, M.M.: b. Jan. 13, 1903, New Bedford, Mass.; educ. Holy Cross College (Worcester, Mass.), St. Mary's Seminary (Baltimore, Md.), Maryknoll Seminary (Maryknoll, N. Y.); ord. priest Jan. 29, 1929; ord. titular bishop of Setea and vicar apostolic of Wuchow, China, Sept. 21, 1939; title changed to bishop of Wuchow, Apr. 11, 1946; expelled by Communists.

Donahue, Stephen Joseph: b. Dec. 10, 1893, New York, N. Y.; educ. Cathedral College (New York, N. Y.), St. Joseph's Seminary (Dunwoodie, N. Y.), North American College (Rome); ord. priest May 22, 1918; ord. titular bishop of Medea and auxiliary bishop of New York, May 1, 1934. Retired.

Donnellan, Thomas A.: b. Jan. 24, 1914, New York, N. Y.; educ. Cathedral College and St. Joseph's Seminary (New York, N.Y.), Catholic Univ. (Washington, D. C.); ord. priest June 3, 1939; ord. bishop of Ogdensburg, Apr. 9, 1964; app. archbishop of Atlanta, installed July 16, 1968.

Donnelly, Joseph F.: b. May 1, 1909, Norwich, Conn.; educ. St. Mary's Seminary and Univ. (Baltimore, Md.), Catholic Univ. (Washington, D.C.), Fairfield Univ. (Fairfield, Conn.); ord. priest June 29, 1934; director of Hartford Archdiocesan Labor Institute, 1942-65; chairman of Connecticut State Board of Mediation and Arbitration 1949-65; ord. titular bishop of Nabala and auxiliary bishop of Hartford, Jan. 28, 1965.

Donohoe, Hugh A.: b. June 28, 1905, San Francisco, Calif.; educ. St. Patrick's Preparatory and Major Seminaries (Menlo Park, Calif.), Catholic Univ. (Washington, D. C.); ord. priest June 14, 1930; ord. titular bishop of Taium and auxiliary bishop of San Francisco, Oct. 7, 1947; app. first bishop of Stockton, Jan. 27, 1962; app. bishop of Fresno, Aug. 27, 1969, installed Oct. 7, 1969.

Donovan, John A.: b. Aug. 5, 1911, Chatham, Ont., Canada; educ. Sacred Heart Seminary (Detroit, Mich.), North American College and Gregorian Univ. (Rome); ord. priest Dec. 8, 1935; ord. titular bishop of Rhasus and auxiliary bishop of Detroit, Oct. 26, 1954; app. bishop of Toledo, installed Apr. 18, 1967.

Donovan, Paul V.: b. Sept. 1, 1924, Bernard, Iowa; educ. St. Gregory's Seminary (Cincinnati, Ohio), Mt. St. Mary's Seminary (Norwood, Ohio), Lateran Univ. (Rome); ord. priest May 20, 1950; ord. first bishop of Kalamazoo, Mich., July 21, 1971.

Dougherty, John J.: b. Sept. 16, 1907, Jersey City, N. J.; educ. Seton Hall Univ. (S. Orange, N. J.), Immaculate Conception Seminary (Darlington, N. J.), North American College, Gregorian Univ., Pontifical Biblical Institute (Rome); ord. priest July 23, 1933; ord. titular bishop of Cotenna and auxiliary bishop of Newark, Jan. 24, 1963.

Dozier, Carroll T.: b. Aug. 18, 1911, Richmond, Va.; educ. Holy Cross College (Worcester, Mass.), Gregorian Univ. (Rome); ord. priest, Mar. 19, 1937, Rome; ord. first bishop of Memphis, Jan. 6, 1971.

Driscoll, Justin A.: b. Sept. 30, 1920, Bernard, Ia.; educ. Loras College (Dubuque, Ia.), Catholic Univ. (Washington, D. C.); ord. priest July 28, 1945; president of Loras College, 1967-70; ord. bishop of Fargo, Oct. 28, 1970.

Drury, Thomas J.: b. Jan. 4, 1908, Co. Sligo, Ireland; educ. St. Benedict's College (Atchison, Kans.), Kenrick Seminary (St. Louis, Mo.); ord. priest June 2, 1935; ord. first bishop of San Angelo, Tex., Jan. 24, 1962; app. bishop of Corpus Christi, installed Sept. 1, 1965.

Dudick, Michael J.: b. Feb. 24, 1916, St. Clair, Pa.; educ. St. Procopius College and Seminary (Lisle, Ill.); ord. priest Nov. 13, 1945; ord. bishop of Byzantine Rite Eparchy of Passaic, Oct. 24, 1968.

Duhart, Clarence James, C.SS.R.: b. Mar. 23, 1912, New Orleans, La.; ord. priest June 29, 1937; ord. bishop of Udon Thani, Thailand, Apr. 21, 1966.

Dunn, Francis J.: b. Mar. 22, 1922, Elkader, Ia.; educ. Loras College (Dubuque, Ia), Kenrick Seminary (St. Louis, Mo.), Angelicum (Rome, Italy); ord. priest Jan. 11, 1948; chancellor of Dubuque, Aug. 27, 1960; ord. titular bishop of Turris Tamallani and auxiliary bishop of Dubuque, Aug. 27, 1969, app. vicar general, Aug. 28, 1969.

Durick, Joseph Aloysius: b. Oct. 13, 1914, Dayton, Tenn.; educ. St. Bernard Minor Seminary (St. Bernard, Ala.), St. Mary's Seminary (Baltimore, Md.), Urban Univ. (Rome); ord. priest May 23, 1940; ord. titular bishop of Cerbal and auxiliary bishop of Mobile-Birmingham, Mar. 24, 1955; app. coadjutor bishop of Nashville, Tenn., installed Mar. 3, 1964; apostolic administrator, 1966; bishop of Nashville, Sept. 10, 1969.

Durning, Dennis V., C.S.Sp.: b. May 18, 1923, Germantown, Pa.; educ. St. Mary's Seminary (Ferndale, Conn.); ord. priest June 3, 1949; ord. first bishop of Arusha, Tanzania, May 28, 1963.

Dworschak, Leo F.: b. Apr. 6, 1900, Independence, Wis.; educ. St. John's Univ. (Collegeville, Minn.), Catholic Univ. (Washington, D.C.); ord. priest May 29, 1926; ord. titular bishop of Tium and coadjutor bishop of Rapid City, Aug. 22, 1946; app. auxiliary bishop of Fargo, Apr. 10, 1947; bishop of Fargo, May 10, 1960; retired, 1970.

Dwyer, Robert Joseph: b. Aug. 1, 1908, Salt Lake City, Utah; educ. St. Patrick's Seminary (Menlo Park, Calif.), Catholic Univ. (Washington, D.C.); ord. priest June 11, 1932; ord. bishop of Reno, Aug. 5, 1952; app. archbishop of Portland, Ore., Dec. 14, 1966, installed Feb. 6, 1967.

E

Elko, Nicholas T.: b. Dec. 14, 1909, Donora, Pa.; educ. Duquesne Univ. (Pittsburgh, Pa.), Seminary of Uzhorod (Czechoslovakia); ord. priest Sept. 30, 1934; ord. titular bishop of Apollonias and apostolic administrator of Byzantine-Rite exarchy of Pittsburgh, Mar. 6, 1955; succeeded as exarch of Pittsburgh, Sept. 5, 1955; became eparch when Pittsburgh was raised to eparchy, July, 1963; app. titular archbishop of Dara, 1967, and ordaining prelate for Byzantine Rite in Rome; head of Oriental liturgical commission; app. auxiliary bishop of Cincinnati, Aug. 10, 1971.

Elwell, Clarence E.: b. Feb. 4, 1904, Cleveland, O.; educ. John Carroll Univ. and St. Mary's Seminary (Cleveland, O.), Univ. of Innsbruck (Austria), Western Reserve Univ. (Cleveland, O.), Harvard Univ. (Cambridge, Mass.); ord. priest Mar. 17, 1929; ord. titular bishop of Cone and auxiliary bishop of Cleveland, Dec. 21, 1962; app. bishop of Columbus, 1968, installed Aug. 22, 1968.

Etteldorf, Raymond P.: b. Aug. 12, 1911, Ossian, Ia.; educ. Loras College (Dubuque, Ia.), Gregorian Univ. (Rome); ord. priest Dec. 8, 1937; secretary general of Supreme Council for direction of Pontifical Missionary Works, 1964-68; secretary of Pontifical Commission for Economic Affairs, 1968-69; ord. titular archbishop of Tindari, Jan. 6, 1969; apostolic delegate to New Zealand and the Pacific Islands.

Evans, George R.: b. Sept. 25, 1922, Denver, Colo.; educ. Notre Dame Univ. (Notre Dame, Ind.), St. Thomas Seminary (Denver, Colo.), Apollinare Univ. (Rome, Italy); ord. priest May 31, 1947; ord. titular bishop of Tubyza and auxiliary bishop of Denver, Apr. 23, 1969.

F

Fearns, John M.: b. June 25, 1897, New York, N.Y.; educ. St. Joseph's Seminary (Yonkers, N.Y.), North American College and Gregorian Univ. (Rome); ord. priest Feb. 19, 1922; ord. titular bishop of Geras and auxiliary bishop of New York, Dec. 10, 1957; app. episcopal vicar, 1966.

Fedders, Edward L., M.M.: b. Dec. 4, 1913, Covington, Ky.; educ. Maryknoll Seminary (Maryknoll, N.Y.); ord. priest June 11, 1944; ord. titular bishop of Antiochia ad Meandrum and prelate of Juli, Peru, Dec. 12, 1963.

Federal, Joseph Lennox: b. Jan. 13, 1910, Greensboro, N.C.; educ. Belmont Abbey College (Belmont Abbey, N.C.), Niagara Univ. (Niagara Falls, N.Y.), Univ. of Fribourg (Switzerland), North American College and Gregorian Univ. (Rome); ord. priest Dec. 8, 1934; ord. titular bishop of Appiaria and auxiliary bishop of Salt Lake City, Apr. 11, 1951; app. coadjutor with right of succession, May, 1958; bishop of Salt Lake City, Mar. 31, 1960.

Fitzpatrick, John J.: b. Oct. 12, 1918, Trenton, Ont., Canada; educ. Urban Univ. (Rome), Our Lady of the Angels Seminary (Niagara Falls, N.Y.); ord. priest Dec. 13, 1942; ord. titular bishop of Cenae and auxiliary bishop of Miami, Aug. 28, 1968; bishop of Brownsville, Tex., May 28, 1971.

Flaherty, J. Louis: b. May 13, 1910, Norfolk, Va.; educ. Holy Cross College (Worcester, Mass.), North American College and Gregorian Univ. (Rome), Catholic Univ. (Washington, D.C.); ord. priest Dec. 8, 1936; ord. titular bishop of Tabuda and auxiliary bishop of Richmond, Oct. 5, 1966.

Flanagan, Bernard Joseph: b. Mar. 31, 1908, Proctor, Vt.; educ. Holy Cross College (Worcester, Mass.), North American College (Rome), Catholic Univ. (Washington, D.C.); ord. priest Dec. 8, 1931; ord. first bishop of Norwich, Nov. 30, 1953; app. bishop of Worcester, installed, Sept. 24, 1959.

Flannelly, Joseph F.: b. Oct. 22, 1894, New York, N.Y.; educ. Cathedral College (New York), St. Joseph's Seminary (Dunwoodie, N.Y.); ord. priest Sept. 1, 1918; ord. titular bishop of Metelis and auxiliary bishop of New York, Dec. 16, 1948. Retired.

Flavin, Glennon P.: b. Mar. 2, 1916, St. Louis, Mo.; educ. Kenrick Seminary (St. Louis, Mo.); ord. priest Dec. 20, 1941; ord. titular bishop of Joannina and auxiliary bishop of St. Louis, May 30, 1957; app. bishop of Lincoln, installed Aug. 17, 1967.

Fletcher, Albert Lewis: b. Oct. 28, 1896, Little Rock, Ark.; educ. Little Rock College and St. John's Seminary (Little Rock, Ark.); ord. priest June 4, 1920; ord. titular bishop of Samos and auxiliary bishop of Little Rock, Apr. 25, 1940; bishop of Little Rock, Dec. 7, 1946; resigned July 4, 1972.

Flores, Patrick F.: b. July 26, 1929, Ganado, Tex.; educ. St. Mary's Seminary (Houston, Tex.); ord. priest May 26, 1956; ord. titular bishop of Itolica and auxiliary bishop of San Antonio, May 5, 1970; first Mexican-American bishop.

Foery, Walter Andrew: b. July 6, 1890, Rochester, N.Y.; educ. St. Andrew's Preparatory Seminary and St. Bernard's Seminary (Rochester, N.Y.); ord. priest June 10, 1916; ord. bishop of Syracuse, Aug. 18, 1937; resigned 1970.

Forst, Marion F.: b. Sept. 3, 1910, St. Louis, Mo.; educ. St. Louis Preparatory Seminary (St. Louis, Mo.), Kenrick Seminary (Webster Groves, Mo.); ord. priest June 10, 1934; ord. bishop of Dodge City, Mar. 24, 1960.

Franz, John B.: b. Oct. 29, 1896, Spring-field, Ill.; educ. Quincy College (Quincy, Ill.), Kenrick Seminary (Webster Groves, Mo.), Catholic Univ. (Washington, D.C.); ord. priest June 13, 1920; ord. first bishop of Dodge City, Aug. 29, 1951; app. bishop of Peoria, installed Nov. 4, 1959; resigned May 24, 1971.

Freking, Frederick W.: b. Aug. 11, 1913, Heron Lake, Minn.; educ. St. Mary's College (Winona, Minn.), North American College and Gregorian Univ. (Rome), Catholic Univ. (Washington, D.C.); ord. priest July 31, 1938; ord. bishop of Salina, Nov. 30, 1957; app. bishop of La Crosse, Dec. 30, 1964, installed Feb. 24, 1965.

Frey, Gerard L.: b. May 10, 1914, New Orleans, La.; educ. Notre Dame Seminary (New Orleans, La.); ord. priest Apr. 2, 1938; ord. bishop of Savannah, Aug. 8, 1967.

Frosi, Angelo, S. X.: b. Jan. 31, 1924, Baffano Cremona, Italy; ord. priest May 6, 1948; ord. titular bishop of Magneto, May 1, 1970, and prelate of Abaete do Tocantins, Brazil.

Furey, Francis J.: b. Feb. 22, 1905, Summit Hill, Pa.; educ. St. Charles Borromeo Seminary (Overbrook, Pa.), Pontifical Major Roman Seminary (Rome); ord. priest Mar. 15, 1930; ord. titular bishop of Temnus and auxiliary bishop of Philadelphia, Dec. 22, 1960; app. coadjutor bishop of San Diego with right of succession, July, 1963; bishop of San Diego, 1966-69; archbishop of San Antonio, Aug. 6, 1969.

Furlong, Philip J.: b. Dec. 8, 1892, New York, N.Y.; educ. Cathedral College (New York, N.Y.), St. Joseph's Seminary (Yonkers, N.Y.); ord. priest May 18, 1918; ord. titular bishop of Araxa and auxiliary to military vicar, Jan. 25, 1956.

G

Gabro, Jaroslav: b. July 31, 1919, Chicago, Ill.; educ. St. Procopius College (Lisle, Ill.), St. Charles College (Catonsville, Md.), St. Basil's College (Stamford, Conn.), St. Josaphat's Seminary and Catholic Univ. (Washington, D.C.); ord. priest Sept. 27, 1945; ord. first eparch of the eparchy of St. Nicholas of the Ukrainians, in Chicago, Oct. 26, 1961, installed Dec. 12, 1961.

Gallagher, Raymond J.: b. Nov. 19, 1912, Cleveland, Ohio; educ. John Carroll Univ. and Our Lady of the Lake Seminary (Cleveland, O.); ord. priest Mar. 25, 1939; secretary of the National Conference of Catholic Charities 1961-65; ord. bishop of Lafayette in Indiana, Aug. 11, 1965.

Gelineau, Louis E.: b. 1929, Burlington, Vt.; educ. St. Michael's College (Winooski, Vt.), St. Paul's Univ. Seminary (Ottawa, Ont.), Catholic Univ. (Washington, D.C.); ord. priest June 5, 1954; ord. bishop of Burlington, Jan. 26, 1972.

Gerbermann, Hugo, M.M.: b. Sept. 11, 1913, Nada, Tex.; educ. St. John's Minor and Major Seminary (San Antonio, Tex.), Maryknoll Seminary (Maryknoll, N.Y.); ord. priest Feb. 7, 1943; missionary work in Ecuador and Guatemala; ord. titular bishop of Amathus and prelate of Huehuetenango, Guatemala, July 22, 1962; first bishop of Huehuetenango, Dec. 23, 1967.

Gerety, Peter L.: b. July 19, 1912, Shelton, Conn.; educ. Sulpician Seminary (Paris, France); ord. priest June 29, 1939; ord. titular bishop of Crepedula and coadjutor bishop of Portland, Me., with right of succession, June 1, 1966; app. apostolic administrator of Portland, 1967; bishop of Portland, Sept. 15, 1969.

Gerow, Richard Oliver: b. May 3, 1885, Mobile, Ala.; educ. McGill Institute (Mobile, Ala.), Mt. St. Mary's College (Emmitsburg, Md.), North American College (Rome); ord. priest June 5, 1909; ord. bishop of Natchez-Jackson, Oct. 15, 1924; retired from active administration of diocese, 1966; resigned, 1967.

Gerrard, James J.: b. June 9, 1897, New Bedford, Mass.; educ. St. Laurent College (Montreal, Que.), St. Bernard's Seminary (Rochester, N.Y.); ord. priest May 26, 1923; ord. titular bishop of Forma and auxiliary bishop of Fall River, Mar. 19, 1959.

Gill, Thomas E.: b. Mar. 18, 1908, Seattle, Wash.; educ. St. Joseph's Preparatory Seminary (Mountain View, Calif.), St. Patrick Seminary (Menlo Park, Calif.), Catholic Univ. (Washington, D.C.); ord. priest June 10, 1933; ord. titular bishop of Lambaesis and auxiliary bishop of Seattle, May 31, 1956.

Gleeson, Francis D., S.J.: b. Jan. 17, 1895, Carrollton, Mo.: educ. Mount St. Michael's Scholasticate (Spokane, Wash.), St. Francis Xavier College (Ona, Spain); entered the Society of Jesus, 1912; ord. priest July 29, 1926; ord. titular bishop of Cotenna and vicar apostolic of Alaska, Apr. 5, 1948; first bishop of Fairbanks, Aug. 8, 1962; retired Nov. 15, 1968.

Glenn, Laurence A,: b. Aug. 25, 1900, Bellingham, Wash.; educ. St. John's Univ. (Collegeville, Catholic Univ. (Washington, D.C.); ord. priest June 11, 1927; ord. titular bishop of Tuscamia and auxiliary bishop of Duluth, Sept. 12, 1956; app. bishop of Crookston, Jan. 27, 1960, installed Apr. 20, 1960; resigned 1970.

Glennie, Ignatius T., S.J.: b. Feb. 5, 1907, Mexico City; educ. Mt. St. Michael's Scholasticate (Spokane, Wash.), Pontifical Seminary (Kandy, Ceylon), St. Mary's College (Kurdeong, India); entered Society of Jesus, 1924; ord. priest Nov. 21, 1938; ord. bishop of Trincomalee, Ceylon, Sept. 21, 1947; title of see changed to Trincomalee-Batticaloa, 1967.

Gorman, Thomas Kiely: b. Aug. 30, 1892, Pasadena, Calif.; educ. St. Mary's Seminary (Baltimore, Md.), Catholic Univ. (Washington, D.C.), Louvain Univ. (Belgium); ord. priest June 23, 1917; ord. bishop of Reno, July 22, 1931; installed as titular bishop of Rhasus and coadjutor bishop of Dallas-Fort Worth, with right of succession, May 8, 1952; bishop of Dallas-Fort Worth, Aug. 20, 1954; resigned 1969.

Gossman, F. Joseph: b. Apr. 1, 1930, Baltimore, Md.: educ. St. Charles College (Catonsville, Md.), St. Mary's Seminary (Baltimore, Md.), North American College (Rome), Catholic Univ. (Washington, D.C.); ord. priest Dec. 17, 1955; ord. titular bishop of Agunto and auxiliary bishop of Baltimore, Sept. 11, 1968; named urban vicar, June 13, 1970.

Gottwald, George J.: b. May 12, 1914, St. Louis, Mo.; educ. Kenrick Seminary (Webster Groves, Mo.); ord. priest June 9, 1940; ord. titular bishop of Cedamusa and auxiliary bishop of St. Louis, Aug. 8, 1961.

Gracida, Rene H.: b. 1924, New Orleans, La.; educ. Rice Univ. and Univ. of Houston (Houston, Tex.), Univ. of Fribourg (Switzerland); ord. priest May 23, 1959; ord. titular bishop of Masuccaba and auxiliary bishop of Miami, Jan. 25, 1972.

Grady, Thomas J.: b. Oct. 9, 1914, Chicago, Ill.; educ. St. Mary of the Lake Seminary (Mundelein, Ill.), Gregorian Univ. (Rome), Loyola Univ. (Chicago, Ill.); ord. priest Apr. 23, 1938; ord. titular bishop of Vamalla and auxiliary bishop of Chicago, Aug. 24, 1967.

Graham, John J.: Sept. 11, 1913, Philadelphia, Pa.; educ. St. Charles Borromeo Seminary (Philadelphia, Pa.), Pontifical Roman Seminary (Rome, Italy); ord. priest Feb. 26, 1938; ord. titular bishop of Sabrata and auxiliary bishop of Philadelphia, Jan. 7, 1964.

Graner, Lawrence A., C.S.C.: b. Apr. 3, 1901, Franklin, Pa.; educ. Holy Cross Seminary (Notre Dame, Ind.), Holy Cross Mission Seminary (Washington, D.C.); entered Congregation of the Holy Cross, 1924; ord. priest June 24, 1928; ord. bishop of Dacca, India, Apr. 23, 1947; title changed to archbishop of Dacca, July 15, 1950; retired 1967.

Graves, Lawrence P.: b. May 4, 1916, Texarkana, Ark.; educ. St. John's Seminary (Little Rock, Ark.), North American College (Rome), Catholic Univ. (Washington, D.C.); ord. priest June 11, 1942; ord. titular bishop of Vina and auxiliary bishop of Little Rock, Apr. 25, 1969.

Graziano, Lawrence, O.F.M.: b. Apr. 5, 1921, Mt. Vernon, N.Y.; educ. Mt. Alvernia Seminary (Wappingers Falls, N.Y.); ord. priest Jan. 26, 1947; ord. titular bishop of Limata and auxiliary bishop of Santa Ana, El Salvador, Sept. 21, 1961; app. coadjutor bishop of San Miguel, El Salvador, with right of succession, 1965; bishop of San Miguel, Jan. 10, 1968; resigned, 1969; assigned titular see of Valabria.

Greco, Charles Paschal: b. Oct. 29, 1894, Rodney, Miss.; educ. St. Joseph's Seminary (St. Benedict, La.), Louvain Univ. (Belgium), Dominican Univ. (Fribourg, Switzerland); ord. priest July 25, 1918; ord. bishop of Alexandria Feb. 25, 1946.

Green, Francis J.: b. July 7, 1906, Corning, N.Y.; educ. St. Patrick's Seminary (Menlo Park, Calif.); ord. priest May 15, 1932; ord. titular bishop of Serra and auxiliary bishop of Tucson, Sept. 17, 1953; named coadjutor of Tucson with right of succession, May 11, 1960; bishop of Tucson, Oct. 26, 1960.

Green, Joseph: b. Oct. 13, 1917, St. Joseph, Mich.; educ. St. Joseph Seminary (Grand Rapids, Mich.). St. Gregory Seminary (Cincinnati, O.), St. Mary's Seminary (Norwood, O.), Lateran Univ. (Rome); ord. priest July 14, 1946; ord. titular bishop of Trisipa and auxiliary bishop of Lansing, Aug. 28, 1962; app. bishop of Reno, installed May 25, 1967.

Grellinger, John B.: b. Nov. 5, 1899, Milwaukee, Wis.; educ. Marquette Univ. and St. Francis Seminary (Milwaukee, Wis.), Urban Univ. and Gregorian Univ. (Rome); ord. priest July 14, 1929; ord. titular bishop of Syene and auxiliary bishop of Green Bay, July 14, 1949.

Greteman, Frank H.: b. Dec. 25, 1907, Willey, Ia.; educ. Loras Academy and Loras College (Dubuque, Ia.), North American College (Rome), Catholic Univ. (Washington, D.C.); ord. priest Dec. 8, 1932; ord. titular bishop of Vissalsa and auxiliary bishop of Sioux City, May 26, 1965; bishop of Sioux City, Dec. 9, 1970.

Grutka, Andrew G.: b. Nov. 17, 1908, Joliet, Ill.; educ. St. Procopius College and Seminary (Lisle, Ill.), Urban Univ. and Gregorian Univ. (Rome); ord. priest Dec. 5, 1933; app. moderator of lay activities in Gary diocese, 1955; ord. first bishop of Gary, Feb. 25, 1957; app. member of Pontifical Marian Academy, Jan. 5, 1970; elected president of Catholic Communications Foundation, Jan. 6, 1971.

Guilfoyle, George H.: b. Nov. 13, 1913, New York, N.Y.; educ. Georgetown Univ. (Washington, D.C.), Fordham Univ. (New York City), St. Joseph's Seminary (Dunwoodie, N.Y.), Columbia Univ. (New York City); ord. priest Mar. 25, 1944; ord. titular bishop of Marazane and auxiliary bishop of New York, Nov. 30, 1964; app. bishop of Camden, installed Mar. 4, 1968.

Guilfoyle, Merlin J.: b. July 15, 1908, San Francisco, Calif.; educ. St. Joseph's College (Mountain View, Calif.), St. Patrick's Seminary (Menlo Park, Calif.), Catholic Univ. (Washington, D.C.$; ord. priest June 10, 1933; ord. titular bishop of Bulla and auxiliary bishop of San Francisco, Sept. 21, 1950; app. bishop of Stockton, Nov. 19, 1969, installed Jan. 13, 1970.

Gumbleton, Thomas J.: b. Jan. 26, 1930, Detroit, Mich.; educ. St. John Provincial Seminary, (Detroit, Mich.), Pontifical Lateran Univ. (Rome); ord. priest June 2, 1956; ord. titular bishop of Ululi and auxiliary bishop of Detroit, May 1, 1968.

H

Hacker, Hilary B.: b. Jan. 10, 1913, New Ulm, Minn.; educ. St. Paul Seminary (St. Paul, Minn.), Gregorian Univ. (Rome); ord. priest June 4, 1938; ord. bishop of Bismarck, N. Dak., Feb. 27, 1957.

Hackett, John F.: b. Dec. 7, 1911, New Haven, Conn.; educ. St. Thomas Seminary (Bloomfield, Conn.), Seminaire Ste. Sulpice (Paris); ord. priest June 29, 1936; ord. titular bishop of Helenopolis in Palaestina and auxiliary bishop of Hartford, Mar. 19, 1953.

Hagarty, Paul Leonard, O.S.B.: b. Mar. 20, 1909, Greene, Ia.; educ. Loras College (Dubuque, Ia.), St. John's Seminary and St. John's Univ. (Collegeville, Minn.); entered Order of St. Benedict, 1931; ord. priest June 6, 1936; ord. titular bishop of Arba and vicar apostolic of the Bahamas, Oct. 19, 1950; first bishop of Nassau, July 5, 1960.

Ham, J. Richard, M.M.: b. July 11, 1921, Chicago, Ill.; educ. Maryknoll Seminary (New York); ord. priest June 12, 1948; missionary to Guatemala, 1958; ord. titular bishop of Puzia di Numidia and auxiliary bishop of Guatemala, Jan. 6, 1968.

Hammes, George A.: b. Sept. 11, 1911, St. Joseph Ridge, Wis.; educ. St. Lawrence Seminary (Mt. Calvary. Wis.), St. Louis Preparatory Seminary (St. Louis, Mo.), Kenrick Seminary (Webster Groves, Mo.), Sulpician Seminary, Catholic Univ. (Washington, D.C.); ord. priest May 22, 1937; ord. bishop of Superior, May 24, 1960.

Hannan, Philip M.: b. May 20, 1913, Washington, D.C.; educ. St. Charles College (Catonsville, Md.), Catholic Univ. (Washington, D.C.), North American College (Rome); ord. priest Dec. 8, 1939; ord. titular bishop of Hieropolis and auxiliary bishop of Washington, D.C., Aug. 28, 1956; app. archbishop of New Orleans, installed Oct. 13, 1965.

Harper, Edward, C.SS.R.: b. July 23, 1910, Brooklyn, N.Y.; educ. Redemptorist Houses of Study; ord. priest June 18, 1939; ord. titular bishop of Heraclea Pontica and first prelate of Virgin Islands, Oct. 6, 1960.

Harrington, Timothy J.: b. Dec. 19, 1918, Holyoke, Mass.; educ. Holy Cross College (Worcester, Mass.), Grand Seminary (Montreal, Que.), Boston College School of Social Work; ord. priest Jan. 19, 1946; ord. titular bishop of Rusuca and auxiliary bishop of Worcester, Mass., July 2, 1968.

Harris, Vincent M.: b. Oct. 14, 1913, Conroe, Tex.; educ. St. Mary's Seminary (La Porte, Tex.), North American College and Gregorian Univ. (Rome), Catholic Univ. (Washington, D.C.); ord. priest Mar. 19, 1938; ord. first bishop of Beaumont, Tex., Sept. 28, 1966; app. titular bishop of Rotaria and coadjutor bishop of Austin, Apr. 27, 1971; bishop of Austin, Nov. 15, 1971.

Harrison, Francis J.: b. Aug. 12, 1912; Syracuse, N.Y.; educ. Notre Dame Univ. (Notre Dame, Ind.), St. Bernard's Seminary (Rochester, N.Y.), ord. priest June 4, 1937; ord. titular bishop of Aquae in Numidia and auxiliary bishop of Syracuse, Apr. 22, 1971.

Hastrich, Jerome J.: b. Nov. 13, 1914, Milwaukee, Wis.; educ. Marquette Univ., St. Francis Seminary (Milwaukee, Wis.); ord. priest Feb. 9, 1941; ord. titular bishop of Gurza and auxiliary bishop of Madison, Sept. 3, 1963; app. bishop of Gallup, N.Mex., Sept. 3, 1969.

Hayes, James Thomas Gibbons, S.J.: b. Feb. 11, 1889, New York City; educ. St. Francis Xavier's College (New York City), Jesuit Novitiate (St. Andrew-on-the-Hudson, N.Y.), Jesuit House of Studies (Tronchiennes, Belgium); entered the Society of Jesus, Aug. 14, 1907; ord. priest June 29, 1921; ord. bishop of Cagayan, P.I., June 18, 1933; first archbishop of Cagayan, June 29, 1951; resigned Oct. 13, 1970.

Hayes, Nevin W., O.Carm: b. Feb. 17, 1922, Chicago, Ill.; ord. priest June 8, 1946; prelate nullius of Sicuani, Peru, 1959; ord. titular bishop of Nova Sinna and prelate of Sicuani, Aug. 5, 1965; app. auxiliary bishop of Chicago, Feb. 2, 1971.

Head, Edward D.: b. Aug. 5, 1919, White Plains, N. Y.; educ. Cathedral College, St. Joseph's Seminary, Columbia Univ. (New York City); ord. priest Jan. 27, 1945; director of New York Catholic Charities; ord. titular bishop of Ardsratha and auxiliary bishop of New York, Mar. 19, 1970.

Helmsing, Charles H.: b. Mar. 23, 1908, Shrewsbury, Mo.; educ. St. Louis Preparatory Seminary (St. Louis, Mo.), Kenrick Seminary (Webster Groves, Mo.); ord. priest June 10, 1933; ord. titular bishop of Axomis and auxiliary bishop of St. Louis, Apr. 19, 1949; first bishop of Springfield-Cape Girardeau, Aug. 24, 1956; bishop of Kansas City-St. Joseph, 1962, installed Apr. 3, 1962.

Henry, Harold W., S.S.C.: b. July 11, 1909, Northfield, Minn.; convert, 1922; educ. St. Columban's D.C.); ord. priest June 10, 1933; Seminary (Omaha, Nebr.); ord. priest Dec. 21, 1932; ord. titular bishop of Coridala and vicar apostolic of Kwang Ju, Korea, May 11, 1957; title changed to archbishop of Kwang Ju, 1962, when see was raised to metropolitan rank; transferred to titular see of Thubunae in Numidia, June 28, 1971, and app. first prefect apostolic of Cheju-Do, Korea.

Hermann, Edward J.: b. Nov. 6, 1913, Baltimore, Md.; educ. Mt. St. Mary's Seminary (Emmitsburg, Md.), Catholic Univ. (Washington, D.C.); ord. priest June 12, 1947; ord. titular bishop of Lamzella and auxiliary bishop of Washington, D.C., Apr. 26, 1966.

Heston, Edward L., C.S.C.: b. Sept. 9, 1907, Ravenna, Ohio; educ. Holy Cross and Moreau Seminaries (Notre Dame, Ind.), Gregorian Univ. (Rome); ord. priest Dec. 22, 1934; secretary of Sacred Congregation for Religious and Secular Institutes, 1969-71; president Pontifical Commission for Social Communication, 1971; ord. titular archbishop of Numidia, Feb. 13, 1972.

Hettinger, Edward Gerhard: b. Oct. 14, 1902, Lancaster, O.; educ. St. Vincent's College (Beatty, Pa.); ord. priest June 2, 1928; ord. titular bishop of Teos and auxiliary bishop of Columbus, Feb. 24, 1942.

Hickey, David F., S.J.: b. Dec. 3, 1882, St. Louis, Mo.; educ. St. Louis Univ., Jesuit Scholasticate (St. Louis Province); entered the Society of Jesus, 1902; ord. priest June 27, 1917; ord. titular bishop of Bonitza and vicar apostolic of Belize (British Honduras), Sept. 21, 1948; title changed to bishop of Belize, Feb. 29, 1956; resigned Aug. 1, 1957, assigned titular see of Cabasa.

Hickey, Dennis W.: b. Oct. 28, 1914, Dansville, N. Y.; educ. Colgate Univ. and St. Bernard's Seminary (Rochester, N. Y.); ord. priest June 7, 1941; ord. titular bishop of Rusuccuru and auxiliary bishop of Rochester, N. Y., Mar. 14, 1968.

Hickey, James A.: b. Oct. 11, 1920, Midland, Mich.; educ. Sacred Heart Seminary (Detroit, Mich.), Catholic Univ. (Washington, D. C.), Lateran Univ. and Angelicum (Rome), Michigan State Univ.; ord. priest June 15, 1946; ord. titular bishop of Taraqua and auxiliary bishop of Saginaw, Apr. 14, 1967; app. rector of North American College, Rome, 1969.

Hines, Vincent J.: b. Sept. 14, 1912, New Haven, Conn.; educ. St. Thomas Seminary (Bloomfield, Conn.), St. Sulpice Seminary (Paris), Lateran Univ. Rome); ord. priest May 2, 1937; ord. bishop of Norwich, Conn., Mar. 17, 1960.

Hoch, Lambert A.: b. Feb. 6, 1903, Elkton, S. D.; educ. Creighton Univ. (Omaha, Nebr.), St. Paul Seminary (St. Paul, Minn.); ord. priest May 30, 1928; ord. bishop of Bismarck, Mar. 25, 1952; bishop of Sioux Falls Feb. 20, 1957.

Hodapp, Robert L., S.J.: b. Oct. 1, 1910. Mankato, Minn.; educ. St. Stanislaus Seminary (Florissant, Mo.), St. Louis Univ. (St. Louis, Mo.); ord. priest June 18, 1941; ord. bishop of Belize, Br. Honduras, June 26, 1958.

Hodges, Joseph H.: b. Oct. 8, 1911, Harper's Ferry, W. Va.; educ. St. Charles College (Catonsville, Md.); North American College (Rome); ord. priest Dec. 8, 1935; ord. titular bishop of Rusadus and auxiliary bishop of Richmond, Oct. 15, 1952; named coadjutor bishop of Wheeling with right of succession, May 24, 1961; bishop of Wheeling, Nov. 23, 1962.

Hogan, James J.: b. Oct. 17, 1911, Philadelphia, Pa.; educ. St. Charles College (Catonsville, Md.), St. Mary's Seminary (Baltimore), Gregorian Univ. (Rome), Catholic Univ. (Washington, D.C.); ord. priest Dec. 8, 1937; ord. titular bishop of Philomelium and auxiliary bishop of Trenton, Feb. 25, 1960; app. bishop of Altoona-Johnstown, installed July 6, 1966.

Hogan, Joseph L.: b. Mar. 11, 1916, Lima,

N. Y.; educ. St. Bernard's Seminary (Rochester, N. Y.), Canisius College (Buffalo, N. Y.), Angelicum (Rome); ord. priest June 6, 1942; ord. bishop of Rochester, Nov. 28, 1969.

Howard, Edward Daniel: b. Nov. 5, 1877, Cresco, Ia.; educ. St. Joseph's College (Dubuque, Ia.), St. Mary's College (St. Mary's, Kans.), St. Paul Seminary (St. Paul, Minn.); ord. priest June 12, 1906; ord. titular bishop of Isauropolis and auxiliary bishop of Davenport, Apr. 8, 1924; app. archbishop of Oregon City, Apr. 30, 1926; title changed to archbishop of Portland, Sept. 26, 1928; resigned, 1966; assigned titular see of Albule.

Hunthausen, Raymond G.: b. Aug. 21, 1921, Anaconda, Mont.; educ. Carroll College (Helena, Mont.), St. Edward's Seminary (Kenmore, Wash.), St. Louis Univ. (St. Louis, Mo.), Catholic Univ. (Washington, D.C.), Fordham Univ. (New York City), Notre Dame Univ. (Notre Dame, Ind.); ord. priest June 1, 1946; ord. bishop of Helena, Aug. 30, 1962.

Hurley, Francis T.: b. Jan. 12, 1927, San Francisco, Calif.; educ. St. Patrick's Seminary (Menlo Park, Calif.), Catholic Univ. (Washington, D.C.); ord. priest June 16, 1951; assigned to NCWC in Washington, D.C., 1957; assistant (1958) and later (1968) associate secretary of NCCB and USCC; ord. titular bishop of Daimlaig and auxiliary bishop of Juneau, Alaska, Mar. 19, 1970; app. bishop of Juneau, July 20, 1971.

Hurley, Mark J.: b. Dec. 13, 1919, San Francisco, Calif.; educ. St. Patrick's Seminary (Menlo Park, Calif.), Univ. of California (Berkeley), Catholic Univ. (Washington, D.C.), Lateran Univ. (Rome), Univ. of Portland (Portland, Ore.); ord. priest Sept. 23, 1944; ord. titular bishop of Thunusuda and auxiliary bishop of San Francisco, Jan. 4, 1968; app. bishop of Santa Rosa, Nov. 19, 1969.

I-J

Issenmann, Clarence G.: b. May 30, 1907, Hamilton, O.; educ. St. Joseph's College (Rensselaer, Ind.), St. Gregory's Seminary (Cincinnati, O.), St. Mary of the West Seminary (Norwood, O.); ord. priest June 29, 1932; ord. titular bishop of Phytea and auxiliary bishop of Cincinnati, May 25, 1954; bishop of Columbus, 1957-64; app. titular bishop of Filaca, coadjutor bishop of Cleveland and apostolic administrator *"sede plena,"* 1964; bishop of Cleveland, 1966.

Johnson, William R.: b. Nov. 19, .1918, Tonopah, Nev.; educ. Los Angeles College and St. John's Seminary (Camarillo, Calif.), Catholic Univ. (Washington, D.C.); ord. priest May 28, 1944; ord. titular bishop of Blera and auxiliary bishop of Los Angeles, Mar. 25, 1971

Joyce, Robert F.: b. Oct. 7, 1896, Proctor, Vt.; educ. Univ. of Vermont (Burlington Vt.), Grand Seminary (Montreal, Canada); ord.

priest May 26, 1923; ord. titular bishop of Citium and auxiliary bishop of Burlington, Oct. 28, 1954; installed as bishop of Burlington, Feb. 26, 1957; resigned Dec. 14, 1971.

K

Kearney, James Edward: b. Oct. 28, 1884, Red Oak, Ia.; educ. St. Joseph's Seminary (Dunwoodie, N.Y.), Catholic Univ. (Washington, D.C.); ord. priest Sept. 19, 1908; ord. bishop of Salt Lake, Oct. 28, 1932; app. bishop of Rochester, July 31, 1937; retired Oct. 21, 1966.

Kellenberg, Walter P.: b. June 3, 1901, New York, N.Y.; educ. Cathedral College (New York, City), St. Joseph Seminary (Dunwoodie, N.Y.); ord. priest June 2, 1928; ord. titular bishop of Joannina and auxiliary bishop of New York, Oct. 5, 1953; app. bishop of Ogdensburg, Jan. 19, 1954; app. first bishop of Rockville Centre Apr. 16, 1957, installed May 27, 1957.

Kennally, Vincent, S.J.: b. June 11, 1895, Boston, Mass.; educ. Woodstock College (Woodstock, Md.), Weston College (Weston, Mass.); ord. priest June 20, 1928; ord. titular bishop of Sassura and vicar apostolic of the Caroline and Marshall Islands, Mar. 25, 1957; retired Sept. 20, 1971.

Klonowski, Henry T.: b. Mar. 8, 1898, Scranton, Pa.; educ. Univ. of Scranton (Scranton, Pa.), St. Francis Seminary (St. Francis, Wis.) St. Cyril and Methodius Seminary (Orchard Lake, Mich.), Capranica College, Angelicum and Gregorian Univ. (Rome); ord. priest Aug. 8, 1920; ord. titular bishop of Daldis and auxiliary bishop of Scranton, July 2, 1947.

Kocisko, Stephen: b. June 11, 1915, Minneapolis, Minn.; educ. Nazareth Hall Minor Seminary (St. Paul, Minn.), Pontifical Ruthenian College, Urban Univ. (Rome); ord. priest Mar. 30, 1941; ord. titular bishop of Teveste and auxiliary bishop of apostolic exarchate of Pittsburgh, Oct. 23, 1956; installed as first eparch of the eparchy of Passaic, Sept. 10, 1963; app. eparch of Byzantine-Rite diocese of Pittsburgh, installed Mar. 5, 1968; app. first metropolitan of Munhall, installed June 11, 1969.

Koester, Charles R.: b. Sept. 16, 1915, Jefferson City, Mo.; educ. Conception Academy (Conception, Mo.), St. Louis Preparatory Seminary and Kenrick Seminary (St. Louis, Mo.), North American College (Rome); ord. priest Dec. 20, 1941; ord. titular bishop of Suacia and auxiliary bishop of St. Louis, Feb. 11, 1971.

Krol, John J.: (See Cardinals, Biographies.)

Kupfer, William F., M.M.: b. Jan. 28, 1909, Brooklyn, N.Y.; educ. Cathedral College (Brooklyn, N.Y.) Maryknoll Seminary (Maryknoll, N.Y.); ord. priest June 11, 1933; missionary in China; app. prefect apostolic of Taichung, Formosa, 1951; ord. first bishop of Taichung, July 25, 1962.

L

Lane, Raymond Aloysius, M.M.: b. Jan. 2, 1894, Lawrence, Mass.; educ. St. John's Prep College (Danvers, Mass.), Maryknoll College and Seminary (Maryknoll, N.Y.); ord. priest Feb. 8, 1920; ord titular bishop of Hypaepa and vicar apostolic of Fushun, Manchukuo, June 11, 1940; elected superior general of Maryknoll, Aug. 7, 1946. Retired.

Lardone, Francesco: b. Jan. 12, 1887, Moretta, Italy; educ. Pontifical Schools of Theology and Canon Law and Royal Univ. (Turin); ord. priest June 29, 1910; became an American citizen, 1937; ord. titular archbishop of Rhizaeum and apostolic nuncio to Haiti and the Dominican Republic, June 30, 1949; app. apostolic nuncio to Peru, Nov. 21, 1953; papal representative to Turkey (first apostolic delegate, then internuncio), 1959-66.

Leech, George Leo: b. May 21, 1890, Ashley, Pa.; educ. St. Charles Borromeo Seminary (Overbrook, Pa.), Catholic Univ. (Washington, D.C.); ord. priest May 29, 1920; ord. titular bishop of Mela and auxiliary bishop of Harrisburg, Oct. 17, 1935; bishop of Harrisburg Dec. 19, 1935; resigned Oct. 19, 1971; app. titular bishop of Allegheny.

Leipzig, Francis P.: b. June 29, 1895, Chilton, Wis.; educ. St. Francis Seminary (Milwaukee, Wis.), Mt. Angel Seminary (St. Benedict, Ore.), St. Patrick's Seminary (Menlo Park, Calif.); ord. priest Apr. 14, 1920; ord. bishop of Baker, Sept. 12, 1950; retired June 30, 1971.

Lemay, Leo, S.M.: b. Sept. 23, 1909, Lawrence, Mass.; educ. Marist College (Washington, D.C.), Gregorian Univ. (Rome); ord. priest Apr. 15, 1933; ord. titular bishop of Agbia and vicar apostolic of North Solomon Islands, Sept. 21, 1960; first bishop of Bougainville, Nov. 15, 1966.

Leonard, Vincent M.: b. Dec. 11, 1908, Pittsburgh, Pa.; educ. Duquesne Univ. (Pittsburgh, Pa.), St. Vincent Seminary (Latrobe, Pa.); ord. priest June 16, 1935; ord. titular bishop of Arsacal and auxiliary bishop of Pittsburgh, Apr. 21, 1964; app. bishop of Pittsburgh, installed July 2, 1969.

Leven, Stephen A.: b. Apr. 30, 1905, Blackwell, Okla.; educ. St. Gregory's College (Shawnee, Okla.), St. Benedict's College (Atchison, Kans.), St. Mary's Seminary (La Porte, Tex.), American College (Louvain, Belgium); ord. priest June 10, 1928; ord. titular bishop of Bure and auxiliary bishop of San Antonio, Feb. 8, 1956; app. bishop of San Angelo, Tex., installed Nov. 25, 1969.

Lohmuller, Martin J.: b. Aug. 21, 1919, Philadelphia, Pa.; educ. St. Charles Borromeo Seminary (Philadelphia, Pa.), Catholic Univ. (Washington, D.C.); ord. priest June 3, 1944; ord. titular bishop of Ramsbury and auxiliary bishop of Philadelphia, Apr. 2, 1970.

Losten, Basil: b. May 11, 1930, Chesapeake City, Md.; educ. St. Basil's College (Stamford, Conn.), Catholic University (Washington, D.C.); ord. priest June 10, 1957; ord. titular bishop of Arcadiopolis in Asia and auxiliary bishop of Ukrainian archeparchy of Philadelphia, May 25, 1971.

Lucey, Robert Emmet: b. Mar. 16, 1891, Los Angeles, Calif.; educ. St. Vincent's College (Los Angeles, Calif.), St. Patrick's Seminary (Menlo Park, Calif.), North American College (Rome); ord. priest May 14, 1916; ord. bishop of Amarillo, May 1, 1934; app. archbishop of San Antonio, Jan. 23, 1941; retired June 4, 1969.

Lucker, Raymond A.: b. Feb. 24, 1927, St. Paul, Minn.; educ. St. Paul Seminary (St. Paul, Minn.); University of Minnesota (Minneapolis), Angelicum (Rome); ord. priest June 7, 1952; director of USCC department of education, 1968-71; ord. titular bishop of Meta and auxiliary bishop of St. Paul and Minneapolis, Sept. 8, 1971.

Lynch, George E.: b. Mar. 4, 1917, New York, N.Y.; educ. Fordham Univ. (New York), Mt. St. Mary's Seminary (Emmitsburg, Md.), Catholic Univ. (Washington, D.C.); ord. priest May 29, 1943; ord. titular bishop of Satafi and auxiliary bishop of Raleigh Jan. 6, 1970.

M

McAuliffe, Michael F.: b. Nov. 22, 1920, Kansas City; educ. St. Louis Preparatory Seminary (St. Louis, Mo.), Catholic Univ. (Washington, D.C.); ord. priest May 31, 1945; ord. bishop of Jefferson City, Aug. 18, 1969.

McCafferty, John E.: b. Jan. 6, 1920, New York, N.Y.; educ. St. Andrew's and St. Bernard's Seminaries (Rochester, N.Y.), Catholic Univ. (Washington, D.C.); ord. priest Mar. 17, 1945; ord. titular bishop of Tanudaia and auxiliary bishop of Rochester, Mar. 14, 1968.

McCarthy, Edward A.: b. Apr. 10, 1918, Cincinnati, O.; educ. Mt. St. Mary Seminary (Norwood, O.), Catholic Univ. (Washington, D.C.), Lateran and Angelicum (Rome); ord. priest May 29, 1943; ord. titular bishop of Tamascani and auxiliary bishop of Cincinnati, June 15, 1965; first bishop of Phoenix, Ariz., Dec. 2, 1969.

McCauley, Vincent, C.S.C.: b. Mar. 8, 1906, Council Bluffs, Ia.; educ. Notre Dame Univ. (Notre Dame, Ind.), Holy Cross Seminary (Washington, D.C.); ord. priest June 24, 1943; ord. first bishop of Fort Portal, Uganda, May 18, 1961.

McCormick, J. Carroll: b. Dec. 15, 1907, Philadelphia, Pa.; educ. College Ste. Marie (Montreal), St. Charles Seminary (Overbrook, Pa.), Minor and Major Roman Seminary (Rome); ord. priest July 10, 1932; ord. titular bishop of Ruspae and auxiliary bishop of Philadelphia, Apr. 23, 1947; app. bishop of Altoona-Johnstown, installed Sept. 21, 1960;

app. bishop of Scranton, installed May 25, 1966.

McDevitt, Gerald V.: b. Feb. 23, 1917, Philadelphia, Pa.; educ. St. Charles Seminary (Philadelphia, Pa.), Pontifical Roman Seminary (Rome), Catholic Univ. (Washington, D. C.); ord. priest May 30, 1942; ord. titular bishop of Tigias and auxiliary bishop of Philadelphia, Aug. 1, 1962.

McDonald, Andrew J.: b. Oct. 24, 1923, Savannah, Ga.; educ. St. Mary's Seminary (Baltimore, Md.); Catholic Univ. (Washington, D.C.), Lateran Univ. (Rome); ord. priest May 8, 1948; app. bishop of Little Rock, July 4, 1972.

McDonald, William J.: b. June 17, 1904, Mooncoin, Ireland; educ. St. Kieran's College and Seminary (Kilkenny, Ireland), Catholic Univ. (Washington, D. C.); ord. priest June 10, 1928; rector of Catholic Univ. of America, 1957-67; ord. titular bishop of Aquae Regiae and auxiliary bishop of Washington, May 19, 1964; app. auxiliary bishop of San Francisco, 1967.

McDonough, Thomas J.: b. Dec. 5, 1911, Philadelphia, Pa.; educ. St. Charles Seminary (Overbrook, Pa.), Catholic Univ. (Washington, D. C.); ord. priest May 26, 1938; ord. titular bishop of Thenae and auxiliary bishop of St. Augustine, Apr. 30, 1947; app. auxiliary bishop of Savannah, Jan. 2, 1957; named bishop of Savannah, installed Apr. 27, 1960; app. archbishop of Louisville, installed May 2, 1967.

McDowell, John B.: b. July 17, 1921, New Castle, Pa.; educ. St. Vincent College, St. Vincent Theological Seminary (Latrobe, Pa.), Catholic Univ. (Washington, D.C.); ord. priest Nov. 4, 1945; ord. titular bishop of Tamazuca, and auxiliary bishop of Pittsburgh, Sept. 8, 1966.

McEleney, John J., S.J.: b. Nov. 13, 1895, Woburn, Mass.; educ. Boston College (Boston, Mass.), Jesuit Scholasticate (New England Province); entered Society of Jesus, 1918; ord. priest June 18, 1930; app. provincial of New England Province, 1944; ord. titular bishop of Zeugma and vicar apostolic of Jamaica, Apr. 15, 1950; title changed to bishop of Kingston, Feb. 29, 1956; archbishop of Kingston, Sept. 14, 1967; retired 1970.

McFarland, Norman F.: b. Feb. 21, 1922, Martinez, Calif.; educ. St. Patrick's Seminary (Menlo Park, Calif.), Catholic Univ. (Washington, D. C.); ord. priest June 15, 1946; ord. titular bishop of Bida and auxiliary bishop of San Francisco, Sept. 8, 1970.

McGann, John R.: b. Dec. 2, 1924, Brooklyn, N.Y.; educ. Cathedral College (Brooklyn, N.Y.), Immaculate Conception Seminary (Huntington, L.I.); ord. priest June 3, 1950; ord. titular bishop of Morosbisdus and auxiliary bishop of Rockville Centre, Jan. 7, 1971; vicar general and episcopal vicar.

McGarry, Urban, T.O.R.: b. Nov. 11, 1911, Warren, Pa.; ord. priest Oct. 3, 1942, in India;

prefect apostolic of Bhagalpur, Aug. 7, 1956; ord. first bishop of Bhagalpur, India, May 10, 1965.

McGucken, Joseph T.: b. Mar. 13, 1902, Los Angeles, Calif.; educ. St. Patrick's Seminary (Menlo Park, Calif.), North American College (Rome); ord. priest Jan. 15, 1928; ord. titular bishop of Sanavus and auxiliary bishop of Los Angeles, Mar. 19, 1941; app. coadjutor bishop of Sacramento with right of succession, Oct. 26, 1955; bishop of Sacramento, Jan. 14, 1957; archbishop of San Francisco, installed Apr. 3, 1962.

McGurkin, Edward A., M.M.: b. June 22, 1905, Hartford, Conn.; educ. Maryknoll Seminary (Maryknoll, N. Y.); ord. priest Sept. 14, 1930; ord. first bishop of Maswa, Tanganyika, Oct. 3, 1956; title of see changed to Shinyanga (Tanzania), 1957.

McIntyre, J. Francis L.: (See Cardinals, Biographies.)

McKinney, Joseph C.: b. Sept. 10, 1928, Grand Rapids, Mich.; educ. St. Joseph's Seminary (Grand Rapids, Mich.), Seminaire de Philosophie (Montreal, Canada), Urban Univ. (Rome, Italy); ord. priest Dec. 20, 1953; ord. titular bishop of Lentini and auxiliary bishop of Grand Rapids, Sept. 26, 1968.

McLaughlin, Bernard J.: b. Nov. 19, 1912, Buffalo, N. Y.; educ. Urban Univ. (Rome, Italy); ord. priest Dec. 21, 1935, at Rome; ord. titular bishop of Mottola and auxiliary bishop of Buffalo, Jan. 6, 1969.

McLaughlin, Charles B.: b. Sept. 26, 1913, New York, N. Y.; educ. Cathedral College (New York City), St. Joseph's Seminary (Yonkers, N.Y.), St. John's Seminary (Little Rock, Ark.); ord. priest June 6, 1941; ord. titular bishop of Risinium and auxiliary bishop of Raleigh, Apr. 15, 1964; app. first bishop of St. Petersburg, installed June 17, 1968.

McManus, James E., C.SS.R.: b. Oct. 10, 1900, Brooklyn, N.Y.; educ. Redemptorist Preparatory College (North East, Pa.), Mt. St. Alphonsus Seminary (Esopus, N. Y.), Catholic Univ. (Washington, D. C.); entered Congregation of the Most Holy Redeemer, 1921; ord. priest June 19, 1927; ord. bishop of Ponce, Puerto Rico, July 1, 1947; founder of Catholic Univ. of Ponce; transferred to titular see of Benda and app. auxiliary bishop of New York, Nov. 18, 1963; retired 1970.

McManus, William E.: b. Jan. 27, 1914, Chicago, Ill.; educ. St. Mary of the Lake Seminary (Mundelein, Ill.), Catholic Univ. (Washington, D.C.); ord priest Apr. 15, 1939; ord. titular bishop of Mesarfelta and auxiliary bishop of Chicago, Aug. 24, 1967.

McNabb, John C., O.S.A.: b. Dec. 11, 1925, Beloit, Wis.; educ. Villanova Univ. (Villanova, Pa.), Augustinian College and Catholic Univ. (Washington, D.C.), De Paul Univ. (Chicago, Ill.); ord. priest May 24, 1952; ord. titular bishop of Saia Maggiore and prelate of Chulucanas, Peru, June 17, 1967.

McNaughton, William J., M.M.: b. Dec. 7,

1926, Lawrence, Mass.; educ. Maryknoll Seminary (Maryknoll, N.Y.); ord. priest June 13, 1953; ord. titular bishop of Thuburbo Minus and vicar apostolic of Inchon, Korea, Aug. 24, 1961; title changed to bishop of Inchon, Mar. 10, 1962.

McNicholas, Joseph A.: b. Jan. 13, 1923, St. Louis, Mo.; educ. Cardinal Glennon College, Kenrick Seminary and St. Louis Univ. (all in St. Louis, Mo.); ord. priest June 7, 1949; ord. titular bishop of Scala and auxiliary bishop of St. Louis, Mar. 25, 1969.

McShea, Joseph M.: b. Feb. 22, 1907, Latimer, Pa.; educ. St. Charles Seminary (Philadelphia, Pa.), Major Pontifical Roman Seminary (Rome); ord. priest Dec. 6, 1931; ord. titular bishop of Mina and auxiliary bishop of Philadelphia, Mar. 19, 1952; app. first bishop of Allentown, installed Apr. 11, 1961.

Maginn, Edward J.: b. Jan. 4, 1897, Glasgow, Scotland; educ. Holy Cross College (Worcester, Mass.), St. Joseph's Seminary (Yonkers, N.Y.); ord. priest June 10, 1922; ord. titular bishop of Curium and auxiliary bishop of Albany, Sept. 12, 1957; apostolic administrator of Albany, 1966-69.

Maguire, John J.: b. Dec. 11, 1904, New York, N.Y.; educ. Cathedral College (New York City), St. Joseph's Seminary (Dunwoodie, N.Y.), North American College (Rome); ord. priest Dec. 22, 1928; ord. titular bishop of Antiphrae and auxiliary bishop of New York, June 29, 1959; app. titular archbishop of Tabalta and coadjutor archbishop of New York, Sept. 15, 1965.

Maguire, Joseph F.: b. 1920, Boston, Mass.; educ. Boston College, St. John's Seminary (Boston, Mass.); ord. priest June 29, 1945; ord. titular bishop of Daimlaig and auxiliary bishop of Boston, Feb. 2, 1972.

Maher, Leo T.: b. July 1, 1915, Mount Union, Ia.; educ. St. Joseph's College (Mountain View, Calif.), St. Patrick's Seminary (Menlo Park, Calif.); ord. priest Dec. 18, 1943; ord. first bishop of Santa Rosa, April 5, 1962; bishop of San Diego, Oct. 4, 1969.

Mahoney, James P.: b. Aug. 16, 1925, Kingston, N.Y.; educ. St. Joseph's Seminary (Dunwoodie, N.Y.); ord. priest 1951; app. titular bishop of Ipagro and auxiliary bishop of New York, July 25, 1972.

Malone, James W.: b. Mar. 8, 1920, Youngstown, O.; educ. St. Charles Preparatory Seminary (Catonsville, Md.), St. Mary's Seminary (Cleveland, O.), Catholic Univ. (Washington, D.C.); ord. priest May 26, 1945; ord. titular bishop of Alabanda and auxiliary bishop of Youngstown, Mar. 24, 1960; apostolic administrator, 1966; bishop of Youngstown, installed June 20, 1968.

Maloney, Charles G.: b. Sept. 9, 1912, Louisville, Ky.; educ. St. Joseph's College (Rensselaer, Ind.), North American College (Rome); ord. priest Dec. 8, 1937; ord. titular bishop of Capsa and auxiliary bishop of Louisville, Feb. 2, 1955.

Maloney, David M.: b. Mar. 15, 1912, Littleton, Colo.; educ. St. Thomas Seminary (Denver, Colo.), Gregorian Univ. and Apollinare Univ. (Rome); ord. priest Dec. 8, 1936; ord. titular biahop of Ruspe and auxiliary bishop of Denver, Jan. 4, 1961; app. bishop of Wichita, Kans., Dec. 6, 1967.

Manning, Thomas R., O.F.M.: b. Aug. 29, 1922, Baltimore, Md.; educ. Duns Scotus College (Cincinnati, O.), Holy Name College (Washington, D.C.); ord. priest June 5, 1948; ord. titular bishop of Arsamosata and prelate of Coroico, Bolivia, July 14, 1959.

Manning, Timothy: b. Nov. 15, 1909, Ballingeary, County Cork, Ireland; educ. Mungret College (Limerick, Ireland), St. Patrick's Seminary (Menlo Park, Calif.), Gregorian Univ. (Rome); ord. priest June 16, 1934; became an American citizen, Jan. 14, 1944; ord. titular bishop of Lesvi and auxiliary bishop of Los Angeles, Oct. 15, 1946; app. first bishop of Fresno, installed Dec. 15, 1967; app. titular archbishop of Capraea and coadjutor archbishop of Los Angeles, 1969, archbishop of Los Angeles, Jan. 21, 1970.

Marcinkus, Paul C.: b. Jan. 15, 1922, Cicero, Ill.; ord. priest May 3, 1947; served in Vatican secretariat from 1952; ord. titular bishop of Orta, Jan. 6, 1969; secretary (1968-71) and president (1971-   ) of Institute for Works of Religion (Vatican Bank).

Mardaga, Thomas J.: b. May 14, 1913, Baltimore, Md.; educ. St. Charles College (Catonsville, Md.), St. Mary's Seminary (Baltimore, Md.); ord. priest May 14, 1940; ord. titular bishop of Mutugenna and auxiliary bishop of Baltimore, Jan. 25, 1967; app. bishop of Wilmington, installed Apr. 6, 1968.

Marling, Joseph M., C.Pp.S.: b. Aug. 31, 1904, Centralia, W. Va.; educ. St. Joseph's College (Collegeville, Ind.), St. Charles Seminary (Carthagena, O.), Catholic Univ. (Washington, D.C.); ord. priest Feb. 21, 1929; ord. titular bishop of Thasus and auxiliary bishop of Kansas City, Mo., Aug. 6, 1947; app. first bishop of Jefferson City, Aug. 24, 1956; resigned 1969; assigned titular see of Lesina.

Marshall, John A.: b. Apr. 26, 1928, Worcester, Mass.; educ. Holy Cross College (Worcester, Mass.), Sulpician Seminary (Montreal), North American College and Gregorian Univ. (Rome), Assumption College, (Worcester); ord. priest Dec. 19, 1953; ord. bishop of Burlington, Jan. 25, 1972.

May, John L.: b. Mar. 31, 1922, Evanston, Ill.; educ. St. Mary of the Lake Seminary (Mundelein, Ill.); ord. priest May 3, 1947; general secretary and vice-president of the Catholic Church Extension Society, 1959; ord. titular bishop of Tagarbala and auxiliary bishop of Chicago, Aug. 14, 1967; bishop of Mobile, Ala., Sept. 29, 1969.

Mazzarella, Bernardino N., O.F.M.: b. Apr. 20, 1904, Mirabella Eclano, Italy; educ. St. Anthony Seminary (Catskill, N.Y.), Franciscan Houses of Study (Province of Immaculate Conception); ord. priest June 5, 1931; ord. titular bishop of Hadrianopolis in Pisidia and prelate nullius of Olancho, Honduras, Oct. 18, 1957; installed as first bishop of Comayagua, Honduras, May 17, 1963.

Medeiros, Humberto S.: b. Oct. 6, 1915, Arrifes, S. Miguel, Azores; educ. Catholic Univ. (Washington, D.C.), Gregorian Univ. (Rome); ord. priest June 15, 1946; ord. bishop of Brownsville, Tex., June 9, 1966; app. archbishop of Boston, installed Oct. 7, 1970.

Mendez, Alfred, C.S.C.: b. June 3, 1907, Chicago, Ill.; educ. Notre Dame Univ. (Notre Dame, Ind.), Institute of Holy Cross (Washington, D.C.); ord. priest June 24, 1935; ord. first bishop of Arecibo, Puerto Rico, Oct. 28, 1960.

Metzger, Sidney Matthew: b. July 11, 1902, Fredericksburg, Tex.; educ. St. John's Seminary (San Antonio, Tex.), North American College (Rome); ord. priest Apr. 3, 1926; ord. titular bishop of Birtha and auxiliary bishop of Santa Fe, Apr. 10, 1940; app. coadjutor bishop of El Paso, Dec. 26, 1941; bishop of El Paso, Dec. 1, 1942.

Michaels, James E., S.S.C.: b. May 30, 1926, Chicago, Ill.; educ. Columban Seminary (St. Columban, Neb.), Gregorian Univ. (Rome); ord. priest Dec. 21, 1951; ord. titular bishop of Verbe and auxiliary bishop of Kwang Ju, Korea, Apr. 14, 1966.

Mihalik, Emil J.: b. Feb. 6, 1920, Pittsburgh, Pa.; educ. St. Procopius Seminary (Lisle, Ill.), Duquesne Univ. (Pittsburgh, Pa.); ord. priest Sept. 21, 1945; ord. first bishop of Byzantine Rite diocese of Parma, O., June 12, 1969.

Minder, John, O.S.F.S.: b. Nov. 1, 1923, Philadelphia, Pa.; ord. priest June 3, 1950; ord. bishop of Keimos, South Africa, Jan. 10, 1968.

Minihan, Jeremiah F.: b. July 21, 1903, Haverhill, Mass.; educ. Georgetown Univ. (Washington, D.C.), St. John's Seminary (Brighton, Mass.), North American College (Rome); ord. priest Dec. 21, 1929, at Rome; ord. titular bishop of Paphus and auxiliary bishop of Boston, Sept. 8, 1954.

Moran, William J.: b. Jan. 15, 1906, San Francisco, Calif.; educ. St. Patrick's Seminary (Menlo Park, Calif.); ord. priest June 20, 1931; Army chaplain, 1933; ord. titular bishop of Centuria and auxiliary to the military vicar, Dec. 13, 1965.

Morkovsky, John Louis: b. Aug. 16, 1909, Praha, Tex.; educ. St. John's Seminary (San Antonio, Tex.), North American College, Urban Univ. and Gregorian Univ. (Rome), Catholic Univ. (Washington, D. C.); ord. priest Dec. 5, 1933; ord. titular bishop of Hieron and auxiliary bishop of Amarillo, Feb. 22, 1956; app. bishop of Amarillo, Aug. 27, 1958; titular bishop of Tigava and coadjutor bishop of Galveston-Houston with right of succession, June 11, 1963; apostolic ad-

ministrator; president Texas Conference of Churches, 1970-72.

Morrow, Louis La Ravoire, S. D. B.: b. Dec. 24, 1892, Weatherford, Tex.; educ. Salesian School and Palafox (Puebla, Mexico); professed in Salesians of St. John Bosco, Sept. 29, 1912; ord. priest May 21, 1921; ord. bishop of Krishnagar, India, Oct. 29, 1939; resigned Oct. 31, 1969.

Mueller, Joseph M.: b. Dec. 1, 1894, St. Louis, Mo.; educ. Pontifical College Josephinum (Worthington, O.); ord. priest June 14, 1919; ord. titular bishop of Sinda and coadjutor bishop of Sioux City, Oct. 16, 1947; bishop of Sioux City, Sept. 20, 1948; resigned Oct. 15, 1970.

Mugavero, Francis John: b. June 8, 1914, Brooklyn, N. Y.; educ. Cathedral College (Brooklyn, N. Y.), Immaculate Conception Seminary (Huntington, N. Y.), Fordham Univ. (New York City); ord. priest May 18, 1940; ord. bishop of Brooklyn, Sept. 12, 1968.

Mulrooney, Charles R.: b. Jan. 13, 1906, Brooklyn, N. Y.; educ. Cathedral College (Brooklyn, N. Y.), St. Mary's Seminary (Baltimore, Md.), Sulpician Seminary (Washington, D. C.); ord. priest June 10, 1930; ord. titular bishop of Valentiniana and auxiliary bishop of Brooklyn, April 22, 1959.

Murphy, T. Austin: b. May 11, 1911, Baltimore, Md.; educ. St. Charles College (Catonsville, Md.), St. Mary's Seminary (Baltimore, Md.); ord. priest June 10, 1937; ord. titular bishop of Appiaria and auxiliary bishop of Baltimore, July 3, 1962.

Murphy, Thomas W., C.SS.R. b. Dec. 17, 1917, Omaha, Nebr.; educ. St. Joseph's College (Kirkwood, Mo.); ord. priest June 29, 1943; ord. first bishop of Juazeiro, Brazil, Jan. 2, 1963.

Mussio, John K.: b. June 13, 1902, Cincinnati, O.; educ. Xavier Univ. (Cincinnati, O.), Notre Dame Univ. (Notre Dame, Ind.), St. Gregory Preparatory Seminary (Cincinnati, O.), Mt. St. Mary Seminary (Norwood, O.), Angelicum (Rome); ord. priest Aug. 15, 1935; ord. bishop of Steubenville, May 1, 1945.

N

Nelson, Knute Ansgar, O.S.B.: b. Oct. 1, 1906, Copenhagen, Denmark; educ. Abbey of Maria Laach (Germany), Brown Univ. (Providence, R. I.); professed in the Order of St. Benedict, May 30, 1932; ord. priest May 22, 1937; became an American citizen, Mar. 4, 1941; ord. titular bishop of Bilta and coadjutor bishop of Stockholm, Sweden, Sept. 8, 1947; succeeded as bishop of Stockholm, Oct. 1, 1957; retired; titular bishop of Dura, 1962.

Newell, Hubert M.: b. Feb. 16, 1904, Denver, Colo.; educ. Regis College and St. Thomas Seminary (Denver, Colo.), Catholic Univ. (Washington, D.C.); ord. priest June 15, 1930; ord. titular bishop of Zapara and coadjutor bishop of Cheyenne, Sept. 24, 1947; bishop of Cheyenne, Nov. 10, 1951.

Newman, Thomas A., M.S.: b. Nov. 3, 1903, Waterbury, Conn.; educ. LaSalette Seminary (Ipswich, Mass.), Gregorian Univ. (Rome); ord. priest June 29, 1929; ord. first bishop of Prome, Burma, May 21, 1961.

Neylon, Martin J., S.J.: b. Feb. 13, 1920, Buffalo, N. Y.; ord. priest June 18, 1950; ord. titular bishop of Libertina and coadjutor vicar apostolic of the Caroline and Marshall Islands, Feb. 2, 1970; vicar apostolic of Caroline and Marshall Is., Sept. 20, 1971.

Noa, Thomas L.: b. Dec. 18, 1892, Iron Mountain, Mich.; educ. St. Francis Seminary (St. Francis, Wis.), North American College (Rome); ord. priest Dec. 23, 1916; ord. titular bishop of Salona and coadjutor bishop of Sioux City, Mar. 19, 1946; app. bishop of Marquette, Aug. 25, 1947; resigned 1968.

Nold, Wendelin J.: b. Jan. 18, 1900, Bonham, Tex.; educ. St. Mary's Seminary (La Porte, Tex.), North American College (Rome); ord. priest Apr. 11, 1925; ord. titular bishop of Sasima and coadjutor bishop of Galveston, Feb. 25, 1948, succeeded as bishop of Galveston, Apr. 1, 1950; title of see changed to Galveston-Houston, 1959.

Nolker, Bernard, C.SS.R.: b. Sept. 25, 1912, Baltimore, Md.; educ. St. Mary's College (North East, Pa.), St. Mary's College (Ilchester, Md.), Mt. St. Alphonsus Seminary (Esopus, N. Y.); ord. priest June 18, 1939; ord. first bishop of Paranagua, Brazil, Apr. 25, 1963.

Noser, Adolph A., S. V. D.: b. July 4, 1900, Belleville, Ill.; educ. Quincy College (Quincy, Ill.), St. Mary's Mission House (Techny, Ill.), Angelicum (Rome); received into the Society of the Divine Word, 1921; ord. priest Sept. 27, 1925; ord. titular bishop of Capitolias and vicar apostolic of Accra, Gold Coast, British West Africa, Aug. 22, 1947; title changed to bishop of Accra, Apr. 18, 1950; transferred to titular see of Hierpiniana and vicariate apostolic of Alexishaven, New Guinea, Jan. 8, 1953; first archbishop of Madang, Nov. 15, 1966.

O

O'Boyle, Patrick A.: (See Cardinals, Biographies.)

O'Brien, Henry Joseph: b. July 21, 1896, New Haven, Conn.; educ. St. Thomas Seminary (Hartford, Conn.), St. Bernard's Seminary (Rochester, N. Y.), Louvain Univ. (Belgium); ord. priest July 8, 1923; ord. titular bishop of Sita and auxiliary bishop of Hartford, May 14, 1940; bishop of Hartford, Apr., 1945; first archbishop of Hartford, Aug. 6, 1953; retired Nov. 20, 1968.

O'Connor, Martin J.: b. May 18, 1900, Scranton, Pa.; educ. St. Thomas College (Scranton, Pa.), St. Mary's Seminary (Baltimore, Md.), North American College, Urban Univ. and Apollinaris (Rome); ord. priest Mar. 15, 1924; ord. titular bishop of Thespia and auxiliary bishop of Scranton,

Jan. 27, 1943; rector of North American College 1946-1964; app. titular archbishop of Laodicea in Syria, Sept. 5, 1959; apostolic nuncio to Malta, 1965-69; president emeritus Pontifical Commission for Social Communication.

O'Connor, William A.: b. Dec. 27, 1903, Chicago, Ill.; educ. Quigley Seminary (Chicago, Ill.), St. Mary of the Lake Seminary (Mundelein, Ill.), Urban Univ. (Rome); ord. priest Sept. 24, 1927; ord. bishop of Springfield, Ill., Mar. 7, 1949.

O'Connor, William Patrick: b. Oct. 18, 1886, Milwaukee, Wis.; educ. St. Francis Seminary (St. Francis, Wis.), Marquette Univ. (Milwaukee, Wis.), Catholic Univ. (Washington, D. C.); ord. Priest Mar. 10, 1912; ord. bishop of Superior, Mar. 7, 1942; app. first bishop of Madison, Jan. 15, 1946; retired Feb. 22, 1967.

O'Donnell, Cletus F.: b. Aug. 22, 1917, Waukon, Ia.; educ. St. Mary Seminary (Mundelein, Ill.), Catholic Univ. (Washington, D.C.); ord. priest May 3, 1941; ord. titular bishop of Abritto and auxiliary bishop of Chicago, Dec. 21, 1960; app. bishop of Madison, Feb. 22, 1967, installed Apr. 25, 1967.

O'Flanagan, Dermot: b. Mar. 9, 1901, Lahinch, County Clare, Ireland; educ. Belvedere College and Milltown Park (Dublin), Ignatiuskolleg (Valkenburg, Holland); ord. priest Aug. 27, 1929; became an American citizen, Nov. 26, 1943; ord. first bishop of Juneau, Oct. 3, 1951; resigned 1968.

O'Keefe, Gerald: b. Mar. 30, 1918, St. Paul, Minn.; educ. College of St. Thomas, St. Paul Seminary (St. Paul, Minn.); ord. priest Jan. 29, 1944; ord. titular bishop of Candyba and auxiliary bishop of St. Paul July 2, 1916; bishop of Davenport, installed Jan. 4, 1967.

O'Leary, Edward C.: b. Aug. 21, 1920, Bangor, Me.; educ. Holy Cross College (Worcester, Mass.), St. Paul's Seminary (Ottawa, Canada); ord. priest June 15, 1946; ord. titular bishop of Moglena and auxiliary bishop of Portland, Me., Jan. 25, 1971.

O'Meara, Edward T.: b. Aug. 3, 1921, St. Louis, Mo.; educ. Cardinal Glennon College and Kenrick Seminary (St. Louis, Mo.), Angelicum (Rome); ord. priest Dec. 21, 1946; app. national director of Society for the Propagation of the Faith, 1967; ord. titular bishop of Thisiduo and auxiliary bishop of St. Louis, Feb. 13, 1972.

O'Neill, Arthur J.: b. Dec. 14, 1917, East Dubuque, Ill.; educ. Loras College (Dubuque, Ia.), St. Mary's Seminary (Baltimore, Md.); ord. priest Mar. 27, 1943; ord. bishop of Rockford, Oct. 11, 1968.

O'Rourke, Edward W.: b. Oct. 31, 1917, Downs, Ill.; educ. St. Mary's Seminary (Mundelein, Ill.), Aquinas Institute of Philosophy and Theology (River Forest, Ill.); ord. priest May 28, 1944; exec. dir. National Catholic Rural Life Conference, 1960-71; ord. and installed bishop of Peoria, July 25, 1971.

P

Pardy, James V., M.M.: b. Mar. 9, 1898, Brooklyn, N. Y.; educ. St. Francis College (Brooklyn), Fordham Univ. (New York City), Catholic Univ. (Washington, D. C.); ord. priest. Jan. 26, 1930; ord. titular bishop of Irenopolis and first vicar apostolic of Cheong Ju, Korea, Sept. 16, 1958; title changed to bishop of Cheong Ju, Mar. 10, 1962; retired 1969; assigned titular see of Umbriatico.

Paschang, John L.: b. Oct. 5, 1895, Hemingford, Nebr.; educ. Conception College (Conception, Mo.), St. John Seminary (Collegeville, Minn.), Catholic Univ. (Washington, D. C.); ord. priest June 12, 1921; ord. bishop of Grand Island, Oct. 9, 1951; resigned July 25, 1972.

Pearce, George H., S.M.: b. Jan. 9, 1921, Brighton, Mass.; educ. Marist College and Seminary (Framington, Mass.); ord. priest Feb. 2, 1947; ord. titular bishop of Attalea in Pamphylia and vicar apostolic of the Samoa and Tokelau Islands, June 29, 1956; title changed to bishop of Apia, 1966; app. archbishop of Suva, Fiji Islands, June 22, 1967.

Pechillo, Jerome, T.O.R.: b. May 16, 1919, Brooklyn, N. Y.; educ. Catholic Univ. (Washington, D. C.); ord. priest June 10, 1947; ord. titular bishop of Novasparsa and prelate of Coronel Oviedo, Paraguay, Jan. 25, 1966.

Pernicone, Joseph M.: b. Nov. 4, 1903, Regalbuto, Sicily; educ. Cathedral College (New York City), St. Joseph's Seminary (Dunwoodie, N. Y.), Catholic Univ. (Washington, D. C.); ord. priest Dec. 18, 1926; ord. titular bishop of Hadrianapolis and auxiliary bishop of New York, May 5, 1954; app. episcopal vicar, 1966.

Perry, Harold R., S. V. D.: b. Oct. 9, 1916, Lake Charles, La.; educ. St. Augustine Seminary (Bay St. Louis, Miss.), St. Mary's Seminary (Techny, Ill.); ord. priest Jan. 6, 1944; app. provincial of southern province of Society of the Divine Word, 1964; ord. titular bishop of Mons in Mauretania and auxiliary bishop of New Orleans, Jan. 6, 1966.

Pinger, Henry A., O.F.M.: b. Aug. 16, 1897, Lindsay, Nebr.; educ. Our Lady of Angels Seminary (Cleveland, O.), St. Anthony's Seminary (St. Louis, Mo.); professed in the Order of Friars Minor, June 18, 1918; ord. priest June 27, 1924; ord. titular bishop of Capitolias and vicar apostolic of Chowtsun, China, Sept. 21, 1937; title changed to bishop of Chowtsun, Apr. 11, 1946; imprisoned by Reds in 1951, released in 1956; expelled.

Povish, Kenneth J.: b. Apr. 19, 1924, Alpena, Mich.; educ. St. Joseph's Seminary (Grand Rapids, Mich.), Sacred Heart Seminary (Detroit, Mich.), Catholic Univ. (Washington, D. C.); ord. priest June 3, 1950; ord. bishop of Crookston, Sept. 29, 1970.

Power, Cornelius M.: b. Dec. 18, 1913, Seattle, Wash.; educ. St. Patrick's College (Menlo Park, Calif.), St. Edward's Seminary (Kenmore, Wash.), Catholic Univ. (Washington, D. C.); ord. priest June 3, 1939; ord. bishop of Yakima, May 1, 1969, installed May 29, 1969.

Primeau, Ernest J.: b. Sept. 17, 1909, Chicago, Ill.; educ. Loyola Univ. (Chicago, Ill.), St. Mary of the Lake Seminary (Mundelein, Ill.), Lateran Univ. (Rome); ord. priest Apr. 7, 1934; ord. bishop of Manchester, Feb. 25, 1960.

Prost, Jude, O.F.M.: b. Dec. 6, 1915, Chicago, Ill.; educ. Our Lady of the Angels Seminary (Cleveland, O.), St. Joseph's Seminary (Teutopolis, Ill.); ord. priest June 24, 1942; ord. titular bishop of Fronta and auxiliary bishop of Belem do Para, Brazil, Nov. 1, 1962.

Pursley, Leo A.: b. Mar. 12, 1902, Hartford City, Ind.; educ. Mt. St. Mary's Seminary (Cincinnati, O.); ord. priest June 11, 1927; ord. titular bishop of Hadrianapolis in Pisidia and auxiliary bishop of Fort Wayne, Sept. 19, 1950; app. apostolic administrator of Fort Wayne, Mar. 9, 1955; installed as bishop of Fort Wayne, Feb. 26, 1957; title of see changed to Fort Wayne-South Bend, 1960.

Q

Quinn, John R.: b. Mar. 28, 1929, Riverside, Calif.; educ. St. Francis Seminary (El Cajon, Calif.), North American College (Rome); ord. priest July 19, 1953; ord. titular bishop of Thisiduo and auxiliary bishop of San Diego, Dec. 12, 1967; bishop of Oklahoma City and Tulsa, Nov. 30, 1971.

R

Raya, Joseph M.: b. July 20, 1917, Zahle, Lebanon; educ. St. Louis College (Paris, France), St. Anne's Seminary (Jerusalem); ord. priest July 20, 1941; came to US, 1949, became US citizen; ord. archbishop of Acre, Israel, of the Melkites, Oct. 20, 1968.

Regan, Joseph W., M.M.: b. Apr. 5, 1905, Boston, Mass.; educ. Boston College (Boston, Mass.), St. Bernard's Seminary (Rochester, N. Y.), Maryknoll Seminary (Maryknoll, N.Y.); ord. priest Jan. 27, 1929; missionary in China 15 years; in Philippines since 1952; ord. titular bishop of Isinda and prelate of Tagum, Philippine Islands, Apr. 25, 1962.

Reh, Francis F.: b. Jan. 9, 1911, New York, N.Y.; educ. St. Joseph's Seminary (Dunwoodie, N.Y.), North American College and Gregorian Univ. (Rome); ord. priest Dec. 8, 1935; ord. bishop of Charleston, S.C., June 29, 1962; named titular bishop of Macriana in Mauretania, 1964; rector of North American College, 1964-68; bishop of Saginaw, installed Feb. 26, 1969.

Rehring, George John: b. June 10, 1890, Cincinnati, O.; educ. Mt. St. Mary of the West Seminary (Cincinnati, O.), Collegium

Angelicum (Rome); ord. priest Mar. 28, 1914; ord. titular bishop of Lunda and auxiliary bishop of Cincinnati, Oct. 7, 1937; app. bishop of Toledo, July 26, 1950; retired 1967.

Reicher, Louis J.: b. June 14, 1890, Piqua, O.; educ. St. Mary's Seminary (Cincinnati, O.), St. Mary's Seminary (La Porte, Tex.): ord. priest Dec. 6, 1918; ord. first bishop of Austin, Apr. 14, 1948; resigned Nov. 15, 1971.

Reilly, Thomas F., C.SS.R.: b. Dec. 20, 1908, Boston, Mass.; educ. Mt. St. Alphonsus Seminary (Esopus, N.Y.), Catholic Univ. (Washington, D.C.); ord. priest June 10, 1933; ord. titular bishop of Themisonium and prelate of San Juan de la Maguana, Dominican Republic, Nov. 30, 1956; first bishop of San Juan de la Maguana, Nov. 21, 1969.

Reiss, John C.: b. May 13, 1922, Red Bank, N.J.; educ. Catholic Univ. (Washington, D.C.), Immaculate Conception Seminary (Darlington, N.J.); ord. priest May 31, 1947; ord. titular bishop of Simidicca and auxiliary bishop of Trenton, Dec. 12, 1967.

Riley, Lawrence J.: b. 1915, Boston, Mass.; educ. Boston College and St. John's Seminary (Boston, Mass.); ord. priest Sept. 21, 1940; ord. titular bishop of Mactaris and auxiliary bishop of Boston, Feb. 2, 1972.

Riley, Thomas J.: b. Nov. 30, 1900, Waltham, Mass.; educ. Boston College (Boston, Mass.), St. John's Seminary (Brighton, Mass.), Louvain Univ. (Belgium); ord. priest May 20, 1927; ord. titular bishop of Regiae and auxiliary bishop of Boston, Dec. 21, 1959.

Roach, John R.: b. July 31, 1921, Prior Lake, Minn.; educ. St. Paul Seminary (St. Paul, Minn.); Univ. of Minnesota (Minneapolis); ord. priest June 18, 1946; ord. titular bishop of Cenae and auxiliary bishop of St. Paul and Minneapolis, Sept. 8, 1971.

Rudin, John J., M.M.: b. Nov. 27, 1916, Pittsfield, Mass.; educ. Maryknoll Seminary (Maryknoll, N.Y.), Gregorian Univ. (Rome); ord. priest June 11, 1944; ord. first bishop of Musoma, Tanzania, Oct. 3, 1957.

Russell, John J.: b. Dec. 1, 1897, Baltimore, Md.; educ. St. Charles College (Catonsville, Md.), St. Mary's Seminary (Baltimore, Md.), North American College (Rome); ord. priest July 8, 1923; ord. bishop of Charleston, Mar. 14, 1950; bishop of Richmond, July 3, 1958.

Ryan, James C., O.F.M.: b. Nov. 17, 1912, Chicago, Ill.; educ. St. Joseph's Seraphic Seminary (Westmont, Ill.), Our Lady of the Angels Seminary (Cleveland, O.); ord. priest June 24, 1938; ord. titular bishop of Margo and prelate of Santarem, Brazil, April 9, 1958.

Ryan, Joseph T.: b. Nov. 1, 1913, Albany N.Y.; educ. Manhattan College (New York City); ord. priest June 3, 1939; national secretary of Catholic Near East Welfare Assn. 1960-65; ord. first archbishop of Anchorage, Alaska, Mar. 25, 1966.

S

Salatka, Charles A.: b. Feb. 26, 1918, Grand Rapids, Mich.; educ. St. Joseph's Seminary (Grand Rapids, Mich.), Catholic Univ. (Washington, D.C.), Lateran Univ. (Rome); ord. priest Feb. 24, 1945; ord. titular bishop of Cariana and auxiliary bishop of Grand Rapids, Mich., Mar. 6, 1962; app. bishop of Marquette, installed Mar. 25, 1968.

Scanlan, John J.: b. May 24, 1906, County Cork, Ireland; educ. National Univ. of Ireland (Dublin), All Hallows College (Dublin); ord. priest June 22, 1930; US citizen 1938; ord. titular bishop of Cenae and auxiliary bishop of Honolulu, Sept. 21, 1954; bishop of Honolulu installed May 1, 1968.

Schad, James L.: b. July 20, 1917, Philadelphia, Pa.; educ. St. Mary's Seminary (Baltimore, Md.); ord. priest Apr. 10, 1943; ord. titular bishop of Panatoria and auxiliary bishop of Camden, Dec. 8, 1966.

Schexnayder, Maurice: b. Aug. 13, 1895, Wallace, La.; educ. Chenet Institute (New Orleans, La.), St. Joseph's Seminary (St. Benedict, La.), St. Mary's Seminary (Baltimore, Md.), North American College (Rome); ord. priest Apr. 11, 1925; ord. titular bishop of Tuscamia and auxiliary bishop of Lafayette, La., Feb. 22, 1951; bishop of Lafayette, La., May 24, 1956.

Schierhoff, Andrew B.: b. Feb. 10, 1922, St. Louis, Mo.; ord. priest Apr. 14, 1948; missionary in Bolivia from 1956; ord. titular bishop of Cerenza and auxiliary of La Paz, Bolivia, Jan. 6, 1969.

Schladweiler, Alphonse: b. July 18, 1902, Milwaukee, Wis.; educ. St. Joseph College (Teutopolis, Ill.), St. Paul's Seminary (St. Paul, Minn.), Univ. of Minnesota (Minneapolis, Minn.); ord. priest June 9, 1929; ord. first bishop of New Ulm, Jan. 29, 1958.

Schlaefer, Salvator, O.F.M. Cap.: b. June 27, 1920, Campbellsport, Wis.; ord. priest June 5, 1946; missionary in Bluefields, Nicaragua from 1947; ord. titular bishop of Fiumepiscense and vicar apostolic of Bluefields, Nicaragua, Aug. 12, 1970.

Schlotterback, Edward F., O.S.F.S.: b. Mar. 2, 1912, Philadelphia, Pa.; educ. Catholic Univ. (Washington, D.C.); ord. priest Dec. 17, 1938; ord. titular bishop of Balanea and vicar apostolic of Keetmanshoop, Southwest Africa, June 11, 1956.

Schmidt, Firmin M., O.F.M.Cap.: b. Oct. 12, 1918, Catherine, Kans.; educ. Catholic Univ. (Washington, D.C.); ord. priest June 2, 1946; app. prefect apostolic of Mendi, Papua-New Guinea, Apr. 3, 1959; ord. titular bishop of Conana and first vicar apostolic of Mendi, Dec. 15, 1965; first bishop of Mendi, Nov. 15, 1966.

Schmidt, Mathias, O.S.B.: b. 1931, Wortonville, Kans.; ord. priest 1957; missionary in Brazil; app. titular bishop of Matugenna and auxiliary bishop of Jatai, Brazil, June 19, 1972.

Schmitt, Adolph G., C.M.M.: b. Apr. 20, 1905, Bimpar, Bavaria; educ. Aloysianum Preparatory Seminary (Lehr, Bavaria), Mariannhill Seminary, and University of Wuerzburg (Bavaria); entered Mariannhill Mission Society, 1926; ord. priest Mar. 19, 1931; became US citizen, 1945; ord. titular bishop of Nasai and vicar apostolic of Bulawayo, Rhodesia, Apr. 2, 1951; bishop of Bulawayo, Jan. 1, 1955.

Schmitt, Mark: b. Feb. 14, 1923, Algoma, Wis., educ. Salvatorian Seminary (St. Nazianz, Wis.), St. John's Seminary (Collegeville, Minn.); ord. priest May 22, 1948; ord. titular bishop of Ceanannus Mor and auxiliary bishop of Green Bay, June 24, 1970.

Schmondiuk, Joseph: b. Aug. 6, 1912, Wall, Pa.; educ. St. Joseph's Preparatory College High School (Philadelphia, Pa.), Pontifical Ruthenian College, Angelicum and Urban Univ. (Rome); ord. priest Mar. 29, 1936; ord. titular bishop of Zeugma in Syria and auxiliary bishop of apostolic exarchate of Philadelphia, Nov. 8, 1956; title of see changed to metropolitan, 1958; app. eparch of Stamford, 1961.

Schoenherr, Walter J.: b. Feb. 28, 1920, Detroit, Mich.' educ. Sacred Heart Seminary (Detroit, Mich.), Mt. St. Mary Seminary (Norwood, O); ord. priest Oct. 27, 1945; ord. titular bishop of Timidana and auxiliary bishop of Detroit, May 1, 1968.

Schuck, James A., O.F.M.: b. Jan. 17, 1913, Treverton, Pa.; educ. St. Joseph's Seminary (Callicoon, N.Y.), St. Bonaventure's University (St. Bonaventure, N.Y.), Holy Name College (Washington, D.C.); ord. priest June 11, 1940; ord. titular bishop of Avissa and prelate of Cristalandia, Brazil, Feb. 24, 1959; member of Holy Name Franciscan province.

Schulte, Paul Clarence: b. Mar. 18, 1890, Fredericktown, Mo.; educ. St. Francis Solanus College (Quincy, Ill.), Kenrick Seminary (Webster Groves, Mo.); ord. priest June 11, 1915; ord. bishop of Leavenworth, Sept. 21, 1937; archbishop of Indianapolis, July 27, 1946; resigned Jan. 14, 1970; assigned titular see of Elicrora.

Schuster, Eldon B.: b. Mar. 10, 1911, Calio, N. Dak.; educ. Loras College (Dubuque, Ia.), Catholic Univ. (Washington, D.C.), Oxford Univ. (England), St. Louis Univ. (St. Louis, Mo.); ord. priest May 27, 1937; ord. titular bishop of Amblada and auxiliary bishop of Great Falls, Mont., Dec. 21, 1961; app. bishop of Great Falls Dec. 2, 1967, installed Jan. 23, 1968.

Senyshyn, Ambrose, O.S.B.M.: b. Feb. 23, 1903, Stary Sambor, Galicia; educ. Monastery Colleges at Krechiev and Iawriev, Dobromil and Crystynopol (Galicia); ord. priest Aug. 23, 1931; ord. titular bishop of Maina and auxiliary bishop of the Ukrainian-Greek Catholic Diocese of the United States, Oct.

22, 1942; app. first bishop of Byzantine Ukrainian Rite exarchate of Stamford, Aug. 8, 1956; eparch of Stamford, 1958; app. metropolitan of Ukrainian archeparchy of Philadelphia, 1961.

Shea, Francis R.: b. Dec. 4, 1913, Knoxville, Tenn.; educ. St. Mary's Seminary (Baltimore, Md.), North American College (Rome), Peabody College (Nashville, Tenn.); ord. priest Mar. 19, 1939; ord. bishop of Evansville, Ind., Feb. 3, 1970.

Sheehan, Daniel E.: b. May 14, 1917, Emerson, Nebr.; educ. Creighton Univ. (Omaha, Nebr.), Kenrick Seminary (Webster Groves, Mo.), Catholic Univ. (Washington, D.C.): ord. priest May 23, 1942; ord. titular bishop of Capsus and auxiliary bishop of Omaha, Mar. 19, 1964; app. archbishop of Omaha, installed Aug. 11, 1969.

Sheen, Fulton J.: b. May 8, 1895, El Paso, Ill.; educ. St. Viator College (Kankakee, Ill.), St. Paul seminary (St. Paul, Minn.), Catholic Univ. (Washington, D.C.), Louvain Univ. (Belgium), Collegium Angelicum (Rome); ord. priest Sept. 20, 1919; app. national director of the Pontifical Society for the Propagation of the Faith, 1950; ord. titular bishop of Caesariana and auxiliary bishop of New York, June 11, 1951; app. bishop of Rochester, installed Dec. 15, 1966; resigned Oct. 15, 1969; titular archbishop of Newport.

Shehan, Lawrence Joseph: (See Cardinals, Biographies.)

Smith, Eustace J., O.F.M.: b. Aug. 22, 1908, Medford, Mass.; educ. St. Joseph's Seraphic Seminary (Callicoon, N.Y.), Holy Name College (Washington, D.C.). Antonianum, Pontifical Biblical Institute (Rome), Franciscan Biblical Institute (Jerusalem); ord. priest June 12, 1934; ord. titular bishop of Apamea Cibotus and vicar apostolic of Beirut, Feb. 2, 1956.

Soenneker, Henry J.: b. May 27, 1907, Melrose, Minn.; educ. Pontifical Josephinum College (Worthington, O.), Catholic Univ. (Washington, D.C.); ord. priest May 26, 1934; ord. bishop of Owensboro, Apr. 26, 1961.

Sowada, Alphonsus A., O.S.C.: b. June 23, 1933, Avon, Minn.; educ. Holy Cross Scholasticate (Fort Wayne, Ind.), Catholic Univ. (Washington, D.C.); ord. priest May 31, 1958; missionary in Indonesia from 1958; bishop of Agats, Indonesia, Nov. 23, 1969.

Speltz, George H.: b. May 12, 1912, Altura, Minn.; educ. St. Mary's College, St. Paul's Seminary (St. Paul, Minn.), Catholic Univ. (Washington, D.C.); ord. priest June 2, 1940; ord. titular bishop of Claneus and auxiliary bishop of Winona, Mar. 25, 1963; app. coadjutor bishop of St. Cloud, Apr. 4, 1966; bishop of St. Cloud, Jan. 31, 1968.

Spence, John S.: b. May 1, 1909, Baltimore, Md.; educ. Loyola College and St. Mary's Seminary (Baltimore, Md.), North American College (Rome); ord. priest Dec. 5, 1933; ord.

titular bishop of Aggersel and auxiliary bishop of Washington, May 19, 1964.

Stanton, Martin W.: b. Apr. 17, 1897, Jersey City, N.J.; educ. St. Peter's College (Jersey City, N.J.), Immaculate Conception Seminary (Darlington, N.J.), Fordham Univ. (New York City); ord. priest June 14, 1924; ord. titular bishop of Citium and auxiliary bishop of Newark, Sept. 24, 1957.

Stemper, Alfred M., M.S.C.: b. Jan. 2, 1913, Black Hammer, Minn.; ord. priest June 26, 1940; ord. titular bishop of Eleutheropolis and vicar apostolic of Kavieng, New Guinea, Oct. 28, 1957; first bishop of Kavieng, Nov. 15, 1966.

Strecker, Ignatius J.: b. Nov. 23, 1917, Spearville, Kans.; educ. St. Benedict's College (Atchison, Kans.), Kenrick Seminary (Webster Groves, Mo.), Catholic Univ. (Washington, D.C.); ord. priest Dec. 19, 1942; ord. bishop of Springfield-Cape Girardeau, Mo., JJune 20, 1962; archbishop of Kansas City, Kans., Oct. 28, 1969.

Sullivan, James S.: b. July 23, 1929, Kalamazoo, Mich.; ord. priest 1955; app. titular bishop of Siccessi and auxiliary bishop of Lansing, July 25, 1972.

Sullivan, John J.: b. July 5, 1920, Horton, Kans.; educ. Kenrick Seminary (St. Louis, Mo.); ord. priest Sept. 23, 1944; vice-president of Catholic Church Extension Society and national director of Extension Lay Volunteers, 1961-69; app. bishop of Grand Island, July 25, 1972.

Sullivan, Joseph V.: b. Aug. 15, 1919, Kansas City, Mo.; educ. Sulpician Seminary (Washington, D.C.), Catholic Univ. (Washington, D.C.); ord. priest June 1, 1946; ord. titular bishop of Tagamuta and auxiliary bishop of Kansas City-St. Joseph, Apr. 3, 1967.

Sullivan, Walter F.: b. June 10, 1928, Washington, D.C.; ord. priest May 9, 1953; ord. titular bishop of Selsea and auxiliary bishop of Richmond, Va., Dec. 1, 1970.

Swanstrom, Edward E.: b. Mar. 20, 1903, New York, N.Y.; educ. Fordham Univ. (New York City), St. John's Seminary (Brooklyn, N.Y.), New York School of Social Work; ord. priest June 2, 1928; director of Catholic Relief Services; ord. titular bishop of Arba and auxiliary bishop of New York, Oct. 28, 1960.

Szoka, Edmund C.: b. Sept. 14, 1927, Grand Rapids, Mich.; educ. Sacred Heart Seminary (Detroit, Mich.), St. John's Provincial Seminary (Plymouth, Mich.), Lateran Univ. (Rome); ord. priest June 5, 1954; ord. first bishop of Gaylord, Mich., July 20, 1971.

T-V

Tanner, Paul F.: b. Jan. 15, 1905, Peoria, Ill.; educ. Marquette Univ. (Milwaukee, Wis.), Kenrick Seminary (Webster Groves, Mo.), St. Frances Seminary (Milwaukee, Wis.), Catholic Univ. (Washington, D.C.):

ord. priest May 30, 1931; assistant director NCWC Youth Department 1940-45; aassistant general secretary of NCWC 1945-58; general secretary of NCWC (now USCC) 1958-68; ord. titular bishop of Lamasba, Dec. 21, 1965; bishop of St. Augustine, Mar. 27, 1968.

Tawil, Joseph: b. Dec. 25, 1913, Damascus, Syris; ord. priest July 20, 1936; ord. titular archbishop of Mira and patriarchal vicar for eparchy of Damascus of the Patriarchate of Antioch for the Melkites, Jan. 1, 1960; apostolic exarch for faithful of the Melkite rite in the US, Oct. 31, 1969.

Taylor, John E., O.M.I.: b. Nov. 15, 1914, East St. Louis, Ill.; educ. Angelicum Univ., Gregorian Univ. (Rome), Univ. of Ottawa (Ottawa, Canada); ord. priest May 25, 1940; ord. bishop of Stockholm, Sept. 21, 1962.

Toolen, Thomas Joseph: Feb. 28, 1886, Baltimore, Md.; educ. Loyola College and St. Mary's Seminary (Baltimore, Md.), Catholic Univ. (Washington, D.C.); ord. priest Sept. 27, 1910; ord. bishop of Mobile, May 4, 1927; personal title of archbishop conferred, July 14, 1954; retired 1969; assigned titular see of Glastonbury.

Topel, Bernard J.: b. May 31, 1903, Bozeman, Mont.; educ. Carroll College (Helena, Mont.), Grand Seminary (Montreal), Catholic Univ. (Washington, D.C.), Harvard Univ. (Cambridge, Mass.), Notre Dame Univ. (Notre Dame, Ind.); ord. priest June 7, 1927; ord. titular bishop of Binda and coadjutor bishop of Spokane, Sept. 21, 1955; bishop of Spokane, Sept. 25, 1955.

Tracy, Robert E.: b. Sept. 14, 1909, New Orleans, La.; educ. St. Joseph's Preparatory Seminary (St. Benedict, La.), Notre Dame Seminary (New Orleans); ord. priest June 12, 1932; national chaplain of Newman Federation; 1954-56; ord. titular bishop of Sergentiza and auxiliary bishop of Lafayette, La., May 19, 1959; app. first bishop of Baton Rouge, Aug. 10, 1961.

Treinen, Sylvester: b. Nov. 19, 1917, Donnelly, Minn.; educ. Crosier Seminary (Onamia, Minn.), St. Paul Seminary (St. Paul, Minn.); ord. priest June 11, 1946; ord. bishop of Boise, July 25, 1962.

Tschoepe, Thomas: b. Dec. 17, 1915, Pilot Point, Tex.; educ. Pontifical College Josephinum (Worthington, O.); ord. priest May 30, 1943; ord. bishop of San Angelo, Tex., Mar. 9, 1966; app. bishop of Dallas, Tex., Aug. 27, 1969.

Unterkoefler, Ernest L.: b. Aug. 17, 1917, Philadelphia, Pa.; educ. Catholic Univ. (Washington, D.C.); ord. priest May 18, 1944; ord. titular bishop of Latopolis and auxiliary bishop of Richmond, Va., Feb. 22, 1962; app. bishop of Charleston, 1964, installed Feb. 22, 1965.

Vath, Joseph G.: b. Mar. 12, 1918, New Orleans, La.; educ. Notre Dame Seminary (New Orleans, La.), Catholic Univ. (Washington, D.C.); ord. priest June 7, 1941; ord. titular bishop of Novaliciana and auxiliary bishop of Mobile-Birmingham, May 26, 1966; app. first bishop of Birmingham, Oct. 8, 1969.

Vehr, Urban John: b. May 30, 1891, Cincinnati, O.; educ. Mt. St. Mary of the West Seminary (Norwood, O.), Catholic Univ. (Washington, D.C.), Collegium Angelicum (Rome); ord. priest May 29, 1915; ord. bishop of Denver, June 10, 1931; app. archbishop of Denver, Nov. 15, 1941; retired 1967.

Veigle, Adrian J.M., T.O.R.: b. Sept. 15, 1912, Lilly, Pa.; educ. St. Francis College (Loretto, Pa.), Pennsylvania State College; ord. priest May 22, 1937; ord. titular bishop of Gigthi and prelate of Borba, Brazil, June 9, 1966.

Vogel, Cyril J.: b. Jan. 15, 1905, Pittsburgh, Pa.; educ. Duquesne Univ. (Pittsburgh, Pa.), St. Vincent's Seminary (Latrobe, Pa.); ord. priest June 7, 1931; ord. bishop of Salina, June 17, 1965.

Vonesh, Raymond J.: b. Jan. 25, 1916, Chicago, Ill.; educ. St. Mary of the Lake Seminary (Mundelein, Ill.). Gregorian Univ. (Rome); ord. priest May 3, 1941; ord. titular bishop of Vanariona and auxiliary bishop of Joliet, Ill., Apr. 3, 1968.

W

Walsh, James Edward, M.M.: b. Apr. 30, 1891, Cumberland, Md.; educ. Mt. St. Mary's College (Emmitsburg, Md.), Maryknoll Foreign Mission Seminary (Maryknoll, N.Y.); entered Catholic Foreign Mission Society (Maryknoll, N.Y.), 1912; ord. priest Dec. 7, 1915; ord. titular bishop of Sata and vicar apostolic of Kongmoon, China, May 22, 1927; superior general of Maryknoll, July 21, 1936, until Aug. 7, 1946; app. general secretary, Catholic Central Bureau, Shanghai, China, Aug. 24, 1948; placed under house arrest in October, 1958, detained in Shanghai hospital; sentenced to 20 years' imprisonment for "espionage," Mar., 1960; released 1970.

Ward, John J.: b. Sept. 28, 1920, Los Angeles, Calif.; educ. St. John's Seminary (Camarillo, Calif.), Catholic Univ. (Washington, D.C.); ord. priest May 4, 1946; ord. titular bishop of Bria and auxiliary of Los Angeles, Dec. 12, 1963.

Waters, Vincent S.: b. Aug. 15, 1904, Roanoke, Va.; educ. Belmont Abbey College (Belmont, N.C.), St. Charles College (Catonsville, Md.), St. Mary's Seminary (Baltimore, Md.), North American College (Rome); ord. priest Dec. 8, 1931; ord. bishop of Raleigh, May 15, 1945.

Watson, Alfred M.: b. July 11, 1907, Erie, Pa.; educ. St. Mary's Seminary (Baltimore, Md.), Catholic Univ. (Washington, D.C.); ord. priest May 10, 1934; ord. titular bishop of National and auxiliary bishop of Erie, June 29, 1965; app. bishop of Erie, 1969, installed May 13, 1969.

Watters, Loras J.: b. Oct. 14, 1915, Dubuque, Ia.; educ. Loras College (Dubuque, Ia.), Gregorian Univ. (Rome), Catholic Univ. (Washington, D.C.); ord. priest June 7, 1941; ord. titular bishop of Fidoloma and auxiliary bishop of Dubuque, Aug. 26, 1965; bishop of Winona, installed Mar. 13, 1969.

Weldon, Christopher J.: b. Sept. 6, 1905, New York, N.Y.; educ. Montreal College (Canada), St. Joseph's Seminary (Dunwoodie, N.Y.), Catholic Univ. (Washington, D.C.); ord. priest Sept. 21, 1939; ord. bishop of Springfield, Mass., Mar. 24, 1950.

Welsh, Thomas J.: b. Dec. 20, 1921, Weatherly, Pa.; educ. St. Charles Borromeo Seminary (Philadelphia, Pa.), Catholic Univ. (Washington, D.C.); ord. priest May 30, 1946; ord. titular bishop of Scattery Island and auxiliary bishop of Philadelphia, Apr. 2, 1970.

Whealon, John F.: b. Jan. 15, 1921, Barberton, O.; educ. St. Charles College (Catonsville, Md.), St. Mary's Seminary (Cleveland, O.); ord. priest May 26, 1945; ord. titular bishop of Andrapa and auxiliary bishop of Cleveland, July 6, 1961; app. bishop of Erie, Dec. 9, 1966; installed Mar. 7, 1967; archbishop of Hartford, installed Mar. 19, 1969.

Whelan, Robert L., S.J.: b. Apr. 16, 1912, Wallace, Ida.; educ. St. Michael's College (Spokane, Wash.), Alma College (Alma, Calif.); ord. priest June 17, 1944; ord. titular bishop of Sicilibba and coadjutor bishop of Fairbanks, Alaska, with right of succession, Feb. 22, 1968; bishop of Fairbanks, Nov. 30, 1968.

Wildermuth, Augustine F., S.J.: b. Feb. 20, 1904, St. Louis, Mo.; educ. St. Stanislaus Seminary (Florissant, Mo.), St. Michael's Scholasticate (Spokane, Wash.), Sacred Heart College (Shembaganur, S. India), St. Mary's College (Kurseong, India), Gregorian Univ. (Rome); entered Society of Jesus, 1922; ord. priest July 25, 1935; ord. bishop of Patna, India, Oct. 28, 1947.

Willinger, Aloysius Joseph, C.SS.R.: b. Apr. 19, 1886, Baltimore, Md.; educ. St. Mary's College (North East, Pa.), Mount St. Alphonsus House of Studies (Esopus, N.Y.); professed in Redemptorist Congregation, Aug. 2, 1906; ord. priest July 2, 1911; ord. bishop of Ponce, Puerto Rico, Oct. 28, 1929; app. titular bishop of Bida and coadjutor bishop of Monterey-Fresno, Dec. 11, 1946; bishop of Monterey-Fresno, Jan. 3, 1953; retired, 1967, assigned the titular see of Tiguola.

Wright, John J.: (See Cardinals, Biographies.) Prefect of the Sacred Congregation for the Clergy.

Wycislo, Aloysius John: b. June 17, 1908, Chicago, Ill.; educ. St. Mary's Seminary (Mundelein, Ill.), Catholic Univ. (Washington, D.C.); ord. priest Apr. 4, 1934; ord. titular bishop of Stadia and auxiliary bishop of Chicago, Dec. 21, 1960; app. bishop of Green Bay, installed Apr. 16, 1968.

Z

Zaleski, Alexander M.: b. June 24, 1906, Laurel, N.Y.; educ. St. Mary's College and Sts. Cyril and Methodius Seminary (Orchard Lake, Mich.), American College (Louvain, Belgium), Biblical Institute (Rome); ord. priest July 12, 1931; ord. titular bishop of Lyrbe and auxiliary bishop of Detroit, May 23, 1950; app. coadjutor bishop of Lansing and apostolic administrator "sede plena," 1964; bishop of Lansing, Dec. 1, 1965.

Zayek, Francis: b. Oct. 18, 1920, Manzanillo, Cuba; ord. priest Mar. 17, 1946; ord. titular bishop of Callinicum and auxiliary bishop for Maronites in Brazil, Aug. 5, 1962; named apostolic exarch for Maronites in US, with headquarters in Detroit; installed June 11, 1966; first eparch of St. Maron of Detroit, Mar. 25, 1972.

Zuroweste, Albert R.: b. Apr. 26, 1901, East St. Louis, Ill.; educ. St. Francis College (Quincy, Ill.), Kenrick Seminary (Webster Groves, Mo.), Catholic Univ. (Washington, D.C.); ord. priest June 8, 1924; ord. bishop of Belleville, Jan. 29, 1948.

US BISHOPS OVERSEAS

Cardinal John J. Wright, prefect of the Congregation for the Clergy; Archbishop Raymond P. Etteldorf, apostolic delegate to New Zealand and the Pacific Islands; Archbishop Edward L. Heston, president, Pontifical Commission for Social Communications; Bishop Anthony J. Deksnys, pastoral work among Lithuanians in Western Europe; Bishop James A. Hickey, rector of the North American College; Bishop Paul C. Marcinkus, president of Institute for Works of Religion (Vatican Bank).

RETIRED US PRELATES

Information includes name of the prelate and see held at the time of retirement; archbishops are indicated by an asterisk.

The preferred form of address of retired prelates is *Former Archbishop* or *Bishop of* (last see held).

Karl J. Alter* (Cincinnati), Peter W. Bartholome (St. Cloud), Mark K. Carroll (Wichita), Thomas P. Collins, M.M. (Pando, vicar apostolic), James L. Connolly (Fall River),

Stephen J. Donahue (New York, auxiliary), Leo P. Dworschak (Fargo), Joseph F. Flannelly (New York, auxiliary), Albert L. Fletcher (Little Rock), Walter A. Foery (Syracuse), John B. Franz (Peoria),

Richard O. Gerow (Natchez-Jackson), Francis D. Gleason, S.J. (Fairbanks), Lawrence A. Glenn (Crookston), Thomas K. Gorman (Dallas-Ft. Worth), Lawrence L. Graner* (Dacca, Bangladesh), Lawrence Graziano, O.F.M. (San Miguel, El Salvador), James T. Hayes, S.J.* (Cagayan, Philip-

pines), David F. Hickey, S.J. (Belize, Br. Honduras), Edward D. Howard* (Portland, Ore.), Robert F. Joyce (Burlington), James E. Kearney (Rochester),

Vincent Kennally, S.J. (Caroline and Marshall Islands, vicar apostolic), Raymond A. Lane, M.M. (titular bishop, Hypaepa), George L. Leech (Harrisburg), Francis P. Leipzig (Baker), Robert E. Lucey* (San Antonio),

William T. McCarty, C.SS.R. (Rapid City), Cardinal J. Francis McIntyre* (Los Angeles), John J. McEleney, S.J.* (Kingston, Jamaica), James F. McManus, C.SS.R. (New York, auxiliary), Joseph M. Marling, C.PP.S. (Jefferson City),

Louis La Ravoire Morrow, S.D.B. (Krishnagar, India), Joseph M. Mueller (Sioux City), Knute Ansgar Nelson, O.S.B. (Stockholm, Sweden), Thomas L. Noa (Marquette), Henry J. O'Brien* (Hartford),

Martin J. O'Connor* (Prefect Emeritus, Pontifical Commission for Social Communications), William P. O'Connor (Madison), Dermot O'Flanagan (Juneau), James V. Pardy, M.M. (Cheong Ju, Korea), John L. Paschang (Grand Island),

George J. Rehring (Toledo), Louis J. Reicher (Austin), Paul C. Schulte* (Indianapolis), Fulton J. Sheen* (Rochester; titular archbishop, Newport), Thomas J. Toolen* (Mobile-Birmingham; personal title of archbishop),

Urban J. Vehr* (Denver), James E. Walsh, M.M. (Kongmoon, China, vicar apostolic), Aloysius J. Willinger, C.SS.R. (Monterey-Fresno).

BISHOP-BROTHERS

See separate entries for biographical data.

The asterisk indicates brothers who were bishops at the same time.

There have been nine pairs of brother-bishops in the history of the US hierarchy.

Most recently: Francis T. Hurley* of Juneau and Mark J. Hurley* of Santa Rosa, both living; Coleman F. Carroll* present archbishop of Miami, and the late Howard Carroll* of Altoona-Johnstown.

The others, all deceased, were: Francis Blanchet* of Oregon City (Portland) and Augustin Blanchet* of Walla Walla; John S. Foley of Detroit and Thomas P. Foley of Chicago; Francis P. Kenrick,* apostolic administrator of Philadelphia, bishop of Philadelphia and Baltimore, and Peter R. Kenrick* of St. Louis; Matthias C. Lenihan of Great Falls and Thomas M. Lenihan of Cheyenne; James O'Connor, vicar apostolic of Nebraska and bishop of Omaha, and Michael O'Connor of Pittsburgh and Erie; Jeremiah F. and John W. Shanahan, both of Harrisburg; Sylvester J. Espelage, O.F.M.,* of Wuchang, China, who died 10 days after the ordination of his brother, Bernard T. Espelage,* O.F.M., of Gallup.

AMERICAN BISHOPS OF THE PAST

Information includes dates, place of birth if outside the US, date of ordination to the priesthood, sees held, and, in the case of non-residential bishops, the name of the titular see in parentheses.

A

Adrian, William H. (1883-1972): ord. Apr. 15, 1911; bp. Nashville, 1936-69 (ret.).

Albers, Joseph (1891-1965): ord. June 17, 1916; aux. bp. Cincinnati (Lunda), 1929-37; first bp. Lansing, 1937-65.

Alemany, Joseph Sadoc, O.P. (1814-1888): b. Spain; ord. Mar. 11, 1837; bp. Monterey, (now Los Angeles), 1850-53; first abp. San Francisco, 1853-84 (res.).

Alencastre, Stephen P., S.S.CC. (1876-1940): b. Madeira; ord. Apr. 5, 1902; coad. v.a. Sandwich Is. (Arabissus), 1924-36; v.a. Sandwich (now Hawaiian Is.,) 1936-40.

Alerding, Herman J. (1845-1924): b. Germany; ord. Sept. 22, 1869; bp. Fort Wayne, 1900-24.

Allen, Edward P. (1853-1926): ord. Dec. 17, 1881; bp. Mobile, 1897-1926.

Althoff, Henry (1873-1947): ord. July 26, 1902; bp. Belleville, 1914-47.

Amat, Thaddeus, C.M. (1811-1878): b. Spain; ord. Dec. 23, 1837; bp. Monterey (now Los Angeles), 1854-78.

Anderson, Joseph (1865-1927): ord. May 20, 1892; aux. bp. Boston (Myrina), 1909-27.

Annabring, Joseph (1900-1959): b. Hungary; ord. May 3, 1927; bp. Superior, 1954-59.

Appelhans, Stephen A., S.V.D. (1905-1951): ord. May 5, 1932; v.a. East New Guinea (Catula), 1948-51.

Armstrong, Robert J. (1884-1957): ord. Dec. 10, 1910; bp. Sacramento, 1929-57.

Arnold, William R. (1881-1965): ord. June 13, 1908; delegate of US military vicar (Phocaea), 1945-65.

Atkielski, Roman R. (1898-1969): ord. May 30, 1931; aux. bp. Milwaukee (Stobi), 1947-69.

B

Babcock, Allen J. (1898-1969): ord. Mar. 7, 1925; aux. bp. Detroit (Irenopolis), 1947-54; bp. Grand Rapids, 1954-69.

Bacon, David W. (1815-1874): ord. Dec. 13, 1838; first bp. Portland, Me., 1855-74.

Baltes, Peter J. (1827-1886): b. Germany; ord. May 31, 1852; bp. Alton (now Springfield), Ill., 1870-86.

Baraga, Frederic: See Index.

Barron, Edward (1801-1854): b. Ireland; ord. 1829; v.a. The Two Guineas (Constantina), 1842-44 (res.) missionary in US.

Barry, John (1799-1859): b. Ireland; ord. Sept. 24, 1825; bp. Savannah, 1857-59.

Barry, Patrick J. (1868-1940): b. Ireland;

ord. June 9, 1895; bp. St. Augustine, 1922-40.

Baumgartner, Apollinaris, O.F.M. Cap. (1899-1970): ord. May 30, 1926; v.a. Guam (Joppa), 1945-65; first bp. Agana, Guam, 1965-70.

Bayley, James Roosevelt: See Index.

Bazin, John S. (1796-1848): b. France; ord. July 22, 1822; bp. Vincennes (now Indianapolis), 1847-48.

Beaven, Thomas D. (1851-1920): ord. Dec. 18, 1875; bp. Springfield, Mass., 1892-1920.

Becker, Thomas A. (1832-1899): ord. June 18, 1859; first bp. Wilmington, 1868-86; bp. Savannah, 1886-99.

Beckman, Francis J. (1875-1948): ord. June 20, 1902; bp. Lincoln, 1924-30; abp. Dubuque, 1930-46 (res.).

Benjamin, Cletus J. (1909-1961): ord. Dec. 8, 1935; aux. bp. Philadelphia (Binda), 1960-61.

Bennett, John G. (1891-1957): ord. June 27, 1914; first bp. Lafayette, Ind., 1944-57.

Bergan, Gerald T. (1892-1972): ord. Oct. 28, 1915; bp. Des Moines, 1934-38; abp. Omaha, 1948-69 (ret.).

Bidawid, Thomas M. (1910-1971): b. Iraq; ord. May 15, 1935; US citizen; first abp. Ahwaz, Iran (Chaldean Rite), 1968-70: Chaldean patriarchal vicar for United Arab Republic, 1970-71.

Blanc, Anthony (1792-1860): b. France; ord. July 22, 1816; bp. New Orleans, 1835-50; first abp. New Orleans, 1850-60.

Blanchet (brothers): **Augustin M.** (1797-1887): b. Canada; ord. June 3, 1821; bp. Walla Walla, 1846-50; first bp. Nesqually (now Seattle), 1850-79 (res.). **Francis N.** (1795-1883): b. Canada; ord. July 19, 1819; v.a. Oregon Territory (Philadelphia, Adrasus), 1843-46; first abp. Oregon City (now Portland), 1846-80 (res.)

Blenk, James H., S.M. (1856-1917): b. Germany; ord. Aug. 16, 1885; bp. San Juan, 1899-1906; abp. New Orleans, 1906-17.

Boeynaems, Libert H., SS.CC. (1857-1926): b. Belgium; ord. Sept. 11, 1881; v.a. Sandwich (now Hawaiian) Is. (Zeugma), 1903-26.

Bohachevsky, Constantine (1884-1961): b. Austrian Galicia; ord. Jan. 31, 1909; ap. ex. Ukrainian Byzantine Catholics in US (Amisus), 1924-58; first metropolitan of Byzantine Rite archeparchy of Philadelphia, 1958-61.

Boileau, George, S.J. (1912-1965): ord. June 13, 1948; coad. bp. Fairbanks (Ausuccura), 1964-65.

Bona, Stanislaus (1888-1967): ord. Nov. 1, 1912; bp. Grand Island, 1932-44; coad. bp. Green Bay (Mela), 1944-45; bp. Green Bay, 1945-67.

Bonacum, Thomas (1847-1911): b. Ireland; ord. June 18, 1870; first bp. Lincoln, 1887-1911.

Borgess, Caspar H. (1826-1890): b. Germany; ord. Dec. 8, 1848; coad. bp. and ap. admin. Detroit (Calydon), 1870-71; bp. Detroit, 1871-87 (res.).

Bourgade, Peter (1845-1908): b. France; ord. Nov. 30, 1869; v.a. Arizona (Thaumacus), 1885-97; first bp. Tucson, 1897-99; abp. Santa Fe, 1899-1908.

Boylan, John J. (1889-1953): ord. July 28, 1915; bp. Rockford, 1943-53.

Boyle, Hugh C. (1873-1950): ord. July 2, 1898; bp. Pittsburgh, 1921-50.

Bradley, Denis (1846-1903): b. Ireland; ord. June 3, 1871; first bp. Manchester, 1884-1903.

Brady, John (1842-1910): b. Ireland; ord. Dec. 4, 1864; aux. bp. Boston (Alabanda), 1891-1910.

Brady, Matthew F. (1893-1959): ord. June 10, 1916; bp. Burlington, 1938-44; bp. Manchester, 1944-59.

Brady, William O. (1899-1961): ord. Dec. 21, 1923; bp. Sioux Falls, 1939-56; coad. abp. St. Paul (Selymbria), June-Oct. 1956; abp. St. Paul, 1956-61.

Brennan, Andrew J. (1877-1956): ord. Dec. 17, 1904; aux. bp. Scranton (Thapsus), 1923-26; bp. Richmond, 1926-45 (res.).

Brennan, Thomas F. (1853-1916): b. Ireland; ord. July 14, 1880; first bp. Dallas, 1891-92; aux. bp. St. John's, Newfoundland (Usula), 1893-1905 (res.).

Broderick, Bonaventure (1868-1943): ord. July 26, 1896; aux. bp. Havana, Cuba (Juliopolis), 1903-05 (res.).

Brondel, John B. (1842-1903): b. Belgium; ord. Dec. 17, 1864; bp. Vancouver Is., 1879-84: first bp. Helena, 1884-1903.

Brossart, Ferdinand (1849-1930): b. Germany; ord. Sept. 1, 1892; bp. Covington, 1916-23 (res.).

Brute, Simon G. (1779-1839): b. France; ord. June 11, 1808; first bp. Vincennes (now Indianapolis), 1834-39.

Buddy, Charles F. (1887-1966): ord. Sept. 19, 1914; first bp. San Diego, 1936-66.

Burke, Joseph A. (1886-1962): ord. Aug. 3, 1912; aux. bp. Buffalo (Vita), 1943-52; bp. Buffalo, 1952-62.

Burke, Maurice F. (1845-1923): b. Ireland; ord. May 22, 1875; first bp. Cheyenne, 1887-93; bp. St. Joseph, 1893-1923.

Burke, Thomas M. (1840-1915): b. Ireland; ord. June 30, 1864; bp. Albany, 1894-1915.

Busch, Joseph F. (1866-1953): ord. July 28, 1889; bp. Lead (now Rapid City), 1910-15; bp. St. Cloud, 1915-53.

Byrne, Andrew (1802-1862): b. Ireland; ord. Nov. 11, 1827; first bp. Little Rock, 1844-62.

Byrne, Christopher E. (1867-1950): ord. Sept. 23, 1891; bp. Galveston, 1918-50.

Byrne, Edwin V. (1891-1963): ord. May 22, 1915; first bp. Ponce, 1925-29; abp. San Juan, 1929-43; abp. Santa Fe, 1943-63.

Byrne, Patrick J., M.M. (1888-1950): ord. June 23, 1915; apostolic delegate to Korea (Gazera), 1949-50.

Byrne, Thomas S. (1841-1923): ord. May 22, 1869; bp. Nashville, 1894-1923.

C

Canevin, J. F. Regis (1853-1927): ord. June 4, 1879; coad. bp. Pittsburgh (Sabrata), 1903-04; bp. Pittsburgh, 1904-21 (res.).

Cantwell, John J. (1874-1947): b. Ireland; ord. June 18, 1899; bp. Monterey-Los Angeles, 1917-22; bp. Los Angeles, 1917-36; first abp. Los Angeles, 1936-47.

Carrell, George A., S. J. (1803-1868): ord. Dec. 20, 1827; first bp. Covington, 1853-68.

Carroll, Howard J. (1902-1960): ord. Apr. 2, 1927; bp. Altoona-Johnstown, 1958-60.

Carroll, James J. (1862-1913): ord. June 15, 1889; bp. Nueva Segovia, P. I., 1908-12 (res.).

Carroll, John: See Index.

Carroll, John P. (1864-1925): ord. July 7, 1886; bp. Helena, 1904-25.

Cartwright, Hubert J. (1900-1958): ord. June 11, 1927; coad. bp. Wilmington (Neve), 1956-58.

Cassidy, James E. (1869-1951): ord. Sept. 8, 1898; aux. bp. Fall River (Ibora), 1930-34; bp. Fall River, 1934-51.

Chabrat, Guy Ignatius, S.S. (1787-1868): b. France; ord. Dec. 21, 1811; coad. bp. Bardstown (Bolina), 1834-47 (res.).

Chanche, John J., S.S. (1795-1852): ord. June 5, 1819; bp. Natchez (now Natchez-Jackson), 1841-52.

Chapelle, Placide L. (1842-1905): b. France; ord. June 28, 1865; coad. abp. Santa Fe (Arabissus), 1891-94; abp. Santa Fe, 1894-97; abp. New Orleans, 1897-1905.

Chartrand, Joseph (1870-1933): ord. Sept. 24, 1892; coad. bp. Indianapolis (Flavias), 1910-18; bp. Indianapolis, 1918-33.

Chatard, Francis S. (1834-1918): ord. June 14, 1862; bp. Vincennes (now Indianapolis—title changed in 1898), 1878-1918.

Cheverus, John Lefebvre de (1768-1836): b. France; ord. Dec. 18, 1790; bp. Boston, 1810-23 (returned to France, made cardinal 1836).

Christie, Alexander (1848-1925): ord. Dec. 22, 1877; bp. Vancouver Is., 1898-99; abp. Oregon City (now Portland), 1899-1925.

Clancy, William (1802-1847): b. Ireland; ord. May 24, 1823; coad. bp. Charleston (Oreus). 1834-37; v.a. British Guiana, 1837-43.

Collins, John J., S.J. (1856-1934): ord. Aug. 29, 1891; v.a. Jamaica (Antiphellus), 1907-18.

Colton, Charles H. (1848-1915): ord. June 10, 1876; bp. Buffalo, 1903-15.

Conaty, Thomas J. (1847-1915): b. Ireland; ord. Dec. 21, 1872; rector of Catholic University, 1896-1903; tit. bp. Samos, 1901-03; bp. Monterey-Los Angeles, 1903-15.

Concanen, Richard L., O.P. (1747-1810): b. Ireland; ord. Dec. 22, 1770; first bp. New York. 1808-10 (detained in Italy, never reached his see).

Condon, William J. (1895-1967): ord. Oct. 14, 1917; bp. Great Falls, 1939-67.

Connolly, John, O.P. (1750-1825): b. Ireland; ord. Sept. 24, 1774; bp. New York, 1814-25.

Conroy, John J. (1819-1895): b. Ireland; ord. May 21, 1842; bp. Albany, 1865-77 (res.).

Conroy, Joseph H. (1858-1939): ord. June 11, 1881; aux. bp. Ogdensburg (Arindela), 1912-21; bp. Ogdensburg, 1921-39.

Conwell, Henry (1748-1842): b. Ireland; ord. 1776; bp. Philadelphia, 1820-42.

Corbett, Timothy (1858-1939): ord. June 12, 1886; first bp. Crookston, 1910-38 (res.).

Corrigan, Joseph M. (1879-1942): ord. June 6, 1903; rector of Catholic University, 1936-42; tit. bp. Bilta, 1940-42.

Corrigan, Michael A. (1839-1902): ord. Sept. 19, 1863; bp. Newark, 1873-80; coad. abp. New York (Petra), 1880-85; abp. New York, 1885-1902.

Corrigan, Owen (1849-1929): ord. June 7, 1873; aux. bp. Baltimore (Macri), 1908-29.

Cosgrove, Henry (1834-1906): ord. Aug. 27, 1857; bp. Davenport, 1884-1906.

Cote, Philip, S.J. (1896-1970): ord. Aug. 14, 1927; v. a. Suchow, China (Polystylus), 1935-46; first bp. Suchow, 1946-70 (imprisoned by Chinese Communists, 1951; expelled from China, 1953; ap. admin. Islands of Quemoy and Matsu, 1969-79).

Cotter, Joseph B. (1844-1909): b. England; ord. May 3, 1871; first bp. Winona, 1889-1909.

Cotton, Francis R. (1895-1960): ord. June 17, 1920; first bp. Owensboro, 1938-60.

Crane, Michael J. (1863-1928): ord. June 15, 1889; aux. bp. Philadelphia (Curium), 1921-28.

Cretin, Joseph (1799-1857): b. France; ord. Dec. 20, 1823; bp. St. Paul, 1851-57.

Crimont, Joseph R., S.J. (1858-1945): b. France; ord. Aug. 26, 1888; v. a. Alaska (Ammaedara), 1917-45.

Crowley, Timothy J., C.S.C. (1880-1945): b. Ireland; ord. Aug. 2, 1906; coad. bp. Dacca (Epiphania), 1927-29; bp. Dacca, 1929-45.

Cunningham, John F. (1842-1919): b. Ireland; ord. Aug. 8, 1865; bp. Concordia, 1898-1919.

Curley, Daniel J. (1869-1932): ord. May 19, 1894; bp. Syracuse, 1923-32.

Curley, Michael J. (1879-1947): b. Ireland; ord. Mar. 19, 1904; bp. St. Augustine, 1914-21; abp. Baltimore, 1921-39; title changed to abp. Baltimore and Washington, 1939-47.

Curtis, Alfred A. (1831-1908): convert, 1872; ord. Dec. 19, 1874; bp. Wilmington, 1886-96 (res.).

Cusack, Thomas F. (1862-1918): ord. May 30, 1885; aux. bp. New York (Temiscyra), 1904-15; bp. Albany, 1915-18.

Cushing, Richard J.: See Index.

D

Daeger, Albert T., O.F.M. (1872-1932): ord. July 25, 1896; abp. Santa Fe, 1919-32.

Daly, Edward C., O.P. (1894-1964): ord.

June 12, 1921; bp. Des Moines, 1948-64.

Damiano, Celestine (1911-1967): ord. Dec. 21, 1935; apostolic delegate to South Africa (Nicopolis in Epiro), 1952-60; bp. Camden, 1960-67.

Danehy, Thomas J., M.M. (1914-1959): ord. Sept. 17, 1939; ap. admin. v. a. Pando, Bolivia (Bita), 1953-59.

David, John B., S.S. (1761-1841): b. France; ord. Sept. 24, 1785; coad. bp. Bardstown (Mauricastrum), 1819-32; bp. Bardstown (now Louisville), 1832-33 (res.).

Davis, James (1852-1926): b. Ireland; ord. June 21, 1878; coad. bp. Davenport (Milopotamus), 1904-06; bp. Davenport, 1906-26.

De Cheverus, John L.: See Cheverus, John.

De Goesbriand, Louis (1816-1899): b. France; ord. July 13, 1840; first bp. Burlington, 1853-99.

De la Hailandiere, Celestine (1798-1882): b. France; ord. May 28, 1825; bp. Vincenes (now Indianapolis), 1839-47 (res.).

Delany, John B. (1864-1906): ord. May 23, 1891; bp. Manchester, 1904-06.

Demers, Modeste, (1809-1871): b. Canada; ord. Feb. 7, 1836; bp. Vancouver Is., 1846-71.

De Neckere, Leo, C.M. (1799-1833): b. Belgium; ord. Oct. 13, 1822; bp. New Orleans, 1829-33.

De Saint Palais, Maurice (1811-1877): b. France; ord. May 28, 1836; bp. Vincennes (now Indianapolis), 1849-77.

Desmond, Daniel F. (1884-1945): ord. June 9, 1911; bp. Alexandria, 1933-45.

Dinand, Joseph N., S.J. (1869-1943): ord. June 25, 1903; v. a. Jamaica (Selinus), 1927-29 (res.).

Dobson, Robert (1867-1942): ord. May 23, 1891; aux. bp. Liverpool, Eng. (Cynopolis), 1922-42.

Domenec, Michael, C.M. (1816-1878): b. Spain; ord. June 30, 1839; bp. Pittsburgh, 1860-76; bp. Allegheny, 1876-77 (res.).

Donahue, Joseph P. (1870-1959): ord. June 8, 1895; aux. bp. New York (Emmaus), 1945-59.

Donahue, Patrick J. (1849-1922): b. England; ord. Dec. 19, 1885; bp. Wheeling, 1894-1922.

Donnelly, George J. (1889-1950): ord. June 12, 1921; aux. bp. St. Louis, (Coela), 1940-46; bp. Leavenworth (now Kansas City — title changed in 1947), 1946-50.

Donnelly, Henry E. (1904-1967): ord. Aug. 17, 1930; aux. bp. Detroit (Tymbrias), 1954-67.

Doran, Thomas F. (1856-1916): ord. July 4, 1880; aux. bp. Providence (Halicarnassus), 1915-16.

Dougherty, Dennis (1865-1951): ord. May 31, 1890; bp. Nueva Segovia, P.I., 1903-08; bp. Jaro, P.I., 1908-15; bp. Buffalo, 1915-18; abp. Philadelphia, 1918-1951; cardinal, 1921.

Dougherty, Joseph P. (1905-1970): ord. June 14, 1930; first bp. Yakima, 1951-69; aux. bp. Los Angeles (Altino), 1969-70.

Dowling, Austin (1868-1930): ord. June 24, 1891; first bp. Des Moines, 1912-19; abp. St. Paul, 1919-30.

Drossaerts, Arthur J. (1862-1940): b. Holland; ord. June 15, 1889; bp. San Antonio 1918-26; first abp. San Antonio, 1926-40.

Drumm, Thomas W. (1871-1933): b. Ireland; ord. Dec. 21, 1901; bp. Des Moines, 1919-33.

Dubois, John, S.S. (1764-1842): b. France; ord. Sept. 28, 1787; bp. New York, 1826-42.

Dubourg, William L., S.S. (1766-1833): b. Santo Domingo; ord. 1788; bp. Louisiana and the Two Floridas (now New Orleans), 1815-25; returned to France; bp. Montauban, 1826-33; abp. Besancon 1833.

Dubuis, Claude M. (1817-1895): b. France; ord. June 1, 1844; bp. Galveston, 1862-92 (res.).

Dufal, Peter, C.S.C. (1822-1898): b. France; ord. Sept. 29, 1852; v.a. Eastern Bengal (Delcon), 1860-78; coad. bp. Galveston, 1878-80 (res.).

Duffy, James A. (1873-1968): ord. May 27. 1899; bp. Kearney 1913-31 (res.).

Duffy, John A. (1884-1944): ord. June 13, 1908; bp. Syracuse, 1933-37; bp. Buffalo, 1937-44.

Duggan, James (1825-1899): b. Ireland; ord. May 29, 1847; coad. bp. St. Louis (Gabala), 1857-59; bp. Chicago, 1859-80 (res.). Inactive from 1869 because of illness.

Dunn, John J. (1869-1933): ord. May 30, 1896; aux. bp. New York (Camuliana), 1921-33.

Dunne, Edmund M. (1864-1929): ord. June 24, 1887; bp. Peoria, 1909-29.

Dunne, Edward (1848-1910): b. Ireland; ord. June 29, 1871; bp. Dallas, 1893-1910.

Durier, Anthony (1832-1904): b. France; ord. Oct. 28, 1856; bp. Natchitoches (now Alexandria), La., 1885-1904.

Dwenger, Joseph, C.Pp.S. (1837-1893): ord. Sept. 4, 1859; bp. Fort Wayne, 1872-93.

E

Eccleston, Samuel, S.S. (1801-1851): ord. Apr. 24, 1825; coad. bp. Baltimore (Thermae), Sept.-Oct., 1834; abp. Baltimore, 1834-51.

Egan, Michael, O.F.M. (1761-1814): b. Ireland; first bp. Philadelphia, 1810-14.

Eis, Frederick (1843-1926): b. Germany; ord. Oct. 30, 1870; bp. Sault Ste. Marie and Marquette, 1899-1922 (res.).

Elder, William (1819-1904): ord. Mar. 29, 1846; bp. Natchez, 1857-80; coad. bp. Cincinnati, 1880-83; apb. Cincinnati, 1883-1904.

Emmet, Thomas A., S.J. (1873-1950): ord. July 30, 1909; v.a. Jamaica (Tuscamia), 1930-49 (res.).

England, John: See Index.

Escalante, Alonso Manuel, M.M. (1906-1967): b. Mexico; ord. Feb. 1, 1931; v.a. Pando, Bolivia (Sora), 1943-60 (res.).

Espelage (brothers): **Bernard T., O.F.M.**

(1892-1971): ord. May 16, 1918; bp. Gallup, 1940-69 (res.). **Sylvester J., O.F.M.** (1877-1940): ord. Jan. 18, 1900; v.a. Wuchang, China (Oreus), 1930-40.

Eustace, Bartholomew J. (1887-1956): ord. Nov. 1, 1914; bp. Camden, 1938-56.

F

Fahey, Leo F. (1898-1950): ord. May 29, 1926; coad. bp. Baker City (Ipsus), 1948-50.

Farley, John: See Index.

Farrelly, John P. (1856-1921): ord. Mar. 22, 1880; bp. Cleveland, 1909-21.

Feehan, Daniel F. (1855-1934): ord. Dec. 29, 1879; bp. Fall River, 1907-34.

Feehan, Patrick A. (1829-1902): b. Ireland; ord. Nov. 1, 1852; bp. Nashville, 1865-80; first abp. Chicago, 1880-1902.

Feeney, Daniel J. (1894-1969): ord. May 21, 1921; aux. bp. Portland, Me. (Sita), 1946-52; coad. bp. Portland, 1952-55; bp. Portland, 1955-69.

Feeney, Thomas J., S.J. (1894-1955): ord. June 23, 1927; v.a. Caroline and Marshall Is. (Agnus), 1951-55.

Fenwick, Benedict J., S.J. (1782-1846): ord. June 11, 1808; bp. Boston, 1825-46.

Fenwick, Edward D., O.P. (1768-1832): ord. Feb. 23, 1793; first bp. Cincinnati, 1822-32.

Fink, Michael, O.S.B. (1834-1904): b. Germany; ord. May 28, 1857; coad. v.a., 1871-74, and v.a., 1874-77, Kansas and Indian Territory (Eucarpia); first bp. Leavenworth (now Kansas City), 1877-1904.

Finnigan, George, C.S.C. (1885-1932): ord. June 13, 1915; bp. Helena, 1927-32.

Fitzgerald, Edward (1833-1907): b. Ireland; ord. Aug. 22, 1857; bp. Little Rock, 1866-1907.

Fitzgerald, Edward A.: (1893-1972): ord. July 25, 1916; aux, bp. Dubuque (Cantanus), 1946-49; bp. Winona, 1949-69 (res.).

Fitzgerald, Walter J., S.J. (1883-1947): ord. May 16, 1918; coad. v.a. Alaska (Tymbrias), 1939-45; v.a. Alaska, 1945-47.

Fitzmaurice, Edmond (1881-1962): b. Ireland; ord. May 28, 1904; bp. Wilmington, 1925-60 (res.).

Fitzmaurice, John E. (1837-1920): b. Ireland; ord. Dec. 21, 1862; coad. bp. Erie (Amisus), 1898-99; bp. Erie, 1899-1920.

Fitzpatrick, John B. (1812-1866): ord. June 13, 1840; aux. bp. Boston (Callipolis), 1843-46; bp. Boston, 1846-66.

Fitzsimon, Laurence J. (1895-1958): ord. May 17, 1921; bp. Amarillo, 1941-58.

Flaget, Benedict, S.S.: See Index.

Flasch, Kilian C. (1831-1891): b. Germany; ord. Dec. 16, 1859; bp. La Crosse, 1881-91.

Floersh, John (1886-1968): ord. June 10, 1911; coad. bp. Louisville (Lycopolis), 1923-24; bp. Louisville, 1924-37; first abp. Louisville, 1937-67 (res.).

Foley (brothers): **John S.** (1833-1918): ord. Dec. 20, 1856; bp. Detroit, 1888-1918. **Thom-**

as (1822-1879): ord. Aug. 16, 1846; coad. bp. and ap. admin. Chicago (Pergamum), 1870-79.

Foley, Maurice P. (1867-1919): ord. July 25, 1891; bp. Tuguegarao, P.I., 1910-16; bp. Jaro, P.I., 1916-19.

Ford, Francis X., M.M.: See Index.

Forest, John A. (1838-1911): b. France; ord. Apr. 12, 1863; bp. San Antonio, 1895-1911.

Fox, Joseph J. (1855-1915): ord. June 7, 1879; bp. Green Bay, 1904-14 (res.).

G

Gabriels, Henry (1838-1921): b. Belgium; ord. Sept. 21, 1861; bp. Ogdensburg, 1892-1921.

Galberry, Thomas, O.S.A. (1833-1878): b. Ireland; ord. Dec. 20, 1856; bp. Hartford, 1876-78.

Gallagher, Michael J. (1866-1937): ord. Mar. 19, 1893; coad. bp. Grand Rapids (Tiposa in Mauretania), 1915-16; bp. Grand Rapids, 1916-18; bp. Detroit, 1918-37.

Gallagher, Nicholas (1846-1918): ord. Dec. 25, 1868; coad. bp. Galveston (Canopus), 1882-92; bp. Galveston, 1892-1918.

Gannon, John M. (1877-1968): ord. Dec. 21, 1901; aux. bp. Erie (Nilopolis), 1918-20; bp. Erie, 1920-66 (res.).

Garcia Diego y Moreno, Francisco, O.F.M. (1785-1846): b. Mexico; ord. Nov. 14, 1808; bp. Two Californias (now Los Angeles), 1840-46.

Garriga, Mariano S. (1886-1965): ord. July 2, 1911; coad. bp. Corpus Christi (Syene), 1936-49; bp. Corpus Christi, 1949-65.

Garrigan, Philip (1840-1919): b. Ireland; ord. June 11, 1870; first bp. Sioux City, 1902-19.

Gartland, Francis X. (1808-1854): b. Ireland; ord. Aug. 5, 1832; first bp. Savannah, 1850-54.

Garvey, Eugene A. (1845-1920): ord. Sept. 22, 1869; first bp. Altoona (now Altoona-Johnstown), 1901-20.

Gercke, Daniel J. (1874-1964): ord. June 1, 1901; bp. Tucson, 1923-60 (res.).

Gerken, Rudolph A. (1887-1943): ord. June 10, 1917; first bp. Amarillo, 1927-33; abp. Santa Fe, 1933-43.

Gibbons, Edmund F. (1868-1964): ord. May 27, 1893; bp. Albany, 1919-54 (res.).

Gibbons, James: See Index.

Gilfillan, Francis (1872-1933): b. Ireland; ord. June 24, 1895; coad. bp. St. Joseph (Spiga), 1922-23; bp. St. Joseph 1923-33.

Gilmore, Joseph M. (1893-1962): ord. July 25, 1915; bp. Helena, 1936-62.

Gilmour, Richard (1824-1891): b. Scotland; ord. Aug. 30, 1852; bp. Cleveland, 1872-91.

Girouard, Paul J., M.S. (1898-1964): ord. July 26, 1927; first bp. Morondava, Madagascar, 1956-64.

Glass, Joseph S., C.M. (1874-1926): ord.

Aug. 15, 1897; bp. Salt Lake City, 1915-26.

Glennon, John: See Index.

Glorieux, Alphonse J. (1844-1917): b. Belgium; ord. Aug. 17, 1867; v.a. Idaho (Apollonia), 1885-93; bp. Boise, 1893-1917.

Goesbriand, Louis J. de (1816-1899): b. France; ord. July 13, 1840; first bp. Burlington, 1853-99.

Gorman, Daniel (1861-1927): ord. June 24, 1893; bp. Boise, 1918-27.

Grace Thomas (1841-1921): b. Ireland; ord. June 24, 1876; bp. Sacramento, 1896-1921.

Grace, Thomas L., O.P. (1814-1897): ord. Dec. 21, 1839; bp. St. Paul, 1859-84 (res.).

Granjon, Henry (1863-1922): b. France; ord. Dec. 17, 1887; bp. Tucson, 1900-22.

Griffin, James A. (1883-1948): ord. July 4, 1909; bp. Springfield, Ill., 1924-48.

Griffin, William A. (1885-1950): ord. Aug. 15, aux. bp. Newark (Sanavus), 1938-40; bp. Trenton, 1940-50.

Griffin, William R. (1883-1944): ord. May 25, 1907; aux. bp. La Crosse (Lydda), 1935-44.

Griffiths, James H. (1903-1964): ord. Mar. 12, 1927; aux. bp. New York and delegate of US military vicar (Gaza), 1950-64.

Grimes, John (1852-1922): b. Ireland; ord. Feb. 19, 1882; coad. bp. Syracuse (Hemeria), 1909-12; bp. Syracuse, 1912-22.

Grimmelsman, Henry J. (1890-1972): ord. Aug. 15, 1915; first bp. Evansville, 1945-65 (res.).

Gross, William H., C.SS.R. (1837-1898): ord. Mar. 21, 1863; bp. Savannah, 1873-85; abp. Oregon City (now Portland), 1885-98.

Guertin, George A. (1869-1932): ord. Dec. 17, 1892; bp. Manchester, 1907-32.

Guilfoyle, Richard T. (1892-1957): ord. June 2, 1917; bp. Altoona (now Altoona-Johnstown), 1936-57.

Gunn, John E., S.M. (1863-1924); b. Ireland; ord. Feb. 2, 1890; bp. Natchez (now Natchez-Jackson), 1911-24.

H

Haas, Francis J. (1889-1953): ord. June 11, 1913; bp. Grand Rapids, 1943-53.

Hafey, William (1888-1954): ord. June 16, 1914; first bp. Raleigh, 1925-37; coad. bp. Scranton (Appia), 1937-38; bp. Scranton, 1938-54.

Hagan, John R. (1890-1946): ord. Mar. 7, 1914; aux. bp. Cleveland (Limata), 1946.

Haid, Leo M., O.S.B. (1849-1924): ord. Dec. 21, 1872; v.a. N. Carolina (Messene), 1888-1910; abbot Mary Help of Christians abbacy, 1910-24.

Hallinan, Paul J. (1911-1968): ord. Feb. 20, 1937; bp. Charleston, 1958-62; first abp. Atlanta, 1962-68.

Hanna, Edward J. (1860-1944): ord. May 30, 1885; aux. bp. San Francisco (Titiopolis), 1912-15; abp. San Francisco, 1915-35 (res.).

Hannan, Jerome D. (1896-1965): ord. May 22, 1921; bp. Scranton, 1954-65.

Harkins, Matthew (1845-1921): ord. May 22, 1869; bp. Providence, 1887-1921.

Hartley, James J. (1858-1944): ord. July 10, 1882; bp. Columbus, 1904-44.

Harty, Jeremiah J. (1853-1927): ord. Apr. 28, 1878; abp. Manila, 1903-16; abp. Omaha, 1916-27.

Hayes, Patrick J.: See Index.

Hayes, Ralph L. (1884-1970): ord. Sept. 19, 1909; bp. Helena 1933-35; rector North American College, 1935-44; bp. Davenport, 1944-66 (res.).

Healy, James A. (1830-1900): ord. June 10, 1854; bp. Portland 1875-1900.

Heelan, Edmond (1868-1948): b. Ireland: ord. June 24, 1890; aux. bp. Sioux City (Gerasa), 1919-20; bp. Sioux City, 1920-48.

Heffron, Patrick (1860-1927): ord. Dec. 22, 1884; bp. Winona, 1910-27.

Heiss, Michael (1818-1890): b. Germany; ord. Oct. 18, 1840; bp. La Crosse, 1868-80; coad. abp. Milwaukee, 1880-81; abp. Milwaukee, 1881-90.

Hendrick, Thomas A. (1849-1909): ord. June 7, 1873; bp. Cebu, P.I., 1904-09.

Hendricken, Thomas F. (1827-1886): b. Ireland; ord. Apr. 25, 1853; bp. Providence, 1872-86.

Hennessy, John (1825-1900): b. Ireland; ord. Nov. 1, 1850; bp. Dubuque, 1866-93; first abp. Dubuque, 1893-1900.

Hennessy, John J. (1847-1920): b. Ireland; ord. Nov. 28, 1869; first bp. Wichita, 1888-1920; ap. admin. Concordia (now Salina), 1891-98.

Henni, John M. (1805-1881): b. Switzerland; ord. Feb. 2, 1829; first bp. Milwaukee, 1844-75; first abp. Milwaukee, 1875-81.

Heslin, Thomas (1845-1911): b. Ireland; ord. Sept. 8, 1869; bp. Natchez (now Natchez-Jackson), 1889-1911.

Hickey, Thomas F. (1861-1940): ord. Mar. 25, 1884; coad. bp. Rochester (Berenice), 1905-09; bp. Rochester, 1909-28 (res.).

Hickey, William A. (1869-1933): ord. Dec. 22, 1893; coad. bp. Providence (Claudiopolis), 1919-21; bp. Providence, 1921-33.

Hillinger, Raymond P. (1904-1971): ord. Apr. 2, 1932; bp. Rockford, 1953-56; aux. bp. Chicago (Derbe), 1956-71.

Hoban, Edward F. (1878-1966): ord. July 11, 1903; aux. bp. Chicago (Colonia), 1921-28; bp. Rockford, 1928-42; coad. bp. Cleveland (Lystra), 1942-45; bp. Cleveland, 1945-66.

Hoban, Michael J. (1853-1926): ord. May 22, 1880; coad. bp. Scranton (Halius), 1896-99; bp. Scranton, 1899-1926.

Hogan, John J. (1829-1913): b. Ireland; ord. Apr. 10, 1852; first bp. St. Joseph, 1868-80; first bp. Kansas City, 1880-1913.

Horstmann, Ignatius (1840-1908): ord. June 10, 1865; bp. Cleveland, 1892-1908.

Howard, Francis W. (1867-1944): ord. June 16, 1891; bp. Covington, 1923-44.

Hughes, John J.: See Index.

Hunkeler, Edward J. (1894-1970): ord. June 14, 1919; bp. Grand Island, 1945-51; bp. Kansas City, Kans. 1951-52; first abp. Kansas City, 1952-69 (res.).

Hunt, Duane G. (1884-1960): ord. June 27, 1920; bp. Salt Lake City, 1937-60.

Hurley, Joseph P. (1894-1967): ord. May 29, 1919; bp. St. Augustine, 1940-67.

Hyland, Francis E. (1901-1968): ord. June 11, 1927; aux. bp. Savannah-Atlanta (Gomphi), 1949-56; bp. Atlanta, 1956-61 (res.).

Hyle, Michael W. (1901-1967): ord. Mar. 12, 1927; coad bp. Wilmington, 1958-60; bp. Wilmington, 1960-67.

I

Ireland, John: See Index.

Ireton, Peter L. (1882-1958): ord. June 20, 1906; coad. bp. Richmond (Cyme), 1935-45; bp. Richmond, 1945-58.

J

Janssen, John (1835-1913): b. Germany; ord. Nov. 19, 1858; first bp. Belleville, 1888-1913.

Janssens, Francis A. (1843-1897): b. Holland; ord. Dec. 21, 1867; bp. Natchez, 1881-88; abp. New Orleans, 1888-97.

Jeanmard, Jules B. (1879-1957): ord. June 10, 1903; first bp. Lafayette, La., 1918-56 (res.).

Johannes, Francis (1874-1937): b. Germany; ord. Jan. 3, 1897; coad. bp. Leavenworth (Thasus), 1928-29; bp. Leavenworth (now Kansas City), 1929-37.

Jones, William A., O.S.A. (1865-1921): ord. Mar. 15, 1890; bp. San Juan, 1907-21.

Junger, Aegidius (1833-1895): b. Germany; ord. June 27, 1862; bp. Nesqually (now Seattle), 1879-95.

K

Kain, John J. (1841-1903): ord. July 2, 1866; bp. Wheeling, 1875-93; coad. abp. St. Louis (Oxyrynchus), 1893-95; abp. St. Louis, 1895-1903.

Katzer, Frederick X. (1844-1903): b. Austria; ord. Dec. 21, 1866; bp. Green Bay, 1886-91; abp. Milwaukee, 1891-1903.

Keane, James J. (1856-1929): ord. Dec. 23, 1882; bp. Cheyenne, 1902-11; abp. Dubuque, 1911-29.

Keane, John J. (1839-1918): b. Ireland; ord. July 2, 1866; bp. Richmond, 1878-88; rector of Catholic University, 1888-97; consultor of Congregation for Propagation of the Faith, 1897-1900; abp. Dubuque, 1900-11 (res.).

Keane, Patrick J. (1872-1928): b. Ireland; ord. June 20, 1895; aux. bp. Sacramento (Samaria), 1920-22; bp. Sacramento, 1922-28.

Kearney, Raymond A. (1902-1956): ord. Mar. 12, 1927; aux. bp. Brooklyn (Lysinia), 1935-56.

Keiley, Benjamin J. (1847-1925): ord. Dec. 31, 1873; bp. Savannah, 1900-22 (res.).

Kelleher, Louis J. (1889-1946): ord. Apr. 3, 1915; aux. bp. Boston (Thenae), 1945-46.

Kelley, Francis C. (1870-1948): b. Canada; ord. Aug. 23, 1893; bp. Oklahoma (now Oklahoma City and Tulsa — title changed in 1930), 1924-48.

Kelly, Edward D. (1860-1926): ord. June 16, 1886; aux. bp. Detroit (Cestrus), 1911-19; bp. Grand Rapids, 1919-26.

Kelly, Edward J. (1890-1956): ord. June 2, 1917; bp. Boise, 1928-56. ea

Kelly, Francis M. (1886-1950: ord. Nov. 1, 1912; aux. bp. Winona (Mylasa), 1926-28; bp. Winona, 1928-49 (res.).

Kelly, Patrick (1779-1829): b. Ireland; ord. July 18, 1802; first bp. Richmond, 1820-22 (returned to Ireland; bp. Waterford and Lismore, 1822-29).

Kennedy, Thomas F. (1858-1917): ord. July 24, 1887; rector North American College, 1901-17; tit. bp. Hadrianapolis, 1907-15; tit. abp. Seleucia, 1915-17.

Kenny, William J. (1853-1913): ord. Jan 15, 1879; bp. St. Augustine, 1902-13.

Kenrick (brothers): **Francis P.** (1796-1863): b. Ireland; ord. Apr. 7, 1821; coad. bp. Philadelphia (Aratha), 1830-42; bp. Philadelphia, 1842-51; abp. Baltimore, 1851-63. **Peter** (1806-1896): b. Ireland; ord. Mar. 6, 1932; coad. bp. St. Louis (Adrasus), 1841-43; bp., 1843-47, and first abp. 1847-95, St. Louis (res.).

Keough, Francis P. (1890-1961): ord. June 10, 1916; bp. Providence, 1943-47; abp. Baltimore, 1947-61.

Keyes, Michael, S.M. (1876-1959): b. Ireland; ord. June 21, 1907; bp. Savannah, 1922-35 (res.).

Kiley, Moses E. (1876-1953): b. Nova Scotia; ord. June 10, 1911; bp. Trenton, 1934-40; abp. Milwaukee, 1940-53.

Kogy, Lorenz S., O.M. (1895-1963): b. Georgia, Russia; ord. Nov. 15, 1917; U.S. citizen, 1944; patriarchal vicar for Armenian diocese of Beirut (Comana), 1951-63.

Koudelka, Joseph (1852-1921): b. Austria; ord. Oct. 8, 1875; aux. bp. Cleveland (Germanicoplis), 1908-11; aux. bp. Milwaukee, 1911-13; bp. Superior, 1913-21.

Kowalski, Rembert, O.F.M. (1884-1970): ord. June 22, 1911; v.a. Wuchang, China (Ipsus), 1942-46; first bp. Wuchang, 1946-70 (in exile from 1953).

Kozlowski, Edward (1860-1915): b. Poland; ord. June 29, 1887; aux. bp. Milwaukee (Germia), 1914-15.

Krautbauer, Francis X. (1824-1885): b. Germany; ord. July 16, 1850; bp. Green Bay, 1875-85.

Kucera, Louis B. (1888-1957): ord. June 8, 1915; bp. Lincoln, 1930-57.

L

Lamb, Hugh (1890-1959): ord. May 29, 1915; aux. bp. Philadelphia (Helos), 1936-51; bp. Greensburg, 1951-59.

Lamy, Jean B.: See Index.

Lane, Loras (1910-1968): ord. Mar. 19, 1937; aux. bp. Dubuque (Bencenna), 1951-56; bp. Rockford, 1956-68.

Laval, John M. (1854-1937): b. France; ord. Nov. 10, 1877; aux. bp. New Orleans (Hierocaesarea), 1911-37.

Lavialle, Peter J. (1819-1867): b. France; ord. Feb. 12, 1844; bp. Louisville, 1865-67.

Lawler, John J. (1862-1948): ord. Dec. 19, 1885; aux. bp. St. Paul (Hermopolis), 1910-16; bp. Lead (now Rapid City), 1916-48.

Le Blond, Charles H. (1883-1958): ord. June 29, 1909; bp. St. Joseph, 1933-56 (res.).

Ledvina, Emmanuel (1868-1952): ord. Mar. 18, 1893; bp. Corpus Christi, 1921-49 (res.).

Lefevere, Peter P. (1804-1869): b. Belgium; ord. Nov. 30, 1831; coad. bp. and admin. Detroit (Zela), 1841-69.

Leibold, Paul F. (1914-1972): ord. May 18, 1940; aux. bp. Cincinnati (Trebenna), 1958-66; bp. Evansville, 1966-69; abp. Cincinnati, 1969-71.

Lenihan (brothers): **Mathias C.** (1854-1943): ord. Dec. 20, 1879; bp. Great Falls, 1904-30 (res.). **Thomas M.** (1844-1901): b. Ireland; ord. Nov. 19, 1868; bp. Cheyenne, 1897-1901.

Leray, Francis X. (1825-1887): b. France; ord. Mar. 19, 1852; bp. Natchitoches (now Alexandria, La.), 1877-79; coad. bp. New Orleans and admin. of Natchitoches (Jonopolis), 1879-83; abp. New Orleans, 1883-87.

Ley, Felix, O.F.M. Cap. (1909-1972): ord. June 14, 1936; ap. admin. Ryukyu Is., (Caporilla), 1968-72.

Lillis, Thomas F. (1861-1938): ord. Aug. 15, 1885; bp. Leavenworth (now Kansas City, Kans.), (Cibyra), 1910-13; bp. Kansas City, Mo., 1913-38.

Lootens, Louis (1827-1898): b. Belgium; ord. June 14, 1851; v. a. Idaho and Montana (Castabala), 1868-76 (res.).

Loras, Mathias (1792-1858): b. France; ord. Nov. 12, 1815; first bp. Dubuque, 1837-58.

Loughlin, John (1817-1891): b. Ireland; ord. Oct. 18, 1840; first bp. Brooklyn, 1853-91.

Lowney, Denis M. (1863-1918): b. Ireland; ord. Dec. 17, 1887; aux. bp. Providence (Hadrianopolis), 1917-18.

Ludden, Patrick A. (1838-1912): b. Ireland; ord. May 21, 1865; first bp. Syracuse, 1887-1912.

Luers, John (1819-1871): b. Germany; ord. Nov. 11, 1846; first bp. Fort Wayne, 1858-71.

Lynch, Joseph P. (1872-1954): ord. June 9, 1900; bp. Dallas (Dallas-Fort Worth, 1953), 1911-54.

Lynch, Patrick N. (1817-1882): b. Ireland; ord. Apr. 5, 1840; bp. Charleston, 1858-82.

M

McAuliffe, Maurice F. (1875-1944): ord. July 29, 1900; aux. bp. Hartford (Dercos), 1925-34; bp. Hartford, 1934-44.

McCarthy, Joseph E. (1876-1955): ord. July 4, 1903; bp. Portland, Me., 1932-55.

McCarthy, Justin J. (1900-1959): ord. Apr. 16, 1927; aux. bp. Newark (Doberus), 1954-57; bp. Camden, 1957-59.

McCarty, William T., C.SS.R. (1889-1972): ord. June 10, 1915; military delegate (Anea), 1943-47; coad. bp. Rapid City, 1947-48; bp. Rapid City, 1948-69 (res.).

McCloskey, James P. (1870-1945): ord. Dec. 17, 1898, bp. Zamboanga, P.I., 1917-20; bp. Jaro, P.I., 1920-45.

McCloskey, John: See Index.

McCloskey, William G. (1823-1909): ord. Oct. 6, 1852; bp. Louisville, 1868-1909.

McCormick, Patrick J. (1880-1953): ord. July 6, 1904; aux. bp. Washington (Atenia), 1950-53.

McCort, John J. (1860-1936): ord. Oct. 14, 1883; aux. bp. Philadelphia (Azotus), 1912-20; bp. Altoona, 1920-36.

McDevitt, Philip R. (1858-1935): ord. July 14, 1885; bp. Harrisburg, 1916-35.

McDonnell, Charles E. (1854-1921): ord. May 19, 1878; bp. Brooklyn, 1892-1921.

McDonnell, Thomas J. (1894-1961): ord. Sept. 20, 1919; aux. bp. New York (Sela), 1947-51; coad. bp. Wheeling, 1951-61.

McEntegart, Bryan (1893-1968): ord. Sept. 8, 1917; bp. Ogdensburg, 1943-53; rector Catholic University (Aradi), 1953-57; bp. Brooklyn, 1957-68.

McFadden, James A. (1880-1952): ord. June 17, 1905; aux. bp. Cleveland (Bida), 1932-43; first bp. Youngstown, 1943-52.

MacFarland, Francis P. (1819-1874): ord. May 1, 1845; bp. Hartford, 1858-74.

McFaul, James A. (1850-1917): b. Ireland; ord. May 26, 1877; bp. Trenton, 1894-1917.

McGavick, Alexander J. (1863-1948): ord. June 11, 1887; aux. bp. Chicago (Marcopolis), 1899-1921; bp. La Crosse, 1921-48.

McGeough, Joseph F. (1903-1970): ord. Dec. 20, 1930; internuncio Ethiopia, 1957-60; apostolic delegate (Hemesa) S. Africa, 1960-67; nuncio Ireland, 1967-69.

McGill, John (1809-1872): ord. June 13, 1835; bp. Richmond, 1850-72.

MacGinley, John B. (1871-1969): b. Ireland; ord. June 8, 1895; bp. Nueva Caceres, 1910-24; first bp. Monterey-Fresno, 1924-32 (res.).

McGolrick, James (1841-1918): b. Ireland; ord. June 11, 1867; first bp. Duluth, 1889-1918.

McGovern, Patrick A. (1872-1951): ord. Aug. 18, 1895; bp. Cheyenne, 1912-51.

McGovern, Thomas (1832-1898): b. Ireland; ord. Dec. 27, 1861; bp. Harrisburg, 1888-98.

McGrath, Joseph F. (1871-1950): b. Ireland; ord. Dec. 21, 1895; bp. Baker City (now Baker), 1919-50.

McGuinness, Eugene (1889-1957): ord. May 22, 1915; bp. Raleigh, 1937-44; coad. bp. Oklahoma City and Tulsa (Ilium), 1944-48; bp. Oklahoma City and Tulsa, 1948-57.

McLaughlin, Thomas H. (1881-1947): ord. July 26, 1904; aux. bp. Newark (Nisa), 1935-37; first bp. Paterson, 1937-47.

McMahon, John J. (1875-1932): ord. May 20, 1900; bp. Trenton, 1928-32.

McMahon, Lawrence S. (1835-1893): ord. Mar. 24, 1860; bp. Hartford, 1879-93.

McManaman, Edward P. (1900-1964): ord. Mar. 12, 1927; aux. bp. Erie (Floriana), 1948-64.

McMullen, John (1832-1883): b. Ireland; ord. June 20, 1858; first bp. Davenport, 1881-83.

McNamara, John M. (1878-1960): ord. June 21, 1902; aux. bp. Baltimore (Eumenia), 1928-47; aux. bp. Washington, 1947-60.

McNamara, Martin D. (1898-1966): ord. Dec. 23, 1922; first bp. Joliet, 1949-66.

McNeirny, Francis (1828-1894): ord. Aug. 17, 1854; coad. bp. Albany (Rhesaina), 1872-77; bp. Albany, 1877-94.

McNicholas, John T., O.P. (1877-1950): b. Ireland; ord. Oct. 10, 1901; bp. Duluth, 1918-25; abp. Cincinnati, 1925-50.

McNulty, James A. (1900-1972): ord. July 12, 1925; aux. bp. Newark (Methone), 1947-53; bp. Paterson, 1953-63; bp. Buffalo, 1963-72.

McQuaid, Bernard J.: See Index.

McSorley, Francis J., O.M.I. (1913-1971): ord. May 30, 1939: v.a. Jolo, P.I. (Sozusa), 1958-71.

McVinney, Russell J. (1898-1971): ord. July 13, 1924; bp. Providence, 1948-71.

Machebeuf, Joseph P. (1812-1889): b. France; ord. Dec. 17, 1836; v. a. Colorado and Utah (Epiphania), 1868-1887; first bp. Denver, 1887-89.

Maes, Camillus P. (1846-1915): b. Belgium; ord. Dec. 19, 1868; bp. Covington, 1885-1915.

Magner, Francis (1887-1947): ord. May 17, 1913; bp. Marquette, 1941-47.

Mahoney, Bernard (1875-1939): ord. Feb. 27, 1904; bp. Sioux Falls, 1922-39.

Maloney, Thomas F. (1903-1962): ord. July 13, 1930; aux. bp. Providence (Andropolis), 1960-62.

Manogue, Patrick: See Index.

Manucy, Dominic (1823-1885): ord. Aug. 15, 1850; v. a. Brownsville (Dulma), 1874-84; bp. Mobile. Mar.-Sept., 1884: (res.); reappointed v. a. Brownsville (Maronea), 1884-85.

Marechal, Ambrose, S.S. (1766-1828): b. France; ord. June 2, 1792; abp. Baltimore, 1817-28.

Markham, Thomas F. (1891-1952): ord. June 2, 1917; aux. bp. Boston (Acalissus), 1950-52.

Martin, Augustus M. (1803-1875): b. France; ord. May 31, 1828; first bp. Natchitoches (now Alexandria), 1853-75.

Marty, Martin, O.S.B. (1834-1896): b. Switzerland; ord. Sept. 14, 1856; v. a. Dakota (Tiberias), 1880-89; first bp. Sioux Falls, 1889-95; bp. St. Cloud, 1895-96.

Marx, Adolph, (1915-1965): b. Germany;

ord. May 2, 1940; aux. bp. Corpus Christi (Citrus), 1956-65; first bp. Brownsville, 1965.

Matz, Nicholas C. (1850-1917): b. France; ord. May 31, 1874; coad. bp. Denver (Telmissus), 1887-89; bp. Denver, 1889-1917.

Meerschaert, Theophile (1847-1924): b. Belgium; ord. Dec. 23, 1871; v. a. Oklahoma and Indian Territory (Sidyma), 1891-1905; first bp. Oklahoma (now Oklahoma City and Tulsa), 1905-24.

Melcher, Joseph (1806-1873): b. Austria; ord. Mar. 27, 1830; first bp. Green Bay, 1868-73.

Messmer, Sebastian (1847-1930): b. Switzerland; ord. July 23, 1871; bp. Green Bay, 1892-1903; abp. Milwaukee, 1903-30.

Meyer, Albert (1903-1965): ord. July 11, 1926; bp. Superior, 1946-53; abp. Milwaukee, 1953-58; abp. Chicago, 1958-65; cardinal, 1959.

Michaud, John S. (1843-1908): ord. June 7, 1873; coad. bp. Burlington (Modra), 1892-99; bp. Burlington, 1899-1908.

Miege, John B., S.J. (1815-1884): b. France; ord. Sept. 12, 1844; v. a. Kansas and Indian Territory (now Kansas City) (Messene), 1851-74 (res.).

Miles, Richard P., O.P. (1791-1860): ord. Sept. 21, 1816; first bp. Nashville, 1838-60.

Misner, Paul B., C.M. (1891-1938): ord. Feb. 23, 1919; v.a. Yukiang, China (Myrica), 1935-38.

Mitty, John J. (1884-1961): ord. Dec. 22, 1906; bp. Salt Lake, 1926-32; coad. abp. San Francisco (Aegina), 1932-35; abp. San Francisco, 1935-61.

Moeller, Henry (1849-1925): ord. June 10, 1876; bp. Columbus, 1900-03; coad. abp. Cincinnati (Aeropolic), 1903-04); abp. Cincinnati, 1904-25.

Molloy, Thomas E. (1884-1956): ord. Sept. 19, 1908; aux. bp. Brooklyn (Lorea), 1920-21; bp. Brooklyn, 1921-56.

Monaghan, Francis J. (1890-1942): ord. May 29, 1915; coad. bp. Ogdensburg (Mela), 1936-39; bp. Ogdensburg, 1939-42.

Monaghan, John J. (1856-1935): ord. Dec. 18, 1880; bp. Wilmington, 1897-1925 (res.).

Montgomery, George T. (1847-1907): ord. Dec. 20, 1879; coad. bp. Monterey-Los-Angeles (Thmuis), 1894-96; bp. Monterey-Los Angeles (now Los Angeles), 1896-1903; coad. abp. San Francisco (Auxum), 1903-07.

Mooney, Edward (1882-1958): ord. Apr. 10, 1909; ap. del. India (Irenopolis), 1926-31; ap. del. Japan, 1931-33; bp. Rochester, 1933-37; first abp. Detroit, 1937-58; cardinal, 1946.

Moore, John (1835-1901): b. Ireland; ord. Apr. 9, 1860; bp. St. Augustine, 1877-1901.

Mora, Francis (1827-1905): b. Spain; ord. Mar. 19, 1856; coad. bp. Monterey-Los Angeles (Mosynopolis), 1873-78; bp. Monterey-Los Angeles, 1878-96 (res.).

Morris, John (1866-1946): ord. June 11, 1892; coad. bp. Little Rock (Acmonia), 1906-07; bp. Little Rock, 1907-46.

Mrak, Ignatius (1810-1901): b. Austria; ord. July 31; 1837; bp. Sault Ste. Marie and Marquette (now Marquette), 1869-78 (res.).

Muench, Aloysius: See Index.

Muldoon, Peter J. (1862-1927): ord. Dec. 18, 1886; aux. bp. Chicago (Tamasus), 1901-08; first bp. Rockford, 1908-27.

Mullen, Tobias (1818-1900): b. Ireland; ord. Sept. 1, 1844; bp. Erie, 1868-99 (res.).

Mulloy, William T. (1892-1959): ord. June 7, 1916; bp. Covington, 1945-59.

Mundelein, George (1872-1939): ord. June 8, 1895; aux. bp. Brooklyn (Loryma), 1909-15; abp. Chicago, 1915-39; cardinal, 1924.

Murphy, Joseph A., S.J. (1857-1939): b. Ireland; ord. Aug. 26, 1888; v. a. Belize, Br. Honduras (Birtha), 1923-39.

Murphy, William F. (1885-1950): ord. June 13, 1908; first bp. Saginaw, 1938-50.

Murray, John G. (1877-1956): ord. Apr. 14, 1900; aux. bp. Hartford (Flavias), 1920-25; bp. Portland, 1925-31; abp. St. Paul, 1931-56.

N

Navagh, James J. (1901-1965): ord. Dec. 21, 1929; aux. bp. Raleigh (Ombi), 1952-57; bp. Ogdensburg, 1957-63; bp. Paterson, 1963-65.

Neale, Leonard (1746-1817): ord. June 5, 1773; coad. bp. Baltimore (Gortyna), 1800-15; abp. Baltimore, 1815-17.

Neraz, John C. (1828-1894): b. France; ord. Mar. 19, 1853; bp. San Antonio, 1881-1894.

Neumann, John, Bl.: See Index.

Niedhammer, Matthew A., O.F.M. Cap. (1901-1970): ord. June 8, 1927; v. a. Bluefields, Nicaragua (Caloe), 1943-70.

Nilan, John J. (1855-1934): ord. Dec. 2, 1878; bp. Hartford, 1910-34.

Noll, John F.: See Index.

Northrop, Henry P. (1842-1916): ord. June 25, 1865; v.a. North Carolina (Rosalia), 1881-83; bp. Charleston, 1883-1916.

Nussbaum, Paul J., C.P. (1870-1935): ord. May 20, 1894; first bp. Corpus Christi, 1913-20 (res.); bp. Sault Ste. Marie and Marquette (now Marquette), 1922-35.

O

O'Brien, William D. (1878-1962): ord. July 11, 1903; aux. bp. Chicago (Calynda), 1934-62.

O'Connell, Denis J. (1849-1927): b. Ireland; ord. May 26, 1877; aux. bp. San Francisco (Sebaste), 1908-12; bp. Richmond, 1912-26 (res.).

O'Connell, Eugene (1815-1891): b. Ireland; ord. May 21, 1842; v. a. Marysville (Flaviopolis), 1861-68; first bp. Grass Valley, 1868-84 (res.).

O'Connell, William H. (1859-1944): ord. June 7, 1884; bp. Portland, 1901-06; coad. bp. Boston (Constantia), 1906-07; abp. Boston, 1907-44; cardinal, 1911.

O'Connor (brothers), **James** (1823-1890): b. Ireland; ord. Mar. 25, 1848; v. a. Nebraska

(Dibon), 1876-85; first bp. Omaha, 1885-90.
Michael, S.J. (1810-1872): b. Ireland; ord.
June 1, 1833; first bp. Pittsburgh, 1843-53;
first bp. of Erie, 1853-54; bp. Pittsburgh,
1854-60 (resigned, joined Jesuits).
O'Connor, John J. (1855-1927): ord. Dec.
22, 1877; bp. Newark, 1901-27.
O'Dea, Edward J. (1856-1932): ord. Dec.
23, 1882; bp. Nesqually (now Seattle — title
changed in 1907), 1896-1932.
Odin, John M., C.M. (1800-1870): b.
France; ord. May 4, 1823; v. a. Texas (Claudiopolis), 1842-47; first bp. Galveston, 1847-
61; abp. New Orleans, 1861-70.
O'Donaghue, Denis (1848-1925): ord. Sept.
6, 1874; aux. bp. Indianapolis (Pomaria),
1900-10; bp. Louisville, 1910-24 (res.).
O'Dowd, James T. (1907-1950): ord. June
4, 1932; aux. bp. San Francisco (Cea), 1948-
50.
O'Farrell, Michael J. (1832-1894): b. Ireland; ord. Aug. 18, 1855; first bp. Trenton,
1881-94.
O'Gara, Cuthbert, C.P. (1886-1968): b.
Canada; ord. May 26, 1915; v.a. Yuanling,
China (Elis), 1934-46; first bp. Yuanling,
1946-68 (imprisoned, 1951, and then expelled,
1953, by Chinese Communists).
O'Gorman, James, O.C.S.O. (1804-1874):
b. Ireland; ord. Dec. 23, 1843; v.a. Nebraska
(now Omaha) (Raphanea), 1859-74.
O'Gorman, Thomas (1843-1921): ord. Nov.
5, 1865; bp. Sioux Falls, 1896-1921.
O'Hara, Edwin V.: See Index.
O'Hara, Gerald P. (1888-1963): ord. Apr.
3, 1920; aux. bp. Philadelphia (Heliopolis),
1929-35; bp. Savannah (title changed to Sa-
vannah-Atlanta in 1937), 1935-59 (res.); regent of Rumania nunciature, 1946-50 (expelled); nuncio to Ireland, 1951-54; ap. del. to
Great Britain, 1954-63.
O'Hara, John F., C.S.C. (1886-1960): ord.
Sept. 9, 1916; delegate of US military vicar
(Mylasa), 1940-45; np. Buffalo, 1945-51; abp.
Philadelphia, 1951-60; cardinal, 1958.
O'Hara, William (1816-1899): b. Ireland;
ord. Dec. 21, 1842; first bp. Scranton, 1868-
99.
O'Hare, William F., S.J. (1870-1926): ord.
June 25, 1903; v.a. Jamaica (Max-
imianopolis), 1920-26.
O'Hern, John F. (1874-1933): ord. Feb. 17,
1901; bp. Rochester, 1929-33.
O'Leary, Thomas (1875-1949): ord. Dec.
18, 1897; bp. Springfield, Mass., 1921-49.
Olwell, Quentin, C.P. (1898-1972); ord.
Feb. 4, 1923; prelate Marbel, P.I. (Thabraca),
1961-69 (ret.).
O'Regan, Anthony (1809-1866): b. Ireland;
ord. Nov. 29, 1834; bp. Chicago, 1854-58
(res.).
O'Reilly, Bernard (1803-1856): b. Ireland;
ord. Oct. 16, 1831; bp. Hartford, 1850-56.
O'Reilly, Charles J. (1860-1923): b. Canada; ord. June 29, 1890; first bp. Baker City
(now Baker), 1903-18; bp. Lincoln, 1918-23.

O'Reilly, James (1855-1934): b. Ireland;
ord. June 24, 1880; bp. Fargo, 1910-34.
O'Reilly, Patrick T. (1833-1892): b. Ireland; ord. Aug. 15, 1857; first bp. Springfield,
Mass., 1870-92.
O'Reilly, Peter J. (1850-1924): b. Ireland;
ord. June 24, 1877; aux. bp. Peoria (Lebedus),
1900-24.
O'Reilly, Thomas C. (1873-1938): ord. June
4, 1898; bp. Scranton, 1928-38.
Ortynsky, Stephen, O.S.B.M. (1866-1916):
b. Poland; ord. July 18, 1891; first Ukrainian
Byzantine Rite bishop in US (Daulia), 1907-
16.
O'Shea, John A., C.M. (1887-1969): ord.
May 30, 1914; v.a. Kanchow, China (Midila),
1928-46; first bp. Kanchow, 1946-69 (expelled
by Chinese Communists, 1953).
O'Shea, William F., M.M. (1884-1945):
ord. Dec. 5, 1917; v.a. Heijo, Japan (Naissus),
1939-45; prisoner of Japanese 1941-42.
O'Sullivan, Jeremiah (1842-1896): b. Ireland; ord. June 30, 1868; bp. Mobile, 1885-96.

P

Paschang, Adolph J., M.M. (1895-1968):
ord. May 21, 1921; v.a. Kong Moon, China
(Sasima), 1937-46; first bp. Kong Moon,
1946-68 (expelled by Communists, 1951.)
Pellicer, Anthony (1824-1880): ord. Aug.
15, 1850; first bp. San Antonio, 1874-80.
Penalver y Cardenas, Luis (1749-1810): b.
Cuba; ord. Apr. 4, 1772; first bp. Louisiana
and the Two Floridas (now New Orleans),
1793-1801; abp. Guatemala, 1801-06 (res.).
Perche, Napoleon J. (1805-1883): b. France;
ord. Sept. 19, 1829; abp. New Orleans, 1870-
83.
Persico, Ignatius, O.F.M. Cap. (1823-1895):
b. Italy; ord. Jan. 24, 1846; bishop from 1854;
bp. Savannah-Atlanta, 1870-72; cardinal,
1893.
Peschges, John H. (1881-1944): ord. Apr.
15, 1905; bp. Crookston, 1938-44.
Peterson, John B. (1871-1944): ord. Sept.
15, 1899; aux. bp. Boston (Hippos), 1927-32;
bp. Manchester, 1932-44.
Phelan, Richard (1828-1904): b. Ireland;
ord. May 4, 1854; coad. bp. Pittsburgh (Cibyra), 1885-89; bp. Pittsburgh, 1889-1904.
Pitaval, John B. (1858-1928): b. France;
ord. Dec. 24, 1881; aux. bp. Santa Fe (Sora),
1902-09; abp. Santa Fe, 1909-18 (res.).
Plagens, Joseph C. (1880-1943): b. Poland;
ord. July 5, 1903; aux. bp. Detroit (Rhodia-
polis), 1924-35; bp. Sault Ste. Marie and Marquette (title changed to Marquette, 1937),
1935-40; bp. Grand Rapids, 1941-43.
Portier, Michael (1795-1859): b. France;
ord. May 16, 1818; v.a. Two Floridas and
Alabama (Olena), 1826-29; first bp. Mobile,
1829-59.
Prendergast, Edmond (1843-1918): b. Ireland; ord. Nov. 17, 1865; aux. bp. Philadelphia Scilium), 1897-1911; abp. Philadelphia,
1911-18.

Purcell, John B. (1800-1883): b. Ireland; ord. May 20, 1826; bp., 1833-50, and first abp., 1850-83, Cincinnati.

Q

Quarter, William (1806-1848): b. Ireland; ord. Sept. 19, 1829; first bp. Chicago, 1844-48.

Quigley, James E. (1855-1915): b. Canada; ord. Apr. 13, 1879; bp. Buffalo, 1897-1903; abp. Chicago, 1903-15.

Quinlan, John (1826-1883): b. Ireland; ord. Aug. 30, 1852; bp. Mobile, 1859-83.

Quinn, William Charles, C.M. (1905-1960): ord. Oct. 11, 1931; v.a. Yukiang, China (Halicarnassus), 1940-46; first bp. Yukiang, 1946-60 (expelled by Chinese Communists, 1951).

R

Rademacher, Joseph (1840-1900): ord. Aug. 2, 1863; bp. Nashville, 1883-93; bp. Fort Wayne, 1893-1900.

Rappe, Louis Amadeus (1801-1877): b. France; ord. Mar. 14, 1829; first bp. Cleveland, 1847-70 (res.).

Ready, Michael J. (1893-1957): ord. Sept. 14, 1918; bp. Columbus, 1944-57.

Reed, Victor J. (1905-1971): ord. Dec. 21, 1929; aux. bp. Oklahoma City and Tulsa (Limasa), 1957-58; bp. Oklahoma City and Tulsa, 1958-71.

Reilly, Edmond J. (1897-1958): ord. Apr. 1, 1922; aux. bp. Brooklyn (Nepte), 1955-58.

Rese, Frederic (1791-1871): b. Germany; ord. Mar. 15, 1823; first bp. Detroit, 1833-71. Inactive from 1841 because of ill health.

Reverman, Theodore (1877-1941): ord. July 26, 1901; bp. Superior, 1926-41.

Reynolds, Ignatius A. (1798-1855): ord. Oct. 24, 1823; bp. Charleston, 1844-55.

Rhode, Paul P. (1871-1945): b. Poland; ord. June 17, 1894; aux. bp. Chicago (Barca), 1908-15; bp. Green Bay, 1915-45.

Rice, Joseph J. (1871-1938): ord. Sept. 29, 1894; bp. Burlington, 1910-38.

Rice, William A., S. J.(1891-1946): ord. Aug. 27, 1925; v.a. Belize, Br. Honduras (Rusicade), 1939-46.

Richter, Henry J. (1838-1916): b. Germany; ord. June 10, 1865; first bp. Grand Rapids, 1883-1916.

Riordan, Patrick W. (1841-1914): b. Canada; ord. June 10, 1865; coad. abp. San Francisco (Cabasa), 1883-84; abp. San Francisco, 1884-1914.

Ritter, Joseph E.: See Index.

Robinson, Pascal C., O. F. M. (1870-1948): b. Ireland; ord. Dec. 21, 1901; ap. visitor to Palestine, Egypt, Syria and Cyprus (Tyana), 1927-29; ap. nuncio to Ireland, 1929-48.

Rohlman, Henry P. (1876-1957): b. Germany; ord. Dec. 21, 1901; bp. Davenport, 1927-44; coad. abp. Dubuque (Macra), 1944-46; abp. Dubuque, 1946-54 (res.).

Rooker, Fraderick Z. (1861-1907): ord. July 25, 1888; bp. Jaro, P.I., 1903-07.

Ropert, Gulstan F., SS. CC. (1839-1903): b. France; ord. May 26, 1866; v.a. Sandwich (now Hawaiian) Is. (Panopolis), 1892-1903.

Rosati, Joseph, C. M.: See Index.

Rosecrans, Sylvester (1827-1878): ord. June 5, 1853; aux. bp. Cincinnati (Pompeiopolis), 1862-68; first bp. Columbus, 1868-78.

Rouxel, Gustave A. (1840-1908): b. France; ord. Nov. 4, 1863; aux. bp. New Orleans (Curium), 1899-1908.

Rummel, Joseph (1876-1964): b. Germany; ord. May 24, 1902; bp. Omaha, 1928-35; abp. New Orleans, 1935-64.

Russell, William T. (1863-1927): ord. June 21, 1889; bp. Charleston, 1917-27.

Ryan, Edward F. (1879-1956): ord. Aug. 10, 1905; bp. Burlington, 1945-56.

Ryan, James (1848-1923): b. Ireland; ord. Dec. 24, 1871; bp. Alton (now Springfield), Ill., 1888-1923.

Ryan, James H. (1886-1947): ord. June 5, 1909; rector Catholic University, 1928-35; tit. bp. Modra, 1933-35; bp., 1935-45, and first abp. Omaha, 1945-47.

Ryan, Patrick J. (1831-1911): b. Ireland; ord. Sept. 8, 1853; coad. bp. St. Louis (Tricomia), 1872-84; abp. Philadelphia, 1884-1911.

Ryan, Stephen, C. M. (1826-1896): b. Canada; ord. June 24, 1849; bp. Buffalo, 1868-96.

Ryan, Vincent J. (1884-1951): ord. June 7, 1912; bp. Bismarck, 1940-51.

S

Salpointe, John B. (1825-1898): b. France; ord. Dec. 20, 1851; v.a. Arizona (Dorylaeum), 1869-84; coad. abp. Santa Fe (Anazarbus), 1884-85; abp. Santa Fe, 1885-94 (res.).

Scanlan, Lawrence (1843-1915): b. Ireland; ord. June 28, 1868; v.a. Utah (Laranda), 1887-91; bp. Salt Lake (now Salt Lake City), 1891-1915.

Scannell, Richard (1845-1916): b. Ireland; ord. Feb. 26, 1871; first bp. Concordia (now Salina), 1887-91; bp. Omaha, 1891-1916.

Schenk, Francis J. (1901-1969): ord. June 13, 1926; bp. Crookston, 1945-60; bp. Duluth, 1960-69.

Scher, Philip G. (1880-1953): ord. June 6, 1904; bp. Monterey-Fresno, 1933-53.

Schinner, Augustine (1863-1937): ord. Mar. 7, 1886; first bp. Superior, 1905-13; first bp. Spokane, 1914-25 (res.).

Schlarman, Joseph H. (1879-1951): ord. June 29, 1904; bp. Peoria, 1930-51.

Schott, Lawrence F. (1907-1963): ord. July 15, 1935; aux. Harrisburg (Eluza), 1956-63.

Schrembs, Joseph (1866-1945): b. Germany; ord. June 29, 1889; aux. bp. Grand Rapids (Sophene), 1911; bp. Toledo, 1911-21; bp. Cleveland, 1921-45.

Schuler, Anthony J., S. J. (1869-1944): ord. June 27, 1901; first bp. El Paso, 1915-42 (res.).

Schwebach, James (1847-1921): b. Luxembourg; ord. June 16, 1870; bp. La Crosse, 1892-1921.

Schwertner, August J. (1870-1939): ord. June 12, 1897; bp. Wichita, 1921-39.

Scully, William (1894-1969): ord. Sept. 20, 1919; coad. bp. Albany (Pharsalus), 1945-54; bp. Albany, 1954-69.

Sebastian, Jerome D. (1895-1960): ord. May 25, 1922; aux. bp. Baltimore (Baris in Hellesponto), 1954-60.

Seghers, Charles J.: See Index.

Seidenbusch, Rupert, O. S. B. (1830-1895): b. Germany; ord. June 22, 1853; v.a. Northern Minnesota (Halia), 1875-88 (res.).

Seton, Robert J. (1839-1927): b. Italy; ord. Apr. 15, 1865; tit. abp. Heliopolis, 1903-27. Grandson of Bl. Elizabeth Seton.

Shahan, Thomas J. (1857-1932): ord. June 3, 1882; rector, Catholic University of America, 1909-27; tit. bp. Germanicopolis, 1914-32.

Shanahan (brothers): **Jeremiah F.** (1834-1886): ord. July 3, 1859; first bp. Harrisburg, 1868-86. **John W.** (1846-1916): ord. Jan. 2, 1869; bp. Harrisburg, 1899-1916.

Shanley, John (1852-1909): ord. May 30, 1874; first bp. Jamestown (see transferred to Fargo in 1897), 1889-1909.

Shanley, Patrick H., O.C.D. (1896-1970): b. Ireland; ord. Dec. 21, 1930; US citizen; prelate Infanta, P.I. (Sophene), 1953-60 (res.).

Shaughnessy, Gerald, S.M. (1887-1950): ord. June 20, 1920; bp. Seattle, 1933-50.

Shaw, John W. (1863-1934): ord. May 26, 1888; coad. bp. San Antonio (Castabala), 1910-11; bp. San Antonio, 1911-18; abp. New Orleans, 1918-34.

Sheehan, Edward T., C.M. (1888-1933): ord. June 7, 1916; v. a. Yukiang, China (Calydon), 1929-33.

Sheil, Bernard J. (1886-1969): ord. May 21, 1910; aux. bp. Chicago (Pegae), 1928-59; tit. abp. Selge, 1959-69 (res.). Founder of Catholic Youth Organization.

Smith, Alphonse (1883-1935): ord. Apr. 18, 1908; bp. Nashville, 1924-35.

Smith, Leo R. (1905-1963): ord. Dec. 21, 1929; aux. bp. Buffalo (Marida), 1952-63; bp. Ogdensburg, 1963.

Smyth, Clement, O.C.S.O. (1810-1865):b. Ireland; ord. May 29, 1841; coad. bp. Dubuque (Thennesus), 1857-58; bp. Dubuque, 1858-65.

Spalding, John L.: See Index.

Spalding, Martin J.: See Index.

Spellman, Francis J.: See Index.

Stang, William (1854-1907): b. Germany; ord. June 15, 1878; first bp. Fall River, 1904-07.

Stariha, John (1845-1915): b. Austria; ord. Sept. 19, 1869; first bp. Lead (now Rapid City), 1902-09 (res.).

Steck, Leo J. (1898-1950): ord. June 8, 1924; aux. bp. Salt Lake City (Ilium), 1948-50.

Stock, John (1918-1972): ord. Dec. 4, 1943; aux. bp. Philadelphia (Ukrainian Rite) (Pergamum), 1971-72.

Stritch, Samuel: See Index.

Sullivan, Bernard, S.J. (1889-1970): ord. June 26, 1921; bp. Patna, India, 1929-46 (res.).

Sweeney, James J. (1898-1968): ord. June 20, 1925; first bp. Honolulu, 1941-68.

Swint, John J. (1879-1962): ord. June 23, 1904; aux. bp. Wheeling (Sura), 1922; bp. Wheeling, 1922-62.

T

Takach, Basil (1879-1948): b. Austria-Hungary; ord. Dec. 12, 1902; first ap. ex. Pittsburgh Byzantine Rite exarchy (Zela), 1924-48.

Thill, Francis A. (1893-1957): ord. Feb. 28, 1920; bp. Concordia (title changed to Salina in 1944), 1938-57.

Tief, Francis J. (1881-1965): ord. June 11, 1908; bp. Concordia (now Salina), 1921-38 (res.).

Tierney, Michael (1839-1908): b. Irland; ord. May 26, 1866; bp. Hartford, 1894-1908.

Tihen, J. Henry (1861-1940): ord. Apr. 26, 1886; bp. Lincoln, 1911-17; bp. Denver, 1917-31 (res.).

Timon, John, C. M. (1797-1867): ord. Sept. 23, 1826; first bp. Buffalo, 1847-67.

Toebbe, Augustus M. (1829-1884): b. Germany; ord. Sept. 14, 1854; bp. Covington, 1870-84.

Treacy, John P. (1890-1964): ord. Dec. 8, 1918; coad. bp. La Crosse (Metelis), 1945-48; bp. La Crosse, 1948-64.

Trobec, James (1838-1921): b. Austria; ord. Sept. 8, 1865; bp. St. Cloud, 1897-1914 (res.).

Tuigg, John (1820-1889): b. Ireland; ord. May 14, 1850; bp. Pittsburgh, 1876-89.

Turner, William (1871-1936): b. Ireland; ord. Aug. 13, 1893; bp. Buffalo, 1919-36.

Tyler, William (1806-1849): ord. June 3, 1829; first bp. Hartford, 1844-49.

V

Van de Velde, James O., S.J. (1795-1855): b. Belgium; ord. Sept. 16, 1827; bp. Chicago, 1849-53; bp. Natchez, 1853-55.

Van de Ven, Cornelius (1865-1932): b. Holland; ord. May 31, 1890; bp. Natchitoches (title changed to Alexandria in 1910), 1904-32.

Van de Vyver, Augustine (1844-1911): b. Belgium; ord. July 24, 1870; bp. Richmond, 1889-1911.

Verdaguer, Peter (1835-1911): b. Spain; ord. Dec. 12, 1862; v. a. Brownsville (Aulon), 1890-1911.

Verot, Augustin, S.S. (1805-1876): b. France; ord. Sept. 20, 1828; v. a. Florida (Danaba), 1858-61; bp. Savannah, 1861-70; bp. St. Augustine, 1870-76.

Vertin, John (1844-1899): b. Austria; ord. Aug. 31, 1866; bp. Sault Ste. Marie and Marquette (now Marquette), 1879-99.

W

Wade, Thomas, S. M. (1893-1969): ord.

June 15, 1922; v. a. Northern Solomons (Barbalissus), 1930-69.

Wadhams, Edgar (1817-1891): convert, 1846; ord. Jan. 15, 1850; first bp. Ogdensburg, 1872-91.

Walsh, Emmet (1892-1968): ord. Jan. 15, 1916; bp. Charleston, 1927-49; coad. bp. Youngstown (Rhaedestus), 1949-52; bp. Youngstown, 1952-68.

Walsh, James A., M.M. (1867-1936): ord. May 20, 1892; co-founder with Thomas F. Price of Maryknoll, first US-established foreign mission society and first sponsor of a US foreign mission seminary; superior of Maryknoll, 1911-36; tit. bp. Syene, 1933-36.

Walsh, Louis S. (1858-1924): ord. Dec. 23, 1882; bp. Portland, Me., 1906-24.

Walsh, Thomas J. (1873-1952): ord. Jan. 27, 1900; bp. Trenton, 1918-28; bp., 1928-37, and first abp., 1937-52, Newark.

Ward, John (1857-1929): ord. July 17, 1884; bp. Leavenworth (now Kansas), 1910-29.

Watterson, John A. (1844-1899): ord. Aug. 9, 1868; bp. Columbus, 1880-99.

Wehrle, Vicent, O.S.B. (1855-1941): b. Switzerland; ord. Apr. 23, 1882; first bp. Bismarck, 1910-39 (res.).

Welch, Thomas A. (1884-1959): ord. June 11, 1909; bp. Duluth, 1925-59.

Whelan, James, O. P. (1822-1878): b. Ireland; ord. Aug. 2, 1846; coad. bp. Nashville (Marcopolis), 1859-60; bp. Nashville, 1860-64 (res.).

Whelan, Richard V. (1809-1874): ord. May 1, 1831; bp. Richmond, 1841-50; bp. Wheeling, 1850-74.

White, Charles (1879-1955): ord. Sept. 24, 1910; bp. Spokane, 1927-55.

Whitfield, James (1770-1834): b. England; ord. July 24, 1809; coad. bp. Baltimore (Apollonia), 1828; abp. Baltimore, 1828-34.

Wigger, Winand (1841-1901): ord. June 10, 1865; bp. Newark, 1881-1901.

Willging, Joseph C. (1884-1959): ord. June 20, 1908; first bp. Pueblo, 1942-59.

Williams, John J. (1822-1907): ord. May 17, 1845; bp., 1866-75, and first abp., 1875-1907, Boston.

Winkelmann, Christian H. (1883-1946): ord. June 11, 1907; aux. bp. St. Louis (Sita), 1933-39; bp. Wichita, 1939-46.

Wood, James F. (1813-1883): convert, 1836; ord. Mar. 25, 1844; coad. bp. Philadelphia (Antigonea), 1857-60; bp., 1860-75, and first abp., 1875-83, Philadelphia.

Woznicki, Stephen (1894-1968): ord. Dec. 22, 1917; aux. bp. Detroit (Peltae), 1938-50; bp. Saginaw, 1950-68.

Y-Z

Young, Josue (1808-1866): ord. Apr. 1, 1838; bp. Pittsburgh, 1853-54; bp. Erie, 1854-66.

Zardetti, Otto (1847-1902): b. Switzerland; ord. Aug. 21, 1870; first bp. St. Cloud, 1889-94; abp. Bucharest, Rumania, 1894-95 (res.).

North American College

The North American College was founded by the bishops of the United States in 1859 as a residence and house of formation for US seminarians and graduate students in Rome. The first ordination of an alumnus took place June 14, 1862. Pontifical status was granted the college by Leo XIII Oct. 25, 1884.

Students living at the college study theology and related subjects in the various seminaries in Rome, principally at the Pontifical Gregorian University.

The college is directed by an American rector and staff, and operates under the auspices of a US bishops' committee which was set up in 1924.

The present rector, the 13th, is the Most Rev. James A. Hickey, titular bishop of Taraqua and the former auxiliary of Saginaw.

Fides

International Fides Service, the news agency of the Congregation for the Evangelization of Peoples, issues a periodic service of news, comment and background information concerning the missions. By the end of 1972, it had issued some 2,500 releases.

The office address is Via di Propaganda, 1 C, 00187, Rome, Italy.

INTER COM

The Inter-Community Association of Missioners is a post-Vatican II professional organization of Catholic priests engaged in the full-time ministry of renewal through the preaching of missions and retreats. Established in 1967, it maintains a central office at 323 Franklin Street, Manchester, N.H. 03101.

The association's membership exceeds 400 priests, representing 24 religious orders.

According to the mind of the Second Vatican Council and its frequent insistence on preaching the Word of God, INTER COM is a service and research organization. The apostolate of parish missions is maintained and enhanced by improving the image of the missioner, by in-service training of veteran missioners and improving their sermon content and presentation, by recruiting younger members of the clergy to this apostolate, by demonstrating cooperation among preaching orders, and by annual seminars for ongoing education, shared experiences, and experimentation on new formats and presentations.

The association also plans and fosters general area missions, makes available potential resources of preachers, and has originated a bold and innovative program for the certification of preachers for whose who qualify.

The episcopal moderator of INTER COM is the Most Rev. Edward L. Heston, C.S.C., titular archbishop of Numida, and president of the Pontifical Commission for Social Communications, Vatican City.

The general chairman is Father Jude Mead, C.P.

Religious

Religious orders and congregations, collectively called **religious institutes,** are special societies in the Church. Their members, called **religious,** live a community kind of life according to rules and constitutions approved by Church authority and strive for Christian perfection not only by fulfilling the obligations common to all the faithful but also through the profession and observance of public vows of obedience, chastity and poverty. In church law, their way of life is called the state of perfection or the religious life.

Religious Institutes

The particular goal of each institute and the means of realizing it in practice are stated in the rule and constitutions proper to the institute. Local bishops, with permission of the Holy See, can give approval for rules and constitutions of **institutes of diocesan rank. Pontifical rank** belongs to institutes approved by the Holy See. General jurisdiction over all religious is exercised by the Congregation for Religious and Secular Institutes. General legislation concerning religious is contained in Canons 487 to 681 of the Code of Canon Law and in subsequent enactments, especially since the Second Vatican Council.

All religious institutes are commonly called religious orders, despite the fact that there are differences between orders and congregations. The best known **orders** include the Benedictines, Trappists, Franciscans, Dominicans, Carmelites and Augustinians, for men; and the Carmelites, Poor Clares, Dominicans of the Second Order and Visitation Nuns, for women. Members of the orders have solemn vows; their communities have papal enclosure and exemption, and are bound to perform the Liturgy of the Hours (Divine Office) in choir as a common practice. Members of the **congregations** have simple vows. The orders are older than the congregations, which did not appear until the 16th century.

Contemplative institutes devote themselves exclusively to divine worship by prayer, penance and other spiritual exercises in a life of retirement. They do not engage in the active ministry. Examples are the Trappists and Carthusians, the Carmelite and Poor Clare nuns. **Active institutes** are geared primarily for the ministry and many kinds of apostolic work. **Mixed institutes** combine elements of the contemplative and active ways of life. While most institutes of men and women can be classified as active, all of them have some contemplative aspects

Historical Development

The basis of the life of religious institutes was the invitation Christ extended to men (Mt. 19:16ff.) to follow him with special dedication in a life like his own, which was that of a poor and chaste man under obedience to the Father.

In the earliest years of Christianity, some men and women dedicated themselves to the service of God in a special manner. Among them were holy women, deaconesses and virgins mentioned in the Acts of the Apostles, and confessors and ascetics like St. Clement of Rome, St. Ignatius of Antioch and St. Polycarp.

In the third and fourth centuries, there were traces of a kind of religious profession, and the root idea of the life began to produce significant results in the solitary and community hermitages of Egypt and Syria under the inspiration of men like St. Paul of Thebes, St. Anthony the Abbot and St. Pachomius.

St. Basil, "Father of Monasticism in the East," exerted a deep and still continuing influence on the development of religious life among men and women. His opposite number in the West was St. Benedict, whose rule or counsels, dating from about 530, set the pattern of monastic life for men and women which prevailed for nearly six centuries and which still endures. Before his time, St. Augustine framed guidelines for community life which are still being followed by some men and women religious.

Mendicant orders, whose members were freer than the monks for works of the active ministry, made their appearance early in the 13th century and began to change some of the established aspects of religious life. Religious women, however, continued to live in the monastic manner.

A significant change in religious life developed in the 16th century when several communities of men with simple rather than solemn vows were approved; among them were **clerics regular** like the Jesuits and Barnabites. Some of these communities are considered to be orders, although they differ in some respects from the older orders.

The Sisters of Charity, in 1633, were the first community of women with simple vows to gain Church approval. Since that time, the number and variety of female communities have greatly increased. Women religious, no longer restricted to the hidden life of prayer, became engaged in many kinds of work including education, health and social service, and missionary endeavor.

Clerical communities of men—i. e., those whose membership is predominantly composed of priests — are similarly active in many types of work. Their distinctive fields are education, home and foreign missions, retreats, special assignments and the communications media, as well as the internal life and conduct of their own communities. They also engage in the ordinary pastoral ministry which is the principal work of diocesan or secular priests.

They are generally called **regular clergy** because of the rule of life (*regula* in Latin) they follow.

Non-clerical or lay institutes of men are the various brotherhoods whose non-ordained members (called **lay brothers,** or simply **brothers**) are engaged in educational and hospital work, missionary endeavors, and other special fields.

Some of the institutes of men listed below have a special kind of status because their members, while living a common life like that which is characteristic of religious, do not profess the vows of religious. Examples are the Maryknoll Fathers, the Oratorians of St. Philip Neri, the Paulists and Sulpicians. They are called **societies of the common life without vows.**

RENEWAL OF RELIGIOUS LIFE

Following are key excerpts from the *Decree on the Appropriate Renewal of Religious Life* promulgated by the Second Vatican Council.

Norms

"A life consecrated by a profession of the counsels (of poverty, chastity and obedience) is of surpassing value. Such a life has a necessary role to play in the circumstances of the present age. That this kind of life and its contemporary role may achieve greater good for the Church, this sacred Synod issues the following decrees. They concern only the general principles which must underlie an appropriate renewal of the life and rules of religious communities. These principles apply also to societies living a community life without the exercise of vows, and to secular institutes, though the special character of both groups is to be maintained. After the Council, the competent authority will be obliged to enact particular laws opportunely spelling out and applying what is legislated here" (No. 1).

"The appropriate renewal of religious life involves two simultaneous processes: (1) a continuous return to the sources of all Christian life and to the original inspiration behind a given community and (2) an adjustment of the community to the changed conditions of the times. . . .

"(a) Since the fundamental norm of the religious life is a following of Christ as proposed by the gospel, such is to be regarded by all communities as their supreme law.

"(b) It serves the best interests of the Church for communities to have their own special character and purpose. Therefore loyal recognition and safekeeping should be accorded to the spirit of founders, as also to all the particular goals and wholesome traditions which constitute the heritage of each community.

"(c) All communities should participate in the life of the Church. According to its individual character, each should make its own and foster in every possible way the enterprises and objectives of the Church in such fields as these: the scriptural, liturgical, doctrinal, pastoral, ecumenical, missionary, and social.

"(d) Communities should promote among their members a suitable awareness of contemporary human conditions and of the needs of the Church. . . .

"(e) Since the religious life is intended above all else to lead those who embrace it to an imitation of Christ and to union with God through the profession of the evangelical counsels, the fact must be honestly faced that even the most desirable changes made on behalf of contemporary needs will fail of their purpose unless a renewal of spirit gives life to them. Indeed such an interior renewal must always be accorded the leading role even in the promotion of external works" (No. 2).

"The manner of living, praying, and working should be suitably adapted to the physical and psychological conditions of today's religious and also, to the extent required by the nature of each community, to the needs of the apostolate, the requirements of a given culture, the social and economic circumstances anywhere, but especially in missionary territories."

Allowance should be made for prudent experimentation in the direction of renewal and adaptation (No. 3).

". . . The hope of renewal must be lodged in a more diligent observance of rule and of constitution rather than in a multiplication of individual laws" (No. 4).

Various Communities

"The members of each community should recall above everything else that by their profession of the evangelical counsels they have given answer to a divine call to live for God alone not only by dying to sin (cf. Rom. 6:11) but also by renouncing the world. They have handed over their entire lives to God's service in an act of special consecration which is deeply rooted in their baptismal consecration and which provides an ampler manifestation of it.

"Inasmuch as their self-dedication has been accepted by the Church, they should realize that they are committed to her service as well.

". . . The members of each community should combine contemplation with apostolic love. By the former they adhere to God in mind and heart; by the latter they strive to associate themselves with the work of redemption and to spread the Kingdom of God" (No. 5).

"Members of those communities which are totally dedicated to contemplation give themselves to God alone in solitude and silence and through constant prayer and ready penance. No matter how urgent may be the needs of the active apostolate, such communities will always have a distinguished part to play in Christ's Mystical Body. . . . Their manner of living should be revised according to the aforementioned principles and standards of appropriate renewal, though their withdrawal from the world and the practices of their contemplative life should be maintained at their holiest" (No. 7).

Communities geared for apostolic action "should skillfully harmonize their observances and practices with the needs of the apostolate to which they are dedicated," with due regard for diversity (No. 8). This norm applies to monastic institutes, which should preserve their special character; to communities which "closely join the apostolic life with choral prayer and monastic observances"; and to "the lay religious life, for both men and women" (Nos. 9 and 10).

[See Secular Institutes for a quotation from the decree on the subject.]

The Vows, Authority

"That chastity which is practiced 'on behalf of the heavenly Kingdom' (Mt. 19:12), and which religious profess, deserves to be esteemed as a surpassing gift of grace. For it liberates the human heart in a unique way (cf. 1 Cor. 7:32-35) and causes it to burn with greater love for God and all mankind. It is therefore an outstanding token of heavenly riches, and also a most suitable way for religious to spend themselves readily in God's service and in works of the apostolate. . . .

"Since the observance of total continence intimately involves the deeper inclinations of human nature, candidates should not undertake the profession of chastity nor be admitted to its profession except after a truly adequate testing period and only if they have the needed degree of psychological and emotional maturity" (No. 12).

"Poverty voluntarily embraced in imitation of Christ provides a witness which is highly esteemed, especially today. Let religious painstakingly cultivate such poverty, and give it new expressions if need be. . . .

". . . Members of a community ought to be poor in both fact and spirit, and have their treasures in heaven (cf. Mt. 6:20).

". . . Communities as such should aim at giving a kind of corporate witness to their own poverty. . . .

"To the degree that their rules and constitutions permit, religious communities can rightly possess whatever is necessary for their temporal life and their mission. Still, let them avoid every appearance of luxury, of excessive wealth, and accumulation of possessions" (No. 13).

"Through the profession of obedience, religious offer to God a total dedication of their own wills as a sacrifice of themselves; they thereby unite themselves with greater steadiness and security to the saving will of God. . . . Under the influence of the Holy Spirit, religious submit themselves to their superiors, whom faith presents as God's representatives, and through whom they are guided into the service of all their brothers in Christ. . . . In this way . . . religious assume a firmer commitment to the ministry of the Church and labor to achieve the mature measure of the fullness of Christ (cf. Eph. 4:13).

"Therefore, in a spirit of faith and of love for God's will, let religious show humble obedience to their superiors in accord with the norms of the rule and constitution. . . . Let them bring to the execution of commands and to the discharge of assignments entrusted to them the resources of their minds and wills, and their gifts of nature and grace. Lived in this manner, religious obedience will not diminish the dignity of the human person but will rather lead it to maturity in consequence of that enlarged freedom which belongs to the sons of God.

". . . Each superior should himself be docile to God's will in the exercise of his office. Let him use his authority in a spirit of service for the brethren. . . . Governing his subjects as God's own sons, and with regard for their human personality, a superior will make it easier for them to obey gladly. Therefore he must make a special point of leaving them appropriately free with respect to the sacrament of penance and direction of conscience. Let him give the kind of leadership which will encourage religious to bring an active and responsible obedience to the offices they shoulder and the activities they undertake. Therefore a superior should listen willingly to his subjects and encourage them to make a personal contribution to the welfare of the community and of the Chruch. Not to be weakened, however, is the superior's authority to decide what must be done and to require the doing of it.

"Let chapters and councils faithfully acquit themselves of the governing role given to them; each should express in its own way the fact that all members of the community have a share in the welfare of the whole community and a responsibility for it" (No. 14).

Vicars' Conference

Sixty vicars and associate vicars for religious elected Father William Hughes of Rockville Centre, N.Y., president of the newly formed Conference of Vicars for Religious at an early May, 1972, meeting in Cleveland.

They also approved a constitution committing the conference: to assist vicars with cooperation, communications services and continuing education; to increase the service of dioceses to religious, and to respond to the needs of religious on regional, national and international levels; to carry on liaison with the Congregation for Religious and Secular Institutes, the National Conference of Catholic Bishops and other organizations concerned with religious.

EXHORTATION TO RELIGIOUS

The most recent authoritative document on the religious life is Pope Paul's "Exhortation on Renewal of the Religious Life according to the Teaching of the Second Vatican Council."

The Exhortation concerns general principles of the religious life, with more reference to the internal life and practice of religious institutes and their members than to their apostolic orientations and functions. While strongly traditional, the document is positive and open to the possibilities of centemporary developments in religious life.

[The following excerpts are from the text published in *L'Osservatore Romano* July 15, 1971.]

Purpose: "The evangelical witness of the religious life clearly manifests to men the primacy of the love of God . . . with a force for which we must give thanks to the Holy Spirit. . . . We would like to tell you what hope is stirred up in us . . . by the spiritual generosity of those men and women who have consecrated their lives to the Lord in the spirit and practice of the evangelical counsels. We wish also to assist you to continue in your path of following Christ in faithfulness to the (Second Vatican) Council's teaching." (This teaching was stated in the *Decree on the Appropriate Renewal of Religious Life* and other documents.)

"By doing this, we wish to respond to the anxiety, uncertainty and instability (regarding religious life) shown by some; at the same time we wish to encourage those who are seeking the true renewal of the religious life. The boldness of certain arbitrary transformations, exaggerated distrust of the past — even when it witnesses to the wisdom and vigor of ecclesial traditions — and a mentality excessively preoccupied with hastily conforming to the profound changes which disturb our times, have succeeded in leading some to consider as outmoded the specific forms of religious life."

The Pope observed that appeal had even been made to the Second Vatican Council "to cast doubt on the very principle of religious life," although "it is well known that the Council recognized 'this specific gift' as having a choice place in the life of the Church."

The Pope recalled the long history and tradition of religious life in the Church, and asked rhetorically: "Who would venture to hold that such a calling today no longer has the same value and vigor (it had in the past)? That the Church could do without these exceptional witnesses of the transcendence of the love of Christ? Or that the world, without damage to itself, could allow these lights to go out? They are lights which announce the kingdom of God with a liberty which knows no obstacles and is daily lived by thousands of sons and daughters of the Church."

Renewal: "Certainly, many exterior elements, recommended by founders of religious orders or congregations, are seen today to be outmoded. Various encumbrances or rigid forms accumulated over the centuries need to be curtailed. Adaptations must be made. New forms can even be sought and instituted with the approval of the Church. For some years now the greater part of religious institutes have been generously dedicating themselves to the attainment of this goal, experimenting — sometimes too hardily — with new types of constitutions and rules. We know well and we are following with attention this effort at renewal which was desired by the Council."

Discernment: "How can we assist you to make the necessary discernment in this dynamic process itself, in which there is the constant risk that the spirit of the world will be intermingled with the action of the Holy Spirit? How can what is essential be safeguarded or attained? How can benefit be obtained from past experience and from present reflection, in order to strengthen this form of evangelical life? . . . We would like to encourage you to proceed with greater sureness and with more joyful confidence along the way that you have chosen. In the 'pursuit of perfect charity,' which guides your existence, what attitude could you have other than a total surrender of the Holy Spirit who, working in the Church, calls you to the freedom of the sons of God?"

Religious Life

Nature of Religious Life: In summary comment on teaching of the Second Vatican Council, Pope Paul said: "The evangelical counsels of chastity vowed to God, of poverty and obedience" are the essential law of religious life. "The Council reminds us that 'the authority of the Church has taken care, under the inspiration of the Holy Spirit, to interpret these evangelical counsels, to regulate their practice, and also to establish stable forms of living according to them.' In this way, the Church recognizes and authenticates the state of life established by the profession of the evangelical counsels."

"It is precisely for the sake of the kingdom of heaven that (religious) have vowed to Christ, generously and without reservation, that capacity to love, that need to possess and that freedom to regulate one's own life, which are so precious to man. Such is (the) consecration (of religious), made within the Church and through her ministry."

Forms of Life

Forms of Life and the Spirit of Founders: Whatever the type of religious life — contemplative, apostolic, a combination of the two — "the Council rightly insists on the obligation of religious to be faithful to the spirit of their founders, to their evangelical intentions and to the example of their sanctity. In this it finds one of the principles for the present renewal and one of the most secure criteria for judging what each institute should undertake. In reality, the charism of the religious life . . . is the fruit off the Holy Spirit, who is always at work within the Church."

."It is precisely here that the dynamism proper to each religious family finds its origin. For, while the call of God renews itself and expresses itself in different ways according to changing circumstances of place and time, it nevertheless requires a certain constancy of orientation. The interior impulse which is the response to God's call stirs up in the depth of one's being certain fundamental options. Fidelity to the exigencies of these fundamental options is the touchstone of authenticity in religious life."

The Ultimate Norm: "Through the variety of forms which give each institute its own individual character and which have their root in the fullness of the grace of Christ, the supreme rule of the religious life and its ultimate norm is that of following Christ according to the teaching of the Gospel."

Essential Commitments

Consecrated Chastity: "Without in any way undervaluing human love and marriage . . . consecrated chastity evokes (the) union (of Christ and the Church) in a more immediate way and brings that surpassing excellenct to which all human love should tend. Thus, at the moment when human love is more than ever threatened by a 'ravaging eroticism,' consecrated chastity must be today more than ever understood and lived with uprightness and generosity. Chastity is decisively positive, it witnesses to preferential love for the Lord and symbolizes in the most eminent and absolute way the mystery of the union of the Mystical Body with its Head. . . . Finally, it reaches, transforms and imbues with a mysterious likeness to Christ man's being in its most hidden depths."

"It is necessary for (religious) to restore to the Christian spirituality of consecrated chastity its full effectiveness."

"The value aand the fruitfulness of chastity observed for the love of God in religious celibacy find their ultimate basis in nothing other than the Word of God, the teachings of Christ, the life of his Virgin Mother, and also the apostolic tradition, as it has been unceasingly affirmed by the Church."

Consecrated Poverty: Religious desire "to live in poverty in the use of this world's goods which are necessary for . . . daily sustenance."

Response to Poor

Practically, the poverty professed by religious must be a response to the cry of the poor. "That cry must . . . bar you from whatever would be a compromise with any form of social injustice. It obliges you also to awaken consciences to the drama of misery and to the demands of social justice. . . . It leads some of you to join the poor in their situation and to share their bitter cares . . . it calls many of your institutes to rededicate for the good of the poor some of their works . . . it enjoins on you a use of goods limited to what is required for the fulfillment of the functions to which you are called. It is necessary that in your daily lives you should give proof, even externally of authentic poverty."

Meaning of Work: "It will . . . be an essential aspect of your poverty to bear witness to the human meaning of work which is carried out in liberty of spirit and restored to its true nature as the source of sustenance and of service. . . . But your activities cannot derogate from the vocation of your various institutes, nor habitually involve work which would take the place of their specific tasks. Nor should these activities in any way lead you tooward secularization, the detriment of your religious life."

"Poverty really lived by pooling goods, including pay, will testify to the spiritual communion uniting you. . . . The legitimate desire of exercising personal responsibility will not find expression in enjoyment of one's own income but in fraternal sharing in the common good. The forms of poverty of each person and of each community will depend on the type of institute and on the form of obedience practiced in it. Thus will be brought to realization, in accordance with particular vocations, the character of dependence which is inherent in every form of poverty."

"Poverty cannot be purely and simply a conformity to the manners of (one's) surroundings. Its witness value will derive from a generous response to the exigencies of the Gospel, in total fidelity to your vocation — not just from an excessively superficial preoccupation for appearing to be poor — and in avoiding those ways of life which would denote a certain affectedness and vanity."

Sign of Consecration

Religious Habit: "While we recognize that certain situations can justify the abandonment of a religious type of dress, we cannot pass over in silence how appropriate it is that the dress of religious men and women should be, as the Council wishes, a sign of their consecration, and that it should be in some way different from the forms that are purely secular."

Consecrated Obedience: Through the profession of obedience, "you (religious) make a total offering of your will and enter more decisively and more clearly into (God's) plan of salvation."

Authority and Obedience: "Authority and obedience are exercised in the service of the common good as two complementary aspects of the same participation in Christ's offering. For those in authority, it is a matter of serving in their brothers the design of the Father's love; while, in accepting their directions, the religious follow our Master's example and cooperate in the work of salvation."

Freedom and Obedience: "You will observe (the) precept" of losing life to follow Christ "by accepting the directives of your superiors as a guarantee of your religious profession, through which you offer to God a total dedication of your own wills as a sacrifice of yourselves. Christian obedience is unconditional submission to the will of God. But your obedience is more strict because you have made it the object of a special giving, and the range of your choices is limited by your commitment. It is a full act of your freedom that is at the origin of your present position. Your duty is to make that act ever more vital, both by your own initiative and by the cordial assent you give the directives of your superiors."

Conscience and Obedience: "Is it possible to have conflicts between the superior's authority and the conscience of the religious . . .? Need we repeat that conscience on its own is not the arbiter of the moral worth of the actions which it inspires? It must take account of objective norms and, if necessary, reform and rectify itself. Apart from an order manifestly contrary to the laws of God or the constitutions of the institute, or one involving a serious and certain evil — in which case there is no obligation to obey — the superior's decisions concern a field in which the calculation of the greater good can vary according to the point of view. To conclude from the fact that a directive seems objectively less good that it is unlawful and contrary to conscience would mean an unrealistic disregard of the obscurity and ambivalence of many human realities. Besides, refusal to obey involves an often serious loss for the common good. A religious should not easily conclude that there is a contradiction between the judgment of his conscience and that of his superior. This exceptional situation will sometimes involve true interior suffering, after the pattern of Christ Himself 'who learned obedience through suffering.'"

Life Style and Witness

Life Style: "At the present moment it is difficult to find a life style (for religious) in harmony with (the) exigency (of the cross). Too many contrary attractions lead one to seek, first of all, for a humanly effective activity. But is it not for you to give an example of joyful, well-balanced austerity, by accepting the difficulties inherent in work and in social relationships and by bearing patiently the trials of life . . . as renunciations indispensable for the fullness of the Christian life?"

"Along (the) path (of Christ's example) a precious aid is offered you by the forms of life

which experience, faithful to the charisms of the various institutes, has given rise to. Experience has varied the combinations of these forms, never ceasing to put forward new developments. . . . An excessive desire for flexibility and creative spontaneity (however) can in fact give rise to accusations of rigidity directed against that minimum of regularity in activities which community life and personal maturity ordinarily require. Disorderly outbursts, which appeal to fraternal charity or to what one believes to be inspirations of the Spirit, can also lead to the breakup of communities."

"The importance of the surroundings in which one lives should not be underestimated either in relation to the habitual orientation of the whole person . . . in the direction of God's call, or in relation to the spiritual integration of the person's tendencies. . . . Many of you will in fact be obliged to lead your lives, at least in part, in a world which tends to exile man from himself and to compromise both his spiritual unity and his union with God. You must therefore learn to find God even under those conditions of life which are marked by an increasingly accelerated rhythm and by the noise and the attraction of the ephemeral."

Witness: "In the present it is especially necessary for religious to give witness as persons whose vital striving to attain their goal — the living God — has effectively created unity and openness in the depth and steadfastness of all their faculties, the purification of their thoughts and the spiritualization of their senses."

"In view of the hectic pace and tensions of modern life, it is appropriate to give particular importance — over and above the daily rhythm of prayer — to those more prolonged moments of prayer which can be variously spread out in the different periods of the day, according to the possibilities and the nature of your vocation."

Rule and Doctrine of Life

Doctrine of Perfection: "The Council considers 'a proven doctrine of acquiring perfection' as one of the inherited riches of religious institutes and one of the greatest benefits that they must guarantee. . . . It is necessary to understand this doctrine in a very concrete way, that is, as a doctrine of life that must be effectively lived. This means that the pursuit to which the institutes devote themselves cannot consist only in certain adaptations to be carried out in relation to the changing circumstances of the world; they must instead assist the fruitful rediscovery of the means essential for leading a life completely permeated with love of God and of men."

Communities, Small and Large: "Small communities can . . . favor the development of closer relationships between the religious and a shared and more fraternal undertaking of responsibility. Nevertheless, while a certain structure can in fact favor the creation of a spiritual environment, it would be vain to imagine that it is sufficient for making it develop. Small communities, instead of offering an easier form of life, prove on the contrary to make greater demands on their members."

"Communities containing many members particularly suit many religious. Communities of this sort may likewise be called for by the nature of a charitable service, by certain tasks of an intellectual nature, or by the contemplative or monastic life."

"Whatever their size, communities large or small will not succeed in helping their members unless they are constantly animated by the Gospel spirit, nourished by prayer and distinguished by generous mortification of the old man, by the discipline necessary for forming the new man, and by the fruitfulness of the sacrifice of the cross."

On Ingredients of Renewal: The Pope said in the exhortation that the basic ingredients of renewal and spiritual growth start with prayer, "the test of the vitality or decadence of the religious life." He underlined the importance of deep interior life, the liturgy, the central significance of the Eucharist, and participation in the mission of the Church.

Recapitulation

At the start of a concluding appeal for the authentic renewal of religious life, Pope Paul recapitulated this central concern.

"The religious life, if it is to be renewed, must adapt its accidental forms to certain changes which are affecting with growing rapidity and to an increasing extent the conditions of life of every human being. But how is this to be attained while maintaining those 'stable forms of living' recognized by the Church, except by a renewal of the authentic and integral vocation of your institutes? For a living being, adaptation to its surrounding does not consist in abandoning its true identity, but rather in asserting itself in the vitality that is its own. Deep understanding of present tendencies and of the needs of the modern world should cause your own sources of energy to spring up with renewed vigor and freshness. It is a sublime task in the measure that it is a difficult one."

RELIGIOUS INSTITUTES OF MEN IN THE UNITED STATES

(Sources: *Official Catholic Directory, 1972;* Catholic Almanac survey.)

The number of priests and brothers is given at the end of entries.

African Missions, Society of, S.M.A.: Founded 1856, at Lyons, France, by Bishop Melchior de Marion Bressilac. General motherhouse, Rome, Italy; American provincialate, 23 Bliss Ave., Tenafly, N.J. 07670. Missionary work in West Africa and inner city parishes. 81 priests.

Assumptionists (Augustinians of the Assumption), AA.: Founded 1845, at Nimes, France, by Rev. Emmanuel d'Alzon; in US, 1946. General motherhouse, Rome, Italy; US province, 329 W. 108th St., New York, N.Y. 10025. Educational, parochial, ecumenical, retreat, foreign mission work. 102 priests, 47 brothers.

Atonement, Franciscan Friars of the, S.A.: Founded 1898, at Garrison, N.Y., by Fr. Paul James Francis. General motherhouse, Graymoor, Garrison, N.Y. 10524. Ecumenical, charitable, mission work. 129 priests, 90 brothers.

Augustinians (Order of St. Augustine), O.S.A.: Established canonically in 1256 by Pope Alexander IV; in US, 1796. General motherhouse, Rome, Italy.

St. Thomas of Villanova Province (1796), Villanova, Pa. 19085. 344 priests, 18 brothers.

Our Mother of Good Counsel Vice-Province, 1200 Forest Ave., Evanston, Ill. 60202. 159 priests, 32 brothers.

St. Augustine Province, 2060 N. Vermont Ave., Los Angeles, Calif. 90027. 42 priests.

Our Mother of Good Counsel Vice Province, St. Augustine Preparatory School, Richland, N.J. 08350, 23 priests, 3 brothers.

Augustinian Recollects, O.A.R.: Founded 1588; in US, 1944. General motherhouse, Rome, Italy; US provincial residence, 57 Ridgeway Ave., West Orange, N.J. 07052. Missionary, parochial, education work. 80 priests, 12 brothers.

Barnabites (Clerics Regular of St. Paul), C.R.S.P.: Founded 1530, in Milan, Italy, by St. Anthony M. Zaccaria. Generalate, Rome, Italy; American headquarters, 40 Agassiz Circle, Buffalo, N.Y. 14214. Parochial, educational, mission work. 16 priests, 1 brother.

Basilian Fathers (Congregation of the Priests of St. Basil), C.S.B.: Founded 1822, at Annonay, France. General motherhouse, 95 St. Joseph St., Toronto 5, Ont., Canada. Educational, parochial work. 169 priests.

Basil the Great, Order of St. (Ukrainian), O.S.B.M.: General motherhouse, Rome, Italy; US province, 31-12 30th St., Long Island City, N.Y. 11106. Parochial work among Byzantine Ukrainian Rite Catholics. 45 priests, 4 brothers.

Basilian Salvatorian Fathers: Founded 1684, at Saida, Lebanon, by Eftimios Saifi; in US, 1953. General motherhouse, Saida, Lebanon; American headquarters, East and Pleasant Sts., Methuen, Mass. 01844. Educational, parochial work among Eastern Rite peoples. 25 priests.

Benedictines (Order of St. Benedict), O.S.B.: Founded 529, in Italy, by St. Benedict of Nursia; in US, 1846.

American Cassinese Federation (1855), Rt. Rev. Martin Burne, O.S.B., pres., St. Mary's Abbey, Morristown, N.J. 07960. 15 abbeys, 2 priories and 2 monasteries in the US. 1,146 priests, 264 brothers.

Benedictine Federation of the Americans (formerly Swiss-American Congregation) (1870), Rt. Rev. David Melancon, O.S.B., pres., St. Joseph Abbey, St. Benedict, La. 70457. 10 abbeys, 1 priory, 1 monastery in US. 532 priests, 186 brothers.

English Benedictine Congregation: St. Anselm's Abbey, S. Dakota Ave. and 14th St. N.E., Washington, D.C. 20017. 29 priests, 2 brothers; Abbey of St. Gregory, Cory's Lane, Portsmouth, R.I. 02871. 31 choir religious; Priory of St. Mary and St. Louis, 500 S. Mason Rd., St. Louis, Mo. 63141. 12 priests.

Congregation of St. Ottilien for Foreign Missions, St. Paul's Abbey, Newton, N.J. 07860. 27 priests, 9 brothers. Benedictine Mission House, Schuyler, Nebr. 68661. 2 priests, 9 brothers.

Hungarian Congregation, Woodside Priory, 032 Portola Rd., Portola Valley, Calif. 94025. 10 priests, 8 brothers.

Congregation of the Annunciation, St. Andrew Priory, Valyermo, Calif. 93563. 23 choir monks.

Houses not in Congregations: Mount Savior Monastery, Pine City, N.Y. 14871. 24 monks; Conventual Priory of St. Gabriel the Archangel, Weston, Vt. 05161. 4 priests, 12 choir monks.

Benedictines, Sylvestrine, O.S.B.: Founded 1231, in Italy by Sylvester Gozzolini. General motherhouse, Rome, Italy; US headquarters, 17320 Rosemont Rd., Detroit, Mich. 48219. 27 priests, 5 brothers.

Bethlehem Missionaries, Society of, S.M.B.: Founded 1921, at Immensee, Switzerland, by Rt. Rev. Canon Peter Bondolfi. General motherhouse, Immensee, Switzerland; US headquarters, 5630 E. 17th Pkwy., Denver, Colo. 80220. Foreign mission work. 13 priests, 1 brother.

Blessed Sacrament, Congregation of the, S.S.S.: Founded 1856, at Paris, France, by St. Pierre Julien Eymard; in US, 1900. General motherhouse, Rome, Italy; US headquarters, 184 E. 76th St., New York, N.Y. 10021. Perpetual adoration and Eucharistic apostolate. 127 priests, 73 brothers.

Camaldolese Congregation, Cam. O.S.B.: Founded 1012, at Camaldoli, near Arezzo, Italy, by St. Romuald; in US, 1958. General motherhouse, Arezzo, Italy; US foundation, Immaculate Heart Hermitage, Big Sur, Calif. 93920. 12 priests, 6 brothers.

Camaldolese Hermits of the Congregation of Monte Corona, Er. Cam.: Founded 1520, from Camaldoli, Italy, by Bl. Paul Giustiniani. General motherhouse, Frascati (Rome), Italy; US foundation, Bloomingdale, O. 43910. 5 priests.

Camillians (Clerics Regular, Ministers of the Sick), O.S.Cam.: Founded 1582, at Rome, by St. Camillus de Lellis; in US, 1923.

General motherhouse, Rome, Italy; North American province, 10100 W. Blue Mound Rd., Wauwatosa, Wis. 53226. 14 priests, 19 brothers.

Carmelites (Order of Our Lady of Mt. Carmel), O. Carm.: General motherhouse, Rome, Italy. Educational, charitable work.

Most Pure Heart of Mary Province (1864), 45 E. Dundee Rd., Barrington, Ill. 60010. 315 priests, 58 brothers.

St. Elias Province (1931), 329 E. 28th St., New York, N.Y. 10016. 87 priests, 6 brothers.

Carmelites, Order of Discalced, O.C.D.: Established 1562, a Reform Order of Our Lady of Mt. Carmel; in US, 1935. General motherhouse, Rome, Italy. Parochial, foreign mission work.

St. Therese of Oklahoma Province (1935), 1125 S. Walker St., P.O. Box 26127, Oklahoma City, Okla. 73126. 34 priests, 4 brothers.

Immaculate Heart of Mary Province (1947), Holy Hill, Hubertus, Wis. 53033. 82 priests, 22 brothers.

Anglo-Irish Province, P.O. Box 446, Redlands, Calif. 92373. 36 priests, 7 brothers.

Polish Province, 1962 Ridge Rd., Munster, Ind. 46321. 8 priests, 2 brothers.

Carthusians, Order of, O. Cart.: Founded 1084, in France, by St. Bruno; in US, 1951. General motherhouse, St. Pierre de Chartreuse, France; US charterhouse, Arlington, Vt. 05250. Cloistered, contemplatives. 5 priests, 5 brothers.

Charity, Grey Franciscan Friars of, C.F.C.: Founded 1859, in Italy. General motherhouse, Rome, Italy; US foundations, 179 Emmet St., Newark, N.J. 07114; 3616 15th St., N.E., Washington, D. C. 20017. 3 priests.

Christ, Society of, S.Ch.: Founded 1932, General Motherhouse, Poznan, Poland; US address, 15 Asselin St., Warren, R.I. 02885.

Cistercians, Order of, S.O. Cist.: Founded 1098, by St. Robert. Headquarters, Rome, Italy.

Our Lady of Spring Bank Abbey, 34639 W. Fairview Rd., Oconomowoc, Wis. 53066. 12 priests, 4 brothers.

Our Lady of Gerowval Monastery, Rose Hill, Miss. 39356.

Our Lady of Dallas Monastery, Rt. 2, Box 1, Irving, Tex. 75060. 35 priests.

Our Lady of Fatima Monastery, Moorestown P.O. 295, N.J. 08057.

Cistercians of the Strict Observance, Order of (Trappists), O.C.S.O.: Founded 1098, in France, by St. Robert; in US, 1848. General motherhouse, Rome, Italy. Number in each community is given at end of each entry.

Our Lady of Gethsemani Abbey (1848), Trappist P.O., Ky. 40073. 100.

Our Lady of New Melleray Abbey (1849), Dubuque, Iowa 52001. 87.

St. Joseph's Abbey (1825), Spencer, Mass. 01562. 94.

Holy Spirit Monastery (1944), Conyers, Ga. 30207. 52.

Our Lady of Guadalupe Abbey (1947), Lafayette, Ore. 97127. 40.

Our Lady of the Holy Trinity Abbey (1947), Huntsville, Utah 84317. 47.

Our Lady of Genesee Abbey (1951), Piffard, N.Y. 14533. 37.

Our Lady of Mepkin Abbey (1949), Moncks Corner, S. Car. 29461. 30.

Our Lady of the Holy Cross Abbey (1950), Berryville, Va. 22611. 33.

Our Lady of the Assumption Abbey, Rt. 5, Ava, Mo. 65608. 16.

Our Lady of New Clairvaux Abbey (1955), Vina, Calif. 96092. 28.

St. Benedict's Monastery (1956), Snowmass, Colo. 81654. 21.

Claretians (Missionary Sons of the Immaculate Heart of Mary), C.M.F.: Founded 1849, at Vich, Spain, by St. Anthony Mary Claret. General motherhouse, Rome, Italy. Mission, parochial, educational work.

Western Province, 1119 Westchester Pl., Los Angeles, Calif. 90019. 88 priests, 21 brothers.

Eastern Province, 400 N. Euclid Ave., Oak Park, Ill. 60302. 47 priests, 7 brothers.

Clerics Regular Minor (Adorno Fathers) C.R.M.: Founded 1589, at Naples, Italy, by St. Francis Caracciolo. General motherhouse, Rome, Italy; US address, 575 Darlington Ave., Ramsey, N.J. 07446. 7 priests.

Columban Fathers (St. Columban's Foreign Mission Society): Founded 1918, by Most Rev. Edward J. Galvin. US headquarters, St. Columbans, Nebr. 68056. Foreign mission work. 157 priests.

Consolata Society for Foreign Missions, I.M.C.: Founded 1901, at Turin, Italy, by Father Joseph Allamano. General motherhouse, Turin, Italy; US headquarters, P.O. Box C, Lincoln Hwy., Somerset, N.J. 08873. 35 priests, 1 brother.

Crosier Fathers (Canons Regular of the Order of the Holy Cross), O.S.C.: Founded 1210, in Belgium by Bl. Theodore De. Celles. Generalate, Amersfoort, Netherlands; US province, 2620 E. Wallen Rd., Fort Wayne, Ind. 46825. Mission, retreat, educational work. 106 priests, 49 brothers.

Cross, Congregation of Holy, C.S.C.: Founded 1837, in France; in US, 1841 Generalate, Rome, Italy. Educational, home, and foreign mission work.

Indiana Province (1841), 1304 E. Jefferson Blvd., South Bend, Ind. 46617. 422 priests, 46 brothers.

Eastern Province (1952), 835 Clinton Ave., Bridgeport, Conn. 06604. 163 priests, 29 brothers.

Southern Province (1968), 812 Audubon St., New Orleans, La. 70118. 64 priests, 3 brothers.

Divine Word, Society of the, S.V.D.: Founded 1875, in Holland, by Fr. Arnold Janssen; in US, 1897. General motherhouse, Rome, Italy.

Northern Province of the Blessed Virgin (1964), Techny, Ill. 60082. 100 priests, 54 brothers.

Sacred Heart Province (Eastern Province) (1940), 1025 Michigan Ave. N.E., Washington, D.C. 20017. 71 priests, 38 brothers.

St. Augustine's Province (Southern Province) (1940), 201 Ruella Ave., Bay St. Louis, Miss. 39520. 60 priests, 10 brothers.

St. Therese Province (Western Province) (1964), 2181 W. 25th St., Los Angeles, Calif. 90018. 50 priests, 10 brothers.

Dominicans (Order of Friars Preachers), O.P.: Founded early 13th century, in France by St. Dominic. General motherhouse, Rome, Italy. Preaching, literary, scientific pursuits.

St. Joseph Province (1806), 869 Lexington Ave., New York, N.Y. 10021. 401 priests, 45 brothers.

Holy Name of Jesus Province (1912), 416 Stanyan St., San Francisco, Calif. 94117. 137 priests, 25 brothers.

St. Dominic Province (1873), 5375 Notre Dame de Grace Ave., Montreal 260, Canada. 34 priests, 12 brothers (in US).

St. Albert the Great Province (1939), 1909 S. Ashland Ave., Chicago, Ill. 60608. 350 priests, 51 brothers.

Spanish Province, US foundation (1926), P.O. Box 277, San Diego, Tex. 78384. 7 priests.

Edmund, Society of St., S.S.E.: Founded 1843, in France, by Fr. Jean Baptiste Muard. General motherhouse, Edmundite Generalate, Winooski, Vt. 45404. Educational, missionary work. 103 priests, 16 brothers.

Eudists (Congregation of Jesus and Mary), C.J.M.: Founded 1643, in France, by St. John Eudes. General motherhouse, Rome, Italy; Canadian province, 6125 Lere Ave., Charlesbourg, Quebec 7, P. Q., Canada. Educational, missionary work. 9 priests in Buffalo diocese.

Francis, Third Order Regular of St., T.O.R.: Founded 1221, in Italy; in US, 1910. General motherhouse, Rome, Italy. Educational, missionary work.

Most Sacred Heart of Jesus Province (1910), 601 Pitcairn Pl., Pittsburgh, Pa. 15232. 189 priests, 48 brothers.

Immaculate Conception Province, 2006 Edgewater Parkway, Silver Springs, Md. 20903. 66 priests, 10 brothers.

Commissariat of the Spanish Province of the Immaculate Conception (1924), 205 East Jersey St., Elizabeth, N.J. 07206. 37 priests, 2 brothers.

Croatian Commissariat, House of Studies, 1359 Monroe St., N.E., Washington, D.C. 20017. 8 priests, 1 brother.

Francis de Sales, Oblates of St., O.S.F.S.: Founded 1871, by Fr. Louis Brisson. General motherhouse, Rome, Italy. Educational work.

Wilmington-Philadelphia Province (1906),

2200 Kentmere Parkway, Box 1452, Wilmington, Del. 19899. 280 priests, 53 brothers.
Toledo-Detroit Province (1966), 2109 Richmond Rd., Box 3322, Toledo, Ohio 43607. 104 priests, 23 brothers.
Franciscans (Order of Friars Minor), O.F.M.: Founded 1209, in Italy, by St. Francis of Assisi; in US, 1844. General motherhouse, Rome, Italy. Preaching, missionary, educational, parochial, charitable work.
St. John the Baptist Province (1844), 1615 Vine St., Cincinnati, Ohio 45210. 366 priests, 119 brothers.
Sacred Heart Province (1858), 3140 Meramec St., St. Louis, Mo. 63118. 474 priests, 126 brothers.
Assumption of the Blessed Virgin Mary Province (1887), Pulaski, Wis. 54162. 217 priests, 121 brothers.
Most Holy Name of Jesus Province (1901), 135 W. 31st St., New York, N.Y. 10001. 700 priests, 131 brothers.
St. Barbara Province (1915), 1500 34th Ave., Oakland, Calif. 94601. 239 priests, 80 brothers.
Immaculate Conception Province, 147 Thompson St., New York, N.Y. 10012. 195 priests, 42 brothers.
Holy Cross Custody (1912), 1400 Main St., P.O. Box 608, Lemont, Ill. 60439. 29 priests, 3 brothers.
Most Holy Savior Custody, 232 S. Home Ave., Pittsburgh, Pa. 15202. 31 priests, 5 brothers.
St. John Capistran Commissariat (1928), 1290 Hornberger Ave., Roebling, N.J. 08554. 20 priests, 11 brothers.
St. Stephen Transylvanian Commissariat (1948), 517 S. Belle Vista Ave., Youngstown, Ohio 44509. 14 priests, 4 brothers.
Holy Family Croatian Custody, (1927), 4848 S. Ellis Ave., Chicago, Ill. 60615. 46 priests.
St. Casimir Lithuanian Custody, Kennebunkport, Me. 04046. 33 priests, 7 brothers.
Holy Gospel Province (Mexico), US foundation, 2400 Marr St., El Paso, Tex. 79903. 13 priests, 4 brothers.
Saints Francis and James Province (Jalisco, Mexico), US foundation, Box 85, Hebbronville, Tex. 78361. 2 brothers.
Eastern District, Commissariat of the Holy Land, Mt. St. Sepulchre, 14th and Quincy Sts. N.E., Washington, D.C. 20017. 14 priests, 22 brothers.
St. Mary of the Angels Custody, Byzantine Slavonic Rite, P.O. Box 70, Sybertsville, Pa. 18251.
Academy of American Franciscan History, 9901 Carmelita Dr., P.O. Box 34440, Washington, D.C. 20034. 7 priests, 1 brother.
Franciscans (Order of Friars Minor Capuchin), O.F.M. Cap.: Established in 1528 as a separate jurisdiction of the order founded in 1209 by St. Francis of Assisi; first US prov-ince established after 1873. General motherhouse, Rome, Italy. Missionary, parochial work.
St. Joseph Province (1857), 1740 Mt. Elliott Ave., Detroit, Mich. 48207. 258 priests, 79 brothers.
St. Augustine Province (1873), 220 37th St., Pittsburgh, Pa. 15201. 247 priests, 37 brothers.
St. Mary Province (1952), 30 Gedney Park Dr., White Plains, N.Y. 10605. 212 priests, 48 brothers.
New Jersey Provincial Commissariate (1918), 754 Gunhill Rd., Bronx, N.Y. 10567. 61 priests, 17 brothers.
California Custody (St. Patrick's Province of Ireland), 1721 Hillside Dr., Burlingame, Calif. 94010. 50 priests.
Sts. Adalbert and Stanislaus Province (Warsaw, Poland), Manor Dr., Oak Ridge, N.J. 07438. 13 priests, 1 brother.
Franciscans (Order of Friars Minor Conventual), O.F.M.Conv.: Established in 1517 as a separate jurisdiction of the order founded in 1209 by St. Francis of Assisi; first US foundation, 1852. General curia, Rome, Italy. Missionary, educational, parochial work.
Immaculate Conception Province (1852), 812 N. Salina St., Syracuse, N.Y. 13208. 235 priests, 32 brothers.
St. Anthony of Padua Province (1903), 1300 Dundalk Ave., Baltimore, Md. 21222. 213 priests, 24 brothers.
St. Bonaventure Province (1939), 955 E. Ringwood Rd., Lake Forest, Ill. 60045. 87 priests, 35 brothers.
Our Lady of Consolation Province (1926), Mt. St. Francis, Ind. 47146. 146 priests, 46 brothers.
Glenmary Missioners (The Home Missioners of America): Founded 1939, in US. General headquarters, State Rt. 4 and Crescentville Rd., Fairfield, Ohio 45014. Home mission work. 74 priests, 31 brothers.
Holy Family, Congregation of the Missionaries of the, M.S.F.: Founded 1895, in Holland, by Rev. John P. Berthier. General motherhouse, Rome, Italy; US headquarters, 10415 Midland Blvd., St. Louis, Mo. 63114. Belated vocations for the missions. 54 priests, 12 brothers.
Holy Family, Sons of the, S.F.: Founded 1864, at Barcelona, Spain, by Joseph Manyanet; in US, 1920. General motherhouse, Barcelona, Spain; US address, P.O. Box 1228, Santa Cruz, N. Mex. 87567. 14 priests.
Holy Ghost Fathers, C.S.SP.: Founded 1703, in Paris, by Claude Francois Poullart des Places; in US, 1872. General motherhouse, Rome, Italy. Missions, Education.
Eastern Province (1872), 915 Dorseyville Rd., Pittsburgh, Pa. 15238. 220 priests, 26 brothers.
Western Province (1964), 4626 Pennsylvania St., Denver, Colo. 80216. 85 priests, 3 brothers.

Holy Ghost, Missionaries of the, M.Sp.S.: Founded 1914, at Mexico City, Mexico, by Felix Rougier. General motherhouse, Mexico City; US headquarters, 4433 Santa Fe Ave., Vernon, Calif. 90058. Missionary work. 5 priests, 2 brothers.

Immaculate Heart Missioners (Congregation of the Immaculate Heart of Mary—Scheut Fathers), C.I.C.M.: Founded 1862, by Very Rev. Theophile Verbist. General motherhouse, Rome, Italy; US province, 4651 N. 25th St., P.O. Box BB, Arlington, Va. 22207. Home and foreign mission work. 98 priests, 1 brother.

Jesuits (Society of Jesus), S.J.: Founded 1534, in France, by St. Ignatius Loyola; in US, 1833. Generalate, Rome, Italy. Missionary, educational, literary work.

Maryland Province (1833), 5704 Roland Ave., Baltimore, Md. 21210. 506 priests, 62 brothers.

New York Province (1943), 501 E. Fordham Rd., Bronx, N.Y. 10458. 869 priests, 89 brothers.

Missouri Province (1863), 4511 W. Pine Blvd., St. Louis, Mo. 63108. 437 priests, 67 brothers.

New Orleans Province (1907), 6301 Strafford Pl., P.O. Box 6378, New Orleans, La. 70114. 320 priests, 50 brothers.

California Province (1909), College at Prospect Aves., P.O. Box 519, Los Gatos, Calif. 95030. 471 priests, 56 brothers.

New England Province (1926), 297 Commonwealth Ave., Boston, Mass. 02115. 769 priests, 57 brothers.

Chicago Province, 509 N. Oak Park Ave., Oak Park, Ill. 60302. 369 priests, 41 brothers.

Oregon Province (1932), 2222 N.W. Hoyt, Portland, Ore. 97210. 388 priests, 50 brothers.

Detroit Province (1955), 602 Boulevard Center Blvd., Cass at W. Grand Blvd., Detroit, Mich. 48202. 283 priests, 61 brothers.

Wisconsin Province (1955), 2120 W. Clybourn St., Suite 200, Milwaukee, Wis. 53233. 452 priests, 50 brothers.

Joseph, Congregation of St., C.S.J.: General motherhouse, Rome, Italy; US vice province, P.O. Box 2064, Albuquerque, N.M. 87103. Parochial, missionary, educational work. 15 priests, 5 brothers.

Joseph, Oblates of St., O.S.J.: Founded 1878, in Italy, by Bishop Joseph Marello. General motherhouse, Rome, Italy. Parochial, educational work.

Eastern Province, 28 Memorial Ave., Exeter, Pa. 18643. 14 priests, 3 brothers.

Western Province, 1333 58th St., Sacramento, Calif. 95819. 22 priests, 6 brothers.

Josephite Fathers, C.J.: General motherhouse, Ghent, Belgium; US foundation, 989 Brookside Ave., Santa Maria, Calif. 93454. 12 priests.

Josephite Fathers (St. Joseph's Society of the Sacred Heart), S.S.J.: Founded 1866, in England, by Cardinal Vaughan; in US, 1871.

General motherhouse, 1130 N. Calvert St. Baltimore Md. 21202. Work in Negro missions, 213 priests, 32 brothers.

LaSalette, Missionaries of Our Lady of, M.S.: Founded 1852, by Msgr. de Bruillard; in US, 1892. Motherhouse, Rome, Italy.

Our Lady of Seven Dolors Province (1933), 120 Mountain Ave., Bloomfield, Conn. 06002. 130 priests, 31 brothers.

Immaculate Heart of Mary Province (1945), P.O. Box 538, Attleboro, Mass. 02703. 110 priests, 41 brothers.

Mary Queen Province (1958), 4650 S. Broadway, St. Louis, Mo. 63111. 92 priests, 9 brothers.

Mary Queen of Peace Vice Province (1967), 5270 N. Lake Dr., Milwaukee, Wis. 53217. 35 priests, 10 brothers.

Legionaries of Christ (Missionaries of the Sacred Heart of Jesus and the Sorrowful Virgin), L.C.: Founded 1941, in Mexico, by Rev. Maracial. General motherhouse, Rome, Italy; US foundation, 393 Derby Ave., Orange, Conn. 06477. 6 priests.

Marian Fathers, M.I.C.: Founded 1673; US foundation, 1913. General motherhouse, Rome, Italy. Educational, parochial, mission work.

St. Casimir Province (1930), 6336 S. Kilbourn Ave., Chicago, Ill. 60629. 55 priests, 7 brothers.

St. Stanislaus Kostka Province (1948), Eden Hill, Stockbridge, Mass. 01262. 24 priests, 13 brothers.

Marianists (Society of Mary; Brothers of Mary), S.M.: Founded 1817, at Bordeaux, France, by Rev. William-Joseph Chaminade; in US, 1849. General motherhouse, Rome, Italy. Educational work.

Cincinnati Province (1849), 2765 Ridgeway Rd., Dayton, Ohio. 45419. 89 priests, 349 brothers.

St. Louis Province (1908), Marycliff, Glencoe, Mo. 63038. 81 priests, 335 brothers.

Pacific Province (1948), Cupertino, Calif. 95014. 34 priests, 148 brothers.

New York Province (1961), 4301 Roland Ave., Baltimore, Md. 21210. 36 priests, 120 brothers.

Mariannhill, Congregation of the Missionaries of, C.M.M.: Trappist monastery, begun in 1882 by Abbot Francis Pfanner in Natal, South Africa, became an independent modern congregation in 1909; in US, 1920. Generalate, Rome, Italy; US-Canadian headquarters, 23715 Ann Arbor Trail, Dearborn Heights, Mich. 48127. Foreign mission work. 20 priests, 7 brothers.

Marist Fathers (Society of Mary), S.M.: Founded 1816, at Lyons, France, by Jean Claude Colin; in US, 1863. General motherhouse, Rome, Italy. Educational work.

Washington Province (1924), 220 Taylor St. N.E., Washington, D.C. 20017. 134 priests, 5 brothers.

Northeastern Province (1924), 518 Pleasant

St., Framingham, Mass. 01701. 125 priests, 16 brothers.

San Francisco Western Province (1961), 625 Pine St., San Fancisco, Calif. 94108. 36 priests, 10 brothers.

Mary Immaculate, Oblates of, O.M.I.: Founded 1816, in France, by Charles Joseph Eugene de Mazenod; in US, 1849. General motherhouse, Rome, Italy. Educational, mission work.

Southern US Province (1904), 5722 Blanco Rd., San Antonio, Tex. 78216. 260 priests, 24 brothers.

Our Lady of Hope, Eastern Province (1883), 350 Jamaicaway, Boston, Mass. 02130. 227 priests, 13 brothers.

St. John the Baptist Province (1921), 216 Nesmith St., Lowell, Mass. 01852. 175 priests, 24 brothers.

Central Province (1924), 104 N. Mississippi River Blvd., St. Paul, Minn. 55104. 175 priests, 25 brothers.

Western Province (1953), 290 Lenox Ave., Oakland, Calif. 94610. 62 priests, 9 brothers.

Italian Province, US foundation, St. Nicholas Church, Palisades Park, N.J. 07650. 5 priests.

Maryknoll Fathers (Catholic Foreign Mission Society of Ameris), M.M.: Founded 1911, in US, by Frs. Thomas F. Price and James A. Walsh. General Center, Maryknoll, N.Y. 10545. 881 priests, 129 brothers.

Mekhitarist Order of Vienna, C.M.Vd.: Established 1773. General headquarters, Vienna, Austria; US addresses, Our Lady Queen of Martyrs Church, 1327 Pleasant Ave., Los Angeles, Calif. 90033 and Holy Cross Church, 100 Mt. Auburn St., Cambridge, Mass. 02138. Work among Armenians in US.

Mercedarians (Order of Our Lady of Mercy), O D.M.: Founded 1218, in Spain, by St. Peter Nolasco. General motherhouse, Rome, Italy; US headquarters, LeRoy, N.Y. 14482. 4 priests, 1 brother.

Mercy, Congregation of Priests of (Fathers of Mercy), C.P.M.: Founded 1808, in France, by Rev. Jean Baptiste Rauzan; in US, 1839. General motherhouse, Cold Spring, N.Y. 10516. Mission work.

Mill Hill Missionaries (St. Joseph's Society for Foreign Missions), M.H.M.: Founded 1866, in England, by Cardinal Vaughan; in US, 1951. General motherhouse, London, England; American headquarters, Albany, N.Y. 12203. 28 priests, 5 brothers.

Missionary Fathers of St. Charles, Congregation of the, C.S.: Founded 1887, at Piacenza, Italy, by Bishop John Baptist Scalbrini. General motherhouse, Rome, Italy.

St Charles Borromeo Province (1888), 27 Carmine St., New York, N.Y. 10014. 86 priests, 5 brothers.

St. John Baptist Province (1903), 546 N. East Ave., Oak Park, Ill. 60302. 74 priests, 4 brothers.

Missionaries of the Holy Apostles, M.Ss A.:

Founded 1962, Washington, D.C., by Eusebe M. Menard. General motherhouse, 1335 Quincy St. N.E., Washington, D.C. 20017. 11 priests.

Monks of the Brotherhood of St. Francis (Monks of New Skete, Byzantine Rite): Founded 1966, in US. New Skete Monastery, Cambridge, N.Y. 12816. 12 monks.

Montfort Fathers (Missionaries of the Company of Mary), S.M.M.: Founded 1715, by St. Louis Marie Grignon de Montfort; in US, 1948. General motherhouse, Rome, Italy; US headquarters, 101-18 104th St., Ozone Park, N.Y. 11416. Mission Work. 63 priests, 7 brothers.

Oratorian Fathers (Congregation of the Oratory of St. Philip Neri(, C.O.: Founded 1575, at Rome, by St. Philip Neri. Central administration, Rome, Italy; American procure, P.O. Box 55, Yarnell, Ariz. 85362. 24 priests, 2 brothers.

Pallottines (Society of the Catholic Apostolate), S.A.C.: Founded 1835, at Rome, by St. Vincent Pallotti. General motherhouse, Rome, Italy. Charitable, educational, parochial, mission work.

Immaculate Conception Province (1952), 309 N. Paca St., Baltimore, Md. 21201. 34 priests, 12 brothers.

Mother of God Province (1946), 5424 W. Blue Mound Rd:, Milwaukee, Wis. 53208. 42 priests, 9 brothers.

Irish Province, US address: 3352 4th St., Wyandotte, Mich. 48192. 30 priests.

Christ the King Province (Poland), 303 Goundry St., North Tonawanda, N.Y. 14120. 9 priests, 1 brother.

Queen of Apostles Province (1909), 448 E. 116th St., New York, N.Y. 10029. 16 priests.

Paraclete, Servants of the, s.P.: Founded 1947, Santa Fe, N.M., archdiocese. General motherhouse, Rome, Italy; US motherhouse, Jemez Springs, N.M. 87025. Devoted to care of priests. 48 priests, 9 brothers.

Paris Foreign Missions Society, M.E.P.: Founded 1662, at Paris, France. Headquarters, Paris, France; US establishment, 930 Ashbury St., San Francisco, Calif. 94117. Mission work and training of native clergy. 3.

Passionists (Congregation of the Passion), C.P.: Founded 1720, in Italy, by St. Paul of the Cross. General motherhouse, Rome, Italy.

St. Paul of the Cross Province (1852), 1901 West St., Union City, N.J. 07087. 403 priests, 60 brothers.

Holy Cross Province (Western Province), 5700 N. Harlem Ave., Chicago, Ill. 60631. 198 priests, 27 brothers.

Patrick's Missionary Society, St., S.P.S.: Founded 1932, at Wicklow, Ireland, by Msgr. Patrick Whitney; in US, 1953. International headquarters, Kiltegan Co., Wicklow, Ireland. US foundations: 35 S. 29th St., Camden, N.J. 08105; 70 Edgewater Rd., Cliffside Park, N.J. 07010; 19536 Eric Dr., Saratoga,

Calif. 95070; 1347 W. Granville Ave., Chicago, Ill. 60626; 721 St. Ferdinand St., New Orleans, La. 70117. 26 priests.

Pauline Fathers (Order of St. Paul the First Hermit), O.S.P.: Founded 1215; established in US, 1955. General motherhouse, Czestochowa, Jasna Gora, Poland; US headquarters, P.O. Box 151, Doylestown, Pa. 18901. 14 priests, 6 brothers.

Pauline Fathers (Society of St. Paul for the Apostolate of Communications), S.S.P.: Founded 1914, by Very Rev. James Alberione; in US, 1932. Motherhouse, Rome, Italy; American province, Old Lakeshore Rd., Derby, N.Y. 14047. 16 priests, 36 brother.

Paulists (Society of Missionary Priests of St. Paul the Apostle), C.S.P.: Founded 1858, in New York, by Fr. Isaac Thomas Hecker. General offices, 86 Dromore Rd., N.Y. 10583. Convert, ecumenical missionary work. Scarsdale, 249 priest.

Piarists (Order of the Pious Schools), Sch.P.: Founded 1617, at Rome, Italy, by St. Joseph Calasanctius. General motherhouse, Rome, Italy. American headquarters, 1339 Monroe St. N.E., Washington, D.C. 20017. Educational work. 58 priests, 2 brothers.

Pontifical Institute for Foreign Missions, P.I.M.E.: Founded 1850, in Italy, at request of Pope Pius XI. General motherhouse, Rome, Italy; US headquarters, 9800 Oakland Ave., Detroit, Mich. 48211. Foreign mission work. 42 priests, 4 brothers.

Precious Blood, Society of, C.Pp.S.: Founded 1815, in Italy, by St. Gaspare del Bufalo. General motherhouse, Rome, Italy.

Cincinnati Province, 3500 Montgomery Rd., Cincinnati, Ohio. 45207. 283 priests, 73 brothers.

Kansas City Province, Ruth Ewing Rd., Liberty, Mo. 64068. 107 priests, 8 brothers.

Pacific Province, 24 Ursuline Rd., Santa Rosa, Calif. 95401. 30 priests, 2 brothers.

Atlantic Vicariate, 65 Highland Ave., Rochester, N.Y. 14620. 17 priests, 2 brothers.

Premonstratensians (Order of the Canons Regular of Premontre; Norbertines), O. Praem.: Founded 1120, at Premontre, France, by St. Norbert. General motherhouse, Rome, Italy. Educational, parish work.

St. Norbert Abbey, 1016 N. Broadway, DePere, Wis. 54115. 132 priests, 11 brothers.

Daylesford Abbey, 220 S. Valley Rd., Paoli, Pa. 19301. 55 priests, 6 brothers.

St. Michael's Seminary and Novitiate, 1042 Star Route, Orange, Calif. 92667. 8 priests.

Providence, Sons of Divine, F.D.P.: Founded 1893, at Tortona, Italy; by Don Aloysius Orione; in US, 1933. General motherhouse, Tortona, Italy; US address, Jasper, Ind. 47546. Parish work. 2 priests.

Redemptorists (Congregation of the Most Holy Redeemer), C.SS.R.: Founded 1732, in Italy, by St. Alphonsus Mary Liguori. General motherhouse, Rome, Italy. Mission work.

Baltimore Province (1850), 7509 Shore Rd., Brooklyn, N.Y. 1209. 627 priests, 76 brothers.

St. Louis Province (1875), Box 6, Glenview, Ill. 60025. 370 priests, 61 brothers.

Oakland Province (1952), 3696 Clay St., San Francisco, Calif. 94118. 96 priests, 15 brothers.

New Orleans Vice-Province, 1527 3rd St., New Orleans, La., 70130.

Resurrectionists (Priests of the Congregation of the Resurrection), C.R.: Founded 1836, in France, under direction of Bogdan Janski. Motherhouse, Rome, Italy; US address, 3601 N. California Ave., Chicago, Ill. 60618. Parochial, educational, mission work. 124 priests, 7 brothers.

Rosminians (Institute of Charity), I.C.: Founded 1828, in Italy, by Antonio Rosmini-Serbati. General motherhouse, Rome, Italy; US address, 2327 W. Heading Ave., Peoria, Ill. 61604. Charitable work. 30 priests.

Sacred Heart of Jesus, Missionaries of the, M.S.C.: Founded 1854, by Rev. Jules Chevalier. General motherhouse, Rome, Italy; US province, 305 S. Lake St., P.O. Box 270, Aurora, Ill. 60507. 109 priests, 37 brothers.

Sacred Heart of Jesus, Priests of the, S.C.J.: Founded 1877, in France. General motherhouse, Rome, Italy; US headquarters, 407 Glenview Ave., Milwaukee, Wis. 53213. Educational, preaching, mission work. 129 priests, 61 brothers.

Sacred Hearts, Fathers of the (Picpus Fathers), SS.CC.: Founded 1805, in France, by Fr. Coudrin. General motherhouse, Rome, Italy. Mission, educational work.

Eastern Province (1946), 1 Main St. Fairhaven, Mass. 02719. 99 priests, 9 brothers.

Western Province (1970), 1425 S. Dunsmuir Ave., Los Angeles, Calif. 90019. 39 priests, 3 brothers.

Hawaiian Province, Box 797, Kaneoke, Oahu, Hawaii 96744. 72 priests, 10 brothers.

Sacred Hearts of Jesus and Mary, Missionaries of the, M.SS.CC.: Founded at Naples, Italy, by Ven. Gaetano Errico. General motherhouse, Rome, Italy; US headquarters, 522 State St., Camden, N.J. 08100. 8 priests.

Salesians of St. John Bosco (Society of St. Francis de Sales), S.D.B.: Founded 1841, by St. John (Don) Bosco. General motherhouse, Rome, Italy.

St. Philip the Apostle Province (1902), 148 Main St., New Rochelle, N.Y. 10802. 177 priests, 71 brothers.

San Francisco Province (1926), 1100 Franklin St., San Francisco, Calif. 94109. 96 priests, 55 brothers.

Salvatorians (Society of the Divine Savior), S.D.S.: Founded 1881, in Rome, by Fr. Francis Jordan; in US, 1896. General motherhouse, Rome, Italy; US province, 1735 Hii-Mount Blvd., Milwaukee, Wis. 53208. Educational, parochial, mission work; campus ministries, chaplaincies. 153 priests, 86 brothers.

Scalabrinians: See Missionary Fathers of St. Charles, Congregation of the.

Servites (Order of the Servants of Mary), O.S.M.: Founded 1233, by seven youths of Florence. Generalate, Rome, Italy. Educational work.

Eastern Province (1967) 3401 S. Home Ave., Berwyn, Ill. 60402. 131 priests, 32 brothers.

Western Province (1967), 5210 Somerset St., Buena Park, Calif. 90620. 58 priests, 16 brothers.

Somascan Fathers, C.R.S.: Founded 1534, at Somasca, Italy, by St. Jerome Emilian. General motherhouse, Rome, Italy; US address, 628 Hanover St., Manchester, N.H. 03104. 4 priests, 3 brothers.

Sons of Mary Missionary Society: Founded 1952, in the Boston archdiocese, by Rev. Edward F. Garesche, S.J. Headquarters, 567 Salem End Rd., Framingham, Mass. 01701. Dedicated to health of the sick; medical, pastoral and social work in home and foreign missions. 24 professed members.

Stigmatine Fathers and Brothers (Congregation of the Sacred Stigmata), C.S.S.: Founded 1816, by Ven. Gaspare Bertoni. General motherhouse, Rome, Italy; US headquarters, 554 Lexington St., Waltham, Mass. 01254. Parish work, Christian living center, information center. 93 priests, 11 brothers.

Sulpicians (Society of Priests of St. Sulpice), S.S.: Founded 1641, at Paris, by Rev. Jean Jacques Olier. General motherhouse, Paris, France; US province, 5408 Roland Ave., Baltimore, Md. 21210. 180 priests.

Theatines (Congregation of Clerics Regular): C.R.: Founded 1524, at Rome, by St. Cajetan. General motherhouse, Rome, Italy; US headquarters, 1050 S. Birch St., Denver, Colo. 80222. 32 priests.

Trappists: See Cistercians of the Strict Observance.

Trinitarians (Order of the Most Holy Trinity), O.SS.T.: Founded 1198, by Sts. John Matha and Felix of Valois. General motherhouse, Rome, Italy; US headquarters, Park Heights Ave., Box 5742, Baltimore, Md. 21208. 37 priests, 18 brothers.

Trinity, Missionary Servants of the Most Holy, S.T.: Founded 1929, by Fr. Thomas Augustine Judge. Generalate, 503 Rock Creek Church Rd. N.W., Washington, D.C. 20010. Home mission work. 162 priests, 51 brothers.

Verona Fathers (Sons of the Sacred Heart of Jesus), F.S.C.J.: Founded 1885, in Italy. General motherhouse, Rome, Italy; US headquarters, 8108 Beechmont Ave., Cincinnati, Ohio 45230. Mission work. 45 priests, 4 brothers.

Viatorian Fathers (Clerics of St. Viator), C.S.V.: Founded 1831, in France, by Fr. Louis Joseph Querbes. General motherhouse,

Rome, Italy; US headquarters, 1100 Forest Ave., Evanston, Ill. 60202. Educational work. 154 priests, 26 brothers.

Vincentians (Congregation of the Mission; Lazarists), C.M.: Founded 1625, in Paris, by St. Vincent de Paul; in US, 1867. General motherhouse, Rome, Italy. Educational work.

Eastern Province (1867), 500 E. Chelten Ave., Philadelphia, Pa. 19144. 341 priests, 17 brothers.

Western Province (188), 1849 Cass Ave., St. Louis, Mo. 63106. 229 priests, 24 brothers.

Utica Vice-Province (1903), 10475 Cosby Manor Rd., Utica, N.Y. 13502. 55 priests, 7 brothers.

American Italian Branch, Our Lady of Pompei Church, 3600 Claremont St., Baltimore, Md. 21224. 6 priests.

American Spanish Branch (Barcelona, Spain), St. Peter's Rectory, 117 Warren St., Brooklyn, N.Y. 11201. 12 priests.

American Spanish Branch (Madrid, Spain), Holy Agony Church, 1834 3rd Ave., New York, N.Y. 10029. 16 priests.

Los Angeles Vice-Province (1958), 649 W. Adams Blvd., Los Angeles, Calif. 90007. 72 priests, 3 brothers.

New Orleans Vice-Province (1958), 1802 Tulane Ave., New Orleans, La. 70116. 63 priests, 2 brothers.

Vocationist Fathers (Society of Divine Vocations), S.D.V.: Founded 1920, in Italy; in US, 1962. General motherhouse, Naples, Italy; US address, 170 Broad St., Newark, N.J. 07104.

White Fathers, W.F.: Founded 1868, at Algiers, by Cardinal C.M.A. Lavigerie. General motherhouse, Rome, Italy; US headquarters, 777 Belvidere Ave., Plainfield, N.J. 07062. Foreign missions. 55 priests, 11 brothers.

Xaverian Missionary Fathers, S.X.: Founded 1895, by Archbishop Conforti, at Parma, Italy. General motherhouse, Rome, Italy. US province, 12 Helene Ct., Wayne, N.J. 07470. Foreign mission work. 25 priests, 1 brother.

INSTITUTES OF BROTHERS

Alexian Brothers, C.F.A.: Founded 1365, at Brabant, Belgium, by Bro. Tobias. Motherhouse, Aachen, Germany; generalate, Signal Mountain, Tenn. 37377. Hospital work. 123.

Charity, Brothers of, F.C.: Founded 1807, in Belgium, by Canon Peter J. Triest. General motherhouse, Rome, Italy; American District House, 7720 Doe Lane, Philadelphia, Pa. 19118. Charitable, educational work.

Christian Brothers, Congregation of, C.F.C. (formerly Christian Brothers of Ireland): Founded 1802 at Waterford, Ireland, by Edmund Ignatius Rice. General motherhouse, Rome, Italy. Educational work.

American Province, Eastern US (1916), 21 Pryor Terr., New Rochelle, N.Y. 10801. 354.

American Province, Western US (1966),

935 Iverson St., Salinas, Calif. 93901. 185.

Christian Instruction, Brothers of (La Mennais Brothers), F.I.C.: Founded 1817, at Ploermel, France, by Abbe Jean Marie de la Mennais and Abbe Gabriel Deshayes. General motherhouse, Jersey Island, England; American province, Notre Dame Institute, Alfred, Me. 04002. 123.

Christian Schools, Brothers of the (Christian Brothers), F.S.C.: Founded 1680, at Reims, France, by St. Jean Baptiste de la Salle. General motherhouse, Rome, Italy; US Conference, 100 De La Salle Dr., P.O. Box 356, Lockport, Ill. 60141. Educational, charitable work. 2,021.

Cross, Congregation of Holy, C.S.C.: Founded 1837, in France, by Rev. Basil Moreau; US province, 1841. Generalate, Rome, Italy. Educational work.

Midwest Province (1841), Box 460, Notre Dame, Ind. 46556. 372.

Southwest Province (1956), St. Edward's University, Austin, Tex. 78704. 193.

Eastern Province (1956), 24 Ricardo St., West Haven, Conn. 06516. 225.

Francis, Brothers of Poor of St., C.F.P.: Founded 1857. Motherhouse, Aachen, Germany; US province, Mt. Alverno School, Price Hill, Cincinnati, Ohio 45238. Educational work, especially with poor and emotionally disturbed youth. 90.

Francis Xavier, Brothers of St. (Xaverian Brothers), C.F.X.: Founded 1839, in Belgium, by Theodore J. Ryken. Generalate, Rome, Italy. Educational work.

Sacred Heart Province, 10516 Summit Ave., Kensington, Md. 20795. 265.

St. Joseph Province, 704 Brush Hill Rd., Milton, Mass. 02186. 242.

Franciscan Brothers of Brooklyn, O.S.F.: Founded in Ireland; established at Brooklyn, 1858. Generalate, 135 Remsen St., Brooklyn, N.Y. 11201. Educational work. 206.

Franciscan Brothers of the Holy Cross, F.F.S.C.: Founded 1862, in Germany. Generalate, Hausen, Linz Rhein, Germany; US region, St. James Trade School, R.R. 1, Springfield, Ill. 62707. Educational work. 22.

Franciscan Missionary Brothers of the Sacred Heart of Jesus, O.S.F.: Founded 1927, in the St. Louis, Mo., archdiocese. Motherhouse, R.R. 3, Eureka, Mo. 63025. Care of aged, infirm, homeless men and boys.

Good Shepherd, Society of Brothers of the, B.G.S.: Founded 1951, by Bro. Mathias Barrett. Motherhouse, P.O. Box 389, Albuquerque, N.M. 87103. Operate shelters and refuges for aged and homeless men; homes for handicapped men and boys, alcoholic rehabilitation center. 57.

Holy Eucharist, Brothers of the, F.S.E.: Founded in US, 1957. Generalate, P.O. Box 356, Cottonport, La. 71327. 17.

Immaculate Heart of Mary, Brothers of the, F.I.C.M.: Founded 1948, at Steubenville, Ohio, by Bishop John K. Mussio. Motherhouse, 609 N. 7th St., Steubenville, Ohio 43952. Educational, charitable work. 18.

Immaculate Heart of Mary, Brothers of Charity: Founded 1958, in US. Motherhouse, P.O. Box 804, Beaumont, Calif. 92228. 13.

John of God, Hospitaller Order of St., O.H.: Founded 1537, in Spain. General motherhouse, Rome, Italy; US headquarters, 2035 W. Adams Blvd., Los Angeles, Calif. 90018. Nursing work and related fields. 34.

Joseph, Brothers of St., F.S.J.: Founded 1962, in US. Motherhouse, Rt. 2, Box 767, Oklahoma City, Okla. 73114. 3.

Marist Brothers, F.M.S.: Founded 1817, in France, by Bl. Marcellin Champagnat. General motherhouse, Rome, Italy; US address for information, 1044 Northern Blvd., Roslyn, N.Y. 11576. Educational work. 478.

Mercy, Brothers of, F.M.M.: Founded 1856, in Germany. General motherhouse, Montabaur, Germany. American headquarters, 4520 Ransom Rd., Clarence, N.Y. 14031. Hospital work. 39.

Mercy, Brothers of Our Lady of, C.F.M.M.: Founded 1844, in The Netherlands by Abp. J. Zwijsen. Generalate, Tilburg, The Netherlands; US region, 2336 South "C" St., Oxnard, Calif. 93030. 17.

Patrician Brothers (Brothers of St. Patrick), F.S.P.: Founded 1808, in Ireland, by Bishop Daniel Delaney; US novitiate, 7820 Bolsa Ave., Midway City, Calif. 92655. Educational work. 20.

Pius X, Brothers of St.: Founded 1952, at La Crosse, Wis., by Bishop John P. Treacy. Motherhouse, Box 438, De Soto, Wis. 54624. Teaching, nursing, farming, charitable work. 14.

Rosary, Brothers of the Holy, F.S.R.: Founded 1956, in US. Address, 101 Boynton Lane, Reno, Nev. 89502. 9.

Sacred Heart, Brothers of the, S.C.: Founded 1821, in France, by Rev. Andre Coindre. General motherhouse, Rome, Italy, Educational work.

New Orleans Province (1847), P.O. Box 89, Bay St. Louis, Miss. 39520. 143.

New England Province (1945), "Cor Jesu Terrace," Pascoag, R.I. 02859. 302.

New York Province (1960), R.D. 1, Box 215, Belvidere, N.J. 07823. 85.

MEN SUPERIORS

The Conference of Major Superiors of Men of the USA is a consultative board for discussion of the affairs of men religious in this country, and a liaison body for establishing and maintaining contact among religious institutes and with the Holy See, bishops, diocesan clergy, and Catholic associations. The conference, which was formed in 1956, was officially established Mar. 23, 1960, by decree of the Congregation for Religious and Secular Institutes.

The general objective of the conference is to promote the spiritual and apostolic welfare of religious priests and brothers in the US.

Conference membership consists of superiors of 94 institutes with a combined total of approximately 30,000 members.

The Rev. Paul M. Boyle, C.P., is president of the conference. The Rev. Francis X. Gokey, S.S.E., is national executive secretary, with offices at 1330 New Hampshire Ave. N.W., Suite 114, Washington, D.C. 20036.

More than 200 provincial superiors, abbots and superiors general pledged themselves to a program of action affecting their congregations and institutions and the nation, at a general assembly of the CMSM June 18 to 22, 1972, in Washington.

A number of resolutions called for "simplicity" of life styles within the Church, "full disclosure" of church resources, and "implementation of the rights of women" in the Church. During discussions, the delegates called for the "fullest possible" participation of lay persons in Church affairs, including the selection of bishop candidates.

Under resolutions concerning the "external world," the conference committed itself to press for "a shift of our national priorities away from the present military to person-oriented priorities."

Father Francis X. Gokey, S.S.E., executive secretary of the conference, said the resolutions represented a continuation of a trend in development for the previous two or three years. He commented that the CMSM "is becoming more people-oriented, more concerned with the needs of the Church, the poor and needy...."

BROTHERS' ASSOCIATION

Representatives of 39 institutes of men religious in the United States attended the charter meeting of the National Association of Religious Brothers early in March, 1972, in Clarkston, Mich.

The primary objectives of the association are "to establish realistic and effective means of communication and cooperation" with the National Conference of Catholic Bishops and the Conference of Major Superiors of Men, and to seek "effective representation for its members in matters concerning their religious and professional lives."

The desirability and need for such a national organization emerged in the course of brothers' meetings over a period of some six years. More than 73 per cent of 700 respondents to a questionnaire favored the establishment of the group, and about 4,000 of nearly 10,000 brothers in the country signified interest in becoming members.

Officers elected at the first meeting were Xaverian Brother Bonaventure Scully of Wheaton, Md., president; Atonement Brother Raymond Saville of Chappaqua, N. Y., vice-president; Brother Damian Carroll, C.P., of Springfield, Mass., secretary-treasurer.

MEMBERSHIP OF RELIGIOUS INSTITUTES OF MEN

Below are world membership statistics from *Annuario Pontificio, 1972* of institutes of men of pontifical right with 500 or more members; the number of priests is in parentheses. Also listed are institutes with less than 500 members with houses in the US.

Jesuits (20,772)	31,745
Franciscans (Friars Minor) (16,304)	24,501
Salesians (11,471)	20,423
Brothers of Christian Schools	14,517
Franciscans (Capuchins) (9,370)	13,403
Benedictines (7,058)	10,819
Dominicans (6,568)	9,399
Marist Brothers	8,737
Redemptorists (5,747)	8,095
Oblates of Mary Immaculate (5,330)	7,176
Society of the Divine Word (3,229)	5,538
Vincentians (4,207)	5,528
Holy Spirit, Congregation (3,566)	4,578
Augustinians (2,979)	4,170
Franciscans (Conventuals) (2,808)	4,104
Passionists (2,700)	3,767
Discalced Carmelites (2,538)	3,689
White Fathers (3,011)	3,542
Christian Brothers	3,517
Claretians (2,022)	3,416
Priests of the Sacred Heart (2,023)	3,046
Trappists (1,705)	3,031
Missionaries of the Sacred Heart of Jesus (2,100)	3,014
Marianists (588)	2,827
Holy Cross Fathers (1,077)	2,638
Brothers of the Sacred Heart	2,522
Carmelites (Ancient Observance) (1,775)	2,433
Marists (1,701)	2,266
Hospitallers of St. John of God (108)	2,215
Pallottines (1,430)	2,104
Piarists (1,563)	2,063
Brothers of Christian Instruction of Ploermel (1,459)	1,885
Picpus Fathers (1,459)	1,881
Scheut Fathers (1,490)	1,822
Premonstratensians (1,251)	1,791
Verona Fathers (1,059)	1,724
Brothers of Christian Instruction of St. Gabriel	1,703
Montfort Fathers (1,258)	1,683
Society of African Missions (1,420)	1,670
Assumptionists (1,340)	1,658
Cistercians (Common Observance) (1,001)	1,553
Viatorians (505)	1,474
Servants of Mary (1,016)	1,467
Blessed Sacrament Fathers (912)	1,399
Augustinians (Recollects) (1,068)	1,399
Salvatorians (851)	1,299
Pious Society of St. Paul (509)	1,254
Brothers of Charity	1,238
Oblates of St. Francis de Sales (762)	1,197

RELIGIOUS INSTITUTES OF WOMEN IN THE UNITED STATES

(Sources: *Official Catholic Directory, 1972*; Catholic Almanac survey.)

The number in parentheses indicates the number of professed members of each institute.

Adorers, Handmaids of the Blessed Sacrament and of Charity, Sisters, A.E.S.C.: Founded 1850, in Spain, in US, 1961. General motherhouse, Madrid, Spain; US foundation, 2637 Homedale St., San Diego, Calif. 92139.

Africa, Missionary Sisters of Our Lady of (White Sisters), S.A.: Founded 1869, at Algiers, Algeria, by Cardinal Lavigerie; in US, 1929. General motherhouse, Frascati, Italy; US headquarters, 5335 16th St., N.W., Washington, D.C. 20011. Medical, educational, catechetical and social work in Africa. (50)

African Sisters of Our Lady of Good Counsel, O.L.G.S.: Founded 1939, in Africa; in US, 1962. General motherhouse, Uganda; US foundation, 23 Mt. Pleasant St., North Brookfield, Mass. 01535. (8)

Agnes, Sisters of St., C.S.A.: Founded 1858, in US, by Caspar Rehrl. General motherhouse, 390 E. Division St., Fond du Lac, Wis. 54935. Educational, hospital, social work. (786)

Ann, Sisters of St., S.S.A.: Founded 1834, in Italy; in US, 1952. General motherhouse, Turin, Italy; US headquarters, Mount St. Ann, Ebensburg, Pa. 15931. (15)

Anne, Sisters of St., S.S.A.: Founded 1850, at Vaudreuil, Que., Canada; in US, 1867. General motherhouse, Lachine, Que., Canada; US address, 720 Boston Post Rd., Marlboro, Mass. 01752. Educational, social work. (308)

Anthony, Missionary Servants of St., M.S.S.A.: Founded 1929, in US, by Rev. Peter Baque. General motherhouse, 100 Peter Baque Rd., San Antonio, Tex. 78209. Social work. (16)

Apostolate, Sisters Auxiliaries of the, A.A.: Founded 1903, in Canada; in US, 1911. General motherhouse, 689 Maple Terr., Monongah, W. Va. 26554. Educational, social work. (18)

Assumption, Congregation of the R.A.: Founded 1839, in France; in US, 1919. General motherhouse, Paris, France; US novitiate, 3480 W. Schoolhouse Lane, Germantown, Philadelphia, Pa. 19144. Educational work. (56)

Assumption, Little Sisters of the, L.S.A.: Founded 1865, in France; in US, 1891. General motherhouse, Paris, France; US motherhouse, 1195 Lexington Ave., New York, N.Y. 10028. Social work. (77)

Assumption, Oblate Sisters of the, O.A.: Founded in France; in US, 1956. US address, 1015 Pleasant St., Worcester, Mass. 01602 (9)

Assumption of the Blessed Virgin, Sisters of the, S.A.S.V.: Founded 1853, in Canada; in US, 1891. General motherhouse, Nicolet, Que., Canada; American province, North Main St., Petersham, Mass. 01366. Educational, mission, social work. (257)

Basil the Great, Sisters of the Order of St. (Munhall Byzantine Rite), O.S.B.M.: Founded fourth century, by St. Basil the Great. Motherhouse, Mount St. Macrina. West National Pike, Uniontown, Pa. 15401. Educational, social work. (140)

Basil the Great, Sisters of the Order of St. (Ukrainian Byzantine Rite), O.S.B.M.: Founded fourth century, in Cappadocia, by St. Basil the Great; in US, 1911. Generalate, Rome, Italy; US motherhouse, 710 Fox Chase Rd., Philadelphia, Pa. 19111. Educational, social work. (119)

Benedictine Nuns of the Primitive Observance, O.S.B.: Founded c. 529, in Italy; in US, 1948. US motherhouse, Regina Laudis Monastery, Bethlehem, Conn. 06751. Cloistered. (33)

Benedictine Sisters, O.S.B.: Founded c. 529, in Italy; in US, 1852. General motherhouse, Eichstatt, Bavaria, Germany. US addresses: St. Vincent's Archabbey, Latrobe, Pa. 15650; St. Walburga Convent, Boulder, Colo. 80302. (60)

Benedictine Sisters (Bedford, N.H.), O.S.B.: Founded in US, 1957. 75 Wallace Rd., Bedford, N.H. 03102. (6)

Benedictine Sisters, Missionary, O.S.B.: Founded 1885. General motherhouse, Tutzing, Bavaria; US motherhouse, 300 N. 18th St., Norfolk, Nebr. 68701. (90)

Benedictine Sisters, Olivetan, O.S.B.: Founded 1887, in US. General motherhouse, 223 E. Jackson Ave., Jonesboro, Ark. 72401. Educational, hospital work. (117)

Benedictine Sisters of Perpetual Adoration of Pontifical Jurisdiction, Congregation of the, O.S.B.: Founded 529, in Italy; in US, 1874. General motherhouse, 8300 Morganford Rd., St. Louis, Mo. 63123. (252)

Benedictine Sisters of Pontifical Jurisdiction, O.S.B.: Founded c. 529, in Italy. No general motherhouse in US. Three congregations:

Congregation of St. Scholastica (1922). Pres., Sister Joan Chittister, O.S.B., St. Benedict Convent, 6101 E. Lake Rd., Erie, Pa. 16511. Seventeen motherhouses in US. (2,061)

Congregation of St. Gertrude the Great (1937). St. Scholastica Convent, Fort Smith, Ark. 72901. Thirteen motherhouses in US. (1,907)

Congregation of St. Benedict (1947). St. Benedict's Priory, St. Joseph, Mo. 56374. Seven motherhouses in US. (1,938)

Bethany, Congregation of Oblates of, C.O.B.: Founded 1902 in France; in US, 1959. Motherhouse, Canada; U.S. address: 4538 Lindell Blvd., St. Louis, Mo. 63108. (11)

Bethany, Sisters of, C.V.D.: Founded 1928, in El Salvador; in U.S., 1949. US address: 850 N. Hobart Blvd., Los Angeles, Calif. 90029. (21)

Bethlemita Sisters, Daughters of the Sacred Heart of Jesus, S.C.I.F.: Founded 1861, in Guatemala. Motherhouse, Bogota, Colombia; US address, 330 W. Pembroke St., Dallas, Tex. 75208. (8)

Blessed Virgin Mary, Institute of the (Loreto Sisters), I.B.V.M.: Founded 17th century in Bavaria; in US, 1954. General motherhouse, Dublin, Ireland; US address. 6351 N. 27th Ave., Phoenix, Ariz. 85017. (11)

Blessed Virgin Mary, Institute of the (Sisters of Loretto), I.B.V.M.: Founded 1609, in Belgium; in US, 1880. US address, Box 508, Wheaton, Ill. 60187. Educational work. (181)

Bon Secours, Sisters of, C.B.S.: Founded 1824, in France; in US, 1881. General motherhouse, Rome, Italy; US motherhouse, Marriottsville Rd., Marriottsville, Md. 21104. Hospital work. (101)

Bridgettine Sisters (Order of the Most Holy Savior), O.SS.S.: Founded 1344, at Vadstena, Sweden, by St. Bridget; in US, 1957. General motherhouse, Rome, Italy; US address, Vikingsborg, Darien, Conn. 06820.

Brigid, Congregation of St., C.S.B.: Founded 1807, in Ireland; in US, 1953. American foundation, 402 John Adams Dr., San Antonio, Tex. 78201. (24)

Carmel Congregation of Our Lady of Mount, O. Carm.: Founded 1825, in France; in US, 1833. General motherhouse, P.O. Box 476, Lacombe, La. 70445. Educational work. (168)

Carmel, Institute of Our Lady of Mount, O. Carm.: Founded 1854, in Italy; in US, 1947. General motherhouse, Florence, Italy; US motherhouse, 5 Wheatland St., Peabody, Mass. 01960. Domestic work. (22)

Carmelite Missionaries, C.M.: Founded Barcelona, Spain; in US, 1962. General motherhouse, Rome, Italy; US foundation, 106 Abbey St., Winters, Calif. 95694.

Carmelite Missionaries of St. Theresa, C.M.S.T.: Founded 1903, in Mexico. General motherhouse, Mexico City, Mexico; US novitiate, 10910 Old Katy Rd., Houston, Tex. 77043. (76)

Carmelite Sisters for the Aged and Infirm, O. Carm.: Founded 1929, at New York, by Cardinal Patrick Hayes. Motherhouse, Avila-on-Hudson, Germantown, N.Y. 12526. Social work. (427)

Carmelite Sisters of Charity, C.a.Ch.: Founded by St. Joaquina de Vedruna. General motherhouse, Rome, Italy; US address, 19950 Anita Ave., Castro Valley, Calif. (25)

Carmelite Sisters of Corpus Christi, O.Carm.: Founded 1908, in England; in US 1920. US address, 21 Battery St., Newport, R.I. 02840. Home and foreign mission work. (145)

Carmelite Sisters of St. Therese of the In-

fant Jesus, C.S.T.: Founded 1917, in US. General motherhouse, 1300 Classen Dr., Oklahoma City, Okla. 73103. Educational, social work. (49)

Carmelite Sisters of the Divine Heart of Jesus, C.D.C.J.: Founded 1891, in Germany; in US, 1912. General motherhouse, Sittard, Holland. US provincial houses, 1230 Kavanagy Pl., Milwaukee, Wis. 52313; 10341 Manchester Rd., St. Louis, Mo. 63122; 4130 Alameda St., Corpus Christi, Tex. 78416. Educational, social, mission work. 184 in US and Canada.

Carmelite Sisters of the Sacred Heart: Founded 1904, in Mexico. General motherhouse, Guadalajara, Mexico; US motherhouse, 920 E. Alhambra Rd., Alhambra, Calif. 91801. Educational, hospital work, day nurseries. (125)

Carmelites, Calced, O.Carm.: Founded 1536, at Naples, Italy; in US, 1930. Five monasteries in US. Cloistered. (47)

Carmelites, Discalced, O.C.D.: Founded 1562, Spain; in US, 1790. Sixty-six independent monasteries throughout the US. Cloistered. (831)

Casimir, Sisters of St., S.S.C.: Founded 1907, in US. General motherhouse, 2601 W. Marquette Rd., Chicago, Ill. 60629. Educational, hospital, social work. (430)

Cenacle, Congregation of Our Lady of the Retreat in the, R.C.: Founded 1826; in US, 1892. General motherhouse, Rome, Italy. US provinces: the Cenacle, Mt. Kisco, N.Y. 10549; 200 Lake St., Brighton, Mass. 02135; 513 Fullerton Pkwy., Chicago, Ill. 60614. (395)

Charity, Daughters of Divine, F.D.C.: Founded 1868, at Chanty, Austria; in US, 1913. General motherhouse, Rome, Italy. US provinces: 56 Meadowbrook Rd., White Plains, N.Y. 10605; 39 N. Portage Path, Akron, O. 44303. Educational, hospital work. (243)

Charity, Irish Sisters of, R.S.C.: Founded 1815, in Ireland; in US, 1953. Motherhouse, Dublin, Ireland; US headquarters, 12555 Westlake St., Garden Grove, Calif. 92640. (52)

Charity, Little Missionary Sisters of, P.M.C.: Founded 1915, in Italy; in US, 1949. General motherhouse, Rome, Italy; US headquarters, 120 Orient Ave., E. Boston, Mass. 02128. (18)

Charity, Sisters of (of Seton Hill), S.C.: Founded 1870, at Altoona, Pa., from Cincinnati foundation. Generalate, Mt. Thor Rd., Greensburg, Pa. 15601. Educational, hospital, social work. (682)

Charity, Sisters of (Grey Nuns of Montreal), S. G. M.: Founded 1738, in Canada; in US, 1855. General motherhouse, Pierrefonds, Roxboro 910, Que., Canada; US motherhouse, 10 Pelham Rd., Lexington, Mass. 02173. (151)

Charity, Sisters of (of Leavenworth), **S. C. L.:** Founded 1858, in US. General motherhouse, Leavenworth, Kans. 66048. (801)

Charity, Sisters of (of Nazareth), S.C.N.: Founded 1812, in US. General motherhouse, Nazareth P. O., Nelson Co., Ky. 40048. (1,319)

Charity, Sisters of (of St. Augustine), C. S. A.: Founded 1851, at Cleveland, O. General motherhouse, 5232 Broadview Rd., Richfield, O. 44286. (282)

Charity, Sisters of Christian, S. C. C.: Founded 1849, in Germany; in US, 1873. General motherhouse, Rome, Italy. US provinces; Mallinckrodt Convent. Mendham, N.J. 07945; Maria Immaculata Convent, Ridge Rd. at Walnut, Wilmette, Ill. 60011, Educational, other work. (988)

Charity, Vincentian Sisters of, V.S.C.: Founded 1835, in Austria; in US, 1902. General motherhouse, 8200 McKnight Rd., Pittsburgh, Pa. 15237. (336)

Charity, Vincentian Sisters of, V.S.C.: Founded 1928, at Bedford, O. General motherhouse, 1160 Broadway, Bedford, O. 44146. (114)

Charity of Cincinnati, Ohio, Sisters of, S.C.: Founded 1809. General motherhouse, Mt. St. Joseph, Ohio 45051. Educational, hospital, social work. (1,285)

Charity of Ottawa, Sisters of (Grey Nuns of the Cross), S.C.O.; S.G.C.: Founded 1845, at Ottawa, Canada; in US, 1857. General motherhouse, Ottawa, Canada; US provincial house, 975 Varnum Ave., Lowell, Mass. 01854. Educational, hospital work, extended health care. (163)

Charity of Our Lady, Mother of Mercy, Sisters of, S.C.M.M.: Founded 1832, in Holland; in US, 1874. General motherhouse, Rome, Italy; US provincialate, East Haven, Conn. 06512. (38)

Charity of Our Lady of Mercy, Sisters of, O.L.M.: Founded 1829, in US. General motherhouse, Charleston, S. C. 29412. Educational, hospital work. (87)

Charity of Quebec, Sisters of (Grey Nuns), S.C.Q.: Founded 1849, at Quebec; in US, 1890. General motherhouse, Ave. de'Estimauville, Quebec 5, P. Q., Canada. Social work. (78)

Charity of St. Elizabeth, Sisters of, Convent, N. J., S.C.: Founded 1859, at Newark, N. J. Generalate, Convent, N. J. 07961. Educational, hospital work. (1,404)

Charity of St. Hyacinthe, Sisters of (Grey Nuns), S.C.S.H.: Founded 1840, at St. Hyacinthe, Canada; in US, 1878. General motherhouse, 665 Ste-Anne, La Providence (S. Hyacinthe), P. Q., Canada. (171)

Charity of St. Joan Antida, Sisters of, S.C.S.J.A.: Founded 1799, in France; in US, 1932. General motherhouse, Rome, Italy; US motherhouse, 8560 N. 76th Pl., Milwaukee, Wis. 53223. (64)

Charity of St. Louis, Sisters of, S.C.S.L.:

Founded 1803, in France; in US, 1910. General motherhouse, Rome, Italy; US provincial house, 146 S. Catherine St., Plattsburgh, N.Y. 12901. (59)

Charity of St. Vincent de Paul, Daughters of, D. C.: Founded 1633, in France; in US 1809, at Emmitsburg, Md., by Bl. Elizabeth Ann Seton. General motherhouse, Paris, France. US provinces: Emmitsburg, Md. 21727; 7800 Natural Bridge Rd., Normandy, St. Louis, Mo. 63121; P. O. Box 5205, Evansville, Ind. 47715; 96 Menands Rd., Albany, N.Y. 12204; P. O. Box 4069, San Jose, Calif. 95126. (2,225)

Charity of St. Vincent de Paul, Sisters of, Halifax, S.C.H.: Founded 1856, at Halifax, N. S., from Emmitsburg, Md., foundation. Generalate, Mt. St. Vincent, Halifax, N. S., Canada. Educational, hospital, social work. (650)

Charity of St. Vincent de Paul, Sisters of, New York, S.C.: Founded 1817, from Emmitsburg, Md. General motherhouse, Mt. St. Vincent on Hudson, New York, N. Y. 10471. Educational, hospital work. (1,138)

Charity of St. Vincent de Paul, Sisters of (Tyrol), C.S.V.P.: Founded 1825, at Tyrol, Austria. General motherhouse, Zams, Oberintal, Tyrol, Austria; US motherhouse, 705 Clyman St., Watertown, Wis. 53094. (28)

Charity of the Blessed Virgin Mary, Sisters of, B.V.M.: Founded 1833, in US. General motherhouse, Mt. Carmel, Dubuque, Ia. 52001. Educational work. (1,891)

Charity of the Incarnate Word, Congregation of the Sisters of, C.C.V.L.: Founded 1869, at San Antonio, Tex., by Bishop C. M. Dubuis. General motherhouse, 4515 Broadway, San Antonio, Tex. 78209. (668)

Charity of the Incarnate Word, Congregation of the Sisters of (Houston, Tex.), C.C.V.I.: Founded 1866, in US, by Bishop C. M. Dubuis. General motherhouse, 6510 Lawndale Ave., Houston, Tex. 77023. Educational, hospital, social work. (444)

Charity of the Sacred Heart, Daughters of, F.C.S.C.J.: Founded 1823, at LaSalle de Vihiers, France; in US, 1905. General motherhouse, La Salle de Vihiers, France; US motherhouse, Littleton, N. H. 03561. (139)

Charles Borromeo, Missionary Sisters of St. (Scalabrini Srs.): Founded 1895, in Italy; in US, 1941. American novitiate, 1414 N. 37th Ave., Melrose Park, Ill. (49)

Child Jesus, Sisters of the Poor, P.C.J.: Founded 1844, at Aix-la-Chapelle, Germany; in US, 1924. General motherhouse, Simpelveld, Holland; American Provincialate, 4567 Olentangy River Rd., Columbus, O. 43214. (46)

Chretienne, Sisters of Ste., S.S.CH.: Founded 1807, in France; in US, 1903. General motherhouse, Metz, France; American provincial house, 297 Arnold St., Wrentham, Mass. 02093. Educational, hospital, mission, work. (150)

Christ, Adorers of the Blood of, A.S.C.: Founded 1834, in Italy; in US, 1870. General motherhouse, Rome, Italy. US provinces: Ruma (P.O. Red Bud R.R.I.), Ill. 62278; 1165 Southwest Blvd., Wichita, Kans. 67213; Columbia, Pa. 17512. Educational, hospital work. (909)

Christ the King, Sister Servants of, S.S.C.K.: Founded 1936, in US. General motherhouse, Mt. Calvary, Wis. 53057. (18)

Christ the Teacher, Sisters of (Byzantine Rite): Founded 1960, at Pittsburgh, Pa. General motherhouse, 66 Riverview Ave., Pittsburgh, Pa.

Christian Doctrine, Sisters of Our Lady of, R.C.D.: Founded 1910, at New York. Motherhouse, Marydell, Suffern, N.Y. 10901. (58)

Christian Education, Religious of, R.C.E.: Founded 1817, in France; in US, 1905. General motherhouse, Paris, France; US provincial residence, 8 Old Mystic St., Arlington, Mass. 02174. (87)

Cistercian Nuns: Established in US, 1958. Motherhouse, Frauenthal, Switzerland; in US, Valley of Our Lady Monastery, Rt. 1, Prairie du Sac, Wis. 53378. (13)

Cistercian Nuns of the Strict Observance, Order of, O.C.S.O.: Founded 1125, in France, by St. Stephen Harding; in US, 1949. General motherhouse France. US abbeys: Arnold St. (R.F.D. Box 500), Wrentham, Mass. 02093; Whitethorn, Calif. 95489; R.R. 3, Dubuque, Ia. 52001. (61)

Clergy, Congregation of Our Lady, Help of the, C.L.H.C.: Founded 1961, in US. Motherhouse, Maryvale Convent, Maple Ave., Higganum, Conn. 06441. (6)

Clergy, Servants of Our Lady Queen of the, S.R.C.: Founded 1929, in Canada; in US, 1936. General motherhouse, Lac-au-Saumon, Que., Canada. (34)

Colettines: See Franciscan Poor Clare Nuns.

Columban, Missionary Sisters of St., S.S.C.: Founded 1922, in Ireland; in US, 1930. General motherhouse, Wicklow, Ireland; US region, 950 Metropolitan Ave., Hyde Park, Mass. 01236. (74)

Consolata Missionary Sisters, M.C.: Founded 1910, in Italy; in US, 1954. General motherhouse, Turin, Italy; US headquarters, 6801 Belmont Rd., Belmont, Mich. 49306. (20)

Cordi-Marian Missionary Sisters, M.C.M.: Founded 1921, in Mexico; in US, 1926. General motherhouse, 1100 S. May St., Chicago, Ill. 60607. (76)

Cross, Daughters of the, D.C.: Founded 1640, in France; in US, 1855. General motherhouse, 1135 St. Vincent Ave., Shreveport, La. Educational work. (47)

Cross, Daughters of, of Liege, F.C.: Founded 1883, in Liege, Belgium; in US, 1958. US address, 165 W. Eaton Ave., Tracy, Calif. 95376. (12)

Cross, Sisters of the Holy, C.S.C.: Founded

1841, at Le Mans, France; in US, 1843. General motherhouse, Notre Dame, Ind. 46556. Educational, hospital work. (1,277)

Cross and of the Seven Dolors, Sisters of the Holy, C.S.C.: Founded 1847, in Canada; in US, 1881. General motherhouse, Montreal, Que., Canada; US provincial house, Pittsfield, N.H. 03263. Educational work. (458)

Cross and Passion, Sisters of the (Passionist Sisters), C.P.: Founded 1852; in US, 1924. General motherhouse, Bolton, England; US address: Mt. St. Joseph, Wakefield, R.I. 02878. (94)

Cross and Passion of Our Lord Jesus Christ, Nuns of the (Passionist Nuns), C.P.: Founded 1771, in Italy, by St. Paul of the Cross; in US, 1910. Five convents in the US. Contemplatives. (84)

Crucified, Augustinian Sisters, Daughters of the: Founded 1840, in Italy. General motherhouse, Rome, Italy; US novitiate, 420 Lincoln Hwy., Malvern, Pa. 19355. (23)

Cyril and Methodius, Sisters of Sts., SS.C.M.: Founded 1909, in US, by Rev. Matthew Jankola. General motherhouse, Danville, Pa. 17821. Educational, hospital work. (416)

Disciples of the Divine Master, P.D.D.M.: Founded 1924; in US, 1948. General motherhouse, Rome, Italy; US headquarters, 3700 N. cornelia Ave., Fresno, Calif. 93705. (50

Divine Compassion, Sisters of, R.D.C.: Founded 1886, in US. General motherhouse, 52 N. Broadway, White Plains, N.Y. 10603. Educational work. (220)

Divine Love, Oblates to, Sisters, R.O.D.A.: Founded 1923, in Italy; in US, 1947. General motherhouse, Rome, Italy; US novitiate, Beckman Rd., Hopewell Junction, N.Y. 12533. (48)

Divine Spirit, Congregation of the, C.D.S.: Founded 1956, in US, by Archbishop John M. Gannon. Motherhouse, 409 W. 6th St., Erie, Pa. 16507. Educational, social work; care of aged. (57)

Dominicans

Dominican Nuns of the Second Order of Perpetual Adoration, O.P.: Founded 1206, in France; in US, 1880. Twelve independent monasteries. Cloistered. (391)

Dominican Oblates of Jesus, D.O.J.: Founded 1946 in Spain. General motherhouse, Madrid, Spain; US foundation, La Salette Convent, 85 New Park Ave., Hartford, Conn. 06106.

Dominican Rural Missionaries, O.P.: Founded 1932, in France; in US, 1951, at Abbeyville, La. General motherhouse, Luzarches, France; US motherhouse, 1318 S. Henry St., Abbeville, La. 70510. (6)

Dominican Sisters of Bethany, O.P.: Founded 1914. The Netherlands; in US, 1961. General motherhouse, Bracciano, Italy; US headquarters, 1501 W. Touhy Ave., Chicago, Ill. 60626. Social service work. (14)

Dominican Sisters of Bethany, Congregation, O.P.: Founded 1866, in France. Motherhouse, France; US novitiate, 204 Ridge St., Millis, Mass. 02054. (10)

Dominican Sisters of the Perpetual Rosary, O.P.: Founded 1880, at Calais, France. Eight independent monasteries. Contemplative. (121)

Dominican Sisters of the Presentation, O.P.: Founded 1684, in France; in US, 1906. General motherhouse, Tours, France; US headquarters, 3012 Elm St., Dighton, Mass. 02715. Hospital work. (72)

Dominican Sisters of the Roman Congregation of St. Dominic, O.P.: Founded 1621, in France; in US, 1904. General motherhouse, Rome, Italy; US province, 200 Ivy St., Brookline, Mass. 02146. Educational work. (90)

Eucharistic Missionaries of St. Dominic, O.P.: Founded 1927, in Louisiana. General motherhouse, 1101 Aline St., New Orleans, La. 70115. Parish mission work. (59)

Maryknoll Sisters of St. Dominic, M.M.: Founded 1912, in New York. Center, Maryknoll, N.Y. 10545. (1,170)

Religious Missionaries of St. Dominic, O.P.: General motherhouse, Rome, Italy; US foundations; 808 S. Wright St., Alice, Texas 78332; 1123 N. Staples St., Corpus Christi, Tex. 78401. 432 N. Oak St., Santa Paula, Calif. 93060. (14).

Sisters of the Third Order of St. Dominic, O.P.: Thirty congregations in the US. Educational, hospital work. Names of Congregations are given below, followed by the date of foundation, location of motherhouse and number of professed Sisters.

St. Catharine of Siena, 1822. St. Catharine, Ky. 40061. (688).

St. Mary of the Springs, 1830. Columbus, Ohio 43219. (666).

Most Holy Rosary, 1849. Sinsinawa, Wis. 53824. (1,719).

Most Holy Name of Jesus, 1850. San Rafael, Calif. 94901. (284).

Holy Cross, 1853. Albany Ave., Amityville, N.Y. 11701. (1,373).

Most Holy Rosary, 1859. Mt. St. Mary on Hudson, Newburgh, N.Y. 12550. (483).

St. Cecilia, 1860. Eighth Ave. N. and Clay St., Nashville, Tenn. 37208. (123).

St. Mary, 1860. 7214 St. Charles Ave., New Orleans, La. 70118. (154).

St. Catherine of Siena, 1862. 5635 Erie St., Racine, Wis. 53402. (492).

Our Lady of the Sacred Heart, 1873. 1237 W. Monroe St., Springfield, Ill. 62704. (530).

Our Lady of the Rosary, 1876. Sparkill, N.Y. 10976. (804).

Queen of the Holy Rosary, 1876. Mission San Jose, Calif. 94538. (494).

Most Holy Rosary, 1877. Adrian, Mich. 49221. (2,040).

Our Lady of the Sacred Heart, 1877. 2025 E. Fulton St., Grand Rapids, Mich. 49503. (668).

St. Dominic, 1878. Blauvelt, N. Y. 10913. (433).

Immaculate Conception (Dominican Sisters of the Sick Poor), 1879. P. O. Box 231, Ossining, N. Y. 10562. Social work. (129).

St. Catherine de Ricci, 1880. 2850 N. Providence Rd., Media, Pa. 19063. (153).

Sacred Heart of Jesus, 1881. Mt. St. Dominic, Caldwell, N. J. 07006. (497).

Sacred Heart, 1882. 6501 Almeda Rd., Houston, Tex. 77021. (313).

St. Thomas Aquinas, 1888. 423 E. 152nd St., Tacoma, Wash. 98445. (187).

Most Holy Cross, 1890. P. O. Box 280, Edmonds, Wash. 98020. (157).

St. Catherine of Siena, 1891. 37 Park St., Fall River, Mass. 02721. (130).

St. Rose of Lima (Servants of Relief for Incurable Cancer), 1896. Hawthorne, N. Y. 10532. (121).

Immaculate Conception, 1902. 3600 Broadway, Great Bend, Kans. 67530. Pontifical Institute. (240).

St. Catherine of Siena, 1911. 4600 93rd St., Kenosha, Wis. 53140. (103).

St. Rose of Lima, 1923. 775 Drahner Rd., Oxford, Mich. 48051. (100).

Immaculate Conception, 1929. Biala Nizna, Poland: US provincial house, 9000 W. 81st St., Justice, Ill. 60458. (25).

Immaculate Heart of Mary, 1929. Akron, Ohio 44313. (203).

Immaculate Heart of Mary, W. 3102 Fort George Wright Dr., Spokane, Wash. 99204. (75).

St. Catherine of Siena of Oakford, Republic of South Africa, 1955. General motherhouse, Natal, Republic of South Africa; US motherhouse, 1855 Miramonte Ave., Mountain View, Calif. 94040. (24).

(End, Listing of Dominicans)

Dorothy, Institute of the Sisters of St., S.S.D.: Founded 1834, in Italy; in US, 1911. General motherhouse, Rome, Italy; US motherhouse, Villa Fatima, Taunton, Mass. 02780. (81).

Eucharistic Missionary Sisters of the Little Flower, M.E.T.: Founded 1949, in Mexico. General motherhouse, Mexico; US foundation, Warrenton, Mo. 63383. (93).

Family, Congregation of the Sisters of the Holy, S.S.F.: Founded 1842, in US. General motherhouse, 6901 Chef Menteur Hway., New Orleans, La. 70126. Educational, hospital work. (288).

Family, Little Sisters of the Holy, P.S.S.F.: Founded 1880, in Canada; in US, 1900. General motherhouse, Sherbrooke, Que., Canada. Domestic work. (117).

Family, Sisters of the Holy, S.H.F.: Founded 1872, in US. General motherhouse, P. O. Box 3248, Mission San Jose, Calif. 94538, Mission San Jose, Calif. 94538. Educational, social work. (289).

Family of Nazareth, Sisters of the Holy,

C.S.F.N.: Founded 1875, in Italy; in US, 1885. General motherhouse, Rome, Italy. US provinces: 353 N. River Rd., Des Plaines, Ill. 60616; Grant and Frankford Aves., Torresdale, Philadelphia, Pa. 19114; 285 Bellevue Rd., Pittsburgh, Pa. 15229; Marian Heights, 1428-1, Monroe Turnpike, Monroe, Conn. 06868; 1600 11th St., Wichita Falls, Tex. 76301. (1,528).

Filippini, Religious Teachers, M.P.F.: Founded 1692, in Italy; in US, 1910. General motherhouse, Rome, Italy; US interprovincial motherhouse, Villa Walsh, Morristown, N. J. 07960. Educational work. (480).

Francis de Sales, Oblate Sisters of St., O.S.F.S.: Founded 1866, in France; in US, 1951. General motherhouse, Troyes, France; US headquarters, Childs, Md. 21916. Educational, social work. (13).

Franciscans

Bernardine Sisters of the Third Order of St. Francis, O.S.F.: Founded 1457, at Cracow, Poland; in US, 1894. General motherhouse, 647 Spring Mill Rd., Villanova, Pa. 19085. Educational, hospital, social work. (1,029).

Congregation of the Servants of the Holy Infancy of Jesus, O.S.F.: Founded 1855, in Germany; in US, 1929. General motherhouse, Wuerzburg, Germany; American motherouse, P. O. Box 708, Plainfield, N. J. 07061. (84).

Congregation of the Third Order of St. Francis of Mary Immaculate, O.S.F.: Founded 1865, in US, by Fr. Pamphilus da Magliano, O.F.M. General motherhouse, 520 Plainfield Ave., Joliet, Ill. 60435. Educational work. (666).

Conventuals of the Third Order of St. Francis of the Mission of the Immaculate Virgin, O.S.F.: Founded 1893, in New York. General motherhouse, Hastings-on-Hudson, N. Y. 10706. Educational, hospital work. (201).

Daughters of St. Francis of Assisi, D.S.F.: Founded 1890, in Austria-Hungary; in US, 1946. Provincial motherhouse, 507 N. Prairie St., Lacon, Ill. 61540. Nursing, CCD work. (35)

Felician Sisters (Congregation of the Sisters of St. Felix), C.S.S.F.: Founded 1855, in Poland; in US, 1874. General motherhouse, Rome, Italy. US provinces: 36800 Schoolcraft Rd., Livonia, Mich. 48150; 600 Doat St., Buffalo, N.Y. 14211; 3800 Peterson Ave., Chicago, Ill. 60645; South Main St., Lodi, N.Y. 07644; 1500 Woodcrest Ave., Coraopolis, Pa. 15108; 1315 Enfield St., Enfield, Conn. 06082; Monument Rd., Ponca City, Okla. 74601. (3,386).

Franciscan Handmaids of the Most Pure Heart of Mary, F.H.M.: Founded 1917, in US. General motherhouse, 15 W. 124th St., New York, N.Y. 10027. Educational, social work. (50)

Franciscan Hospitaller Sisters of the Immaculate Conception, F.H.I.C.: Founded

1876, in Portugal; in US, 1960. General motherhouse, Oporto, Portugal; US foundation, 1395 E. Santa Clara St., San Jose, Calif. 95116. (19)

Franciscan Missionaries of Mary, F.M.M.: Founded 1877, in India; in US, 1904. General motherhouse, Rome, Italy; US provincialate, 225 E. 45th St., New York, N.Y. 10017. Foreign mission work. (283)

Franciscan Missionaries of Our Lady, O.S.F.: Founded 1854, at Calais, France; in US, 1913. General motherhouse, Desvres, France; US motherhouse, 4200 Essen Lane, Baton Rouge, La. 70809. Hospital work. (51)

Franciscan Missionaries of St. Joseph (Mill Hill Sisters), F.M.S.J.: Founded 1883, at Rochdale, Lancashire, England; in US, 1952. General motherhouse, Eccleshall, Stafford, England; US headquarters, 1903 New Scotland Rd., Slingerlands, N.Y. 12159. (17)

Franciscan Missionaries of the Divine Motherhood, F.M.D.M.: Founded 1935, in England; US foundations: East Greenbush, N.Y. 12061; Croghan, N.Y. 13327. (14)

Franciscan Missionary Sisters for Africa, O.S.F.: American foundation, 1953. Generalate, Ireland; US headquarters, 172 Foster St., Brighton, Mass. 02135.

Franciscan Missionary Sisters of Giglio, S.F.M.G.: First foundation in US, 1961. General motherhouse, Assisi, Italy; US address, St. Hyacinth College and Seminary, Granby, Mass. 01033. (11)

Franciscan Missionary Sisters of Our Lady of Sorrows, O.S.F.: Founded 1937, in China, by Bishop R. Palazzi, O.F.M.; in US, 1849. US address, 2385 Laurel Glen Rd., Santa Cruz, Calif. 95060. Educational, social, domestic, retreat and foreign mission work. (42)

Franciscan Missionary Sisters of the Divine Child, F.M.D.C.: Founded 1927, at Buffalo, N.Y., by Bishop William Turner. General motherhouse, 6380 Main St., Williamsville, N.Y. 14221. Educational, social work. (79)

Franciscan Missionary Sisters of the Immaculate Conception, O.S.F.: Founded 1874, in Mexico; in US, 1927. US provincial house, 1519 Woodworth St., San Fernando, Calif. 91340. (97)

Franciscan Missionary Sisters of the Sacred Heart, F.M.S.C.: Founded 1860, in Italy; in US, 1865. Generalate, Rome, Italy; US provincialate, 120 Franklin St., Peekskill, N.Y. 10566. Educational and social welfare apostolates and specialized services. (364)

Franciscan Poor Clare Nuns (Poor Clares, Order of St. Clare, Poor Clares of St. Colette), P.C., O.S.C., P.C.C.: Founded 1212, at Assisi, Italy, by St. Francis of Assisi; in US, 1875. Proto-Monastery, Assisi, Italy; twenty-four autonomous monasteries in the US. (452)

Franciscan Sisters, Daughters of the Sacred Hearts of Jesus and Mary, O.S.F.: Founded 1860, in Germany; in US, 1872. Generalate, Rome, Italy; US motherhouse, P.O. Box 667,

Wheaton, Ill. 60187. Educational, hospital, social work. (308)

Franciscan Sisters of Allegany, N.Y., O.S.F.: Founded 1859, at Allegany, N.Y., by Fr. Pamphilus da Magliano, O.F.M. General motherhouse, Allegany, N.Y. 14706. Educational, hospital, foreign mission work. (773)

Franciscan Sisters of Baltimore, O.S.F.: Founded 1868, in England; in US, 1881. General motherhouse, 3725 Ellerslie Ave., Baltimore, Md. 21218. Educational work. (84)

Franciscan Sisters of Chicago, O.S.F.: Founded 1894, in US. General motherhouse, 1220 Main St., Lemont, Ill. 60439. Educational, hospital, social work. (342)

Franciscan Sisters of Christian Charity, O.S.F.: Founded 1869, in US. Motherhouse, Rt. 1, Manitowoc, Wis. 54220. Educational, hospital work. (990)

Franciscan Sisters of Little Falls, Minn., O.S.F.: Founded 1891, in US. General motherhouse, Little Falls, Minn. 56345. Health, education, social services. (400)

Franciscan Sisters of Mary Immaculate of the Third Order of St. Francis of Assisi, F.M.I.: Founded 16th century, in Switzerland; in US, 1932. General motherhouse, Rome, Italy; US provincial house, Box 5664, Amarillo, Tex. 79107. (84)

Franciscan Sisters of Our Lady of Perpetual Help, O.S.F.: Founded 1901, in US, from Joliet, Ill., foundation. General motherhouse, 201 Brotherton Lane, St. Louis, Mo. 63135. Educational, hospital work. (326)

Franciscan Sisters of Our Lady of the Holy Angels, B.M.V.A.: Founded 1863, at Neuwied, Germany; in US, 1923. General motherhouse, Rhine, Germany; US motherhouse, 1925 Norfolk Ave., St. Paul, Minn. 55116. Educational, hospital, social work. (40)

Franciscan Sisters of Ringwood, F.S.R.: Founded 1927, at Passaic, N.J. General motherhouse, Mt. St. Francis, Ringwood, N.J. 07456. Educational work. (68)

Franciscan Sisters of St. Elizabeth, F.S.S.E.: Founded 1866, at Naples, Italy; in US, 1919. General motherhouse, Rome; US address, 449 Park Rd., Parsippany, N.J. 07054. (45)

Franciscan Sisters of St. Joseph, F.S.S.J.: Founded 1897, in US. General motherhouse, 5286 S. Park Ave., Hamburg, N.Y. 14075. Educational, hospital work. (460)

Franciscan Sisters of the Atonement, Third Order Regular of St. Francis (Graymoor Sisters), S.A.: Founded 1898, in US, as Anglican community; entered Church, 1909. General motherhouse, Graymoor, Garrison P.O., N.Y. 10524. Mission work. (337)

Franciscan Sisters of the Immaculate Conception, O.S.F.: Founded in Germany; in US, 1928. General motherhouse, Kloster, Bonlanden, Germany; US province, N. Davis Rd., E. Aurora, N.Y. 14052. (30)

Franciscan Sisters of the Immaculate Conception, O.S.F.: Founded 1901, in US. General motherhouse, 1000 30th St., Rock Island, Ill. 61201. Hospital work. (42)

Franciscan Sisters of the Immaculate Conception and St. Joseph for the Dying, O.S.F.: Founded 1919, in US. General motherhouse, 485 Church St., Monterey, Calif. 93940. (25)

Franciscan Sisters of the Immaculate Conception, Missionary, O.S.F.: Founded 1873, in US. General motherhouse, Rome, Italy; US address, 790 Centre St., Newton, Mass. 02158. Educational work. (456)

Franciscan Sisters of the Poor, S.F.P.: Founded 1845, at Aix-la-Chapelle, Germany, by Mother Frances Schervier; in US, 1858. Community service center, 23 Middagh St., Brooklyn, N.Y. 11201. Hospital, social work. (403)

Franciscan Sisters of the Sacred Heart, O.S.F.: Founded 1876, in US. General motherhouse, Mokena, Ill. 60448. Educational, hospital, mission work. (415)

Franciscan Sisters of the Third Order of the Immaculate Conception, F.S.I.C.: Founded 1879, in Spain; in US, 1958. General motherhouse, Murcia, Spain; US foundation, 1525 N. 18th St., Philadelphia, Pa. 19121.

Hospital Sisters of the Third Order of St. Francis, O.S.F.: Founded 1844, in Germany; in US, 1875. General motherhouse, Muenster, Germany; US motherhouse, Box 42, Springfield, Ill. 62705. Hospital work. (665)

Little Franciscan Sisters of Mary, P.F.M.: Founded 1889, in US. General motherhouse, Baie St. Paul, Que., Canada. US province, 43 Thorne St., Worcester, Mass. Educational, hospital, social work.

Missionaries of the Third Order of St. Francis of Our Lady of the Prairies, O.L.P.: Founded 1960, in US. General motherhouse, Powers Lake, N. Dak. 58773.

Missionary Sisters of the Immaculate Conception of the Mother of God, S.M.I.C.: Founded 1910, in Brazil; in US, 1922. Generalate, P.O. Box 204, 662 East Dr., Oradell, N.J. 07649. Mission, educational, hospital work. (145)

Mothers of the Helpless, M.D.: Founded 1873, in Spain; in US, 1916. General motherhouse, Valencia, Spain; US address: 432 W. 20th St., New York, N.Y. 10011. (26)

Philip Neri Missionary Teachers, Sisters of St. R.F.: Founded 1858, in Spain; in US, 1956. Motherhouse, Barcelona, Spain; US novitiate, Route 4, Box 131, Stuart, Fla. 33494. (32)

Poor Clares of Perpetual Adoration, P.C.P.A.: Founded 1854, at Paris, France; in US, 1921, at Cleveland, Ohio. Four monasteries. Contemplative, cloistered, perpetual adoration. (75)

School Sisters of St. Francis, O.S.F.: Founded 1874, in US. General motherhouse, 1501 S. Layton Blvd., Milwaukee, Wis. 53215. (1,323)

School Sisters of St. Francis (Bethlehem, Pa.), O.S.F.: Founded 1843, in Austria; in US, 1913. General motherhouse, Rome, Italy; US province, Bethlehem, Pa. 18017. Educational work. (96)

School Sisters of St. Francis (Pittsburgh, Pa.), O.S.F.: Founded 1913, in US. Provincial motherhouse, 934 Forest Ave., Pittsburgh, Pa. 15202. Educational, nursing work. (151)

School Sisters of the Third Order of St. Francis (Savannah, Mo.), O.S.F.: Founded 1842, in Austria; in US, 1924. Provincial house, La Verna Hts., Savannah, Mo. 64485. Educational, hospital work. (50)

School Sisters of the Third Order of St. Francis (Panhandle, Tex.), O.S.F.: Founded 1845, in Austria; in US, 1942. General motherhouse, Vienna, Austria; center and novitiate, Sancta Maria Convent, Panhandle, Tex. 79068. Educational, social work. (38)

Sisters of Charity of Our Lady, Mother of the Church, S.C.M.C.: Established 1970, in US. Motherhouse, Baltic, Conn. 06330. Teaching, nursing, care of aged, and dependent children. (87)

Sisters of Mercy of the Holy Cross, S.C.S.C.: Founded 1856, in Switzerland; in US, 1912. General motherhouse, Ingenbohl, Switzerland; US provincial house, Merrill, Wis. 54452. (94)

Sisters of St. Elizabeth, S.S.E.: Founded 1931, at Milwaukee, Wis. General motherhouse, 745 N. Brookfield Rd., Brookfield, Wis. 53005. (20)

Sisters of St. Elizabeth of the Third Order of St. Francis, O.S.E.: General motherhouse, Humboldt, Sask., Canada; US foundation, Holy Infant Hospital, Hoven, S. Dak. 57450.

Sisters of St. Francis (Clinton, Iowa), O.S.F.: Founded 1868, in US. General motherhouse, Bluff Blvd. and Springdale Dr., Clinton, Ia. 57232. Educational, hospital, social work. (250)

Sisters of St. Francis (Millvale, Pa.), O.S.F.: Founded 1865, Pittsburgh, Pa. General motherhouse, 146 Hawthorne Rd., Millvale P. O., Pittsburgh, Pa. 15209. Educational, hospital work. (443)

Sisters of St. Francis of Christ the King, O.S.F.: Founded 1869, in Austria. General motherhouse, Rome, Italy; US provincial house, Lemont, Ill. 60439. Educational work, home for aged. (150)

Sisters of St. Francis of Penance and Christian Charity, O.S.F.: Founded 1835, in Holland; in US, 1874. General motherhouse, Rome, Italy. US provinces: 4421 Lower River Rd., Stella Niagara, N.Y. 14144; 2851 W. 52nd Ave., Denver, Colo. 80221; 3910 Bret Harte Dr., P.O. Box 1028, Redwood City, Calif. 94064. (731)

Sisters of St. Francis of the Holy Eucharist, O.S.F.: Founded 1424, in Switzerland; in US, 1893. General motherhouse, Ashland and Prewitt Sts., Nevada, Mo. 64772. Educational, social work. (55)

Sisters of St. Francis of the Congregation of

Our Lady of Lourdes, O.S.F.: Founded 1916, in US. General motherhouse, 6832 Convent Blvd., Sylvania, O. 43560. Educational hospital work. (510)

Sisters of St. Francis of the Holy Cross, O.S.F.: Founded 1881, in US, by Rev. Edward Daems, O.S.C. General motherhouse, Rt. 1, Green Bay (Bay Settlement), Wis. 54301. Educational, nursing work; home for aged. (180)

Sisters of St. Francis of the Holy Eucharist, O.S.F.: Founded 1424, in Switzerland; in US, 1893. General motherhouse, Ashland and Prewitt Sts., Nevada, Mo. 64772. Educational, social work. (55)

Sisters of St. Francis of the Immaculate Conception, O.S.F.: Founded 1890, in US. General motherhouse, 2408 W. Heading Ave., Peoria, Ill. 61604. Educational, social work. (118)

Sisters of St. Francis of the Immaculate Heart of Mary, O.S.F.: Founded 1241, in Bavaria; in US, 1913. General motherhouse, Rome, Italy; US motherhouse, Hankinson, N.D. 58041. Educational, hospital work. (144)

Sisters of St. Francis of the Martyr St. George, O.S.F.: Founded 1859, in Germany; in US, 1923. General motherhouse, Thuine, Hanover, Germany; US motherhouse, Alton, Ill. 62002. Social, hospital, foreign mission work. (60)

Sisters of St. Francis of the Perpetual Adoration, O.S.F.: Founded 1863, in Germany; in US, 1875. General motherhouse, Olpe, Germany. US provinces: Box 766, Mishawaka, Ind. 46544; P.O. Box 1060, Colorado Springs, Colo. 80901. Educational, hospital work. (792)

Sisters of St. Francis of the Providence of God, O.S.F.: Founded 1922, in US, by Msgr. M. L. Krusas. General motherhouse, Grove and McRoberts Rds., Pittsburgh, Pa. 15234. Educational, hospital work. (238)

Sisters of St. Joseph of the Third Order of St. Francis, S.S.J.: Founded 1901, in US. General motherhouse, 107 S. Greenlawn Ave., South Bend, Ind. 46617. Educational, hospital work. (1,060)

Sisters of St. Mary of the Third Order of St. Francis, S.S.M.: Founded 1872, in US. General motherhouse, 1100 Bellevue Ave., St. Louis, Mo. 63117. Hospital, social work. (431)

Sisters of the Holy Infant Jesus, H.I.J.: Founded 1662, at Rouen, France; in US, 1950. General motherhouse, Paris, France. US addresses: 20 Reiner St., Colma, Calif. 94014; St. John the Baptist School, Healdsburg, Calif. 95458; St. Veronica's School, South San Francisco, Calif. 94015. (23)

Sisters of the Sorrowful Mother (Third Order of St. Francis), S.M.M.: Founded 1883, in Italy; in US, 1889. General motherhouse, Rome, Italy. US provinces: 6618 N. Teutonia Ave., Milwaukee, Wis. 53209; 9

Pocono Rd., Denville, N.J. 07834; Rt. 3, Box 97, Broken Arrow, Okla. 74012. Educational, hospital work. (543)

Sisters of the Third Franciscan Order Minor Conventuals, O.S.F.: Founded 1860, at Syracuse, N.Y. General motherhouse, 1024 Court St., Syracuse, N.Y. 13208. Educational, hospital work. (560)

Sisters of the Third Order of St. Francis, O.S.F.: Founded 1877, in US, by Bishop John L. Spalding. Motherhouse, Edgewood Hills, E. Peoria, Ill. 61611. Hospital work. (214)

Sisters of the Third Order of St. Francis, O.S.F.: Founded 1894, in US. Motherhouse, Maryville, Mo. 64468. Hospital work. (75)

Sisters of the Third Order of St. Francis, O.S.F.: Founded 1861, at Buffalo, N.Y., from Philadelphia foundation. General motherhouse, 400 Mill St., Williamsville, N.Y. 14221. Educational, hospital work. (350)

Sisters of the Third Order of St. Francis (Oldenburg, Ind.), O.S.F.: Founded 1851, in US. General motherhouse, Oldenburg, Ind. 47036. Educational work. (776)

Sisters of the Third Order of St. Francis of Assisi, O.S.F.: Founded 1849, in US. General motherhouse, 3221 S. Lake Dr., Milwaukee, Wis. 53207. Educational work. (810)

Sisters of the Third Order of St. Francis of Penance and Charity, O.S.F.: Founded 1869, in US, by Rev. Joseph Bihn. Motherhouse, St. Francis Ave., Tiffin, O. 44883. Educational, hospital work. (230)

Sisters of the Third Order of St. Francis of the Holy Family, O.S.F.: Founded 1875, in US. General motherhouse, Dubuque, Ia. 52001. Education, hospital work. (838)

Sisters of the Third Order of St. Francis of the Perpetual Adoration, F.S.P.A.: Founded 1849, in US. General motherhouse, 912 Market St., La Crosse, Wis. 54601. Educational, health care. (1,031).

Sisters of the Third Order Regular of St. Francis of the Congregation of Our Lady of Lourdes, O.S.F.: Founded 1877, in US. General motherhouse, Assisi Heights, Rochester, Minn. 55901. Education, hospitals. (812)

(End, Listing of Franciscans)

Good Shepherd Sisters (Servants of the Immaculate Heart of Mary), S.C.I.M.: Founded 1850, in Canada; in US, 1882, General motherhouse, Quebec, Canada; Provincial House, Bay View, Saco, Maine 04072. Educationa, social work. (226).

Good Shepherd, Sisters of Our Lady of Charity of the, R.G.S.: Founded 1641, in France; in US, 1843. Generalate, Rome, Italy. US provinces: 575 N. Bend Rd., Cincinnati, O. 45224; Mt. St. Florence, Peekskill, N.Y. 10566; 3601 Reservoir Rd. N. W., Washington, D.C. 10007; 7654 Natural Bridge Rd., Normandy, Mo. 63121; 5100 Hodgson Rd., St. Paul, Minn. 55112. (1,447) (including 536 Contemplatives of the Cross).

Graymoor Sisters: See Franciscan Sisters of the Atonement.

Grey Nuns of the Sacred Heart, G. N. S. H.: Founded 1921, in US. General motherhouse, Quarry Rd., Yardley, Pa. 19067. (374).

Guadalupe, Sisters of, O.L.G.: Founded 1946, in Mexico City. General motherhouse, Mexico City, Mexico; US address, St. Mary's College, Winona, Minn. 55987. (60).

Guardian Angels, Sisters of the Holy, S.A.C.: Founded 1839, in France. General motherhouse, Madrid, Spain; US foundation, 1245 S. Van Ness, Los Angeles, Calif. 90019.

Handmaids of Mary Immaculate, A.M.I.: Founded 1952, in Helena, Montana. Motherhouse, Carroll College, Helena, Mont. 59601.

Handmaids of the Precious Blood, Congregation of, H.P.B.: Founded 1947, at Jemez Springs, N. M. General motherhouse, Villa Cor Jesu, Jemez Springs, N. M. 87025. (39).

Helpers, Society of, H.H.S.: Founded 1856, in France; in US, 1892. General motherhouse, Paris, France; US motherhouse, 303 Barry Ave., Chicago, Ill. 60657.

Hermanas Catequistas Guadalupanas, H.C.G.: Founded 1923, in Mexico; in US, 1950. General motherhouse, Mexico; US foundation, 7815 Somerset Rd., San Antonio, Tex. 78211. (22).

Holy Child Jesus, Society of the, S. H. C. J.: Founded 1846, in England; in US, 1862. General motherhouse, Rome, Italy. US provinces. 1341 Montgomery Ave., Rosemont, Pa. 19010; Westchester Ave., Rye, N. Y. 10580; 500 Bellefontaine St., Pasadena, Calif. 91105. (508).

Holy Faith, Sisters of the, S.H.F.: Founded 1856, in Ireland; in US, 1953. General motherhouse, Dublin, Ireland; US address, 1050 N. Texas St., Fairfield, Calif. 94533.

Holy Ghost, Sisters of the, C.H.G.: Founded 1913, in US, by Most Rev. J. F. Regis Canevin. General motherhouse, 5246 Clarwin Ave., West View, Pittsburgh, Pa. 15229. Educational, nursing work; care of aged. (122).

Holy Ghost and Mary Immaculate, Sister Servants of, S.H.G.: Founded 1893, in US. General motherhouse, 301 Yucca St., San Antonio, Tex. 78203. Education, hospital work. (243).

Holy Heart of Mary, Servants of the, S.S.C.M.: Founded 1860, in France; in US, 1889. General motherhouse, Montreal, Que., Canada; US motherhouse, 145 S. 4th St., Kankakee, Ill. 60901. Educational, hospital, social work. (142).

Holy Names of Jesus and Mary, Sisters of the, S.N.J.M.: Founded 1843, in Canada; in US, 1859. General motherhouse, 1420 Mt. Royal Blvd., Outremont, Montreal, Canada; four provinces in US. (1,569).

Holy Spirit, Daughters of the, F.S.E.: Founded 1706, in France; in US, 1902. General motherhouse, Bretagne, France; US motherhouse, 72 Church St., Putnam, Conn. 06260. Educational work, district nursing.

(419).

Holy Spirit, Mission Sisters of the, M.S.Sp.: Founded 1932, at Cleveland, O. Motherhouse, 1030 N. River Rd., Saginaw, Mich. 48603.

Holy Spirit, Missionary Sisters, Servants of the: Founded 1889, in Holland; in US, 1901. Generalate, Rome, Italy; US motherhouse, Techny, Ill. 60082. (320).

Holy Spirit, Sisters of the, C.S.Sp.: Founded 1890, in Rome, Italy; in US, 1929. General motherhouse, 10102 Granger Rd., Garfield Hts., Ohio 44125. Educational, social, nursing work. (18).

Holy Spirit of Perpetual Adoration, Sister Servants of the: Founded 1896, in Holland; in US, 1915. General motherhouse, Steyl, Holland; US motherhouse, 2212 Green St., Philadelphia, Pa. 19130. (75).

Home Mission Sisters of America (Glenmary Sisters): Founded 1952, in US. Motherhouse, 4580 Colerain Ave., Cincinnati, O. 45223. (18).

Home Visitors of Mary, Sisters, H.V.M.: Founded 1949, in Detroit, Mich. Motherhouse, 356 Arden Park, Detroit, Mich. 48002. (20).

Humility of Mary, Congregation of, C.H.M.: Founded 1854, in France; in US, 1864. US address, Ottumwa, Ia. 52501. (347).

Humility of Mary, Sisters of the, H.M.: Founded 1854, in France; in US, 1864. US address Villa Maria, Pa. 16155. (470).

Immaculate Conception, Little Servant Sisters of the: Founded 1850, in Poland; in US, 1926. General motherhouse, Poland; US motherhouse, 184 Amboy Ave., Woodbridge, N. J. 07095. (36).

Immaculate Conception, Sisters of the C.I.C.: Founded 1874, in US. General motherhouse, 5205 Avron Blvd., Metairie, La. 70002. (34).

Immaculate Conception of the Blessed Virgin Mary, Sisters of the (Lithuanian), M.I.C.: Founded 1918, at Mariampole, Lithuania; in US, 1936. General motherhouse, Mariampole, Lithuania; US headquarters, Putnam, Conn. 06260. (43).

Immaculate Heart of Mary, Daughters of the, I.H.M.: Founded 1952, in US. General motherhouse, Wintersville, Steubenville P.O., Ohio 43952.

Immaculate Heart of Mary, Missionary Daughters of the: Founded 1848, in Spain; in US, 1878. General motherhouse, Barcelona, Spain. US province, 35 E. 15th St., Tucson, Ariz. 85700. Educational work. (98).

Immaculate Heart of Mary, Missionary Sisters, I.C.M.: Founded 1897, in India; in US, 1919. Generalate, Rome, Italy; US address, 1710 N. Glebe Rd., Arlington, Va. 22207. Educational social, foreign mission work. (86).

Immaculate Heart of Mary, Sisters of the (California Institute of the Most Holy and Immaculate Heart of the B.V.M.), I.H.M.:

Founded 1848, in Spain; in US, 1871. Generalate, 3431 Waverly Dr., Los Angeles, Calif. 90027. (68).

Immaculate Heart of Mary, Sisters, Servants of the, I.H.M.: Founded 1845 in US, by Rev. Louis Florent Gillet. US jurisdictions: 610 W. Elm St., Monroe, Mich. 48161; Villa Maria, Immaculata, Pa. 19345; Marywood, Scranton, Pa. 18509; 2857 Palmerston St., Troy, Mich. 48084; 8961 Laurence St., Allen Park, Mich. 48101. Educational work. (5,337).

Incarnate Word and Blessed Sacrament, Congregation of, I. W. B. S., S. I. W.: Founded 1625, in France; in US, 1853. US motherhouses: 6618 Pearl Rd., Parma Heights, Cleveland, O. 44130; 4600 Bissonnet St., Bellaire, Tex. 77401; 1101 Northeast Water St., Victoria, Tex. 77901; 2930 S. Alameda St., Corpus Christi, Tex. 78404. Educational, hospital work. (598).

Infant Jesus, Sisters of the (Nursing Sisters of the Sick Poor), C.I.J.: Founded 1835, in France; in US, 1905. General motherhouse, 310 Prospect Park W., Brooklyn, N.Y. 11215. (165).

Jeanne d'Arc, Sisters of Ste.: Founded 1914, in America, by Rev. Marie Clement Staub, A.A. General motherhouse, 1681 Chemin St. Louis, Quebec, Canada; US novitiate, 29 Whitman Rd., Worcester, Mass. 01609. Spiritual and temporal service of priests, 282 (in US and Canada).

Jesus, Congregation of Daughters of, F. J.: Founded 1834, in France; in US, 1904. General motherhouse, Kermaria, Locmine, France; American motherhouse, 9040 84th Ave., Edmonton, Alberta, Canada. Educational, hospital work. 10.

Jesus, Daughters of, F. I.: Founded 1871, in Spain; in US, 1950. General motherhouse, Rome, Italy; US convent, 6020 St. Charles Ave., New Orleans, La. 70118. 51.

Jesus, Little Sisters of: Founded 1939, in Sahara; in US, 1952. General motherhouse, Rome, Italy; US headquarters, 700 Irving St. N. W., Washington, D.C. 20017. 20.

Jesus, Society of the Sisters, Faithful Companions of, F. C. J.: Founded 1820, in France; in US, 1896. General motherhouse, Kent, England. US convents: Columbus St., Fitchburg, Mass. 01420; 20 Atkins St., Providence, R. I. 02908; 5 Lincoln St., Centredale, R.I. 02911; Corys Lane, Portsmouth, R. I. 02871. 64.

Jesus Crucified, Congregation of: Founded 1930, in France; in US, 1955. General motherhouse, Brou, France; US foundations: Regina Mundi Priory, Devon, Pa. 19333; St. Paul's Priory, 61 Narragansett, Newport, R.I. 35.

Jesus Crucified and the Sorrowful Mother, Poor Sisters of, C.J.C.: Founded 1924, in US, by Rev. Alphonsus, C.P. General motherhouse, Thatcher St., Brockton, Mass. 02402. Educational, home nursing work. 97.

Jesus-Mary, Religious of, R. J. M.: Founded 1818, at Lyons, France; in US, 1877. General motherhouse, Rome, Italy; US province, 8908 Riggs Rd., Hyattsville, Md. 20782. Educational Work. 319.

Jesus, Mary and Joseph, Missionaries of, M. J. M. J.: Founded 1939, in Spain; in US, 1956. General motherhouse, Madrid, Spain; US regional house, 12940 Up River Rd., Corpus Christi, Tex. 78410. 30.

Jesus the Priest, Oblate Sisters of, O. J. S.: Founded 1937, in Mexico City; in US, 1950. Motherhouse, Mexico City, Mexico; US address, La Salle Institute, Glencoe, Mo. 63038.

John the Baptist, Sisters of St., C. S. J. B.: Founded 1878, in Italy; in US, 1906. General motherhouse, Rome, Italy; US provincialate, Anderson Hill Rd., Puschase, N.Y. 10577. Educational work. 192.

Joseph, Little Daughters of St., L. D. S. J.: Founded 1857, in Canada; in US, 1931. General motherhouse, 2333 W. Sherbrooke St., Montreal, Que., Canada. Spiritual and temporal welfare of priests 4.

Joseph, Missionary Servants of St., M. S. S. J.: Founded 1874, in Spain; in US, 1957. General motherhouse, Salamanca, Spain; US address, 203 N. Spring St., Falls Church, Va. 22046. 11.

Joseph, Religious Daughters of St., F. S. J.: Founded 1875, in Spain. General motherhouse, Spain; US foundation, 328 N. Humphreys Ave., Los Angeles, Calif. 90022. 13.

Joseph, Religious Hospitallers of St., R. H. S. J.: Founded 1636, in France; in US, 1894. General motherhouse, 251 Pine Ave. W., Montreal, Que., Canada. Hospital work. 88.

Joseph, Sisters of St., C. S. J.: Founded 1650, in France; in US, 1836, at St. Louis. US motherhouses (Number of professed members is given in parentheses):

637 Cambridge St., Brighton, Mass. 02135 (1,601); 1515 W. Ogden Ave., La Grange Park, Ill. 60525 (229); 480 S. Batavia St., Orange, Calif. 92666 (426); Mt. St. Joseph Convent, Chestnut Hill, Philadelphia, Pa. 19118 (2,525).

St. Joseph Convent, Brentwood, N.Y. 11717 (1,744); 23 Agassiz Circle, Buffalo, N.Y. 14214 (353); Mt. St. Joseph's Convent, Rutland, Vt. 05701 (121); 3430 Rocky River Dr. N.W., Cleveland, O. 44111 (335); 819 W. 8th St., Erie, Pa. 16502 (354); Main St. and Division Rd., Tipton, Ind. 46072 (129); Nazareth, Mich. 49074 (612); 362 W. Main St., Watertown, N.Y. 13601 (161); Mt. Gallitzin Motherhouse, Baden, Pa. 15005 (539)

4095 East Ave., Rochester, N.Y. 14610 (771); 13th and Washington Sts., Concordia, Kans. 66901 (539); Holyoke, Mass. 01040 (770); 1412 E. 2nd St., Superior, Wis. 54880 (38); Pogue Run Rd., Wheeling, W. Va. 26003 (243); 3700 E. Lincoln St., Wichita, Kans. 67218 (362).

Joseph, Sisters of St., S. S. J.: Founded 1650, at Le Puy, France; in US, 1902. General motherhouse, Le Puy, France; US motherhouse, 127 Howland St. Fall River, Mass. 02724. Educational, hospital work. 105.

Joseph, Sisters of St., C. S. J.: Founded 1823, in France; in US, 1855. General motherhouse, Bourg, France. US provinces: Marywood Rd., Crookston, Minn. 56716; 1200 Mirabeau Ave., New Orleans, La. 70122; 6532 Beechmont Ave., Cincinnati, O. 45230. 359.

Joseph, Sisters of St. (Lyons, France), C. S. J.: Founded 1650, in France; in US, 1906. General motherhouse, Lyons, France; US motherhouse, 93 Halifax St., Winslow, Me. 04901. Educational, hospital work. 125.

Joseph, Sisters of St., of Peace, C. S. J.: Founded 1884, in England. General executive office, 1325 Massachusetts Ave., Washington, D.C. 20005. Educational, hospital, social service work. 509.

Joseph of Carondelet, Sisters of St., C. S. J.: Founded 1650, in France; in US, 1836, at St. Louis, Mo. US headquarters, 2307 S. Lindbergh Blvd., St. Louis, Mo. 63131. 4,205.

Joseph of Chambery, Sisters of St.: Founded 1650, in France; in US, 1885. General motherhouse, Rome, Italy; US motherhouse, 27 Park Rd., West Hartford, Conn. 06119. Educational, hospital, social work. 394.

Joseph of Cluny, Sisters of St., S. J. C.: Fonded 1807, in France. General motherhouse, Paris, France; US provincial house, Cluny Convent, Brenton Rd., Newport, R. I. 02840. 54.

Joseph of St. Augustine, Fla., Sisters of St., S. S. J.: General motherhouse, 241 St. George St., St. Augustine, Fla. 32084. Educational, hospital, social work. 195.

Joseph of St. Mark, Sisters of St., S. S. J. S. M.: Founded 1845, in France; in US, 1937. General motherhouse, Alsace-Lorraine, France; US motherhouse, 21800 Chardon Rd., Euclid, Cleveland, O. 44117. Social, domestic work. 58.

Lamb of God, Sisters of the, A.D.: Founded 1945, in France; in US, 1958. General motherhouse, France; US foundation, 1516 Parish Ave., Owensboro, Ky. 42301. 5.

Little Sisters of the Workers of the Sacred Heart of Jesus and Mary: Founded 1902, in Italy; in US, 1948. General motherhouse, Rome, Italy; US address, 201 Taylor St. N. E., Washington, D. C. 20017. 21.

Loretto at the Foot of the Cross, Sisters of, S. L.: Founded 1842, in France; in US, 1949. General motherhouse, Monaghan, Ireland; US novitiate, 22300 Mulholland Dr., Woodland Hills, Calif. 91364. Educational work. 104.

Love of God, Sisters of the, R. A. D.: Founded 1864, in Spain; in US, 1958. Motherhouse, Spain; US address, Fairhaven, Mass. 02719.

Marian Sisters of the Diocese of Lincoln: Founded 1954. Motherhouse, 68462 Marycrest, Waverly, Nebr. 68462. 25.

Marian Society of Dominican Catechists, O. P.: Founded 1954. General motherhouse, Boyce, La. 71409. Diocesan community. 8.

Marianites of Holy Cross, Congregation of the Sisters, M. S. C.: Founded 1841, in France; in US, 1843. General motherhouse, Sarthe, France; US provinces: 4123 Woodland Dr., New Orleans, La. 70114; Great Rd., Princeton, N.J. 08540. 355.

Marist Sisters, Congregation of Mary, S.M.: Founded 1824, in France. General motherhouse, Rome, Italy; US convents: Dearborn Hts., Mich. 48125; Detroit, Mich.; Wheeling, W. Va. 26002. 25.

Maronite Antonine Sisters: Established in US, 1966; US address: Box 519 N. Lipkey Rd., R. D. 1, North Jackson, Ohio 44451. 5.

Martha of Prince Edward Island, Sisters of St., C.S.M.: Founded 1916, in Canada; in US, 1961. General motherhouse, 141 Mt. Edward Rd., Charlottetown, P.E.I., Canada.

Marthe, Sisters of Sainte (of St. Hyacinthe), S.M.S.H.: Fonded 1883, in Canada; in US, 1929. General motherhouse, St. Joseph de Hyacinthe, Que., Canada (24)

Mary, Company of, O.D.N.: Founded 1607, in France; in US, 1926. General motherhouse, Rome, Italy; US motherhouse, 16791 E. Main St., Tustin, Calif. 92680. (86)

Mary, Daughters of the Heart of, D.H.M.: Founded 1790, in France; in US, 1851. General motherhouse, Paris, France; US motherhouse, 103 E. 20th St., New York, N.Y. 10003. Educational work. (288)

Mary, Little Company of, Nursing Sisters, L.C.M.: Founded 1877, in England; in US, 1893. General motherhouse, Rome, Italy; US provincial house, 95th and California Aves., Evergreen Park, Ill. 60642. (80)

Mary, Mantellate Sisters Servants of, O.S.M.: Founded 1861, in Italy; in US, 1916. General motherhouse, Rome, Italy; US motherhouse, 13811 S. Western Ave., Blue Island, Ill. 60406. Educational, hospital work. (70)

Mary, Missionary Sisters of the Society of (Marist Sisters), S.M.S.M.: Founded 1845, at St. Brieuc, France; in US, 1922. General motherhouse, Rome, Italy; US provincialate, 591 Springs Rd., Bedford, Mass. 01730. Foreign missions. (63)

Mary, Servants of, O.S.M.: Founded 13th century, in Italy; in US, 1893. General motherhouse, Louvain, Belgium; US provincial motherhouse, 7400 Military Ave., Omaha, Nebr. (236)

Mary, Servants of (Servite Sisters), O.S.M.: Founded 1894, in Austria; in US, 1952. General motherhouse, Louvain, Belgium; US novitiate, Sublimity, Ore. 97385. Nursing work.

Mary, Servants of (Servite Sisters), O.S.M.: Founded 13th century, in Italy; in US, 1912. General motherhouse, Ladysmith, Wis. 54848. (143)

Mary, Sisters of St., of Oregon, S.S.M.O.: Founded 1886, in Oregon, by Bishop William H. Gross, C.Ss.R. General motherhouse, 4440 S.W. 148th Ave., Beaverton, Ore. 97005. Educational, nursing work. (245)

Mary, Sisters Servants of (Trained Nurses), S.deM.: Founded 1851, at Madrid, Spain; in US, 1914. General motherhouse, Rome, Italy; US motherhouse, 800 N. 18th St., Kansas City, Kans. 66102. Home nursing. (339)

Mary and Joseph, Daughters of, D.M.J.: Founded 1817, in Belgium; in US, 1926. General motherhouse, Rome, Italy; American provincial house, 3832 Jasmine Ave., Culver City, Calif. 90230. (104)

Mary Help of Christians, Daughters of (Salesian Sisters of St. John Bosco), F.M.A.: Founded 1872, in Italy, By St. John Bosco, in US, 1908. General motherhouse, Rome, Italy; US motherhouse, North Haledon, N.J. 07508. Education, youth work. (270)

Mary of Namur Sisters of St., S.S.M.N.: Founded 1819, at Namur, Belgium; in US, 1863. General motherhouse, Namur, Belgium. US provinces: 7110 Lake Shore Rd., Derby, N.Y. 14097; Irving, Tex. 75060. (398)

Mary of Providence, Daughters of St., D.S.M.P.: Founded 1872, at Como, Italy; in US, 1913. General motherhouse, Como, Italy; US provincial house, 4200 N. Austin Ave., Chicago, Ill. 60634. Educational work. (105)

Mary of the Catholic Apostolate, Sisters of the, S.A.C.: Founded 1926 at Schoenstatt, Germany; in US, 1949. General motherhouse, Schoenstatt, Germany. US addresses: Star Route 1, Box 100, Rockport, Tex. 78382; 5831 Cottage Grove Rd., Madison, Wis. 53716. Cottage Grove Rd., Madison, Wis, 53716. (66)

Mary of the Immaculate Conception, Daughters of, D.M.: Founded 1904, in US, by Msgr. Lucian Bojnowski. General motherhouse, New Britain, Conn. 06053. Educational, hospital work. (163)

Mary Immaculate, Daughters of (Marianist Sisters), F.M.L.: Founded 1816, in France, by Very Rev. William-Joseph Chaminade. General motherhouse, Rome, Italy; US motherhouse, Tex. 78228. Educational work. (27)

Mary Immaculate, Religious of, R.M.I.: Founded 1876, in Spain; in US, 1954. General motherhouse, Rome, Italy; US foundation 719 Augusta St., San Antonio, Tex. 78215. (27)

Mary Immaculate, Sisters Servants of, S.S.M.I.: Founded 1892, in Austria; in US, 1935. General motherhouse, Rome, Italy; US province: 209 W. Chestnut Hill Ave., Philadelphia, Pa. 19118. Educational, hospital work. (90)

Mary Immaculate of Mariowka, Sister Servants of, S.S.M.I.: Founded 1878 in Poland. General motherhouse, Poland; American provincialate, 1220 Tugwell Dr., Catonsville, Md. 21228. (22)

Mary Reparatrix, Society of, S.M.R.: Founded 1857, in France; in US, 1908. General motherhouse, Rome, Italy; US motherhouse, 14 E. 29th St., New York, N.Y. 10016. (77)

Medical Mission Sisters (Society of Catholic Medical Missionaries, Inc.), S.C.M.M.: Founded 1925, in US. Generalate, Rome, Italy; American motherhouse, 8400 Pine Rd., Philadelphia, Pa. 19111. Medical work, especially in mission areas. (160)

Medical Missionaries of Mary, M.M.M.: Founded 1937, in Ireland, by Mother Mary Martin, M.M.M.; in US, 1950. General motherhouse, Drogheda, Ireland; US motherhouse, 1 Arlington St., Winchester, Mass. 01890. Medical aid in missions. (41)

Mercedarian Missionaries of Berriz, M.M.B.: Founded 1930, in Spain; in US, 1946. General motherhouse, Berriz, Spain; US vice provincial house, 918 E. 9th St., Kansas City, Mo. 64106. (113)

Mercy, Daughters of Our Lady of, D.M.: Founded 1837, in Italy, by St. Mary Joseph Rosello; in US, 1919. General motherhouse, Savona, Italy; US motherhouse, Catawba Ave., Newfield, N.J. 08344. Educational, hospital work. (108)

Mercy, Missionary Sisters of Our Lady of, M.M.O.M.: Founded 1938, in Brazil; in US, 1955. General motherhouse, Brazil; US address, 388 Franklin St., Buffalo, N.Y. 14202. (5)

Mercy, Sisters of, R.S.M.: Founded 1831, in Ireland, by Mother Mary Catherine McAuley. US motherhouses (number of professed members is given in parentheses):

634 New Scotland Ave., Albany, N.Y. 12208 (352); 273 Willoughby Ave., Brooklyn, N.Y. 11205 (448); S. 5245 Murphy Rd., Orchard Park, N.Y. 14127 (400); Mansfield Ave., Burlington, Vt. 05401 (157): 1125 Prairie Dr., N.E., Cedar Rapids, Ia. 52402 (238): 444 E. Grandview Blvd., Erie, Pa. 16504 (189); 249 Steele Rd., W. Hartford, Conn. 06117 (609);

Windham, N.H. 03087 (401); Merion, Pa. 10968 (684); 3333 Fifth Ave., Pittsburgh, Pa. 15213 (421); 605 Stevens Ave., Portland, Me. 04103 (329); Belmont, N. Car. 28012 (197); 1437 Blossom Rd., Rochester, N.Y. 14610 (376); Rt. 3, Box 3216, Auburn, Calif. 95603 (153);

2300 Adeline Dr., Burlingame, Calif. 94010 (417); US Route 22 at Tirrell Rd., North Plainfield, N.J. 07061 (577); 46 High St., Worcester, Mass. 01608 (116).

Mercy, Sisters of, of the Union in the United States of America, R.S.M.: Founded 1831 in Ireland, by Mother M. Catherine McAuley; union formed in 1929. General motherhouse, 10000 Kentsdale Dr., Box 3446, Bethesda, P.O., Washington, D.C. 20034. (5,826)

Mercy, Sisters of, Daughters of Christian

Charity of St. Vincent de Paul, S.M.D.C.: Founded 1842, in Hungary; US foundation, Rt. 1, Box 353, Hewitt, N.J. 07421.

Mercy of the Blessed Sacrament, Sisters of, R.M.S.S.: Founded 1910 in Mexico City. General motherhouse, Mexico; US foundation, 555 E. Mountain View, Barstow, Calif. 92311.

Mill Hill Sisters: See Franciscan Missionaries of St. Joseph.

Minim Daughters of Mary Immaculate, C.F.M.M.: Founded 1886, in Mexico; in US, 1926. General motherhouse, Leon, Guanajuato, Mexico. US address, Box 1865, Nogales, Ariz. 85621. (50)

Misericorde Sister, S.M.: Founded 1848, in Canada; in US, 1887. General motherhouse, 12435 Ave. Misericorde, Montreal 9, Canada. Hospital work. (67)

Mission Helpers of the Sacred Heart, M.H.S.H.: Founded 1890, in US. General motherhouse, 1001 W. Joppa Rd., Towson, Md. 21204. Religious education, social work. (199)

Missionary Catechists of the Sacred Hearts of Jesus and Mary (Violetas), M.C.: Founded 1927, in Mexico; in US, 1943. Motherhouse, Tlalpan, Mexico; US address, 209 W. Murray St., Victoria, Tex. 77901. (136)

Missionary Sisters of the Catholic Apostolate (Pallottine Sisters), S.A.C.: Founded in Rome, 1843; in US, 1912. Generalate, Rome, Italy; US provincialate, Rt. 2, Box 390, Florissant, Mo. 63031. (115)

Most Pure Virgin Mary, Missionary Daughters of the: Founded 1903, at Mexico City; in US, 1916. General motherhouse, Aguascalientes, Mexico. Educational work.

Mother of God, Missionary Sisters of the, M.S.M.G.: Byzantine, Ukrainian Rite, Stamford. Motherhouse, 711-719 N. Franklin St., Philadelphia, Pa. 19123 (17)

Mother of God, Sisters Poor Servants of the, S.M.G.: Founded 1869, at London, England; in US, 1947. General motherhouse, Maryfield, Roehampton, London; US addresses: High Point, N.C. 27260; Norton, Va. 24273; 1800 Geary St., Philadelphia, Pa. 19145. Hospital work. (26)

Nazareth, Poor Sisters of: Founded 1924, in US. General motherhouse, Hammersmith, London, England; US novitiate, 3333 Manning Ave., Los Angeles, Calif. 90064. (54)

Notre Dame, School Sisters de: Founded 1853, in Czechoslovakia; in US, 1910. General motherhouse, Horazdovice, Czechoslovakia; US motherhouse, 3501 State St., Omaha, Nebr. 68112. Educational work. (135)

Notre Dame, School Sister of, S.S.N.D.: Founded 1833, in Germany; in US, 1847. General motherhouse, Rome, Italy. US provinces: 700 W. Highland Rd., Mequon, Wis. 53092; 6401 N. Charles St., Baltimore, Md. 21212; 320 E. Ripa Ave., St. Louis, Mo. 63125; Good Counsel Hill, Mankato, Minn.

56011; Wilton, Conn. 06897; Rt. 2, Box 4, Irving, Tex. 75060; R.R. 1, DeKalb, Ill. 60115. (5,917)

Notre Dame, Sisters of, S.N.D.: Founded 1850, 1850, at Coesfeld, Germany; in US, 1874. General motherhouse, Rome, Italy. US 13000 Auburn Rd., Chardon, O. 44024; 1601 Dixie Highway, Covington, Ky. 41011; 3837 Secor Rd., Toledo, O. 43623; 624 W. Potrero Rd., Thousand Oaks, Calif. 91360. (1,556)

Notre Dame, Sisters of the Congregation of, C.N.D.: Founded 1653, in Canada; in US, 1860. General motherhouse, Montreal, Que., Canada; US motherhouse, 223 West Mountain Rd., Ridgefield, Conn. 06877. Education. (360)

Notre Dame de Namur, Sisters of, S.N.D.: Founded 1803, in France; in US, 1840. General motherhouse, Rome, Italy. US provinces: Jeffrey's Neck Rd., Ipswich, Mass. 01938; 1561 N. Benson Rd., Fairfield, Conn. 06430; Ilchester, Md. 21083; 701 E. Columbia Ave., Reading, Cincinnati, O. 45215; Bohlman Rd., Saratoga, Calif. 95070. Educational work. (2,691)

Notre Dame de Sion, Congregation of, N.D.S.: Founded 1843, in France; in US, 1892. Generalate, Rome, Italy; US provincial house, 3823 Locust St., Kansas City, Mo. 64109. Creation of better understanding and relations between Christians and Jews. (29)

Notre Dame des Anges, Missionary Sisters of, M.N.D.A.: Founded 1922, in Canada; in US, 1949. General motherhouse, Lennoxville, Canada; US headquarters, 320 N. Main St., Union City, Conn. 06770.

Our Lady of LaSalette, Sisters of, S.M.S.: Founded 1930, in France. General motherhouse, France; US novitiate, Attleboro, Mass. 02703. (6)

Our Lady of Sorrows, Sisters of, O.L.S.: Founded 1839, in Italy; in US, 1947. General motherhouse, Rome, Italy. Staff five schools in Alexandria, La., diocese. Educational, social work; schools for retarded children. (27)

Pallottine Sisters of the Catholic Apostolate, C.S.A.C.: Founded 1843, at Rome, Italy; in US, 1889. General motherhouse, Rome; US motherhouse, Harriman Heights, Harriman, N.Y. 10926. Educational work. (178)

Parish Visitors of Mary Immaculate, P.V.M.I.: Founded 1920, in New York. General motherhouse, Box 658, Monroe, Orange Co., N.Y. 10950. Mission work. (128)

Passionist Sisters: See Cross and Passion, Sisters of the.

Paul, Daughters of St., Missionary Sisters of the Catholic Editions, D.S.P.: Founded 1915, at Alba, Piedmont, Italy; in US, 1932. General motherhouse, Rome, Italy; US provincial house, 50 St. Paul's Ave., Jamaica Plain, Mass. 02130. Apostolate of the communications arts. (114)

Peter Claver, Missionary Sisters of St., S.S.P.C.: Founded 1894; in US, 1914. General motherhouse, Rome, Italy; US address Rt. 2, Box 393, Chesterfield, Mo. 63017. (18)

Pious Schools, Sisters of, Sch., P.: Founded 1829 in Spain; in US, 1954. General motherhouse, Rome, Italy; US headquarters, 12500 N. Maclay St., Sylmar, Calif. 91342. (45)

Poor, Little Sisters of the, P.S.D.P.: Founded 1839, in France; in US, 1868. General motherhouse, St. Pern, France. US provinces: 110-30 221st St., Queens Village, N.Y. 11429; 601 Maiden Choice Lane, Baltimore, Md. 21228; 80 W. Baldwin Rd., Palatine, Ill. 60067. Social work. (730)

Poor Clare Missionary Sisters (Misionaras Clarisas), M.C.: Founded Mexico. General motherhouse, Rome, Italy; US novitiate, 11712 Stuart Dr., Garden Grove, Calif. 92640.

Poor Clare Nuns: See Franciscan Poor Clare Nuns.

Poor Clare Nuns of the Holy Eucharist, P.C.H.E.: Motherhouse, 5817 Old Leeds Rd., Birmingham, Ala. 35210. (9)

Poor Clares of Ireland, P.C.: General motherhouse, Newry, Ireland; US foundation, 37 E. Emerson, Chula Vista, Calif. 92011.

Poor Handmaids of Jesus Christ (Ancilla Domini Sisters), P.H.J.C.: Founded 1851, in Germany; in US, 1868. General motherhouse, Dernbach, Westerwald, Germany; US motherhouse, Donaldson, Ind. 46513. Educational, hospital work. (492)

Precious Blood, Daughters of Charity of the Most: Founded 1872, at Pagani, Italy; in US, 1908. General motherhouse, Rome, Italy; US novitiate, 46 Preakness Ave., Paterson, N.J. 07502. Social work. (30)

Precious Blood, Missionary Sisters of the, C.P.S.: Founded 1885, at Mariannhill, South Africa; in US, 1925. Generalate, Rome, Italy; US motherhouse, New Holland Ave., P.O. Box 43, Shillington, Pa. 19607. Home and foreign mission work. (52)

Precious Blood, Sisters Adorers of the, A.P.B.: Founded 1861, in Canada; in US, 1890. General motherhouses: 2520, rue Girouard, St. Hyacinthe, Que., Canada (French); 667 Talbot St., London 12, Ont., Canada (English). Contemplatives. (115)

Precious Blood, Sisters of the, C.Pp.S.: Founded 1834, in Switzerland; in US, 1844. Generalate, 4000 Denlinger Rd., Dayton, Ohio 45426. Educational, hospital work. (641)

Precious Blood, Sisters of the Most, C.Pp.S.: Founded 1845, in Steinerberg, Switzerland; in US, 1870. General motherhouse, 204 N. Main St., O'Fallon, Mo. 63366. Educational work. (575)

Presentation, Sisters of St. Mary of the S.M.P.: Founded 1829, in France; in US, 1903. General motherhouse, Broons, Cotesdu-Nord, France. US motherhouse, Valley City, N. Dak. 58072. Educational, hospital work. (112)

Presentation of Mary, Sisters of the, P.M.: Founded 1796, in France; in US, 1873. General motherhouse, Rome, Italy. US provinces: Manchester, N.H. 03104; Methuen, Mass. 01844. (813)

Presentation of the B.V.M., Sisters of the, P.B.V.M.: Founded 1777, in Ireland; in US, 1854. US motherhouses: 2360 Carter Rd., Dubuque, Ia. 52001; R.D. 2, Box 101, Newburgh, N.Y. 12550; 8931 Callaghan Rd., San Antonio, Tex. 78230; 2340 Turk St., San Francisco, Calif. 94118; Watervliet, N.Y. 12189.

Route 1, Fargo, N. Dak. 58102; 250 S. Davis Dr., P.O. Box 1113, Warner Robbins, Ga. 31093; Aberdeen, S. Dak. 57401; 1300 E. Cedar, Globe, Ariz. 85501; 1555 E. Dana, Mesa, Ariz. 85201; 366 South St., Fitchburg, Mass. 01420. (1,433)

Providence, Daughters of Divine, F.D.P.: Founded 1832, Italy; in US, 1964. General motherhouse, Rome, Italy; US foundation, 1029 N. Atlanta St., Metairie, La. 70003.

Providence, Missionary Catechists of Divine, M.C.D.P.: Founded 1930, as a filial society; adjunct branch of Sisters of Divine Providence (San Antonio). Formation house, 2318 Castroville Rd., San Antonio, Tex. 78237. (65)

Providence, Oblate Sisters of, O.S.P.: Founded 1829, in US. General motherhouse, 701 Gun Rd., Baltimore, Md. 21227. Educational work. (262)

Providence, Sisters of, S.P.: Founded 1861, in Canada; in US, 1873. General motherhouse, Brightside, Holyoke, Mass. 01040. (362)

Providence, Sisters of, S.P.: Founded 1843, in Canada; in US, 1854. General motherhouse, Montreal, Canada. US provinces: Providence Hts., Pine Lake, Issaquah, Wash. 98027; 9 E. 9th Ave., Spokane, Wash. 99202. (598)

Providence, Sisters of (of St. Mary-of-the-Woods), S.P.: Founded 1806, in France; in US, 1840. General motherhouse, St. Mary-of-the-Woods, Ind. 47876. (1,329)

Providence, Sisters of Divine, C.D.P.: Founded 1762, in France; in US, 1866. General motherhouse, Box 197, Helotes, Tex. 78023. Educational, hospital work. (669)

Providence, Sisters of Divine, C.D.P.: Founded 1851, in Germany; in US, 1876. General motherhouse, Rome, Italy. US provinces: 9000 Babcock Blvd., Allison Park, Pa. 15101; 8351 Florissant Rd., Normandy, Mo. 63121; Box 2, Rte. 80, Kingston, Mass. 02360. Educational, hospital work. (698)

Providence, Sisters of Divine (of Kentucky), C.D.P.: Founded 1762, in France; in US, 1889. General motherhouse, Moselle, France; US province, Melbourne, Ky. 41059. Educational, hospital work, domestic work. (406)

Providence and of the Immaculate Conception, Sisters of, S.P.I.C.: Founded 1837, in Belgium. General motherhouse, Belgium; US novitiate, 350 Smith Lane, Concord, Calif. 94520.

Redeemer, Oblates of the Most Holy, O.SS.R.: Founded 1864 in Spain. General motherhouse, Spain; US foundation, 60-80 Pond St., Jamaica Plain, Mass. 02130. (6)

Redeemer, Order of the Most Holy, O.SS.R.: Founded 1731, by St. Alphonsus Liguori; in US, 1957. US addresses: Esopus, N.Y. 12429; Liguori, Mo. 63057. (22)

Redeemer, Sisters of the Divine, S.D.R.: Founded 1849 in Niederbronn, France; in US, 1912. General motherhouse, Rome, Italy; US motherhouse, 999 Rock Run Road, Elizabeth, Pa. 15037. Educational, hospital work; care of the aged. (135)

Redeemer, Sisters of the Holy, S.H.R.: Founded 1849, in Alsace; in US, 1924. General motherhouse, Wuerzburg Germany; US regional house, Huntingdon Valley, Pa. 19006. Personalized medical care in hospitals, homes for aged and private homes. (127)

Refuge, Sisters of Our Lady of Charity of, O.L.C.R.: Founded 1641 at Caen, France; in US, 1855. US federation, P.O. Box 327, Wisconsin Dells, Wis. 53965. Social work. (257)

Religious Conceptionist Missionaries, R.C.M.: Founded 1892, in Spain; in US, 1962. General motherhouse, Madrid, Spain; US foundation, 867 Oxford, Clovis, Calif. 93612.

Reparation of the Congregation of Mary, Sisters of, S.R.C.M.: Founded 1904, in US. Motherhouse, Monsey, N.Y. 10952. (25)

Resurrection, Sisters of the, C.R.: Founded 1891, in Italy; in US, 1900. General motherhouse, Rome, Italy. US provinces: 7432 Talcott Ave., Chicago, Ill. 60631; Castleton-on-the Hudson, N.Y. 12033. Educational work. (363)

Rita of the Immaculate Heart, Daughters of St., D.S.R.: Motherhouse, P.O. Box 129, Versailles, Ky. 40383. (11)

Rosary, Congregation of Our Lady of the Holy, R.S.R.: Founded 1874, in Canada; in US, 1899. General motherhouse, C.P. 2020, Rimouski, Que., Canada. Educational work.

Rosary, Missionary Sisters of Our Lady of the Holy, H.R.S.: Founded 1924, in Ireland; in US, 1954. Motherhouse, Killeshandra, Co. Cavan, Ireland. US novitiate, 214 Ashwood Rd., Villanova, Pa. 19085. African missions.

Sacrament, Missionary Sisters of the Most Blessed,M.SS.S.: General motherhouse, Madrid, Spain; US foundations: 1111 Wordin Ave., Bridgeport, Conn. 06605; 121 Congress St., Newark, N.J. 07105.

Sacrament, Nuns of the Perpetual Adoration of the Blessed, A.P.: Founded 1807, in Rome, Italy; in US, 1925. US monasteries: 145 N. Cotton Ave., El Paso, Tex. 79901; 771 Ashbury St., San Francisco, Calif. 94117. (48)

Sacrament, Oblate Sisters of the Blessed, O.S.B.S.: Founded 1935, in US; motherhouse, Marty, S.D. 57361. Care of American Indians. (16)

Sacrament, Religious Mercedarians of the Blessed, R.M.S.S.: Founded 1910, in Mexico; in US, 1926. General motherhouse, Mexico City, Mexico; US convent, 222 W. Cevallos St., San Antonio, Tex. 78204. (12)

Sacrament, Servants of the Blessed, S.S.S.: Founded 1858, in France, by St. Pierre Julien Eymard; in US 1947. General motherhouse, Rome, Italy; US motherhouse, 101 Silver St., Waterville, Me. 04901. Contemplative. (33)

Sacrament, Sisters of Perpetual Adoration of the Blessed (of Guadalupe), A.P.: Founded 1879, in Mexico; in US, 1925. General motherhouse, Mexico City, Mexico. (12)

Sacrament, Sisters of the Blessed, for Indians and Colored People, S.B.S.: Founded 1891, in US. General motherhouse, Cornwell Heights, Pa. 19020. (504)

Sacrament, Sisters of the Most Holy, M.H.S.: Founded 1851, in France; in US, 1872. General motherhouse, 409 W. St. Mary Blvd. (P.O. Box 2429), Lafayette, La. 70501. (135)

Sacrament, Sisters Servants of the Blessed, S.S.B.S.: Founded 1904, in Mexico. General motherhouse, Guadalajara, Mexico. US address, 536 Rockwood Ave., Calexico, Calif. 92231.

Sacramentine Nuns (Religious of the Order of the Blessed Sacrament and Our Lady), O.SS.: Founded 1639, in France; in US, 1912. US monasteries: 23 Park Ave., Yonkers, N.Y. 10703; US 31, Conway, Mich. 49722. Perpetual adoration of the Holy Eucharist. (51)

Sacred Heart, Daughters of Our Lady of the: Founded 1882, in France; in US, 1955. General motherhouse, Rome, Italy; US address, 424 E. Browning Rd., Bellmawr, N.J. 08031. Educational work. (24)

Sacred Heart, Missionary Sisters of the (Cabrini Sisters), M.S.C.: Founded 1880, in Italy, by St. Frances Xavier Cabrini; in US, 1889. General motherhouse, Rome, Italy; US provincialate, 227 E. 19th St., New York, N.Y. 10003. Educational, health, social and catechetical work. (391)

Sacred Heart, Religious of the Apostolate of the, R.A.: General motherhouse, Madrid, Spain; US address, 1120 6th St., Miami Beach, Fla., 33139.

Sacred Heart, Society Devoted to the, S.D.S.H.: Founded 1940, in Hungary; in US, 1956. US motherhouse, 728 S. Hudson Ave., Los Angeles, Calif. 90005. Educational work. (33)

Sacred Heart, Society of the, R.S.C.J.: Founded 1800, in France; in US, 1818. General motherhouse, Rome, Italy. US provinces: 1177 King St., Greenwich, Conn. 06830; 4940 S. Greenwood Ave., Chicago, Ill. 60615; 13550 Conway Rd., St. Louis, Mo. 63141; 2259 Vallejo St., San Francisco, Calif. 94123; 885 Centre St., Newton, Mass. 02159. Educational work. (913)

Sacred Heart of Jesus, Apostles of,

A.S.C.J.: Founded 1894, in Italy; in US, 1902. General motherhouse, Rome, Italy; US motherhouse, 265 Benham St., Hamden, Conn. 06514. Educational, social work. (266)

Sacred Heart of Jesus, Congregation of Oblates of, O.S.C.: Founded 1843, in France; in US, 1955. US address, 314 S. 4th St., Camden, N.J. 08103. (10)

Sacred Heart of Jesus, Handmaids of the, A.C.J.: Founded 1877, in Spain. General motherhouse, Rome, Italy; US province. 2025 Church Rd., Wyncote, Pa. 19095. Educational, retreat work. (60)

Sacred Heart of Jesus, Missionary Sisters of the Most, M.S.C.: Founded 1899, in Germany; in US, 1908. General motherhouse, Rome, Italy; US province, Hyde Park, Reading, Pa. 19605. Educational, hospital, social work. (325)

Sacred Heart of Jesus, Oblate Sisters of the, O.S.H.J.: Founded 1894; in US, 1949. General motherhouse, Rome, Italy; US motherhouse, 50 Warner Rd., Hubbard, Ohio 44425. Educational, social work. (26)

Sacred Heart of Jesus, Servants of the Most: Founded 1894, in Poland; in US, 1959. General motherhouse, Cracow, Poland; in US, 231 Arch St., Cresson, Pa. 16630. (11)

Sacred Heart of Jesus, Sisters of the S.S.C.J.: Founded 1816, in France; in US, 1903. General motherhouse, St. Jacut, Britany, France; US provincial house, 5922 Blanco Rd., San Antonio, Tex. 78216. Educational, hospital, domestic work. (91)

Sacred Heart of Jesus and of the Poor, Servants of the (Mexican), S.S.H.J.P.: Founded 1885, in Mexico; in US, 1907. General motherhouse, Apartado 92, Puebla, Pue, Mexico. (70)

Sacred Heart of Jesus for Reparation, Congregation of the Handmaids of the: Founded 1918, in Italy; in US, 1958. US address, Sunshine Park, R.D. 3, Steubenville, Ohio 43952.

Sacred Heart of Mary, Religious of the, R.S.H.M.: Founded 1848, in France; in US, 1877. Generalate, Rome, Italy. US provinces: 15 E. 81st St., New York, N.Y. 10028; 945 Tremonto Rd., Santa Barbara, Calif. 93103. (634)

Sacred Hearts, Religious of the Holy Union of the, S.U.S.C.: Founded 1826, in France; in US, 1886. Generalate, Rome, Italy. US provinces: 492 Rock St., Fall River, Mass. 02720; Main St., Groton, Mass. 01450. Educational work. (376)

Sacred Hearts and of Perpetual Adoration, Sisters of the, SS.CC.: Founded 1797, in France; in US, 1908. General motherhouse, Rome, Italy; US motherhouse, 330 Main St., N. Fairhaven, Mass. 02719. Educational work. (38)

Sacred Hearts of Jesus and Mary, Sisters of the, S.S.H.J.M.: Established 1953, in US. General motherhouse, Essex, England; US address, 515 Boden Way, Oakland, Calif. 94607. (36)

Savior, Company of the, C.S.: Founded 1952, in Spain; in US, 1962. General motherhouse, Barcelona, Spain; US foundation, 820 Clinton Ave., Bridgeport, Conn. 06608. (56)

Savior, Sisters of the Divine, S.D.S.: Founded 1888, in Italy; in US, 1895. General motherhouse, Rome, Italy; US motherhouse, 4311 N. 100th St., Milwaukee, Wis. 53222. Educational, hospital work. (247)

Saviour, Daughters of Most Holy: Founded 1849, in Germany; in US, 1951. American province, 547 B St., Santa Rosa, Calif. 95401. (5)

Social Service, Sisters of, S.S.S.: Founded 1908, in Hungary; in US, 1926. General motherhouse, 1120 Westchester Pl., Los Angeles, Calif. 90019. (137)

Social Service, Sisters of, S.S.S.: Founded in Hungary, 1923. US motherhouse, 440 Linwood Ave., Buffalo, N.Y. 14209. Social work. (38)

Teresa of Jesus, Society of St., S.T.J.: Founded 1876, in Spain; in US, 1910. General motherhouse, Rome, Italy; US provincial house, 4018 S. Presa St., San Antonio, Tex. 78223. (110)

Thomas of Villanova, Congregation of Sisters of St., S.S.T.V.: Founded 1661, in France; in US, 1948. General motherhouse, Neuilly-sur-Seine, France; US motherhouse, Norwalk, Conn. 06851.

Trinity, Missionary Servants of the Most Blessed, M.S.B.T.: Founded 1912, in US, by Very Rev. Thomas A. Judge. General motherhouse, 3501 Solly St., Philadelphia, Pa. 19136. Educational, social work. (462)

Trinity, Sisters of the Most Holy, O.Ss.T.: Founded 1198, in Rome; in US, 1920. General motherhouse, Rome, Italy; US motherhouse, 21320 Euclid Ave., Euclid, Ohio 44117. Educational work. (44)

Ursula of the Blessed Virgin, Society of the Sisters of St., S.U.: Founded 1606, in France; in US, 1902. General motherhouse, Tours, France; US address: 168 W. 79th St., New York, N. Y. 10024. Educational work. (73)

Ursuline Nuns (Roman Union), O.S.U.: Founded 1535, in Italy; in US, 1727. Generalate, Rome, Italy. US provinces: 1 Berrian Rd., New Rochelle, N.Y. 19804; Crystal Heights Rd., Crystal City, Mo. 63019; 639 Angela Dr., Santa Rosa, Calif. 95401; 71 Lowder St., Dedham, Mass. 02026; 401 Findley St., Toronto, O. 43694. (1,180)

Ursuline Nuns of the Congregation of Paris, O.S.U.: Founded 1535, in Italy; in US, 1727. US motherhouses: St. Martin, O. 45170; East Miami St., Paola, Kans. 66071; 3115 Lexington Rd., Louisville, Ky. 40206; 2600 Lander Rd., Cleveland, O. 44124; Maple Mount, Ky. 42356; 2413 Collingwood Blvd., Toledo, 43620; 4250 Shields Rd., Canfield, O. 44406; 1339 E. McMillan St., Cincinnati, O. 45206. (2,011)

Ursuline Nuns of the Congregation of Tildonk, Belgium, R.U.: Founded 1535, in Italy;

in US, 1924. Generalate, Haecht, Belgium; US address, Blue Point, L. I., N. Y. 11715. Educational, foreign mission work. (130)

Ursuline Sisters, O.S.U.: General motherhouse, Blackrock, Cork, Ireland; US address, Torch Hill Rd., Columbus, Ga. 31903. (6)

Ursuline Sisters of Mount Calvary, O.S.U.: Founded 1535, in Italy; in US, 1910. General motherhouse, Mount Calvary, Germany; US motherhouse, 1026 N. Douglas Ave., Belleville, Ill. 62221. Educational work. (44)

Venerini Sisters, Religious, M.P.V.: Founded 1685, in Italy; in US, 1909. General motherhouse, Rome, Italy; US provincialate, 23 Edward St., Worcester, Mass. 01605. (70)

Verona, Missionary Sisters of, M.S.V.: Founded 1875, in Italy; in US, 1950. US motherhouse 1307 Lakeside Ave., Richmond, Va. 23228. Hospital, social, educational work. (40)

Victory Missionary Sisters, Our Lady of, O.L.V.M.: Founded 1922, in US. Motherhouse, Victory Noll, Box 109, Huntington, Ind. 46750. Educational, social work. (356)

Vincent de Paul, Sisters: See Charity of St. Vincent de Paul, Sisters of.

Visitation Nuns, V.H.M.: Founded 1610, in France; in US, 1799. North American federations: 2002 Bancroft Pkwy., Wilmington, Del. 19806 (Pres., Mother Mary Gabriella Muth); Visitation Monastery, Springfield, Mo. 65804 (Pres., Mother Anne Madeleine Ernstmann). Contemplative. Educational work. (570)

Visitation of the Congregation of the Immaculate Heart of Mary, Sisters of the, S.V.M.: Founded 1952, in US. Motherhouse, 900 Alta Vista St., Dubuque, Ia. 52201. Educational work. (28)

Vocationist Sisters (Sisters of the Divine Vocations): Founded 1921, in Italy. General motherhouse, Naples, Italy; US foundation, 172 Broad St., Newark, N. J. 07103. (5)

White Sisters: See Africa, Missionary Sisters of Our Lady of.

White Sisters of Charity of St. Vincent de Paul of Zagreb: Founded 1845, in Croatia; in US, 1955. General motherhouse, Zagreb, Yugoslavia; US motherhouse, 1619 Abbott Rd., Lackawanna, N.Y. 14218. (31)

Wisdom, Daughters of, D.W.: Founded 1703, in France, by St. Louis Marie Grignon de Montfort; in US, 1904. General motherhouse, Vendee, France; US motherhouse, 385 S. Ocean Ave., Islip, N. Y. Educational, hospital work. (253)

Xaverian Missionary Society of Mary, Inc., M.M.: Founded 1945, in Italy; in US, 1954. General motherhouse, Parma, Italy; US address, 242 Salisbury St., Worcester, Mass. 01609. (10)

Xavier Mission Sisters (Catholic Mission Sisters of St. Francis Xavier), X.M.S.: Founded 1946, at Warren, Mich., by Cardinal Edward Mooney. General motherhouse, 35750 Moravian Dr., Fraser, Mich. 48026. Educational, hospital, social work in missions. (12)

ORGANIZATIONS OF WOMEN RELIGIOUS

Leadership of Women

The Leadership Conference of Women Religious in the United States of America is an association of the major superiors of religious communities of women, with the purpose of promoting the spiritual and apostolic welfare of the sisterhoods of the US.

Organized in the late 50's and approved by the Congregation for Religious and Secular Institutes June 13, 1962, it has a membership of approximately 600. Its original name, changed in 1971, was the Conference of Major Superiors of Women. With its formerly affiliated Sister Formation Conference, it inaugurated measures for the religious and professional development of sisters and has contributed greatly to the renewal of religious life in this country.

The officers are: Sister Thomas Aquinas Carroll, R.S.M., national president, 3333 Fifth Ave., Pittsburgh, Pa. 15213; Sister Margaret Brennan, I.H.M., national vice president, 610 W. Elm St., Monroe, Mich. 48161; Sister Charitas Marcotte, R.S.M., national secretary-treasurer, Rte. 22 and Terrill Rd., N. Plainfield, N.J. 07061; Sister Mary Daniel Turner, S.N.D.deN., executive director.

The national secretariat is located at 1325 Massachusetts Ave., N.W., Washington, D.C. 20005.

Formation Conference

The Sister Formation Conference was organized in 1952 for the purpose of promoting the spiritual and professional formation of sisters belonging to American institutes. In 1970 it became independent of the Leadership Conference of Women Religious with which it had been affiliated.

Sister M. Annette Scofield, S.M., is national head of the conference. Her address is 2300 Adeline Dr., Burlingame, Calif. 94010.

Sister Eileen Kelly, P.B.V.M., is executive secretary. Sister Kathleen McDonough, S.N.J.M., is associate executive secretary.

The national secretariat is located at 1325 Massachusetts Ave. N.W., Washington, D.C. 20005.

National Assembly

More than 2,000 delegates attending a convention in Cleveland Apr. 17 to 19, 1970, voted overwhelmingly in favor of a proposal to establish the National Assembly of Women Religious and to make it "a voice" of sisters in the United States.

The assembly's primary goat is "to challenge women religious to communicate a valid concept of the role of the consecrated celibate women in the Church today, and to study, evaluate, establish priorities and make recommendations concerning areas in which women religious are critically needed."

The proposal to organize the assembly originated at a meeting of 400 sisters from 41 dioceses held in Portland, Me., in 1968. Fifteen hundred sisters meeting in Chicago in May, 1969, advanced the proposal and set up a task force to put it into final shape for the decisive action taken at the Cleveland convention.

The assembly is intended to be a forum for communication among women religious and "a voice through which they can speak to the Church and to the world."

Other objectives are to: promote unity within the Church by working in close collaboration with bishops and major superiors; represent the interests of the "grass roots" sister; provide a means by which women religious can participate in decision-making and implementing at the national, regional and local levels; provide a channel for sharing of personnel, resources and research; give impetus and direction to the organizing of local-igroups; encourage women religious to use their competence and expertise for the service of the Church and society.

Membership in the NAWR is open to individual sisters, councils of sister (official organization of sisters in a diocese), organizations of women religious (de facto groups of sisters which are not official diocesan bodies), and associates.

Programs are developed locally and in 10 NAWR regions, according to priorities determined at those levels. The programs are generally related to the categories of standing committees on social action, religious life, pastoral ministry, council and structures.

Five hundred sisters at the second NAWR convention Apr. 27 to 30, 1972, in Minneapolis, took action on a variety of proposals, including a resolution in favor of the ordination of women to the priesthood.

Sister Ethne Kennedy, head of the assembly, said that the resolution went beyond one passed in 1971 which called only for the ordination of women deacons. She commented: "It shows that we are not looking for gradualism. Since the Synod (of Bishops in 1971) it has been clear that there are no reasons against the ordination of women except sociological ones."

Delegates also voted to have the assembly's executive board "establish official channels of communication with the Vatican's Congregation for Religious" concerning "decisions and directives pertinent to the lives of women religious in the United States."

The proposal was related to a February directive from the congregation requiring sisters to wear religious habits. "That was one example of what we're talking about," Sister Ethne said; "but it is broader than that. It concerns all that affects the lives of religious."

Broad inclusive proposals — like one committing the NAWR to work actively "to promote respect for all human life and to insure effective participation of people in the decisions that affect their lives" — were brought to the assembly floor for enactment rather than clusters of individual resolutions.

Behind the resolution above, however, were a variety of suggestions including: participation in legislative processes; support of the Equal Rights Amendment for women; endorsing peace candidates; examining the stock portfolios of religious groups; working to change the priorities of government budgets to emphasize health and welfare; efforts to protect life at all stages.

The delegates also decided to place greater emphasis than before on regional activities.

NAWR had a reported membership of 68 diocesan councils and two other groups of sisters, representing about 70,000 of more than 140,000 sisters in the country. There were 3,000 individual members, as compared with 4,600 reported in the summer of 1971.

The principal officers of NAWR are: Sister Ethne Kennedy, chairlady, and Sister Helen Marie Neal, treasurer.

Offices are located at 720 N. Rush St., Chicago, Ill. 60611.

Black Sisters

(Source: Sister M. Martin de Porres Grey, R.S.M., conference president.)

The National Black Sisters' Conference was organized in August, 1968, for the express purpose of enabling the sisters to determine their priorities in relation to their black people. Four years after its founding, 75 per cent of its 325 members had apostolates in black communities. The conference includes black sisters from 123 religious congregations in the United States and Islands, as well as 30 women who have left their congregations but have remained with the conference.

A major concern of the conference is the development of continuance of black vocations to religious life in the unique contemporary black life style, for fulfillment in bringing about the liberation of black people. Control of vocation increases and the placement of the new ready black women is being implemented by a narrative slide presentation — "A New World Picture. Click," — which promotes a new image of black nuns in special programs for high school and college students.

The conference foresees the establishment of a house of formation as a center for the initial formation of black sisters in the black life style. It has initiated efforts to make it possible for black sisters to transfer from the congregations to which they belong to other institutes in which they might find greater opportunities for personal and apostolic fulfillment. Evaluations are being made of the priorities of various congregations in terms of their apostolates, life styles and formation. Only the names of those congregations which meet the conference's criteria will be circulated among black women interested in religious life.

Toward the further development of its members, an annual, week-long educational conference is held, as well as national and regional retreats and workshops on the black apostolate. A Tribunal for Black Religious Affairs has been formed, consisting of black sisters and priests — canon lawyers, attorneys and psychologists — for legal protection for sisters in temporary vows. A workshop is held annually for white superiors and formation personnel.

A new black congregation, composed of ex-nuns, was established in August, 1971, following the National Black Sisters' Conference's annual conference.

An educational service, called DESIGN (Development of Educational Services in the Growing Nation) has been established as one of the priorities of the conference, for the purpose of maximizing community control of black schools and developing educational excellence for black students. The conference has set up a nine-session minicourse to develop parent participation in schools and has initiated a 14-month teacher training program for community schools. The program enables participants to obtain a master's degree in administration or education from an accredited university. The conference has been acting as a placement service for inner-city parochial schools wishing black sister teachers.

At the time of writing, the results of the conference's 18-month practicability study for determining the effects of black sisters on the black community, the church, and religious life, were being computerized for final dissemination and publication.

Other priorities include work with the National Office for Black Catholics and efforts to bring about a redistribution of black sisters to meet the demands of the black community in a better way and to unify the total work of the Church in focusing on the most productive channels of freedom for black people.

The conference is concerned with national and local social issues and is committed to public stands and concrete action where these may be indicated. Immediate concerns are black community schools, alternative black educational systems, prison reform, and community organization.

The conference publishes a newsletter, *Signs of Soul*, three times a year, and has published the following: "Black Religious Women as Part of the Answer," "Celibate Black Commitment," and "Black Survival: Past, Present and Future."

Sister M. Martin de Porres Grey, R.S.M., is president of the National Black Sisters' Conference. Headquarters are located at 3333 Fifth Ave., Pittsburgh, Pa. 15213.

National Coalition

The 17-member executive board of the National Coalition of American Nuns, meeting in the spring of 1972 in Chicago, issued a new "Declaration of Independence" which advocated full equality for women by 1976, the bicentennial year of American independence.

Other priorities listed in the declaration were: reformation of existing economic and power systems; austerity and simplicity of life styles; a board-based research program in human sexuality.

Full equality for women in the Church, according to the declaration, meant the ordination of women to the priesthood and elected proportional representation in church voting bodies.

NCAN, organized in July, 1969, in Chicago, has a membership of approximately 2,000 sisters. Sister Margaret Traxler, S.S.N.D., is president.

Sisters Uniting

Sisters Uniting, formed in March, 1971, in Chicago, describes itself as a group that works "to facilitate cooperation and coordination" of six national associations: the Association of Contemplative Sisters, the National Sister Foundation Conference, the National Sister Vocation Conference, the National Coalition of American Nuns, the Leadership Conference of Women Religious, and the National Association of Women Religious.

Representatives of the participating organizations, at a council meeting held in June, 1972, in Chicago, recommended that sisters: support the Equal Rights Amendment for women; cooperate with a United Farm Workers' boycott of non-union lettuce; question political candidates regarding their stance on the issues of justice and peace; encourage their institutes to examine their investments in view of renewed fighting in Vietnam; cooperate with "Network," an organization for the education of nuns in social justice and needs for social legislation.

Consortium

The Consortium Perfectae Caritatis ("Association of Perfect Love"), named after the Latin title of the Second Vatican Council's *Decree on the Appropriate Renewal of Religious Life*, was organized in March, 1971, at a Washington, D.C., meeting of nearly 120 sisters from 48 communities in the United States and Canada.

The stated purposes of the association are: (1) to bring together those who accept the conciliar documents of Vatican Council II regarding religious life, subsequent papal statements, and interpretations and directives emanating from the Congregation for Religious and Secular Institutes; (2) to communicate and share with each other experiences in implementing the conciliar plan of renewal.

Delegates attending a three-day conference of the year-old association in March, 1972, in Arlington, Va., pledged themselves to the pursuit of authentic renewal, with renewed promises of loyalty and obedience to the pope and commitment to cooperation with directives from the Congregation for Religious and Secular Institutes.

Mother Mary Elise, S.N.D., of Chardon, O., is head of the group's national council.

The association publishes *Consortium* bimonthly.

The mailing address of the magazine is P.O. Box 1092, Washington, D.C. 20013.

Las Hermanas

Las Hermanas ("The Sisters") is a coalition of Spanish-speaking sisters (Mexican-, Hispano-American) formed in April, 1971. According to a constitution adopted seven months later at a national meeting held in Santa Fe, N.M., its purpose is "to actively present the ever-changing needs of the Hispanos so that, aware of our cultural heritage, we may function effectively in the community, thus developing that Christian humanism which is so essential to the People of God."

Resolutions passed by the 100 delegates from 41 communities called for: the formation of teams to sensitize religious communities and their members to the characteristics and needs of Mexican-American (Chicano) and Hispano culture; organizing team ministries to Chicanos; study of a proposal to form a community of Mexican-American ex-sisters. Delegates also looked forward hopefully to setting up a center for the religious formation of Chicana candidates for the sisterhood.

Officers elected at the meeting were: Sister Gloria Gallardo, pioneer of Las Hermanas, president; Sister Gregoria Ortega of Houston, vice president; Sister Maria Eloisa Rodriguez of Los Angeles, secretary; Sister Blanca Rosa Rodriguez, treasurer.

Contemplatives

The Association of Contemplative Sisters was founded by nearly 140 representatives of 57 communities in the US and Canada who took part in a two-week seminar for contemplatives held in August, 1969, at Woodstock College, Md. Its membership, in June, 1971, consisted of 850 sisters belonging to more than 100 communities in this country and Canada. A year later, the membership had increased to 1,000.

The purposes of the association are to encourage and foster healthy development of the contemplative life so that contemplative women may serve the Church more effectively, and to provide a vehicle of communication between the nuns, their communities and the Church at large.

In 1972, June 8 to July 20, the association sponsored an institute of contemplative studies in affiliation with Marquette University at Mt. St. Mary College, Milwaukee; it also conducted a three-phase leadership training program for contemplatives, between February and September, to assist entire communities through the sisters themselves.

The primary concerns of the annual meeting of the delegate assembly Oct. 25 to 30, 1972, in Adrian, Mich., were evaluation of the provisional set-up of the association and the establishment of goals for the next year.

Officers in 1972 were: Sister Vilma Seelaus, O.C.D., president, and coordinating committee members, Sisters: M. Jane Flynn, O.C.D.; Perrone Thibeaut, V.H.M.; Elizabeth Enoch, O.S.C.; Gertrude Wilkinson, O.SS.R. Sister Jean Alice McGoff, O.C.D., was chairlady of the delegate assembly.

The executive secretary was Sister Ann Ryan, 2475 Dodd Road, St. Paul, Minn. 55118.

ACS has offices in Esopus, N.Y. 12429.

Carmelites

Representatives of 24 of the nation's 65 communities of cloistered Carmelite nuns met in February, 1970, in Marriottsville, Md., for discussion of ways to foster cooperation and communication among themselves. Results of the four-day meeting at Bon Secours motherhouse were the formation of a loose association of independent Carmelite monasteries and the creation of an interim committee to obtain ideas for future developments and plans for follow-up meetings.

A statement of purpose issued by the 45 nuns at the meeting declared that "the member monasteries through corporate effort, study and sharing seek to collaborate in the work of renewal and adaptation."

The sisters set four aims for the member monasteries:

"(1) to facilitate mutual assistance and purposeful communication among themselves and with other related organizations; (2) to provide efficient representation with those in authority; (3) to make possible collaboration in the updating and revision of laws; (4) to accept and foster unity in diversity."

Other Conferences

International Organizations: The Union of Superiors General (Men), which was established in 1957, had its statutes approved by the Congregation for Religious and Secular Institutes in 1967, and has Pedro Arrupe, S.J., as president; the International Union of Superiors General (Women), which was established in 1965, had its statutes approved in 1967, and has M. Mary Linscatts, of the Sisters of Our Lady of Namur, as president.

Regional Organization: The Latin American Confederation of Religious, which was established in 1959, had its statutes approved in 1967, and has Manuel Edwards, SS.CC., as president.

Other Conferences: National conferences of superiors of religious, generally separate for

SECULAR INSTITUTES

(Sources: Almanac survey; *The Official Catholic Directory, 1972; Annuario Pontificio;* Conference of the Life of Total Dedication in the World, Rev. Stephen Hartdegen, O.F.M., Executive Secretary, 14th and Shepherd Sts. N.E., Washington, D.C. 20017.)

Secular institutes are societies of men and women living in the world who dedicate themselves by vow or promise to observe the evangelical counsels and to carry on apostolic works suitable to their talents and opportunities in the areas of their everyday life.

"Secular institutes are not religious communities but they carry with them in the world a profession of evangelical counsels which is genuine and complete, and recognized as such by the Church. This profession confers a consecration on men and women, laity and clergy, who reside in the world. For this reason they should chiefly strive for total self-dedication to God, one inspired by perfect charity. These institutes should preserve their proper and particular character, a secular one, so that they may everywhere measure up successfully to that apostolate which they were designed to exercise, and which is both in the world and, in a sense, of the world" *(Decree on the Appropriate Renewal of Religious Life,* No. 11; Second Vatican Council).

A secular institute reaches maturity in several stages. It begins as an association of the faithful, technically called a pious union, with the approval of a local bishop. Once it has proved its viability, he can give it the status of an institute of diocesan right, in accordance with norms and permission emanating from the Congregation for Religious and Secular Institutes. On issuance of a separate decree from this congregation, an institute of diocesan right becomes an institute of pontifical right.

Secular institutes, which originated in the latter part of the 18th century, were given full recognition and approval by Pius XII Feb. 2, 1947, in the apostolic constitution *Provida Mater Ecclesia.* On Mar. 25 of the same year a special commission for secular institutes was set up within the Congregation for Religious. Institutes were commended and confirmed by Pius XII in a motu proprio of Mar. 12, 1948, and were the subject of a special instruction issued a week later, Mar. 19, 1948.

Institutes in the US

Caritas Christi (Cultural Crossroads, Inc.): Originated in Marseilles, 1937; for women. Established as a secular institute of pontifical right Mar. 19, 1955. Address: Rev. Austin Green, O.P., national priest-assistant, 2131 Rowley Ave., Madison, Wis. 53705.

men and women, have been established in 17 countries in Europe, 14 in North and Central America, 10 in South America, 17 in Africa, and 18 in Asia and Australia.

Community of the Cenacle (Opus Cenaculi): Originated in Italy, 1952; for priests and laymen. Received formal decree of approval from the Congregation for Religious and Secular Institutes Oct. 29, 1953. Address: Via Aurelia 183, 00165, Rome, Italy. Msgr. Georges Roche, general superior; Msgr. Pedro Lopez-Gallo, general vicar and secretary; US superior, Rev. William Royce Hughes, Rt. 1, Jarrell, Tex. 76737.

Cordimarian Filiation (Daughters of the Immaculate Heart of Mary): Originated in Spain, 1850, by St. Anthony M. Claret; for women. Final approval by the Holy See, Dec. 8, 1959. Address, Rev. Joseph Gallego, C.M.F., 4541 S. Ashland Ave., Chicago, Ill. 60609. International membership of approximately 2,000.

Diocesan Laborer Priests: Approved as a secular institute of pontifical right. The specific aim of the institute is the promotion, sustenance and cultivation of apostolic, religious and priestly vocations. Delegate for US, Rev. John Queralt, 3706 15th St. N.E., Washington, D.C. 20017.

Handmaids of Jesus and Mary (Ancelles de Jesus-Maria): Originated in Versailles, France, 1947; for women. Recognized as a secular institute, 1961. Address: Madame la Superieure Generale des Ancelles de Jesus-Marie, Le Couarail, 46 bis rue Louis-Bleriot, Buc 78, France. International membership.

Institute of the Heart of Jesus: Originated in France Feb. 2, 1791; restored Oct. 29, 1918; for diocesan priests. Received final approval from the Holy See as a secular institute of pontifical right Feb. 2, 1952. Canon Jean Canivez, superior general. Addresses: Central House, 202 Avenue du Maine, Paris 14me, France; US address, Rev. Stewart Platt, 124 Keystone Ave., Campbell, O. 44405. International membership of approximately 1,900.

Missionaries of the Kingship of Christ: Originated in Assisi, Italy, 1919; for women. Established as an institute of pontifical right with decree of praise July 12, 1948; received final approbation Aug. 3, 1953. American establishment originated, 1950; first members received, Oct. 4, 1951; separate territory in the USA established May 9, 1970. Address: Rev. Stephen Hartdegen, O.F.M., Holy Name College, 14th and Shepherd Sts. N.E., Washington, D.C. 20017. International membership of women, approximately 4,000. Separate divisions for women, men, diocesan priests. In keeping with the Franciscan spirit of the institute, members belong to the Third Order of St. Francis.

Oblate Missionaries of Mary Immaculate: Founded, 1952, and approved as a secular institute Feb. 2, 1962; for women. Addresses: Oblate Missionaries of Mary Immaculate, 1510 West Church St., P.O. Box 650, Jeanerette, La. 70544; 7535 Boulevard Parent, Trois Rivieres, P. Q., Canada. International membership of approximately 1,000.

Rural Parish Workers of Christ the King: Originated in Cottleville, Mo., 1942; for women. An approved secular institute of the Archdiocese of St. Louis. Dedicated to the service of neighbor, especially in rural areas. Address: Box 300, Rt. 1, Cadet, Mo. 63630.

Schoenstatt Sisters of Mary: Originated in Schoenstatt, Germany, 1926; for women. Established as a secular institute of diocesan right May 20, 1948; of pontifical right Oct. 18, 1948. Addresses: Schoenstatt Sisters of Mary, 5831 Cottage Grove Rd., Madison, Wis. 53716; House Schoenstatt, Star Rt. 1, Box 100, Rockport, Tex. 78382. International membership of more than 2,500.

Secular Institute of Pius X: Originated in Manchester, N.H., 1940; for priests and laymen. Approved as a secular institute, 1959 (first secular institute of diocesan right founded in the US to be approved by the Holy See). Rev. Rosaire Dugas, director. Addresses: P.O. Box 357, Manchester, N.H. 03101; P.O. Box 1815, Quebec City, P.Q., Canada.

Society of Our Lady of the Way: Originated, 1936; for women. Approved as a secular institute of pontifical right Jan. 3, 1953. Address: Society of Our Lady of the Way, 2339 N. Catalina Ave., Los Angeles, Calif. 90027. International membership of more than 400.

Teresian Institute: Originated in Spain; for women. Approved as a secular institute of pontifical right. US address: 15500 N.W. 32nd Ave., Opa Locka, Fla. 33054.

Voluntas Dei: Originated in Canada, 1958; for secular priests and laymen. Approved as a secular institute May 6, 1965. Address: Institute Voluntas Dei, 7385, Blvd. Parent, Trois-Rivieres, Que., Canada. International membership of approximately 150.

The *Annuario Pontificio* (1972) lists the following **secular institutes of pontifical right which are not established in the US:**

For men: Company of St. Paul (originated Nov. 17, 1920; decree of praise, June 30, 1950). Institute of Prado (originated Dec. 25, 1856; decree of praise, Oct. 28, 1959). Soldiers of Christ the King (originated, 1936; decree of praise, Oct. 27, 1963).

For women: Alliance in Jesus through Mary, Apostles of the Sacred Heart, Catechists of the Sacred Heart of Jesus (Ukrainian), Daughters of the Sacred Heart, Daughters of the Queen of the Apostles, Institute of the Blessed Virgin Mary (della Strada), Missionaries of the Sick, Institute of Notre Dame du Travail, Institute of Our Lady of Life, Company of St. Ursula, Oblates of Christ the King, Workers of Divine Love, Faithful Servants of Jesus.

Associations

Caritas: Originated in New Orleans, 1950; for women. Address: 3316 Feliciana St., New Orleans, La. 70126.

Daughters of Our Lady of Fatima: Originated in Lansdowne, Pa., 1949; for women. Received diocesan approval, Jan., 1952. Address: Miss Mary C. Long, Fatima House, Rolling Hills Rd., Ottsville, Pa. 18942.

Focolare Movement: Inaugurated in Trent, Italy, in 1943, by Chiara Lubich and a small group of companions; for men and women. Approved as an association of the faithful, 1962. It is not a secular institute by statute, but vows are observed by many single persons among its totally dedicated core membership of 1,500. Centers are located in 26 countries throughout the world. US centers are located in Boston, Chicago (where it was introduced in 1955), and New York. National headquarters and publication office of the bimonthly *Living City:* 360 E. 65th St., New York, N.Y. 10021.

Jesus Caritas Fraternity of Fr. Charles de Foucauld: Originated in Ars, France, 1952; for women. Established as an association of perfection May 31, 1962. Address: Miss A. M. de Commaille, 185 Claremont Ave., New York, N. Y. 10027. International membership of approximately 550.

Little Brothers of the Poor (Friends of the Elderly): Originated in Paris, 1946. The group has the status of a pious union and was given permission in 1959 by Cardinal Albert Meyer to establish a fraternity in Chicago. Dedicated to service of the poor, especially the elderly. US address: 1658 W. Belmont St., Chicago, Ill. 60657.

Madonna House Apostolate: Originated in Toronto, Canada, 1930; for priests and lay persons. The constitutions of Madonna House were approved on a diocesan basis in July, 1956. Address: Madonna House, Combermere, Ontario, Canada—Catherine Doherty (women), Louis Stoekle (men), Rev. J. T. Callahan (priests). International membership. **Pax Christi** (St. Francis Center): Originated in Greenwood, Miss., 1952; for women. Received diocesan approval, 1957. Kate Jordan, director, Central House, 708 Avenue I, Greenwood, Miss. 38930.

Pax Christi: Lay institute of men and women dedicated to witnessing to Christ, with special emphasis on service to the poor in Mississippi. Mis Genevieve Feyen, president, 2108 Altawoods Blvd., Jackson, Miss. 39204.

Anniversary

The 25th anniversary of the apostolic constitution *Provida Mater Ecclesia,* the charter for secular institutes, was marked in 1972. One feature of the observance was the establishment by institute representatives of an international liasion network.

THIRD ORDERS SECULAR

Third orders secular are societies of the faithful living in the world who seek to deepen their Christian life and apostolic commitment in association with and according to the spirit of various religious institutes. Members are called Tertiaries, Lay Franciscans, etc. The orders are called "third" because their foundation followed the establishment of the first (for men) and second (for women) religious orders with which they are associated.

Augustine, Third Order Secular of St.: Founded, 13th century; approved Nov. 7, 1400.

Carmel, (The Lay Carmelite Order) (Calced): Founded, 13th century; approved by Pope Nicholas V, Oct. 7, 1452. Address: Aylesford, National Scapular Center, Rt. 66 and Cass Ave. N. Westmont, Ill. 60559. Approximately 15,000 members in US.

Carmel, Third Order Secular of Our Blessed Lady of Mt., and St. Teresa of Jesus (Discalced): Rule based on the Carmelite reform established by St. Teresa and St. John of the Cross, 16th century; approved Mar. 23, 1594. Addresses of provincial directors: 514 Warren St., Brookline, Mass. 02146; Marylake, Star Route, Little Rock, Ark. 72206; P.O. Box 3079 San Jose, Calif. 95116. Approximately 3,150 members in US.

Dominic, Third Order Secular of St. (The Dominican Laity): Founded in the 13th century. Addresses of provincial directors: 141 E. 65th St., New York, N.Y. 10021; 1909 S. Ashland Ave., Chicago, Ill. 60608; St. Albert's College, 5890 Birch Ct., Oakland, Calif. 94618.

Francis, Third Order Secular of St. (Secular Franciscans): Founded, 1209 by St. Francis of Assisi; approved Aug. 30, 1221. Address: National Secretary, Third Order of St. Francis, 1615 Vine St., Cincinnati, Ohio 45210. Approximately 2.2 million in the world, 62,000 English speaking in North America.

Mary, Third Order of: Founded, Dec. 8, 1850; rule approved by the Holy See, 1857. Addresses of provincial directors: 87 Lacy St., Marietta, Ga. 30060; 27 Isabella St., Boston, Mass. 02117; 1675 Grand Ave., San Raphael, Calif. Approximately 14,000 in the world, 6,600 in US.

Mary, Third Order Secular of Servants of (Servite): Founded, 1233; approved, 1424. Address: Director of Third Order, 323 W. Illinois St., Chicago, Ill. 60610. Approximately 3,500 in US.

Mercy, Secular Third Order of Our Lady of (Mercedarian): Founded, 1219 by St. Peter Nolasco; approved the same year.

Norbert, Third Order of St.: Founded, 1122 by St. Norbert; approved by Pope Honorius II, 1126. Address: St. Norbert Abbey, De Pere, Wis. Approximately 5,300 in US and Canada.

Trinity, Third Order Secular of the Most

Holy: Founded, about 1198; approved, 1219. Address: Bro. Mathew Stephan, St. John de Matha, Monastery, 4301 Madison St., Hyattsville, Md. 20781.

Oblates of St. Benedict are lay persons affiliated with a Benedictine abbey or monastery who strive to direct their lives, as circumstances permit, according to the spirit and Rule of St. Benedict.

Franciscan Congress

Prayer, poverty and peace were the principal themes of a "statement of commitment" adopted by some 500 delegates to the Lay Franciscan Congress at Santa Clara University in August, 1972.

Delegates from the North American Federation of the Third Order of St. Francis called for the "prayer and presence" of its members to be "more open, joyful, personal, sensitive, frequent, Gospel-centered and repentant."

Acknowledging that the Franciscan movement allows "diversity in prayer forms and styles," the delegates declared:

"The goals of the Catholic Charismatic Movement — namely, repentance, faith, commitment to Jesus Christ as Lord and Savior, and an openness to the gifts of the Spirit to the glory of the Father — are goals essential to the life of the Church and are in harmony with the personal and communal vocation of Franciscans."

On poverty, they said: "We must be prophetic witnesses against the materialism of our society and light the lamp of evangelical poverty in order to project and radiate the spirit of servanthood."

The congress declared that members "must be ready to give of ourselves and truly to be of personal service to our brothers and sisters — not as lords but as servants. That this servanthood is incompatible with capitalism is not certain to some of us, but we are united in our determination to resist comsumerism."

The lay Franciscans also noted their commitment "to follow the path of reconciliation, the path to unity, peace and fraternity . . . to reverse the process by which men are divided . . . to become aware of those prejudices and learned emotional responses which divide us and make worlds of brotherhood a mockery."

Calling for a total effort of non-violence, reconciliation and peace, the congress acknowledged its responsibility "for the issues of world justice and peace and to educating ourselves to the sins of exploitation and violence, seeking to awaken our government and our society to the injustices and evils that are perpetrated in the administration of justice to the poor, abortion and the right to life, unjust welfare and tax laws, denial of adequate housing, unjust treatment of prisoners and the injustice of war."

The congress elected William E. Corcoran of Cincinnati president.

Missionary Activity of the Church

The following excerpts concerning the Church's missionary activity are from the decree of the same name promulgated by the Second Vatican Council.

Doctrine

"The pilgrim Church is missionary by her very nature" (No. 2).

Christ "founded His Church as the sacrament of salvation, and sent His apostles into all the world just as He Himself had been sent by His Father (cf. Jn. 20:21). He gave them this command: 'Go, therefore, and make disciples of all nations, baptizing them in the name of the Father, and of the Son, and of the Holy Spirit, teaching them to observe all that I have commanded you' (Mt. 28:19ff). 'Go into the whole world; preach the gospel to every creature. He who believes and is baptized shall be saved, but he who does not believe shall be condemned' (Mk. 16:15ff).

". . . The mission of the Church . . . is fulfilled by that activity which makes her fully present to all men and nations" (No. 5).

" 'Missions' is the term usually given to those particular undertakings by which the heralds of the gospel are sent out by the Church and go forth into the whole world to carry out the task of preaching the gospel and planting the Church among peoples or groups who do not yet believe in Christ. These undertakings are brought to completion by missionary activity and are commonly exercised in certain territories recognized by the Holy See" (and placed under the general direction of the Congregation for the Evangelization of Peoples) (No. 6).

Distinctive Purpose

"The specific purpose of this missionary activity is evangelization and the planting of the Church among those peoples and groups where she has not yet taken root. Thus from the seed which is the Word of God, particular native Churches can be adequately established and flourish the world over, endowed with their own vitality and maturity. Thus too, sufficiently provided with a hierarchy of their own which is joined to a faithful people, and adequately fitted out with requisites for living a full Christian life, they can make their contribution to the good of the Church universal.

". . . Missionary activity among the nations differs from pastoral activity exercised among the faithful, as well as from undertakings aimed at restoring unity among Christians. And yet these two other activities are most closely connected with the missionary zeal of the Church, because the division among Christians damages the most holy cause of preaching the gospel to every creature and blocks the way to the faith for many. Hence, by the same mandate which makes missions necessary, all the baptized are called to be gathered into one flock, and thus to be able to bear unanimous witness before the nations to Christ their Lord. And if they are not yet capable of bearing full witness to the same faith, they should at least be animated by mutual esteem and love" (No. 6).

"Missionary activity is nothing else and nothing less than a manifestation or epiphany of God's will, and the fulfillment of that will in the world and in world history. In the course of this history God plainly works out the history of salvation by means of mission. By the preaching of the word and by the celebration of the sacraments, whose center and summit is the most holy Eucharist, missionary activity brings about the presence of Christ, the Author of salvation" (No. 9).

The three phases of missionary activity are:

• **Christian Witness,** to establish the presence of the Church: "The Church must be present in these groups of men through those of her children who dwell among them or are sent to them. For, wherever they live, all Christians are bound to show forth, by the example of their lives and by the witness of their speech, that new man which they put on at baptism, and that power of the Holy Spirit by whom they were strengthened at confirmation. Thus other men, observing their good works, can glorify the Father (cf. Mt. 5:16) and can better perceive the real meaning of human life and the bond which ties the whole community of mankind together" (No. 11).

• **Preaching the Gospel and Gathering Together the People of God,** through proclamation of the Gospel to conversion and on to transition to full Christian life. In this process: "The Church strictly forbids forcing anyone to embrace the faith, or alluring or enticing people by unworthy techniques. By the same token, she also strongly insists on a person's right not to be deterred from the faith by unjust vexations on the part of others" (No. 13).

• **Forming the Christian Community,** with the objective of developing, sustaining and self-supporting churches in mission lands through the various ministries of lay persons, bishops, priests, deacons and religious (Nos. 15 to 18).

Concerning the role of lay persons, the decree said: "Laymen cooperate in the Church's work of evangelization. As witnesses and at the same time as living instruments, they share in her saving mission. This is especially so if they have been called by God and have been accepted by the bishop for this work" (No. 41).

UNITED STATES FOREIGN MISSIONARIES

Data on US foreign missionary personnel in the following tables were gathered by, and are reproduced with permission of, the United States Catholic Mission Council, 1325 Massachusetts Ave. N.W., Washington, D.C., 20005.

The last detailed compilation of statistics on US priests, religious and lay persons in overseas assignments was completed and published in 1968.

(For additional information about the Church in mission areas, see News Events and other Almanac entries.)

Field Distribution, 1972

Area Country	Men	Women	Total
Africa	**636**	**471**	**1,107**
Afars and Issas		2	2
Algeria		1	1
Botswana		3	3
Burundi	1		1
Cameroon	2	16	18
Dahomey	1		1
Ethiopia	20	6	26
Ghana	61	51	112
Ivory Coast		1	1
Kenya	59	68	127
Lesotho	12	20	32
Liberia	32	29	61
Malagasy Rep.	15		15
Malawi	32	41	73
Morocco	1	1	2
Mozambique		1	1
Nigeria	33	35	68
Rhodesia	12	6	18
Rwanda		1	1
Senegal	2	1	3
Sierra Leone	5	4	9
South Africa	34	12	46
South-West Africa	3		3
Swaziland	2	3	5
Tanzania	163	78	241
Tunisia	1	1	2
Uganda	75	43	118
Upper Volta	2	2	4
Zaire	6	20	26
Zambia	62	25	87
Near East	**43**	**16**	**59**
Afghanistan		3	3
Bahrain	1		1
Egypt	7	5	12
Iran	1		1
Israel	12	2	14
Jordan		1	1
Lebanon	19	5	24
Saudi Arabia	1		1
Syria	1		1
Yemen	1		1

Area Country	Men	Women	Total
Far East	**1,324**	**631**	**1,955**
Bangladesh	45	19	64
Burma	9		9
Hong Kong	41	70	111
India	118	82	200
Indonesia	42	10	52
Japan	230	125	355
Korea	120	55	175
Laos	2	1	3
Malaysia	3	8	11
Nepal	18		18
Pakistan	26	39	65
Philippines	477	120	597
Singapore	3	2	5
Sri Lanka (Ceylon)	15	3	18
Taiwan	125	84	209
Thailand	37	8	45
Vietnam	13	5	18
Oceania	**329**	**497**	**826**
Australia	10	36	46
Caroline Islands	44	15	59
Fiji Islands	10	23	33
Guam	32	118	150
Hawaii	35	172	207
Mariana Islands	5	3	8
Marshall Islands	4	7	11
New Caledonia	2	1	3
New Guinea	153	80	233
New Hebrides	3	2	5
New Zealand	1	3	4
Ryukyu Islands	17	4	21
Samoa	8	11	19
Solomon Islands	4	13	17
Tonga Islands	1	9	10
Europe	**20**	**19**	**39**
Cyprus	4		4
Denmark	6	1	7
Finland		11	11
Greece		2	2
Italy	2	2	4
Norway	1		1
Sweden	6	2	8
Turkey	1	1	2
North America	**98**	**136**	**234**
Alaska	76	66	142
Canada	21	70	91
Greenland	1		1
Caribbean Islands	**389**	**430**	**819**
Antigua		2	2
Bahamas	10	32	42
Barbados		10	10
Cayman	1		1
Cuba		1	1
Dominica		3	3

Area Country	Men	Women	Total
Dominican Rep.	31	2	33
Grenada	1	6	7
Haiti	35	18	53
Jamaica	116	79	195
Puerto Rico	180	245	425
St. Lucia	2	5	7
Trinidad		2	2
Virgin Islands	13	25	38
Central America	**444**	**284**	**728**
Br. Honduras	31	21	52
Costa Rica	13	22	35
El Salvador	29	19	48
Guatemala	111	88	199
Honduras	47	22	69
Mexico	133	57	190
Nicaragua	48	30	78
Panama	32	25	57
South America	**1,024**	**858**	**1,882**
Argentina	25	9	34
Bolivia	154	139	293
Brazil	352	182	534
Chile	85	132	217
Colombia	34	61	95
Ecuador	14	12	26
Guyana	1	11	12
Paraguay	29	5	34
Peru	287	261	548
Uruguay	1	3	4
Venezuela	42	43	85
Totals 1972	**4,307**	**3,342**	**7,649**

US Priests and Brothers, 1972

Listed below are 78 mission-sending groups, the number of priests and brothers each had in overseas assignments, and areas of service. The total number of US priests and brothers serving abroad was 3,902.

Maryknoll Fathers 713
Bolivia, 62; Chile, 48; Colombia, 3; El Salvador, 9; Guatemala, 45; Hawaii, 33; Hong Kong, 32; Japan, 75; Kenya, 18; Korea, 61; Mexico, 30; Peru, 56; Philippines, 60; Taiwan, 71; Tanzania, 89; Uganda, 2; Venezuela, 19.

Jesuits 702
Alaska, 38; Argentina, 7; Australia, 1; Brazil, 17; Br. Honduras, 28; Carolines, 44; Cayman Island, 1; Chile, 10; Colombia, 2; Dominican Republic, 1; Ecuador, 3; Egypt, 6; Guam, 4; Honduras, 17; Hong Kong, 1; India, 102; Jamaica, 88; Japan, 21; Korea, 22; Lebanon, 14; Malawi, 2; Marshall Islands, 4; Mexico, 10; Nepal, 18; Nigeria, 4; Peru, 29; Philippines, 116; Puerto Rico, 20; Rhodesia, 1; Saudi Arabia, 1; Sri Lanka (Ceylon), 15; Syria, 1; Taiwan, 28; Tanzania, 1;

Thailand, 3; Uganda, 2; Venezuela, 2; Vietnam, 2; Zambia, 16.

Franciscans (Friars Minor) 267
Bolivia, 24; Brazil, 98; Cyprus, 4; Egypt, 1; El Salvador, 8; Guatemala, 10; Honduras, 17; Hong Kong, 4; Israel, 11; Jamaica, 3; Japan, 27; Korea, 1; Lebanon, 3; Mexico, 4; Peru, 2; Philippines, 45; Puerto Rico, 4; Singapore, 1.

Divine Word Missionaries 205
Argentina, 2; Australia, 4; Brazil, 2; Chile, 1; Ecuador, 1; Ghana, 37; India, 5; Indonesia, 10; Japan, 8; Mexico, 7; New Guinea, 78; Paraguay, 2; Philippines, 44; Taiwan, 4.

Redemptorists 197
Brazil, 89; Dominican Republic, 8; Honduras, 1; Paraguay, 11; Puerto Rico, 52; Thailand, 27; Virgin Islands, 9.

Oblates of Mary Immaculate 172
Alaska, 2; Bolivia, 3; Brazil, 28; Canada, 6; Chile, 2; Denmark, 6; Greenland, 1; Haiti, 30; Hong Kong, 2; Japan, 18; Laos, 2; Lesotho, 1; Mexico, 28; Philippines, 36; South Africa, 1; Sweden, 6.

Franciscans (Capuchins) 155
Bahrain, 1; Guam, 22; Honduras, 6; Marianas, 5; Nicaragua, 37; Papua-New Guinea, 38; Puerto Rico, 23; Ryukyu, 17; Zambia, 6.

Benedictines 106
Bahamas, 8; Brazil, 17; Br. Honduras, 3; Colombia, 9; El Salvador, 2; Guatemala, 16; Japan, 4; Mexico, 7; Peru, 12; Puerto Rico, 20; Taiwan, 8.

Marianists 99
Australia, 2; Chile, 1; Japan, 10; Kenya, 11; Lebanon, 2; Malawi, 14; Nigeria, 3; Peru, 32; Puerto Rico, 17; Zambia, 7.

Columbans 93
Australia, 2; Burma, 1; Fiji, 6; Japan, 5; Korea, 24; Peru, 9; Philippines, 42; Vietnam, 1; Virgin Islands, 3.

Dominicans 85
Bolivia, 14; Ghana, 4; Mexico, 4; Nigeria, 23; Pakistan, 25; Peru, 14; Philippines, 1.

Passionists 70
Italy, 1; Jamaica, 15; Japan, 9; Korea, 4; Philippines, 41.

Holy Cross Brothers 67
Bangladesh, 18; Brazil, 19; Ghana, 12; Liberia, 8; Uganda, 10.

Brothers of Christian Schools 66
Ethiopia, 17; Guatemala, 11; Hong Kong, 1; Kenya, 3; Nicaragua, 10; Philippines, 21; Singapore, 1; Tanzania, 1; Uganda, 1.

Holy Ghost Fathers 64
Mexico, 4; Puerto Rico, 25; Tanzania, 34; Uganda, 1.

Franciscans (Conventuals) 56

Brazil, 19; Costa Rica, 12; Honduras, 1; Japan, 7; Malawi, 1; Zambia, 16.
Holy Cross Fathers 55
Bangladesh, 26; Peru, 1; Puerto Rico, 1; Uganda, 27.
La Salette Fathers 53
Argentina, 10; Burma, 8; Malagasy, 13; Philippines, 22.
Sacred Heart Brothers 43
Kenya, 4; Lesotho, 10; Rhodesia, 6; Uganda, 11; Zambia, 12.
Vincentians 39
Hong Kong, 1; Iran, 1; Malagasy, 1; Nigeria, 1; Panama, 22; Taiwan, 12; Vietnam, 1.
White Fathers 35
Australia, 1; Dahomey, 1; Ghana, 5; Malawi, 4; Tanzania, 10; Uganda, 6; Upper Volta, 1; Zaire, 3; Zambia, 4.
Marist Fathers 29
Fiji, 4; New Caledonia, 2; New Guinea, 11; New Hebrides, 3; Samoa, 4; Solomons, 4; Tonga, 1.
Missionaries of the Sacred Heart 27
Colombia, 5; New Guinea, 21; Swaziland, 1.
Society of African Missions 25
Liberia, 24; Nigeria, 1.
Franciscans (Third Order Regular) 25
Brazil, 13; India, 5; Paraguay, 6; Turkey, 1.
Marist Brothers 24
Japan, 7; Malaysia, 1; Malawi, 2; Philippines, 13; Singapore, 1.
Augustinians 24
Japan, 6; Peru, 18.
Xaverian Brothers 23
Bolivia, 8; Kenya, 15.
Atonement Friars 22
Brazil, 10; Japan, 12.
Salvatorians 22
Mexico, 1; Tanzania, 21.
Precious Blood Fathers 20
Chile, 15; Peru, 5.
Oblates of St. Francis de Sales 20
Brazil, 7; South Africa, 10; South-West Africa, 3.
Crosier Fathers 19
Indonesia.
Immaculate Heart Missioners 16
Brazil, 1; Dominican Republic, 12; Guatemala, 1; Haiti, 1; Japan, 1.
Priests of the Sacred Heart 16
Indonesia, 7; South Africa, 8; Zaire, 1.
Blessed Sacrament Fathers 16
Philippines, 10; Tanzania, 1; Uganda, 5.
Trinitarians 16
Puerto Rico.
Christian Brothers 13
Peru, 11; South Africa, 2.
Salesians 13
Chile, 1; Dominican Republic, 2; Ecuador, 2; India, 1; Japan, 2; Korea, 4; Peru, 1.
Sacred Hearts Fathers 13
Japan.

Claretians 12
Guatemala, 5; Philippines, 7.
Viatorians 12
Colombia, 7; Japan, 3; Taiwan, 2.
Discalced Carmelites 12
Philippines.
Xaverian Fathers 12
Bangladesh, 1; Brazil, 3; Japan, 1; Mexico, 1; Sierra Leone, 5; Zaire, 1.
Verona Fathers 11
Ecuador, 1; Ethiopia, 1; Mexico, 1; Peru, 1; South Africa, 2; Uganda, 5.
Carmelites 11
Chile, 1; Peru, 10.
Stigmatines 11
Brazil, 3; Canada, 1; Thailand, 7.
Servites 9
South Africa, 8; Swaziland, 1.
Brothers of Christian Instruction 7
Pakistan, 1; Tanzania, 1; Uganda, 5.
Sons of Mary 6
Peru.
Norbertines 6
Peru.
Montfort Fathers 6
Haiti, 1; Indonesia, 4; Malawi, 1.
Edmundites 6
Venezuela.
Sulpicians 6
Argentina, 1; Guatemala, 1; Hawaii, 2; Japan, 1; Mexico, 1.
Mariannhill Fathers 5
New Guinea, 1; Rhodesia, 2; South Africa, 2.
Mill Hill Missionaries 5
Kenya, 1; Malaysia, 1; Philippines, 2; W. Cameroon, 1.
Missionaries of the Holy Family 5
Mexico.
Missionaries of the Holy Apostles 5
Brazil, 3; Peru, 2.
Augustinian Recollects 5
Dominican Republic, 3; Mexico, 2.
Assumptionists 4
Chile, Mexico, New Zealand, Zaire.
Consolata Fathers 4
Ethiopia, 1; Kenya, 3.
Marian Fathers 4
Argentina.
Basilian Fathers 3
Mexico.
Glenmary Home Missioners 2
Colombia.
Franciscan Brothers 2
Canada, Mexico.
PIME Missionaries 2
Brazil, Philippines.
Quebec Foreign Missions 2
Philippines.
Hospitaller Brothers 1
Korea.
Josephites (SSJ) 1
Bahamas.

Patrons of the Missions are Sts. Francis Xavier and Therese of Lisieux.

US Diocesan Priests, 1972

Listed below are 91 US dioceses, the number of priests each had in overseas assignments, and areas of service. The total number of US diocesan priests serving abroad was 244.

Agana (Guam): 1.
Albany, N.Y.: 3 (Alaska, 2; Peru, 1).
Allentown, Pa.: 1 (Guam).
Altoona-Johnstown, Pa.: 1 (Paraguay).
Amarillo, Tex.: 1 (Mexico).
Atlanta,* Ga.: 1 (Peru).

Baltimore,* Md.: 1 (Peru).
Baton Rouge, La.: 1 (Guatemala).
Belleville, Ill.: 1 (Guatemala).
Birmingham, Ala.: 2 (Peru, Brazil).
Boise, Ida.: 2 (Colombia).
Boston,* Mass.: 27 (Alaska, 2; Puerto Rico, 1; Peru, 16; Virgin, Is., 1; Bolivia, 5; Ecuador, 2).
Bridgeport, Conn.: 6 (Brazil, 2; Peru, 3; Philippines, 1).
Brooklyn, N.Y.: 6 (Korea, 1; Norway, 1; Paraguay, 4).
Buffalo, N.Y.: 5 (Bolivia, 2; Peru, 2; Puerto Rico, 1).
Burlington, Vt.: 3 (Bolivia, 1; Peru, 2).

Camden, N.J.: 8 (Brazil).
Charleston, S.C.: 1 (Peru).
Chicago,* Ill.: 6 (Bolivia, 1; Panama, 5).
Cincinnati,* O.: 1 (Brazil).
Cleveland, O.: 6 (El Salvador).

Dallas, Tex.: 1 (Peru).
Denver,* Colo.: 1 (Latin America).
Des Moines, Iowa: 1 (Bolivia).
Detroit,* Mich.: 2 (Brazil).
Dodge City, Kans.: 1 (Venezuela).
Dubuque,* Iowa: 3 (Bolivia).

Fall River, Mass.: 1 (Bolivia).
Fargo, N.D.: 2 (Peru).
Fort Wayne-S. Bend, Ind.: 1 (Panama).

Galveston-Houston, Tex.: 4 (Korea, 1; Guatemala, 3).
Grand Island, Neb.: 1 (Brazil).
Green Bay, Wis.: 3 (Dominican Republic, 2; Mexico, 1).

Helena, Mont.: 4 (Guatemala, 3; Mexico, 1).

Indianapolis,* Ind.: 1 (Bolivia).

Jefferson City, Mo.: 8 (Peru).
Joliet, Ill.: 1 (Ecuador).

Kansas City-St. Joseph, Mo.: 7 (Bolivia).
Kansas City,* Kans.: 1 (Brazil).

La Crosse, Wis.: 4 (Bolivia, 3; Peru, 1).
Lafayette, Ind.: 1 (Peru).
Lafayette, La.: 1 (Mexico).

Lansing, Mich.: 1 (Peru).
Lincoln, Neb.: 1 (Venezuela).
Little Rock, Ark.: 1 (Mexico).
Los Angeles,* Calif.: 2 (Panama, Peru).
Louisville,* Ky.: 1 (Peru).

Manchester, N.H.: 2 (Colombia).
Marquette, Mich.: 1 (Panama).
Miami,* Fla.: 1 (Peru).
Milwaukee,* Wis.: 4 (Grenada, 1; Paraguay, 3).
Mobile, Ala.: 2 (Bolivia, Peru).

Natchez-Jackson, Miss.: 3 (Mexico).
Newark,* N.J.: 3 (Argentina, Brazil, Panama).
New Orleans,* La.: 1 (Mexico).
New Ulm, Minn.: 2 (Guatemala).

Ogdensburg, N.Y.: 5 (Peru).
Oklahoma City-Tulsa, Okla.: 3 (Guatemala).
Orlando, Fla.: 1 (Ecuador).

Paterson, N.J.: 2 (Bolivia).
Peoria, Ill.: 1 (Mexico).
Philadelphia,* Pa.: 5 (Italy, 1; Venezuela, 3; Vietnam, 1).
Phoenix, Ariz.: 1 (Mexico).
Pittsburgh, Pa.: 5 (Peru).
Portland, Me.: 1 (Tanzania).
Pueblo, Colo.: 1 (Guam).

Raleigh, N.C.: 2 (Mexico).
Richmond, Va.: 1 (Peru).
Rockford, Ill.: 2 (Peru).

Sacramento, Calif.: 1 (Korea).
Saginaw, Mich.: 1 (Mexico).
St. Cloud, Minn.: 6 (Venezuela, 4; Guam, 1; Malawi, 1).
St. Louis,* Mo.: 14 (Bolivia, 11; Venezuela, 1; Chile, 2).
St. Paul-Minneapolis,* Minn.: 3 (Alaska, 1; Venezuela, 2).
St. Petersburg, Fla.: 1 (Kenya).
San Antonio,* Tex.: 1 (Guatemala).
San Diego, Calif.: 1 (Bolivia).
San Francisco,* Calif.: 1 (Guatemala).
Santa Rosa, Calif.: 1 (Zambia).
Sioux City, Iowa: 2 (Peru).
Spokane, Wash.: 2 (Guatemala).
Steubenville, O.: 1 (Peru).
Syracuse, N.Y.: 2 (Ecuador, Peru).

Trenton, N.J.: 2 (Bolivia, Peru).

Wheeling, W. Va.: 1 (Guatemala).
Wichita, Kans.: 4 (Venezuela, 3; Mexico, 1).
Winona, Minn.: 3 (Bahamas, Bolivia, Peru).
Worcester, Mass.: 2 (Peru).

Yakima, Wash.: 1 (Guatemala).
Youngstown, O.: 5 (El Salvador, 2; Guatemala, Mexico, Tanzania).

Melkite Exarchate: 1 (Israel).

US Sisters, 1972

Listed below are 107 mission-sending groups, the number of sisters each had in overseas mission assignments, and areas of service; also listed are five sisters whose group affiliation was unspecified. The total number of sisters serving abroad was 3,127.

Maryknoll Sisters 611
Bolivia, 45; Carolines, 6; Chile, 50; Dominican Republic, 1; El Salvador, 3; Guatemala, 36; Hawaii, 91; Hong Kong, 63; Japan, 30; Kenya, 19; Korea, 32; Marianas, 1; Marshalls, 7; Mexico, 11; Nicaragua, 12; Panama, 12; Peru, 30; Philippines, 71; Taiwan, 29; Tanzania, 56; Uganda, 3; Zambia, 3.

Franciscans 295
Bolivia, 12; Brazil, 37; Chile, 8; Colombia, 9; Costa Rica, 10; Ecuador, 1; Guatemala, 4; Hawaii, 42; Honduras, 4; Hong Kong, 1; India, 1; Indonesia, 1; Jamaica, 29; Japan, 10; Kenya, 5; Mexico, 8; New Guinea, 14; Nicaragua, 4; Peru, 23; Philippines, 5; Puerto Rico, 39; Taiwan, 11; Tanzania, 2; Uganda, 6; Venezuela, 8; Zambia, 1.

Sisters of St. Joseph (C.S.J.) 157
Alaska, 2; Brazil, 9; Cameroon, 1; India, 8; Japan, 18; Liberia, 3; New Guinea, 10; Panama, 4; Peru, 32; Philippines, 6; Puerto Rico, 62; Sweden, 2.

Sisters of Mercy 137
Alaska, 3; Argentina, 2; Bahamas, 1; Br. Honduras, 15; Chile, 6; Colombia, 2; Costa Rica, 2; Guam, 52; Guatemala, 2; Guyana, 8; Honduras, 11; India, 6; Jamaica, 6; Panama, 8; Peru, 7; Philippines, 7.

School Sisters of Notre Dame 123
Argentina, 3; Bolivia, 5; Brazil, 1; Chile, 7; Guam, 47; Guatemala, 6; Honduras, 4; Japan, 13; Liberia, 4; Paraguay, 3; Puerto Rico, 26; Ryukyu Is., 4.

Dominicans 119
Alaska, 1; Bahamas, 11; Bolivia, 8; Canada, 1; Colombia, 4; Ecuador, 2; El Salvador, 2; Guatemala, 3; India, 2; Jamaica, 21; Kenya, 8; Malawi, 1; Mexico, 8; Nigeria, 9; Pakistan, 9; Peru, 22; Puerto Rico, 6; Upper Volta, 1.

Marists 119
Australia, 13; Fiji, 23; Hawaii, 1; Jamaica, 13; New Caledonia, 1; New Guinea, 16; New Hebrides, 2; New Zealand, 3; Peru, 15; Samoa, 10; Solomons, 13; Tonga, 9.

Servants of Immaculate Heart of Mary 94
Brazil, 7; Chile, 11; India, 1; Peru, 38; Puerto Rico, 33; Uganda, 4.

Catholic Medical Missionaries 92
Afghanistan, 2; Bangladesh, 1; Ghana, 21; India, 17; Kenya, 2; Pakistan, 19;

Swaziland, 1; Uganda, 12; Venezuela, 16; Vietnam, 1.

Franciscan Missionaries of Mary 80
Australia, 13; Colombia, 2; Ghana, 1; India, 11; Indonesia, 5; Israel, 1; Japan, 8; Korea, 2; Liberia, 8; Malaysia, 6; Mexico, 2; Mozambique, 1; New Guinea, 2; Pakistan, 6; Peru, 1; Senegal, 1; Singapore, 1; South Africa, 5; Sri Lanka (Ceylon), 3; Upper Volta, 1.

Benedictines 73
Bahamas, 6; Brazil, 10; Chile, 8; Colombia, 21; Guatemala, 8; Japan, 5; Korea, 1; Peru, 2; Puerto Rico, 5; Taiwan, 5; Tanzania, 2.

Notre Dame Sisters 70
Brazil, 7; Hawaii, 4; India, 14; Japan, 13; Kenya, 16; New Guinea, 13; Zaire, 3.

Daughters of Charity 66
Bolivia, 32; Cameroon, 1; Japan, 10; Puerto Rico, 12; Taiwan, 5; Thailand, 1; Zaire, 5.

Ursulines 60
Alaska, 3; Barbados, 1; Botswana, 3; Brazil, 3; Chile, 5; Denmark, 1; El Salvador, 2; Greece, 2; Guyana, 2; Indonesia, 3; Mexico, 10; Peru, 6; Puerto Rico, 4; Taiwan, 1; Thailand, 7; Venezuela, 4; Zambia, 3.

Holy Cross Srs. (Notre Dame) 42
Bangladesh, 15; Brazil, 19; Uganda, 8.

Servants of the Holy Spirit 42
Australia, 9; Ghana, 13; India, 4; New Guinea, 6; Philippines, 4; Taiwan, 4; Japan, 2.

Most Precious Blood Srs. 34
Bolivia, 5; Chile, 10; Finland, 11; Peru, 8.

Srs. of Charity of St. Vincent de Paul 34
Bahamas, 9; Bolivia, 3; Canada, 1; Guatemala, 2; Japan, 1; Korea, 4; Peru, 4; Virgin Is., 10.

Srs. of St. Joseph (Carondelet) 31
Bolivia, 1; Colombia, 1; Guatemala, 4; Lebanon, 1; Peru, 9; Puerto Rico, 15.

Bernardines 30
Brazil, 12; Liberia, 9; Puerto Rico, 9.

Graymoor Sisters 30
Brazil, 7; Canada, 19; Japan, 4.

Srs. of Holy Child Jesus 30
Chile, 5; Ethiopia, 1; Ghana, 9; Nigeria, 15.

Franciscans of Perpetual Adoration 26
El Salvador, 10; Guam, 14; Taiwan, 2.

Missionary Srs. of Most Sacred Heart 25
Bangladesh, 3; Lebanon, 1; New Guinea, 17; Nicaragua, 4; Swaziland, 2.

White Srs. of Africa 24
2; Kenya, 2; Malawi, 8; Tanzania, 4; Tunisia, 1; Uganda, 3; Zambia, 4.

Daughters of Wisdom 24
Haiti, 4; Malawi, 19; Zaire, 1.

Adorers of Blood of Christ 23

Bolivia, 1; Brazil, 6; Guatemala, 3; Korea, 2; Liberia, 5; Puerto Rico, 5; Tanzania, 1.

Franciscans of Sorrowful Mother 22
Barbados, 9; Brazil, 5; Grenada, 4; St. Lucia, 2; Trinidad, 2.

Srs. of St. John the Baptist 22
Brazil, 5; Chile, 5; Zambia, 12.

Felician Sisters 22
Brazil.

Srs. of Notre Dame de Namur 20
Brazil, 7; Hawaii, 4; Kenya, 6; Mexico, 2; Zaire, 1.

Srs. of the Holy Names 19
Lesotho, 9; Peru, 10.

Immaculate Heart of Mary Srs. 18
Antigua, 2; Dominica, 3; Guatemala, 2; Jamaica, 2; Philippines, 1; Virgin Is., 7; Zaire, 1.

Missionary Srs. of St. Columban 18
Hong Kong, 1; Korea, 9; Peru, 1; Philippines, 7.

Medical Missionaries of Mary 17
Ethiopia, 2; Kenya, 2; Nigeria, 4; Taiwan, 2; Tanzania, 5; Uganda, 2.

Little Srs. of the Poor 17
Algeria, 1; Australia, 1; Colombia, 2; Hong Kong, 1; India, 2; Kenya, 2; Korea, 1; Malaysia, 2; Singapore, 1; Samoa, 1; Taiwan, 2; Turkey, 1.

Srs. of Divine Providence 16
Korea, 2: Puerto Rico, 14.

Srs. of Holy Family of Nazareth 16
Peru, 7; Puerto Rico, 9.

Mercedarians 15
Carolines, 9; Guam, 4; Marianas, 2.

Society of the Sacred Heart 15
Chile, 2; Zaire, 1; Japan, 2; Korea, 2; Lebanon, 1; Peru, 2; Philippines, 1; Taiwan, 1; Uganda, 3.

Srs. of Assumption of Bl. Virgin 15
Brazil, 1; Canada, 11; Japan, 3.

Srs. of Charity (Leavenworth) 15
Bolivia, 5; Peru, 10.

Srs. of Divine Savior 15
Colombia, 2; Taiwan, 7; Tanzania, 6.

Srs. of Holy Family (S.H.F.) 15
Hawaii.

Srs. of Providence 15
Alaska, 1; Argentina, 2; Bolivia, 1; Peru, 6; Taiwan, 5.

Srs. of St. Agnes 12
Ecuador, 4; Nicaragua, 8.

Srs. of Presentation of Mary (P.M.) 12
Philippines.

Srs. of Loretto 12
Bolivia, 6; Chile, 4; Peru, 2.

Mission Helpers of Sacred Heart 11
Venezuela.

Srs. of Charity of Nazareth 10
India.

Franciscan Srs. of Poor (Brazil) 10

Srs. of Ste. Chretienne 10
Afars and Issas, 2; Canada, 8.

Srs. of Charity of BVM (Dubuque) 9
Ecuador, 3; Hawaii, 6.

Daughters of the Holy Spirit 9
Cameroon, 1; Chile, 8.

Oblate Srs. of Providence 9
Costa Rica, 8; Cuba, 1.

Srs. of Presentation (P.B.V.M.) 9
Mexico, 7; Peru, 1; Venezuela, 1.

Religious of Jesus and Mary 9
Colombia, 1; India, 2; Lebanon, 3; Pakistan, 3.

Srs. of St. Mary of Namur 9
Rwanda, 1; Zaire, 8.

Srs. of Charity of Incarnate Word 8
Guatemala, 6; Peru, 2.

Poor Clares 8
Bolivia, 1; Cameroon, 7.

Srs. of Social Service (Los Angeles) 8
Mexico, 2; Taiwan, 6.

Religious of the Cenacle 7
Argentina, 2; Peru, 5.

Religious of Sacred Heart of Mary 7
Colombia, 3; Rhodesia, 4.

Grey Nuns of Montreal 7
Nigeria.

Srs. of St. Anne 7
Alaska, 3; Canada, 1; Chile, 1; Haiti, 2.

Srs. of Holy Cross (Pittsfield) 6
Afghanistan, 1; Haiti, 4; Ivory Coast, 1.

Daughters of Mary 6
Colombia.

Srs. of Charity of Sacred Heart 6
Lesotho.

Holy Rosary Srs. 6
Cameroon, 1; Kenya, 1; Sierra Leone, 1; South Africa, 1; Zambia, 2.

Srs. of Holy Family (S.S.F.) 6
Br. Honduras.

Nursing Srs. of Sick Poor 5
Bahamas.

Grey Nuns of Sacred Heart 5
Peru.

Missionary Srs. of Notre Dames des Anges .. 5
Hong Kong, 3; Peru, 2.

Carmelites (O. Carm.) 5
Philippines.

Srs. of Mercy (Burlingame) 5
Peru.

Missionaries of Immaculate Conception 5
Philippines, 1; Taiwan, 4.

Srs. of Holy Union of Sacred Hearts 5
Cameroon.

Congregation of Humility of Mery 4
Ecuador, 2; Mexico, 2.

Congregation of the Passion 4
Japan.

Missionaries of Precious Blood 4
South Africa.

Daughters of Heart of Mary 4
Ethiopia, 1; India, 1; Pakistan, 2.

Daughters of Mary and Joseph 4
Brazil, 2; Canada, 1; Mexico, 1.

Franciscans of Mary Immaculate 4
Canada, 1; Costa Rica, 2; Panama, 1.

Franciscans of Sacred Heart 4
Bolivia.

Servants of Most Bl. Trinity 4
Puerto Rico.
Good Shepherd Srs. (Saco, Me.) 4
Lesotho.
Srs. of St. Mary of Oregon 4
Peru.
Our Lady of Victory Missionary Srs. 3
Bolivia.
Srs. of Christian Charity 3
Uruguay.
Society of Helpers 3
Colombia, 2; Hong Kong, 1.
Carmelites (D.C.J.) 2
Nicaragua.
Franciscans of St. Joseph 2
Brazil.
Srs. of Charity of St. Joan Antida 2
Paraguay.
Srs. of St. Ursula 2
Zaire.
Xavier Mission Srs. 2
Japan.
Carmelites of St. Therese (C.S.T.) 1
Guatemala.
Srs. of Humility of Mary 1
El Salvador.
Filippini Srs. 1
Ethiopia.
Poor Handmaids of Jesus Christ 1
Philippines.
Ursulines (Tildonk) 1
India.
Srs. of Mercy of Holy Cross 1
Brazil.
Srs. of Charity of St. Hyacinth 1
Brazil.
Srs. of Incarnate Word 1
Guatemala.
Srs. of Mary of Presentation (S.M.P.) 1
Cameroon.
Servants of Holy Heart of Mary 1
Cameroon.
Srs. of Social Service (Buffalo) 1
Puerto Rico.
Society of St. Teresa of Jesus 1
Nicaragua.
Religious, Unspecified Affiliation 5
Alaska, 2; Brazil, 1; Venezuela, 2.

Lay Volunteers, 1972

Listed below are 37 sponsoring organizations, the number from each in overseas mission assignments, and areas of service. The total number of lay volunteers was 376.

Jesuit Volunteer Corps 82
Alaska.
Catholic Relief Services 74
Bolivia, 1: Braxil, 3: Burundi, 1; Cameroon, 1; Chile, 2; Colombia, 1; Costa Rica, 1; Dominican Republic, 2; Ecuador, 2; El Salvador, 2; Ghana, 3; Guatemala, 5; Haiti, 1; Honduras, 2; India, 7; Indonesia, 2; Italy, 2; Jordan, 1; Kenya, 2; Laos, 1; Lesotho, 1; Malagasy, 1; Malaysia, 1; Mexico, 2;

Morocco, 2; Nicaragua, 1; Nigeria, 1; Panama, 1; Paraguay, 2; Peru, 2; Philippines, 1; Senegal, 2; Tanzania, 1; Tunisia, 1; Upper Volta, 1; Uruguay, 1; Vietnam, 10; Yemen, 1.
Catholic Medical Mission Board 54
Bolivia, 1; Colombia, 3; Dominican Republic, 2; Ghana, 4; Guatemala, 3; Guyana, 2; Haiti, 10; Honduras, 2; Kenya, 2; Lesotho, 1; Malawi, 9; Mexico, 1; Peru, 1; Rhodesia, 1; St. Lucia, 5; Sierra Leone, 1; Tanzania, 2; Uganda, 2; Vietnam, 2.
Lay Mission Helpers 40
Cameroon, 4; Canada, 7; Ghana, 1; Jamaica, 2; Kenya, 4; Malawi, 10; New Guinea, 5; Rhodesia, 1; Sierra Leone, 2; South Africa, 2; Tanzania, 2.
Frontier Apostolate 27
Canada.
Regis College Lay Apostolate 19
Canada, 2; Hawaii, 9; Virgin Is., 8.
Jesuit Missions of Boston 15
Jamaica.
Milwaukee Latin American Office 7
Brazil, 2; Colombia, 2; Honduras, 1; Jamaica, 1; Peru, 1.
Madonna House Apostolate 6
Grenada, 2; Honduras, 2; Israel, 1; Peru, 1.
Kansas City-St. Joseph Diocese 4
Ethiopia, 2; Peru, 1; Brazil, 1.
Capuchin Fathers (N.Y.) 4
Guam, 3; Honduras, 1.
Marist Brothers (N.Y) 4
Samoa.
Mission Doctors Association 4
Malawi, 1; Rhodesia, 3.
International Liaison 3
Canada, 2; Lesotho, 1.
Kansas City, Kans., Archdiocese 3
Brazil, Canada, Venezuela.
La Crosse Diocese 3
Brazil, 1; Mexico, 2.
Norbertine Fathers 2
Peru.
Baltimore Archdiocese 2
Peru.
Erie Diocese 2
Mexico.
Rockford Diocese 2
Guatemala, Mexico.
San Francisco Archdiocese 2
Guatemala, Mexico.
Worcester Diocese 2
Colombia, Mexico.
Consolata Missioners 1
Colombia.
Holy Cross Sisters (Notre Dame) 1
Brazil.
Loretto Community (Natchez) 1
Chile.
Boston Archdiocese 1
Brazil.
Brooklyn Diocese 1
Peru.

Burlington Diocese (Chile) 1
Cleveland Diocese 1
  El Salvador.
Columbus Diocese 1
  New Guinea.
Detroit Archdiocese 1
  Guatemala.
Duluth Diocese (Nicaragua) 1

Galveston-Houston Diocese 1
  Guatemala.
Hartford Archdiocese................................. 1
  Chile.
New Ulm Diocese 1
  Indonesia.
Scranton Diocese (Brazil) 1
Seattle Archdiocese (Canada) 1

US Foreign Missionaries, 1951-1972

Year	Diocesan Priests	Religious Priests	Religious Brothers	Religious Sisters	Seminarians	Lay Persons	Total
1951		2474		1903			4377
1953		2771		1984			4755
1956		2914		2212			5126
1958	19	3477		2532		96	6124
1960	14	3018	575	2827	170	178	6782
1962	31	3172	720	2764	152	307	7146
1964	80	3438	782	3137	157	532	8126
1966	215	3731	901	3706	201	549	9303
1966	282	3727	869	4150	208	419	9655
1970	373	3117	666	3824	90	303	8373
1972	244	3171	634	3127	97	376	7649

Field Distribution by Areas, 1951-1972

	1951	1953	1956	1958	1960	1962	1964	1966	1968	1970	1972
Africa	312	379	445	617	781	901	1025	1184	1157	1141	1107
Far East.....................	1432	1481	1555	1809	1959	2110	2332	2453	2470	2137	1955
Near East....................	56	79	103	110	111	75	122	142	128	39	59
Oceania......................	593	730	809	951	986	992	846	953	1027	900	826
Europe	47	81	102	153	203	93	69	38	33	38	39
North America	277	225	168	357	337	224	220	211	251	233	234
Caribbean Islands........	800	800	887	928	991	967	1056	1079	1198	1067	819
Central America	280	326	329	392	433	537	660	857	936	738	728
South America.............	580	654	728	807	981	1247	1796	2386	2455	2080	1882
TOTALS	4377	4755	5126	6124	6782	7146	8126	9303	9655	8373	7649

US Mission Council

The United States Catholic Mission Council, which took over and expanded functions of the former Mission Secretariat, started operations Sept. 1, 1970, "to provide a forum and organ for the evaluation, coordination and fostering, in the United States, of the worldwide missionary effort of the Church."

Structurally, the council is made up of five seven-member committees representing the National Conference of Catholic Bishops, the Conference of Major Superiors of Men, the Leadership Conference of Women Religious, the laity, and mission agencies. Heads of the committees form the executive board which meets at least quarterly to oversee the implementation of policies and programs determined at annual meetings of the whole committee.

Typical activities of the council are educational efforts related to the Church's teaching about its missionary nature, the sponsorship of conferences on theological and pastoral foundations of missionary endeavor, liaison and cooperation with missionary bodies of other Christian churches, the encouragement of mission studies, training programs and refresher courses for departing and returning missionaries, gathering data on missionary activity, and general mission animation.

In 1972, the council sponsored a National Mission Animation Conference Nov. 13 to 16 in Washington, and completed compilation of a comprehensive personnel inventory of US priests, religious and lay persons in foreign mission service.

Father Joseph M. Connors, S.V.D., is executive secretary of the council, with offices at 1325 Massachusetts Ave. N.W., Room 500, Washington, D.C. 20005.

Mission Committees: Diocesan mission committees may be greatly assisted by local mission committees in parishes, religious communities, universities, colleges, high schools, and other centers of Catholic life and action. Through such local committees the vision of the whole missionary Church can be more effectively brought to the individual person. This is already demonstrated by the success of existing mission clubs and circles.

ANNIVERSARY, REPORT

A "Mass of the Nations" celebrated by Pope Paul VI on Pentecost Sunday, May 21, and the worldwide observance of Mission Sunday, Oct. 22, 1972, marked the 350th anniversary of the Congregation for the Evangelization of Peoples.

The Congregation "de Propaganda Fide" was established by Pope Gregory XV Jan. 6, 1622, to further missionary activity and to maintain its ecclesial and spiritual character.

The aims of the congregation were, and still are: to work for the conversion of people to the Catholic faith, to promote the formation of local clergies and establish indigenous hierarchies, to respect the cultures and customs of the various nations, to see that missionaries learn native languages and adapt themselves to native cultures, to keep missionaries out of politics.

Three hundred and 50 years after its foundation, the congregation has supervisory responsibility for missionary work among some 57 million people in the majority of countries in Asia and Africa, in all of Oceania, and in 80 jurisdictions in America and Europe.

A partial fact sheet reflecting developments in these mission areas indicates:

• From Jan. 1, 1950, to Jan. 1, 1972, the number of jurisdictions under the supervision of the congregation increased from 587 to 840 (365 in Asia, 315 in Africa, 80 in America, 61 in Oceania, 19 in Europe).

• Between 1949 and 1969, the number of Catholics in Asia (exclusive of Mainland China, Mongolia, North Korea, North Vietnam) increased from 6,079,092 to 14,149,823; in Africa, from 10,999,552 to 32,097,164.

• During the same period, the number of priests in Asia (as above) increased from 6,868 to 15,258; in Africa, from 7,500 to 15,100. The number of Asian and African priests increased from 3,447 to 9,811 and from 1,080 to 3,633, respectively.

• In 1972, there were 38,611 priests, 15,000 brothers, 85,000 sisters and 250,000 catechists in territories entrusted to the congregation.

• Also in 1972, there were 147 African and 141 Asian bishops, and the Church on both continents was administered in large part by native bishops. Thirty-one of 36 metropolitan sees in Black Africa were held by Africans, and 33 of 38 metropolitan sees in Asia had Asian archbishops.

By contrast, the first African bishop in modern times was ordained only in 1939. The first Asian bishop, an Indian, was ordained in 1923; the first Chinese, in 1926; the first Japanese, in 1927; the first Vietnamese, in 1933.

HOME MISSIONS

The expression "home missions" is applied to places in the US where the local Church is not fully established, i.e., where it does not have resources, human and otherwise, which are needed to begin or, if begun, to survive and grow. These areas share the name "missions" with their counterparts in foreign lands because they too need outside help to provide the personnel and means for making the Church present and active there in carrying out its mission for the salvation of men.

Dioceses in the Southeast, the Southwest, and the Far West are most urgently in need of outside help to carry on the work of the Church. Millions of persons live in counties in which there are no resident priests. Many others live in rural areas beyond the reach and influence of a Catholic center. According to the most recent statistics compiled by the Town and Country Religious Research Center of CARA (Center for Applied Research in the Apostolate), there are 643 priestless counties in the United States, and the leadership of a priest is lacking in over 5,000 US cities and towns. Many states generally thought to be well off from a pastoral standpoint include areas in which the Catholic Church and the ministry of priests are virtually unknown.

About 20 per cent of the total US population and less than three per cent of the Catholic population live within the boundaries of the 17 "most missionary" dioceses of the country. A "Survey of the Catholic Weakness" conducted by the National Catholic Rural Life Conference disclosed that the Catholic Church ranked 33rd among 38 religious bodies in percentage of rural membership.

Mission Workers

A number of forces are at work to meet the pastoral needs of these missionary areas and to establish permanent churches and operating institutions where they are required. In many dioceses, one or more missions and stations are attended from established parishes and are gradually growing to independent status. Priests, brothers and sisters belonging to scores of religious institutes are engaged full-time in the home missions. Lay persons, some of them in affiliation with special groups and movements, are also involved.

Group 7 was organized by the Glenmary Home Missioners for this purpose in 1971. Membership is open to Catholic adults, 21-years-old and older, willing to make a minimum commitment of two years. Five groups of individuals and families are currently members of Group 7 and are working in Georgia, New Jersey, Ohio and West Virginia.

The Society for the Propagation of the Faith, which conducts an annual collection for mission support in all parishes of the US, allocates 40 per cent of this sum for disbursement to home missions through the American Board of Catholic Missions.

The Catholic Church Extension Society provides one million dollars or more a year for the building of mission installations and related needs.

Special mission support is the purpose of the Commission for the Catholic Missions among the Colored People and the Indians. Diocesan, parochial and high school mission societies frequently undertake projects in behalf of the home missions.

Glenmary Missioners

The Glenmary Home Missioners, founded by Father W. Howard Bishop in 1939, is the only home mission society established for the sole purpose of carrying out the pastoral ministry in small towns and the rural districts of the United States. With 76 priests and 26 professed brothers as of Jan. 1, 1972, the Glenmary Missioners has 38 mission bases in the archdioceses of Atlanta and Cincinnati, and in the dioceses of Altoona-Johnstown, Charlotte, Covington, Dallas, Harrisburg, Little Rock, Nashville, Natchez-Jackson, Oklahoma City-Tulsa, Owensboro, Savannah and Wheeling.

The Rev. Charles M. Hughes is president.

National headquarters are located in Fairfield, O. The mailing address is P. O. Box 46404, Cincinnati, O. 45246.

Regional offices for promotion are at 429 Unquowa Rd., Fairfield, Conn. 06430, and P. O. Box 8, Techny, Ill. 60082.

Sisters

The Glenmary Home Mission Sisters of America, founded July 16, 1952, had 20 professed members engaged in work in four social and catechetical centers, one home nursing center, one house of study and one promotional center, in the archdioceses of Cincinnati and St. Louis, and the dioceses of Columbus, Dallas, Owensboro and Raleigh. Much of this work was concentrated in rural areas where poverty was prevalent. In September, 1971, members of the community began work in religious education research in Nashville and in campus ministry in the Savannah diocese.

Sister Mary Joseph Wade, elected in 1967, is superior general. The community has headquarters at 4580 Colerain Ave., Cincinnati, Ohio 45223.

Negro Missions

The Commission for Catholic Missions among the Colored People and the Indians reported the following (1971) statistics for 68 dioceses in which it supplied financial assistance: 853,500 Catholics, 616 churches, 896 priests, 25,963 infant baptisms, 8,226 adults received into the Church, 368 schools, 111,511 students. The total number of black Catholics was estimated to be more than 900,000.

The report noted that the principal areas of ministry were in 48 large cities in northern and northwestern states and California, where about one-half of the total black population and two-thirds of the Catholic black population were living. Two-thirds (some 600) of the priests engaged in ministry to the blacks were in these areas.

Two hundred and ninety-four parishes and missions were reported in 27 dioceses of the South, with 289 priests, some 300,000 Catholics, 150 elementary schools and three high schools. Nineteen churches and 11 schools were closed in 1971. The black Catholic population in the South decreased by some 20 per cent between 1961 and 1971.

The commission report, which was limited in scope, did not cover all aspects of the Church's ministry to the black population, which was estimated to number more than 22 million.

Indian Missions

The Commission for Catholic Missions among the Colored People and the Indians reported the following (1971) statistics for 42 dioceses in which it supplied financial assistance: 146,980 Catholics, 409 churches and mission stations, 250 priests, 4,630 infant baptisms, 732 adults received into the Church, 45 schools, 7,407 students.

Missions were located in 25 states: 157 in the Southwest, 63 in the Northwest, 60 in the Dakotas, 45 in Alaska, 36 in the Great Lakes area, and 40 in other states. One hundred and twenty of the missions had one or more resident priests who served outstations as well as base missions.

Ten of the schools had high school departments; 12 provided board, lodging and care for neglected and dependent children; 33 were day schools. Six hundred and fifty men and women religious and lay persons were on school staffs.

Figures in the report pertained to Indian ministry on government reservations.

According to preliminary figures of the 1970 US Census, about 500,000 Indians lived on or near reservations in more than 20 states; more than 200,000 were urban and living elsewhere. An estimated 25,000 Catholic Indians were not on reservations.

Support Bodies

The Catholic Church Extension Society: This society was established for the purpose of preserving and extending the Church in the US and its dependencies principally through the collection and disbursement of funds for missions. Since the time of its founding in 1905, more than $50 million have been received and expended for this purpose. Disbursements in 1971 amounted to $2.4 million.

Works of the society are supervised by a board of governors consisting of twelve members: Cardinal John Cody, archbishop of Chicago, chancellor; Rev. Joseph A. Cusack, president; five bishops or priests, and five laymen. Society headquarters are located at 1307 S. Wabash Ave., Chicago, Ill. 60605.

Commission for Catholic Missions among the Colored People and the Indians: Organized in 1886, this commission provided financial support ($2,365,000 in 1971) for religious works among Negroes and Indians in the United States. Funds are raised by an annual collection in all parishes of the country.

Cardinal Lawrence Shehan is head of the board of directors. Rev. J. B. Tennelly, S.S., D.D., is secretary. Commission headquarters are located at 2021 H St. N.W., Washington,

MINISTRY TO THE SPANISH-SPEAKING

Spanish-speaking peoples, the greater percentage of whom have been baptized in the Church, are the largest Catholic minority in the United States.

The 1970 US Census, without reference to religious affiliation, reported 5,073,000 Mexican-Americans. The Migration Division of the Commonwealth of Puerto Rico reported 1.8 million persons of Puerto Rican birth or parentage, as of Jan. 1, 1971. There are additional numbers of Spanish-speaking from Cuba, Central and South America, and other Hispanic origin. Estimates of the total number of Spanish-speaking in this country range as high as 10 million.

Variable Conditions

Pastoral ministry to the Spanish-speaking in the United States varies, depending on differences among the people and the availability of personnel to carry it out.

The pattern in cities with large numbers of Spanish-speaking is built around special churches, centers or other agencies where pastoral and additional forms of service are provided in a manner suited to the needs, language and culture of the people. Services in some places are extensive and include legal advice, job placement, language instruction, recreational and social assistance, specialized counseling, replacement services. In many places, however, even where there are special ministries, the needs are generally greater than the means required to meet them.

Most of the Puerto Rican segment of the Spanish-speaking population are located in urban areas. The highest concentrations in 1967, according to the Migration Division of the Commonwealth of Puerto Rico, were in New York City (1 million), Chicago (120,000), Philadelphia (45,000), Newark (40,500) and Paterson (25,500), N. J.

Similarly, most of the Cuban segment, including the more than 325,000 who have entered the country since 1959, are city dwellers.

Some of the urban dwellers have been absorbed into established parishes and routines of church life and activity. Many Spanish-speaking communities, especially those with transients, remain in need of special ministries.

An itinerant form of ministry best meets the needs of the scores of thousands of migrant workers who follow the crops in various areas of the country. Some of these ministries are carried out from centers and include other services — health, instruction for children, etc. — in addition to opportunities for attending Mass and receiving the sacraments.

Nearly 80 per cent of Mexican-Americans are in California (2.2 million), Texas (1,630,000), New Mexico (265,000), Arizona (225,000) and Colorado (180,000). Some of them have been more or less absorbed into the mainstream of church and civic life for generations. Many others, however, labor under serious pastoral, economic, educational and social handicaps.

Increasing demands have been made by these Chicanos in recent years for greater representation in affairs of the Church and the allocation of more personnel and church funds for programs of assistant.

Diocesan Ministries

Dioceses with special ministries for the Spanish-speaking include: Allentown, Baltimore, Boston, Bridgeport (also Portuguese), Buffalo, Chicago, Cincinnati, Cleveland, Columbus, Corpus Christi, Detroit, El Paso, Fall River (also Portuguese), Galveston-Houston, Grand Rapids, Harrisburg, Hartford, Miami, Milwaukee, Nashville, Newark, New York, Paterson, Philadelphia.

Portland (Me.), Pueblo, Richmond, Rochester, Rockville Centre, Sacramento, Saginaw, St. Augustine, Salt Lake City, San Angelo, San Antonio, San Diego, San Francisco, Santa Fe, Springfield (Mass.), Toledo, Trenton, Washington, Worcester, Yakima, Youngstown.

Dioceses with migrant ministries include: Boise, Camden, Crookston, Denver, Duluth, Fargo, Gary, Harrisburg, Kansas City (Kan.), La Crosse, Lafayette (Ind.), New Ulm, St. Petersburg. Such ministries have been in operation for a long time in the Southwest.

Organizations

The USCC Division of Spanish-Speaking: In 1968, the former Bishops' Committee for the Spanish-Speaking was reorganized, included in the United States Catholic Conference structure, and given this new title. It is one of the divisions of the USCC Department of Social Development.

The USCC Division of Spanish-Speaking, which expanded its range of operations in 1969, functions to assist the Church in dealing more effectively with issues and problems that affect the Spanish-speaking, especially Mexican-Americans, and to assist them in acquiring the capabilities necessary for individual and cooperative participation in the problem-solving processes of the total community.

Paul Sedillo, Jr., is director of the division, which has offices at 1312 Massachusetts Ave. N.W., Washington, D.C. 20005. Regional offices are located in San Antonio, Tex., Lansing, Mich., and San Jose, Calif.

In the Southwest, 55 Mexican-American priests organized **PADRES** in October, 1969, to help the Church identify more closely with the social, economic and educational needs of the Spanish-speaking. PADRES is the abbreviation of the Spanish title, "Padres Asociados para Derechos Religiosos, Educativos y Sociales." Bishop Patrick F. Flores is the national chairman. Father Roberto S. Flores, O.F.M., is the executive director. Offices are located at 2518 W. Commerce St., San Antonio, Tex. 78207.

An analogous organization of Chicano sisters, *Las Hermanas,* was organized in 1971 (see separate entry).

Miami Apostolate

The Spanish-Speaking Apostolate in metropolitan Miami is one of the most extensive in the country. It serves a population of well over 400,000 people: more than 250,000 Cubans who have established residence there since Fidel Castro rose to power Jan. 1, 1959; a permanent Latin population of more than 45,000; and some 100,000 migrant workers. Directly involved in the apostolate are 80 Spanish-speaking priests and 88 religious brothers and sisters. Spanish-speaking priests are assigned to 32 parishes.

Centro Hispano Catholic (Spanish Catholic Center), founded by Archbishop Coleman F. Carroll in October, 1959, provides many forms of assistance to new arrivals from Latin countries, including: pastoral counseling, orientation to life in the US, employment services, medical out-patient clinical and dental services, medicine-food-clothing distribution, day nursery and kindergarten care, recreational programs for senior residents, and home visits. Located in the center are Archdiocesan Offices for Immigration Services and the Latin American Affairs Office which fosters cultural relations with Latin American countries.

The staff of the center consists of a chaplain, one Sister of the Daughters of Charity, one Sister of St. Philip Neri, four Sisters of Social Service, and more than a score of lay persons. Sister Nikoletta, S.S.S., is the supervisor. Msgr. Bryan O. Walsh is executive director of the center and episcopal vicar for Spanish-speaking peoples in the archdiocese. The center is located at 130 N. E. 2nd St., Miami, Fla. 33132.

Officers of the Migration and Refugee Service, US Catholic Conference, in Miami figured largely in the work of receiving and resettling many of the refugees who have come to this country via the Cuban airlift.

All told, 325,355 persons were resettled between 1961 and the end of 1971. The states with the highest numbers of resettled Cubans were New York (76,200), New Jersey (44,721), California (32,680), and Illinois (17,750).

Appalachian Industries

Appalachian Industries, specializing in woodworking, was started in 1967 by Father Patrick O'Donnell, a Glenmary Missioner assigned to Lewis and Carter Counties in northeastern Kentucky.

Its purposes are to attract new businesses and to develop local enterprises, thereby giving people of the area reasons to remain in local employment rather than moving to cities for the sake of higher income. The training of craftsmen and their establishment as independent contractors is a primary objective.

Industries has a market outlet in Appalachian Studios and runs a retail gift shop in Vanceburg.

Appalachian Studios is located on Route 59 north of Vanceburg. The mailing address is Route 1, Box 6-A, Vanceburg, Ky. 41179.

Bearings

Bearings for Reestablishment, since it became operational in 1966, has provided counseling and employment services for well over 3,000 priests, clergymen of other faiths, sisters and brothers in transition to secular life and work.

In 1972, it established Manhattan Career Development to offer career counseling for active church personnel.

Bearings has more than 11 branches in the United States, Canada, England and Australia.

Malcolm Pennington is president.

The New York City office is located at 235 W. 49th St.

Credit Unions

The Credit Union National Association, Inc., reported in July, 1972, that there were 913 Catholic credit unions in the United States and 287 in Canada, with a combined membership of 889,000.

John XXIII Center

The John XXIII Center for Eastern Christian Studies was established in 1951 by Father Feodor Wilcock and a group of other Eastern-Rite Jesuits. It operates a wide variety of ecumenical activities related to Eastern Christian studies. One of its projects is the John XXIII Institute, believed to be the only academic institution outside of Rome offering a degree in the theology of the Eastern tradition of Christianity.

Father James H. McCarthy, S.J., is head of the Center, which is located on the campus of Fordham University, New York City.

Education

Following are a résumé and excerpts of the principal themes stated in the Declaration on Christian Education issued by the Second Vatican Council.

All men have an inalienable right to education for personal and social development, and for attainment of their ultimate end (salvation). Christians have a right to a Christian education.

Parents are the primary and principal educators, and the first school is the family in which children learn to live in the society of men and of the Church.

Parents, who entrust others with a share in the work of educating their children, need the help of the community. Civil society, therefore, has the responsibility of aiding parents and secondary educators, as the common good demands, by building schools and providing other educational institutions.

Roles in Education

"The office of educating belongs by a unique title to the Church, not merely because she deserves recognition as a human society capable of educating, but most of all because she has the responsibility of announcing the way of salvation to all men, of communicating the life of Christ to those who believe, and of assisting them with ceaseless concern so that they may grow into the fullness of that same life" (No. 3).

"In discharging her educative function, the Church is preoccupied with all appropriate means to that end. But she is particularly concerned with the means which are proper to herself, of which catechetical training is foremost. . . . The Church seeks to penetrate and ennoble with her own spirit those other means which belong to the common heritage of mankind, and which contribute mightily to the refinement of spirit and the molding of men. Among these are the media of social communication, many groups devoted to spiritual and physical development, youth associations, and especially schools" (No. 4).

"Parents, who have the first and the inalienable duty and right to educate their children, should enjoy true freedom in their choice of schools. Consequently, public authority, which has the obligation to oversee and defend the liberties of citizens, ought to see to it, out of a concern for distributive justice, that public subsidies are allocated in such a way that, when selecting schools for their children, parents are genuinely free to follow their consciences.

"For the rest, it is incumbent upon the state to provide all citizens with the opportunity to acquire an appropriate degree of cultural enrichment, and with the proper preparation for exercising their civic duties and rights. Therefore, the state itself ought to protect the right of children to receive an adequate schooling. . . . But . But it must keep in mind the principle of subsidiarity, so that no kind of school monopoly arises. For such a monopoly would militate against the native rights of the human person, the development and spread of culture itself, the peaceful association of citizens, and the pluralism which exists today in very many societies" (No. 6).

"The Church is keenly aware of her very grave obligation to give zealous attention to the moral and religious education of all her children. To those large numbers of them who are being trained in schools which are not Catholic, she needs to be present with her special affection and helpfulness. This she does through the living witness of those who teach and direct such students, through the apostolic activity of their schoolmates, but most of all through the services of the priests and laymen who transmit to them the doctrine of salvation in a way suited to their age and circumstances, and who afford them spiritual assistance through programs which are appropriate under the prevailing conditions of time and setting.

"The Church reminds parents of the serious duty which is theirs of taking every opportunity — or of making the opportunity — for their children to be able to enjoy these helps and to pace their development as Christians with their growth as citizens of the world. For this reason, the Church gives high praise to those civil authorities and civil societies that show regard for the pluralistic character of modern society, and take into account the right of religious liberty, by helping families in such a way that in all schools the education of their children can be carried out according to the moral and religious convictions of each family" (No. 7).

Catholic School Purposes

"The Church's involvement in the field of education is demonstrated especially by the Catholic school. No less than other schools does the Catholic school pursue cultural goals and the natural development of youth. But it has several distinctive purposes.

• "It aims to create for the school community an atmosphere enlivened by the gospel spirit of freedom and charity.

• "It aims to help the adolescent in such a way that the development of his own personality will be matched by the growth of that new creation he became by baptism.·

• "It strives to relate all human culture eventually to the news of salvation, so that the light of faith will illumine the knowledge which students gradually gain of the world, of life, and of mankind."

"The Catholic school retains its immense importance in . . . our times." (No. 8).

CATHOLIC SCHOOLS AND STUDENTS IN THE UNITED STATES

(Source: *The Official Catholic Directory, 1972.* Figures are as of Jan. 1, 1972.)
Archdioceses are indicated by an asterisk. For dioceses marked +, see Dioceses with Interstate Lines.

Section, State Diocese	Elementary Schools	Students	High Schools	Students	Universities Colleges	Students
NEW ENGLAND	**741**	**227,254**	**168**	**76,931**	**34**	**43,490**
Maine, Portland	33	9,352	6	1,373	2	911
New Hampshire, Manchester	61	15,834	8	3,664	4	3,161
Vermont, Burlington	16	4,326	4	1,787	4	2,260
Massachusetts	351	115,328	96	42,877	13	26,853
*Boston	206	73,603	67	27,070	8	20,108
Fall River	51	12,772	8	4,603	1	1,591
Springfield	52	16,984	9	5,642	1	501
Worcester	42	11,969	12	5,562	3	4,653
Rhode Island, Providence	88	23,967	16	6,749	4	3,217
Connecticut	192	58,447	38	20,481	7	7,088
*Hartford	102	32,285	17	10,862	4	1,510
Bridgeport	64	19,422	13	6,188	2	5,162
Norwich	26	6,740	8	3,431	1	416
MIDDLE ATLANTIC	**2,473**	**1,015,268**	**470**	**311,387**	**78**	**130,675**
New York	**1,083**	**482,616**	**219**	**142,018**	**39**	**55,898**
*New York	315	137,210	78	48,019	18	17,825
Albany	97	25,933	20	8,189	3	3,244
Brooklyn	201	151,006	37	34,034	4	17,675
Buffalo	177	52,403	34	15,813	10	13,751
Ogdensburg	34	7,507	6	1,804	1	116
Rochester	94	28,444	9	9,222	—	—
Rockville Centre	95	58,050	17	16,429	1	1,157
Syracuse	70	22,063	18	8,508	2	2,130
New Jersey	**503**	**202,506**	**102**	**61,489**	**13**	**19,526**
*Newark	233	94,996	50	27,138	6	17,071
Camden	73	28,105	14	9,680	—	—
Paterson	75	22,610	16	7,199	6	1,751
Trenton	122	56,795	22	17,472	1	704
Pennsylvania	**887**	**330,146**	**149**	**107,880**	**26**	**55,251**
*Philadelphia	317	171,914	52	62,908	10	26,759
Allentown	89	20,478	10	6,531	2	888
Altoona-Johnstown	42	10,092	3	2,750	2	2,084
Erie	55	17,294	12	5,041	3	4,945
Greensburg	56	11,681	4	1,398	2	1,618
Harrisburg	63	16,250	11	6,304	—	—
Pittsburgh	180	64,053	44	16,884	3	9,897
Scranton	85	18,384	13	6,064	4	9,060
SOUTH ATLANTIC	**591**	**207,830**	**148**	**62,357**	**20**	**33,595**
Delaware, Wilmington +	33	12,246	11	4,270	—	—
Maryland, *Baltimore +	105	44,669	27	13,486	6	6,219
District of Columbia, *Washington +	89	33,602	31	12,656	5	21,427
Virginia, Richmond +	60	21,004	19	5,980	1	580
West Virginia, Wheeling +	36	7,287	12	2,852	1	683
North Carolina	44	10,750	3	625	2	1,036
Belmont Abbey	—	—	—	—	1	718
Charlotte	21	4,998	3	625	1	318
Raleigh	25	5,752	—	—	—	—
South Carolina, Charleston	32	6,595	4	1,501	—	—
Georgia	34	11,290	8	3,295	—	—
*Atlanta	16	5,285	3	1,524	—	—

Section, State Diocese	Elementary Schools	Students	High Schools	Students	Universities Colleges	Students
Savannah	18	6,005	5	1,771	—	—
Florida	**158**	**60,387**	**33**	**17,692**	**5**	**3,650**
*Miami	63	28,390	17	9,292	4	2,497
Orlando	27	9,529	5	2,492	—	—
St. Augustine	29	9,171	3	2,092	—	—
St. Petersburg	39	13,297	8	3,816	1	1,153
EAST NORTH CENTRAL	**2,380**	**806,138**	**388**	**243,928**	**53**	**103,594**
Ohio	**580**	**207,428**	**104**	**71,046**	**13**	**26,457**
*Cincinnati	143	53,402	29	22,549	4	17,096
Cleveland	185	77,732	30	23,576	4	5,605
Columbus	58	16,736	15	6,512	1	965
Steubenville	22	4,544	5	1,854	1	1,217
Toledo	100	31,571	19	10,030	2	675
Youngstown	72	23,443	6	6,525	1	899
Indiana	**239**	**67,940**	**38**	**17,511**	**9**	**16,741**
*Indianapolis	94	25,907	14	6,383	2	1,315
Evansville	33	8,730	7	2,536	—	—
Ft. Wayne-S. Bend	47	14,410	9	4,493	5	12,564
Gary	46	14,860	5	3,394	1	1,665
Lafayette	19	4,033	3	705	1	1,197
Illinois	**733**	**283,909**	**121**	**90,019**	**12**	**38,391**
*Chicago	412	196,264	76	66,258	6	31,056
Belleville	70	15,373	6	4,044	1	742
Joliet	70	22,510	9	6,312	3	3,968
Peoria	61	16,624	10	4,534	—	—
Rockford	56	15,306	9	4,578	—	—
Springfield	64	17,832	11	4,293	2	2,625
Michigan	**370**	**124,940**	**84**	**42,170**	**8**	**14,542**
*Detroit	172	76.586	56	29,094	5	12,450
Gaylord	22	4,990	5	1,268	—	—
Grand Rapids	46	11,186	7	3,882	1	1,013
Kalamazoo	24	5,178	3	1,636	1	432
Lansing	45	12,952	8	3,928	1	647
Marquette	16	3,902	—	—	—	—
Saginaw	45	10,146	5	2,362	—	—
Wisconsin	**458**	**121,921**	**41**	**23,182**	**11**	**7,463**
*Milwaukee	183	57,218	18	12,114	5	3,982
Green Bay	108	28,753	11	5,081	2	2,258
La Crosse	83	18,934	9	4,523	1	485
Madison	58	12,298	3	1,464	1	430
Superior	26	4,718	—	—	2	308
EAST SOUTH CENTRAL	**320**	**78,908**	**63**	**24,774**	**10**	**8,567**
Kentucky	**177**	**42,283**	**34**	**14,212**	**5**	**5,641**
*Louisville	84	23,422	14	7,237	3	2,872
Covington	63	12,930	15	5,114	1	1,812
Owensboro	30	5,931	5	1,861	1	957
Tennessee	**45**	**12,258**	**10**	**5,004**	**2**	**1,173**
Memphis	19	5,868	5	2,802	1	864
Nashville	26	6,390	5	2,202	1	309
Alabama	**57**	**14,756**	**6**	**3,176**	**3**	**1,753**
Birmingham	27	6,063	2	1,157	2	823
Mobile	30	8,693	4	2,019	1	930
Mississippi, Natchez-Jackson	**41**	**9,611**	**13**	**2,382**	—	—
WEST NORTH CENTRAL	**1,042**	**274,172**	**199**	**84,084**	**36**	**43,260**
Minnesota	**258**	**71,005**	**36**	**17,020**	**8**	**9,208**
*St. Paul and Minneapolis	117	41,443	17	10,994	2	3,855

Section, State Diocese	Elementary Schools	Students	High Schools	Students	Universities Colleges	Students
Crookston	14	2,582	2	481	—	—
Duluth	17	2,845	1	673	1	914
New Ulm	33	6,583	4	970	—	—
St. Cloud	43	10,102	5	1,475	3	2,400
Winona	34	7,450	7	2,427	2	2,039
Iowa	**183**	**44,369**	**37**	**15,885**	**8**	**6,809**
*Dubuque	83	21,715	15	6,891	3	2,806
Davenport	25	5,901	8	2,242	4	2,907
Des Moines	27	5,959	3	2,122	—	—
Sioux City	48	10,794	11	4,630	1	1,096
Missouri	**309**	**89,717**	**55**	**28,267**	**8**	**16,732**
*St. Louis	198	65,761	39	21,513	6	13,563
Jefferson City	38	7,600	2	839	—	—
Kansas City-St. Joseph	49	12,873	11	5,199	2	3,169
Springfield-Cape Girardeau	24	3,483	3	716	—	—
North Dakota	**37**	**7,961**	**9**	**2,849**	**2**	**694**
Bismarck	21	4,403	7	2,117	1	658
Fargo	16	3,558	2	732	1	36
South Dakota	**32**	**6,994**	**8**	**2,015**	**2**	**882**
Rapid City	6	1,284	3	454	—	—
Sioux Falls	26	5,710	5	1,561	2	882
Nebraska	**115**	**29,652**	**35**	**10,789**	**2**	**4,732**
*Omaha	74	23,085	22	8,070	2	4,732
Grand Island	12	2,141	7	1,021	—	—
Lincoln	29	4,426	6	1,698	—	—
Kansas	**108**	**24,474**	**19**	**7,259**	**6**	**4,203**
*Kansas City	47	13,450	8	4,011	3	2,517
Dodge City	15	2,207	—	—	1	468
Salina	12	2,390	7	1,235	1	594
Wichita	34	6,427	4	2,013	1	624
WEST SOUTH CENTRAL	**550**	**167,667**	**137**	**52,680**	**13**	**20,162**
Arkansas, Little Rock	**41**	**6,539**	**7**	**2,376**	**—**	**—**
Louisiana	**202**	**83,691**	**67**	**28,944**	**4**	**7,566**
*New Orleans	105	50,554	32	18,921	4	7,566
Alexandria	27	7,282	8	2,162	—	—
Baton Rouge	26	11,062	8	3,182	—	—
Lafayette	44	14,793	19	4,679	—	—
Oklahoma, Oklahoma City-Tulsa	**34**	**6,080**	**5**	**2,095**	**1**	**512**
Texas	**273**	**71,357**	**58**	**19,265**	**8**	**12,084**
*San Antonio	60	17,102	19	5,515	3	7,557
Amarillo	13	1,918	2	537	1	4
Austin	19	4,157	2	294	1	1,234
Beaumont	11	2,830	2	692	—	—
Brownsville	10	2,246	2	694	—	—
Corpus Christi	29	5,716	5	1,528	—	—
Dallas	33	11,152	7	2,950	1	1,403
El Paso+	29	6,226	5	1,671	—	—
Fort Worth	17	4,029	3	1,083	—	—
Galveston-Houston	46	14,688	10	4,252	2	1,886
San Angelo	6	1,293	1	69	—	—
MOUNTAIN	**224**	**55,471**	**50**	**16,977**	**7**	**8,417**
Montana	**31**	**5,912**	**11**	**2,913**	**2**	**2,110**
Great Falls	20	3,866	6	1,477	1	1,031
Helena	11	2,046	5	1,436	1	1,079
Idaho, Boise	**13**	**2,333**	**1**	**415**	**1**	**200**
Wyoming, Cheyenne+	**9**	**2,163**	**1**	**165**	**—**	**—**

Section, State Diocese	Elementary Schools	Students	High Schools	Students	Universities Colleges	Students
Colorado	62	15,931	15	4,963	2	2,360
*Denver	49	14,020	12	4,451	2	2,360
Pueblo	13	1,917	3	512	—	—
New Mexico	36	7,853	5	1,708	2	3,747
*Santa Fe	24	5,880	4	1,583	2	3,747
Gallup+	12	1,973	1	125	—	—
Arizona	54	16,146	12	4,780	—	—
Phoenix	28	10,070	9	3,553	—	—
Tucson	26	6,076	3	1,227	—	—
Utah, Salt Lake City	8	2,081	3	913	—	—
Nevada, Reno	11	3,046	2	1,120	—	—
PACIFIC	828	261,271	188	87,630	20	36,889
Washington	99	25,414	19	7,319	4	6,639
*Seattle	66	17,911	14	5,176	2	3,744
Spokane	25	5,240	4	1,675	2	2,895
Yakima	8	2,263	1	468	—	—
Oregon	64	14,197	13	4,224	2	2,495
*Portland	60	13,440	12	4,092	2	2,495
Baker	4	757	1	132	—	—
California	630	210,321	146	71,795	13	26,846
*Los Angeles	276	109,414	70	37,254	5	7,171
*San Francisco	113	36,064	30	14,908	5	15,304
Fresno	24	5,682	3	1,141	—	—
Monterey	16	3,423	3	974	—	—
Oakland	57	17,125	11	6,501	2	2,090
Sacramento	41	11,688	10	3,485	—	—
San Diego	77	20,816	11	4,901	1	2,281
Santa Rosa	13	2,994	6	1,609	—	—
Stockton	13	3,115	2	1,022	—	—
Alaska	4	554	2	320	—	—
Anchorage	1	113	—	—	—	—
Fairbanks	2	299	2	320	—	—
Juneau	1	142	—	—	—	—
Hawaii, Honolulu	31	10,785	8	3,972	1	909
EASTERN RITES	57	11,438	7	1,248	2	204
*Philadelphia	20	3,597	1	308	1	180
*Munhall	8	2,129	—	—	—	—
St. Nicholas of Chicago	4	1,038	1	204	—	—
Parma	7	1,244	1	514	—	—
Passaic	9	1,762	—	—	—	—
Stamford	9	1,668	4	222	1	24
St. Maron of Detroit	—	—	—	—	—	—
Melkite Exarchate	—	—	—	—	—	—
TOTALS 1972	9,206	3,105,417	1,815	961,996	273	428,853
Totals 1971	9,606	3,413,610	1,954	1,015,713	283	426,205
Totals 1962	10,630	4,451,893	2,435	955,785	278	336,604

REPORT ON CATHOLIC EDUCATION

The status of Catholic educational institutions in the US in 1972 and several previous years was reflected in figures (as of Jan. 1) from editions of *The Official Catholic Directory* and from reports issued by the National Catholic Educational Association, the US Office of Education and the US Census Bureau.

Statistics

Colleges and Universities: 273 in 1972 (10 less than in 1971 and 31 less than in 1965). The decreases were due not only to closings but also to some changes of status, from claimed religious affiliation to institutional independence. Students: 428,853 in 1972 (2,648 more than in 1971 and 44,327 more than in 1965). Enrollment increased from 1965 to 1969 and decreased by 4,853 in 1970, and 4,658 in 1971. The 1972 figure was higher than that registered in the previous year but was lower than the 1969 total of 435,716.

High Schools: 1,815 in 1972 (139 less than in 1971, and a decrease of 650 since 1965). Students: 961,996 in 1972 (53,717 less than in 1971, and a decrease of 133,523 since 1965).

Elementary Schools: 9,206 in 1972 (400 less than in 1971, and a decrease of 1,725 since 1965. Students: 3,105,417 in 1972 (308,193 less than in 1971, and a decrease of 1,461,392 since 1965).

Public School Students receiving religious instruction: 5,579,060 (94,562 more than in 1971), including 1,327,331 high school students (24,299 more) and 4,251,729 elementary school students (70,263 more). The figures reflect an increase since 1965 (23,103 and 965,830 more high and elementary school students, respectively), but are out of proportion to the decline in Catholic school enrollment.

Enrollment Trends: Elementary and high school enrollments boomed in the peak years from 1945 to 1965 but have decreased steadily since that time. College and university enrollments have fluctuated.

The US Office of Education reported in September, 1972, that total nonpublic school enrollment decreased from 1961 to 1971 while public school enrollment increased 22.5 per cent. The overall decline in Catholic school enrollment for the period was 17 per cent. The highest percentage of decrease (21.8) was registered in the Great Lakes and Plains regions.

Teachers: 188,527 in 1972 (11,911 less than in 1971), including: priests, 8,700 (1,104 less); scholastics, 625 (120 more); brothers, 4,302 (612 less); sisters, 70,664 (7,707 less); lay teachers, 104,236 (2,608 less).

Lay teachers comprised 55 per cent of the total faculty in 1972 and 53.4 per cent in 1971. They comprised only 8.25 per cent of the faculty in 1944 when their number was first reported by *The Official Catholic Directory.*

They outnumbered priest and religious teachers for the first time in 1971.

Professionalism: According to estimates in the 1971-1972 report of the National Catholic Educational Association, the percentage of elementary religious teachers with less than a B.A. degree dropped in one year from 17.3 to 5.2. The corresponding lay teacher percentage also dropped in one year, for 34.5 to 17.5.

Costs: Tuition and fees in Catholic grade schools in 1971 averaged $100 to $150, an amount which represented only part of per-student costs, the balance being made up by parish or other subsidy. Indicated 1970-1971 budgets for elementary schools, in terms of national averages, were 17.5 per cent greater than they were for 1969-1970. Indicated budgets for 1971-1972 showed in increase of 30 per cent.

Per-pupil tuition in diocesan and parish high schools in 1971-1972 averaged more than $250, an amount which was supplemented by parish or diocesan subsidy. Private high school tuition averaged nearly $450. (Corresponding per pupil expenditures in public school systems were much higher.)

Aside from construction and maintenance expenses, the costliest budget items were salaries for lay teachers whose pay scales were higher than those of priests and religious. Salaries for the latter were rising, however, for a variety of reasons; one of them was the need of religious communities for greater income to provide for the care of their retired teachers.

Sisters Remain Committed

Trends behind the decrease (7,245 in 1971 and 7,707 in 1972) in the number of sisters teaching in Catholic schools were smaller numbers of young women joining religious communities, the departure of sisters from religious life, and the withdrawal of some sisters from teaching to take up other forms of apostolic work. By and large, however, the decrease does not indicate any wholesale lack of interest on the part of women religious in Catholic education and schools.

Lay Teachers

The most apparent effect of the increase in the number of lay teachers who outnumbered priests and religious teachers for the second time in 1972 and made up 55 per cent of the total staff, was financial. They got higher salaries than priests and religious, whose lower-costing services amounted to a living endowment to Catholic education.

Another effect was loss of confidence on the part of some parents who had come to identify Catholic schools so closely with religious teachers that they found it difficult to conceive how the schools could remain Catholic without them or with less of them.

Minority Enrollment

The NCEA reported 183,844 black students in Catholic elementary and high schools in 1971. They amounted to five per cent of the Catholic school enrollment; many of them were not Catholics. Spanish surnamed students — nearly 186,000, slightly over five per cent of the total enrollment — made up the largest minority group in the schools. Less than one per cent of students were American Indians and Orientals.

More than 5,000 of the total number of teachers were from minority groups.

Problems and Causes

Symptomatic of the financial problems troubling Catholic schools were the statements of bishops and administrators pressing for constitutional public aid programs, the closing of 1,725 elementary and 650 high schools since 1965, and the withdrawal of students by parents because of rising tuition costs.

Causes of enrollment drops included rising costs, population shifts from cities to suburban areas, lower birth rates, and attitudinal changes of parents wondering whether the schools will survive, whether they are worth what they cost, and whether they are really so important for religious as well as general education.

School spokesmen, however, have reaffirmed again and again that Catholic schools will not be phased out of existence.

Questioning continues about the high percentage (60 to 75) of church funds allocated to schools in which less than 50 per cent, overall, of Catholic children are enrolled while much less is available for religious education programs for public school students and adults.

New Programs Needed

Educators have called attention to past emphasis on the role of Catholic schools in education and the neglect of other aspects of the Church's total teaching function. Programs like the Green Bay Plan, introduced in 1971, envisage extension of the Church's educational effort in more effective forms to involve the total community—adults, parents as cooperators in the religious development of their children, college and university students through the campus ministry, lower-level students not in Catholic schools.

Doctrinal Concern

Opinions of parents and educators, as well as bishops who have the prime magisterial responsibility in the Church, remain divided over the merits of some aspects of current religious education programs — the orthodoxy of content, the thrust of methods, the soundness of materials, and the definiteness of aims. At the extremes are those who resist any change at all in traditional catechetical programs and those who appear to be more concerned about ecumenical, psychological and sociological relevance than wholeness of the doctrine which is essential to Catholic belief, practice, experience and witness.

This state of affairs has produced chain reactions of confusion in religious education and, for some parents, lack of confidence in Catholic schools. Some observers regard this morale problem as more basic than widely publicized problems of a financial nature.

US bishops and educators are taking steps to resolve problems of religious education and to provide directives for the teaching of doctrine in line with the *General Catechetical Directory* issued by the Congregation for the Clergy in 1971.

LEGAL STATUS OF CATHOLIC EDUCATION

The right of private schools to exist and operate in the United States is recognized in law. It was confirmed by the US Supreme Court in 1925 when the tribunal ruled (Pierce v. Society of Sisters, see Church-State Decisions of the Supreme Court) that an Oregon state law requiring all children to attend public schools was unconstitutional.

Private schools are obliged to comply with the education laws in force in the various states regarding such matters as required basic curricula, periods of attendance, and standards for proper accreditation.

The special curricula and standards of private schools are determined by the schools themselves. Thus, in Catholic schools, the curricula include not only the subject matter required by state educational laws but also other fields of study, principally, education in the Catholic faith.

The Supreme Court has ruled that the First Amendment to the US Constitution, in ac-

cordance with the No Establishment of Religion Clause of the First Amendment, prohibits direct federal and state aid from public funds to church-affiliated schools. (See several cases in Church-State Decisions of the Supreme Court.)

This prohibition does not extend to child-benefit and public-purpose programs of aid under federal or state laws, even though some incidental and secondary benefit accrues to church-related schools.

Catholic schools are exempt from real estate taxation in all of the states. Since Jan. 1, 1959, nonprofit parochial and private schools have also been exempt from several federal excise taxes.

Shared Time

In a shared time program of education, students enrolled in Catholic or other church-related schools take some courses (e.g., religion, social studies, fine arts) in their own schools and others (e.g., science, mathematics, industrial arts) in public schools. Such a program, outlined in 1956 by Dr. Erwin L. Shaver of the Massachusetts Council of Churches, has been given serious consideration in recent years by Catholic and other educators. Its constitutionality has not been seriously challenged, but practical problems — relating to teacher and student schedules, transportation, adjustment to new programs, and other factors — are knotty.

Limited shared time programs involving Catholic school students have been in operation since 1927 in Caledonia, Minn., since 1945 in Rutland, Vt., and for a number of years in several communities in Connecticut, Illinois, Michigan, Minnesota, Pennsylvania and Ohio. Since 1964, programs have also been reported operative in Iowa, New Jersey, Oregon, Washington and Wisconsin.

Released Time

Several million children of elementary and high school age of all denominations have the opportunity of receiving religious instruction on released time. Under released time programs they are permitted to leave their public schools during school hours to attend religious instruction classes held off the public school premises. They are released at the request of their parents. Public school authorities merely provide for their dismissal, and take no part in the program.

The first released time program was set up at Gary, Ind., in 1914. In 1905 a proposal had been made by Dr. George U. Wenner, to the Interfaith Conference on Federation, that public school pupils be given a day off a week for religious instruction in their churches. In 1876 a court decision in Vermont left to the discretion of local school boards whether they would release public school students for religious instruction.

In New York, where released time began in 1917, a law was passed in 1940 which authorized school boards to permit the release of public school pupils from class, at the request of their parents, to attend religious instruction off public school premises. The US Supreme Court upheld the constitutionality of the measure in the case of Zorach v. Clauson in 1952.

Released time programs are operative in most states at this time.

ESEA

The first major federal aid to education program in US history containing provisions benefitting parochial school students was enacted by the first session of the 89th Congress and signed into law by President Lyndon B. Johnson on Apr. 11, 1965. The 1965 Elementary and Secondary School Aid Law was passed by the House of Representatives (263 to 153) on Mar. 26 and by the Senate (73 to 18) on Apr. 9.

Provisions

The principal provisions of the $1.3 billion program were stated in three of the eight titles of the law.

• 1. One billion dollars was allocated to public school districts under a formula based chiefly on the number of children in schools who came from families earning less than $2,000 a year. The grant was intended to cover half of the cost of education for each eligible pupil.

Parochial and other private school pupils in the same low-income bracket were to benefit by extensions to them by local public school districts of shared services or facilities. Public school districts were required to take these children into account when making plans to aid needy students.

• 2. About $100 million was provided to buy textbooks for pupils, materials and volumes for school libraries, and some instructional equipment. All were to be owned by a public agency, such as a local school district or library, but they could be loaned to children attending nonpublic schools.

• 3. Another $100 million was to be used to establish educational centers to benefit both public and private school pupils with cultural enrichment programs and other special services. Public agencies would operate these centers, but the legislation required that private school educators and others from outside the public schools take part in planning for them.

Avoids Impasse

President Johnson presented his program to the Congress on Jan. 12, 1965, in a special message which indicated his intention of avoiding the separation of Church and State impasse which had blocked all earlier aid proposals pertaining to nonpublic, and especially church-affiliated, schools. The aim of the program, under public control, is to serve the public purpose by aiding disadvantaged pupils in public and nonpublic schools.

Program Regulations

Regulations for the administration of programs under the new law were issued Sept. 15, 1965, by the US Office of Education. The leading norms are as follows.

• Participation of Nonpublic School Children: Must be "substantially comparable" to that of public school children.   • Special Projects: Can include "broadened healh services, school breakfasts for poor children, and guidance and counseling services" in addition to strictly educational offerings.

Public school teachers can go to private schools to offer special services, and mobile or portable equipment can be placed on private school premises temporarily.

• Aid for Textbooks and Library Resources: Materials are to be loaned by public agencies to private school teachers and pupils, not to the schools themselves.

To be distributed to private school pupils on an equal basis with public school student numbers, the materials must be approved for use in public schools and can include books, periodicals, documents, pamphlets, photographic works, musical scores, maps, charts, globes, sound recordings, films and video tapes.

If constitutional restrictions prevent a state from allowing its agencies to act as channels for aid to teachers and pupils in private schools, the regulations provide that the US Commissioner of Education can provide for the distribution of the books and materials himself.

Amendment, Benefits

ESEA, since its passage, has been refunded in several stages and amended in some respects but has remained substantially the same as enacted.

The law has benefitted many disadvantaged pupils in public and nonpublic schools. Spokesmen for Catholic education, however, have called attention of the Congress to the fact that provisions of the law have not been applied to a disproportionately large number of eligible students in Catholic schools.

AID TO NONPUBLIC EDUCATION

Financial pressure on Catholic and public school systems focused new emphasis in 1972 on the possibility and the exploration of ways and means of providing programs of public aid to nonpublic education that would be both constitutional and beneficial to both systems.

Court Tests

Father Charles M. Whelan, S.J., constitutional lawyer and professor of law at Fordham University, told a meeting of diocesan attorneys in March that any statute providing public aid to nonpublic schools, parents with children in such schools or students themselves would have to meet three tests developed by the US Supreme Court.

Accordingly, a statute must:

• have a "secular legislative purpose";

• neither inhibit nor advance religion as its "principal or primary effect";

• not foster "excessive government entanglement with religion."

Constitutional Programs

Among forms of aid which Father Whelan categorized as "certainly constitutional" are bus transportation, textbook loans, school lunches and health services, and "secular, neutral or non-ideological services, facilities and materials provided in common to all school children," public and nonpublic.

Programs of these types were in operation in about 36 states.

Aid was provided most commonly in the form of auxiliary services such as transportation to and from school (24 states), health and welfare services (13 states), textbook loans (seven or eight states), aid to disadvantaged children (six states), and driver education (four states). Several states offered free lunch programs and testing services, vocational training and even cooperative central purchasing arrangements.

Other permissible forms of aid are dual enrollment and shared time programs (encouraged in seven states) and "payments for record keeping and testing required by law."

Unconstitutional Aid

"Clearly unconstitutional" programs include "any form that requires a general audit of the nonpublic school books to categorize all expenditures as either 'secular' or 'religious.'"

Also forbidden, Father Whelan said, are tuition payments, "whether to parents, students or schools" which are not based on need and are not restricted to the costs of secular education.

He stated that the Supreme Court would definitely not ratify reimbursing nonpublic schools or teachers for part or all of salaries paid "for the basic instruction of ordinary parochial school students during the secular school year."

Debatable Programs

Forms of aid which "may or may not be constitutional" include "general voucher systems" — granting parents educational vouchers to be used at either public or nonpublic schools — and "tax benefits limited to nonpublic schools, students, teachers, parents or sponsors."

Various mixtures of aid forms figured in legislative and judicial action in 1972, in California, Illinois, Iowa, Kentucky, Minnesota, New Jersey, New York, Ohio, Pennsylvania and other states.

A number of bills in the may-or-may-not-be-constitutional category were enacted but placed under almost immediate challenge in the courts where they were enjoined in effect, if not judged unconstitutional. Two possible exceptions were statutes in Illinois and Iowa.

A report released in February by the American Jewish Congress said that 32 suits on nonpublic school aid issues were pending in state and federal courts. The total was higher by the end of the year.

Tax Credit Bill

Catholic educators and other supporters of public aid to nonpublic education were hopeful in 1972 of eventual passage of a federal tax credit bill introduced in the House of Representatives by Wilbur Mills, chairman of the Ways and Means Committee, and Hugh Casey of New York. Their hopes were shaded, however, by June 30, 1971, rulings of the Supreme Court against the constitutionality of a salary supplement statute in Rhode Island and a purchase-of-services act in Pennsylvania. (See Church-State Decisions of the Supreme Court.)

The proposed Public and Private Assistance Act (H.R. 16141), as introduced, would provide:

• $2.25 billion a year for five years to states in order to relieve school districts and boards from dependence on property taxes for the support of public education;

• a federal income tax credit of up to $200 to parents for each of their children in a nonpublic elementary or secondary school.

Hearings on the bill opened in August.

Pro and Con

The measure had the support of the Nixon administration as well as the US Catholic Conference, most Catholic educators, and a number of organizations including Parents for Nonpublic Education and Citizens Relief for Education by Income Tax.

It was opposed by the National Education Association, numerous organizations of teachers, the American Civil Liberties Union, Americans United for Separation of Church and State, the Committee for Public Education and Religious Liberty, the National Jewish Community Relations Advisory Council and other groups with significant influence.

Some Catholic educators were opposed to the bill because, as presented, it would not benefit the poor. They also agreed with others that the bill, if enacted, might have the effect of freezing students of poor families in second-rate public schools while providing tax-credited students with opportunities of access to superior—and perhaps segregated—nonpublic schools.

Arguments against the bill were of the general against-separation-of-Church-and-state type coupled with specifics of the Rhode Island, Pennsylvania and other decisions of the Supreme Court. An additional argument was that tax relief to parents with children in nonpublic schools would result in less tax support for public schools.

Arguments for the bill claimed that the right of parents to send children to schools of their choice — and thereby satisfy their education obligation — is hollow and void if exercise of the right is hindered and/or prevented because of the heavy economic burden of taxes for the support of schools which their children do not attend. (See statement of the US bishops, Parental Rights.)

Proponents of the bill also contended that the tax credit is in line with constitutional, statutory or traditional tax exemption for churches and for contributions to nonprofit educational and other institutions.

PARENTAL RIGHTS AND NONPUBLIC SCHOOLS

Following is the text of a statement adopted unanimously by the National Conference of Catholic Bishops Nov. 15, 1971, declaring that parents of nonpublic school students have a constitutional right to tax aid. In a related action, the bishops endorsed the concept of tax credits to parents for a portion of the educational expenses of their children in nonpublic schools.

[This text was circulated by the NC Documentary Service, *Origins*.]

The Constitution of the United States guarantees religious and political liberty to every citizen. Precisely for this reason, we, the Catholic Bishops of the United States, feel compelled to speak to our fellow citizens about certain implications of the recent United States Supreme Court decision relating to government assistance for teachers' salaries in parochial schools. Our purpose is not to discuss the particular programs upon which the Court ruled, nor indeed the related tax and educational crisis affecting the citizens of many states. Rather we address ourselves to features of the decision which, left unchecked, would affect basic freedoms of all. These freedoms relate to parental rights, the free exercise of religion, and the liberty of every citizen to speak, assemble, petition and vote on matters affecting the public role of religion in American life.

Right Guaranteed

The fundamental right of parents to educate their children in nonpublic schools is guaranteed by our Constitution and was recognized a half century ago in the *Pierce* case, wherein the Supreme Court said: "The child is not the mere creature of the State."

But today the highest Court of the land — dealing with a case intimately related to parents — makes no explicit mention of that right. Instead, by its decision this well recognized right could become an illusion if it results in a state educational monopoly in which parental rights — if acknowledged at all — will be enjoyed only by the wealthy, by those who can bear both the burden of school taxes and of the separate added cost of nonpublic schooling.

Government Obligation

Today the effects of taxation, inflation and rising governmental cost make it increasingly impossible for parents to exercise their constitutional freedoms in education without enabling assistance. Government plainly has an obligation in justice to make those accommodations necessary to secure parental rights in education. In order to exercise this right today, parents need and are entitled to a measure of economic help — a share of the tax dollars they pay. Government should not tip the economic scales so heavily in favor of the public schools that parents can exercise their right to choose nonpublic schools only with severe personal sacrifice.

We are hopeful and confident that the Congress and the states will promptly enact legislation, in conformity with the Constitution, which will aid parents in the exercise of their rights in education. In no way, however, should such legislation be construed as contributing to the creation or support of racially segregated schooling. Furthermore, we trust that the Supreme Court will use its vast powers, in appropriate cases, to emphasize parental rights in education and to repudiate every effort to make the child a "mere creature of the State."

Unacceptable Reasoning

The Supreme Court has said that the public discussion and political activity required to achieve enactment of certain types of state aid to church-related education must be kept out of the public forum because they present "hazards of religion intruding into the political area." This kind of reasoning is unacceptable.

The Supreme Court has also stated that "religion must be a private matter for the individual, the family and the institutions of private choice." Religion is indeed a private matter, but it is for more than that. Since the founding of the Republic it has been deemed, in an important sense, a very public matter. The separation of church and state is a wise policy. The separation of religion from public life is dangerous folly. We Americans have always known that religious liberty demands, by its very nature, that it be exercised publicly.

Danger to Liberty

There can be no political liberty in a society in which religious groups and individual believers, as such, may not speak out on public issues. There can be no religious liberty in a society in which public issues may not be discussed in their religious dimension.

We trust that citizens concerned for the protection of parental rights, religious liberty, diversity and excellence in education, and the avoidance of the increased taxation resulting from a state monopoly of education, will not work, peaceably and with renewed vigor, for viable programs of aid to the education of *all* children.

We trust that religious-minded citizens of all faiths will continue to bear public witness to the truths they hold, so that — as always before in American history — religion will continue to have its proper role in the life of our nation.

GENERAL CATECHETICAL DIRECTORY

A General Catechetical Directory compiled under the direction of the Congregation for the Clergy was approved by Pope Paul VI Mar. 18, 1971, and published several months later.

[The following excerpts, with boldfaced lines added, are from the English translation approved by the Congregation for the Clergy and published by the Publications Office, United States Catholic Conference.

[The excerpts are limited to the nature and functions of catechesis, a listing of doctrines to be regarded as its basic contents, and a citation from the Addendum concerning first reception of the sacraments of Penance and the Eucharist. Additional passages concerning catechetical methods are not covered here.]

Purpose: "The intent of this *Directory* is to provide the basic principles of pastoral theology which pastoral action in the ministry of the word can be more fittingly directed and governed."

Primary emphasis: "Those things which are said about divine revelation, the criteria according to which the Christian message is to be expounded, and the more outstanding elements of that same message, are to be held by all."

For: "The *Directory* is chiefly intended for bishops, Conferences of Bishops, and in general all who under their leadership and direction have responsibility in the catechetical field . . . to provide assistance in the production of catechetical directories and catechisms."

Portions of the *Directory* dealing with methods are subject to adaptation and variation in line with age and developmental levels, cultural and social conditions, and other factors, under the direction of the concerned bishops.

Catechetics

Aims: "Steps which are effective and indeed of the greatest importance for good results must be taken: promoting the growth of the customary forms of the ministry of the word and stimulating new ones; evangelizing and catechizing men of lower cultural levels; reaching the educated classes and taking care of their needs; improving the traditional forms of the Christian presence and finding new ways; gathering together all the practical aids of the Church and at the same time avoiding forms which are not in accord with the Gospel" (No. 9).

Ministry of the Word: "The ministry of the word takes many forms, including catechesis, according to the different conditions under which it is practiced and the ends which it strives to achieve.

• "There is the form called evangelization, or missionary preaching. This has as its purpose the arousing of the beginnings of faith, so that men will adhere to the word of God.

• "Then there is the catechetical form,

'which is intended to make men's faith become living, conscious, and active, through the light of instruction.'

• "And then there is the liturgical form, within the setting of a liturgical celebration, especially that of the Eucharist. . . .

• "Finally, there is the theological form, that is, the systematic treatment and the scientific investigation of the truths of faith."

The *Directory* notes that "in the concrete reality of the pastoral ministry, they (all four forms) are closely bound together" (No. 17).

Varied Forms: "In a word, catechetical activity can take on forms and structures that are quite varied, that is to say, it can be systematic or occasional, for individuals or for communities, organized or spontaneous" (No. 19).

Catechesis for Adults: "Catechesis for adults, since it deals with persons who are capable of an adherence that is fully responsible, must be considered the chief form of catechesis. All other forms, which are indeed always necessary, are in some way oriented to it" (No. 20).

Maturity of Faith: "Within the scope of pastoral activity, catechesis is the term to be used for that form of ecclesial action which leads both communities and individual members of the faithful to maturity of faith" (No. 21).

"Catechesis performs the function of disposing men to receive the action of the Holy Spirit and to deepen their conversion. It does this through the word, to which are joined the witness of life and prayer" (No. 22).

Communion with God: "Catechesis performs the functions of helping men make . . . communion with God a reality, and of presenting the Christian message in such a way that it is clear that the highest value of human life is safeguarded by it. All this requires that catechesis keep in mind the legitimate aspirations of men, as also the progress and success of the values contained in these aspirations" (No. 23).

The Whole Truth: "It is not . . . sufficient for catechesis merely to stimulate a religious experience, even if it is a true one; rather, catechesis should contribute to the gradual grasping of the whole truth about the divine plan by preparing the faithful for the reading of Sacred Scripture and the learning of tradition" (No. 24).

Liturgy and Prayer: "Catechesis must promote an active, conscious, genuine participation in the liturgy of the Church. . . ."

"Catechesis must also train the faithful to meditate on the word of God and to engage in private prayer" (No. 25).

Christian Interpretation: "Catechesis has the task . . . of emphasizing this function (of a person mature in the faith to work toward the fulfillment of the divine plan of salvation) by teaching the faithful to give a Christian interpretation to human events,

especially the signs of the times, so that all 'will be able to test and interpret all things in a wholly Christian spirit' " (No. 26).

"The order or hierarchy of the truths of Catholic teaching should be kept" (No. 27).

Other and This Worldly Purposes: "Catechesis . . . performs the function of directing the hope of men in the first place to the future goods which are in the heavenly Jerusalem. At the same time, it calls men to be willing to cooperate in the undertakings of their neighbors and of the human race for the improvement of human society" (N0. 29).

"Catechesis has the function of lending aid for the beginning and the progress of this life of faith throughout the entire course of a man's existence, all the way to the full explanation of revealed truth and the application of it to man's life" (No. 30).

"At one and the same time it (catechesis) performs the functions of initiation, education and formation" No. 31).

Methods: "Catechesis . . . should convey the word of God, as it is presented by the Church, in the language of the men to whom it is directed" (No. 32).

"The function of catechesis . . . cannot be restricted to repetition of traditional formulas; in fact, it demands that these formulas be understood, and be faithfully expressed in language adapted to the intelligence of the hearers, using even new methods when necessary. The language will be different for different age levels, social conditions of men, human cultures, and forms of civil life" (No. 34).

Witness: "Catechesis . . . demands the witness of faith, both from the catechists and from the ecclesial community, a witness that is joined to an authentic example of Christian life and to a readiness for sacrifice" (No. 35).

Prophetic Ministry: "Catechesis, as a most excellent opportunity for the prophetic ministry of the Church, must not only foster strong and continuous contact with the various forms of life in the ecclesial community, but it must strive to promote a greater accord between the possible formulations of the divine message and the various cultures and diverse languages of peoples" (No. 37).

Approach: "Catechesis begins, therefore, with a rather simple presentation of the entire structure of the Christian message (using also summary or global formulas), and it presents this in a way appropriate to the various cultural and spiritual conditions of those to be taught. By no means, however, can it stop with this first presentation, but it must be interested in presenting the content in an always more detailed and developed manner, so that individuals among the faithful and the Christian community may arrive at an always more profound and vital acceptance of the Christian message, and may judge the concrete conditions and practices of Christian life by the light of revelation" (No. 38).

Guidance of Magisterium: "This task of catechesis, not an easy one, must be carried out under the guidance of the Magisterium of the Church, whose duty it is to safeguard the truth of the divine message, and to watch that the ministry of the word uses appropriate forms of speaking and prudently considers the help which theological research and the human sciences can give" (No. 38).

Contents

Structure: "The structure of the whole content of catechesis must be theocentric and trinitarian: through Christ, to the Father, in the Spirit.

"Through Christ: The entire economy of salvation receives its meaning from the incarnate Word. It prepared his coming; it manifests and extends his kingdom on earth from the time of his death and resurrection up to his second glorious coming, which will complete the work of God. So it is that the mystery of Christ illumines the whole content of catechesis. The diverse elements — biblical, evangelical, ecclesial, human, and even cosmic — which catechetical education must take up and expound are all to be referred to the incarnate Son of God.

"To the Father: The supreme purpose of the incarnation of the Word and of the whole economy of salvation consists in this: that all men be led to the Father. Catechesis, therefore, since it must help to an ever-deeper understanding of this plan of love of the heavenly Father, must take care to show that the supreme meaning of human life is this: to acknowledge God and to glorify him by doing his will, as Christ taught us by his words and the example of his life, and thus to come to eternal life.

"In the Spirit: The knowledge of the mystery of Christ and the way to the Father are realized in the Holy Spirit. Therefore, catechesis, when expounding the content of the Christian message, must always put in clear light this presence of the Holy Spirit, by which men are continually moved to have communion with God and men and to fulfill their duties.

"If catechesis lacks these three elements or neglects their close relationship, the Christian message can certainly lose its proper character" (No. 41).

Hierarchy of Truths: "In the message of salvation there is a certain hierarchy of truths which the Church has always recognized when it composed creeds or summaries of the truths of faith. This hierarchy does not mean that some truths pertain to faith itself less than others, but rather that some truths are based on others as of a higher priority, and are illumined by them.

"On all levels catechesis should take account of this hierarchy of the truths of faith.

"These truths may be grouped under four basic heads: the mystery of God the Father, the Son, and the Holy Spirit, Creator of all things; the mystery of Christ the incarnate Word, who was born of the Virgin Mary, and who suffered, died, and rose for our salvation; the mystery of the Holy Spirit, who is present in the Church, sanctifying it and guiding it until the glorious coming of Christ, our Savior and Judge; and the mystery of the Church, which is Christ's Mystical Body, in which the Virgin Mary holds the pre-eminent place" (No. 43).

Contents: The basic content of catechetics covers the principal truths of faith (Nos. 47 to 69):

the mystery of the Trinity;

creation and the economy of salvation;

Jesus Christ, Son of God, the firstborn of all creation, the center of the whole economy of salvation, true God and true man in the unity of his divine Person, Savior and Redeemer of the world;

the sacraments, actions of Christ in the Church, the primordial sacrament;

the Eucharist, the center of sacramental life;

the catechesis of matrimony, in need of emphasis;

human and Christian freedom;

sin;

the moral life of Christians;

the perfection of charity, "in a way of life in which love reigns in the keeping of the commandments";

the Church, People of God, communion and saving institution;

Mary, the Mother of God, the Mother and model of the Church;

final communion with God.

Obedience, Freedom, Conscience: "The docility with which the Holy Spirit must be obeyed entails a faithful observance of the commandments of God, the laws of the Church, and just civil laws.

"Christian freedom still needs to be ruled and directed in the concrete circumstances of human life. Accordingly, the conscience of the faithful, even when informed by the virtue of prudence, must be subject to the Magisterium of the Church, whose duty it is to explain the whole moral law authoritatively, in order that it may rightly and correctly express the objective moral order.

"Further, the conscience itself of Christians must be taught that there are norms which are absolute, that is, which bind in every case and on all people. That is why the saints confessed Christ through the practice of heroic virtues; indeed, the martyrs suffered even torture and death rather than deny Christ" (No. 63).

After Death: "Catechesis cannot pass over in silence the judgment after death of each man, or the expiatory punishments of purgatory, or the sad and lamentable reality of eternal death, or the final judgment" (No. 69).

Dogmatic Formulas: "It must not be forgotten that dogmatic formulas are a true profession of Catholic doctrine, and are accordingly to be accepted as such by the faithful in the sense in which the Church has understood and does understand them. ... The traditional formulas for professing the faith and for praying, such as the Apostles' Creed, the Lord's Prayer, the Hail Mary, and the like, are to be taught with special care" (No. 73).

Catechetics for Adolescents: "Adolescents and young adults are less exposed to the danger of violently opposing the Church than they are to the temptation of leaving it" (No. 82).

"The principal task of catechesis in adolescence will be to further a genuinely Christian understanding of life. It must shed the light of the Christian message on the realities which have greater impact on the adolescent, such as the meaning of bodily existence, love and the family, the standards to be followed in life, work and leisure, justice and peace" (No. 84).

Rational Foundations for Faith: "To make firm the inner coherence of . . . religious thinking, witnessing is not enough. Today scientific strictness is demanded everywhere; hence, catechesis must also provide the rational foundations for faith with the greatest care" (No. 88).

"Catechesis, which should encourage personal experience of faith and at the same time well-ordered reflection on religious matters, is brought to perfection when it leads to the fulfillment of religious duties" (No. 89).

Catechesis for Adults:— Its aims are to:
• "Teach them to evaluate correctly, in the light of faith, the sociological and cultural changes in contemporary society. . . .
• "Explain contemporary questions in religious and moral matters. . . .
• "Shed light on the relations between temporal action and ecclesial action. . . .
• "Develop the rational foundations of faith" (No. 97).

First Penance, Eucharist

In an Addendum on the first reception of the sacraments of Penance and the Eucharist, the *Directory* said, in part:

"In very recent times in certain regions of the Church experiments relative to the first reception of the sacraments of Penance and of the Eucharist have been made. These have given rise to doubt and confusion.

"So that the Communion of children may be appropriately received early, and so that psychological disturbances in the future Christian life which can result from a too early use of Confession may be avoided, and so that better education for the spirit of penance and a more valid catechetical preparation for Confession itself may be fostered, it has seemed to some that children should be admitted to first Communion without first receiving the sacrament of Penance.

"In fact, however, going to the sacrament of Penance from the beginning of the use of reason does not in itself harm the minds of the children, provided it is preceded, as it should be, by a kind and prudent catechetical preparation. The spirit of penance can be developed more fully by continuing catechetical instruction after first Communion; likewise, there can be growth in knowledge and appreciation of the great gift that Christ has given to sinful men in the sacrament of the pardon they will receive and of reconciliation with the Church.

"These things have not prevented the introduction in certain places of a practice in which some years regularly elapse between first Communion and first Confession. In other places, however, the innovations made have been more cautious, either because first Confession was not so much delayed, or because consideration is given the judgment of the parents who prefer to have their children go to the sacrament of Penance before first Communion" (No. 4).

Common Practice Favored

"The Supreme Pontiff, Pius X, declared, 'The custom of not admitting children to Confession or of never giving them absolution, when they have arrived at the use of reason, must be wholly condemned' (Decree *Quam singulari,* VII, *Acta Apostolicae Sedis,* 1910, p. 583). One can scarcely have regard for the right that baptized children have of confessing their sins, if at the beginning of the age of discretion they are not prepared and gently led to the sacrament of Penance.

"One should also keep in mind the usefulness of Confession, which retains its efficacy even when only venial sins are in question, and which gives an increase of grace and of charity, increases the child's good dispositions for receiving the Eucharist, and also helps to perfect the Christian life. Hence, it appears the usefulness of Confession cannot be dismissed in favor of those forms of penance or those ministries of the word, by which the virtue of penance is aptly fostered in children, and which can be fruitfully practiced together with the sacrament of Penance, when a suitable catechetical preparation has been made. The pastoral experience of the Church, which is illustrated by many examples even in our day, teaches her how much the so-called age of discretion is suited for effecting that the children's baptismal grace, by means of a well-prepared reception of the sacraments of Penance and of the Eucharist, shows forth its first fruits, which are certainly to be augmented afterwards by means of a continued catechesis.

"Having weighed all these points, and keeping in mind the common and general practice which *per se* cannot be derogated without the approval of the Apostolic See, and also having heard the Conferences of Bishops, the Holy See judges it fitting that the practice now in force in the Church of putting Confession ahead of first Communion should be retained. This in no way prevents this custom from being carried out in various ways, as, for instance, by having a communal penitential celebration precede or follow the reception of the sacrament of Penance.

"The Holy See is not unmindful of the special conditions that exist in various countries, but it exhorts the bishops in this important matter not to depart from the practice in force without having first entered into communication with the Holy See in a spirit of hi-erarchical communion. Nor should they in any way allow the pastors or educators or religious institutes to begin or to continue to abandon the practice in force.

"In regions, however, where new practices have already been introduced . . . the Conferences of Bishops will wish to submit these experiments to a new examination. If after that they wish to continue these experiments for a longer time, they should not do so unless they have first communicated with the Holy See, which will willingly hear them, and they are at one mind with the Holy See" (No. 5).

UNIVERSITIES AND COLLEGES IN THE UNITED STATES

Listed below are institutions of higher learning established under Catholic auspices. Some of them are now independent.

Information includes: name of each institution; indication of male (m), female (w), co-educational (c) student body; name of founding group or group with which the institution is affiliated; year of foundation; number of students, in parentheses.

Albertus Magnus College (w): 700 Prospect St., New Haven, Conn. 06511. Dominican Sisters; 1925 (500).

Albuquerque, University of (c): St. Joseph Pl. N. W., Albuquerque, N. M. 87105. Sisters of St. Francis; 1940 (843).

Allentown College of St. Francis de Sales (c); Center Valley, Pa. 18034. Oblates of St. Francis de Sales; 1965 (633).

Alvernia College (w): Reading, Pa. 19607. Franciscan Sisters; 1958 (285).

Alverno College (w): 3401 S. 39th St. Milwaukee, Wis. 53215. School Sisters of St. Francis; 1936; independent (1,101).

Anna Maria College (w): Sunset Lane, Paxton, Mass. 01612. Sisters of St. Anne; 1946 (580).

Annhurst College (w): R. R. 2 Woodstock, South Woodstock, Conn. 06281. Daughters of the Holy Spirit; 1941 (416).

Aquinas College (c): 1607 Robinson Rd. S. E. Grand Rapids, Mich. 49506. Sisters of St. Dominic; 1922 (1,354).

Assumption College (c): 500 Salisbury St., Worcester, Mass. 01609. Assumptionist Fathers; 1904 (1,581).

Avila College (c): 11901 Wornall Rd., Kansas City, Mo. 64145. Sisters of St. Joseph of Carondelet; 1867 (754).

Barat College (w): 700 Westleigh Rd., Lake Forest, Ill. 60045. Religious of the Sacred Heart; 1919 (571).

Barry College (w): 11300 N. E. 2nd Ave., Miami, Fla. 33161. Dominican Sisters; 1940 (1,248).

Bellarmine College (c): 2000 Norris Pl. Louisville, Ky. 40205; Louisville archdiocese, 1950 (1,655).

Belmont Abbey College (m): Belmont, N. C. 20812. Benedictine Fathers; 1878 (718).

Benedictine College (formerly St. Benedict and Mt. St. Scholastica Colleges) (c): Atchi-son, Kans. 66002. Benedictines (1,288).

Biscayne College (m): 16400 N. W. 32nd Ave., Miami, Fla. 33054. Augustinian Fathers; 1962 (400).

Boston College (University Status) (c): Newton, Mass. 02167. Jesuit Fathers; 1863 (13,444).

Brescia College (c): 120 W. 7th St. Owensboro, Ky. 42301. Ursuline Sisters; 1925 (957).

Briar Cliff College (c): W. 33rd and Rebecca Sts., Sioux City, Ia. 51104. Sisters of St. Francis of the Holy Family; 1930 (1,096).

Cabrini College (w): Radnor, Pa. 19088. Missionary Srs. of Sacred Heart; 1957 (418).

Caldwell College (w): Caldwell, N. J. 07006. Dominican Sisters; 1939 (841).

Canisius College (c): 2001 Main St., Buffalo, N. Y. 14208. Jesuit Fathers; 1870; independent (3,912).

Cardinal Cushing College (w): 129 Fisher Ave., Brookline, Mass. 02146. Sisters of the Holy Cross; 1952 (295).

Cardinal Stritch College (c): 6801 N. Yates Rd., Milwaukee, Wis. 52317. Sisters of St. Francis of Assisi; 1932 (843).

Carlow College (w): 3333 5th Ave., Pittsburgh, Pa. 15213. Sisters of Mercy; 1929 (1,045).

Carroll College (c): Helena, Mont. 59601. Diocesan Clergy; 1910 (1,094).

Catholic University of America (c): Fourth St. and Michigan Ave. N. E., Washington, D. C. 20017. Hierarchy of the United States; 1889. Pontifical University. (6,257).

Catholic University of Puerto Rico (c): Ponce, P. R. Hierarchy of Puerto Rico (6,595).

Chaminade College (c): 3140 Waialae Ave., Honolulu, H. I. 96816. Marianists; 1955 (909).

Chestnut Hill College (w): Philadelphia, Pa. 19118. Sisters of St. Joseph; 1871 (626).

Christian Brothers College (c): 650 E. Parkway S., Memphis, Tenn. 38104. Brothers of the Christian Schools; 1871 (864).

Clarke College (w): 1550 Clarke Dr., Dubuque, Iowa. 52001. Sisters of Charity; 1843 (731).

Creighton University (c): 2500 California St., Omaha, Neb. 68131. Jesuit Fathers; 1878 (4,234).

Dallas, University of (c): Irving, Tex. 75060. Diocesan; 1956 (1,403).

Dayton, University of (c): 300 College Park, Dayton, Ohio 45409. Marists; 1850 (7,153).

De Paul University (c): 2323 N. Seminary Ave., Chicago, Ill. 60614. Vincentians; 1898 (9,404).

Detroit, University of (c): McNicholas Rd. at Livernois, Detroit, Mich. 48221. Jesuit Fathers; 1877 (8,058).

Dominican College (w): 2401 E. Holcombe Blvd., Houston, Tex. 77021. Dominican Sisters; 1964 (375).

Dominican College (c): 5915 Erie St., Racine, Wis. 53402. Dominican Sisters; 1935; independent (828).

Dominican College of Blauvelt (c): Blauvelt, N. Y. 10913. Dominican Sisters; 1952 (636).

Dominican College of San Rafael (w): San Rafael, Calif. 94901. Dominican Sisters; 1890 (953).

Don Bosco College (m): P.O. Box 6, Newton, N.J. 07860. Salesian Fathers; 1928 (116).

Dunbarton College (w): 2935 Upton St. Washington, D. C. 20008. Sisters of the Holy Cross; 1935 (328).

Duquesne University (c): 801 Bluff St., N.W., Pittsburgh, Pa. 15219. Holy Ghost Fathers; 1878 (8,427).

D'Youville College (w): 320 Porter Ave., Buffalo, N. Y. 14201. Grey Nuns of the Sacred Heart; 1908 (1,253).

Edgecliff College (c): Edgecliff Victory Pkwy., Cincinnati, Ohio 45206. Sisters of Mercy; 1935 (800).

Edgewood College (c): 855 Woodrow St. Madison, Wis. 53711. Dominican Sisters; 1927 (430).

Emmanuel College (w): 400 The Fenway, Boston, Mass. 02115. Sisters of Notre Dame de Namur; 1919 (1,343).

Fairfield University (c): Fairfield, Conn. 96433. Jesuit Fathers; 1942 (3,762).

Felician College (w): S. Main St., Lodi, N. J. 07644. Felician Sisters; 1923 (505).

Fontbonne dcollege (w): Wydown and Big Bend Blvds., St. Louis, Mo. 63105. Sisters of St. Joseph of Carondelet; 1923 (778).

Fordham University (C): Fordham Rd. and Third Ave., New York, N. Y. 10458. Jesuit Fathers; 1841; independent (11,226).

Fort Wright College (c): W. 4000 Randolph Rd., Spokane, Wash. 99204. Sisters of the Holy Names of Jesus and Mary; 1939 (410).

Gannon College (c): 109 W. 6th St., Erie, Pa. 16501. Diocesan Clergy; 1944 (3,568).

Georgetown University (c): 37th and O Sts. N. W., Washington, D. C. 20007. Jesuit Fathers; 1789 (7,730).

Georgian Court College (w): Lakewood, N. J. 08701. Sisters of Mercy; 1908 (704).

Gonzaga University (c): Spokane, Wash. 99202. Jesuit Fathers; 1887 (2,770).

Great Falls, College of (c): 1301 20th St. S., Great Falls, Mont. 59401. Sisters of Charity of Providence; 1932 (1,016).

Gwynedd-Mercy College (w): Gwynedd Valley, Pa. 19437. Sisters of Mercy; 1948 (663).

Holy Cross College (m): Worcester, Mass. 01610. Jesuit Fathers; 1843 (2,492).

Holy Family College (c): R.F.D. 5, Manitowoc, Wis. 54220. Franciscan Srs. of Christian Charity; 1935 (606).

Holy Family College (w): Grant and Frankford Aves., Philadelphia, Pa. 19114. Srs. of Holy Family of Nazareth; 1954 (370).

Holy Names, College of the (w): 3500 Mountain Blvd., Oakland, Calif. 94619. Sisters of the Holy Names of Jesus and Mary; 1800 (813). Coed in graduate division.

Illinois Benedictine College (c): Lisle, Ill. 60532. Benedictine Fathers; 1890 (1,022).

Immaculata College (w): Immaculata, Pa. 19345. Sisters, Servants of the Immaculate Heart of Mary; 1920. (916).

Incarnate Word College (c): 4301 Broadway, San Antonio, Tex. 78209. Sisters of Charity of the Incarnate Word; 1881 (1,530).

Iona College (c): 715 North Ave., New Rochelle, N. Y. 10801. Congregation of Christian Brothers; 1940 (3,415).

John Carroll University (c): North Park and Miramar Blvds. Cleveland, Ohio. 44118. Jesuit Fathers; 1886 (3,964).

King's College (c): Wilkes-Barre, Pa. 18702. Holy Cross Fathers; 1946 (2,669).

Ladycliff College (c): Highland Falls, N. Y. 10928. Franciscan Sisters: 1933; independent (457).

La Roche College (c): 9000 Babcock Blvd., Allison Park, Pittsburgh, Pa. 15101. Sisters of Divine Providence; 1963 (425).

La Salle College (c): 20th St. and Olney Ave., Philadelphia, Pa. 19141. Brothers of the Christian Schools; 1863 (3,732).

Le Moyne College (c): Syracuse, N. Y. 13214. Jesuit Fathers; 1946 (2,569).

Lewis College (c): Lockport, Ill. 60441. Christian Brothers; 1930 (2,119).

Lone Mountain College (c): 2800 Turk St., San Francisco, Calif. 94118. Religious of the Sacred Heart; 1930 (774).

Loras College (c): 1450 Alta Vista St., Dubuque, Ia. 52001. Archdiocese of Dubuque; 1839 (1,426).

Loretto Heights College (c): 3001 S. Federal Blvd., Denver, Colo. 80236. Sisters of Loretto; 1918; independent (846).

Loyola College (c): 4501 N. Charles St., Baltimore, Md. 21210. Jesuits; 1852 (3,028).

Loyola University (c): 820 N. Michigan Ave., Chicago, Ill. 60611. Jesuit Fathers; 1870 (16,720).

Loyola University (c): 6363 St. Charles Ave., New Orleans, La. 70118. Jesuit Fathers; 1904 (4,866).

Loyola University of Los Angeles (c): 7101 W. 80th St., Los Angeles, Calif. 90045. Jesuit Fathers; 1911 (3,820).

Madonna College (w): Livonia Mich. 48150. Felician Sisters; 1937 (727).

Manhattan College (m): 4513 Manhattan College Pkwy., New York, N. Y. 10471. Brothers of the Christian Schools; 1853; independent (4,714). Coed arrangements with Mt. St. Vincent College.

Marian College (w): Fond du Lac, Wis. 54935. Sisters of St. Agnes; 1936 (450).

Marian College (c): 3200 Cold Springs Rd., Indianapolis, Ind. 46222. Sisters of St. Francis (Oldenburg, Ind.); 1937 (923).

Marillac College (w): 7804 Natural Bridge Rd., Normandy, Mo. 63121. Sister Formation College (246).

Marist College (c): Poughkeepsie, N. Y. 12601. Marist Brothers of the Schools; 1946; independent (1,790).

Marquette University (c): 615 N. 11th St., Milwaukee, Wis. 53233. Jesuit Fathers; 1881; independent (11,034).

Mary College (c): Route 2, Box 119, Bismarck, N. D. 58501. Benedictine Sisters; 1959 (658).

Mary Manse College (c): 2436 Parkwood Ave., Toledo, Ohio 43620. Ursuline Nuns; 1922 (840).

Marycrest College (c): 1607 W. 12th St., Davenport, Iowa 52804. Sisters of the Humility of Mary; 1939 (1,025).

Marygrove College (w): 8425 W. McNicholas Rd., Detroit, Mich. 48221. Sisters, Servants of the Immaculate Heart of Mary; 1910 (1,102).

Marylhurst College (w): Marylhurst, Ore. 97036. Sisters of the Holy Names of Jesus and Mary; 1930 (550).

Marymount College (w): 7750 Fordham Rd., Los Angeles, Calif. 90045. Religious of the Sacred Heart of Mary; 1933 (812).

Marymount College (c): Salina, Kan. 67401. Sisters of St. Joseph of Concordia; 1922 (594).

Marymount College (w): Tarrytown, N. Y. 10592. Religious of the Sacred Heart of Mary; 1907; independent (1,007).

Marymount Manhattan College (w): 221 E. 71st St., New York N. Y. 10021. Religious of the Sacred Heart of Mary; 1948; independent (724).

Maryville College (w): 13550 Conway Rd., St. Louis, Mo. 63141. Religious of the Sacred Heart; 1872 (576).

Marywood College (c): Scranton, Pa. 18509. Sisters, Servants of the Immaculate Heart of Mary; 1915 (2,214).

Mater Dei College (w): Riverside Dr., Ogdensburg, N. Y. 13669. Sisters of St. Joseph; 1960 (117).

Medaille College (c): 18 Agassiz Circle. Buffalo, N. Y. 14214. Srs. of St. Joseph; 1937 (497).

Mercy College (c): 555 Broadway, Dobbs Ferry, N. Y. 10522. Sisters of Mercy; 1950; independent (952).

Mercy College (c): 8200 W. Outer Dr., Detroit, Mich. 48219. Sisters of Mercy; 1941 (1,620).

Mercyhurst College (c): 501 E. 38th St. Erie, Pa. 16501. Sisters of Mercy; 1926 (850).

Merrimack College (c): North Andover, Mass. 01845. Augustinians. 1947 (2,130).

Misericordia (w): Dallas, Pa. 18612. Sisters of Mercy; 1932 (919).

Molloy College (w): 1000 Hempstead Ave., Rockville Centre, N.Y. 11570. Dominican Sisters; 1955 (1,157).

Mount Angel College (c): Mt. Angel, Ore. 97362. Benedictine Sisters; 1954; independent (232).

Mount Marty College (c): Yankton, S. D. 57078. Benedictine Sisters; 1950 (524).

Mt. Mary College (w): 2900 N. Menomonee River Pkwy., Milwaukee, Wis. 53222. School Sisters of Notre Dame; 1913 (760).

Mt. Mercy College (c): Cedar Rapids, Ia. 52402. Sisters of Mercy; 1928 (649).

Mt. St. Agnes College: Merged with Loyola College (Maryland).

Mt. St. Joseph College (w): 670 Tower Hill Rd., Wakefield, R. I. 02879. Passionist Sisters; 1953 (250).

Mt. St. Joseph on the Ohio, College of (w): St. Joseph, Ohio 45051. Sisters of Charity; 1920 (793).

Mt. St. Mary College (w): Hooksett, N. H. 03106. Sisters of Mercy; 1934; independent (301).

Mt. St. Mary College (c): Newburgh, N. Y. 12550. Dominican Sisters; 1954 (743).

Mt. St. Mary College (m): Emmitsburg, Md. 21727. Diocesan Clergy; 1808 (1,129).

Mt. St. Mary's College (w): 12001 Chalon Rd., Los Angeles, Calif. 90049. Sisters of St. Joseph of Carondelet; 1925 (1,168).

Mt. St. Vincent, College of (w): Mt. St. Vincent-on-Hudson, New York, N. Y. 10471. Sisters of Charity; 1847; independent (984). Coed arrangements with Manhattan College.

Mount Senario College (c): Ladysmith, Wis. 54848. Servants of Mary (228).

Mundelein College (w): 6363 N. Sheridan Rd., Chicago, Ill. 60626. Sisters of Charity of the Blessed Virgin Mary; 1929 (979).

Nazareth College (c): Kalamazoo, Mich. 49074. Sisters of St. Joseph; 1924 (404).

Nazareth College (w): East Ave., Rochester, N. Y. 14610. Sisters of St. Joseph; 1924; independent (1,253).

New Rochelle, College of (w): 29 Castle Pl., New Rochelle, N. Y. 10805. Ursuline Nuns; 1904; independent (957).

Newton College of the Sacred Heart (w): 885 Centre St., Newton, Mass. 02159. Religious of the Sacred Heart; 1946; independent (867).

Niagara University (c): Niagara Falls, N. Y. 14109. Vincentian Fathers; 1856 (3,341).

Notre Dame, College of (c): Belmont, Calif. 94002. Sisters of Notre Dame de Namur; 1868 (1,393).

Notre Dame College (w): 4545 College Rd., Cleveland, Ohio 44121. Sisters of Notre Dame; 1922 (392).

Notre Dame College (c): Manchester, N. H. 03104. Sisters of the Holy Cross; 1950 (361).

Notre Dame College (w): 320 E. Ripa Ave., St. Louis, Mo. 63125. School Sisters of Notre Dame; 1896 (334).

Notre Dame College of Staten Island (w): 300 Howard Ave., Staten Island, N. Y. 10301. Sisters of Notre Dame; 1931 (425).

Notre Dame of Maryland, College of (c): 4701 N. Charles St., Baltimore, Md. 21210. School Sisters of Notre Dame; 1873 (705).

Notre Dame University (c): Notre Dame, Ind. 46556. Holy Cross Fathers; 1842 (7,526).

Ohio Dominican College (c): Columbus, Ohio 43219. Dominican Srs.; 1911 (965).

Our Lady of Holy Cross College (c): 4123 Woodland Dr., New Orleans, La. 70114. Congregation of Sisters Marianites of Holy Cross (287).

Our Lady of the Elms College (w): Chicopee, Mass. 01013. Sisters of St. Joseph; 1928 (501).

Our Lady of the Lake College (w): 411 S.W. 24th St., San Antonio, Tex. 78285. Sisters of Divine Providence; 1912 (1,869).

Portland, University of (c): Willamette Blvd. at Fiske St., Portland, Ore. 97203. Holy Cross Fathers; 1901; independent (2,035).

Providence College (m): River Ave. and Eaton St. Providence, R. I. 02918. Dominican Fathers; 1917 (2,350).

Quincy College (c): 1831 College Ave., Quincy, Ill. 62301. Franciscan Fathers; 1860 (2,164).

Regis College (c): W. 50th Ave. and Lowell Blvd. Denver, Colo. 80221. Jesuit Fathers; 1888 (1,424).

Regis College (w): Wellesley St., Weston, Mass. 02193. Sisters of St. Joseph; 1927 (849).

Rivier College (w): Nashua, N. H. 03060. Sisters of the Presentation of Mary; 1933; independent (825).

Rockhurst College (c): 5225 Troost Ave., Kansas City, Mo. 64110. Jesuit Fathers 1910 (2,469).

Rogers College (c): Maryknoll, N.Y. 10545. Maryknoll Sisters; 1931 (226).

Rosary College (w): 7900 Division St., River Forest, Ill. 60305. Dominican Sisters; 1901 (1,291).

Rosary Hill College (c): 4380 Main St., Buffalo, N.Y. 14226. Sisters of St. Francis of Penance and Christian Charity; 1947; independent (1,262).

Rosemont College (w): Rosemont, Pa. 19010. Society of the Holy Child Jesus; 1921 (670).

Sacred Heart College (w): Belmont, N.C. 28012. Sisters of Mercy; 1935 (318).

Sacred Heart College (c): 3100 McCormick Ave., Wichita, Kan. 67213. Sisters Adorers of the Most Precious Blood; 1933 (624).

Sacred Heart University (c): Bridgeport, Conn. 06604. Diocese of Bridgeport; 1963; independent (1,400).

St. Ambrose College (c): Davenport, Ia.

52803. Diocese of Davenport; 1882 (1,410).

St. Anselm's College (c): Manchester N.H. 03102. Benedictine Fathers; 1889 (1,674).

St. Basil's College (m): 195 Glenbrook Rd., Stamford, Conn. 06902. Byzantine Rite Diocese of Stamford; 1939 (23).

St. Benedict College (w): St. Joseph, Minn. 56374. Benedictine Sisters; 1913 (896).

St. Bernard College (c): St. Bernard, Ala. 35138. Benedictine Fathers; 1892 (632).

St. Bonaventure University (c): St. Bonaventure, N.Y. 14778. Franciscan Fathers; 1856 (2,637).

St. Catherine College (w): 2004 Randolph St., St. Paul, Minn. 55116. Sisters of St. Joseph of Carondelet; 1905 (1,367).

St. Edward's University (c): Austin, Tex. 78704. Holy Cross Brothers; 1885 (1,003).

St. Elizabeth, College of (w): Convent Station, N.J. 07961. Sisters of Charity; 1899; independent (761).

St. Francis College (c): 605 Pool Rd., Biddeford, Me. 04005. Franciscan Fathers; 1943; independent (564).

St. Francis College (c): 180 Remsen St., Brooklyn, N.Y. 11201. Franciscan Brothers; 1884 (2,580).

St. Francis College (c): 2701 Spring St., Fort Wayne, Ind. 46808. Sisters of St. Francis; 1937 (2,001).

St. Francis College (c): 500 Wilcox 60435. Joliet, Ill. Franciscan Sisters; 1925 (829).

St. Francis College (c): Loretto, Pa. 15940. Franciscan Fathers; 1847 (1,604).

St. John College (w): Cleveland, Ohio 44114. Diocesan College; 1928 (849).

St. John Fisher College (m): 3690 East Ave., Rochester, N.Y. 14618. Basilian Fathers; 1951; independent (1,340).

St. John's University (c): Grand Central and Utopia Pkwys., Jamaica, N.Y. 11432. Vincentian Fathers; 1870 (13,735).

St. John's University (m): Collegeville, Minn. 56321. Benedictine Fathers; 1857 (1,604).

St. Joseph College (w): Emmitsburg, Md. 21727. Daughters of Charity of St. Vincent de Paul; 1809 (508).

St. Joseph College (w): 1678 Asylum Ave., West Hartford, Conn. 06117. Sisters of Mercy; 1932 (936). Coed in graduate school.

St. Joseph's College (w): Standish (P.O. N. Windham), Me. 04062. Sisters of Mercy; 1915 (347). Coed in summer session.

St. Joseph's College (c): Rensselaer, Ind. 47978; 4721 Indianapolis Blvd., East Chicago, Ind. 46312. Society of the Precious Blood; 1889 (1,366 at Rensselaer; 1,665 at East Chicago).

St. Joseph's College (c): City Ave. at 54th St. Philadelphia, Pa. 19131. Jesuit Fathers; 1851 (2,827).

St. Joseph's College (c): 245 Clinton Ave., Brooklyn, N.Y. 11205. Sisters of St. Joseph; 1916; independent (528).

St. Joseph the Provider, College of (c):

Clement Rd., Rutland, Vt. 05701. Sisters of St. Joseph; 1954 (142).

St. Leo College (c): St. Leo, Fla. 33574. Benedictine Fathers; 1889; independent (1,153).

St. Louis University (c): 221 N. Grand Blvd., St. Louis, Mo. 63103. Jesuit Fathers; 1818 (11,076).

St. Martin's College (c): Olympia, Wash. 98501. Benedictine Fathers; 1895 (574).

St. Mary, College of (w): 1901 S. 72nd St., Omaha, Neb. 68124. Sisters of Mercy; 1923; independent (560).

St. Mary College (w): Xavier P.O., Kan. 66098. Sisters of Charity of Leavenworth; 1923 (602).

St. Mary of the Plains College (c): Dodge City, Kans. 67801. Sisters of St. Joseph of Wichita; 1952 (468).

St. Mary-of-the-Woods College (w): St. Mary-of-the-Woods, Ind. 47876. Sisters of Providence; 1840 (392).

St. Mary's Collegejt1 (w): Notre Dame, Ind. 46556. Sisters of the Holy Cross; 1844 (1,851).

St. Mary's College (m): Orchard Lake, Mich. 48034. Secular Clergy (95).

St. Mary's College (c): St. Mary's College, Calif. 94575. Brothers of the Christian Schools; 1863 (1,265).

St. Mary's College (c): Winona, Minn. 55987. Brothers of teh Christian Schools; 1913 (1,052).

St. Mary's Dominican College (w): 7214 St. Charles Ave., New Orleans, La. 70118. Dominican Sisters; 1910 (859).

St. Mary's University (c): 2700 Cincinnati Ave., San Antonio, Tex. 78228. Society of Mary (Marianists); 1852 (4,211).

St. Michael's College (c): Winooski Park, Vt. 05404. Society of St. Edmund; 1904 (1,468).

St. Norbert College (c): West de Pere, Wis. 54178. Norbertine Fathers; 1898 (1,613).

St. Peter's College (c): 2641 Kennedy Blvd., Jersey City, N.J. 07306. Jesuit Fathers; 1872 (4,900).

St. Rose, College of (c): 432 Western Ave., Albany, N.Y. 12203. Sisters of St. Joseph of Carondelet; 1920; independent (1,505).

St. Scholastica, College of (c): College St. and Kenwood Ave., Duluth, Minn. 55811. Benedictine Sisters; 1912 (914).

St. Teresa, College of (c): Winona, Minn. 55987. Sisters of St. Francis; 1907 (987).

St. Thomas, College of (m): St. Paul, Minn. 55101. Archdiocese of St. Paul; 1885 (2,488).

St. Thomas, University of (College Status) (c): 3812 Montrose Blvd., Houston, Tex. 77006. Basilian Fathers; 1947 (1,551).

St. Thomas Aquinas College (c): Sparkill, N.Y. 10976. Dominican Sisters (660).

St. Vincent's College (m): Latrobe, Pa. 15650. Benedictine Fathers; 1846 (986).

St. Xavier College (c): 3700 W. 103rd St., Chicago, Ill. 60655. Sisters of Mercy; chartered 1846 (1,103).

Salve Regina College (w): Ochre Point Ave., Newport, R.I. 02840. Sisters of Mercy; 1934 (617).

San Diego, University of (c): Alcala Park, San Diego, Calif. 92110. Diocesan clergy; 1954. Coordinate colleges for men and women (804 men; 667 women).

San Francisco University of (c): 2131 Fulton St., San Francisco, Calif. 95053. Jesuit Fathers; 1851 (6,085).

Santa Fe, College of (c): Santa Fe, N. Mex. 87501. Brothers of the Christian Schools; 1947 (1,271).

Scranton University of (c): Scranton, Pa. 18510. Jesuit Fathers; 1888 (2,832).

Seattle University (c): Broadway and East Madison, Seattle, Wash. 98122. Jesuit Fathers; 1891 (3,170).

Seton Hall University (c): South Orange, N.J. 07079. Diocesan Clergy; 1856 (9,628).

Seton Hill College (w): Greensburg, Pa. 15601. Sisters of Charity of Mother Seton; 1883 (632).

Siena College (c): Loudonville, N.Y. 12211. Franciscan Fathers; 1937 (1,892).

Siena Heights College (c): Adrian, Mich. 49221. Dominican Sisters; 1919 (647).

Spalding College (c): 851 S. 4th St., Louisville, Ky. 40203. Srs. of Charity of Nazareth; 1920 (1,067).

Spring Hill College (c): Mobile, Ala. 36608. Jesuit Fathers; 1830 (930).

Steubenville, College of (c): Steubenville, Ohio 43952. Franciscan Fathers; 1946 (1,304).

Stonehill College (c): North Easton, Mass. 02356. Holy Cross Fathers; 1948 (1,591).

Thomas More College (c): Turkey Foot Rd., Box 85, Fort Mitchell, Covington, Ky. 41017. Diocese of Covington; 1921 (1,812).

Trinity College (w): Colchester Ave., Burlington, Vt. 05401. Sisters of Mercy; 1925 (500).

Trinity College (w): Michigan Ave. and Franklin St. N.E., Washington, D.C. 20017. Sisters of Notre Dame de Namur; 1897 (618).

Ursuline College (w): Lander Rd. and Fairmont Blvd., Cleveland, Ohio 44124. Ursuline Nuns; 1871 (400).

Villa Maria College (w): 2551 W. Lake Rd., Erie, Pa. 16505. Sisters of St. Joseph; 1925 (527).

Villanova University (c): Villanova, Pa. 19086. Augustinian Fathers; 1842 (9,993).

Viterbo College (w): La Crosse, Wis. 54601. Franciscan Sisters; 1931 (485).

Walsh College (c): 2020 Easton St. N.W., Canton, Ohio 44720. Brothers of Christian Instruction; 1951 (899).

Wheeling College (c): 316 Washington Ave., Wheeling, W. Va. 26003. Jesuit Fathers; 1954 (689).

White Plains, College of (w): 52-78 N. Broadway, White Plains, N.Y. 10603. Sisters of the Divine Compassion; 1923; independent (479).

Xavier University (c): Victory Pkwy. and Dana Ave., Cincinnati, Ohio 45207. Jesuit Fathers; 1831 (6,139).

Xavier University (c): Palmetto and Pine Sts., New Orleans, La. 70125. Sisters of the Blessed Sacrament; 1925 (1,554).

Catholic Junior Colleges

Alphonsus College (c): 87 Overlook Dr., Woodcliff Lake, N.J. 07680. Sisters of St. John the Baptist. (300).

Ancilla Domini College (w): Donaldson, Ind. 46513. Ancilla Domini Sisters; 1937 (185).

Aquinas Junior College (c): Harding Rd., Nashville, Tenn. 37205. Dominican Sisters; 1961 (102).

Cullman College (c): Cullman, Ala. 35055. Benedictine Sisters; 1940 (191).

Donnelly College (c): Sandusky Ave., Kansas City, Kan. 66102. Diocesan College. Benedictine Sisters; 1949 (627).

Elizabeth Seton College (c): 1061 N. Broadway, Yonkers, N. Y. 10701. Sisters of Charity; 1960 (400).

Englewood Cliffs College (c): Englewood Cliffs, N.J. 07632. Sisters of St. Joseph of Peace (897).

Harriman College (w): Harriman Heights Rd., Harriman, N.Y. 10926. Sisters of the Catholic Apostolate (168).

Hilbert College (c): 5200 S. Park Ave., Hamburg, N.Y. 14075. Franciscan Sisters; 1960 (619).

Holy Cross Junior College (c): Notre Dame, Ind. 46556. Brothers of Holy Cross; 1966 (290).

Immaculata College of Washington (w): 4300 Nebraska Ave. N.W., Washington, D.C. Sisters of Providence; 1922 (147).

Lourdes Junior College (w): Sylvania, 43560. Franciscan Srs. (92).

Manor Junior College (w): Fox Chase Manor, Jenkintown, Pa. 19046. Sisters of St. Basil the Great; 1947 (180).

Maria College (w): 700 New Scotland Ave., Albany, N.Y. 12208. Sisters of Mercy; 1963 (376).

Maria Regina College (w): 1024 Court St., Syracuse, N.Y. 13208. Franciscan Srs.; 1963 (407).

Marymount College (w): 2807 N. Glebe Rd., Arlington, Va. 22007. Religious of the Sacred Heart of Mary; 1950 (675).

Marymount College (c): 6717 Palos Verdes Dr., South Palos Verdes Estates, Calif. 90274. Religious of the Sacred Heart of Mary (200).

Mt. Aloysius Junior College (c): Cresson, Pa. 16630. Sisters of Mercy; 1939 (480).

Mt. St. Clare College (c): Bluff Blvd., and Springdale Dr., Clinton, Ia. 52732. Sisters of Third Order of St. Francis; 1918 (355).

Ottumwa Heights College (c): Grandview Ave., Ottumwa, Ia. 52501. Sisters of the Humility of Mary; 1925 (335).

Our Lady of Angels College (w): Glen Rid-

dle, Pa. 19037. Sisters of St. Francis; 1965 (128).

Presentation College (w): Aberdeen, S.D. 57401. Sisters of the Presentation; 1951 (358).

St. Catharine College (c): St. Catharine, Ky. 40061. Dominican Sisters; 1931 (150).

St. Gertrude, College of (c): Cottonwood, Ia. 83522. Benedictine Sisters (200).

St. Gregory's Junior College (c): Shawnee, Okla. 74801. Benedictine Fathers; 1876 (510).

St. Joseph College of Florida (c): 720 S. Indian River, Jensen Beach, Fla. 33457. Sisters of St. Joseph (318).

St. Joseph's College (c): Bennington, Vt. 05201. Sisters of St. Joseph (150).

St. Mary's College (c): 200 N. Main St., O'Fallon, Mo. 63366. Sisters of the Most Precious Blood; 1921 (350).

St. Mary's College (c): 2600 S. 5th St., Minneapolis, Minn. 55406 (707).

Salesian College (w): 659 Belmont Ave., N. Haledon, N.J. 07508. Salesian Sisters (65).

Springfield College in Illinois (c): 1500 N. Fifth St., Springfield, Ill. 62702. Ursuline Nuns; 1929 (461).

Tombrock College (w): New St., P.O. Box 628, Paterson, N.J. 07424. Missionary Srs. of the Immaculate Conception; 1964 (436). Coed in evening division.

Trocaire College (w): 110 Red Jackett Pkwy., Buffalo, N.Y. 14220. Sisters of Mercy; 1958 (450).

Villa Julie College (w): Valley Rd., Stevenson, Md. 21153. Sisters of Notre Dame de Namur; 1952 (245).

Villa Maria College of Buffalo (c): 240 Pine Ridge Rd., Buffalo, N.Y. 14225. Felician Srs.; 1960 (424).

CAMPUS MINISTRY

"Campus ministry is a pastoral apostolate of service to the members of the entire college community through concern and care for persons, the proclamation of the Gospel, and the celebration of the liturgy," according to a set of guidelines drawn up by an eight-member commission of the National Catholic Educational Association. The general purpose of the ministry is to make the Church present and active in the academic community.

Ideally, according to the guidelines, elements of the ministry — carried on by teams of priests, men and women religious, and lay persons — include liturgical leadership; pastoral counseling; coordination of expressions and energies for religious life on campus; Christian witness on social and moral issues; objective and independent mediation between various groups on campus; participation in religious aspects of the work of the administration, faculty and students.

Status, Agencies

The dimensions and challenge of the campus ministry are evident from estimates that approximately 75 to 80 per cent of 1.8

million Catholics in colleges and universities in 1971-72 were on secular or non-Catholic private campuses. Serving them were about 750 full-time and 1,000 part-time campus ministry personnel.

Developments in recent years led to dismantling of virtually the whole Newman structure and its replacement by other organizations and programs considered better related to existing conditions on campuses and in the Church and society in general.

The Division of Higher Education, under the Department of Education of the US Catholic Conference, has responsibility for continuing support of ministry in this field. Rev. Laurence T. Murphy, M.M., is director of the division, with offices at 1312 Massachusetts Ave. N.W., Washington, D.C. 20005.

Information and services are furnished by the National Committee of Diocesan Directors of Campus Ministry. This is a committee of members elected from each of the 12 ecclesiastical regions of the US, and is an advisory body to the Division of Higher Education.

The autonomous Catholic Campus Ministry Association, whose former equivalent was the National Newman Chaplains' Association is headed by the Rev. Kean Cronin, 761 University Center, Wayne State University, Detroit, Mich. 48202.

Training Programs

Frank J. Lewis Chaplains' Schools for Campus Ministry Orientation, held in June, 1972, in Detroit and San Diego, provided orientation and direction for men and women new to the ministry. Forty campus ministers attended each of the schools, which were funded by the Frank J. Lewis Foundation.

The National Center for Campus Ministry, for specialized ministerial training and education, serves as a national focus for religious and moral concern in higher education.

Designed by an ecumenical team of chaplains and educators active on public, private and church-related campuses, it is sponsored by the Catholic bishops of the US and is funded by Catholic and non-Catholic individual donors and foundations. It is governed by a board of directors representing major American religious and academic traditions.

The center conducts a year-long program of intensive professional training open to men and women of all faiths; shorter programs or institutes for active campus ministers; research projects meeting the needs of clergymen, professional educators, and others dedicated to building up moral and religious influences in academic institutions.

The year-long program, open in 1972-73 to a maximum of 30 participants, is being conducted in Cambridge, Mass., in conjunction with the seven divinity schools of the Boston Theological Institute, the Church Society for College Work, and the various campus ministries of the surrounding area.

The Rev. John Whitney Evans is director of the center, which is located at 1430 Massachusetts Ave., Cambridge, Mass. 02138.

Newman Background

Special ministry on secular campuses in the US began in 1893 when the first student unit of the Newman movement or apostolate was formed at the University of Pennsylvania. Similar units were formed later at other colleges and universities, and in 1915 various groups throughout the country organized a national student federation. Father John Keough of Philadelphia, who became the first national chaplain of the federation in 1917, was a prime mover in publicizing and developing the movement.

The bishops of the US formally recognized the movement in 1941, and in 1962 approved a National Newman Apostolate structure consisting of: the National Newman Student Federation (dating from 1915), the John Henry Cardinal Newman Honorary Society (1938), the National Newman Chaplains' Association (1950), the National Newman Alumni Association (1957), the National Newman Association of Faculty and Staff (1959), and the National Newman Foundation (1959).

LAY THEOLOGY INSTITUTE

The Institute of Lay Theology, established in 1960 at the University of San Francisco by Rev. Eugene Zimmers, S.J., prepares mature individuals for full-time, salaried positions in the field of Christian adult education. Through its School of Applied Theology, now an affiliate of the Graduate Theological Union, Berkeley, Calif., it is authorized to grant the degree of Master of Applied Theology to candidates on the completion of a two-year program of study and in-service practice.

The school also recruits clergy and religious as students for the purpose of theological updating, renewal or career change.

Graduates, receiving professional salaries, are working at national and diocesan levels; most of them serve in the parish apostolate as directors of adult education or in Confraternity of Christian Doctrine programs, and some are directors of Catholic information centers. The number of such directors is steadily increasing.

There has been an increase also, since 1960, in the number of Catholic colleges and universities which have put into operation programs similar to those developed by the institute for the training of directors of religious education.

Address: School of Applied Theology, 2450 LeConte Ave., Berkeley, Calif. 94709.

The National Association of Boards of Education (1970), with a membership of 1,200, is a commission of the National Catholic Educational Association.

DIOCESAN AND INTERDIOCESAN SEMINARIES

Information, according to states, includes names of archdioceses and dioceses, and names and addresses of seminaries. Types of seminaries, when not clear from titles, are indicated in most cases. Interdiocesan seminaries are generally conducted by religious orders for candidates for the priesthood from several dioceses. The list does not include houses of study only for members of religious communities.

Arizona: Tucson — Regina Cleri Seminary (minor), 8800 E. 22nd St. 85710.

California: Los Angeles — St. John's Seminary (major), 5012 E. Seminary Rd., Camarillo. 93010; St. John's Seminary College, 5118 E. Seminary Rd., Camarillo. 93010; Our Lady Queen of Angels (minor), Box 1071, San Fernando. 91341.

Sacramento — St. Pius X Seminary (minor), Twin Cities Rd. and Midway Ave., Galt. 95632.

San Diego — St. Francis Seminary, 5102 San Pedro Ave. 92111.

San Francisco — St. Patrick's Seminary (major), 320 Middlefield Rd., Menlo Park. 94025; St. Patrick's College Seminary, P.O. Box 151, Menlo Park. 94040; St. Joseph High School (minor), Menlo Park. 94040.

Colorado: Denver — St. Thomas Theological Seminary (major), 1300 S. Steele St. 80210.

Connecticut: Hartford — St. Thomas Seminary (minor), 467 Bloomfield Ave., Bloomfield. 06002.

Stamford Byzantine Rite — Ukrainian Catholic Seminary (major), 161 Glenbrook Rd. 06902; St. Basil's Preparatory School, Clovelly Rd. 06902.

District of Columbia: Washington — Theological School of Catholic University of America, 401 Michigan Ave., N.E. 20017.

Florida: Miami — St. John Vianney Minor Seminary, 2900 S.W. 87th Ave. 33165; St. Vincent de Paul Seminary (major), Military Trail, P.O. Box 460, Boynton Beach. 33435.

Hawaii: Honolulu — St. Stephen's Seminary, P.O. Box 698, Kaneohe. 96744.

Illinois: Belleville — St. Henry's Preparatory Seminary, 5901 W. Main St. 62223.

Chicago — Quigley Preparatory Seminary, 103 East Chestnut St. 60611 (North), 7740 South Western Ave. 60620 (South); St. Mary of the Lake Seminary, Mundelein. 60060; Niles Campus of St. Mary of the Lake Seminary, 7135 N. Harlem Ave. 60631.

Joliet — St. Charles Borromeo Seminary, High School and College, Tr. 53A and Airport Rd. 60441.

Springfield — Immaculate Conception Seminary, 1903 E. Lakeshore Dr. 62707.

Indiana: Evansville — Magister Noster Preparatory Seminary, 921 Hesmer Rd. 47711.

Gary — Bishop Noll Institute, 1519 Hoffman St., Hammond. 46320.

Indianapolis — St. Meinrad Major and Minor Seminary (interdiocesan), St. Meinrad. 47577.

Iowa: Davenport — St. Ambrose Seminary, 518 W. Locust St. 52803.

Dubuque — Seminary of St. Pius X, Loras College. 52001.

Kansas: Kansas City — Savior of the World Seminary, 126th and Parallel, P.O. Bonner Springs. 66012.

Kentucky: Covington — Seminary of St. Pius X, Erlanger. 41018.

Louisville — St. Thomas Seminary (preparatory), 1816 Norris Pl. 40205.

Louisiana: Baton Rouge — St. Joseph Cathedral Prep School, 3300 Hundred Oaks Ave. 70821.

Lafayette — Immaculata Seminary (preparatory), Carmel Ave. 70501. Box 3847. 70501.

New Orleans — Notre Dame Seminary, 2901 S. Carrollton Ave. 70118; St. John Vianney Preparatory School, 3810 Monroe St. 70118.

Maryland: Baltimore — St. Mary's Seminary and University, 5400 Roland Ave. 21210; Mt. St. Mary's Seminary, Emmitsburg. 21727.

Massachusetts: Boston — St. John's Seminary, Brighton. 02135; Pope John XXIII National Seminary, 558 South Ave., Weston. 02193.

Melkite Exarchate — St. Basil's Seminary for Eastern Rites, 30 East St., Methuen. 01844.

Michigan: Detroit — Sacred Heart Seminary College, Inc., 2701 Chicago Blvd. 48206; Sts. Cyril and Methodius Seminary, Orchard Lake. 48034; St. John's Provincial Seminary, P.O. Box 298, Plymouth. 48170.

Grand Rapids — St. Joseph's Minor Seminary, 600 Burton St., S.E., 49507.

St. Maron of Detroit Eparchy — Our Lady of Lebanon Maronite Seminary, 7164 Alaska Ave. N.W., Washington, D.C. 20012.

Minnesota: St. Cloud — St. John's Seminary, Collegeville. 56321.

St. Paul and Minneapolis — St. Paul Seminary, 2260 Summit Ave., St. Paul. 55101; St. John Vianney Seminary, 2260 Summit Ave., St. Paul. 55101.

Winona — Immaculate Heart of Mary Seminary, Terrace Heights. 55987.

Missouri: Jefferson City — St. Thomas Aquinas Preparatory Seminary, 245 N. Levering Ave. 63401.

Kansas City-St. Joseph — Immaculate Conception Seminary (interdiocesan), Conception. 64433; St. John's Diocesan Seminary 2015 E. 72nd St. Kansas City. 64132.

St. Louis — St. Louis Roman Catholic Theological Seminary (Kenrick Seminary), 7800 Kenrick Rd. 63119; Cardinal Glennon College, (major), 5200 Glennon Dr. 63119;

St. Louis Preparatory Seminary, 5200 Glennon Dr. 63119 (South), 3500 St. Catherine St., Florissant 63033 (North).
Springfield-Cape Girardeau — Sacred Heart House of Studies, 625 E. Locust St. 65803.
Montana: Helena — Diocesan Preparatory Seminary, Carroll College. 59601.
New Jersey: Newark — Immaculate Conception Seminary (major), Darlington. 07446; Seton Hall Divinity School, South Orange. 07079.
New Mexico: Gallup — Cristo Rey Minor Seminary, 406 W. Aztec. 87301.
Santa Fe — Immaculate Heart of Mary Seminary, Mt. Carmel Rd. 87501.
New York: Albany — Mater Christi College Seminary, 1134 New Scotland Rd. 12208.
Brooklyn — Cathedral Preparatory Seminary of the Immaculate Conception, 555 Washington Ave. 11238; Cathedral College of the Immaculate Conception, 7200 Douglaston Parkway, Douglaston. 11362; Cathedral Preparatory Seminary of the Immaculate Conception, 56-25 92nd St., Elmhurst. 11373.
Buffalo — Diocesan Preparatory Seminary, 564 Dodge St. 14208; St. John Vianney Seminary (major), East Aurora. 14052; Christ the King Seminary (interdiocesan), Allegany, P.O. St. Bonaventure. 14778.
New York — St. Joseph's Seminary (major), Dunwoodie, Yonkers. 10704: Cathedral College (minor), 555 West End Ave. 10024.
Ogdensburg — Wadhams Hall, Riverside Dr. 13669.
Rochester — St. Bernard's Seminary, 2260 Lake Ave. 14612.
Rockville Centre — Immaculate Conception Diocesan Seminary, Lloyd Harbor, Huntington, L.I. 11743; St. Pius X Preparatory Seminary, 1220 Front St., Uniondale, L.I. 11553.
North Dakota: Fargo — Cardinal Muench Seminary, RFD 2. 58102.
Ohio: Cincinnati — Mt. St. Mary's Seminary of the West, 5440 Moeller Ave., Norwood. 45212; St. Gregory's Minor Seminary, 6616 Beechmont Ave., Cincinnati. 45230.
Cleveland — St. Mary's Seminary, 1227 Ansel Rd. 44108; Borromeo Seminary, 28700 Euclid Ave. Wickliffe. 44092.
Columbus — College of St. Charles Borromeo, 2010 E. Broad St. 43209; Pontifical College Josephinum (interdiocesan), Worthington. 43085.
Steubenville — St. John Vianney Seminary (major and minor), Bloomingdale. 43910.
Toledo — Seminary of the Holy Spirit, 5201 Airport Highway. 43615.
Pennsylvania: Erie — St. Mark's Seminary, 429 E. Grandview Blvd. 16504.
Munhall Greek Rite — Byzantine Catholic Seminary of Sts. Cyril and Methodius, 3605 Perrysville Ave., Pittsburgh.
Philadelphia — Theological Seminary of St. Charles Borromeo, Overbrook. 19151.
Philadelphia Ukrainian Rite — St. Josaphat's Seminary, 201 Taylor St. N.E., Washington, D.C. 20017.
Pittsburgh — St. Paul Seminary, 2900 Noblestown Rd. 15205.
Scranton — St. Pius X Seminary, Dalton. 18414.
Rhode Island: Providence — Our Lady of Providence Seminary (major), Warwick Neck Ave., Warwick. 02889.
South Dakota: Sioux Falls — Minor Seminary, 3100 W. 41st St. 57105.
Texas: Corpus Christi — Corpus Christi Minor Seminary, Rt. 1, Box 500. 78415.
Dallas — Holy Trinity Seminary (major), P.O. Drawer 5378, Irving. 75062.
El Paso — St. Charles Seminary High School, P.O. Box 17548. 79917.
Galveston-Houston — St. Mary's Seminary, 9845 Memorial Dr. 77024.
San Antonio — The Assumption Seminary 2600 W. Woodlawn Ave. 78228.
Virginia: Richmond — St. John Vianney Minor Seminary, Rt. 2, Box 389. 23233.
Washington: Seattle — St. Thomas the Apostle (major, for provinces of Seattle, Portland in Oregon and Anchorage, Alaska), Kenmore. 98028; St. Edward's Seminary (minor), Kenmore. 98028.
Spokane — Bishop White Seminary, E. 429 Sharp Ave. 99202; Mater Cleri Seminary, Colbert. 99005.
West Virginia: Wheeling — St. Joseph Preparatory Seminary, Rt. 6, Vienna. 26101; Seminary House of Studies, 1252 National Rd., Wheeling. 26003.
Wisconsin: Green Bay — Sacred Heart Diocesan Seminary, Oneida. 54155.
Madison — Holy Name Seminary (minor), High Point Rd., R.R. 2. 53711.
Milwaukee — St. Francis School of Pastoral Ministry, 3257 S. Lake Dr. 53207; St. Francis de Sales College, 3501 S. Lake Dr. 53207; De Sales Seminary High School, 3501 S. Lake Dr. 53207.

NCEA

The National Catholic Educational Association, founded in 1904, is a voluntary organization of educational institutions and individuals concerned with Catholic education in the US. Its objectives are to promote and encourage the principles and ideals of Christian education and formation by suitable service and other activities.

The NCEA has 16,000 institutional and individual members. Its official publication is *Momentum.* Numerous service publications are issued to members.

Bishop Raymond J. Gallagher of Lafayette, Ind., is chairman of the association. The Rev. C. Albert Koob, O.Praem., is president.

Headquarters are located at: Suite 350, One Dupont Circle, Washington, D.C. 20036.

REPORT ON SEMINARIES

Guidelines

The Congregation for Catholic Education, in a 10,000-word document entitled *Ratio Fundamentalis* and issued Mar. 16, 1970, provided bishops and other church authorities with a basic draft of norms and prinicples on the education and formation of candidates for the priesthood.

The guidelines were drawn from the *Decree on Priestly Formation* promulgated by the Second Vatican Council, and from suggestions and proposals forwarded to the congregation from episcopal conferences throughout the world. They all add up to the most significant single document on the subject of seminaries and seminary training since the Council of Trent ordered and blueprinted the organization of formal seminaries in the 16th century.

The document noted that its norms are to be regarded as pattern-setting directives within whose framework episcopal conferences are free to move for purposes of local adaptation with respect to effective programs of formal education, personal and spiritual formation, and apostolic experience.

Cardinal Gabriele Garrone, prefect of the congregation, acknowledged the difficulty of adapting seminaries and their programs for the best possible accomplishment of their purposes in contemporary circumstances of great change. He said that the magnitude of the challenge to seminary renewal is so staggering as to all but discourage attempts to cope with it. It must be coped with, however, he added in an accompanying statement — and in such a way that the future of the Church will not be jeopardized by what he called "reckless adventures."

A statement on philosophical studies by seminarians, drawn up by a group of philosophers under the auspices of the US Bishops' Committee on Priestly Formation, was endorsed by the committee and forwarded to the Congregation for Catholic Education in the summer of 1972. The statement was a response to a letter on the same subject circulated by the congregation among bishops the previous January.

The philosophers recommended the spread of philosophical studies over a period of six, rather than the customary two, years; more time for such studies; the integration of philosophical with other studies; and that the philosophy program be "coordinated in its parts rather than dependent upon random courses."

Philosophy must be adequate to promote serious and effective study of theology, the statement said. It should also be "closely related to the personal growth of the individual student. For the future priest, it is an indispensable aid to the implementation of his own decision to open his life to God, to discover the religious meaning of the work and to develop a capacity to mediate this to others as a religious leader."

Major Seminaries

Self-contained, independent seminaries — in each diocese, in each religious institute and in different jurisdictions of the same religious institutes — have been phased out of existence in some places in favor of joint schools with combined faculties and student bodies.

Examples are the Theological Coalition in Washington, D.C., in which more than five religious communities are participants; the Union Theological complex in New York City, with participation by the Jesuit Woodstock College; the Chicago cluster of theological schools, the interdenominational amalgamation of seminaries centered at Berkeley, California.

Some religious institutes have initiated programs which place their candidates for the priesthood on college and university campuses for exposure to curricula and the use of facilities which the institutes cannot supply from their own resources.

The ecumenical dimension of major seminary training is being expanded.

Self-contained, independent seminaries, which continue in operation in a considerable number of US dioceses, have modified many of their structures, gearing their formation programs more on personalistic lines than in the past, extending study programs beyond the scope of manual theology, concentrating on the educative and formational potential of community, and providing students with greater opportunities for apostolic experience in in-service types of programs.

FEDERATION OF SEMINARIANS

The National Federation of Catholic Seminarians was established by 134 delegates from 43 seminaries at an April, 1973, meeting in New Orleans. The organization had been in prospect for several years.

Its purposes, as stated in the constitution, are to promote unity through communication among seminarians, "to provide a forum for the sharing of seminary programs," to allow seminarians "to speak with a representative voice . . . to promote and cooperate in programs of pastoral research and action . . . to work for the implementation of norms for the renewal of priestly formation in seminaries . . . to foster our present ministerial role in the Church," and to cooperate with other existing organizations in the Church.

Besides ratifying a constitution, delegates passed a number of related enabling resolutions and elected Ray Diesbourg and Greg Commella, of the Catholic Theological Union in Chicago, president and vice president, respectively.

US SEMINARIES AND STUDENTS, 1962-1972

(Source: *The Official Catholic Directory.*)

Year	Dioc. Seminaries	Total Dioc. Students	Religious Seminaries Scholasticates	Total Rel. Students	Total Seminarians
1962	98	23,662	447	22,657	46,319
1963	107	25,247	454	22,327	47,574
1964	112	26,701	459	22,049	48,750
1965	117	26,762	479	22,230	48,992
1966	126	26,252	481	21,862	48,114
1967	123	24,293	452	21,086	45,379
1968	124	22,232	437	17,604	39,836
1969	122	19,573	407	14,417	33,990
1970	118	17,317	383	11,589	28,906
1971	110	14,987	340	10,723	25,710
1972	106	13,554	326	9,409	22,963

Breakdown

The peak enrollment year for diocesan seminaries was 1965, when they had a total of 26,792 students. The comparative figure at the beginning of 1972 was 13,554, a decrease of more than 50 per cent.

The peak year for seminaries of religious institutes was 1962, when the total enrollment was 22,657. The comparative figure at the beginning of 1972 was 9,409, a decrease of 58 per cent.

The total all-time high enrollment of 48,992 in 1965 was down to 22,963 at the beginning of 1972, a decrease of 53 per cent.

Reasons

Many reasons have been advanced for the decline in the number of candidates for the priesthood and religious life.

Obvious ones are defections from both ways of life; the impact of changes rightly or wrongly attributed to the Second Vatican Council; the slow pace of institutional renewal in the priesthood, the religious life and the Church in general, coupled with confused expectations; opportunities for apostolic service in other vocations; the problem of adjusting personalist strivings with the needs for institutional commitment; the difficulty of submitting oneself to the other-as well as this-worldly demands of these vocations in the contemporary cultural and social climate.

The basic reason, however, is a crisis of faith. So stated Cardinal Gabriel Garrone, prefect of the Congregation for Catholic Education, in a Vatican Radio interview in April, 1972.

He said that the progressive decrease in vocations "is in direct relation to the crisis in the priesthood" and religious life.

This crisis in turn, he added, is "linked to the crisis of faith, and the crisis of faith is linked to the absolutely unprecedented conditions of the present-day life of men and of society."

The Cardinal said: "Our fundamental concern must spring from the fact that we live in a very complex and very new environment; and that we, therefore, run the risk of remaining passive, either through discouragement or cowardice, or else we lose sight of the most fundamental impulse of all in the matter of vocations — faith."

PONTIFICAL UNIVERSITIES

(Principal source: *Annuario Pontificio.*)

These universities, listed according to country of location, have been canonically erected and authorized by the Sacred Congregation for Catholic Education to award degrees in stated fields of study.

Argentina: Catholic University of S. Maria of Buenos Aires (June 16, 1960). Theology, philosophy, psychology, pedagogy, letters, law and political science, economic and social science, physics and mathematics, engineering, fine arts (with music). Rector, Most Rev. Octavio N. Derisi, titular bishop of Raso.

Belgium: Catholic University of Louvain (Dec. 9, 1425; 1834). Theology, canon law, philosophy, letters, psychology and educational science, law, economics and social science, medicine, science. Rector, Most Rev. Albert Descamps, Titular Bishop of Tunes.

Brazil: Pontifical Catholic University of Rio de Janeiro (Jan. 20, 1947). Philosophy, science and letters, law, social institute, industrial and civil engineering. Rector, Ormindo Viveiros de Castro, S.J.

Pontifical Catholic University of Rio Grande do Sul, Porto Alegre (Nov. 1, 1950). Philosophy, science and letters, law, political and economic science, engineering, odontology. Rector, Prof. Jose Otao Stefani.

Pontifical Catholic University of Sao Paulo (Jan. 25, 1947). Theology, law, philosophy, science and letters, industrial engineering, economic and social science, medicine, journalism. Rector, Prof. Oswaldo Aranha Bandeira de Mello.

University of Campinas (Sept. 8, 1956). Philosophy, science, letters, law, economics, odontology, music. Rector, Prof. Benedito Jose Barreto Fonseca.

Canada: Laval University, Quebec (Mar.

15, 1876). Theology, philosophy, arts and letters, law, commerce, medicine and pharmacy, science, social science, agriculture and forestry. Rector, Msgr. Albert Vachon.

St. Paul University, Ottawa (Feb. 5, 1889). Theology, canon law, philosophy, missiology. Rector, Rev. Marcel Patry, O. M. I.

University of Sherbrooke (Nov. 21, 1957). Theology, art, law, science, commerce, medicine. Rector, Msgr. Roger Maltais.

Central America: Central American Catholic University—

El Salvador Division: José Simeón Cañas University (Sept. 15, 1965). Economic Science; mechanical, electronic, chemical engineering.

Guatemala Division: Rafael Landivar University (Oct. 18, 1961). Letters, law, administrative science. Rector, Prof. José Falla Arís.

Nicaragua (1961). Law, civil and electronic engineering; administrative economic science, veterinary science. Rector. Arturo Dibar, S.J.

Panama Division: University of S. Maria la Antigua (May 27, 1965). Letters, philosophy and pedagogy, science, administration and commerce. Rector, Carlos Ariz, C. M. F.

Chile: Catholic University of Chile, Santiago (June 21, 1888). Theology, philosophy, letters, education, juridical, political and social science, physics and mathematics, architecture, agronomy, economics, medicine, technology. Rector, Prof. Fernando Castillo Velasco.

Catholic University of Valparaiso (Nov. 1, 1961). Philosophy and pedagogy, juridical and social science, commerce, physics and mathematics, chemical engineering, polytechnics, architecture, agriculture. Rector, Dr. Raul Allard Neumann.

Colombia: Bolivarian Pontifical Catholic University, Medellin (Aug. 16, 1945). Law, social and political science, pedagogy, philosophy, economics and commerce, letters, mechanical, electrical and chemical engineering, architecture and civic planning, fine arts. Rector, Msgr. Felix Henao Botero.

Pontifical Xaverian University, Bogota (July 31, 1937). Theology, canon law, philosophy, letters, pedagogy, law, economics, social science, medicine, dentistry, engineering, architecture. Rector, Rev. Alfonso Borrero, S.J.

Cuba: Catholic University of St. Thomas of Villanueva, Havana (May 4, 1957). Philosophy and letters, pedagogy and figurative art, law, commercial science, art and economics, science and technology. Taken over by the Castro government in May, 1961.

Ecuador: Catholic University of Ecuador, Quito (July 16, 1954). Law and economics, philosophy, pedagogy and letters, engineering, agriculture. Rector, Rev. Hernan Malo Gozalez, S.J.

Ethiopia: University of Asmara (Sept. 8, 1960). Letters and pedagogy, juridic, political and economic sciences, mathematics, engineering and architecture. President, Sr. Marianora Onnis.

France: Catholic Faculties of Lille (Nov. 18, 1875). Theology, law, letters, medicine and pharmacy, science, engineering. Rector, Msgr. Gerard Leman.

Catholic Faculties of Lyons (Nov. 22, 1875). Theology, canon law, philosophy, law and economics, letters, science. Rector, Canon Paul Chevallier.

Catholic Institute of Paris (Aug. 11, 1875). Theology, canon law, philosophy, pedagogy, economic and social science, letters, science. Rector, Msgr. Paul Poupard.

Catholic Institute of Toulouse (Nov. 15, 1877). Theology, canon law, philosophy, letters and science, Rector, Msgr. Xavier Ducros.

Catholic University of the West, Angers (Sept. 16, 1875). Theology (philosophy), law, economics, letters, science. Rector, Msgr. Jean Honore.

Ireland: St. Patrick's College, Maynooth (Mar. 29, 1896). Theology, canon law, philosophy, arts and science, sociology, education, Celtic studies. Rector, Msgr. Jeremiah Newman.

Italy: Catholic University of the Sacred Heart, Milan (Dec. 25, 1920). Jurisprudence, political and social science, economics and commerce, letters and philosophy, medicine and surgery, pedagogy, agriculture. Rector, Prof. Giuseppe Lazzati.

Japan: *Jochi Daigaku* (University of Sophia), Tokyo (Mar. 29, 1913). Theology, philosophy, letters, languages, law, economics and commerce, science and polytechnics. Rector, Rev. Giuseppe Pittau, S. J.

Lebanon: St. Joseph University of Beirut (Mar. 25, 1881). Theology, Oriental letters, law, engineering, economics, medicine and pharmacy. Rector, Rev. Abdallah Dagher, S.J.

Netherlands: Roman Catholic University, Nijmegen (June 29, 1923). Theology, law, letters, philosophy, medicine, natural science. Rectors: Dr. G. Brenninkmeijer, W. C. L. Van der Grinten, Dr. C. Kuyper.

Paraguay: Catholic University of Our Lady of the Assumption, Asuncion (Feb. 2, 1965). Philosophy and pedagogy, law, political and social science, administrative science. Rector, Rev. Juan Oscar Usher.

Peru: Catholic University of Peru, Lima (Sept. 30, 1942). Theology, philosophy, history and letters, jurisprudence and political science, economic and commercial science, civil engineering, education, agriculture. Rector, Felipe MacGregor, S.J.

Philippine Islands: University of Santo Tomas, Manila (Nov. 20, 1645). Theology, canon law, philosophy, pedagogy, law, letters, science, engineering and architecture, fine arts, medicine and surgery, pharmacy, commerce and administration, music. Rector, Rev. Leonardo Legazpi, O.P.

Poland: Catholic University of Lublin (July 25, 1920). Theology, philosophy, canon law, social-economic science, letters. Rector, Msgr. Albert Krapiec, O.P.

Spain: Catholic University of Navarra, Pamplona (Aug. 6, 1960). Theology, canon law, philosophy and letters, jurisprudence, medicine, science, pharmacy, political, economic and commercial science, industrial engineering, agriculture, journalism, Superior Institute of Business Studies. Rector, Prof. Francisco Ponz-Piedrafita.

Pontifical University of Comillas (Mar. 29, 1904). Theology, canon law, philosophy. Rector, Rev. Francisco Belda, S.J.

Pontifical University of Salamanca (Sept. 25, 1940). Theology, canon law, social sciences, philosophy. Rector, Rev. Fernando Sebastian Aguilar, C. M. F.

University of Deusto, Bilbao (Aug. 10, 1963). Theology, law, economics and social science, philosophy and letters, science. Rector, Rev. Pedro Pi Ferrer, S.J.

Taiwan: Fu Jen Catholic University (Nov. 15, 1923, at Peking; reconstituted at Taipeh, Sept. 8, 1961). Theology, art, law, economics, science. Rector, Cardinal Paul Yu Pin.

United States: Catholic University of America, Washington, D. C. (Mar. 7, 1889). Pontifical faculties of theology, canon law, philosophy. Rector, Prof. Clarence C. Walton.

De Paul University, Chicago (June 28, 1957). Arts and science, jurisprudence, commerce, music, physical education. Rector, Rev. John Cartelyou, C. M.

Georgetown University, Washington, D.C. (Mar. 30, 1833). Arts and science, language, law, economics, diplomatic and consular science, medicine and odontology. Rector, Rev. Gerald J. Campbell, S. J.

Niagara University, Niagara Falls (June 21, 1956). Arts and science, economics, education. Rector, Kenneth T. Slattery, C.M.

Venezuela: Catholic University "Andres Bello," Caracas (Sept. 29, 1963). Letters and education, law, economics, social science, physical and natural science, pharmacy, civil and industrial engineering, architecture. Rector, Rev. Pio Bello, S. J.

Zaire: University of Kinshasa, Kinshasa (Apr. 25, 1957). Theology, law, medicine, letters and philosophy, science, political, social and economic science. Rector, Most Rev. Tharcisse Tshibangu, titular bishop of Scampa.

Faculties of Ecclesiastical Studies

(Source *Annuario Pontificio*)

These faculties in Catholic seminaries and universities, listed according to country of location, have been canonically erected and authorized by the Sacred Congregation for Catholic Education to award degrees in stated fields of study. In addition to those listed here, there are other faculties of theology or philosophy in state universities and for members of certain religious orders only.

Australia: Faculty of Theology, Sydney (Feb. 2, 1954). Pres., Rev. Patrick Murphy.

Canada: Institute of Medieval Studies, Toronto (Oct. 18, 1939). Pres., Very Rev. Lawrence K. Shook, C. S. B.

Germany: Theological Faculty, Paderborn (June 11, 1966). Pres., Rev. Eduard Stakemeier.

Theological Faculty of the Major Episcopal Seminary, Trier (June 5, 1950). Pres., Rev. Wilhelm Bartz.

Philosophical Faculty, Munich (1925; Oct. 25, 1971). Pres., Very Rev. Albert Keller, S. J.

Great Britain: Heythrop Athenaeum of Ecclesiastical Studies (Nov. 1, 1964). Theology, philosophy. Pres., Rev. Frederick Copleston, S.J.

India: Pontifical Athenaeum of Poona (July 27, 1926). Theology, philosophy. Rector, Rev. Eriberto Alphonso, S.J.

Italy: Interregional Theological Faculty, Milan (Aug. 8, 1935). Pres. Most Rev. Carlo Colombo, titular bishop of Vittoriana.

Pontifical Theological Faculty of the Most Sacred Heart of Jesus, Cuglieri, of the Pontifical Regional Seminary of Sardinia (July 5, 1927). Pres., Rev. Giuseppe Bosio.

Pontifical Ambrosian Institute of Sacred Music, Milan (Mar. 12, 1940). Pres., Msgr. Ernesto Moneta Caglio.

Theological Faculty for the Archdiocese of Naples, of the Major Archiepiscopal Seminary (Oct. 31, 1941). Pres., Msgr. Antonio Ambrosanio.

Spain: Theological Faculty of Barcelona, of the Major Seminary of Barcelona and the College of St. Francis Borgia of San Cugat del Valles (Mar. 7, 1968). Pres., Rev. Pedro Ribas, S.J.

Theological Faculty of the North, of the Metropolitan Seminary of Burgos and the Diocesan Seminary of Vitoria (Feb. 6, 1967). Pres., Very Rev. Jose Zunzunegui.

United States: St. Mary's Faculty of Theology, Baltimore (May 1, 1822). Pres., Rev. John F. Dede, S.S.

St. Mary of the Lake Faculty of Theology, Chicago (Sept. 30, 1929). Pres., Rev. William LeSaint, S.J.

Vietnam: Theological Faculty, Dalat (July 31, 1965). Pres., Rev. Giuseppe Raviolo, S.J.

The Pontifical College Josephinum (Theological Seminary and Preparatory Department) at Worthington, Ohio, is a regional pontifical seminary. Established Sept. 1, 1888, it is immediately subject to the Holy See. Rector, Msgr. Thomas P. Campbell.

In recent years, formal seminary training has included and been supplemented by programs of in'service training which provide students with ministerial experience during preparation for ordination.

Institutes of Higher Studies in Rome
(Source: *Annuario Pontificio.*)

Pontifical Gregorian University (1552). Theology, canon law, philosophy, psychology, science of religion, church history, missiology, social sciences. Rector, Very Rev. Herve Carrier. Associated with the university are:

The **Pontifical Bible Institute** (May 7, 1909), with faculties of Scripture and ancient Oriental studies. Rector, Rev. C. Martini.

The **Pontifical Institute of Oriental Studies** (Oct. 15, 1917), with faculties of Oriental ecclesiastical studies and Oriental canon law. Rector, Very Rev. Ivan Zuzek.

Pontifical Lateran University (1773). Theology, canon law, civil law, philosophy, moral theology, literature. Rector, Msgr. Pietro Pavan.

Pontifical Urban University (1627). Theology, philosophy, missiology. Rector, Rev. Pietro Chiocchetta.

Pontifical University of St. Thomas Aquinas (**Angelicum**) (1580), of the Order of Preachers. Theology, canon law, philosophy, social sciences, spirituality. Rector, Very Rev. Paul Gundolf Gieraths, O.P.

Pontifical Athenaeum of St. Anselm (1687), of the Benedictines. Theology, philosophy, liturgy, monastic studies. Rector, Very Rev. Basil Studer, O.S.B.

Pontifical Athenaeum Antonianum (of St. Anthony) (May 17, 1933), of the Order of Friars Minor. Theology, canon law, philosophy, and the affiliated School of Biblical Studies in Jerusalem. Rector, Rev. Roberto Zavelloni, O.F.M.

Pontifical Athenaeum Salesianum (May 3, 1940), of the Salesians of Don Bosco. Canon law, theology, philosophy, pedagogy, Higher Latin Studies (Feb. 22, 1964). Rector, Rev. Antonio Javierra, S.D.B.

Pontifical Institute of Sacred Music (1911). President, Msgr. Ferdinand Haberl.

Pontifical Institute of Christian Archeology (Dec. 11, 1925). Rector, Prof. Vittore Saxer.

Pontifical Theological Faculty "St. Bonaventure" (Dec. 18, 1587), of the Order of Friars Minor Conventual. President, Very Rev. Aifonso Pompei, O. F. M. Conv.

Pontifical Theological Faculty of Sts. Teresa of Jesus and John of the Cross (Teresianum) (July 16, 1935), of the Carmelites. Theology, spirituality. President, Very Rev. Tommaso della Croce, O. Carm.

Pontifical Theological Faculty "Marianum" (1398), of the Servants of Mary. President, Very Rev. Salvatore M. Meo.

Pontifical Institute of Arabic Studies (1926), of the White Fathers. President, Very Rev. Joseph Gelot, P. A.

PONTIFICAL ACADEMY OF SCIENCES

(Sources: *Annuario Pontificio,* NC News Service.)

The Pontifical Academy of Sciences was constituted in its present form by Pius XI Oct. 28, 1936, in virtue of *In Multis Solaciis,* a document issued on his own initiative.

The academy is the only supranational body of its kind in the world, with a pope-selected, life-long membership of outstanding mathematicians and experimental scientists from many countries. The normal complement of members is 70; the total number, however, includes additional honorary and supernumerary members. Non-Catholics as well as Catholics belong to the academy.

Purposes of the academy are to honor pure science and its practitioners, to promote the freedom of pure science and to foster research.

The academy originated as the Accademia Linceorum (lynxes) in Rome Aug. 17, 1603. Pius IX reorganized this body and gave it a new name — Pontificia Accademia dei Nuovi Lincei — in 1847. It was taken over by the Italian state in 1870 and called the Accademia Nationale dei Lincei, Leo XIII reconstituted it with a new charter in 1887. Pius XI designated the Vatican Gardens as the site of academy headquarters in 1922 and gave it its present title and status in 1936. Four years later he gave the title of Excellency to its members.

In addition to four supernumerary members, membership as of Aug. 1, 1972, numbered 55 in the following countries: US, 8; England, 7; France, 6; Italy, 4; Canada, 3; Germany, Japan, Netherlands, Spain, Sweden and Switzerland, 2 each; Argentina, Australia, Austria, Belgium, Brazil, Chile, Greece, Finland, Mexico, Monaco, Pakistan, Peru, Portugal, Vatican City and Venezuela.

Scientists from the US who presently hold membership in the Academy are: Edward Adalbert-Doisy, professor of biochemistry at St. Louis University School of Medicine (May 29, 1948); Franco Rasetti, professor emeritus of physics at John Hopkins University, Baltimore, Md. (Oct. 28, 1936); George Speri Sperti, director of the Institutum Divi Thomae in the Athanaeum of Ohio (Oct. 28, 1936); Hugh Stott Taylor, professor of chemistry at Princeton University (Oct. 28, 1936); Veikho A. Heiskanen, director of Geodesic Institute at Ohio State University (Sept. 24, 1964); William Wilson Morgan, director of Yerkes Observatory, Williams Bay, Wis. (Sept. 24, 1964); Sir John Carew Eccles, professor at the neurological laboratory of the State University of New York at Buffalo (Apr. 8, 1961); Albert Szent-Gyorgyi, director of muscle research at the Marine Biological Laboratory, Woods Hole, Mass. (Apr. 10, 1970).

Deceased US members of the Academy

were: George D. Birkhoff, Alexis Carrel, Herbert Sidney Langfeld, Robert A. Millikan, Thomas H. Morgan, Theodore von Karman, Victor F. Hess, Peter Debye.

Other members of the Academy and the dates of their selection are as follows:

Argentina: Luis F. Leloir (Apr. 22, 1968).

Australia: Keith E. Bullen (Apr. 22, 1968).

Austria: Hans Tuppy (Apr. 10, 1970).

Belgium: Christian de Duve (Apr. 16, 1970).

Brazil: Charles Chagas Filho (Aug. 18, 1961).

Canada: Herbert Charles Best (Apr. 5, 1955); Ernesto Gherzi, S.J. (Oct. 28, 1936); Gerhard Herzberg (Sept. 24, 1964).

Chile: Eduardo Cruz-Coke (May 29, 1948).

England: Hermann Alexander Bruck (Apr. 5, 1955); Sir James Chadwick (Apr. 8, 1961); Paul Adrien Dirac (Aug. 18, 1961); Alan Lloyd Hodgkin (Apr. 22, 1968); Alfred R. Ubbelohde (Apr. 22, 1968); Peter C. C. Garnham (Apr. 10, 1970); Robert Stoneley (Apr. 10, 1970).

Finland: Arthur Ilmari Virtanen (Apr. 5, 1955).

France: Louis de Broglie (Apr. 5, 1955); Gaston Maurice Julia (Apr. 5, 1955); Jean Lecomte (Sept. 24, 1964); Pierre Raphael Lepine (Sept. 24, 1964); Louis Leprince-Ringuet (Aug. 18, 1961); Georges Chaudron (April 10, 1970).

Germany: Werner Carl Heisenberg (Apr. 5, 1955); Wolfgang Gentner (Apr. 10, 1970).

Greece: George Joakimoglou (Apr. 10, 1970).

Italy: Giovanni Battista Bonino (May 23, 1942); Betolo Giovanni Battista Marini (Apr. 22, 1968); Domenico Marota (Apr. 8, 1961); Mauro Picone (Apr. 10, 1970).

Japan: Paul San-Ichiro Mizushima (Aug. 18, 1961); Hideki Yukawa (Apr. 8, 1961).

Mexico: Manuel Sandoval Vallarta (Aug. 18, 1961).

Monaco: Rudolf L. Mossbauer (Apr. 10, 1970).

Netherlands: F. J. J. Buytendijk (Oct. 28, 1936); Jan Hendrik Oort (Aug. 18, 1961).

Pakistan: Salimuzzanam Siddiqui (Sept. 24, 1964).

Peru: Alberto Hurtado (Aug. 18, 1961).

Portugal: Antonio De Almeida (Apr. 8, 1961).

Spain: Jose Garcia Sineriz (May 23, 1942); Manuel Lora Tomayo (Sept. 24, 1964).

Sweden: Sven Horstadius (Aug. 18, 1961); Arne W. K. Tiselius (Apr. 5, 1955).

Switzerland: Walter Rudolf Hess (Apr. 5, 1955); Leopold Ruzioka (Dec. 5, 1942).

Vatican City: Daniel J. Kelly O'Connell, S.J. (Sept. 24, 1964).

Venezuela: Marcel Roche (Apr. 10, 1970).

Supernumerary members are: Patrick Treanor, S.J., directory of the Vatican Observatory; Joseph Junkes, S.J., prefect of the Astrophysics Laboratory of the Vatican Observatory; Alfons Stickler, S.D.B., prefect of the Vatican Library; Msgr. Martino Giusti, prefect of the Secret Vatican Archives.

President of the Academy is Daniel J. Kelly O'Connell, S.J.

PONTIFICAL URBAN UNIVERSITY

The Pontifical Urban University was founded by Pope Urban VIII Aug. 1, 1627, for the express purpose of training priests from mission countries.

In the nearly 350 years of its existence, the university has had great influence on the missionary activity of the Church. At the present time, many of the more than 250 native bishops in mission countries are among its alumni, as well as a large number of their priests.

UNION PRO DEO

The International Union Pro Deo was inaugurated in Belgium by Father Felix Morlion, O.P., in a series of courses in political and social philosophy, and subsequently spread to other parts of Europe, North and South America. At the invitation of Pope Pius XII, an international study center was established in Rome in 1944. Four years later, the Pro Deo International University of Social Studies was founded, and has since been the headquarters of the movement.

The Congregation for Catholic Education has supervisory authority over the Union, which was given the status of a moral entity Jan. 25, 1965.

CATHOLIC ALUMNAE

The International Federation of Catholic Alumnae, established in 1914, has its office in the Administration Building (Room 416), Catholic University of America, Washington, D.C. 20001. Its purpose is to work for the extension of Catholic education and community services, and to provide scholarships for teaching sisters. Its membership consists of graduates of Catholic high schools, colleges and universities, and other institutions of higher learning.

CORRESPONDENCE COURSES

Religious correspondence courses are available to persons who wish to investigate the teachings of the Catholic Church privately or are unable to receive personal instructions. Both Catholics and non-Catholics can apply. National courses offered include:

CCD Correspondence Courses for Adults, 424 North Broadway, Wichita, Kans. 67202.

Confraternity Home Study Service, 3473 S. Grand Blvd., St. Louis, Mo. 63118.

Paulist Home Study Service, 21 E. Van Buren St., Chicago, Ill. 60605.

The Catholic Centre, Saint Paul University, 1 Stewart St., Ottawa, 2 Ont., Canada.

See also Knights of Columbus for its participation in advertising Catholic beliefs and correspondence courses.

Social Services

Catholic Charities is the ordinary title of an umbrella-type of agency which supervises social work under the auspices of archdioceses and dioceses in the United States.

The first central, over-all diocesan agency in the US was established in 1903. There are now more than 500 diocesan and branch agencies of Catholic Charities in this country.

The principal fields of service in which diocesan organizations and their member agencies are engaged are family counseling, child welfare, health services for unmarried mothers, community services, day care centers, neighborhood center programs, and care of the aged. Community organization and social action are also functions of Catholic Charities.

National Conference

The National Conference of Catholic Charities, organized in 1910, serves diocesan organizations by providing a field service, developing a literature, providing an informational service, promoting research, assisting with organization, improving standards, and representing agencies of Catholic Charities among other national organizations and offices, both voluntary and governmental. It has over 500 institutional, 1,500 individual and 650 organizational members.

Closely affiliated with the conference is the National Association of Directors of Catholic Charities and the Conference of Religious, an organization of religious engaged in social and charitable work. Also affiliated are the Society of St. Vincent de Paul of the US, the Association of Ladies of Charity of the US, and the National Christ Child Society.

The conference is the representative of the International Conference of Catholic Charities before the UN Economic and Social Council and before UNICEF. It has consultative status with both agencies.

NCCC initiated self-study in 1972 of proposals for re-focusing its goals, overall reorganization, and substantial increases in staff and budget. Practical effect of the proposals, if translated into action, would be greater emphasis on social action and advocacy, with maintenence of the social services traditionally associated with the conference.

The conference, as presently constituted, "cannot meet the expectations of the Church or the demands made on it by church organizations," Msgr. Lawrence J. Corcoran told a three-state meeting of Catholic Charities officials in April. He said: "We must make changes that will permit us to meet those demands and growing expectations. We must develop a national outlook, a national identity and focus."

Participants in the Indianapolis meeting, like others in similar gatherings during the year, were in general agreement concerning the spirit and process of renewal within the national organization but voiced some serious considerations regarding budget and structural proposals. How to raise money to finance changes in a time of shrinking budgets, and functioning state conferences into regional ones, were key issues to be resolved.

Mrs. Dorothy B. Daly is president of the conference. Msgr. Lawrence J. Corcoran is the secretary.

Offices are located at 1346 Connecticut Ave. N.W., Washington, D.C. 20036.

Vincent de Paul Society

The Society of St. Vincent de Paul, originally called the Conference of Charity, is an association of Catholic laymen devoted to personal service of the poor through the spiritual and corporal works of mercy. The first conference was formed at Paris in 1833 by Frederic Ozanam and his associates.

The first conference in the US was organized in 1845 at St. Louis. There are now approximately 4,900 units of the society in this country, with a membership of about 45,000.

In the past 50 years, members of the society in this country have distributed among poor persons financial and other forms of assistance valued at approximately $150 million.

US Vincentian councils and conferences participating in "twinning" programs assist their poorer counterparts abroad by sending them correspondence, information and financial aid on a continuing basis.

Under the society's revised regulations, women are being admitted to membership. Increasing emphasis is being given to store and rehabilitation workshops of the society through which persons with marginal income can purchase refurbished goods at minimal cost. Handicapped persons are employed in renovating goods and store operations.

Henri Jacob of Paris, France, is president of the Council General, the governing body of the society. There are approximately 600,000 members in the world.

The office of the US Superior Council is located at 611 Olive St., St. Louis, Mo. 63101.

Service Organizations

Catholic Hospital Association: Founded in 1915, is a service organization for 853 Catholic-sponsored health care facilities located throughout the United States.

Through research, its monthly *Hospital Progress,* annual meetings and conferences, it keeps institutional and individual members up-to-date on unique Catholic apostolic aspects of medical, moral, educational and professional developments in the health field.

The Catholic Health Services Leadership

Program, a major CHA activity, is designed to develop the relationships and maximize the potential strengths and resources of religious congregations, dioceses and their multi-faceted health care facilities and services.

The Catholic Health Assembly (annual meeting) offers CHA constituents the opportunity to dialogue the best methods to strengthen and unify the corporate health commitment of religious congregations and dioceses — the sponsoring groups that operate Catholic hospitals and nursing homes.

Sister Irene Kraus, D.C., is president of the association. Sister Mary Maurita, R.S.M., is the executive vice-president.

Executive offices are located at 1438 S. Grand Boulevard, St. Louis, Mo. 63104.

National Association of Catholic Chaplains: Founded in 1965, it operates under the auspices of the Department of Health Affairs, US Catholic Conference. Membership in 1972 was approximately 1,000.

The association conducts two pastoral institutes for general hospital chaplains annually, one in Washington, D.C., and another in Menlo Park, Calif. By the summer of 1972, nearly 600 chaplains had attended these institutes.

Father Frank J. Weber, chaplain of Metropolitan State Hospital, Norwalk, Calif., is president of the association. Father Michael J. McManus is the executive secretary.

The office of the association is located at 1312 Massachusetts Ave. N. W., Washington, D.C. 20005.

FACILITIES FOR RETIRED AND AGED PERSONS

Sources: Sister Marie M. Gaffney, M.S.B.T., consultant to the National Conference of Catholic Charities, Commission on Aging; *1972 Guidebook* of the Catholic Hospital Association; *The Official Catholic Directory, 1972.*

This list covers residence, health care and other facilities for retired and aged.

Information includes name, type of facility if not evident from the title, address, total capacity (in parentheses).

Alabama: Allen Memorial Home, 170 N. Catherine St., Mobile 36604 (50).

Good Samaritan Hospital Nursing Home, 1107 Voeglin St., Selma 36701 (26).

Sacred Heart Home of the Little Sisters of the Poor, 1655 McGill Ave., Mobile 36604 (108). Villa Mercy, Daphne 36526 (45).

Arizona: Sacred Heart Home for the Aged, 1110 N. 16th St., Phoenix 85006 (170).

Villa Maria de Guadalupe Home for the Aged, 701 E. Adams St., Tucson 85719 (25).

Arkansas: Benedictine Manor (Retirement Home), 2nd and Grand Sts., Hot Springs 71901 (50).

St. Joseph's Home, Brinkley 72021 (28). Joseph's Home for the Aged, Camp Robinson Rd., N. Little Rock 72118 (9).

California: Casa Manana Inn, 3700 N. Sutter St., Stockton 95204 (175).

Catholic Women's Center (Hotel for Elderly Single Women), 195 E. San Fernando St., San Jose 95112 (30).

Little Flower Haven, 8585 La Mesa Blvd., La Mesa 92041 (94).

Little Sisters of the Poor, 2700 E. First St., Los Angeles 90033 (160).

Little Sisters of the Poor, 2647 E. 14th St., Oakland 94601 (110).

Little Sisters of the Poor, 300 Lake St., San Francisco 94118 (186).

Madonna Residence (for women over 60), 270 McAllister St., San Francisco 94102 (82).

Marian Residence, 124 S. College Dr., Santa Maria 93454 (44).

Nazareth House, 2121 N. 1st St., Fresno 93703 (64).

Nazareth House, 3333 Manning Ave., Los Angeles 90064 (107).

Nazareth House, 245 Nova Albion Way, Terra Linda, San Rafael 94903 (109).

Our Lady of Fatima Villa (nursing home, women), 20400 Saratoga-Los Gatos Rd., Saratoga 95070 (85).

Our Lady's Home, 3431 Foothill Blvd., Oakland 94601 (200).

St. Francis Home, 1718 W. 6th St., Santa Ana 92703 (71).

Villa Siena, 1855 Miramonte, Mountain View 94040 (23).

Colorado: Little Sisters of the Poor, 3630 W. 30th Ave., Denver 80211 (100).

St. Elizabeth Retreat, 2825 W. 32nd Ave., Denver 80211 (95).

Connecticut: Notre Dame Convalescent Home, West Rocks Rd., Norwalk 06851 (60).

Regina Pacis Villa, RFD No. 1, Pomfret 06258 (12).

St. Andrew's Home for the Aged, 238 Winthrop Ave., New Haven 06511 (99).

St. Joseph Guest Home (Women, Employed and Retired), 311 Greene St., New Haven 06511 (93).

St. Joseph's Home for the Aged, 88 Jackson St., Willimantic 06226 (37).

St. Joseph's Manor, 6448 Main St., Trumbull 06611 (285).

St. Lucian's Home of the Aged, 532 Burritt St., New Britain 06053.

St. Mary's Home, 291 Steele Rd., W. Hartford 06117 (177).

Villa Maria Rest Home for the Aged, West St., Thompson 06277 (30).

Delaware: St. Joseph's Home, Little Sisters of the Poor, 401 N. Bancroft Pkwy., Wilmington 19805 (97).

District of Columbia: St. Joseph's Home, Little Sisters of the Poor, 220 H St., N.E., Washington 20002 (160).

Florida: All Saints Home, 2040 Riverside Ave., Jacksonville 32204 (53).

Cor Jesu Home for the Aged, 4918 N. Habana Ave., Tampa 33614 (90).

Florida Manor, P.O. Box 5577, Orlando 32805.

Haven of Our Lady of Peace, 5203 9th Ave., Pensacola 32504 (88).

Lourdes Residence, 305 S. Flagler Dr., W. Palm Beach 33401 (142).

Marian Towers, Inc., 620 N.E. 63rd St., Miami 33138.

The Pennsylvania, 208 Evernia St., W. Palm Beach 33401 (230).

St. Elizabeth Gardens, 801 N. E. 33rd St., Pompano Beach 33064.

St. Joseph's Residence, 3485 N.W. 30th St., Ft. Lauderdale 33311.

St. Joseph's Manor, 2335 Lakeview Ave. S., St. Petersburg 33712 (64).

Villa Maria (Residence), 1050 N.E. 123rd St., N. Miami 33161.

Villa Maria Nursing and Rehabilitation Center, 1050 N.E. 125th St., N. Miami 33161 (180).

Idaho: St. Benedict's Hospital Home for the Aged, Jerome 83338 (40).

Illinios: Addolorato Villa, Highway 83, McHenry Rd., Wheeling 60090 (104).

Holy Family Villa, Lemont 60439 (108).

Huber Memorial Home, 1000 30th St., Rock Island 61201 (22).

Loretto Home, 417 Prospect St., Alton 62002 (57).

Marianjoy, Inc., (Nursing and Extended Care, P.O. Box 667, Wheaton 60187 (89).

Maryhaven-West (Residence, Nursing Care), 1700 E. Lake St., Glenview 60025 (148)).

Mayslake Retirement Village (Apartment Retirement Project), 1801 35th St., Oak Brook 60521 (325).

Meredith Memorial Home, Public Square, Belleville 62220 (86).

Mother Theresa Home, 1270 Main St., Lemont 60439 (56).

Our Lady of Angels Retirement Home, 1201 Wyoming, Joliet 60435 (90).

Our Lady of the Snows Apartment Community Retirement Home, 9500 Route 460, Belleville 62223 (175).

Rosary Hill Convalescent Home, 9000 W. 81st St., Justice 60458 (60).

St. Andrew Home, 7000 N. Newark Ave., Chicago 60648 (199).

St. Ann Home and Infirmary, Waukegan and Techny Rds., Techny 60082 (175).

St. Ann's Home for the Aged, 770 State St., Chester 62233 (45).

St. Augustine's House, Little Sisters of the Poor, 2358 Sheffield Ave., Chicago 60614 (116).

St. Benedict's Home, 6930 W. Touhy Ave., Niles 60648 (50).

St. Joseph's Home, 80 W. Baldwin Rd., Palatine 60067 (208).

St. Joseph's Home, 2650 N. Ridgeway Ave., Chicago 60647 (175).

St. Joseph's Home, 2223 W. Heading Ave., Peoria 61604 (200).

St. Joseph's Home, 649 E. Jefferson St., Freeport 61032 (118).

St. Joseph's Home, S. 6th St. Rd., Springfield 62703 (93).

St. Patrick's Residence, 22 E. Clinton St., Joliet 60431 (207).

Villa Scalabrini, Northlake 60161 (146).

Villa Saint Cyril, 1111 St. John's Ave., Highland Park 60035 (80).

5 **Indiana:** Providence Home of Our Lady of the Holy Rosary, Jasper 47546 (37).

Providence Retirement Home, 703 E. Spring St., New Albany 47150 (73).

Regina Pacis Home, 3900 Washington Ave., Evansville 47715 (51).

Sacred Heart Home, R.R. 2, Avilla 46710 (130).

St. Anne Home, 1900 Randalia Dr., Ft. Wayne 46805 (119).

St. Anthony's Rest Home, 201 Franciscan Rd., Crown Point 46307 (122).

St. Augustine Home, Little Sisters of the Poor, 2345 W. 86th St., Indianapolis 46260 (184).

St. John and St. Gertrude Home, Little Sisters of the Poor, 1236 Lincoln Ave., Evansville 47714 (105).

St. Paul Hermitage, 501 N. 17th ST., Beech Grove 46107.

Iowa: The Alverno Residence for Retired Citizens, Clinton 52732 (120).

Bishop Drumm Home for the Aged, 1409 Clark St., Des Moines 50314 (145).

Holy Spirit Retirement Home, 1701 W. 25th St., Sioux City 51103 (78).

Kahl Home for the Aged and Infirm, 1101 W. 9th St., Davenport 52802 (130).

The Marian Home, 23 N. 7th St., Fort Dodge 50501 (50).

Mary of the Angels Home (Women, Employed and Retired), 605 Bluff St., Dubuque 52001 (92).

Ritter Home for Retired Women, 1837 Sunnyside Ave., Burlington 52601 (10).

St. Anthony Nursing Home, 406 E. Anthony St., Carroll 51401 (78).

St. Francis Home, 901 Davis Ave., Dubuque 52001 (101).

St. Monica's Home, 4500 Perry Creek Rd., Sioux City 51104 (38).

Kansas: Mt. St. Joseph Home for the Aging, 2601 Ridge Ave., Kansas City 66102 (47).

St. Ann's Home, 323 E. 5th St., Concordia 66901 (76).

St. John's Rest Home, Victoria 67671 (45).

St. Joseph's Home for the Aging, 924 N. Topeka, El Dorado 67042 (58).

Villa Maria, 116 S. Central, Mulvane 67110 (57).

Kentucky: Carmel Home, Old Hartford Rd., Owensboro 42301 (82).

Carmel Manor, Carmel Manor Ave., Ft. Thomas, 41075 (103).

Cardome Residence Home for Women, Georgetown 40324 (30).

Home for Senior Citizens, P.O. Box R. 1, Philpot 42366 (61).

Madonna Manor Nursing Home, 2344 Amsterdam Rd., Covington 41016 (Cottages for Senior Citizens, 8).

St. Charles Nursing Home, Kyles Lane, Covington 41011 (143).

St. Joseph's Home for the Aged Poor, 622 S. 10th St., Louisville 40203 (195).

St. Margaret of Cortona Home, 1310 Leestown Pike, Lexington 40508 (20).

Taylor Manor Nursing Home, Versailles 40383 (78).

Louisiana: Bethany M.H.S. Nursing Home, P.O. Box 2308, Lafayette 70501 (40).

Consolata Home (Extended Care Facility), New Iberia 70560 (74).

Lafon Home of the Holy Family, 1125 N. Tonti St., New Orleans 70119 (75).

Little Sisters of the Poor, 1501 N. Johnson St., New Orleans 70116 (135).

Ollie Steele Burden Manor (Nursing Home), 4200 Essen Lane, Baton Rouge 70809 (44).

Our Lady of Prompt Succor Home, 751 E. Prudhomme Lane, Opelousas 70570.

St. Joseph's Home, 2301 Sterlington Rd., Monroe 71201 (110).

St. Margaret's Daughters' Home, 504 Tricou St., New Orleans 70117 (82).

Wynhoven Apartments (Residence for Senior Citizens), 4600 - 10th St., Marrero 70072.

Maine: Marcotte Nursing Home, 100 Campus Ave., Lewiston 04240.

Mt. St. Joseph Home, Highwood St., Waterville 04901 (76).

Northern Maine Security Home (Nursing Home), Eagle Lake 04789 (71).

St. John Valley Security Home (Boarding-Nursing Home), Madawaska 04756 (81).

St. Joseph Home for Women, 10 Locust St., Portland 04103 (6).

Villa Muir, Home for Women, Bay View, Saco, 04072 (15).

Maryland: Carroll Manor (Residence and Nursing Home), 4922 La Salle Rd., Hyattsville 20782 (210).

Little Sisters of the Poor, 601 Maiden Choice Lane, Baltimore 21228 (250).

Sacred Heart Home, 5805 Queens Chapel Rd., Hyattsville 20782 (102).

Stella Maris Hospice, 2300 Dulaney Valley Rd., Towson 21204 (317).

Villa Rosa, Lottsford Vista Rd., Mitchellville 21109 (53).

Massachusetts: Beaven-Kelly Home for Aged Men, 1245 Main St., Brightside, Holyoke 01040 (55).

Catholic Memorial Home, 2446 Highland Ave., Fall River 02720 (290).

Don Orione Home, 111 Orient Ave., East Boston 02128 (180).

D'Youville Manor, 981 Varnum St., Lowell 01854 (207).

Little Sisters of the Poor, 424 Dudley St., Boston 02119 (115).

Little Sisters of the Poor, 186 Highland Ave., Somerville 02143 (148).

Madonna Manor, Washington St., N. Attleboro 02760 (129).

Marian Manor, 40 Old Harbor St., S. Boston, 02127 (250).

Marian Manor, 33 Summer St., Taunton 02780 (129).

Maristhill Nursing Home, 66 Newton St., Waltham 02154 (120).

Our Lady's Haven, 71 Center St., Fairhaven 02719 (131).

Protectory of Mary Immaculate (Nursing Home), 189 Maple St., Lawrence 01841 (123).

Sacred Heart Home, 359 Summer St., New Bedford 02740 (192).

St. Francis Home for Aged, 37 Thorne St., Worcester 01604 (60).

St. Joseph's Manor for Aged Women, 321 Centre St., Dorchester 02122 (95).

St. Joseph's Manor Nursing and Rest Home, 261 Thatcher St., Brockton 02154 (56).

St. Luke's Home, 85 Springfield St., Springfield 01105 (108).

St. Patrick's Manor, 863 Central St., Framingham 01701 (280).

Michigan: Bishop Noa Home for Senior Citizens, Escanaba 49829 (107).

Burtha M. Fisher Home, 17550 Southfield Rd., Detroit 48235 (183).

Carmel Hall, 2560 Woodward Ave., Detroit 48201.

Kundig Center, 2936 Ash St., Detroit 48208 (140).

Lourdes Nursing Home, 2380 Watkins Lake Rd., Pontiac 48054 (108).

Marian Hall, 529 Detroit St., Flint 48502 (75).

Marycrest Manor, 15475 Middlebelt Rd., Livonia 48154 (92).

Marydale, 3147 Tenth Ave., Port Huron 48060 (44).

St. Ann's Home, 2161 Leonard St. N.W., Grand Rapids 49304 (113).

St. Catherine Cooperative House for Elderly Women, 1641 Webb Ave., Detroit 48206 (13).

St. Elizabeth Briarbank, 1315 N. Woodward Ave., Bloomfield Hills 48013 (55).

St. Francis Home for the Aged, 915 N. River Rd., Saginaw 48603 (100).

St. John Vianney Cooperative House for Men, 4806 Mt. Elliot, Detroit 48207 (30).

St. Joseph's Home for the Aged, 4800 Cadieux Rd., Detroit 48224 (120).

Stapleton Center, 1439 Parkway, Detroit 48214 (20).

Villa Elizabeth, 2100 Leonard St. N.E. Grand Rapids 49505 (109).

Villa Franciska, 565 W. Long Lake Rd., Bloomfield Hills 48013 (18).

Minnesota: Assumption Nursing Home, Cold Spring 56320 (67).

Divine Providence Community Home, Sleepy Eye 56085 (40).

Divine Providence Home, Ivanhoe 56142 (51).

Holy Trinity Home for Aged, Graceville 56240 (17).

Madonna Towers, 4001 19th Ave. N.W., Rochester 55901 (145).

Mary Randorf Home of Sacred Heart Parish, 222 5th St. N., Staples 56479 (84).

Mother of Mercy Nursing Home, Albany 56307 (62).

Regina Nursing Home and Residence, Hastings, 55033 (60).

Sacred Heart Hospice, 1200 Twelfth St. S.W., Austin 55912 (60).

St. Alexander Home, 1500 5th St. N., New Ulm 56073 (61).

St. Ann's Home, 330 E. 3rd St., Duluth 55805 (200).

St. Ann's Hospice, 1347 W. Broadway, Winona 55987 (111).

St. Elizabeth's Home for the Aged, Campbell Ave. Wabasha 55981 (69).

St. Francis Home, W. 4th Ave., Shakopee 55379 (35).

St. Francis Home for Aged and Chronically Ill, Breckenbridge 56520 (132).

St. Joseph's Home, 1824 Minnesota Blvd. S.E., St. Cloud 56301 (118).

St. Joseph's Home for Aged, 215 Broadway N.E., Minneapolis 55413 (116).

St. Mary's Extended Care Center, 2511 S. 7th St., Minneapolis 55406 (242).

St. Mary's Home, Winsted 55395 (74).

St. Mary's Home, 1925 Norfolk Ave., St. Paul 55116 (90).

St. Mary's Villa, Pierz 56364 (66).

St. Otto's Home for the Aged, Little Falls 56345 (159).

St. Paul's Home for the Aged Poor, 90 Wilkin St., St. Paul 55102 (116).

St. Raphael's Home, 511 9th Ave. N., St. Cloud 56301 (92).

St. Theresa Home, 8000 Bass Lake Rd., New Hope 55428 (200).

St. Vincent's Rest Home, 223 E. 7th St., Crookston 56716 (73).

St. William's Rest Home, Parkers Prairie 56361 (73).

Villa of St. Francis Nursing Home, Morris 56267 (69).

Missouri: Chariton Apartments (Retirement Apartments), 4249 Michigan St., St. Louis 63117 (122 apts.; 150 residents).

Convent of the Immaculate Heart (Women), 7626 Natural Bridge Rd., Normandy 63121 (128).

Hotel Alverne (Retirement Home), 1014 Locust St., St. Louis 63101 (222).

LaVerna Heights Retirement Home, 104 E. Park Ave., Savannah 64485 (60).

Little Sisters of the Poor, 5331 Highland Ave., Kansas City 64110 (240).

Little Sisters of the Poor, 3225 N. Florissant Ave., St. Louis 63107 (135).

Little Sisters of the Poor, St. Charles Home, 3400 S. Grand Blvd., St. Louis 63118 (165).

Mercy Villa (Nursing Home), 1015 N. Main St., Springfield 65802 (205).

Mother of Good Counsel Home for Chronic Sick, 6825 Natural Bridge Rd., St. Louis 63121 (110).

Our Lady of Mercy Home, 918-24 E. 9th St., Kansas City 64106 (126).

Our Lady of Perpetual Help Nursing Home, 3419 Gasconada St., St. Louis 63118 (141).

St. Agnes Home, 10341 Manchester Rd., Kirkwood 63122 (130).

St. Anne Home (Nursing Home), 5351 Page Blvd., St. Louis 63112 (190).

St. Joseph Hill Infirmary (Nursing Home for Men), RR 1, Box 339, Eureka 63025 (125).

St. Joseph's Home for the Aged, 1550 W. Main St., Jefferson City 65101 (70).

St. Joseph's Home for the Aged, First Capitol Dr., St. Charles 63301 (101).

Montana: Holy Family Hospital Home for the Aged, St. Ignatius 59865 (10).

St. Joseph Hospital Home for the Aged, Polson 59860 (40).

Nebraska: Madonna Professional Care Center (Nursing Care), 2200 S. 52nd St., Lincoln 68502 (182).

Mt. Carmel Home, Keens' Memorial, 18th St., and 5th Ave., Kearney 68847 (73).

St. Joseph's Home, 401 N. 18th St., Norfolk 68701 (62).

St. Joseph's Home, 320 E. Decatur St., West Point 68788 (50).

St. Joseph's Villa, David City 68632 (44).

St. Vincent's Home, 4500 Ames Ave., Omaha 68104 (259).

New Hampshire: Mount Carmel Home for the Aged, 235 Myrtle St., Manchester 03104 (118).

Notre Dame Hospital, Geriatrics Department, Manchester 03102 (28).

St. Ann Home, 201 Dover Point Rd., Dover 03820 (52).

St. Francis Home, Laconia 03246 (49).

St. Teresa Manor, 519 Bridge St., Manchester 03104 (50).

St. Vincent de Paul Nursing Home, Providence Ave., Berlin 03570 (70).

New Jersey: Holy Family Residence, New St., P.O. Box 536, W. Paterson 07424 (60).

Little Sisters of the Poor, 70 Dey St., Paterson 07503 (141).

Mater Dei Nursing Home, Rt. 40, P.O. Newfield, Upper Pittsgrove Township 08344 (64).

Morris Hall, Home for the Aged, 1253 Lawrenceville Rd., Lawrenceville 08532 (96).

Mount St. Andrew Villa, 55 W. Midland Ave., Paramus 07652 (58).

Our Lady's Residence (Nursing Home), Glendale and Clematis Aves., Pleasantville 08232 (104).

St. Ann's Home for the Aged, 198 Old Bergen Rd., Jersey City 07305 (105).

St. Joseph's Rest Home for Aged Women, 46 Preakness Ave., Paterson 07502 (30).

St. Joseph's Villa, Peapack 07977 (12).

St. Mary's Nursing Home, Kresson Rd., Cherry Hill 08034 (94).

St. Rose of Lima Home, 1 S. 8th St., Newark 07107 (170).

Villa Maria, 641 Somerset St., N. Plainfield 07061 (75).

New Mexico: Good Shepherd Manor (Shelter Care Home for Aged Men), Little Brothers of the Good Shepherd, P.O. Box 10248, Albuquerque 87114 (24).

New York: Bernardine Apartments, 240 E. Onondaga St., Syracuse 13202 (temporary address).

Ferncliff Residence, 47 River Rd., Rhinebeck 12572 (19).

Frances Schervier Home and Hospital, 2975 Independence Ave., New York 10453 (364).

Holy Family Home, 410 Mill St., Williamsville 14221 (96).

Josephine Baird Home, 340 W. 55th St., New York 10019 (175).

Little Sisters of the Poor, 391 Central Ave., Albany 12206 (103).

Little Sisters of the Poor, 660 E. 183rd St., Bronx 10458 (200).

Little Sisters of the Poor, 1608 8th Ave., Brooklyn 11215 (152).

Little Sisters of the Poor, 135 W. 106th St., New York 10025 (137).

Little Sisters of the Poor, 110-30 221st St., Queens Village 11429.

Little Sisters of the Poor, 192 9th St., Troy 12180 (110).

Loretto Rest, E. Brighton and Glen Aves., Syracuse 13205 (206).

Madonna Home of Mercy Hospital (Nursing Home), Watertown 13601 (120).

Madonna Residence for the Elderly, 1 Prospect Park W., Brooklyn 11215 (290).

Marillac Home, 240 E. Onondaga St., Syracuse 13202 (temporary address).

Mary Manning Walsh Home, 1339 York Ave., New York 10021 (347).

Mercy Hospital Nursing Home Unit, Tupper Lake 12986 (14).

Mt. Carmel Home for the Aged and Infirm, 539 W. 54th St., New York 10019 (92).

Mt. Loretta Convalescent and Rest Home, R.D. 3, Amsterdam 12010 (87).

Nazareth Nursing Home and Convent, 291 W. North St., Buffalo 14201 (102).

Our Lady of Consolation Residence, Albany and Schlegel Aves., Amityville 11701 (108).

Ozanam Hall for the Elderly, 42-41 301st St., Bayside 11361.

Providence Rest Home, 3304 Waterbury Ave., Bronx 10465 (154).

Resurrection Rest Home, Castleton 12033 (54).

Sacred Heart Nursing Home, 8 Mickle St., Plattsburgh 12901 (74).

St. Ann's Home for the Aged, 1500 Cortland Ave., Rochester 14621 (354).

St. Anthony's Home for the Aged, 5285 S. Park Ave., Hamburg 14075 (68).

St. Columban's Home, Silver Creek 14136 (50).

St. Elizabeth Home, 5539 Broadway, Lancaster 14086 (100).

St. Francis Home, 147 Reist St., Williamsville 14221 (97).

St. Joseph's Guest House, 350 Cuba Hill Rd., Huntington 11743.

St. Joseph's Home, 420 Lafayette St., Ogdensburg 13669 (82).

St. Joseph's Nursing Home, 2535 Genesee St., Utica 13501.

St. Luke Manor for Chronically Ill, 17 Wiard St., Batavia 14020 (20).

St. Mary of the Angels Home for the Aged, 400 Mill St., Williamsville 14221 (14).

St. Patrick's Home for the Aged and Infirm, 65 Van Cortland Park S., Bronx 10463 (214).

St. Teresa's Guest House, 120 Highland Ave., Middletown 10940 (92).

St. Vincent's Home for the Aged, 319 Washington Ave., Dunkirk 14048 (36).

St. Zita's Home, 143 W. 14th St., New York 10011.

Uihlein Mercy Center (Nursing Home), Lake Placid 12946 (100).

North Carolina: Maryfield Nursing Home, Greensboro Rd., High Point 27260 (60).

North Dakota: Holy Family Guest Home, Carrington 58421 (40).

Manor St. Joseph, Edgeley 58533 (50).

St. Anne's Guest Home, 813 Lewis Blvd., Grand Forks 58201 (100).

St. Olaf Guest (Retirement) Home, Powers Lake 58773 (20).

Ohio: Alvernia Rest Home, 6765 State Rd., Cleveland 44134 (143).

Assumption Nursing Home, 550 Chalmers Ave., Youngstown 44511 (84).

Franciscan Terrace, 60 Compton Rd., Cincinnati 45215 (33).

House of Loreto, 2812 Harvard Ave. N.W., Canton 44709 (95).

Jennings Hall, 10204 Granger Rd., Garfield Heights, Cleveland 44125 (121).

Kirby Manor, 11500 Detroit Ave. 44102 (202 suites).

Little Sisters of the Poor, 476 Riddle Rd., Cincinnati 45220 (112).

Little Sisters of the Poor, 4291 Richmond Rd., Cleveland 44122 (212).

Maria-Joseph Home for the Aged, 4950 Salem Ave., Dayton 45416 (50).

Mercycrest, 100 W. McCreight Ave., Springfield 45504 (150).

Mt. St. Joseph, 21800 Chardon Rd., Euclid 44117 (95).

Sacred Heart Home, 4900 Navarre Ave., Oregon 43616 (180).

St. Augustine Manor (Nursing Home), 7818 Detroit Ave., Cleveland 44102 (175).

St. Edward's Home, 3131 Smith Rd., Akron 44313 (95).

St. Francis Home for the Aged, 182 St. Francis Ave., Tiffin 44883 (106).

St. Joseph's Home for the Aged Poor, 2024 Florence Ave., Cincinnati 45206 (120).

St. Joseph's Hospice for the Aged, 219 N. Chapel St., Louisville 44641 (34).

St. Margaret's Hall, 1960 Madison Rd., Cincinnati 45206 (148).

St. Mary's Home for the Aged, 278 Broadway, Youngstown 44504 (53).

St. Raphael Home for the Aged, 1550 Roxbury Rd., Columbus 43212 (80).

St. Rita Home for the Aged, 880 Greenlawn Ave., Columbus 43223 (97).

St. Theresa Home for the Aged, 6760 Belkenton Ave., Cincinnati 45236 (118).

Schroder Manor, 1802 Millville Ave., Hamilton 45012.

The Siena Home for Aged, 235 W. Orchard Spring Dr., Dayton 45415 (98).

Villa Maria Nursing Home, Green Springs 44836 (110).

Villa Maria Rest Home, 609 N. 7th St., Steubenville 43952 (26).

Villa Sancta Anna Home for Aged, 25000 Chagrin Blvd., Cleveland 44122 (68).

Oklahoma: St. Ann's Home, 3825 N.W. 19th St., Oklahoma City 73107 (82).

Oregon: Benedictine Center for Nursing and Rehabilitation, S. Main St., Mt. Angel 97362 (106).

Marysville Nursing Home, 14645 S. W. Farmington Rd., Beaverton 97005 (120).

Mt. St. Joseph's Rest Home and Extended Care Center, 3060 S.E. Stark St., Portland 97214 (317).

St. Anthony's Hospital Home for the Aged, Pendleton 97801 (65).

St. Catherine's Residence and Nursing Center, 3959 Sheridan Ave., North Bend 97459 (102).

St. Elizabeth's Nursing Home, Baker 97814 (49).

Pennsylvania: Ascension Manor, 911 N. Franklin St., Philadelphia 19123 (140 units).

Blessed John Neumann Nursing Home, 10400 Roosevelt Blvd., Philadelphia 19116 (196).

Christ the King Manor, 1100 W. Long Ave., Du Bois 15801 (40).

Corpus Christi Residence for Women, 7165 Churchland St., Pittsburgh 15206.

Drueding Infirmary, Master and Lawrence Sts., Philadelphia 19122 (50).

Garvey Manor, Logan Blvd., Hollidaysburg, 16648 (152).

Holy Family Manor, 1200 Spring St., Bethlehem 18018 (200).

Little Flower Manor, Springfield and Providence Rds., Darby 19023 (75).

Little Sisters of the Poor, 602 E. Church Lane, Philadelphia 19144 (180).

Little Sisters of the Poor, 5324 Pennsylvania Ave., Pittsburgh 15224 (115).

Little Sisters of the Poor, 1028 Benton Ave., Pittsburgh 15212 (118).

Little Sisters of the Poor, 2500 Adams Ave., Scranton 18509 (67).

Maria Joseph Manor, Danville 17821 (87).

Marian Manor, 2695 Winchester Dr., Pittsburgh 15220 (180).

Mt. Trexler Skilled Nursing Unit of Sacred Heart Hospital, Limeport 18060 (65).

Our Lady Help of Christians Convalescent Home, 56th St. and City Line Ave., Philadelphia 19131 (17).

Sacred Heart Home for the Aged, St. Clara House, 429 Pine St., Allentown 18102 (21).

Sacred Heart Manor, 6445 Germantown Ave., Philadelphia 19119 (169).

St. Ann Home — Villa Laboure, 449 E. Locust Ave., Philadelphia 19144 (16).

St. Anne Home, R.R. 2, Columbia 17512 (100).

St. Anne Home for the Elderly, 685 Angela Dr., Greensburg, 15601 (125).

St. Basil's Home for Women, Uniontown 15401 (18).

St. Bernadette Home for the Aged and Convalescent, 1525 N. 18th St., Philadelphia 19121 (174).

St. Ignatius Nursing Home, 4401 Haverford Ave., Philadelphia 19104 (176).

St. Joseph Home, Newtown 18940 (75).

St. Joseph Manor, 1616 Huntingdon Pike, Meadowbrook 19046 (102).

St. Leonard's Guest Home, 601 N. Montgomery St., Hollidaysburg 16648 (24).

St. Mary's Home for the Aged, 607 E. 26th St., Erie 16504 (122).

St. Mary's Manor for Sighted and Unsighted, 701 Lansdale Ave., Lansdale 19446 (160).

St. Mary's Villa (Nursing Home), Elmhurst 18416 (122).

Shenango Valley Home for Senior Citizens, 2250 Shenango Freeway, Sharon 16146 (80).

Sisters of the Holy Ghost, Home for Aged Women, Hampton Heights, Allison Park 15101 (17).

Villa de Marillac Nursing Home, 5300 Stanton Ave., Pittsburgh 15206 (50).

Villa St. Elizabeth, 1301 Museum Rd., Reading 19602 (49).

Villa Teresa, Old Union Deposit Rd., Harrisburg 17111.

Vincentian Home for the Chronically Ill, Perrymount Rd., Pittsburgh 15237 (152).

Rhode Island: Bishop Scalabrini Home for the Aged (Italian), 860 Quidnessett Rd., North Kingstown 02852 (55).

L'Hospice St. Antoine, Mendon Rd. (P.O. Woonsocket), North Smithfield 02895 (249).

Little Sisters of the Poor, 964 Main St., Pawtucket 02860 (135).

The St. Clare Home for Aged People, 309 Spring St., Newport 02840 (38).

South Carolina: Carter Mary Home, 1660 Ingram Rd., Charleston 29407 (8).

South Dakota: Brady Memorial Home, 500 S. Ohlman St., Mitchell 57301 (60).

Maryhouse, Pierre 57501 (47).

Mother Joseph Manor, 1002 North Jay St., Aberdeen 57401 (60).

St. William's Home for the Aged, 101 Viola St., Milbank 57252 (35). Tekakwitha Nursing Home, Sisseton 57262 (102).

Tennessee: Alexian Brothers Rest Home (Retired Men and Women), Signal Mountain 37377 (97).

Ave Maria Home for the Aged, 2805 Charlie Bryan Rd., Memphis 38128 (36).

St. Mary's Nursing Home, Humboldt 38343 (50).

Texas: Home for Aged Women, 920 S. Oregon St., El Paso 79901 (24).

Luearlam Manor, 844 Central Blvd., Brownsville 78520 (56).

Mt. Carmel Home, 4130 S. Alameda St., Corpus Christi 78411 (92).

Our Mother of Perpetual Help Rest Home, 319 E. Madison Ave., Brownsville 78520 (46).

Regis Retirement Home and Infirmary, 400 Austin Ave., Waco 76701 (260).

St. Ann's Home for the Aged, P.O. Box 833, Panhandle 79068 (52).

St. Anthony's Center, 6301 Almeda Rd., Houston 77021 (279).

St. Benedict's Nursing Home, Alamo and Johnson Sts., San Antonio 78204 (160).

St. Francis Home (Women), 2506 Mobile Ave., El Paso 77930 (14).

St. Francis Village, Inc. (Retired and Elderly), Crowley. Mailing address — P.O. Box 16310, Ft. Worth 76133 (400).

St. Joseph Residence, 330 W. Pembroke St., Dallas 75208 (49).

Virgen de San Juan Nursing Home, San Juan 78589 (46).

Utah: St. Joseph Villa, 474 Westminster Ave., Salt Lake City 84115 (89).

Vermont: Loretto Home for Aged, 59 Meadow St., Rutland 05701 (55).

Michaud Memorial Manor, Derby Line 05830 (24).

St. Joseph's Home for Aged, 243 N. Prospect St., Burlington 05401 (55).

Virginia: Fulton Catholic Home, Inc., 810 Louisiana St., Richmond 23231.

St. Sophia's Home for the Aged, 16 N. Harvie St., Richmond 23220 (114).

Washington: Cathedral Plaza Apartments, W. 1120 Sprague Ave., Spokane 99201 (150).

The De Paul, 4831 35th Ave. S.W., Seattle 98126 (113).

Fahy Garden Apartments, Dean and Cedar Sts., Spokane 99201 (30).

Fahy West Apartments, W. 1517 Dean Ave., Spokane 99201 (55).

Highline Nursing Home, 609 Highline Dr., E. Wenatchee 98802 (80).

The Josephinum, 1902 2nd Ave., Seattle 98101 (228).

Mt. St. Vincent Nursing Home, 4831 35th Ave., N.W., Seattle 98126 (198).

St. Joseph Nursing Home, 1006 North H St., P.O. Box 229, Aberdeen 98520 (34).

St. Joseph Nursing Home, 707 E. Mission Ave., Spokane 99202 (83).

West Virginia: Knights of St. George Home, Wellsburg 26070 (30).

St. Barbara's Memorial Nursing Home, P.O. Box 86, Mononagh 26554 (50).

Welty Memorial Home for the Aged, 21 Washington Ave., Wheeling 26003 (42).

Wisconsin: Divine Savior Nursing Home, 715 W. Pleasant St., Portage 53901 (115).

The Henry Boyle Catholic Home for the Aged, 271 N. Park Ave., Fond du Lac 54935 (35).

Hope Nursing Home, 438 Ashford Ave., Lomira 53048 (40).

McCormick Memorial Home for the Aged, 212 Iroquois St., Green Bay 54301 (70).

Marycrest (Women), 600 Third Ave., Durand 54736 (14).

Maryhill Manor Nursing and Retirement Home, 973 Main St., Niagara 54151 (47).

Milwaukee Catholic Home for the Aged, 2301 E. Bradford Ave., Milwaukee 53211 (50).

Nazareth House, Stoughton 53589 (100).

Sacred Heart Hospital Nursing Home, Tomahawk 54487 (22).

St. Ann Rest Home, 2020 S. Muskego Ave., Milwaukee 53204 (57).

St. Anne's Home for the Elderly, 3800 N. 92nd St., Milwaukee 53222 (220).

St. Camillus Health Center, 10100 W. Bluemound Rd., Wauwatosa 53226 (186).

St. Catherine Infirmary, 5635 Erie St., Racine 53402 (33).

St. Elizabeth's Home, Brookfield 53035.

St. Francis Home, 709 S. 10th St., La Crosse 54601 (69).

St. Francis Home for the Aged, 2325 E. 3rd St., Superior 54880 (49).

St. Joan Antida Home, 6640 W. Beloit Rd., W. Allis 53219 (79).

St. Joseph's Home, 705 Clyman St., Watertown 53094 (88).

St. Joseph's Home, 9244 29th Ave., Kenosha 53140 (82).

St. Joseph's Home, 5301 W. Lincoln Ave., W. Allis 53219 (130).

St. Joseph's Home, and Hospital, River Falls 54022 (55).

St. Joseph's Hospital Home for the Aged, Arcadia 54612 (61).

St. Joseph's Nursing Home, 2415 Cass St., La Crosse 54601 (73).

St. Joseph's Nursing Home, 106 Water Ave., Hillsboro 54634 (39).

St. Joseph on the Flambeau Nursing Home, Ladysmith 54848 (104).

St. Joseph Residence, Inc., 1925 Division St., New London 54961 (106).

St. Mary's Home for the Aged, 2005 Division St., Manitowoc 54220 (140).

St. Mary's Nursing Home, 3516 W. Center St., Milwaukee 53210 (126).

St. Mary's Residential Care Home, 203 W. Wisconsin St., Sparta 54656 (30).

St. Mary's Ringling Manor, 1208 Oak St., Baraboo 53913 (88).

St. Monica's Senior Citizens Home, 3920 N. Green Bay Rd., Racine 53404 (85).

South Milwaukee Nursing Home, 3601 S. Chicago Ave., S. Milwaukee 53172 (94).

St. Paul Home (Nursing Home), 509 W. Wisconsin Ave., Kaukauna 54130 (54).

Villa St. Vincent, 610 S. Pearl St., New London 54961 (52).

Villa Clement (Nursing and Convalescent Center), W. Allis 53214 (190).

Villa Loretto Nursing Home, Mt. Calvary 53057 (52).

Organizations for Handicapped

(See the article following for a listing of facilities for the handicapped.)

Blind

The Carroll Rehabilitation Center for the Visually Impaired (formerly the Catholic Guild for All the Blind): Located at 770 Centre St., Newton, Mass. 02158, it conducts St. Paul's Rehabilitation Center for the Blind, St. Raphael's Geriatric Adjustment Center, and programs in research, community mobility, volunteer and special services, casework and counseling, and professional training. It maintains a large program of services for trainees not in residence on campus. It also publishes a quarterly newspaper, *Listen,* with a circulation of approximately 30,000. The executive director is Frederick Picard.

American Federation of Catholic Workers for the Blind: The Federation, founded in 1954 in Pittsburgh, Pa., is an association of independent agencies which work for and with the blind in their own local areas. It acts as a clearinghouse for ideas and as a spokesman of Catholic principles on a national level. It holds a convention biennially, and has a membership of about 14 agencies and numerous individuals. The president is Paul Sauerland, Special Services Division, Catholic Charities, 75 Post Ave., Westbury, N.Y. 11590.

Xavier Society for the Blind: The Society is located at 154 E. 23rd St., New York, 10010. Founded in 1900 by Rev. Joseph Stadelman, S.J., it is a center for publications for the blind and maintains a circulating library of approximately 7,000 volumes in Braille, along with a growing list of titles in large type and on tape. Its many publications include *The Catholic Review,* a monthly selection of articles of current interest from the Catholic press presented for the visually handicapped both in Braille and on tape. Xavier maintains the National Catholic Educational Index, listing all transcribed and recorded textbooks used currently in the overall Catholic educational system. The director of Xavier is Rev. Anthony F. La Bau, S.J.

The Deaf

Approximately 250 priests, 120 sisters and 30 brothers are engaged in special work among some 60,000 deaf persons in the U.S.

International Catholic Deaf Association: Established in 1949, the association has more than 6,000 members in 105 chapters, mostly in the US. It is affiliated with the Council of Organizations Serving the Deaf, the recognized official organization of all national associations working with the deaf in this country. In 1971, the ICDA cooperated with the National Association for the Deaf in conducting a census of the deaf funded by the US Department of Health, Education and Welfare. New data was sought regarding the number — greatly increased since rubella outbreaks from 1963 to 1965 — location and needs of the deaf, for service planning and programming. The ICDA publishes *The Deaf Catholic,* a bimonthly. The ICDA chaplain is Rev. Lawrence Murphy, St. John's School for the Deaf, Milwaukee, Wis. 53207.

Mentally Retarded

National Apostolate for the Mentally Retarded: Established in 1968, the apostolate is located at St. Joseph College, 1678 Asylum Ave., West Hartford, Conn. 06117. It publishes the quarterly *NAMR Journal* and a monthly newsletter, and has available a bibliography on the religious education of the retarded. Rev. Joseph C. Gengras is president of the apostolate.

Service Agency

Special Educational Department, National Catholic Educational Association: Established in 1954 to coordinate under one agency information and service functions for all areas of special education under Catholic auspices. Prior to 1954, its functions were carried out by a special office of the NCEA. Rev. Msgr. E. H. Behrmann is executive secretary of the department, with offices at 4472 Lindell Blvd., St. Louis, Mo. 63108.

YOUTH SURVEY

An increasing number of Catholic young people considered social involvement more important than traditional religious practices, according to findings of a survey of 2,182 Catholic high school seniors in New York. Seventy per cent of those polled considered "helping the poor" and "working for interracial harmony" the most important indices of "the good Catholic life."

The study, "Catholics and the Practice of the Faith, 1967 and 1971," was conducted by Msgr. George A. Kelly, of St. John's University. Msgr. Kelly also reported that 30 per cent of the boys and 38 per cent of the girls attended Mass every Sunday in 1971, as compared with 65 per cent and 80 per cent, respectively, in 1967.

FACILITIES FOR HANDICAPPED CHILDREN AND ADULTS

Source: *Directory of Catholic Special Facilities and Programs in the United States for Handicapped Children and Adults,* 1971 edition, published by the National Catholic Educational Association, One Dupont Circle — Suite 350, Washington, D. C. 20036; edited by the Rev. Msgr. Elmer H. Behrmann, Ph. D., and Sister Ann Dolores Moll, S. L., executive secretary and secretary, respectively, of the Special Education Department, NCEA.

This listing covers facilities and programs with an educational or training concept. Information about other services for the handicapped can generally be obtained from the Catholic Charities Office or its equivalent (c/o Chancery Office) in any diocese. (See Index for listing of addresses of chancery offices in the US.)

Abbreviation code: b, boys; c, coeducational; d, day; g, girls; r, residential. Other information includes chronological age for admission. The number in parentheses at the end of an entry indicates total capacity or enrollment.

Deaf and Hard of Hearing

California: St. Joseph's Center for Deaf and Hard of Hearing, 4025 Grove St., Oakland. 94609.

Illinois: Holy Redeemer Day Classes for Deaf (c; 6-13 yrs.), 9536 S. Millard Ave., Evergreen Park. 60642 (30).

Holy Trinity Day Classes for the Deaf (c; 3-14 yrs.), 1910 W. Taylor, Chicago. 60612 (50).

St. Mary of Perpetual Help High School (day classes, c; 14-20 yrs.), 1023 W. 32nd St., Chicago. 60608 (18).

St. Timothy Day Classes for the Deaf (c; 3-14 yrs.), 6330 N. Washtenaw, Chicago. 60645 (24).

Louisiana: Chinchuba Institute (r&d,c; 2-16 yrs.), P.O. Box 187, Marrero. 70072 (73).

Massachusetts: Boston School for the Deaf (r&d,c; 4 yrs. and older), 800 N. Main St., Randolph. 02368 (304).

Missouri: St. Joseph Institute for the Deaf (r&d,c; 3½-15 yrs.), 1483 82nd Blvd., University City. 63132 (170).

New Jersey: Mt. Carmel Guild Pre-School Deaf Program (d.c.), 17 Mulberry St., Newark. 07102 (80).

New York: Cleary School for Deaf Children (d.c; 2½ yrs. and older), 301 Smithtown Blvd., Lake Ronkonkoma, L.I. 11779 (72).

Nassau Day Classes (c; 3-14 yrs.), 75 Post Ave., Westbury. 11590 (54).

St. Francis de Sales School for the Deaf (d.c; 3-16 yrs.), 697 Carroll St., Brooklyn. 11215 (170).

St. Joseph's School for the Deaf (d,c; 3-10 yrs.), 1000 Hutchinson River Pkwy, Bronx. 10465 (270).

St. Mary's School for the Deaf (r&d,c; 3-21 yrs.), 2253 Main St., Buffalo. 14214 (390).

Ohio: St. Rita School for the Deaf (r,c; 4 yrs. and older), 1720 Glendale-Milford Rd., Cincinnati. 45215 (150).

Pennsylvania: Abp. Ryan Memorial Institute for Deaf (r&d,c; pre-school through 8th grade), 3509 Spring Garden St., Philadelphia. 19104 (80).

De Paul Institute (r&d,c; 2-18 yrs.), Castlegate Ave., Pittsburgh. 15226 (173).

Wisconsin: St. John's School for the Deaf (r&d,c; 3-20 yrs.), 3680 S. Kinnickinnic Ave., Milwaukee. 53207 (160).

Emotionally And/Or Socially Maladjusted

Arizona: Good Shepherd School for Girls (r; 12-21 yrs.), 1820 W. Northern Ave., Phoenix. 85021 (189). Also has after care off-campus division.

Arkansas: Monastery of Our Lady of Charity (r,g; 6 yrs. and older), 1125 Malvern Ave., Hot Springs. 71901 (50).

California: Boys Town of the Desert (r; 12-16 yrs.), 14700 Manzanita Park Rd., Beaumont. 92223 (80).

Hanna Boys Center (r; 10-15 yrs.), Box 100, Sonoma. 95476 (120).

Junipero Serra Boys Club (r; 16-18 yrs.), 316 N. Union Ave., Los Angeles. 90026 (32).

Pelletier High School (r,g; 12-18 yrs.), 1500 S. Arlington Ave., Los Angeles. 90019 (105).

Rancho San Antonio (r,b; 12-16 yrs.), 21000 Plummer St., Chatsworth. 91311 (93).

University Mound School for Girls (r; 13-17 yrs.), 501 Cambridge St., San Francisco. 94134 (96).

Colorado: Mt. St. Vincent Home (r,c; 5-14 yrs.), 4159 Lowell Blvd., Denver. 80211 (48).

Neuville Center (r,g; 8th-12th grade), 15151 E. Quincy Ave., Denver. 80232 (60).

Connecticut: Highland Heights—St. Francis Home for Children (r,c; 8-12 yrs.), 651 Prospect St. 06505 (28).

Marion Hall (r,g; 12-17 yrs.), 170 Sisson Ave., Hartford. 06105 (60).

Mt. St. John (r,b; 11-16 yrs.), Kirtland St., Deep River. 06417 (95).

Georgia: Village of St. Joseph (r&d,c; 6-16 yrs.), 2969 Butner Rd. S.W., Atlanta. 30331.

Hawaii: Child Development Center (therapeutic day treatment center; preschool), 2345 Nuuanu Ave., Honolulu. 96817 (10).

Illinois: Group Home—Dominican Sister of Bethany (r,g; 13-16 yrs.), 1434 W. Estes Ave., Chicago. 60626 (8).

Group Home, The Marcella Residence (g; 14-18 yrs.), 4633 N. Dover, Chicago. 60640 (10).

House of the Good Shepherd, Heart of Mary High School (r,g; 13-18 yrs.), 1126 W. Grace St., Chicago. 60613 (90).

St. Joseph Carondelet Child Center (r,c; 5-14 yrs.), 739 E. 35th St., Chicago. 60616 (48).

Indiana: Father Gibault School for Boys (r; 10-16 yrs.), 5901 Dixie Bee Rd., Terre Haute. 47802 (108).

Hoosier "Boys" Town (r; 10-15 yrs.), Schererville. 46375 (80).

St. Vincent Villa (r.c; 6-13 yrs.), 2000 N. Wells St., Ft. Wayne. 46808 (60).

St. Vincent Villa Pre-School (d,c), 2000 N. Wells St., Ft. Wayne. 46808 (37).

Kentucky: Boys' Haven (r; 14-19 yrs.), 3201 Bardstown Rd., Louisville. 40205 (51).

Maryhurst School (r,g; 13-17 yrs.), 2214 Bank St., Louisville. 40212.

Our Lady of the Highlands (r,g; teen-age high school age), 938 Highland Ave., Ft. Thomas. 41075 (60).

Louisiana: Our Lady of the River School (r,g), 3225 River Rd., Bridge City. 70094 (60).

Maryland: Christ Child Institute for Children (d,c), Edson Lane, Rockville. 20852 (28).

Good Shepherd Center (r,g; 14-18 yrs.), 4100 Maple Ave., Baltimore. 21227 (120).

Massachusetts: Cushing Hall (r,b; 13-16 yrs.), 279 Tilden Rd., Scituate. 02066 (40). Diagnostic treatment center.

McAuley Nazareth Home for Boys (r; 6-10 yrs.), 77 Mulberry St., Leicester. 01524 (30).

Nazareth Child Study Center (r&d,c; 18 mo.-14 yrs.), 420 Pond St., Jamaica Plain, Mass. 02130 (160).

Our Lady of Lourdes School (r,g; 12-16 yrs.), 280 Tinkham Rd., Springfield. 01129 (80).

Our Lady of Providence Children's Center (r,c; 6-12 yrs.), 2112 Riverdale St., W. Springfield. 01089 (40).

Michigan: Barat House, League of Catholic Women (r,g; 12-16 yrs.), 5250 John R. St., Detroit. 48202 (24).

Boysville of Michigan, Inc. (r; 13-18 yrs.), 8744 Clinton-Macon Rd., Clinton. 49236 (180).

Don Bosco Hall (r,b; 13-17 years.), 10001 Petoskey Ave., Detroit. 48204 (52).

Villa Maria, Sisters of the Good Shepherd (r,g; 13-18 yrs.), 1315 Walker St. N.W., Grand Rapids. 49504 (50).

Vista Maria School (r,g; 12-17 yrs.), 20651 W. Warren Ave., Detroit. 48223 (125).

Minnesota: Carmel Heights (r,g; 13-19 yrs.), 1600 Eighth Ave. East, Duluth. 55805 (20).

Oak Grove High School (r,g; 14-17 yrs.), 5100 Hodgson Rd., St. Paul. 55112 (60).

St. Cloud Children's Home (r,c; 12-16 yrs.), 1726 7th Ave. S., St. Cloud. 56301 (60).

Missouri: Child Center of Our Lady of Grace (r&d,c; 4-12 yrs.), 7900 Natural Bridge Rd., St. Louis. 63121 (100).

Marillac School (r&d,c; 7-11 yrs.), 310 W. 106th St., Kansas City. 64114 (115 day, 30 boarders).

Marygrove School for Girls (r; 12-17 yrs.), 2705 Mullanphy Lane, Florissant. 63031 (70).

Nebraska: Father Flanagan's Boys' Home (r; 10-16 yrs.), Boys Town, Nebr. 68010 (820).

Girls Town (r; 13-18 yrs.), 653 S. 40th St., Omaha. 68105 (70).

Nevada: St. Yves High School (r,g; 13-17 yrs.), 7000 North Jones Blvd., Las Vegas, 89106 (60).

New Jersey: Collier School (r,g; 12-17 yrs.), Rest Hill, Wickatunk. 07765 (60).

New York: The Astor Home for Children (r,c; 6-11 yrs., boys; 6-9 yrs., girls), 36 Mill St., Rhinebeck. 12572 (52).

Baker Hall (r,b; 12-17 yrs.), 150 Martin Rd., Lackawanna. 14218 (90).

Holy Angels Home (r,g; 11-17 yrs.), 1326 Winton Rd. N., Rochester. 14609 (39).

LaSalle School for Boys (r&d; 11-18 yrs.), 391 Western Ave., Albany. 12203 (145).

Lincoln Hall (r,b; 12-16 yrs.), Lincolndale. 10540 (270).

Madonna Heights School for Girls (r; 12-16 yrs.), Burrs Lane, Huntington. 11743 (98).

Our Lady of Charity School (r,g; 12-18 yrs.), Hamburg. 14075 (50).

Saint Anne Institute (r,g; 12-18 yrs.), 25 W. Lawrence St., Albany. 12206 (190).

St. Helena's Residence (r,g; 12-17 yrs.), 337 E. 17th St., New York. 10003 (20).

St. John's of Rockaway Beach (r,b; 10-14 yrs.), 144 Beach 111th St., Rockaway Park. 11694 (112). Also conducts group homes in Rockaway and Richmond Hill.

Villa Loretto (r,g; 15½-18 yrs.), Peekskill. 10566 (140).

North Dakota: Home on the Range for Boys (r; 12-18 yrs.), Sentinel Butte. 58654 (49).

Ohio: Carmelita Hall (r,g; 14-19 yrs.), 2903 Ridgewood Dr., Parma. 44134 (16).

Children's Village of St. Vincent de Paul (Parmadale) (r,c; 3-16 yrs.), 6753 State Rd., Parma. 44134 (240).

Marycrest School for Girls (r,g; 14-18 yrs.), 7800 Brookside Rd., Independence. 44131 (70).

Mount Alverno School (r,b; 12-15 yrs.), Mount Alverno Rd., Cincinnati. 45238 (84).

Our Lady of the Woods School, Girls Town of America (r; 13-18 yrs.), 575 N. Bend Rd., Cincinnati. 45224 (80).

Rosemont School (r,g; 12-18 yrs.), 2440 Dawnlight Ave., Columbus. 43211 (92).

St. Anthony Home for Boys (r; 13-17 yrs.), 8301 Detroit Ave. N.W., Cleveland. 44102 (60).

Oklahoma: Tulsa Vianney Girls Residence (r; 12-17 yrs.), 4001 E. 101st St., Tulsa. 74135 (59).

Oregon: Christie School (r,g; 9-16 yrs.), Marylhurst. 97036 (40).

St. Mary's Home for Boys (r; 8-18 yrs.), 16535 S.W. Tualatin Valley Highway, Beaverton. 97005 (40).

Villa St. Rose School for Girls (r; 12-18 yrs.), 597 N. Dekum St., Portland. 97217 (65).

Pennsylvania: Claver School for Girls (r; 13-17 yrs.), 5301 Chew Ave., Philadelphia. 19138 (45).

Gannondale School for Girls (r; 12-17 yrs.), 4635 E. Lake Rd., Erie. 16511 (48).

Gilmary School for Girls (r; 14-18 yrs.), Flagherty Run Rd., Coraopolis. 15108 (96).

Harborcreek School for Boys (r; 10-15 yrs.), 5712 Iroquois Ave., Harborcreek. 16421 (65).

Lourdesmont School (r,g; 14-17 yrs.), 537 Venard Rd., Clarks Summit. 18411 (60-75).

Pauline Auberle Foundation (r,b; 13-19 yrs.), 1101 Hartman St., McKeesport. 15132 (55).

St. Gabriel Hall (r,b; 10-17 yrs.), P.O. Box 390, Phoenixville. 19460 (177).

St. Michael's School for Boys (r,b; 12-15 yrs.), Hoban Heights. 18620 (100).

Tekakwitha Hills School (r,g; 13-18 yrs.), 8550 Verree Rd., Philadelphia. 19111 (70).

Toner Institute (r,b; 9-13 yrs.), Castlegate Ave., Pittsburgh. 15226 (66).

Tennessee: DeNeuville Heights School for Girls (r; 13-18 yrs.), 3060 Baskin St., Memphis. 38127 (52).

Texas: Mt. St. Michael Jr. and Sr. High School (r,g; 12-18 yrs.), 4500 W. Davis St., Dallas. 75211 (120).

St. Joseph Center (r&d,c; 10-15 yrs.), 901 S. Madison St., Dallas. 75219 (60).

Washington: Good Shepherd Home (r,g; 13-17 yrs.), 4649 Sunnyside Ave. N., Seattle. 98103 (70).

Marian Heights High School (r,g; 13-18 yrs.), 3754 W. Indian Trail Rd., Spokane. 99208 (60). Also conducts a group home.

Morning Star Boys Ranch (r,b; 11-14 yrs.), Box 781-A Route 3, Spokane. 99203 (30).

Wisconsin: Cedarcrest Girls Residence (r,g; 12-16 yrs.), 8830 W. Bluemound Rd., Milwaukee. 53226 (55).

Our Lady of Charity High School (r,g; 12-21 yrs.), 2640 West Point Rd., Green Bay. 54303 (102).

St. Aemilian Child Care Center, Inc. (r&d,b; 6-12 yrs.), 8901 W. Capitol Dr., Milwaukee. 53222 (47).

St. Charles Boys Home (r; 12-18 yrs.), 151 S. 84th St., Milwaukee. 53214 (56).

St. Joseph's Children's Home (r,c; 6-15 yrs., boys; 6-12 yrs., girls), 1200 15th Ave. E., Superior. 54880 (40).

St. Michael's Home for Children (r,c; 9-18 yrs.), 3222 South Ave., La Crosse. 54601 (83).

St. Vincent Group Home (r,g; 13-21 yrs.), 3310 N. Dousman St., Milwaukee. 53212 (22).

Wyoming: St. Joseph's Children's Home (r,c; 6-13 yrs.), South Main, Torrington. 82240 (45).

Mentally Retarded

California: Helpers of the Mentally Retarded, Inc., 2626 Fulton St., San Francisco. 94118. Conducts two facilities: Helpers Home for Girls (permanent home; 18 years and older), 2626 Fulton St., San Francisco. 94118 (6); Helpers Home for Boys (permanent home; 18 years and older), 383 14th Ave., San Francisco. 94118 (6).

Kennedy Child Study Center (d,c; 5-13 yrs.), 1339 - 20th St., Santa Monica. 90404 (80). Also conducts a developmental nursery (18 mos.-3 yrs.) and a preschool for children from culturally deprived areas (3-5 yrs.).

St. Madeleine Sophie's Preschool Training Center (c; 2-9 yrs.), 2111 E. Madison Ave., El Cajon. 92021 (60).

St. Vincent School (r&d,g; 8-14 yrs.), P.O. Drawer V, 4300 Calle Real, Santa Barbara. 93102 (175).

Tierra del Sol (d,c; 12 yrs. and older), 9919 Sunland Blvd., Sunland. 91040 (100).

Connecticut: Special Education Department, 162 Oak St., Bridgeport. 06604.

Sacred Heart Educational Center (d,c; 5 yrs. to adult), Holy Family Academy, Baltic. 06330 (45).

District of Columbia: Lt. Joseph P. Kennedy Jr. Institute (d,c; 6-18 yrs.), 801 Buchanan St. N.E., Washington. 20017 (120).

St. Gertrude's School of Arts and Crafts (r&d,g; 6-12 yrs.), 4801 Sargent Rd. N.E., Washington. 20017 (48).

Florida: Department of Special Education, 1325 W. Flagler St., Miami. 33135.

Marian Center School for Exceptional Children (r&d,c; 3-14 yrs.), 15701 Northwest 37th Ave., Opa Locka. 33054 (140).

Morning Star School (d,c; 4-15 yrs.), 725 Mickler Rd., Jacksonville. 32211 (70).

Morning Star School (d,c; 4-18 yrs.), 954 Leigh Ave., Orlando. 32804 (45).

Morning Star School (d,c; 4-16 yrs.), 4660 - 80th Ave., N., Pinellas Park. 33565 (50).

Morning Star School (d,c; 4-16 yrs.), 302 E. Linebaugh Ave., Tampa. 33612 (50).

Hawaii: Special Education Center of Oahu (d,c; 4-21 yrs.), 5275 Kalanianole Hwy., P. O. Box 7028, Honolulu. 96821 (80).

Illinois: Bartlett Developmental Learning Center (r&d,c; 6-16 yrs.), 801 W. Bartlett Rd., Bartlett. 60103 (80).

Good Shepherd Manor (permanent home for men; 18 yrs. to death), P.O. Box 260, Momence. 60954 (125).

Kennedy Job Training Center (c; 16 yrs. and older), 123rd and Wolf Rd., Palos Park. 60464 (110).

Lt. Joseph P. Kennedy, Jr., School (r&d,b; 6-12 yrs.), 123rd & Wolf Rd., Palos Park. 60464 (164).

Misericordia Home (r,c; 1 mo.-6 yrs.), 2916 W. 47th St., Chicago. 60632 (136).

Mt. St. Joseph (sheltered care home for older retarded girls and women; 20-45 yrs.), Route 3, Box 261, Lake Zurich. 60047 (158; long waiting list).

St. Agnes Special Education Classes (d,c; 5½-10 yrs.), 3835 S. Washtenaw, Chicago. 60632 (15).

St. Francis School for Exceptional Children (r,c; 6-12 yrs.), 1209 S. Walnut Ave., Freeport. 61032 (27).

St. Jude School (d,c; 6-16 yrs.), 2nd & Spring Ave., Aviston. 62216 (30).

St. Mary of Providence (r&d,g; 4-14 yrs.), 4200 N. Austin Ave., Chicago. 60634 (190).

St. Rose Center (d,g; 6-15 yrs.), 4911 S. Hoyne Ave., Chicago. 60609 (60).

Special Education Program of the East St. Louis Deanery (d,c; 6-16 yrs.), 8213 Church Lane, East St. Louis. 62203 (45).

Indiana: Cara Pre-School (d,c; 4-8 yrs.), 18th and Poplar Sts., Terre Haute. 47803 (13).

Marian Day School (d,c; 6-16 yrs.), 625 Bellemeade Ave., Evansville. 47713 (56).

St. Bavo Special Class (d,c; 6-15 yrs.), 512 W. 8th St., Mishawaka. 46544 (12).

St. Mary Child Center School (d,c; 6-16 yrs.), 311 N. New Jersey St., Indianapolis. 46204 (32).

Trainable and Educable Special Education Classes (d,c; 6-18), P.O. Box 121, Batesville. 47006 (30).

Kansas: Department of Special Education, Diocese of Wichita, 619 S. Maize Rd., Wichita. 67209.

Holy Family Center (d,c; 6-18 yrs.), 619 S. Maize Rd., Wichita. 67209 (65).

Hope, Inc. (d,c; 16 yrs. and older), 1500 Polk, Great Bend. 67530 (35).

Lakemary Center, Inc. (r&d,c; 3-16 yrs.), 100 Lakemary Dr., Paola. 66071 (60r,60d).

Kentucky: Good Counsel School (d,c; 6-16 yrs.), 116 W. 6th St., Covington. 41011 (120).

Laboratory Classes for the Mentally Retarded, Ursuline College (d,c; 4½-15 yrs.), 3105 Lexington Rd., Louisville. 40206 (35-40).

Msgr. Pitt Learning Center (d,c; 5 yrs. and older), 1202 S. Shelby, Louisville. 40203 (70).

Msgr. Pitt Pre-Job Training and Work Study Program (d,c; 16-20 yrs.), 1202 S. Shelby, Louisville. 40203 (20).

Louisiana: Department of Special Education, Archdiocese of New Orleans, 1522 Chippewa St., New Orleans. 70130. Conducts day classes, a special day school, and a vocational rehabilitation center for the mentally retarded.

Department of Special Education, Diocese of Baton Rouge, 555 N. 23rd St., Baton Rouge. 70805. Conducts 12 classes in 6 special centers and a vocational rehabilitation center.

Holy Angels Institute (r,c; teen-age, 14 yrs. and older; nursery, 2 mo. to kindergarten age), 10450 Ellerbe Rd., Shreveport. 71106 (140).

Regina Caeli Center (d,c; 6-16 yrs.), 3903 Kingston, Lake Charles. 70601 (45).

St. Mary's Training School (r,c; 4-16 yrs.), P.O. Box 295, Clarks. 71415 (172).

Maryland: The Benedictine School for Exceptional Children (r,c; 6-16 yrs.), Ridgely. 21660 (100). Also conducts Habilitation Center (r,c; 17-25 yrs.) and a half-way house.

The Education Center (d,c; 6-16 yrs.), 7027 Bellona Ave., Baltimore. 21212 (150).

St. Bernardine Special Education School (d,c; 6-12 yrs.), 3814 Edmondson Ave., Baltimore. 21229 (55).

St. Elizabeth School for Special Education (d,c; 12 yrs. and older), 801 Argonne Dr., Baltimore. 21218 (160).

St. Francis School for Special Education (d,c; 5-13 yrs.), 2226 Maryland Ave., Baltimore. 21218 (92).

St. Maurice Day School (d,c; 5-16 yrs.), 10100 Kendale Dr., Potomac. 20854 (108).

Massachusetts: Cardinal Cushing School and Training Center for Exceptional Children (r&d,c; 6 yrs. and older), Hanover. 02339 (165).

Nazareth Hall on the Cape (d,c; 6-15 yrs.), 261 South St., Hyannis. 02601 (25).

Nazareth Hall for Exceptional Children (d,c; 7-14 yrs.), 887 Highland Ave., Fall River, 02720 (70).

Nazareth Hall School (d,c; 5-16 yrs.), 204 Commonwealth Ave., Attleboro Falls. 02763.

Nazareth Vocational Center (c; 14-21 yrs.), 707 Highland Ave., Fall River. 02720 (24).

Our Lady of Mercy School (d,c; 7-16 yrs.), 25 West Chester St., Worcester. 01605 (90).

St. Coletta Day School (d,c; 7-12 yrs., admission age), 85 Washington St., Braintree. 02184 (58).

Michigan: Department of Special Education, Archdiocese of Detroit, 305 Michigan Ave., Detroit. 48222. Conducts 10 educable classes in 5 centers.

Felician Sisters Home for Mentally Retarded Infants (from birth to 5 yrs.), 1012 S. Jefferson St., Saginaw. 48601. A demonstration project.

Our Lady of Providence School (r&d,g; 6-16 yrs.), 16115 Beck Rd., Northville. 48167 (130).

Robert F. Kennedy High School (c; 14-18 yrs.), 5930 McClellan Ave., Detroit. 48213 (90).

St. Louis School (r,b; 8-14 yrs.), 16195 Old U.S. 12, Chelsea. 48118 (60).

Work Evaluation Program (c; 17 yrs. and older), Holy Trinity School, Lacrosse and 6th Sts., Detroit. 48226. (10). Vocational program sponsored by Detroit Special Education Dept.

Minnesota: Christ Child School for Exceptional Children (d,c; 4-21 yrs.), 2078 Summit Ave., St. Paul. 55103 (124).

St. Gertrude's School (d,c; 7-16 yrs.), 30 Eighth Ave. S., St. Cloud. 56301 (23).

Missouri: Department of Special Education, Archdiocese of St. Louis, 4472 Lindell Blvd., St. Louis. 63108. Conducts 22 special day classes (c; 6-16 yrs.) and 2 day classes for pre-school children.

Good Shepherd Manor (custodial care facility for boys and men; 16-40 yrs.), 3220 E. 23rd St., Kansas City. 64127 (40).

St. Joseph's Vocational Center (c; 16-21 yrs.), 5341 Emerson Ave., St. Louis. 63120 (124).

St. Mary's Special School (r,c; 6-16 yrs.), 5341 Emerson Ave., St. Louis. 63120 (137).

St. Peter's Special Classes (d,c; 6-15 yrs.), 314 W. High St., Jefferson City. 65101 (30).

Universal Sheltered Workshop, 4208 W. Florissant Ave., St. Louis. 63115. Provides sheltered terminal employment to adult mentally retarded.

Nebraska: Villa Marie School (r&d,c; 7-16 yrs.), Rt. 1, Box 109, Waverly. 68462 (25).

New Jersey: Alhambra Pavilion Day Care and Child Study Center (c; 4-8 yrs.), 21 Centre St., Newark. 07102 (40).

Archbishop Damiano School (d,c; 3½-15 yrs.), 532 Delsea Dr., Westville Grove. 08093 (90).

Child Study Center (d,c; 4-8 yrs.), 272 Main St., Ridgefield Park. 07660 (17).

Department of Special Education, Diocese of Camden, 721 Cooper St., Camden, N.J. 08101. Conducts day classes.

Department of Special Education, Diocese of Paterson (d,c; 3-9 yrs.), 16 Jackson St., Paterson. 07505 (18).

Immaculate Conception Special Class (d,c; 6 yrs. and older), 171 Division St., Trenton. 08611 (11).

McAuley School for Exceptional Children (d,c; 5-9 yrs.), Rt. 22 at Terrill Rd., N. Plainfield. 07061 (30).

Marian Center (d,c; 7-14 yrs.), Delsea Dr. and Chestnut St., Vineland. 08360 (30).

Mount Carmel Guild — Department of Special Education, Archdiocese of Newark, 17 Mulberry St., Newark. 07102. Conducts day classes for the mentally retarded. Also conducts work training programs.

St. Cecilia Special Class (c; 7-13 yrs.), 21 Vernon St., Iselin. 08830 (30).

New Mexico: Notre Dame on the Rio Grande (custodial facility for males, 13 yrs. and older; no maximum age), 305 Lagunita Rd. S.W., Albuquerque. 87105 (15).

St. Joseph's Manor (custodial facility for males, 16 years and older; no maximum age), P.O. Box 487, Bernalillo. 87004. (24).

New York: Cantalician Center for Learning (d,c; 6-18 yrs.), 3233 Main St., Buffalo. 14214 (200).

Catholic Charities Learning Center for Exceptional Children (d,c; 3-6 yrs.), 305 Garfield Pl., Brooklyn. 11215 (18).

Cobb Memorial School (r,c; 6-10 yrs.), Altamont. 12009 (50).

Immaculate Heart of Mary Children's Home (r,c; 6-12 yrs.), William and Kennedy Sts., Buffalo. 14206. Conducts special class for retarded children in the home.

Marianne Hall — Special Education (d,c; 3-15 yrs.), 114 Michaels Ave., Syracuse, 13208 (12).

Maryhaven School for Exceptional Children (r&d,c; 7-16 yrs.), 450 Myrtle Ave., Port Jefferson. 11777 (90). Also conducts a vocational rehabilitation center (d,c; 16 yrs. and older).

St. Catherine Child Care Center (r,c; birth to 5 yrs.), 30 N. Main St., Albany. 12203 (20).

St. Joseph School for Exceptional Children (r&d,c; 7-14 yrs.), Bennett Rd., Dunkirk. 14048 (30).

St. Rita's Home for Children (r,c; birth to 3 yrs.), 2110 Millersport Hwy., Buffalo. 14221 (64).

School for the Disabled (d,c; 5 yrs. and older), Maxwell Rd. — Rt. 9, Newtonville. 12128 (40). For mentally retarded and cerebral palsied.

School of the Holy Childhood (d,c; 7-18 yrs.), 215 Andrews St., Rochester. 14604 (85).

Special Education Department, Diocese of Brooklyn, 345 Adams St., Brooklyn, 11201. Conducts 14 special day classes in 7 parish schools.

Special Education Department, Archdiocese of New York, 451 Madison Ave., New York. 10022. Conducts 13 special day classes in 9 parish schools.

North Carolina: Holy Angels Nursery (r,c; birth to 6 yrs.), Belmont. 28012 (72).

Ohio: Department of Mental Retardation, Diocese of Cleveland, 2346 W. 14th St., Cleveland. 44113.

Good Shepherd Manor (permanent care of men 18 years and older), P.O. Box 387, Wakefield. 45687 (104).

Mary Immaculate School for Exceptional Children (d,c; 6-16 yrs.), 3837 Secor Rd., Toledo. 43623 (100).

Marymount Rehabilitation Services (vocational rehabilitation; 16 yrs. and older), 12215 Granger Rd., Cleveland. 44125.

Mt. Aloysius (r,b; 10-21 yrs.), Tile Plant Rd., New Lexington. 43764 (100).

Our Lady of Angels Special School (d,c; 7-21 yrs.), 3570 Rocky River Dr., Cleveland. 44111. Also conducts Seton High School Work Study Program (c; 16-21 yrs.).

Our Lady of the Elms Special Education (d,c; 6-14 yrs.), 1230 W. Market St., Akron. 44313 (64).

Rose Mary, The Johanna Graselli Rehabilitation and Education Center (r,c; 2-15 yrs.), 19350 Euclid Ave., Cleveland. 44117 (40).

St. John's Villa (d,c; 6-14 yrs.), W. Main St., Carrollton. 44615 (150).

St. Joseph Center (d,c; 7-16 yrs.), 2346 W. 14th St., Cleveland. 44113 (75).

Sheltered Workshop and Training Center (c; 16 yrs. and older), 1904 W. 22nd St., Cleveland. 44143 (25).

Oregon: Emily School for Retarded Children (d,c; 4-18 yrs.), 830 N. E. 47th Ave., Portland. 97213 (30).

Our Lady of Providence Children's Nursing Center (r; nursing care), 830 N. E. 47th Ave., Portland. 97213.

Pennsylvania: Clelian Heights School for Exceptional Children (r&d,c; 6-16 yrs.), R.D. 3, Box 304A, Greensburg. 15601 (100). Also conducts re-socialization program (r&d,g; 16-20 yrs.).

Department of Special Education, Diocese of Pittsburgh, 162 Steuben St., Pittsburgh. 15220. Conducts a program consisting of eight special day classes.

Don Guanella School (r,b; 7-14 yrs.), Sproul Road, Route 27, Springfield. 19064 (200).

McGuire Memorial (r&d,c; infancy to 7 yrs.), 2119 Mercer Rd., New Brighton. 15066 (150).

Mercy Day School: Center for Special Learning (d,c; 6-18 yrs.), 830 S. Woodward St., Allentown. 18103 (80).

Our Lady of Confidence Day School (c; 3-21 yrs.), 1099 W. Luzerne St., Philadelphia. 19140 (240).

St. Anthony School for Exceptional Children (r&d,c; 6-16 yrs.), 13th St. and Hulton Rd., Oakmont. 15139 (150). Also conducts a work adjustment center (c; 16 yrs. and older).

St. Joseph Day School (c; 6-18 yrs.), 619 Mahantongo St., Pottsville. 17901 (40).

St. Joseph's Children and Maternity Hospital Day School (c), 2010 Adams Ave., Scranton. 18509 (24).

St. Katherine School (d,c; 7-17 yrs.), Lancaster and Bowman Ave., Philadelphia. 19151 (270).

St. Mary of Providence Institute (r&d,g; 6-14 yrs.), Elverson. 19520 (120).

Rhode Island: St. Joseph's Pine Harbor (r,c; 3-16 yrs.), Singleton Rd., Pascoag. 02859 (70).

Tennessee: Madonna Day School for Retarded Children (d,c; 7-16), 4189 Leroy, Memphis. 38108 (50).

Texas: Katherine A. Ryan Center for Mentally Retarded Children (d,c), 4301 Broadway, San Antonio. 78209 (40).

Notre Dame of Dallas Special School (d,c; 6-12 yrs.), yrs.), Rt. 2, Box 4, Irving. 75062. (108).

Virginia: St. Coletta School (d,c; 5-18 yrs.), 1305 N. Jackson, Arlington. 22201 (45).

St. Mary's Infant Home (r,c; 3 days-9 yrs.), 317 Chapel St., Norfolk. 23504 (50).

Washington: Antonian School for Special Children (r&d,c; 6-18 yrs.), Cheney Rural Rt. 3, Box 14B, Cheney. 99004 (31).

Marian School (d,c; 6-18 yrs.), Fort Wright College, Spokane. 99204. (45).

Wisconsin: St. Coletta School, Jefferson. 53549. Offers the following programs:

a complete program of special education from kindergarten through elementary and advanced levels (r&d,c);

a work training center in preparation for job placement (r,c; 17-20 yrs.)'

a custodial care center (r,c; 45-85 yrs.);

a half-way house to give guidance and assist with problems (r,c; 18-24 yrs.);

a sheltered workshop to provide employment for the mentally retarded in a sheltered environment (r,c; 25-45 yrs.).

St. Coletta Day School (c; 8-16 yrs.), 1725 N. 54th St., Milwaukee. 53208 (16).

Orthopedically Handicapped

Alabama: Father Purcell Memorial (r,c; birth to 14 yrs.), 1918 Fairview Ave., Montgomery. 36108 (54).

Kentucky: Redwood School and Rehabilitation Center, United Cerebral Palsy of Northern Kentucky, Inc., (d,c; 18 mo. and older), 71 Orphanage Rd., Fort Mitchell, 41017 (77).

Pennsylvania: St. Edmond's Home for Crippled Children (r,c; 2-10 yrs.), 320 S. Roberts Rd., Rosemont. 19010 (50).

Visually Handicapped

Illinois: Department of Vision and Hearing (itinerant program for the visually handicapped; 6-20 yrs.), 126 N. Desplaines St., Chicago. 60606.

St. Raphael Day School for the Blind (c), 6011 S. Justine St., Chicago. 60636 (6).

Maine: Blind Children's Resource Center, Sacred Heart School (d,c; 6-14 yrs.), 273 Minot Ave., Auburn (15).

Blind Children's Resource Center, Cathedral School (d,c; grades 1-8), 14 Locust St., Portland. 04111 (17).

New Jersey: Mt. Carmel Guild Special Education, Department for the Visually Handicapped (itinerant teaching program for grade and high school children), 17 Mulberry St., Newark. 07102 (56).

St. Joseph's School for the Multiple Handicapped Blind (r&d,c; 4-21 yrs.), 253 Baldwin Ave., Jersey City. 07306 (37).

New York: Catholic Charities Special Services Division (itinerant program, c; 6-20 yrs.), 75 Post Ave., Westbury. 11590 (42).

Catholic Guild for the Blind (itinerant teaching program, c; 5-17 yrs.), 191 Joralemon St., Brooklyn. 11201.

Lavelle School for the Blind (r&d,c; 3-20 yrs.), 221st St. and Paulding Ave., Bronx. 10469 (220).

St. Peter's School Resource Room (c; kindergarten through 8th grade), 2331 Fifth Ave., Troy. 12180 (15).

Pennsylvania: St. Lucy Day School (d,c; 5-14 yrs.), 929 S. Farragut St., Philadelphia. 19143 (49).

OTHER SOCIAL SERVICES

Cancer Hospitals or Homes: The following homes or hospitals specialize in the care of cancer patients. They are listed according to state.

Our Lady of Perpetual Help Free Cancer Home, Servants of Relief for Incurable Cancer, 760 Washington St., S.W., Atlanta, Ga. 20315 (75).

Rose Hawthorne Lathrop Home, Servants of Relief for Incurable Cancer, 1600 Bay St., Fall River, Mass. 02724 (40).

Our Lady of Good Counsel Free Cancer Home, Servants of Relief for Incurable

Cancer, 2076 St. Anthony Ave., St. Paul, Minn. 55104 (49).

Calvary Hospital, Dominican Sisters of the Sick Poor, 1600 Macombs Ave., Bronx, N.Y. 10452 (111).

St. Rose's Free Home for Incurable Cancer, Servants of Relief for Incurable Cancer, 71 Jackson St., New York, N.Y. 10002 (94).

Rosary Hill Home, Servants of Relief for Incurable Cancer, Hawthorne, N.Y. 10532 (82).

Holy Family Home, Dominican Sisters, 6707 State Rd., Cleveland, O. 44134.

Penrose Cancer Hospital, Sisters of Charity of Cincinnati, 2215 N. Cascade Ave., Cincinnati, Ohio.

Sacred Heart Free Home for Incurable Cancer, Dominican Sisters, 1315 W. Hunting Park Ave., Philadelphia, Pa. 19140 (60).

Drug Addiction: A national office was established in the framework of the US Catholic Conference in 1972: Catholic Office of Drug Education (CODE), 1312 Massachusetts Ave. N.W., Washington, D.C. 20005. Director, Rev. Roland Melody, S.T.

Rehabilitation centers have been established in several dioceses.

Alcoholics: Some priests and religious throughout the US are committed in a special way to the personal rehabilitation and pastoral care of alcoholics through participation in Alcoholics Anonymous and other programs. Facilities for the rehabilitation of alcoholics include: St. Christopher's Inn, conducted by the Atonement Friars, Graymoor, Garrison, N.Y. 10524; Matt Talbot Inn, 9305 Superior Ave., Cleveland, Ohio 44106; Mt. Carmel Hospital for Alcoholism, 396 Straight St., Paterson, N.J. 07501.

The National Clergy Conference on Alcoholism was established to conduct workshops in various dioceses to instruct priests on ways of dealing with problem drinkers.

Convicts: Priests serve as full-or part-time chaplains in penal and correctional institutions throughout the country. Limited efforts have been made to assist in the rehabilitation of released prisoners in Halfway House establishments.

Facilities for Homeless Men: Representative of places where meals are provided, and in some cases lodging and other services as well, are: St. Francis of Assisi Refuge, 470 Albany St., Boston, Mass., where 600 men are fed daily by the St. Vincent de Paul Society; the U.S. foundation of the Little Brothers of Notre Dame, 500 West Division St., Chicago, Ill., for the elderly; St. Christopher's Inn, Graymoor, N.Y.; the St. Anthony Dining Room, San Francisco, where more than seven million meals have been served since 1950; four places run by the Little Brothers of the Good Shepherd — St. John's Hospice for Men, 1221 Race St., Phila., Pa. 19107; Good Shepherd Refuge, 601 2nd St., Albuquerque,

N.M.; Ozanam Inn, 843 Camp St., New Orleans, La. 70130, under the sponsorship of the St. Vincent de Paul Society; Good Samaritan Inn, 1450 E. Broad St., Columbus, O. 43205; also — St. Joseph's House of Hospitality, 61 Tannehill St., Pittsburgh, Pa. 15219; St. Vincent's Dining Room, 205 E. 2nd St., Reno, Nev.; St. Vincent's Dining Room, 821 N. H St., Las Vegas, Nev.; Holy Name Centre for Homeless Men, Inc., 18 Bleeker St., New York, N.Y. 10012.

Unwed Mothers: Residential and care services for unwed mothers are the specific work of Sisters of the Good Shepherd in their numerous convents in the US.

PRISONERS' RIGHTS

Seventy-seven Catholic bishops were among 450 civic and religious leaders who signed a statement in February, 1972, calling for the recognition of prisoners' human rights.

Sponsored by the National Alliance on Shaping Safer Cities, the statement called attention to "the abysmal conditions that make life intolerable for both guards and prisoners at institutions throughout the nation." It commended the "Bill of Rights for Prisoners" put into effect by Attorney General J. Shane Creamer of Pennsylvania, and called on attorneys general of the United States and the other 49 states "to follow this example."

The prisoners' "Bill of Rights" was recommended in the statement was based on the Standard Minimum Rules for the Treatment of Prisoners adopted by the Economic and Social Council of the United Nations in 1955. The statement recommended that the UN General Assembly endorse the rules and urge member states to implement them.

"The standard minimum rules prohibit racial or religious discrimination, require separation of untried and convicted inmates as well as separating youthful offenders from hardened criminals," the statement noted. "They prohibit corporal punishment as well as punishment by 'handcuffs, chains, irons or straitjackets.' They declare that no punishment shall be imposed unless the inmate has 'been informed of the offense alleged against him and given a proper opportunity of presenting his defense.' They clearly state that untried prisoners are 'presumed to be innocent and should be treated as such.'

"We must not allow the tragedy of Attica to move us to repression. Instead, we must intensify speedy reforms, so that prisons will no longer create embittered, angry, hopeless people, but rather be a real force in the process of rehabilitation. Adoption of the United Nations Standard Minimum Rules for the Treatment of Prisoners would safeguard both correctional officers and inmates, and would provide America with a unique opportunity to assert its moral leadership among the nations of the world."

Retreats

There is great variety in retreat and renewal programs, with orientations ranging from the traditional to teen encounters. Central to all of them are celebration of the liturgy and deepening of a person's commitment to faith and witness in life.

Features of many of the forms are as follows.

Traditional Retreats: Centered around conferences and the direction of a retreat master; oriented to the personal needs of the retreatants; including such standard practices as participation in Mass, reception of the sacraments, private and group prayer, silence and meditation, discussions.

Team Retreat: Conducted by a team of several leaders or directors (priests, religious, lay persons) with division of subject matter and activities according to their special skills and the nature and needs of their group.

Closed Retreat: Involving withdrawal for a period of time — overnight, several days, a weekend — from everyday occupations and activities.

Open Retreat: Made without total disengagement from everyday involvements, on a part-time basis.

Private Retreat: By one person, on a kind of do-it-yourself basis with the one-to-one assistance of a director.

Special Groups: With formats and activities geared to particular groups; e.g., members of Alcoholics Anonymous, vocational groups and apostolic groups.

Marriage Encounters: Usually weekend periods of husband-wife reflection and dialogue; introduced into the US from Spain in 1967.

Charismatic Renewal: Featuring elements of the movement of the same name; "Spirit-oriented"; communitarian and flexible, with spontaneous and shared prayer, personal testimonies of faith and witness.

Christian Community: Characterized by strong community thrust.

Teen Encounters, SEARCH: Formats adapted to the mentality and needs of youth, involving experience of Christian faith and commitment in a community setting.

Christian Maturity Seminars: Similar to teen encounters in basic concept but different to suit persons of greater maturity.

Cursillo: see separate entry.

Movement for a Better World: see separate entry.

Conferences

Retreats International: The first organization for promoting retreats in the US was started in 1904 in California. Its initial efforts and the gradual growth of the movement led to the formation in 1928 of the National Catholic Laymen's Retreat Conference, the forerunner of Retreats International. The president is Lyle M. Becker, P. O. Box 1123, Appleton, Wis. 54911. Father Thomas F. Middendorf is executive secretary. Mailing address: Donaldson Rd., Erlanger, Ky. 41018.

Retreats International-Women's Division: Successor to the National Laywomen's Retreat Movement, which was founded in 1936 in Chicago as an association of retreat houses, retreat leagues, diocesan organizations, schools and convents conducting or sponsoring retreats for women. Mary Jeanne Farrell is the president. Coadjutor Archbishop Leo C. Byrne of St. Paul and Minneapolis is the episcopal advisor. Mailing address: 438 S. Geyer Rd., Kirkwood, Mo. 63122.

HOUSES OF RETREAT AND RENEWAL

(Sources: Almanac survey: *The Official Catholic Directory, 1972.*)

Abbreviation code: m, men; w, women; mc, married couples. Houses and centers without code generally offer facilities to all groups. An asterisk after an abbreviation indicates that the facility is primarily for the group designated but that special groups are also accommodated. The number at the end of an entry indicates the total number making closed retreats as reported in an Almanac survey conducted in 1972; some houses included in their total numbers participating in days of prayer and recollection.

Houses furnish information concerning the types of programs they offer.

Alabama: Blessed Trinity Shrine Retreat, P.O. Holy Trinity, Holy Trinity 36859 (1,800).

Visitation Sacred Heart Retreat House, 2300 Spring Hill Ave., Mobile 36607 (1,000).

Alaska: Holy Spirit Retreat House, Star Route A, Box 388, Anchorage 99502 (800).

Arizona: Franciscan Renewal Center, Casa de Paz y Bien, 5802 E. Lincoln Dr., Box 220, Scottsdale 85252 (3,000).

Picture Rocks Retreat — A Christian Renewal Center, P.O. Box 5276, Tucson 85703.

California: Apostolic Oblates, 8113 Fillmore Dr., Stanton 90680.

Cenacle Retreat House (w*), 5340 Fair Oaks Blvd., Carmichael 95608 (1,200).

Christ the King Retreat Center, Box 156, Citrus Heights 95610 (670).

Christian Brothers Retreat House, 2233 Sulphur Springs Rd., St. Helena 94574.

El Carmelo Retreat House, 926 E. Highland Ave., P.O. Box 446, Redlands 92373.

El Retiro San Inigo, Box 128, Los Altos 94022 (2,600).

Holy Spirit Retreat House, 4316 Lanai Rd., Encino 91316 (3,246).

Immaculate Heart Retreat House (w), 3431 Waverly Dr., Los Angeles 90027.

La Casa de Maria, 888 San Ysidro Lane, Santa Barbara 93108.

Manresa Retreat House, P.O. Box K, Azusa 91702 (29,500).

Mary and Joseph Retreat House, 5300 Crest Rd. Palos Verdes 90274.

Mater Dolorosa Retreat House (m), 700 N. Sunnyside Ave., Sierra Madre 91024 (3,000).

Monastery of the Angels (w), 2021 Gower St., Los Angeles 90068.

New Camaldoli Immaculate Heart Hermitage (m, private), Big Sur 93920 (300-350).

Poverello of Assisi Retreat House, 1519 Woodworth St., San Fernando 91340.

Retreat House of the Sacred Heart (w), 920 E. Alhambra Rd., Alhambra 91801.

St. Andrew's Priory Retreat House, Valyermo 93563 (1,000).

St. Andrew's Priory Youth Center (y), Valyermo 93563 (2,000).

St. Anthony's Retreat House, P.O. Box 248, Three Rivers 93271 (3,000).

St. Charles Priory, Benet Hill, Oceanside 92054 (1,000).

St. Clare's Retreat, 2381 Laurel Glen Rd. Santa Cruz 95060 (2,900).

St. Francis Retreat (m*), P.O. Box 68, San Juan Bautista 95045.

St. Raymond's Dominican Retreat, 1666 Valley Rd., Thousand Oaks 91360.

San Damiano Retreat, P.O. Box 767, Danville 94526 (3,700).

Serra Retreat, P.O. Box 127, Malibu 90265 (2,500).

Sisters of Social Service, 1120 Westchester Pl., Los Angeles 90019 (885).

Vallombrosa Center (w*), 250 Oak Grove Ave., Menlo Park 94025.

Villa Maria del Mar, East Cliff Dr., Santa Cruz 95060 (25,000).

Colorado: El Pomar Retreat Center, 1661 Mesa Ave., Colorado Springs 80906 (1,300).

Sacred Heart Retreat House (m), Box 185, Sedalia 80135.

St. Scholastica Academy (w), 615 Pike Ave., Canon City 81212.

Connecticut: Cenacle Center for Meditation and Spiritual Renewal (w*), Wadsworth St., Middletown 06457.

Holy Family retreat (m*), 303 Tunxis Rd., West Hartford 06107 (5,000).

Holy Ghost Retreat House (m), Box 607, New Canaan 06840.

Immaculata Retreat House, Route 32, Windham Rd., Willimantic 06547 (1,600).

Our Lady of Calvary Retreat League, Cotton Rd., Farmington 06032 (1,700).

Villa Marie Retreat House, 159 Sky Meadow Dr., Stamford 06903.

Delaware: St. Francis Renewal Center, 1901 Prior Rd., Wilmington 19809.

District of Columbia: Washington Retreat House (w*), 4000 Harewood Rd. N.E., Washington 20017.

Florida: Cenacle Retreat House (w*), 1400 S. Dixie Highway, Lantana 33462 (1,200).

Franciscan Center (ecumenical), 3010 Perry Ave., Tampa 33603.

Holy Name Priory, San Antonio 33576.

Mary Queen of Apostoles Dominican Retreat House, 7275 S.W. 124th St., Kendall 33156.

Our Lady of Florida Retreat House (m*), 1300 US Hwy. No. 1, North Palm Beach 33408 (3,778).

St. Francis Friary (m), P.O. Box 421, Gulf Breeze 32561.

St. Leo's Abbey, St. Leo 33574 (80-100).

Georgia: Ignatius House, 6700 Riverside Dr. N.W., Atlanta 30328.

Monastery of the Holy Spirit (m), R.R. 1, Conyers 30207.

Illinois: Aylesford Renewal Center, US 66 at Cass Ave., N, Westmont 60559.

Bellarmine Hall (m*), Box 268, Barrington 60010 (3,000).

Bishop Lane Retreat House, R.R. 2, Box 214 A, Rockford 61102.

Cabrini Contact Center, 9430 Golf Rd., Des Plaines 60016.

Cenacle Retreat House (w*), Box 349, Warrenville 60555.

Childerley Retreat House (university students), 506 McHenry Rd., Wheeling 60090.

Congregation of Our Lady of the Retreat in the Cenacle (w), 513 Fullerton Parkway, Chicago 60614.

Congregation of Our Lady of the Retreat in the Cenacle (w), 11600 Longwood Dr., Chicago 60643.

Holy Spirit Retreat House, Techny 60082 (400-500).

King's House, N. 66th St., Belleville 62223 (3,500).

King's House of Retreats, Box 313, Henry 61537 (2,294).

La Salle Manor (y), Plano 60545 (3,700).

St. Francis Retreat, Mayslake, 1717 31st St., Oak Brook 60521 (4,500).

St. Mary's Retreat House, P.O. Box 608, 1400 W. Main St., Lemont 60439.

St. Peter's Friary (m), 110 W. Madison St., Chicago 60602.

Viatorian Villa, 3015 N. Bayview Lane, McHenry 60050 (1,400).

Villa Redeemer, Box 6, Glenview 60025.

Indiana: Alverna Retreat House, 8140 Spring Mill Rd., Indianapolis 46260 (3,000).

Franciscan Retreat, 12921 Parrish St., P.O. Box 164, Cedar Lake 46303.

Lourdes Retreat House, Box 156, Cedar Lake 46303 (600).

Our Lady of Fatima Retreat House, 5353 E. 56th St., Indianapolis 46226 (1,000).

Our Lady of Fatima Retreat House, Notre Dame 46556 (5,000).

St. Jude Guest House, St. Meinrad 47577 (625).

Sarto Retreat House, 4200 N. Kentucky Ave., Evansville 47711.

Seven Dolors Shrine Retreat House, R.R. 12, Box 28, Valparaiso 46383.

Iowa: American Martyrs Retreat House, P.O. Box 605, Cedar Falls 50613 (3,400).

Colfax Interfaith Spiritual Center, Box 37, Colfax, 50054.

Kansas: Villa Christi Retreat House, 3033 W. Second St., Wichita 67203.

Kentucky: Marydale Center, Donaldson Rd., Erlanger 41018 (6,000).

Our Lady of Gethsemani (m, private), The Guestmaster, Abbey of Gethsemani, Trappist 40073.

Louisiana: Abbey Christian Life Center, St. Joseph's Abbey, St. Benedict 70457.

Ave Maria Retreat House, Route 1, Box 0368 AB, Marrero 70072 (1,800).

Cenacle Retreat House (w), 5500 St. Mary St., Metairie 70004 (1,600).

Manresa House of Retreats (m), P.O. Box 89, Convent 70723 (3,000).

Maryhill Retreat House (Christian Life Center), 600 Maryhill Rd., Pineville 71360 (2,000).

Our Lady of the Oaks Retreat House, P.O. Box D, Grand Coteau 70541 (1,800).

Maine: St. Paul's Center, Oblate Fathers Retreat House, 135 State St., Augusta 04330 (12,000).

Maryland: CYO Retreat House (y*), Box 211, Sparks 21152 (4,000).

Christian Brothers Retreat House (y), Rt. 15 South, Adamstown 21712.

Loyola Retreat House-on-Potomac (m*), Faulkner 20632 (2,800). City Office, 1028 Connecticut Ave. N.W., Washington, D.C. 20036.

Manresa-on-Severn, Annapolis 21404 (5,000).

Marian Retreat House (w), 4400 Forest Hill Rd., Baltimore 21207.

Marriottsville Spiritual Center, Marriottsville 21104.

Pine Lane Spiritual Center, Winchester Rd., Annapolis 21404.

St. Joseph Spiritual Center, 3800 Frederick Ave., Baltimore 21229 (3,000).

Massachusetts: Calvary Monastery Retreat House, Passionist Fathers, 59 South St., Shrewsbury 01545 (6,804).

Campion Hall Jesuit Retreat House, Great Pond Rd., North Andover 01845 (2,000).

Cenacle Retreat House, 200 Lake St., Brighton, Boston 02135 (2,000).

Cenacle Retreat House (w), George Hill Rd., Lancaster 01523.

Christian Formation Center, River Rd., Andover 01810.

Don Bosco Retreat House (boys), P.O. Box 271, Ipswich 01938.

Eastern Point Retreat House, Gonzaga Hall, Gloucester 01930.

Espousal Center, 554 Lexington St., Waltham 02154.

Holy Cross Fathers Retreat House, Washington St., N. Easton 02356.

La Salette Center of Christian Living, 947 Park St., Attleboro 02703.

Loretto Retreat House (y), Jeffrey's Neck Rd., Ipswich 01938.

Marian Center, 1365 Northampton St., Holyoke 01040.

Miramar Retreat House, Duxbury, 02332 (2,200).

Mother of God Retreat House (boys), Old Groveland Rd., Bradford 01830 (500).

Our Lady of Mt. Carmel Retreat House, Oblong Rd., Williamstown 01267.

Round Hills Centre for Renewal, P.O. Box P-A, Smith Neck Rd., South Dartmouth 02748 (3,000).

St. Gabriel's Retreat House, 159 Washington St., Brighton, Boston 02135 (2,000).

St. Joseph's Center, Sullivan Square, Charlestown, Boston 02129.

Michigan: Blessed Sacrament Retreat House, Sacramentine Sisters, Conway 49722 (1,000).

Capuchin Retreat, Box 188, Washington 48094 (1,635).

Christian Commune House (y), 1975 N. River Rd., St. Clare 48079.

Manresa Jesuit Retreat House, 1390 Quarton Rd., Bloomfield Hills 48013 (4,000).

Mary Reparatrix Retreat Center, 17330 Quincy Ave., Detroit 48221 (1,500-2,500).

Marygrove Renewal Center, Garden 49835 (1,200).

Portiuncula in the Pines, P.O. Box 250, De Witt 48820 (1,800).

Queen of Angels Retreat, 3400 S. Washington Blvd., Saginaw (1,819).

St. Basil's Center, 3990 Giddings Rd., Pontiac 48057.

St. Lazare Retreat House, W. Spring Lake Rd., Spring Lake 49456 (1,400).

St. Mary's Retreat House (w*); 775 W. Drahner Rd., Oxford 48051 (1,500).

St. Paul of the Cross Retreat House, 23333 Schoolcraft, Detroit 48223.

Minnesota: Cenacle Retreat House (w*), 1221 Wayzata Blvd., Wayzata 55391 (2,000).

Christian Brothers Retreat Center, Rt. 1, Box 18, Marine-on-St. Croix 55047 (3,500).

Christian Community Center, Assisi Heights, Rochester 55901 (1,880).

Fiat Retreat House, 621 First Ave. S., Minneapolis 55404.

Franciscan Retreats, Conventual Franciscan Friars, Prior Lake 55372 (2,500).

Immaculate Heart of Mary Seminary, Terrace Heights, Winona 55987 (300).

Jesuit Retreat House (m), 3900 Demontreville Rd., North St. Paul 55109 (2,000).

King's House of Retreats, 621 S. First Ave., Buffalo 55313 (4,000).

Maryhill Retreat House, 260 Summit Ave., St. Paul 55102.

St. John Abbey (mc), Collegeville 56321 (300, includes children).

The Welch Center, 605 N. Central Ave., Duluth 55811 (500).

Mississippi: St. Augustine's Seminary (m*), Divine Word Missionaries, Box 311, Bay St. Louis 39520.

Missouri: Cenacle Retreat House, 900 S. Spoede Rd., St. Louis 63131 (4,200).

Family Life Center, St. Pius X Abbey, Box 39, Pevely 63070 (3,000).

Holy Family Retreat House, Conception 64432.

Immacolata Retreat House, RFD 4, Box 434, Liberty 64068.

Marianist Apostolic Center, Glencoe 63038 (4,000).

Our Lady of Assumption Abbey (m), Rt. 5, Ava 65608 (250).

Pallottine Renewal Center, Old Halls Ferry Rd., Florissant 63033 (3,000).

Passionist Retreat of Our Lady, Retreat House, Passionist Fathers and Brothers, Warrenton 63383 (3,000).

The White House Retreat (m), 7400 Christopher Dr., St. Louis 63129 (4,200).

Montana: St. Joseph Retreat House, P.O. Box 336, Deer Lodge 59722.

Nebraska: Catholic Women's Retreat League, 3862 Frances St., Omaha 68105 (170).

Good Counsel, R.R. 1, Box 110, Waverly 68462 (1,200).

St. Columbans Foreign Mission Society, St. Columbans 68056 (300).

New Hampshire: The Common - St. Joseph Monastery, Peterborough 03458.

New Hampshire Monastery, New Boston 03070.

Oblate Fathers Retreat House, Hudson 03051 (2,400).

St. Francis Friary and Retreat House, 860 Central Rd., Rye Beach 03871.

New Jersey: Blackwood Center, St. Pius X House, Box 216, Blackwood 08012.

Blessed Trinity Missionary Retreat Cenacle (w*), 1190 Long Hill Rd., Stirling 07980 (725).

Carmel Retreat House, 1071 Ramapo Valley Rd., Mahwah; mailing address, P.O. Box 285, Oakland 07436 (3,500).

Cenacle Retreat House (w*), River Rd., Highland Park 08904.

Loyola House of Retreats, 161 James St., Morristown 07960 (3,200).

Queen of Peace Retreat House, St. Paul's Abbey, Newton 07860 (3,300).

St. Bonaventure Retreat House (m), 174 Ramsey St., Paterson 07501.

St. Joseph's Villa (w), Srs. of St. John the Baptist, Peapack 07977 (1,200).

San Alfonso Retreat House, 755 Ocean Ave., Long Branch 07740 (6,200).

Stella Maris Convent, 981 Ocean Ave., Elberon 07741.

Villa Pauline Retreat House (w), Hilltop Rd., Mendham 07945 (969).

New Mexico: Holy Cross Retreat House, P.O. Box 158, Mesilla Park 88047 (1,200).

Our Lady of Guadalupe Monastery (families - pentecostal), Pecos 87552 (3,000).

Our Lady Queen of Peace, 5825 Coors Rd. S.W., Albuquerque 87105 (3,000).

New York: Bishop Molloy Retreat House, 178th and Wexford Terr., Jamaica, L.I. 11432 (6,000).

Cardinal Spellman Retreat House, Passionist Fathers, 5801 Palisade Ave., Bronx (Riverdale) 10471 (9,000).

Cenacle Retreat House, Mt. Kisco 10549 (1,877).

Cenacle Retreat House, 693 East Ave., Rochester 14607 (1,200).

Christ the King Retreat House, 500 Rockford Rd., Syracuse 13224.

Christ the King Seminary (m), St. Bonaventure 14778.

Congregation of the Cenacle, Cenacle Rd., Lake Ronkonkoma, L.I. 11779.

Cormaria Retreat House (w*), Sag Harbor, L.I. (1,600).

Dominican Retreat House, 1945 Union St., Schenectady 12309 (4,000).

Gonzaga Retreat House (y), Monroe 10950.

Grace House, Genesee St., Alden 14004 (1,000).

Holy Cross Passionist Apostolic Center, Rt. 5, Dunkirk 14048 (5,000).

Jesuit Retreat House, Auriesville 12016 (1,500).

John XXIII Center (Retreat House and Ecumenical Center), Assumptionists, Cassadaga 14718 (2,500).

Marian Shrine, Don Bosco Retreat House, Filor's Lane, West Haverstraw 10993 (5,000).

Monastery of the Precious Blood (w), Ft. Hamilton Parkway and 54th St., Brooklyn 11219.

Mount Alvernia Retreat House, Wappingers Falls 12590 (673).

Mount Augustine Retreat House, 144 Campus Rd., Staten Island 10301 (10,000).

Mount Manresa Retreat House, 239 Fingerboard Rd., Staten Island 10305 (3,000).

Notre Dame Retreat House, Box 74, Foster Rd., Canandaigua 14424 (3,500).

Queen of Apostles Retreat House, North Haven, Sag Harbor 11963.

Regina Maria Retreat House (w), 77 Brinkerhoff St., Plattsburgh 12901.

Retreat House of Mary Reparatrix, 14 E. 29th St., New York 10016 (950).

St. Andrew's House, Walden 12586.

St. Columban's Retreat House (m), Derby 14047.

St. Francis Retreat House, Capuchin Fathers, Garrison 10524 (2,000).

St. Gabriel (y), Burns Rd., Shelter Island Heights 11965 (2,200).

St. Ignatius Retreat House, Strickler Rd., Clarence Center (2,800).

St. Ignatius Retreat House, Inisfada, Manhasset, L.I. 11030.

St. Josephat's Retreat House (mc), Box 231, Glen Cove 11542.

St. Joseph Center (Spanish Center), 523 W. 142nd St., New York 10031.

Stella Maris Retreat House (w), Skaneateles 13152.

North Carolina: Maryhurst Retreat House (w*), P.O. Box 1390, Pinehurst 28374.

North Dakota: Queen of Peace Retreat, 1310 N. Broadway, Fargo 58102 (1,200).

Ohio: Catholic Women's Retreat League, c/o Miss Josephine Roundtree, president, 92 S. 4th St., Newark 43055.

Dominican Retreat House, Our Lady of Good Counsel (w*), 1130 Harman Ave., Dayton 45419 (1,350).

Franciscan Renewal Center, 320 West St., Carey 43316.

Friarhurst Retreat House, 8136 Wooster Pike, Cincinnati 45227.

Holy Cross Center, Passionist Community, 1055 St. Paul Pl., Cincinnati 45202 (400).

Jesuit Retreat House, 5629 State Rd., Cleveland 44134 (2,000).

Loyola of the Lakes, 700 Killinger Rd., Clinton 44216 (2,000).

Loyola Retreat House, P.O. Box 289, Milford 45150 (3,600).

Maria Stein Retreat-Renewal Center, Box 128, Maria Stein 45860 (1,557).

Marianist Center, 4435 East Patterson Rd., Dayton 45430 (1,250).

Mary Reparatrix Retreat House (w), 3350 Ruther Ave., Cincinnati 45220 (1,300).

Men of Milford Retreat House (m), Box 348, Milford 45150 (2,500).

Monastery and Retreat House of the Precious Blood (w, private), 173 Main St., Norwalk 44857.

Our Lady of the Pines (w), 1250 Tiffin St., Fremont 43420.

Sacred Heart, 3014-3128 Logan Ave., Box 3902, Youngstown 44505 (2,000).

St. Joseph Christian Life Center, 18485 Lake Shore Blvd., Cleveland 44119.

Shrine Center for Renewal, Diocese of Columbus, 5277 E. Broad St., Columbus 43213.

Oklahoma: Jesuit Retreat, P.O. Box 949, Cushing 74023 (1,000).

Oregon: Loyola Jesuit Retreat House, 3220 S.E. 43rd St., Portland 97206.

Mt. Angel Abbey, St. Benedict 97373 (1,200).

Our Lady of Peace Retreat, 3600 S. W. 170th Ave., Beaverton 97005 (1,500).

Trappist Abbey Retreat (m, y, private), P.O. Box 97, Lafayette 97127.

Pennsylvania: Bl. Raphaela Mary Retreat House, Haverford 19041 (3,601).

Byzantine Catholic Seminary (m), 3605 Perrysville Ave., Pittsburgh 15214 (100).

Cenacle Retreat House (w), 4721 Fifth Ave., Pittsburgh 15212.

Convent of the Precious Blood, New Holland Ave., Shillington 19607.

Dominican Retreat House (w*), Ashbourne Rd. and Juniper Ave., Elkins Park 19117 (12,311).

Mt. St. Ann Retreat, (w, y), P.O. Box 328, Ebensburg 15931 (200-250).

Nativity Retreat House (w), 711 N. Franklin St., Philadelphia 19123.

St. Alphonsus Retreat House (m*), Box 218, Tobyhanna 18466 (1,200).

St. Emma Retreat House, Five Point Rd., Greensburg 16601.

St. Fidelis Seminary, Herman 16039 (1,200).

St. Francis College (m*), Herman 15940 (750-800).

St. Francis Retreat House, 291 Chipman Rd., Easton 18042 (1,500).

St. Francis Retreat House (w), Monocacy Manor, Bethlehem 18017.

St. Francis Retreat House, 1201 Beechwood Blvd., Pittsburgh 15206.

St. Gabriel's Retreat House (w), 631 Griffin Pond Rd., Clarks Summit 18411 (1,000).

St. Joseph Academy—Marian Hall (w, summer only), RD 2, Columbia 17512 (400).

St. Joseph's-in-the-Hills (m*), Malvern 19355 (13,500).

St. Mark's Seminary, 429 E. Grandview Blvd., Erie 16504 (200).

St. Paul of the Cross Retreat House, 148 Monastery Ave., Pittsburgh 15203 (6,561).

St. Vincent Retreat House (m*, summer), Latrobe 15650 (1,500).

Villa Maria Retreat House, Box 218, Wernersville 19585.

Villa of Our Lady of the Poconos (w*), Mt. Pocono 18344 (1,800).

Rhode Island: Corpus Christi Carmel Retreat House, (w*), 21 Battery St., Newport 02840 (1,000).

Ephpheta House — A Center for Renewal, 10 Manville Hill Rd; mailing address, P.O. Box 1, Manville 02838 (2,000).

Immaculate Heart of Mary Retreat House (w, y), 11 North Rd., Peace Dale 02883 (3,300).

Our Lady of Peace Retreat House, Ocean Rd., Narragansett 02882.

South Carolina: Springbank Christian Center, Dominican Retreat House, Kingstree 29556.

Texas: Cenacle Retreat House, 420 N. Kirkwood, Houston 77024 (3,000).

Christian Holiday House (ecumenical), Oblate Fathers, P.O. Box 635, Dickinson 77539 (2,550).

Holy Name Retreat House, 430 Bunker Hill Rd., P.O. Box 19306, Houston 77024.

Montserrat Jesuit Retreat House, Lake Dallas 75065.

Our Lady of the Pillar Christian Renewal Center, 2507 N.W. 36th St., San Antonio 78228 (1,600).

Saint Joseph Retreat House, 127 Oblate Dr., San Antonio (3,000).

San Juan Retreat House, Diocese of Brownsville, P.O. Box 998, San Juan 78589.

Utah: Our Lady of the Holy Trinity Retreat House (m), Huntsville 84317 (350).

Virginia: Dominican Retreat, 7103 Old, McLean 22101 (2,000).

Holy Family Retreat House, Box 3151, Hampton 23363 (1,800).

St. Ann Retreat House, Bristow 22013.

Washington: Camp Field Retreat Center, P.O. Box 128, Leavenworth 98826.

Immaculate Heart Retreat House, Route 3, Box 653, Spokane 99203 (2,000).

Palisades Retreat, P.O. Box 2214, Tacoma (2,500).

St. Peter the Apostle Diocesan Retreat Center, P.O. Box 86, Cowiche 98923.

Wisconsin: Cenacle Retreat House (w*), 3288 N. Lake Dr., Milwaukee 53211.

Holy Hill Retreat Center, Hubertus 53033.

Holy Name Retreat House, Chambers Island; mailing address, 131 S. Madison St., P.O. Box 337, Green Bay 54305 (1,000).

Jesuit Retreat House (m), 4800 Fahrnwald Rd., Oshkosh 54901 (1,300).

Monte Alverno Retreat House, 1000 N. Ballard Rd., Appleton 54911 (4,000).

Our Lady of Perpetual Help, 1800 N. Timber Trail Lane, Oconomowoc 53066 (2,000).

Our Lady of Spring Bank Manor, Cistercian Fathers, Oconomowoc 53066 (230).

St. Benedict Center for Christian Unity (ecumenical), P.O. Box 5070, Madison 53705 (550).

St. Vincent Pallotti Center, Rt. 3, Box 47, Elkhorn 53121 (1,000).

Siena Center, 5635 Erie St., Racine 53402.

Wyoming: St. Stephen's Indian Mission (two retreats annually), St. Stephen's 82524 (96).

CANA, PRE-CANA CONFERENCES

These special-purpose conferences are not a part of retreat programs, and the movement they represent is not related to the retreat movement. With the latter, however, they share the purpose of deepening religious experience.

Cana Conferences: Cana Conferences for married couples focus on four general areas: the relationships between husband and wife, parents and children, God and the family, society and the family. Treatment of these subjects, techniques of presentation, methods of discussion, and integrated religious activities are determined by the ordinary or special interests of different conference groups. Priests, medical doctors, marriage experts from other disciplines, and married couples may serve as lecturers or discussion leaders. Most conference groups are open to mixed-religion couples.

The movement, called Cana after the marriage feast at Cana (Jn. 2:1-11), traces its origin to Family Renewal Days given in 1943 in New York City by Father John P. Delaney, S.J. The name was changed to Cana Conference by Father Edward Dowling, S.J. The bishops of the United States, in their annual statement in 1949, commended the conferences and urged their promotion throughout the country.

The movement is autonomous and has no central headquarters. It is serviced nationally by the Family Life Division of the US Catholic Conference.

Pre-Cana Conferences: These pre-marriage conferences for engaged couples are analogous to Cana Conferences for married couples. Their purpose is a spiritual, intellectual, emotional, and practical preparation for Christian marriage.

Christopher Awards

(The Following Christopher Awards for television and films are additional to other awards listed on pp. 700 and 701.)

"Circus Town" — David A. Tapper, producer, director and writer (NBC).

"The Eagle and the Hawk" — Robert Riger, producer, director and writer (ABC).

"Heroes and Heroin: An ABC News Special" — Av Westin, executive producer, director and writer; David Buksbaum, producer (ABC).

"The Homecoming: A Christmas Story" — Lee Rich, executive producer; Robert L. Jacks, producer; Fielder Cook, director; Earl Hamner, Jr., writer (CBS).

"The Impatient Heart" — William Sackheim, producer; John M. Badham, director; Alvin Sargent, writer (NBC).

"The International Weapons Trade" (segment of "First Tuesday") — Robert Rogers, producer, director and writer (NBC).

"Jane Eyre" — Frederick H. Brogger, producer; Delbert Mann, director; Jack Pulman, adaptation (NBC).

"Julie and Carol at Lincoln Center" — Joe Hamilton, producer; Dave Powers, director; Bob Ellison and Marty Farrell, writers; Mitzie and Ken Welch, special musical materials and lyrics (CBS).

"Justice in America" (Major Investigative CBS News Series in Three Parts, Focusing on the Courts) — Burton Benjamin, executive producer; John Sharnik, producer, director and writer (CBS).

"They've Killed President Lincoln!" — Warren V. Bush, executive producer; Robert Guenette, producer and director; Robert Guenette and Theodore H. Strauss, writers (NBC).

"This Child is Rated X: An NBC News White Paper on Juvenile Justice" — Martin Carr, producer, director and writer (NBC).

"When Johnny Comes Marching Home" — Ernest Pendrell, producer, director and writer (ABC).

Films

General: "The Railway Children" — Robert Lynn, producer; Lionel Jeffries, director and writer of screenplay (Universal Release).

For adults and adolescents: "Clare's Knee" — Pierre Cottrell, producer; Eric Rohmer, director and writer (Columbia Pictures).

Lay Persons and Their Apostolate

The identity and role of lay persons in the life and mission of the Church were defined in two documents issued by the Second Vatican Council.

According to the *Dogmatic Constitution on the Church* (No. 31):

"The term laity is here understood to mean all the faithful except those in holy orders and those in a religious state sanctioned by the Church. These faithful are by baptism made one body with Christ and are established among the People of God. They are in their own way made sharers in the priestly, prophetic, and kingly functions of Christ. They carry out their own part in the mission of the whole Christian people with respect to the Church and the world.

"A secular quality is proper and special to laymen. . . .

"The laity, by their very vocation, seek the kingdom of God by engaging in temporal affairs and by ordering them according to the plan of God. They live in the world, that is, in each and in all of the secular professions and occupations. They live in the ordinary circumstances of family and social life, from which the very web of their existence is woven.

"They are called there by God so that by exercising their proper function and being led by the spirit of the gospel they can work for the sanctification of the world from within, in the manner of leaven. In this way they can make Christ known to others, especially by the testimony of a life replendent in faith, hope, and charity. The layman is closely involved in temporal affairs of every sort. It is therefore his special task to illumine and organize these affairs in such a way that they may always start out, develop, and persist according to Christ's mind, to the praise of the Creator and the Redeemer."

Call to the Apostolate

In its *Decree on the Lay Apostolate*, the council developed these concepts and outlined the principal features of this apostolate.

"Incorporated into Christ's Mystical Body through baptism and strengthened by the power of the Holy Spirit through confirmation, they are assigned to the apostolate by the Lord Himself. They are consecrated into a royal priesthood and a holy people (cf. 1 Pt. 2:4-10) in order that they may offer spiritual sacrifices through everything they do, and may witness to Christ throughout the world. . . .

"The apostolate is carried on through the faith, hope, and charity which the Holy Spirit diffuses in the hearts of all members of the Church. Indeed, the law of love, which is the Lord's greatest commandment, impels all the faithful to promote God's glory through the spread of His kingdom and to obtain for all men that eternal life which consists in knowing the only true God and Him whom He sent, Jesus Christ (cf. Jn. 17:3). On all Christians therefore is laid the splendid burden of working to make the divine message of salvation known and accepted by all men throughout the world.

"For the exercise of this apostolate, the Holy Spirit who sanctifies the People of God through the ministry and the sacraments gives to the faithful special gifts as well (cf. 1 Cor. 12:7), 'alloting to everyone according as he will' (1 Cor. 12:11). Thus may the individual, 'according to the gift that each has received, administer it to one another' and become 'good stewards of the manifold grace of God' (1 Pt. 4:10), and build up thereby the whole body in charity (cf. Eph. 4:16). From the reception of these charisms or gifts . . . there arise for each believer the right and duty to use them in the Church and in the world for the good of mankind and for the upbuilding of the Church. In so doing, believers need to enjoy the freedom of the Holy Spirit who 'breathes where he wills' (Jn. 3:8). At the same time, they must act in communion with their brothers in Christ, especially with their pastors" (No. 3).

"The layman's religious program of life should take its special quality from his status as a married man and a family man, or as one who is unmarried or widowed, from his state of health, and from his professional and social activity. He should not cease to develop earnestly the qualities and talents bestowed on him in accord with these conditions of life, and he should make use of the gifts which he has received from the Holy Spirit" (No. 4).

Goals and Methods

"The mission of the Church is not only to bring to men the message and grace of Christ, but also to penetrate and perfect the temporal sphere with the spirit of the gospel" (No. 5).

"The mission of the Church concerns the salvation of men, which is to be achieved by belief in Christ and by His grace. Hence the apostolate of the Church and of all her members is primarily designed to manifest Christ's message by words and deeds and to communicate His grace to the world. . . .

(The lay apostolate) "does not consist only in the witness of one's way of life; a true apostle looks for opportunities to announce Christ by words addressed either to nonbelievers with a view to leading them to faith, or to believers with a view to instructing them, strengthening them, and motivating them toward a more fervent life" (No. 6).

"The temporal order must be renewed in such a way that, without the slightest detriment to its own proper laws (and values), it can be brought into conformity with the higher principles of the Christian life and adapted to the shifting circumstances of time, place, and person. Outstanding among the works of this type of apostolate is that of Christian social action. This sacred Synod desires to see it extended now to the whole temporal sphere, including culture" (No. 7).

"The apostolate of the social milieu, that is, the effort to infuse a Christian spirit into the mentality, customs, laws, and structures of the community in which a person lives, is so much the duty and responsibility of the laity that it can never be properly performed by others" (No. 13).

"The individual apostolate . . . is the origin and condition of the whole lay apostolate, even in its organized expression, and admits of no substitute" (No. 16).

"The group apostolate is highly important also because the apostolate must often be implemented through joint action, in both the church communities and various other spheres. For the associations established to carry on the apostolate in common sustain their members, form them for the apostolate, and rightly organize and regulate their apostolic work so that much better results can be expected than if each member were to act on his own" (No. 18).

"Deserving of special honor and commendation in the Church are those lay people, single or married, who devote themselves and their professional skill, either permanently or temporarily, to the service of associations and their activities" (No. 22).

Apostolic Vocation of Christians

This was the subject of an address delivered by Pope Paul VI May 24, 1972, during a general audience.

[The following excerpts are from the text which appeared in the June 1 English edition of L'Osservatore Romano.]

The Pope said, in part:

"We can call the apostolate the exterior witness prompted by the Holy Spirit.

"You know, in this connection, two obvious things, especially since the recent (Second Vatican) Council.

"Under the name of apostolate is understood the whole exterior activity of the Church with regard to her primary purpose, salvation by means of Christ. Today this activity had become all the more conscious and urgent."

"And then you know that the Christian vocation itself is by its very nature also a vocation to the apostolate. That is, the apostolate has been recognized as an activity inherent in the very fact of being a Christian; hence the promotion of the concept of the Catholic layman as a collaborator of the hierarchical apostolate properly speaking."

"We all know too that this apostolic, missionary, outgoing awareness of the Christian called to faith and assisted by grace is not yet duly acquired by many people who call themselves Christians. This is a sign that the efficacy of Pentecost has not yet been understood and experienced for what it is, as it was at the beginning of Christianity; namely, an impulse to bear witness to own one's own faith, to defend it and spread it."

"The apostolate, in its innumerable forms, is the positive work of building up the Church: it becomes the visible, and hence the social and historical, sign of the authentic motion of the Spirit in the hearts of those who appeal to the Spirit to consider themselves Christians.

"Here a very serious reflection on the apostolate is necessary. It has become a very fruitful subject of thought and action among Catholics today. A general reflection: How is the apostolate getting on in our sphere today?"

Many Activities

"We must thank the Lord on seeing a very rich flourishing of activities of every kind among the People of God for the proclamation and affirmation of the Christian name. And praise be to those who offer their talent, action, name, means, prayer, sufferings, solidarity and interest in the present effort of the Catholic apostolate. . . . We would like one and all to know that they are appreciated by the Church, particularly by those with special responsibilities in the Church. May they all be thanked, encouraged, blessed.

"We pray to the Holy Spirit to pour out his gifts upon them, so that all those engaged in the apostolate, inside or outside the ecclesial structure, may feel energy within them and be all inwardly sustained by the conviction and joy of positive and militant Christian profession.

"But we must all remember that the consistent, constant and courageous attitude of Christian profession — that is, of the apostolate — is always threatened in our complex human existence by many forms of renascent and crafty weakness. The Christian, the apostle especially, is obliged to be strong and courageous, to be frank and free, as becomes a follower of Christ. But there always exists, even in the most committed . . . an incurable frailty. . . .

"This frailty often causes our personality to slip imperceptibly into that magnetic field around us and overwhelming us which is called self-consciousness, conformity with fashion, paralyzing fear of the judgment or irony of others or of the press.

"We were thinking during the past days of Pascal's remark about public opinion, which wears one down. And today, as this public atmosphere gains the upper hand over personal autonomy, we must remember how liable we are to shirk the external appeal of the Church and the internal appeal of conscience to observe the Christian commitment. We proclaim that we are free but often, afraid what people will say, we are far from being so."

Counterfeit Apostolate

"Moreover, a form of habitual confrontation, often harmful and sometimes irresponsible, which has become fashionable today in the Christian profession, causes so many fine energies that should serve the constructive apostolate to deviate from charity and sometimes even from truth. The attitude of habitu-

USCC-RELATED AGENCIES

The following agencies are engaged in carrying out programs of the United States Catholic Conference. Additional agencies are reported in other Almanac entries.

Division of Religious Education/CCD: (Confraternity of Christian Doctrine): Its objective is the religious education of Catholic children who are not in Catholic schools, out-of-school youths and adults. Recent figures indicate that some five and one-half million Catholic children and youths participate in CCD programs from pre-kindergarten through high school. An adult religious education program is carried out through group discussions of texts or films, forums, and particularly in extensive catechist training courses for all academic levels.

The modern revival and expansion of the confraternity dates from publicaion of the encyclical *Acerbo Nimis* by St. Pius X in 1905. His directive that the CCD be established in every parish was incorporated in the Code of Canon Law and reaffirmed by the Second Vatican Council in the *Decree on the Bishops' Pastoral Office in the Church.*

The CCD is a parish-based organization operating under a priest-director and a board of commission of lay persons.

Responsibility for many details of a local CCD unit ideally rests with a lay coordinator or administrator who is a trained professional in theology and/or religious education. This is a recent development in religious education outside the parish school system. Another noteworthy new development in CCD programs is growing emphasis on training parents to prepare their children for reception of First Communion, penance and confirmation.

On the diocesan level, CCD work is directed by a priest appointed by the bishop, with a staff of assistants — priests, religious, lay persons. In some dioceses, the program operates under an office of religious education or other agency with a similar title. The diocesan office oversees the work of local and regional units, conducts teacher-training courses, issues guidelines for a unified program, conducts diocesan or regional meetings for CCD teachers and other workers.

On the national level, the Division of Religious Education/CCD (formerly called the

al contestation, which unfortunately characterizes not a few initiatives today, is a counterfeit of the apostolate.

"We wish that the Spirit, by whom they claim to be guided — perhaps to withdraw themselves from the harmony of ecclesial communion and the obedience due to him who is a minister of authority — would restore them to the honor of their function, which is to stimulate real ecclesial and social renewal, and to the real charity of fellowship characteristic of the Christian spirit."

National Center of the Confraternity of Christian Doctrine and since 1969 under the Department of Education, US Catholic Conference) contributes in many ways to the operation of religious education programs throughout the country. On the international level, it participates in programs of the Congregation of the Clergy in the religious education field.

Father Charles C. McDonald is director of the division.

Offices are located at 1312 Massachusetts Ave. N.W., Washington, D.C. 20005.

National Council of Catholic Laity: Organized in 1971 under the auspices of the National Council of Catholic Men and the National Council of Catholic Women. In line with plans initiated early in 1970, the council is a coalition in which the parent organizations have integrated budgeting, national staff and office operations, and greater opportunities for collaboration in wider and more flexible ranges of field and program activities.

Under the first phase of development of the umbrella-like NCCL, the conferences of men and women keep their identities and structures. Autonomy is retained by their affiliates — some 70 diocesan councils, 18 national organizations, 20 Knights of Columbus state councils, 1,700 parish and overseas military groups of men; approximately 10,000 organizations of women. Joseph F. Carroll is executive director of the National Council of Catholic Men. Mrs. Thomas J. Burke is president of the National Council of Catholic Women.

The NCCL is governed by a 24-member board.

H. G. Rountree of Rogers, Ark., is the president. Margaret Mealey is the executive director.

Offices are located at 1312 Massachusetts Ave. N.W., Washington, D.C. 20005.

National Catholic Rural Life Conference: Founded in 1923 through the efforts of Bishop Edwin V. O'Hara for the purpose of promoting the general welfare of rural people by a program of extensive services, publications and rural-related activities. Publications include the official monthly *Catholic Rural Life.*

The conference has approximately 5,000 members among rural pastors, farmers, teachers, sociologists, economists, agricultural agents and officials. There are 95 officially appointed diocesan rural life directors.

St. Isidore the Farmer is patron of the conference.

Bishop George H. Spelty of St. Cloud is president. Co-directors are Msgr. John G. Weber and Father John J. McRaith.

National headquarters are located at 3801 Grand Ave., Des Moines, Ia. 50312.

National Catholic Community Service: Established by the US hierarchy in November, 1940, to serve members of the armed forces, defense production workers and their families. It has continued since then to serve the spiritual, social, welfare and recreational needs of the nation's defense forces, and patients in Veterans' Administration hospitals.

NCCS has directly related responsibility for USO services through staff in 46 locations in the United States and overseas — in Rome and Naples, Italy; Athens, Greece; Rota, Spain; Frankfurt, Germany; Keflavik, Iceland; Manila, Philippines; Okinawa, Thailand, Vietnam. A VA program is in operation in 166 hospitals throughout the country, and 100 NCCS-VA diocesan hospital committees are assisting in this work.

During World War II, in cooperation with the United Service Organizations, NCCS conducted over 500 operations in this country and abroad. It is a member agency of the USO and of the VA Voluntary Service National Advisory Committee.

The organization is under the direction of a board of trustees composed of the officers, three other members of the USCC administrative board, and the military vicar. NCCS works closely with departments of the USCC.

NCCS publications include prayerbooks and pamphlets for members of the armed services, NCCS newsletters, and several publications issued jointly with other member organizations of USO.

National staff members include acting executive director, Dr. Maurice M. Hartmann, and director of program and field service, Michael E. Menster.

Headquarters are located at 1312 Massachusetts Ave. N.W., Washington, D.C. 20005.

Catholic Relief Services—USCC: The official overseas aid and development agency of the American Catholic Church.

CRS was founded in 1943 by the bishops of the United States to help civilians in Europe and North Africa caught in the disruption and devastation of World War II.

Initially, CRS collected, purchased and shipped to war-torn countries huge quantities of food, clothing, medicines and other relief supplies which were distributed to hundreds of thousands of displaced persons, prisoners of war, bombed-out families, widows, orphans and other war victims.

As conditions in Europe improved in the late 1940s and early 1950s, the works conducted by CRS spread to other continents and areas — Asia, Africa and Latin America, wherever people were in want or distress — helping all in need, regardless of race, religion or color.

Since CRS started operations, over 10 million tons of supplies valued in excess of $2.22 billion, have been shipped overseas by the agency and distributed to the impoverished. Today, CRS is the largest private voluntary relief agency in the world. Its programs benefit an estimated 30 million persons in more than 70 countries each year.

CRS has brought aid and comfort to helpless victims of many floods, hurricanes, earthquakes and famines. More recently, the agency has concentrated substantial portions of its overall aid programs in areas where armed conflict and natural disasters have driven innocent victims from their homes and created new and staggering refugee populations and problems, specifically in Vietnam and Bangladesh. In Latin America, CRS distributes food, clothing, medicines and other relief supplies. In Africa, it helps newly independent countries with their mounting problems of social and economic development and dire human need.

In addition to alleviating immediate needs of the poverty-stricken by direct relief, the programs of CRS also encompass long-range development projects designed to help individuals, families and entire communities raise their standards of living and attain economic viability. Such projects run the gamut from simple road-clearing projects that link isolated villages with better marketplaces and building crude dams to digging intricate irrigation systems, providing potable water sources, establishing small industries, and constructing schools and community centers.

Another function of CRS is to cooperate with international and governmental relief agencies as well as help to establish local counterpart welfare agencies in each of the countries where CRS operates.

Funds for CRS operations are raised through an annual nationwide drive in all parishes of the US, held on Laetare Sunday. Contributions to the annual Catholic Bishops' Thanksgiving Clothing Campaign are processed and shipped overseas for distribution tto the needy by CRS.

Bishop Edward E. Swanstrom, auxiliary of New York, is the executive director.

CRS headquarters are located at 350 Fifth Avenue, New York, N.Y. 10001.

Family Life Division — USCC: Established in 1931 as a central service agency for assisting, developing and coordinating family life programs throughout the United States. Since 1969 it has expanded its scope of interest and concern to the whole social mission of the Church.

Until this change was made, the division's activities were largely educational, with respect to: growth of the Christian person, preparation for marriage, husband-wife relationships, parent-children relationships, family-Church-community relationships, and services to family life programs. Accordingly, it promoted Cana and Pre-Cana conferences, couple-centered groups, and the development of marriage courses in secondary and higher education. It also carried out representative functions for the bishops of the US in matters pertaining to family life. The division is continuing many of these and other services.

The recent thrust of the division's wide concern and activity has been in the direction of exerting pressure on the social structure to improve circumstances for a decent family life.

Approximately 130 US dioceses have family life directors who are associated with the division.

Rev. James T. McHugh is the director.

Division headquarters are located at 1312 Massachusetts Ave. N.W., Washington, D.C. 20005.

SPECIAL APOSTOLATES AND GROUPS

Apostleship of the Sea: An international Catholic organization for the moral, social and spiritual welfare of seafarers, founded in 1922 in Glasgow, Scotland. Approved by the Holy See in 1922, it is under the top-level direction of the Pontifical Commission for Migrants and Other Travellers, Piazza San Calisto 16, Rome, Italy—00153. The US unit is the National Catholic Apostleship of the Sea Conference, founded in 1947. It serves 80 chaplains in 73 US ports on seacoasts and the Great Lakes. Conference operations include a hospitality and welcoming program carried on through 14 maritime centers inb; Chicago, Ill.; Houston, Tex.; Jacksonville, Fla.; Lake Charles and New Orleans, La.; Milwaukee, Wis.; Mobile, Ala.; New York, N.Y.; Oakland, San Francisco, San Pedro and Wilmington, Calif.; Seattle, Wash.; Tampa, Fla. Combined attendance at the clubs in 1972 was 481,308. Recent developments include emphasis on interfaith cooperation on the port level in seamen's work, and investigations on how the Apostleship of the Sea can assist in all phases of the various apostolates for people on the move. Bishop Robert E. Tracy of Baton Rouge is the episcopal promoter and national director of the conference. The Rev. James P. Keating, of Chicago is secretary. The national office is located at 10513 S. Torrence Avenue, Chicago, Ill. 60617.

Catholic Central Union of America (1855): One of the oldest Catholic lay organizations in the US, the Union is devoted to the development and vigor of Christian principles in personal, social, cultural, economic and civic life. It was the first society ever given an official mandate for Catholic Action by a committee of the American bishops, in 1936. A bureau in St. Louis is the center for the separate but coordinated direction of the Union. The headquarters is also a publishing house (the monthly *"Social Justice Review, The Catholic Woman's Journal,* other publications), a library of German-Americana and Catholic Americana, a clearing-house for information, and a center for works of charity. Aid is given to home and foreign missions, and maintenance and direction are provided for St. Elizabeth's Settlement and Day Nursery in St. Louis. Union membership is approximately 22,000. Joseph Gervais of Rochester, N. Y. is president; Harvey J. Johnson is director of the Central Bureau located at 3835 Westminster Place, St. Louis, Mo. 63108. (See also: National Catholic Women's Union.)

Catholic Medical Mission Board (1928): Founded by Dr. Paluel Flagg and the Rev. Edward Garesche, S.J. Its purposes are to gather and ship medical supplies, and to recruit and assign medical and paramedical personnel to overseas mission hospitals and dispensaries. In 44 years it has shipped more than 30 million pounds of supplies. In 1971 more than $8 million in medicines were shipped to 2,590 mission distribution centers in 69 countries. Also in 1971, 111 medical volunteers were placed in 18 countries; 34 additional volunteers were similarly assigned during the first three months of 1972. The Rev. Joseph J. Walter, S.J., is the director. Office: 10 W. 17th Street, New York, N. Y. 10011.

Center for Applied Research in the Apostolate (CARA): A research and development agency in the field of the Church's worldwide religious and social mission. Its purpose is to gather information for the use of decision-makers in evaluating the present status of the Church's mission of service and in planning programs of development toward greater effectiveness of its multiphased ministry in the futurs. CARA has research and planning programs focused on: church personnel (recruitment, selection, training, utilization, effectiveness, retirement, health, due process); town and country, formed in 1967 when the Glenmary Home Missioners merged their research center with CARA; overseas areas, with respect to Africa, Oceania, Asia and Latin America; the campus ministry; urban affairs; social theology, and other subjects. CARA was incorporated as a non-profit corporation in the District of Columbia Aug. 5, 1964. The Rev. Louis J. Luzbetak, S.V.D., is executive director. Cardinal John Carberry is chairman of the board of directors. Offices are located at Massachusetts Ave. and 13th St. N.W., Washington, D.C. 20005.

Christian Family Movement (CFM) (1947): Originating in Chicago and having a membership of married couples, its purpose is to

Christianize family life and create communities conducive to Christian family life. Since 1968, CFM in the US has included couples from all Christian churches. The International Confederation of Christian Family Movements has a membership of 135,000 couples. Ray and Dorothy Maldoon are the US national president couple. National and international headquarters: 1655 Jackson Blvd., Chicago, Ill. 60612. Spanish-speaking CFM, organized in 1969 under the title **Movimiento Familiar Cristiano (MFC)**, serves some 2,000 couples in 42 major cities. Headquarters: 1655 Jackson Blvd., Chicago, Ill. 60612.

Christian Life Communities: Formerly known as Sodalities of Our Lady, they are groups of men and women, adults and youth, joined with other people who are involved or wish to be involved in living their full Christian vocation and commitment in the world. The governing principles and operating norms of Sodalities were revised in the spirit of documents of the Second Vatican Council by the General Council of the World Federation of Sodalities in October, 1967. The new principles were confirmed, on an experimental basis, by Paul VI Mar. 25, 1968. In August, 1970, they were amended by the General Council and submitted to the Holy See for approval. The communities (5,000 in the world, 184 in the US) have greater freedom than previous rules permitted with respect to overall structure, spiritual program (although the Spiritual Exercises of St. Ignatius remain a specific source and characteristic of the spirituality), and apostolic endeavor. The US National Federation functions under lay officers and a board of directors composed of lay persons, priests and religious, with Bishop Maurice J. Dingman of Des Moines as episcopal moderator. The World Federation office is located in Rome. National office: 3109 S. Grand Blvd., St. Louis, Mo. 63118.

Cursillo Movement: An instrument of Christian renewal designed to form and stimulate persons to engage in apostolic action individually and in the organized apostolate, in accordance with the mission which individuals have to transform the environments in which they live into Christian environments. The movement originated in Spain, where the first cursillo was held near Palma, Mallorca, in 1949. It was introduced in the US in 1957 and by the beginning of 1972 was reported to be functioning in 124 dioceses. It was then estimated that probably 250,000 persons in this country had made a cursillo. The method of the movement involves a three-day weekend called a cursillo and a follow-up program known as the post-cursillo.

The weekend is an intensive experience in Christian community living centered on Christ and built around 15 talks (10 by laymen, five by priests), active participation in discussions and related activities, the celebra-

tion of the liturgy. The follow-up program focuses on small weekly reunions of three to five persons and larger group reunions, called ultreyas, in which participants share experiences and insights derived from their prayer life, study and apostolic action. The movement operates within the framework of diocesan and parish pastoral plans, and functions autonomously in each diocese under the direction of the bishop. Responsibility for growth and effectiveness rests with a diocesan leaders' school, a diocesan secretariat, or both. Bishop Joseph Green of Reno is episcopal advisor to the movement. Gerry Hughes is coordinator of the National Cursillo Center, P.O. Box 21226, Dallas, Tex. 75211.

Frontier Apostles (1956): Volunteers for a year of service in their professional line in the Diocese of Prince George, British Columbia, Canada. Some 900 have served since the start of the corps by Bishop Fergus O'Grady; about 80 per cent of 180 now serving teach in schools of the diocese.

Grail, The (1921): An international movement of women concerned about the full development of all peoples, working in education, social and cultural areas. Founded by Rev. Jacques van Ginneken, S.J., in The Netherlands, it was introduced in the US in 1940. Working in 22 countries, Grail participants include women from Australia, Brazil, Canada, East Africa, Egypt, France, Germany, India, Indonesia, Italy, Japan, Mexico, The Netherlands, Portugal, Scotland, South Africa, Surinam, United States, West Africa. Chairman of the Co-ordinating Committee, US Grail: Mary A. Kane. US headquarters: Grailville, Loveland, Ohio 45140. International Secretariat: 5, rue Sayed Sokkar, Matareya, Cairo, Egypt.

Group 7 (1971): Started by the Glenmary Home Missioners to recruit Catholic men and women 21 years of age and older for periods of two years or more in the US home mission apostolate, particularly in the 17-state area of Appalachia, the South and Southeast. The purpose of participants is to give individual and group witness to Christian faith in personal and family life, work of their own choice, and community activities. The sponsoring Missioners prepare members for the apostolate, assist them with ongoing educational and instructional programs, and keep them in touch with each other through regular communications. Father John McNearney is director of Group 7. Headquarters: Box 46404, Cincinnati, O. 45246.

International Liaison (1965): A placement office for volunteer lay personnel sponsored by the Archdiocese of Newark. It provides liaison services between volunteers and programs in operation in the US and abroad, and has working relations with the UN Development Program, VISTA, Catholic missions and other agencies. Father George Mader is the director. Office: 39 Lackawanna Pl., Bloomfield, N.J. 07003.

Jesuit Volunteer Corps (1956): Established by the Oregon Province of the Jesuits, for service to the underprivileged. In the fall of 1972, 250 volunteers were working among Eskimos and Indians in Alaska; Indians in the Western states; in inner-city areas, primarily in the Northwest; in Zambia, Ponape and Truk, Caroline Islands; with Spanish-speaking peoples in migrant areas in the Northwest and in El Paso; and in some Northwest Jesuit high schools. The Rev. W. Davis, S.J., is the director. Headquarters: P.O. Box 4408, Portland Ore. 97208.

Movement for a Better World (1952): A group of 26 persons (men and women religious, lay persons) who travel all over the English-speaking world conducting retreats. The retreats have a distinctive communitarian thrust and are geared to motivating Christian witness and action for making a better world. In 1971, MBW reached a total of approximately 8,500 retreatants. The founder and general director of worldwide MBW is Father Riccardo Lombardi, S.J. US office: 127 R St. N.E., Washington, D.C. 20002. The movement publishes *Atmosphere* eight times a year.

New England Jesuit College Lay Apostolate (1959): The program recruits men and women from Boston College, Fairfield University, the College of the Holy Cross and other New England colleges and universities for one to two years of work with Jesuit missionaries, especially in Jamaica, West Indies. Headquarters: 297 Commonwealth Ave., Boston, Mass. 02115.

Opus Dei: An association of Catholic faithful who strive to practice the Christian virtues, in accordance with a fully secular spirit, in their own states in life and through the exercise of their own professions or occupations in order to carry on an apostolate of witness to Christ. Since the purpose is strictly spiritual, members are free to hold the most diverse views on temporal matters, thus assuring a real pluralism of opinions in all cultural, economic, political and similar areas. Founded by Msgr. Josemaria Escriva in 1928 in Spain, it received final approval from the Holy See June 16, 1950. Members of more than 70 nationalities from all continents form separate branches for men and women. In the US, Opus Dei conducts corporate works in the East, Midwest and on the West coast. The directors' offices are located at 9 East 96th Street (15A), New York, N.Y. 10028. Information office: 415 W. 120 St., New York, N.Y. 10027. Elsewhere, the association conducts universities, training schools for farmers and workers, and numerous educational and charitable centers.

Regis College Lay Apostolate (1950): Founded by Sister Mary John, C.S.J., it enlists college graduates for a year of teaching service in home and overseas missions. Three hundred and 85 lay apostles from Regis College and more than 300 from other colleges have served since the beginning of the program. Headquarters: Regis College, Weston, Mass. 02193.

Southwest Volunteer Apostolate: In the process of development, it aims to recruit and place volunteers for work in the Diocese of Gallup principally among Indians and the Spanish-speaking. Robert Myschka is the executive secretary. Headquarters: Propagation of the Faith Office, 415 E. Green St., Gallup, N.M. 87301.

Young Christian Movement (YCM) (1812): an international apostolic movement, formerly known as the Young Christian Workers, which seeks to train and involve young adults, single and between the ages of 18 and 30, in a variety of people-oriented situations. Groups meet weekly to discuss social and moral issues and to become involved in the solution of problems affecting their individual lives and the community. Membership is international, in 91 countries. The assistant national chaplain is Father Patrick J. O'Connor. The national office is located at 1655 W. Jackson Blvd., Chicago, Ill. 60612. International headquarters: Brussels, Belgium.

LAOS: An ecumenical agency for training and recruiting volunteers with professional skills for work in developing nations and in areas of need in the US. LAOS aims to increase public awareness of forces which dehumanize people and to promote action for a world of justice, brotherhood and peace. Address: 4920 Piney Branch Rd. N.W., Washington, D.C. 20011.

CATHOLIC YOUTH ORGANIZATIONS

Angelic Warfare Confraternity (1727): 141 E. 65th St., New York, N.Y. 10021. Apostolic organization for youth who wish to pledge themselves to guard the virtue of purity, seek the truth, and honor the Queen of the Holy Rosary. Director, Brendan Larnen, O.P.

Black Christian Students (1968): 720 N. Rush St., Chicago, Ill. For black youth in high schools and parishes in the Chicago area, with emphasis on the Christian dimension of black identity, awareness, culture and future directives. BCS, with plans to spread elsewhere, originated from a group in Young Christian Students, with which it maintains liaison. National Coordinator, Maurice Blackwell; liaison (with YCS), Rev. Vincent J. Giese.

Boy Savior Youth Movement (1874): 30 W. 16th St., New York, N.Y. 10011; 18,000 in 55 schools.

Boy Scouts in the Catholic Church: The National Catholic Committee on Scouting, an affiliate of the Division of Youth Activities of the USCC, works in cooperation with the Boy Scouts of America, North Brunswick, N.J., in promoting the basic principles of Catholicism among more than one million Catholics among the BSA membership of six million. *Boy's Life.* Committee Chairman, Thomas F. Hawkins, Oak Brook, Ill.

Camp Fire Girls, Inc. (1910): 1740 Broadway, New York, N.Y. 10019. The Division of Youth Activities of the USCC acts as advisor in matters pertaining to Catholic participation in the Camp Fire Girls program. To help young people learn and grow in their individual ways through participation in enjoyable activities. Open to girls from six through high school and high school boys. Membership: over 650,000 (no exact statistics available on number of Catholic girls participating).

Catholic Central Youth Union of America: 3835 Westminster Pl., St. Louis, Mo. 63108. To develop lay leadership in Catholic social action. Membership: 12-25 age group—approximately 200.

Catholic Youth Organization (CYO): Name of official, parish-centered diocesan Catholic youth programs throughout the country. The National CYO Federation is a constituent member of the Division of Youth Activities of the USCC; 1312 Massachusetts Ave. N.W., Washington, D.C. 20005. CYO promotes a program of spiritual, social and physical activities. The original CYO was organized by Bishop Bernard Sheil of Chicago in 1930.

Columbian Squires (1925): P. O. Drawer 1670, New Haven, Conn. 06507. Junior organization of the Knights of Columbus. To train and develop leadership through active participation in well-organized four-point program of activities. Membership: 13- to 18-year-old Catholic boys. More than 700 circles (local units) active in 44 states and in Canada, Puerto Rico, Mexico, Philippines and Guatemala. *Columbian Squires,* monthly. Director, William L. Piedmont.

Forest Rangers, Catholic Order of Foresters: 305 W. Madison St., Chicago, Ill. 60606. To develop physical, mental and moral lives of members. *Catholic Forester.* Membership: youth up to 16 years of age—approximately 42,000 in 1,183 subordinate courts in US and Canada. High Chief Ranger, Louis E. Caron.

Girl Scouts of the U.S.A.: 830 Third Ave., New York, N.Y. 10022. Girls from all archdioceses and dioceses in the US and its possessions participate in Girl Scouting. The Division of Youth Activities of the USCC is affiliated with Girl Scouts of the U.S.A. *Girl Scout Leader; The American Girl.* Membership: nearly four million (no exact statistics available on number of Catholic girls participating).

Junior Catholic Daughters of America: 10 W. 71st St., New York, N.Y. 10023. A major department of the Catholic Daughters of America. Promote spiritual, cultural and recreational activities under proper leadership; develop articulate Catholic leadership. Membership: Juniors (11 to 18 years old) — approximately 9,000 in 252 courts; Juniorettes (7 to 11 years old) — approximately 4,500 in 150 courts. National Director, Miss Ada E. O'Connor. National Chaplain, Bishop Bernard J. Flanagan of Worcester.

Junior Daughters of Isabella: 375 Whitney Ave., New Haven, Conn. 06511. To promote religious, educational, civic and athletic training of Catholic girls. Membership: Catholic girls 10-22 in junior circles in 11 states and one foreign country.

League of Tarcisians of the Sacred Heart (1917): 3 Adams St., Fairhaven, Mass. 02719. Organize children in their schools as junior apostles of the Sacred Heart. Director, Rev. Francis Larkin, SS. CC.

National Catholic Forensic League (1952): To develop articulate Catholic leaders through an inter-diocesan program of speech and debate activities. *Newsletter,* quarterly. Membership: 900 schools; membership open to Catholic, private and public schools through the local diocesan league. President (1972-74), Rev.Frederick J. Easterly, C.M., St. John Vianney Seminary, 2900 S.W. 87th Ave., Miami, Fla. 33165.

National Christ Child Society Inc. (1886): 5151 of Philadelphia is director. of Philadelphia is director. D.C. 20016. Founder, Mary V. Merrick. A welfare organization for the care of underprivileged children. Membership: approximately 10,000 adult and junior members in 33 cities in US. President, Mrs. Robert Rasmussen.

Pontifical Association of the Holy Childhood (1843): 800 Allegheny Ave., Box 6758, Pittsburgh, Pa. 15212. *Annals of the Holy Childhood,* 8 times a year, National Director, Rev. Vernon F. Gallagher, C.S.Sp.

St. Dominic Savio Classroom Club: 148 Main St., New Rochelle, N. Y. To promote a program of spiritual, intellectual and recreational activities. *Notes to Savios,* monthly. Membership: students in fifth grade in elementary school through second year of high school — 500,000 members, 2,500 moderators and one million crusaders throughout the world.

Young Christian Students: 1655 W. Jackson Blvd., Chicago, Ill. 60612. A student movement for Christian social change. Membership: 3,000 students in high schools.

Fraternities and Sororities

Alpha Delta Gamma (1924): P. O. Box 54321, Los Angeles, Calif. 90054. Fraternity, *Alphadelity,* MembershipL 6,000 in 18 college, chapters and 10 alumni associations.

Delta Epsilon Sigma (1939): Loras College, Dubuque, Ia. 52001. National scholastic honor society for students, faculty and alumni of Catholic colleges and universities. Membership: 17,099 in 99 chapters. Secretary, Rev. R. L. Ferring.

Kappa Gamma Pi (1926): A national Catholic college women's honor society for graduates who, in addition to academic excellence, have shown outstanding leadership in extracurricular activities. *Kappa Gamma Pi News*, quarterly. Membership: approximately 16,000 in 123 colleges; 40 alumnae chapters in metropolitan areas. National Moderator, Rev. Cyril F. Meyer, C.M., St. John's Univ., Jamaica, N.Y. 11432. President, Dr. Sally Ann Vonderbrink, 5747 Colerain Ave., Cincinnati, O. 45239.

Phi Kappa Theta (1959): 544 Main St., Suite 400, Worcester, Mass. 01608. National collegiate fraternity with a Catholic heritage. Continuation of Phi Kappa Fraternity, founded at Brown Univ. in 1889, and Theta Kappa Phi Fraternity, founded at Lehigh Univ. in 1919. *The Temple Magazine* quarterly, and newsletter, *The Sun.* Membership: 4,000 undergraduate and 24,000 alumni in 75 collegiate and 25 alumni chapters. President,

CATHOLIC CAMPS

(Source: The *1972 Directory of Catholic Camps,* published by the National Catholic Camping Association, Division of Youth Activities, US Catholic Conference. The association is an advisory and service agency for member camps.)

Alabama

Cullen, Mobile Bay, Battle Wharf: boys and girls 6 to 14; P.O. Box D, Mobile 36601.

California

CYO Day Camps, Los Angeles: boys and girls 5 to 12 in sites located in unserved, low income neighborhoods; 1400 W. 9th St., Los Angeles 90015.

Don Bosco, Arrowbear Lake: boys 8 to 14; 13640 Bellflower Rd., Bellflower 90706.

Imelda, Monte Rio; girls 8 to 12; 1212 Guerrero St., San Francisco 94110.

Junipero Serra, Los Angeles County: boys 7 to 15; 200 North Ave. 21, Los Angeles 90031.

Mariastella, Wrightwood: girls 8 to 16; 1120 Winchester Pl., Los Angeles 90019.

New Divine Word, Riverside: girls 7 to 12, boys 7 to 14; 11316 Cypress Ave., Riverside 92550.

Oliver, Descanso: boys 6 to 10, girls 7 to 12, 13 to 15; 226 W. Date, San Diego 92101.

Pendola, Camptonville: boys and girls 8 to 14; CYO, 1101 K St., Sacramento 95814.

St. Francis, Watsonville: boys 9 to 14; P.O. Box 720, Watsonville 95076.

St. Pius, Galt: boys and girls 7 to 14; Twin Cities Rd., Galt 95632.

St. Vincent de Paul, Los Angeles County: boys 7 to 13; 200 North Ave. 21, Los Angeles 90031.

Salesian, Middletown: boys 8 to 13; 2851 Salesian Ave., Richmond 94804.

Teresita Pines, Wrightwood: girls 7 to 14; 926 S. Detroit, Los Angeles 90036.

Rev. J. Raymond Favret. Executive Director, Robert L. Wilcox.

Youth Division, USCC

The Division of Youth Activities of the United States Catholic Conference, established in 1940, is a coordinating and service agency for Catholic youth work throughout the country. The Rev. Msgr. Thomas J. Leonard of Philadelphia is director of the division.

The organizations within the division are the National CYO Federation, which serves diocesan organizations, and the National Catholic Camping Association.

The Division of Youth Activities maintains liaison with the US Youth Council, the World Assembly of Youth, the World Federation of Catholic Youth, and other groups.

The division has offices at 1312 Massachusetts Ave.N.W., Washington, D.C. 20005.

Colorado

Camp Holy Cross, Canon City: boys 8 to 14; Canon City 81212.

Our Lady of the Rockies, Evergreen: girls 8 to 15; Catholic Daughters of America, 1296 West Littleton Blvd., Littleton 80120.

Camp St. Malo, Allenspark: boys 8 to 16; 940 Fillmore St., Denver 80206.

Connecticut

Lakeville Manor, Lakeville: girls 7 to 12; 61 W. Cedar St., Newington 06111.

Camp Palmer, Oxford: boys 9 to 14; 1 Columbus Pl., 17th Fl., New Haven 06510.

Villa Ferretti, Winsted: girls 7 to 14; 25 St. John's Pl., Torrington 06790.

District of Columbia

Abbey Day Camp, Washington: boys 6 to 14; 14th St. and South Dakota Ave. N.E., Washington 20017.

Florida

Good Counsel, Floral City: boys and girls 8 to 15; P.O. Box 551, Venice 33595.

St. John, Switzerland; boys and girls 7 to 14; Orangedale Route, Green Cove Springs 32043, or St. Ambrose Church, Elkton 32033 (before June 1).

Illinois

Bethlehem, LaGrange Park: girls 7 to 13; 1515 W. Ogden Ave., LaGrange Park 60525.

CYO Star of the Sea, Lake Springfield: boys and girls 9 and over; 423 N. 7th St., Springfield 62702.

Ondessonk, Ozark: boys and girls 6th to 10th grades; 8022 Church Lane, East St. Louis 62203.

St. Joseph, LaGrange Park: boys 6 to 12; 1209 W. Ogden Ave., LaGrange Park 60525.

Villa Marie, Pestakee Bay, McHenry: boys

and girls; 645 W. Randolph St., Chicago 60606.

Indiana

CYO Camp Christina, Brown County: boys 10 to 15, girls 9 to 15; 1502 W. 16th St., Indianapolis 46202.

CYO Camp Rancho Framasa, Brown County: boys 8 to 12, girls 8 to 15; 1502 W. 16th St., Indianapolis 46202.

Fort Wayne-South Bend Diocesan CYO Camp: boys and girls 8 to 14; R. R. 4, Box 311A, Syracuse 46567.

Lawrence CYO Camp, Valparaiso: boys and girls 8 to 14; Box 2038, Gary 46408.

Kentucky

Marydale, Erlanger: boys and girls, families; Donaldson Rd., Erlanger 41018.

Maine

Gregory, Dry Mills: boys 7 to 14; 87 High St., Portland 04101.

Pesquasawasis, Danville Junction: girls 7 to 15; 87 High St., Portland 04101.

Maryland

Aviat, Childs: girls 6 to 12; Childs 21916.

Brisson, Northeast: boys 9 to 15; Northeast 21901.

Christ Child, Island Creek: girls 8 to 16; Christ Child Settlement House and Camp, 608 Massachusetts Ave. N.E., Washington, D.C. 20002.

Georgetown Prep Day Camp, Rockville; boys 6 to 14; 10900 Rockville Pike, Rockville 20852.

Maria on Breton Bay, Leonardtown: girls 5 to 16; R. F. D. 1, Leonardtown 20650.

Trinity Day Camp, Pikesville: boys 6 to 13; P.O. Box 5742, Baltimore 21208.

Massachusetts

Cathedral, East Freetown: boys 6 to 15; P.O. Box 63, Middleboro Rd., East Freetown 02717.

Elm Bank, Wellesley: boys 6 to 13; 900 Washington St., Wellesley 02181.

Holy Cross, Goshen: boys 8 to 14; Cathedral High School, Springfield 01118.

La Salette, Ipswich: boys 7 to 14; Topsfield Rd., Ipswich 01938.

Manomet Hill-Takwita, Manomet; boys 5 to 14, girls 5 to 16; 122 Russell Ave., Watertown 02171.

Mishannock, Kingston: girls 6 to 15; Box 152, Route 80, Kingston 02360.

Our Lady of the Lake Day Camp, East Freetown: girls 6 to 15; Box 63, Middleboro Rd., East Freetown 02717.

Stella Maris, West Gloucester: girls 9 to 15; 27 Sheridan Circle, Winchester 01890.

Many dioceses have camp programs.

Michigan

CYO Boys' Camp near Pt. Sanilac: boys 8 to 14; 305 Michigan Ave., Detroit 48226.

CYO Girls' Camp, near Pt. Sanilac; girls 8 to 14; 305 Michigan Ave., Detroit 48226.

De Sales, Brooklyn: boys 7 to 14; 1150 Ventura Dr., Brooklyn 49230.

Guardian Angel, Holly: girls 7 to 12; 18307 Taylor Lake Rd., Holly 48442.

Marquette Diocesan Summer Camp, near Land o' Lakes, Wis.: girls 7 to 17, boys 7 to 11; Catholic Rectory, Watersmeet 49969.

Ozanam, Lake Huron: boys 10 to 14; Society of St. Vincent de Paul, 2629 Lenox, Box 7936, Detroit 48215.

Stapleton, Lexington: girls 8 to 13; Society of St. Vincent de Paul, 2629 Lenox, Box 7936, Detroit 48215.

Villanova, Holland: boys 8 to 14; R. R. 1, Holland 49423.

Minnesota

Catholic Order of Foresters, near Anoka: boys and girls 8 to 15; 2800 Wayzata Blvd., Minneapolis 55405.

CYC Boys' Camp, Big Sandy Lake: boys 9 to 15; 150 N. Smith Ave., St. Paul 55102.

Foley, Pine River: boys 8 to 16; Box 26, St. Paul 55102.

Villa Maria, Frontenac: girls 9 to 18; Frontenac 55026.

Mississippi

St. Mary of the Pines, Chatawa: boys 6 to 12, girls 6 to 16; Chatawa 39362.

Missouri

CYC Soccer Camp (Mater Dei), Hillsboro: boys 10 and over; Rt. 2, Hillsboro 63050.

Don Bosco Camp for Boys, Hillsboro: boys from 1st to 10th grades; Rt. 2, Hillsboro 63050.

Little Flower, Kansas City: boys and girls 7 to 14; 1026 Forest Ave., Kansas City 64106.

Mater Dei Camp for Girls, Hillsboro: girls from 1st to 10th grades; Rt. 2, Hillsboro 63050.

Nebraska

Christ Child, Blair: mentally retarded boys and girls; 1248 S. 10th St., Omaha 63108.

New Hampshire

Bernadette, Wolfeboro: girls 7 to 16; 153 Ash St., Manchester 03105.

Don Bosco, East Barrington: boys 9 to 14; Byron and Horace Sts., E. Boston, Mass. 02128.

Fatima, Gilmanton, I.W.: boys 7 to 16; 153

Ash St., Manchester 03105.

Leo, near Laconia: boys 7 to 17; Berlin, Conn. 06037.

Marist, Center Ossipee: boys 7 to 15; St. Mary's High School, Manhasset, N.Y. 11030.

Pius, Enfield: boys 6 to 15; Enfield 03748.

New Jersey

Alvernia, Ringwood: girls 5 to 13, boys 5 to 10; Mt. St. Francis, Ringwood 07456.

Auxilium, Newton: girls 6 to 14; R.D. 6, Box 598, Newton 07860.

Basilian, Matawan Township: boys 7 to 14; Fuhrmann Rd., Matawan 07747.

CYO Camp Tegakwitha, Landing: girls 7 to 13; 101 University Ave., Newark 07102.

CYO Day Camp, Blackwood: boys and girls 7 to 13; 1845 Haddon Ave., Camden 08103.

Delbarton, Morristown: boys 6 to 13; St. Mary's Abbey, Morristown 07960.

Don Bosco, Newton: boys 9 to 14; Newton 07860.

Mother Mazzarello, Paterson: girls 6 to 14; 659 Belmont Ave., N. Haledon 07508.

St. Benedict, Newton: boys 7 to 15; St. Paul's Abbey, Newton 07860.

St. John, Gladstone: boys 6 to 10, girls 6 to 14; Gladstone 07934.

New York

Acadia, Livingston Manor: boys 6 to 18; 472 W. 142nd St., New York 10031.

Alvernia, Centerport, Long Island: boys 6 to 14; Box CC, Centerport, L.I. 11721.

Bishop Foery Day Camp, Jordan: boys and girls 7 to 14; 529 N. Salina St., Syracuse 13208.

Broadlea, Goshen: girls 6 to 17; Goshen 10294.

Clare Vue Day Camp, Hastings-on-Hudson: girls 6 to 13; St. Clare Academy, Hastings-on-Hudson 10706.

CYO Day Camp, Coney Island: boys and girls 6 to 12; 2720 Surf Ave., Brooklyn 11224.

CYO Girls' Camp, Putnam Valley: girls 8 to 14; 122 East 22nd St., New York 10010.

Dineen, New Paltz: boys 8 to 14; 122 E. 22nd St., New York 10010.

Dominican, Staatsburg: boys 6 to 16; Dominican Camp, 869 Lexington Ave., New York 10021.

Dominican Day Camp, Staatsburg: boys 6 to 15; Dominican Day Camp, 869 Lexington Ave., New York 10021.

Hayes, Godeffroy: boys 8 to 14; 122 E. 22nd St., New York 10010.

Henry Kaufmann CYO Camp, Stony Point: boys and girls 6 to 12; R.F.D. 1. Stony Point 10980.

Immaculata, Mattituck, Long Island: girls 6 to 16; CYO, 50 N. Park Ave., Rockville Centre 11571.

Jeanne D'Arc, Merrill: girls 6 to 18; 253 Dorchester Rd., Scarsdale 10583.

Lourdes, Skaneateles: boys 7 to 15, girls 7

to 16; 255 E. Onondaga St., Syracuse 13202.

Marian Lodge, Paradox: girls 8 to 17; 340 First St., Albany 12206.

Marydale CYO Day Camp, Melville, Long Island: boys and girls 5 to 12; CYO, 50 N. Park Ave., Box X, Rockville Centre 15571.

Marydell, Nyack: girls 6 to 16; Nyack 10960.

Maryglen, East Eden: girls 8 to 15; 100 S. Elmwood Ave., Buffalo 14202.

Namunkura, West Haverstraw: boys 8 to 14; West Haverstraw 10993.

Nazareth, Woodgate: boys and girls 7 to 15; 1408 Genesee St., Utica 13502.

Our Lady of Lourdes, Livingston Manor: girls 6 to 18; 472 W. 142 St., New York 10031.

Sacred Heart of Mary, Sag Harbor: Sag Harbor 11963.

St. Francis for Girls, Putnam Valley: girls 6 to 13; P.O. Box 789, Peekskill 10566.

St. Helene, Palenville: boys and girls 7 to 10; 225 E. 45th St., New York 10017.

St. Joseph for Boys, Putnam Valley: boys 6 to 13; P.O. Box 789, Peekskill 10566.

St. Joseph for Boys, Sullivan County: boys 6 to 16; St. Joseph's, Sullivan County 12777.

St. Joseph for Girls, Sullivan County: girls 6 to 16; St. Joseph's, Sullivan County 12777.

St. Vincent, Sag Harbor: boys 6 to 14; North Haven, Sag Harbor 11963.

St. Vincent de Paul, Glen Wild: boys and girls 6 to 11; 122 E. 22nd St., New York 10010.

St. Vincent de Paul Health Camp, Angola: boys and girls 9 to 13; 100 S. Elmwood Ave., Buffalo 14202.

Stella Maris, Livonia: boys 7 to 14, girls 8 to 14; 50 Chestnut St., Rochester.

Sunnyside Day Camp, Troy: boys and girls 3 to 14; Villa Maturana, Troy 12180.

Taconic Lodge, Cold Spring-on-Hudson: boys 7 to 14; Rt. 301, Cold Spring-on-Hudson 10516.

Tekakawitha, Lake Luzerne: boys 9 to 15; 340 First St., Albany 12206.

Turner, Allegany State Park: boys 8 to 15; 100 S. Elmwood Ave., Buffalo 14202.

North Carolina

Our Lady of the Hills, Hendersonville: boys and girls 7 to 16; Hendersonville 28739.

North Dakota

Dominic Savio, Riverdale: boys and girls 7 to 14; Riverdale 58565.

Ohio

CYO Camp Christopher, Akron: boys and girls, families; 138 Fir Hill, Akron 44303.

CYO Camp Isaac Jogues, North Madison: boys and girls 8 to 16; 1027 Superior Ave., Cleveland 44114.

Dominican Camp for Girls, Kelleys Island: girls 6 to 14; 3011 Carskaddon Ave., Toledo 43606.

Fort Scott Camp for Boys, New Baltimore:

boys 8 to 15; Vernon Manor Hotel, Cincinnati 45219.

Gilmour Day Camp, Gates Mills: boys 8 to 13; Gilmour Academy, Gates Mills 44040.

Knights of Columbus Youth Camp, Bloomingdale: boys and girls 8 to 16; 148 S. 4th St., Steubenville 43952.

Ladyglen, Grand Rapids: girls 6 to 14; 2413 Collingwood Blvd., Toledo 34620.

Oregon

Howard, Troutdale: boys and girls 8 to 16; CYO, 603 Dekum Bldg., Portland 87204.

Pennsylvania

Akenac at Pinecrest, Dingmans Ferry: girls 12 to 16; Mt. St. Florence, Peekskill, N.Y. 10566.

Frederick Ozanam, Westtown: boys and girls 6 to 11; 1606 N. 21st St., Philadelphia 19121.

Glinodo, Erie: girls 6 to 16; 6101 East Lake Rd., Erie 16511.

Newmann CYO Camp, Jamison: boys and girls 7 to 13; Jamison 18929.

Notre Dame, Fairview (Erie): boys 7 to 15; 233 W. 8th St., Erie 16501.

St. Andrew, Tunkhannock: boys 6 to 17; Box G. Tunkhannock 18701.

St. Monica, Mohnton: boys and girls 8 to 14; 2422 S. 17th St., Philadelphia 19145.

Tegawitha, Tobyhanna: girls 6 to 16; Tobyhanna 18466.

Treweryn-Mercy, Gwynned Valley: boys and girls 4 to 13; Gwynned Valley 19437.

Rhode Island

Mater Spei Day Camp, Glocester: boys and girls 5 to 13; Cathedral Square, Providence 02903.

Tennessee

Marymount, Fairview: boys and girls 8 to 18; 2015 West End Ave., Nashville 37203.

Texas

Texas Catholic Boy's Camp, Mountain Home: boys 8 to 14; 1403 N. St. Mary's St., San Antonio 78215.

Vermont

Holy Cross, Mallets Bay: boys 5 to 15; 131 Main St., Burlington 05401.

Marycrest, Grand Isle: girls 6 to 16; 100 Mansfield Ave., Burlington 05401.

Neringa, Marlboro: boys and girls of grade and high school age (camp centered on Lithuanian culture); RFD 4, Box 134C, W. Brattleboro 05301.

Virginia

Linton, Bristow: boys 6 to 14; 9535 Linton Hall Rd., Bristow 22013.

Parater, Penola: boys 7 to 14 and girls; 813 Cathedral Pl., Richmond 23220.

New York has the most camps.

Washington

Blanchet, Gig Harbor: grade school boys and girls 10 to 15: 500 Aurora Ave., Seattle 98109.

West Virginia

Rolling Hills, Mount St. George, Wellsburg: boys and girls 8 to 14; 709 Brighton Rd., Pittsburgh, Pa. 15233.

Tygart, Huttonsville: boys and girls 8 to 14; Box 40, Huttonsville 26273.

Wisconsin

Gray, Baraboo: boys 8 to 15; Box 181, Baraboo 53913.

Our Lady of Sunset Point, Eagle River: girls 6 to 13; 10024 S. Central Park Ave., Chicago, Ill. 60642.

Ray Meyers' Boys' Camp, Three Lakes: boys 6 to 16; 321 S. Cuyler, Oak Park, Ill. 60602.

Richards, East Troy: boys 9 to 13; Divine Word Seminary, East Troy 53120.

Tekawitha, Loon Lake, Shawano: girls 7 to 16; 721 Eliza St., Green Bay 54301.

Tivoli, Cecil, Shawano Lake: boys 8 to 14; St. Norbert Abbey, De Pere 54115.

Villa Jerome, Hubertus: boys 7 to 14; 8901 W. Capitol Dr., Milwaukee 53222.

We-Ha-Kee, Winter: girls 7 to 17; Rt. 1, Winter 54896.

Canadian Camps listed in the *Directory* were Coselen Camp, South Portage, Lake-of-Bays, Ontario; Marygrove, District-Georgian Bay; Mere M. L. Clarac, St. Donat, Montcalm, Quebec; Olalondo, Arva, Ontario.

Catholic Camping Association

The National Catholic Camping Association, founded in 1951, is an organization in the Division of Youth Activities, US Catholic Conference. Its objectives are to promote Catholic action, thought and philosophy through an organized camping program; to emphasize the need of Catholic camping as an integral part of a Catholic youth program; to develop standards among member camps; to act in a liaison capacity with government agencies on camping; to promote and publicize member camps.

The association publishes *Trail Signs Newsletter* bimonthly from November to August and an annual *Directory of Catholic Camps*; sponsors an awards program for camps, boys and girls; holds a national convention every two years and regional meetings in non-convention years.

Membership consists of camps, organizations and individuals, in six categories.

The director of the association is the Rev. Msgr. Thomas J. Leonard, director of the Division of Youth Activities, USCC.

Association headquarters are located at 1312 Massachusetts Ave. N.W., Washington, D.C. 20005.

CATHOLIC ASSOCIATIONS, MOVEMENTS, SOCIETIES

(Principal Source: Almanac survey.)
See Index for other associations, movements and societies covered elsewhere.

Many of the following organizations, traditional in style, have adapted themselves to renewal changes in the Church.

A

Academy of American Franciscan History (1944), Box 34440, Washington, D.C. 20034. Dir., Rev. Antonine Tibesar, O.F.M.

Academy of California Church History (1946), P.O. Box 1668, Fresno, Calif. 93717. Pres., Msgr. James Culleton.

Albertus Magnus Guild (1953). Society of Catholic scientists. Pres., Thomas J. Killian, Portland State Univ., Portland, Ore.

American Benedictine Academy (1947), 2nd and Division Sts., Atchison, Kans. 66002. Scholarly Benedictine society; *The American Benedictine Review,* edited by Timothy Fry, O.S.B.

American Catholic Correctional Chaplains Association (1952), 275 in 475 institutions. Pres., Rev. Howard Johnson, P.O. Box 31, Plymouth, Wis. 53073.

American Catholic Historical Association (1919), The Catholic University of America, Washington, D.C. 20017. *The Catholic Historical Review,* quarterly. Pres., Albert C. Outler (1972), Sec., Rev. Robert Trisco.

American Catholic Philosophical Association (1926), Catholic University of America, Washington, D.C. 20017; 1,600. *New Scholasticism,* quarterly, *Proceedings,* annually. Pres., Gerald F. Kreyche, Nat. Sec., George F. McLean, O.M.I.

American Committee on Italian Migration (1952), 9 E. 35th St., New York, N.Y. 10016; 32,000. *ACIM Dispatch,* 4 times a year. Sec., Rev. Joseph A. Cogo, C.S.

American Slovenian Catholic Union (KSKJ) (1894), 351-353 N. Chicago St., Joliet, Ill. 60431; 46,000. *Glasilo,* weekly. Sup. Sec., Louis Zeleznikar.

Ancient Order of Hibernians in America, Inc. (Hibernians) (AOH) (1836), 4444 N. College Ave., Indianapolis, Ind. 46205. *National Hibernian Digest,* 6 times a year. Pres., Edward J. Fay.

Apostleship of Prayer (1849-France; 1861-US): 114 E. 13th St., New York, N.Y. 10003. *Monthly Leaflet,* 1,400,000. Promotes Daily Offering and Sacred Heart devotion.

Apostolate of Christian Action, P.O. Box 24, Fresno, Calif. 93707. *Divine Love,* quarterly. Pres., Stephen Oraze.

Archconfraternity of Christian Mothers (Christian Mothers) (1881), 220 37th St., Pittsburgh, Pa. 15201; over 3,400 branches. Monthly newsletter and quarterly bulletin. Dir. Gen., Very Rev. Bertin Roll, O.F.M. Cap.

Archconfraternity of Our Lady of Perpetual Help and St. Alphonsus (1871), 526 59th St., Brooklyn, N.Y. 11220. 1,250 branches.

Archconfraternity of Perpetual Adoration

(1893), St. John's Abbey, Collegeville, Minn. 56321. Dir. Gen., Rt. Rev. John Eidenschink, O.S.B.

Archconfraternity of the Holy Ghost (1912), Holy Ghost Preparatory School, Cornwells Heights, Pa. 19020 (US headquarters). Nat. Dir., Very Rev. Henry J. Brown, C.S.Sp.

Association for Social Economics (formerly the Catholic Economic Association) (1941), De Paul University, 2323 N. Seminary Ave., Chicago, Ill. 60614; 800. *Review of Social Economy,* semiannually. Pres., Richard J. Ward.

Association for the Sociology of Religion (formerly the American Catholic Sociological Society) (1938), 1403 N. St. Mary's St., San Antonio, Tex. 78215; 300. *Sociological Analysis,* quarterly. Exec. Sec., Bro. Eugene Janson, S.M.

Association of Catholic Trade Unionists (1937), 13 E. 30th St., New York, N.Y. 10016. Pres., Kenneth G. Haag.

Association of Marian Helpers (1946), Stockbridge, Mass. 01262; 525,000, mostly in US. *The Marian Helpers Bulletin,* quarterly.

Association of Romanian Catholics of America (1948), 4309 Olcott Ave., E. Chicago, Ind. 46312.

B

Block Rosary Lay Apostolate (1945), 651 Marlborough Ave., Detroit, Mich. 48215. World Dir., Nicholas J. Schorn.

Blue Army of Our Lady of Fatima (1946), Ave Maria Institute, Washington, N.J. 07882; world-wide membership. *Soul,* bimonthly. Pres., Bishop Joao Pereira Venancio of Leiria, Portugal.

C

Calix Society (1947), 21 Prince St. S.E. Minneapolis, Minn. 55414; 2,000. *The Chalice,* quarterly. For the spiritual rehabilitation of alcoholics.

Canon Law Society of America (1939), 134 Farmington Ave., Hartford, Conn. 06105. To further research and study in canon law; 1,300. Pres., Rev. Raymond E. Goedert.

Catechetical Guild Educational Society (1932), Noll Plaza, Huntington, Ind. 46750 Pres., Harold Siepel.

Catholic Accountants Guilds (1947), 611 8th Ave., Brooklyn, N.Y. 11215 (first Guild was formed in Brooklyn); independent Guilds in 8 other cities; 1,500. Moderator, Very Rev. Thomas G. Hagerty.

Catholic Aid Association (1878), 49 W. Ninth St., St. Paul, Minn. 66102; 70,000. *Catholic Aid News,* monthly. Fraternal life insurance society. Pres., Michael F. Ettel.

Catholic Alumni Clubs International (1957), 5320 Centinela Ave., Apt. 4, Los Angeles, Calif. 90066; 8,000 in 53 clubs in the US and Canada. To advance social, cultural and spiritual well-being of members. Pres., Robert P. Casper.

Catholic Apostolate of Radio, Television and Advertising (1954), 457 Madison Ave., New York, N.Y. 10022; 1,700 in New York City. Pres., Michael J. Donovan.

Catholic Art Association (1937), Box 113, Rensselaerville, N.Y. 12147; 800. Pres., Rev. Thomas W. Phelan.

Catholic Audio-Visual Educators Association (CAVE) (1953), Pres., Rev. Bernard F. Wetzel, O.S.F.S., College of St. Francis de Sales, Center Valley, Pa. 18034.

Catholic Aviation League of Our Lady of Loreto (1949), O'Hare International Airport, P.O. Box 66123, Chicago, Ill. 60666. Pres., Arthur Fennell.

Catholic Bible Society of America, Inc. (1957), P.O. Box 2296, Dallas, Tex. 75221. Place Bibles in hospitals of Diocese of Dallas and elsewhere. Pres. Mrs. James S. Adams.

Catholic Biblical Association of America (1936), Catholic University of America, Washington, D.C. 20017; 950, *The Catholic Biblical Quarterly.* Pres., Rev. Raymond E. Brown, S.S.

Catholic Big Brothers, Inc. (of Archdiocese of New York) (1918), 122 E. 22nd St., New York, N.Y. 10010; Newsletter, quarterly. To provide opportunities for male identification to fatherless boys, 8-15 years of age, through services of qualified adult male volunteers.

Catholic Big Sisters, Inc., of the Archdiocese of New York), 135 E. 22nd St., New York, N.Y. 10010. Voluntary organization providing adjunctive services to Family Court, for girls up to 16 and boys up to 10 years of age. Dir., Hortense Baffa.

Catholic Business and Professional Men's Club (1950), 2440 Saratoga Dr., Louisville, Ky. 40205. Pres., Lee J. Steiden.

Catholic Business Education Association (1945); 2,001. *Business Education Review,* quarterly. Pres., Sister Mary Matthew McCloskey, R.S.M., St. Joseph School, Greenville, Miss. 38702.

Catholic Classical Association of Greater New York (1949). Pres., Prof. J. Roger Dunkle, Dept. of Classics and Comparative Literature, Brooklyn College, Brooklyn, N.Y. 11210.

Catholic Commission on Intellectual and Cultural Affairs (CCICA) (1946), 620 Michigan Ave. N.E., Washington, D.C. 20017; 325. Exec. Dir., Rev. William J. Rooney.

Catholic Council on Working Life, 1307 S. Wabash Ave., Chicago, Ill. 60605. Pres., Martin Burns.

Catholic Daughters of America (1903), 10 W. 71st St., New York, N.Y. 10023; over 200,000. *Share Magazine.* Nat. Regent, Judge Mary C. Kanane, presiding officer.

Catholic Evidence Guild (1918, in England; 1931, in US), c/o 127 W. 31st St., New York, N.Y. 10001. Lay movement for spread of Catholic truth by means of outdoor speaking.

Catholic Family Life Insurance (1868), 1572 E. Capitol Dr., Milwaukee, Wis. 53211; 42,135. *The Family Friend,* quarterly. Pres., David L. Springob.

Catholic Guardian Society (1913), 122 E. 22nd St., New York, N.Y. 10010. Exec. Dir., James P. O'Neill.

Catholic Home Bureau for Dependent Children (1898), 130 E. 22nd St., New York, N.Y. 10010. Exec. Dir., Rev. Msgr. G. Howard Moore.

Catholic Institute of the Food Industry, Inc. (1946), 59 Park Ave., New York, N.Y. 10016; 325. Quarterly newsletter. Pres., Frank W. Heffernan.

Catholic Institute of the Press (1944), c/o Rev. Msgr. Eugene V. Clark, Chap., 457 Madison Ave., New York, N.Y. 10022. To foster Christian principles and action among working members in the communications fields.

Catholic Interracial Council of New York, Inc. (1934), 55 liberty St., New York, N.Y. 10005. *Interracial Review,* quarterly. Pres., Robert F. Wagner, Exec. Dir., Arthur D. Wright.

Catholic Interracial Councils: See National Catholic Conference for Interracial Justice.

Catholic Knights of America (1877), 3525 Hampton Ave., St. Louis, Mo. 63139; 18,966. *Catholic Knights of America Journal,* monthly. Fraternal insurance society.

Catholic Knights of St. George (1881), 709 Brighton Rd., Pittsburgh, Pa. 15233; 67,000. *Knight of St. George,* monthly. Fraternal insurance society. Pres., Joseph J. Miller.

Catholic Kolping Society (1923), 125 N. Stratton La., Mt. Prospect, Ill. 60056; 2,205, *Kolping Banner,* monthly. Fraternal society.

Catholic Lawyers' Guild. Organization usually on a diocesan basis, under different titles.

Catholic League (1943), 1200 N. Ashland Ave., Chicago, Ill. 60622 *Liga,* quarterly. Exec. Dir., Most Rev. Alfred Abramowicz.

Catholic Library Association (1921), 461 W. Lancaster Avenue, Haverford, Pa., 19041; 4,000. *Catholic Library World,* monthly (Sept.-April), bimonthly (May-June, July-Aug.); *Catholic Periodical and Literature Index.* Pres., Rev. Joseph P. Browne, C.S.C., Exec. Dir., Matthew R. Wilt.

Catholic Near East Welfare Association (Near East Missions) (1926), 330 Madison Ave., New York, N.Y. 10017. *Near East Missions,* weekly column in 70 diocesan newspapers. Aids missionary activity in 18 countries (under jurisdiction of the Sacred Congregation for the Oriental Church) in Europe, Africa and Asia, including the Holy Land. Nat. Sec., Rev. Msgr. John G. Nolan.

Catholic Negro-American Mission Board (1907), 335 Broadway, Room 1102, New York, N.Y. 10013; 18,000. *Educating in Faith,* monthly. Dir., Rev. Benjamin M. Horton, S.S.J.

Catholic One Parent Organization (COPO) (1961), 39 Lackawanna Pl., Bloomfield, N.J. 07003. To give widows and widowers an opportunity to meet others in the same situation, blending social and spiritual programs. Moderator, Rev. Joseph M. Doyle.

Catholic Order of Foresters (1883), 305 W. Madison St., Chicago, Ill. 60606; 195,489 in 28 states and Canada. *The Catholic Forester,* bimonthly. Fraternal and insurance society. High Chief Ranger, Louis E. Caron.

Catholic Pamphlet Society (1938), 2171 Fillmore Ave., Buffalo, N.Y. 14214. Sec., Rev. Msgr. Eugene H. Selbert.

Catholic Peace Fellowship (1964), North Broadway, Upper Nyack, N.Y. 10960; 6,500, *CPF Bulletin.* Peace education and action, development of the pacifist tradition within the Catholic Church. Nat. Sec., Thomas C. Cornell.

Catholic Press Association of the US, Inc. (1911), 432 Park Ave. S., New York, N.Y. 10016; 378. *The Catholic Journalist* bimonthly; *Catholic Press Director,* annually. Pres., Rev. Louis G. Miller, C.SS.R.: Exec. Dir., James A. Doyle.

Catholic Renascence Society (1940), c/o Exec. Sec., Sister Celestine Cepress, Viterbo College, La Crosse, Wis. 54601. *Renascense,* quarterly.

Catholic Scholarships for Negroes, Inc. (1946), 254 Union St., Springfield, Mass. 01105. Pres., Mrs. Roger Putnam.

Catholic School Press Association (1931), 1135 W. Kilbourn Ave., Milwaukee, Wis. 53233. *Catholic School Editor,* quarterly. Dir., Warren G. Bovee.

Catholic Theological Society of America (1946), Office of Secretary, St. Mary of the Lake Seminary, Mundelein, Ill. 60060; 1,183, *Proceedings* annually. Pres., Rev. John H. Wright, S.J. (1972-73).

Catholic Truth Society (1922), 2816 E. Burnside St., Portland, Ore. 97214; Exec. Dir., Gorman Hogan.

Catholic Union of the Sick in America, Inc. (CUSA) (1947), 184 E. 76th St., New York, N.Y. 10021; 1,200. Interim Admin. Leader, Rev. Joseph La Montague, S.S.S.

Catholic War Veterans (1935), 2 Massachusetts Ave. N.W., Washington, D.C. 20001; 2,000 posts, *Catholic War Veteran,* bimonthly. National Commander Aldo Di Chiari.

Catholic Women's Benevolent Legion (1895), 353 W. 57th St., New York, N. Y. 10019; 4,000. *Bulletin,* quarterly. Fraternal and insurance society.

Catholic Worker Movement (1933), 36 E. First St., New York, N.Y. 10003. *The Catholic Worker,* 9 times a year. Lay apostolate founded by Dorothy Day; has Houses of Hospitality in 17 US cities. Promotes pacifism and anarchism in that it is decentralist, and believes in what the popes have termed the principle of subsidiarity, urging decentralization in the school system, community control, and in the economic field credit unions, cooperatives and unions of workers and mutual aid.

Catholic Workman (Katolicky Deinik) (1891), New Prague, Minn. 56071; 18,487; *Catholic Workman,* monthly. Fraternal and insurance society. Pres. Rudy G. Faimon.

Catholic Writers' Guild of America (1919), 65 East 89th St., New York, N. Y. 10028; 200. Exec. Sec., Rev. Bernard J. McMahon.

Central Association of the Miraculous Medal (1915), 475 E. Chelten Ave., Philadelphia, Pa. 19144. *Miraculous Medal,* quarterly. Dir., Rev. Donald L. Doyle, C.M.

Chaplains' Aid Association, Inc. (1917), 29 E. 50th St., New York, N.Y. 10022. Pres., Most Rev. Philip J. Furlong.

Christopher Movement (1945), 12 E. 48th St., New York, N. Y. 10017. Without formal organization or meetings, the movement stimulates personal initiative and responsible action in line with Christian principles, particularly in the fields of education, government, industrial relations and communications. Christopher radio and TV programs are broadcast by 3,200 stations; a million and one-quarter copies of *Christopher News Notes* are distributed seven times a year without subscription fee; 38 daily newspapers carry the syndicated column *Three Minutes a Day;* over two million copies of 26 Christopher books are in circulation. Dir., Rev. Richard Armstrong, M.M.

Church Music Association of America (1964). Pres., Dr. Roger Wagner; Gen. Sec., Rev. Robert A. Skeris, De Sales Prep Seminary, 3501 S. Lake Dr., Milwaukee, Wis. 53207.

Composers' Forum for Catholic Worship, Inc. (1970), P.O. Box 8554, Sugar Creek, Mo. 64054; 1,000. Research center for the creation of new music for the liturgy. Exec. Dir., Robert I. Blanchard.

Confraternity of the Immaculate Conception of Our Lady of Lourdes (1874), Box 561, Notre Dame, Ind. 46556.

Confraternity of the Most Holy Rosary: See Rosary Altar Society.

Convert Makers of America (1944), 268 W. Pike St., Pontiac, Mich. 48053; 1,200 graduate members, 100 trainees a year under direction of priest-advisers, *Convert Making Our Apostolate,* monthly bulletin. Nat. Dir., Rev. E. A. Juraschek.

Crusade for a More Fruitful Preaching and Hearing of the Word of God, Inc. (1937), Allendale, N.J.; *Voices from the Pew,* 2 times a year for seminarians. Pres., Mrs. Barbara Durbin.

Czech Catholic Union of Texas (K.J.T.)

(1889), 113 Colorado St., La Grange, Tex. 78945; 14,855. *Nasinec,* weekly, and *K. J. T. News,* monthly. Fraternal and insurance society. Pres., I. C. Parma.

D

Damien-Dutton Society (1944), P.O. Box 1222, New Brunswick, N.J. 08903; 18,000. *Damien Dutton Call,* quarterly. Provides medicine, rehabilitation and research for conquest of leprosy. Dir., Howard E. Crouch.

Daughters of Isabella (1897), 375 Whitney Ave., New Haven, Conn. 06511; 120,000. Supreme Reg., Mrs. Marie Heyer.

E

Edith Stein Guild, Inc. (19 5), Promotes Judaeo-Christian understanding and assists Jewish converts; 860. *ESG Newsletter* bimonthly. Address, 144-80 Sanford Ave., Flushing, N. Y. 11355.

Enthronement of the Sacred Heart in the Home (1907), 3 Adams St., Fairhaven, Mass. 02719; over 2,000,000. Nat. Dir., Rev. Francis Larkin, SS.CC.

Eucharistic Guard for Nocturnal Adoration (1938), National Center, 800 North Country Club Rd., Tucson, Ariz. 85716. Dir., Rev. James T. Weber.

Eymard League (1948), 194 E. 76 St., New York, N.Y. 10021; approximately 26,000. *Eymard League Bulletin,* quarterly. Nat. Dir., Rev. Ralph A. Lavigne, S.S.S.

F

Family Communion Crusade, Inc. (1950), Barre, Mass. 01005. Pres., Dr. Henry Rendich. Exec. Dir., Rev. Hector C. Lemieux, S.S.S.

Family Rosary Crusade (1942), and **Crusade for Family Prayer,** 773 Madison Ave., Albany, N.Y. 12208. Dir., Rev. Patrick Peyton, C.S.C.

Federation of Diocesan Liturgical Commissions (1969), 225 Clark, Pueblo, Colo. 81003. *Federation Notes.* Exec. Dir., Rev. John R. Beno.

First Catholic Slovak Ladies' Association, USA (1892), 24950 Chagrin Blvd., Beachwood, Ohio 44122; 100,000. *Fraternally Yours,* monthly. Fraternal insurance society. Exec. Sec., Frances L. Mizenko.

First Catholic Slovak Union (Jednota) (1890), 3289 E. 55th St., Cleveland, Ohio 44127; 115,097. *Jednota,* weekly. Exec. Sec., Stephen F. Ungvarsky.

First Friday Clubs (1936). Organized on local basis; about 90 clubs in US, others elsewhere. Objectives are to spread devotion to the Sacred Heart, encourage members to receive Holy Communion on First Fridays and to meet at breakfast, luncheon or dinner for discussions of Catholic interest.

Franciscan Apostolate of the Way of the Cross (1949), 174 Ramsey St., Paterson, N.J. 07501. Stations Crucifix available on request.

Dir., Rev. Cassian J. Kirk, O.F.M.

Friendship House (1938), 21 E. Van Buren St., Chicago, Ill. 60605. *Community,* quarterly. Religious-oriented group, lay and clergy, working in human relations and social problems. Nat. Dir., John Kearney.

G

Gabriel Richard Institute, (1949), 2315 Orleans Ave., Detroit, Mich. 48207. Conducts leadership technique courses in 15 dioceses.

Gregorian Institute of America (1942), 2115 W. 63rd St., Chicago, Ill. 60636. Pres., Edward J. Harris.

Guard of Honor of the Immaculate Heart of Mary (1932), 135 West 31st St., New York, N.Y. 10001. A pious association whose members cultivate and foster devotion to the Blessed Virgin Mary.

Guild of Catholic Lawyers (1928), Empire State Bldg., 350 Fifth Ave., Room 316, New York, N.Y. 10001; 600. Pres., Albert E. del Vecchio.

Guild of Our Lady of Ransom (1948), 409 W. Broadway (Room No. 5), S. Boston, Mass. 02117. For aid to inmates and former inmates of Massachusetts prisons. Exec. Dir., and Treas., Rev. John J. Foley, Catholic Chaplain, Massachusetts State Prison.

Guild of St. Paul (1937), 601 Hill'n Dale, Lexington, Ky. 40503; 13,542; Nat. Spir. Dir., Rt. Rev. Msgr. Leonard Nienaber; Pres., Robert Parks.

H

Holy Name Society (in US) (1909), 141 E. 65th St., New York, N.Y. 10021; 5,000,000. Promote reverence for and devotion to the Holy Name of Jesus and develop lay apostolate programs in line with renewal aims of the Second Vatican Council. Nat. Dir., Rev. Brendan Larnen, O.P.

Holy Name Society, National Association (1970), 141 E. 65th St., New York, N.Y. 10021. Association of diocesan and parochial Holy Name Societies. Pres., Stephen Andrusisian.

Hungarian Catholic League of America, Inc. (1945), 30 E. 30th St., New York, N.Y. 10016; local branches in 15 states. *Catholic Hungarian Sunday,* weekly.

I

Illinois Club for Catholic Women (1920), 820 North Michigan, Chicago, Ill. 60611. *Triune,* quarterly. Pres., Mrs. Lydon Wild.

International Catholic Truth Society (1899); 407 Bergen St., Brooklyn, N.Y. 11217. Propagate and preserve the Faith by distribution of Catholic literature. Pres., Rev. Edward Lodge Curran.

International Food Research and Educational Center, Stonehill College, North Easton, Mass. 02356. Internat. Dir,, Bro. Herman E. Zaccarelli, C.S.C.

Italian Catholic Federation of California,

Central Council (1924), 678 Green St., San Francisco, Calif. 94133; 20,000. *Bollettino,* monthly. Sec., Armand De Martini.

J

John Carroll Society, The (1951), 1721 Rhode Island Ave., N.W. Washington, D.C. 20036. 600. *The John Carroll Society,* quarterly. Sec., Dr. Paul F. Jaquet.

Judean Society, Inc. (1966), 1075 Space Park Way No. 336, Mt. View, Calif. 94040; over 700; *The Challenge,* 6-8 times a year. To offer divorced Catholic women friendship and self-help activities; to educate concerning rights under Canon law; to inform the public regarding the life style of divorced Catholic women. Nat. Dir., Frances A. Miller.

K

Knights of Lithuania (1913), 1467 Force Dr., Mountainside, N.J. 07092; over 5,000. *Vytis,* monthly. Pres., Dr. J. J. Stukas.

Knights of Peter Claver (1909), Claver Bldg., 1821 Orleans Ave., New Orleans, La. 70116; 17,000. *The Claverite,* bimonthly. Fraternal and aid society. Sup. Knight, Ernest Granger, Sr.

Knights of St. John, Supreme Commandery (1886), 1603 S. Bedford Ave., Evansville, Ind. 47713. Sup. Sec., Brig. Gen. Clarence J. Schu.

Knights of St. John, Supreme Ladies' Auxiliary (1900), 831 Emmett St., Schenectady, N.Y. 1t307; 20,000. Sup. Sec., Miss Adelaide Mahoney.

L

Ladies of Charity in the United States, Association of (1960), 1849 Cass Ave., St. Louis, Mo. 63106; 34,000. International Association founded by St. Vincent de Paul in 1617. Pres., Mrs. Fred N. Eckhardt.

League of St. Dymphna, National Shrine of St. Dymphna, Massillon, Ohio 44646. For persons with mental and nervous disorders. Director, Rev. M. M. Herttna.

League of Shut-Ins (1945), Marcus, Ia. 51035; 2,100. *Seconds Sanctified,* quarterly.

Lithuanian Catholic Religious Aid, Inc. (1961), 64-09 56th Rd. Maspeth, N.Y. 11378; 194. To assist the persecuted Church in Lithuania. Pres., Most Rev. Vincent Brizgys.

Lithuanian Roman Catholic Alliance of America (1889), 73 S. Washington St., Wilkes-Barre, Pa. 18701; 160 branches. *Garsas,* bimonthly. Fraternal insurance organization. Pres., Leonard Simutis.

Little Flower Mission League (1957), P.O. Box 178, Cottonport, La. 71327. Sponsored by the Brothers of the Holy Eucharist.

Little Flower Society (1923), 11343 S. Michigan Ave., Chicago, Ill. 60628; 40,000, *Little Flower News,* monthly. Nat. Dir., Rev. Quentin Duncan, O. Carm.

Liturgical Conference, The, 1330 Massachusetts Avenue N.W., Washington, D.C. 20005. *Liturgy, Living Worship, Homily Serv-*

ice, monthlies. Education, research and publication programs for vitalizing and enriching Christian liturgical life. Pres., Matthew H. Ahmann, Exec. Dir., George A. Moudry.

Loval Christian Benefit Association (1890), 305 W. 6th St., Erie, Pa. 16507; 67,268. *The Fraternal* Leader, bimonthly. Pres., Miss Bertha M. Leavy.

M

Mariological Society of America (1949), 350. *Marian Studies,* annually. St. Joseph Hospital, 601 N.E. Garbor Blvd., Port Charlotte, Fla. 33950.

Markham Prayer Card Apostolate (Apostolate To Aid the Dying) (1931), Franciscan Sisters of the Poor, 60 Compton Rd., Cincinnati, Ohio 45215. Dir., Rev. Herman H. Kenning.

Melkite Association of North America (1958), 5804 Tanglewood Dr., Bethesda, Md. 20034; 20,000. Promote and stimulate the spiritual and social welfare of Greek Catholic Melkites in America. Pres., Baddia J. Rashid.

Militia of Mary Immaculate (1917), 8000 39th Ave., Kenosha, Wis. 53141. A pious association founded by Bl. Maximilian Kolbe for the conversion of unbelievers and sanctification of all under sponsorship of the Blessed Virgin.

Missionary Association of Catholic Women (1916), 1425 N. Prospect Ave., Milwaukee, Wis. 53202. Pres., Msgr. Joseph Gockel.

Missionary Cenacle Apostolate (M.C.A.) (1909), 149 E. 39th St., New York, N.Y. 10016; about 1,000.

Missionary Union of the Clergy in the USA (1936), 366 Fifth Ave., New York, N.Y. 10001; *Worldmission,* quarterly. Nat. Dir., Most Rev. Edward T. O'Meara.

Morality in Media, Inc. (1962), 487 Park Ave., New York, N.Y. 10022; 35,000. Newsletter, 8 times a year. To counteract traffic in obscenity and pornography by promoting principles of love, truth and taste in the media. Pres., Rev. Morton A. Hill, S.J.

N

National Alliance of Czech Catholics (1917), 2636 S. Central Park, Chicago, Ill. 60623; 450 parishes. Pres., Mrs. Victoria Voller.

National Apostolate for Mentally Retarded (1968), 1678 Asylum Ave., W. Hartford, Conn. 06117. *NAMR Quarterly Publication.*

National Catholic Bandmasters' Association (1953), Notre Dame University, Notre Dame, Ind. 46556. *Score,* at intervals. Natl. Coordinator, Robert O'Brien.

National Catholic Cemetery Conference (1949), 710 N. River Rd., Des Plaines, Ill. 60010. *The Catholic Cemetery,* monthly. Pres., Rev. Francis H. Niehaus.

National Catholic Conference for Interracial Justice (1960), 1307 S. Wabash Ave., Chicago, Ill. 69605. *Commitment,* monthly. Serves 150 Catholic human relations and urban affairs groups; sponsors educational and health services.

National Catholic Development Conference (1968), 130 E. 40th St., New York, N.Y. 10016. Professional association of fund-raising administrators. Pres., Rev. Edward J. Gorry, C.S.P., Exec. Dir., George T. Holloway.

National Catholic Guidance Conference (1962), Department of Graduate Studies in Education, Box 638, Univ. of Notre Dame, Notre Dame, Ind. 46556; 38 diocesan councils, 441 institutions, 1,002 individuals. *Counseling and Values,* and *Newsletter,* quarterlies. Exec. Dir., Willis E. Bartlett.

National Catholic Music Educators Association (1942), 4637 Eastern Ave. N.E., Washington, D.C. 20018; affiliate of NCEA; 4,583. *Musart,* bimonthly during school year; *Overtones,* bimonthly; *Now!,* quarterly. Pres., Rev. William A. Volk, C.PP.S., Exec. Dir., Vincent P. Walter, Jr.

National Catholic Pharmacists Guild of the United States and Canada (1962 in US), 500 in US. *The Catholic Pharmacist.* Exec. Sec., Ursula E. Heyer, 1311 White Ave., Baltimore, Md. 21214.

National Catholic Society of Foresters (1891), 59 E. Van Buren St., Chicago, Ill. 60605; 103,278. *National Catholic Forester,* bimonthly. A fraternal insurance society. Pres., Mrs. Lucy Domino.

National Catholic Stewardship Council (1962), P.O. Box 733, Kansas City, Mo. 64141; 650. To exchange ideas on ways and means of assisting those engaged in promotion of stewardship and support of the Church. Exec. Sec., Rev. Robert N. Deming.

National Catholic Women's Union (1916), 3835 Westminster Pl., St. Louis, Mo. 63108; 29,500. *The Catholic Woman's Journal,*10 times a year. Auxiliary of the Catholic Central Union of America.

National Center for Church Vocations (1969), 305 Michigan Ave., Detroit, Mich. 48226. Established by National Conference of Catholic Bishops and the Conferences of Major Superiors of men and women to coordinate Church vocations work in the US. Exec. Dir., Rev. Edward J. Baldwin.

National Church Goods Association, 6469 N. Nokomis Ave., Chicago, Ill. 60646. Pres., Jack M. O'Connor.

National Clergy Conference on Alcoholism, 2749 N. Marshfield Ave., Chicago, Ill. 60614. Exec. Sec., Rev. John P. Cunningham.

National Federation of Catholic Physicians' Guilds (1927), 2825 N. Mayfair Rd., Milwaukee, Wis. 53222; 6,700 in 88 autonomous guilds in US and Canada, *Linacre Quarterly.* Pres., Charles Pfister, M.D.

National Guild of Catholic Psychiatrists, Inc. (1950), 41 Church St., Waterbury, Conn. 06720; *The Newsletter,* quarterly; *The Bulletin,* yearly. Pres., Donato J. Alamprese, M.D.

National Sisters Vocation Conference (1970), 1307 S. Wabash Ave., Chicago, Ill. 60605. Nat. Dir., Sr. Margaret Mary Modde, O.S.F.

Nocturnal Adoration Society of the United States (1882), 194 E. 76th St., New York, N. Y. 10021; 38,000 in 555 units. Nat. Dir., Rev. Hector C. Lemieux, S.S.S.

O

Order of the Alhambra, International (1904), 4200 Leeds Ave., Baltimore, Md. 21229. 11,000 in US and Canada. Fraternal society dedicated to assisting retarded children. Supreme Cmdr. Michael Kranson.

P

Paulist League (1924), 415 W. 59th St., New York, N. Y. 10019; 28,750. Dir., Rev. Edward J. Gorry, C.S.P.

Pious Union of Prayer (1898), St. Joseph's Home, P.O. Box 288, Jersey City, N.J. 07303; 96,000.*Orphans' Messenger* and *Advocate of the Blind,* quarterly.

Pious Union of St. Joseph for Dying Sinners (1942), 110 W. Madison St., Chicago, Ill. 60602; 300,000. Dir., Rev. Cuthbert Malone, O.F.M.

Pious Union of the Holy Spirit (1900), 262 Blackstone Blvd., Providence, R.I. 02906. Pres., Rev. Jerome McHugh, O.F.M. Cap.

Pontifical Mission for Palestine (1949), c/o Catholic Near East Welfare Association, 330 Madison Ave., New York, N.Y. 10017. Field offices in Beirut, Lebanon, Jerusalem and Amman, Jordan. The papal relief agency for 1.5 million Palestinian refugees in Lebanon, Syria, Jordan, and the Gaza Strip. Distributes food, clothing, other essentials; maintains medical clinics, orphanages, libraries, refugee camp schools and chapels, the Pontifical Mission Center for the Blind (Gaza), the Pontifical Mission Libraries (Jerusalem, Bethlehem, Nazareth), the Epheta Institute for Deaf-Mutes (Bethlehem). Pres., Rev. Msgr. John G. Nolan.

Priests' Eucharistic League (1887), 194 E. 76th St., New York, N.Y. 10021; 20,500. *Emmanuel,* monthly. Nat. Dir., Rev. Raymond A. Tartre, S.S.S.

Pro Maria Committee (1952), 22 Second Ave., Lowell, Mass. 01854. Promote devotion to Our Lady of Beauraing (See Index). Dir., Rev. J. Debergh, O.M.I.

The Providence Association of the Ukrainian Catholics in America (Ukrainian Catholic Fraternal Benefit Society) (1912), 817 N. Franklin St., Philadelphia, Pa. 19123. *America* (Ukrainian-English).

R

Raskob Foundation for Catholic Activities, Inc. (1945), 1205 Hotel Du Pont, Wilmington, Del. 19898. Exec. Sec., Gerard S. Garey.

Reparation Society of the Immaculate Heart of Mary, Inc. (1946), 100 E. 20th St., Baltimore, Md. 21218. *Fatima Findings,* monthly. Dir. Rev. John Ryan, S.J.

Rosary Altar Society (Confraternity of the

Most Holy Rosary) (1891, in US), 141 E. 65th St., New York, N. Y. 10021; 3,000,000. *The Rosary Bulletin,* monthly. Prov. Dir., Rev. Brendan Larnen, O.P.

Rosary League (1901), Franciscan Sisters of the Atonement, Graymoor, Garrison, N.Y. 10524. 1,600. *Sparks,* quarterly.

S

Sacred Heart Auto League, Walls, Miss. 38680; 400,000. To promote careful, prayerful driving. Dir., Rev. Gregory Bezy, S.C.J.

St. Ansgar's Scandinavian Catholic League (1910), 40 W. 13th St., New York, N.Y. 10011; 2,000. *St. Ansgar's Bulletin,* annually.

St. Anthony's Guild (1924), Paterson, N.J. 07509. *Anthonian,* quarterly. Dir., Rev. Salvator Fink, O.F.M.

St. Apollonia Guild (1958), 2186 Draper Ave., St. Paul, Minn. 55113. For Catholic dentists. Pres., Dr. Ronald W. Pfleger.

St. Boniface Mission League, Inc. (1913), Box 4174, Milwaukee, Wis. 53210. Pres., Teresa E. Muench.

St. Jude League (1928), 221 W. Madison St., Chicago, Ill. 60606. *St. Jude journal,* bimonthly. Dir., Rev. Robert J. Leuver, C.M.F.

St. Margaret of Scotland Guild, Inc. (1938), Graymoor, Garrison, N.Y. 10524; 2,200. Founder and Moderator, Rev. Colman Gallacher.

St. Martin de Porres Guild (1936), 141 E. 65th St., New York, N.Y. 10021. Gen. Dir., Rev. Timothy Shea, O.P.

St. Paul Center, Byzantine Information Apostolate (1965), 1125 Varnum St. N.E., Washington, D.C. 20017. Promotes Christian unity by furthering knowledge of the liturgy and art of the Eastern Church; ecumenical contacts with Orthodox clergy and laity. US press office for the Patriarchate of Antioch for the Melkites. Nat. Dir., Very Rev. Archpriest Armand J. Jacopin.

St. Paul Guild, Inc. (1901), c/o St. Patrick's Information Center, 31 E. 50th St., New York, N.Y. 10022. *The Epistle,* semiannually. Spir. Dir. and Exec. Sec., Rev. Msgr. Francis X. Duffy.

St. Thomas Aquinas Foundation of the Dominican Fathers of the Unite States (STAF), 141 E. 65th St., New York, N.Y. 10021. Nat. Mod., Very Rev. Thomas H. McBrien, O.P.

Scapular Apostolate (1941), 329 E. 28th St., New York, N.Y. 10016.

Seraphic Society for Vocations (1944), St. Joseph Franciscan Seminary, P.O. Box 245, Westmont, Ill. 60559. Dir., Bro. Quentin Holmes, O.F.M.

Serra International (1938), 22 W. Monroe St., Chicago, Ill. 60603; 12,500 members in 360 clubs in more than 27 countries. *Serran,* bimonthly. Fosters vocations to the priesthood, trains Catholic lay leadership. Formally aggregated to the Pontifical Society for Priestly Vocations, 1951. Pres., Samuel D'Anna, Jr.

Slovak Catholic Federation of America (1911), 2430 California Ave., Pittsburgh, Pa. 15212; 300,000. *Good Shepherd (Dobry Pastier)* monthly. The following fraternal organizations hold continuous membership: First Catholic Slovak Union, First Catholic Slovak Ladies Assn.; Slovak Catholic Sokol; Penna. Slovak Catholic Union; Ladies Penna. Slovak Catholic Union; First Slovak Wreath of the Free Eagle.

Slovak Catholic Sokol (1905), 205 Madison St., Passaic, N.J. 07055; 51,965. *Katolicky Sokol,* weekly; *Priatel Dietok,* monthly.

Society for the Propagation of the Faith (1822), 366 Fifth Ave., New York, N.Y. 10001; 3,000,000 in 156 dioceses in US. *Mission,* bimonthly; *Worldmission,* quarterly. Is subject to direction of Sacred Congregation for the Propagation of the Faith. Nat. Dir., Most Rev. Edward T. O'Meara.

Society of St. Peter the Apostle for Native Clergy (1898), 366 Fifth Ave., New York, N.Y. 10001; 156 branches. Organized as the Pope's own mission aid society for the maintenance of diocesan seminaries and diocesan seminarians in mission countries.

Spiritual Life Institute of America (1961), Star Route One, Sedona, Arizona 86336. *Desert Call,* seasonal. An ecumenical movement to foster the contemplative spirit in America. Founder, Rev. William McNamara, O.C.D.

T

Te Deum International (1940), 611 S. 6th St., Springfield, Ill. 62701; 27 chapters. For Catholic adult education on current and international affairs.

Theresians of America (1961), 5326 E. Pershing Ave., Scottsdale, Ariz. 85254; 6,000. Spiritual, intellectual and apostolic organization concerned with the vocation to Christian womanhood in both religious and lay states. Nat. Dir. and founder, Very Rev. Msgr. Elwood C. Voss.

U

United States Catholic Historical Society (1885), Office of Executive Secretary, St. Joseph's Seminary, Yonkers, N.Y. 10704; 360. *Historical Records and Studies* and a monograph series, annually. Pres., J. G. E. Hopkins.

V

Vernacular Society (1946), P.O. Box 207, Passaic, N.J. 07055; 500. *Vernacular,* newsletter. Pres., Reinhold Kissner.

W-Y

Western Catholic Union (1877), W.C.U. Bldg., 506-510 Maine St., Quincy, Ill. 62301; 27,614 in 126 branches in 9 states. *Western Catholic Union Record,* monthly.

William J. Kerby Foundation (1941), The Catholic University of America, Washington, D.C. 20017. Pres., Charles Cronin.

Wisconsin Council of Catholic Women (1915), 30 Hattie Ct., Marinette, Wis. 54143; 20,000. Pres., Miss Frances L. Powers.

Young Ladies' Institute (1887), 50 Oak St., San Francisco, Calif. 94102. Grand Sec,, Mrs. Valda Britschgi.

Young Men's Institute (1883), 50 Oak St., San Francisco, Calif. 94102; 7,690. *Institute Journal,* bimonthly. Grand Sec., B. G. Merdinger.

Knights of Columbus

The Knights of Columbus, which originated as a fraternal benefit society of Catholic men, was founded by Father Michael J. McGivney and chartered by the General Assembly of Connecticut Mar. 29, 1882.

In line with their general purpose to be of service to the Church, the Knights are active in many apostolic works and community programs.

Since January, 1947, the Knights have sponsored a program of Catholic advertising in secular publications with national circulation. This has brought almost 6 million inquiries and led to some 600,000 enrollments in courses in the Catholic faith. In recent years the Knights have broadened this program to include other media for spreading Christian and religious ideals. As a result substantial contributions have been made to support the work of the John LaFarge Institute in New York, the Catholic Communications Foundation in New York, and the Center for Applied Research in the Apostolate (CARA) in Washington.

K. of C. scholarship funds — two at the Catholic University of America, another for disbursement at other Catholic colleges in the US, and one at Canadian colleges — have provided college educations for more than 1,200 students since 1914.

The order promotes youth activity through sponsorship of the Columbian Squires and through cooperation with other organized youth groups.

K. of C. membership, as of Apr. 30, 1972, was 1,148,925 in 5,751 councils in the US, Canada, the Philippines, Cuba, Mexico, Puerto Rico, Panama, Guatemala, Guam and the Virgin Islands. Insurance assets, as of Dec. 31, 1971 amounted to $441,384,768 and total insurance in force, $2,047,813,685.

The Knights; publication, *Columbia,* has the greatest circulation (almost 1.2 million) of any Catholic monthly in the US.

John W. McDevitt is Supreme Knight. Virgil C. Dechant is Supreme Secretary.

International headquarters are located at One Columbus Plaza, New Haven, Conn. 06507.

The 1972 convention of the Knights of Columbus was held Aug. 15 to 17 in Toronto.

Post-Vatican II Associations

National Association of Laity: The National Association of Laity (NAL) was formally established in June, 1967, by delegates representative of independent lay associations already organized or in the process of formation.

Its chartered purposes are: (1) to promote and encourage continual renewal in the Church; (2) to stimulate an authentic, free, and responsible lay voice in the Church; (3) to assist the renewal efforts of individuals and local organizations; (4) to encourage the exchange of ideas on every level inside and outside the Christian community; (5) to encourage initiatives for seeking solutions to problems affecting the community of men; (6) to establish and maintain effective liaison with the National Conference of Catholic Bishops and other national organizations.

The NAL had 32 affiliates across the country as of July, 1972, and was in communication with 51 additional groups.

Jack Yorke is president of the NAL.

NAL headquarters are located at Suite 21-D, 7 E. 14th St., New York, N.Y. 10003.

National Federation of Laymen, Inc.: The stated purpose of the National Federation of Laymen, Inc., is "to work for the restoration of Christ's Kingship over temporal society, basing itself on the natural law and Catholic social doctrine."

The federation is organized on the following principles: "(1) Uncompromising fidelity to the orthodox social doctrine of the teaching of the Church. (2) Unhesitating rejection of all varieties of neo-modernism. (3) Determined active opposition to all forms of atheism within society. (4) Acceptance of the Constitutions, Decrees and Declarations of Vatican II as the context within which to launch lay initiatives designed to penetrate and perfect the temporal order with the Spirit of the Gospel."

The immediate objective of the federation, as its officers informed the bishops of the US in April, 1968, is to reinstate the use of orthodox religion textbooks in Catholic educational systems. This is in line with the federation motto, "Catholic Religious Education Demands Orthodoxy" (CREDO).

The federation has representatives in 31 regions across the country.

Edward J. Kraus of Chicago is chairman of the federation. Arthur J. Allen is the executive secretary.

The address of national headquarters is P.O. Box 56058, Chicago, Ill. 60656.

Catholics United for the Faith: CUF was founded in August, 1968, by a group of Catholic laymen who pledged themselves "to support, defend and enthusiastically advance the efforts of the teaching Church," and to combat the tendency among some Catholics "to break the doctrinal bonds that unite the Papacy with the Universal Church."

CUF's membership, in 83 chapters in the US and two in Rome, Italy, numbers approximately 9,000.

The efforts of CUF's membership are largely directed to research and to distribution of information concerning sex education courses, catechetics, abortion, private Catholic educational institutions now being founded, and other related areas. They are also engaged in promoting the development of a renewal of lay spirituality by devotion to the Blessed Sacrament, meditation on the lives of saints and devotion to Mary, advocating all-night vigils, prayer rallies, and recitation of the Rosary.

H. Lyman Stebbins is the president of CUF. Kirby M. Sheridan is executive director.

CUF headquarters are located at 1291 North Avenue, New Rochelle, New York 10804.

Two national groups resembling CUF in nature and purpose are: **Catholic Laymen of America, Inc.,** formed in 1968, with a mailing address at P. O. Box 5826, Denver, Colo., 80217; and **Una Voce,** older and with international ties, with a mailing address at P. O. Box 446, Grand Central Station, New York, N. Y. 10017. Una Voce's prime concern is retention of the Tridentine Latin Mass, with Gregorian Chant; it has 19 units in Europe, Australia and Latin America, and a membership of more than 5,000 in the United States.

Convention and Forum

Differences of concern among segments of lay persons were obvious in the actions and resolutions of the 1972 National Association of Laity Convention and the Wanderer Forum.

NAL Convention

About 175 delegates attending the fifth national convention of the National Association of Laity July 7 to 9, 1972, in Detroit, continued the trend of the association's pressure tactics to bring about change in the Church.

They censured Cardinal John J. Krol and Bishop Joseph L. Bernardin "for a series of acts abdicating their role of moral responsibility" with respect to escalation of the war in Vietnam. They also indicted the entire US Catholic Conference "as (an) accessory to the crime of genocide of the Vietnamese people and destroyers of their country."

The delegates praised five bishops for their peace efforts and three others for simplicity of life style, personal identification with the poor, the openness to lay participation in church affairs.

These bishops, together with the heads of 11 national Catholic organizations were invited to a November meeting with NAL personnel to discuss agendas for 1973.

In other actions and resolutions, the convention called on the Internal Revenue Service to check the financial reports of funds spent by bishops for lobbying, especially for educational aid, and to prosecute violations; favored the ordination of women to holy orders; rejected recent norms issued by the Vatican for the nomination of bishop candidates; urged the Church to restructure society; accepted busing as a means of desegregating schools; backed the United Farm Workers and their boycott of California and Arizona head lettuce; said it would investigate the social responsibility of corporations and would urge stockholders to vote for social-purpose investment and development.

The convention failed to articulate any clear position on the abortion issue. One paper, accepted for discussion purposes, appeared to endorse abortion in most instances. A four-member human life committee produced four minority reports on the subject.

Jack Yorke, who was reelected president, said the NAL would continue its work for peace, women's rights, the right of conscientious objection to military service, equitable distribution of Catholic educational funds for religious education, opposition to state aid for church-related schools, financial accountability, and the "coversion" of members of the hierarchy, according to the *National Catholic Reporter.*

Wanderer Forum

More than 500 persons attending the eighth annual Wanderer Forum June 16 to 18, 1972, in Minneapolis mixed discussion of their traditional concerns with resolutions of a political nature. The convention was sponsored by *The Wanderer,* a Catholic conservative weekly published in St. Paul.

The Forum took a strong stand against the Equal Rights Amendment, stating that it "threatens to degrade the stature of women . . . remove the safeguards which Christian society has erected for their protection." They blamed "falst representation" of the amendment for "its precipitous ratification by 19 states."

Conventioneers also rejected all recommendations of the Commission on Population Growth and the American Future, and asked bishops not to limit criticism of the recommendations to those dealing just with abortion.

The delegates called for a halt to "continuing agitation for novelty in the liturgy," and claimed that the new liturgy is not meeting the spiritual needs of many Catholics. They opposed in-hand reception of Holy Communion and the reception of first Communion before first confession. They endorsed a reemphasis of traditional devotion.

Describing the current religious textbook situation as "a profound scandal," they called for immediate work, under the direction of the bishops, on a national, uniform catechism and asked for a strong statement on the fundamental doctrines of the Catholic faith. They supported the establishment of pontifical catechetical centers across the country, and appealed to bishops to "more faithfully observe" the tradition of visits to diocesan facilities in efforts to stop "serious liturgical and pastoral abuses."

Delegates urged the bishops to insure the orthodoxy of all priests and administrative officials of the US Catholic Conference.

They voiced opposition to any efforts for Catholic membership in the National Council of Churches.

The Forum, in connection with its reaffirmation of belief in "the sacredness of all life," called on "all citizens to firmly resist the adoption of . . . legislation encroaching upon the stability and independence of the family."

INTERNATIONAL CATHOLIC ORGANIZATIONS

Guidelines

International organizations wanting to call themselves "Catholic" are required to meet standards set by the Vatican's Council of the Laity and to register with and get the approval of the Papal Secretariat of State, according to guidelines published in *Acta Apostolicae Sedis* under date of Dec. 23, 1971. The guidelines were made public in March, 1972.

Among conditions for the right of organizations to "bear the name Catholic" are:
• leaders "will always be Catholics," and candidates for office will be approved by the Secretariat of State;
• adherence by the organization to the Catholic Church, its teaching authority and teachings of the Gospel;
• evidence that the organization is really international with a universal outlook and that it fulfills its mission through its own management, meetings and accomplishments.

The guidelines also stated that leaders of the organizations "will take care to maintain necessary reserve as regards taking a stand or engaging in public activity in the field of politics or trade unionism. Abstention in these fields will normally be the best attitude for them to adopt during their term of office."

The guidelines were in line with a provision stated by the Second Vatican Council in the *Decree on the Apostolate of the Laity*: "No project may claim the name 'Catholic' unless it has obtained the consent of the lawful church authority."

They made it clear that all organizations are not obliged to apply for recognition, but that the Church "reserves the right to recognize as linked with her mission and her aims those organizations or movements which see fit to ask for such recognition."

Rosemary Goldie, vice-secretary of the laity council, said that the guidelines had not been issued to stem any abuses by organizations but only to clarify which are international Catholic organizations.

She also stated that "many organizations do not want full recognition by the Holy See. . . . Neverthelsss, we want to keep in contact with such organizations because the Holy See is interested in every one with a worthy cause."

It was not clear at the time of writing which of the organizations listed below had complied with the standards for recognition as international Catholic organizations.

Conference

Conference of International Catholic Organizations: A permanent body for collaboration among various organizations which seek to promote the development of international life along the lines of Christian principles. Eleven international Catholic organizations participated in its foundation and first meeting in 1927 at Fribourg, Switzerland. In 1951, the conference established its general secretariat and adopted governing statutes which were approved by the Vatican Secretariat of State in 1953.

The general secretariat is located at 1, route du Jura, Fribourg, Switzerland.

Permanent bodies of the conference which depend upon the general secretariat are the: Information Center on UN Affairs, 1, rue de Varembé, Geneva, Switzerland; International Catholic Coordinating Center for UNESCO, 98, rue de l'Université, Paris VII, France.

Permanent commissions are: Family Welfare, 68, rue Philippe le Bon, Brussels 4, Belgium; Church, Witness Commission, 12, rue de l'Orme, Brussels 4, Belgium; Health Commission, 20, Place Mgr. Ladeuze, Louvain, Belgium; Social Questions, 127, rue de la Loi, Brussels 4, Belgium; Commission for Catholic International Organizations having Consultative Status with ECOSOC or UN Specialized Agencies.

Conference Members

Apostolatus Maris International Council, International Secretariat, Permanent Bureau, Via della Scrofa 70, Rome, Italy.

Catholic International Federation for Physical Education, 5, Place St.-Thomas d'Aquin, Paris VII, France.

Catholic International Hospital Federation, 72, Badhuisweg, The Hague, Netherlands.

Catholic International Union for Social Service, 111, rue de la Poste, Brussels 3, Belgium.

Conference of International Catholic Organizations, 1, route du Jura, Fribourg, Switzerland.

International Association of Ladies of Charity of St. Vincent de Paul, 10, avenue Constant Coquelin, Paris VII, France.

International Catholic Association for

Radio and Television (UNDA), 5, rue de Romont, Gare, Fribourg, Switzerland.

International Catholic Child Bureau, 63, Largo Brancaccio, Rome, Italy.

International Catholic Education Office, 9, rue Guimard, Brussels 4, Belgium.

International Catholic Film Office, 8, rue de l'Orme, Brussels 4, Belgium.

International Catholic Girls' Society, 1, route du Jura, Fribourg, Switzerland.

International Catholic League Against Alcoholism, 3, Löwenstrasse, Lucerne, Switzerland.

International Catholic Migration Commission, 65, rue de Lausanne, Geneva, Switzerland.

International Catholic Press Union, 43, rue St.-Augustin, Paris II, France. Three Federations belong to the Union:

    International Federation of Catholic Journalists, 43, rue St.-Augustin, Paris II, France;

    International Federation of Catholic Newspaper Publishers, 22, Cours Albert 1, Paris VIII, France;

    International Federation of Catholic Press Agencies, c/o KNP, 48 Anna Paulownastraat, The Hague, Netherlands.

International Committee of Catholic Nurses, 32, rue Joseph II, Brussels 4, Belgium.

International Federation of Catholic Men, 4, Via della Conciliazione, Rome, Italy.

International Federation of Catholic Universities, rue de Grenelle, Paris VII, France.

International Federation of Catholic Youth, 94, Via Torre Rossa, Rome, Italy.

International Federation of Christian Workers' Movements, 127, rue de la Loi, Brussels 4, Belgium.

International Study Centre for Religious Education, 184, rue Washington, Brussels, Belgium.

International Union of Catholic Employers' Associations, 49, Avenue d'Auderghem, Brussels 4, Belgium.

Legion of Mary, International Council, De Montfort House, North Brunswick Street, Dublin 7, Ireland.

Pax Romana, International Catholic Movement for Intellectual and Cultural Affairs, 1, route du Jura, Fribourg, Switzerland.

Pax Romana, International Movement of Catholic Students, 1, route du Jura, Fribourg, Switzerland.

Society of St. Vincent de Paul, 5, rue de Pré-aux-Clercs, Paris VII, France.

World Federation of Catholic Young Women and Girls, 31, Av. de l'Hopital Francais, Brussels 8, Belgium.

World Federation of Christian Life Communities, 8, Borgo Santo Spirito, Rome, Italy.

World Union of Catholic Teachers, 3, Via della Conciliazione, Rome, Italy.

World Union of Catholic Women's Organizations, 98, rue de l'Universite 98, Paris VII, France.

Young Christian Workers, 78, Boulevard Poincaré, Brussels 7, Belgium.

Associate Organizations

Apostleship of Prayer, Borgo Santo Spirito 5, Rome, Italy.

Catholic Union for Interracial Cooperation, consisting of:

    Ad Lucem, 12, rue Guy-de-la-Brosse, Paris V, France;

    International Catholic Auxiliaries, 84, rue Gachard, Brussels, Belgium;

    The Grail, 30 Konigslaan, Amsterdam, Netherlands.

International Federation of Christian Trade Unions, 148, rue de la Loi, Brussels, Belgium.

International Federation of Institutes for Social and Socio-Religious Research, 116, rue des Flamands, Louvain, Belgium.

International Movement of Catholic Rural Youth, Diestsevest 24, Leuven, Belgium.

International Union for Social Studies, 19, avenue d'Yser, Brussels, Belgium.

International Young Christian Students, rue de Rennes, Paris VI, France.

Pax Christi, 26, rue Barbet-de-Jouy, Paris VII, France.

Sword of the Spirit, Hinsley House, 38, King St., London W. C. 2, England.

World Union of Catholic Philosophical Societies, 25, Aignerstrasse, Salsburg-Aigen, Austria.

Others

Catholic Union (to aid Catholics of the Eastern rites), Fribourg, Switzerland.

Inter American Catholic Social Action Confederation, 1312 Massachusetts Avenue N.W., Washingtonn 5, D. C., U.S.A.

International Association of Catholic Doctors, 3, Av. des Deux Eglises, Brussels 4, Belgium.

International Christian Social Union, 127, rue de la Loi, Brussels, Belgium.

International Federation of Little Singers ("Pueri Cantores"), 1420 Avenue of the Americas, New York, N. Y., U.S.A.

International Federation of Middle Class Catholics, Venlo, Netherlands.

International Institute of Liturgical Art, Rome, Italy.

International Marian Academy, Rome, Italy.

International Union of Catholic Esperantists, 81, Utrechtsweg, Vleuten (Utrecht), Netherlands.

International Union "Pro Deo," 89, Via Nazionale, Rome, Italy.

International Unitas Society, Rome, Italy.

Permanent Committee for International Congresses of the Apostolate of the Laity, Palazzo delle Congregazioni, 16, Piazza San Calisto, Rome, Italy.

Some of the international Catholic organizations hold congresses in Rome.

Communications

Following are excerpts from a 23,000-word Pastoral Instruction on the Mass Media written by the Pontifical Commission for Social Communications and made public June 3, 1971. The most extensive document on the subject ever issued by the Vatican, it supplements and applies the contents of the much shorter Decree on the Instruments of Social Communication promulgated by the Second Vatican Council Dec. 4, 1963. The Latin title of the Instruction is Communio et Progressio ("Unity and Advancement"), from its first two words.

[These excerpts are from the text circulated by NC News Service.]

Purpose of the Media; "The unity and advancement of men living in society: these are the chief aims of social communication and of all the means it uses. These means include the press, the cinema, radio and television."

"In the Christian faith, the unity and brotherhood of man are the chief aims of all communication."

The Common Good: "The total output of the media in any given area should be judged by the contribution it makes to the common good."

Requirements of Communication: "Every communication must comply with certain essential requirements, and these are sincerity, honesty and truthfulness. Good intentions and a clear conscience do not thereby make a communication sound and reliable. A communication must state the truth. It must accurately reflect the situation with all its implications. The moral worth and validity of any communication does not lie solely in its theme or intellectual content. The way in which it is presented, the way in which it is spoken and treated, and even the audience for which it is designed — all these factors must be taken into account."

Every Man a Partner: "The torrent of information and opinion pouring through (the) channels (of communication) makes every man a partner in the business of the human race. This interchange creates the proper conditions for that mutual and sympathetic understanding which leads to universal progress."

Questions: "How can we ensure that (the) swift and haphazard and endless stream of news is properly evaluated and understood? The media are bound to seek a mass audience, and so they often adopt a neutral stance in order to avoid giving offense to any section of their audience. How, in a society that is committed to the rights of dissent, is the distinction between right and wrong, true and false, to be made?"

"How, in the face of competition to capture a large popular audience, are the media to be prevented from appealing to and inflaming the less admirable tendencies in human nature? How can one avoid the concentration of the power to communicate in too few hands, so that any real dialogue is killed? How can one avoid allowing communications made indirectly and through machinery to weaken direct human contact — especially when these communications take the form of pictures and images? When the media invite men to escape into fantasy, what can be done to bring them back to present reality? How can one stop the media from encouraging mental idleness and passivity? And how can one be certain that the incessant appeal to emotion does not sap reason?"

Public Opinion: "The means of social communication are a public forum where every man may exchange ideas. The public expression and the confrontation of different opinions that occur within this dialogue influence and enrich the development of society and further its progress."

"Public opinion is an essential expression of human nature organized in society."

"If public opinion is to emerge in the proper manner, it is absolutely essential that there be freedom to express ideas and attitudes. In accordance with the express teaching of the Second Vatican Council, it is necessary to declare unequivocally that freedom of speech for individuals and groups must be permitted so long as the common good and public morality are not endangered."

Propaganda: "The process of promoting — in what is sometimes referred to as a 'propaganda campaign' — with a view to influencing public opinion is justified only when it serves the truth, promotes causes that are in the public interest, and its objectives and methods accord with the dignity of man."

Weight of Opinions: "Not every opinion that is given publicity should be taken as a true expression of that public opinion which is held by a significant number of people. A number of differing opinions can flourish at the same time in the same area, although one usually has a greater following than the others. The opinion of the majority, however, is not necessarily the best or the closest to the truth."

"Views openly and commonly expressed which reflect the aspirations of the people should always be carefully considered. This is especially binding on those in authority, whether civil or religious."

Right To Be Informed and To Inform: "If public opinion is to be formed in a proper manner, it is necessary that, right from the start, the public be given free access both to the sources and channels of information, and be allowed freedom to express its own views. Freedom of opinion and the right to be informed go hand in hand."

"With the right to be informed goes the

duty to seek information. Information does not simply occur; it has to be sought."

"The right to information is not merely the prerogative of the individual; it is essential to the public interest."

Safety of Correspondents: "The safety of (news) correspondents should be ensured in every possible way because of the service they render to man's right to know about what is happening. This is particularly true in the case of wars, which involve and concern the whole human race. The Church utterly condemns the use of violence against newsmen or against anyone in any way involved in the passing on of news."

Privacy and secrecy: "The right to information is not limitless. It has to be reconciled with other existing rights. There is the right of privacy which protects the private life of families and individuals. There is the right of secrecy which obtains if necessity or professional duty or the common good itself requires it. Indeed, whenever public good is at stake, discretion and discrimination and careful judgment should be used in the preparation of news."

Advertising: Advertising must respect the truth, taking into account accepted advertising conventions."

"If harmful or utterly useless goods are touted to the public, if false assertions are made about goods for sale, if less admirable human tendencies are exploited, those responsible for such advertising harm society and forfeit their good name and credibility. More than this, unremitting pressure to buy articles of luxury can arouse false wants that hurt both individuals and families by making them ignore what they really need. And those forms of advertising which, without shame, exploit the sexual instincts simply to make money, or which seek to penetrate into the subconscious recesses of the mind in a way that threatens the freedom of the individual, these forms of advertising must be shunned. It is desirable that advertisers make definite rules for themselves lest their sales methods affront human dignity or harm the community."

"Serious harm can be done (to developing countries) if advertising and commercial pressure become so irresponsible that communities seeking to rise from poverty to a reasonable standard of living are persuaded to seek this progress by satisfying wants that have been created artificially."

News Reporting: "Not only must news reporting keep to the facts and bear down on the most important ones, but the meaning of what is reported should be brought out by explanation."

Censorship: "Censorship should be used only in the very last extremity."

Communication in the Church: "The Church looks for ways of multiplying and strengthening the bonds of union between her members. For this reason, communication and dialogue among Catholics are indispensable. The Church lives her life in the midst of the whole community of man. She must therefore maintain contacts and lines of communication in order to keep a relationship with the whole human race. This is done both by giving information and by listening carefully to public opinion inside and outside the Church. By holding a continuous discussion with the contemporary world, she tries to help in solving the problems that men face at the present time."

Dialogue and Public Opinion: "Since the Church is a living body, she needs public opinion in order to sustain a giving and taking between her members."

"Catholics should be fully aware of the real freedom to speak their minds which stems from a 'feeling for the faith' and from love."

"Those who exercise authority in the Church will take care to ensure that there is responsible exchange of freely held and expressed opinion among the People of God. More, they will set up norms and conditions for this to take place."

Freedom of Expression: "While the individual Catholic follows the magisterium (teaching authority of the Church), he can and should engage in free research so that he may better understand revealed truths or explain them to a society subject to incessant change."

Constructive Dialogue: "Free dialogue within the Church does no injury to her unity and solidarity. It nurtures concord and the meeting of minds by permitting the free play of the variations of public opinion. But, in order that this dialogue may go on in the right direction, it is essential that charity be in command even when there are differing views. Everyone in this dialogue should be animated by the desire to serve and to consolidate unity and cooperation. There should be a desire to build, not to destroy. There should be a deep love for the Church and a compelling desire for its unity."

Scientific Investigation and Doctrine: "Distinction must be borne in mind between, on the one hand, the area that is devoted to scientific investigation and, on the other, the area that concerns the teaching of the faithful. In the former area, experts enjoy the freedom required by their work and are free to communicate to others in books and commentaries the fruits of their research. In the second area, only those doctrines may be attributed to the Church which are declared to be such by her authentic teaching authority. These doctrines, obviously, can be aired in public without fear."

"It sometimes happens, however, because of the very nature of social communication, that new opinions circulating among theologians at times circulate too soon and in the wrong places. Such opinions, which might be confused with the authentic doctrine of the Church, should be examined critically. It must also be remembered that the real significance of such theories is often badly distorted by popularization and by the style of presentation used in the media."

Flow of Information in the Church: "Since the development of public opinion within the Church is essential, individual Catholics have the right to all the information they need to play their active role in the life of the Church."

The normal flow of life and the smooth functioning of government within the Church requires a steady two-way flow of information between the ecclesiastical authorities at all levels and the faithful as individuals and as organized groups. This applies to the whole world. To make this possible, various institutions are required. These might include news agencies, official spokesmen, meeting facilities, pastoral councils, all properly financed."

Attitude on Secrecy: "On those occasions when the affairs of the Church require secrecy, rules normal in civil affairs apply.

"On the other hand, the spiritual riches which are an essential attribute of the Church demand that the news she gives out . . . be distinguished by integrity, truth and openness. When ecclesiastical authorities are unwilling to give information or are unable to do so, then rumor is unloosed; and rumor is not a bearer of the truth but of dangerous half-truths. Secrecy should therefore be restricted to matters that involve the good name of individuals or that touch upon the rights of people, whether singly or collectively."

Church-World Dialogue: "The Church needs to know contemporary reactions to ideas and events, whether they be Catholic or not. The greater the extent to which the means of social communication reflect these reactions, the more they contribute toward this knowledge required by the Church."

"It is the mission of those with responsible positions in the Church to announce without fail or pause the full truth by the means of social communication, so as to give a true picture of the Church and her life. Since the media are often the only channels of information that exist between the Church and the world, a failure to use them amounts to 'burying the talent given by God.' "

Media and the Gospel: "During his life on earth, Christ showed himself to be the perfect Communicator, while the Apostles used what means of communication were available in their time. It is now necessary that the same message be carried by the means of social communication that are available today. Indeed, it would be difficult to suggest that Christ's command was being obeyed unless all the opportunities offered by the . . . media to extend to vast numbers of people the announcement of his Good News were being used."

The Catholic Press: "The Catholic press . . . can be marvelously effective in bringing a knowledge of the Church to the world and a knowledge of the world to the Church. It does this by imparting information and by stimulating those processes by which public opinion is formed. There is, however, no advantage in founding new publications if quantity is achieved at the cost of quality and if the new injure the old."

"That part of the Catholic press which is of general interest published news and opinions and background articles about all the facets and the problems and worries of modern life. This it does in the light of Christian principles. It is the task of the Catholic press to balance, to complete and, if necessary, to correct the news and comments about religion and the Christian life."

UNITY IN THE MEDIA

The Pontifical Commission for Social Communications approved General Criteria for Ecumenical Collaboration in the Area of Social Communications, Nov. 15, 1971.

[The following text, made public by the National Conference of Catholic Bishops Jan. 3, 1972, was circulated by NC News Service.]

1. The ways and forms of Catholic collaboration with projects launched by Christian non-Catholic Associations should be inspired by the principles outlined in the II Ecumenical Vatican Council *(Decree on Ecumenism, especially No. 12).*

2. The Pontifical Commission for Social Communications encourages all these efforts at ecumenical collaboration with a view to better carrying out the task of the integral development of man through more effective use of the means of social communication (cf. Pastoral Instruction, *Communio et Progressio,* pp. 96-100). An effort must be made to do together everything which our faith does not oblige us to do separately.

3. In the practical application of this general principle, this collaboration can be worked out only on a loyal, reciprocal "partnership" basis.

4. It is helpful to point out that the Pastoral Instruction cites certain possible applications of this collaboration. In No. 99: "There is almost no end to the opportunities for such collaboration. Some are obvious joint programs of radio and television; education projects and services, especially for parents and young people; meetings and discussions between professionals that may be on an international level; recognition of achievement in these fields by annual awards; cooperation in research in the media, especially in professional training and education. All these can help towards the fair and equal advancement of all peoples" *(Decree on Ecumenism,* No. 12). The above is inspired by the following sentences in the conciliar *Decree on Ecumenism:* "Cooper-

ation between Christians shows openly the unity that already binds them together and is a splendid manifestation of Christ's own mission at the service of all mankind" (No. 12).

5. Out of concern for fidelity to its doctrine, the Catholic Church must always maintain its own institutions which are directly related to its pastoral action in the area of social communications.

6. It is advisable to encourage institutions and Catholic specialists in the area of SCM to join Catholic organizations (OIC/SCM, National Offices, National Catholic Associations . . .) through which they will be able to contribute to a more effective and more or-derly, ecumenical collaboration. Thus they will approach ecumenical collaboration as groups.

7. Should anyone feel that a different approach should be adopted, this should be done only in agreement with competent ecclesiastical authority.

The document stated in a footnote: "All joint undertakings in the field of social communications must leave the Catholic Church free to express, without any spirit of animosity, her own positions in matters of doctrine, such as family and social ethics (marriage, divorce, birth control, abortion and euthanasia)."

CATHOLIC NEWSPAPERS AND MAGAZINES IN THE US

(Sources: Almanac Survey, *Catholic Press Directory 1972*, NC News Service.)

Abbreviation code: a, annual; bm, bimonthly; m, monthly; q, quarterly; w, weekly.

Newspapers
A-B

Advocate, The, w; 37 Evergreen Pl., E. Orange, N.J. 07018; Newark archdiocese; 68,712.

Alamo Messenger, w; P.O. Drawer 12459, San Antonio, Tex. 78212; San Antonio archdiocese; 23,760.

Alive, m; 400 East Monroe, Phoenix, Ariz. 85004; Phoenix diocese.

Anchor, The, w; 410 Highland Ave., Fall River, Mass. 02722; Fall River diocese; 26,184.

Arizona Register, 64 W. Ochoa St., Tucson, Ariz. 85701; 20,067.

Beacon, The, w; Box A, Pequannock, N.J. 07440; Paterson diocese; 51,722.

Byzantine Catholic World, w; 3643 Perrysville Ave., Pittsburgh, Pa. 15214; Munhall Byzantine archdiocese; 12,844.

C

Catholic Accent, w; 723 E. Pittsburgh St., Greensburg, Pa. 45601; Greensburg diocese; 50,133.

Catholic Advance, The, w; 424 N. Broadway, Wichita, Kans. 67202; Wichita diocese; 12,329.

Catholic Banner, w; 119 Broad St., Charleston, S.C. 29401; Charleston diocese; 6,506.

Catholic Bulletin, w; 244 Dayton Ave., St. Paul, Minn. 53102; St. Paul and Minneapolis archdiocese, New Ulm diocese; 54,993.

Catholic Chronicle, w; 1933 Spielbusch Ave., Toledo, O. 43624; Toledo diocese; 39,120.

Catholic Commentator, The, w; P.O. Box 14746, Baton Rouge, La. 70808; Baton Rouge diocese; 40,673.

Catholic Crosswinds, w; P.O. Box 194, Pueblo, Colo. 81002; Pueblo diocese; 20,186.

Catholic Exponent, w; PO. Box 779, Youngstown, O. 44501; Youngstown diocese; 23,786.

Catholic Free Press, w; 247 Mill St., Worcester, Mass. 01602; Worcester diocese; 27,721.

Catholic Herald, The, w; 5890 Newman Ct., Sacramento, Calif. 95819; Sacramento diocese; 13,466.

Catholic Herald Citizen, w; P.O. Box 736, Milwaukee, Wis. 53201; Milwaukee archdiocese, Madison diocese; 180,112.

Catholic Herald Citizen — Superior Edition, w; 1512 N. 12th St., Superior, Wis. 54880.

Catholic Hungarian's Sunday, w; 517 S. Belle Vista Ave., Youngstown, O. 44509; 3,400.

Catholic Light, w; 300 Wyoming Ave., Scranton, Pa. 18503; Scranton diocese; 53,524.

Catholic Messenger, w; 407 Brady St., Davenport, Ia. 52805; Davenport diocese; 26,523.

Catholic Mirror, w; 306 Securities Bldg., Des Moines, Ia. 50309; 16,000.

Catholic Missourian, w; 600 Clark Ave., Jefferson City, Mo. 65101; Jefferson City diocese; 16,153.

Catholic News, The, w; 68 W. Broad St., Mt. Vernon, N.Y. 10552; New York archdiocese; 69,996.

Catholic News-Register, w; 425 Summit St., Joliet, Ill. 60435; Joliet diocese; 10,721.

Catholic Northwest Progress, w; 907 Terry Ave., Seattle, Wash. 98104; Seattle archdiocese, Yakima diocese; 43,000.

Catholic Observer, w; 50 Observer St., Springfield, Mass. 01104; Springfield diocese; 15,870.

Catholic Post, The, w; 409 N. Monroe Ave., Peoria, Ill. 61603; Peoria diocese; 36,186.

Catholic Register, w; 1406 12th Ave., Altoona, Pa. 16603; Altoona-Johnstown diocese.

Catholic Review, w; 320 Cathedral St., Baltimore, Md. 21203; Baltimore archdiocese; 66,571.

Catholic Sentinel, w; 2816 E. Burnside St., Portland, Ore. 97214; Portland archdiocese; 21,251. (Serves Baker diocese also which uses one or two pages in Portland edition.)

Catholic Spirit, The, bw; P.O. Box 230, Wheeling, W. Va. 26603; Wheeling diocese; 24,000.

Catholic Standard, w; 1711 N. St., N.W., Washington, D.C. 20036; Washington archdiocese; 44,426.

Catholic Standard and Times, w; 222 N. 17th St., Philadelphia, Pa. 19103; Philadelphia archdiocese; 65,700.

Catholic Star Herald, w; 101 N. Seventh St., Camden, N.J. 08102; Camden diocese; 45,216.

Catholic Sun, The, w; 204 E. Jefferson St., Syracuse, N.Y. 13202; Syracuse diocese; 50,000.

Catholic Telegraph, w; 326 W. 7th St., Cincinnati, O. 45202; Cincinnati archdiocese; 54,055.

Catholic Times, w; 197 E. Gay St., Columbus, O. 43216; Columbus diocese; 11,116.

Catholic Transcript, w; 785 Asylum Ave., Hartford, Conn. 06105; Hartford archdiocese, Bridgeport and Norwich dioceses; 52,461.

Catholic Universe Bulletin, w; 1027 Superior Ave. N.E., Cleveland, O. 44114; Cleveland diocese; 79,949.

Catholic Virginian, w; 14 N. Laurel St., Richmond, Va. 23220; Richmond diocese; 36,209.

Catholic Voice, The, w; 2918 Lakeshore Ave., Oakland, Calif. 94610; Oakland diocese; 92,135.

Catholic Week, w; P.O. Box 349, Mobile, Ala. 36601; Mobile diocese; 9,900.

Catholic Weekly, The, w; P.O. Box 1405, Saginaw, Mich. 48605; (diocese), 21,185

Catholic Weekly, The, w; P.O. Box 167, Flint, Mich. 48501; Lansing diocese; 18,780.

Catholic Witness, The, w; 2300 Market St., Harrisburg, Pa. 17103; Harrisburg diocese; 49,596.

Church Today, m; P.O. Box 5047, Alexandria, La. 71301; Alexandria diocese; 14,913.

Church World, w; 19 Commercial St., Portland, Me. 04104; Portland diocese; 14,349.

Clarion Herald, w; 523 Natchez St., New Orleans, La. 70130; New Orleans archdiocese; 108,270.

Community, biweekly; P.O. Box 8625, Jacksonville, Fla. 32211; Jacksonville diocese (one page published every other Sunday in four area newspapers).

Concern, m (exec. July); 153 Ash St., Manchester, N.H. 03105; Manchester diocese; 14,000.

Courier, The, w; 270 Hamilton St., Winona, Minn. 55987; Winona diocese; 12,800.

Courier Journal, w; 67 Chestnut St., Rochester, N.Y. 14604; Rochester diocese; 73,480.

Criterion, The, w; P.O. Box 174, Indianapolis, Ind. 46306; Indianapolis archdiocese; 41,716.

Crociato, Il (Ital.-Eng.), w; 1 Hanson Pl., Brooklyn, N.Y. 11217; 4,360.

D-F

Delmarva Dialog, w; 1626 N. Union St., Wilmington, Del. 19899; Wilmington diocese; 30,000.

Denver Catholic Register, w; 934 Bannock St., Denver, Colo. 80201; Denver archdiocese; 30,000.

Draugas (Lithuanian), daily; 4545 W. 63rd St., Chicago, Ill. 60629; Lithuanian Catholic Press Society.

Eastern Catholic Life, w; 101 Market St., Passaic, N.J. 07055; Passaic Byzantine eparchy; 13,821.

Eastern Kansas Register, The, w; P.O. Box 2329, Kansas City, Kans. 66110; Kansas City archdiocese; 32,864.

Eastern Montana Catholic Register, w; 725 Third Ave. N., Great Falls, Mont. 59401; Great Falls diocese; 8,687.

Evangelist, The, w; 39 Philip St., Albany, N.Y. 12207; Albany diocese; 97,649.

Florida Catholic The, w; 620 N. Magnolia Ave., Orlando, Fla. 32802; Orlando and St. Petersburg dioceses; 42,694.

Fort Wayne-South Bend Edition of Our Sunday Visitor, w; Noll Plaza, Huntington, Ind. 46750; 23,505.

G-L

Gary Edition of Our Sunday Visitor, w; P.O. Box 445, Gary, Ind. 46401; 39,198.

Georgia Bulletin, w; 756 W. Peachtree St. N.W., Atlanta, Ga. 30308; Atlanta archdiocese; 24,345.

Globe, The, w; P.O. Box 1678, Sioux City, Ia. 51102; Sioux City diocese; 24,345.

Guardian, The, 2500 N. Tyler St., Little Rock, Ark. 72207; Little Rock diocese; 10,215.

Hawaii Catholic Herald, w; 1184 Bishop St., Honolulu, H.I. 96813; Honolulu diocese; 9,350.

Idaho Register, w; 420 Idaho St., Boise, Idaho 83702; Boise diocese; 11,816.

Inland Register, w; 1023 W. Riverside, Spokane, Wash. 99210; Spokane diocese; 10,300.

Intermountain Catholic Register, The, w; P.O. Box 2489, Salt Lake City, Utah 84110; Salt Lake City diocese; 6,082.

Jednota (Slovak-Eng.), w; 1655 W. Harrisburg Pike, Middletown, Pa. 17057; 37,714.

Kansas City-St. Joseph Key to the News, w; P.O. Box 1037, Kansas City, Mo. 64141.

Lafayette Edition of Our Sunday Visitor, w; 610 Lingle Ave., Lafayette, Ind. 47901; 12,107.

Lake Shore Visitor, w; 2-M Commerce Bldg., Erie, Pa. 16512; Erie diocese; 15,290.

Liberte, La (French-English), w; 275 Rollstone St., Fitchburg, Mass. 01421; 2,000.

Long Island Catholic, The, w; 53 N. Park Ave., Rockville Centre, N.Y. 11570; Rockville Centre diocese; 189,913.

(Most dioceses in the US have newspapers.)

M

Magnificat, w; 501 Virginia St., Buffalo, N.Y. 14202; Buffalo diocese; 132,561.

Message, The, w; 208 N.W. Third St., Evansville, Ind. 47708; Evansville diocese; 12,780.

Messenger, The, w; 224 W. Washington St., Belleville, Ill. 62220; Belleville diocese; 24,481.

Messenger, The, w; 1044 Scott St., Covington, Ky. 41012; Covington diocese; 12,678.

Michigan Catholic, The, w; 644 Selden St., Detroit, Mich. 48201; Detroit archdiocese; 131,748.

Mirror, The, w; P.O. Box 847, Springfield, Mo. 65801; Springfield-Cape Girardeau diocese; 11,200.

Mississippi Today, w; P.O. Box 2130, Jackson, Miss. 39206; Natchez-Jackson diocese; 10,775.

Monitor, The, w; 441 Church St., San Francisco, Calif. 94114; San Francisco archdiocese; 35,308.

Monitor, The, w; 139 N. Warren St., Trenton, N.J. 08607; Trenton diocese; 82,687.

Montana Catholic Register (Western), w; P.O. Box 1729, Helena, Mont. 59601; Helena diocese; 10,044.

Morning Star, The, w; P.O. Box 3223, Lafayette, La. 70501; Lafayette diocese; 26,027.

N

Narod Polski (Polish-Eng.), semi-monthly; 1331 Augusta Blvd., Chicago, Ill. 60622; 55,000.

Nasa Nada (Eng.-Croatian), w; 1414 W. 119th St., Crown Point, Ind. 46307; 6,500.

National Catholic Register, w; P.O. Box 281, 1348, Fort Worth, Tex. 76101; national edition and 15 diocesan editions; 300,438.

National Catholic Reporter, The, w; P.O. Box Kansas City, Mo. 64141; published by laymen; 51,083.

National Hibernian Digest, The, bm; 63 Lafayette Ave., Trenton, N.J. 08610; Ancient Order of Hibernians; 19,700.

Nebraska Register, The, w; 607 W. Division St., Grand Island, Nebr. 68801; Grand Island diocese; 4,033.

Nevada Register, w; P.O. Box 1989, Reno, Nev. 89505; Reno diocese; 5,000.

New Day, The, w; 202 Morningside Dr. S.E., Albuquerque, N.M. 87108; Albuquerque diocese; 3,000.

New Star, The, w; 2208 W. Chicago Ave., Chicago, Ill. 60622; St. Nicholas of Chicago Ukrainian diocese; 4,205.

New World, The, w; 109 N. Dearborn St., Chicago, Ill. 60602; Chicago archdiocese; 228,934.

North Carolina Catholic, w; P.O. Box 10686, Raleigh, N.C. 27605; Raleigh diocese; 4,300.

North Country Catholic, w; 615 Washington St., Ogdensburg, N.Y. 12403; Ogdensburg diocese; 14,106.

Northwestern Kansas Register, w; P.O. Box 958, Salina, Kans. 67401; 8,325.

O-R

Observer, The, w; 580 Fremont St., Monterey, Calif. 93940; Monterey diocese; 9,600.

Observer, The, w; 1260 N. Church St., Rockford, Ill. 61101; Rockford diocese; 12,790.

One Voice, w; P.O. Box 10822, Birmingham, Ala. 35202; Birmingham diocese; 10,060.

Our Northland Diocese; m; 1200 Memorial Dr., Crookston, Minn. 56716; Crookston diocese; 11,929.

Our Sunday Visitor, w; Noll Plaza, Huntington, Ind. 46750; national edition and official publication for 6 dioceses; Our Sunday Visitor, Inc. 436,666.

Outlook, m (Sept.-June); 215 W. 4th St., Duluth, Minn. 55806; Duluth diocese; 25,000.

Pilot, The w; 49 Franklin St., Boston, Mass. 02110; Boston archdiocese; 130,850.

Pittsburgh Catholic, The, w; 110 Third Ave., Pittsburgh, Pa. 15222; Pittsburgh diocese; 65,813.

Polish American Journal, biweekly; 413 Cedar Ave., Scranton, Pa. 18505; 26,751.

Priests — USA, m; 1307 S. Wabash Ave., Chicago, Ill. 60605; National Federation of Priests' Councils; 8,000.

Providence Visitor, w; 184 Broad St., Providence, R.I.; Providence diocese; 44,747.

Record, The, w; 433 S. 5th St., Louisville, Ky. 40202; Louisville archdiocese; 18,367.

S

St. Cloud Visitor, w; 810 Germain St., St. Cloud, Minn. 56301; St. Cloud diocese; 27,333.

St. Joseph's-Blatt (German), bm; St. Benedict, Ore. 97373; Manfred F. Ellenberger; 2,300.

St. Louis Review, w; 462 N. Taylor Ave., St. Louis, Mo. 63108; St. Louis archdiocese; 85,466.

Shlakh — The Way, w; 805 N. Franklin St., Philadelphia, Pa. 19123; Philadelphia archeparchy. Stamford and Chicago eparchies; 11,673.

Southern Cross, The, w; Alcala Park, San Diego diocese; 26,319.

Southern Cross, The, w; P.O. Box 10027; Savannah, Ga. 31402; Savannah diocese; 9,435.

Southern Nebraska Register, w; P.O. Box 80329, Lincoln, Nebr. 68501; Lincoln diocese; 14,284.

Southwest Kansas Register, w; P.O. Box 1317, Dodge City, Kans. 67801; Dodge City diocese; 7,785.

Spirit, The, 203 S. Monroe Ave., Green Bay, Wis. 54305; Green Bay diocese; 41,251.

T

Tablet, w; 1 Hanson Pl., Brooklyn, N.Y. 11217; Brooklyn diocese; 107,404.

Tennessee Register, The, w; 421 Charlotte Ave., Nashville, Tenn. 37219; Nashville diocese; 11,701.

Texas Catholic, w; 3915 Lemmon Ave., Dallas, Tex. 75219; Dallas and Fort Worth dioceses; 23,557.

Texas Catholic Herald, The, w; 1700 San Jacinto St., Houston, Tex. 77002; Galveston-Houston diocese; 82,777.

Texas Catholic Herald — Austin Edition, w; 1212 Guadalupe, Austin, Tex. 78701; Austin diocese; 7,300.

Texas Catholic Herald — Beaumont, w; P.O. Box 3944, Beaumont, Tex. 77704; Beaumont diocese; 15,400.

Texas Concho Register, w; 116 S. Oakes, San Angelo, Tex. 76901; San Angelo diocese; 3,375.

Texas Gulf Coast Catholic, w; P.O. Box 2584, Corpus Christi diocese; 7,827.

Tidings, The, w; 1530 W. 9th St., Los Angeles, Calif. 90015; Los Angeles archdiocese; 71,951.

Times-Review, The, w; P.O. Box 991, La Crosse, Wis. 54601; La Crosse diocese; 16,500.

True Voice, The, w; 6060 N.W. Radial, Omaha, Nebr. 68104; Omaha archdiocese; 21,659.

Twin Circle — The National Catholic Press, w; P.O. Box 25986, Los Angeles, Calif. 90025; 84,895.

U-W

U.P. Catholic, w; Locker Drawer 548, Marquette, Mich. 49855; Marquette diocese; 7,311.

Vermont Catholic Tribune, w; 209 College St., Burlington, Vt. 05401; Burlington diocese; 28,537.

Voice, The, w; 6201 Biscayne Blvd., Miami, Fla. 33138; Miami archdiocese; 62,672.

Voice of the Southwest, w; P.O. Box 68, Lumberton, N. Mex. 87547; Gallup diocese; 1,596.

Wanderer, The, w; 128 E. 10th St., St. Paul, Minn. 55101; 46,474.

West Texas Register, w; 1800 N. Spring, Amarillo, Tex. 79107; Amarillo diocese; 3,300.

Western Catholic Edition of Our Sunday Visitor, w; 514 E. Lawrence Ave., Springfield, Ill. 62705; Springfield diocese; 40,814.

Witness, The, w; 845 Bluff St., Dubuque, Ia. 52001; Dubuque archdiocese; 25,475.

Wyoming Catholic Register, w; 214 W. 26th St., Cheyenne, Wyo. 82001; 5,512.

(The *Visitor* and *Register* (National) are the only chains of Catholic newspapers in the United States. Their combined circulations are more than one million copies.)

Magazines, Other Periodicals

A

Act, 10 times a year; 1655 Jackson Blvd., Chicago, Ill. 60512; 2,500.

ACTU Newsletter, m; 13 E. 30th St., New York, N.Y. 10016; 3,500.

Alumnae News, q; 29 Castle Pl., New Rochelle, N.Y. 10801.

America, w; 106 W. 56th St., New York, N.Y. 10019; 54,060.

American Benedictine Review, q; 2nd and Division Sts., Atchison, Kans. 66002; 2,300.

American Ecclesiastical Review, m; 620 Michigan Ave. N.E., Washington, D.C. 20017; 3,081.

American Midland Naturalist, q; Notre Dame, Ind. 46556.

Americas, The, q; Box 34440, Washington, D.C. 20034; Academy of American Franciscan History.

Amerikanski Slovenec (Slovenian), w; 6117 St. Clair Ave., Cleveland, O. 44103; Slovenian Catholic Union; 16,200.

Annals of Our Lady of the Angels, m; 253 Knickerbocker Rd., Tenafly, N.J. 07670; 25,500.

Annals of the Holy Childhood, 8 times a year; P.O. Box 6758, Pittsburgh, Pa. 15212; Pontifical Association of the Holy Childhood; 365,000.

Anthonian, q; Paterson, N.J. 07509; St. Anthony's Guild; 201,000.

Anthropological Quarterly, q; 620 Michigan Ave. N.E., Washington, D.C. 20017; Catholic Anthropological Conference; 785.

Apostolate of Our Lady, m; Carey, O. 43316; Our Lady of Consolation National Shrine.

Apostolate of the Little Flower, bm; P.O. Box 5280, 906 Kentucky Ave., San Antonio, Tex. 78201; Discalced Carmelite Fathers; 35,180.

Ave Maria (Polish), 6 times a year; 600 Doat St., Buffalo, N.Y. 14211; Felician Srs.; 5,844.

B

Bells of St. Ann, bm; Belcourt, N.D. 58316; St. Ann's Indian Mission; 24,429.

Benedictine Orient, bm; 2400 Maple Ave., Lisle, Ill. 60532; 8,349.

Benedictines, q; Mt. St. Scholastica, Atchison, Kans. 66002; 650.

Bernardine, The, bm (Oct.-June); Maryview, 647 Spring Mill Rd., Villanova, Pa. 19085; Bernardine Srs.; 14,000.

Best Sellers, semimonthly; Univ. of Scranton Library, Scranton, Pa, 18510; 2,668.

Better World, q; Belford, N.J. 07718; Mary Productions Guild; 10,000.

Bible Today, The, 6 times a year; Liturgical Press, Collegeville, Minn. 56321.

Bishop's Bulletin, The, m; 1900 S. Lake Ave., Sioux Falls, S.D. 57105; 23,500.

Brothers' Newsletter, q; Passionist Monastery, P.O. Box 150, West Springfield, Mass. 01089; for religious Brothers; 4,500.

C

Call Board, The, 5 times a year; 227 W. 45th St., New York, N.Y. 10036; Catholic Actors' Guild; 1,000.

Catechist, The, m (exc. Dec., June-Aug.); 38 W. 5th St., Dayton, O. 45402; 31,000.

Catholic Action News, m; 608 Broadway, Fargo, N. Dak. 58102; Fargo diocese; 22,064.

Catholic Aid News, m; 49 W. 9th St., St. Paul, Minn. 55102; 22,100.

Catholic Apostolate Newsletter, m (exc. July and Aug.); 5424 Blue Mound Rd., Milwaukee, Wis. 53208; Pallottine Fathers; 13,500.

Catholic Biblical Quarterly, q; 620 Michigan Ave., Washington, D.C. 20017; Catholic Biblical Assn.; 3,865.

Catholic Cemetery, The, m; 710 N. River Rd., Des Plaines, Ill. 60016; 1,676.

Catholic Charities Review, m (exc. July-Aug.), 1346 Connecticut Ave. N.W., Washington, D.C. 20036; 7,000.

CCH Echoes, q; 1400 State St., Alton, Ill. 62002; Catholic Children's Home; 250.

Catholic Digest, The, m; P.O. Box 3090, St. Paul, Minn. 55165; 533,677.

Catholic Family Leadej, bm; 1312 Massachusetts Ave. N.W., Washington, D.C. 20005; Family Life Division, USCC; 10,805.

Catholic Forester Magazine, bm; 305 W. Madison St., Chicago, Ill. 60606; Catholic Order of Foresters: 137

Catholic Historical Review, q; 620 Michigan Ave. N.E., Washington D.C. 20017; American Catholic Historical Assn.; 2,200.

Catholic Institutional Management, bm; 6305 Brookside Plaza, Kansas City, Mo. 64113; 39,458.

Catholic Journalist, The, bm; 432 Park Ave. S., New York, N.Y. 10016; Catholic Press Association; 1,736.

C.K. of A. Journal, m; 217 E. 8th St., Cincinnati, O. 45202; Catholic Knights of America; 18,500.

C.L. of C. Index, m; 195 E. Broad St., Columbus, O. 43215.

Catholic Lawyer, q; 96 Schermerhorn St., Brooklyn, N.Y. 11201; St. Thomas More Institute for Legal Research; 3,500.

Catholic Library World, m; 461 W. Lancaster Ave., Haverford, Pa. 19041; Catholic Library Association; 3,430.

Catholic Life Magazine, m (exc. July-Aug.); 9800 Oakland Ave., Detroit, Mich. 48211; PIME Missionaries; 15,746.

Catholic Mind, The, 10 times a year; 106 W. 56th St., New York, N.Y. 10019; 9,700.

Catholic Periodical and Literature Index, by; 461 W. Lancaster Ave., Haverford, Pa. 19041; Catholic Library Association; 1,978.

Catholic Press Directory, a; 432 Park Ave. S., New York, N.Y. 10016; Catholic Press Assn.; 2,225.

Catholic Quote, m; Dwight, Nebr. 68635; 5,670.

Catholic Review (Braille), m; 154 E. 23rd St., New York, N.Y. 10010; Xavier Society for the Blind; 1,780.

Catholic School Editor, The, q; 1135 W. Kilbourn Ave., Milwaukee, Wis. 53233; Catholic School Press Assn.; 600.

Catholic University of America Law Review, q; 620 Michigan Ave. N.E., Washington, D.C. 20017; 745.

Catholic War Veteran, bm; 2 Massachusetts Ave. N.W., Washington, D.C. 20001; 50,000.

Catholic Woman's Journal, m; 3835 Westminster Pl., St. Louis, Mo. 63108; 1,428.

Catholic Worker, 9 times a year; 36 E. First St., New York, N.Y. 10003; Dorothy Day; 85,000.

Catholic Workman, m; 107 N. Central Ave., New Prague, Minn. 56071; 8,250.

Catholic Youth Work Annual, a; 1312 Massachusetts Ave. N.W., Washington, D.C. 20005; 7,000.

Chicago Studies, 3 times a year; P.O. Box 665, Mundelein, Ill. 60060; 5,000.

Christopher News Notes, 7 times a year; 12 E. 48th St., New York, N.Y. 10017; The Christophers, Inc.; 1,250,000.

Classical Bulletin, 6 times a year; 221 N. Grand Blvd., St. Louis, Mo. 63103; 1,750.

Classical Folia, biennial; College of Holy Cross, Worcester, Mass. 01610; Institute of Early Christian Iberian Studies.

Claverite, The, bm; P.O. Box 1254, Birmingham, Ala. 35201; Knights of Peter Claver; 8,000.

Columban Mission, m (exc. June, Aug.); St. Columbans, Nebr. 68056; Columban Fathers; 280,000.

Columbia, m; One Columbus Plaza, New Haven, Conn. 06507; Knights of Columbus; 1,038,241.

Columbian, The, w; 188 W. Randolph St., Chicago, Ill. 60601; 26,337.

Columbian Squires, m; Columbus Plaza, New Haven, Conn. 06507; 24,518.

Comment/Media Today, 9 times a year; 39 Lackawanna Pl., Bloomfield, N.J. 07003; Christian Communications Apostolate; 2,500.

Commitment, q; 1307 S. Wabash Ave., Chicago, Ill. 60605; National Catholic Conference for Interracial Justice.

Commonweal, w; 232 Madison Ave., New York, N.Y. 10016; 31,111.

Community, q; 21 E. Van Buren St., Chicago, Ill. 60605; Friendship House; 1,700.

Consolata Missions, q; P.O. Box C, Somerset, N.J. 08873; 25,000.

Cord, The, m; St. Bonaventure University, St. Bonaventure, N.Y. 14778; 1,339.

Critic, The, bm; 180 N. Wabash Ave., Chicago, Ill. 60601; Thomas More Association; 31,215.

Cross and Crown, q; P.O. Box 627, Oak

Park, Ill. 60303; 8,745.

Cross My Heart, m; 62 Newton St., Waltham, Mass. 02154; Marist Missionary Sisters; 44,000.

Crossroads Radio, bm; 1089 Elm St., W. Springfield, Mass. 01089; 5,100.

Crusader's Almanac, The, q; 1400 Quincy St. N.E., Washington, D.C. 20017; Commissariat of the Holy Land; 105,000.

Cursillo Newsletter, m; P.O. Box 304, Reno, Nev. 89504; 1,500.

D

Dakota Catholic Action, m; 420 Raymond St., Bismarck, N. Dak. 58501; Bismarck diocese; 15,000.

Damien-Dutton Call, q; P.O. Box 1222; New Brunswick, N.J. 08903; 15,000.

Daystar, q; 172 Foster St., Brighton, Mass. 02135; Franciscan Missionary Sisters of Africa; 1,600.

De Sales World, The, q; 2200 Kentmere Pky., Wilmington, Del. 19899; 31,000.

Diakonia, q; Fordham Univ., Bronx, N.Y. 10458; John XXIII Center for Eastern Christian Studies; 1,021.

Divine Love, q; P.O. Box 24, Fresno, Calif. 93707.

Divine Word Messenger, q; Bay St. Louis, Miss. 39520; 15,000.

Divine Word Missionaries, q; Techny, Ill. 60082.

E

Educating in Faith, m; 335 Broadway, New York, N.Y. 10013; Catholic Negro-American Mission Board; 16,500.

Edmundite Newsletter, bm; 1428 Broad St., Selma, Ala. 36701; 71,709.

Emmanuel, m (bm July-Aug.); 194 E. 76th St., New York, N.Y. 10021; Priests' Eucharistic League; 20,560.

Encounter, q; 200 Lake St., Boston, Mass. 02135; Religious of the Cenacle; 9,000.

Eucharist, bm; 194 E. 76th St., New York, N.Y. 10021; 15,636.

Extension, m; 1307 S. Wabash Ave., Chicago, Il. 60605; Catholic Church Extension Society.

F

Family, m; 50 St. Paul's Ave., Boston, Mass. 02130; Daughters of St. Paul; 160,520.

Family Digest, m; Noll Plaza, Huntington, Ind. 46750; 160,520.

Family Friend, q; P.O. Box 5663, Milwaukee, Wis. 53211; 18,900.

Fatima Findings, m; 100 E. 20th St., Baltimore, Md. 21218; Reparation Society of the Immaculate Heart of Mary; 5,000.

Franciscan Herald, m; 1434 W. 51st St., Chicago, Ill. 60609; Third Order of St. Francis; 5,100.

Franciscan Message, m (exc. July-Aug.); Franciscan Publishers, Pulaski, Wis. 54162; 3,500.

F.M.A. Focus, q; P.O. Box 598, Mt. Vernon, N.Y. 10550; Franciscan Mission Associates; 406,251.

Franciscan Studies, a; St. Bonaventure, N.Y. 14778; Franciscan Institute; 694.

Fraternal Leader, bm; 305 W. 6th St., Erie, Pa. 16507; Loyal Christian Benefit Association; 59,204.

Freeing the Spirit, q; 1325 Massachusetts Ave. N.W., Washington, D.C. 20005; National Office for Black Catholics.

Friar, m; Butler, N.J. 07405; Franciscan Fathers; 22,700.

G-I

Glenmary's Challenge, q; 4119 Glenmary Terrace, Fairfield, Ohio 45014; Glenmary Home Missioners; 100,000.

Good Shepherd (Slovak and English), m; 205 Madison St., Passaic, N.J. 07055; Slovak Catholic Federation of America.

Grain and Fire, q; P.O. Box 178, Cottonport, La. 71327; Brothers of the Holy Eucharist; 600.

Guide, m; 2852 Broadway, New York, N.Y. 10025; Paulist Fathers; 5,500.

Homiletic and Pastoral Review, m; 86 Riverside Dr., New York, N.Y. 10024; 16,238.

Hospital Progress, m; 1438 S. Grand Blvd., St. Louis, Mo. 63104; Catholic Hospital Association; 11,916.

Immaculata, m; 8000 39th Ave., Kenosha, Wis. 53141; Franciscan Fathers.

Impact, 6 times a year; 1325 Massachesetts Ave. N.W., Washington, D.C. 20005; National Office for Black Catholics; 5,000.

Institute Journal, bm; 50 Oak St., San Francisco, Calif. 94102; Young Men's Institute; 10,000.

J-K

Jesuit, The, q; 39 E. 83rd St., New York, N.Y. 10028; 67,000.

Jesuit, The (New Orleans Edition), q; 1607 Pere Marquette Bldg., New Orleans, La. 70112; 36,000.

Jesuit Blackrobe, q; 3601 W. Fond du Lac Ave., Milwaukee, Wis. 53216; 55,000.

Jesuit Bulletin, 4 times a year; 4511 W. Pine Blvd., St. Louis, Mo. 63108; Jesuit Seminary and Mission Bureau; 67,000.

Josephite Harvest, The, bm; 1130 N. Calvert St., Baltimore, Md. 21202; Josephite Missionaries; 73,070.

Jurist, The, q; Catholic University of America, Washington, D.C. 20017; School of Canon Law; 2,200.

Katolicky Sokol (Catholic Falcon) (Slovak-English), w; 205 Madison St., Passaic, N.J. 07055; Slovak Catholic Sokol; 19,400.

Katolik, w; 1637 S. Allport St., Chicago, Ill. 60608; 5,000.

Kenosis, published irregularly; 82 Ponus Ridge Rd., New Canaan, Conn. 06840; Byzantine Franciscan Fathers.

Kinship, q; 4580 Colerain Ave., Cincinnati,

O. 45223; Glenmary Home Mission Sisters; 17,600.

Knights of St. John, q; 1603 S. Bedford Ave., Evansville, Ind. 47713; 8,000.

Kolping Banner, m; 125 N. Stratton Lane, Mt. Prospect, Ill. 60056; Catholic Kolping Society; 2,162.

L

Laivas (Lithuanian), biweekly; 4545 W. 63rd St., Chicago, Ill. 60629.

Lamp, The / A Christian Unity Magazine, m; Graymoor, Garrison, N.Y. 10524; Friars of the Atonement; 34,000.

Land of Cotton, q; 2048 W. Fairview Ave., Montgomery, Ala. 36108; 74,897.

Latin America Calls, 9 times a year; P.O. Box 6066, Washington, D.C. 20005; Division of Latin America, USCC; 124,000.

Leaves, bm; 23715 Ann Arbor Trail, Dearborn Heights, Mich. 48127; Mariannhill Fathers; 196,000.

Liguorian, m; 1 Liguori Rd., Liguori, Mo. 63057; Redemptorist Fathers; 362,734.

Linacre Quarterly, q; 2825 N. Mayfair Rd., Milwaukee, Wis. 53222; Federation of Catholic Physicians Guilds; 9,720.

Listen, bm; 770 Centre St., Newton, Mass. 02158; Catholic Guild for All the Blind.

Little Bronzed Angel, m; St. Paul's Indian Mission, Marty, S.D. 53761; Benedictine Fathers; 38,500.

Little Flower Magazine, bm; 1125 S. Walker, Oklahoma City, Okla. 73126; Discalced Carmelite Fathers; 18,000.

Liturgical Arts, q; 521 Fifth Ave., New York, N.Y. 10017; Liturgical Arts Society, Inc.; 2,400.

Living Light, The, q; Our Sunday Visitor, Inc., Huntington, Ind. 46750, publisher; edited by National Center of Religious Education — CCD, USCC; 5,500.

M

Marian, The, m; 45 W. 63rd St., Chicago, Ill. 60629; Marian Fathers.

Marian Helpers Bulletin, q; Stockbridge, Mass. 01262; Association of Marian Helpers and of the Congregation of Marian Fathers; 520,000.

Maronite Newsletter, bm; 11470 Kercheval, Detroit, Mich. 48214; St. Maron of Detroit diocese; 4,500.

Marquette University Magazine, q; 1834 W. Wisconsin Ave., Milwaukee, Wis. 53233; 55,000.

Marriage, m; Abbey Press, St. Meinrad, Ind. 47577; 72,996.

Mary Magazine and Aylesford News, bm; Cass Ave. N. at I-55, Westmont, Ill. 60559; Carmelite Fathers; 22,575.

Maryknoll Magazine, m; Maryknoll, N.Y. 10545; Catholic Foreign Mission Society; more than 300,000.

Master's Work, q; Waukegan and Willow Rds., Techny, Ill. 60082; Holy Spirit Missionary Sisters; 8,500.

Mediatrix, q; 6301 12th Ave., Brooklyn, N.Y. 11219; 6,000.

Medical Mission News, bm; 10 W. 17th St., New York, N.Y. 10011; Catholic Medical Mission Board, Inc. 35,000.

Men of Malvern, bm; Malvern, Pa. 19355; 24,000.

Mercy Profile, q; 2303 Grandview Ave., Cincinnati, O. 45206; Sisters of Mercy; 17,000.

Messenger, The, m; 16010 Detroit Ave., Lakewood, O. 44107; 11,000.

Messenger of the Holy Family, bm; 2500 Ashby Rd., St. Louis, Mo. 63114; 4,600.

MHS Review, bm; 232 S. Home Ave., Pittsburgh, Pa. 15202.

Miesiecznik Franciszkanski (Polish), m; Franciscan Printery, Pulaski, Wis. 54162; Franciscan Fathers; 14,100.

Mill Hill World, q; Albany, N.Y. 12203; 9,000.

Miraculous Medal, The, q; 475 E. Chelten Ave., Philadelphia, Pa. 19144; Central Association of the Miraculous Medal; 111,522.

Mission, bm; 366 Fifth Ave., New York, N.Y. 10001; Society for Propagation of the Faith; 3,000,000.

Mission, bm; Red Lion and Knight Rds., Philadelphia, Pa. 19114; Sisters of the Blessed Sacrament; 7,400.

Mission Helper, The, q; 1001 W. Joppa Rd., Baltimore, Md. 21204; Mission Helpers of the Sacred Heart; 7,400.

Missionhurst, 9 times a year; 4651 N. 25th St., Arlington, Va. 22207; Immaculate Heart of Mary Mission Society, Inc.; 433,000.

Mission Intercom, 10 times a year; 1325 Massachusetts Ave. N.W., Washington, D.C. 20005; US Catholic Mission Council; 3,000.

Modern Schoolman, The, q; 3700 W. Pine Blvd., St. Louis, Mo. 63108; St. Louis University; 800.

Momentum, 4 times a year; Suite 350, One Dupont Circle, Washington, D.C. 20036; National Catholic Educational Association; 16,800.

Mother Cabrini Messenger, bm; 2520 Lakeview Ave., Chicago, Ill. 60614; Mother Cabrini League; 70,000.

Mount Loretto Review, a; 6581 Hylan Blvd., Staten Island, N.Y. 10309; 200,000.

Musart, bm; 4637 Eastern Ave. N.E., Washington, D.C. 20018; National Catholic Music Educators Association; 4,837.

Mwangaza, q; 172 Foster St., Brighton, Mass. 02135; Franciscan Missionary Sisters for Africa; 1,600.

My Daily Visitor, m; Noll Plaza, Huntington, Ind. 46750; Our Sunday Visitor, Inc.; 21,572.

N

Narod (Czech), w; 1637 S. Allport St., Chicago, Ill. 60608; Benedictine Abbey Press; 5,000.

National Catholic Forester, bm; 59 E. Van Buren St., Chicago, Ill. 60605; 60,000.

New Catholic World, bm; 1865 Broadway, New York, N.Y. 10023; 16,000.

New Covenant, m; P.O. Box 102, Main St. Station, Ann Arbor, Mich. 48107; Charismatic Renewal Services.

New Scholasticism, q; Notre Dame, Ind. 46556; American Catholic Philosophical Association; 2,650.

News and Views, q; 3900 Westminster Pl., St. Louis, Mo. 63108; Sacred Heart Program; 200,000.

North American Voice of Fatima, m; 1023 Swann Rd., Youngstown, N.Y. 14174; 18,013.

Notre Dame Focus, q; Jeffrey's Neck Rd., Ipswich, Mass. 01938; Sisters of Notre Dame de Namur; 3,963.

O

Oblate World and Voice of Hope, bm; 350 Jamaica Way, Boston, Mass. 02130; Oblates of Mary Immaculate; 35,000.

Official Guide to Catholic Educational Institutions, a; 200 Sunrise Highway, Rockville Centre, L.I., N.Y. 11570; 51,121.

OMI Missions, bm; P.O. Box 96, San Antonio, Tex. 78291; 25,000.

Orphan's Messenger and Advocate of the Blind, q; P.O. Box 288, Jersey City, N.J. 07303; St. Joseph's Home; 94,701.

Our Lady of the Snows, bm; 15 S. 59th St., Belleville, Ill. 62223; Shrine of Our Lady of the Snows; 305,541.

Our Lady's Digest, bm; Olivet, Ill. 61860; La Salette Fathers.

Our Lady's Missionary, m; La Salette Shrine, Ipswich, Mass. 01938; La Salette Fathers; 60,000.

P

Pacemaker, bm; 500 17th Ave., Seattle, Wash. 98020; Providence Hospital; 1,800.

Padre's Trail, 10 times a year; St. Michael's Mission, St. Michael, Ariz. 86511; Franciscan Fathers; 6,707.

Paraclete, 5 times a year; P.O. Box 2000, Wheaton, Md. 20902; Holy Ghost Fathers. 175,000.

Parent-Educator, m (during school year); Twenty-Third Publications, P.O. Box 180, West Mystic, Conn. 06388.

Parish Visitor, q; P.O. Box 658, Monroe, N.Y. 10950; Parish Visitors of Mary Immaculate; 3,000.

Passionist Orbit, q; 5700 N. Harlem Ave., Chicago, Ill. 60631; Passionist Fathers; 1,832.

Pastoral Life, m; Route 224, Canfield, Ohio 44406; Society of St. Paul; 6,652.

Paulist Fathers News, bm; 415 W. 59th St., New York, N.Y. 10019; 15,950.

People, m; 1312 Massachusetts Ave. N.W., Washington, D.C. 20005; National Council of Catholic Laity; 30,000.

Perpetual Help World, q; 294 E. 150th St., Bronx, N.Y. 10451; Redemptorists.

Philosophy Today, q; Carthagena Station, Celina, Ohio 48522; 1,325.

Pilgrim, q; Jesuit Fathers, Auriesville, N.Y. 12016; Shrine of Our Lady of Martyrs; 25,000.

Pope Speaks, The, q; 3622 12th St. N.E., Washington, D.C. 20017; John O'Neill; 6,185.

Priatel Dietok (Children's Friend) (Slovak), m; 205 Madison St., Passaic, N.J. 07055; Junior Catholic Sokol; 7,600.

Priest, The m; Noll Plaza, Huntington, Ind. 46750; Our Sunday Visitor, Inc.; 12,255.

Professional Placement Newsnotes, bm; 10 W. 17th St., New York, N.Y. 10011; 5,500.

Providence Sister, The, 4 times a year; Providence Heights, Issaquah, Wash. 98027; Sisters of Charity of Providence; 15,000.

Q-R

Queen, bm; 40 S. Saxon Ave., Bay Shore, N.Y. 11706; Montfort Fathers; 12,000.

Reign of the Sacred Heart, m; Hales Corners, Wis. 53130; 90,000.

Religion Teacher's Journal, 9 times a year; P.O. Box 180, W. Mystic, Conn. 06388; 40,100.

Religious Book Guide, bm; 200 Sunrise Highway, Rockville Centre, N.Y. 11570; 9,747.

Renascence, q; Marquette University, Milwaukee, Wis. 53233; Catholic Renascence Society; 782.

Response, The, bm; (Sept.-June); 39 Lackawanna Pl., Bloomfield, N.J. 07003; International Liaison of Newark archdiocese; 500.

Review for Religious, bm; 539 N. Grand Blvd., St. Louis, Mo. 63103; 21,784.

Review of Politics, q; Univ. of Notre Dame, Notre Dame, Ind. 46566; 2,500.

Review of Social Economy, semiannual; 2323 N. Seminary Ave., Chicago, Ill. 60614; Association for Social Economics; 750.

Roses and Gold from Our Lady of the Ozarks, m; 1749 Grand Ave., Carthage, Mo. 64336; 37,500.

Roze Maryi (Polish). b; Eden Hill, Stockbridge, Mass. 01262; 8,400.

S

Sacred Music, q; Route 2, Box 1, Irving, Tex. 75060; 1,800.

St. Anthony Messenger, m; 1615 Republic St., Cincinnati, O. 45210; Franciscan Fathers; 236,854.

Salesian Bulletin, bm; 148 Main St., New Rochelle, N.Y. 10802; Salesian Fathers; 78,000.

Salesian Missions, bm; 148 Main St., New Rochelle, N.Y. 10802; Salesians of St. John Bosco; 750,000.

Salvatorian, The, q; Society of the Divine Savior, Salvatorian Center, Wis. 53061; 183,414.

Sandal Prints, bm; 1820 Mt. Elliott Ave.,

Detroit, Mich. 48207; Capuchin Fathers; 10,327.

School Guide for Catholic Students, a; 68 W. Broad St., Mt. Vernon, N.Y. 10552; 110,000.

School Sister, The, q; Notre Dame of the Lake, Mequon, Wis. 53092; 45.119.

Science Studies, a; St. Bonaventure University, St. Bonaventure, N.Y. 14778.

Scouting Bulletin of the Catholic Committee on Scouting, q; North Brunswick, N.J. 08902; 8,500.

Serenity, q; 601 Maiden Choice Lane, Baltimore, Md. 21228; Little Sisters of the Poor.

Share, m (Sept.-June); Maryknoll, N.Y. 10545; Maryknoll Junior Edition.

Shepherd's Call, The, q; 601 Second St. S.W., Albuquerque, N.M. 87103; 7,750.

Sign, The, m; Monastery Place, Union City, N.J. 07087; Passionist Fathers; 155,000.

Silent Advocate, 6 times a year; St. Rita School for the Deaf, 1720 Glendle-Milfort Rd., Cincinnati, O. 45215.

Sister Formation Bulletin, q; 1325 Massachusetts Ave. N.W., Washington, D.C. 20005; 11,000.

Sisters Today, M; St. John's Abbey, Collegeville, Minn. 65321; 22,511.

Social Justice Review, m (exc. July-Aug.); 3835 Westminster Pl., St. Louis, Mo. 63108; Catholic Central Union of America; 1,850.

Sociological Analysis, q; 1403 North St. Mary's St., San Antonio, Tex. 78215.

Sodalis, 9 times a year; St. Mary's College, Orchard Lake, Mich. 48033; Sts. Cyril and Methodius Seminary; 1,546.

Sons of Mary Missionary Society, 4 times a year; 567 Salem End Rd., Framingham, Mass. 01701; 3,000.

Sophia, bm (exc. July-Aug.); 19 Dartmouth St., West Newton, Mass. 02165; Melkite Exarchate in US; 6,900.

Soul, bm; Ave Maria Institute, Washington, N.J. 07882; Blue Army; 71,000.

Spirit, q; Seton Hall University, South Orange, N.J. 07079; poetry magazine; 831.

Spirit and Life, m; Clyde, Mo. 64432; Benedictine Convent of Perpetual Adoration; 8,732.

Spiritual Book News, 7 times a year; Notre Dame, Ind. 46556; 5,011.

Spiritual Life, q; 2131 Lincoln Rd. N.E., Washington, D.C. 20002; Discalced Carmelites; 9,000.

Spotlite, 6 times a year; Aurora, Ill. 60507; Missionaries of the Sacred Heart; 50,000.

Squires Newsletter, m; Columbus Plaza, New Haven, Conn. 06507; Columbian Squires; 14,550.

T

Theological Studies, q; 475 Riverside Dr., New York, N.Y.; Jesuit Fathers; 5,863.

Theology Digest, 4 times a year; 3701 Lindell Blvd., St. Louis, Mo. 63108; 8,956.

Theresian, The, 3 times a year, 5326 E.

Pershing Ave., Scottsdale, Ariz. 85254; 8,000.

Thomist, The, q; 487 Michigan Ave. N.E., Washington, D.C. 20017; Dominican Fathers; 1,100.

Thought, q; 441 E. Fordham Rd., Bronx, N.Y. 10458; Fordham University; 1,815.

Today's Catholic Teacher, m (Sept.-May); 38 W. 5th St., Dayton, O. 45402; 70,000.

Today's Parish, bm (Jan.-Nov.); Twenty-Third Publications, P.O. Box 180, West Mystic, Conn. 06388.

Trinity Missions, 5 times a year; P.O. Box 30, Silver Spring, Md. 20910; more than 350,000.

Triumph, m; 278 Broadview Ave., Warrenton, Va. 22186; 8,000.

U-V

L'Union (French), q; 1 Social St., Woonsocket, R.I. 02895; 35,000.

UNIREA, The Union (Romanian and English), m; 4309 Olcott Ave., East Chicago, Ind. 46312; 2,000.

U.S. Catholic/Jubilee, m; 221 W. Madison St., Chicago, Ill. 60606; Claretian Fathers; 45,444.

Verona Fathers Missions, bm; 2104 St. Michael's St., Cincinnati, O. 45204; 26,000.

Victorian, q; 780 Ridge Rd., Lackawanna, N.Y. 14218; Our Lady of Victory Homes for Charity; 25,987.

Vox Regis, 2 times a year; St. Bonaventure, N.Y. 14778; Christ the King Seminary; 900.

W-Z

Waif's Messenger, m; 1140 W. Jackson Blvd., Chicago, Ill. 60607; Mission of Our Lady of Mercy; 48,752.

Way — Catholic Viewpoints, 10 times a year; 109 Golden Gate Ave., San Francisco, Calif. 94102; Franciscan Fathers of California, Inc.; 8,404.

Western Catholic Union Record, m; 906 W.C.U. Bldg., Quincy, Ill. 62301; Western Catholic Union; 19,428.

White Fathers Magazine, bm; 1622 21st St. N.W., Washington, D.C. 20009; Society of Missionaries of Africa (White Fathers); 15,571.

Word of God, The, w; 2187 Victory Blvd., Staten Island, N.Y. 10314; Society of St. Paul; 40,000.

Working for Boys, q; 601 Winchester St., Newton Highlands, Mass. 02161; Xaverian Brothers; 28,789.

Worldmission, q; 366 5th Ave., New York, N.Y. 10001; Society for the Propagation of the Faith; 2,000.

Worship, 10 times a year; St. John's Abbey, Collegeville, Minn. 56321; 9,643.

Xaverian, The, q; 10516 Summit Ave., Kensington, Md. 20795; Xaverian Brothers; 19,000.

Xaverian Missions Newsletter, 9 times a year; 12 Helene Ct., Wayne, N.J. 07470; Xaverian Missionary Fathers; 16,500.

Youth — Program Service, bm; 1312 Massachusetts Ave. N.W., Washington, D.C. 20005; 7,500.

Zeal, q; St. Elizabeth Mission Society of the Sisters of St. Francis, Allegany, N.Y. 14706; 18,000.

Books

The Official Catholic Directory, annual, P.J. Kenedy and Sons, 866 Third Ave., New York, N.Y. 10022; circulation 15,239. First edition, 1817.

The Catholic Almanac, annual; Our Sunday Visitor, Inc., Huntington, Ind. 46750, publisher; editorial offices, 620 Route 3, Clifton, N.J. 07013. First edition, 1904. (See publication history.)

The American Catholic Who's Who, biennial; NC Publications, Inc., Press Bldg., Suite 932, Washington, D.C. 20004. First volume, 1934-35.

International English Language Periodicals

Australasian Catholic Record, q; St. Patrick's Seminary, Manly, New South Wales, Australia.

Biblical Theology, tri-annual; Silverlea, 9 Hazelwood Park, Newtonabbey, County Antrim, Ireland.

Canadian Journal of Theology, q; University of Toronto Press, Toronto 5, Ontario, Canada.

Christ to the World; Via G, Nicoterra 31, 00195, Rome, Italy.

Clergy Review, m; 48 Great Peter St., London, S.W. 1, England.

Doctrine and Life, m; Dominican Publications, St. Saviour's, Dublin 1, Ireland.

Downside Review, q; Newman Bookshop, 87 St. Aldates, Oxford, England.

Dublin Review, q; 14 Howick Place, London, S.W. 1, England.

Eastern Churches Review, semi-annual; 9 Alfred St., Oxford, England.

Furrow, m; St. Patrick's College, Maynooth, Ireland.

Heythrop Journal q; Heythrop College, Oxon, England (US agent, Fordham University, Bronx, N.Y. 10458).

IDOC International, 22 times a year; 432 Park Ave. S., New York, N.Y. 10016.

International Philosophical Quarterly, q; Fordham University, Bronx, N.Y. 10458.

Irish Ecclesiastical Record, m; Browne and Nolan, Ltd., Richview Press, Clonskeogh, Dublin 4, Ireland.

Irish Theological Quarterly, q; St. Patrick's College, Maynooth, Ireland.

Liturgy, q; M. Lamigeon, 55 Station Road, Beaconsfield, Bucks, England.

L'Osservatore Romano, w; Vatican City.

Louvain Studies, Semi-annual; Naamsestraat 100, Louvain, Belguim.

Lumen Vitae, q; International Center for Studies in Religious Education, 184, rue Washington, Brussels 5, Belgium.

Month, m; 114 Mount St., London, W. 1, England.

New Blackfriars, m; St. Dominic Priory, South Hampton Rd., London, N.W. 5, England.

One in Christ, q; Benedictine Convent, Priory Chase, London N. 14, England.

Philosophical Studies, annual; St. Patrick's College, Maynooth, Ireland.

Recusant History, tri-annual; Catholic Record Society, 114 Mount St., London, W. 1, England.

Religion and Society, q; Christian Institute for the Study of Religion and Society, 19 Miller Rd., Bangalore 6, South India.

Sursum Corda, bm; 47 Victoria St., Waverly, N.S.W., Australia 2024.

Tablet, w; 48 Great Peter St., London, S.W. 1, England.

Teaching All Nations, q; East Asian Pastoral Institute, Box 1815, Manila, Philippines.

Theology, m; S.P.C.K. Holy Trinity Church, Marylebone Rd., London, N.W. 1, England.

Catholic News Agencies

(Source: The Catholic Press Association.)

Argentina: Agencia Informativa Catolica Argentina (AIC), Rodriguez Pena 846, Casilla de Correo Central 2886, Buenos Aires.

Austria: Katholische Presse-Agentur (Kathpress), Wollzeile 2a, Vienna 1.

Belgium: Centre d'Information de Presse (CIP), 9, rue Guimard, Brussels.

Germany: Katholische Nachrichten Agentur (KNA), Kaiser Friedrichstrasse, 9, Bonn.

Hong Kong: Catholic Centre Press Bureau, P.O. Box 2984, Hong Kong.

India: Catholic News of India (CNI), 4 Rajnivas Marg, Delhi 6.

Indonesia: Agence "PAX," Dj. Kramat Raya 134, Djakarta IV/5.

Japan: TO-SEI, 10, 6-Brancho, Chiyoda-ku, Tokyo.

Mexico: Documentacion e Informacion Catolica, Aristoteles 239, Mexico 1.

Central National de Communicacion Social (CENCOS(, Medellin 33, Mexico 7.

Netherlands: Katholiek Nederlands Persbureau (KNP), Anna Paulownastraat 48, The Hague.

Pakistan: Catholic News Service (CNSP), 111 Depot Lines, Karachi 3.

Peru: Noticias Aliadas, Apartado 5377, Lima.

Spain: Prensa Asociada (PA), Alfonso XI, 4—Apartado 14530, Madrid 14.

Switzerland: Katholische Internationale Presse-Agentur (KIPA), Case Postale 443, Fribourg 1.

Taiwan: Catholic I-Shi News Agency, 120 Yun-Ho St., Taipeh.

Tanzania: News Letter, P.O. Box 3133, Dar-es-Salaam.

Uganda: Catholic News Bulletin, P.O. Box 2886, Kampala.

United States of America: NC News Service (NC), 1312 Massachusetts Ave. N.W., Washington, D.C. 20005.

Yugoslavia: Aktuslnosti Krscanska Sadasnjost (AKSA), Yugoslav Catholic Center for Documentation and Information, Belgrade.

Zaire: Documentation et Information Africaine (DIA), B.P. 2598, Kinshasa.

Missions: Agenzia Internationale Fides (AIF), Palazzo di Propagande Fide, Via di Propaganda I-c, Rome, Italy.

Agencies distributing news related to Catholicism as well as other news are:

France: Agence France Presse (AFP), 13 Place de la Bourse, Paris 2e.

Italy: Agenzia Nazionale Stampa Associata (ANSA), Via Propaganda 27, Rome.

Spain: LOGOS, Mateo Inurria 15, Apartado 466, Madrid—16.

United States of America: Religious News Service (RNS), 43 W. 57th St., New York, N.Y. 10019.

US Press Services

NC News Service (NC), established in 1920, provides a worldwide daily news report, fea-

ture and photo services to more than 200 Catholic publications in the US and abroad; "Origins," documentary and text service; "Catholic Trends," a fortnightly newsletter to church administrators; "Know Your Faith," a weekly religious education package. NC is represented in all US dioceses and more than 20 foreign countries. It is a division of the Communications Department, United States Catholic Conference, with offices at 1312 Massachusetts Ave. N.W., Washington, D.C. 20005. The director is A.E.P. Wall.

Religious News Service (RNS) provides Catholic and other religious news in daily foreign and domestic reports, photos and features; "The Religious News Reporter," a weekly 15-minute radio and/or TV package; "The Week in Religion," a feature. RNS was inaugurated in 1933 by the National Conference of Christians and Jews as an independent news agency. Its offices are located at 43 W. 57th St., New York, N.Y. 10019. Lillian R. Block is managing editor.

Eastern Rite Information Service (ER), for Eastern Church news; 2208 W. Chicago Ave., Chicago, Ill. 60622.

Catholic Press Features (CPF), for articles and columns; Boston Rd., Bellrose, N.Y. 11426.

CATHOLIC WRITERS' MARKET

(Source: Almanac survey.)

Editors call the following suggestions to the attention of writers:

Manuscripts should be typewritten, double-spaced, on one side of the page.

Writers should know the editorial policy, purpose and style of the publication to which they submit manuscripts. Sample copies may easily be obtained, often for the mere cost of postage. Some editors suggest that writers send outlines of proposed material, in order to facilitate editorial decision and direction. "Timely" copy should be submitted considerably in advance of the date of proposed publication; some editors advise a period of three months. Authors are urged to avoid sermonizing. Writers should not expect extensive criticism of their work, although they should profit from advice and direction when these are given. Editors are not required to state their reasons for rejecting manuscripts. Replies regarding the acceptance or rejection of copy are usually made within a few weeks.

All writers should send to editors stamped, self-addressed envelopes for the return of material. Those who write to Canadian editors may use international reply coupons, not US stamps.

Payment is made on acceptance or publication. Rates are sometimes variable because of the reputation of the writer, the quality and length of the manuscript, the amount of editorial work required for its final preparation.

America: 106 W. 56th St., New York, N.Y.

10019. Ed., Rev. Donald R. Campion, S.J. Weekly, circulation 65,000; $10 per year.

ARTICLES on important public issues evaluated scientifically and morally; serious and authenticated articles on family life, education, religion; occasionally, "thought" pieces; 1,000-2,000 words—3¢ a word. VERSE, short and modern, befitting a Catholic publication but not necessarily religious —$7.50 and up. No fiction.

American Ecclesiastical Review: 620 Michigan Ave. N.E., Washington, D.C. 20017. Editor-in-chief, Bro. James P. Clifton, C.F.X. Monthly, exc. July-Aug., circulation 3,000; $10 per year.

ARTICLES, mostly theological: 3,000 words—$4 per page.

Annals of Good St. Anne de Beaupre, The: Basilica of St. Anne, Quebec, Canada. Ed., Rev. J. C. Nadeau, C.SS.R. Monthly, circulation 78,000; $2 per year.

FICTION: Stories of general Catholic interest, preferably with slant on devotion to St. Anne; 1,500-1,800 words — 2¢ a word. ARTICLES of solid general interest to Catholics: on aspects of devotion to St. Anne, relative to history of the devotion in North America or elsewhere: on educational or social problems, or situations that should be of concern to all — especially Christians: 1,200-1,800 words — 2¢ a word, Payment on acceptance; report within a month.

Annals of the Holy Childhood: P.O. Box 6758, Pittsburgh, Pa. 15212. Ed., Rev. Vernon F. Gallagher, C.S.Sp. Eight issues a year, circulation 360,000; $1 per year.

FICTION and ARTICLES with mission themes suitable for children: 600-800 words — usual rates.

Catechist, The: 38 W. Fifth St., Dayton, O. 45402. Ed., Rod Brownfield. Monthly Sept. through May (exc. Dec.), circulation 31,000; $5 per year.

ARTICLES of interest to teachers of religion in parochial schools and CCD programs: 1,500-1,800 words — rate varies. PHOTOGRAPHS, black and white — rate varies.

Catholic Digest: P.O. Box 3090, St. Paul, Minn. 55165. Mss. to Rev. Kenneth Ryan, editor. Monthly, circulation 580,000; $3.97 per year.

ARTICLES, factual, of interest to Catholics: 1,500-2,500 words — $200 and up !reprint magazine, uses only two or three original ms per month). PICTURE STORIES, $75 and up. SPECIAL DEPARTMENTS — Open Door, In Our Parish, Hearts Are Trumps, Flights of Fancy, In Our House: short incidents — nominal prices paid to contributors. No fiction or verse.

Catholic Free Press: 247 Mill St. Worcester, Jr. Weekly, circulation 37,469; $5 per year. Official newspaper of the Diocese of Worcester.

ARTICLES on liturgical subjects, domestic and world affairs, etc.; illustrated features and human interest articles: 500-3,000 words $7-$25. No fiction.

Columban Mission: St. Columbans, Nebr. 68056. Exec. Ed., James Feely. Monthly (exc. June, Aug.); circulation 280,000; $1 per year.

ARTICLES mostly staff written: occasionally accept feature or factual articles on social and religious aspects of Oriental and Latin American life: 2,000 words — $70-$100. PHOTOGRAPHS of Oriental and Latin American subjects and photo stories — $5 each.

Columbia: Columbus Plaza, New Haven, Conn. 06507. Ed., Elmer Von Feldt. Monthly, circulation 1,038,241; $2 per year. Official organ of the Knights of Columbus.

ARTICLES dealing with current events, social problems, Catholic apostolic activities: 1,000-3,000 words (must be accompanied by glossy photos) — $100 to $300. FICTION, Christian viewpoint: up to 3,000 words — up to $300. SATIRE: 1,000 words — $100. CARTOONS, pungent, wordless humor — $25. COVERS — $500.

Commonweal: 232 Madison Ave., New York, N.Y. 10016. Ed., James O'Gara. Weekly, circulation 30,000; $14 per year.

FICTION, seldom: up to 2,500 words — 2¢ a word. ARTICLES, political, religious and literary subjects: 1,000-3,000 words — 2¢ a word. VERSE, serious poetry of high literary merit — about 40¢ a line.

Cross and Crown: 6851 S. Bennett Ave., Chiago, Ill. 60649. Ed., Very Rev. John J.

McDonald, O.P. Quarterly, circulation 8,371; $4 per year.

ARTICLES concerning any phase of the spiritual life: minimum 3,000 words—$4 a page. No fiction or poetry.

Crusader's Almanac: Franciscan Monastery, 1400 Quincy St. N.E., Washington, D.C. 20017. Ed., Rev. Paschal Kinsel, O.F.M. Quarterly, circulation 105,000; 50¢ per year.

ARTICLES about the Holy Land, Bible and Crusades given preference — 1¢ a word.

Divine Word Messenger: 201 Ruella Ave., Bay Saint Louis, Miss. 39520. Ed., Rev. George G. Wilson, S.V.D. Quarterly, circulation 15,000; $2 per year.

Review Catholic Church's progress in southern missions of Divine Word Missionaries, to win support for this apostolate.

ARTICLES: Catholic Church and American Negro; also general, social, religious, pious, moral themes: 500-1,500 words — 2¢ a word.

Emmanuel; 194 E. 76th Street, New York, N.Y. 10021. Editor-in-Chief, Rev. Raymond A. Tartre, S.S.S. Monthly, bimonthly July-Aug., circulation 20,560; $3 per year.

ARTICLES, clerical spirituality, Eucharistic, pastoral, theological, Scriptural: 2,000-3,000 words — $40.

Eucharist: 194 E. 76th St., New York, N.Y. 10021. Ed., Rev. William J. O'Halloran, S.S.S. Bimonthly, circulation 15,636; $3 per year.

ARTICLES, presenting meaning of Eucharist in Catholic spirituality: average length 1,500 words — 2-3¢ a word.

Family Digest: Noll Plaza, Huntington, Ind. 46750. Ed., John F. Laughlin. Monthly, circulation 160,520; $5 per year.

ARTICLES oriented to the young and growing Catholic family; personality profiles, social concerns, education, but especially family interrelationships; 1,000-1,200 words maximum — 4¢ a word and up. PHOTOS, professional quality b/w and limited color — $5 each and up; PHOTO STORIES — same rates. CARTOONS — $10 each for exclusives.

Franciscan Message: Franciscan publishers, Pulaski, Wis. 54162, Ed., Rev. Richard Tulko, O.F.M. Monthly (except July-Aug.), circulation 3,500; $3 per year.

ARTICLES, factual, current Catholic events, educational, spiritual: 1,500-1,800 words 1¢-2¢ a word.

Friar: Butler, N.J. 07405. Ed., Rev. Rudolf Harvey, O.F.M. Monthly (bimonthly July-Aug.), circulation 22,700; $5 per year.

FICTION, Franciscan themes either historical or current: 2,000 words. ARTICLES, Franciscan themes, current events, biography, popular instruction: 2,000 words. Rates vary. CARTOONS.

Hospital Progress: 1438 S. Grand Blvd., St. Louis, Mo. 63104. Ed., H. R. Bryden. Monthly, circulation 17,000; $7 per year.

Official organ of the Catholic Hospital Association.

ARTICLES, hospital-oriented; administrative procedures and theories; hospital departmental services: 1,500-5,000 words — $1 per column inch. BOOK REVIEWS, hospital oriented — payment by agreement.

Institute Journal: 50 Oak St., San Francisco, Calif. 94102. Ed., James R. Mullen. Bimonthly, $1 per year.

FICTION — no fixed rate. PHOTOGRAPHS — $15.

Josephite Harvest, The: 1130 N. Calvert St., Baltimore, Md. 21202. Ed., Rev. John G. Barnett, S.S.J. Bimonthly; circulation 73,070; $1 per year.

ARTICLES concerning the missions: 1¢ a word, and up — by previous arrangement only.

The Lamp/A Christian Unity Magazine: Graymoor, Garrison, N.Y. 10524. Ed., Rev. Charles Angell. Monthly, circulation 34,000; $4 per year.

ARTICLES: Nonfiction dealing with ecumenism on popular level: 1,500-2,000 words — 2½¢ a word. No fiction, poetry or art.

Living Light, The: Published by Our Sunday Visitor, Huntington, Indiana 46750. Editorial offices, National Center of Religious Education-CCD, 1312 Massachusetts Ave. N.W., Washington D.C. 20005. Quarterly, circulation 5,500; $8 per year.

ARTICLES on religious education, catechetics, Scripture: under 2,000 words — 5¢ per word. BOOK REVIEWS: 500 words — 3¢ per word.

Marian Helpers Bulletin: Eden Hill, Stockbridge, Mass. 01262. Ed., Bro. Robert M. Doyle, M.I.C. Quarterly, circulation over 525,000; $1 per year.

ARTICLES of general interest on devotional, spiritual, moral and social topics: 300-1,200 words — $25-$35 per articls.

Marriage: Abbey Press, St. Meinrad, Ind. 47577. Ed., John J. McHale, Monthly, circulation 63,000; $5 per year.

FICTION: Use only about 10 a year. Should deal with the relationship between husband and wife: up to 2,000 words. ARTICLES: Interviews with marriage authorities and interesting couples, profiles, personal essays on marriage: maximum 2,500 words — 5¢ a word minimum.

Maryknoll: Maryknoll, N.Y. 10545. Ed., Rev. Donald J. Casey, M.M. Monthly, circulation more than 300,000; $1.00 per year.

ARTICLES must apply in some way to the hopes and aspirations, the culture, the problems and challenges of peoples in Asia, Africa and Latin America: 1,000-1,500 words — average payment, $100. Outline wanted before submission of material. PHOTOS: More interested in photo stories than in individual black and whites and color transparencies. Photo stories — up to $150, black and white; up to $200, color. Individual photos — $15,

black and white; $25, color. Transparencies returned after use. Query to be made before sending photos.

Messenger of the Sacred Heart, The: 68 Broadview Ave., Toronto 8, Ont., Canada. Ed., Rev. F. J. Powers, S.J. Monthly, circulation 18,000; $2.50 per year.

FICTION: stories which appeal to men, written with humor—good family reading: maximum, 2,000 words — 2¢ a word. ARTICLES of Catholic interest: 2,500 words — 2¢ a word Payment upon acceptance.

Miraculous Medal, The: 475 E. Chelten Ave., Philadelphia, Pa. 19144. Ed., Rev. Donald L. Doyle, C.M. Quarterly, circulation 112,000.

FICTION, of general interest. Catholic in principle: 1,500-2,000 words — 2¢ a word and up. VERSE, religious in theme or turn; preferably about Our Lady: maximum 20 lines — 50¢ a line and up. Payment on acceptance. No articles.

My Daily Visitor: Noll Plaza, Huntington, Ind. 46750. Mng. Ed., Paul A. Manoski. Monthly, circulation 21,572; $3 per year.

A pocket-sized booklet of reflections for each day of the month, combined with Mass prayers for the Sundays and holy days of the month.

MATERIAL: Daily reflections based on the feast of the day or the liturgical season: maximum 165 words per page (each day's reflection is printed on a separate page) — $100 for series of reflections.

New Catholic World: 1865 Broadway, New York, N.Y. 10023. Mng. Ed., Robert Heyer. Bimonthly, circulation 16,000; $4.50 per year. Thematic issues.

FICTION, anything but pietistic: 1,800-2,000 words. ARTICLES, related to themes of issue. 1973 themes — Property, Children and the Church, Aging, Communications, Normality/Abnormality, Human Liberations. All perspectives except historical and technical on these themes: about 1,800-2,000 words. VERSE, not over 22 lines. Rates of payment not supplied.

O.M.I. Missions Magazine: P.O. Box 96, San Antonio, Tex. 78206. Ed., Theresa Cademartori; Dir., Rev. Cullen F. Deckert, O.M.I. Bimonthly, circulation 10,000; $3 per year.

ARTICLES: Photo and mission stories of Oblate Fathers in their missionary work; profiles of Oblate priests and brothers; articles of general Catholic interest — 1½-2¢ a word. Finished manuscripts only.

Orphan's Messenger and Advocate of the Blind: St. Joseph's Home, P.O. Box 288, Jersey City, N.J. 07303. Ed., Sr. Eleanor Quin. Quarterly, circulation 94,701; $1 per year.

FICTION, all types, family problems and themes with good morals: 1,000-1,500 words — 1¢ to 2¢ a word. ARTICLES, timely topics or religious: 500-1,000 words — 1¢ to 3¢ a word. PHOTOGRAPHS and DRAWINGS accepted occasionally — rate varies.

Our Family: Box 249, Battleford, Sask., Canada SOM OEO. Ed., Rev. A. J. Materi, O.M.I. Monthly, circulation 4,784; $3 per year.

FICTION, adult only; stories that reflect lives, problems and concerns of audience; love, romance, adventure, intrigue; 1,800-3,000 words — 1¢-2¢ a word. ARTICLES related to family living; religion, education, social, biographical, marriage, courtship, domestic, institutional: 1,800-3,000 words — 1¢-2¢ a word. POETRY, in the market for many more poems; should deal with man in search for himself, for God, for others, for love, for meaning in life, for commitment: 8-30 lines — $3-$10. PHOTOS — $3-$10, more if used on cover. Usually buys first North American serial rights; will consider purchasing second or reprint rights.

Our Sunday Visitor: Noll Plaza, Huntington, Ind. 46750. Ed., Richard B. Scheiber. Weekly newspaper-magazine, circulation 436,666; $6 per year.

ARTICLES, no limitation on subjects other than those imposed by good taste and orthodoxy. Picture and text stories, profiles of individuals and organizations; articles that reflect moral, cultural, historical, social, economic and certain political concerns about the US and the world; articles on current problems. Practical, factual and anecdotal material is sought: 1,200-2,000 words—$75-$100, usual payment. Queries are preferred to unsolicited completed manuscripts. PHOTOGRAPHS, picture stories preferred rather than individual photos. Picture stories—$125 and up, color; $75 and up, black and white. Individual photos—$25, color; $10, black and white. No fiction or poetry.

Priest, The: Noll Plaza, Huntington, Ind. 46750. Ed., Rev. Jordan Aumann, O.P. (Mss. to the Editor, 1111 N. Richmond St., Chicago, Ill. 60622.) Monthly, circulation 12,255; $7 per year.

ARTICLES of benefit to priests and seminarians in any of the following areas: priestly spirituality, contemporary theology, liturgy, apostolate and ministry, pastoral notes, Scripture. Controversial subject matter acceptable provided it does not go beyond the realm of orthodoxy or respect for authority or demands of fraternal charity: 6-15 double-spaced pages—$25 to $100 (about $5 per manuscript page).

Queen of All Hearts: 40 S. Saxon Ave., Bay Shore, N.Y. 11706. Ed., Rev. James Mc-Millan, S.M.M.; Mng. Ed., Rev. Roger M. Charest S.M.M. Bimonthly; circulation 12,000; $3 per year.

FICTION: short stories, preferably with a Marian theme: 1,000-2,000 words. ARTICLES that bring out the importance of devotion to Mary. PHOTOGRAPHS with human interest, especially relating to the Madonna. VERSE with Marian theme. Payment varies. No artwork or fillers.

Review for Religious: 612 Humboldt Bldg., 539 N. Grand Blvd., St. Louis, Mo. 63103. Ed., R. F. Smith, S.J. Bimonthly, circulation 21,784; $6 per year.

ARTICLES, of interest to religious: 3,000-10,000 words—$5 per printed page.

St. Anthony Messenger: 1615 Republic St., Cincinnati, O. 45210. Ed., Rev. Jeremy Harrington, O.F.M. Monthly, circulation 250,000; $5 per year.

FICTION: Written out of a totally Christian background, illuminating the truth of human nature for adults. No preachiness, sentimentality. FACT ARTICLES: 3,000-3,500 words. Outstanding personalities. Information and comment on major movements in the Church: application of Christian faith to daily life; real-life solutions in the areas of a) family life, education; b) personal living (labor, leisure, art, psychology, spirituality). Human interest narrative. Humor. Photos and picture stories. Query letters welcome.

Salesian Missions: 148 Main St., New Rochelle, New York. Ed., Rev. Edward J. Cappelletti, S.D.B. Bi-monthly, circulation 825,000; $2 per year.

ARTICLES: mission interest; pertaining to Salesian Society, life, spirit and educational system of St. John Bosco; adolescent interest and education—2¢ a word and up. PHOTOGRAPHS—$5-$6. Suggest queries before submitting material. Payment on acceptance. Early report.

Sign, The: Monastery Pl., Union City, N.J. 07087. Ed., Rev. Augustine P. Hennessy, C.P. Monthly, circulation 155,000; $5 per year.

FICTION of general Catholic interest: 1,000-3,500 words—$200-$300. ARTICLES of Catholic and general interest: 1,000-3,000 words — $200-$300. PHOTOGRAPHS, DRAWINGS **Social Justice Review:** 3835 Westminster Pl., St. Louis, Mo. 63108. Ed., Harvey J. Johnson, Monthly, exc. July-Aug., circulation 1,850; $6 per year.

ARTICLES: research, editorial and review: 2,000-4,000 words—$3 per column. No fiction.

Spiritual Life: 2131 Lincoln Rd., N.E., Washington, D.C. 20013; Ed., Rev. Christopher Latimer, O.C.D. Quarterly, circulation 10,000; $4 per year.

ARTICLES, must follow scope of magazine: about 2,000 words—rate varies. Sample copy and instructions for writers sent upon request.

Today's Catholic Teacher: 38 W. Fifth St., Dayton, O. 45402. Ed., Ruth A. Matheny. Monthly Sept. through May (exc. Dec.), circulation 70,000; $6 per year.

ARTICLES of professional and personal interest to teachers, administrators, and members of school boards in Catholic schools and CCD programs: 600-800 words, 1,500-3,000 words—$20-$75. Premium payment for superior content and writing presentation.

Triumph: 278 Broadview Ave., Warrenton, Va. 22186. Ed., Michael Lawrence. Monthly, circulation, 8,000; $10 per year.
ARTICLES: Should follow general scope of the magazine: 1,000-3,500 words—2½¢ per word on publication. BOOK REVIEWS, inquire of editor first: 1,000-2,500 words—2½¢ per word on publication.
Triumph also publishes a newsletter, **Catholic Currents,** semimonthly; circulation, 5,000. ARTICLES accepted for centerfold: approx. 1,500-1,600 words—2½¢ per word.
WAY—Catholic Viewpoints: 109 Golden Gate Ave., San Francisco, Calif. 94102. Ed., Rev. Simon Scanlon, O.F.M. Ten times a year, circulation 8,404; $4 per year.
ARTICLES, in keeping with the purpose of the magazine, to bear effective witness to the ideals and aims of the Order of St. Francis: to view the world through Christian eyes; to point up the relationship between abstract belief and concrete action in the modern world: 1,500-2,200 words—$30 to $50. PHOTOGRAPHS: bought with articles.
Working for Boys: 601 Winchester St., Newton Highlands, Mass. 02161. Ed.,

Brother Jerome, C.F.X. (Mss. to Bro. Jason, C.F.X., Assoc. Ed., Xaverian Brothers High School, Westwood, Mass, 02090.) Quarterly, circulation 28,567; 25¢ per year.
To support the educational program of St. Joseph Province of the Xaverian Brothers.
FICTION, preferably seasonal: 800-1,000 words—3¢ a word. ARTICLES, preferably seasonal: All Souls, Christmas, Easter, Summer: 800-1,000 words—3¢ a word. VERSE, seasonal, 4-16 lines—25¢-50¢ a line.
Worship: St. John's Abbey, Collegeville, Minn. 56321. Ed., Rev. Aelred Tegels, O.S.B. Monthly, exc. July-Aug.), circulation 10,271; $6.50 per year.
ARTICLES related to the engagement of the magazine in ongoing study of both the theoretical and pastoral dimensions of liturgy; examines historical traditions of worship in their doctrinal context, the experience of worship in Christian churches, the findings of contemporary theology, psychology, communications, cultural anthropology, and sociology insofar as they have a bearing on public worship: 3,000-5,000 words—2¢ a word for commissioned articles. No fiction or poetry.

DIRECTORY OF PUBLISHERS

This list includes Catholic publishers, some major Protestant publishers, other publishing houses which issue Catholic titles.
Abbey Press, St. Meinrad, Ind. 47577.
Abingdon Press, Nashville, Tenn. 37203.
Abrams, Harry A., 110 E. 59th St., New York, N.Y. 10022.
Academy Guild Press, 2430 E. McKinley St., Fresno, Calif. 93621.
Alba House, 2187 Victory Blvd., Staten Island, N. Y. 10314.
Alleluia Press, Allendale, N.J. 07401.
Allyn and Bacon, Inc., Rockleigh, N.J. 07647.
American Press, 106 W. 56th St., New York, N. Y. 10019.
Association Press, 291 Broadway, New York, N.Y. 10007.
Augsburg Publishing House, 426 S. 5th St., Minneapolis, Minn. 55415.
Ave Maria Institute, Washington, N. J. 07882.
Ave Maria Press, Notre Dame, Ind. 46556.
Bantam Books, Inc., 666 Fifth Ave., New York, N.Y. 10019.
Barnes and Noble, Inc., 105 Fifth Ave., New York, N. Y. 10003.
Beacon Press, 25 Beacon St., Boston, Mass. 02108.
Benziger, Inc., 866 Third Ave., New York, N.Y. 10022.
Bobbs-Merrill, Inc., 4300 W. 62nd St., Indianapolis, Ind. 42668.
Brown, William C., Co., 135 S. Locust St., Dubuque, Ia. 52001.
Bruce Books, 866 3rd Ave., New York, N.Y. 10022.

Carmelite Press, 6413 Dante Ave., Chicago, Ill. 60637.
Carmelite Third Order Press, Aylesford Priory, Downers Grove, Ill. 60515.
Catechetical Guild, Noll Plaza, Huntington, Ind. 46750.
Catholic Bible House, Box 2651, Charlotte, N. C. 28201.
Catholic Book Publishing Co., 257 W. 17th St., New York, N. Y. 10011.
Catholic Library Association, 461 W. Lancaster Ave., Haverford, Pa. 19041.
Catholic Press, Inc. 1725 S. Indiana Ave., Chicago, Ill. 60616.
Catholic University of America Press, 620 Michigan Ave. N.E., Washington, D. C. 20017.
Cistercian Publications, Spencer, Mass. 01562.
Claretian Publications, 221 W. Madison St., Chicago, Ill. 60606.
Come Publishers, 335 W. Prospect Ave., Appleton, Wis. 54911.
Conception Abbey Press, Conception, Mo. 64433.
Concordia Publishing House, 3558 S. Jefferson Ave., St. Louis, Mo. 63118.
Confraternity of the Precious Blood, 5300 Fort Hamilton Parkway, Brooklyn, N.Y. 11219.
Corpus Publications, 1330 Massachusetts Ave. N. W., Washington, D. C. 20005.
Crawley, John J. and Co., Inc., 336 Mountain Rd., Union City, N.J. 07087.
Crowell-Collier and Macmillan, Inc., 866 Third Ave., New York, N. Y. 10022.
Daughters of St. Paul, 78 Fort Pl., Staten Is., N.Y. 10301.

Delaney Publications, 720 N. Rush St., Chicago, Ill. 60611.

Dell Publishing Co., Inc., 750 Third Ave., New York, N. Y. 10017.

Devin-Adair Co., 1 Park Ave., Greenwich, Conn. 06870.

Dimension Books, Inc., Box 811, Denville, N. J. 07834.

Divine Word Publications, Techny, Ill. 60082.

Dodd, Mead and Co., 79 Madison Ave., New York, N. Y. 10016.

Donohue, M. A., and Co., 711 S. Dearborn St., Chicago, Ill. 60605.

Doubleday and Co., Inc., 277 Park Ave., New York, N. Y. 10017.

Duquesne University Press, Pittsburgh, Pa. 15219.

Eerdmans Publishing Co., 255 Jefferson Ave. S.E., Grand Rapids, Mich. 49502.

Englewood Cliffs College Press, Hudson Terr., Englewood Cliffs, N.J. 07632.

Farrar, Straus and Giroux, Inc., 19 Union Sq. W., New York, N. Y. 10003.

Fawcett Publications, Fawcett Pl., Greenwich, Conn. 06830.

Fides Publishers, Inc., Box F. Notre Dame, Ind. 46556.

Fordham University Press, 441 E. Fordham Rd., Bronx, N. Y. 10458.

Fortress Press, 2900 Queen Lane, Philadelphia, Pa. 19129.

Franciscan Herald Press, 1434 W. 51st St. Chicago, Ill. 60609.

Franciscan Publishers, Pulaski, Wis. 54162.

Golden Press, Inc., 850 Third Ave., New York, N. Y. 10022.

Harcourt, Brace, Jovanovitch, Inc., 757 Third Ave., New York, N. Y. 10017.

Harper and Row, 49 E. 33rd St., New York, N. Y. 10016.

Harvard University Press, Cambridge, Mass. 02138.

Hawthorn Books, Inc., 70 Fifth Ave., New York, N. Y. 10011.

Herder, B., Book Co., 314 N. Jefferson, St. Louis, Mo. 63103.

Herder and Herder, 232 Madison Ave., New York, N. Y. 10016.

Hi-Time Publishers, Inc., Box 7337, Milwaukee, Wis. 53213.

Holt, Rinehart and Winston, Inc., 383 Madison Ave., New York, N.Y. 10017.

Houghton Mifflin Co., 110 Tremont St., Boston, Mass. 02107.

Image Books (see Doubleday and Co.).

Immaculata Press, Putnam, Conn. 06260.

John Day Co., 257 Park Ave. S., New York, N.Y. 10010.

John Knox, Press, Box 1176, Richmond, Va. 23209.

K. of C. Information Bureau, P.O. Box 1971, New Haven, Conn. 06509.

Kenedy, P.J., and Sons, 866 3rd Ave., New York, N. Y. 10022.

Knopf, Alfred A., Inc., 201 E. 50th St., New York, N. Y. 10022.

Liguorian Books, Liguori, Mo. 63057.

Lippincott, J. B., Co., E. Washington Sq., Philadelphia, Pa. 19105.

Little, Brown and Co., 34 Beacon St., Boston, Mass. 02108.

Liturgical Conference, 1330 Massachusetts Ave. N. W., Washington, D. C. 20005.

Liturgical Press, Collegeville, Minn. 56321.

Loyola University Press, 3441 N. Ashland Ave., Chicago, Ill. 60657.

Lumen Christi Press, P. O. Box 13176, Houston, Tex. 77019.

McGraw-Hill Book Co., 330 W. 42nd St., New York, N. Y. 10036.

Macmillan Company, 866 Third Ave., New York, N. Y. 10022.

McKay Co., David, 750 Third Ave., New York, N. Y. 10017.

Marian Library, University of Dayton, Dayton, O. 45409.

Marquette Univ. Press, 1131 W. Wisconsin Ave., Milwaukee, Wis. 53233.

Maryknoll Publications, Maryknoll, N. Y. 10545.

Marytown Press, Kenosha, Wis. 53140.

Mine Publications, 25 Groveland Terrace, Minneapolis, Minn. 55403.

Mission Helpers of the Sacred Heart, 1001 W. Joppa Rd., Baltimore, Md. 21204.

NC Publications, 1312 Massachusetts Ave. N.W. Washington, D.C. 20005.

National Center of Religious Education— CCD, 1312 Massachusetts Ave. N.W., Washington, D.C.

Nelson, Thomas Inc. 407 Seventh Ave. S., Nashville, Tenn. 37203.

New American Library, 1301 Ave. of the Americans, New York, N. Y. 10019.

Newman Press (see Paulist/Newman).

Notre Dame University Press, Notre Dame, Ind. 46556.

Orbis Books, Maryknoll, N.Y. 10524.

Our Sunday Visitor, Inc., Noll Plaza, Huntington, Ind. 46750.

Oxford University Press, Inc., 200 Madison Ave., New York, N. Y. 10016.

Paulist/Newman Press, 400 Sette Dr., Paramus, N. J. 07652.

Penguin Books, Inc., 7110 Ambassador Rd., Baltimore, Md. 21207.

Pflaum/Standard, 38 W. 5th St., Dayton, O. 45402.

Philosophical Library, 15 E. 40th St., New York, N. Y. 10016.

Pio Decimo Press, Box 53, Baden Sta., St. Louis, Mo. 63147.

Pocket Books, Inc., 630 Fifth Ave., New York, N. Y. 10020.

Popular Library, Inc., 355 Lexington Ave., New York, N. Y. 10017.

Prentice-Hall, Inc., Englewood Cliffs, N. J. 07632.

Provincial Press, 43 Zurich Way, Tell City, Ind. 47586.

Putnam's, G. P. Sons, 200 Madison Ave., New York, N. Y. 10016.

Random House, Inc., 201 E. 50th St., New York, N. Y. 10022.

Regina Press, Midland Ave., Hicksville, N.Y. 11801.

Regenery, Henry, 114 W. Illinois St., Chicago, Ill. 60610.

Romig, Walter, 979 Lakepointe Rd., Grosse Pointe, Mich. 48230.

Sadlier, William H., 11 Park Pl., New York, N. Y. 10007.

St. Anthony Messenger Press, 1615 Republic St., Cincinnati, O. 45210.

St. Charles House, St. Charles, Ill. 60174.

St. John's University Press, Grand Central and Utopia Pkwys., Jamaica, N. Y. 11432.

St. Martin's Press, 175 Fifth Ave., New York, N.Y. 10010.

St. Norbert Abbey Press, Box 192, De Pere, Wis. 54115.

St. Paul Editions, 50 St. Paul's Ave., Boston, Mass. 02130.

Scepter Publishers, 30 N. La Salle St., Chicago, Ill. 60602.

Schocken Books, Inc., 67 Park Ave., New York, N. Y. 10016.

Scott, Foresman and Co., 99 Bauer Dr,, Oakland, N. J. 07436.

Scribner's, Chas., Sons, 597 Fifth Ave., New York, N. Y. 10017.

Seminar Press, 111 Fifth Ave. New York, N.Y. 10003.

Sentinel Press, 194 E. 76th St., New York, N. Y. 10021.

Sheed and Ward, 64 University Pl., New York, N. Y. 10003.

Silver Burdett Co., Park Ave. and Columbia Rd., Morristown, N. J. 07960.

Simon and Schuster, Inc., 630 Fifth Ave., New York, N. Y. 10020.

Tan Books and Publishers, P.O. Box 424, Rockford, Ill. 61105.

Taplinger Publishing Co., 200 Park Ave. S., New York, N. Y. 10003.

Templegate, 719 E. Adams St., Springfield, Ill. 62705.

Twenty-Third Publications, P.O. Box 180, W. Mystic, Conn. 06388.

Twin Circle Guild, 86 Riverside Dr., New York, N. Y. 10024.

United States Catholic Conference, 1312 Massachusetts Ave. N.W., Washington, D.C. 20005.

US Center for the Catholic Biblical Apostolate, 1312 Massachusetts Ave. N.W., Washington, D.C. 20005.

Universal Publications, P.O. Box 722, Patagonia, Ariz. 85624.

Viking Press, 625 Madison Ave., New York, N. Y. 10022.

Westminster Press, Juniper and Walnut Sts., Philadelphia, Pa. 19107.

BOOK CLUBS

Catholic Book Club (1928), 106 W. 56th St., New York, N. Y. 10019. Sponsors Campion Award.

Catholic Digest Book Club (1954), Suite 337, 405 Lexington Ave., New York, N.Y. 10017.

Herald Book Club (1958), Franciscan Herald Press, 1434 W. 51st St., Chicago, Ill. 60609.

Thomas More Book Club (1939), Thomas More Association, 180 N. Wabash Ave., Chicago, Ill. 60601. The Association sponsors the Thomas More Association Award.

DIRECTORY OF AUDIO-VISUAL AID SOURCES

Following are sources of audio-visual aids for religious instructional use and related purposes.

Abbey Press, St. Meinrad, Ind. 47577. Posters.

Alba House Communications, Society of St. Paul, Canfield, Ohio 44406. Filmstrips, records, tapes, audio-visual equipment.

ALESCO (American Library and Educational Service Co.), 404 Sette Dr., Paramus, N. J. 07652.

AVE, Audio Visual Education, C.P.A.S. Buying Service and Co-op Filmstrip Lending Library, 15924 Grand River Ave., Detroit, Mich. 48217.

Argus Communications, 3505 N. Ashland Ave., Chicago, Ill. 60657. Filmstrips, tapes.

Avant Garde Records, Inc., 250 W. 57th St., New York, N.Y. 10019. Records.

Biblical Films, Box 373, Rockville, Conn. 06066.

Cassette Productions, Inc., Suite 2817, 420 Lexington Ave., New York, N.Y. 10017. Tapes.

Catechetical Guild, Noll Plaza, Hunting-ton, Ind. 46750. Sound filmstrips, pamphlets, pictures, records.

Catholic Audio Visual Association, Our Lady of Angels College, Glen Riddle, Pa. 19031. Posters, slides.

Catholic Film Center, 29 Salem Way, Yonkers, N. Y. 10703.

Catholic Information Society, 214 W. 31st St., New York, N. Y. 10001. Posters.

Catholic Near East Welfare Association, 330 Madison Ave., New York, N.Y. 10017. Pictures, slides.

The Catholic Record Shop, 73 W. Main St., Westminster, Md. Religious records.

Catholic Visual Aid Service, 422 S. Kenmore Ave., Los Angeles, Cal. 90005. Filmstrips.

Catholic Visual Education, 136 W. 32nd St., New York, N. Y. 10001. Filmstrips.

Church World Press, Inc., 2969 W. 25th St., Cleveland, O. 44113. Pictures.

Cinema Guild, Inc., 10 Fiske Place, Mount Vernon, N. Y.

Contemporary Communications, Techny, Ill. 60082.

David C. Cook Publishing Co., 850 N. Grove Ave., Elgin, Ill. 60120.

Daughters of St. Paul, 50 St. Paul's Ave., Jamaica Plain, Boston, Mass. 02130. Filmstrips.

Divine Word Films, Girard, Penn.

Don Bosco Films and Filmstrips, 148 Main St., New Rochelle, N.Y. 10802.

Encyclopedia Britannica Films, Inc., 1150 Wilmette Ave., Wilmette, Ill.

Eye Gate House, 146-01 Archer Ave., Jamaica, N.Y. 11435.

Family Filmstrips, 5823 Santa Monica Blvd., Hollywood, Calif. 90038.

Family Theater Films, 7201 Sunset Blvd., Hollywood, Cal. 90046.

Franciscan Communications Center, 1229 S. Santee St., Los Angeles, Calif. 90015 Films, sound tapes, records.

Full Circle Associates, 426 E. 119th St., New York, N.Y. 10035. Posters.

Fullvue Products, 693 W. 130th St., New York, N. Y. 10027. Slides.

G.I.A. Publications, Inc., 2115 W. 63rd St., Chicago, Ill. 60636.

Gregorian Institute of America, 2115 W. 63rd St., Chicago, Ill. 60636.

Hi-Time Visual Aids, Box 7337, Milwaukee, Wis. 53213. Posters.

Janus Film Library, 55th and 7th Ave., New York, N. Y. 10019.

Jesuit Foreign Missions, Province of New England, 126 Newbury St. Boston, Mass. 02116. Films.

Josephite Pastoral Center, 1200 Varnum St. N.E., Washington, D.C. 20017. Filmstrips.

Thomas L. Klise Co., P.O. Box 3418, Peoria, Ill. 61614. Tapes and sound filmstrips.

Life of Christ Film Library, 40 S. Monterey, Villa Park, Ill. Films.

Liturgical Press, Collegeville, Minn. 56321 Wall charts.

Loyola Films, 80th and Loyola Blvd., Los Angeles, Cal.

Loyola University Press, 3441 N. Ashland Ave., Chicago, Ill. 60613. Charts.

Marian Guild, St. Joseph Central House, Emmitsburg, Md. Filmstrips.

Maryknoll Publications, Maryknoll, N.Y. Filmstrips, movies, slides, sound tapes.

Mass Media Ministries, 2116 N. Charles St., Baltimore, Md. 21218. Films.

Mission Helpers of the Sacred Heart, 1001 W. Joppa Rd., Baltimore, Md. 21204. Charts.

Mt. Carmel Guild Audio Visual Library, 300 Broadway, Newark, N. J. 07104.

National Audiovisual Center, Washington, D.C. 20409. Government-sponsored audio/visual materials.

National Council of Catholic Men Film Center, 405 Lexington Ave., New York, N.Y. 10017.

National Geographic Magazine, 16th and M St. N. W., Washington, D. C. Biblical maps.

N C News Service, 1312 Massachusetts Ave., N. W., Washington, D. C. 20005. Filmstrips, bulletin board cards, weekly quizzes.

A. J. Nystrom Co., 3333 Elston Ave., Chicago, Ill. 60618. Biblical maps.

Paulist Press, 400 Sette Dr., Paramus, N. J. 07652. Slides, posters.

PIME Missionaries of Sts. Peter and Paul, 121 E. Boston Blvd., Detroit, Mich. 48202. Films.

Pflaum/Standard Publishing Co., 38 West 5th St., Dayton, O. 45402. Posters, filmstrips.

Postal Church Service, Inc. 8401 Southern Blvd., Youngstown, O.

Religion Teachers Association of Chicago, 430 N. Michigan Ave., Chicago, Ill. Tapes.

Religious Slides, P.O. Box 3776, San Diego, Calif.

Roa's Films, 1696 N. Astor St., Milwaukee, Wis. 53202. Filmstrips, motion pictures.

Sacra-Disc Music Society, Suite 1823, 250 W. 57th St., New York, N. Y. 10019. Records.

Saint Columban Sisters, 950 Metropolitan Ave., Hyde Park, Mass. Films.

Saint John Bosco Film Library, Box P., New Rochelle, N. Y. Filmstrips.

Saint Leo Bulletin, Box 577, Newport, R. I. Calendar poster.

Salesiana Publishers, 148 Main St., New Rochelle, N.Y. 10802. Filmstrips.

Simplex, 1564 Broadway, New York, N. Y. 10036. Films.

Scripture Press Publications, 1825 College, Wheaton, Ill. 60187. Suedegraphs, teaching pictures.

Robert Slye Electronics, Inc., 725 15th St., N. W., Washington, D.C. Records.

Society for Visual Education, Inc., 1345 W. Diversey Parkway, Chicago, Ill. 60614. Filmstrips.

Tele-Vue Productions, 24 S. Illinois St., Belleville, Ill. 62220. Films, tapes.

Twenty-Third Publications, P.O. Box 180, W. Mystic, Conn. 06388. Filmstrips, records.

Twyman Films, 329 Salem Way, Dayton, O. 45401.

Universal Color Slides, 424 E. 89th St., New York, N. Y. 10028.

White Fathers Film Center, 1624 21st St., Washington, D. C. 20009.

White Sisters of Africa, 319 Middlesex Ave., Metuchen, N. J. Films.

World Library of Sacred Music, 2145 Central Pkway., Cincinnati, O. 45214. Records.

Audio-visual aids have increased in value and use as teaching tools in recent years and have had significant effects in religious as well as general education. As their popularity has grown, so has the number of their producers and suppliers. One of the Catholic sources is the Catechetical Guild.

The "Know Your Faith" program of religious instruction, coupled with audio-visual aids, is in wide use across the country.

RADIO, TELEVISION, THEATRE

Radio

Christian in Action: Originated in 1941, produced in cooperation with the Division for Film and Broadcasting, NCCB/USCC. A 15-minute weekly program currently employing a youth-oriented music and commentary format; heard on more than 50 stations (ABC).

Christopher Radio Program: Produced by Rev. Richard Armstrong, M.M. Features 15-minute interview-discussion series, weekly, on 900 stations; a one-minute Christopher "Thought for Today," daily, on more than 2,200 stations. Address: 12 E. 48th St., New York, N.Y. 10017.

Crossroads: Originated in 1954 as the Hour of the Crucified, produced by the Passionist Fathers and Brothers. Weekly, on nearly 325 stations and Armed Forces Radio. Director: Rev. Cyril Schweinberg, C.P. Address: 1089 Elm St., West Springfield, Mass. 01089.

Guideline: Produced in cooperation with the Division for Film and Broadcasting, NCCB/USCC. Weekly program designed to set forth the teachings of the Catholic Church and to discuss issues the Church faces in the contemporary world; heard on approximately 90 stations (NBC).

Sacred Heart Program: Originated in 1939, produced by the Jesuit Fathers. Features five 15-minute programs and one half-hour program weekly on radio, and one 15-minute TV program weekly. Director, Rev. Denis E. Daly, S.J. Address: 3900 Westminster Place, St. Louis, Mo. 63108.

Television

Directions: Originated in 1960, this weekly half-hour program sustains a news-oriented approach to reporting social, moral and religious issues within a Catholic context. The Division for Film and Broadcasting, NCCB/USCC, cooperates in the production of some 11 segments a year, which are carried at variable dates on more than 100 stations (ABC).

Look Up and Live: Originated in 1954, this half-hour series sustains a variety of formats from dramatizations to studio discussions. The Division for Film and Broadcasting, NCCB/USCC, cooperates in producing 14 half-hours a year, in addition to interfaith and seasonal specials; carried on approximately 120 stations (CBS).

Religious Specials: The Division for Film and Broadcasting, NCCB/USCC, cooperates in the production of four one-hour Catholic specials a year and occasional seasonal or tri-faith presentations. These programs offered a varied format: film, dramatizations, panel discussions, music and commentary, etc. Catholic portions are telecast on approximately 175 stations (NBC).

Theatre

The Blackfriars Theatre: The oldest experimental theatre under Catholic auspices in the United States, suspended operations in March, 1972, 32 years after it became the first off-Broadway theatre in New York City. Founded in 1931 in Washington, D.C., under the sponsorship of the Blackfriars Guild, it produced 75 original plays in 41 years; the last one, which opened Feb. 23, 1972, was *The Red Hat.* The Guild founders and long-time promoters of the theatre were Dominican Fathers Urban Nagle (1905-65) and Thomas F. Carey (1904-72.)

Catholic University Speech and Drama Department: Established in 1937. Offers degree courses in theatre arts, produces six plays a year in The Hartke Theatre, has touring company of graduates (see National Players). Head of the department, Rev. Gilbert V. Hartke, O.P. Address: Catholic University of America, Washington, D.C. 20017.

National Players: Originated in 1948, is the professional touring company of graduates of the Catholic University Speech and Drama Department; oldest classical touring company in the US. Operates a theatre at Olney, Md.

Catholic Actors' Guild of America, Inc.: Established in 1914 to provide varied services to people in the theatre. Has more than 1,200 members, publishes *The Call Board* bimonthly. President, Cyril Ritchard. Address: Piccadilly Hotel, 227 W. 45th St., New York, N.Y. 10036. The Actors' Chapel is located in St. Malachy's Church, 239 W. 49th St., New York, N.Y.

National Theatre Arts Conference: Originated in 1937. It is primarily a program service organization; membership, 750. President and Director, Sister Honor Murphy, Dominican College, Racine, Wis. 53402.

Communications Services

Christopher TV Series: Originated in 1951. Half-hour and quarter-hour interviews in color, weekly, on more than 210 stations. Address: 12 E. 48th St., New York, N.Y. 10017.

Family Theater: Films for TV. Address: 7201 Sunset Blvd., Hollywood, Calif. 90046.

Franciscan Communications Center: A media center for coordinating activities of the First Order (O.F.M.) and Third Order of St. Francis in the field of mass communications. Creators and producers of TeleSPOTS and AudioSPOTS, 30- and 60-second public service messages for radio and TV; TeleKETICS, religious education materials. Address: 1229 South Santee St., Los Angeles, Calif. 90015.

Mary Productions "Airtime": Originated in 1950. Offers royalty-free scripts for stage, film, radio and tape production. Address:

Mary Productions Guild, 58 Lenison Ave., Belford, N.J. 07718.

Paulist Communications Services: Contracts with dioceses and parishes to provide public service programs free to radio stations and scripts to priest-broadcasters; contacts stations for dioceses. Address: 17575 Pacific Coast Highway, Pacific Palisades, Calif. 90272.

Paulist Productions: Producers and distributors of the INSIGHT Film Series. Available for TV at no charge. Purchase and rental information available. Address: P.O. Box 1057, Pacific Palisades, Calif. 90272.

Sacred Heart Program — TV: Originated in 1954, produced by the Jesuit Fathers. Director, Rev. Denis E. Daly, S.J. Address: 3900 Westminster Pl., St. Louis, Mo. 63108.

St. Bernardine Communicators Guild: Offers vocation tapes to individuals and organizations for broadcast on local stations. Address: 6801 N. Yates Rd., Milwaukee, Wis. 53217.

Tele-Vue Productions: Films for TV, mostly educational, for sale and rental. Address: Rev. Paul W. Stauder, 24 S. Illinois St., Belleville, Ill. 62220.

The Catholic Broadcasters Association of America (CBA): Founded in 1948 to recognize, promote and honor programming designed to foster the dissemination of Judaeo-Christian principles through broadcasting; membership, 150. Presents "Gabriel Awards" to programs, syndicators, individuals and producers for products in competition in English-speaking countries. Is exploring the formation, possibly in 1973, of a US branch of the Catholic International Association for Radio and TV (UNDA), to be known as UNDA/USA. publishes the *CBA Newsletter* five times a year. Address: 136 W. George St., Indianapolis, Ind. 46225. President, Rev. Kenny Sweeney.

Division for Film and Broadcasting (DFB): A unit of the Department of Communications of the National Conference of Catholic Bishops and the United States Catholic Conference, was formed in January, 1972, through a reorganization of the former National Catholic Office for Motion Pictures and the National Catholic Office for Radio and Television.

DFB provides a national service of information, training and cooperation for diocesan communications offices throughout the country. It sponsors workshops, seminars and institutes in film and broadcasting, and publishes SHARE, a packet of film and broadcasting information, twice monthly.

For the motion picture medium, DFB publishes the twice-monthly *Catholic Film Newsletter* which reviews all current nationally released 35 mm films and provides information about resources for film utilization and education (16 mm films, books, magazines, festivals). The critical reviews are addressed to

the moral as well as artistic dimensions of motion pictures and are the result of a consensus based on the reactions of DFB's professional staff and board of consultors. All films reviewed are also classified according to the DFB rating system. Film classification supplements appear every two months as part of the *Newsletter*. In addition, the publication carries information and evaluative studies on trends and issues pertinent to television, with an emphasis on educational material.

The division maintains a 16mm film library of Catholic program material and a consultation service for educational and religious film program directors.

For the broadcast media, DFB is responsible for cooperating with the three major networks (NBC, ABC, and CBS) in the production of all regularly scheduled network radio and television programs involving Catholic participation: (See Radio and Television).

For the Catholic press, DFB publishes a weekly film/broadcast service consisting of reviews, information, articles and photos. Special projects are undertaken with individual publications, religious and general.

DFB also plays a liaison role for the NCCB/USCC with the film and broadcasting industries, national media, and religious agencies and organizations. It is a member of OCIC and UNDA, the international Catholic organizations for film and broadcasting, respectively. Consultations and information services are also provided for the Pontifical Commission for Social Communications and the communications offices of national episcopal conferences throughout the world.

Rev. Patrick J. Sullivan, S.J., is the director.

Address: Suite 4200, 405 Lexington Ave., New York, N. Y. 10017.

Foundation

The Catholic Communications Foundation (CCF) was established by the Catholic Fraternal Benefit Societies in 1968 in New York to lend support and assistance to development of the broadcasting apostolate.

The CCF, in addition to making financial grants (more than $210,000 from 1969 to 1971) for religious programs and programming services, has promoted the development of diocesan communications capabilities and has funded scholarship programs at the Institute for Religious Communications at Loyola University, New Orleans.

CCF officers are Bishop John A. Donovan, chairman of the board; Bishop Andrew A. Grutka, president and treasurer; John B. Heinz and Charles E. Reilly, Jr., executive vice president and secretary, respectively. Serving on the board are several US bishops, communications executives, and representatives of the fraternal societies.

Address: Suite 1450, 500 Fifth Ave., New York, N.Y. 10036.

DIOCESAN COMMUNICATIONS OFFICES, DIRECTORS

(Source: *The Official Catholic Directory*, 1972. Archdioceses designated by asterisk.)

Albany, N.Y.: Rev. William H. Kennedy, 30 N. Main Ave. 12203 (Radio-TV).

Allentown, Pa.: Msgr. Vincent E. Lewellis, 1729 Turner St. 18104 (Information).

Altoona-Johnstown, Pa.: Msgr. Edward O'Malley, Logan Blvd., Hollidaysburg, Pa. 16648 (Information).

Amarillo, Tex.: Msgr. Richard F. Vaughan, Box 5644. 79107 (Radio-TV).

Anchorage,* Alaska: Rev. Francis J. Fish, P.O. Box 2239. 99501 (Information).

Baltimore,* Md.: James E. Shaneman (Information), Rev. Casimir Pugevicius (Radio-TV), 320 Cathedral St. 21201.

Baton Rouge, La.: Jim Falkner, P.O. Drawer 14746. 70808 (Radio-TV).

Belleville, Ill.: Rev. William F. Rensing, 108 S. Third St. 62220 (Information); Msgr. L. A. Bauer, 5520 W. Main St. 62223 (Radio-TV).

Birmingham, Ala.: Rev. Martin Muller, P.O. Box 6147. 35209 (Radio-TV).

Bismarck, N. Dak.: Rev. John J. Owen, Douglas, N. Dak. 58735 (Radio-TV).

Boise, Ida.: Rev. Perry W. Dodds, Box 2835. 83701 (Information); Rev. David J. Kundtz, Box 129, Pocatello, Ida. 83201 (Idaho Catholic Office of Radio and Television).

Boston,* Mass.: George E. Ryan, 49 Franklin St. 02110 (News Bureau); Msgr. Walter L. Flaherty, 25 Granby St. 02115 (Radio-TV).

Bridgeport, Conn.: Rev. Alfred Sienkiewicz, Holy Spirit Rectory, 403 Scofieldtown Rd., Stamford. 06903 (Radio-TV).

Brooklyn, N.Y.: Rev. Robert F. Hurley, 11 De Sales Pl. 11207 (Catholic Information Centers); Rev. Thomas J. Flanagan, (Public Information Bureau), Frank De Rosa (Press Relations), Frank Bianco (Public Affairs), 75 Greene Ave. 11238; Confraternity Office, 345 Adams St. 11201 (Radio-TV).

Brownsville, Tex.: Rev. Joseph P. Delaney, P.O. Box 2279, Brownsville, Tex. 78520.

Buffalo, N.Y.: Msgr. Anthony J. Caligiuri, 35 Lincoln Pkwy. 14222 (Communications); Msgr. John J. McMahon, 100 S. Elmwood Ave. 14202 (Radio).

Burlington, Vt.: Msgr. W. John Fradet, 323 Pearl St. 05401 (Information Center); Rev. Joseph T. Nugent, Fairfax, Vt. 054054 (Radio-TV).

Camden, N.J.: Charles Germain, 1845 Haddon Ave. 08101 (Information).

Charleston, S.C.: Rev. Charles J. Molony, P.O. Box 818. 29402 (Radio-TV).

Cheyenne, Wyo.: Rev. Philip Colibraro, Box 163, Evanston, Wyo. 82930 (Radio-TV).

Chicago,* Ill.: Rev. James P. Roache (Communications), Rev. John Banahan (Radio-TV), P.O. Box 1979. 60690.

Cincinnati,* Ohio: Msgr. Earl L. Whalen, 426 E. 5th St. 45202 (Information, Radio-TV).

Cleveland, Ohio: Rev. Joseph H. Kraker, 1027 Superior Ave. 44114 (Communications, Radio-TV).

Corpus Christi, Tex.: John Foley, 818 Antelope, 78401 (Information).

Covington, Ky.: Rev. James E. Quill, Seminary of St. Pius X, Erlanger, Ky. 41018 (Radio-TV.

Crookston, Minn.: Rev. John O'Toole, Box 605. 56716 (Press).

Dallas, Tex.: Norman D. Phillips, P.O. Box 19347. 75219 (Information); Eddie Hallack, KDFW-TV).

Davenport, Iowa: Rev. Francis C. Henricksen, 407 Brady St. 52801 (Communications).

Denver,* Colo.: Rev. C. B. Woodrich, 934 Bannock St. 80204 (Information).

Des Moines, Iowa: Rev. Frank E. Bognanno (Radio-TV), Sr. Janet Michael, O.P. (Information), P.O. Box 1816. 50306.

Detroit,* Mich.: William Coughlin (Communications), Harold Chisholm (Information), 305 Michigan Ave. 48226.

Dodge City, Kans.: Msgr. A. J. Felling, Box 849. 67801 (Radio-TV).

Dubuque,* Iowa: 1229 Mt. Loretta Ave. 52001 (Information).

Duluth, Minn.: Rev. George M. Schroeder, 215 W. 4th St. 55812 (Public Relations. Radio-TV).

El Paso, Tex.: Andrew Sparke, 912 Myrtle St. 79901 (Information, Radio-TV).

Erie, Pa.: Rev. E. James Caldwell, Box 4047 (Publicity, Information, Radio-TV).

Evansville, Ind.: Rev. Joseph Ziliak, 219 W. third St. 47708 (Radio-TV).

Fairbanks, Alaska: Rev. James E. Poole, S.J., P.O. Box 101, Nome, Alaska 99762 (Radio-TV).

Fort Wayne-South Bend, Ind.: Rev. Msgr. James P. Conroy, Noll Plaza, Huntington, Ind. 46750 (Information).

Fort Worth, Tex.: Chancery Office, 1206 Throckmorton St. 76118 (Information, Public Relations); Frank Mills, 2343 Mistletoe Blvd. 76104 (Radio-TV).

Fresno, Calif.: Joseph Jasmin, P.O. Box 1668. 93717 (Information).

Gallup, N. Mex.: Rev. Cormac Antram, O.F.M., P.O. Box 48, Houck, Ariz. 85606 (Radio-TV).

Galveston-Houston, Tex.: Rev. Jacques Weber, S.J., 1900 San Jacinto St., Houston. 77002 (Radio-TV).

Gaylord, Mich.: Rev. Ronald V. Gronowsky, P.O. Box 700, 49735 (Information).

Grand Rapids, Mich.: Msgr. Hugh Beahan, 423 First St. N.W. 49504 (Information, Radio-TV).

Great Falls, Mont.: Rev. Richard Hopkins,

725 Third Ave. North, P.O. Box 2107. 59403 (Radio-TV).

Green Bay, Wis.: Reiny Wessing, P.O. Box 909, 54305 54305 (Communications).

Greensburg, Pa.: Rev. John J. Garred, 723 E. Pittsburgh St. 15601 (Information, Radio-TV).

Harrisburg, Pa.: David T. McAndrew, P.O. Box 787. 17108 (Communications); Rev. Stephen J. Hribick, 420 E. Simpson Ferry Rd., Mechanicsburg, Pa. 17055 (Information).

Hartford,* Conn.: Rev. Edmund Nadolyn, 477 Connecticut Blvd., East Hartford, Conn. 06108 (Communications).

Indianapolis, Ind.: Rev. Msgr. Cornelius B. Sweeney (Information, Public Relations), Rev. Kenny C. Sweeny (Radio-TV), 136 W. Georgia St. 46225.

Jefferson City, Mo.: Rev. John Long, Rt. 4. 65101 (Radio-TV).

Joliet, Ill.: Rev. Edwin Joyce, 425 Summit St. 60435 (Public Relations, Information).

Juneau, Alaska: Robert Mihelyi (Communications), Lawrence Sullivan (TV), 329 5th St., 99801.

Kansas City-St. Joseph, Mo.: Rev. James Hart, P.O. Box 1037, Kansas City, Mo. 64141 (Information, Radio-TV).

Lafayette, Ind.: Rev. James J. O'Neill, 1907 W. Sycamore St., Kokomo, Ind. 46901 (Radio-TV).

Lafayette, La.: Msgr. Richard Mouton, P.O. Drawer E. 70501 (Information); Msgr. Marcel Murie, P.O. Box 156, Lawtell, La. 70550 (Radio-TV).

Lincoln, Nebr.: Rev. James D. Dawson, P.O. Box 80328. 68501. (Information, Radio-TV).

Little Rock, Ark.: Msgr. B. Francis McDevitt, 617 Louisiana St. 72201 (Radio-TV).

Los Angeles,* Calif.: Rev. John C. Urban, 1531 W. 9th St. 90015 (Radio-TV).

Louisville,* Ky.: Rev. John H. Morgan, 1305 W. Market St. 40203 (Radio-TV).

Madison, Wis.: Msgr. Raymond E. Klaas, P.O. Box 111. 53701 (Information).

Manchester, N.H.: Rev. Philip P. Bruni, 153 Ash St. 03105 (Communications).

Marquette, Mich.: Rev. Raymond Moncher, 310 W. Washington St. 49855 (Radio-TV).

Miami,* Fla.: Rev. Donald F. X. Connolly (Information), Msgr. John H. O'Shea (Radio-TV), 6301 Biscayne Blvd. 33138.

Milwaukee,* Wis.: Rev. Msgr. Ralph R. Schmit, 12666 W. Beloit Rd., New Berlin, Wis. 53151 (Communications—Instructional TV).

Mobile, Ala.: Rev. James G. Walsh, C.S.P., 557 Dauphin St. 36602; Msgr. William R. James, 2048 W. Fairview Ave., Montgomery, Ala. 36108 (Radio-TV).

Nashville, Tenn.: Joseph Sweat, 421 Charlotte Ave. 37219 (Communications).

Natchez-Jackson, Miss.: James E. Bonney, P.O. Box 2248, Jackson, Miss. 39205 (Communications).

Newark,* N.J.: Msgr. Paul J. Hayes, 39 Lackawanna Pl., Bloomfield, N.J. 07003 (Communications); Rev. James A. Pindar, Seton Hall Univ., South Orange, N.J. 07079 (Radio-TV).

New Orleans,* La.: Rev. Lanaux J. Rareshide (Public Information), Thomas M. Finney (Public Relations), Rev. Jean C. Meyer (Radio-TV), 7887 Walmsley Ave. 70125.

New York, N.Y.: Msgr. Eugene C. Clark, 453 Madison Ave. 10022 (Information, Radio-TV); Msgr. John J. Healy, St. Joseph's Seminary, Yonkers, N.Y. 10704 (Instructional TV).

Oakland, Calif.: Rev. Richard Mangini, 2900 Lakeshore Ave. 94610 (Radio-TV).

Ogdensburg, N.Y.: Rev. David W. Stinebrickner, P.O. Box 88. 13669 (Information); Rev. John L. Downs, Redwood, N.Y. 13679 (Radio-TV).

Oklahoma City and Tulsa, Okla.: Miss Mary Kay Dyer, 7121 N.W. 7th St. 73187 (Communications).

Orlando, Fla.: Rev. David E. Page, P.O. Box 865, Maitland, Fla. 32751 (Information).

Paterson, N.J.: Gerald A. Costello, Box A, Pequannock, N.J. 07470 (Information); Rev. William W. Lindgren, 24 De Grasse St. 07505 (Radio-TV).

Philadelphia,* Pa.: Edward F. Devenney, 222 N. 17th St. 19103 (Press, Radio-TV, Public Affairs).

Philadelphia,* Pa. (Byzantine Rite): 815 N. Franklin St. 19123 (Public Relations).

Phoenix, Ariz.: Jerry Burns, 400 E. Monroe. 85004 (Communications).

Pittsburgh, Pa.: Rev. Msgr. Daniel H. Brennan (Communications), Joseph Williams (Information, Public Relations), 111 Blvd. of the Allies. 15222.

Portland, Me.: Clarence F. McKay, 510 Ocean Ave. 04103 (Information).

Portland,* Ore.: Gorman Hogan, 2818 E. Burnside St. 97214 (Information); Rev. Leo Remington, 2838 Burnside St. 97207 (Radio-TV).

Providence, R.I.: Rev. David J. Coffey, Cathedral Square, 02903 (Radio-TV).

Pueblo, Colo.: Edward P. Nichols, Jr., 225 Clark St. 81003 (Information).

Raleigh, N.C.: Rev. Robert T. Lawson, P.O. Box 1949. 27602 (Radio-TV).

Richmond, Va.: James D. Hetzer, 16 N. Laurel St. 23220 (Information).

Rochester, N.Y.: Rev. Louis J. Hohman, 67 Chestnut St. 14604 (Communications).

Rockford, Ill.: Rev. Thomas J. Monahan, 1260 N. Court St. 61101 (Information); Rev. Richard E. Kramer, 390 Fulton St., Elgin, Ill. 60120 (Radio-TV).

Rockville Centre, N.Y.: Rev. Daniel S. Hamilton, P.O. Box 395. 11570 (Information); Rev. Edward J. Molloy, 253 Sunrise Highway. 11570 (Radio-TV).

Sacramento, Calif.: Rev. James F. Church, 1121 K St. 95814 (Radio-TV).

Saginaw, Mich.: Rev. Howard M. Brown, 2555 Wieneke Rd. 48603 (Communications).

St. Augustine, Fla.: Msgr. Harold F. Jordan, Assumption Seminary, 2403 Atlantic Blvd., P.O. Box 5040, Jacksonville, Fla. 32207 (Radio-TV).

St. Cloud, Minn: Rev. Rosemary Borgert, P.O. Box 1068, 56301 (Information, Radio-TV).

St. Louis,* Mo.: Rev. Joseph M. O'Brien, 4140 Lindell Blvd. 63108 (Radio-TV).

St. Nicholas in Chicago (Ukrainians): Msgr. Jaroslav Swyschuk, 2238 W. Rice St. 60622 (Information, Radio-TV).

St. Paul and Minneapolis,* Minn.: Rev. Robert Nygaard, 226 Summit Ave., St. Paul. 55102

St. Petersburg, Fla.: Rev. J. Keith Symons, P.O. Box 13133. 33733 (Communications Media).

Salina, Kans.: Rev. Lawrence E. Pierce, P.O. Box 958. 07401 (Information, Radio-TV).

Salt Lake City, Utah: Msgr. William H. McDougall, 331 E. S. Temple. 84111 (Information); Rev. Thomas J. Meersman, P.O. Box 477, Kearns, Utah 84118 (Radio-TV).

San Antonio,* Tex.: Rev. Emil Wesselsky, P.O. Box 12429. 78212 (Social Communications).

San Diego, Calif.: Michael Newman, Alcala Park. 92110 (Communications).

San Francisco,* Calif.: Rev. Miles O'B. Riley, 50 Oak St. 94102 (Communications); Msgr. Francis A. Quinn, 441 Church St. 94114 (Public Relations).

Santa Rosa, Calif.: Msgr. Walter J. Tappe, 398 10th St., P.O. Box 1499. 95403 (Information, Public Relations).

Savannah, Ga.: Rev. Francis Donohue, P.O. Box 10065. 31402 (Communications).

Seattle,* Wash.: Rev. James Eblen, 907 Terry Ave. 98104 (Information, Radio-TV).

Sioux City, Ia.: Rev. Francis J. Brady, 3715 Ridge Ave. 51106 (Radio-TV).

Sioux Falls, S. Dak.: 423 N. Duluth Ave. 57104 (Information, Radio-TV).

Spokane, Wash.: Rev. Ralph H. Schwemin, Assumption Church, W. 3405 Weile 65806 (Information, Radio-TV).

Springfield, Mass.: Rev. Cyril Schweinberg, C.P., Bro. Damian Carroll, C.P., 1089 Elm St., W. Springfield, Mass. 01089 (Radio-TV).

Springfield-Cape Girardeau, Mo.: Rev. Justin D. Monaghan, 410 Landers Bldg. 65806 (Information, Radio-TV).

Steubenville, Ohio: P.O. Box 969. 43952 (Information); Rev. Donald Happe, St. Stanislaus Church. 43952 (Radio-TV).

Superior, Wis.: Rev. Robert M. Urban, 1512 N. 12th St. 54880 (Information, Radio-TV).

Syracuse, N.Y.: Msgr. William Shannon,

259 E. Onondaga St. 13202 (Radio-TV).

Toledo, Ohio: Mr. James Richards, 2544 Parkwood Ave. 43610 (Communications).

Tucson, Ariz.: Rev. Mason W. Borgman, P.O. Box 31. 85702 (Information).

Washington,* D.C.: Rev. Msgr. Leonard F. Hurley, 1425 V St. N.W. 20009 (Radio-TV).

Wheeling, W. Va.: Frank L. Sweeney, P.O. Box 220. 26003 (Communications); Rev. Victor Seidel, S.T., P.O. Box 301. 26003 (Radio-TV); Rev. Robert E. Lee, Mt. Olivet. 26003 (Radio-TV).

Wichita, Kans.: Rev. William M. Carr, 424 N. Broadway. 67202 (Radio-TV).

Wilmington, Del.: F. Eugene F. Donnelly, 1626 N. Union St. 19806 (Public Relations); Rev. James T. Delaney, 2505 Centerville Rd. 19808 (Radio-TV).

Winona, Minn.: Rev. Msgr. William T. Magee, Box 949. 55987 (Information).

Worcester, Mass.: Rev. John J. Kelliher, Christ the King Rectory, 1052 Pleasant St. 01602 (Radio-TV).

Yakima, Wash.: Rev. Robert J. Shields, P.O. Box 366, White Salmon. 98672 (Radio-TV).

Youngstown, Ohio: Msgr. J. Paul O'Connor, 144 W. Wood St. 44503 (Information, Radio-TV).

National Office

The National Catholic Office for Information, successor to the NCWC Bureau of Information, serves as the official spokesman for both the United States Catholic Conference and the National Conference of Catholic Bishops in relating to the news media.

The office prepares and distributes news releases; handles inquiries from the press; arranges news media coverage of bishops' meetings; offers public information and public relations counsel on a day-to-day basis to the office of the general secretary of the USCC and the NCCB, and to other agencies and staff members; performs a number of special research and writing functions on behalf of the conferences and their staffs.

The office also provides services and coordination for diocesan information offices.

Russell Shaw is director of the office, which is located at 1312 Massachusetts Ave. N. W., Washington, D.C. 20005.

Condition of Catholic Press: Nc News Service and the Catholic Press Association, reporting on a survey of 111 diocesan newspapers in September, 1972, stated:

"Things are bad in some areas of the Catholic press, but not disastrously so." There is "no evidence that the Catholic press is in danger of expiring. It seems, rather, to have taken to bed with a bad virus. In some individual instances the virus has been complicated by a feeling of depression or malaise. . . . Yet, there has never been a time when an alert diocesan press was more essential to the vigor of the Church.

Honors and Awards

Pontifical Orders

The Pontifical Orders of Knighthood are secular orders of merit whose membership depends directly on the pope. Details regarding the various orders are handled by a special agency in the Secretariat of Briefs, an office in the Papal Secretariat of State.

Supreme Order of Christ (Militia of Our Lord Jesus Christ): The highest of the five pontifical orders of knighthood, the Supreme Order of Christ was approved Mar. 14, 1319, by John XXII as a continuation in Portugal of the suppressed Order of Templars. Members were religious with vows and a rule of life until the order lost its religious character toward the end of the 15th century. Since that time it has existed as an order of merit. Paul VI, in 1966, restricted awards of the order to Christian heads of state.

Order of the Golden Spur (Golden Militia): Although the original founder is not certainly known, this order is one of the oldest knighthoods. Indiscriminate bestowal and inheritance diminished its prestige, however, and in 1841 Gregory XVI replaced it with the Order of St. Sylvester and gave it the title of Golden Militia. In 1905 St. Pius X restored the Order of the Golden Spur in its own right, separating it from the Order of St. Sylvester. Paul VI, in 1966, restricted awards of the order to Christian heads of state.

Order of Pius IX: Founded by Pius IX June 17, 1847, the order is awarded for outstanding services for the Church and society, and may be given to non-Catholics as well as Catholics. The title to nobility formerly attached to membership was abolished by Pius XII in 1939. In 1957 Pius XII instituted the Class of the Grand Collar as the highest category of the order; in 1966, Paul VI restricted this award to heads of state "in solemn circumstances." The other three classes are of Knights of the Grand Cross, Knights of the Second Class or Commanders, and Knights of the Third Class. The new class was created to avoid difficulties in presenting papal honors to Christian or non-Christian leaders of high merit.

Order of St. Gregory the Great: First established by Gregory XVI in 1831 to honor citizens of the Papal States, the order is conferred on persons who are distinguished for personal character and reputation, and for notable accomplishment. The order has civil and military divisions, and three classes of knights.

Order of St. Sylvester: Instituted Oct. 31, 1841, by Gregory XVI to absorb the Order of the Golden Spur, this order was divided into two by St. Pius X in 1905, one retaining the name of St. Sylvester and the other assuming the title of Golden Militia. Membership consists of three degrees: Knights of the Grand Cross, Knight Commanders with and without emblem, and simple Knights.

Ecclesiastical Order

Order of the Holy Sepulchre: Critical opinion is divided regarding various details of the history of the order. It is certain, however, that these knights first appeared in the Holy Land and were in existence at the end of the 11th century. Some assign earlier dates or origin, claiming as founders St. James the Apostle, first bishop of Jerusalem, and St. Helena, builder of the Basilica of the Holy Sepulchre. Others hold that Godfrey of Bouillon instituted the order in 1099 and that it took its name from the Holy Sepulchre where its members were knighted.

The order lost a great deal of prestige after the fall of the Latin Kingdom of Jerusalem and the consequent departure of the knights from the Holy Land. It was united with the Knights of St. John in 1489, came under the grand mastership of Alexander VI in 1496 and shortly thereafter was split into three national divisions, German, French and Spanish. Pius IX re-established the Latin patriarchate of Jerusalem in 1847 and gave the patriarch the faculty of conferring the order of knighthood. This right had been held by the Franciscan custos following the appointment of the Friars as guardians of the Holy Land in 1342. Three classes of membership were designated in 1868. Leo XIII later instituted the Cross of Honor (which does not confer knighthood) in three classes — gold, silver and bronze — and also the Dames of the Holy Sepulchre. From 1907 to 1928 the pope was grand master, an office now held by a cardinal. Revised statutes for the order went into effect in 1949, 1962 and 1967. The 1949 constitution enjoined the knights "to revive in modern form the spirit and ideal of the Crusades with the weapons of faith, the apostolate, and Christian charity."

The Order of the Holy Sepulchre now has five classes: 12 Knights of the Collar and four degrees, with separate divisions of each for men and women — Grand Cross, Commanders with Plaque, Commanders and Knights. Three honorary decorations are awarded, vis., Palm of the Order, Cross of Merit (which may be bestowed on non-Catholics), and the Pilgrim's Shell.

Investiture ceremonies combine a profession of faith with the ancient ritual of knighthood dubbing. Candidates do not take monastic vows but pledge an upright Christian life and loyalty to the pope.

The grand master of the order is Cardinal Maximilien de Furstenberg.

There are three lieutenancies of the order in the United States.

Knights of Malta

The Sovereign Military Hospitaller Order of St. John of Jerusalem of Rhodes and of Malta traces its origin to a group of men who maintained a Christian hospital in the Holy Land in the 11th century. The group was approved as a religious order — the Hospitallers of St. John — by Paschal II in 1113.

The order, while continuing its service to the poor, principally in hospital work, assumed military duties in the following century and included knights, chaplains and sergeants-at-arms among its members. All the knights were professed monks with the vows of poverty, chastity and obedience. Headquarters were located in the Holy Land until the last decade of the 13th century and on Rhodes after 1308 (whence the title, Knights of Rhodes).

After establishing itself on Rhodes, the order became a sovereign power like the sea republics of Italy and the Hanseatic cities of Germany, flying its own flag, coining its own money, floating its own navy, and maintaining diplomatic relations with many nations.

The order was forced to abandon Rhodes in 1522 after the third seige of the island by the Turks under Sultan Suliman I. Eight years later, the Knights were given the island of Malta, where they remained as a bastion of Christianity until near the end of the 18th century. Headquarters have been located in Rome since 1834.

The title of Grand Master of the Order, in abeyance for some time, was restored by Leo XIII in 1879. A more precise definition of both the religious and the sovereign status of the order was embodied in a new constitution of 1961 and a code issued in 1966.

Religious aspects of the order are subject to regulation by the Holy See. At the same time the sovereignty by the order, which is based on international law, is recognized by the Holy See and by 38 countries with which full diplomatic relations are maintained.

The four main classifications of members are: Knights of Justice, who are religious with the vows of poverty, chastity and obedience; Knights of Obedience, who make a solemn promise of obedience to superiors of the order; Knights of Honor and Devotion, of noble lineage; and Knights of Magistral Grace. There are also three other groups of members.

The order, with five grand priories, two sub-priories and 32 national associations, is devoted to hospital and charitable work of all kinds in some 60 countries.

The Grand Master, who is the sovereign head of the order, has the title of Most Eminent Highness with the rank of Cardinal. He must be of noble parentage and under solemn vows for a minimum period of 10 years.

The present grand Master is Fra' Angelo de Mojana di Cologna, a lawyer of Milan, who was elected for life May 8, 1962, by the Council of State.

The address of headquarters of the order is Via Condotti, Palazzo Malta, 00187 Roma, Italia.

Papal Medals

Pro Ecclesia et Pontifice: This decoration ("For the Church and the Pontiff") had its origin in 1888 as a token of the golden sacerdotal jubilee of Leo XIII; he bestowed it on those who had assisted in the observance of his jubilee and on persons responsible for the success of the Vatican Exposition. The medal bears the likeness of Leo XIII on one side; on the other, the tiara, the papal keys, and the words *Pro Ecclesia et Pontifice.* Originally, the medal was issued in gold, silver or bronze. St. Pius X ordered that it be of gold only. It is awarded in recognition of service to the Church and the papacy.

Benemerenti: Several medals ("To a well-deserving person") have been conferred by popes for exceptional accomplishment and service. The medals, which are made of gold, silver or bronze, bear the likeness and name of the reigning pope on one side; on the other, a laurel crown and the letter "B."

These two medals may be given by the pope to both men and women. Their bestowal does not convey any title or honor of knighthood.

AMERICAN CATHOLIC AWARDS

Aquinas Medal, by the American Catholic Philosophical Association for outstanding contributions to the field of Catholic philosophy.

Jacques Maritain (1951), Etienne Gilson (1952), Gerald Smith, S.J. (1955), Gerald B. Phelan (1959), Rudolf Allers (1960), James A. McWilliams, S.J. (1961) Charles De Koninck (1964), James Collins (1965).

Martin C. D'Arcy (1967), Dr. Josef Pieper (1968), Leo R. Ward (1969), Bernard Lonergan, S.J. (1970), Henry B. Veatch (1971), Joseph Owens, C.SS.R. (1972).

Bellarmine Medal (1955), by Bellarmine College (Louisville, Ky.), to persons in national or international affairs who, in controversial matters, exemplify the characteristics of St. Robert Bellarmine in charity, justice and temperateness.

Jefferson Caffrey (1955), Gen. Carlos Romulo (1956), US Rep. John W. McCormack (1957), Frank M. Folsom (1958), Robert D. Murphy (1959), James P. Mitchell (1960), Frederick H. Boland (1961);

Gen. Alfred M. Gruenther (1962), Henry Cabot Lodge (1963), R. Sargent Shriver (1964), Irene Dunne (1965), Sen. Everett M. Dirksen (1966), Nicholas Katzenbach (1967), Danny Thomas (1968), J. Irwin Miller (1969), Theodore M. Hesburgh, C.S.C. (1970), Sen. John Sherman Cooper (1971).

Borromeo Award (1960), by Carroll College

(Helena, Mont.), for zeal, courage and devotion in the spirit of St. Charles Borromeo.

William D. Murray (1960), Robert E. Sullivan (1961), Vincent H. Walsh (1962), Leo V. Kelly (1963), Joseph A. Kimmet (1964), Dr. W. E. Long (1965), Frank E. Blair (1968), Gough, Booth, Shanahan and Johnson (1971).

Campion Award (1955), by the Catholic Book Club for distinguished service in Catholic letters.

Jacques Maritain (1955), Helen C. White (1956), Paul Horgan (1957), James Brodrick, S.J. (1958), Sister M. Madeleva (1959), Frank J. Sheed and Maisie Ward (1960), John La Farge, S.J. (1961), Harold C. Gardiner, S.J. (1962);

T. S. Eliot (1963), Barbara Ward (1964), Msgr. John T. Ellis (1965), John Courtney Murray, S.J. (1966), Phyllis McGinley (1967), Dr. George N. Shuster (1968), G. B. Harrison (1970), Walter and Jean Kerr (1971).

Cardinal Gibbons Medal (1949) by the Alumni Association of the Catholic University of America for distinguished and meritorious service to the Church, the United States or the Catholic University.

Carlton J. H. Hayes (1949), Gen. Carlos P. Romulo (1950), Fulton Oursler (1951), Most Rev. Fulton J. Sheen (1953), J. Edgar Hoover (1954), Gen. J. Lawton Collins (1955), US Sen. John F. Kennedy and Ignatius Smith, O.P. (1956), Most Rev. Bryan J. McEntegart (1957), Thomas E. Murray (1958);

Gen. Alfred M. Gruenther (1959), Karl F. Herzfeld (1960), Charles G. Fenwick (1961), Luke E. Hart (1962), John W. McCormack (1963), John A. McCone (1964), R. Sargent Shriver (1965), James J. Norris (1967), Danny Thomas (1968), Theodore Hesburgh, C.S.C. (1969), Dr. Carroll Hochwalt (1970), Danny Thomas (1971).

Cardinal Spellman Award (1947), by the Catholic Theological Society for outstanding achievement in the field of theology.

Revs. Francis J. Connell, C.SS.R., Emmanuel Doronzo, O.M.I., Gerald Yelle, S.S., William R. O'Connor, John C. Murray, S.J. (1947); Eugene Burke, C.S.P. (1948), Bernard J. J. Lonergan, S.J. (1949), John C. Murray, S.J. (1950), Msgr. William R. O'Connor (1951), Emmanuel Doronzo, O.M.I. (1952), Gerald Kelly, S.J. (1953), Francis J. Connell, C.SS.R. (1954), Edmond D. Benard (1955), John C. Ford, S.J. (1956);

Gerard Yelle, S.S. (1957), Msgr. Joseph C. Fenton (1958), Juniper Carol, O.F.M. (1959), Rev. John Quasten (1960), Cyril C. Vollert, S.J. (1961), Walter J. Burghardt, S.J. (1962), Rev. Francis Dvornik (1963), Barnabas Ahern, C.P. (1964), Godfrey Diekmann, O.S.B. (1965), Paul K. Meagher, O.P. (1966), John L. McKenzie, S.J. (1967), Dr. Martin R. P. McGuire (1968), Richard J. McCormick, S.J. (1969), Avery Dulles, S.J. (1970), Raymond E. Brown, S.S. (1971).

Catholic Action Medal (1934), by St. Bonaventure University (Allegany, N. Y.).

Alfred E. Smith (1934), Michael Williams (1935), Joseph Scott (1936), Patrick Scanlan (1937), George J. Gillespie (1938), William F. Montavon (1939), John J. Craig (1940), John S. Burke (1941), Dr. George Speri Sperti (1942), Francis P. Matthews (1943);

Jefferson Caffrey (1944), John A. Coleman (1945), David Goldstein (1946), Clement Lane (1947), Paul W. Weber (1948), Bruce M. Mohler (1949), Edward M. O'Connor (1950), Richard F. Pattee (1951), James M. O'Neill (1952), John E. Swift (1953);

Frank M. Folsom (1954), Walter L. McGuiness (1955), Carlton J. H. Hayes (1956), Thomas E. Murray (1957), Paul V. Murray (1958), Dr. John L. Madden (1959), Christopher H. Dawson (1960), Stephen Kuttner (1961), Charles De Koninck (1962), Lt. Gen. G. Trudeau (1963), Frank J. Sheed (1964), Danny Thomas (1965), Walter and Jean Kerr (1966), Sir Hugh Stott Taylor (1967), Maurice Lavanoux (1968).

CIP Award (1948), by the Catholic Institute of the Press for service in the communications media.

Bob Considine (1948), Neil MacNeil (1949), Fulton Oursler (1950), Leo McCarey (1951), Dr. James M. O'Neill (1952), H. I. Phillips (1953), Martin Quigley (1954), Gene Lockhart (1955), Jim Bishop (1956), Arthur Daley and Red Smith (1957);

Clare Boothe Luce (1958), John La Farge, S.J. (1959), Phyllis McGinley (1960), Edwin O'Connor (1961), Barrett McGurn (1962), Paul Horgan (1963), Daniel Callahan (1964), NBC-TV and CBS-TV (1965), Gary MacEoin (1966).

Catholic Press Association Award (1959), by the Catholic Press Association for distinguished contribution to Catholic journalism.

Dale Francis (1959), Frank A. Hall (1960), John C. Murray, S.J. (1961), Albert J. Nevins, M.M. (1962), Floyd Anderson (1963), Rev. Patrick O'Connor (1964), John Cogley (1965), Joseph Breig (1966), John Reedy, C.S.C. (1967), Bishop James P. Shannon (1968), no award (1969), Msgr. Robert G. Peters (1970), Francis A. Fink (1971), Jeremy Harrington (1972).

Cecilia Medal (1952), by the Music Department of Boys Town (Nebr.) for outstanding work in liturgical music.

Winifred T. Flanagan (1952), Dom Francis Missia (1953), Omer Westendorf (1954), Dom Ermin Vitry (1955), William A. Reilly (1956), Flor Peeters (1957), Roger Wagner (1958), Most Rev. Gerald T. Bergan (1959), Francis T. Brunner, C.SS.R. (1960), Jean Langlois (1961);

James B. Welch (1962), W. Ripley Dorr (1963), C. Alexander Peloquin (1964), Dr. Louise Cuyler (1965), Dr. Eugene Selhorst (1966), Dr. Paul Manz (1967), Myron J. Roberts (1968), Norman T. Letter (1969), Rev.

Elmer Pfeil (1969), Rev.˙ Richard Schuler (1970).

Christian Culture Award (1941), by Assumption University (Canada) to outstanding exponents of Christian ideals.

Sigrid Undset (1941), Jacques Maritain (1942), Philip Murray (1943), Frank J. Sheed (1944), Arnold M. Walter (1945), Henry Ford II (1946), George S. Sperti (1947), Richard Pattee (1948), Etienne Gilson (1949), Paul Doyon (1950), Christopher Dawson (1951), John C.H. Wu (1952);

Charles Malik (1953), Ivan Mestrovic (1954), F. W. Foerster (1955), Paul Martin (1956), Robert Speaight (1957), Allen Tate (1958), Barbara Ward (1959), John Cogley (1960), Peter Drucker (1961), Benjamin E. Mays (1962), John Quincy Adams (1963);

William Foxwell Albright (1964), Dr. Karl Stern (1965), John Howard Griffin (1966), Edith K. Peterkin (1967), Dr. Mircea Eliade (1968), Dr. James D. Collins (1969), Dorothy Day (1970), Dr. Marshall McLuhan (1971), James M. Cameron (1972).

Christian Wisdom Award (1958), by Loyola University (Chicago) to outstanding American or European theologians.

John C. Murray, S.J. (1958), Martin C. D'Arcy, S.J. (1959), Gustave A. Weigel, S.J. (1960), Etienne Gilson (1962).

Chrysostom Award (1966), by the St. Paul Center Byzantine Information Bureau for work toward reunion of the Orthodox and Roman Catholic Churches.

Cardinal Lawrence Shehan (1966), Patriarch Maximos IV Sayegh, posthumously (1967), Rev. John Meyendorff (1968), Catholicos Khouren I (1969), Patriarch Athenagoras (1970).

Collegian Award (1949), by "The Collegian," weekly student newspaper of La Salle College (Phila.), for public service in the field of communications.

Ed Sullivan (1949), Morley Cassidy (1950), Bob Considine (1951), Red Smith (1952), George Sokolsky (1953), Edward R. Murrow (1954), David Lawrence (1955), Jim Bishop (1956), Richard W. Slocum (1957), Chet Huntley (1958);

John C. O'Brien (1959), Walter Cronkite (1960), David Brinkley (1961), James Reston (1962), Charles Collingwood (1963), Art Buchwald (1964), Nancy Dickerson (1965), Charles Schulz (1966), Sandy Grady (1967), Harrison E. Salisbury (1968), Ralph W. Howard (1969).

Damien-Dutton Award (1953), by the Damien-Dutton Society for service toward conquest of leprosy or for the promotion of better understanding of social problems connected with the disease.

Stanley Stein (1953), Joseph Sweeney, M.M. (1954), Sister Marie Suzanne (1955), Dr. Perry Burgess (1956), John Farrow (1957), Dr. H. Windsor Wade (1958), Sister Hilary Ross (1959), Msgr. Louis J. Mendelis

(1960), Dr. Kensuke Mitsuda (1961), Pierre d'Orgeval, SS.CC. (1962);

Eunice Weaver (1963), Dr. Robert Cochrane (1964), John F. Kennedy, posthumously (1965), The Peace Corps (1966), Dr. Howard A. Rusk (1967), Dr. Frans Hemerijckx (1968), Dr. Victor G. Heiser (1969), Dr. Dharmendra (1970), Dr. Chapman H. Binford (1971), Dr. Patricia Smith (1972).

Dinneen Award (1957), by the National Theatre Arts Conference.

Emmett Lavery (1957), Euphemia Van Rensselaer Wyatt (1958), Therese M. Cuny (1959), Urban Nagle, O.P. (1961), George Schaefer (1964), Walter Kerr (1965), Alfred Lunt and Lynn Fontanne (1966), Roger Stevens (1967), Pearl Bailey (1969), Gabriel V. Hartke, O.P. (1970), John Michael Tedelak (1971).

Edith Stein Award (1955), by the Edith Stein Guild for service toward better understanding between Christians and Jews.

Sister Noemi de Sion (1956), Authur B. Klyber, C.SS.R. (1957), Rev. John M. Oesterreicher (1958), John J. O'Connor (1959), Victor J. Donovan, C.P. (1960), Jacques and Raissa Maritain (1961), Gerard E. Sherry (1962), Mother Kathryn Sullivan, R.S.C.J. (1963), Paulist Press (1964), Rev. Edward N. Flannery (1965), Mother Katherine Hargrove, R.S.C.J. (1966), Gregory Baum, O.S.A. (1967), Sr. Rose Albert Thering (1968), Msgr. Vincent O. Genova (1969), Dr. Joseph Lichten (1970), Philip Scharper (1971).

Emmanuel D'Alzon Medal (1954), by Assumption College (Worcester, Mass.) to persons exemplifying the ideals of the founder of the Assumptionists.

Jacques Maritain (1954), Michael F. Doyle (1955), Cardinal Richard J. Cushing (1956), Mother Mary St. Elizabeth (1956), Most Rev. John J. Wright (1959), Paolino Gerli (1960), Most Rev. Honoré van Waeyenbergh (1961), J. Peter Grace (1963), Danny Thomas (1967), Miss Mary Dowd, posthumously (1970).

Father McKenna Award (1950), by the national headquarters of the Holy Name Society, for outstanding service to the society's ideals.

Msgr. John J. Murphy, Msgr. Henry J. Watterson, Msgr. Frederic J. Allchin (1950), Eustace Struckhoff, O.F.M., Msgr. Joseph A. McCaffrey, Msgr. Francis P. Connelly, Rev. Raymond E. Jones, Msgr. Joseph E. Maguire, Msgr. Edward J. Kelly, Msgr. J. Frederick Kriebs, Rev. Thomas E. O'Connell, Very Rev. Charles L. Elslander, Rev. Joseph J. Heim, Msgr. F. Borgias Lehr (1951);

Rev. Francis J. Hannegan (1954), Rev. Charles A. Hoot, Rev. Louis A. Hinnebusch, O.P., Rev. John O. Purcell, Rev. Paul M. Lackner (1955), Msgr. F. J. Timoney (1958), Rev. Thomas F. McNicholas (1960), James A. Quinn, O.P., and Rev. John C. Griffith (1961), Msgr. Joseph A. Aughney (1962),

Msgr. Cornelius P. Higgins (1963), Msgr. Charles P. Mynaugh (1964), Msgr. Charles P. Muth, Rev. Patrick J. Foley (1971).

Franciscan International Award (1958), by the Conventual Franciscans (Prior Lake, Minn.) for outstanding contributions to the American way of life.

Mr. and Mrs. Ignatius A. O'Shaughnessy (1959), Archbishop William O. Brady (1960), Lawrence Welk (1961), Charles Kellstad (1962), Dr. Finn J. Larsen (1963), Dr. Charles W. Mayo (1964), Ara Parseghian (1965), F. K. Weyerhaueser (1966);

Alcoholics Anonymous (1967), James T. Griffin (1968), George S. Harris (1969), Baroness Catherine DeHueck Doherty (1970), Harry Reasoner (1971), Dr. Billy Graham (1972).

Good Samaritan Award (1968), by the National Catholic Development Conference to recognize the concern for one's fellowman exemplified by the Good Samaritan.

Bishop Edward E. Swanstrom (1968), Berard Scarborough, O.F.M. (1969), Bishop Joseph B. Whelan, C.S.Sp. (1970).

Hoey Awards (1942), by the Catholic Interracial Council of New York (55 Liberty St., New York, N.Y. 10004) for the promotion of interracial justice.

Frank A. Hall and Edward La Salle (1942), Philip Murray and Ralph H. Metcalfe (1943), Mrs. Edward V. Morrell and John L. Yancey (1944), Paul D. Williams and Richard Barthe (1945), Richard Reid and Charles L. Rawlings (1946), Julian J. Reiss and Clarence T. Hunter (1947), Mrs. Anna McGarry and Ferdinand L. Rousseve (1948), John J. O'Connor and M. C. Clarke (1949), J. Howard McGrath and Lou Montgomery (1950), Mrs. Roger L. Putnam and Francis M. Hammond (1951);

Charles F. Vatterot, Jr., and Joseph J. Yancey (1952), Joseph J. Morrow and John B. King (1953), Mrs. Gladys D. Woods and Collins J. Seitz (1954), Millard F. Everett and Dr. James W. Hose (1955), Frank M. Folsom and Paul G. King (1956), George Meany and James W. Dorsey (1957), James T. Harris and Robert S. Shriver, Jr. (1958), Percy H. Steele, Jr., and John P. Nelson (1959);

William Duffy, Jr., and George A. Moore (1960), Ralph Fenton and Mrs. Osma Spurlock (1961), Benjamin Muse and Dr. Eugene T. Reed (1962), James T. Carey and Percy H. Williams (1963), Arthur J. Holland and Frederick O'Neal (1964), Gerard E. Sherry and James R. Dumpson (1965), Jane M. Hoey and Mrs. Roy Wilkins (1966), Dr. Frank Horne and Lt. Gov. Malcolm Wilson (1967), E. H. Molisani and John Strachan (1968);

Harold E. McGannon and Hulan E. Jack (1969), George P. McManus, Alfred B. Del Bello, Maceo A. Thomas and Cleo Joseph L. Froix, M.D. (1970), Most Rev. Francis J. Mugavero and Most Rev. Harold R. Perry (1971).

Honor et Veritas Award (1959), by the Catholic War Veterans to outstanding Americans.

Gen. Douglas MacArthur (1961), U. S. Sen. Thomas J. Dodd (1962), Gen. William Westmoreland (1966), Dean Rusk (1967), Col. Martin T. Riley (1968), Theodore M. Hesburgh (1969), Kenneth D. Wells (1970), Danny Thomas (1971), Thomas V. Cuite (1972).

Insignis Medal (1951), by Fordham University for extraordinary distinction in the service of God through excellence in professional performance.

Dr. Carlos Espinosa Davila, Arthur H. Hayes (1955), Pierre Harmel, Victor Andres Belaunde (1956), M. E. Michelet (1957), Daniel Linehan, S.J., Dr. Victor F. Hess (1958), Dr. George N. Shuster, John H. Tully, Albert Conway (1959), Charles F. Vatterot, Cardinal Agagianian, Charles Norman and Lucy W. Shaffer, David C. Cronin, S.J. (1960);

Cardinal Spellman (1961), Edward P. Gilleran (1962), Joseph A. Martino, William J. Tracy (1963), Brother James M. Kenny, S.J., and Austin Ripley (1966), Vincent T. Lombardi (1967), Melkite Patriarch Maximos V Hakim of Antioch (1968), Joseph and Marian Kaiser (1970).

John F. Kennedy Award (1963), by the Catholic Interracial Council of Chicago (21 W. Superior St.) for service in the cause of interracial justice; originally (1961) the Award of Merit.

R. Sargent Shriver, Jr. (1961), Vice President Lyndon B. Johnson (1962), Rev. Dr. Eugene Carson Blake (1963), Rev. Dr. Martin Luther King, Jr. (1964), Rev. Richard F. Morrisroe (1965), Msgr. Daniel F. Cantwell (1966), Edwin C. Berry (1967), Gov. Otto Kerner (1968), A. Phillip Randolph (1969), Sen. Paul H. Douglas (1970).

John Gilmary Shea Prize (1944), by the American Catholic Historical Association for scholarly works on the history of the Catholic Church broadly considered.

Carlton J. H. Hayes (1946), John H. Kennedy (1950), George W. Pare (1951), Rev. Philip Hughes (1954), Annabelle M. Melville (1955), Rev. John Tracy Ellis (1956), Rev. Thomas J. McAvoy, C.S.C. (1957), Rev. John M. Daley, S.J. (1958), Rev. Robert A. Graham, S.J. (1959);

Rev. Maynard Geiger, O.F.M. (1960), Rev. John C. Murray, S.J. (1961), Francis Dvornik (1962), Oscar Halecki (1963), Helen C. White (1964), John T. Noonan (1965), Rev. Robert I. Burns, S.J. (1966 and 1967), Rev. Edward S. Surtz, S.J. (1968), Robert Brentano (1969), David M. Kennedy (1970), Jaroslav Pelikan (1971).

Laetare Medal (1883), by the University of Notre Dame for distinguished accomplishment for Church or nation by an American Catholic.

John Gilmary Shea (1883), Patrick J. Kee-ley (1884), Eliza Allen Starr (1885), Gen. John Newton (1886), Edward Preuss (1887), Patrick V. Hickey (1888), Mrs. A. H. Dorsey (1889), William J. Onahan (1890), Daniel Dougherty (1891), Henry F. Brownson (1892);

Patrick Donahoe (1893), Augustin Daly (1894), Mrs. James Sadlier (1895), Gen. William S. Rosecrans (1896), Dr. Thomas A. Emmet (1897), Timothy E. Howard (1898), Mary G. Caldwell (1899), John Creighton (1900), Wm. B. Cochran (1901), Dr. J. B. Murphy (1902);

Charles J. Bonaparte (1903), Richard C. Kerens (1904), Thomas B. Fitzpatrick (1905), Dr. Francis Quinlan (1906), Katherine E. Conway (1907), James C. Monaghan (1908), Frances Tiernan (Christian Reid) (1909), Maurice F. Egan (1910), Agnes Repplier (1911), Thomas M. Mulry (1912);

Charles G. Hebermann (1913), Edward Douglass White (1914), Mary V. Merrick (1915), Dr. James J. Walsh (1916), Admiral William S. Benson (1917), Joseph Scott (1918), George Duval (1919), Dr. Lawrence F. Flick (1920), Elizabeth Nourse (1921), Charles P. Neil (1922);

Walter G. Smith (1923), Charles D. Maginnis (1924), Dr. Edward F. Zahm (1925), Edward N. Hurley (1926), Margaret Anglin (1927), Jack J. Spalding (1928), Alfred E. Smith (1929), Frederick P. Kenkel (1930), James J. Phelán (1931), Dr. Stephen J. Maher (1932);

John McCormack (1933), Mrs. Nicholas F. Brady (1934), Frank Spearman (1935), Richard Reid (1936), Jeremiah Ford (1937), Dr. Irvin Abell (1938), Josephine Brownson (1939), Gen. Hugh A. Drum (1940), William T. Walsh (1941), Helen C. White (1942);

Thomas F. Woodlock (1943), Anne O'Hare McCormick (1944), G. Howland Shaw (1945), Carlton J. H. Hayes (1946), William B. Bruce (1947), Frank C. Walker (1948), Irene Dunne (Mrs. Francis Griffin) (1949), (1951), Thomas E. Murray (1952);

I. A. O'Shaughnessy (1953), Jerrerson Caffrey (1954), George Meany (1955), Gen. Alfred M. Gruenther (1956), Clare Boothe Luce (1957), Frank M. Folsom (1958), Robert D. Murphy (1959), George N. Shuster (1960), Pres. John F. Kennedy (1961), Dr. Francis J. Braceland (1962);

Adm. George W. Anderson, Jr. (1963), Phyllis McGinley (1964), Frederick D. Rossini (1965), Mr. and Mrs. Patrick F. Crowley (1966), J. Peter Grace (1967), R. Sargent Shriver (1968), Justice William J. Brennan, Jr. (1969), Dr. William D. Walsh (1970), Walter and Jean Kerr (1971), Dorothy Day (1972).

McAuliffe Medal Awards, by the Hartford Archdiocesan Labor Institute (1620 Whitney Ave., Hamden, Conn.) to representatives of management and labor for promoting good industrial relations in the State of Connecticut.

Keith T. Middleton and Frank S. Petela (1960), James A. Walsh and Joseph M. Tone (1961), Benjamin Bogin and Michael E. La Rose (1962), Stanley J. Cullen and George Froelich (1963), Joseph B. Burns and Wiley C. Wheeler (1964), Most Rev. Joseph F. Donnelly (1965, only one recipient), Gilbert R. Boutin and Edward L. Crowley (1966), Edward W. Rice and Rufus C. Stillman (1967).

Magnificat Medal (1947), by Mundelein College (Chicago) to Catholic college alumnae for leadership in social action.

Mrs. Henry Mannix (1948), Mrs. Felix H. Lapeyre (1949), Mrs. Mary B. Finan (1950), Mrs. John J. Daly (Mary Tinley) (1951), Mrs. K. Cary Clem (1952), Mrs. Robert E. Garritty (1953), Dr. Jeannette E. Vidal (1954), Mrs. Ben Regan (1955), Marion McCandless (1956), Mrs. Donald Gunn (1957);

Ellen Collins (1958), Ruth M. Fox (1959), Margaret J. Mealey (1960), Mrs. George Vergara (1961), Josephine Sobrino (1962), Mrs. Patrick F. Crowley (1963), Ann M. Lally (1964).

Marianist Award (1949), by the University of Dayton for outstanding contributions to Mariology (until 1966); for outstanding contributions to mankind (from 1967).

Juniper Carol, O.F.M. (1950), Daniel A. Lord, S.J. (1951), Patrick J. Peyton, C.S.C. (1952), Roger Brien, S.G.G. (1953), Emil Neubert, S.M. (1954), Joseph A. Skelly, C.M. (1955), Frank Duff (1956), Eugene F. Kennedy and John McShain (1957), Winifred A. Feely (1958), Eamon R. Carroll, O. Carm. (1960), Coley Taylor (1961), Abbe Rene Laurentin (1963), Philip C. Hoelle, S.M. (1964), Cyril O. Vollert, S.J. (1965), Eduardo Frei Montalvo (1967).

Marian Library Medal (1953), by the Marian Library of the University of Dayton for books in English on the Blessed Virgin Mary. Starting in 1971, the medal will be awarded every four years, at the time of an International Mariological Congress, to a scholar for Mariological studies.

Most Rev. Fulton J. Sheen (1953), Msgr. John S. Kennedy (1954), Rev. William G. Most (1955), Ruth Cranston (1956), Juniper Carol, O.F.M. (1957), Donald C. Sharkey and Joseph Debergh, O.M.I. (1958);

Edward O'Connor, C.S.C. (1959), John J. Delaney (1960), Sister Mary Pierre, S.M. (1961), Marion A. Habig, O.F.M. (1962), Titus F. Cranny, S.A. (1963), Hilda C. Graef (1964), Edward Schillebeeckx, O.P. (1965), Cyril Vollert, S.J. (1966), Thomas O'Meara, O.P. (1967), Charles Balic, O. F. M. (1971).

Mater et Magistra Award (1963), by the College of Mt. St. Joseph on the Ohio to women for social action in the pattern and spirit of the encyclical *Mater et Magistra.*

Jane Hoey (1963), Mary Dolan (1964), Mrs. Anne Fremantle (1966), Margaret Mealey (1967), Mrs. Arthur L. Zepf, Sr. (1968), Alice R. May (1969).

Mendel Medal (1928), by Villanova University for scientists.

Dr. John A. Kolmer (1929), Dr. Albert F. Zahm (1930), Dr. Karl F. Herzfeld (1931), Dr. Francis P. Garvan (1932), Dr. Hugh Stott Taylor (1933), Abbe Georges Lemaitre (1934), Dr. Francis Owen Rice (1935), Rev. Julius A. Nieuwland, C.S.C. (1936), Pierre Teilhard de Chardin, S.J. (1937), Dr. Thomas Parran (1938); Rev. John M. Cooper (1939), Dr. Peter J. W. Debye (1940), Dr. Eugene M. K. Geiling (1941), Dr. Joseph A. Becker (1942), Dr. George Speri Sperti (1943), Dr. John C. Hubbard (1946), Frank N. Piasecki (1954), James B. Macelwane, S.J. (1955), Dr. William J. Thaler (1960), Dr. James A. Shannon (1961), Maj. Robert M. White (1963), Dr. Charles A. Hufnagel (1965), Dr. Alfred M. Bongiovanni (1968).

Msgr. John P. Monaghan Social Action Award by the Assn. of Catholic Trade Unionists; originally (1948), the Quadragesimo Anno Medal.

John Quincy Adams (1948), Brother Justin, F.S.C. (1949), Joseph Bierne (1950), Rev. Raymond A. McGowan (1951), Philip Murray (1952), Charles M. Halloran (1953), US Sen. Robert F. Wagner, Sr. (1954), Rev. John P. Monaghan (1955), John C. Cort (1956), Msgr. Joseph F. Connolly (1957);

George Meany (1958), Robert F. Kennedy (1959), Thomas Carey (1960), James B. Carey (1961), Rev. Joseph Hammond (1966), Paul Jennings (1967), Matthew Guinan (1968), David Sullivan (1969), Vincent McDonnell (1970).

Our Lady of Guadalupe Medal (1942), by Pi Alpha Sigma (Pan-American Fraternity of St. John's University, Brooklyn, N. Y.), for promoting understanding among peoples of the Americas; originally, the Pan-American Medal.

Rev. Joseph F. Thorning (1942), Sister Helen Patricia, I. H. M. (1943), Charles G. Fenwick (1944), Hector D. Castro (1945), Richard Pattee (1946), Rev. James A. Magner (1947), Roderick P. Wheeler, O. F. M. (1948), Rev. William R. McCarthy (1949), Ellen Collins (1950), Alfredo Antonini (1951), Henry Grattan Doyle (1952), Cardinal Manuel Arteaga Y Betancourt (1953);

Juniper B. Carol, O. F. M. (1954), Leandro Mayoral, C. M. (1955), Antonini Jurgelaitis, O. P. (1957), Vera Villegas (1958), Eugenio Florit (1959), Luis Felipe Letelier Icaza (1960), John J. Considine, M. M. (1961), Most Rev. Mark G. McGrath, C. S. C. (1962), the John J. Falls Family (1963), Michael Mullen, C. M. (1964), Felicia Rincon de Gautier (1965), Cardinal Richard Cushing (1967).

Peace Award (1950), by the Third Order Secular of St. Francis.

Myron C. Taylor (1950), John Foster Dulles (1951), John W. McCormack (1952), John C. Wu (1953), Ralph Bunche (1954), John R. Gariepy (1956), Most Rev. Richard J. Cushing (1957), Patrick McGeehan, Sr. (1958), Victor Andres Belaunde (1959), J. Edgar Hoover (1960), George K. Hunton (1961);

Mrs. Lester Auberlin (1962), Rev. Martin Luther King (1963), Most Rev. John J. Wright (1964), Pope Paul VI (1965), Cardinal Wyszynski (1966), Bishop Fred Pierce Corson (1967), Robert F. Kennedy, posthumously (1968), Msgr. Robert Fox (1969), Bishop James Walsh, M. M. (1970).

Pierre Charles Award (1960), by the Institute of Mission Studies (Fordham University) for the best mission book of the year.

Vincent Cronin (1960), John J. Considine, M. M. (1961), Horacio de la Costa, S. J. (1962), George H. Dunne, S. J. (1963), Louis Luzbetak, S. V. D. (1964), Eugene Hillman, C. S. Sp. (1965), Robert Burns, S. J. (1966).

Pius XII Marian Award (1955), by the Montfort Fathers for promotion of the devotion of consecration to the Immaculate Heart of Mary.

Denis M. McAuliffe, O. P. (1955), James M. Keane, O. S. M. (1956), Rev. John Cantwell Waltham (1957), Delicia Undson (1958), Rev. Herman J. Vincent of St. Henry's Parish, Bridge City, Tex., and parishioners of St. Helen's Mission, Orangefield, Tex. (1959), Leo Dillon (1960), Rev. Nicholas Norman (1961), De Montfort Groups of Detroit, Mich., and Rev. Thomas Kerwin, their spiritual director (1962), Frank Duff (1965).

Poverello Medal (1949), by The College of Steubenville (Ohio), "in recognition of great benefactions to humanity, exemplifying in our age the Christ-like spirit of charity which filled the life of St. Francis of Assisi."

Alcoholics Anonymous Fellowship (1949), Edward F. Hutton (1950), the Court of Last Resort, New York, N. Y. (1951), The Lions International (1952), Variety Clubs International (1953), Llewellyn J. Scott (1954), Dr. Jonas E. Salk and Associates (1955), Mother Anna Dengel (1956), Catherine de Hueck Doherty (1957), D. M. Hamill (1958);

Daniel W. Egan, T. O. R. (1959, posthumously), Mrs. Emma C. Zeis (1960), Donald H. McGannon (1961), Jane Wyatt (1962), Birgit Nilsson (1963), Arthur Joseph Rooney (1964), Joe E. Brown (1965), Project Hope (1966), Lena F. Edwards (1967), VISTA (1968), Jack Twyman (1969), The Salvation Army (1970), Most Rev. John K. Mussio (1971).

Regina Medal (1959), by the Catholic Library Association for outstanding contributions to children's literature.

Eleanor Farjeon (1959), Anne Carroll Moore (1960), Padraic Colum (1961), Frederick G. Melcher (1962), Ann Nolan Clark (1963), May Hill Arbuthnot (1964), Ruth Sawyer Durand (1965), Leo Politi (1966), Bertha Mahoney Miller (1967), Marguerite de Angeli (1968), Lois Lenski (1969), Ingri and Edgar Parin d'Aulaire (1970), Tasha Tudor (1971) Miendert DeJong (1972).

Rerum Novarum Award (1949), by St. Peter's College (Jersey City, N. J.) for outstanding work in the interests of industrial peace.

Raymond Reiss (1949), Justin McAghon (1950), Frederick W. Mansfield (1951), Most Rev. Karl J. Alter (1952), Martin P. Durkin (1953), Christopher W. Hoey (1954), James P. Mitchell (1955), George Meany (1956), Henry Ford II (1957), Hugh E. Sheridan (1958);

Joseph F. Finnegan (1959), Cardinal Richard Cushing (1960), Joseph D. Keenan (1961), (no award 1962), Louis C. Seaton (1963).

Richard Reid Memorial Award (1963), by the Catholic Institute of the Press in memory of its cofounder.

Thomas A. Brennan (1963), James A. Connolly (1964), John J. Sheehan (1965), Arthur Hull Hays (1966), Victor L. Ridder (1968), Bob Considine, (1969).

The Saint De La Salle Medal, by Manhattan College, for contribution to Catholic education.

John F. Brosnan (1951), Cardinal Francis Spellman (1952), Most Rev. Joseph P. Donahue (1953), Most Rev. Edwin V. O'Hara, posthumously (1950), Sr. Mary Emil, I.H.M. (1957), Msgr. Joseph E. Schieder (1958), Very Rev. Bro. Bertrand, O. S. F. (1959), Dr. Roy J. Deferrari (1960).

John Courtney Murray, S.J. (1961), Bro. Clair Stanislaus, F.S.C. (1962), Most Rev. Bryan J. McEntegart (1963), Sr. M. Rose Eileen, C.S.C. (1964), Mother Kathryn Sullivan, R.S.C.J. (1965), Bro. Bernard Peter, F.S.C. (1966), Dr. William Hughes Mulligan (1967), C. Alfred Koob, O. Praem. (1968), Theodore M. Hesburgh, C.S.C. (1970), Most Rev. Edwin B. Broderick (1971).

St. Francis Xavier Medal (1954), by Xavier University (Cincinnati) to persons exemplifying the spirit of St. Francis Xavier.

Most Rev. Fulton J. Sheen, Rev. Leo Kampsen, Msgr. Frederick G. Hochwalt (1954), James Keller, M.M. (1955), Gen. Carlos P. Romulo (1956), Stan Musial, Aloysius A. Breen, S.J., Edwin G. Becker (1957), Msgr. (Maj. Gen.) Patrick J. Ryan, Msgr. (Maj. Gen.) Terrence P. Finnegan, Msgr. (Rear Adm.) George A. Rosso (1958);

Neal Ahern and T. L. Bouscaren, S.J. (1959), Celestine J. Steiner, S.J. (1960), Philip J. Scharper (1961), Charles Dismas Clark, S.J. (1962), Pres. John F. Kennedy (posthumously) and J. Paul Spaeth (1963), James B. Donovan (1964), Charles H. Keating, Jr. (1965), Frank Blair (1967), Martin H. Work (1968), Lt. Col. William A. Anders (1969), Bishop James E. Walsh, M.M. (1970), Lawrence Welk, Rev. Msgr. Ralph N. Beiting (1971).

St. Vincent de Paul Medal (1948), by St.

John's University (Brooklyn, N.Y.), for outstanding service to Catholic charities.

Francis D. McGarey (1948), John A. Coleman (1949), Aloysius L. Fitzpatrick (1950), Frank J. Lewis (1951), Howard W. Fitzpatrick (1952), Richard F. Mulroy (1953), Harry J. Kirk (1954), Bernard J. Keating (1955), John M. Nolan (1956), John R. Gariepy (1957);

Charles E. McCarthy (1958), Frederick V. Goess (1959), Maurice J. Costello (1960), Thomas F. Hanley (1961), John J. Lynch (1962), William A. Walters (1963), George E. Heneghen (1964), James A. Quigney (1965), Henry J. Shields (1966);

Eugene McGovern (1967), George J. Krygier (1968), James A. Cousins (1969), Edward T. Reilly (1970), T. Raber Taylor (1971).

Serra Award of the Americas (1947), by the Academy of American Franciscan History for service to Inter-American good will.

Sumner Welles (1947), Pablo Martinez del Rio (1948), Dr. Herbert E. Bolton (1949), Gabriela Mistral (1950), Carlos E. Castaneda (1951), Victor A. Belaunde (1952), Clarence Haring (1953), Alceu Amoroso Lima (1954), France V. Scholes (1956);

Silvio Zavala (1957), John Tate Lanning (1958), John Basadre (1959), Arthur Preston Whitaker (1960), Marcel Bataillon (1961), Javier Malagon y Barcelo (1962), Dr. George P. Hammond (1964), Augustin Millares Carlo (1970).

Signum Fidei Medal (1942), by the Alumni Association of La Salle College (Phila.) for contribution to the advancement of Christian principles.

Brother E. Anselm, F.S.C. (1942), Karl H. Rogers (1943), Very Rev. Edward V. Stanford, O.S.A. (1944), Mrs. Edward V. Morrell (1945), Cardinal Dennis Dougherty (1946), Max Jordan (1947), John J. Sullivan (1948), Dr. Louis H. Clerf (1949), Most Rev. Gerald P. O'Hara (1950), Most Rev. Fulton J. Sheen (1951);

John H. Harris (1952), James Keller, M.M. (1953), John M. Haffert (1954), Dr. Francis J. Braceland (1955), Matthew H. McCloskey (1956), Henry Viscardi, Jr. (1957), no award (1958), Dr. Joseph J. Toland, Sr. (1959), Luke E. Hart (1960), Joseph E. McCafferty (1961);

Martin H. Work (1962), R. Sargent Shriver (1963), Mother M. Benedict, M.D. (1964), Sen. Eugene McCarthy (1965), William B. Ball (1966), Frank Folsom (1967), Rev. Leon H. Sullivan (1968), Rev. William J. Finley (1969);

Dr. James W. Turpin (1970), Lisa A. Richette, Esq. (1971), Rev. Melvin Floyd (1972).

Soteriological Award (1967), by the Confraternity of the Passion (Third Order of the Passionists, St. Michael's Monastery, Union City, N. J.) for outstanding exemplification of sharing in the Passion of Christ in contemporary society.

Most Rev. Cuthbert M. O'Gara, C.P. (1967), Mrs. Martin Luther King, Jr. (1968), Veronica's Veil Players (1969), Mother Mary Teresa Benedetti, C.P. (1970), Dr. Billy Graham (1971), Flo Kuhn (1972).

Stella Maris Medal (1960), by Mary Manse College (Toledo, O.) for service.

Alice R. May (1960), Emma Endres Kountz (1961), Elizabeth M. Zepf (1962), Judge Geraldine F. Macelwane (1963), Ven. Mother Mary Adelaide, O.S.F. (1964), Marian Rejent, M.D. (1966), Mrs. Irene Hubbard McCarthy (1967), Sr. Ruth Hickey, S.G.M. (1969), Mrs. Ella Phillips Stewart (1970), Sr. M. Lawrence Wilson (1971).

Thanksgiving Award (1962), by Clarke College (Dubuque, Iowa) for meritorious service to the nation and its citizens.

Dr. William A. Walsh (1963), Henry Viscardi, Jr. (1964), Laurence Jones (1965), Sara Spencer (1966), R. Buckminster Fuller (1967), Harry Golden (1968).

Thomas More Association Medal (1954), by the Thomas More Association for distinguished contribution to Catholic literature during the year.

Doubleday and Co., Inc. (1954), Alfred A. Knopf, Inc. (1955), P. J. Kenedy and Sons, Inc. (1956), Farrar, Straus and Cudahy, Inc. (1957), Hawthorn Books (1958), Sheed and Ward, Inc. (1959), J. B. Lippincott Co.

(1960), Doubleday and Co., Inc. (1961), Random House, Inc. (1962);

William Morrow and Co., Inc. (1963), Harper and Row (1964), Farrar, Straus and Giroux (1965), Doubleday and Co., Inc. (1966), Herder and Herder (1967), Hans Kueng (1968), John L. McKenzie, S.J. (1969), Daniel Callahan (1970), Daniel Berrigan, S.J. (1971).

Vercelli Medal (1947), by the Holy Name Society for distinguished service to ideals of the society.

William Bruce, Paul M. Brennan, Joseph Scott, Stephen Barry, Patrick Kennedy (1947), R. W. Hoogstraet (1948), William H. Collins (1949), Ward D. Hopkins (1950), Charles A. Burkholder, James C. Connell, James T. Vocelle, Edwin J. Allen, Fred A. Muth, Austin J. Roche, Michael Lawlor (1951), Michael L. Roche (1953), Maurice J. O'Sullivan, Lucien T. Vivien, Jr. (1954);

John A. Lee, Sr., Daniel M. Hamill, Clarence F. Boggan, Louis J. Euler, Henry J. McGreevy, Ralph F. Nunlist (1955), James J. McDonnell (1957), Joseph J. Wilson (1958), William J. Meehan (1959), Paul Meade (1960), William T. Tavares (1961), David M. Martin (1962), Bert M. Walz (1963), Herbert Michelbrook (1964), Alfred A. McGarraghy (1965), Frank J. Beuerlein (1968), Humbert J. Campana (1970), Richard Asmus (1971).

CATHOLIC PRESS ASSOCIATION AWARDS

Catholic Press Association Awards for material published in 1971 were presented May 11, 1972, during the 62nd CPA convention, at Banff, Alberta, Canada.

Magazines

General excellence: *St. Anthony Messenger* (general interest magazine); *Paulist Fathers News* (religious order magazine); *Maryknoll* (mission magazine); *Mediatrix* (professional and special interest magazine); *Homiletic and Pastoral Review* (magazine for the clergy); *Thought: A Review of Culture and Ideas* (scholarly magazine); *Annals of Good St. Anne de Beaupre* (devotional magazine).

Best cover: *St. Anthony Messenger*, November, Lawrence Zink (four-color); *Queen*, May-June, photographer uncredited (two- or-three color); *Glenmary's Challenge*, summer, Rev. Patrick O'Donnell (single color).

Best short story: *U.S. Catholic and Jubilee*, for "Walter, the Cosmic Lover," by John O'Donnell.

Best original article: *Mercy Profile*, for "The Excitement of Harvard," by Sister Kyran Joyce Lawless, R.S.M.

Best editorial: *Commonweal*, for "Saga of Shame."

Best regular column: *Columbia*, for "Will Next Tax Laws Penalize Large Families" by Russell Shaw.

Best photo story originating with a magazine: *Lamp/ A Christian Unity Magazine*, for

"New Hope Manor" by Sue Cribari.

Best single photo originating with a magazine: *St. Anthony Messenger*, fro "Racism Wears a Lodge Pin" by Lawrence Zink.

Best illustration for an article or story: *Glenmary's Challenge*, for "No One Knocked" by Rev. Patrick O'Donnell.

Best poetry: *Liguorian*, for "Only Once" by Leo R. Ward, C.S.C.

Best single issue: *Maryknoll*, January, for "Hunger, Every Nation's Problem."

Best single piece of promotion: *Mediatrix*, for its introductory booklet.

Newspapers

Awards were presented to newspapers in three categories of circulation: small — 17,000 and under; medium — 17,001 to 40,000; large — more than 40,000.

General excellence: *The Southern Cross*, Savannah, Ga. (small circulation); *St. Cloud Visitor*, St. Cloud, Minn. (medium circulation); *The Tablet*, Brooklyn, N.Y. (large circulation).

Best front page: *Central California Register*, Fresno (small circulation); *The Southern Cross*, San Diego, Calif. (medium circulation); *Catholic Universe Bulletin*, Cleveland, O. (large circulation).

Best campaign in the public interest: *The Church World*, Portland, Me. (small circulation), for a year-long series of articles on social legislation at the state level; *The Vermont*

Catholic Tribune, Burlington (medium circulation), on the issue of public aid to private education; *The Catholic Bulletin,* St. Paul, Minn. (large circulation), for a campaign in support of the state's Income Tax Credit Law.

Best news story originating with the paper: *The Southern Cross,* San Diego, Calif., for Beryl Newman's "Report on the Pentecostals."

Best background, in-depth or interpretive reporting: *The Evangelist,* Albany, N.Y., for "The Church in the Albany Diocese Ten Years after the Call of the Spirit."

Best editorial: *The Monitor,* St. John's Newfoundland, for "The Teachers' Strike" by Rev. Patrick J. Kennedy, editor.

Best editorial page or section: *The Evangelist,* Albany, N.Y.

Best human interest feature story: *The Church World,* Portland, Me., for "Does Man Have a Moral Right to Voluntarily Demand to be Killed?" series by Dr. Frank Ayd, Jr.

Best single column originating with the paper: *The Catholic Voice,* Oakland, Calif., for "Even the Clergy have Fallen" by Ray Orrock.

Best youth coverage: *Western Catholic Reporter,* Edmonton, Alberta.

Best photo story originating with a newspaper: *Tennessee Register,* Nashville, Tenn., for "A Walk Through the Tennessee Hills," a story by Rev. Owen F. Campion, editor; photos by Jack Corn; layout by Bill Langdon.

Best photograph originating with a newspaper: *Clarion Herald,* New Orleans, La., for "Chile in School" by Frank Methe.

Best special issue, section or supplement: *The Catholic Voice,* Oakland, Calif., for "The Welfare Question."

Best example of circulation promotion: *Catholic Northwest Progress,* Seattle, Wash., for "Know-Your-Faith" contest.

Best example of effective advertising promotion: *The Pilot,* Boston, Mass., for "Travel Adventures, 1971."

Books

National Catholic Book Awards for works published in 1971 were announced by the Catholic Press Association May 18, 1972. The categories and books were:

History: *Christianity in the Twentieth Century,* by John A. Hardon; Doubleday and Co.

Scholarship: *The Populus of Augustine and Jerome,* by Edward Peters; Yale University Press.

Popular Theology: *The End of Religion,* by Dom Aelred Graham; Harcourt, Brace, Jovanovich.

Social Issues: *The Assault on Authority,* by William W. Meissner; Orbis Books.

Fiction: *Love in the Ruins,* by Walker Percy; Farrar, Straus and Giroux.

Paperback: *The Pentecostal Movement,* by E. D. O'Connor, C.S.C.; Ave Maria Press.

CHRISTOPHER AWARDS

Sixty-two producers, directors and writers were honored by the Christophers Feb. 24, 1972, for 1971 achievements in the fields of film, books and television. A total of 15 books, 15 television specials and two films were cited during an awards presentation in New York City. In addition, a special award was presented to Geraldo Rivera of WABC-TV for investigative reporting on institutions for the mentally handicapped.

"These awards," noted Father Richard Armstrong, M.M., director of the Christophers, "pay tribute to individuals who have used their God-given talents to provide high quality literature and entertainment for the general public." Award winners were selected on the basis of their affirmation of the highest values of the human spirit, artistic and technical accomplishment, and a significant degree of public acceptance of their work.

Books, Adults

Anonymous, *Go Ask Alice;* Prentice Hall.

Dee Brown, *Bury My Heart at Wounded Knee — An Indian History of the American West;* Holt, Rinehart and Winston.

Ernesto Cardenal, *The Psalms of Struggle and Liberation;* Herder and Herder.

Dr. Henry Clark, *Ministries of Dialogue;* Association Press.

Avery Dulles, S.J., *The Survival of Dogma;* Doubleday.

Admiral Samuel Eliot Morison, *The European Discovery of America, the Northern Voyages, A.D. 500-1600;* Oxford University Press.

Malcolm Muggeridge, *Something Beautiful for God* (black and white photographs by S.K. Dutt); Harper and Row.

Eudora Welty, *One Time, One Place;* Random House.

Dr. Gordon C. Zahn, Editor, *Thomas Merton on Peace;* McCall.

Books, Youth

Russell Hoban, *Emmet Otter's Jug-Band Christmas,* illustrated by Lillian Hoban; Parents' Magazine Press; ages 4 to 7.

Arnold Lobel, *On the Day Peter Stuyvesant Sailed into Town;* Harper and Row Junior Books; ages 4 to 7.

Clyde Robert Bulla, *Pocahontas and the Strangers,* illustrated by Peter Burchard; Crowell; ages 8 to 11.

Miska Miles, *Annie and the Old One,* illustrated by Peter Parnall; Atlantic-Little Brown; ages 8 to 11.

Elaine and Walter Goodman, *The Rights of the People — The Major Decisions of the Warren Court;* Farrar, Straus and Giroux; ages 12 and up.

Zilpha Keatley Synder, *The Headless Cupid,* illustrated by Alton Raible; Atheneum; ages 12 and up.

Television

"Aesop's Fables" — Lee Rich, executive producer; Lou Scheimer and Norm Prescott, producers; Hal Sutherland, director; Earl Hamner, Jr., writer (CBS).

"Alcoholism: Out of the Shadows" — David A. Tapper, director; James Benjamin, producer and writer (ABC).

"Beethoven's Birthday: A Celebration in Vienna with Leonard Bernstein" — Schuyler G. Chapin, entire productions supervisor; James Krayer, executive producer; Humphrey Burton, producer and director; Humphrey Burton and Leonard Bernstein, writers (CBS).

ABBREVIATIONS

A.A.: Augustinianus Assumptionis; Augustinians of the Assumption (Assumptionists).

A.A.S.: "Acta Apostolicae Sedis"; Acts of the Apostolic See.

A.B.: Artium Baccalaureus; Bachelor of Arts.

Abb.: abbacy.

Abp.: Archbishop.

A.D.: Anno Domini; in the year of the Lord.

ad lib.: ad libitum; at your own choice.

A.M.: Artium Magister; Master of Arts.

A.M.D.G.: Ad majorem Dei gloriam; to the greater glory of God.

AOH: Ancient Order of Hibernians.

Ap.: Apostle.

A.U.C.: Ab Urbe Condita; from the founding of the city.

A.V.: Authorized Version (of the Bible).

b: born.

B.A.: Bachelor of Arts.

B.C.: before Christ.

B.C.L.: Bachelor of Canon (Civil) Law.

Bl.: Blessed.

Bp.: Bishop.

Bro.: brother.

B.S.: Bachelor of Science.

B.V.M: Blessed Virgin Mary.

c.: circa; about.

CARA: Center for Applied Research in the Apostolate.

C.E.: Common or Christian Era.

CCC: Canadian Catholic Conference.

CCD: Confraternity of Christian Doctrine.

CEF: Citizens for Educational Freedom.

C.F.A.: Congregatio Fratrum Cellitarum seu Alexianorum; Alexian Brothers.

CFM: Christian Family Movement.

C.F.X.: Congregatio Fratrum S. Francisci Xaverii; Xaverian Brothers.

C.I.C.: Codex Iuris Canonici; Code of Canon Law.

C.I.C.M: Congregatio Immaculati Cordis Mariae; Congregation of the Immaculate Heart of Mary (Scheut Fathers).

CICOP: Catholic Inter-American Cooperation Program.

C.J.: Congregatio Josephitarum Gerardimontensium; Josephite Fathers (of Belgium).

C.J.M.: Congregation of Jesus and Mary (Eudists).

C.M.: Congregation of the Mission (Vincentians or Lazarists).

C.M.F.: Cordis Mariae Filius; Missionary Sons of the Immaculate Heart of Mary.

C.M.M.: Congregatio Missionariorum de Mariannhill; Missionaries of Mariannhill.

CMSM: Conference of Major Superiors of Men.

C.O.: Congregatio Oratorii; Oratorian Fathers.

COCU: Consultation on Church Union.

C.P.: Congregation of the Passion.

CPA: Catholic Press Association.

CPF: Catholic Press Features.

C.P.M.: Congregatio Presbyterorum a Misericordia; Congregation of the Fathers of Mercy.

C.PP.S.: Congregatio Missionariorum Pretiosissimi Sanguinis; Society of the Precious Blood.

C.R.: Congregation of the Resurrection.

C.R.M.: Clerics Regular Minor.

CRS: Catholic Relief Service.

C.R.S.P.: Clerics Regular of St. Paul (Barnabite Fathers).

C.S.: Missionaries of St. Charles (Scalabrinians).

C.S.B.: Congregation of St. Basil (Basilians).

C.S.C.: Congregatio Sanctae Crucis; Congregation of Holy Cross.

C.S.P.: Paulist Fathers.

C.S.S.: Congregation of the Sacred Stigmata: (Stigmatine Fathers and Brothers).

C.SS.R.: Congregatio Sanctissimi Redemptoris; Congregation of the Most Holy Redeemper (Redemptorists).

C.S.Sp.: Congregatio Sancti Spiritus; Congregation on the Holy Ghost (Holy Ghost Fathers).

C.S.V.: Clerks of St. Viator (Viatorians).

C.Y.O.: Catholic Youth Organization.

D.C.L.: Doctor Canonicae (Civilis) Legis; Doctor of Canon (Civil) Law.

Doctor Divinitatis; Doctor of Divinity.

D.N.J.C.: Dominus noster Jesus Christus; Our Lord Jesus Christ.

Doct.: Doctor.

D.O.M.: Deo Optimo Maximo; To God, the Best and Greatest.

D.V.: Deo volente; God willing.

e.g.: exempli gratia; for example.

ER: Eastern Rite News Service.

Er. Cam.: Congregatio Monachorum Eremitarum Camaldulensium; Monk Hermits of Camaldoli.

et al.: et alii or et aliae; and others.
exc.: except.

f., ff.: following.
F.D.P.: Filii Divini Providenciae; Sons of Divine Providence.
F.M.S.: Fratris Maristarum a Scholis; Marist Brothers.
F.M.S.I.: Filii Mariae Salutis Infirmorum; Sons of Mary, Health of the Sick.
Fr.: Father, or Friar.
F.S.C.: Fratres Scholarum Christianorum; Brothers of the Christian Schools (Christian Brothers).
F.S.C.J.: Congregatio Filiorum S. Cordis Jesu; Sons of the Sacred Heart (Verona Fathers).

I.C.: Institute of Charity (Rosminians).
ICEL: International Committee on English in the Liturgy.
i.e.: id est; that is.
IHS: Iesus Hominem Salvator; Jesus, the Savior of Men.
I.M.C.: Institutum Missionum a Consolata; Consolata Society for Foreign Missions.
I.N.R.I.: Iesus Nazarenus, Rex Iudaeorum; Jesus of Nazareth, King of the Jews.

J.C.D.: Juris Canonici Doctor; Doctor of Canon Law.
J.C.L.: Juris Canonici Licentiatus; Licentiate in Canon Law.
J.M.J.: Jesus, Mary, Joseph.
J.U.D.: Juris Utriusque Doctor; Doctor of Both Civil and Canon Laws.

K. of C.: Knights of Columbus.
K.H.S.: Knight of the Holy Sepulchre.
K.P.: Knight of Pius IX.
K.S.G.: Knight of St. Gregory.
K.S.S.: Knight of St. Sylvester.

LCWR: Leadership Conference of Women Religious.
LL.B.: Legum Baccalaureus; Bachelor of Laws.
LL.D.: Legum Doctor; Doctor of Laws.
LWF: Lutheran World Federation.

M.E.P.: Societe des Missions Etrangeres de Paris; Paris Foreign Missions Society.
M.H.M.: Mill Hill Missionaries.
M.I.C.: Congregatio Clericorum Regularium Marianorum sub titulo Immaculatae Conceptionis Beatae Mariae Virginis; Marian Fathers.
MM: Martyrs.
M.M.: Catholic Foreign Mission Society (Maryknoll Missioners).
M.S.: Missionaries of Our Lady of La Salette.
M.S.C.: Missionaries of the Sacred Heart.
M.S.F.: Congregatio Missionarorum a Sancta Familia; Missionaries of the Holy Family.
Msgr.: Monsignor.

NAB: New American Bible.
NAWR: National Association of Women Religious.
NC: National Catholic News Service.
NCC: National Council of Churches.
NCCB: National Conference of Catholic Bishops.
NCCL: National Catholic Council of the Laity.
NCCM: National Council of Catholic Men.
NCCS: National Catholic Community Service.
NCCW: National Council of Catholic Women.
NCEA: National Catholic Educational Association.
NCRLC: National Catholic Rural Life Conference.
NEB: New English Bible.
NFPC: National Federation of Priests' Councils.
NOBC: National Office for Black Catholics.
N.T.: New Testament.

O.A.R.: Order of Augustinian Recollects.
O.Carm.: Ordo Carmelitarum; Order of Calced Carmelites (Carmelites).
O.Cart.: Ordo Cartusiensis; Carthusian Order.
O.C.D.: Ordo Carmelitarum Discalceatorum; Order of Discalced Carmelites.
O.C.S.O.: Order of Cistercians of the Strict Observance (Trappists). Other Cistercisions are of the Common Observance.
O.D.M. or L. de M.: Ordo B. Mariae de Merced; Order of Mercy (Mercedarians).
O.F.M.: Order of Friars Minor (Franciscans).
O.F.M.Cap.: Order of Friars Minor Capuchin (Capuchins).
O.F.M. Conv.: Order of Friars Minor Conventual (Conventuals).
O.H.: Ordo Hospitalarius S. Joannis de Deo; Hospitaller Order of St. John of God.
O.M.I.: Oblates of Mary Immaculate.
O.P.: Order of Preachers (Dominicans).
O. Praem: Order of Premonstratensians (Norbertines).
O.S.A.: Order of Hermits of St. Augustine (Augustinians).

O.S.B.: Order of St. Benedict (Benedictines).
o.s.b.; order of St. Basil the Great.
O.S.C.: Ordo S. Cruis: Order of the Holy Cross (Crosier Fathers).
O.S.Cam: Order of St. Camillus (Camillians).
O.S.F.: Order of St. Francis; Franciscan Brothers; also various congregations of Franciscan Sisters.
O.S.F.S.: Oblates of St. Francis de Sales.
O.S.J.: Oblates of St. Joseph.
O.S.M.: Order of Servants of Mary (Servites).
O.S.P. Order of St. Paul the First Hermit (Pauline Fathers).
O.SS.T.: Ordo Sanctissimae Trinitatis Redemptionis Captivorum; Order of the Most

Holy Trinity (Trinitarians).
O.T.: Old Testament.

P.A.: Protonotary Apostolic.
PAVLA: Papal Volunteers for Latin America.
Ph.D.: Philosophiae Doctor; Doctor of Philosophy.
P.I.M.E.: Pontificium Institutum pro Missionibus Exteris; Pontifical Institute for Foreign Missions; Missionaries of Sts. Peter and Paul.
Pont. Max.: Pontifex Maximus; Supreme Pontiff.
PP., Pp.: Papa (Pope).

R.C.: Roman Catholic.
R.I.P.: Requiescat in pace; may he [she] rest in peace.
RNS: Religious News Service.
R.P.: Reverendus Pater (Reverend Father).
R.V.: Revised Version (of the Bible).

S.A.: Societas Adunationis (Franciscan Friars of the Atonement).
S.A.C.: Societatis Apostolatus Catholici; Society of the Catholic Apostolate (Pallottines).
Sch.P. or S.P.: Ordo Clericorum Regularum Pauperum Matris Dei Scholarum Piarum; Piarist Fathers.
S.C.J.: Congregatio Sacerdotum a Corde Jesu; Congregation of Priests of the Sacred Heart.
S.D.B.: Salesians of Don Bosco.
S.D.S.: Society of the Divine Savior (Salvatorians).
S.D.V.: Society of Divine Vocations.
S.F.: Congregatio Filiorum Sacrae Familiae; Sons of the Holy Family.
S.J.: Society of Jesus (Jesuits).
S.M.: Society of Mary (Marists); Society of Mary (Marianists).
S.M.A.: Societas Missionum as Afros; Society of African Missions.
S.M.B.: Societas Missionaria de Bethlehem; Society of Bethlehem Missionaries.
S.M.M.: Societas Mariae Montfortana; Company of Mary (Montfort Fathers).
S.O.Cist: Sacer Ordo Cisterciensis; Cistercians of the Common Observance.
SODEPAX: Joint Commission for Society, Development and Peace.
S.P.: Piarist Fathers; Servants of the Holy Paraclete.
Sr.: Sister.
S.S.: Society of St. Sulpice (Sulpicians).
SS.CC.: Congregatio Sacrorum Cordium; Fathers of the Sacred Hearts.
S.S.E.: Society of St. Edmund.
S.S.J.: Societas Sancti Joseph SSmi Cordis; St. Joseph's Society of the Sacred Heart (Josephites).
S.S.L.: Sacrae Scripturae Licentiatus; Licentiate in Sacred Scripture.
S.S.P: Society of St. Paul.

S.S.S.: Sacerdoti del Sanctissimo Sacramento; Congregation of the Blessed Sacrament.
S., St.; SS., Sts.: Saint; Saints.
S.T.: Missionarii Servi Sanctissimae Trinitates; Missionary Servants of the Most Holy Trinity.
S.T.B.: Sacrae Theologiae Baccalaureus; Bachelor of Sacred Theology.
S.T.D.: Sacrae Theologiae Doctor; Doctor of Sacred Theology.
S.T.L.: Sacrae Theologiae Licentiatus; Licentiate in Sacred Theology.
S.T.M.: Sacrae Theologiae Magister; Master of Sacred Theology.
S.V.D.: Societas Verbi Divini; Society of the Divine Word.
S.X.: Xaverian Missionary Fathers.

T.O.R.: Third Order Regular of St. Francis.
T.O.S.F.: Tertiary of Third Order of St. Francis.

UN: United Nations.
UNCTAD: United Nations Conference on Trade and Development.
UNESCO: United Nations Educational, Scientific and Cultural Organization.
UNICEF: United Nations Children's Fund.
USCC: United States Catholic Conference.

V.A.: Vicar Apostolic.
Ven.: Venerable.
V.F.: Vicar Forane.
V.G.: Vicar General.
V.T.: Vetus Testamentum; Old Testament.

WCC: World Council of Churches.
WICS: Women in Community Service.
W.F.: White Fathers.

Y.C.M.: Young Christian Movement.

Zip Codes

These abbreviations have been approved for use with ZIP Code numbers.
Alabama, AL; California, CA; Colorado, AR; California, CA; Colorado, CO; Connecticut, CT; Delaware, DE; District of Columbia, DC; Florida, FL;
Georgia, GA; Guam, GU; Hawaii, HI; Idaho, ID; ILLINOIS, IL; Indiana, IN; Iowa IA; Kansas, KS; Kentucky, KY; Louisiana, LA;
Maine, ME; Maryland, MD; Massachusetts, MA; Michigan, MI; Minnesota, MN; Mississippi, MS; Missouri, MO; Montana, MT; Nebraska, NB; Nevada, NV;
New Hampshire, NH; New Jersey, NJ; New Mexico, NM; New York, NY; North Carolina, NC; North Dakota, ND; Ohio, OH; Oklahoma, OK; Oregon, OR; Pennsylvania, PA;
Puerto Rico, PR; Rhode Island, RI; South Carolina, SC; South Dakota, SD; Tennessee, TN; Texas, TX; Utah, UT; Vermont, VT; Virginia, VA; Virgin Islands, VI;
Washington, WA; West Virginia, WV; Wisconsin, WI; Wyoming, WY.